Praise for Reformed Systematic Theology, *Volume 2*

"In volume 2 of *Reformed Systematic Theology*, Joel Beeke and his theological Barnabas, Paul Smalley, continue their massive exposition of Christian doctrine. Like the first volume, it is marked by constant use of Scripture coupled with references to the great theologians, and is written for all of the people of God in language that is more pastoral than metaphysical. This second volume covers the vital areas of anthropology and Christology, and continues in the style of a true 'church dogmatics' reminiscent of the work of the great pastor-theologians of the church. A model of clarity, it will promote doxology, maturity, and further inquiry. Here is catechesis at its best, instructing the student of theology, providing pastors with a sermon-enriching manual, and giving growing Christians a resource book that will both inform and nourish them, as well as provide endless theological enjoyment!"

   Sinclair B. Ferguson, Chancellor's Professor of Systematic Theology, Reformed
   Theological Seminary; Teaching Fellow, Ligonier Ministries

"The scholarship and devotion of this volume are truly impressive and must reflect the result of many years of rigorous study and careful teaching of the themes pursued. I have not read a systematic theology that impressed me to the same extent. This is a work that not only instructs but also speaks to the heart. It is a presentation of orthodox Reformed theology that reflects the Puritan tradition, but also presents that tradition in the context of the flow of Christian theology from the Bible through the church fathers and the medieval expositors, the Reformation challenges, and on to the contemporary scene."

   Robert Oliver, Pastor Emeritus, Old Baptist Chapel, Bradford on Avon,
   UK; Emeritus Lecturer in Church History and Historical Theology, London
   Theological Seminary

"Written with great clarity and thoughtful simplicity, this volume can be confidently relied upon for study and teaching. This is how systematic theology should be done— by having in mind both the pastor in the pulpit and the people in the pews. The authors are to be commended for giving us this top-rate, scholarly-yet-accessible, God-honoring volume."

   Rob Ventura, Pastor, Grace Community Baptist Church, North Providence,
   Rhode Island; coauthor, *A Portrait of Paul* and *Spiritual Warfare*

"This volume continues the heart-warming approach of volume 1. I particularly admire the authors' insightful and scrupulously fair exposition of positions with which they disagree. Their work offers a quite comprehensive approach to different readings throughout the history of the subjects dealt with."

   Jonathan F. Bayes, UK Director, Carey Outreach Ministries; Pastor, Stanton
   Lees Chapel, Derbyshire, England; author, *Systematics for God's Glory* and *The
   Weakness of the Law*

Praise for the Reformed Systematic Theology Series

"*Reformed Systematic Theology* not only takes readers into the depths of our triune God, but also shows what these great truths have to do with the Christian life. No contemporary systematic theology will bring the reader to a greater understanding of how theology blossoms into doxology than this one."

Matthew Barrett, Associate Professor of Christian Theology, Midwestern Baptist Theological Seminary; Executive Editor, Credo Magazine

"*Reformed Systematic Theology* is the ripe fruit of Joel Beeke's lifelong engagement as a preacher and as a teacher of preachers. This is not a systematic theology written by an ivory-tower theologian, but rather by a seasoned preacher for whom the doctrines he expounds have become, by the grace of God, an experiential reality."

Bartel Elshout, Pastor, Heritage Reformed Congregation, Hull, Iowa; translator, *The Christian's Reasonable Service* and *The Christian's Only Comfort in Life and Death*

"Beeke and Smalley have written a work useful to the church at large that teaches Christians what they should believe and how they should love, but they have not sacrificed academic rigor to achieve these goals."

J. V. Fesko, Professor of Systematic and Historical Theology, Reformed Theological Seminary, Jackson, Mississippi

"Joel Beeke has continued his decades-long service to Christ and his church by presenting us with his mature reflections on the nature of systematic theology. This work is fully reliable, well written, easily understood, and thoroughly researched."

Richard C. Gamble, Professor of Systematic Theology, Reformed Presbyterian Theological Seminary

"Joel Beeke is a rare gift to the church, a noted Christian leader who combines the skills of a learned theologian, master teacher, noted historian, and yet also a caring pastor. *Reformed Systematic Theology* is a virtual gold mine of biblical doctrine that is systematically arranged, carefully analyzed, historically scrutinized, and pastorally applied."

Steven J. Lawson, President, OnePassion Ministries; Professor of Preaching, The Master's Seminary; Teaching Fellow, Ligonier Ministries

"'Oh, the depth of the riches and wisdom and knowledge of God!' This expression of praise from Paul's great doxology is a fitting response to reading this wonderful work of doctrine and devotion. Though the Reformed faith is often caricatured as merely intellectual, this work demonstrates that Reformed theology is also profoundly experiential, as no chapter fails to move from theology to doxology."

John MacArthur, Pastor, Grace Community Church, Sun Valley, California; Chancellor Emeritus, The Master's University and Seminary

"Here is theology functioning as it ought to function—calling us to worship. You will not need to agree with the authors at every point to believe and to hope that this work will serve Christ's church well in our generation and for generations to come."

Jeremy Walker, Pastor, Maidenbower Baptist Church, Crawley, UK

REFORMED
SYSTEMATIC
THEOLOGY

REFORMED SYSTEMATIC THEOLOGY

Volume 2:
Man and Christ

Joel R. Beeke and Paul M. Smalley

:: CROSSWAY®

WHEATON, ILLINOIS

Reformed Systematic Theology, Volume 2: Man and Christ

Copyright © 2020 by Joel R. Beeke and Paul M. Smalley

Published by Crossway
        1300 Crescent Street
        Wheaton, Illinois 60187

Cover design: Jordan Singer

First printing 2020

Printed in the United States of America

Unless otherwise indicated, Scripture quotations are from the *King James Version* of the Bible.

Scripture quotations marked ESV are from the ESV® Bible (The Holy Bible, English Standard Version®), copyright © 2001 by Crossway, a publishing ministry of Good News Publishers. Used by permission. All rights reserved.

Scripture texts marked NAB, revised edition, are taken from the New American Bible, revised edition © 2010, 1991, 1986, 1970 Confraternity of Christian Doctrine, Washington, DC, and are used by permission of the copyright owner. All Rights Reserved. No part of the New American Bible may be reproduced in any form without permission in writing from the copyright owner.

All emphases in Scripture quotations have been added by the authors.

Hardcover ISBN: 978-1-4335-5987-7
ePub ISBN: 978-1-4335-5990-7
PDF ISBN: 978-1-4335-5988-4
Mobipocket ISBN: 978-1-4335-5989-1

Library of Congress Cataloging-in-Publication Data

Names: Beeke, Joel R., 1952– author. | Smalley, Paul M., author.
Title: Reformed systematic theology / Joel R. Beeke and Paul M. Smalley.
Description: Wheaton, Illinois: Crossway, [2020] | Includes bibliographical references and index.
Identifiers: LCCN 2018029011 (print) | LCCN 2018047407 (ebook) | ISBN 9781433559884 (pdf) | ISBN 9781433559891 (mobi) | ISBN 9781433559907 (epub) | ISBN 9781433559877 (hardcover) | ISBN 9781433559907 (ePub) | ISBN 9781433559891 (mobipocket)
Subjects: LCSH: Reformed Church—Doctrines.
Classification: LCC BX9422.3 (ebook) | LCC BX9422.3 .B445 2019 (print) | DDC 230/.42—dc23
LC record available at https://lccn.loc.gov/2018029011

Crossway is a publishing ministry of Good News Publishers.

SH		28	27	26	25	24	23	22	21	20
14	13	12	11	10	9	8	7	6	5	4	3	2	1

For
Stephen Myers, Adriaan Neele,
Greg Salazar, and Daniel Timmer
treasured brothers, colleagues, and friends,
professors in the PhD program at Puritan
Reformed Theological Seminary,
who live out the motto:
"The things that thou hast heard of me among many witnesses,
the same commit thou to faithful men,
who shall be able to teach others also" (2 Tim. 2:2).
—Joel R. Beeke

And for
Tom Nettles and John Woodbridge
two seminary professors who taught me to love Christian history
and to read the great books of Christ-exalting
theologians from centuries past;
and
John Owen (1616–1683)
the first Puritan theologian whose writings I read,
herald of the glory of Christ, our Prophet, Priest, and King.
"How beautiful upon the mountains are the feet
of him that bringeth good tidings,
that publisheth peace; that bringeth good tidings
of good, that publisheth salvation;
that saith unto Zion, Thy God reigneth!" (Isa. 52:7).
—Paul M. Smalley

Contents

Section B: The Doctrine of the Person of Christ

Section C: The Doctrine of the Work of Christ

Abbreviations

ACCS/OT

Ancient Christian Commentary on Scripture, Old Testament. Edited by Thomas Oden. 15 vols. Downers Grove, IL: InterVarsity Press, 2001–2005.

ANF

The Ante-Nicene Fathers. Edited by Alexander Roberts and James Donaldson. Revised by A. Cleveland Coxe. 9 vols. New York. Charles Scribner's Sons, 1918.

LW

Luther's Works. Edited by Jaroslav Pelikan et al. 79 vols. St. Louis, MO: Concordia, 1958–2016.

NIDNTTE

The New International Dictionary of New Testament Theology and Exegesis. Edited by Moisés Silva. 5 vols. Grand Rapids, MI: Zondervan, 2014.

NIDOTTE

The New International Dictionary of Old Testament Theology and Exegesis. Edited by Willem A. VanGemeren. 5 vols. Grand Rapids, MI: Zondervan, 1997.

NPNF[1]

A Select Library of Nicene and Post-Nicene Fathers of the Christian Church, First Series. Edited by Philip Schaff. 14 vols. New York: Christian Literature Co., 1888.

NPNF[2]	*A Select Library of Nicene and Post-Nicene Fathers of the Christian Church*, Second Series. Edited by Philip Schaff and Henry Wace. 14 vols. New York: Christian Literature Co., 1894.
The Psalter	*The Psalter, with Doctrinal Standards, Liturgy, Church Order, and Added Chorale Section.* Preface by Joel R. Beeke and Ray B. Lanning. 1965; repr., Grand Rapids, MI: Eerdmans for Reformation Heritage Books, 2003.
RCS/OT	*Reformation Commentary on Scripture, Old Testament.* Edited by Timothy George. 15 vols. Downers Grove, IL: IVP Academic, 2012–.
Reformed Confessions	*Reformed Confessions of the 16th and 17th Centuries in English Translation: 1523–1693.* Compiled by James T. Dennison Jr. 4 vols. Grand Rapids, MI: Reformation Heritage Books, 2008–2014.
RST	Joel R. Beeke and Paul M. Smalley. *Reformed Systematic Theology.* 4 vols. Wheaton, IL: Crossway, 2019–.
TDNT	*Theological Dictionary of the New Testament.* Edited by Gerhard Kittel, Geoffrey W. Bromiley, and Gerhard Friedrich. 10 vols. Grand Rapids, MI: Eerdmans, 1964.
The Three Forms of Unity	*The Three Forms of Unity.* Introduction by Joel R. Beeke. Birmingham, AL: Solid Ground, 2010.
Trinity Hymnal—Baptist Edition	*Trinity Hymnal—Baptist Edition.* Revised by David Merck. Suwanee, GA: Great Commission Publications, 1995.
WJE	*The Works of Jonathan Edwards.* 26 vols. New Haven, CT: Yale University Press, 1957–2008.

Tables

Preface to Volume 2

Jesus Christ came so that people would know the truth (John 8:31–32; 18:37). As the cross loomed on the horizon, our Lord Jesus prayed to his Father, "This is life eternal, that they might know thee the only true God, and Jesus Christ, whom thou hast sent," and interceded for the people whom the Father had given him, "Sanctify them through thy truth: thy word is truth" (17:3, 17). Christ brought us truth—life-giving, holiness-producing knowledge of God. Through this true word, God applies to our lives Christ's saving work on the cross.

The work of a systematic theologian is to gather the truth from the Holy Scriptures and present it in a way that, by the Holy Spirit's power, both illuminates the mind and ignites the heart to direct the whole life to the glory of God. The publication of this second volume marks the halfway point in our attempt to produce a systematic theology that is biblical, doctrinal, experiential, and practical. Here we address the topics of creation, human nature, sin, God's covenants, and the person and work of Christ.

We are profoundly grateful to the Lord for his blessing on this project. We never could have produced this systematic theology without the help of other men and women who are instruments in the Lord's hands. We are indebted to the many pastors and theologians (past and present) whose teachings have nourished our souls over the years. We thank Justin Taylor for his support of the project, Greg Bailey for his skillful editing of the manuscript, and the rest of the staff at Crossway for their assistance in publishing and promoting this set of books. Our writing has often been clarified by the editorial suggestions of Ray Lanning and Scott Lang. We also want to thank the following theologians for suggesting refinements of portions of the book: Robert Oliver, Steve Wellum, and Stephen Myers. And we are greatly indebted to the love and prayers of our dear wives,

Mary Beeke and Dawn Smalley, both of whom are women who put Christian theology into practice.

Most of all, we thank the triune God for the Mediator. Writing about the person and work of Jesus Christ has impressed upon us afresh that God dwells in unapproachable light, and our attempt to describe Christ's glory is but the stammering of children. Soli Deo gloria!

Joel R. Beeke and Paul M. Smalley

PART 3

ANTHROPOLOGY:
THE DOCTRINE OF MAN

Analytical Outline: Anthropology

I. Introduction to Anthropology
  A. What Is Theological Anthropology?
  B. Why Study Anthropology?
    1. Its Importance in the Bible
    2. Its Integral Relation to Other Doctrines
    3. Its Value to Other Academic Disciplines
    4. Its Implications for Contemporary Existential Crises
    5. Its Impact upon Practical Ministry
  C. How Does the World Approach Anthropology?
    1. Man Defined by Philosophical Idealism
    2. Man Defined by Physical Biology
    3. Man Defined by Sexual Desires
    4. Man Defined by Material Wealth
    5. Man Defined by Individual Freedom
    6. Man Defined by Social Relationships
    7. Man Defined by Emotional Health
    8. Man Undefined by Existential Absurdity
  D. How Does the Bible Approach Anthropology?
    1. The State of Original Innocence
    2. The State of Fallen Nature
    3. The State of Grace
    4. The State of Glory

Section A: The Doctrine of Creation

II. The Creation of the World
  A. False Theories of Origins
    1. Polytheism
    2. Pantheism

3. Genesis 2 Contradicts Genesis 1
4. Serpents Do Not Talk
B. Adam and Biblical Doctrine
1. The Historical Adam Is the Basis of Mankind's Nobility
2. The Historical Adam Is the Root of Mankind's Unity
3. The Historical Adam Is the Foundation of Gender Relationships
4. The Historical Adam Is the Agent of Mankind's Fall
5. The Historical Adam Is a Type of Mankind's Savior
C. Adam and Biblical Authority
1. The Danger of Subjecting God's Word to Human Skepticism
2. The Danger of Subordinating God's Word to Human Science
3. The Danger of Shrinking God's Word to Human Experience
V. The Image of God
A. Exegetical and Biblical Theology
1. The Created Image of God
    a. Images of God's Attributes
    b. Images for God's Worship
    c. Images of God's Reign
    d. Images for God's Family
2. The Continuing Image of God
3. The Incarnate Image of God
4. The Renewed Image of God
5. The Completed Image of God
B. Historical and Polemical Theology
1. Constitutional Perspectives on God's Image
    a. A Physical Image
    b. A Mental Image
    c. A Mental Image versus a Moral Likeness
    d. A Moral Image
2. Functional Perspectives on God's Image
    a. A Royal Image
    b. A Relational Image
    c. A Righteous-Dynamic Image
C. Systematic and Practical Theology
1. Summary of Exegetical and Biblical Theology

2. A Holistic Reformed Theology of God's Image
   a. Classic Reformed Teachings on the Holistic Image
   b. William Ames: A Model of Systematic Reflection on the Image
   c. The Unity of the Holistic Image
3. Practical Implications of Man as God's Image
   a. Sanctity
   b. Spirituality
   c. Rationality
   d. Dignity
   e. Integrity
   f. Equality
   g. Benevolence
   h. Authority
   i. Stewardship
   j. Morality
   k. Atrocity
   l. Destiny

VI. The Gender and Sexuality of Man
  A. Modern Controversies over Gender and Sexuality
    1. Feminism
    2. The Homosexual-Rights Movement
    3. Transgenderism
  B. Basic Biblical Teaching on Gender
    1. Gender Identity and the Two Biological Sexes
    2. Man as Authoritative Leader, Woman as Empowering Helper
  C. Basic Biblical Teaching on Sex
    1. Sexual Activity and Reproduction
    2. Sexual Activity and the Marriage Relationship
  D. Basic Biblical Teaching on Homosexuality
    1. Old Testament Teaching on Homosexuality
    2. New Testament Teaching on Homosexuality
    3. The Modern Concept of Sexual Orientation

VII. The Constitution of Man
  A. Unity and Duality
    1. Biblical Terminology for Aspects of the Human Constitution
       a. Breath (Hebrew *neshamah*)
       b. Soul (Hebrew *nephesh*; Greek *psychē*)

B. The Essential and Common Elements of Covenants
   1. Essential Elements
      a. A Solemn Promise
      b. A Verbal, Legal Instrument to Define a Relationship of Loyalty
   2. Common (but Not Essential) Elements
      a. Subordination to Another's Lordship
      b. Laws to Obey
      c. The Authorization of the Performance of an Office
      d. Parties Are Representatives of a Larger Group in Union with Them
      e. An Observable Sign
C. The Essential Elements of a Covenant in Genesis 2
   1. A Solemn, Legal, Verbal Revelation
   2. An Implicit Promise
   3. Mutual Loyalty and Love
D. Other Common Covenantal Elements in Genesis 2
   1. A Name of Covenantal Lordship
   2. The Office of Prophet, Priest, and King
   3. Adam's Representation of His Natural Descendants
   4. Observable Tokens of Faithfulness
E. Other Scripture Passages That Reveal the Covenant of Works
   1. Hosea 6:6–7
   2. Isaiah 24:5–6
   3. Romans 5:12–19
F. The Foundational Position of Covenants in God's Relationships to Man
G. Historical Roots of the Reformed Orthodox Doctrine
   1. Patristic, Medieval, and Counter-Reformation Theology
   2. Reformed Theology in the Sixteenth Century
H. Systematic Analysis of the Reformed Orthodox Doctrine
   1. Covenants in General
      a. The Doctrinal Centrality of Covenants
      b. A Variety of Kinds of Covenants
      c. The Requisite Human Response
      d. Personal and Loving Fidelity
   2. Introduction to the Covenant with Adam
      a. The Implicit Revelation of a Covenant with Adam

        i. Worship the Holy Lord

        ii. Keep God's Worship Holy

   c. The Kingly Servant

        i. Use Our Freedom to Enjoy God's World

        ii. Own Our Responsibility to Do God's Will

3. The Covenant of Works Clarifies the Servant's Apostasy from the Lord

   a. The Adamic Apostasy

        i. Acknowledge Man's Changeability at His Best

        ii. Recognize Our Solidarity with Adam in Sin

   b. The Legal Apostasy

        i. Understand Man's Quest for External Legal Righteousness

        ii. Be Humbled under the Law's Righteous Verdict

   c. The Heinous Apostasy

        i. Grieve over the Gravity of Man's Ingratitude and Treason

        ii. Renounce All False Hopes of Saving Ourselves

4. The Covenant of Works Foreshadows the Redeeming Lord and Servant

   a. The Lord and Servant of Our Life

        i. Believe in Christ as the Lord and Life Giver

        ii. Believe in Christ as the Last and Life-Giving Adam

   b. The Lord and Servant of Our Location

        i. Serve the Lord Christ in Our Daily Vocations

        ii. Follow Christ through the Trials of This World

   c. The Lord and Servant of Our Law

        i. Obey Christ as the Lawgiver

        ii. Rest in Christ as the Surety of His People

4. The Lord and Servant of Our Love

        i. Rejoice in Christ's Love as the Husband of His Bride

        ii. Live in Christian Freedom, Not under the Covenant of Works

Section C: The Doctrine of Sin

IX. Introduction to the Doctrine of Sin

   A. Foundational Theological Truths about Sin

      1. Sin Is Not an Illusion

  c. Rebellion against Divine Authority—Consequence: Guilt

 C. Theological Definitions of Sin's Center and Root

  1. Sensuality versus Rationality

  2. Pride versus Humility

  3. Selfishness versus Love

  4. Idolatry versus the Worship of God

  5. Unbelief versus Faith in God's Word

  6. Rebellion against God's Law versus Obedience

 D. A Reflection on the Complex Meaning of Sin

 E. An Experiential Application of Sin's Definition: What Have I Done?

X. The Fall of Man into Sin and Misery

 A. The Transgression of Creatures against Their God

  1. The Rebellion of the Devil and His Angels

  2. Satan's Deceit regarding God's Word

   a. Doubt about God's Word

   b. Distortion of God's Word

   c. Denial of God's Word

  3. Man's Defiance of God's Word

 B. The Righteousness of God toward Sinners

  1. God's Silence during the Temptation

  2. God's Secret Judgments on Sinners

   a. Bitter Shame

   b. Guilt and Fear

  3. God's Patient Confrontation of Sinners

  4. God's Spoken Judgments upon Sinners

   a. God Spoke His Supreme Curse on Satan

   b. God Afflicted the Woman in Her Domestic Relationships

   c. God Punished the Man with Hard Labor and Death

 C. The Severity and Goodness of God

  1. God's Sanction of Threefold Death for Sin

   a. Spiritual Death

   b. Physical Death

   c. Eternal Death

  2. God's Seed-Promise of the Victor

   a. The Application of Salvation

   b. The Accomplishment of Salvation

   c. The Agent of Salvation

XI. The State of Sin
   A. Historical Theology of Original Sin
      1. The Early and Medieval Church
         a. The Early Church on Original Sin
         b. The Medieval Church on Original Sin
      2. Reformation Churches
         a. The Lutheran Churches on Original Sin
         b. The Early Reformed Churches on Original Sin
         c. Tridentine and Modern Roman Catholicism on Original Sin
         d. Other Streams of Sixteenth-Century Thought
            i. Socinians
            ii. Anabaptists
      3. Post-Reformation Churches
         a. Arminianism on Original Sin
         b. Reformed Orthodoxy on Original Sin
         c. Modern Attacks on the Doctrine of Original Sin
      4. Summary Reflection on the Historical Doctrine of Original Sin
   B. Biblical Teaching on Original Sin
      1. The Universal State of Sin
      2. The Deadly Dimensions of Original Sin
      3. The Imputation of Sin: The Guilt of Adam's First Sin
         a. The Apostle Paul's Doctrine of Adam and Christ
         b. God's Justice and Man's Guilt regarding Adam
      4. The Absence of Life: The Lack of Original Righteousness
      5. Total Depravity: The Corruption of Man's Whole Nature
         a. The Depravity of the Heart
         b. The Depravity of the Entire Life
      6. Total Inability: The Dominion of Sin
      7. The Amazing Patience and Mercy of God to Sinners
   C. The Free Choice of the Will
      1. The Terminology and Concept of Free Will
         a. The Biblical Terminology of Freedom and Will
         b. The Philosophical and Theological Concept of Free Will
      2. Free Will in the Fourfold State of Man
         a. The State of Innocence: Changeable Ability to Choose God

1. Suffering in Solidarity with Their Fallen Race
2. Suffering God's Judgments against Their Nation

B. God's Fatherly Purposes for Affliction upon His Saints
   1. God Humbles Them Deeply
   2. God Exposes Their Sins
   3. God Purges Their Corruption
   4. God Draws Them Near to Him
   5. God Conforms Them to Christ
   6. God Expands Their Joy
   7. God Increases Their Faith
   8. God Weans Them from This World
   9. God Prepares Them for Their Heavenly Inheritance

C. The Saints' Communion with Christ in Affliction
   1. The Piety of Christ
   2. The Perseverance of Christ
   3. The Power of Christ
   4. The Prayers of Christ
   5. The Presence of Christ
   6. The Plan of Christ

1

Introduction to Anthropology

It was part of Christ's wisdom that "he knew what was in man" (John 2:25). This knowledge enabled our Lord Jesus to deal skillfully with people ranging from Pharisees to prostitutes. Christ understood people. As the light of the world, he both revealed himself to us and revealed us to ourselves (John 3:19; cf. 15:22). Our Lord Jesus not only said many "I am" statements, but also made some very pointed "Ye are" statements.[1]

A true anthropology is foundational for right and wise ethical decisions. Much of the confusion of our age arises from false anthropologies. Stephen Wellum frames the matter provocatively: "Are we creatures of dignity because we are created in God's image? Or are we merely animals, by-products of an impersonal evolutionary process, things that can be, technologically speaking, manipulated and re-fashioned for whatever ends we deem best?"[2]

Of course, man is not the greatest subject for our minds to contemplate. There is a reason why the first of the loci considered in theology is the doctrine of God (theology proper). However, the Bible does reflect back to us an image of ourselves, just as a mirror reflects the face of a man so that he can see himself and make appropriate changes (James 1:23–24). This is the function of anthropology: to use the Word of God as a mirror in which to see what we are, so that, by grace, we may become what we should be.

---

1. Matt. 10:31; Luke 16:15; John 8:23, 44, 47; 10:26.
2. Stephen J. Wellum, "Editorial: The Urgent Need for a Theological Anthropology Today," *Southern Baptist Theological Journal* 13, no. 2 (Summer 2009): 2 (full article, 2–3).

What Is Theological Anthropology?

"What is man?" So asks more than one biblical writer. It is a question that has stirred the hearts of men, women, and children since the earliest days. Who am I? What are we, and why are we here? Human beings are unique among the creatures that walk upon this earth in their self-consciousness and reflection upon the meaning of their identity. The ancient philosophers considered it to be a maxim of wisdom, "Know thyself."[3]

There are many legitimate ways to study human life. For example, a medical doctor studies the anatomy of the human body in order to understand its functioning and remedy its illnesses. An athletic trainer might study the performance of people in a sport in order to help his clients play as well as possible. Likewise, we might study the behavior of groups of people in relationship to each other as an exercise in sociology and political science.

When the biblical writers ask, "What is man?" it is notable that they address the question to God. Job said in his pain, "What is man, that thou shouldest magnify him? And that thou shouldest set thine heart upon him?" (Job 7:17). David gazed up at the stars in wonder and exclaimed, "What is man, that thou art mindful of him? And the son of man, that thou visitest him?" (Ps. 8:4; cf. 144:3). In the biblical perspective, the question of man's identity cannot be separated from God and our relationship with him. John Calvin (1509–1564) said, "Nearly all the wisdom we possess, that is to say, true and sound wisdom, consists of two parts: the knowledge of God and of ourselves. But, while joined by many bonds, which one precedes and brings forth the other is not easy to discern."[4]

The theological discipline of anthropology seeks to address this question: What is man, especially in relation to God? The term *anthropology* derives from a combination of the Greek word for "man" or "human being" (*anthrōpos*) and the term for "speech," "thought," or "word" (*logos*). Theology, in general, is the knowledge and wisdom derived from meditating upon and obeying the word of God.[5] There-

---

3. This was one of the maxims inscribed at Delphi and often quoted by Greek philosophers. See Pausanias, *Description of Greece*, trans. W. H. S. Jones and H. A. Ormerod (Cambridge, MA: Harvard University Press; London: William Heinemann Ltd., 1918), 10.24.1, Perseus Digital Library, http://www.perseus.tufts.edu/hopper/text?doc=Paus.+10.24&fromdoc=Perseus%3Atext%3A1999.01.0160.
4. John Calvin, *Institutes of the Christian Religion*, ed. John T. McNeill, trans. Ford Lewis Battles, 2 vols. (Philadelphia: Westminster, 1960), 1.1.1.
5. For a study in what theology is and how it is rightly done, see *RST*, 1:39–173 (chaps. 1–9).

fore, theological anthropology is the submissive study of God's Word to learn about ourselves.

Why Study Anthropology?

Theology is both an academic discipline and a spiritual discipline. For this reason, it demands much of us. It is worthwhile, therefore, to start our study of anthropology by asking why this labor deserves our time and trouble. Why should we study the doctrine of man?[6]

Its Importance in the Bible

The Lord devotes much of the Bible to teaching us about who and what we are. Louis Berkhof (1873–1957) wrote "that man occupies a place of central importance in Scripture and that the knowledge of man in relation to God is essential to its proper understanding," for "man is not only the crown of creation, but also the object of God's special care."[7]

Since it is good to study the works of God (Pss. 92:4–5; 111:2), much more we should consider the climax of God's creative work, which is the creation of man (8:4), whom he has placed over all his other works (v. 6). Such a study enables us to adoringly exclaim, "O LORD, our Lord, how excellent is thy name in all the earth!" (vv. 1, 9). Calvin said about the study of man, "Among all God's works here is the noblest and most remarkable example of his justice, wisdom, and goodness."[8]

God's Word models for us a healthy attention to anthropology. Large tracts of the Scriptures consist of historical narratives and personal vignettes that expose us to the character of men and nations. Entire books, such as Ruth and Esther, describe no miracles and contain no prophetic revelations (though the secret providence of God looms in the background), but report only the faithful actions of godly people, whether peasant or queen. Proverbs focuses largely upon human life in God's world, offering pithy sayings that illuminate human nature and identify different kinds of people. The Bible also contains major doctrinal statements about man, such as "And God said, Let us make man in our image" (Gen. 1:26) and "You . . . were dead in trespasses and sins" (Eph. 2:1).

---

6. We are indebted for several thoughts in this chapter to Millard J. Erickson, *Christian Theology*, 3rd ed. (Grand Rapids, MI: Baker, 2013), 424–35.
7. Louis Berkhof, *Systematic Theology* (Edinburgh: Banner of Truth, 1958), 181.
8. Calvin, *Institutes*, 1.15.1.

We need self-knowledge for our salvation. Consider the epistle to the Romans, perhaps the preeminent exposition of the gospel in the Holy Scriptures. It is full of teaching about the work of Jesus Christ, how God applies that work by the Spirit and faith, and what response we should offer in thankful love. However, most of the first three chapters of Romans consist of the dark truths about human sin and its consequences. Evidently, anthropology is a crucial part of the gospel. We should appreciate its place in the Bible and study it carefully.

Its Integral Relation to Other Doctrines

Much of systematic theology consists of linking particular biblical truths so that we develop a biblical system of thought. Anthropology is part of this web of knowledge. It sheds light on the doctrine of God, for man was created in God's image (Gen. 1:26). Understanding humanity helps us to understand the person of our Lord Jesus Christ, for God's Son became "like unto his brethren" in all things human except sin (Heb. 2:17; 4:15). What God originally made us to be points ahead to what we will become if we are united to Christ, for the new creation will be like paradise—only better, because of the Lamb of God (Rev. 22:1–5).

Our origin as God's creation reinforces our moral obligation to obey his commandments. Anthropology, therefore, lays a foundation upon which we build our ethics. What is right or wrong in our treatment of others largely depends on who they are. Murder, adultery, theft, lying— these violations of the Ten Commandments are sins because of the nature of those against whom we commit them. The same is true of ethical questions regarding genetic engineering, cloning, abortion, euthanasia, racism, and economic oppression.

The doctrine of anthropology interfaces with every major teaching of the Christian faith. Right views of anthropology significantly strengthen our overall system of belief. Wrong views of anthropology unravel that system of belief and can undermine the very gospel of salvation.

Its Value to Other Academic Disciplines

Anthropology touches on the earthliest of topics in theology, so it overlaps to some degree with academic disciplines outside of the field of theology, such as biology, psychology, and sociology. In medicine, scientists are increasingly recognizing the close relationship between a healthy mind and a healthy body—and good mental health arises from functioning according to our human nature as God created us to be.

Anthropology answers pressing questions about the roots of human malice and suffering, and enables us to form a practical worldview by which we can live wisely in this world. It guards us from treating people like mere animals or trash. Calvin quoted Bernard of Clairvaux (1090–1153): "How can he upon whom God has set his heart be nothing?"[9] Yet anthropology also protects us from naively viewing human beings like angels on earth—despite how cute babies may be or how righteous we may seem in our own eyes. Calvin said, "We always seem to ourselves righteous and upright and wise and holy—this pride is innate in all of us—unless by clear proofs we stand convinced of our own unrighteousness. . . . We are not thus convinced if we look merely to ourselves and not also to the Lord, who is the sole standard by which this judgment must be measured."[10] A biblical view of man will make us not only better Christians, but also better parents and children, better friends, better neighbors, better citizens, and better employees and employers.

The doctrine of man touches a matter of vital concern for all people, because it is about each one of us. Millard Erickson writes, "The doctrine of humanity is one point where it is possible to get a toehold in the mind of the modern secular person."[11] Whether we are preaching or in a personal conversation with an unbeliever, anthropology provides ways to approach people through matters that they value highly, and then to lead them to God to find answers that an unbelieving worldview cannot provide.

Its Implications for Contemporary Existential Crises

As the nations in Europe and North America reap the bitter fruit of rejecting their Christian heritage, we see a disintegration of human culture all around us, whether we consider public morality, education, crime and safety, or media and the arts. This disintegration produces considerable anxiety and sometimes despair. Cultural forces erode our sense of personal identity and dissolve relationships into superficiality. Anthony Hoekema (1913–1988) said, "The growing supremacy of technology; the growth of

---

9. Quoted in Calvin, *Institutes*, 3.2.25.
10. Calvin, *Institutes*, 1.1.2.
11. Erickson, *Christian Theology*, 427.

bureaucracy; the increase of mass-production methods; and the growing impact of mass media . . . tend to depersonalize humanity."[12]

Profound and searching questions disturb those not lulled to sleep by pleasure, leisure, and entertainment, such as:

- Who am I? What are my roots? Do I belong to something bigger than myself?
- Why is my life so painful and confusing?
- What does it mean to be human? How are we different from animals?
- How can I know what is right and wrong? Are all things merely relative?
- Why are we in the mess that we are in?
- Why is it that despite our remarkable technology and information systems, we cannot solve basic problems such as social justice and world peace?
- Why do people who are not so different from us commit atrocities such as genocide, terrorism, human trafficking, and ethnic oppression?
- Where is our world going? Do I have any cause for hope?

The Bible offers us a perspective on human life that answers such questions in a manner that is *realistic* (so that we can deal wisely with ourselves and other people), *idealistic* (so that we can aim for high and worthy goals), and *optimistic* (so that we can keep striving for what is good and right with a solid hope of making a difference).

Its Impact upon Practical Ministry

Pastors need to understand and believe what the Bible teaches them about the people whom they serve. Shepherds must know their sheep (Prov. 27:23). While this requires personal relationships as pastors watch over the souls entrusted to them (Heb. 13:17), it also requires a deep knowledge of God's Word, which is sufficient to equip God's servants for their work (2 Tim. 3:17).

As Erickson points out, an imbalanced view of human nature can distort the way we do ministry.[13] If we view people as mere minds, we

---

12. Anthony A. Hoekema, *Created in God's Image* (Grand Rapids, MI: Eerdmans, 1986), 2.
13. Erickson, *Christian Theology*, 429.

will focus on intellectual ministry and expect teaching in itself to change them. If we believe that people are driven by emotions, then we will seek to motivate them by counseling them through past experiences and creating new emotional experiences. If we reduce people to their relationships, then our ministry might minimize doctrine and maximize fellowship. If we overspiritualize our understanding of people, we will treat physical problems as moral failures. We need a biblically balanced perspective on man in order to exercise a wise, balanced, holistic ministry.

Anthropology benefits all Christians in ministry. The Word of God reveals much about human nature that guides us in how to relate to other people. How can we serve people in Christ's name if we do not know who they are or what their deepest needs and problems are? Let us never forget that when we serve mankind, we care for "the masterpiece of the lower creation," as Thomas Boston (1676–1732) said.[14]

How Does the World Approach Anthropology?

The only thing more dangerous than the church being in the world is the world being in the church. Christians must resist the efforts of this wicked world to conform us to its mindset (Rom. 12:2). Therefore, before beginning our study of what the Bible teaches about mankind, we will review how people in this world commonly define man so that we can examine ourselves for how worldliness may have infiltrated our minds.

1. *Man defined by philosophical idealism.* In this perspective, the most real thing about human beings is their mind or spirit. The fleshly body is demeaned and viewed at best as a shell around the person and at worst as an evil to be escaped. Hoekema wrote, "We find this view in ancient Greek philosophy; according to Plato [427–347 BC], for example, what is real about man is his or her intellect or reason, which is actually a spark of the divine within the person that continues to exist after the body dies."[15] Idealism may result in an unhealthy emphasis upon the intellect, ascetic mistreatment of the body, or careless indulgence of physical desires. Though not as common in our present materialistic society, this elevation of spirit and degradation of body persists in some groups today and can infect the church. Paul writes that the Holy Spirit foretold the apostasy of people

---

14. Thomas Boston, *An Illustration of the Doctrines of the Christian Religion,* in *The Complete Works of the Late Rev. Thomas Boston, Ettrick,* ed. Samuel M'Millan (1853; repr., Stoke-on-Trent, England: Tentmaker, 2002), 1:177.
15. Hoekema, *Created in God's Image,* 2.

into demonic doctrines: "Forbidding to marry, and commanding to abstain from meats, which God hath created to be received with thanksgiving of them which believe and know the truth" (1 Tim. 4:3; cf. Col. 2:20–23).

2. *Man defined by physical biology.* Naturalism, with its denial of the invisible world, reduces all things to their scientifically measurable, physical being. Human beings, then, consist entirely of the material and processes of their physical bodies, and their minds are but the electrochemical interchanges of their brains. This belief has the practical implication that our problems are all rooted in biology and solved by physical mechanics and chemistry. In a culture dominated by the theory of evolution, it is common for people to view human beings as just highly developed animals or, in the case of some radical environmentalists, the worst of all animals. Man is no more, in the words of Desmond Morris, than "the naked ape."[16] Those who treat human life on a merely biological level nurture their bodies but neglect their souls. Christ warned, "For what shall it profit a man, if he shall gain the whole world, and lose his own soul?" (Mark 8:36).

3. *Man defined by sexual desires.* This form of naturalism, developed especially by psychologist Sigmund Freud (1856–1939), asserts that inner psychological conflict generally arises out of the frustration of one's desires for sexual satisfaction.[17] If man is essentially an evolved animal, then, it is claimed, his primary drive is the libido or energy that strives for survival and sexual fulfillment. As Erickson notes, this theory is adopted in its crudest form by prostitution and the pornography industry, which treat people as animals that exist only to give and receive sexual pleasure.[18] In popular media, lack of sexual fulfillment is often portrayed as the most pitiful of all conditions. In more recent times, people have also defined themselves by their perceived "sexual orientation," so that any criticism of their sexual practices is seen as an act of violence against their very persons. This definition of man is used to justify living to gratify "the lust of the flesh" (1 John 2:16).

4. *Man defined by material wealth.* No one can deny that food, clothing, and other necessities are essential to life or that the desire for money and possessions strongly motivates people (cf. Matt. 6:24–26). However, in

---

16. Desmond Morris, *The Naked Ape: A Zoologist's Study of the Human Animal* (London: Jonathan Cape, 1967).

17. Sigmund Freud, *A General Introduction to Psychoanalysis*, trans. G. Stanley Hall (New York: Horace Liveright, 1920), 259–60, 267–68.

18. Erickson, *Christian Theology*, 431.

this perspective, men are explicitly or implicitly defined by what they own. People often measure one another by their possessions or by their usefulness for increasing their own wealth—the kind of attitude rebuked by the apostle James (James 2:1–5). This is the theoretical perspective of Marxism, which interprets history according to economic factors and the struggle for wealth, though it also may be the practical perspective of capitalism. The Lord Jesus warned, "Take heed, and beware of covetousness: for a man's life consisteth not in the abundance of the things which he possesseth" (Luke 12:15). Only God can be that portion that satisfies us in life and in death (Ps. 73:24–28). Thomas Brooks (1608–1680) said, "The more money is increased, the more the love of money is increased; and the more the love of money is increased, the more the soul is unsatisfied. 'Tis only an infinite God, and an infinite good that can fill and satisfy the precious and immortal soul of man."[19]

5. *Man defined by individual freedom.* The Reformers sought to restore the freedom of the Christian from bondage to man's religious laws and doctrines. Later, the Puritans and various other movements struggled for freedom against what they perceived as political tyranny. However, in modern culture, *freedom* has been redefined as the liberty of the individual to do whatever he pleases without constraint, restraint, or rebuke, so long as it does not harm others. As Jean-Jacques Rousseau (1712–1778) said, "Obedience to a self-prescribed law is liberty."[20] Oppression, then, is the imposition of a standard that we did not choose for ourselves. William Ernest Henley (1849–1903) boldly captured the spirit of this assertion in his poem "Invictus":

> Out of the night that covers me,
> Black as the Pit from pole to pole,
> I thank whatever gods may be
> For my unconquerable soul. . . .
>
> It matters not how strait the gate,
> How charged with punishments the scroll,

---

19. Thomas Brooks, *London's Lamentations: or, a Serious Discourse Concerning that Late Fiery Dispensation that Turned Our (Once Renowned) City into a Ruinous Heap* (London: for John Hancock and Nathaniel Ponder, 1670), 194; cf. *The Works of Thomas Brooks* (Edinburgh: Banner of Truth, 1980), 6:259.

20. Jean-Jacques Rousseau, *The Social Contract, or Principles of Political Right*, trans. H. J. Tozer, Wordsworth Classics of World Literature (Ware, Hertfordshire, England: Wordsworth, 1998), 1.8 (20). Rousseau recognized that ideal liberty may be limited by the necessities of living in society.

I am the master of my fate:

I am the captain of my soul.[21]

Relativism and postmodernism take this principle to its logical end, asserting that each person has the right to construct his own reality, and that teaching absolute truth and morality is a form of hatred. In fact, teaching absolute truth and morality is an act of love (1 Cor. 13:6; Eph. 4:15).

6. *Man defined by social relationships.* In this view, man is less like individual birds than like a flock, whether geese flying in V formation or starlings swirling as one cloud. Family dynamics and social structures determine who we are and how we act. We find this idea illustrated in an extreme and speculative form in the Foundation series of books by science fiction author Isaac Asimov (1920–1992), who postulated a world where scientists could predict future history by a mathematical model of the behavior of large groups of people.[22] The Scriptures recognize that relationships affect behavior (Prov. 22:24; 1 Cor. 15:33), but emphasize individual responsibility before God (2 Cor. 5:10).

7. *Man defined by emotional health.* In our present culture, which is pervasively influenced by therapeutic psychology, people commonly believe that "the central goal of life is to be happy and to feel good about oneself."[23] This mindset appears in the lines sung by Whitney Houston (1963–2012): "Learning to love yourself—it is the greatest love of all."[24] People with this mindset search for jobs and relationships that provide emotional satisfaction and believe that the most important principle for life is to accept themselves and follow their hearts. The Christian worldview acknowledges the central place of joy in life (Neh. 8:10), but it subordinates immediate personal satisfaction to repentance from sin, self-denial, and sacrificial service for the sake of loving God and others in hope of ultimate life and joy in God's glory (Luke 9:23–26).

8. *Man undefined by existential absurdity.* Some people view human life with profound agnosticism and even cynicism. They regard life as mean-

21. William Ernest Henley, "Invictus," *Modern British Poetry*, ed. Louis Untermeyer (1920), http://www.bartleby.com/103/7.html.

22. Isaac Asimov, *The Foundation Trilogy: Three Classics of Science Fiction* (Garden City, NY: Doubleday, 1951–1953). Asimov was an atheistic humanist raised in Judaism.

23. Christian Smith with Melina Lundquist Denton, *Soul Searching: The Religious and Spiritual Lives of American Teenagers* (Oxford: Oxford University Press, 2005), 163.

24. Whitney Houston, "The Greatest Love of All," lyrics by Linda Creed, music by Michael Masser, *Whitney Houston* (Arista Records, February 14, 1985).

ingless and purposeless (nihilism). In the words of William Shakespeare's (1564–1616) Macbeth:

> Life's but a walking shadow, a poor player,
> That struts and frets his hour upon the stage,
> And then is heard no more: it is a tale
> Told by an idiot, full of sound and fury,
> Signifying nothing.[25]

Atheistic existentialism embraces this nihilistic perspective and irrationally calls people to forge their own meaning by being authentic to themselves. However, man is too small and transient to act as his own creator; he must find his reference point in the Lord who created all things for his pleasure and works all things according to the counsel of his will (Eph. 1:11; Rev. 4:11).

In each of the above definitions, a real component of human life has been elevated to a position it cannot sustain. Even existentialism reflects man's sense of mystery and alienation in a fallen world. This explains why each definition resonates with us to some extent, and yet ultimately fails to explain who we are. Hoekema observed, "One way of evaluating these views would be to say that they are one-sided; that is, they emphasize one aspect of the human being at the expense of others." However, he perceptively noted the deeper problem: "Since each of these above-named views of man considers one aspect of the human being to be ultimate, apart from any dependence on or responsibility to God the Creator, each of these anthropologies is guilty of idolatry: of worshiping an aspect of creation in the place of God."[26]

How Does the Bible Approach Anthropology?

The Word of God has a well-developed anthropology. We might summarize the Bible's approach to the question "What is man?" with the terms *theological* and *redemptive-historical*. It is *theological* anthropology because it understands man in a manner inseparable from his relationship with God. Man's purpose is inextricably bound up in the God who created him. The Westminster Shorter Catechism states it beautifully in its first question and answer: "What is the chief end of man? Man's chief end is to glorify God (1 Cor. 10:31; Rom. 11:36), and to enjoy him for ever (Ps. 73:25–28)."[27]

---

25. William Shakespeare, *Macbeth*, act 5, scene 5.
26. Hoekema, *Created in God's Image*, 4.
27. *Reformed Confessions*, 4:353.

Samuel Willard (1640–1707) explained that though we cannot add to God's essential glory, "to glorify God is to shew forth his glory, to declare him to be most glorious." We glorify God by thinking rightly of him and having hearts of adoration, fear, and trust toward him, with submission under his commands and quietness under his providence.[28]

The Bible's anthropology is also *redemptive-historical* because it considers man's condition according to the stages of human existence from creation and the fall to redemption and the new creation. Augustine of Hippo (354–430) contrasted the first stage with the last by saying that in paradise man was able to sin or not to sin against God, but in glory man will not be able to sin.[29] Augustine posited four stages for man's condition after the fall: (1) "before the law," when the sinner lives contentedly in wickedness; (2) "under the law," when the sinner is agitated by the law, but only to greater guilt and sin; (3) "under grace," when God gives faith and love so that the person fights against lust and grows in holiness; and (4) "full and perfect peace,"[30] which is glory itself.

Later, theologians reformulated this scheme, following the redemptive-historical pattern of creation, fall, redemption, and completion. Medieval theologians consolidated the first and second of Augustine's steps, "before the law" and "under the law," into the one spiritual state of sin and included man's state before the fall in their schema. The result, presented in the *Sentences* of Peter Lombard (c. 1096–1160)[31] and found in the writings of Reformed theologians such as Johannes Wollebius (1586–1629) and Francis Turretin (1623–1687), was the doctrine of human nature in its fourfold state.[32] Its most famous exposition may well have been by Boston.[33] In brief, these states are:

1. *The state of original innocence.* God created man in his image, which made man the pinnacle and ruler of a world that was very good (Gen.

---

28. Samuel Willard, *A Compleat Body of Divinity in Two Hundred and Fifty Expository Lectures on the Assembly's Shorter Catechism* (Boston: by B. Green and S. Kneeland for B. Eliot and D. Henchman, 1726), 5–6.

29. Augustine, *Enchiridion*, chap. 105, in NPNF[1], 3:271. See also Augustine, *On Rebuke and Grace*, chap. 33, in NPNF[1], 5:485; and *The City of God*, 22.30, in NPNF[1], 2:510.

30. Augustine, *Enchiridion*, chap. 118, in NPNF[1], 3:275. We note here the importance of legal conviction in Augustinian theology, a theme taken up in Lutheran and Reformed theology.

31. Peter Lombard, *The Sentences*, trans. Giulio Silano, 4 vols. (Toronto: Pontifical Institutes of Mediaeval Studies, 2007–2010), 2.25.5–6 (2:118).

32. Johannes Wollebius, *Compendium Theologiae Christianae*, 1.8.xii, in *Reformed Dogmatics*, ed. and trans. John W. Beardslee III, A Library of Protestant Thought (New York: Oxford University Press, 1965), 65. Henceforth cited as Wollebius, *Compendium*, 1.8.xii (65). See also Francis Turretin, *Institutes of Elenctic Theology*, trans. George Musgrave Giger, ed. James T. Dennison Jr., 3 vols. (Phillipsburg, NJ: P&R, 1992–1997), 8.1.9 (1:571).

33. Thomas Boston, *Human Nature in Its Fourfold State* (Edinburgh: Banner of Truth, 1964).

1:26, 31). In this state, man was free to do the good that pleased God and had the ability to not sin (Latin *posse non peccare*). However, he was also able to sin (*posse peccare*) against God.

2. *The state of fallen nature.* After Adam's sin, man's heart continuously generates moral evil and nothing but moral evil in all its motions (Gen. 6:5). Consequently, "there is none that doeth good" (Ps. 14:1). Fallen mankind, apart from Christ, does not have the ability to do anything pleasing to God, and so is unable to not sin (*non posse non peccare*).

3. *The state of grace.* Those sinners united to Christ by a Spirit-worked faith have been saved from the ruling power of sin (Romans 6), but not its presence in their souls (Rom. 7:14–25). Consequently, they are able to not sin (*posse non peccare*) and free to do good, but not perfectly.

4. *The state of glory.* When Christ comes and brings his people into his glory, they will be like him and see him as he is (1 John 3:2). Their complete salvation and perfect communion with him will make them unable to sin (*non posse peccare*).

We will refer to all four states, but our focus will be on the states of original innocence and fallen nature, for they are the burden of anthropology.[34] Calvin said, "This knowledge of ourselves is twofold: namely, to know what we were like when we were first created and what our condition became after the fall of Adam."[35]

Let us then proceed with our study of anthropology for the glory of God. Too often we have thought of ourselves without thinking of God. David Dickson (c. 1583–1662) said, "Oh, how great is our atheism! The Lord rub it off! Let us meditate on our making, that we may fall in love with our Maker."[36] Before you read any further, stop and pray for God to show himself to you as you learn more about yourself and your fellow human beings, and to cause you to love your Maker.

Sing to the Lord

God's Teaching and Guidance for Those Who Trust Him

To Thee I lift my soul,

In Thee my trust repose;

---

34. The state of grace is the subject of soteriology, and the state of glory, eschatology.

35. Calvin, *Institutes*, 1.15.1; cf. 2.1.1.

36. David Dickson, *Exposition of the Tenth Chapter of Job*, in *Select Practical Writings of David Dickson* (Edinburgh: The Committee of the General Assembly of the Free Church of Scotland for the Publication of the Works of Scottish Reformers and Divines, 1845), 1:37.

My God, O put me not to shame
Before triumphant foes.

None shall be put to shame
That humbly wait for Thee,
But those that willfully transgress,
On them the shame shall be.

Show me Thy paths, O Lord,
Teach me Thy perfect way,
O guide me in Thy truth divine,
And lead me day by day.

For Thou art God that dost
To me salvation send,
And patiently through all the day
Upon Thee I attend.

Recall Thy mercies, Lord,
Their tenderness untold,
And all Thy lovingkindnesses,
For they have been of old.

Psalm 25
Tune: Dennis
The Psalter, No. 60

Questions for Meditation or Discussion

1. What is theological anthropology?
2. What are several reasons why we should study theological anthropology?
3. How can an understanding of theological anthropology help us to minister to people?
4. What are some ways the world defines us merely by physical things?
5. Of these, what is one that you personally have embraced or encountered? How does that way of looking at people affect one's life?
6. What are some other (nonphysical) ways that the world tends to define us?
7. Choose one of the ways listed in your answer to question 6 and explain how it might shape a nation's culture if accepted by many people.

8. What is the fourfold state of man? What is the relation of each state to sin?

9. In which state would you consider yourself to be? Why?

Questions for Deeper Reflection

10. What does it mean that biblical anthropology is (1) theological and (2) redemptive-historical? Why is it important?

11. With regard to the four states of man, what harm might it do if we viewed and treated

- a person in the second state as if he were in the first?
- a person in the second state as if he were in the third?
- a person in the third state as if he were in the second?
- a person in the third state as if he were in the fourth?

Section A

The Doctrine of Creation

2

The Creation of the World, Part 1

God the Creator

The Bible roots our understanding of man in creation. Human life has purpose and meaning because we did not come into being by accident or by our own will, but by the will of God, who created both us and the world in which we live. Therefore, we belong to him and exist for him (Pss. 95:6; 100:3). All that we are and have is from him, through him, and to him as the God of the decree and creation (Rom. 11:36). The doctrine of creation anchors our worldview in God, directs our lives to his glory, and protects us against idolatry (Acts 14:15; Rev. 4:11). Herman Bavinck (1854–1921) underlined the importance of this doctrine for our view of God: "God is the sole, unique, and absolute cause of all that exists."[1]

William Perkins (1558–1602) summarized the doctrine of creation: "God made all things very good of nothing."[2] Wilhelmus à Brakel (1635–1711) put it in historical and theological perspective: "In traveling reversely through time, one will ultimately arrive at the beginning, beyond

---

1. Herman Bavinck, *Reformed Dogmatics*, ed. John Bolt, trans. John Vriend, 4 vols. (Grand Rapids, MI: Baker Academic, 2003–2008), 2:407. This, of course, does not mean God causes sin, for sin is not a being, but a distortion and perversion.
2. William Perkins, *A Golden Chain*, chap. 7, in *The Works of William Perkins*, ed. Joel R. Beeke, Derek W. H. Thomas, et al., 10 vols. (Grand Rapids, MI: Reformation Heritage Books, 2015–2020), 6:26.

which one cannot proceed. Beyond this there is nothing but God only who inhabits eternity." Brakel continued, "The eternal God, being desirous to reveal Himself and to communicate His goodness, has according to His eternal purpose and by His wisdom and omnipotence, created the universe and all things belonging to it."[3]

The doctrine of creation plays a crucial role in systematic theology.[4] Creation initiates the execution of God's decree and launches history. It is the starting point for the Bible and the beginning of God's self-revelation. It lays the foundation for ethics and worship, and anchors the gospel of Jesus Christ in the nature of God, the nature of man, and their inescapable relation as Creator and creature.[5] Second only to redemption by the incarnate Lord, creation is the greatest manifestation of the glory of God. It was also a doctrine that was attacked early in the history of the church, resulting in the opening affirmation of the Apostles' Creed: "I believe in God the Father, Almighty, Maker of heaven and earth."[6]

Theologians often discuss the doctrine of creation under the doctrine of God (theology proper), and understandably so. The study of who God is naturally leads to the study of his acts. God's acts include his eternal decree, the creation of the world in the beginning, and his providence over all things through the ages.

However, there are good reasons to discuss creation under anthropology as well. Biblically, the primary Scripture passage on the creation of the world (Genesis 1) reaches its high point with the creation of man in God's image (vv. 26–28) and leads directly into a more detailed revelation of man's callings and relationships (2:4–25). Theologically, God's purpose to glorify himself in the created world centers upon Christ Jesus our Lord, who is a man and the Savior of the new humanity (Eph. 3:9–11). Since we are men, we have a practical interest in understanding how the creation revolves around us as creatures and our relationships to the Creator and other creatures.

Therefore, our first step in answering the question "What is man?" is to answer the question "What is the origin of all things?"

---

3. Wilhelmus à Brakel, *The Christian's Reasonable Service*, ed. Joel R. Beeke, trans. Bartel Elshout, 4 vols. (Grand Rapids, MI: Reformation Heritage Books, 1992–1995), 1:265.
4. On the importance of the doctrine of creation, see Erickson, *Christian Theology*, 338–40.
5. Bavinck, *Reformed Dogmatics*, 2:407.
6. *The Three Forms of Unity*, 5.

False Theories of Origins

Every system of belief, or worldview, includes some explanation of the existence of the universe. Such an explanation is called a *cosmogony*, from the Greek phrase for how "the world has come to be" (*kosmos gegonen*). Monotheism asserts that the entire universe is the result of the creative work of the one true and living God. Bavinck noted, "The doctrine of creation is known only from revelation and is understood by faith." He cited Hebrews 11:3, "Through faith we understand that the worlds were framed by the word of God," explaining that non-Christian religions that posit a divine creation, such as Judaism and Islam, do so only because they are influenced by the testimony of God's Word.[7] God's general revelation makes known the Creator, but apart from special revelation, man's religions and philosophies significantly deviate from the doctrine of creation.

False views of creation spring from belief in false gods. There are many false belief systems in this world regarding God, including polytheism, pantheism, panentheism, and atheistic materialism.[8] *Polytheism* posits two or more first causes of the world. For instance, according to ancient pagan religions, the world (and many of its gods) arose from two or more gods in a process often involving either sexual reproduction or warfare. Consequently, though one god may be the highest, each deity has its own domain and none rules over all things. Polytheism may also appear as a fundamental dualism, such as the notion that both God and matter are eternal, and God's creation consists of his shaping and arranging preexisting matter that he did not make. Augustus Strong (1836–1921) said, "It contradicts our fundamental notion of God as absolute sovereign to suppose the existence of any other substance to be independent of his will. This second substance . . . not only limits God's power, but destroys his blessedness."[9]

A second category of explanations for the origin of the universe arises from *pantheism*, such as in Hinduism, where all being is part of the One. Consequently, even if this universe (and others) came into existence at a particular point in time, all things participate in unending cycles of expansion and contraction of the One. There is no real distinction between God and creation, for the One produced all by multiplying itself and said,

---

7. Bavinck, *Reformed Dogmatics*, 2:408.
8. On these false belief systems and their gods, see *RST*, 1:584–605 (chap. 31).
9. Augustus H. Strong, *Systematic Theology*, 3 vols. (Philadelphia: Griffith and Rowland, 1909), 2:381.

"I indeed am this creation."[10] Other pantheistic religions, such as ancient Gnosticism, teach that God produced the world through a sequence of emanations from his being, with each emanation descending to a lower level of being, resulting in a shared divinity within a spiritual hierarchy of being.[11]

In *panentheism*, God is the soul of the universe, and the world is like his body. In the ancient world, panentheism was promoted by Neo-Platonists such as Plotinus (d. 270). In the seventeenth century, Thomas Goodwin (1600–1679) complained that some men taught that all things were "but pieces and parcels of God himself." In the panentheistic error that Goodwin opposed, God has two aspects, one distinct from the world and another as the substance of the world and its parts.[12] Friedrich Schleiermacher (1768–1834), the father of theological liberalism, believed we cannot attribute to Genesis 1–2 "a genuine historical character," and regarded the doctrine of creation as irrelevant to the feeling of absolute dependence upon the divine (his central concept of religion).[13] Deeply influenced by Neo-Platonism and the pantheistic philosophy of Baruch Spinoza (1632–1677), Schleiermacher opened the door for panentheism to flood into modern theological liberalism.[14] In the twentieth century, process theologians developed a view of God in which he consists of two poles: an eternal absolute and the temporal world. Such a deity did not create the world and he does not rule it, but is one with it, suffers with it, develops with it, and seeks to persuade it to develop toward good.[15]

Pantheism and panentheism are distant concepts from the "God that made the world and all things therein, seeing that he is Lord of heaven and earth" (Acts 17:24). As Goodwin pointed out, such views have no place for a God who relates to the world like a potter to the clay (Rom. 9:21), who will not give his glory to another and rebukes idolatry (Isa. 42:8), who

---

10. Brihadaranyaka Upanishad, 1.4.1–5, cited in *The Upanishads*, trans. F. Max Müller, 2 vols. (Oxford: Oxford University Press, 1884), 2:85–86.

11. Strong, *Systematic Theology*, 2:383–84.

12. Thomas Goodwin, *Of the Creatures, and the Condition of Their State by Creation*, in *The Works of Thomas Goodwin*, 12 vols. (1861–1866; repr., Grand Rapids, MI: Reformation Heritage Books, 2006), 7:3–4.

13. Friedrich Schleiermacher, *The Christian Faith*, ed. H. R. Mackintosh and J. S. Stewart, 2 vols. (New York: Harper and Row, 1963), 36, 40 (1:143, 151).

14. On Schleiermacher's views, see *The Christian Faith*, 8.2, 51 (1:39, 201); Bavinck, *Reformed Dogmatics*, 2:411; and John W. Cooper, *Panentheism—The Other God of the Philosophers: From Plato to the Present* (Grand Rapids, MI: Baker Academic, 2006), 80–88.

15. John S. Feinberg, *No One Like Him: The Doctrine of God*, Foundations of Evangelical Theology (Wheaton, IL: Crossway, 2001), 160–70.

obliges men to obedience and judges the wicked, and who redeems sinners, for they erase the distinction between God and his creations.[16]

A fourth category of unbiblical cosmogony is *materialism*. In this perspective, the physical matter and energy of the universe has always existed, and it is all that has ever existed. In Epicureanism, as taught by Epicurus (341–270 BC), all things are thought to consist of many indivisible atoms whose random collisions over time produced the universe and all things in it, including human beings.[17] Consequently, the driving force in the universe is random physical interactions. This philosophical view experienced a revival in the Renaissance and was opposed by the Reformers.[18] Materialism is often associated with atheism.

Charles Darwin (1809–1882) proposed the materialistic theory of evolution to explain the origin of all living creatures by the mindless natural selection of those organisms most fit to survive and propagate themselves. His theory was adapted by later scientists into Neo-Darwinism, with the further explanation of evolution through gradual change prompted by random genetic mutations over millions of years. The extremely long time required by evolution fits with the "big bang" theory that the universe arose spontaneously out of a singularity of inconceivable density and energy about fourteen billion years ago, with the earth forming about four and a half billion years ago. The big bang and evolutionary theories presently form the dominant perspective on origins in Europe and North America. We will examine these theories in relation to the Christian faith in more detail in a later chapter.[19]

In reality, the categories of polytheism, pantheism, panentheism, and materialism overlap. Polytheism on a popular level often goes hand in hand with pantheism on a more philosophical level. Pantheism and panentheism encourage the worship of the creature. Materialists, while they deny the existence of God, tend to divinize the world. Popular astronomer Carl Sagan (1934–1996) claimed, "The universe is all that is or ever was or ever will be," which is materialism, but he also spiritualized secular science into a kind of religious devotion, saying, "Our feeblest contemplations

---

16. Goodwin, *Of the Creatures*, in *Works*, 7:4–6.

17. S. R. Obitts, "Epicureanism," in *Evangelical Dictionary of Theology*, ed. Walter A. Elwell (Grand Rapids, MI: Baker, 1984), 358; and Susan E. Schreiner, *The Theater of His Glory: Nature and the Natural Order in the Thought of John Calvin* (Grand Rapids, MI: Baker Academic, 1991), 16–21.

18. Nicolaas H. Gootjes, "Calvin on Epicurus and the Epicureans: Background to a Remark in Article 13 of the Belgic Confession," *Calvin Theological Journal* 40 (2006): 34–35 (full article, 33–48).

19. See chap. 5.

of the cosmos stir us. . . . We know we are approaching the greatest of mysteries."[20] If the universe has no Creator, then it becomes our god. As the apostle Paul explained, those who refuse to glorify God and give him thanks exchange "the glory of the uncorruptible God" for the visible things of creation (Rom. 1:21–23).

God's Work of Creation

Having reviewed alternative views of the universe, we now turn to the Word of God. Whereas mankind can only speculate about the origin of the world, not having been there to witness it (Job 38:4), the eternal God is able to speak from direct knowledge of these events. The words of the Bible are the pure and trustworthy words of God (Prov. 30:5).

The doctrine of creation is taught in many places in the Bible, but it is good for us to begin "in the beginning," with the foundational text on creation—indeed, the foundation of the whole Bible—Genesis 1:1–2:3.[21] The text is well known, so we simply summarize it:

- *Day one*: In the beginning, God created the heavens and the earth, and made light, resulting in the sequence of day and night.
- *Day two*: God divided the waters above the earth, most likely the clouds, from the waters below the earth—that is, the seas, rivers, lakes, and subterranean aquifers.[22]
- *Day three*: God gathered the waters so that the dry land appeared, naming the former "seas" and the latter "earth." God also made the plants.
- *Day four*: God created lights in the heaven to distinguish days, seasons, and years.
- *Day five*: God created sea creatures and flying creatures, and blessed them with the call to be fruitful and multiply.
- *Day six*: God created land animals. God then created man and woman in his image and blessed them with the call to be fruitful, multiply, and rule over the other living creatures.

---

20. Carl Sagan, *Cosmos* (1980; repr., New York: Ballantine Books, 2013), 1.

21. Genesis 2:4 begins a new section in Genesis that focuses on man's creation. The beginning of the new section is marked by the phrase "These are the generations," and it employs the distinctive name "the Lord God," whereas Gen. 1:1–2:3 always refers to "God."

22. See Ps. 148:4, 8. The ancient people of Israel understood that rain came from clouds (Judg. 5:4; 1 Kings 18:44–45; Job 26:8; 36:27–28; Pss. 77:16; 147:8; Eccles. 11:3). See John Calvin, *Commentaries* (repr., Grand Rapids, MI: Baker, 2003), on Gen. 1:6–8; and Geerhardus Vos, *Reformed Dogmatics*, trans. and ed. Richard B. Gaffin et al., 5 vols. (Bellingham, WA: Lexham Press, 2012–2016), 1:170.

- *Day seven*: God ceased from his creative work, and blessed and sanctified the day.

The creation account of Genesis draws attention to the uniqueness and universality of God's creative work, as well as to the glory of the One who performed it.

The Uniqueness of the Work of Creation

The work of creation marked the "beginning" of the universe (Gen. 1:1). The week of Genesis 1:1–2:3 is "the beginning of the creation" (Mark 10:6; cf. 13:19). God invented the sequence of days, so that the first day of the creation week marks the first day of history (Gen. 1:5). Prior to that day, there was no time, but only God.[23] Paul writes that God decreed his purpose of grace in Christ "before the ages began" (2 Tim. 1:9; Titus 1:2 ESV); that is, before God initiated temporal history with his act of creating the heavens and the earth.[24] As Augustine said, God did not make the world "in time," as if creation fell upon some point in an already existing stream of time, but he made the world "with time"—that is, he created the world and time together.[25] Bavinck said, "Before that moment there is nothing but the deep silence of eternity." Eternity does not consist of empty ages of inactivity, but of no ages at all. "In the absence of the world there is no time, and therefore no empty time."[26] God is not the Lord in time, but the Lord before time and the Lord over time, because he is the Creator of time.[27] Our time-bound language fails us, and we must bow in worship before the God who transcends time itself.

The work of creation is also unique because it does not continue, for "on the seventh day God ended his work"—that is, "all his work which God created and made" (Gen. 2:2–3). God continues to work in providence, but his work of creation was completed in the first week. As Peter Lombard, drawing from the Augustinian tradition, said, "He ceased making new creatures."[28] The basic categories of God's creatures were established in that first week.

---

23. Tertullian, *Against Marcion*, 2.3, in *ANF*, 3:299.
24. See Ps. 90:2; Prov. 8:22–31; Matt. 13:35; 25:34; John 17:5, 24; Rom. 16:25; Eph. 1:4; 1 Pet. 1:20; Rev. 13:8; 17:8.
25. Augustine, *The City of God*, 11.6, in *NPNF*[1], 2:208.
26. Bavinck, *Reformed Dogmatics*, 2:426–27.
27. Lombard, *The Sentences*, 2.2 (2:10).
28. Lombard, *The Sentences*, 2.12.5.4 (2:53); cf. his citations of Augustine and Bede in 2.15.7 (2:66).

The Universality of the Work of Creation

The statement that "God created the heaven and the earth" (Gen. 1:1) indicates that God made all parts or places in the universe.[29] Consequently, God is the universal God. The Bible often identifies the Lord as the God who made heaven and earth in order to assert his universal dominion.[30] All things are his creations, and he is "the most high God, the possessor of heaven and earth" (14:19, 22), the "God of heaven and earth" (Ezra 5:11; cf. Gen. 24:3). He is "the living God, which made heaven, and earth, and the sea, and all things that are therein" (Acts 14:15). The New Testament states several times that God created "all things."[31]

"Heaven" includes the special dwelling place of God and the angels.[32] Though Genesis focuses attention upon the earth (1:2), other texts in the Bible elaborate that God created the heavenly realm, including the invisible angelic powers (Ps. 148:1–6; Col. 1:16).[33]

God also created all things in the visible universe. It is evident from the rest of Genesis 1 that God created everything from the stars above to the seas below, and all things in them. The scope of creation is comprehensive. Therefore, the Bible knows only two categories of being: God and what God made. There is no third alternative. We may say of everything that is not God, "God made that. It belongs to him." The universality of God's creation implies that all things that are not God, material or spiritual, have their beginning in creation. God did not make the world out of any preexisting substance, but out of nothing (Latin *ex nihilo*).[34] Hebrews 11:3 says, "Through faith we understand that the worlds were framed by the word of God, so that things which are seen were not made of things which do appear." This is an important doctrine because it implies that no substance exists in the universe apart from God's will. Millard Erickson writes, "The doctrine of creation is first and rather obviously a statement that there is no ultimate reality other than God. There is no room for dualism . . . two ultimate principles."[35] All is either God or from God.

---

29. For examples of heaven and earth representing all places, see Deut. 3:24; 4:39; 2 Chron. 6:14; Job 20:27; 28:24; Ps. 73:25.

30. Ex. 20:11; 2 Kings 19:15; 2 Chron. 2:12; Neh. 9:6; Pss. 115:15; 121:2; 124:8; 134:3; 146:6; Isa. 37:16; Jer. 32:17; 51:15; Acts 4:24; 14:15; 17:24; Col. 1:16; Rev. 10:6; 14:7; cf. Gen. 24:3; 1 Kings 8:23; 2 Chron. 36:23; Ezra 1:2; 5:11; Ps. 95:4–5; Jonah 1:9.

31. John 1:3; 1 Cor. 8:6; Eph. 3:9; Col. 1:16; Rev. 4:11.

32. Gen. 28:12, 17; cf. 1 Kings 22:19; 2 Cor. 12:2.

33. Wollebius, *Compendium*, 1.5.(1).viii.1 (55). For the doctrine of angels, see *RST*, 1:1109–32 (chap. 54).

34. For a more detailed defense of creation *ex nihilo*, see the next chapter.

35. Erickson, *Christian Theology*, 345.

Creation and the Glory of God

God revealed his work of creation to his people in order to manifest his glory as the Creator and Lord of all things.[36] The Westminster Confession of Faith (4.1) says, "It pleased God the Father, Son, and Holy Ghost, for the manifestation of the glory of His eternal power, wisdom, and goodness, in the beginning, to create, or make of nothing, the world, and all things therein whether visible or invisible, in the space of six days; and all very good."[37] John Calvin compared creation to a theater of God's glory, saying, "Let us not be ashamed to take pious delight in the works of God open and manifest in this most beautiful theater."[38]

The Uniqueness of the Creator

Creation is the work of a unique agent. The Hebrew verb translated as "create" (*qal* of *bara*) is used "always of divine activity."[39] Throughout the text, God is the One speaking and working. Derek Kidner (1913–2008) commented, "It is no accident that *God* is the subject of the first sentence of the Bible, for this word dominates the whole chapter and catches the eye at every point of the page: it is used some thirty-five times in as many verses of the story. The passage, indeed the Book, is about Him first of all; to read it with any other primary interest (which is all too possible) is to misread it."[40]

Genesis 1 sharply distinguishes God from all other things that exist. "In the beginning," God already is, but the world was first coming to be. Genesis 1 reveals a world with no effective competitors to God. Unlike the ancient Babylonian creation myth of the Enuma Elish, Genesis depicts no battle among the gods, but only the quiet progress of a world subject to the will of its sovereign Maker. Whereas the sun and moon were often worshiped in the ancient world, Genesis does not even name them, but only calls them "lights" (vv. 14–16) and depicts them as subject to God.

Therefore, the doctrine of creation reveals God as the eternal and only Creator. God alone is eternal (Ps. 90:2; Isa. 57:15). Goodwin noted, "The

---

36. The doctrine of God, including his attributes and Trinity, is explored in detail in *RST*, vol. 1. Here we deal specifically with how his work of creation manifests his glory.

37. *Reformed Confessions*, 4:239.

38. Calvin, *Institutes*, 1.14.20.

39. Francis Brown, Samuel Rolles Driver, and Charles Augustus Briggs, *Enhanced Brown-Driver-Briggs Hebrew and English Lexicon* (Oxford: Clarendon, 1977), 135.

40. Derek Kidner, *Genesis*, Tyndale Old Testament Commentaries (Downers Grove, IL: InterVarsity Press, 1967), 43.

best of creatures have but half an eternity, they are to everlasting, but not from everlasting. This is proper to God only."[41] God alone is Creator, and this role distinguishes him from all other gods (Neh. 9:6; Jer. 10:10–12).[42] Psalm 96:5 says, "For all the gods of the nations are idols: but the LORD made the heavens." In Isaiah 44:24, God says, "I am the LORD that maketh all things; that stretcheth forth the heavens alone; that spreadeth abroad the earth by myself." The words "by myself" emphasize that no creature could share in this work; God alone creates. In stark contrast to the worthless idols of the nations (vv. 9–20), the Lord uses his act of creating the world to demonstrate his uniqueness: "Is there a God beside me? Yea, there is no God; I know not any" (v. 8).

This unique work by a unique Being leads to the unique honor belonging to the Creator. Hezekiah confessed, "O LORD of hosts, God of Israel, that dwellest between the cherubims, thou art the God, even thou alone, of all the kingdoms of the earth: thou hast made heaven and earth" (Isa. 37:16). Johannes Wollebius rightly stated, "The work and honor of creation ought not to be attributed to any creature, even the angels, but only to God."[43] We must reject the teaching that creatures can become cocreators with God or even instruments of God's creative work, a false doctrine used to wrongly exalt angels and men.[44] God works through means in providence, but not in creation.

The doctrine of creation lays the foundation for a basic element of the Christian worldview: the difference between the Creator and the creation.[45] Louis Berkhof wrote, "The world is not God nor any part of God, but something absolutely distinct from God." Yet he also noted, "The world is always dependent on God." Therefore, Berkhof said, "God is not only the transcendent God, infinitely exalted above all His creatures; He is also the immanent God, who is present in every part of His creation, and whose Spirit is operative in all the world."[46]

We must give our worship and supreme allegiance to no other being than the Creator of heaven and earth. Calvin said, "It was his will that the history

---

41. Goodwin, *Of the Creatures*, in *Works*, 7:7.
42. Bavinck, *Reformed Dogmatics*, 2:421.
43. Wollebius, *Compendium*, 1.5.(1).ii (54).
44. Turretin, *Institutes*, 5.2 (1:433–36). Turretin attributed this error to some medieval Catholics in their doctrine of transubstantiation (Lombard, Gabriel Biel, Francisco Suarez; *contra* Thomas Aquinas, Bonaventure, etc.), as well as to Remonstrants and Socinians in their doctrine of creation through the angels. In more recent times, the idea of our being cocreators with God has been advocated by process theologians and open theists.
45. Willard, *A Compleat Body of Divinity*, 109.
46. Berkhof, *Systematic Theology*, 134.

of Creation be made manifest, in order that the faith of the church, resting upon this, might seek no other God but him who was put forth by Moses as the Maker and Founder of the universe."[47] In worshiping God alone, we must approach him as the Holy One who is infinitely exalted above us and all our places and acts of worship, for he made all things (Isa. 66:1–2).[48] The thought of being alienated from this Creator-God and under his wrath should be unbearable to us. Brakel wrote, "The contemplation of God as Creator first of all makes it very evident that all your security, freedom, rest, peace, and happiness consist in the goodness and love of your Maker toward you."[49]

The Trinity of the Creator

God progressively revealed through his Word that he is one God who eternally exists in three persons. God is most fully made known in the New Testament as the Father, the Son, and the Holy Spirit.[50] Genesis 1 contains references to plurality in God that we may cautiously receive as early, partial revelations of what God would later make known in the doctrine of the Trinity. When the text says, "God created the heaven and the earth" (Gen. 1:1), the verb "created" is in the singular form, indicating one subject. However, we read next, "And the earth was without form, and void; and darkness was upon the face of the deep. And the Spirit of God moved upon the face of the waters" (v. 2). The phrase "the Spirit of God" is the same expression used elsewhere for the Holy Spirit, who empowers God's servants.[51] We interpret the image of the Spirit's activity according to Deuteronomy 32:10–12: "He found him in a desert land, and in the waste [tohu, the same word as "without form"] howling wilderness; he led him about, he instructed him, he kept him as the apple of his eye. As an eagle stirreth up her nest, fluttereth [rakhaph, the same word as "moved"] over her young, spreadeth abroad her wings, taketh them, beareth them on her wings: so the LORD alone did lead him, and there was no strange god with him." Therefore, we interpret Genesis 1:2 not as speaking of "the wind of God," but as revealing that the Spirit of God acted upon the primeval creation like a tender mother bird over

---

47. Calvin, Institutes, 1.14.1.
48. See the exposition of this text in Goodwin, Of the Creatures, in Works, 7:10–21.
49. Brakel, A Christian's Reasonable Service, 1:278.
50. On the doctrine of the Trinity, see RST, 1:876–953 (chaps. 45–47).
51. Ex. 31:3; 35:31; Num. 24:2; 2 Chron. 15:1; 24:20.

its children in a wilderness, nurturing God's work.[52] Calvin said, "The eternal Spirit had always been in God, while with tender care he supported the confused matter of heaven and earth, until beauty and order were added."[53]

The strongest suggestion of plurality in God appears in Genesis 1:26: "Let *us* make man in *our* image." Both the pronouns and the verb translated as "make" are plural in the Hebrew text.[54] Since there is no hint in the Bible that man is the image of any being except God, this text pictures God in conversation with God as a plurality of persons. The angels did not create man. Some theologians have proposed that this is the plural of majesty, the royal "we" that kings and queens sometimes use. However, there does not appear to be evidence of such a practice by royalty recorded in the Old Testament Scriptures.[55] It is best to take this text to indicate a plurality of persons in God.[56]

Are there hints in Genesis of what that plurality might entail? We have already noted the agency of the Spirit in creation (cf. Job 26:13; 33:4). Genesis coordinates the agency of the Spirit in creation with the agency of God's Word, such as, "And God said, Let there be light: and there was light" (Gen. 1:3).[57] In the Old Testament, God's Word sometimes acts as an agent sent by God to do his will with divine power, somewhat like the divine angel of the Lord.[58] The Word of the Lord has supernatural qualities, and the godly praise God's Word with reverence.[59] John gives further clarity to the distinct personality of the Word when he writes, "In the beginning was the Word, and the Word was with God, and the Word was God. The same was in the beginning with God. All things were made by him; and without him was not any thing made that was made. . . . And the Word was made flesh, and dwelt among us" (John 1:1–3, 14). Therefore, Christ is the Creator of the world along with the Father and the Spirit (Heb. 1:10). Christ and the Spirit are not merely

---

52. Sinclair B. Ferguson, *The Holy Spirit*, Contours in Christian Theology (Downers Grove, IL: InterVarsity Press, 1996), 19–20.

53. Calvin, *Institutes*, 1.13.22.

54. For similar constructions used of God, see Gen. 3:22; 11:7; Isa. 6:8.

55. Stephen Charnock, *The Existence and Attributes of God*, in *The Works of Stephen Charnock*, 6 vols. (Edinburgh: Banner of Truth, 2010), 2:130; and Vos, *Reformed Dogmatics*, 1:40–41.

56. Calvin, *Commentaries*, on Gen. 1:26; and Feinberg, *No One Like Him*, 450–51.

57. See also Gen. 1:6, 9, 11, 14, 20, 22, 24, 26, 28; cf. Ps. 33:6.

58. Pss. 107:20; 147:15, 18; Isa. 55:11.

59. Pss. 56:4, 10; 119:89, 120, 129, 160–62; Isa. 66:2. See John M. Frame, *The Doctrine of God*, A Theology of Lordship (Phillipsburg, NJ: P&R, 2002), 473.

instruments of the Creator[60] or co-Creators subordinate to the Father, but are one Creator.[61]

The Creator is the triune God. Let us reverence all three persons of the triune God as worthy of our praise (Rev. 4:11). Worthy is the Father! Worthy is the Son! Worthy is the Spirit! Let us praise him, three in one.

The Power of the Creator

Creation was a work of immense power, as is evident from the vast size of the universe. However, a striking feature of the creation account is the ease with which God performed it. There is no hint of hard labor. Rather, the Bible reveals creation by divine fiat (compare the Latin words *fiat lux*, or, "Let there be light," Gen. 1:3 Vulgate). God's creation of the universe by his word implies that the universe did not come from him by some necessity, like streams from a spring, but was made according to the freedom of God's will, like a building from a builder.[62] Therefore, God always relates to the created world freely according to his will (Pss. 115:3, 15; 135:6).

God created the world by the mere expression of his will brought into effect by his Spirit (Ps. 33:6, 9).[63] Samuel Willard said, "His omnipotent will gave the being of all things, and this is called his powerful word."[64] When we consider that our sun is over three hundred thousand times more massive than the earth and that God created innumerable stars with a mere word, the power of the Creator should fill us with awe and astonishment.[65]

Genesis does not depict the work of creation as a long process or struggle, but as a series of effectual acts. John Gill (1697–1771) said, "He

---

60. The Scriptures say that all things were made "by" or "through" (*en* and *dia*) the Son (John 1:3; Col. 1:16; Heb. 1:2). However, Charnock pointed out that those two prepositions do not always indicate an instrument, but sometimes agency or effective cause. Charnock, *The Existence and Attributes of God*, in *Works*, 2:167–68. See *dia* in Rom. 11:36; 1 Cor. 1:9; Eph. 1:1; 1 Thess. 4:2; Heb. 2:10; and *en* in Acts 20:19; Gal. 1:24; Eph. 3:13; Heb. 10:10.

61. On the special attribution of the work of creation to the Father as the first person of the Trinity, see Johannes Polyander, Antonius Walaeus, Antonius Thysius, and Andreas Rivetus, *Synopsis Purioris Theologiae, Synopsis of a Purer Theology: Latin Text and English Translation, Volume 1, Disputations 1–23*, trans. Riemer A. Faber, ed. Dolf te Velde, Rein Ferwerda, Willem J. van Asselt, William den Boer, Riemer A. Faber (Leiden: Brill, 2014), 10.7 (1:249).

62. Turretin, *Institutes*, 5.1.1 (1:431); and William Ames, *A Sketch of the Christian's Catechism*, trans. Todd M. Rester (Grand Rapids, MI: Reformation Heritage Books, 2008), 51.

63. Note, "God said" (Gen. 1:3, 6, 9, 11, 14, 20, 24, 26, 28–29) and "it was so" (vv. 7, 9, 11, 15, 24, 30).

64. Willard, *A Compleat Body of Divinity*, 110.

65. Scientists calculate that the sun's mass is about 4×10^{30} pounds (4 followed by 30 zeroes). Scientists estimate that our galaxy alone contains 100 billion stars, and the universe may contain many billions of galaxies.

gave the word, and every creature started [came suddenly] into being in a moment. . . . Let there be light, and there was light."[66] We find the power of divine fiat illustrated in Christ's commanding supernatural healings, casting out demons, and calming stormy seas—all with a mere word.[67] The latter miracle identifies Christ as the Lord of heaven and earth, for it is God who calms the sea (Pss. 65:7; 107:29; Jonah 1:4–16). The mere word of God immediately accomplishes his will.

Creation by divine fiat demonstrates the ability of God to work apart from any means.[68] Calvin pointed out that the order of creation teaches us this lesson: God made the light before the sun, moon, and stars to prove that he can supply our needs apart from any instrument.[69] Similarly, God made the plants before the sun to demonstrate that "God acts through the creatures, not as if he needed external help, but because it was his pleasure."[70] Stephen Charnock (1628–1680) said, "The carpenter cannot work without his rule, and axe, and saw, and other instruments. . . . But in creation there is nothing necessary to God's bringing forth a world but a simple act of his will."[71]

Some of the prophets encourage the faith of God's people with the reminder that God is the One whose power was able to create the universe. Zechariah declares that the almighty power by which God created the world guarantees the final victory of his people over their enemies (Zech. 12:1–9). Jeremiah, anticipating the deliverance of Israel from exile, exclaimed, "Ah Lord GOD! Behold, thou hast made the heaven and the earth by thy great power and stretched out arm, and there is nothing too hard for thee" (Jer. 32:17). The infinite power of the Creator should move us to trust confidently in his ability to save people from their sins (Matt. 19:25–26). Salvation is a new creation,[72] and therefore it exhibits the supernatural freedom of God to do his will. As Perkins said, "By His word He created man's heart when it was not. And He can and will as easily create in us all new hearts."[73]

---

66. John Gill, *A Complete Body of Doctrinal and Practical Divinity* (Paris, AR: The Baptist Standard Bearer, 1995), 261. Henceforth cited as Gill, *Body of Divinity*.
67. Matt. 8:2–3, 5–13, 16, 23–27. We are indebted to Andy McIntosh, retired professor of thermodynamics at Leeds University, for this thought.
68. Perkins, *An Exposition of the Symbol*, in *Works*, 5:47.
69. Calvin, *Commentaries*, on Gen. 1:3.
70. Calvin, *Commentaries*, on Gen. 1:11–13.
71. Charnock, *The Existence and Attributes of God*, in *Works*, 2:130.
72. 2 Cor. 5:17; Gal. 6:15; Eph. 2:10, 15; 4:24.
73. Perkins, *An Exposition of the Symbol*, in *Works*, 5:47.

The Authority of the Creator

God's authority, or right to rule, arises logically from the fact that he made all things, and therefore, he owns them. David says in Psalm 24:1–2, "The earth is the LORD's, and the fulness thereof; the world, and they that dwell therein. For he hath founded it upon the seas, and established it upon the floods." This shows that God is "the King of glory," who must be honored and obeyed by those who would draw near to him (vv. 3–10). Therefore, the proper use of all God's creatures is to glorify the Creator, and not any idol, for idols created nothing and can claim nothing as truly their own (1 Cor. 10:25–31; cf. Ps. 115). We must worship God as the King over all, for he made all things (Ps. 95:1–6).

The Creator demonstrated his ownership and authority by interpreting his creation through the acts of naming it and evaluating its goodness.[74] Genesis 1 repeatedly states, "And God called" (vv. 5, 8, 10), when he assigned names to aspects of his world: day, night, heaven, earth, and sea. It was God who gave the name "man" (*adam*) to the human race (5:2). Genesis also implies God's authority in the statement "And God saw . . . it was good."[75] The first instances of things being counted as "good" in the Bible are found in God's evaluation. The Bible often says that someone's conduct was good or evil "in the sight of the LORD."[76] God is the primary observer of his creatures, and his judgment carries supreme weight.

The authority of God as the Creator undergirds our obligation to obey his commandments. Since the Creator is the Lord and owner of all that he made, all creatures stand in relation to him as servants. Psalm 119:90–91 says, "Thy faithfulness is unto all generations: thou hast established the earth, and it abideth. They continue this day according to thine ordinances: for all are thy servants." This truth should move us to study God's laws and depend upon him for illumination. Psalm 119:73 says, "Thy hands have made me and fashioned me: give me understanding, that I may learn thy commandments."

God's universal authority over all places and peoples also lays the foundation for the kingdom of Christ over all nations. Psalm 89 is a song about the royal Son of David, and it says, "The heavens are thine,

---

74. Frame, *The Doctrine of God*, 294.
75. Gen. 1:4, 10, 12, 18, 21, 25; cf. v. 31.
76. Gen. 38:7; Lev. 10:19; Num. 32:13; Deut. 6:18; 9:18; 12:25, 28; etc., including dozens of times in Kings and Chronicles. Literally, "sight" is "eyes."

the earth also is thine: as for the world and the fulness thereof, thou hast founded them. The north and the south thou hast created them" (Ps. 89:11–12). Thus, the risen Lord, about to take his rightful seat as supreme King, declared, "All power [*exousia*, literally, "authority"] is given unto me in heaven and in earth" (note the allusion to Gen. 1:1), and commanded his church to make obedient disciples of all nations (Matt. 28:18–20).

The supreme authority of the Creator demonstrates his right to be sovereignly gracious in his acts of election, whether the national election of Israel (Ex. 19:5; Deut. 10:14–15) or the personal election of individuals to salvation (Rom. 9:18–21). The Creator has the right to do what he pleases with his works, even to give to some the damnation that they deserve for their sins and to give to others mercy and glory that they do not deserve (vv. 22–23).

The Wisdom of the Creator

The creation account in Genesis shines with order and beauty that testify to the wisdom of the Creator. Jeremiah 51:15 says, "He hath made the earth by his power, he hath established the world by his wisdom, and hath stretched out the heaven by his understanding." Proverbs 3:19 says, "The LORD by wisdom hath founded the earth; by understanding hath he established the heavens." Charnock compared the creation of the world to the skillful crafting of a musical instrument that is then tuned to play beautiful music. He said, "There is nothing so mean, so small, but glitters with a beam of divine skill."[77]

Although God could have created the world fully functional in an instant, he chose to create the heavens and earth, and then develop them over six days. In its initial condition, the earth was "without form" (*tohu*) and "void" (*bohu*), terms for an uninhabited wilderness that cannot sustain human life.[78] God proceeded to structure the world by creating a series of distinctions: daylight versus the darkness of night (day one), waters below versus waters above (day two), and the dry land versus the seas (day three). There is a parallel between days one to three and days four to six (one and four: light; two and five: water and sky; three and six: land) that some commentators have summarized as "forming"

---

77. Charnock, *The Existence and Attributes of God*, in *Works*, 2:21.
78. Deut. 32:10; Job 12:24; Isa. 34:11; 45:18; Jer. 4:23.

(days one–three) and "filling" (days four–six).[79] God worked in a wise and orderly manner to prepare a proper environment that he populated with living creatures.

The wisdom of the Creator appears also in the vast diversity of the living creatures, each made according to its "kind" (*min*).[80] Solomon showed his wisdom by his ability to speak intelligently about various trees, plants, animals, birds, insects, and fish (1 Kings 4:30–34). How much more should we admire the wisdom of God, who invented each kind of living creature! Willard wrote, "There are more mysteries of wisdom in the most despicable plant, than human wisdom can dive into."[81]

The harmony and mutual interdependence of these incredibly diverse kinds of living creatures in a "very good" world (Gen. 1:31) also demonstrates the wisdom of the Creator. Biological life does not consist only of isolated organisms, but a complex and carefully balanced ecological system that includes the inanimate aspects of the earth's biosphere. The psalmist surveys God's provision of water and food for the various plants, animals, and men, and says, "O Lord, how manifold are thy works! In wisdom hast thou made them all: the earth is full of thy riches" (Ps. 104:24). Charnock compared the variety, beauty, fitness, and organic connections of the parts of creation to the members of a marvelous body in which each part contributes to the life of the whole.[82] The wisdom of God appears particularly in his crafting of the world to be a home for man: "he created it not in vain [*tohu*], he formed it to be inhabited" (Isa. 45:18). Calvin said, "He has so wonderfully adorned heaven and earth with as unlimited abundance, variety, and beauty of all things as could possibly be, quite like a spacious and splendid house, provided and filled with the most exquisite and at the same time most abundant furnishings."[83]

Recognizing God's wisdom in creation should move Christians to trust his decree and providence for their lives today as he executes his fatherly will.[84] Our Lord Jesus points anxious believers to consider the birds and the flowers, and to see how God gives them food and beauty

---

79. See Kidner, *Genesis*, 46. The account does not strictly follow this form-fill pattern: God filled the earth with plants on the *third* day.
80. Gen. 1:11–12, 21, 24–25; cf. 6:20; 7:14.
81. Willard, *A Compleat Body of Divinity*, 118.
82. Charnock, *The Existence and Attributes of God*, in *Works*, 2:22–26.
83. Calvin, *Institutes*, 1.14.20.
84. The Heidelberg Catechism (LD 9, Q. 26), in *The Three Forms of Unity*, 75–76.

(Matt. 6:25–34). If the wise Creator has arranged his world so well that animals that engage in no agriculture still find their food, much more we can expect him to work out his good plan for our lives (Rom. 8:28). Even when Christians suffer, God remains "a faithful Creator" (1 Pet. 4:19).

The Goodness of the Creator

Another pattern of repetition in Genesis 1 is the statement that "God saw . . . it was good,"[85] culminating in the statement "God saw every thing that he had made, and, behold, it was very good" (Gen. 1:31). Moses most likely wrote these words while Israel was in a barren wilderness. The picture of "grass" springing up under God's blessing (cf. Deut. 32:2; 2 Sam. 23:4; Ps. 23:2) would have made the Israelites think of verdant pasture for their livestock. The "herb" and "fruit tree" would have appealed to their hunger for fresh food (cf. Gen. 1:29–30). This paves the way for the description of the lush garden of Eden in Genesis 2. God also demonstrates his goodness by speaking his blessing on his creatures (1:22, 28; 2:3), a blessing that empowers them to reproduce, work, and rest. It is astonishing to consider, but God created mankind in order to bless them. Truly, the earth is full of God's faithful love (Pss. 33:5; 119:64; cf. 145:9).

Geerhardus Vos (1862–1949) wrote, "The doctrine of creation secures for the creature a certain measure of glory." He explained, "The finger of God has touched and formed it, and in the midst of all its defection and sin the imprint of God's finger clings to it."[86]

Creation is a doctrine of delight. The goodness of creation teaches us, in contrast to dualistic and ascetic beliefs, that "every creature of God is good, and nothing to be refused, if it be received with thanksgiving: for it is sanctified by the word of God and prayer" (1 Tim. 4:4–5). In the context of that statement, Paul particularly warned against demonic doctrines that slandered the goodness of marriage and required abstinence from various kinds of food (vv. 1–3). We should not feel guilty about enjoying God's creation if we do so according to his revealed will for his glory, for God "giveth us richly all things to enjoy" (6:17). God himself modeled the enjoyment of creation in the repeated statement that he saw the goodness

---

85. Gen. 1:4, 10, 12, 18, 21, 25.
86. Vos, *Reformed Dogmatics*, 1:159.

of his world. This appears, too, in the last day of the creation week, when God ceased his work and "rested," or "sabbathed" (Gen. 2:2). Another text says that God "was refreshed" (Ex. 31:17). This does not mean that he was tired, for the Creator does not grow weary (Isa. 40:28). Rather, it means that he stopped the work of creation and simply enjoyed what he had made.[87]

The excellent goodness of creation shows us that God is "the overflowing fountain of all good," as the Belgic Confession (Art. 1) so beautifully puts it.[88] Augustine said, "It is enough for the Christian to believe that the only cause of all created things, whether heavenly or earthly, whether visible or invisible, is the goodness of the Creator, the one true God."[89] God did not create the world because he needed something from it, for "he giveth to all life, and breath, and all things" (Acts 17:25), and, "Who hath first given to him?" (Rom. 11:35). Rather, "every good gift and every perfect gift is from above, and cometh down from the Father of lights, with whom is no variableness, neither shadow of turning" (James 1:17).

God is the best and supreme good, since he made all other good things. Thomas Watson (c. 1620–1686) said, "Did God make this glorious world? Did he make everything good? Was there in the creature so much beauty and sweetness? Oh! Then what sweetness is there in God?"[90] William Ames (1576–1633) said that this doctrine is useful for admonition, "that we may not allow our souls to cling to this world but that we may lift them higher and cling to the One who made the world."[91]

Knowing and Celebrating the Glory of the Creator

Therefore, we conclude that God created the universe for his declarative glory, to display the beauty of his attributes. The fiery spirits of heaven constantly declare, "The whole earth is full of his glory" (Isa. 6:3).[92] Calvin said, "You cannot in one glance survey this vast and beautiful system of the universe, in its wide expanse, without being completely overwhelmed by the boundless force of its brightness." He wrote, "This skillful ordering

---

87. Vos, *Reformed Dogmatics*, 1:176.
88. *The Three Forms of Unity*, 17.
89. Augustine, *Enchiridion*, chap. 9, in *NPNF*[1], 3:240; cf. Polyander, Walaeus, Thysius, and Rivetus, *Synopsis Purioris Theologiae*, 10.18 (1:253).
90. Thomas Watson, *A Body of Divinity* (Edinburgh: Banner of Truth, 1965), 117.
91. Ames, *A Sketch of the Christian's Catechism*, 50.
92. For the doctrine of general revelation, see *RST*, 1:185–86, 195–263.

of the universe is for us a sort of mirror in which we can contemplate God, who is otherwise invisible."[93]

Therefore, we should use all things for God's glory. Calvin wrote in his catechism, "What is the chief end of human life?" and answered, "To know God." He went on, "Why do you say that?" and replied, "Because He created us and placed us in this world to be glorified in us. And it is indeed right that our life, of which He Himself is the beginning, should be devoted to His glory."[94]

The greatest tragedy of mankind is that we refuse to know our Creator and make him known (Rom. 1:19–21). By God's grace in Christ, creation should move us to glorify him. The angels joyfully sang God's praises when he founded the earth (Job 38:7). Psalm 148 calls upon every aspect of creation, from stars to cattle, from angels to children, to praise the Lord. Through the prophet Isaiah, the Lord said of each of his people, "I have created him for my glory" (Isa. 43:7). In the last book of the Bible, we hear the heavenly worshipers declare, "Thou art worthy, O Lord, to receive glory and honour and power: for thou hast created all things, and for thy pleasure they are and were created" (Rev. 4:11). This grand vision for God's creation is fulfilled in Jesus Christ, the Lamb who redeemed people from every nation to worship and serve the Lord (Rev. 5:9–10).

Therefore, let us be what God made us to be. Let us live for the glory of God through Jesus Christ. If by grace we do so, then we fulfill the very purpose for which God created the world, "to glorify God, and to enjoy him for ever."[95]

Sing to the Lord

Praise the Almighty Creator

> I sing th' almighty pow'r of God,
> That made the mountains rise,
> That spread the flowing seas abroad,
> And built the lofty skies. (repeat line)
>
> I sing the wisdom that ordained
> The sun to rule the day;

---

93. Calvin, *Institutes*, 1.5.1.
94. Calvin's Catechism of 1545 (Q. 1–2), in *Reformed Confessions*, 4:469.
95. Westminster Shorter Catechism (Q. 1), in *Reformed Confessions*, 4:353.

The moon shines full at his command,
And all the stars obey. (repeat line)

I sing the goodness of the Lord
That filled the earth with food;
He formed the creatures with his word,
And then pronounced them good. (repeat line)

Lord! how thy wonders are displayed
Where'er I turn mine eye!
If I survey the ground I tread,
Or gaze upon the sky. (repeat line)

Isaac Watts
Tune: Ortonville
Trinity Hymnal—Baptist Edition, No. 106 (with additional second stanza)
Or Tune: Ellacombe (without repeated line)

Questions for Meditation or Discussion

1. Why is the doctrine of creation crucial for systematic theology?
2. How do the following worldviews tend to explain the origin of all things: (1) polytheism, (2) pantheism, (3) panentheism, and (4) materialism?
3. What did God create or institute on each of the days of the first week?
4. What do the authors mean by "the universality of the work of creation"?
5. How does God's work of creation show his uniqueness?
6. What hints of the Trinity do we find in Genesis 1? How do other Scripture passages reveal that the Creator is triune?
7. How did God display his (1) power, (2) authority, (3) wisdom, and (4) goodness in the work of creation?
8. How has studying God's work of creation encouraged you to trust him more?

Questions for Deeper Reflection

9. What do the authors mean when they say that God is "the Creator of time"? Do you agree? Why or why not?
10. What does it mean to view God's creation as a theater for his glory? How should that belief shape how we live and relate to the world around us?

11. A friend of yours is a pantheistic environmentalist, believing that we must care for the world because we are one with all things. She asks you how Christian beliefs about creation compare to hers. What do you say?

3

The Creation of the World, Part 2

Historical and Theological Questions

In the last two centuries, the Christian doctrine of creation has been challenged by theories that propose alternative models of our origin. Some theologians have responded to this challenge by assigning Genesis 1 to the category of myth.[1] The term *myth* has a range of meanings.[2] It might refer to a traditional story that functions as part of a holistic explanation of reality (a worldview). With that meaning, a myth may or may not be true, and the term is used in a relatively neutral way regarding the historicity of an account. However, most often myths are associated with religious legends that might have some historical basis but that contain significant fictional additions and embellishments.[3] *Myth* may even be used as a synonym for *legend* or *fable*, something entirely fictitious. It is in this sense that the New Testament uses the related Greek word (*mythos*).[4]

---

1. Peter Enns, "Inerrancy, However Defined, Does Not Describe What the Bible Does," in *Five Views on Biblical Inerrancy*, ed. J. Merrick and Stephen M. Garrett, Counterpoints: Bible and Theology (Grand Rapids, MI: Zondervan, 2013), 83–116. For a response to Enns's views on inerrancy, in addition to those of the other contributors to *Five Views on Biblical Inerrancy*, see G. K. Beale, *The Erosion of Inerrancy in Evangelicalism: Responding to New Challenges to Biblical Authority* (Wheaton, IL: Crossway, 2008).

2. Feinberg, *No One Like Him*, 574–76.

3. Enns states that "the historical core for the exodus story" might be "a small band of slaves who left or escaped Egypt and migrated over land (or across a shallow lake), and later generations retold this historical core in mythic language." Enns, "Inerrancy, However Defined," in *Five Views on Biblical Inerrancy*, 97.

4. 1 Tim. 1:4; 4:7; 2 Tim. 4:4; Titus 1:14; 2 Pet. 1:16.

To call Genesis 1 a myth in the latter sense is to relegate it to the realm of ancient ideas that we now regard as fiction, like Greek or Norse mythology, of interest perhaps to historians and intriguing to the imagination, but of little significance for our understanding of the universe. However, Genesis 1 is part of the Holy Scriptures, which are not the mere words of men, but the Word of God, which is always true in its teaching and profitable in its application (Prov. 30:5; 2 Tim. 3:16). When the Pharisees pressed our Lord Jesus Christ for his view of divorce, he replied, "Have ye not read," quoted from Genesis 1 and 2, and said, "What therefore God hath joined together, let not man put asunder" (Matt. 19:4–6). God's Son regarded Genesis not as myth, but as the true history of creation and the solid foundation of God's moral law.

Though there are some parallels between Genesis and other ancient Near Eastern documents, the Genesis account differs significantly from other creation stories. For example, the Enuma Elish postulates creation through sexual reproduction and warfare among various gods.[5] Genesis presents the Creator and his work with unparalleled simplicity, purity, and majesty. Edward Young (1907–1968) said, "Genesis one is a document *sui generis* [in a category of its own]; its like or equal is not to be found anywhere in the literature of antiquity. And the reason for this is obvious. Genesis one is a divine revelation to man concerning the creation of heaven and earth."[6]

Some people object that the biblical writers embraced an ancient view of the universe that is incompatible with modern science. It is said that the Bible teaches a *three-tier view of the universe* consisting of heaven, earth, and sea/underworld (Phil. 2:10; Rev. 5:3, 13), in which the sky is a solid dome holding up a heavenly sea (Gen. 1:6–8; cf. Ps. 148:4). The term translated as "firmament" (*raqiya'*) in Genesis 1 is said to refer to "a solid surface like metal" because the related verb (*raqa'*) is used for "pounding metals into thin sheets" (cf. Ex. 39:3; Job 37:18; Isa. 40:19). Therefore, they argue that the biblical authors embraced ancient, mythological cosmology, so we cannot rely on the Bible for accurate views of science or history, but only for spiritual truths.[7]

---

5. Paul Copan and William Lane Craig, *Creation Out of Nothing: A Biblical, Philosophical, and Scientific Exploration* (Grand Rapids, MI: Baker, 2004), 30–36.

6. Edward J. Young, *Studies in Genesis One* (Phillipsburg, NJ: Presbyterian and Reformed, 1964), 82; cf. "The Days of Genesis: Second Article," *Westminster Theological Journal* (May 1963): 148 (full article, 143–71).

7. Denis O. Lamoureux, "No Historical Adam: Evolutionary Creation View," in *Four Views on the Historical Adam*, ed. Matthew Barrett and Ardel B. Caneday (Grand Rapids, MI: Zondervan, 2013), 47–54.

In response to this objection, we argue that the objector is reading ancient cosmology into the biblical text. The Bible is remarkably restrained in matters of astronomy, but speaks in "popular style" and "common usage" about phenomena as they appear to our senses,[8] as John Calvin noted.[9] When the Bible uses the language of "every creature which is in heaven, and on the earth, and under the earth" (Rev. 5:13), it is using all-inclusive language for the whole creation. The Bible does not teach us much about the structure of the universe. For example, the Bible speaks of "the circle of the earth" (Isa. 40:22), but also of "the four corners of the earth" (11:12; Acts 10:11; Rev. 7:1). The point is not whether the world is a circle or a square. It is that God rules over the entire world that he created.

The "waters which were above the firmament" are probably best understood as a reference to the clouds.[10] The ancient peoples understood that there were waters above us, for they knew, as the Bible attests, that rain came from clouds.[11] As to the argument that "firmament" (*raqiya'*) means a solid object, we cannot deduce that the noun refers to something like metal simply because the verb is often used for spreading out metals. This is an error in linguistics. The basic meaning of the word is not solidity, but being "spread out."[12] The Bible also uses other words to communicate that God spread or stretched out the skies, sometimes comparing the sky not with hard metal but with soft material, such as a curtain or tent.[13] The Bible does not aim to describe the material of the universe, either from an ancient or modern perspective, but does accurately report historical events about God's works in creating it.

Therefore, as evangelical and Reformed Christians, we should not call Genesis 1 a myth, but regard it as theological, historical literature. It is theological in that its main points pertain to the revelation of God and his works. It is historical in that its words truly describe real events, people, and things. It is literature, for God crafted it with skill and wisdom to communicate its truth to men. Genesis is the word of God.[14]

---

8. On the Bible's description of reality from an ordinary human point of view, not a technical, scientific perspective, see the clarification of the doctrine of inerrant veracity in *RST*, 1:374.

9. Calvin, *Commentaries*, on Gen. 1:6–8, 15–16.

10. Calvin, *Commentaries*, on Gen. 1:6–8.

11. Judg. 5:4; 1 Kings 18:44–45; Job 26:8; 36:27–28; Pss. 77:16; 147:8; Eccles. 11:3.

12. Victor P. Hamilton, *The Book of Genesis, Chapters 1–17*, The New International Commentary on the Old Testament (Grand Rapids, MI: Eerdmans, 1990), 122.

13. Ps. 104:2; Isa. 40:22; cf. Job 9:8; Isa. 42:5; 44:24; 45:12; 51:13; Jer. 10:12; 51:15; Zech. 12:1.

14. Feinberg, *No One Like Him*, 577–78.

Given that Genesis is not a myth, we face a number of important questions about the text. In this chapter, we will examine a historical question about the genre and historicity of Genesis, and a theological question about creation out of nothing. In the next two chapters, we will consider exegetical and scientific questions related to Genesis.

Is Genesis 1–2 Historical Narrative?

The Bible sometimes uses metaphorical language to communicate historical truth, as David does in Psalm 18.[15] Some people have said that Genesis 1 is a kind of poetry or extended metaphor intended to communicate the truth that God created the world but not to present a historical account of how he did so. As evidence, the objector might point to the rhythmic parallelism of the text, as did Johann Herder (1744–1803).[16]

However, the early chapters of Genesis present themselves as history, albeit history written with theological intent.[17] We conclude this for the following reasons. First, the text reads like *historical narrative* as found in other parts of the Bible, not like poetry.[18] For example, Hebrew poetry is characterized by parallelism of thought, where one line repeats the same thought in somewhat different words or states its antithesis.[19] We see examples of parallelism in the lines of the psalm referenced above, such as:

Then the earth shook and trembled; the foundations also of the hills moved. (v. 7)

And he rode upon a cherub, and did fly: yea, he did fly upon the wings of the wind. (v. 10)

We do not find such linear parallelism in Genesis 1. Instead, the text is written with a string of sentences in the grammatical form commonly used

---

15. Eric Lane, *Psalms 1–89: The Lord Saves*, Focus on the Bible (Fearn, Ross-shire, Scotland: Christian Focus, 2006), 93.

16. J. G. Herder, *The Spirit of Hebrew Poetry*, trans. James Marsh, 2 vols. in one (Burlington: Edward Smith, 1833), 1:58; cf. Bavinck, *Reformed Dogmatics*, 2:491.

17. Parts of this section are adapted from Joel R. Beeke, "The Case for Adam," in *God, Adam, and You: Biblical Creation Defended and Applied*, ed. Richard D. Phillips (Phillipsburg, NJ: P&R Publishing, 2015), chap. 2, pp. 18–26, with permission of P&R Publishing Co., PO Box 817, Phillipsburg, NJ, 08865, www.prpbooks.com.

18. Richard P. Belcher Jr., *Genesis: The Beginning of God's Plan of Salvation*, Focus on the Bible (Fearn, Ross-shire, Scotland: Christian Focus, 2012), 31.

19. Parallelism in Hebrew poetry can take various forms, including synonymous, antithetic, comparative, climactic, or synthetic. See Michael P. V. Barrett, "Introduction to the Poetic and Wisdom Books," in *The Reformation Heritage KJV Study Bible*, ed. Joel R. Beeke, Michael P. V. Barrett, Gerald M. Bilkes, and Paul M. Smalley (Grand Rapids, MI: Reformation Heritage Books, 2014), 707.

in Hebrew to describe a series of events in historical narrative.[20] This form stands behind the English translation of phrases such as "And God said," "And God saw," "And God called," and "And God made."[21]

When we peruse the first four chapters of Genesis, we find that they naturally read as historical narrative. As we continue to read through Genesis, we find that the early chapters are part of a larger narrative. In Genesis 13:10, we find a reference to the garden of Eden as a place, one just as real as the land of Egypt.[22] This is an account of real history. As Francis Schaeffer (1912–1984) noted, the Bible presents the "concept of creation as a fact of space-time history" on the same level as other "points of history" that it records.[23]

Second, the Bible links creation to later history through *genealogies*. Though American culture does not place a very high value on genealogies, other cultures treasure them as important links between the present and the past. We cannot detach the first two chapters of Genesis from the rest of it and treat them as nonhistorical myths or allegories without damaging the structure of Genesis and its integrity as a historical document. In Genesis 5, we read a genealogy tracing Adam's descendants to Noah's sons. Later genealogies continue to follow the family line to Abram (chap. 11) and the grandchildren of Jacob (chap. 46). The book of Chronicles picks up the genealogical family tree and carries it through the descendants of David beyond the exile (1 Chron. 1–3). Richard Pratt writes, "The Chronicler wrote to give his readers a true historical record of Israel's past."[24] The New Testament traces the genealogy of Jesus Christ back to Adam (Luke 3:23–38).

Therefore, the Bible presents the Genesis accounts of creation as real history, of one piece with the history of God's redeeming acts in Jesus Christ. This means that we must not dismiss them as legends, for they are part of the Word of God. Geerhardus Vos wrote, "The creation narrative is interwoven like a link in the chain of God's saving acts. God does not make a chain of solid gold, in which the first link is a floral wreath."[25]

---

20. The technical term for such Hebrew constructions is *wayyiqtol* (or *waw*-consecutive plus imperfect).

21. See Robert L. Reymond, *A New Systematic Theology of the Christian Faith* (Nashville: Thomas Nelson, 1998), 117.

22. For other references to the garden of Eden, see Isa. 51:3; Ezek. 28:13; 31:9, 16, 18; 36:35; Joel 2:3.

23. Francis A. Schaeffer, *Genesis in Space and Time* (Downers Grove, IL: InterVarsity Press, 1972), 15.

24. Richard L. Pratt Jr., *1 and 2 Chronicles* (Fearn, Ross-shire, Scotland: Christian Focus, 1998), 11.

25. Vos, *Reformed Dogmatics*, 1:161.

Third, as we noted earlier, *Christ* treated Genesis as true history. Our ultimate authority as Christians is the Lord Jesus Christ. What do we find when we examine how Christ viewed the history of the Old Testament? John Wenham (1913–1996) wrote, "He consistently treats the historical narratives as straight-forward records of fact."[26] Christ spoke specifically of Adam: "But from the beginning of creation, 'God made them male and female.' 'Therefore a man shall leave his father and mother and hold fast to his wife, and the two shall become one flesh.' So they are no longer two but one flesh" (Mark 10:6–8 ESV). Here Christ referred to Genesis 1:27 and 2:24, and he located the events described in those texts as "from the beginning of creation." We also note that Christ held together Genesis 1 and 2 as complementary accounts, not contradictory ones. It is difficult to avoid the conclusion that God's Son viewed the first two chapters of Genesis as a historical account of God's creation of the world and mankind.

We also see that Jesus Christ affirmed the historicity of the early chapters of Genesis in Luke 11:50–51: "That the blood of all the prophets, which was shed from the foundation of the world, may be required of this generation; from the blood of Abel unto the blood of Zacharias, which perished between the altar and the temple: verily I say unto you, It shall be required of this generation." Here again Christ referred to the earliest days of creation: "from the foundation of the world." And he spoke of the first martyr, Abel, the son of Adam (Genesis 4). Clearly Christ treated the accounts of Genesis as real history. If Christ Jesus, God's Son, our Lord, believed in the historical creation of the world and the first human beings as described in the early chapters of Genesis, then so should we.

Did God Create *ex Nihilo*?

The major theological question about creation concerns whether God made the universe out of material that already existed and thus was not created by him, or whether the things he made came from no existing material, but he created their entire substance by his word. Did the universe have an absolute beginning at some point of time or is the "material" underlying its present form eternal?

---

26. John Wenham, *Christ and the Bible*, 3rd ed. (Grand Rapids, MI: Baker, 1994), 17.

A major competitor in the ancient world to the biblical view of origins was Platonism.[27] Plato wrote in his book *Timaeus* that a divine craftsman (*dēmiourgos*) shaped and ordered preexisting matter according to eternal ideas to produce the world. Platonic ideas of creation influenced some early Christian writers, such as Justin Martyr (c. AD 100–165), who erroneously thought that Plato had borrowed his teaching from the books of Moses.[28]

In contrast to Greek Platonic teaching, various Hebrew traditions, reflecting a biblical worldview, asserted that God did not merely shape materials that were already available, but made all things when they did not yet exist.[29] In one ancient Jewish writing, a mother addressed her soon-to-be-martyred son: "I beseech thee, my son, look upon the heaven and the earth, and all that is therein, and consider that God made them of things that were not" (2 Macc. 7:28). The phrase "of things that were not" (Greek *ouk ex ontōn*) was rendered by the Latin *ex nihilo* in the Vulgate. Christian theologians often speak of creation *ex nihilo* to summarize the teaching of Genesis and other parts of the Bible. Irenaeus (fl. 180) and Tertullian (fl. 200) taught it, Augustine asserted it, the Fourth Lateran Council (1215) affirmed it, and the Reformed confessional tradition perpetuated it.[30] Herman Bavinck said, "The Christian church unitedly held fast to the confession: 'I believe in God the Father, Almighty, Creator of heaven and earth.' And by creation it meant that act of God through which, by his sovereign will, he brought the entire world out of nonbeing into a being that is distinct from his own being."[31]

---

27. Another competitor was Stoicism, but its pantheistic identification of God with the world was sufficiently different from the biblical worldview that it did not threaten the church's doctrine of creation as much as Platonism.

28. Justin Martyr, *First Apology*, chap. 59, in *ANF*, 1:182. Wisdom 11:17 says that God "made the world of matter without form" (*ex amorphou hulēs*). See Paul Copan, "Is *Creatio ex Nihilo* a Post-Biblical Invention? An Examination of Gerhard May's Proposal," *Trinity Journal* 17NS (1996): 82–83 (full article, 77–93). However, for other, balancing statements by Justin Martyr, see Bavinck, *Reformed Dogmatics*, 2:409.

29. The Dead Sea Scrolls, Community Rule (1QS 3:15). Jubilees 2:2 states that God created the darkness and the deep of Gen. 1:2. See Copan and Craig, *Creation Out of Nothing*, 100, 105. When challenged by a philosopher, Rabban Gamaliel II denied that God created the world out of materials but said that he made its most elemental materials, such as space, water, air, and even darkness. Genesis Rabbah 1:9, cited in Jacob Neusner, *The Rabbis and the Prophets*, Studies in Judaism (Lanham, MD: University Press of America, 2011), 11.

30. Irenaeus, *Against Heresies*, 2.1.1; 2.10.4, in *ANF*, 1:359, 370; Tertullian, *Against Heretics*, 13, in *ANF*, 3:249; Augustine, *Confessions*, 12.7, in *NPNF*[1], 1:177; Fourth Lateran Council, Canon 1, in *Creeds of the Churches: A Reader in Christian Doctrine from the Bible to the Present*, ed. John H. Leith, 3rd ed. (Louisville: Westminster/John Knox, 1982), 57; Belgic Confession (Art. 12) and Heidelberg Catechism (LD 9, Q. 26), in *The Three Forms of Unity*, 27, 75; and Westminster Confession of Faith (4.1), in *Reformed Confessions*, 4:239.

31. Bavinck, *Reformed Dogmatics*, 2:416.

The doctrine of creation *ex nihilo* asserts that all things owe their entire being to the creative word of God. Stephen Charnock wrote, "When we say the world was made of nothing, we mean that there was no matter existent for God to work upon, but what he raised himself in the first act of creation."[32] Apart from God himself, nothing exists that was not made by God's powerful will, neither the most basic components of physical matter and energy, nor the spirits of men and angels, nor their relationships in time and space.

The doctrine of creation out of nothing has been attacked by some theologians and philosophers on the grounds that it is a philosophical accretion to Christianity not taught by the Bible.[33] Gerhard May (1940–2007) argued that the doctrine "was not demanded by the text of the Bible," but arose as early Christian apologists engaged philosophically with Greek thought and sought to defend their notion of the omnipotence and freedom of God.[34]

Though there is no Scripture passage that explicitly states creation *ex nihilo*, the doctrine is well established on several biblical grounds.

First, Genesis 1:1 begins the creation account with the statement "In the beginning God created the heaven and the earth." Here, heaven and earth act as a merism, or figure of speech, for all that exists. Therefore, God created all that is. When Genesis proceeds to tell how God illuminated and shaped various aspects of the dark and watery earth, it is saying that he was working with the material he had just created. Bavinck wrote, "At no time or place is there even the slightest reference to an eternal formless matter. God alone is the Eternal and Imperishable One. He alone towers above processes of becoming and change."[35]

Some scholars object that Genesis 1:1–3 should be translated, "In the beginning, when God created the heavens and the earth—and the earth was without form or shape, with darkness over the abyss and a mighty wind sweeping over the waters—then God said: Let there be light, and there was light" (NAB, revised edition). The NAB notes that

---

32. Charnock, *The Existence and Attributes of God*, in *Works*, 2:127.

33. For a discussion and response, see Copan, "Is *Creatio ex Nihilo* a Post-Biblical Invention," 77–93. Copan lists Langdon Gilkey, Arthur Peacocke, Ian Barbour, and Gerhard May as critics of creation *ex nihilo*. See also Thomas Jay Oord, ed., *Theologies of Creation: Creatio Ex Nihilo and Its New Rivals* (London: Routledge, 2014). The Latter-Day Saints (Mormon) church also teaches creation out of preexisting chaos, in line with its founding prophet, Joseph Smith.

34. Gerhard May, *Creatio ex Nihilo: The Doctrine of "Creation Out of Nothing" in Early Christian Thought*, trans. A. S. Worrall (Edinburgh: T&T Clark, 1994), 24, 180.

35. Bavinck, *Reformed Dogmatics*, 2:417.

verse 2 presents "the pre-creation state symbolized by the chaos out of which God brings order."[36] This is essentially a modern form of the Platonic creation story.[37] However, while this reading is grammatically possible,[38] it makes for very awkward syntax, especially in a chapter marked by short, crisp statements.[39] The most natural reading of the text is that the "earth" in verse 2 is the same "earth" said to be created by God in verse 1.[40] John Currid notes that the traditional rendering "is found in every ancient translation without exception."[41] Consequently, we should understand the text to teach that God created the universe *ex nihilo*, with the result that the earth was initially created to be a dark mass covered in water, which God then used as the raw materials to form all earthly things.[42]

Second, the Bible denies the preexistence of matter by asserting that God made all things. Genesis 1 teaches a comprehensive and universal work of creation. It includes every kind of creature that exists, excluding none, in the category of what God made.[43] Genesis is utterly silent regarding any prime matter from which God formed the universe. However, many Scripture passages state that God created "all things."[44] Psalm 146:6, which Paul quoted in Acts 14:15, states that the extent of "all things" consists of everything in every realm of the universe: "heaven and earth, the sea, and all that is in them" (ESV). Since creation implies a beginning,[45] all things have a beginning and originated from God's mighty work, and he did not make anything from something that existed prior to that.

---

36. New American Bible, revised edition (2011), Gen. 1:1–3, United States Conference of Catholic Bishops, http://www.usccb.org/bible/genesis/1. See also the NJPS translation of the Jewish Publication Society (http://www.taggedtanakh.org/Chapter/Index/english-Gen-1).

37. An early exponent of this interpretation was the Jewish commentator Abraham Ibn Ezra (d. c. 1167)—a thinker heavily influenced by Greek philosophy, especially Neo-Platonism. See John Peter Lange, *A Commentary on the Holy Scriptures*, trans. Tayler Lewis and A. Gosman (Bellingham, WA: Logos Bible Software, 2008), 1:161; and Tzvi Langermann, "Abraham Ibn Ezra," in *The Stanford Encyclopedia of Philosophy* (Winter 2016 ed.), ed. Edward N. Zalta, https://plato.stanford.edu/archives/win2016/entries/ibn-ezra/.

38. "In the beginning" (*bereshit*) is, in this view, taken to be in the construct before a relative clause. J. C. L. Gibson, *Davidson's Introductory Hebrew Grammar*, 4th ed. (Edinburgh: T&T Clark, 1994), sec. 13 (12).

39. Lange, *A Commentary on the Holy Scriptures*, 1:161–62.

40. Belcher, *Genesis*, 42.

41. John D. Currid, *A Study Commentary on Genesis: Genesis 1:1–25:18*, EP Study Commentary (Darlington, England: Evangelical Press, 2003), 58.

42. For an extended discussion of the relationship between Genesis 1:1 and 1:2, see Copan and Craig, *Creation Out of Nothing*, 36–49.

43. See the discussion of creation's universality in chap. 2.

44. Neh. 9:6; John 1:3; Acts 14:15; 17:24; 1 Cor. 8:6; Eph. 3:9; Col. 1:16; Rev. 4:11.

45. Gen. 1:1; Mark 10:6; 13:19; Eph. 3:9; 2 Pet. 3:4.

Third, Hebrews 11:3 denies that God made the universe out of anything visible: "By faith we understand that the universe was created by the word of God, so that what is seen was not made out of things that are visible" (ESV).[46] The phrase "by the word of God" plainly alludes to the creation account in Genesis. The words "not made out of things that are visible" tap into the theme of Hebrews 11 that faith appropriates realities that we cannot see (vv. 1, 7–8, 13, 27). William Lane (1931–1999) commented, "It denies that the creative universe originated from primal material or anything observable" in a manner that "would seem to exclude any influence from Platonic . . . cosmology."[47] The point is not that God made the universe out of invisible matter, but that God did not make the world out of any matter, and so we must not base our view of the world's origin upon empirical observation and reasoning, but receive the doctrine of creation "through faith." F. F. Bruce (1910–1990) paraphrased Hebrews 11:3 as saying, "The visible universe . . . was not made out of equally visible raw material; it was called into being by divine power." He went on to say, "The writer to the Hebrews . . . affirms the doctrine of *creatio ex nihilo*, a doctrine uncongenial to Greek thought."[48]

Fourth, Colossians 1:16 states that by Christ "were all things created, that are in heaven, and that are in earth, visible and invisible." There is no person, material, or substance, not even something undetectable by our senses, that was not created by God. What then could have existed already "in the beginning" from which God could have formed the world and its inhabitants? Nothing existed except God. God did not make the world out of his own substance, for he is immutable and cannot change (Ps. 102:25–27; Mal. 3:6). His essence is of an entirely different nature from anything he created (Isa. 40:18, 25; Acts 17:29; Gal. 4:8).[49] Therefore, God made the universe out of nothing.

Fifth, Romans 4:17 affirms that God "calls into existence the things that do not exist" (ESV). At the very least, this verse attributes to God the power to create *ex nihilo*. Leon Morris (1914–2006) said, "Paul is

---

46. Although the verb *katartizō*, which is translated as "created" or "framed" (KJV), means "to give order or bring to perfection" (cf. Matt. 4:21), the verb translated as "was . . . made" (perfect *ginomai*) means "to become," and so here "come into being" (cf. John 1:3).

47. W. L. Lane, *Hebrews*, Word Biblical Commentary (Dallas, TX: Word, 1991), 2:332, cited in Copan, "Is *Creatio ex Nihilo* a Post-Biblical Invention," 91.

48. F. F. Bruce, *Hebrews*, New International Commentary on the New Testament (Grand Rapids, MI: Eerdmans, 1964), 280–81.

49. Cf. Perkins, *An Exposition of the Symbol*, in *Works*, 5:48.

speaking of God as creating something out of nothing by his call."[50] The context refers to Abraham's faith that God would give a son to him and his wife despite their old age and barrenness (Genesis 17). However, Paul could very well be connecting Abraham's faith to creation. God's promises to Abraham of fruitfulness, multiplied offspring, and fatherhood over nations (see Gen. 17:4–6, the text Paul cites in Rom. 4:17) allude to God's blessing on the first man and woman in Genesis 1.[51] The first creation had fallen under death by Adam's sin (Rom. 5:12), but Abraham trusted in "God, who quickeneth the dead" (4:17), to renew creation. Therefore, Paul discussed Abraham's faith in a manner that both affirmed God's ability to create out of nothing and may have implicitly linked that faith to creation and new creation.

Sixth, the doctrine of creation *ex nihilo* is essential to a biblical view of God. If the universe consists of material not created by God, then we are faced with three possibilities: the universe is an eternal entity independent of and alongside God; the universe is God; or there is no God. Consequently, the biblical view of God as the sovereign Lord over all would collapse,[52] and in its place would arise one of the alternative views discussed in the previous chapter: polytheism, pantheism, panentheism, or materialism.[53] None of these views is compatible with the Bible. Attempts to mingle them with Christianity end up with a substantially different view of God. The biblical view of God requires creation out of nothing. Bavinck said, "The teaching of creation out of nothing maintains that there is a distinction in essence between God and the world."[54] This distinction is definitive for a proper view of God's relation to the world. If God did not make everything, how would he have the power to rule over all things to do all his will? Why would God have authority over all things if they had their existence apart from him? Isaiah's polemic against the false gods of the nations rests upon the assertion that the Lord alone is "the first" and "the last," and that he is the Lord "from the beginning" because he created all things.[55]

The doctrine of God's creation of the universe out of nothing establishes the complete dependence of the world upon God (Col. 1:16–17; Heb.

---

50. Leon Morris, *The Epistle to the Romans*, The Pillar New Testament Commentary (Grand Rapids, MI: Eerdmans, 1988), 209.
51. Kenneth A. Mathews, *Genesis 11:27–50:26*, The New American Commentary 1B (Nashville: Broadman & Holman, 2005), 202.
52. Lange, *A Commentary on the Holy Scriptures*, 1:162.
53. For a consideration of these alternative views, see chap. 2.
54. Bavinck, *Reformed Dogmatics*, 2:419.
55. Isa. 37:16; 40:21–22, 26, 28; 41:4; 42:5, 12; 44:6; 45:5–7, 12, 18; 46:10; 48:12–13.

1:2–3). Robert Letham writes, "Everything that exists was brought into being by God; this was a free act of God's will, not an emanation from his being, and there was no preexisting material. Consequently, all that is not God is contingent, dependent on him for its existence and continuation."[56]

Therefore, we conclude that the doctrine of creation *ex nihilo* is derived from biblical statements and is necessary for a biblical view of God and his relation to the world.

God's creation of the universe out of nothing greatly magnifies his power and asserts his absolute sovereignty over the world. Charnock said, "Greater power cannot be imagined than that which brings something out of nothing."[57] Therefore, God's creation of the world out of nothing should fill us with awe, reverence, and fear. Psalm 33:6 reminds us that God made the heavens by his word. Verses 8 and 9 then say, "Let all the earth fear the LORD: let all the inhabitants of the world stand in awe of him. For he spake, and it was done; he commanded, and it stood fast." When we watch builders construct a large and beautiful building with their power tools, equipment, and stacks of building materials, we feel a certain admiration for what they accomplish. How much more should we admire, adore, and worship the God who made the heavens, the earth, and all that is in them, and that with no tools or materials, but simply by commanding them into existence!

This doctrine should also humble us. Thomas Watson said, "Our beginning was of nothing. Some brag of their birth and ancestry; but how little cause have they to boast who came from nothing."[58] What do we have that we did not receive? And if we received it all from God, then why do we boast? Let us boast only in the Lord, who made heaven and earth.

Sing to the Lord

Let All Creation Praise Its Creator

Praise the Lord in heav'nly places,
Ye His hosts and angels bright;
Sun and moon declare His glory,
Praise Him, all ye stars of light.

Let the sky and clouds forever
Praise His glorious majesty;

---

56. Robert Letham, *Systematic Theology* (Wheaton, IL: Crossway, 2019), 271.
57. Charnock, *The Existence and Attributes of God*, in *Works*, 2:128.
58. Watson, *A Body of Divinity*, 114; cf. Perkins, *An Exposition of the Symbol*, in *Works*, 5:48.

At His word they were created,
Ordered by His firm decree.

In the earth let all things praise Him,
Seas and all that they contain,
Stormy winds that do His pleasure,
Hail and lightning, snow and rain.

Hills and mountains, praise your Maker,
Praise Him, all ye flocks and herds,
Woods and fields and fruitful vineyards,
Creeping things and flying birds.

Kings and princes bow before Him,
Earthly judges, give Him praise,
All ye people, tell His glory,
Old and young, your voices raise.

Psalm 148
Tune: Lydia
The Psalter, No. 105

Questions for Meditation or Discussion

1. What does it mean to call Genesis 1 a "myth"? Why is that not a wise way for a Christian to approach the Scriptures?
2. How do the authors refute the idea that the Bible teaches that the sky is a solid dome holding up a sea of waters?
3. What are three reasons why we should view the early chapters of Genesis as historical narrative, not a poetic metaphor?
4. What is the doctrine of creation *ex nihilo*?
5. What reasons may be gathered from Genesis 1 to support the doctrine of creation *ex nihilo*?
6. How do the following texts support the doctrine of creation *ex nihilo*: (1) Hebrews 11:3, (2) Colossians 1:16, and (3) Romans 4:17?
7. Why is the doctrine of creation *ex nihilo* crucial for the biblical doctrine of God?
8. What practical implications does the doctrine of creation *ex nihilo* have for our right to boast in ourselves and our ability to trust in the Lord?

Questions for Deeper Reflection

9. You tell a friend that the early chapters of Genesis must be true history because Christ treated them as such. Your friend says, "Maybe Jesus made a mistake about Genesis. After all, to err is human." How do you respond?

10. Someone objects to the doctrine of creation *ex nihilo* by saying that it is nonsense. "Both science and everyday experience teach us," he says, "that nothing comes from nothing." How do you respond? Base your answer on the Holy Scriptures.

4

4

The Creation of the World, Part 3

Exegetical Questions

One principle that unites evangelical and Reformed Christians is that they believe that all of Scripture is God's Word. However, even among those who agree that Genesis 1 is part of the Word of God, there is disagreement about its interpretation. How are we to understand the six days of creation? This matter of interpretation was raised before modern science, but has become especially pressing given the dominant scientific model that the universe is billions of years in age. We will survey the main categories of interpretation, though we recognize that there are nuances and variations in each category.[1]

Whereas the denial of creation *ex nihilo* has fatal effects on our doctrine of God,[2] variant interpretations of the days of Genesis are held by Christians who have an orthodox view of God and salvation. Nevertheless, this is a matter of right interpretation and faithfulness to the Word of God. It has important implications for our faith, and so we must consider it carefully.

It is crucial that our interpretation of the Bible be controlled by the Bible itself, not by outside considerations such as scientific theories. John

---

1. We do not review here the specific views of John Collins, John Sailhamer, or Gordon Gray. For a summary and evaluation, see Belcher, *Genesis*, 34–45.
2. See chap. 3.

Feinberg says, "We should not ignore the data of disciplines such as science, but as evangelicals we must determine our views insofar as possible on the basis of biblical teaching."[3] This is because the Bible is God's Word. This chapter focuses on the exegetical question of how to interpret the days of Genesis 1.

Augustine: Instantaneous Creation, Allegorical Days, Young Earth

Augustine taught instantaneous creation with allegorical days. In other words, God created all things in a moment. The idea of instantaneous creation arose from Sirach or Ecclesiasticus 18:1: "The One who lives forever created all things together."[4] The Latin Vulgate has *simul* or "at the same time" for "together," but the Greek reads *koinē* or "in common." The Latin translation led to the assumption that creation took place in an instant. In Augustine's view, the sequence of days in Genesis 1 reflects a process of revelation by which God unveiled his work, so the chapter should be read as a theological allegory or symbolic story. The angels, Augustine said, "are that light which was called 'Day,' and whose unity Scripture signalizes by calling that day not the 'first day,' but 'one day.' For the second day, the third, and the rest are not other days; but the same 'one' day is repeated to complete the number six or seven, and the six days are one day repeated for the sake of numerical completeness."[5]

We note, however, that Augustine did not believe that the universe was created millions or billions of years ago, but that, according to the Scriptures, it was about six thousand years old.[6] In other words, Augustine regarded Genesis 1 as a spiritual allegory for creation in a moment, but otherwise derived his chronology from the biblical history and genealogies of the following chapters. He did not believe that Genesis 1 spanned long ages of time or that creation could be located eons ago. Therefore, Augustine cannot be appealed to as a forerunner of various old-earth creation views, such as the gap, day-age, or framework views.

This first interpretative approach to the days of Genesis founders on two errors. It builds doctrine upon a proof text from the Apocrypha,

---

3. Feinberg, *No One Like Him*, 578.
4. Augustine, *The Literal Meaning of Genesis*, 4.33.52, cited in Louis Lavallee, "Augustine on the Creation Days," *Journal of the Evangelical Theological Society* 32, no. 4 (December 1989): 460 (full article, 457–64).
5. Augustine, *The City of God*, 11.9, 30, in NPNF¹, 2:210, 222.
6. Augustine, *The City of God*, 12.10–12, in NPNF¹, 2:232–33.

which is not part of the written Word of God. The "Wisdom" of Joshua ben Sirach is not part of the Hebrew Bible or the Greek New Testament. Therefore, it does not have divine authority to establish doctrine. Furthermore, as noted above, the Greek text of Sirach tends to a different meaning from the Latin translation used by Augustine.

This approach also treats a biblical text that is written as historical narrative as if it were an allegory. One of the fundamental errors of the medieval church was ascribing multiple meanings to a biblical text, whereas the Reformers restored the literal sense of Scripture to the church. Martin Luther (1483–1546) was aware of Augustine's view, but bluntly said,

> Therefore, as the proverb has it, he [Moses] calls "a spade a spade," i.e., he employs the terms "day" and "evening" without allegory, just as we customarily do. . . . Moses spoke in the literal sense, not allegorically or figuratively, i.e., that the world, with all its creatures, was created within six days, as the words read. If we do not comprehend the reason for this, let us remain pupils and leave the job of teacher to the Holy Spirit.[7]

The Gap View: Long Ages In Genesis 1:1–2

Some Christians propose a gap between the first two verses of Genesis.[8] Thomas Chalmers (1780–1847) promoted this viewpoint as early as 1804 among Reformed Christians, arguing that the Bible tells us the age of the human race but not the age of the earth, for there could be "an interval of many ages betwixt the first act of creation, described in the first verse of the book of Genesis . . . and those more detailed operations the account of which commences at the second verse."[9] This is sometimes called the "ruin-reconstruction view" because the condition of the earth as "without form, and void" is said to be the result of a massive catastrophe after the initial creation. The gap allows for long geological ages, while the catastrophe allows for the fossil record. *The Scofield Reference Bible* popularized this doctrine in the early twentieth century by comparing the language of Genesis 1:2 to that used by the prophets for divine judgment (Isa. 24:1;

---

7. Martin Luther, *Lectures on Genesis*, in *LW*, 1:4–5 (Genesis 1).
8. Herman Bavinck wrote that the seed of this view can be found in the teaching of Remonstrant theologians Simon Episcopius and Philipp van Limborch that the angels fell during a time period between Genesis 1:1 and 1:2, but the full theory did not emerge until the eighteenth century. Bavinck, *Reformed Dogmatics*, 2:492.
9. Quoted in William Hanna, *Memoirs of the Life and Writings of Thomas Chalmers* (Edinburgh: Thomas Constable, 1842), 1:81, 386.

45:18; Jer. 4:23) and speculating that the judgment was connected to the "fall of angels."[10] This view continues to have advocates among evangelical Christians.[11]

The gap view suffers from a lack of biblical evidence. There is nothing in Genesis 1:2 that indicates an unspoken interval of billions of years, the fall of angels, or a catastrophic judgment. Herman Bavinck pointed out, "There is nothing in this verse that supports this position. The text does not say that the earth *became* waste and void, but that it was so."[12] The use of the terminology "without form, and void" in prophetic oracles of judgment does not allow us to read judgment back into Genesis 1 when it is not present in that context,[13] but indicates that God's judgments are acts of uncreation in which he partially reverses his creative blessing, thereby demonstrating that he is the Lord. There is nothing in the entire Bible about the worldwide catastrophe proposed in the gap view.[14] That makes this doctrine highly unlikely, and certainly not one to be taught with authority.

Further, the gap view is inconsistent with biblical teaching on creation. The tone of Genesis 1 runs entirely contrary to any idea of strife or judgment, but emphasizes the sovereign ease with which God acted in making the world in perfect harmony with his will. It is difficult to see how a world already marred by Satan's rebellion could be viewed as "very good" by God (v. 31). The entire work of creation took place in six days. Exodus 20:11 states, "For in six days the LORD made heaven and earth, the sea, and all that in them is, and rested the seventh day." That does not seem to allow us to separate the creation of heaven and earth (Gen. 1:1) from the six days.[15]

The ages postulated before man's existence also seem contrary to our Lord's assertions that God created man "from the beginning of creation" (Mark 10:6) and that the blood of martyrs such as Abel was shed "from the foundation of the world" (Luke 11:50; cf. Heb. 4:3; 9:26). Such statements locate the creation of man in close proximity to the creation of the heavens and the earth (cf. Ps. 102:25; Isa. 48:13; Heb. 1:10).

---

10. *The Scofield Reference Bible*, ed. C. I. Scofield (New York: Oxford University Press, 1909), on Gen. 1:2 (3).

11. For a detailed argument in favor of the gap view, see Arthur C. Custance, *Without Form and Void* (Brockville, Canada: n.p., 1970). For a critical response, see Weston W. Fields, *Unformed and Unfilled: A Critique of the Gap Theory* (1976; repr., Green Forest, AR: Master Books, 2005).

12. Bavinck, *Reformed Dogmatics*, 2:496.

13. Feinberg, *No One Like Him*, 586.

14. Douglas F. Kelly, *Creation and Change: Genesis 1.1–2.4 in the Light of Changing Scientific Paradigms* (Fearn, Ross-shire, Scotland: Christian Focus, 1997), 96.

15. Belcher, *Genesis*, 44–45.

The Day-Age View: Six Days as a Sequence of Six Long Ages

Another attempt to interpret Genesis 1 in a manner consistent with an old earth involves reading the six days as representative of ages. Thus, the creation account is taken to present a series of divine acts spread across long periods of time. This approach attempts to preserve the truth of Genesis 1 and the order of the days, but interprets them in a manner consistent with the prevailing scientific view of the age of the universe.

Benjamin Silliman (1779–1864), lecturer on the physical sciences at Yale, proposed in 1829 a perspective that "differs from the common understanding of the Mosaic account of creation . . . not in the order of the events, but in the amount of time, which they are supposed to have occupied before the creation of man."[16] Hugh Miller (1802–1856), a geologist and believer in the inerrancy of the Bible, found himself dissatisfied with the gap view advocated by Chalmers, but accepted Chalmers's belief that "the days of the Mosaic creation may be regarded . . . as successive periods of great extent."[17] The day-age view may be wedded to theistic evolution or to progressive creationism. The latter is the idea that God acted supernaturally to create new kinds of creatures at points in a very long geological time span.[18] Two recent advocates for the day-age view are Hugh Ross and Gleason Archer (1916–2004).[19]

Some of the evidence presented for the day-age view consists of arguments against reading the six days as literal calendar days. Proponents of this view argue that theirs is a natural reading, for days sometimes represent ages in the Bible. Psalm 90:4 says, "For a thousand years in thy sight are but as yesterday when it is past, and as a watch in the night." Peter wrote, "One day is with the Lord as a thousand years, and a thousand years as one day" (2 Pet. 3:8). The day-age interpretation is said to have been common among the theologians of the early church, such as Irenaeus.[20]

The day-age doctrine represents a sincere attempt to embrace both science and the biblical witness to creation. However, we believe that it

---

16. Benjamin Silliman, *Outline of the Course of Geological Lectures Given in Yale College* (New Haven, CT: Hezekiah Howe, 1829), 126.

17. Hugh Miller, *The Testimony of the Rocks: Or, Geology in Its Bearings on the Two Theologies, Natural and Revealed* (Boston: Gould and Lincoln, 1857), 157–58.

18. Silliman, *Outline of the Course of Geological Lectures Given in Yale College*, 7, 50, 65, 121.

19. Hugh Ross and Gleason L. Archer, "The Day-Age View," in *The Genesis Debate: Three Views on the Days of Creation*, ed. David G. Hagopian (Mission Viejo, CA: Crux Press, 2001), 123–63. See Hugh Ross, *Creation and Time: A Biblical and Scientific Perspective on the Creation-Date Controversy* (Colorado Springs: NavPress, 1994). Ross is the founder of Reasons to Believe (www.reasons.org).

20. Ross and Archer, "The Day-Age View," in *The Genesis Debate*, ed. Hagopian, 125–26, 158n15. See Irenaeus, *Against Heresies*, 5.23.2, in *ANF*, 1:551–52.

imposes upon the text of Genesis 1 an unnatural and unnecessary interpretation. Scripture passages that identify a day as an age are not interpretations of Genesis but are making other points, such as God's eternity (Ps. 90:2–4) or his patience (2 Pet. 3:8–9). We have no basis in Scripture to import this metaphorical use of "day" into the Genesis account.

The day-age view was not the predominant view of the early church, claims to the contrary notwithstanding.[21] Although some early theologians such as Origen (185–c. 254) and Augustine allegorized Genesis 1, they did not interpret it in a day-age fashion, but believed the world was only several thousand years old.[22] Irenaeus did not teach the day-age view, but instead taught that there would be six ages of history that corresponded to the six literal days of creation—a view also held by others.[23]

The day-age view sets a dangerous precedent for hermeneutics or biblical interpretation, because it encourages us to use "a science-driven approach to the text."[24] For example, though the Bible indicates that God created light on the first day and the stars on the fourth day, Ross and Archer state that God made light and stars at the very beginning, and the events of days one and four refer to God making the atmosphere increasingly clear so that light reached the earth and the stars became distinctly visible.[25] This is a plain example of reading scientific theory into the Bible. Such modern theories would have been foreign to the original readers of Scripture, but the text was written to communicate with them.[26] Though we believe that scientific reality agrees with the Word of the Creator, we must not let the current theory control our exegesis or we will ultimately surrender the authority and clarity of God's Word.

The Framework View: Six Days as Structured Metaphor

The framework hypothesis affirms that Genesis 1 is the true Word of God, but claims that it is not historical narrative or a presentation of events in

---

21. On early church interpretations of Genesis, see William VanDoodewaard, *The Quest for the Historical Adam* (Grand Rapids, MI: Reformation Heritage Books, 2015), 21–33. See also Robert Bradshaw, "Creationism & the Early Church" (online book), https://robibradshaw.com/contents.htm.

22. Origen, *Against Celsus*, 1.19–20, in *ANF*, 4:404; and Augustine, *The City of God*, 12.10–12, in *NPNF*[1], 2:232–33.

23. Irenaeus, *Against Heresies*, 5.28.3, in *ANF*, 1:557.

24. Lee Irons with Meredith G. Kline, "The Framework Response [to the Day-Age View]," in *The Genesis Debate*, ed. Hagopian, 180.

25. Ross and Archer, "The Day-Age View," in *The Genesis Debate*, ed. Hagopian, 135.

26. Feinberg, *No One Like Him*, 612.

chronological sequence, but theological proclamation instead.[27] Whereas the gap and day-age approaches preserve the historical order of the Genesis days, this interpretation of the days sees them as following a topical arrangement. It is called the "framework" approach because it argues that the text is a literary framework designed to communicate theological truth through an extended metaphor or parable. The framework hypothesis was articulated at Princeton Theological Seminary in 1892 by John D. Davis (1854–1926).[28] It was popularized by Arie Noordtzij (1871–1944), Nicholas H. Ridderbos (1910–1981), and Meredith Kline (1922–2007).[29] It has rapidly grown in popularity among Reformed and evangelical Christians in the last few decades.

As with the day-age view, much of the support for the framework view rests upon arguments that the days of Genesis 1 cannot be literal calendar days. Advocates for the framework view also argue that we should not take the text as a literal sequence of historical days because Genesis depicts creation topically in a parallel framework:

Realms	Inhabitants
Day 1: Light, Day, Night	Day 4: Shining Objects in the Sky
Day 2: Sky, Waters Below, Waters Above	Day 5: Sea Creatures, Flying Creatures
Day 3: Dry Land, Seas, Plants	Day 6: Animals, Man
Creator—Day 7: The Lord's Holy Rest	

Though there are two sets of days, each set refers to the same creative acts when God formed each kingdom and filled it with its inhabitants. Genesis presents them in a pattern of six and seven for literary purposes. The seventh day of God's rest is depicted by analogy to human rest, and so the first six days are also anthropomorphic analogies to God's creative acts.[30]

---

27. Lee Irons with Meredith G. Kline, "The Framework View," in *The Genesis Debate*, ed. Hagopian, 217–56.

28. John D. Davis, "The Semitic Tradition of Creation," *Presbyterian and Reformed Review* 3, no. 11 (1892): 457–59 (full article, 448–61), at Princeton Theological Seminary Library, http://journals.ptsem.edu/id/BR1892311/dmd004. Davis believed that Genesis 1 was a Hebrew adaptation of ancient myths to their own monotheistic belief system rather than direct revelation from God.

29. Irons with Kline, "The Framework View," in *The Genesis Debate*, ed. Hagopian, 225; and Young, *Studies in Genesis One*, 44.

30. Irons with Kline, "The Framework View," in *The Genesis Debate*, ed. Hagopian, 224, 245–49. Kline spoke of "creation kingdoms" and "creation kings," but we have followed the language of John Frame because it is not clear from the text that sea creatures, flying creatures, and

We respond to these arguments as follows. Structured narrative in the Bible does not prove that a text is not a historical account. Consider the highly structured accounts of the ten plagues on Egypt (Exodus 7–12) or the six sets of seven in the genealogy of Jesus Christ (Matt. 1:1–17). Are these also nonhistorical and nonsequential? Feinberg rightly cautions, "Once you treat a piece whose literary genre seems to involve history as though it does not, that also raises serious questions about other texts that appear to be history of some sort."[31]

Genesis 1 presents us with a unique historical situation—the time before the rebellion of sinners and God's curse upon the earth. It is not surprising that we find a beautiful harmony and order to the works of creation. Jean-Marc Berthoud writes, "What difficulty would it be for [the Author of the universe] to cause the most complex, refined literary form to coincide with the very way in which he himself created all things in six days? Artistic form is in no sense opposed to the actual relation of facts, especially since the Author of the account is none less than the actual Creator of the facts."[32]

Furthermore, the proposed parallel between the first three days and the next three is not exact. God set the celestial objects "in the firmament of the heaven" on day four (Gen. 1:14), but that place is not mentioned on day one for it was created on the second day. Day five is supposed to run parallel to day two, but the birds created on the fifth day "multiply in the earth" (1:22), which God made on the third day.[33] Rather than collapsing days one and four, two and five, and three and six together into three nonchronological theological topics, it makes much more sense to read Genesis 1 as a chronological sequence of days in which each act of creation prepares for what follows it.[34] For example, God created the earth (day one), and later dry land and plants (day three), and later birds that would build nests on the dry land and eat the plants (day five). If adherents to the framework view reply that we must dispense with all notions of chronology in Genesis 1, then they must surrender basic truths such as the creation of man after plants and animals, which they seem hesitant to do.[35]

---

other animals rule as kings over their environments. Note that Frame is not advocating this view, but sympathetically describing it. Frame, *The Doctrine of God*, 303–4.

31. Feinberg, *No One Like Him*, 614.

32. Translated from French and cited in Kelly, *Creation and Change*, 115.

33. Young, *Studies in Genesis One*, 72.

34. Wayne Grudem, *Systematic Theology: An Introduction to Biblical Doctrine* (Grand Rapids, MI: Zondervan, 1994), 302–3.

35. Note that Irons and Kline still desire to assert from Genesis 1 that "the six days constitute a closed period" of special creative activity (implying a progression from six to seven) and that

As to the seventh day, while it is true that the text depicts God resting in an anthropomorphic manner (perhaps to highlight our responsibility to imitate him by keeping the Sabbath), it is an interpretive leap to conclude that the sequence of days is itself an anthropomorphism. Does the presence of anthropomorphism or metaphor in other narratives imply that they are also nonhistorical? What, then, about Genesis 2:7? The rest of Genesis? The rest of the Bible? Again, we find that interpreting Genesis 1 as something other than historical narrative introduces a dangerous hermeneutic. Contrary to such an approach, we agree with Edward Young: "From the presence of 'anthropomorphic' words or expressions in Genesis one, it does not follow that the mention of the days is anthropomorphic nor does it follow that the days are to be understood in a topical or non-chronological order rather than chronologically."[36]

In reality, the seventh day provides a powerful argument against the framework view, for the seventh day is the ground of the weekly pattern in which man works six days and then spends the seventh in holy rest. Young said, "The whole structure of the week is rooted and grounded in the fact that God worked for six consecutive days and rested a seventh."[37] However, under the framework interpretation, God did not work for a series of six days and then rest on the seventh. The entire sequence upon which the fourth commandment stands dissolves.

The Calendar Day View: Six Literal Days in Chronological Sequence

The *prima facie* reading of Genesis 1—that is, the interpretation that arises most immediately from a first reading of the text—is a historical sequence of six actual days. The repetition of the phrase "the evening and the morning" with each of the six days suggests an ordinary cycle of night and day. As Robert Reymond (1932–2013) said, given that the "overwhelming preponderance" of this terminology in Scripture refers to "the ordinary daily cycle," that understanding "should be maintained unless contextual considerations force one to another view."[38] The calendar day view also finds support in the literal reading of Genesis 1:5, "And the evening and the morning were

---

"man was created at the end of the process." Irons with Kline, "The Framework Response [to the Day-Age View]," in *The Genesis Debate*, ed. Hagopian, 182.

36. Young, *Studies in Genesis One*, 58.
37. Young, *Studies in Genesis One*, 78.
38. Reymond, *A New Systematic Theology of the Christian Faith*, 393.

one day."[39] As far back as the fourth century, Basil the Great (c. 329–379) commented that the intent may have been to define the measure of "the space of one day" in this context as "twenty-four hours."[40] The use of the numerical sequence of days to ground the Sabbath commandment also depends on taking the text at its face value and confirms that Moses regarded the period of creation as a literal week (Ex. 20:11; 31:17).

Christians who interpret Genesis 1 as six calendar days often see this interpretation as self-evident from the text itself and may find it puzzling that any Christian would question it. However, Christians who hold to views such as the day-age or framework approaches argue that we cannot accept this literal interpretation for the following reasons:

1. God is said to have created light on the first day, but the sun on the fourth. It is not reasonable to consider the first three days to be literal days without a sun or to think that God would make one source of light and then replace it with another.[41]

2. Too many events take place on the sixth day (Gen. 1:24–31) to fit into a twenty-four-hour day, including the creation of animals, the creation of man, man's naming of the animals, the creation of woman, and man's speech about her (cf. Genesis 2).[42]

3. The seventh day has no reference to evening and morning, and therefore is an age or "eternal day" that continues to the present time (Gen. 2:1–3; cf. Heb. 4:3–11).[43]

4. Genesis 2:4 says God created all things in a day: "In the day that the LORD God made the earth and the heavens." Therefore, the days are not literal.[44]

5. Genesis 2:5–6 shows that God did not sustain his world by supernatural acts during the creation process, but by ordinary, natural providence, and so did not create plants before the sun, dry the earth in a single day after separating it from the waters, and so on.[45]

---

39. The Hebrew text does not say "the first day," using ordinal numerals, but the cardinal "one" (*ekhad*).

40. Basil, *Hexaemeron*, 2.8, in *NPNF²*, 8:64.

41. Irons with Kline, "The Framework View," in *The Genesis Debate*, 221, 229; and Kenneth R. Samples, "The Nature and Duration of Creation Day Six," December 4, 2007, *Reasons to Believe*, https://www.reasons.org/explore/publications/rtb-101/read/rtb-101/2007/12/04/the-nature-and-duration-of-creation-day-six.

42. Samples, "The Nature and Duration of Creation Day Six."

43. Ross and Archer, "The Day-Age View," in *The Genesis Debate*, 146–47; and Irons with Kline, "The Framework View," in *The Genesis Debate*, ed. Hagopian, 245.

44. Miller, *The Testimony of the Rocks*, 158.

45. Irons with Kline, "The Framework View," in *The Genesis Debate*, ed. Hagopian, 232–33.

Therefore, some Christians have concluded that, without denying the truth of the Holy Scriptures, the text of Genesis itself drives us to read the six days as six ages, as a literary framework, or as some other kind of metaphor.

However, we believe that, despite these objections, the text of Genesis is still best interpreted as a historical narrative about a sequence of six calendar days followed by the seventh. In reply to the arguments above, we state that:

1. The absence of the sun prior to the fourth day does not hinder a cycle of day and night; all that is needed is a light source from a particular direction (created on the first day) and the rotation of the earth. The text bases these events on the supernatural power of the Creator to create and rule at his mere word, not the natural order we observe in the world today. John Calvin anticipated this objection when he wrote, "The Lord, by the very order of creation, bears witness that he holds in his hand the light, which he is able to impart to us without the sun and moon."[46] God operated without the sun for days one, two, and three to show he did not need it or any earthly means to provide for his creation.[47] Therefore, we do not depend ultimately on any created thing, much less worship it, but give our trust and worship to God alone.

2. The objection against the sixth day containing all the events of Genesis 2 is based on speculative assumptions about the detail and duration of Adam's naming of the animals. We simply do not know how specific the naming was or how long it took. We should not, therefore, take Genesis 2:19–20 as a contradiction of the literal reading of Genesis 1. The point of the text, rather, is to demonstrate Adam's authority over the animals and his need for a helper suitable for him.

3. Genesis 2:1–3 does not state or imply that the seventh day continues to the present. Since it is the last day in the creation week, we would not expect it to bear the same features of the first six days. To appeal to the lack of a reference to "the evening and the morning" is an argument from silence, and such arguments are notoriously inconclusive. If the seventh day were perpetual, it would

---

46. Calvin, *Commentaries*, on Gen. 1:3.
47. John Calvin, *Sermons on Genesis: Chapters 1:1–11:4*, trans. Rob Roy McGregor (Edinburgh: Banner of Truth, 2009), 25–26.

make nonsense of the command to keep one day out of seven as the Sabbath, as God did (Ex. 20:11). We would be keeping the Sabbath perpetually. Hebrews 4:3–11 deals with the Sabbath rest from the perspective of typology, just as that epistle treats Aaron, Melchizedek, the sacrifices, and the land of Canaan as types of Christ and his kingdom. It is not saying that the seventh day *is* the eternal rest, but that the Sabbath foreshadows the heavenly rest that we obtain by faith in Christ.

4. The expression "in the day that the LORD God made the earth and the heavens" (Gen. 2:4) uses a Hebrew idiom that means "when, at the time."[48] It may be translated, "When the LORD God made . . ." The syntax of the six creation days is significantly different, being a numbered sequence of days in a narrative. A similar sequence appears in Numbers 7:12–83, which speaks of a series of offerings on the "first day," "second day," "third day," and so on through the twelfth day. Like Genesis 1, Numbers 7 is highly repetitive, but is clearly intended to communicate a historical sequence of literal days.

5. The argument from Genesis 2:5–6 is puzzling, for it attempts to deduce a universal principle from a specific situation. The text prepares the reader for the narrative that follows, in which God assigns man the vocation of keeping and guarding the garden.[49] Why should we read these verses as a hidden clue that chapter 1 is not literal history? Even if Genesis 2:5 describes an ordinary providential work (and some aspects of the text are difficult to interpret),[50] how does it prove God did not act supernaturally in other situations to preserve his creation in the first week?[51] Both Genesis 1 and 2 ascribe an overwhelmingly supernatural character to God's works during this time. When God's world was not fully formed and finished, we might expect it not to function as the stable system it became and presently is under God's ordinary providence, but to need the continual supernatural nurturing of the Holy Spirit (1:2).

---

48. Belcher, *Genesis*, 28. The Hebrew consists of *beyom* in construct relation to the infinitive verb "to make" (*'asot*). On this syntax, see Brown, Driver, and Briggs, *Enhanced Brown-Driver-Briggs Hebrew and English Lexicon*, 400, defn. 7d(1).

49. J. Ligon Duncan III and David W. Hall, "The Twenty-Four-Hour Response [to the Framework View]," in *The Genesis Debate*, ed. Hagopian, 262.

50. See Belcher, *Genesis*, 32–33.

51. Young, *Studies in Genesis One*, 64.

In the end, we find the plain and simple reading of Genesis 1 as a historical narrative to be the most compelling. When the Reformers called the church back to the Word of God, they taught God's people to follow the literal sense of the history recorded in Genesis, not an allegorical reading of it.[52] Calvin said of chapter 1, "Moses wanted to indicate that one entire day was made up of two parts: from evening till morning, and from morning till the following evening"—that is, "the day and the night," or "twenty-four hours."[53]

The sophisticated arguments used to deny this are, in a sense, self-defeating, for if the days were not literal, how would Genesis 1 have communicated clearly to its ancient Hebrew audience? Could they have accused Moses of writing in a deceitful manner if the actual meaning of the text is hidden in subtle clues or assumptions about light, the sun, and other aspects of the text? Conversely, we must ask how many people would interpret Genesis 1 in any other way than a literal series of days if they were not influenced by other factors, whether it be apocryphal writings (as was Augustine) or scientific theories (as are modern theologians).

We have noted that our stance on the six days of Genesis 1 has significant implications for how we interpret the whole Bible and for the authority of the Scriptures relative to the sciences. We must state again, however, that we should not view Christians with different views of the creation days as heretics. Though the doctrine of creation is essential for orthodox Christianity, this aspect of the doctrine is not.[54] Therefore, let us debate it earnestly but not condemn one another over it. We are not calling for a theological truce to "live and let live." Rather, we are calling for brothers to speak the truth in love so that we may all grow up into the Head, the Lord Jesus Christ, by whom all things were made.

Sing to the Lord

The Beauty of God's Creation

Each little flow'r that opens,
Each little bird that sings,
God made their glowing colors,
He made their tiny wings.

---

52. Joel R. Beeke, *What Did the Reformers Believe about the Age of the Earth?* (Petersburg, KY: Answers in Genesis, 2014).
53. Calvin, *Sermons on Genesis*, 29, 60.
54. Vos, *Reformed Dogmatics*, 1:169; and Feinberg, *No One Like Him*, 578.

Refrain:
Yes, all things bright and beautiful,
All creatures great and small,
And all things wise and wonderful,
The Lord God made them all.

The purple-headed mountain,
The river running by,
The sunset and the morning
That brightens up the sky.

He gave us eyes to see them,
And lips that we might tell
How great is God Almighty,
Who doeth all things well.

Cecil Frances Alexander
Tune: All Things Bright and Beautiful
Trinity Hymnal—Baptist Edition, No. 636

Questions for Meditation or Discussion

1. What view of the six days in Genesis 1 did Augustine hold?
2. How do the authors argue against Augustine's view?
3. What is the "gap" or "ruin-reconstruction" view of Genesis 1?
4. What arguments do the authors present against the gap theory?
5. What is the "day-age" view of Genesis 1?
6. What claim do advocates of the day-age view make about historical views of creation in the church? Is this claim true or false?
7. How does the day-age view exemplify "a science-driven approach to the text" of Scripture?
8. What is the "framework" interpretation of Genesis 1?
9. For what reasons do the authors disagree with the framework interpretation?
10. What is the "calendar day" interpretation of Genesis 1? What is its greatest strength?
11. How are the following points or texts used as objections to the calendar day interpretation? How do the authors answer each objection?

    • the creation of the sun on the fourth day
    • the several events of the sixth day

- the seventh day
- Genesis 2:4
- Genesis 2:5–6

Questions for Deeper Reflection

12. The authors indicate that one reason they find the calendar day interpretation most compelling is that it is "the plain and simple reading of Genesis 1." What do they mean? Do you agree? Why or why not?

13. How is it that faithful Christians, including such theologians as Augustine, John Calvin, Thomas Chalmers, and Meredith Kline, can disagree about how to read Genesis 1? What lessons can we learn from this disagreement among believers in God's Word?

5

The Creation of the World, Part 4

Scientific Questions

When it comes to relating the Bible to science, we can fall into two fundamental errors. One ditch into which we can fall is treating the Bible as if it were a science textbook. Herman Bavinck quoted Augustine as saying, "We do not read in the Gospel that the Lord said: 'I will send you a Paraclete who will teach you about the course of the sun and the moon!'"[1] The purpose of the Bible is not to teach astronomy, geology, or biology, but to make us wise unto salvation by faith in Christ and to turn us from sin to a life of righteousness (2 Tim. 3:15–16).

The other ditch is the error of saying the Bible has no authority to speak to matters pertaining to science. If that were the case, then we would have no doctrine of creation from the Scriptures. Parts of the Bible asserting such a doctrine would have to be treated as something less than the Word of God. Bavinck said, "When Scripture, from its own perspective precisely as the book of religion, comes into contact with other sciences and also sheds its light on them, it does not all at once cease to be the Word of God but remains that Word."[2] Whatever the Bible says,

---

1. Augustine, *Proceedings against Felix the Manichee*, 1.10, cited in Bavinck, *Reformed Dogmatics*, 2:495.
2. Bavinck, *Reformed Dogmatics*, 2:495.

including its teachings about history or the origin of the universe, is truth revealed by God.

Though we assert the supreme authority of the Bible, we do not demean science, but value it highly as a noble, God-glorifying enterprise (1 Kings 4:30, 33; Prov. 25:2). Many eminent scientists have believed the Bible to be the Word of God.[3] Christians should esteem science as part of our stewardship from God to subdue the earth and exercise dominion over its creatures (Gen. 1:28). At the same time, we are royal stewards, not supreme kings, so all our investigations and actions must be done in a spirit of submission to our God and Creator. With this mindset, we are prepared to consider questions about science and creation.

Does Science Prove That the World Is Billions of Years Old?

The age of the earth has been an apologetic issue for Christianity since ancient times. Aristotle (384–322 BC) argued that the world and its motions had no beginning, but were eternal.[4] The Stoics believed that the universe ran through cycles in which it was formed out of fire according to the ordering principle of the immanent Logos, then passed through ages of history before being destroyed in fire and being formed again by the Logos.[5] In schools of Greek philosophy like these, the world was seen as an ever-changing but eternal reality, in sharp contrast to the "in the beginning" of Genesis 1:1.

Today, the doctrine of creation is often compared to scientific theories, which have largely taken the place of philosophical schools in offering explanations of reality. For many years, scientists viewed the universe as existing in a "steady state" forever. Since the mid-twentieth century, the most popular theory is that the universe erupted as a "big bang" from a point of inconceivable density and energy approximately fourteen billion years ago. The stars and planetary systems were formed out of matter and energy as the universe expanded and cooled, with our earth forming about four and a half billion years ago. A less popular alternative is the theory of a "big bounce," in which the universe

---

3. For example, Galileo Galilei, Isaac Newton, Johannes Kepler, Blaise Pascal, Michael Faraday, James Clerk Maxwell, and, more recently, Raymond Damadian, the inventor of the MRI scanner.

4. Aristotle, *Physics*, book 8, cited in Istvan Bodnar, "Aristotle's Natural Philosophy," in *The Stanford Encyclopedia of Philosophy* (Winter 2016 ed.), https://plato.stanford.edu/entries/aristotle-natphil/#4.

5. Dirk Baltzly, "Stoicism," in *The Stanford Encyclopedia of Philosophy* (Spring 2014 ed.), ed. Edward N. Zalta, https://plato.stanford.edu/entries/stoicism/#Phys.

periodically contracts to a point and then rebounds again to expand and form stars and planets.[6]

Those who believe that the world is billions of years old appeal to two major arguments: radioactive dating and the traversal of starlight across the vast regions of space. Radioactive dating (or radiometric dating) uses the rate of radioactive decay of some elements' unstable isotopes to determine the age of the material in which the elements are found. The rate of decay is exponential and measured by a half-life, which is the time for half of the isotope to decay into another element. Scientists say that radioactive dating of meteorite rock has produced results of about four and a half billion years. As to starlight, astronomers estimate that our galaxy is so large that light takes a hundred thousand years to cross it, and that galaxies billions of light-years from earth have been observed. The argument, then, is that the universe must be billions of years old in order for light to travel those distances. This, we are told, is a plain fact that we must accept, or we are irrational.

In reply, we note that science gives us not simple measurements of plain facts but interpretations of facts based on complex, humanly constructed theories that stand in tension with unexplained data. How certain are these theories? Even the big bang theory itself, though presently dominant in astrophysics, has many skeptics in the scientific community because it must hypothesize the existence of vast quantities of "dark matter" and "dark energy" in order for the theory to match observational data.[7]

As to the specific matters of dating the universe, we would make four points.

First, the Scriptures indicate that God created the world, at least in some respects, with the appearance of age.[8] God made Adam and Eve not as infants, but as adults capable of marriage and mature responsibilities in the garden. The Lord created trees already grown and bearing fruit for people and animals to eat. Presumably, these trees were rooted in soil. Over the first six days, the Lord brought the world into being as a fully

6. See Steffen Gielen and Neil Turok, "Perfect Quantum Cosmological Bounce," *Physical Review Letters*, 117, no. 2 (July 8, 2016), http://journals.aps.org/prl/abstract/10.1103/PhysRevLett.117.021301.

7. Eric Lerner, "Bucking the Big Bang," *New Scientist*, May 22, 2004, https://www.newscientist.com/article/mg18224482-900-bucking-the-big-bang/. This protest against the dominance of big bang theory in the scientific community was signed by more than two hundred scientists and engineers. See "An Open Letter to the Scientific Community," *New Scientist*, May 22, 2004, http://web.archive.org/web/20090823063418/http://www.cosmologystatement.org/.

8. Reymond, *A New Systematic Theology of the Christian Faith*, 396.

functional and integrated system. Under ordinary circumstances, people, trees, and ecological systems would have taken many years to form. But being formed instantly, creation looked older than it was.

Could the creation of the universe in a mature state explain the apparent age reflected in geological and astronomical measurements? It might explain some phenomena, such as God creating the galaxies with immediately existing gravitational fields and light in the space around them.[9] However, we need to be careful not to portray God as if he made a world that was deceptively old in its appearance, as would be the case if he created fossils where no plant or animal had ever been. Another phenomenon that is difficult to explain by the appearance of age is observable light from stellar events such as the explosion of a supernova.

The valid point of this argument is that science cannot trace the age of a supernatural act, such as creation, by comparing it to present, natural processes. If a scientist analyzed the wine that Christ miraculously made from water (John 2:1–11), he probably would conclude that it came from the juice of grapes harvested at some past time, which then had fermented over some weeks or months—though Christ made it in an instant.

Second, it is important to note that dating the world is not a matter of taking a simple measurement. There is no "clock" inside a rock. Radioactive dating involves theories about the relative amounts of elements present in rocks ages ago, the addition or removal of material over time, the intensity of radiation from outside the material, and so on. Similarly, there is no giant yardstick by which we can measure the distance to stars. The distance to stars relatively near the earth can be calculated with accurate observation and geometry, but the distance of more distant objects is estimated through indirect methods that rely on theories about astrophysics.

Third, methods of dating the universe are based on assumptions that certain quantities are constant at all times and in all places. But how do we know that the rate of radioactive decay has remained constant throughout all ages? Scientists have made a systematic study of radioactivity for only about a century.[10] What do we know for sure about interstellar space and

---

9. If God had created the sun and other stars in a moment without also creating appropriate energy fields (gravitational, electromagnetic, etc.) extending through space around them, then the sudden appearance of these radiant masses might have formed a shock wave of energy that could have harmed or destroyed the planets around them.

10. For an explanation of radiometric dating and evidence that decay rates may have been much higher in the past, see Paul A. Garner, *The New Creationism: Building Scientific Theories on a Biblical Foundation* (Darlington, England: Evangelical Press, 2009), 89–104.

the motion of light through it, given that the most distant space probe launched from earth (Voyager 1) is less than one hundredth of a light-year away? How do we know that the speed of light has never been higher than it is now? Some scientists have proposed that the speed of light is variable and was once several orders of magnitude greater than it is today.[11] How do we know how light, space, and time have interacted in regions far beyond any place we have explored and in times long before we were born?

Fourth, current astrophysics posits that space itself is expanding. The fabric of space-time is said to be expanding at such a rate that the observable universe has a radius of about 4.6 billion light years, though it is only about 14 billion years old. Therefore, how can we deduce the age of the universe from the speed of light? This may seem strange to us, but we are increasingly realizing that the laws and structure of the universe, even space and time, are an interconnected system. For example, time moves at different rates depending on one's relative velocity, especially noticeable at speeds over a tenth of the speed of light. Intense gravity can also change the passage of time.[12]

In raising these questions, we do not intend to attack the scientific fields of geology and astronomy as if they were not valid human endeavors. Instead, we are calling for humility in scientific conclusions. Scientists also live with mysteries they cannot presently explain, such as the fact that light behaves like both waves (periodic fluctuations in electromagnetic fields) and particles (discrete photons). Much more should we approach the origins of the universe with humility. The Lord's words to Job still challenge us today: "Where wast thou when I laid the foundations of the earth?" (Job 38:4). Science excels when it pertains to presently observable patterns. When it seeks to investigate events of the remote past, science must take into account reliable testimony from eyewitnesses. When we consider the creation of the world and some key events in history, we have the testimony of the true and faithful witness, God himself.

---

11. Proponents of variable light speed include noncreationist scientists. See Jean-Pierre Petit, "An Interpretation of Cosmological Model with Variable Light Velocity," *Modern Physics*, Letters A, 3, no. 16 (Nov. 1988), https://www.jp-petit.org/science/f300/modern_physics_letters_a1.pdf; J. W. Moffat, "Superluminary Universe: A Possible Solution to the Initial Value Problem in Cosmology," rev. November 14, 1998, original version published in *International Journal of Modern Physics* D, 2, no. 3 (1993): 351–65, available at Cornell University, https://arxiv.org/abs/gr-qc /9211020; Andreas Albrecht and João Magueijo, "A Time Varying Speed of Light as a Solution to Cosmological Puzzles," November 2, 1998, rev. January 5, 1999, Cornell University, https://arxiv .org/abs/astro-ph/9811018; and João Magueijo, "New Varying Speed of Light Theories," October 15, 2003, Cornell University, https://arxiv.org/pdf/astro-ph/0305457v3.pdf. See also Kelly, *Creation and Change*, 144–55.

12. Garner, *The New Creationism*, 27

If we are going to call scientists to humility, then we must practice humility ourselves as Christians and theologians. What does this mean for us? First, humility about a subject that we cannot directly observe requires us to lean wholeheartedly upon God's Word, and not our own understanding. It is not humility to be skeptical or agnostic about matters on which God has spoken. Second, humility requires us not to confuse the inerrancy of the Bible with the inerrancy of our interpretations of it. We must be willing to reexamine our doctrines and test them by the Word of God. Finally, we need to be careful not to go beyond Scripture and create doctrines about how the universe began that are not taught by God's Word. Creationists can indulge in speculative theories that are loosely based on the Bible, but dogmatism is not warranted in such matters. Theologians must remember that the Bible was written for ordinary people, and, though it is true in all it affirms, it does not speak in technical, scientific terminology.

Is the Bible Compatible with Neo-Darwinian Evolution?

The second scientific question pertinent to the doctrine of creation addresses the origin and development of life. Evolution, though proposed in scientific terms today, is deeply rooted in ancient non-Christian philosophy. People have sought for millennia to explain the universe and life within it by means of entirely natural processes. Centuries before Christ was born, Epicurean philosophers taught that we and everything around us today were formed by the random collisions of atoms over long periods of time.[13]

This atheistic, naturalistic idea was given a scientific form by Charles Darwin, an English geologist and naturalist. Darwin published a book in 1859 with the title *On the Origin of Species by Means of Natural Selection, or the Preservation of Favoured Races in the Struggle for Life*.[14] As the title suggests, Darwin proposed that the various kinds of biological life had developed by a process of natural selection whereby those living things whose characteristics best fit them to their particular environments survived and propagated themselves. The word *selection* is misleading, since the process took place not by intelligent direction but by the blind laws of nature. Species are, therefore, not immutable, but descended from other species that are generally now extinct.[15]

---

13. Obitts, "Epicureanism," in *Evangelical Dictionary of Theology*, 358.
14. Charles Darwin, *On the Origin of Species by Means of Natural Selection, or the Preservation of Favoured Races in the Struggle for Life* (London: John Murray, 1859).
15. Darwin, *On the Origin of Species*, 5–6.

Darwin's theory was widely promoted by Thomas Henry Huxley (1825–1895), especially with respect to man's descent from species of apes. Scientists in the early twentieth century synthesized the theory with newly discovered principles of genetics to form the neo-Darwinian theory of evolution, which postulated that genetic mutations introduced new characteristics that proved more advantageous to living organisms. We may distinguish between microevolution (small changes in a species or genus of organisms) and macroevolution (development of entirely new kinds of organisms). Few dispute microevolution; it is macroevolution that makes grand claims about the origin of man and all biological life.

The theory of evolution proposes that all life developed by natural processes from the elements of the earth beginning three or four billion years ago.[16] For many eons, life consisted of very simple, single-celled organisms, but these led to more complex plant life and the sudden appearance of many forms of animal life in what is called the Cambrian explosion (dated approximately 550 million to 500 million years ago). Such animals gradually advanced to the highly sophisticated organisms, including man, that are alive today.

Some Christians have embraced what is known as theistic evolution, in which the basic tenets of evolution are accepted while the atheistic philosophy that generally accompanies it is replaced by belief in the providence of God or at least the initial creation of the world by God. Thus, while God guided evolution, he did so through laws of nature. C. S. Lewis (1898–1963) proposed that God used evolution to raise up advanced animals and then granted mind and spirit to some of them to make man.[17] Thus, Adam was not a historical person as Genesis 2 depicts him. Other theistic evolutionists, such as Tim Keller, say that evolution is compatible with a literal view of Genesis 2 and the account of Adam and Eve, albeit with a nonliteral view of Genesis 1.[18] However, other Christians have raised serious objections to theistic evolution on scientific, philosophical, and biblical grounds.[19]

---

16. Technically speaking, the term for the emergence of biological life out of inanimate matter is not *evolution* but *abiogenesis*. However, abiogenesis is a crucial piece of the evolutionary explanation for life, so we speak of it here under the umbrella term of *evolution*.

17. C. S. Lewis, *The Problem of Pain* (New York: HarperCollins, 2001), 72. See David Williams, "Surprised by Jack, Part 4: Mere Evolution," December 13, 2012, Biologos blog, http://biologos.org/blogs/archive/surprised-by-jack-part-4-mere-evolution. The same approach is proposed as a possible solution in Thomas H. McCall, *Against God and Nature: The Doctrine of Sin*, Foundations of Evangelical Theology (Wheaton, IL: Crossway, 2019), 389–93.

18. Tim Keller, "Creation, Evolution, and Christian Laypeople," 3–5, 7–9, Biologos, https://biologos.org/articles/creation-evolution-and-christian-laypeople/.

19. J. P. Moreland, Stephen C. Meyer, Christopher Shaw, Ann K. Gauger, and Wayne Grudem, eds., *Theistic Evolution: A Scientific, Philosophical, and Theological Critique* (Wheaton, IL: Crossway, 2017).

Rational and Empirical Problems with Evolution

Evolution is subject to serious empirical and rational objections.[20] The fossil record does not display a smooth transition of development from one kind of living being to another. The overwhelming pattern in fossils is the stability of distinct kinds of creatures.[21] Darwin recognized this problem.[22] Despite extensive investigation of the fossil record over the last century and a half, the lack of visible transitions has grown only more acute.[23] Consequently, some evolutionary scientists, such as Niles Eldredge and Stephen Jay Gould (1941–2002), proposed a major revision to the theory called "punctuated equilibrium," which states that macroevolution is not a gradual process, but takes place in a rapid and isolated manner, and thus leaves no fossil record.[24] This dramatic reversal of the standard evolutionary theory makes it even less likely that random mutations could develop one kind of organism into another kind.

Evolution is poorly supported by biological observations or models.

- We have observed adaptation, and mankind has bred animals to produce different kinds of pets and livestock, but we have not observed macroevolution across major classifications of living things. Breeding dogs still produces dogs.
- Microbiology has uncovered a world of marvels in the smallest biological structures, tiny molecular machines with an irreducible complexity necessary to perform important functions in the life of the individual cell.[25]

20. An excellent summary of these may be found in Phillip E. Johnson, *Darwin on Trial* (Downers Grove, IL: InterVarsity Press, 1991). A new edition was published by InterVarsity Press in 2010.

21. One evolutionary geologist writes, "In four of the biggest climatic-vegetational events of the last 50 million years, the mammals and birds show no noticeable change in response to changing climates. No matter how many presentations I give where I show these data, no one (including myself) has a good explanation yet for such widespread stasis despite the obvious selective pressures of changing climate." Donald R. Prothero, "Darwin's Legacy," *eSkeptic*, February 15, 2012, http://www.skeptic.com/eskeptic/12-02-15/#feature. See Denyse O'Leary, "Stasis: Life Goes On but Evolution Does Not Happen," *Evolution News and Views*, October 12, 2015, http://www.evolutionnews.org/2015/10/stasis_when_lif100011.html.

22. Darwin, *On the Origin of Species*, 279.

23. Norman C. Nevin, "The Nature of the Fossil Record," in *Should Christians Embrace Evolution? Biblical and Scientific Responses*, ed. Norman C. Nevin (Phillipsburg, NJ: P&R, 2011), 145–46.

24. Niles Eldredge and Stephen Jay Gould, "Punctuated Equilibria: An Alternative for Phyletic Gradualism," in *Models in Paleobiology*, ed. Thomas J. M. Schopf (San Francisco: Freeman, Cooper, 1972), 82–115, http://www.blackwellpublishing.com/ridley/classictexts/eldredge.asp. See Stephen Jay Gould, *The Structure of Evolutionary Theory* (Cambridge, MA: Harvard University Press, 2002).

25. See Michael J. Behe, *Darwin's Black Box: The Biochemical Challenge to Evolution* (New York: Simon & Schuster, 1996).

- The possibility of random forces assembling living organisms out of raw materials can be compared to the probability that a tornado touching down in a junkyard would assemble a fully functional Boeing 747 jet aircraft with its engines running.[26]
- Each organism's genetic code (DNA) houses enormous amounts of information. Random chemical reactions do not create information, but, instead, tend to break it down. New information, such as the writing of sentences in a language or a computer program in code, requires intelligence, not just energy.[27]

A final rational objection to the theory of evolution pertains to its moral consequences. The Humanist Manifesto III states, "Humans are an integral part of nature, the results of unguided evolutionary change." Yet it also states, "We are committed to treating each person as having inherent worth and dignity."[28] This is commendable, but we must ask, "Why?" If human beings are animals, then why not kill them if we find it useful? If some people are weaker and less productive than the rest of the population, why should we care for them with costly compassion? People who believe in evolution may think that we should conduct ourselves in an ethical and kind manner, but they have no rational basis to do so. Moral obligation implies a transcendent standard, and such a standard can come only from our Creator.

Evolution and Biblical Truth

While we acknowledge that it is possible for a person to believe in evolution and yet be a Christian, we argue that evolution is inconsistent with the Holy Scriptures. Christian theistic evolution is personally possible but internally incoherent, and ultimately harmful for faith.

First, as we argued in the previous chapter, Genesis 1 teaches that God created the universe, plants, animals, and man in the space of six days. This literal historical account rules out the possibility of the long ages of time necessary for evolution.

Second, Genesis 1 indicates that plants, animals, and mankind came into existence by supernatural acts of God. The chapter presents creation

---

26. See Johnson, *Darwin on Trial*, 104.

27. Andy McIntosh, "Information and Thermodynamics," in *Should Christians Embrace Evolution?*, 160–65. See Werner Gitt, *In the Beginning Was Information* (Green Forest, AR: Master Books, 2005).

28. "Humanism and Its Aspirations: Humanist Manifesto III, a Successor to the Humanist Manifesto of 1933," American Humanist Association, https://americanhumanist.org/what-is -humanism/manifesto3/.

by divine fiat: "And God said, Let there be light: and there was light" (Gen. 1:3). The same kind of language is used for the creation of plants (v. 11), sea creatures and flying creatures (v. 20), and land animals (v. 24). As Stephen Charnock observed, the immediate connection between God's speaking and creation's coming forth is even more evident in the Hebrew text, where the words translated as "let there be light" and "and there was light" are identical, with the only difference being the addition of the Hebrew conjunction translated as "and," as if to say that God's speaking of the word is the accomplishment of God's will.[29] This does not communicate slow, natural development over long ages, but effectual divine action with immediate results. By contrast, evolution indicates that random natural processes produced many varieties of things, most of which failed to survive, with relatively few thriving and developing over millions of years into the kinds of organisms we have today. As Wayne Grudem says, trying to force the two ideas together results in something like this: "And God said, 'Let the earth bring forth living creatures according to their kinds.' And after three hundred eighty-seven million four hundred ninety-two thousand eight hundred seventy-one attempts, God finally made a mouse that worked."[30]

Third, Genesis 1 says that God made each plant or animal "according to its kind" (vv. 11–12, 21, 25 ESV). The term rendered as "kind" (*min*), while not identical to biological taxonomic terms such as *genus* or *species*, refers to a relatively specific classification of a living creature such as a subcategory of flying creatures (Lev. 11:13–19). God originally created biological life in many differentiated forms, not in one very simple form that mutated into the dazzling variety we observe today.

Fourth, the order of the creation days in Genesis 1 does not match the order presented by evolutionary theory. The creation of birds (day five) falls before that of land animals (day six). Even if one were to interpret the days as long ages, this order contradicts the evolutionary scheme that birds evolved from reptiles, specifically a kind of small dinosaur.

Fifth, evolution's basic principle of natural selection, popularly known as "survival of the fittest," presumes that animals have suffered and died for millions of years, often by being killed by other animals for food. However, Genesis indicates that God originally gave the plants to man and the

---

29. Charnock, *The Existence and Attributes of God*, in *Works*, 2:132.
30. Grudem, *Systematic Theology*, 277.

animals to eat for their food (Gen. 1:29–30). At the end of the six days, "God saw every thing that he had made, and, behold, it was very good" (v. 31). It was only after the fall of man by his sin that God pronounced a curse upon the earth and subjected man to death (3:17–19). Death came into the world by Adam's sin (Rom. 5:12; 1 Cor. 15:21).

A theistic evolutionist might object that the entrance of death through Adam pertains only to mankind and not to animals. We reply by noting that if mankind evolved from previous life forms, then we are animals and we cannot make such a distinction: their physical mortality must be ours as well. Further, Paul indicates that the fall of man brought suffering and death to all creation: "For the creature [or creation, Greek *ktisis*] was made subject to vanity, not willingly, but by reason of him who hath subjected the same in hope, because the creature itself also shall be delivered from the bondage of corruption into the glorious liberty of the children of God. For we know that the whole creation groaneth and travaileth in pain together until now" (Rom. 8:20–22). This text does not refer to the original condition of creation, but to a condition of "vanity" to which the world was subjected by God—a reference to the consequences of man's fall. This condition will be lifted when God's children are glorified. It is also referred to as "corruption" (*phthora*), a term that means death, destruction, decay, or moral corruption.[31] As John Feinberg says, animals and plants do not suffer moral corruption, so this term must refer to physical death and decay.[32] Therefore, the groaning of creatures under pain and death arose from the fall of man. This makes evolution by natural selection impossible before God created man, and man sinned against God.

Sixth, Genesis 2:7 states that God made Adam "of the dust of the ground, and breathed into his nostrils the breath of life; and man became a living soul." The "breath of life" refers to the biological life possessed by mankind and all land animals (7:21–22; cf. Job 27:3).[33] The phrase "living soul" is the same term used for every "living creature," including animals (Gen. 2:19; 9:10–16). This indicates that prior to God's special creative act, man was not a living, breathing creature of any kind, but mere earth. The Bible affirms this repeatedly.[34] To claim that this is metaphorical

---

31. Rom. 8:21; 1 Cor. 15:42, 50; Gal. 6:8; Col. 2:22; 2 Pet. 1:4; 2:12, 19.
32. Feinberg, *No One Like Him*, 622.
33. A similar expression, though using somewhat different Hebrew terminology, also appears in Gen. 6:17; 7:15.
34. Gen. 3:19; 18:27; Ps. 103:14; 1 Cor. 15:47.

speech for man's development out of an animal is to make nonsense out of the text and to reduce Genesis 2 to a fable. The text teaches that God made man by a supernatural act. This is confirmed by the word translated as "create" with respect to man's origin (1:27); it is a work of divine energy, not a natural development. Johannes Wollebius noted, "There was no quality or disposition in the dust that would have produced the human body, which was formed unnaturally and miraculously from it."[35] What is at stake is whether we will reduce events which the Bible depicts as supernatural to natural processes.

Seventh, Genesis 2:21–23 teaches that God made Adam first, and then made the woman out of part of Adam's body. Adam later named her Eve "because she was the mother of all living" (3:20). The apostle Paul affirms the historical truth of Genesis 2 that God made Adam first, and then made woman out of the man (1 Tim. 2:13; 1 Cor. 11:8–9). Our Lord Jesus Christ quoted Genesis 2:24 and asserted in accordance with the account that God "joined together" man and woman in the first marriage (Matt. 19:5–6). Therefore, we must take Genesis 2 as a true, literal, historical account. However, this directly contradicts the idea that Adam and Eve were two individuals taken out of a group of highly evolved primates, or that there were no literal Adam and Eve, but mankind evolved as a group of individuals.

We conclude that it is impossible to embrace evolution without doing violence to the text of Scripture. To pull out this thread is to begin to unravel the fabric of God's Word. If taken to its logical conclusions, it will lead to grave doubts about the trustworthiness of the New Testament. Therefore, we call upon the church to stand against evolution. This is not a stance against science but a stance against unbelief toward the Word.

Was the Flood Global or Local?

The third question pertains to the narrative of the flood (Genesis 6–9), which is not strictly part of the creation account but is closely related to the doctrine of creation. The destruction of the earth and its inhabitants was a partial act of uncreation by God, and the bringing of Noah's family and representatives of the animals and birds through the flood by the ark was like a renewed creation. Thus, the Lord renewed the call upon man to be fruitful, multiply, and fill the earth after Noah emerged from the ark (9:1).

---

35. Wollebius, *Compendium*, 1.5.(1).iv (54).

The nations of the world can be traced back to their origin in the sons of Noah (Genesis 10). Their descendants built the Tower of Babel, and the Lord confused their language to divide them into the various linguistic and ethnic groups of the nations (Genesis 11). Noah's flood and the events that immediately followed are foundational to the Bible's explanation for the origins of mankind as we exist today.

However, some people regard the flood as a legend that may have grown out of the historical seed of a local flood but then took on epic proportions. They point out that other ancient cultures included a flood story in their mythology, such as the Epic of Gilgamesh.[36] They also argue that the geological record does not bear testimony to a global flood. Some Christians have responded to these arguments by conceding that the flood of Genesis was only a local event and may even have mythological elements, but it still communicates the inspired message that God judges sin and saves people by grace.[37] In this manner, they seek to conform to scientific conclusions but maintain a posture of faith in the Word of God. However, other Christians have proposed alternative geological explanations that support a worldwide flood.[38]

Most significant from a theological perspective is the question of whether Genesis can be interpreted as teaching a local flood or a global flood. We affirm the last position. The flood account was written as narrative with no indications that it is anything other than a historical account. In fact, Genesis 7 and 8 refer to specific dates and periods of time, as if drawn from a diary.[39] Treating the text as a legendary shell to communicate a theological message undermines both the authority of God's Word and

---

36. For a study of the Gilgamesh flood story and how it relates to Genesis, see Nozomi Osanai, "A Comparative Study of the Flood Accounts in the Gilgamesh Epic and Genesis," Answers in Genesis, August 3, 2005, https://answersingenesis.org/the-flood/flood-legends/flood-gilgamesh-epic /introduction/.

37. "How Should We Interpret the Genesis Flood Account?," Biologos, updated Feb. 11, 2019, http://biologos.org/common-questions/biblical-interpretation/genesis-flood.

38. One theory popular in the mid-twentieth century was the collapse of a water canopy above the atmosphere. See John C. Whitcomb and Henry M. Morris, *The Genesis Flood: The Biblical Record and Its Scientific Implications* (Philadelphia: Presbyterian and Reformed, 1961), 77, 240, 255–57. This is an interpretation of Gen. 1:6–7 that asserted that "the waters which were above the firmament" were a vapor canopy in the upper atmosphere that came down during the flood. The theory was proposed in 1874 by a Quaker scientist, Isaac Newton Vail (1840–1912). See Isaac N. Vail, *The Waters above the Firmament: or, The Earth's Annular System*, 2nd ed. (Philadelphia: Ferris and Leach, 1902). It seems, however, to be contrary to Scripture, which portrays the waters above the heavens as remaining after the flood (Ps. 148:4). It also proved to be difficult to sustain scientifically. For a more recent theory called catastrophic plate tectonics, see Garner, *The New Creationism*, 183–93; and Andrew A. Snelling, *Earth's Catastrophic Past: Geology, Creation, and the Flood*, 2 vols. (Petersburg, KY: Answers in Genesis, 2010).

39. Gen. 7:11, 17, 24; 8:3–6, 10, 12–14.

its theological message. But there are good reasons to conclude that the flood was worldwide in scope.

First, Genesis 6–9 teaches that God destroyed all living creatures on the surface of the earth in the flood (7:4). The Lord did not say that he would destroy a group of people, but "I will destroy man whom I have created from the face of the earth; both man, and beast, and the creeping thing, and the fowls of the air" (6:7). The reason was that "all flesh had corrupted his way upon the earth" (v. 12). The text says six times that this judgment would come on "all flesh."[40] In fact, the flood narrative places great emphasis upon the totality of the judgment: "The waters prevailed exceedingly upon the earth . . . and the mountains were covered. And all flesh died that moved upon the earth . . . and Noah only remained alive, and they that were with him in the ark" (Gen. 7:19–23).

Second, the narrative does not make sense if it describes only a local flood. Why did Noah need to save representatives of all the animals if only a region were to be flooded? Why bring birds into the ark when they could fly away? In fact, why did Noah need to build a boat, especially one of such large proportions (450 feet by 75 feet by 45 feet)? Why did he not simply move to a safe location or climb a mountain? If, however, the flood covered all the mountains that existed at that time, but just in one area, how did the waters remain high for five months (Gen. 7:24), resulting in conditions that kept Noah in the ark for more than a year? The point of these questions is that trying to read a local flood into Genesis makes the account ludicrous.

Third, the text indicates that the flood was an unusual catastrophe involving a geological disturbance, not just a large flood produced by rain. Genesis 7:11 says, "The same day were all the fountains of the great deep broken up, and the windows of heaven were opened" (cf. 8:2). The "fountains of the great deep" might refer to the bottom of the oceans (cf. Prov. 8:28–29) or to "subterranean waters."[41] The verb translated as "broken up" (*baqʻa*) means to forcefully divide, split, or violently tear.[42] Therefore, heavy rain from above was accompanied by violent eruptions of water from below. While this does not prove that the flood was worldwide, it does indicate that it was a cataclysmic event that disrupted the geological formations of the earth.

---

40. Gen. 6:12–13, 17; 7:21; 9:11, 15; cf. Gen. 6:19; 7:15–16; 8:17; 9:15–17.
41. Belcher, *Genesis*, 95.
42. Gen. 22:3; Ex. 14:16, 21; Num. 16:31; etc.

Fourth, the presence of flood stories in other documents of the ancient Near East does not prove that Genesis 6–9 is legendary. In fact, it can be argued the other way around. Flood stories are found all over the world, including African, European, Russian, Chinese, Indian, Native American, and Pacific Island cultures. They do differ in details, and some contain fantastic elements that contradict Genesis. However, this is what one would expect if there had been a global flood: memories preserved in stories recounted in many nations.

Fifth, if we sweep aside the explicit statements of Genesis in order to assert that the text refers to a local flood with a mixture of hyperbole and legend, then we overthrow the authority of God's Word. We silence the Bible's ability to instruct us about any historical event. If it is argued that Noah's flood is a special case because it does not accord with the conclusions of scientists, then we have set a precedent to treat any narrative of a miraculous event as a myth—including the resurrection of Jesus Christ from the dead—if the culture contradicts it.

Sixth, we cannot reduce the flood narrative to a legend with a theological point without undermining the theology of its message. The theology of the flood is not merely a message of judgment and grace, but of *total* judgment and *exclusive* grace: "Noah only remained alive, and they that were with him in the ark" (Gen. 7:23). If the flood was merely local, the point is lost, for many people would have survived without making use of God's means of salvation. Christ and Peter used the flood as a foreshadowing of the Lord's coming to judge the world (Matt. 24:37–38; 2 Pet. 2:5; cf. 3:6). The application is clear: God's judgment fell upon the whole world with the flood, and it will fall upon all the world again, and no one will escape unless they are saved by Jesus Christ (Acts 4:12). If we regard the flood as a mere legend with no historical basis at all, then the theological message it conveys falls to the ground.

Seventh, interpreting the flood as a local event raises serious doubts about the trustworthiness of God's covenants. After God called Noah out of the ark, the Lord made a covenant with him, his family, and all birds and animals: "Neither shall all flesh be cut off any more by the waters of a flood; neither shall there any more be a flood to destroy the earth" (Gen. 9:11). If the flood refers to a local inundation, then God did not keep his promise, for many such floods have taken place, including the coastal flood caused by the 2004 tsunami in the Indian Ocean, which swept more than two hundred thousand people to their deaths. We see how serious this matter is when we consider that God asserted that his faithfulness to the covenant with Noah is his faithfulness to the new covenant (Isa. 54:9–10). While compromising on the totality of the flood may seem like a minor historical point, it not only undermines the authority of Scripture, but also the doctrine of salvation in Christ alone.

Sing to the Lord

The Supremacy of God the Creator

> Sing to the Lord, sing His praise all ye peoples,
> New be your song as new honors ye pay;
> Sing of His majesty, bless Him forever,
> Show His salvation from day to day.

> Tell of His wondrous works, tell of His glory,
> Till through the nations His name is revered;
> Praise and exalt Him, for He is almighty,
> God over all let the Lord be feared.

> Vain are the heathen gods, idols and helpless,
> God made the heav'ns, and His glory they tell;
> Honor and majesty shine out before Him,
> Beauty and strength in His temple dwell.

> Make all the nations know God reigns forever;
> Earth is established as He did decree;
> Righteous and just is the King of the nations,
> Judging the people with equity.

Psalm 96
Tune: Wesley
The Psalter, No. 259
Trinity Hymnal—Baptist Edition, No. 65

Questions for Meditation or Discussion

1. What reasons do the authors give to urge scientists not to be dogmatic about the age of the universe based on radioactive dating and starlight from distant galaxies?
2. What is the theory of evolution?

3. What scientific objections have been raised against the theory of evolution?

4. What moral objection has been raised against the theory of evolution?

5. How is the first chapter of Genesis incompatible with evolution?

6. How is the second chapter of Genesis incompatible with evolution?

7. How does Genesis 6–9 refute the idea that Noah's flood was local, not worldwide?

8. How might flood legends in many cultures support the historical reality of Noah's flood?

9. If the flood of Genesis was not worldwide, what does that imply about God's promises? Why?

10. If accidental chemical changes over time produced all life, including you, what difference would it make in what you believe about yourself and how you treat other people?

Questions for Deeper Reflection

11. When you are talking to a friend about creation and evolution, he says, "Don't you see that evolution is a proven scientific fact? How can you cling to the old ideas of the Bible when so many scientists stand against you?" What do you say?

12. Your friend says, "I don't see why I have to take Genesis literally in order to be a Christian. Why can't I accept evolution and still believe in Christ for my salvation?" How do you respond?

Section B

The Doctrine of Man's Creation and Nature

6

The Creation of Man by God

What is man? Sadly, many in this age seek answers to this question merely by studying man's body and behavior in comparison to the animals. This leads to a degraded view of man. In William Shakespeare's drama, Hamlet says,

What is a man,
If his chief good and market of his time
Be but to sleep and feed? A beast, no more.

Hamlet then considers that "he that made us . . . gave us not that capability and god-like reason to fust [rot] in us unused."[1]

Three centuries later, George Bernard Shaw (1856–1950) recognized that "a beast, no more" is indeed the implication of Darwin's theory of evolution. Shaw wrote,

The Darwinian process may be described as a chapter of accidents. As such, it seems simple, because you do not at first realize all that it involves. But when its whole significance dawns on you, your heart sinks into a heap of sand within you. There is a hideous fatalism about it, a ghastly and damnable reduction of beauty and intelligence, of strength and purpose, of honor and aspiration, to such casually picturesque changes as an avalanche may make in a landscape, or a railway accident in a human figure.[2]

---

1. William Shakespeare, *Hamlet*, act 4, scene 4.
2. George Bernard Shaw, *Back to Methuselah: A Metabiological Pentateuch* (New York: Brentano's, 1921), xlvi.

In sharp contrast, the Christian faith teaches that man is no conglomeration of blind accidents, but a fallen masterpiece of God. In order to understand who we are, we must go back to man's creation by God, as it is recorded in the Holy Scriptures. The Bible opens with two complementary accounts of God's creation of mankind. The first presents man as the crown of the cosmos. The second account shows us man's original closeness to the Creator. We will examine both accounts in this chapter.

Man's Special Honor in God's Cosmos (Gen. 1:26–2:3)

Although man is one kind of creature among the many made by God, this creature has a unique place in the world. The first chapter of Genesis contains a number of indications that God created man with a special status.

The Climax of the Creation Account

Over the first six days, God shaped his world with increasing complexity and beauty. From the initial mass of dark earth and water arose the highly structured world of seas and dry land populated with a vast variety of plants. God filled the skies with dazzling points of light to distinguish the days, seasons, and years. At his command, new creatures sprang into motion in the sky and the sea, including the monstrous beasts that swim the depths. Then, on the last day of his creative work, God made the land animals, from creeping insects to lumbering cattle. However, there was one creature that remained for God to make. Man was the crown of creation for whom the world was prepared. The text emphasizes the centrality of man in God's creative acts by repeating the verb that is translated as "create" (*bara*) three times in Genesis 1:27, whereas it appears only twice before (vv. 1, 21).[3] We see a teleology in the process of creation, a systematic method designed to reach this great goal or end (*telos*).[4] John Laidlaw (1832–1906) wrote, "At the summit man appears, the apex of the pyramid of earthly being."[5] Only then, with man and woman on earth, was God's creation done and pronounced "very good" (Gen. 1:31).

The progression of Genesis 1 witnesses to God's love for man. John Calvin said, "We ought in the very order of things diligently to contemplate

---

3. Kenneth A. Mathews, *Genesis 1–11:26*, The New American Commentary 1A (Nashville: Broadman & Holman, 1996), 160.
4. Walther Eichrodt, *Theology of the Old Testament*, trans. J. A Baker, Old Testament Library (Philadelphia: Westminster, 1961–1967), 2:109.
5. John Laidlaw, *Bible Doctrine of Man, or The Anthropology and Psychology of Scripture*, rev. ed. (Edinburgh: T&T Clark, 1895), 28.

God's fatherly love toward mankind, in that he did not create Adam until he had lavished upon the universe all manner of good things."[6] Adam awakened to a world of wonders. Calvin added, "Man was rich before he was born."[7] God gave mankind all things richly so that we may enjoy them and be rich in thanksgiving and good works (1 Tim. 4:4; 6:17). Stephen Charnock wrote, "The world was made for man," noting that "angels have not need of anything in the world," but "the world was made for the support and delight of man, in order to his performing the service due from him to God."[8]

Surely this was the occasion of rejoicing in heaven. The angels sang God's praises when God laid the foundation of the earth (Job 38:4, 7). We can imagine them watching in wonder and joy as God structured and adorned his world with flowers, trees, fruit, fish, birds, beetles, and lions. What must have been their sense of wonder when God created the first man and woman? To this day, the angels watch mankind and marvel over God's goodness to us, especially his saving goodness to the elect in Christ, the last Adam.[9]

The Counsel of God

Another way in which God drew attention to the special honor he was bestowing on mankind was the announcement of divine counsel prior to man's creation. When God made other animate creatures, he said, "Let the waters bring forth," or, "Let the earth bring forth" (Gen. 1:20, 24). However, we read in Genesis 1:26, "And God said, Let us make man." This surprising "let us" reveals God consulting with God, which we recognize in the light of later revelation as a conversation within the Trinity.[10] John Chrysostom (c. 344–407) said that these words suggest "deliberation, collaboration and conference with another person," a unique feature in creation that greatly honors man among God's creatures.[11] Calvin commented, "Hitherto God has been introduced simply as *commanding*; now, when he approaches the most excellent of all his works, he enters into *consultation*. . . . He chose to give this tribute to the excellency of man."[12]

---

6. Calvin, *Institutes*, 1.14.2.
7. Calvin, *Commentaries*, on Gen. 1:26.
8. Charnock, *The Existence and Attributes of God*, in *Works*, 2:310.
9. Luke 15:10; 1 Cor. 4:9; 11:10; Eph. 3:10; Heb. 1:13–14; 1 Pet. 1:12.
10. On the Trinity and creation, see chap. 2.
11. John Chrysostom, *Sermons on Genesis*, 2.1, in *ACCS/OT*, 1:28.
12. Calvin, *Commentaries*, on Gen. 1:26. Calvin went on to say in the same place, "But since the Lord needs no other counsellor, there can be no doubt that he consulted with himself. The Jews make themselves altogether ridiculous, in pretending that God held communication with the earth or with angels."

What does this consultation imply? In a consultation, people take counsel together to make a wise plan.[13] Martin Luther commented, "Man was created by the special plan and providence of God."[14] We should not deduce that God made the other creatures without careful thought, for all creation displays the wisdom of the Creator (Ps. 104:24). However, the words "let us make man" imply that man stands at the center of the wise and eternal counsel of the Trinity. In Proverbs 8, we hear God's Wisdom "rejoicing" at the creation of the world and saying, "My delights were with the sons of men" (Prov. 8:30–31). Literally, the word translated as "rejoicing" (*sakhaq*) means "laughing" or "playing," a vivid word picture that reflects God's joy in his wise purposes for mankind. Mankind was the focal point of God's delightful decree.

We learn from the New Testament that this counsel especially centered upon one man, the God-man, our Lord Jesus Christ, who is Wisdom incarnate. Paul writes that God "hath saved us, and called us with an holy calling, not according to our works, but according to his own purpose and grace, which was given us in Christ Jesus before the world began" (2 Tim. 1:9). This was "the eternal purpose which he purposed in Christ Jesus our Lord" (Eph. 3:11). When the Father, Son, and Holy Spirit made Adam, they had already planned that the Son would become the last Adam to redeem our fallen race. God was forming the human nature to which he would eternally join himself in the incarnation. How marvelous is his love!

The Image of God

The uniqueness of humanity among the creatures further appears in the way God made us to represent him on earth. When God made the plants, sea creatures, flying creatures, and land creatures, the text says ten times he made each "after his kind" or "after their kind."[15] However, Laidlaw noted that "when we come to man, the formula is suddenly and brilliantly altered" to read not "after his kind" but "in our image" (Gen. 1:26).[16] The text emphasizes the divine image in mankind by repetition in the next verse: "So God created man in his own image, in the image of God created he him; male and female created he them" (v. 27).

---

13. Prov. 8:14; 11:14; 12:15; 15:22; 19:20–21; 20:18.
14. Luther, *Lectures on Genesis*, in *LW*, 1:56 (Gen. 1:26).
15. Gen. 1:11–12, 21, 24–25.
16. Laidlaw, *Bible Doctrine of Man*, 30.

It should amaze us that God would form an image of himself in a being of the sort that man is. Man is a creature. He stands in a position of infinite difference from the eternal, all-powerful Creator, to whom no one can be compared (Isa. 40:21–28). However, God created man to stand in the closest possible relation to him. Man is the living image of God, somewhat as a son is the image of his father (Gen. 5:1–3; cf. Luke 3:38). Though mankind has fallen far from his original state, we still see in human beings sparkles of divine glory, like "the ruins of a palace" in which we can discern something of its former majesty, as Charnock said.[17]

We will explore the meaning of this image in detail later,[18] but here we would observe the sharp distinction that it makes between man and all other creatures. Of all earthly things, only man is called the image of God. The Bible approves of man's mastery over animals. After the fall, the Lord apparently killed animals to provide clothing to cover man's nakedness (Gen. 3:21). The Lord was pleased with the sacrifice of animals offered to him in worship (4:4). After the flood, God granted man the right to eat the animals, but he said that "whoever sheds the blood of man, by man shall his blood be shed, for God made man in his own image" (9:2–6 ESV). We must not treat people like animals, for man's creation in God's image makes human life sacred. Animals are God's good creatures, and we should treat them with compassion and wise stewardship.[19] However, we should not treat animals like people; we may control them, kill them, and use them as best benefits mankind and glorifies God in a fallen world.

The Delegation of Dominion

Man's superior position over other earthly creatures received explicit authorization from the Creator. The creation of man in God's image is bracketed by statements of man's "dominion" over all the earth, with its teeming varieties of creatures (Gen. 1:26–28). God had acted, to this point, as the King over all things, whose very word gave them being, structure, life, and activity. Now God granted the right to rule to the creature who bore his image.

This delegation of dominion did not diminish God's kingly sovereignty, but it did empower man to rule the earth for the glory of God. Psalm 115

---

17. Charnock, *The Existence and Attributes of God*, in *Works*, 2:308.
18. See chaps. 8–10.
19. Ex. 23:4–5; Deut. 20:19–20; 25:4; Prov. 12:10; cf. Jonah 4:11.

says that God still does "whatsoever he hath pleased," and yet, "the earth hath he given to the children of men" (vv. 3, 16). The dominion of man does not arise from man's inherent greatness, but is a grant of authority and dignity that serves to glorify God. When we consider the heavens, we should exclaim with Psalm 8, "What is man, that thou art mindful of him?" However, despite man's smallness, the Lord has "put all things under his feet," including domesticated livestock, wild animals, birds, and fish. Our proper response is not to boast in ourselves, but to praise the excellency of God's name (vv. 3–9).

Absolute divine sovereignty and delegated human dominion converge in the exalted Lord Jesus Christ. The writer of Hebrews applies Psalm 8 to Christ (Heb. 2:5–8), who was once put to death, but afterward was "crowned with glory" so that he would bring "many sons unto glory" (vv. 9–10). If we diminish the distinctive dominion granted to man in creation, then we deny the glory that belongs to God's incarnate Son. God made man to reign over the world for the sake of the kingdom of his Son, who is "the image of the invisible God, the firstborn of every creature" (Col. 1:15)—that is, the preeminent King over all the universe (vv. 16–18; cf. Ps. 89:27).

The Consecration of Worship

The seventh day of the creation week also shows us the unique nature of man, though not in as explicit a fashion. When we read that God "rested" on the seventh day (Gen. 2:2–3), the verb (*shabat*) is of the same root as the word translated as "Sabbath," and appears in other texts about the Sabbath.[20] The fourth commandment states that Israel must keep the Sabbath because the Lord rested on the seventh day of creation (Ex. 20:11; 31:17). Let us remember that Moses wrote Genesis, most likely while leading Israel through the wilderness after they received the Ten Commandments.[21]

Genesis also says that God "sanctified" the seventh day (Gen. 2:3)—that is, he set it apart as holy. Luther commented, "To sanctify means to set aside for sacred purposes, or for the worship of God."[22] Israel was familiar with holy days, for the Sabbath was a holy day to the Lord,[23] a

---

20. Ex. 16:30; 23:12; 31:17; 34:21; cf. Lev. 23:32; 25:2; 26:34–35.
21. "Introduction to the Pentateuch," and "Introduction to the Book of Genesis," in *The Reformation Heritage KJV Study Bible*, ed. Beeke, Barrett, Bilkes, and Smalley, 1–3.
22. Luther, *Lectures on Genesis*, in *LW*, 1:79 (Gen. 2:3).
23. Ex. 31:15; 35:2; Neh. 10:31; Isa. 58:13.

day when, like other festive days, Israel was to rest and worship God in "holy convocation."[24] Therefore, God set aside the seventh day as a day for man to cease from his ordinary work and give himself to worshiping God. This helps us to understand the anthropomorphic language of God resting and being refreshed (v. 2; Ex. 31:17). The Creator does not get tired (Isa. 40:28), but he ceased his work of creation after six days in order to set an example for those whom he had made in his image.

Our purpose here is not to defend the abiding significance of the Sabbath for Christians (though that is precious to us), but to demonstrate man's uniqueness. Of all God's earthly creations, man has a special capacity to enter into the holy work of worship.[25] Though all the universe displays God's glory (Ps. 19:1), God created man in a special way to praise him (Isa. 43:7, 21). As Luther said, Genesis 2:1–3 indicates that "man was especially created for the knowledge and worship of God," for that is the special function of "the Sabbath."[26]

In summary, we find that the first chapter of Genesis presents man as a creature of God among other creatures and yet as a creature with a unique identity and position in God's world. Man is the climax and crown of creation, the centerpiece of God's eternal counsel, the image of God on earth, the royal servant who rules God's world for God's glory, and the worshiper who regularly pauses his earthly work to engage with others and by himself in holy adoration. What a wonder man is! We should praise and glorify God for these marvelous privileges.

Man's Special Relationships in God's Covenant (Gen. 2:4–25)

Genesis 2:4 begins, "These are the generations [*elleh toledot*] of the heavens and of the earth," a statement similar to the "these are the generations" statements for Adam, Noah, Noah's sons, Shem, and so on.[27] Just as the Lord generated descendants from the patriarchs, so he generated the first man and woman from the world that he had created.[28] This is the

---

24. Ex. 12:16; Lev. 23:3, 7–8, 21, 27, 35–37; Num. 28:18, 25–26; 29:1, 12. On worship during the Sabbath day, see Psalm 92.

25. Biblical statements about seas and trees joining in worship appear to be figures of speech that personify creation to express how the coming of the King will bless all of his creation and will cause it to radiate his glory as never before (Pss. 69:34; 96:11–13; 98:7–9; Isa. 35:1–2; 44:23; 49:13; 55:12; Luke 19:40). Note the clearly metaphorical language in the words "Let the floods clap their hands" (Ps. 98:8). It is possible, however, that in the new heaven and new earth, God will enable all creation to worship him in a manner we cannot presently understand (Rev. 5:13).

26. Luther, *Lectures on Genesis*, in *LW*, 1:80 (Gen. 2:3).

27. Gen. 5:1; 6:9; 10:1; 11:10, 27; 25:12, 19; 36:1; 37:2.

28. Kelly, *Creation and Change*, 46.

content of the rest of chapter 2. It reveals the special relationship that the Lord had with man in man's original state. It also lays the foundation for understanding the fall of man and his redemption by grace.

"The LORD God": From Cosmic to Covenantal Perspective

Chapter 2 returns to the creation of man as male and female (see Gen. 1:27) and expands upon that event with significantly more detail. There is a marked difference in style between Genesis 1:1–2:3 and 2:4–25. The former follows a highly structured sequence of events in seven days. The latter is more fluid. The former views events from a cosmic perspective, relating the creation of earth, seas, and other things. Here we read of "God" as *Elohim*. The latter is written from a more personal perspective, focusing on the Lord's dealings with two people in the garden of Eden. In it he is always "the LORD God" (*YHWH Elohim*), highlighting the covenantal quality of God's dealings with man. "The LORD" (traditionally rendered as "Jehovah") is the name by which God revealed himself to Israel. As the original audience of Genesis, Israel had recently received a deeper revelation of the divine name "the LORD" as signifying God's infinite, eternal, and unchangeable faithfulness to his covenant (Ex. 3:13–17; 6:2–8).[29] Its repeated use in this context, no less than twenty times in Genesis 2 and 3, suggests that this is a revelation of God's covenantal relationship with man in his original state. This may be the reason why "the LORD God" is used throughout the text from 2:4 onward.[30]

Critical scholars since the eighteenth century have argued that the two texts represent different, even contradictory accounts of creation that were joined by the editor(s) of Genesis.[31] It was popular in the late nineteenth and early twentieth centuries to treat Genesis as a patchwork

---

29. On the meaning of the divine name, see *RST*, 1:549–65 (chap. 29).

30. Belcher, *Genesis*, 61.

31. One alleged contradiction lies in Genesis 2:5, which states that prior to God's creation of man, there had not yet sprung up the "plant of the field" or "herb of the field." This is said to contradict Genesis 1:11–12, which reports that God created the plants on the fourth day before making man on the sixth. However, the Hebrew terms can be understood to refer to specific agricultural conditions that did not exist until after man's creation and fall. Hamilton, *The Book of Genesis, Chapters 1–17*, 154. The word translated as "plant" (*siyakh*) refers to wilderness shrubs (Gen. 21:15; Job 30:4, 7). The phrase rendered as "herb of the field" (*'eseb hasadeh*) is used of cultivated fields in Genesis 3:18: "Thorns also and thistles shall it bring forth to thee; and thou shalt eat the herb of the field" (cf. Ex. 9:22, 25; 10:15). It may be, then, that the text means that God had not yet established a cultivated place in the world for man to inhabit, as he did in the garden. Or the text might be stating the difference in the earth before and after the fall, when man was banished from the garden and labored to cultivate fields out of wild and weedy lands. For these and other possible interpretations, see Belcher, *Genesis*, 32–33. We need not see any contradiction to Genesis 1.

of legendary documents stitched together by a later redactor—a view known as "higher criticism." The scholarly consensus regarding this "documentary hypothesis" disintegrated in the late twentieth century as scholars increasingly recognized that Genesis is a unified and carefully crafted book.[32]

Scholars who subscribe to higher criticism miss the beautiful, complementary relationship between the two chapters. Our Lord Jesus Christ viewed them as a unified testimony to how God made man at "the beginning of the creation" (Mark 10:6–8). Genesis 2 does not present itself as a complete creation account. It depends on chapter 1 to provide an account of how God created the heavens and the earth (see Gen. 2:4). Likewise, Genesis 1 needs chapters 2 and 3 to explain the origin of sin and death in our world.

The Lord of Our Life: God's Supernatural Creation of Man

Paul no doubt had Genesis in mind when he said that the "Lord of heaven and earth . . . giveth to all life, and breath, and all things" (Acts 17:24–25). This is true not only in daily providence, but also was so in the initial creation of man. Genesis 2:7 gives us a very personal account of how God made the first man when it says, "And the LORD God formed man of the dust of the ground, and breathed into his nostrils the breath of life; and man became a living soul."

The text emphasizes man's physical origin from earthly materials, both in the name "man" (*adam*), which sounds like "ground" (*adamah*), and by saying God made him "of the dust of the ground." The word translated as "dust" (*'aphar*) refers to earth or soil (Gen. 26:15; Lev. 17:13).[33] Some Christians have attempted to read theistic evolution into the text by proposing that "dust" represents biological life prior to Adam.[34] John Barton Payne (1922–1979) responded, "The creation context, however, seems to require simple dust and man's connection with this dust as a direct one: Genesis 3:14 speaks of the serpent in the dust, presumably lifeless ground; and man's return to the dust, at death (Gen. 3:19), could hardly be by a process of devolution through intermediate living stages."[35]

---

32. Belcher, *Genesis*, 15–16.
33. "It is taking too much liberty with Heb. *'apar* to render it 'mud' or 'clay'" in order to conform the text to the idea of a potter. Hamilton, *The Book of Genesis, Chapters 1–17*, 156.
34. See the discussion of macroevolution in chap. 5.
35. J. Barton Payne, "Theistic Evolution and the Hebrew of Genesis 1–2," *Bulletin of the Evangelical Theological Society* 8, no. 2 (Spring 1965): 88 (full article, 85–90).

Other interpreters have argued that "dust" is a symbol for "mortality," meaning that man was created in a state of mortality.[36] However, this interpretation does not fit with Genesis 3:14, where the serpent crawls in the dust. It involves a misreading of verse 19, "For dust thou art, and unto dust shalt thou return," for dust does not equal "mortality," but God used man's future decay into real, physical dirt to graphically communicate his loss of immortality. This interpretation also makes nonsense of God's warning in Genesis 2:17 that man would become mortal if he disobeyed the divine command (cf. Rom. 5:12; 1 Cor. 15:21–22).

Therefore, the context in Genesis 2–3 strongly favors interpreting "dust" in a literal sense as the soil or earth under our feet. In a text written in the form of historical narrative, we should interpret its words literally unless there is compelling reason not to do so. We conclude that God formed the body of the first man out of inanimate materials found in the soil on the surface of the earth.[37] This teaching should humble us, for we are of the dust (Gen. 18:27). Our bodies share the same biological life as the animals. God did not make man originally with a heavenly life, but with a natural, earthly life (1 Cor. 15:44–50). We are not semidivine, heavenly beings, but creatures of the earth.

God also gave the "breath of life" (*nishmat khayim*) to that body. Nearly identical phrases are used in Genesis for the biological life of animals: literally, the "breath of spirit of life" (*nishmat ruakh khayim*, Gen. 7:22) and the "spirit of life" (*ruakh khayim*, 6:17; 7:15; cf. Ps. 104:29–30). The same words that are used to say that man became a "living soul" (*nephesh khayyah*) appear later in Genesis 2 for animals, each of which is also a "living creature" (*nephesh khayyah*)[38] formed out of the "ground" (*adamah*, v. 19). This is not to deny the distinct reality of the human soul or spirit as an immaterial substance (Matt. 10:28).[39] Rather, it is to recognize that in Scripture, the phrase translated as "living soul" does not refer so much to the soul as to a living being.

---

36. John H. Walton, *The Lost World of Adam and Eve: Genesis 2–3 and the Human Origins Debate* (Downers Grove, IL: IVP Academic, 2015), 74.

37. Scientists say that over 99 percent of the human body's mass in its present state consists of oxygen, carbon, hydrogen, nitrogen, calcium, phosphorus, potassium, sulfur, sodium, chlorine, and magnesium (in that order, with the first four comprising 96 percent). All these elements are present in soil.

38. We also find the phrase *nephesh khayyah* used of animals in Gen. 1:20–21, 24, 30; 9:10, 12, 15–16.

39. On the soul or spirit in distinction from the body, see chaps. 12–13.

Genesis 2:7 is saying, then, that man's body did not originate in something that was already a living creature, but that man became a living creature only when God created him. This refutes any evolutionary origin of man from previous animals. Payne wrote, "It indicates that Adam did not become alive until God breathed life into His already 'formed' man; he could not have been a continuation of some form of previously existing organic life."[40]

Though man shared much in common with the earth and with the animals, he also was made with a special relationship to God. Though man is a "living creature" like the animals, the manner in which God made man distinguishes him from animals, for the Lord God "breathed into his nostrils the breath of life." Laidlaw explained, "The immediate divine origination of man's breath, spirit, understanding constitutes a special connection between the Creator and this, the chiefest of his works."[41] The imagery of God blowing the breath of life into man suggests that human life originated in face-to-face closeness with God. Derek Kidner wrote, "*Breathed* is warmly personal, with the face-to-face intimacy of a kiss."[42]

The text does not imply the divinity of man, as if Adam shared in God's very breath, but a special creative work of the Holy Spirit, who is the living breath of God. Augustine explained that we should not read the text to say that "a part, as it were, of the nature of God was turned into the soul of man," for "the nature of God is not mutable."[43] Rather, God's breathing the breath of life into man suggests that God's Spirit created man's life and spirit. Elihu reflected upon this divine inbreathing when he said, "But there is a spirit [*ruakh*] in man: and the inspiration [*nishmat*] of the Almighty giveth them understanding," and, "The spirit [*ruakh*] of God hath made me, and the breath [*nishmat*] of the Almighty hath given me life" (Job 32:8; 33:4). The Scriptures thereby suggest an analogy between God and man: God is an eternal Spirit (Gen. 1:2) who made man by God's Spirit to possess a created spirit (2:7). The life of man parallels and images the life of God, but on a finite, dependent level.

This also establishes a parallel between man's original creation and his salvation. The term used in Genesis 2:7 appears again when God "breathed" (*naphakh*) life into dead men in Ezekiel's vision of the dry

---

40. Payne, "Theistic Evolution and the Hebrew of Genesis 1–2," 89.
41. Laidlaw, *The Bible Doctrine of Man*, 35–36.
42. Kidner, *Genesis*, 60.
43. Augustine, *Two Books on Genesis against the Manichaeans*, 2.8.11, in *ACCS/OT*, 1:52.

bones: "Thus saith the Lord GOD; Come from the four winds, O breath [*ruakh*], and breathe [*naphakh*] upon these slain, that they may live" (Ezek. 37:9). The Lord then promised, "[I] shall put my spirit [*ruakh*] in you, and ye shall live" (v. 14)—that is, the Spirit of regeneration and sanctification (36:26–27). We read in John 20:22 that the risen Christ "breathed on them, and saith unto them, Receive ye the Holy Ghost." Our creation began in the Holy Spirit, and our new creation must be worked by the same Spirit.

The Lord of Our Location: God's Rich Provision for Man

The Lord God is the giver of our life, and God's ordained home for man shows this to be an abundant life. The Lord placed man in a garden full of beautiful plants and delicious food (Gen. 2:8–9). The very name of the area, "Eden," is identical in spelling and sound to the Hebrew word for "delight" or "luxury" (*eden*).[44] To people who lived in the arid lands of the ancient Near East, water meant wealth. Eden overflowed with so much water that its river fed the great rivers of the region (vv. 9–14). The area was also noted for its gold and gemstones (vv. 11–12). In the garden, the Lord God spoke with man and communed with him (vv. 15–25). The garden was guarded by angelic cherubim, God's heavenly warriors (3:24).[45]

Reading this text through ancient Israelite eyes helps us to recognize that the garden functioned as a prototypical temple where God dwelt with man.[46] God instructed Israel to make its priests' garments (Exodus 28), its tabernacle (Exodus 25–27), and later its temple (1 Kings 6–7) out of gold and gemstones, and to adorn these structures with artistic images of trees, fruit, and cherubim, and with large basins of water. Ezekiel called Eden "the garden of God" and "the holy mountain of God" (Ezek. 28:13–14; 31:8–9), just as Israel's temple was in Mount Zion, God's "holy mountain" (20:40). The visions of Revelation represent the heavenly Jerusalem both in terms of a magnificent temple-city and as a return to the garden of Eden (Rev. 21:1–22:5). Man's first home was the temple of the Lord.

The physical, historical elements of the garden were visible signs of spiritual communion with the Lord. Geerhardus Vos wrote, "It is a real

---

44. Gen. 18:12; 2 Sam. 1:24; Ps. 36:8; Jer. 51:34.
45. On the cherubim, see Pss. 18:10; 80:1; 99:1; Isa. 37:16; Ezek. 1:5–14; 9:3; 10:1–9, 14–20; 11:22; 28:13–14.
46. G. K. Beale, *The Temple and the Church's Mission: A Biblical Theology of the Dwelling Place of God*, New Studies in Biblical Theology (Downers Grove, IL: InterVarsity Press, 2004), 66–80.

symbolism embodied in the actual things."[47] Proverbs says that God's wisdom is a "tree of life" for his people (Prov. 3:18). Psalm 36 teaches us to say to God, "With thee is the fountain of life," and "thou shalt make them drink of the river of thy pleasures," where "pleasures" is the plural of "Eden" (*eden*) (Ps. 36:8–9). All around Adam and Eve were reminders that life consists of communion with God. Vos said, "The truth is thus clearly set forth that life comes from God, that for man it consists of nearness to God."[48]

This is the humbling and exalting truth of Genesis about mankind. We are but creatures, having much in common with the animals and the very dirt under our feet. However, we were also created for communion with the living God. This communion is our life, and it is found only in relating to him properly as the Lord God. He gave us everything, but because we refused to submit to his lordship, we lost our communion with him. God's superabundant generosity, shining so brightly in the garden, highlights all the more our "shameful ingratitude," as Calvin said.[49]

The Lord of Our Law: God's Personal Communication with Man

After God made the first man, he did not leave him to explore the world and discover his own destiny. "The LORD God" immediately asserted his authority over the man by assigning him a home and a vocation (Gen. 2:15). He also gave man a law to obey, with life and death hanging upon his obedience (vv. 16–17). The covenant name of God suggests that God related to man as his covenant Lord, directing human life by his covenant word. Man may have been king over creation, but he remained the servant of the Creator.

The direct communication of the Lord God with Adam heightens the sense of holy privilege that man enjoyed in his access to God. When the Lord appeared to Moses to speak to him, God warned Moses that he stood on holy ground (Ex. 3:5). When the Lord brought Moses and Israel back to the same mountain, he ordered them to "sanctify" it—that is, to treat it as holy and not venture too close to the glory from which the voice of God spoke (19:23). Then the Lord instructed Moses to build the tabernacle and the ark of the covenant, which would be in the Most Holy

---

47. Geerhardus Vos, *Biblical Theology: Old and New Testaments* (Edinburgh: Banner of Truth, 1948), 27.
48. Vos, *Biblical Theology*, 28.
49. Calvin, *Commentaries*, on Gen. 2:9.

Place: "And there I will meet with thee, and I will commune with thee . . . of all things which I will give thee in commandment unto the children of Israel" (25:22). Likewise, in the garden of Eden, the original holy place, the Lord spoke directly to man.

With this holy privilege came the obligation of covenant faithfulness. This was true of Israel, whom God would count as "a kingdom of priests, and an holy nation" if "ye will obey my voice indeed, and keep my covenant" (Ex. 19:5–6). It was true first of Adam, whom the Lord God commanded, "Of every tree of the garden thou mayest freely eat: but of the tree of the knowledge of good and evil, thou shalt not eat of it: for in the day that thou eatest thereof thou shalt surely die" (Gen. 2:16–17). God established a covenant between himself and mankind.

Therefore, man's relationship with God is characterized by covenant and law. We will explore God's covenant with Adam in later chapters.[50] At this point, we would simply note that the covenant emphasizes the high calling of man: that combination of holy privilege and holy obligation whereby man always stands in the presence of God, whether under blessing or curse. So long as man is man, he cannot escape the law of God (Rom. 2:14–15).

The Lord of Our Love: God's Institution of Marriage for Man

God made man to be a creature in relationships. In the midst of the cosmic creation account, Genesis 1:27 makes this enigmatic statement: "So God created man in his own image, in the image of God created he him; male and female created he them." The second chapter of Genesis expands this statement in a manner rich with implications. We will discuss human gender and sexuality in more detail later.[51] Here, however, we would make some general observations.

The text centers upon Adam's need for a "help meet for him," or a helper that was suitable to him (Gen. 2:18, 20). The term translated as "help" (*'ezer*) is a strong word, referring not to a lesser assistant but to someone who supplies strength, even salvation, to those in need. God is the helper (*'ezer*) of his people.[52] The phrase "meet for him" (*kenegdo*) is composed in Hebrew of the preposition rendered as "according to" (*k-*)

---

50. See chaps. 14–16.
51. See chap. 11.
52. Ex. 18:4; Deut. 33:7, 29; Pss. 70:5; 121:1–2; 124:8; 146:5; Hos. 13:9; cf. Gen. 49:25.

and a term meaning "in front of" (*neged*); it indicates a match able to relate face-to-face on equal terms. This helps us to understand the Lord's surprising comment that "it is not good that the man should be alone" (v. 18). It is not that God is insufficient for man or that paradise was flawed, but that God created man with an inherent incompleteness that could be supplied only by fellowship and partnership with someone who matched and complemented him.[53]

The Lord led Adam through a process of discovery that culminated in God's presentation of the newly formed woman to her husband. We read in Genesis 2:19, "And out of the ground the LORD God formed every beast of the field, and every fowl of the air; and brought them unto Adam to see what he would call them: and whatsoever Adam called every living creature, that was the name thereof."

A contradiction is alleged to exist between Genesis 1:24 and 2:19. In the former, the animals were clearly created *before* man. However, the latter verse is often translated, "And out of the ground the Lord God formed every beast of the field, and every fowl of the air; and brought them unto Adam to see what he would call them," implying that they were made just prior to being brought to the man. However, the verb in 2:19 can be translated as "had formed," which is consistent with 1:24 and resolves the difficulty.

Alternatively, the second account could be interpreted to mean that while God had already created the kinds of animals, he specially created some individual animals out of the earth and brought them to the man.[54] The Lord might have done this so that Adam could witness God's creative power and sovereignty over the animals.

Genesis 2:18–25 teaches us that as part of this process, God gave man authority over the animals, for the Lord granted man the privilege of naming them just as God had named aspects of the world. However, Adam realized that the helper he needed could not come from any mere animal, but required someone who truly matched him as a divine image bearer (1:27). God supplied this helper entirely by his power and love, while Adam was in a condition of complete helplessness ("deep sleep"). God made the woman "of the man" and "for the man" (1 Cor. 11:8–9), miraculously developing her out of flesh and bone removed from the man's

---

53. Cf. Calvin, *Commentaries*, on Gen. 1:27.
54. Hamilton, *The Book of Genesis, Chapters 1–17*, 176.

side. Peter Lombard observed that the woman was not made from his head as if she was "set over man in domination," nor from his foot "as if subject to him in servitude," but from his side, "for the partnership of love."[55] Calvin concluded that marriage is "the best support of life," for God made woman "as a companion and an associate to the man, to assist him to live well."[56]

God presented the woman to the man, initiating the first marriage, and so "God hath joined together" husband and wife (Matt. 19:6). Man received the woman from God to love and cherish her as his own body: "bone of my bones, and flesh of my flesh" (Gen. 2:23). Man's naming the woman implied that, though they were equally human, he exercised God-given authority over her as her loving leader and head of the household. By making her out of him, God also indicated his will that husband and wife be "one flesh" (v. 24), committed and bound together in lifelong unity and partnership. The first man and woman lived together in the garden without fear or shame to separate them, enjoying total openness and intimacy.

The Lord God, then, is the Lord over our relationships of love. God did not design man to function in isolated individuality, but to be part of a network of relationships in which some give authoritative leadership and others give strong help, but all are joined together in bonds of love. The first and foundational human relationship of love is marriage. Husbands and wives have distinct, interdependent roles, so that "neither is the man without the woman, neither the woman without the man, in the Lord" (1 Cor. 11:11). From the root of marriage springs all human relationships, including the spiritual family of God's redeemed people, where we find these same patterns of authority, gifted help, and mutual interdependence (Rom. 12:3–8; 1 Cor. 12).

Marriage is a covenant of mutual faithfulness (Mal. 2:14) that mirrors the relationship between the Lord and his people (Isa. 54:5; Hos. 2:19–20). The man's words to the woman, "bone of my bones, and flesh of my flesh," have covenantal overtones, similar to what the Israelites said when they made a covenant with David to be their king (2 Sam.

---

55. Lombard, *The Sentences*, 2.18.2 (2:77). Matthew Henry would later utilize this insight, writing, "The woman was made of a rib out of the side of Adam; not made out of his head to rule over him, nor out of his feet to be trampled upon by him, but out of his side to be equal with him, under his arm to be protected, and near his heart to be beloved." *Matthew Henry's Commentary on the Whole Bible: Complete and Unabridged in One Volume* (Peabody, MA: Hendrickson, 1994), on Gen. 2:21–25 (10).

56. Calvin, *Commentaries*, on Gen. 2:18.

5:1–3; cf. 19:13).[57] The "deep sleep" (*tardemah*) of Adam is the same term used for Abram's "deep sleep" when the Lord made a covenant with him and his seed (Gen. 15:12). The marriage of the first man and woman foreshadows the covenant relationship between Christ and his church (2 Cor. 11:2–3; Eph. 5:28–32). The holy temple of the garden is a home where love abounds.

Therefore, though the Lord God is the Lord of our love relationships with each other, more importantly he is the Lord of his gracious covenant of love. God created man for a special relationship with him, showering his image bearer with blessings and privileges in order that man might live close to him. How marvelous is his kindness to man! How horribly tragic is man's fall from such a high position! And yet, how glorious is God's grace through the last Adam, Jesus Christ! Knowing that grace experientially puts us on the pathway back to paradise. Along the way, God's grace trains us to turn away from our independent, abusive, rebellious ways, and to live together in spiritual families with submission to authority, appreciative partnerships with other people whose help we need, and close friendships in which we fellowship not just with each other but with the Lord himself.

Sing to the Lord

Invitation to Worship Our Maker

Come, sound his praise abroad,
And hymns of glory sing:
Jehovah is the sovereign God,
The universal King.

He formed the deeps unknown,
He gave the seas their bound;
The wat'ry worlds are all his own,
And all the solid ground.

Come, worship at his throne;
Come, bow before the Lord:
We are his works, and not our own;
He formed us by his word.

---

57. See Walter Brueggemann, "Of the Same Flesh and Bone (Gn 2, 23a)," *The Catholic Biblical Quarterly* 32, no. 4 (October 1970): 535–38 (full article, 532–42); cf. Hamilton, *The Book of Genesis, Chapters 1–17*, 179–80.

Today attend his voice,
Nor dare provoke his rod;
Come, like the people of his choice,
And own your gracious God.

Isaac Watts (cf. Psalm 95)
Tune: Silver Street
Trinity Hymnal—Baptist Edition, No. 102

Questions for Meditation or Discussion

1. In what sense is the creation of man the climax of God's work of creation?
2. How does Genesis 1:26–28 give special honor to the human race among all God's creatures?
3. What does Genesis 2:1–3 reveal about God's purpose for mankind?
4. What do the authors suggest is the significance of the shift from "God" in Genesis 1:1–2:3 to "the LORD God" in Genesis 2:4–25?
5. What does Genesis 2:7 teach us about the origin of the first human being?
6. How does the Bible portray the garden of Eden as a prototypical temple? What does this imply about mankind's purpose?
7. What do God's words to Adam in Genesis 2:15–17 imply about man's relationship to God?
8. What does it mean that God made the woman to be a "help meet for him"—that is, a helper suitable for her husband (Gen. 2:18)?
9. What indications are there in Genesis 2 that marriage is a covenant?
10. What about this chapter do you find most humbling? What shows us God's intent to honor man?

Questions for Deeper Reflection

11. Some scholars have treated Genesis 1 and 2 as contradictory accounts of creation reflecting different traditions. Are there any apparent contradictions between the two chapters? If so, how might they be resolved? If the chapters are not actually contradictory, then how do they relate to each other?
12. Compare the creation of Adam (Gen. 2:7) with the descriptions of God's saving works in Ezekiel 37:9, 14 and John 20:22. What do the parallels imply?

7

The Controversy over
the Historical Adam

Adam has long had his skeptics.[1] Martin Luther commented on God's creation of Adam from the dust: "If Aristotle heard this, he would burst into laughter and conclude that although this is not an unlovely yarn, it is nevertheless a most absurd one."[2] In more recent times, some people have attempted to graft the word *Adam* onto a concept that is quite foreign to the Scriptures. For example, evolutionists speak of "Y-chromosome Adam" and "Mitochondrial Eve," but these genetic constructs are not the same as the biblical persons Adam and Eve.

Some theistic evolutionists view "Adam" as a *group* of highly developed hominids to whom God gave moral and spiritual consciousness. In this view, the human race descended from "a group of several thousand individuals who lived about 150,000 years ago."[3] That first cohort of early humans had evolved from other primates similar to apes.[4] In this view, Genesis 2 is understood to refer not to the literal creation of Adam and Eve, but is "a symbolic allegory of the entrance of the human soul into a previously soulless animal kingdom," as Francis Collins says.[5] Such an interpretation is necessary, Peter

---

1. This chapter is adapted from Joel R. Beeke, "The Case for Adam," in *God, Adam, and You*, ed. Phillips, 15–43.

2. Luther, *Lectures on Genesis*, in *LW*, 1:84 (Gen. 2:7).

3. "Were Adam and Eve Historical Figures?," Biologos, https://biologos.org/common-questions /were-adam-and-eve-historical-figures.

4. See R. J. Berry, "Adam or Adamah?," *Science and Christian Belief* 23, no. 1 (2011): 31 (full article, 23–48).

5. Francis S. Collins, *The Language of God: A Scientist Presents Evidence for Belief* (New York: Free Press, 2006), 207.

Enns tells us, because science "has shown beyond any reasonable scientific doubt that humans and primates share common ancestry."[6] We must adjust our approach to Genesis, we are told, to acknowledge that like other ancient documents it is not a historical account, but myth.[7]

In the face of such claims, some Reformed and evangelical scholars have concluded that the church must abandon the classic doctrine of Adam and Eve and accept evolution.[8] Even some who believe in a historical Adam try to fit Genesis together with the theory of the evolution of man from hominids.[9]

In previous chapters, we discussed the theory of evolution and its incompatibility with the inspiration of the Word of God,[10] and the interpretation and historical verity of Genesis 1–3.[11] A thorough historical study of how the church has understood Adam throughout the ages has been written by William VanDoodewaard.[12] In this chapter, we will focus on the question of whether the Bible presents Adam as a real, historical individual, and why it matters.

There are two main lines of argument for the historical Adam. First, the history revealed by God in the Bible asserts that Adam was a real man and the father of the entire human race. Second, the theology revealed by God in the Bible depends upon Adam's historical reality. Though we cannot separate theology from history in the Scriptures, we can discuss the reality of events recorded in Bible history before we draw conclusions as to their spiritual significance.

Objections to the Historicity of Adam

While the Bible contains various genres of literature and figures of speech, such as metaphors, poems, anthropomorphisms, allegories, symbolic num-

6. Peter Enns, *The Evolution of Adam: What the Bible Does and Doesn't Say about Human Origins* (Grand Rapids, MI: Brazos, 2012), ix.
7. Enns, *The Evolution of Adam*, 35–59. See C. John Collins, *Did Adam and Eve Really Exist? Who They Were and Why You Should Care* (Wheaton, IL: Crossway, 2011), 12.
8. Such as Peter Enns, Bruce Waltke, Richard Colling, and Tremper Longman III. See Charles Honey, "Adamant on Adam: Resignation of Prominent Scholar Underscores Tension over Evolution," *Christianity Today* (June 2010): 14. These views are actively promoted by the Biologos Foundation (www.biologos.org). See also Hans Madueme and Michael Reeves, "Adam under Siege: Setting the Stage," introduction to *Adam, the Fall, and Original Sin: Theological, Biblical, and Scientific Perspectives*, ed. Hans Madueme and Michael Reeves (Grand Rapids, MI: Baker Academic, 2014), vii–viii.
9. Kidner, *Genesis*, 28–29; and John R. W. Stott, *The Message of Romans* (Downers Grove, IL: InterVarsity Press, 1994), 164. For similar approaches, see Collins, *Did Adam and Eve Really Exist?*, 123–31.
10. On evolution, see chap. 5.
11. On Genesis and history, see chap. 3.
12. VanDoodewaard, *The Quest for the Historical Adam.*

bers, and parables, it also contains historical narrative that relates real events in space and time. We have already argued that the early chapters of Genesis present themselves as the narrative of real history, based on Hebrew syntax and style, genealogies from Adam to Christ (Genesis 5; 11; 1 Chronicles 1–3; Luke 3), and the testimony of Christ himself (Mark 10:6–8; Luke 11:50–51).[13] Jude 14 apparently reflects a literal, historical understanding of the genealogies when it identifies Enoch as "the seventh from Adam" (cf. Gen. 5:1–24). The most natural reading of the Bible understands it to assert that Adam and Eve were real, historical persons who were the ancestors of all mankind.

Against this understanding of Adam, some people have raised the following objections.

1. *By noting that God named the man Adam, the generic Hebrew word for "human being," Genesis indicates that he is a symbol for mankind in general or "every-man."*[14]

We respond by observing that God gave this individual the name for the entire human race because Adam was the father and representative of all humanity. However, Scripture distinguishes between mankind in general and Adam as a particular human being. Genesis 5:1–3 literally says, "This is the book of the generations of *man*. In the day that God created *man*, in the likeness of God made he him; male and female created he them; and blessed them, and called their name *man*, in the day when they were created. And *man* lived an hundred and thirty years, and begat a son in his own likeness, after his image, and called his name Seth." So sometimes "man" (or *adam* in Hebrew) refers to the whole race ("and called their name man"), but at other times it refers to the father of the race ("and man lived an hundred and thirty years").

2. *Genesis 1–3 is a statement not so much about human history as it is about Israel's identity, and so "the story of Adam becomes a story for 'every Israelite.'"*[15] Thus, the narrative of Adam's creation is a myth or parable analogous to the history of the election and fall of Israel.

In reply, we acknowledge that Israel's history echoes Adam's history in some respects. The Lord gave Israel an inheritance in a blessed land, which the nation forfeited through disobedience to God's law, resulting in divine curses and banishment from its inheritance (Leviticus 26; Deuteronomy 28).

---

13. See chap. 3.
14. Berry, "Adam or Adamah?," 31.
15. Enns, *The Evolution of Adam*, 141–42.

Hosea drew a parallel between Israel's covenant breaking and Adam's: "they like Adam [*ke-adam*] have transgressed the covenant" (Hos. 6:7 KJV mg.). This should not surprise us, for God designed Israel's experiences to serve as types of mankind's salvation by the last Adam, Jesus Christ. However, the parallel is not exact, for Israel, unlike Adam, was sinful from the start,[16] and the Lord's ways with the nation were always according to the covenant of grace revealed in God's promises to Abraham.[17]

That there are typological parallels between Adam and Israel, Adam and Christ, or Israel and Christ does not mean that we should regard the Bible's historical accounts as mythology. Instead, they show us the sovereign hand of God revealing his ways with man through human beings, institutions, and historical events. Furthermore, the historical narratives and genealogies of Genesis present Adam and Eve as the historical parents of the whole human race. Genesis 3:20 says that Adam named his wife Eve because she was "the mother of all living." Although the creation narrative has implications for Israel, the emphasis of the early chapters of Genesis lies upon "a universal focus rather than a national or ethnic focus," as William Barrick writes.[18]

3. *Genesis 2 contradicts Genesis 1 by saying that God created things in a different order, and therefore we cannot take both accounts literally.*

We respond that Genesis 1 and 2 are not contradictory, but present the same events from complementary perspectives.[19] As we argued in the last chapter, Genesis 1 gives us the big picture—the cosmic perspective on the creation of the whole world, with man as the pinnacle of God's creative work. Genesis 2 zooms in on the creation of man, slowing down the action and focusing our attention on the garden of Eden, to give a covenantal, relational perspective. The two chapters are to be read together in harmony, not set against each other.[20]

4. *Genesis 3:1 tells us that a "serpent" had a clever conversation with the woman, and since we know snakes do not talk, this is obviously a symbolic myth, not a historical account.*[21]

---

16. Ex. 32:1–10; Josh. 24:2, 14–15; Ezek. 20:5–8.

17. Ex. 2:24; 3:6, 15–17; 6:2–8; Lev. 26:42–45.

18. William D. Barrick, "A Historical Adam: Young-Earth Creation View," in *Four Views on the Historical Adam*, ed. Barrett and Caneday, 204.

19. See Collins, *Did Adam and Eve Really Exist?*, 52–54.

20. Specific answers to alleged claims that the order of Gen. 1 contradicts Gen. 2:5, 19 are given in chap. 6.

21. Thus, Herman Gunkel's commentary on Genesis, cited in Collins, *Did Adam and Eve Really Exist?*, 63. A similar objection is that the two trees are magical, and thus, this is fantasy. But the

In answer to this objection, we note that the Bible indicates that "the serpent" was not just a snake, but a creature or form used by an evil spirit. The ancient Israelites would have understood such a connection because in ancient cultures a serpent represented a spiritual power connected to the idols of this world.[22] Rahab, the sea serpent, was an image of the power of Egypt (Ps. 89:10; Isa. 51:9). Isaiah 27:1 foretells that "in that day the LORD with his sore and great and strong sword shall punish leviathan the piercing serpent, even leviathan that crooked serpent; and he shall slay the dragon that is in the sea." Revelation 12:9 envisions that same day of the Lord, declaring, "And the great dragon was cast out, that old serpent, called the Devil, and Satan, which deceiveth the whole world: he was cast out into the earth, and his angels were cast out with him."

Therefore, there is nothing unreasonable about reading Genesis 1–3 as the reliable account of real historical persons and events. The Bible represents Adam as the first individual human being, specially created by God out of the dust, and we should believe that he is such.

Adam and Biblical Doctrine

Adam is not just an interesting figure in history. He is foundational to our beliefs as Christians. Perhaps if someone proved that George Washington never existed, it might change the American one-dollar bill, but it would not change your life very much, if at all. But if Adam disappears into mythology, then we lose the foundation for our views of man's identity, sin, and Savior.

The Historical Adam Is the Basis of Mankind's Nobility

While our bodies share many common characteristics with the animals, the Scriptures insist that man is not just a highly developed animal but a special creation of God, made in his image to rule over the animals (Gen. 1:26). Adam was originally and uniquely formed as the first man (2:7; cf. 1 Cor. 15:45).

If we reject the historicity of Adam, we destroy the basis of the distinction between mankind and the animal kingdom. The evolutionary view of human origins logically leads to a degradation of the dignity and value of

---

two trees named in paradise are never given magical powers according to the text. It is better to see them as sacramental: covenantal signs instituted by God.

22. *NIDOTTE*, 3:85; and Vos, *Biblical Theology*, 34.

man to the level of an animal. In fact, given the impact the human race has on other living things, some evolutionary environmentalists believe that it would be best for the world if the human race was largely exterminated.[23]

A theistic evolutionist might object that the image of God is not in our bodies, but in our spiritual capacity to know God and our commission from God to rule the earth. Therefore, our bodies could have developed by a natural process of evolution, and "God could have used a miraculous process to create our spiritual capacities, or used some combination of natural processes and divine revelation to develop these capacities."[24]

In answer to this objection, Genesis 1 does not say that God gave his image to beings that already existed, but that "God created man in his own image" (Gen. 1:27). The image of God is not something added to us but part of our very constitution. This is so much the case that even after the fall of man into sin and spiritual death, we still are characterized as made in the image of God. In Genesis 9:1–6, we are told that the Lord gave man the right to kill and eat animals, but declared that anyone who murders a human being must die because God created man in his image. However, if men are highly evolved animals endowed with some extra graces from God, then it is hard to understand how we are so different from other animals that we may kill and eat them, but not kill (and eat) each other.

The denial of the historical Adam and the assertion of human evolution blur the difference between mankind and beasts. Only by believing in the historical Adam are we warranted to confess with David in Psalm 8:6–9,

> Thou madest him to have dominion over the works of thy hands; thou hast put all things under his feet: All sheep and oxen, yea, and the beasts of the field; the fowl of the air, and the fish of the sea, and whatsoever passeth through the paths of the seas. O LORD our Lord, how excellent is thy name in all the earth!

The Historical Adam Is the Root of Mankind's Unity

If we deny the historical Adam, we lose the important doctrine that the human race is one race. Acts 17:26 says that God "hath made of one blood

---

23. For example, consider the Voluntary Human Extinction Movement (http://www.vhemt.org/) and the purported remarks of Dr. Eric Pianka to the Texas Academy of Science in March 2006. Rick Pearcey, "Dr. 'Doom' Pianka Speaks," *The Pearcey Report*, http://www.pearceyreport.com /archives/2006/04/transcript_dr_d.php.

24. "How Could Humans Have Evolved and Still Be in the 'Image of God'?," Biologos, https:// biologos.org/common-questions/how-could-humans-have-evolved-and-still-be-in-the-image-of -god.

all nations of men for to dwell on all the face of the earth, and hath determined the times before appointed, and the bounds of their habitation." Some translations even say "of one man."[25] Black or white, Chinese or Russian, Arab or Jew, we are all blood brothers. We have no basis to view other human beings as fundamentally different from ourselves, for we all share a common set of ancestors. John Calvin said, "God could himself indeed have covered the earth with a multitude of men; but it was his will that we should proceed from one fountain, in order that our desire of mutual concord might be the greater, and that each might the more freely embrace the other as his own flesh."[26]

Someone might object that our unity is in Christ, not in Adam (Gal. 3:28). However, not all men are in Christ (Eph. 2:12). Therefore, this relation to Christ cannot be the basis of our view of humanity in general. Furthermore, our unity *in* Christ is based on our union *with* Christ, and our union with him depends on his taking our common human nature to himself in his incarnation. Hebrews 2:11 says that our Savior is not ashamed to call us his brothers because we "are all of one [*ex henos*]." Even our unity in Christ depends upon our common human nature from Adam.

If we treat Genesis as a collection of myths or metaphors, then we seriously damage our ability to stand against ethnic prejudice and hatred. We open the door for the idea that various ethnic groups come from different origins (polygenesis or polygenism), and thus some are superior to others.[27] Voltaire (François-Marie Arouet, 1694–1778), an Enlightenment philosopher who rejected biblical authority, saw Europeans, Africans, and Native Americans as separate species with distinctly different roots.[28] Present mainstream evolutionary theory opposes the polygenesis of man, but it has had advocates in modern times. Also, scientists have recently argued that some genetic features of an ethnic group may be rooted in interbreeding between Homo sapiens and other species of less advanced hominids.[29]

---

25. In Acts 17:26, the Beza uncial text (D) and the majority Byzantine texts read *ex henos haimatos* ("of one blood"), a reading supported by the Latin text of Irenaeus and by Chrysostom, Theodoret, and Bede. The Sinaiticus, Alexandrinus, and Vaticanus uncials (א, A, B), together with some miniscules from the ninth century or later, read *ex henos* ("of one [masculine or neuter singular]"), leading to the translation "of one man."

26. Calvin, *Commentaries*, on Gen. 1:28.

27. VanDoodewaard, *The Quest for the Historical Adam*, 119–21.

28. Thomas F. Gossett, *Race: The History of an Idea in America*, new ed. (Oxford: Oxford University Press, 1997), 44.

29. Todd Charles Wood and Joseph W. Francis, "The Genetics of Adam," in *What Happened in the Garden: The Reality and Ramifications of the Creation and Fall of Man*, ed. Abner Chou (Grand Rapids, MI: Kregel, 2016), 85–86, 88. The evidence of proposed interbreeding between

This idea could easily be twisted into ethnic prejudice. Or, since evolutionary development might take place in a portion of a population, it could be used by some to claim that their people group is a new master race, akin to what the Nazis did with the "Aryan race."[30]

Replacing a historical Adam with mankind's evolution out of other species makes it logically possible for humanity to be viewed as multiple races or a blend of species. In making this statement, we are not accusing all evolutionists of racism. We are thankful for evolutionists who affirm the unity of the race. We also acknowledge the failings of the church in this matter. Sadly, some professing Christians have also been guilty of the great sin of promoting ethnic superiority and oppression. The answer to this problem is to return to the doctrine of our fundamental unity as one human race descended from one human father, Adam.[31]

The Historical Adam Is the Foundation of Gender Relationships

Our Lord Jesus Christ taught us to look to the creation of Adam and Eve as the basis for the Creator's order for gender relationships and human sexuality. When challenged by the Pharisees to state his view of divorce, Christ appealed to Genesis 1:27 and 2:24 (Matt. 19:3–6).

The apostle Paul similarly based his teachings on gender relationships upon the early chapters of Genesis. When explaining how men and women should honor male headship in the meetings of the church, Paul writes in 1 Corinthians 11:8–9, "For the man is not of the woman: but the woman of the man. Neither was the man created for the woman; but the woman for the man." Again, in 1 Timothy 2:13–14, he said that "Adam was first formed, then Eve. And Adam was not deceived, but the woman being deceived was in the transgression."

We must ask ourselves, why did Christ and Paul refer to Adam and Eve when addressing these questions? They grounded their teaching in the Creator's original design for men and women, especially in regard to marriage (Matt. 19:4). God's providence toward Adam in paradise teaches us God's

---

Neanderthals and human beings is said to be found among Europeans and Asians, not southern Africans. This is not good news for white supremacists who are evolutionists!

30. "Victims of the Nazi Era: Nazi Racial Ideology," *Holocaust Encyclopedia*, United States Holocaust Memorial Museum, https://www.ushmm.org/wlc/en/article.php?ModuleId=10007457.

31. The same issue arises with the historicity of Noah, since every human being after the flood descends from him; though Noah does not have the same theological significance as Adam, yet the denial of his historicity imperils our belief in the fundamental equality of all human beings.

will for mankind precisely because Adam truly was God's first human crea-tion. Straight from the Master's hands, pristine and unblemished by sin and the fall, Adam is a revelation of God's will for human relationships.

If we rip the Genesis account out of the flow of history and regard it as a myth, it loses its authority to reveal God's will for all mankind. However, if we view Adam as the first man God created, then we are able to apply the Old Testament in the same way that Jesus and Paul did to illuminate what it means to be male and female. In this age, when the church is so ravaged by moral relativism, militant feminism, and homosexual activism, we are blessed to have a solid basis for our sexual ethics in God's creation ordinances.

The Historical Adam Is the Agent of Mankind's Fall

How do we explain the sin and misery of the human race? Paul writes in Ro-mans 5:12, "Wherefore, as by one man sin entered into the world, and death by sin; and so death passed upon all men, for that all have sinned." Later, in verse 17, he says, "By one man's offence death reigned by one." Robert Yarbrough says that Adam "is as integral to the logic of redemption in this passage as Christ is."[32] Yarbrough also considers Paul's references to Adam in his first epistle to the saints in Corinth (1 Cor. 15:22, 45) when he writes, "At a climactic juncture of this epistle, in chapter 15 with its restatement of the gospel message (vv. 1–9) and insistence on the reality of the resurrec-tion, Paul adduces Adam as a central plank in his rhetorical, apologetic, and theological platform."[33] It is no small matter to deny that "in Adam's fall, we sinned all."[34]

In Romans 5, Paul is elaborating the doctrine of the fall of man, a doctrine attested in Old Testament statements such as Ecclesiastes 7:29: "Lo, this only have I found, that God hath made man upright; but they have sought out many inventions" (cf. Job 31:33; Hos. 6:7 KJV mg.). Paul views Adam's fall as a real event in history (2 Cor. 11:3; 1 Tim. 2:14), and one that determined the shape of all the history that followed.

It has been argued that "the Adam of Paul was not the historical Adam," but that he saw Adam as a literary figure designed to show us

---

32. Robert W. Yarbrough, "Adam in the New Testament," in *Adam, the Fall, and Original Sin,* ed. Madueme and Reeves, 43.

33. Yarbrough, "Adam in the New Testament," in *Adam, the Fall, and Original Sin,* ed. Madueme and Reeves, 47.

34. This was the opening of the alphabetic rhyme in *The New England Primer.* See *The New En-gland Primer: A Reprint of the Earliest Known Edition, and Many Facsimiles and Reproductions, and an Historical Introduction,* ed. Paul Leicester Ford (New York: Dod, Mead, and Co., 1899), 64.

that sin leads to death.[35] However, Paul writes in Romans 5:14 that "death reigned from Adam to Moses." Francis Schaeffer commented, "Adam, it is obvious, is viewed as being just as historic as Moses. If this were not the case, Paul's argument would be meaningless."[36] John Murray (1898–1975) commented that denying "the fall as a literal happening . . . wrecks Paul's whole argument."[37]

The historical fall of man is pivotal to Christianity. The death of men and women was not God's original design for his "very good" creation. Death came from Adam's historical fall. But if there was no Adam, then we have suffered the agonies and grief of death from our beginning as a race.[38] And if death and disaster did not arise from the judgment of God upon Adam's sin, how did they come into God's creation? Did God create a world of evil? Is God perhaps not the all-powerful Creator of all things, but only one limited influence among others? The fall of Adam is a hinge upon which our doctrines of creation and God turn. If we break the hinge, the whole system of biblical doctrine collapses.

Furthermore, without Adam's historical fall, we lose the doctrine of original sin, the teaching that the guilt of Adam's sin is imputed to us and the pollution of sin is inherited by us. We are most likely to replace it with the evolutionary idea that mankind is gradually improving.[39] To affirm such a notion, we must reject the doctrinal heritage of the Christian church and embrace Pelagianism. We must then reject the teaching of the Bible that all men are under sin's dominion (Rom. 3:9; 5:21; 6:14, 17). The consequence is liberalism's so-called gospel, as Richard Niebuhr (1894–1962) described it: "A God without wrath brought men without sin into a kingdom without judgment through the ministrations of a Christ without a cross."[40]

---

35. Dennis R. Venema and Scot McKnight, *Adam and the Genome: Reading Scripture after Genetic Science* (Grand Rapids, MI: Baker, 2017), 188.

36. Schaeffer, *Genesis in Space and Time*, 41.

37. John Murray, *The Epistle to the Romans*, The New International Commentary on the New Testament (Grand Rapids, MI: Eerdmans, 1968), 1:181n18.

38. The Biologos Foundation grossly misuses John Calvin's commentary on Genesis 3:19 at this point, claiming that Calvin taught that even if Adam had not sinned, he would have experienced "a more gentle kind of physical death or 'passing' from life into life." "Did Death Occur before the Fall?," Biologos, https://biologos.org/common-questions/did-death-occur-before-the-fall. But as the very words of Calvin they quote show, Calvin did not teach that an unfallen Adam would have died, but that he would have been glorified without death.

39. For examples of modern theologians denying the fall, see Collins, *Did Adam and Eve Really Exist?*, 44–47.

40. Richard Niebuhr, *The Kingdom of God in America* (1937; repr., New York: Harper & Row, 1959), 193.

The Historical Adam Is a Type of Mankind's Savior

A "type" is a historical person, event, or institution designed by God to foreshadow Christ and his kingdom in a way that is imperfect yet illuminating. The biblical basis for this language is Romans 5:14: "Yet death reigned from Adam to Moses, even over those whose sinning was not like the transgression of Adam, who was a type of the one who was to come" (ESV). Paul goes on in Romans 5 to show that whereas condemnation and death fell on those in Adam because of his sin and disobedience, "much more" did justification and life come to those in Christ because of Christ's obedience.

Paul makes the same comparison in 1 Corinthians 15 when discussing Christ's resurrection. He writes in verses 21–22, "Since by man came death, by man came also the resurrection of the dead. For as in Adam all die, even so in Christ shall all be made alive." In verse 45, he speaks of "the first man Adam" and "the last Adam." In fact, in verse 47, he speaks of "the first man" and "the second man" as if no one else had ever lived. There may also be allusions to Adam in Paul's description of Christ as the Image of God.[41]

Luke indicates that Christ is like Adam when, as we saw, he traces Christ's genealogy back to Adam, "the son of God," just after Christ was proclaimed "my beloved Son" by the Father's heavenly voice (Luke 3:22–23, 38). Just after presenting this genealogy, Luke records the temptation of Christ by the Devil in the wilderness, just as Adam was tempted in the garden. However, Christ stood against all temptation, whereas Adam fell.

The historical Adam is firmly embedded in the Bible's doctrine of Christ.[42] Paul is not using the history of Adam as an instructive parable. He describes the two great figures in history upon whom everything hangs. If there was no real Adam, then Paul's theology collapses. The apostle would then be profoundly mistaken, not just in his understanding of Adam but in his doctrine of Christ's work. On the contrary, we believe that Paul was inspired of God, an apostle whose message did not come from man but was revealed to Paul by Christ himself (Gal. 1:12).

Adam and Biblical Authority

Let us suppose that someone still insists that though he believes the Bible to be God's Word and accepts its doctrines of man and salvation, he does not

---

41. 2 Cor. 4:4; Col. 1:15; cf. Rom. 8:29; Eph. 4:22–24.
42. See Joel R. Beeke, "Christ, the Second Adam," in *God, Adam, and You*, ed. Phillips, 141–68.

believe that Adam was a real, historical figure as Genesis describes him. This position raises serious questions about the Bible itself.

The Danger of Subjecting God's Word to Human Skepticism

The first set of questions pertains to the authority of biblical history. On what basis should we believe that Abraham, Moses, or David was a real person? They also appear in historical narratives in the Bible, they are listed in genealogies, and they are spoken of as real people by our Lord Jesus. If that evidence is insufficient to prove that Adam was a historical figure, why should we believe that any of these people were historical figures?

Once we deny the historicity of Adam, we trigger an earthquake that sends a tsunami of skepticism surging over the Bible, wiping out its historical reliability. Nor can we build a seawall that will keep this tidal wave out of the New Testament. We understand that there are some people who deny Adam but still confess Christ. However, we must ask: On what basis can you say Adam was a myth but be sure Christ was real? If you deny Adam's historicity, what is to keep you from denying Christ's historical birth, life, death, and resurrection?

Biblical history is not like Aesop's fables, charming stories that we can apply to ourselves by way of analogy. Rather, the Bible is telling us *our history* for our good, just as knowing your family history can help you to understand your life today. As one author said, when we read the Bible, "we must understand that we dwell in the same history."[43] C. John Collins says that the Bible gives us "a grand narrative or worldview story," and each of the people of God should see himself as "an *heir* of this story, with all its glory and shame; as a *steward* of the story, responsible to pass it on to the next generation; and as a *participant*, whose faithfulness could play a role, in God's mysterious wisdom, in the story's progress."[44] As both a human being and a fallen sinner, you are what you are because of what Adam was and what Adam did.

We must honestly face what the text of Holy Scripture is claiming, whether or not we like it or can square it with the prevailing views of science. As Edward Young said, it is far more honest to say, "Genesis pur-

---

43. Alan Jacobs, "Leon Kass and the Genesis of Wisdom," *First Things* 134 (June/July 2003): 32, cited in Collins, *Did Adam and Eve Really Exist?*, 40.

44. Collins, *Did Adam and Eve Really Exist?*, 40–41; cf. C. John Collins, "Theology of the Old Testament," in *The ESV Study Bible* (Wheaton, IL: Crossway, 2008), 30.

ports to be a historical account, but I do not believe that account," than it is to say, "I believe that Genesis is true" while actually believing that it is mythology.[45]

The Danger of Subordinating God's Word to Human Science

Calvin said that God gave us the Scriptures as eyeglasses to help us see and properly understand his general revelation of himself and his ways.[46] We need these corrective lenses because our sin-clouded eyes naturally distort what we see in the world. However, those who deny Adam also deny that the Bible speaks authoritatively about scientific matters.[47] Rather, they regard science as the eyeglasses with which we should read Scripture, using scientific knowledge to sift out God's message from the errors of the ancient community of faith.[48]

This results in the view that God did not breathe his truth into the details of Scripture, but inspired only its core theological message.[49] For example, Richard Carlson and Tremper Longman say, "The sacred author was not as concerned about factual details as he was about clearly presenting theological concepts understandable by his intended audience."[50] This is a far cry from the position taken by the Lord Jesus, who said, "The scripture cannot be broken" (John 10:35).

Those who deny that Adam truly existed may affirm that "the Bible is the inspired and authoritative word of God."[51] However, they mean something different from what evangelical and Reformed Christians historically have meant by such a claim. They do not hold to biblical inerrancy, but believe that the Bible contains errors and false teachings derived from the cultures and times in which it was written. They also do not affirm the Bible's supreme authority to resolve religious

---

45. E. J. Young, *In the Beginning: Genesis 1–3 and the Authority of Scripture* (Edinburgh: Banner of Truth, 1976), 19.

46. Calvin, *Institutes*, 1.6.1; 1.14.1.

47. "Christians today misread Genesis when they try to engage it, *even minimally*, in the scientific arena." Enns, *The Evolution of Adam*, 33, emphasis added. The Bible is thus shut out of the scientific world.

48. An example of reading Scripture through the lenses of evolution may be found in Richard F. Carlson and Tremper Longman III, *Science, Creation, and the Bible: Reconciling Rival Theories of Origins* (Downers Grove, IL: IVP Academic, 2010), 122.

49. See B. B. Warfield, *Limited Inspiration*, (Philadelphia, Presbyterian & Reformed, 1962), also available under its original title, "Professor Henry Preserved Smith on Inspiration," *The Presbyterian and Reformed Review* 5, no. 4 (October 1894), 600–653; http://www.archive.org/stream/presbyterianrefo5201warf#page/600/mode/2up.

50. Carlson and Longman, *Science, Creation, and the Bible*, 126.

51. "About Us," Biologos, http://biologos.org/about.

controversies. Instead, they believe that the Bible must submit to the ever-changing theories of science. Ironically, even as they reject some biblical teachings as the notions of ancient cultures, they impose on the Bible other ideas from modern culture. They believe that rather than absolute divine authority governing our faith, we have only the relative authority of human culture and opinion.

For example, Peter Enns readily acknowledges that the apostle Paul believed that Adam must have been just as real as Jesus Christ. But he says that we need not follow Paul's view, for he was an "ancient man," and today we know better.[52] He also teaches that Paul intentionally twisted the meaning of the Old Testament Scriptures in order to fit his gospel message, "reworking the past to speak to the present."[53] Enns says that the Pentateuch was not written by Moses, but was composed piecemeal and brought together after the exile, several centuries after the exodus from Egypt.[54] He rebukes conservative evangelicals for believing that if the Bible is God's Word, then it must "be historically accurate in all its details."[55] Instead, God "adopted mythic categories" from the ancient world, myths we may now discard so long as we retain the spiritual truth they contain.[56] These are clear and sobering examples of how denying the reality of Adam puts a person on a trajectory to denying the full trustworthiness of the Holy Scriptures.

The Danger of Shrinking God's Word to Human Experience

Some who take this route may not realize that they are departing from the path of biblical orthodoxy and are following the unbiblical road of neoorthodoxy. Emil Brunner (1889–1966), a noted neoorthodox theologian, said that the biblical account of creation is "not a theory of the way in which the world came into existence," but only a summons to know God as Lord and Creator.[57] Thus, according to Brunner, the Adam of Genesis 2 cannot be separated from ancient beliefs about the universe, and in light of our modern scientific understanding, we cannot regard

---

52. Enns, *The Evolution of Adam*, xvi–xvii, 139. See also Lamoureux, "No Historical Adam," in *Four Views on the Historical Adam*, ed. Barrett and Caneday, 61–62.

53. Enns, *The Evolution of Adam*, 113.

54. Enns, *The Evolution of Adam*, 23.

55. Peter Enns, *Inspiration and Incarnation: Evangelicals and the Problem of the Old Testament* (Grand Rapids, MI: Baker Academic, 2005), 47.

56. Enns, *Inspiration and Incarnation*, 53.

57. Emil Brunner, *The Christian Doctrine of Creation and Redemption, Dogmatics, Volume 2*, trans. Olive Wyon (Philadelphia: Westminster, 1952), 7–8.

him as a real individual.[58] For Brunner, paradise is "myth," not "historical fact."[59] Likewise, the account of the fall is not about a historical event, but is a revelation of man's conflict with God, a truth not about "a certain man called Adam, who lived so many thousand years ago, but of myself, and of yourself, and of everyone else in the world."[60] Millard Erickson writes, "In many ways Brunner's approach likens the creation account to a parable."[61]

We must recognize that according to neoorthodoxy's approach to divine revelation, the Bible is not the Word of God, but man's fallible witness to God's Word. The Word of God, in this view, is an experience of encountering God in Jesus Christ.[62] This experience results in doctrine. Like theological liberalism, neoorthodoxy reduces divine revelation to human experience. This leaves us uncertain as to what we should believe about the Lord and his ways.[63] It also places us at odds with Jesus Christ, who said that the words of the prophets and his words were all eternal truth (Matt. 5:18; 24:35).[64]

One of the great problems involved in the denial of the historical Adam is that it separates the message of the Word of God from the history it records.[65] This separation destroys the credibility of its message. The Bible tells us the gospel, which means "good news." It is a message about events that happened and their happy consequences. Without the events, there is no news to tell. As Paul writes in 1 Corinthians 15:17, "If Christ be not raised, your faith is vain; ye are yet in your sins." In the end, if we undermine the Bible's historical foundations, then the whole of Christianity

---

58. Brunner, *The Christian Doctrine of Creation and Redemption*, 50; and Emil Brunner, *Man in Revolt*, trans. Olive Wyon (London: RTS-Lutterworth Press, 1939), 86.

59. Brunner, *The Christian Doctrine of Creation and Redemption*, 74. On Brunner and Adam, see Bernard Ramm, *The Christian View of Science and Scripture* (Grand Rapids, MI: Eerdmans, 1954), 318–19.

60. Brunner, *Man in Revolt*, 88.

61. Erickson, *Christian Theology*, 441.

62. Emil Brunner, *Revelation and Reason: The Christian Doctrine of Faith and Knowledge*, trans. Olive Wyon (Philadelphia: Westminster, 1946), 9.1, 4, 8–10 (118–20, 122, 126–31); and Karl Barth, "The Christian Understanding of Revelation," in *Against the Stream: Shorter Post-War Writings, 1946–52*, ed. Ronald Gregor Smith (New York: Philosophical Library, 1954), 210–25.

63. Erickson, *Christian Theology*, 159.

64. For more on the doctrine of revelation in neoorthodoxy, see *RST*, 1:304–9.

65. Lamoureux, "No Historical Adam," in *Four Views on the Historical Adam*, ed. Barrett and Caneday, 50, 62–63. Unlike Brunner, Lamoureux affirms that the spiritual truths of the Bible are inerrant revelation. However, how does one distinguish spiritual truths from incidental science and history in the Bible, especially if those spiritual truths are contradicted by contemporary science? His position is logically unstable and likely to collapse into subjective experientialism.

collapses into subjective opinions and feelings. Feelings, however, cannot save us.

Brunner's approach raises serious questions about the clarity and veracity of the Bible. It is hard to avoid the conclusion that ancient readers and hearers of Scripture would have taken Genesis at face value as a historical narrative. Was that not God's intent? Why else would God have presented matters in this way? If people can explain the basic ideas of evolution to children,[66] surely God could have done the same for the men and women of ancient Israel. He could have revealed that he created life by a long, slow process, that he conferred human souls upon existing animals, and that he made many human beings at first instead of just one. He did not reveal any of this, however, but in direct contradiction to it, he revealed his creation of the first man and woman.

Furthermore, if the Bible is cultural dressing wrapped around divine truth, or a human witness to a divine encounter, then how can we be sure which part is the husk and which is the kernel? What one generation embraces as authentic Christianity could very well be rejected by another generation as merely time-bound human culture. Amid such uncertainty, the Bible is not treated as having divine authority, nor can it be called God's Word without equivocation. Over time, the kernel shrinks and Christianity becomes a hollow shell into which men pour their own ideas. It is far better to submit to the written Word of God and allow it to fill us with the knowledge of the truth.

In summary, both the history and theology taught by the Bible call us to believe in the historical person of Adam as depicted in Genesis. Without Adam, we undermine the doctrinal foundation of such important truths as the nobility, unity, sexuality, and depravity of mankind. Adam's historical fall is the counterpart of Christ's historical work of salvation. Philip Ryken says, "The logical and long-term effect of denying the existence of Adam is to weaken the church's grip on central biblical truths that make a difference in daily life."[67] This is because the denial of Adam's reality as an individual person introduces a hermeneutic of suspicion into our approach to the Bible. It sets aside the plain meaning of the inspired text and subordinates its authority to the opinions of mere men.

---

66. There are a number of illustrated children's books that introduce them to the theory of evolution.

67. Philip G. Ryken, "We Cannot Understand the World or Our Faith without a Real, Historical Adam," in *Four Views on the Historical Adam*, ed. Barrett and Caneday, 270.

Sing to the Lord

Trusting in God's Word in a Deceitful World

O Lord, be Thou my helper true,
For just and godly men are few;
The faithful who can find?
From truth and wisdom men depart,
With flatt'ring lips and double heart
They speak their evil mind.

The lips that speak, the truth to hide,
The tongues of arrogance and pride,
That boastful words employ,
False-speaking tongues that boast their might,
That own no law, that know no right,
Jehovah will destroy.

Because the poor are sore oppressed,
Because the needy are distressed,
And bitter are their cries,
The Lord will be their helper strong;
To save them from contempt and wrong
Jehovah will arise.

Jehovah's promises are sure,
His words are true, His words are pure
As silver from the flame.
Though base men walk on ev'ry side,
His saints are safe, whate'er betide,
Protected by His Name.

Psalm 12
Tune: Bremen
The Psalter, No. 21
Or Tune: Colwyn Bay
Trinity Hymnal—Baptist Edition, No. 45

Questions for Meditation or Discussion

1. Explain and answer the following objections to a historical Adam.
   - the meaning of "Adam"
   - Genesis 1–3 and Israel

- Genesis 1 and 2
- the Serpent's activity

2. Why is the doctrine of a real Adam in history important for our view of the following?

- human nature
- the unity of the human race despite differences of color and ethnicity
- God's design for men and women

3. How would the loss of the historical Adam affect the Christian doctrine of sin?

4. If Adam were not a real man, then what would that imply about Paul's theology of Christ as the last Adam?

5. What would the denial of Adam's historicity logically imply about the rest of the Bible's historical accounts—including the life of Christ?

6. If we interpret Adam to be a myth or metaphor on the basis of scientific theories, then what authority have we given scientists over the Bible? What does that imply about the Bible?

7. What was Emil Brunner's approach to the Bible's account of Adam? How did that fit Brunner's view of divine revelation? If we adopt his approach, where will it lead us?

8. What difference does it make to you personally whether Adam was a real man? If you discovered that he was not real, would it affect your faith and obedience? Why or why not?

Questions for Deeper Reflection

9. How can we discern whether a narrative in the Bible is historical narrative, a parable for spiritual truth, or history expressed in metaphorical language? Give some examples from the Scriptures.

10. When debating this issue with someone, he says, "I don't need to worry about whether Genesis is historical or legendary. I know Jesus Christ. He is enough for me." How do you respond?

8

The Image of God, Part 1

Exegetical and Biblical Theology

The words "God created man in his own image" (Gen. 1:27) summarize the excellence of the human race. Gregory of Nyssa (fl. 375) said, "In what then does the greatness of man consist, according to the doctrine of the Church? Not in his likeness to the created world, but in his being in the image of the nature of the Creator."[1] Nothing could exalt man more than bearing the image of God. The value of all things lies in their manifestation of the glory of God, and God has chosen to concentrate his revealed glory in the human race. Herman Bavinck said, "The entire world is a revelation of God, a mirror of his attributes and perfections. Every creature in its own way and degree is the embodiment of a divine thought. But among creatures, only man is the image of God, God's highest and richest revelation and consequently the head and crown of the whole creation."[2]

Therefore, in order to understand mankind, we must grasp what God has revealed about man's creation in the divine image. Geerhardus Vos highlighted the "great importance" of this doctrine: "By 'image of God' is expressed what is characteristic of man and his relation to God. That he is God's image distinguishes him from animals and all other creatures."[3]

---

1. Gregory of Nyssa, *On the Making of Man*, 16.2, in *NPNF²*, 5:404.
2. Bavinck, *Reformed Dogmatics*, 2:531.
3. Vos, *Reformed Dogmatics*, 2:12.

This concept is crucial to knowing man's nature, identity, function, and relationship to God, his fellow men, and the other creatures.

In this chapter, we will trace the developing revelation of God's image through redemptive history from creation to the new creation in Christ. In the next chapter, we will examine the meaning of the image through the lenses of historical and polemical theology. Finally, in chapter 10, we will employ the lenses of systematic and practical theology to consider the meaning of the image.

The Created Image of God

The foundational text for this doctrine appears at the climax of the creation account in Genesis 1:26–27. There we hear God say, "Let us make man in our image, after our likeness," after which the text tells us, "So God created man in his own image, in the image of God created he him; male and female created he them." Just as the verb *created* appears three times to emphasize that man was the crown of creation (v. 27), we read the word *image* three times (vv. 26–27) and *likeness* once (v. 26), highlighting how central the divine image is to man's created identity and purpose.

We learn from Genesis 2:7 that God gave life to man by breathing the breath of life into his nostrils. There is an analogy between man's created life and God's eternal life.[4] This analogy is similar to man's being created in God's image. This suggests that God's image in man consists of a kind of divine life (Eph. 4:18; 2 Pet. 1:3–4), or more precisely, a life analogous to the life of God. God is self-existent and independent as the "I Am" (Ex. 3:14); man's life depends upon God's Spirit (Job 33:4). Nevertheless, the living image bearers of God were divinely designed to reflect the glorious life of the Creator.

Images of God's Attributes

The term translated as "image" (*tselem*) refers to an artistic depiction,[5] and "likeness" (*demut*) refers to an appearance, pattern, or similarity.[6] Aside from references to the image of God in man (Gen. 1:26; 5:3), the two words appear together only once, and that with apparently the same

---

4. See the discussion of Gen. 2:7 in chap. 6.

5. Num. 33:52; 1 Sam. 6:5, 11; 2 Kings 11:18; 2 Chron. 23:17; Ezek. 7:20; 16:17; 23:14; Amos 5:26. As used in Pss. 39:6 and 73:20, the word seems to contrast a mere appearance with reality.

6. 2 Kings 16:10; 2 Chron. 4:3; Ps. 58:5; Isa. 13:4; 40:18; Ezek. 1:5, 10, 13, 16, 22, 26, 28; 8:2; 10:1, 10, 21–22; 23:15; Dan. 10:16

meaning (Ezek. 23:14–15).[7] Similarly, in Genesis 1, they are used "almost interchangeably," as Anthony Hoekema observed. Sometimes both words are together in parallel construction (Gen. 1:26; 5:1), once just "image" (Gen. 1:27, twice), and once just "the likeness of God" (Gen. 5:1).[8] Therefore, in the phrase "in our image, after our likeness," the two terms appear to explain each other: God made man as an image like himself. Hoekema wrote, "The two words together tell us that man is a representation of God who is like God in certain respects."[9]

The idea, then, behind God's creation of man "in our image, after our likeness" is that the Lord designed human beings to be limited, visible, earthly creatures that resembled God for his glory. The context for this statement is God's creative acts that reveal his attributes. His creative acts distinguish him from man. God revealed his absolute uniqueness and incomparable glory as the only eternal God, Creator of all things out of nothing, and Lord over all. Man is not God, but only an image like God. Francis Turretin wrote that the image "does not consist in a participation of the divine essence," but is a created analogy.[10]

Thus, we expect the image of God to be analogous in a finite way to the infinite power, authority, wisdom, and goodness that God manifested in creating the world.[11] Wilhelmus à Brakel said the divine image "consists in a faint resemblance to the communicable attributes of God."[12] Man has a small sketch of God's attributes imprinted upon him. Genesis does not say that God gave or imparted his image to man, nor that he commissioned man to image him, but that God made man in his image. This implies that in man's original state, aspects of his nature and condition reflected the divine nature and actions.

Thus, the divine image implies personality. The text of Genesis 1 is not just a list of events caused by an impersonal power, but a narrative of the acts of a personal agent. J. I. Packer comments, "Creation, as depicted in Genesis 1, was the work of a mighty mind, forming and executing purposes ('Let there be . . .') and then evaluating its own achievements ('God

---

7. Compare "she saw men pourtrayed upon the wall, the images [*tselem*] of the Chaldeans" with "after the manner [*demut*] of the Babylonians of Chaldea" (Ezek. 23:14–15).
8. Hoekema, *Created in God's Image*, 13. See also Mathews, *Genesis 1–11:26*, 166; and Reymond, *A New Systematic Theology of the Christian Faith*, 427.
9. Hoekema, *Created in God's Image*, 13.
10. Turretin, *Institutes*, 5.10.4 (1:465).
11. On creation as a revelation of God's uniqueness, lordship, and other attributes, see chap. 2.
12. Brakel, *The Christian's Reasonable Service*, 1:323.

saw everything that he had made, and behold it was very good.')"[13] We would add to Packer's statement that God's deliberation ("Let us make man") implies that God is a volitional being. Therefore, man in God's image is also a rational, volitional, personal being. This is not imposing Greek philosophical categories upon the text of Scripture, but simply recognizing what the Bible is communicating. Man could not be the image of God's wisdom and goodness if he lacked the capacity to think and to choose.

An image of God functions to make God known. Given the prominence that Genesis 1 gives to divine speech, one would expect God's human images to make him known, in part, through speaking his words. Therefore, the concept of the image of God suggests one of the covenantal offices or functions of man: to serve as God's prophets to one another. Just as the prophets represented God both in word and deed, so man is to reveal his Creator not only in his speech, but also in the conduct of his life.

Images for God's Worship

God's image serves for God's worship. "Image" (*tselem*) is used several times in the Bible for images of various gods.[14] God forbade the use of images "of any thing that is in heaven above, or that is in the earth beneath, or that is in the water under the earth" to represent him or aid in worship (Ex. 20:4–6). Though this commandment uses a different term for "image" than does Genesis 1, the idea is the same, and the commandment uses language that clearly alludes to creation.[15] Men make inanimate idols to image their false gods, but the true God makes living people to be his image bearers. This suggests that people exist for the worship of God.

The antithesis between God's created image in man and man-made images, or idols, shows how false worship inverts the nature and calling of men to glorify the Creator. God created humans to be creatures who become like the object of their worship. They were made to be like God, but when they turned from him, they were still image-bearing creatures, and thus reflected something in the creation (idols) to which they gave their adoration. Greg Beale has rightly noted that you resemble what you revere either for

---

13. J. I. Packer, *Knowing Man* (Westchester, IL: Cornerstone Books, 1979), 21.
14. Num. 33:52; 2 Kings 11:18; 2 Chron. 23:17; Ezek. 7:20; 16:17; Amos 5:26.
15. Compare Ex. 20:4 to Gen. 1:20; Ex. 20:11; Neh. 9:6.

your ruin or restoration.[16] Rather than being content to reflect the Creator, apostate man tries to reverse the situation and create gods that reflect his corrupt desires.[17] G. C. Berkouwer (1903–1996) said, "The creation of man in God's image is very directly related to the prohibition of images. . . . For in worshipping images, man completely misunderstands God's intentions and no longer realizes the meaning of his humanity in his communion with God."[18] By exchanging the glory of God for images of created things, man falls short of the glory of God that he was made to image and extinguishes his own light and wisdom (Rom. 1:21–23; 3:23). The image of God stands in direct opposition to the soul-blinding gods of this world, for God made it to radiate the light of his glory (2 Cor. 4:4; cf. Rom. 8:29–30; 2 Cor. 3:18).

Sacred images dwell in temples. This, too, suggests a nuance of meaning for Genesis 1 that parallels what we observed about the garden as God's temple in Genesis 2.[19] God created the world in six days and rested on the seventh,[20] and the number seven figures prominently in the tabernacle and temple narratives.[21] Therefore, Genesis 1 may picture creation as a temple, with man as the image of God. It was in the tabernacle and temple that the priests worked, symbolically clothed with God's glory and beauty, garments of the same materials as the tabernacle itself.[22] Divine glory inhabits God's temple.[23] Therefore, God's creation of man in his image suggests that man is the chief feature in God's cosmic temple, created to worship him and promote his worship as priests clothed in his glory.

Images of God's Reign

In Genesis, we find the closest relation between man's creation in God's image and man's kingship over the world. We see this in Genesis 1:26: "And God said, Let us make man in our image, after our likeness: and let

16. G. K. Beale, *We Become What We Worship: A Biblical Theology of Idolatry* (Downers Grove, IL: InterVarsity Press, 2016), 16.
17. See Richard Lints, *Identity and Idolatry: The Image of God and Its Inversion*, New Studies in Biblical Theology (Downers Grove, IL: InterVarsity Press, 2015), 80–81.
18. G. C. Berkouwer, *Man: The Image of God*, Studies in Dogmatics (Grand Rapids, MI: Eerdmans, 1962), 84.
19. See chap. 6.
20. See chap. 4 on the exegesis of creation in six days according to Genesis 1.
21. Ex. 29:30, 35, 37; Lev. 8:33, 35; 2 Chron. 7:9. The instructions to build the tabernacle are given in seven divine speeches, the seventh of which concerns the Sabbath (Ex. 25:1; 30:11, 17, 22, 34; 31:1, 12). Solomon spent seven years building the temple (1 Kings 6:38). Cf. Lints, *Identity and Idolatry*, 52.
22. Ex. 28:2, 5, 40; cf. the use of the same terms "glory" and "beauty" for the Lord in Ps. 96:3, 6.
23. Ex. 29:43; 40:35; 1 Kings 8:10–11.

them have dominion over the fish of the sea, and over the fowl of the air, and over the cattle, and over all the earth, and over every creeping thing that creepeth upon the earth." We see the same connection between image and kingship in verses 27–28: "So God created man in his own image, in the image of God created he him; male and female created he them. And God blessed them, and God said unto them, Be fruitful, and multiply, and replenish the earth, and subdue it: and have dominion over the fish of the sea, and over the fowl of the air, and over every living thing that moveth upon the earth."

Therefore, the divine image in man is closely related to man's status as God's servant-king on earth. In the ancient world, kings often set up sculpted images of themselves to represent their authority; God set up living images to represent his authority on earth.[24] The God of creation exercises supreme authority over his works; as his image bearer, man is granted a measure of authority as well. Though man is a miniscule creature in a vast universe, God gave him dominion over the earth (Ps. 8:4–8).[25]

This idea would have connected well with ancient peoples, but with a radical twist. There are several examples in ancient literature of kings who were called images of their gods.[26] The king was to live in close connection to his god and to represent him on earth. However, in Scripture the divine image was not the exclusive property of society's ruling elite, but extended to all mankind. Whereas ancient society was stratified into royalty, nobility, free men, and slaves, God conferred on every human being the dignity of bearing his image.

Man's dominion was not a curse to the earth, but its glory. Periodically throughout the creation account, we read that God saw that what he had made was "good."[27] It is significant that after creating man in his image and giving man dominion over the plants and animals, "God saw every thing that he had made, and, behold, it was very good" (Gen. 1:31). Hoekema said, "Man, therefore, as he came from the hands of the Creator, was not corrupt, depraved, or sinful; he was in a state of integrity, innocence, and holiness."[28] Man was originally a faithful servant-king over God's world, and man's kingdom was a great blessing to everything God had made.

---

24. Hoekema, *Created in God's Image*, 67.
25. On man's distinction from and dominion over the animals, see chap. 6.
26. D. J. A. Clines, "The Image of God in Man," *Tyndale Bulletin* 19 (1968): 83–85 (full article, 53–103).
27. Gen. 1:4, 10, 12, 18, 21, 25.
28. Hoekema, *Created in God's Image*, 15.

Images for God's Family

The image is also relational. The one God revealed himself in personal plurality ("let *us* make man in *our* image").[29] God made man to dimly reflect God's eternal Trinity through each man's complementary and interdependent relationships with other people. These relationships begin with the family, for God created man in his image "male and female" to "be fruitful, and multiply" (Gen. 1:27–28). Thereby they would fill the earth with a family of divine images.

The concepts of servant-kings and a relational image of God converge in another biblical concept connected to God's image: men were made to be God's created sons. Bible scholar Kenneth Mathews writes, "In the ancient Near East royal persons were considered the sons of the gods or representatives of the gods (cf. 2 Sam 7:13–16; Ps 2:7). Mankind is appointed as God's royal representatives (i.e., sonship) to rule the earth in his place."[30]

We encounter this divine sonship when Genesis returns to the theme of God's image in its first genealogy. It parallels the statement that "God created man, in the likeness of God made he him" with the declaration that Adam "begat a son in his own likeness, and after his image" (Gen. 5:1–3). On the one hand, the text contrasts God's *creating* and Adam's *begetting*, lest we think that the image of God implies that man shares in God's deity. On the other hand, the text compares God's making Adam in his image and Adam's begetting a son in his image. Adam was not a begotten son of God, but he was a created son of God (Luke 3:38).

The idea of sonship captures the ideas we have already observed in connection to the image of God. A son is like his father, and God made man as an image of his attributes. A son should honor his father, and so God made man to worship him. A son shares in his father's authority and works to accomplish his father's will, and God created man to represent him as his servant-king. A son has relationships with his father and the family, and God formed man to walk with God and his fellow men and women in love.

It is not a surprise, then, to discover, as we trace the theme of God's image throughout the rest of the Bible, that it often stands in close relation to God's Son and the sons that he is bringing to glory. However, before

---

29. See chap. 2.
30. Mathews, *Genesis 1–11:26*, 164.

we reach that glad theme, we must consider the terrible wound that sin inflicted upon God's sons.

The Continuing Image of God

The fall of man brought devastating consequences upon our race (Genesis 3). The reader of Genesis naturally wonders what effect the fall had upon the image of God. As he reads on, he learns that mankind became murderers and polygamists, so that some men took whatever women pleased them and filled the earth with violence.[31] God saw "that the wickedness of man was great in the earth, and that every imagination of the thoughts of his heart was only evil continually" (6:5). Can such people be said to exist in the image of God? However, Genesis also testifies that man did not degenerate into a mere animal, but practiced farming, married, raised children, built cities, performed the musical arts, and worked with metal (4:2, 17, 20–22). What then should we think of the image of God in fallen man?

In a text loaded with allusions to creation, the Lord reaffirmed to Noah that man still bore God's image in some sense. God gave the animals to man to kill and eat, but warned that he would call to account anyone who murdered a human being (Gen. 9:5–6). This principle was to be applied not just to the godly, but to mankind in general. God explained the reason: "In the image of God made he man" (v. 6). All human life is sacred, despite the fall of man into sin and misery, because of man's image bearing.[32] It may be that the activities of human civilization that we just noted in Genesis 4 are evidences of the remnants of this image.

James likewise alludes to the image of God when he rebukes men for the inconsistency of blessing God but cursing other people, "who are made in the likeness of God" (James 3:9 ESV). James has just written of man's mastery over the various animals, birds, serpents, and sea creatures (v. 7), an allusion to Genesis 1:26.[33] He also uses the same term "likeness" (homoiōsis), by which the Greek Septuagint rendered demut in Genesis 1:26. Thus, James affirms man's superiority to other living creatures and his sanctity as God's image bearer. We may rule over the beasts and use

---

31. Gen. 4:11, 19, 23; 6:2, 11.
32. Hamilton, The Book of Genesis, Chapters 1–17, 315; and Laidlaw, The Bible Doctrine of Man, 144.
33. Douglas J. Moo, The Letter of James, The Pillar New Testament Commentary (Grand Rapids, MI: Eerdmans, 2000), 160.

them for good purposes, but we must respect and treat human beings differently.

Therefore, the image of God remains in some sense an abiding reality in fallen mankind, with sobering implications for how we treat other human beings. Violence, hateful speech, and rebellion against human authority violate God's holiness, for they assault his image on earth.

The Incarnate Image of God

The supreme image of God is Jesus Christ. Just as Adam was "the son of God," so God said to Christ, the descendant of Adam, "Thou art my beloved Son; in thee I am well pleased" (Luke 3:22, 38). However, whereas Adam disobeyed God when tempted by the Devil, Christ persevered in obedience when the Devil tempted him (Luke 4:1–13). Luke's contrast of Adam's sonship and Christ's raises the expectation that our Lord Jesus is God's image par excellence, the last Adam who will restore the fallen image of God in man.

The epistles of Paul are even more explicit in affirming Christ as the supreme divine image. Paul writes of "the light of the glorious gospel of Christ, who is the image of God" (2 Cor. 4:4). Jesus Christ is nothing less than "the Lord" (v. 5), the radiance of "the glory of God" (v. 6; cf. Heb. 1:3). Paul alludes to the creation of Adam, for the Greek term translated as "image" (*eikōn*) is the same one used in the Septuagint for God's "image" (*tselem*, Gen. 1:26–27). However, he does so in a way that transcends Adam and gives Christ a cosmic significance on the level of the Lord and Creator (cf. 1 Cor. 8:6; Heb. 1:10). Paul compares the shining of Christ's light in men's hearts to God's creative fiat when he "commanded the light to shine out of darkness" (2 Cor. 4:6). The shining of Christ's image-glory in man's soul is nothing less than a new creation.

We find the clearest statement of this truth in Paul's grand Christological confession in Colossians 1:15–17: "[He] is the image of the invisible God, the firstborn of every creature: for by him were all things created, that are in heaven, and that are in earth, visible and invisible, whether they be thrones, or dominions, or principalities, or powers: all things were created by him, and for him: and he is before all things, and by him all things consist." The person in view here is God's Son, the supreme King and Redeemer of God's people (vv. 13–14). Christ fulfills man's original purpose as the Image of God by making visible the invisible. The term "firstborn" does not designate Christ as a part of creation, but as its ruler, just as God said of the son of David: "Also I will make him my firstborn, higher than the kings of the earth" (Ps. 89:27). This is abundantly clear from Colossians 1:16–17, for Christ is the agent of creation and providence. Christ is Lord over all things, even the angelic powers.

Therefore, when the Bible refers to Christ as the Image of God, it both compares and contrasts him to Adam. Like Adam, Christ in his human nature is God's image and King on earth. He is "the last Adam" (1 Cor. 15:45), come to redeem the fallen image bearers of God and restore them for God's glory. However, Adam was only a type of Christ (Rom. 5:14), for Christ is infinitely greater. Whereas Adam was a mere creature on earth given authority to rule other creatures, Christ is the Creator and Lord of heaven and earth. In him dwells the very fullness of God (Col. 1:19; 2:9), for he possesses equality with God (Phil. 2:6). Christ is the Image of God because he is God's eternal Son who shares the Father's divine nature. Turretin wrote, "The Son of God is the essential image of most perfect equality," sharing in the same "essence with the Father," but Adam was the "analogical image of inadequate and imperfect similitude."[34]

The Renewed Image of God

God saves sinners by uniting them to Christ in his death and resurrection by a Spirit-worked faith. The light of Christ, the Image of God, breaks forth in their hearts as an act of new creation through the preaching of the gospel (2 Cor. 4:4–6). United to him who is the Image of God, they are renewed in God's image. Paul writes, "But we all, with open face beholding as in a glass the glory of the Lord, are changed into the same image [*eikōn*] from glory to glory, even as by the Spirit of the Lord" (3:18). Beholding God's image in Christ results in becoming conformed to him as God's image. Paul summarizes the process with the phrase "from glory to glory," for sinners "come short of the glory of God" (Rom. 3:23), but the saints have Christ in them, "the hope of glory" (Col. 1:27).

The glory of the renewed image of God already shines in the spiritual transformation of the saints. Paul says, "Lie not one to another, seeing that ye have put off the old man with his deeds; and have put on the new man, which is renewed in knowledge after the image [*eikōn*] of him that created him" (Col. 3:9–10). The "old man" refers to mankind as fallen in Adam

---

34. Turretin, *Institutes*, 5.10.2 (1:465).

(note the singular "man"); the "new man" refers to the people united to Christ (v. 11). Paul juxtaposes the divine image specifically to lying, and he identifies it with true "knowledge," which in this epistle refers to experiential knowledge of God and his will in Christ (1:9–10; 2:2–3). In the larger context of putting off and putting on, the image of God stands against sexual immorality and sinful anger (3:5, 8), and is linked to humility and love (vv. 12–14). Union with Christ also binds believers together in a manner that overcomes their ethnic and social divisions (v. 11) so that they live in peace as "one body" (v. 15).

In a parallel text in the epistle to the Ephesians, Paul writes that Christians have been taught to "put off . . . the old man," "be renewed in the spirit of your mind," and "put on the new man, which after God is created in righteousness and true holiness" (Eph. 4:21–24). The use of creation language and the parallel with Colossians 3:10 make it likely that the phrase "after God" (*kata theon*)—literally, "according to God"—refers to the divine image. As in Colossians, Paul contrasts this renewed image with "deceitful lusts" (Eph. 4:22) and connects it to "righteousness and true holiness" (v. 24), literally, "righteousness and piety of truth." This is no individualistic, private holiness, but a life of unity and peace as the "one body" of Christ (vv. 3–4; cf. vv. 12, 16), "for we are members one of another" (v. 25). The larger context expands on this idea with the call to rid oneself of malicious anger, sexual filth, and greed, and to embrace honesty, purity, and sacrificial love (4:25–5:6).

Unconverted sinners utterly lack these righteous and holy qualities, being alienated from God, at enmity with him, unable and unwilling to know him or to keep his commandments.[35] Rather than being children of God, sinners are children of the Devil and do Satan's works.[36] In this moral respect, the image of God is destroyed in mankind. It died when Adam sinned.

Therefore, although Paul writes of Christ's image bearing in terms of glory and sonship, when it comes to the renewed image in believers, his emphasis falls upon knowledge, righteousness, and holiness. This has significant implications for our understanding of what it means to be created in God's image. Charles Hodge (1797–1878) commented, "That image did not consist merely in man's rational nature, nor in his

---

35. Rom. 3:10–12; 8:7–8; Eph. 4:17–18; Col. 1:21; Titus 3:3.
36. John 8:44; Eph. 2:1–3; 1 John 3:8–10.

immortality, nor in his dominion, but specially in that righteousness and holiness, that rectitude in all his principles, which are inseparable from the possession of the truth, or true knowledge of God."[37] The fact that Paul can write of God renewing his image in man in the graces of knowledge, righteousness, and holiness—even though regenerated men are not yet restored to outward glory and dominion—implies that the core of God's image consists in the moral image, the spiritual life of the heart.

Image-bearing sons and daughters are called to imitate their Father in his goodness. The image of God forms the infrastructure for the duty of imitation pressed upon God's restored children. Christ commanded them to be "perfect" in their love as the Father is perfect (Matt. 5:48). They must be "merciful" as he is merciful (Luke 6:36). The apostolic injunction to believers is to respond "as obedient children" to the call of their Father: "Be ye holy; for I am holy" (1 Pet. 1:14–17). Since Jesus Christ is the supreme image of God, the pathway of growth into that regenerated image involves the imitation of Christ. This is a very fruitful subject for meditation (cf. John 13:1–15; 1 Cor. 11:1; Phil. 2:1–11). Paul writes, "Be ye therefore followers [imitators] of God, as dear children; and walk in love, as Christ also hath loved us, and hath given himself for us an offering and a sacrifice to God for a sweetsmelling savour" (Eph. 5:1–2). Hoekema concluded that "the heart of the image of God must be love," for this "was central in the life of Christ."[38] This is true, but we must remember that the image of God is larger than love, for it includes the full glory of God's comprehensive restoration of human nature.

The Completed Image of God

Tracing the theme of the divine image through redemptive history leads us ultimately to consider its meaning in the completion of all things in the new heaven and new earth. Paul looks ahead to that day in Romans 8:29: "For whom he did foreknow, he also did predestinate to be conformed to the image [*eikōn*] of his Son, that he might be the firstborn among many brethren." God will bring his people together as one large family ("many brethren"), in which Christ will be the chief and ruler ("firstborn") and God will be the Father.

---

37. Charles Hodge, *Ephesians*, The Geneva Series of Commentaries (Edinburgh: Banner of Truth, 1964), 193. See Charles Hodge, *Systematic Theology*, 3 vols. (Peabody, MA: Hendrickson, 1999), 2:99–102.

38. Hoekema, *Created in God's Image*, 22; cf. 73.

God's predestination aims at the honor of his Son: "that he might be the firstborn." R. C. Sproul (1939–2017) drew attention to this Christ-centered consequence, writing, "The only reason why God has saved me is for the sake of Jesus Christ . . . that Christ might have the pre-eminence."[39] United to Christ, we will be richly blessed by the Father's love for his Son. We will be "glorified" like Christ (Rom. 8:30). John Murray said, "The apostle has in view the conformity to Christ that will be realized when they will be glorified with Christ . . . the final and complete conformity of resurrection glory. . . . It is noteworthy that this should be described as conformity to the image of the Son; it enhances the marvel of the destination."[40]

When we look across Romans 8, we see how rich is Paul's concept of conformity to the image of God's Son. It involves our liberty from both "sin and death" (Rom. 8:2), our transformation from God haters to sin haters and law keepers (vv. 4–8, 13), our adoption as sons of God the Father (vv. 14–16), our being "glorified together" with Christ and sharing in the "the glory which shall be revealed in us" (vv. 17–18), the vivification and redemption of our mortal bodies (vv. 11, 23), and our dwelling in a creation set free from sorrow and corruption, and brought "into the glorious liberty of the children of God" (v. 21). These themes resonate deeply with what we have seen from Genesis about the image of God and associate it with the glory of God's sons.[41] All these rich blessings are actuated by the Holy Spirit, who is the Spirit of Christ.

Just as Christ is greater than Adam, so our image bearing in Christ will be more glorious than Adam's. In Paul's teaching on the resurrection of the dead in 1 Corinthians 15, he contrasts the life that mankind received in "the first man Adam" to what believers will receive in union with "the last Adam" (v. 45). The first is marked by corruption, dishonor, weakness, and the natural life of flesh and blood; the last by incorruption, glory, power, and the life empowered by God's Spirit (vv. 42–44). This life not only will lift Christians above their present condition in this fallen world, but will exalt them higher than Adam ever stood in paradise, for the first man was earthly, but the second man is heavenly (vv. 47–48). Paul says, "And as we have borne the image of the earthy,

---

39. R. C. Sproul, *The Gospel of God: An Exposition of Romans* (Fearn, Ross-shire, Scotland: Christian Focus, 1994), 152.
40. Murray, *The Epistle to the Romans*, 1:319.
41. Mathews, *Genesis 1–11:26*, 170–71.

we shall also bear the image [*eikōn*] of the heavenly" (v. 49). Since Paul speaks here of the resurrection of the body, image bearing has implications for the body as well as the spirit.

Therefore, the image of God spans history from creation to new creation and sums up the destiny of man in Christ. It is a glorious image, an image of sonship, the image of Christ. Therefore, the biblical theme of God's image draws our hearts upward to Christ, seated at the right hand of God. It is not merely about our past and present, but about the future of believers in the Lord Jesus Christ. It is a doctrine of hope.

Sing to the Lord

The Imitation of Christ, God's Image

My dear Redeemer and my Lord,
I read my duty in thy Word;
But in thy life the law appears
Drawn out in living characters.

Such was thy truth, and such thy zeal,
Such def'rence to thy Father's will,
Such love, and meekness so divine,
I would transcribe and make them mine.

Cold mountains and the midnight air
Witnessed the fervor of thy prayer;
The desert thy temptations knew,
Thy conflict and thy vict'ry too.

Be thou my pattern; make me bear
More of thy gracious image here:
Then God the Judge shall own my name
Amongst the foll'wers of the Lamb.

Isaac Watts
Tune: Federal Street
Trinity Hymnal—Baptist Edition, No. 171

Questions for Meditation or Discussion

1. What do the words translated as "image" and "likeness" in Genesis 1:26 mean?

2. What does it mean to say that there is an analogy between finite man and the infinite God?

3. How does the image of God relate to the following concepts in the Bible?
   - the revealed attributes of God
   - the priestly worship of God
   - the royal reign of God
   - the relational family of God

4. How would you prove from Scripture that the image of God continues in man after the fall?

5. What implications does the continuing image of God have for how we treat all human beings?

6. How is Christ the Image of God in a manner similar to Adam as God created him?

7. How is Christ the Image of God in a manner that infinitely transcends Adam?

8. What does Paul say about God's image or likeness when discussing our renewal by the Spirit?

9. How does the ultimate goal of our salvation relate to the image of God?

10. How does the biblical teaching about God's image enhance your sense of the great dignity of the human race? How does it affect your view of yourself?

Questions for Deeper Reflection

11. What does Paul's teaching about the renewal of God's image in Christians imply about the essential core of that image?

12. What does Paul's teaching about the ultimate destiny of Christians imply about the full meaning of being in God's image?

9

The Image of God, Part 2

Historical and Polemical Theology

There is a mystery wrapped around the words "image of God." Gregory of Nyssa said, "What therefore, you will perhaps say, is the definition of the image? How is the incorporeal likened to body? How is the temporal like the eternal? That which is mutable by change like to the immutable?" Gregory went on to say, "The true answer to this question, indeed, perhaps only the very Truth [God himself] knows."[1] Therefore, we must approach this subject with great humility.

In the previous chapter, we laid out an exegetical and biblical theology of God's image in man. Reformed theologians have often systematized this richness by speaking "of the image of God in a broader and narrower sense," as Herman Bavinck explained. In its narrow sense, "the primary content of the image of God" consists of "knowledge, righteousness, and holiness," which man forfeited in his fall. In its broad sense, man remains in the image of God after the fall, for he remains human. Bavinck noted that some Reformed orthodox theologians said that "the image of God consists antecedently in man's spiritual nature, formally in sanctity, and consequently in dominion."[2] But however they formulated it, Reformed theologians have historically emphasized the holistic nature of the image.

---

1. Gregory of Nyssa, *On the Making of Man*, 16.3–4, in NPNF², 5:404.
2. Bavinck, *Reformed Dogmatics*, 2:550; cf. Laidlaw, *The Bible Doctrine of Man*, 154.

For example, Anthony Hoekema stated that the image of God in man "describes him in the totality of his existence."[3]

Other theologians have said that God's image consists especially or exclusively in some aspect of human life. We may categorize their explanations as either constitutional or functional. In this chapter, we will examine the fidelity and balance of their perspectives according to the revelation of God's holy Word. In the following chapter, we will commend a holistic view of God's image that includes all these elements.

Constitutional Perspectives on God's Image

Some theologians have stressed the *constitutional* nature of the image, asserting that it refers to something about human nature, at least in its original state. This takes various forms.

A Physical Image

Some take the image in a physical sense. An ancient heretical sect known as the Anthropomorphites, led by a man named Audaeus in the fourth century, took Genesis 1:26 so literally as to mistakenly conceive of God as having a physical body that man resembles in his outward appearance.[4] The Latter-Day Saints (Mormon) Church perpetuates this heresy today.[5] Some twentieth-century Old Testament scholars of a liberal or modernistic bent also interpreted Genesis according to the pagan idea of man's physical resemblance to the body of a deity.[6] This idea is refuted by the biblical witness that God does not have a body, but is an infinite spirit, so no physical image can represent him.[7] Genesis 1 contains no hint of a physical god, but reveals God's spiritual attributes through his creative actions and speech.

Theologians in the orthodox Christian tradition did recognize, however, that the human body bears marks of nobility and uniqueness. Pagans saw this, too. The Roman poet Ovid (43 BC–c. AD 17) wrote

---

3. Hoekema, *Created in God's Image*, 66. He wrote, "The image of God involves both structure and function" (69), where "function" includes relationships.
4. Theodoret, *Ecclesiastical History*, 4.9, in NPNF[2], 3:114.
5. Former Mormon Church President Gordon B. Hinckley (1910–2008) wrote, "Our bodies are sacred. They were created in the image of God." Cited in "All Human Beings Are Created in the Image of God," The Church of Jesus Christ of Latter-Day Saints, https://www.lds.org/ensign/2008/07/all-human-beings-are-created-in-the-image-of-god?lang=eng. On God's corporality, see *Doctrine and Covenants*, 130.22, The Church of Jesus Christ of Latter-Day Saints, https://www.lds.org/scriptures/dc-testament/dc/130.22.
6. Hermann Gunkel, Gerhard von Rad, and P. Humbert, cited in Clines, "The Image of God in Man," 56.
7. Ex. 20:4–6; Deut. 4:12, 15; 1 Kings 8:27; Ps. 139:7–10; Isa. 31:3; 40:18–26; John 4:24.

that whereas animals look down at the ground, man has a majestic face that looks up at the skies.[8] Christian theologians such as Augustine, Bede (c. 672–735), Peter Lombard, Thomas Aquinas (1225–1274), John Calvin, and Francis Turretin accepted the idea that the human body indirectly expresses the image of God in this and other ways.[9] However, as Aquinas said, the image most properly belongs to the soul of man, not his body.[10]

A Mental Image

More commonly among Christian theologians, the constitutional view of God's image focuses on mental powers and qualities. In this view, man bears God's image because of his self-awareness, ability to reason, free agency of will, conscience, and capacity for moral action. For example, Gregory of Nyssa said that the divine image especially appears in the rational intellect and free decision of man's will, "the power of understanding and deliberating."[11]

The mental view has been charged with being overly speculative, for Genesis does not explain the image in terms of will or intellect.[12] However, Genesis 1 does reveal the wisdom, will, and goodness of the Creator. God's image, therefore, must reflect that wisdom and goodness, and must include the capacity to reason and choose. The mental definition of the image of God also fits well with the sharp distinction that Genesis 1 makes between man and the animals (Gen. 1:26–28; 9:1–6). It properly identifies the primary seat of that difference in man's mind or soul, for the human body has the same life as that of animals (2:7).

There is no denying, however, that theologians of the early and medieval church developed this idea in speculative directions. Pelagius (fl. 380–420) identified the image with man's freedom of the will, writing, "Because man was created in God's image, he is free."[13] Consequently, man possesses

8. Ovid, *Metamorphoses*, trans. Frank Justus Miller, Loeb Classical Library (Cambridge, MA: Harvard University Press, 1921), 1.84–86 (1:8–9).

9. Bede, *Libri quatuor in principium Genesis*, 1.26, cited in Lombard, *The Sentences*, 2.16.4.2 (2:71); Augustine, cited in Thomas Aquinas, *Summa Theologica*, trans. Fathers of the English Dominican Province, 22 vols. (London: R. & T. Washbourne, 1914), Pt. 1, Q. 93, Art. 6, Reply Obj. 3; Calvin, *Institutes*, 1.15.3; and Turretin, *Institutes*, 5.10.5 (1:465).

10. Aquinas, *Summa Theologica*, Pt. 1, Q. 93, Art. 3 and 6.

11. Gregory of Nyssa, *On the Making of Man*, 16.9, 11, 17, in *NPNF²*, 5:405–6.

12. Mathews, *Genesis 1–11:26*, 168.

13. Pelagius, *Expositiones* 188, cited in Martien E. Brinkman, *The Tragedy of Human Freedom: The Failure and Promise of the Christian Concept of Freedom in Western Culture*, trans. Harry Flecken and Henry Jansen (Amsterdam: Rodopi, 2003), 117.

inalienable and indestructible freedom despite the sin of Adam. This is not a deduction warranted by Scripture.[14]

Alternatively, the image was often centered more upon the intellect. Aquinas quoted Augustine as saying, "Man's excellence consists in the fact that God made him to His own image by giving him an intellectual soul, which raises him above the beasts of the field."[15] We note, however, that Aquinas did not exclude the will from the image, but conceptualized the image as the human mind, knowledge, and love.[16] In this he followed Augustine's Trinitarian model of the divine image in man's soul, also expressed as memory, understanding, and will.[17] This, too, involved philosophical speculation beyond the bounds of Scripture.

A reason-centered concept of God's image runs the risk of replacing a biblical view of man with Greek and Roman philosophical ideas. Aristotle taught that man is distinguished from animals by his use of reason.[18] Roman Stoic philosopher Seneca (c. 4 BC–AD 65) said that divinity dwells in man, for "man is a reasoning animal" (*rationale enim animal est homo*).[19] However, the biblical concept of man does not divinize man or reduce God to an immanent principle of rationality, but places man under the personal Lord as his created image. Our understanding of the divine image must be thoroughly centered upon the true God and a right response to him. As Calvin said, our knowledge of man and knowledge of God cannot be separated, and true knowledge of God necessarily involves fear and love toward him.[20]

A Mental Image versus a Moral Likeness

Early in church history, proponents of the mental-image view began to distinguish "image" from "likeness," and identified the mental capacities with "image" and the moral virtues with "likeness." Kenneth Mathews notes, "This may well have been influenced by the erroneous addition in the LXX [Septuagint] where 'and' (*kai*) was written between 'image' and

---

14. On man's freedom of choice and enslavement to sin, see chaps. 20–22.
15. Augustine, *Gen. ad lit.*, 6.12, cited in Aquinas, *Summa Theologica*, Pt. 1, Q. 93, Art. 2.
16. Aquinas, *Summa Theologica*, Pt. 1, Q. 93, Art. 6.
17. Augustine, *On the Trinity*, 9:11–12; 10:11–12, in NPNF[1], 3:132–33, 142–43.
18. Aristotle, *Ethics*, trans. J. A. K. Thomson, rev. Hugh Tredennick (London: Penguin, 1976), 1.7, 13 (75, 88–90).
19. Seneca, *Moral Epistles*, 41.2, 8, in Seneca, *Ad Lucilium Epistulae Morales*, trans. Richard M. Gummere, Loeb Classical Library (Cambridge, MA: Harvard University Press, 1917), 1:272–73, 276–77.
20. Calvin, *Institutes*, 1.1.1–2; 2.1.1.

'likeness.'"[21] This addition obscures the parallelism within the Hebrew phrase "in our image, after our likeness" (Gen. 1:26). Consequently, Irenaeus said that an unspiritual man possesses God's image but lacks his likeness, which must be restored by the Holy Spirit.[22] We find this distinction in Origen and Gregory of Nyssa,[23] John of Damascus (c. 675–749),[24] Lombard,[25] and Aquinas.[26] It was also affirmed by the Roman Catholic Counter-Reformation scholar Robert Bellarmine (1542–1621).[27] However, modern Roman Catholic theology has abandoned the distinction.[28] A recent Roman Catholic Bible says that "image" and "likeness" are "virtually synonyms."[29]

The distinction between "image" and "likeness" is artificial and misleading. Hoekema wrote, "We appreciate the fact that Irenaeus makes a distinction between an aspect of the image of God that we retained after the Fall and an aspect that was lost through the Fall and is regained through Christ. . . . Irenaeus was wrong, however, in associating these two aspects of *image* and *likeness*. . . . These two words are used virtually interchangeably."[30]

One theological consequence of separating "image" and "likeness" was that theologians came to view holiness as a supernatural gift added to human nature (*donum superadditum*) instead of a vital part of human nature as originally created. Man's destiny was to become superhuman through a process of deification—an idea possibly influenced by a Neo-Platonic idea of man's ascent to mystical union with God.[31] If likeness to God is deified, then the "image" of God is reduced to a constitutional

21. Mathews, *Genesis 1–11:26*, 164.
22. Irenaeus, *Against Heresies*, 5.6.1, 5.8.1, in ANF, 1:532–33.
23. Origen, *On First Principles*, 3.6.1; and Gregory of Nyssa, *On the Origin of Man*; both cited in *ACCS/OT*, 1:29, 33.
24. John of Damascus, *An Exact Exposition of the Orthodox Faith*, 2.12, in NPNF², 9.2:31.
25. Lombard, *The Sentences*, 2.16.3.5 (2:70).
26. Aquinas, *Summa Theologica*, Pt. 1, Q. 93, Art. 9.
27. Robert Bellarmine said, "*Adamum peccando non imaginem Dei sed similitudinem perdidisse.*" Bellarmine, *De Gratia Generi Humano in Primo Parente Collata*, 1.2, in *Disputationum Roberti Bellarmini . . . De Controversiis Christianae Fidei, Tomus Quartus* (Milan: Edente Natale Battezzanti, 1862), 4:19; cf. Hodge, *Systematic Theology*, 2:96.
28. A recent statement from the Vatican suggests that this is a point at which "patristic and medieval theology diverged . . . from biblical anthropology." International Theological Commission, *Communion and Stewardship: Human Persons Created in the Image of God*, sec. 15, http://www.vatican.va/roman_curia/congregations/cfaith/cti_documents/rc_con_cfaith_doc_20040723_communion-stewardship_en.html.
29. New American Bible, Revised Edition (2011), Gen. 1:26, United States Conference of Catholic Bishops, http://www.usccb.org/bible/gn/1:26#01001026-1.
30. Hoekema, *Created in God's Image*, 35.
31. Bavinck, *Reformed Dogmatics*, 2:187–91, 539. Bavinck attributed the entrance of this thinking into Christianity in large degree to the writings of Pseudo-Dionysius (fl. c. 500).

similarity to God without a holy relationship to him. Only the "likeness" is able to lift man up to communion with the divine, but this is not native to his humanity.[32] Man's fall robbed him of this superadded gift, but human nature, especially the rational power of the mind, was not severely damaged by the fall. This error gave support to semi-Pelagianism, with its optimistic view of man's intellect and will.

A Moral Image

The Reformers abandoned the Patristic and scholastic distinction between "image" and "likeness" in favor of a more biblical approach that sees righteousness as the heart of God's image.[33] Adam's fall did not merely strip away the supernatural likeness while leaving the natural or essential image intact, so that he could still think and will as he had been created to do. Rather, the fall brought a death that damaged and distorted man's whole being.[34] Since man's whole person was created for God's glory, falling away from God shook man's nature to its depths with "a radical reversal" and "powerful revolution," as Geerhardus Vos said. He wrote, "Man could not remain neutral," for his nature is fundamentally moral and God-related; therefore, "he must either stand for God in original righteousness or against Him in natural unrighteousness."[35]

A recognition of the moral quality of God's image arises in part from Paul's descriptions of that "image" in terms of "knowledge" (Col. 3:10) and "righteousness and holiness of truth" (Eph. 4:24 KJV mg.). The Westminster Shorter Catechism (Q. 10) summarizes Paul's insight into the image of God when it says, "God created man male and female, after his own image, in knowledge, righteousness, and holiness, with dominion over the creatures."[36] Paul's words make it clear that the image of God has moral excellence as a central feature. Reformation theologians restored that feature to the doctrine of God's image after many centuries of confusion during which moral conformity was isolated from the image.

However, Martin Luther argued that God's image and likeness consisted of Adam's original righteousness and glorious reign over the world,

---

32. Vos, *Reformed Dogmatics*, 2:12.
33. Calvin, *Institutes*, 1.15.3.
34. Luther, *Lectures on Genesis*, in *LW*, 1:164–65 (Gen. 3:7). See Bavinck, *Reformed Dogmatics*, 2:548.
35. Vos, *Reformed Dogmatics*, 2:14–15.
36. *Reformed Confessions*, 4:354.

which man lost in his fall.[37] Orthodox Lutheran theologians thus assert that fallen man is destitute of God's image, for original sin destroyed human righteousness and replaced it with corruption.[38]

The Lutheran view of an exclusively moral image rightly rejects the artificial distinction between "image" and "likeness," and recognizes the severity of the spiritual death that has come upon mankind. However, this view encounters serious difficulties with biblical affirmations of the continuation of the image in all men (Gen. 9:6; James 3:9). It also raises questions about how fallen sinners have any possibility of ever relating to God. Lutheranism historically struggled against extreme teachings that arose in its midst, which treated sinners like mere blocks of wood or stone before God.[39] Augustine said, "Although worn out and defaced by losing the participation of God, yet the image of God still remains. For it is His image in this very point, that it is capable of Him, and can be partaker of Him; which so great good is only made possible by its being His image."[40]

Some Reformed theologians have spoken about the image of God with such an emphasis upon man's moral life that it may seem that they followed in the same path as Luther in denying any divine image to fallen man.[41] However, these same theologians also acknowledged "relics of God's image" remaining in fallen man, and affirmed that these remnants reflected the "wider sense" of God's image.[42] As we will see, the mainstream of Reformed orthodoxy followed Calvin in teaching a holistic view that centered upon moral excellence but included more broadly man's whole nature and proper activity.[43]

---

37. Luther, *Lectures on Genesis*, in *LW*, 1:60–65 (Gen. 1:26).

38. Apology of the Augsburg Confession, 2.18–22; Formula of Concord (Solid Declaration, 1.10–11), in *The Book of Concord: The Confessions of the Evangelical Lutheran Church*, ed. Robert Kolb and Timothy J. Wengert, trans. Charles Arand, Eric Gritch, Robert Kolb, William Russell, James Schaaf, Jane Strohl, and Timothy J. Wengert (Minneapolis: Fortress, 2000), 114–15, 533–34.

39. Formula of Concord (Solid Declaration, 2.20, 24, 59), in *The Book of Concord*, 548–49, 555.

40. Augustine, *On the Trinity*, 14.8.11, in *NPNF*[1], 3:189.

41. For example, see Perkins, *An Exposition of the Symbol*, in *Works*, 5:64–65, 71, 90; and Brakel, *The Christian's Reasonable Service*, 1:323–25. Brakel's view that man's rational nature is not the image but the background, or "canvas," on which it was painted was also held by Johannes Cocceius (1603–1669). See Bavinck, *Reformed Dogmatics*, 2:550.

42. Perkins, *An Exposition of the Symbol*, in *Works*, 5:9; *A Golden Chain*, chap. 12, in *Works*, 6:37–40; and Brakel, *The Christian's Reasonable Service*, 1:17–18.

43. Hodge, *Systematic Theology*, 2:98, 102. One apparent exception is Samuel Willard, who wrote, "The image of God on man, was that moral rectitude which was imprinted on his whole nature, making him in his manner and measure fit to resemble, and able to serve God." The image is "not properly man's nature, or the faculties of his rational soul," but consists of the goodness and righteousness which man lost in the fall. Willard, *A Compleat Body of Divinity*, 125, cf. 6, 659, 758–59. Willard regarded dominion as distinct from the image (127).

Functional Perspectives on God's Image

Another approach to understanding God's image does not seek its meaning in what man *is* so much as what man *does*: his divinely assigned function or office in creation. Theologians adhering to a functional perspective on God's image typically focus on a specific human function that they derive from a biblical motif, such as kingship, relationship, or righteousness.

A Royal Image

One view with ancient roots identifies the image with man's office as king and his activity in ruling the world. John Chrysostom said that "the meaning of 'in our image'" is to be discovered not in "the order of being but a similarity of command," citing Genesis 1:26: "And let them have dominion over the fish of the sea, and over the fowl of the air, and over the cattle, and over all the earth, and over every creeping thing that creepeth upon the earth."[44] Another Scripture passage quoted in support of this idea is Psalm 8, where a reference to man's being made "a little lower" than heavenly beings (v. 5) leads to a celebration of human dominion over the creatures (vv. 6–8).

Some early Reformed theologians held a similar view to that of Chrysostom. Wolfgang Musculus (1497–1563) explained the image of God in man as "the power and dignity to rule" as "lord over the earth and all things that are in it."[45] However, Musculus said that this understanding of the divine image "excludeth not the rightness of the inner man," for without righteousness man is no better than a beast, "though he be a prince."[46] Peter Martyr Vermigli (1499–1562) said, "The image of God consists of this, that he should be ruler over all creatures." He regarded the soul and its faculties as "the cause of the image." As to the moral qualities of justice and wisdom, they are necessary to represent God rightly.[47]

---

44. John Chrysostom, *Homilies on Genesis, 1–17*, trans. Robert C. Hill, The Fathers of the Church 74 (Washington, DC: The Catholic University of America Press, 1986), 9.6 (120). He also followed the common Patristic interpretation that "likeness" referred to virtue (9.7 [120]).

45. Wolfgang Musculus, *In Mosis Genesim* (1554), 41–42, cited in *ACCS/OT*, 1:47.

46. Wolfgang Musculus, *Common Places of Christian Religion* (London: n.p., 1563), fol. 12r.

47. Peter Martyr Vermigli, *In Primum Librum Mosis . . . Genesis* (1569), 7r–v, in *The Peter Martyr Library, Volume 4, Philosophical Works*, trans. and ed. Joseph C. McLelland, Sixteenth Century Essays & Studies (Kirksville, MO: Thomas Jefferson University Press and Sixteenth Century Journal Publishers, 1996), 42–43.

Socinians and some Arminians located the divine image exclusively in man's dominion over the earth.[48] Remonstrant theologian Philipp van Limborch (1633–1712) denied that the image consisted of man's original righteousness, but identified it with man's rule over the creatures according to his rational nature and skillful body.[49] Vos explained that Socinian and Arminian theologians could not follow medieval supernaturalism or the holistic Reformed view of the image with its implications for total depravity, thus leaving them to seek a "religiously neutral sense" of the image in dominion.[50] We note, however, that Jacob Arminius (1560–1609) had a holistic view of the image as pertaining in different ways to body and soul, the mental faculties, moral excellence, and dominion over the creatures.[51]

The royal-image interpretation has received support from some modern scholars.[52] David Clines argues for it based on the parallel idea of the image of gods in other ancient literature. He rejects the Patristic view that the image resides in the soul and its faculties because he does not believe the Bible teaches that man was composed of two parts, body and soul.[53] Clines concludes,

> Man is created not *in* God's image, since God has no image of His own, but *as* God's image, or rather *to be* God's image, that is to deputize in the created world for the transcendent God who remains outside the world order. . . . The whole man is the image of God, without distinction of spirit and body. . . . The image is to be understood not so much ontologically as existentially: it comes to expression not in the nature of man so much as in his activity and function. This function is to represent God's lordship to the lower orders of creation.[54]

There is genuine insight in the functional interpretation, for Genesis 1:26–28 intertwines the divine image and dominion. However, Genesis 1:26–28 does not explicitly identify the image as dominion, but dominion

---

48. Turretin, *Institutes*, 5.10.9 (1:467).

49. Philipp van Limborch, *Compleat System, or Body of Divinity, Both Speculative and Practical, Founded on Scripture and Reason*, trans. William Jones (London: for John Taylor and Andrew Bell, 1702), 1:142–45.

50. Vos, *Reformed Dogmatics*, 2:15.

51. Jacob Arminius, *Private Disputations*, 26.7, in *The Works of James Arminius*, trans. James Nichols (vols. 1–2) and W. R. Bagnall (vol. 3), 3 vols. (Auburn: Derby and Miller, 1853), 2:64.

52. Millard Erickson notes Leonard Verduin, Norman Snaith, and Sigmund Mowinckel as proponents of the functional view. Erickson, *Christian Theology*, 466.

53. Clines, "The Image of God in Man," 57, 83–86. We will discuss the constitution of man as body and spirit/soul in chaps. 12–13.

54. Clines, "The Image of God in Man," 101.

was granted in a distinct word from God after he had made man in his image. This suggests that the image of God, or at least some aspects of it, is not merely dominion, but the ground and capacity for dominion. As to Psalm 8, it does not explicitly speak of the image of God.[55]

An exclusively royal interpretation is reductionistic. While Genesis 1 certainly reveals God's power and authority, it also reveals his wisdom, goodness, and relationships. These factors, too, must have some expression in our interpretation of "Let us make man in our image." Furthermore, if the image is entirely functional, then what meaning can it have if mankind, or a particular human being, fails to perform that function? In other words, is man still God's image if he fails to act like it? This question has serious implications for human dignity, especially for people without the fitness to rule.

A Relational Image

A more recent approach to interpreting the image of God focuses on man's personal relationships. Based on the divine "us" in Genesis 1:26 and "male and female" in verse 27, it defines the image of God not as something man is or does, but in man's relationships to God and to his fellow men. For example, we read in a twenty-first-century Roman Catholic document published by the Vatican that the image "is essentially dialogical or relational," a "dynamic orientation to the divine," that is "disrupted" but "cannot be destroyed by sin."[56]

A distinctive form of the relational perspective arose in Protestant neoorthodoxy, where the conception of the image is man's relationship to God through Christ. Karl Barth (1886–1968) said that we cannot define man by what distinguishes him from the animals, but we must "view him in the history which has its basis in God's attitude to him."[57] For Barth, our understanding of man must come from our study of Christ, which reveals real humanity to consist of our relationship to God as our Creator and Lord and our experience of deliverance by God.[58] Erickson summarizes Barth's view: "The image of God is not to be understood in terms of any structural qualities within humans; it is not something a human is or

---

55. Berkouwer, *Man: The Image of God*, 70–71; and Erickson, *Christian Theology*, 468–69.
56. International Theological Commission, "Communion and Stewardship," secs. 45–46, 48.
57. Karl Barth, *Church Dogmatics*, ed. G. W. Bromiley and T. F. Torrance, 4 vols. in 14 (Edinburgh: T&T Clark, 1960), III/2, sec. 44.2 (78).
58. Barth, *Church Dogmatics*, III/2, sec. 44.2 (73–74).

possesses. Rather, the image is a matter of one's relationship with God; it is something a human experiences. Thus, it is dynamic rather than static."[59]

Emil Brunner said, "We would do well to understand 'image' in the sense of reflection," a reflection of God's glory "as a mirror" (cf. 2 Cor. 3:18). Brunner wrote, "Man's meaning and his intrinsic worth do not reside in himself, but in the One who stands 'over against' him, in Christ, the Primal Image, in the Word of God."[60] Brunner explained that man's creation in the image of God means that God made us as rational beings in a love relationship with him, thereby summoning us to respond to God's "Thou art mine" with an answering, "Yes, I am Thine."[61] Man's sin has not destroyed God's image, for man must always be a person in relation to God, but sin has perverted that love relationship into enmity and hatred.[62] In this manner, Brunner apparently retained some sense of an inherent image located in rational personality, but stressed the relational aspect of the image.[63] As Hoekema observed, Barth's view of the image was "purely relational," whereas Brunner retained "the twofold aspect of the image."[64]

Relational perspectives contain a measure of truth. They remind us that we cannot define the image merely in terms of man's mental superiority to the animals; the image of God must be understood in terms of relationship with God. Relational views tap into the biblical stream of thought that flows from the divine image to divine sonship (Gen. 5:1–3). God's image does indeed seem intertwined with man's special relationship to him as one created for face-to-face intimacy and communion with God (2:7, 18–22).

However, relational perspectives also have problems, beginning with their underlying assumptions. Neoorthodoxy's shift away from man's constitutional superiority over the animals may have arisen because of the influence of Darwinian evolutionary thought.[65] Evolution levels the ground between man, beast, and bacteria. Another factor in the shift to relational explanations is modern theology's preference for existentialist categories over ontological and metaphysical ones.[66] Modern theology is

---

59. Erickson, *Christian Theology*, 464–65.
60. Brunner, *Man in Revolt*, 96.
61. Brunner, *Man in Revolt*, 98, 103.
62. Brunner, *Man in Revolt*, 105, 136.
63. See Erickson, *Christian Theology*, 463.
64. Hoekema, *Created in God's Image*, 52, 57.
65. Barth discussed evolution in the immediate context of his treatment of the image. *Church Dogmatics*, III/2, sec. 44.2 (82–83).
66. Erickson, *Christian Theology*, 468.

uncomfortable with analyzing spiritual realities in terms of *what* they are, and focuses instead on *how* we experience them. On the contrary, God's Word reveals spiritual realities, and we can know truths about our souls.

Another problem for relational views is the question of how the relational image remains after man's apostasy from God. To fit a strictly relational view with the doctrine of man's fall requires either the destruction of the image or a denial of the doctrine of total corruption and inability. Barth avoided the problem by denying a historical fall of man in Adam.[67] Barth interpreted Adam as everyman: "We are what Adam was. . . . Adam is what we and all men are."[68] This is a serious departure from the Word of God.[69]

We cannot reduce the image to relationship with God, as Barth did, without neglecting significant strands of the Bible's teaching on this matter. The divine image pertains not only to man's standing before God but also to man's dominion over the creatures (Gen. 1:26). Furthermore, our concept of the image must account for man's continued image bearing after the fall ruptured his relationship with God (9:6). If the image of God consists of nothing more than a reflection in a mirror, as Brunner suggested, then when the mirror turns away, the image disappears. It must, therefore, be more than relationship.

A Righteous-Dynamic Image

Dutch Reformed minister Klaas Schilder (1890–1952) denied the traditional Reformed distinction between the broad and narrow image, and argued that human nature is "the precondition for the image, but not the image itself," according to G. C. Berkouwer. The image consisted "only in dynamic discharge of his calling."[70] Unlike the royal-image view, Schilder's view did not locate that calling primarily in dominion but in righteous living. Therefore, we call it the righteous-dynamic image. This perspective is similar to that of Luther, and like him, Schilder said that the image "vanishes when man rebels against God."[71]

---

67. Karl Barth, *The Epistle to the Romans*, trans. Edwyn C. Hoskyns (London: Oxford University Press, 1933), 181. See Hoekema, *Created in God's Image*, 50–51.
68. Karl Barth, *Christ and Adam: Man and Humanity in Romans 5*, trans. T. A. Smail (Eugene, OR: Wipf and Stock, 2004), 78–79.
69. See chap. 7 on the historicity of Adam.
70. Berkouwer, *Man: The Image of God*, 54.
71. Berkouwer, *Man: The Image of God*, 56. Berkouwer (58) notes that this view was also held by German theologians Edmund Schlink (1903–1984) and Friedrich Karl Schumann (1886–1960).

Berkouwer argued along similar lines to Schilder. He attempted to reconcile this teaching with Genesis 9:6 and James 3:9 by saying that these texts refer to man's humanness and "the original aim of his creation," but not his present state.[72]

Berkouwer presented the following arguments for the righteous-dynamic view.

First, he said, "Scripture is concerned with man in his relation to God, in which he can never be seen as man-in-himself, and surely not with man's 'essence' described as self or person."[73] Any view that connects the image with man's constitution is speculative.

Second, any attempt to unify the constitutional and functional aspects of the image fails, for it "remains stubbornly dualistic, because the image understood in the wider sense has a very different content than the image understood in the narrower sense."[74]

Third, attempts to find God's image in man's constitution inevitably focus upon some part of man, such his reasoning or will, but "Scripture always speaks simply of *man* as created in the image of God, and gives no warrant for considering only a part of man as partaking of the image."[75]

Fourth, speaking of God's image in fallen man easily leads to a mistaken belief in "some remnants of goodness which survive in fallen man," which then opens the way "for the entrance of all sorts of Pelagian and humanistic views."[76]

Fifth, he argued that the real meaning of God's image appears in Paul's description of its renewal (Eph. 4:24; Col. 3:10). That renewal consists of "a new relationship with God" and a "new direction" to life. Therefore, the image is not an analogy between God's nature and human nature but a life of human love responding to divine love.[77]

In response, we acknowledge that Berkouwer's arguments expose some true problems with the Patristic and medieval view of the divine image. By setting mental image against moral life, this view did in many cases become dualistic, unduly focusing upon human intellect or volition, and semi-Pelagian. However, Berkouwer's attack upon the traditional Reformed view is not well founded, as the following responses show.

---

72. Berkouwer, *Man: The Image of God*, 59.
73. Berkouwer, *Man: The Image of God*, 59–60.
74. Berkouwer, *Man: The Image of God*, 61.
75. Berkouwer, *Man: The Image of God*, 63.
76. Berkouwer, *Man: The Image of God*, 64.
77. Berkouwer, *Man: The Image of God*, 99–100.

First, it is a false dichotomy to say that the Bible is concerned with man's relationship with God and not human nature. In fact, the Holy Scriptures speak much about both. When Genesis 1:27 tells us that "God created man in his own image," it invites us to consider God as revealed in that chapter and to see man as a created analogy to him. The first creation account makes known God's power, authority, wisdom, and goodness. Such attributes imply personality, rationality, and moral agency. Therefore, it is not speculation but sound interpretation to understand Genesis as indicating that man is somewhat like God in bearing power, authority, wisdom, and goodness.

Second, the mainstream Reformed view does not set up a dualism between humanness and supernatural gifts of holiness (as Roman Catholicism does), but instead says that the loss of original righteousness implies the distortion and depravity of the entire person. Conversely, holiness is not deification but creaturely likeness to God and fellowship with him. This view of man integrates form and function, being and activity.

Third, we agree with Berkouwer that some perspectives on the image of God are reductionistic and fail to account for the whole man. Ironically, Berkouwer fell into this very trap when he rejected all constitutional dimensions of the image and focused entirely upon man's function of serving God. If the image refers to man himself, then it must include what man is.

Fourth, semi-Pelagianism arises from the doctrine of a multidimensional image only if we fail to recognize how sin has corrupted every aspect of human existence. We can fully affirm that man retains remnants of the image in his fallen nature while denying that any spiritual life or goodness remains in him (Rom. 3:10–12; Eph. 2:1). The remnants consist of the broken and corrupted aspects of our fallen humanity left after righteousness departs, such as our darkened minds (Rom. 1:21–22; Eph. 4:17–18), depraved wills (Rom. 8:7; Eph. 2:3), and diminished reign (Gen. 9:1–6).

Fifth, we agree with Berkouwer that at the heart of God's image is God's gift of holiness in the heart. However, Berkouwer's view fails to properly account for other biblical teaching that the image remains in man (Gen. 9:6; James 3:9) even after that holiness has been corrupted (Gen. 6:5). These Scripture passages do not refer their exhortations to our humanness per se but explicitly to our image bearing. It will not do for us to embrace some biblical statements about the image but reject others because we cannot fit them into our perspective. Rather, we must hold them all together, which implies that in some respects wicked, fallen men are still like God. Therefore, we must honor them and regard their lives as sacred.

In the end, we agree with Hoekema's assessment that while Berkouwer draws upon legitimate biblical themes, "the image of God consists of more than mere functioning; it concerns not only what man does but also what he is," for in Genesis the "image" of God is not a verb but a noun, a noun that "refers to the uniqueness of man's existence, and . . . is inseparable from man's being man."[78]

So far, we have examined approaches to the image of God that emphasize, sometimes exclusively, some aspect of what the Bible associates with that image in Genesis. We have found each of these approaches to touch upon an important biblical theme, but none of them to adequately address the whole body of biblical truth on this question. What remains is to present a holistic approach. This will be the subject of our next chapter, together with practical implications of the image.

Sing to the Lord

God's Kindness in Creating Mankind

Lord, our Lord, Thy glorious Name
All Thy wondrous works proclaim;
In the heav'ns with radiant signs
Evermore Thy glory shines.

Infant lips Thou dost ordain
Wrath and vengeance to restrain,
Weakest means fulfill Thy will,
Mighty enemies to still.

Moon and stars in shining height
Nightly tell their Maker's might;
When Thy wondrous heav'ns I scan,
Then I know how weak is man.

What is man that he should be
Loved and visited by Thee,
Raised to an exalted height,
Crowned with honor in Thy sight?

---

78. Hoekema, *Created in God's Image*, 64–65.

With dominion crowned he stands
O'er the creatures of Thy hands;
All to him subjection yields
In the sea and air and field.

Lord, our Lord, Thy glorious Name
All Thy wondrous works proclaim,
Thine the Name of matchless worth,
Excellent in all the earth.

Psalm 8
Tune: Thanksgiving
The Psalter, No. 15
Trinity Hymnal—Baptist Edition, No. 107

Questions for Meditation or Discussion

1. What mistaken ideas have some people taught concerning God's image and the human body?
2. Where do most Christian theologians locate the main aspects of God's image in man?
3. How did some Christian theologians in the early and medieval church distinguish between "image" and "likeness"? How did the Reformers respond to this distinction?
4. How did Lutheran and some Reformed theologians limit God's image to a specific aspect of man? What did that imply about the continuing image of God in man?
5. What do the authors mean by "constitutional" versus "functional" views of God's image?
6. What is the "royal-image" view? What are the strengths of this view? Its weaknesses?
7. What is the "relational-image" view? What biblical truths does it reflect? What problems does it cause?
8. What view of God's image did G. C. Berkouwer advocate? How did he argue for this view?
9. How do the authors answer Berkouwer's arguments?
10. How would you describe the concept of God's image that prevails in your own church? In what ways, if any, does your church tend to reduce God's image to one aspect of man? What consequences does this produce in how people think and live?

Questions for Deeper Reflection

11. Do the terms translated as "image" and "likeness" in Genesis 1:26–28 refer to two distinct realities, or do the two terms refer to essentially the same truth? Build an argument for your answer.

12. The authors say that one factor driving the shift from constitutional to relational views of God's image is "modern theology's preference for existentialist categories over ontological and metaphysical ones." What does this mean? Do you agree? Why or why not?

10

The Image of God, Part 3

Systematic and Practical Theology

A systematic and practical understanding of God's image in man is essential for a God-centered worldview. Since the fall, mankind has striven to find purpose and meaning apart from God. However, nothing cuts off man's ambition for autonomy more effectively than the doctrine of God's image. Man's purpose is not to be curved in on himself, but to be anchored outside of himself in God. We cannot understand man as man without reference to God. Our quest for meaning and purpose cannot start below and build upward. John Laidlaw said that the Bible "presupposes God, to account for man."[1] Without this divine presupposition, any view of human meaning has no substance, and human beings have no basis for hope. That is simply because man's chief end is to glorify God and to enjoy him forever.

Therefore, this chapter will commend the systematic view of God's image that we find in the mainstream of the Reformed tradition. This is the view that the image consists centrally of inward righteousness and a right relationship to God, but more broadly encompasses man's whole nature along with his divinely ordained function. We will close the chapter with some practical implications of the doctrine.

---

1. Laidlaw, *The Bible Doctrine of Man*, 161.

Summary of Exegetical and Biblical Theology

Before proceeding to systematic theology, we must briefly review the conclusions of our earlier biblical study.[2] The image of God is not something God imparted to man; rather, it is man's identity, and as such, it is a way of describing human nature and activity. The word *image* is linked by its own meaning and by biblical theology to revelation, worship, and reign. God made man to be a limited, temporal revelation of his infinite, eternal attributes, particularly the attributes of God's power, wisdom, and goodness, which the creation account highlights (Genesis 1). Whereas false gods have dead images in idols, the true God created human brings to be living images of himself for his worship (v. 26). The text also links God's image to man's reign over the earth as God's servant-kings (vv. 26, 28). Therefore, God's image is closely related to the covenantal offices of prophet, priest, and king. We will discuss these in more depth under the covenant with Adam.[3]

God's image placed the first man in a relationship to God akin to that between a son and his father (Gen. 5:1–3; Luke 3:38). It also appears to function more broadly in all human relationships, for immediately after the pronouncement of man's creation in God's image, we read, "male and female created he them" (Gen. 1:27). This marriage relationship lays the foundation for the life of the family and the multiplication of God's images in society on earth (v. 28).

Despite the horrendous corruption of man's inner life and outward behavior by the fall (Gen. 6:5), God's image continues to make human life sacred and far more valuable than that of any animal (9:5–6; James 3:9). We see signs of the image's remnants in human agriculture, marriage, child rearing, city building, the arts, and industry (Gen. 4:17–22). The continuing image also provides an important ground for submission to proper human authority (1 Cor. 11:7).

God's image is supremely found in Jesus Christ, God's Son and the last Adam (1 Cor. 15:45; 2 Cor. 4:4). Christ, however, far exceeds Adam and all mankind in glory, for he is God's eternal and coequal Image and the Creator of all things (Col. 1:15–17). By the spiritual union of sinners to Christ, God renews his image from glory to glory (2 Cor. 3:18). This renewed image appears now in the moral transformation of the wicked into people of knowl-

---

2. See chap. 8.
3. See chap. 14.

edge, righteousness, holiness, and unified relationships in the body of Christ (Eph. 4:22–24; Col. 3:9–11). It equips God's people to begin functioning as God's prophets, priests, and kings already.[4] The renewal of God's image will find its completion when all God's elect are fully "conformed to the image of his Son" (Rom. 8:29) and "bear the image of the heavenly" man after their resurrection and glorification with him (1 Cor. 15:49).

A Holistic Reformed Theology of God's Image

How are we to integrate these biblical teachings into a faithful doctrine of God's image? We have already argued that identifying the image specifically with man's mental abilities, moral qualities, dominion, or relationships does not adequately account for what the Scriptures say.[5] We believe that the best approach is the holistic one reflected in the Reformed tradition.

Classic Reformed Teachings on the Holistic Image

John Calvin taught that God's image encompasses the whole person. He regarded the image of God as a summary of "the whole excellence by which man's nature towers over all the kinds of living creatures."[6] The core of the image is the illumination of the mind with truth and righteousness of the heart. Paul implies this when he writes that God renewed the image through Christ's regenerating and sanctifying grace (Eph. 4:24; Col. 3:10).[7] The glory of God's image resides in the mind or soul and radiates outward into the body. Calvin wrote, "And although the primary seat of the divine image was in the mind and heart, or in the soul and its powers, yet there was no part of man, not even the body itself, in which some sparks did not glow."[8]

---

4. Some Reformed theologians have seen a correspondence of the threefold office to the three terms *knowledge*, *righteousness*, and *holiness* that Paul uses of the renewed image (Eph. 4:24; Col. 3:10), though they differ on whether righteousness correlates with priest and holiness with king, or vice versa. The terminology does not lend itself to a clear conclusion. In Paul's usage, "righteousness" (*dikaiosunē*) can refer to the imputed status of justification (Rom. 4:3, 5–6), but in the practical context of Ephesians 4, it more likely refers to actual righteousness of life and conduct (cf. Eph. 5:9). As such, it could be applied either to kings (Heb. 7:2) or priests (Ps. 106:30–31 [105:30–31 LXX]). "Holiness" (*hosiotēs*), though not derived from the root word meaning "sanctified" or "set apart for God" (*hagios*), is a term for sacred or pious service to God (Luke 1:75; cf. 1 Tim. 2:8). Its adjectival form (*hosios*) is used of Christ the royal Son of David (Acts 2:27; 13:35, both citing Ps. 16:10) and of Christ the High Priest (Heb. 7:26).

5. See chap. 9.

6. Calvin, *Institutes*, 1.15.3.

7. Calvin, *Institutes*, 1.15.4.

8. Calvin, *Institutes*, 1.15.3.

As we noted earlier, Martin Luther said that the fall obliterated the image of God from man. Calvin sometimes spoke in the same manner, for he saw spiritual knowledge, righteousness, and holiness as central to the image.[9] However, in other places Calvin wrote that, though the lines of God's image in us are so "maimed, that they may truly be said to be destroyed," nevertheless we may still trace them faintly in fallen man.[10] Therefore, "God's image was not totally annihilated and destroyed" in Adam's fall, but what remains in man is deformed, corrupted, confused, and mutilated. God begins its renewal in man's spiritual rebirth, but this renewal is only partial in this life—"it will attain its full splendor in heaven."[11]

Calvin's holistic view of God's image carried over into the mainstream of Reformed orthodoxy. We find the affirmation of God's image in man's whole nature, his moral righteousness, and his dominion over the creatures in the writings of Antonius Thysius (1565–1640), Johannes Wollebius, James Ussher (1581–1656), Matthew Poole (1624–1679), John Howe (1630–1705), Stephen Charnock, and Francis Turretin.[12]

The holistic approach continues in modern Reformed theology. Thus, in the nineteenth century, we find Charles Hodge and A. A. Hodge (1823–1886) defining the image as man's rational nature, moral perfection, and creaturely dominion.[13] In the twentieth century, the same was taught by Louis Berkhof.[14] G. H. Kersten (1882–1948) and Robert Reymond included human nature and righteousness in the image, but viewed dominion as a consequence of God's image, not the image itself.[15] Even this, however, is a variation of the classic Reformed orthodox holistic view, which regarded the image to exist "antecedently in nature (as to the spirituality and immortality of the soul); formally in rectitude or original righteous-

---

9. Calvin, *Commentaries*, on Gen. 3:1–3; 2 Cor. 3:18; Eph. 4:24; cf. Hoekema, *Created in God's Image*, 43.

10. Calvin, *Commentaries*, on Gen. 1:26.

11. Calvin, *Institutes*, 1.15.4.

12. Polyander, Walaeus, Thysius, and Rivetus, *Synopsis Purioris Theologiae*, 13.36–37, 41 (1:329, 331); Wollebius, *Compendium*, 1.5.(2).ii (56); James Ussher, *A Body of Divinity: Being the Sum and Substance of the Christian Religion*, ed. Michael Nevarr (Birmingham, AL: Solid Ground, 2007), 5th head (92–93); Matthew Poole, *Annotations upon the Holy Bible*, 3 vols. (New York: Robert Carter and Brothers, 1853), 1:4; John Howe, *The Works of the Rev. John Howe* (London: Henry G. Bohn, 1846), 74, 133; Charnock, *The Existence and Attributes of God*, in *Works*, 2:205; and Turretin, *Institutes*, 5.10.5–6 (1:465–66).

13. Hodge, *Systematic Theology*, 2:96–99, 102; A. A. Hodge, *Outlines of Theology* (1879; repr., Grand Rapids, MI: Zondervan, 1973), 300.

14. Berkhof, *Systematic Theology*, 204–5, 207.

15. G. H. Kersten, *Reformed Dogmatics: A Systematic Treatment of Reformed Doctrine*, 2 vols. (Grand Rapids, MI: Netherlands Reformed Book and Publishing Committee, 1980), 1:176; and Reymond, *A New Systematic Theology of the Christian Faith*, 428–29.

ness; consequently in the dominion and immortality of the whole man," as Turretin said.[16]

William Ames: A Model of Systematic Reflection on the Image

We see the beautiful balance and comprehensiveness of the Reformed doctrine of God's image in the systematic theology of William Ames. Ames wrote that this image consisted of the body's "beauty and usefulness conforming to God's will"; the soul's "faculties . . . in the understanding and the will," including its gifts of "wisdom, holiness, and righteousness"; and man's "dominion over other creatures so that he might use them freely to the glory of God and for his own necessity."[17] Even man's placement in paradise "as in his palace" contributed to "the perfection of man" by which he imaged God.[18]

Ames went on to say that with the fall came "spiritual death," which began with "the defacement of the image of God."[19] However, God moderates the effects of the fall through "vestiges of God's image" that remain "in the understanding and in the will."[20] Evidently these are the "very nature of man," which cannot be destroyed without unmanning man. The vestiges in the understanding consist of some theoretical knowledge of God (Rom. 1:20). Though defiled, the conscience retains some ability by which man is able to distinguish between just and unjust actions (2:15). "In the will," according to Ames, "the vestiges appear in a certain inclination to dimly known good," which though dead and unable to produce spiritual good, still moves men to approve "shadows of virtue" (cf. 2 Tim. 3:5) and restrains them from "many grosser sins" (cf. 1 Cor. 5:1).[21] The Christian's love for God moves him to love men, too, "for they are in some sort partakers of the image of God."[22]

Turning to Christ, Ames says that he is "the express image of God," the Father's Word and Wisdom.[23] He is the only "perfect" or complete image of God, for even before the fall, man was only an image "in his measure"; that is to say, God did not grant him the ability to be a full image of God.[24]

---

16. Turretin, *Institutes*, 5.10.6 (1:466).
17. Ames, *The Marrow of Theology*, 1.8.71–74 (106).
18. Ames, *The Marrow of Theology*, 1.8.77–78 (106).
19. Ames, *The Marrow of Theology*, 1.12.35 (119).
20. Ames, *The Marrow of Theology*, 1.14.22 (123).
21. Ames, *The Marrow of Theology*, 1.14.23–29 (123–24).
22. Ames, *The Marrow of Theology*, 2.16.8 (301).
23. Ames, *The Marrow of Theology*, 1.5.16 (89).
24. Ames, *The Marrow of Theology*, 1.8.68–69 (105–6).

Our adoption as sons of God takes place through the Son alone, for "he alone is the bond of the union" by which we share in the inheritance and renewed image of God (Rom. 8:17, 29).[25]

In Christ comes the mortification of sin and vivification of righteousness, which "is the restoration of the image or life of God in man (Col. 3:10; Eph. 4:24)."[26] This image includes both inward affections toward God ("theological virtues") and just, ethical behavior ("moral virtues").[27] Ames's view of the image was also dynamic and relational. The supreme end of human life is "living to God"—that is, living "in accord with the will of God, to the glory of God, and with God working in them."[28] At the end of the world, "then the image of God will be perfected in all the sanctified (Eph. 5:27)."[29] Ames's theology reflects the richness and balance of the Bible's teachings about God's image.

The Unity of the Holistic Image

An important question for any holistic perspective on God's image is how various facets of the image cohere as one. As we saw when considering the righteous-dynamic view of God's image, G. C. Berkouwer challenged the Reformed tradition on this very point.[30] It is a legitimate question, although we must proceed with humility because we do not fully understand human nature, and much less the God whose image we bear.

Part of the answer lies in the inseparable relation of activity and nature. This observation brings us back to Genesis 1, a text full of God's activity. God created, nurtured, spoke, saw, formed, divided, named, deliberated, and blessed his creation. God's works reveal his divine nature (Pss. 19:1; 104:24; Rom. 1:20). His mighty acts distinguish him from "them which by nature are no gods" (Gal. 4:8) and manifest that he is the Lord of righteousness, justice, faithful love, delight, power, and wisdom (Jer. 9:24; 10:10–12). These qualities are not just God's activities but his personal attributes.

Therefore, when we read in Genesis 1 that God made man in his image, we anticipate that man reflects God both in nature and activity. For created beings, activity requires certain capacities. Anthony Hoekema ob-

---

25. Ames, *The Marrow of Theology*, 1.28.11 (165).
26. Ames, *The Marrow of Theology*, 1.29.24 (170).
27. Ames, *The Marrow of Theology*, 2.2.17 (226).
28. Ames, *The Marrow of Theology*, 1.1.5–6 (77).
29. Ames, *The Marrow of Theology*, 1.41.5 (214).
30. See chap. 9.

served, "One cannot function without a certain structure." He offered as an example an eagle's ability to fly, which depends upon its possession of wings. He concluded, "Similarly, human beings were created to function in certain ways: to worship God, to love the neighbor, to rule over nature, and so on. But they cannot function in these ways unless they have been endowed by God with the structural capacities that enable them to do so. So structure and function are both involved when we think of man as the image of God."[31] Part of that structure must include rational personality. Likewise, natural capacities without proper functioning are diseased at best, and a total lack of function is a clear sign of death. Rational personality stripped of wisdom and goodness may continue to act, but its motions are the motions of spiritual death, not life. Therefore, constitution and function belong together.

If we consider the image from the perspective of royal dominion, then the unity and necessity of constitution and function are apparent. Thysius wrote, "Indeed, for someone to exercise dominion, he must be endowed with the gift of a soul that reasons; but to do so fairly and peaceably, he must certainly be wise, holy, and just. And if he would also put his dominion into practice, he must have a body well-prepared for actions that accord with a soul that is sound. And finally, for the dominion to be perpetual, the man must be immortal."[32]

Another way to see the unity of God's image is to compare the idea of an image to a divine temple where God's glory dwells visibly. If, as Genesis suggests,[33] the image of God is like a temple, then we can imagine it like a structure where God's holy glory dwells in the innermost part and radiates outward as the priests perform their sacred service (Exodus 40; Leviticus 9).[34] Even if the priesthood falls into idolatry, the glory departs, and judgment shatters God's sanctuary, the ruins of the temple remain and await their reconstruction, cleansing, reconsecration, and refilling with glory. Though no longer functioning, it remains "thy holy temple" (Ps. 79:1). Similarly, all the parts of man's being and function were woven together to represent God's presence on earth, and even after the fall ruined us, we remain God's image.

---

31. Hoekema, *Created in God's Image*, 69.
32. Polyander, Walaeus, Thysius, and Rivetus, *Synopsis Purioris Theologiae*, 13.41 (1:331).
33. See chap. 8.
34. On the picture of the image as light radiating from within, see Turretin, *Institutes*, 5.10.6 (1:466).

We conclude then that the holistic view of God's image is the best theological formulation of this biblical teaching. Herman Bavinck looked back over the Holy Scriptures and the Reformed confessional tradition, and said, "A human being does not bear or have the image of God but . . . he or she is the image of God." He added, "This image extends to the whole person . . . in soul and body, in all his faculties and powers, in all conditions and relations."[35] In light of the presence of God's image in every facet of human existence, we must seek to glorify God in all that we do (1 Cor. 10:31). Geerhardus Vos said, "There is no sphere of life that lies outside his relationship to God and in which religion would not be the ruling principle."[36]

Practical Implications of Man as God's Image

Life is not absurd and meaningless. People are not disposable things to be used and then discarded when no longer useful. Neither is humanity another link in the chain of evolutionary progress, destined to be replaced by a more advanced creature. God created man in his image. The human race, therefore, is the pinnacle of God's earthly creation. Man has purpose, and that purpose is inseparably intertwined with the God who created him.

It would take many volumes to unpack the implications of God's image in man, but we cannot leave this theological study without briefly considering some of them.

1. *Sanctity*. Over all human life, from the womb to senile old age, flies this glorious banner: "Whoso sheddeth man's blood, by man shall his blood be shed: for in the image of God made he man" (Gen. 9:6). Man is sacred, and to take away his life without just cause is to assault the glory of God. People are not animals. Christ taught his disciples that their heavenly Father cares for the plants and animals, but regards people as far more valuable (Matt. 6:26; 10:29–31; 12:12). We must do likewise, and cherish human life. We must strive to bring to repentance and forgiveness of sins those involved in murder, abortion, unjust war, violent oppression, euthanasia, and all other crimes that wrongfully take human lives.

2. *Spirituality*. God is a spirit (John 4:24). Man, created in his image, reflects that spirituality as a being made to worship and seek transcendent

---

35. Bavinck, *Reformed Dogmatics*, 2:554–55. He included (1) the human soul; (2) the faculties of the soul; (3) knowledge, righteousness, and holiness; (4) the human body; and (5) human happiness (555–61).
36. Vos, *Reformed Dogmatics*, 2:13.

glory. Man has a spiritual and religious aspect to his life that cannot be reduced to the interactions of mere matter and energy. As divine images, we are either glorifying God or engaged in idolatry. Each human being is inescapably religious, either in worshiping the true God or in rebelling against him in order to worship his creatures (Rom. 1:20–23). In a manner of speaking, we are all priests, whether to the Lord or to a false god.

3. *Rationality*. Man is a thinking, personal being, just like the God of Genesis 1. Created in the image of one who acts with power, wisdom, and goodness, he has mental faculties by which he thinks, reasons, chooses, speaks, and acts in the presence of the Lord. Just as God acted in creation according to an orderly plan for the sake of certain goals, so man acts not by mere instinct but out of motives, using means to attain rational goals. Therefore, we must address human beings, even in their fallen state, in a manner that exposes foolish means and wrong goals, and offers reasons and motives to embrace better ones. We must treat people as thinkers.

4. *Dignity*. Despite human wickedness, the image of God remains in some sense in fallen man. Therefore, we may not treat people with contempt and curses (James 3:17). Instead, Peter commands us, "Honour all men. Love the brotherhood. Fear God. Honour the king" (1 Pet. 2:17). By using the same word "honour" (*timaō*) for our duty to "all men" and "the king," Peter subtly reminds us that all mankind, even the poorest peasant, has the same basic warrant to receive honor. All bear the image of God. Proverbs 14:31 says, "He that oppresseth the poor reproacheth his Maker: but he that honoureth him hath mercy on the poor." It is a mark of Babylon, the city of destruction, to count the "bodies and souls of men" among the commodities in which it traffics (Rev. 18:13 KJV mg.). People are not commodities for us to use, but images by which we honor God.

5. *Integrity*. By this term, we do not refer to moral integrity, but to the integrated oneness of human nature. We can speak of man's parts and distinguish aspects of God's image from others, but we must remember that God created man as a whole being in his image. This world tries to drive wedges between our bodies and morality, our intellectual lives and faith, and our emotions and obedience. The result is fragmentation. We must seek to understand and help people in the full complexity of their physical, mental, moral, vocational, and relational lives. Above all, we must teach people to direct every aspect of their lives toward glorifying God.

6. *Equality.* Since the dignity of the divine image was lodged in our first parents (Gen. 1:27), it belongs to both genders, every ethnic group, and all classes within society. The statements that "all men are created equal" and "are endowed by their Creator with certain unalienable rights" are not merely political sentiments, but truths rooted deeply in the soil of the Scriptures.[37] Racism (wrongly so named, for there is only one human race), sexism, classism, and all forms of prejudice are attacks against the honor of the living God, who is the Maker of all (Job 31:13–15). We must stand against bigotry and oppression, and help the oppressed to learn their fundamental equality with all mankind.

7. *Benevolence.* The image of God is a potent motive to do good to all men. Calvin said, "The Lord commands all men without exception 'to do good' [Heb. 13:16]. Yet the great part of them are most unworthy if they be judged by their own merit. But here Scripture helps in the best way when it teaches that we are not to consider that men merit of themselves but to look upon the image of God in all men, to which we owe all honor and love."[38] The most arrogant supervisor, rebellious child, and wicked neighbor have this in common—as we love them, we are loving the God who made them in his image.

8. *Authority.* The right to engage in agriculture and industry arises directly from the dominion of God's image bearers over the world. When human beings breed animals, care for them in controlled environments, put them to work in service to humanity, and kill them to harvest their bodies for food, medicine, and other products, they are not transgressing against the oneness of all life. They are exercising God-given authority over God's earth (Gen. 1:26, 28). Furthermore, when one man exercises proper authority over others, it is not tyranny but an office that bears God's image. Though we owe all men honor, we particularly owe honor and obedience to human authority (Rom. 13:1–7), except when its demand for honor would displace God (Dan. 3:18, 28) or its commands conflict with God's Word (Acts 5:29).

9. *Stewardship.* The image of God is not God. Man rules as God's servant-king, and therefore is a royal steward of God's possessions. His calling is not to be a destroyer of the earth (Rev. 11:18), but to represent

---

37. Preamble to the Declaration of Independence, https://www.archives.gov/founding-docs/declaration-transcript. Though some of the founding fathers were deists, others were Christians, and all drew to some extent upon the Christian heritage that shaped British culture.

38. Calvin, *Institutes,* 3.7.6.

the Lord, who "is good to all: and his tender mercies are over all his works" (Ps. 145:9). The ox should work for man, but the ox should also enjoy the fruit of its work (Deut. 25:4; 1 Cor. 9:9; 1 Tim. 5:18). Therefore, "a righteous man regardeth the life of his beast" (Prov. 12:10). God commanded the Israelites to show compassion for the livestock of their enemies (Ex. 23:4–5), for the merciful Lord has compassion even on the cattle who suffer because of divine judgment on man's sin (Jonah 4:11). Therefore, though we do not idolize animals or treat them like people, we must exercise wise stewardship over them. In the same way, we are to steward the natural environment and avoid polluting it or unnecessarily harming it. Even in times of war, with all the devastation that it requires, God calls us to avoid needless destruction of trees, and so, by implication, other living things (Deut. 20:19–20). Men are God's servants, and the Master will call them to account for what he has entrusted to them (Matt. 25:19).

10. *Morality.* At the heart of the image of God stand knowledge, righteousness, and holiness (Eph. 4:24; Col. 3:10). Though these qualities were destroyed in man's fall, mankind remains a moral agent. As servant-kings, we rule the world either according to God's will for his glory or in rebellion against our Lord and Master (Ps. 2:1–3). The human conscience bears witness in all men that we cannot escape God's sight or accountability (Rom. 2:14–15). Humanistic attempts to deny absolute moral standards and replace them with an amoral, utilitarian approach to life fail to account not only for the reality of God but also for the testimony of man's own conscience. Whatever field of human endeavor we may consider, whether it be politics, medicine, business, family, or any other, moral principles matter. Man cannot escape morality, and therefore his only hope is to be renewed in the moral image of God through the Spirit of Christ.

11. *Atrocity.* The great value of man in God's image clarifies why human wickedness is such an atrocity. We are not offended by the savagery of the tiger or the shark with its prey, although we may grieve because they were not originally creatures of violence. However, when we see men treating men like beasts, something within us says, "These things ought not so to be" (James 3:10). When a human being gives himself over to idolatry, immorality, or greed, it is an abomination. Filth in a latrine is no offense, but in a temple it is blasphemous. Man's corruption and evil deeds are obscene precisely because he was created to be a portrait of God; it is that holy image that he has shattered and defiled with his sin.

12. *Destiny*. Created in God's image, man exists for God's glory. The meaning of this is manifold, but we have seen that a golden thread running through the whole is the idea of sonship. God made us to know him, fellowship with him, obey him, and honor him as his created sons. Amazing condescension! God formed man for the highest of callings. How tragic is the fall that displaced us from God's fatherly favor and placed us under his wrath! God's only begotten Son became a man in order to restore sinners to this high privilege. That is amazing grace. However, whether God glorifies himself by saving us from our sins or by damning us for our sins, mankind will glorify God in the end. It is our inescapable destiny.

As fallen human beings, we are not in a position to understand the image of God completely. We do not fully know what it means to be human. But we will know. The full glory of God's image is a mystery that will be revealed with the coming of God's incarnate Image, Jesus Christ. John says, "Beloved, now are we the sons of God, and *it doth not yet appear what we shall be*: but we know that, when he shall appear, *we shall be like him*; for we shall see him as he is" (1 John 3:2). One day the image will be revealed to those who belong to Jesus Christ and—beyond all dreams and expectations—we will share in it.

Sing to the Lord

The Hope of Being Glorified in God's Image

Who are these like stars appearing,
These before God's throne who stand?
Each a golden crown is wearing;
Who are all this glorious band?
Alleluia! hark, they sing,
Praising loud their heav'nly King.

Who are these of dazzling brightness,
These in God's own truth arrayed,
Clad in robes of purest whiteness,
Robes whose lustre ne'er shall fade,
Ne'er be touched by time's rude hand?
Whence come all this glorious band?

These are they who have contended
For their Saviour's honor long,

Wrestling on till life was ended,
Foll'wing not the sinful throng;
These who well the fight sustained,
Triumph through the Lamb have gained.

These are they whose hearts were riven,
Sore with woe and anguish tried,
Who in prayer full oft have striven
With the God they glorified;
Now, their painful conflict o'er,
God has bid them weep no more.

These like priests have watched and waited,
Off'ring up to Christ their will;
Soul and body consecrated,
Day and night to serve him still:
Now in God's most holy place
Blest they stand before his face.

Heinrich T. Schenk, trans. Frances E. Cox
Tune. All Saints Old
Trinity Hymnal—Baptist Edition, No. 602

Questions for Meditation or Discussion

1. What do the authors mean by the "holistic" view of God's image in man?
2. Who are some Reformed theologians that have affirmed the holistic view?
3. What was William Ames's teaching about God's image in man as created, fallen, and regenerated in Christ?
4. Briefly explain how the image of God has each of these implications for mankind:
   - sanctity
   - spirituality
   - rationality
   - dignity
   - integrity
   - equality
   - benevolence

- authority
- stewardship
- morality
- atrocity
- destiny

5. Of the implications listed above, which do you most need to remember right now? Why?

Questions for Deeper Reflection

6. How can John Calvin say that God's image was "obliterated" in man's fall (*Commentaries*, on Gen. 3:1) and yet say the image was "not annihilated," but "corrupted" (*Institutes*, 1.15.4)? Did Calvin contradict himself? Why or why not?
7. How can God's image be unified if it consists of both human constitution and function?
8. How does 1 John 3:2 help us to live with the mystery surrounding the doctrine of God's image? How does that passage of Scripture give the Christian hope?

11

The Gender and Sexuality of Man

In the study of the doctrine of human nature, we cannot avoid the topics of gender and sexuality.[1] The first two chapters of Genesis lay the foundation for a Christian view of sex, marriage, and family. As God's revelation of his original creation, this part of the Bible is paradigmatic for understanding God's will for humanity.

Few subjects stir up as much controversy today as this one. The most blatant divergence from biblical teaching is the assertion that morals are relative and our only rule for right behavior is love. Under such a moral philosophy, virtually anything is acceptable and should be tolerated if it involves the mutual consent of those involved. This is a wholesale rejection of the moral law of God and its replacement with emotional subjectivism. The cultural shift toward moral relativism is accompanied by and inter-twined with the rise of a new morality regarding gender and sexuality, which may be summarized in three controversies.

Modern Controversies over Gender and Sexuality

First, *feminism* has challenged the biblical perspective on the meaning of gender and how it shapes family, church, and society. The modern feminist movement arose in the nineteenth century, a time when revival-ist preachers, such as Charles Grandison Finney (1792–1875), instilled

---

1. Portions of this chapter are adapted from Joel R. Beeke, *Friends and Lovers: Cultivating Companionship and Intimacy in Marriage* (Adelphi, MD: Cruciform Press, 2012); and Joel R. Beeke and Paul M. Smalley, *One Man and One Woman: Marriage and Same-Sex Relations* (Grand Rapids, MI: Reformation Heritage Books, 2016).

fervent confidence that Christians could transform society and overcome its ills. Finney himself encouraged women to pray publicly in his meetings. Some early feminist leaders, such as Elizabeth Cady Stanton (1815–1902), were openly hostile to the Bible.[2] Early feminism agitated for women's civil rights, such as the right to vote and participate in the political process, own property and receive fair wages, and pursue higher education.[3] These demands and others were enunciated by the hundred signatories of the Declaration of Sentiments (1848) at Seneca Falls, New York.[4] In 1920, the Nineteenth Amendment to the United States Constitution granted women the right to vote, and the feminist controversy became quiet for the next few decades.

However, a new wave of feminism began in the 1960s, prompted by the writings of women such as Simone de Beauvoir (1908–1986) and Betty Friedan (1921–2006).[5] Infused with existentialist and sometimes Marxist thought, representatives of this new feminism viewed traditional women's roles in marriage and motherhood as inherently oppressive, and pursued absolute freedom to express their femininity however they chose.[6]

As in any movement, there is diversity in feminism. A form of feminist thought entered into evangelical churches, resulting in a movement known as evangelical egalitarianism, which argues that the church has misinterpreted or misapplied biblical statements about male headship. Other feminists have sought to entirely reconstruct the ideas of gender and sexuality without reference to biblical or traditional cultural ideas, dovetailing with the next area of controversy.

Second, the *homosexual-rights movement* began in the late 1960s. It has demanded, as a matter of justice, that all members of society accept and affirm homosexual, bisexual, and other orientations and practices as good and healthy. What is particularly relevant for our discussion is the

---

2. Andreas J. Köstenberger and Margaret E. Köstenberger, *God's Design for Man and Woman: A Biblical-Theological Survey* (Wheaton, IL: Crossway, 2014), 295–301.

3. Mary A. Kassian, *The Feminist Mistake: The Radical Impact of Feminism on Church and Culture* (Wheaton, IL: Crossway, 2005), 17–18.

4. "Report of the Woman's Rights Convention," National Park Service, Women's Rights National Historical Park, New York, https://www.nps.gov/wori/learn/historyculture/report-of-the-womans-rights-convention.htm. The document also criticizes churches for excluding women from leadership and attacks the cultural double standard that castigates women for forms of immorality winked at in men.

5. Simone de Beauvoir, *Le Deuxième Sexe* (Paris: Gallimard, 1949), published in English as *The Second Sex*, trans. Howard M. Parshley (London: Jonathan Cape, 1953); and Betty Friedan, *The Feminine Mystique* (New York: Dell, 1964).

6. Kassian, *The Feminist Mistake*, 18–27.

impact of this movement on the church. For nearly two thousand years, churches uniformly opposed same-sex orientation and sexual acts as sinful. Many Reformed and evangelical writers still teach that homosexuality is a violation of the laws of God. It is a sin that Christ must forgive, and its ruling power must be broken if we are to count ourselves as Christians.[7] However, in the last few decades, some denominations have welcomed people practicing same-sex erotic activity into membership and even ordained ministry. An increasing number of people and churches say that one can practice homosexuality and be a Christian.[8]

Third, a distinct but related issue is *transgenderism*, the personal assertion of a different gender identity from one's biological sex at birth. Transgenderism is not identical to homosexuality, and is commonly treated as a distinct matter. *Time* magazine journalist Katy Steinmetz writes, "There is no concrete correlation between a person's gender identity and sexual interests; a heterosexual woman, for instance, might start living as a man and still be attracted to men."[9] Some would go so far as to remove any fixed sense of gender and replace it with an infinite variety of identities, or an "omnigender."[10]

---

7. This is the historic position of the Christian church. Some recent books supporting it include Sam Allberry, *Is God Anti-Gay? And Other Questions about Homosexuality, the Bible and Same-Sex Attraction* (Epsom, Surrey, UK: The Good Book Company, 2013); Michael L. Brown, *Can You Be Gay and Christian? Responding with Love and Truth to Questions about Homosexuality* (Lake Mary, FL: Charisma House, 2014); Rosaria Champagne Butterfield, *Openness Unhindered: Further Thoughts of an Unlikely Convert on Sexual Identity and Union with Christ* (Pittsburgh: Crown and Covenant, 2015); Mark Christopher, *Same-Sex Marriage: Is It Really the Same?* (Leominster, UK: Day One, 2009); Kevin DeYoung, *What Does the Bible Really Teach about Homosexuality?* (Wheaton, IL: Crossway, 2015); Robert A. J. Gagnon, *The Bible and Homosexual Practice: Texts and Hermeneutics* (Nashville: Abingdon, 2001); R. Albert Mohler Jr., *We Cannot Be Silent: Speaking Truth to a Culture Redefining Sex, Marriage, and the Very Meaning of Right and Wrong* (Nashville: Thomas Nelson, 2015); R. Albert Mohler Jr., ed., *God and the Gay Christian? A Response to Matthew Vines* (Louisville: SBTS Press, 2014), free ebook, available from http://sbts.me/ebook, henceforth cited as *Response to Matthew Vines*; Synod of the Reformed Presbyterian Church in North America (RPCNA), *The Gospel and Sexual Orientation*, ed. Michael Lefebvre (Pittsburgh: Crown and Covenant, 2012); James R. White and Jeffrey D. Niell, *The Same Sex Controversy* (Bloomington, MN: Bethany House, 2002); and Donald J. Wold, *Out of Order: Homosexuality in the Bible and the Ancient Near East* (Grand Rapids, MI: Baker, 1998).

8. Books arguing for acceptance of homosexuality among Christians include Tom Horner, *Jonathan Loved David: Homosexuality in Biblical Times* (Philadelphia: Westminster, 1978); David G. Myers and Letha Dawson Scanzoni, *What God Has Joined Together: A Christian Case for Gay Marriage* (New York: HarperCollins, 2005); Pim Pronk, *Against Nature? Types of Moral Argumentation regarding Homosexuality*, trans. John Vriend (Grand Rapids, MI: Eerdmans, 1993); Letha Dawson Scanzoni and Virginia Ramey Mollenkott, *Is the Homosexual My Neighbor? A Positive Christian Response*, rev. ed. (New York: HarperCollins, 1994); Dan O. Via and Robert A. J. Gagnon, *Homosexuality and the Bible: Two Views* (Minneapolis: Augsburg Fortress, 2003); and Matthew Vines, *God and the Gay Christian: The Biblical Case in Support of Same-Sex Relationships* (Colorado Springs: Convergent Books, 2014).

9. Cited in Mohler, *We Cannot Be Silent*, 68.

10. Virginia R. Mollenkott, *Omnigender: A Trans-Religious Approach* (Cleveland: Pilgrim Press, 2001). See the discussion in Mohler, *We Cannot Be Silent*, 72.

These three interconnected movements—feminism, homosexual activism, and transgenderism—have had an enormous impact upon society. As theologians, we cannot respond to all of the scientific, political, legal, and practical questions related to these matters. However, the Bible addresses the fundamental questions about man, woman, and human sexuality. The Word of God provides the truths and directions we need to live wise and godly lives in an impure world.

Basic Biblical Teaching on Gender

What does it mean to be a man or a woman? As in all matters of human nature, we find the biblical teaching to begin at the beginning, in the first two chapters of Genesis.

Gender Identity and the Two Biological Sexes

Immediately after announcing that he would create man in his own image, God created Adam and Eve in two distinct genders. Genesis 1:27 says, "So God created man in his own image, in the image of God created he him; male and female created he them." Gender is not merely a personal mindset or a social construct, but an aspect of God's fixed order in creation. Since the words translated as "male" and "female" are used of animals as well as humans,[11] gender has a biological component firmly rooted in the physical body. This implies that the gender of each person corresponds to his or her physical sex as male or female. Therefore, it is not helpful to assign a person a gender identity different from his or her genitalia because of biological observations about the person's brain or some personality tendencies more commonly found in the opposite sex. Jacob and Esau were quite different in personality and interests, but both were equally male (Gen. 25:27–28).[12]

There are cases in which a person's body lacks the capacity for ordinary sexual functions: "eunuchs, which were so born from their mother's womb" (Matt. 19:12). Some people are born with a mixture of male and female anatomy or genetics (*intersex* people). We acknowledge people in these conditions as truly human beings who should be treated with dignity, justice, and compassion. However, these are rare physical abnormalities resulting from the fall, and most intersex individuals identify as a man or woman. Intersex is not transgenderism.

---

11. Gen. 6:19; 7:3, 9, 16.
12. RPCNA, *Gospel and Sexual Orientation*, 23–28.

God created people of both distinct genders "in the image of God" (Gen. 1:27). This is the ground of the equal dignity of men and women, and the reason it is a grave injustice to harm their lives or verbally abuse them (Gen. 9:6; James 3:9). Although different from each other, men and women share one human nature and have the same value. God reveals his glorious attributes in both men and women. Male and female people enter equally into the worship of God (cf. Gal. 3:28). Men and women share the royal commission to subdue the earth and exercise authority over it (Gen. 1:28). The gender distinction between the two sexes is not an evil or a deficiency, but part of God's "very good" original creation (v. 31). Ray Ortlund writes, "Man was created as royalty in God's world, male and female alike bearing the divine glory equally."[13]

Though different cultures find diverse ways to express gender, gender itself stands upon the biological differences between males and females. As Albert Mohler says, "The binary system of gender is grounded in a biological reality and is not socially constructed. . . . We affirm that biological sex is a gift from God to every individual and to the human community to which that individual belongs."[14]

The biblical doctrine of creation corrects transgenderism. Gender is not something we choose, but a divinely ordained facet of our humanity (Gen. 1:27). It is very good for a man to be a man, and very good for a woman to be a woman (v. 31). People should not try to erase their differences or construct a genderless society, but should live as equals with different genders, a difference visible even in their clothing and hairstyles (Deut. 22:5; 1 Cor. 11:14–16).

Man as Authoritative Leader, Woman as Empowering Helper

We find this combination of different but equal genders elaborated in the second chapter of Genesis. The account highlights the difference in terms of *relative authority*. God created the man first (Gen. 2:7). The apostle Paul interprets the order of creation to indicate a leadership role: "But I suffer not a woman to teach, nor to usurp authority over the man, but to be in silence. For Adam was first formed, then Eve" (1 Tim. 2:12–13). While the man was yet alone, the Lord God assigned him a home and a

---

13. Raymond C. Ortlund Jr., "Male-Female Equality and Male Headship, Genesis 1–3," in *Recovering Biblical Manhood and Womanhood: A Response to Evangelical Feminism*, ed. John Piper and Wayne Grudem (Wheaton, IL: Crossway, 1991), 97.

14. Mohler, *We Cannot Be Silent*, 80.

vocation, and gave his commandment to him (Gen. 2:15–17). This implies that the man was called to teach God's Word to the woman, not vice versa.

The narrative proceeds to relate the making of the woman. The man named each animal as the Lord God brought it to him (Gen. 2:19), just as God named parts of his creation (1:5, 8, 10). God then made the woman in a manner that also served for Paul as a sign that "the head of the woman is the man. . . . For the man is not of the woman: but the woman of the man. Neither was the man created for the woman; but the woman for the man" (1 Cor. 11:3, 8–9). When the Lord God brought the woman to the man, he named her, also implying that he had authority over his wife (Gen. 2:23; cf. 3:20).[15] In Scripture, a greater king shows his authority over a lesser king or official by giving him a new name.[16] The description of marriage that follows Eve's naming emphasizes the man's initiative in leaving and cleaving to form a new bond (2:24).

As the account passes on to the fall of man, we continue to see evidences of distinction. When the Serpent tempted Adam and Eve, he addressed his deception to the woman (Gen. 3:1), which Paul interprets as another argument why women should not teach men or exercise authority over them in the church (1 Tim. 2:14). Paul's assessment did not arise from a prejudiced view of feminine intelligence, but from an understanding of gender roles, for he knew women who were wise and able to teach, such as his friend Priscilla.[17] Satan sought to reverse the divinely ordained roles by addressing the woman. The text of Genesis does not excuse the man, but indicts him with the statement that the woman "gave also unto her husband with her; and he did eat" (Gen. 3:6). Adam's silence in the account is deafening; he had failed to lead his wife and to stand against the Serpent. Paul further indicts the man when he acknowledges that Adam clearly understood that the Serpent was lying, yet he chose his wife over God and ate the fruit she offered him (1 Tim. 2:14).

The Lord God came seeking the fallen couple but specifically "called unto Adam, and said unto him, Where art thou?" (Gen. 3:9).[18] The first to receive the command was the first to be called to account for breaking

---

15. The same verb "call" (*qara*) appears in all of these naming texts (Gen. 1:5, 8, 10; 2:19–20, 23). It is not otherwise used in these two chapters. Wayne Grudem, *Evangelical Feminism and Biblical Truth: An Analysis of More than 100 Disputed Questions* (Sisters, OR: Multnomah, 2004), 31–33.

16. Gen. 41:45; 2 Kings 23:34; 24:17; Dan. 1:7.

17. Acts 18:2, 18, 26; Rom. 16:3; 1 Cor. 16:19; 2 Tim. 4:19.

18. Both "him" and "thou" in Gen. 3:9 are singular.

it—another sign of leadership. God's punishment on the woman aimed at her roles as a mother and wife, but his punishment on the man brought the more global consequence of a curse upon the ground and death upon mankind (vv. 16–19). It was Adam, not Eve, who stood as the representative of the entire race and whose disobedience brought death and condemnation (Rom. 5:12–19). In Genesis 5:2, we read another indication that the man stood as the leader and representative of all mankind: "Male and female created he them; and blessed them, and called their name Adam, in the day when they were created." The entire race is named after the first man, showing his headship.

Christian feminists object that Genesis 3:16 teaches us that a husband's authority over his wife stems from the consequences of the fall.[19] In the text, we hear the Lord God say this to the woman: "And thy desire shall be to thy husband, and he shall rule over thee."

In response, we note that the text does assert man's power over his wife, though it does not indicate whether that rule is a consequence of sin or a continuing reality despite sin. As we have seen, there are many indications in Genesis 2–3 that God gave the man authority over his wife before the fall. The word translated as "rule" (*mashal*) simply means to exercise authority, whether as a servant over a household (24:2) or as a high official over a nation (45:8). The term rendered as "desire" (*teshuqah*) can be positive, as in "I am my beloved's, and his desire [*teshuqah*] is toward me" (Song 7:10). However, we find a close parallel in Genesis 4:7, where the Lord warned Cain, "Sin lieth at the door. And unto thee shall be his desire [*teshuqah*], and thou shalt rule [*mashal*] over him." The Hebrew syntax is the same as Genesis 3:16.[20] God's words portray sin as a predator at the door, desiring to overcome and rule Cain. Similarly, God's words to the woman indicate that in her fallen state she will desire to conquer her husband, but he will rule her despite her efforts. Therefore, the text teaches that with the fall women will enter into strife over the authority of their husbands, not that husbands will unjustly start to oppress their wives.[21]

---

19. Marianne Meye Thompson, "Response," in *Women, Authority, and the Bible*, ed. Alvera Mickelsen (Downers Grove, IL: InterVarsity Press, 1986), 95–96; and Gilbert Bilezikian, *Beyond Sex Roles: A Guide for the Study of Female Roles in the Bible* (Grand Rapids, MI: Baker, 1985), 55–56.

20. Compare a woodenly literal translation of the two texts: "to your husband [will be] your desire, but he will rule over you" (Gen. 3:16) and "to you [will be] its desire, but you shall rule over it" (4:7).

21. James B. Hurley, *Man and Woman in Biblical Perspective* (Grand Rapids, MI: Zondervan, 1981), 219.

However, though Genesis 2–3 teaches the distinct authority of the husband, it also stresses the *equality* of the woman and the man in terms of their humanity. The Lord God prefaced her creation with this observation: "It is not good that the man should be alone" (2:18). This is a startling statement after the repeated "good" of chapter 1. It highlights man's incompleteness without "an help meet for him" (v. 18). The term translated as "help" or "helper" (*'ezer*) is not a demeaning word for a less capable assistant, but a term used many times for the Lord as the One who gives strength and salvation to people in need.[22] The woman has something the man lacks, which empowers him. Paul affirms that man cannot get along without woman (1 Cor. 11:11–12). The phrase "meet for him" (*kenegdo*) literally means "according to one in front of him" and communicates a fitting match for companionship and partnership. No mere bird or beast, not even in paradise itself, will meet man's need (Gen. 2:20). His helper must share his very nature as his equal.

Having one nature in common seems to be one of the reasons for God's peculiar method of making the woman from the man's rib. She was, by the man's glad confession, "bone of my bones, and flesh of my flesh" (Gen. 2:23). She was a part of him, sharing the same human life formed and breathed into him by God (v. 7). As Paul deduces from this text, God intends for husbands to love and cherish their wives as a part of themselves, just as Christ amazingly loves his bride and sacrificed himself for her (Eph. 5:25, 28–31).

Even the narrative of the fall portrays the woman as a rational, morally accountable creature (Gen. 3:1–6). Though the Lord God called to the man first, he did address the woman as a responsible moral agent (vv. 13, 16). He also included her in the first promise of salvation, both as a recipient of grace and as a means of bringing the victorious seed into the world (v. 15; cf. v. 20). It is clear that the woman is of the same essence as the man, fully equal to him in that regard, and a full participant in God's saving grace.

The Scriptures here offer a corrective to both male chauvinism and feminism. Chauvinism is an attitude of superiority over women that may express itself in verbal contempt, oppressive and unjust behavior, or acts of violence. Such an attitude—as well as the conduct it inspires—is despicable and a direct offense against God. Nowhere does the Bible endorse such arrogance. Instead, both Genesis and Paul exhort men to humbly recog-

---

22. Ex. 18:4; Deut. 33:7, 29; Pss. 70:5; 121:1–2; 124:8; 146:5; Hos. 13:9; cf. Gen. 49:25.

nize their need for women and fundamental equality with them. As Peter says, the Christian man who treats his wife without honor and gentleness will find his prayers hindered (1 Pet. 3:7). Peter warns, "God resisteth the proud, and giveth grace to the humble" (5:5).

Likewise, Scripture also corrects feminism. Some of the goals of early feminism addressed injustices against women, such as inequalities in compensation or exclusion from higher education. However, feminism in other respects rebels against God's design for creation. God has established an order within which the two genders must operate, and their roles are not identical. God calls men to be leaders and women to be helpers. This does not give a man universal authority over women, but it does direct relationships in marriage and the church, as Paul teaches. Womanly submission to proper male authority does not degrade women, but releases them to use their competency to empower the men in their lives to fulfill their callings.

The result is a balanced perspective that combines essential equality, mutual interdependence, masculine leadership, and submission to God's authority in all things. Andreas and Margaret E. Köstenberger write, "God's plan for humanity is one of partnership in which the man, as God-appointed leader, and his wife alongside him jointly represent the Creator by exercising dominion over the earth."[23]

Basic Biblical Teaching on Sex

We return now to Genesis 1–2 for a more focused inquiry: What do these texts teach about sexual intimacy? Again, we find a balanced perspective on the matter. The Bible is not shy about sex. It teaches us the Creator's beautiful design and the horrific effects of rebellion against that design.

Sexual Activity and Reproduction

The first perspective on sex found in the Bible is reproductive. In Genesis 1:27–28, "male and female created he them" leads to "Be fruitful, and multiply." This does not reduce sexuality to mere reproduction, for the people in view are images of God and must treat each other as such. They are not to act as mere animals engaged in breeding. However, the text does show that the production of children is one of God's beautiful purposes in sexual union.

For those created in God's image, sexual relationships serve to multiply that image and fill the earth with the glory of God. Though childbirth

---

23. Köstenberger and Köstenberger, *God's Design for Man and Woman*, 35.

became painful and dangerous for women after the fall (Gen. 3:16), having children was not intended to be a burden, for "God blessed them" in this calling (1:28). Even after the fall, believers can affirm that "children are an heritage of the LORD: and the fruit of the womb is his reward" (Ps. 127:3). If you try to enjoy sexual intimacy with your spouse while despising the thought of bearing children, then you are tearing apart what God joined together.

What about birth control? Let us state a few basic guidelines:

1. Any method of birth control that could destroy a life already conceived in the womb should be rejected as potential murder.
2. The Bible does not condemn all birth control, and it may be the best part of wisdom and love to use it in certain situations, such as when a wife is recovering from childbirth or is plagued by medical or psychological problems.
3. We must not legislate or judge each other on the issue of birth control beyond what Scripture says, lest we be guilty of legalism. Rather, we must allow each couple to study God's Word and prayerfully decide for themselves according to their situation.
4. We must not allow selfishness, materialism, or other man-centered motives to drive us to unnecessarily limit the size of our families, but prayerfully seek God's greatest glory in man's greatest good, even at our expense.
5. We are called to let the Lord be Lord over every area of life, including the size of our family.

However, producing children to raise in God's ways is not the only purpose for which God created sexual intimacy.

Sexual Activity and the Marriage Relationship

The second perspective on sexuality that we find in Genesis is relational. We have already observed that God made the woman for the man as a "help meet for him," to be a strong and equal feminine partner for life (Gen. 2:18, 20). Man received her as "bone of my bones, and flesh of my flesh." These words acknowledged her common nature with him as one who had physically originated in his body. Adam's words also pledged covenantal commitment; we find parallel language in political covenants and other pledges of faithfulness.[24] Malachi 2:14 rebukes the unfaithful husband for treachery against "thy companion, and the wife of thy covenant."

This covenant of companionship is God's ordained context for sexual activity. We read in Genesis 2:24, "Therefore shall a man leave his father and his mother, and shall cleave unto his wife: and they shall be one flesh." Man was to enter into relationship with his feminine partner through marriage. Christ attributed these words to the Creator and so taught us to look to this text as the foundation for our understanding of marriage (Matt. 19:4–6). "Leave" implies the public formation of a new household distinct from that of "his father and his mother." "Cleave" (*dabaq*) means to cling to or hold tightly (Ruth 1:14), to adhere as if glued together (2 Sam. 23:10). It is a term used of the covenantal loyalty that Israel should have toward the Lord.[25] Paul indicates that "one flesh" refers primarily to sexual union, for it obtains even in a relationship with a prostitute (1 Cor. 6:16). At the same time, the original "one flesh" in the garden was more than physical, for we read in Genesis 2:25 that the man and woman were "naked" and "were not ashamed," which signifies complete freedom and openness with each other—a relationship without personal barriers. Christ said that this covenantal and physical union is a lasting bond that we cannot violate without sinning against the Creator: "What therefore God hath joined together, let not man put asunder" (Matt. 19:6).

Therefore, God instituted marriage as mankind's blessed context for enjoying sexual intimacy. Sex is not a casual encounter for the sake of pleasure, an exploratory exercise to see how compatible two people are, or a mere expression of affection and attraction. Sex belongs to the covenantal relationship between one man and one woman, a beautiful aspect of their companionship and partnership, guarded by the bond of a solemn lifelong commitment. The Westminster Confession of Faith (24.1) reflects this when it says, "Marriage is to be between one man and one woman."[26]

On the one hand, the biblical view of sex and marriage rebukes those who forbid marriage or look down on marital sex as less spiritual than celibacy. Those are "doctrines of devils," not the teaching of the Holy Spirit (1 Tim. 4:1–3). Sex is a good and beautiful gift from God that, if

---

24. Gen. 29:14; Judg. 9:2; 2 Sam. 5:1–3; 19:13; 1 Chron. 11:1. See Brueggemann, "Of the Same Flesh and Bone (Gn 2, 23a)," 535–38; and Hamilton, *The Book of Genesis, Chapters 1–17*, 179–80. We discussed this briefly in the appropriate place in chap. 6.

25. Deut. 10:20; 11:22; 13:4; 30:20; Josh. 22:5; 23:8.

26. *Reformed Confessions*, 4:263.

shared in the context of committed love, strengthens the marriage relationship. The Westminster Larger Catechism (Q. 138) points out that the seventh commandment requires, by a positive implication, "conjugal love (Prov. 5:19–20), and cohabitation (1 Peter 3:7)."[27]

Proverbs 5:18–19 gives us this remarkably strong counsel: "Let thy fountain be blessed: and rejoice with the wife of thy youth. Let her be as the loving hind and pleasant roe; let her breasts satisfy thee at all times; and be thou ravished always with her love." God calls the husband and the wife to enjoy each other's bodies passionately. William Gouge (1575–1653) wrote, "As the man must be satisfied at all times in his wife, and even ravished with her love; so must the woman be satisfied at all times in her husband, and even ravished with his love."[28]

On the other hand, Scripture rebukes those who practice or promote sex outside of the marriage of one man and one woman. We find both truths in Hebrews 13:4: "Marriage is honourable in all, and the bed undefiled: but whoremongers and adulterers God will judge." The "bed" (*koitē*) is a euphemism for sexual activity (Rom. 13:13). Sex in marriage is not unclean in God's sight. However, sex outside of marriage is forbidden. The term "whoremongers" (plural *pornos*) refers to those who engage in fornication (*porneia*), a broad term for sexual immorality.[29] Adultery is a violation of the marriage covenant by engaging in sexual activity with an outsider. The law of Moses forbade premarital sex (Ex. 22:16–17; Deut. 22:13–21) and demanded the death penalty for adultery, for both the man and the woman (Deut. 22:22–29).[30] In the new covenant, such behavior calls for church discipline (1 Cor. 5:9, 11).

The marriage of one man and one woman remains God's authorized channel where the strong waters of human sexuality should flow. Paul affirms the goodness of celibacy, but writes, "Nevertheless, to avoid fornication, let every man have his own wife, and let every woman have her own husband" (1 Cor. 7:2). Within marriage, the husband and wife should not deny each other sexually for an extended time, but only by mutual consent for a short season of prayer (vv. 4–5). Paul says, "Let the husband

---

27. *Reformed Confessions*, 4:333.
28. William Gouge, *Of Domestical Duties* (1622; repr., Pensacola, FL: Puritan Reprints, 2006), 158 [2/2.4].
29. See the *pornē/porneia/porneuō* word group in its Septuagintal use in Gen. 34:31; 38:24; Lev. 19:29; Num. 25:1 (cf. vv. 6, 14–18); Deut. 22:21; Hos. 3:3; Ezek. 16:15, 34.
30. In ancient Israelite society, betrothal was considered legal marriage prior to consummation, and thus, sexual activity between a betrothed woman and another man was counted as adultery.

render unto the wife due benevolence:[31] and likewise also the wife unto the husband" (v. 3). The Greek words translated as "due benevolence" communicate the idea of loving obligation, a debt that must be paid to a friend. Gouge said, "As it is called benevolence because it must be performed with good will and delight, willingly, readily and cheerfully; so it is said to be due because it is a debt which the wife oweth to her husband, and he to her."[32] Though Paul recognizes the advantages of being single for Christ, he says that "it is better to marry than to burn" with strong sexual desires (v. 9). The Westminster Confession (24.2) offers this summary of the biblical purpose of marriage: "Marriage was ordained for the mutual help of husband and wife (Gen. 2:18), for the increase of mankind with a legitimate issue, and of the Church with an holy seed (Mal. 2:15); and for preventing of uncleanness (1 Cor. 7:2, 9)."[33]

We have found in our study that from the beginning, God created gender and sexuality to be an important aspect of our humanity. Just as there are two complementary creation accounts, so we find complementary pairs of truths in them about this matter.

	Genesis 1:26–28	Genesis 2:4–3:24
Gender Distinction	Two Biological Sexes: Male and Female	Two Relational Roles: Authority and Helper
Gender Equality	Shared Divine Glory: Image of God with Dominion	Common Human Life: Same Flesh/Both Moral Agents
Sexual Union	Reproduction: Be Fruitful and Multiply	Marital Bond: Leave, Cleave, One Flesh

Table 11.1. A Comparison of Genesis 1 and 2–3 on Gender and Sexuality

Basic Biblical Teaching on Homosexuality

So far we have seen that the Bible commends sexual activity in the context of the marriage of one man and one woman. This implicitly rules out homosexuality as contrary to God's creation ordinance. The Bible also speaks

---

31. The Greek phrase translated as "due benevolence" is *opheilēn eunoian*. The latter term, which means "good will, affection, or friendliness," appears in most later manuscripts, but not in several older manuscripts.
32. Gouge, *Of Domestical Duties*, 161 [2/2.9].
33. *Reformed Confessions*, 4:263.

explicitly to homosexuality, and it unequivocally condemns it as a sin from which people must be saved by Christ.[34] There is not a single example of a commendation of homosexuality in Scripture. This is acknowledged even by many who desire to promote same-sex relationships.[35]

Old Testament Teaching on Homosexuality

The best-known historical references to homosexuality in Scripture are those about Sodom, a city noted for its great wickedness (Gen. 13:13; 18:20). The Lord did not find ten righteous people there. Therefore, he destroyed the city in a spectacular outpouring of fire and brimstone, which was visible for miles around (18:32; 19:24–29). The Scriptures reveal two kinds of wickedness that provoked this act of judgment. There was *grave injustice*, as evidenced in the "cry" for help rising up from the city (18:20–21; 19:13; cf. Ezek. 16:49–50),[36] and *sexual perversion*, shown when the men of Sodom demand to "know" Lot's male visitors (Gen. 19:4–5), a euphemism for sexual intercourse (v. 8).[37] Jewish writings outside of the Bible from the second century BC, such as Jubilees and the Testaments of the Twelve Patriarchs, also identified sexual sin as one of the great offenses of Sodom.[38]

The law of Moses clearly prohibited sexual acts between men. Leviticus 18:22 says, "Thou shalt not lie with mankind, as with womankind: it is abomination." Leviticus 20:13 says, "If a man also lie with mankind, as he lieth with a woman, both of them have committed an abomination: they shall surely be put to death; their blood shall be upon them." Kevin DeYoung writes, "The reason the prohibitions are stated so absolutely, is because men were designed to have sex with women, not a man with another

---

34. This argument is developed at some length in Beeke and Smalley, *One Man and One Woman.*

35. "Wherever homosexual intercourse is mentioned in Scripture, it is condemned." Pronk, *Against Nature?*, 279. Via writes, "The biblical texts that deal specifically with homosexual practice condemn it unconditionally." Via and Gagnon, *Homosexuality and the Bible: Two Views*, 93. See also Luke Timothy Johnson and Diarmaid MacCulloch, cited in DeYoung, *What Does the Bible Really Teach about Homosexuality?*, 132.

36. Victor P. Hamilton, *The Book of Genesis, Chapters 18–50*, New International Commentary on the Old Testament (Grand Rapids, MI: Eerdmans, 1995), 20–21.

37. Gen. 4:1, 17, 25; 19:8; 24:16; 38:26; Num. 31:17–18, 35; Judg. 19:25; 1 Sam. 1:19; 1 Kings 1:4. The Septuagint also translates "know" with a Greek word (*syngenōmetha*) used with a sexual meaning in the Scriptures (Gen. 39:10) and outside them. Wold, *Out of Order*, 82, 86–87.

38. Jubilees 16:5–6; Testament of Levi 14:6; Testament of Benjamin 9:1; Testament of Naphtali 3:4, cited in Gagnon, *The Bible and Homosexual Practice*, 88n121. In the first century BC, Philo wrote of Sodom, "Those were men who lusted after one another, doing unseemly things, and not regarding or respecting their common nature . . . and so, by degrees, the man became accustomed to be treated like women." *De Abrahamo*, 135–36, cited in Peter H. Davids, *The Letters of 2 Peter and Jude*, The Pillar New Testament Commentary (Grand Rapids, MI: Eerdmans, 2006), 53.

male."[39] Someone might object that these passages also prohibit sexual relations with a woman during her menstruation (18:19; 20:18), showing that they do not reveal abiding moral principles. In reply, we note that Leviticus shows homosexual acts to be serious violations of the moral law by imposing the death penalty on the perpetrators (20:13), whereas sexual relations during menstruation only make a man ceremonially unclean (15:24).

New Testament Teaching on Homosexuality

The New Testament reaffirms this old covenant law, proving that it has abiding moral significance for all peoples. Paul writes in 1 Timothy 1:9–10 that God's law is contrary to the sins of mankind, including "them that defile themselves with mankind." The phrase translates a single masculine word (*arsenokoitēs*) that combines two Greek terms, "male" and "bed," meaning, "males who go to bed [sexually] with males."[40] The same two terms appear in the ancient Greek translation of both Leviticus 18:22 and 20:13.[41] Therefore, Paul affirms the abiding moral authority of the law's condemnation of homosexual acts.

The New Testament books of Jude and 2 Peter offer divinely inspired commentary on Sodom and Gomorrah. Jude says that those cities suffered God's fiery destruction for "giving themselves over to fornication, and going after strange flesh" (Jude 7). "Strange flesh" cannot refer to the fact that the visitors were angels, for the Sodomites did not regard them as angels but as men (Gen. 19:5), and the same sin is attributed to nearby cities that were not visited by angels. Therefore, we should understand "strange flesh" as condemning the men of Sodom and Gomorrah specifically for their homosexuality because of its violation of the boundaries of God's created order for sexuality.[42] Similarly, 2 Peter 2:7 speaks of "the filthy conversation of the wicked" in Sodom, where "filthy" (*aselgeia*) refers to sexual licentiousness or shameless sensuality.[43]

The longest statement in the Bible about homosexuality is Romans 1:26–27: "For this cause God gave them up unto vile affections: for even

---

39. DeYoung, *What Does the Bible Really Teach about Homosexuality?*, 41.
40. Similar Greek words are formed with the *-koitēs* ending, including "one who sleeps with slaves," "one who sleeps with his mother," and "one who sleeps with many." David F. Wright, "Homosexuals or Prostitutes? The Meaning of ΑΡΣΕΝΟΚΟΙΤΑΙ (1 Cor. 6:9, 1 Tim. 1:10)," *Vigiliae Christianae* 38, no. 2 (June 1984): 130 (full article, 125–53). Vines's argument that the word refers to economic exploitation is remarkably weak. Vines, *God and the Gay Christian*, 122–25.
41. Wright, "Homosexuals or Prostitutes?," 129.
42. Davids, *The Letters of 2 Peter and Jude*, 52–53.
43. Rom. 13:13; Gal. 5:19; Eph. 4:19.

their women did change the natural use into that which is against nature: and likewise also the men, leaving the natural use of the woman, burned in their lust one toward another; men with men working that which is unseemly, and receiving in themselves that recompence of their error which was meet." Given the mention of the two genders and the immediately preceding statements about sexual sin (v. 24), it is clear that Paul wrote of "natural use" with regard to sexual matters here. The word translated as "use" (*chrēsis*) appears frequently in other Greek writings with reference to sexual relations.[44] Like the laws of Leviticus, "homosexual relations in general are indicted," as Tom Schreiner observes.[45]

The apostle teaches us much about homosexuality. Sexual activity between people of the same sex is "against nature," which refers here to God's created order for mankind.[46] John Murray wrote, "The offense of homosexuality is the abandonment of the divinely constituted order in reference to sex."[47] God condemns sexual activity not only between men but also between women. Sexual desires toward the same sex are sin. The problem with these sexual desires is not that they are too strong, but that they are corrupt in desiring satisfaction in a wrong object.[48] Therefore, the Bible teaches that what today are called gay and lesbian desires and acts are sinful, whether they are unusual events or a long-term way of life.

Homosexual desires and actions degrade human beings. They are "vile" (*atimia*), which means that they bring dishonor to those who exercise them. They produce "that which is unseemly" (*aschēmosunē*)—that is, indecency and cause for shame (cf. Rev. 16:15). Paul goes on to say that such people are already receiving the penalty that necessarily accompanies such a wandering from God's ways. Homosexuality particularly manifests itself in an idolatrous people who have turned from the knowledge of the true God. Paul does not say that each individual who engages in such sins is particularly idolatrous, but rather that when a group—such as a people or nation (note the plurals)—turns from the Creator to worship idols, God gives that people over to greater bondage to fornication and homosexual-

---

44. Thomas R. Schreiner, *Romans*, Baker Exegetical Commentary on the New Testament (Grand Rapids, MI: Baker Academic, 1998), 94.

45. Schreiner, *Romans*, 95–96.

46. For references to creation, compare Rom. 1:20, 25 to Gen. 1:1; Rom. 1:23 to Gen. 1:26, 30; Rom. 1:27 to Gen. 1:27; and Rom. 1:32 to Gen. 2:17. See Gagnon, *The Bible and Homosexual Practice*, 289–91.

47. Murray, *The Epistle to the Romans*, 1:47–48.

48. Denny Burk, "Is Homosexual Orientation Sinful?," *Journal of the Evangelical Theological Society* 58, no. 1 (2015): 101 (full article, 95–115).

ity. He is "not talking about an individual's decline into sin," but giving "a typical description of a culture's decline."[49] Homosexuality not only provokes the wrath of God, but is a sign that the wrath of God has already come upon an idolatrous people.

Therefore, the Westminster Larger Catechism (Q. 139) rightly says that "sodomy, and all unnatural lusts (Rom. 1:24, 26–27; Lev. 20:15–16)," are sins "forbidden in the seventh commandment."[50] Both homosexual desire and activity violate God's holy law.[51]

For people who have given themselves over to same-sex erotic desires and practices, Paul's message of law and gospel comes through most clearly in 1 Corinthians 6:9–10: "Know ye not that the unrighteous shall not inherit the kingdom of God? Be not deceived: neither fornicators, nor idolaters, nor adulterers, nor effeminate, nor abusers of themselves with mankind, nor thieves, nor covetous, nor drunkards, nor revilers, nor extortioners, shall inherit the kingdom of God." Paul reiterates the law of God that homosexuality is sin. The phrase "abusers of themselves with mankind" translates the same Greek word seen before in 1 Timothy 1:10, which means "males who go to bed with males" (*arsenokoitēs*). Here again the word echoes the laws of Leviticus in its condemnation of all sexual activity between men, a connection strengthened by the fact that Paul has just written strongly against incest, another sexual sin condemned in Leviticus 18 and 20.[52] The word translated as "effeminate" (*malakos*) literally means "soft"; here it designates "men who are soft." Immediately preceding "males who go to bed with males," it refers to men who seek to attract and please homosexual aggressors.[53] With these two words Paul rebukes the full range of male homosexual behavior as sin incompatible with Christianity.

Some writers object that Paul was ignorant of homosexual relationships involving more equality or affection, so he must have been condemning only the abuse of teenage boys or slaves.[54] We reply that the apostle's

---

49. RPCNA, *Gospel and Sexual Orientation*, 18.

50. *Reformed Confessions*, 4:333.

51. RPCNA, *Gospel and Sexual Orientation*, 54.

52. David E. Garland, *1 Corinthians*, Baker Exegetical Commentary on the New Testament (Grand Rapids, MI: Baker Academic, 2003), 212–13.

53. Gordon D. Fee, *The First Epistle to the Corinthians*, The New International Commentary on the New Testament (Grand Rapids, MI: Eerdmans, 1987), 243–44.

54. Myers and Scanzoni, *What God Has Joined Together*, 84–85; and Vines, *God and the Gay Christian*, 37.

life and ministry in cities steeped in Greco-Roman culture would have acquainted him with the wide variety of male-to-male sexual relationships practiced in the ancient world, including those of mutual affection and admiration.[55] Though there certainly were oppressive relationships, there were also examples in Greek history and literature of homosexual relationships in which both men were regarded as noble.[56] Christ's apostle was aware of lofty views of homosexual relationships, but simply condemned homosexuality without qualification.

Paul warns that people engaged in homosexual sex will not "inherit the kingdom of God" if they do not repent of their sin. In the teaching of Jesus Christ, the only alternative to inheriting the kingdom is being cast into the fires of hell for eternal punishment.[57] Therefore, to pronounce God's blessing on the union of two men or two women is to endanger their souls.[58] However, Paul did not write that if we ever commit such sins then we are surely damned, but he said, "And such were some of you: but ye are washed, but ye are sanctified, but ye are justified in the name of the Lord Jesus, and by the Spirit of our God" (1 Cor. 6:11). Some Corinthian believers had lived as such sinners, but the past tense indicates that they were no longer unrighteous—no longer adulterers, men who slept with men, thieves, or drunkards.[59] Their identity had changed because they were "in Christ Jesus" (1 Cor. 1:2). Union with Christ now defined them, and they could not be the same.[60]

Telling people that Christ can save them from sin is not homophobia. True homophobia is believing that people who practice same-sex sexual relations are so different that they can never turn back to the Lord and his ways.[61] On the contrary, the homosexual man or woman who repents, forsakes sin, and trusts in Christ by grace becomes a saint, washed clean, set apart for God, and counted righteous for Christ's sake. The gospel promise of "such *were* some of you" means there is no such thing as a gay Christian or a lesbian Christian, any more

---

55. Anthony C. Thiselton, *First Epistle to the Corinthians*, New International Greek Testament Commentary (Grand Rapids, MI: Eerdmans, 2000), 452.

56. Gagnon, *The Bible and Homosexual Practice*, 351–52.

57. Matt. 25:34, 41, 46; cf. Rev. 21:7–8.

58. DeYoung, *What Does the Bible Really Teach about Homosexuality?*, 77.

59. The Greek tense is imperfect, implying a condition that continued in the past or actions repeated in the past.

60. RPCNA, *Gospel and Sexual Orientation*, 47.

61. Rosaria Champagne Butterfield, *The Secret Thoughts of an Unlikely Convert: An English Professor's Journey into Christian Faith*, expanded ed. (Pittsburgh: Crown and Covenant, 2015), 169.

than there is a Christian adulterer or a Christian drunkard. To be sure, inner conflict with sin remains (Gal. 5:17), bringing great frustration to the believer (Rom. 7:14–25). The solution is to cling by faith to the promises of Christ and to strive in holy fear to put off all sin and pursue holiness as part of God's living temple and spiritual family, the local church (2 Cor. 6:16–7:1).

The Modern Concept of Sexual Orientation

An objection often raised against the biblical view of homosexuality is that the Scriptures do not speak to the modern understanding of a person's sexual orientation.[62] According to the American Psychological Association, "Sexual orientation refers to an enduring pattern of emotional, romantic, and/or sexual attractions to men, women, or both sexes."[63] Orientation is an unhelpfully broad and indefinite concept based upon a person's experience of social and sexual desires.[64] The Scriptures speak very positively of emotional connections and friendships between people of the same sex. However, though the Bible does not use the term *orientation*, it speaks of male sexual desire toward males and female sexual desire for females, and condemns such desires (Rom. 1:26–27). Thus, Scripture does address the orientation of a person's sexual attractions.

The modern concept of sexual orientation goes beyond a description of our desires; it seeks to set a new definition of identity and personhood based on our emotions and sexual experiences.[65] This fundamental shift in how we define who we are sets the stage for people to claim a homosexual orientation as their basic identity. Rosaria Butterfield writes, "If I self-define as heterosexual or homosexual . . . everything, including nonsexual affection, is subsumed by this new humanity of sexuality."[66] Thus, any attack on the goodness of homosexuality is seen as an attack on homosexuals' persons. We must reject this distorted sense of identity.

---

62. Hendrik Hart, foreword to Pronk, *Against Nature?*, xi; and Vines, *God and the Gay Christian*, 21–41, 129. Mohler says of Vines, "His main argument is that the Bible simply has no category of sexual orientation." Mohler, "God, the Gospel and the Gay Challenge: A Response to Matthew Vines," in *Response to Matthew Vines*, 14.

63. American Psychological Association, *Answers to Your Questions: For a Better Understanding of Sexual Orientation & Homosexuality* (Washington, DC: American Psychological Association, 2008), 1, https://www.apa.org/topics/lgbt/orientation.pdf.

64. Mohler, "God, the Gospel and the Gay Challenge," in *Response to Matthew Vines*, 18.

65. Butterfield, *Openness Unhindered*, 94–95.

66. Butterfield, *Openness Unhindered*, 98.

God is the Creator and Lord of all. Our identity is found in being created in the image of God (Gen. 1:26). Therefore, our lives are defined by how we relate to God and his Word. We must resist the attempt to make our feelings into our identity, and instead learn our identity from our Creator. Rather than saying, "I am a homosexual," or, "I am a heterosexual," we should say, "I am a man or woman created in the image of God for his glory, but fallen into sin." Butterfield says, "You cannot repent of sexual orientation, since sexual orientation is an artificial category built on a faulty premise."[67] Denny Burk writes, "In God's world, we are who God says we are. We are not merely the sum total of our fallen sexual desires."[68]

The most basic questions about our identity are not "How do I feel?" and "What do I want?" but "How am I related to God—as a sinner in Adam or a saint in Christ?" and "How am I representing God as his living image by obeying his Word?" These are questions that transcend the matter of homosexuality, and even sexuality itself, and engage our whole persons for the glory of God. We must remember that sex and marriage are temporary gifts that end with physical death (Rom. 7:3) and will be superceded when Christ raises us from the dead (Matt. 22:30). We were made for something far greater—spiritual union with the God of glory.

Sing to the Lord

The Blessedness of the Godly Family

Blest the man that fears Jehovah,
Walking ever in His ways;
By thy toil thou shalt be prospered
And be happy all thy days.

In thy wife thou shalt have gladness,
She shall fill thy home with good,
Happy in her loving service
And the joys of motherhood.

Joyful children, sons and daughters,
Shall about thy table meet,

---

67. Butterfield, *Openness Unhindered*, 107.
68. Burk, "Is Homosexual Orientation Sinful?," 113.

Olive plants, in strength and beauty,
Full of hope and promise sweet.

Lo, on him that fears Jehovah
Shall this blessedness attend,
For Jehovah out of Zion
Shall to thee His blessing send.

Thou shalt see God's kingdom prosper
All thy days, till life shall cease,
Thou shalt see thy children's children;
On Thy people, Lord, be peace.

Psalm 128
Tune: Jude/Galilee
The Psalter, No. 360
Trinity Hymnal—Baptist Edition, No. 626

Questions for Meditation or Discussion

1. Why are gender and sexuality difficult topics to discuss today?
2. What are three modern movements that have greatly impacted our views of gender and sexuality?
3. How did these movements affect you in your personal background and experience?
4. What is the basic biblical teaching on our gender identity as men or women?
5. How does the Bible describe the roles of men and women in relation to each other, especially in the home?
6. What does Genesis 1 teach us about sexuality in terms of reproduction?
7. What does Genesis 2 teach us about sexuality in terms of relationship?
8. What does the Old Testament teach about homosexuality? (Cite specific texts.)
9. What does the New Testament teach about homosexuality? (Cite specific texts.)
10. What is the modern concept of sexual orientation? How do the authors critique it?
11. How should churches treat homosexual or transgender people who desire to attend their services? If such people desire to become members of the church or are already members, how should the church show them the love and righteousness of God?

Questions for Deeper Reflection

12. What are some ways that your background and traditions have affected how you view what it means to be a "masculine" man or a "feminine" woman? To what extent are those ideas transcendent principles of truth or righteousness, and to what extent merely cultural norms?

13. What are some examples of how churches have fallen into legalism regarding sexuality? What are some examples of how churches have compromised with sexual sin?

14. Imagine that a leader in your church proposes the addition of a gender-neutral, single-occupant restroom to its building out of sensitivity to people with gender confusion. Is this proposal righteous, loving, and wise? Why or why not?

15. In a culture of great confusion about gender and sexuality, how can Christians grow in wisdom and godliness regarding these areas of life?

12

The Constitution of Man, Part 1

Unity and Duality

When God created the heavens and the earth, he made a dual realm populated with spirits above and plants and animals below. However, there is one creature who shares in both realms. Herman Bavinck said, "Creation culminates in humanity where the spiritual and material world are joined together."[1] This is part of the wonder of man: he is a creature both physical and spiritual, with feet planted on the earth and a soul that aspires to heaven.

The biblical view of man, then, contradicts the notion, found in various Greek philosophies, that body and spirit are polar opposites that cannot coexist happily. The Holy Scriptures depict man as body and spirit joined in blessed union by the will of the good Creator. Unlike pantheism or panentheism, this conjunction does not make man divine or his soul a particle of God, but it does qualify him to be a created image of God on earth.[2]

The view that man consists of body and soul is rooted deeply in the orthodox Christian tradition. The Athanasian Creed confesses the incarnate Christ as "perfect God and perfect man, of a reasonable soul and human flesh subsisting," for "the reasonable soul and flesh is one man."[3] The

---

1. Bavinck, *Reformed Dogmatics*, 2:511.
2. See Laidlaw, *The Bible Doctrine of Man*, 59.
3. *The Three Forms of Unity*, 10–11.

Council of Chalcedon also set forth the one person of Jesus Christ as "truly God and truly man, of a reasonable soul and body," for without body and soul he would be less than human.[4] The body-soul view of man, crystallized in the doctrine of the incarnation, continued in the Reformed confessional tradition.[5] The Heidelberg Catechism (LD 22, Q. 57) expresses the Christian hope "that not only my soul after this life shall be immediately taken up to Christ its Head; but also, that this my body, being raised by the power of Christ, shall be reunited with my soul, and made like unto the glorious body of Christ."[6]

Human nature consists of a complex of interconnected parts. How are these parts related? Can we even speak of them as parts? It seems best to see the human constitution as a curious tension between unity of personal function and duality of body and soul.

Biblical Terminology for Aspects of the Human Constitution

The Holy Scriptures use a variety of words to describe the components or dimensions of human existence. Passing by terms for body parts that do not have major significance for the doctrine of anthropology, we list here several of the most important words with their basic meanings (we will explore their theological significance later). We offer only a sampling of Scripture references; for more, please consult the lexicons and theological dictionaries.

1. "Breath" (Hebrew *neshamah*) is a term for biological life in its transience and fragility.[7] However, the word is occasionally used for the inner psychological life (Prov. 20:27).

2. "Soul" (Hebrew *nephesh*) has a wide variety of meanings, ranging from animal life to personhood to inward feelings.[8] A dead "body" can be expressed as a dead "soul" (*nephesh*).[9] "Soul" can refer to someone's life (Ex. 21:23; Judg. 16:16), even to the point of being connected to the blood (Deut. 12:23). In Leviticus 24:17, "killeth any man" is literally "killeth a soul of man." In some texts, the "soul" is the subject of physical appetites,

---

4. Philip Schaff, ed., *The Creeds of Christendom*, 3 vols. (New York: Harper and Brothers, 1877), 2:62.

5. Belgic Confession (Art. 18), in *The Three Forms of Unity*, 34; Heidelberg Catechism (Q. 1, 11, 26, 34, 37, 57, 69, 76, 109, 118, 121), in *The Three Forms of Unity*, 68, 71, 76, 79, 80, 86, 90, 93, 107, 110, 112; Westminster Shorter Catechism (Q. 22), in *Reformed Confessions*, 4:356.

6. *The Three Forms of Unity*, 86.

7. Gen. 2:7; 7:22; cf. Isa. 2:22.

8. Gen. 1:20–21, 24, 30; 2:7, 19; 12:5; 14:21; 23:8; 42:21.

9. Lev. 21:11; Num. 6:6; 9:6–7, 10.

such as hunger and thirst.[10] Even beasts have a *nephesh* in this sense (Prov. 12:10). The New Testament term translated as "soul" (Greek *psychē*) is of similar meaning. Those who aimed to kill the child Jesus sought his "life" (*psychē*, Matt. 2:20), and anxiety about one's "life" (*psychē*) can refer to worry about food and clothing (6:25). The opposite of saving "life" (*psychē*) is to kill (Mark 3:4). However, "soul" (*psychē*) can also refer to something that survives death (Matt. 10:28).

3. "Spirit" (Hebrew *ruakh*) can mean "wind" (Gen. 3:8; 8:1). Or it can refer to the life breath of animals and mankind.[11] However, it can also refer to the inner person, with his feelings or inner strength (Gen. 26:35; 41:8; 45:26–27). Of course, it can also refer to God's Spirit (1:2) or an evil spirit (1 Sam. 16:16; 1 Kings 22:19–23). The corresponding Greek term (*pneuma*) has a similar range of meanings.[12]

4. "Heart" (Hebrew *leb* or *lebab*) refers to the inner person, with its emotions, thoughts, voluntary resolutions, moral condition before God, and spiritual orientation toward God.[13] Likewise, the equivalent term in the New Testament (Greek *kardia*) refers to the center of one's personal existence, with its thoughts, feelings, and choices.[14] From the heart flows the entire life of the person in all its activity (Prov. 4:23; Mark 7:21).

5. "Reins" (plural Hebrew *kilyah*) means kidneys (Ex. 29:13, 22; Lev. 3:4, 10, 15), but is also used of the inward thoughts, feelings, and moral dispositions, much like "heart."[15] This latter usage also appears in the New Testament (Greek *nephros*, Rev. 2:23).

6. "Mind" (Greek *nous*) can translate "heart" (Hebrew *leb* or *lebab*) in the Old Testament, though it is not common.[16] In the New Testament, it refers to the understanding,[17] considered not as bare intellect but as a center of spiritual depravity or godly renewal.[18]

7. "Flesh" (Hebrew *bashar*) means skin, meat, or other soft tissue of the body, or the whole body,[19] but it can also refer more broadly to

---

10. Deut. 12:20; Ps. 107:9; Prov. 25:25; 27:7.
11. Gen. 6:17; 7:15, 22; Job 10:12; 12:10; 27:3; 34:14–15; Pss. 104:29–30; 146:4; Isa. 38:16; 42:5.
12. Matt. 1:18; Mark 1:23, 26; Luke 1:47; John 3:8; 19:30; Rom. 1:9; James 2:26.
13. Gen. 6:5–6; 8:21; 17:17; 20:5–6; 24:45; 27:41; 1 Kings 11:2–4.
14. Matt. 5:28; 9:4; Rom. 2:29; 10:1, 6; 1 Pet. 3:4.
15. Pss. 7:9; 16:7; 26:2; 73:21; Prov. 23:16; Jer. 11:20; 12:2; 17:10; 20:12.
16. Ex. 7:23; Josh. 14:7; Job 7:17; Isa. 10:7, 12.
17. Rom. 14:5; 1 Cor. 14:14; Rev. 13:18; 17:9.
18. Luke 24:45; Rom. 1:28; 7:23, 25; 12:2; Eph. 4:17, 23; cf. Rom. 8:6–8; Col. 1:21.
19. Gen. 2:21, 23–24; 17:11.

humanity or animals in their entirety,[20] often with the connotation of weakness.[21] The New Testament counterpart (Greek *sarx*) embraces these meanings,[22] as well as the idea of humanity in its sinfulness.[23]

8. "Bone" (Hebrew *'etsem*) refers to the hard skeletal matter of the body (Gen. 2:23), but it can also stand for a person's strength (Job 21:24) or emotional condition.[24] The Greek equivalent (*osteon*) in the New Testament refers only to the physical bones.[25]

9. "Body" (Greek *sōma*) in the Septuagint translation of the Old Testament, aside from references to corpses, often renders "flesh" (Hebrew *bashar*).[26] In the New Testament, this term means the physical body composed of eyes, hands, and so on, sustained by food, threatened by illness, and subject to death.[27] However, as we will see, "body" can also refer to the whole person, and plays an important role in spirituality and holiness.[28]

In light of this survey of terms, we find an overlap among words we might suppose to be distinct in meaning. Terms such as "soul" and "spirit" can refer to the physical life, and words such as "bone" and "kidneys" can refer to mental and psychological qualities. How are we to account for these phenomena?

The Functional Unity of the Human Person

The Bible represents human nature as a system that functions with considerable unity. In other words, human activities cannot be neatly parceled up between different parts of the human constitution. For example, Christ taught that God's greatest commandment requires the engagement of every aspect of who we are: "And thou shalt love the Lord thy God with all thy heart, and with all thy soul, and with all thy mind, and with all thy strength: this is the first commandment" (Mark 12:30). Paul similarly prayed for the sanctification of the entire person: "And the very God of peace sanctify you wholly; and I pray God your whole spirit and soul and

---

20. Jer. 32:27. See "all flesh" in Gen. 6:12–13, 17, 19; 7:15–16, 21; 8:17, 21; 9:11, 15–17.
21. 2 Chron. 32:8; Pss. 56:4; 78:39; Isa. 31:3; 40:6; Jer. 17:5.
22. Luke 14:38; John 1:14; Rom. 3:20; 6:19.
23. Rom. 7:5, 18, 25; 8:1, 3–9, 12–13; Gal. 5:13, 16–17, 19, 24; 6:8.
24. Pss. 6:2; 31:10; 32:3; 35:10; 51:8; 102:3; Prov. 15:30.
25. Matt. 23:27; Luke 24:39; John 19:36; Eph. 5:30; Heb. 11:22.
26. Lev. 6:10; 14:9; 15:2, 3, 13, 16; etc. For the Hebrew semantic range of "corpse" translated as *sōma*, see *TDNT*, 7:1044–45. On "flesh" (*bashar*) as the Hebrew equivalent of "body," see Robert H. Gundry, *Sōma in Biblical Theology: With Emphasis on Pauline Anthropology* (Grand Rapids, MI: Zondervan, 1987), 118.
27. Matt. 5:29–30; 6:25; Mark 5:29; 14:8; 15:43.
28. Rom. 6:6, 12; 12:1.

body be preserved blameless unto the coming of our Lord Jesus Christ" (1 Thess. 5:23).

This may surprise people who are accustomed to thinking of holiness solely in terms of the soul or man's spiritual dimension. However, the Bible has a comprehensive approach to spirituality that includes the body. It calls us to cleanse "flesh and spirit" for the sake of holiness (2 Cor. 7:1) and commends a concern for being "holy both in body and in spirit" (1 Cor. 7:34). David wrote in Psalm 63:1, "O God, thou art my God; early will I seek thee: my soul thirsteth for thee, my flesh longeth for thee in a dry and thirsty land, where no water is."

This functional unity of man's constitution explains why the Bible can use the term "soul" to represent the whole person. When we read of man's original creation in Genesis 2:7, the text does not say that man "received" a soul or "possessed" a soul, but that "man became a living soul." In some texts, "soul" is best understood as "self."[29] In other texts, a stated number of "souls" means that number of people.[30]

Conversely, the Bible can use the term "body" to stand for the whole person as well, especially the person as viewed in his concrete existence and practical conduct (James 3:2, 6). When Paul urges believers to "present your bodies" to God as living sacrifices (Rom. 12:1), he does not merely mean for us to offer outward worship to the exclusion of our inner persons, but to offer up all that we are. Christ offered his "body" for our sins, but in so doing he offered his entire human nature as an act of obedience to God's will (Heb. 10:9–10). The body is so closely identified with the person that some Scripture passages speak of burying a person's "body" (Matt. 14:12; Mark 15:43, 45), but others speak of burying the person himself.[31]

The Bible's employment of "body" and "soul" in a holistic manner does not make the terms identical in meaning with each other or with the whole person, but reflects the involvement of the whole man in life, a functional and vital unity in the human constitution—the outer man of the body and the inner man of the heart (Rom. 6:12–14, 17; 12:1).[32]

Therefore, we must view man as a living unity. God did not make man to be a personal soul that merely inhabits a body, but a person who consists of a united body and soul. William Perkins said that, unlike angels,

---

29. See Num. 35:3–12; Jer. 3:11; 37:9; Luke 12:19 in the original languages.
30. Deut. 10:22; Jer. 52:29–30; Acts 2:41; 7:14; 27:37; 1 Pet. 3:20.
31. Matt. 8:21; Luke 16:22; Acts 2:29; 5:9–10; 1 Cor. 15:4.
32. Murray, *The Epistle to the Romans*, 2:110–11; Gundry, *Sōma in Biblical Theology*, 29–30.

men have souls "united with bodies, so as both shall make one whole and entire person."[33] Antonius Thysius said that in speaking of human nature, "We do not mean the body and the soul separately but something that is composed from both, that is from the rational soul and the body which a very tight and close bond binds together into one nature, united in one person."[34]

Recognition of the functional unity of the human constitution allows for the great mutual influence that body and soul have upon each other. Brain injuries, sickness, hormonal changes, and other physical conditions affect our thinking and emotions. It seems significant that the Lord provided Elijah with food and sleep before talking with him about his fear and despair (1 Kings 19:4–7). David Murray writes that depression and anxiety can arise from sin, and yet they "can also be the result, not of personal sin, but of living in a fallen body in a fallen world."[35] From the other side, our mental beliefs influence our attitudes and feelings, which in turn influence our physical health. Proverbs 17:22 observes, "A merry heart doeth good like a medicine: but a broken spirit drieth the bones." Paul says that sexually immoral behavior not only harms our spirituality, but the fornicator "sinneth against his own body" (1 Cor. 6:18). Therefore, we must live integrated lives with an awareness of body and soul. We must serve others with concern for the whole person.

The Duality of Body and Spirit (vs. Anthropological Monism)

Does this mean, then, that there is no duality in human nature, no substantial distinction between body and soul? Perspectives that say yes are called anthropological monism. In some cases, such monism is a form of materialism, a perspective in which all of reality consists of physical matter and forces. An influential early modern philosopher who advocated monistic materialism was Thomas Hobbes (1588–1679), who argued that psychological states are merely effects of physical biology. Another kind of monism says that human nature is one substance with two modes, as was taught by Baruch Spinoza.[36]

---

33. Perkins, *An Exposition of the Symbol*, in *Works*, 5:69.
34. Polyander, Walaeus, Thysius, and Rivetus, *Synopsis Purioris Theologiae*, 13.3 (1:315).
35. David P. Murray, *Christians Get Depressed Too: Hope and Help for Depressed People* (Grand Rapids, MI: Reformation Heritage Books, 2010), 63.
36. On Thomas Hobbes and Baruch Spinoza with regard to anthropological monism, see John W. Cooper, *Body, Soul, and Life Everlasting: Biblical Anthropology and the Monism-Dualism Debate* (Grand Rapids, MI: Eerdmans, 1989), 17–22.

Whereas some liberal modernists embraced an extreme dualism in which the body was not essential to complete humanity,[37] others, such as Rudolf Bultmann (1884–1976) and John A. T. Robinson (1919–1983), argued for monism based on the holistic use of "body" in the Bible.[38] However, after a careful study of the Greek term translated as "body" (*sōma*), Robert Gundry writes,

> We conclude that neither in the Pauline epistles, nor the literature of the NT outside those epistles, nor the LXX, nor extra-Biblical ancient Greek literature does the definition "whole person" find convincing support. This is not to deny that (outside the Platonic tradition) emphasis falls on the unity of man's being. But it is a unity of parts, inner and outer, rather than a monadic unity. . . . The *sōma* may *represent* the whole person simply because the *sōma* lives in union with the soul/spirit.[39]

Neoorthodox theologians also rejected the hyperdualistic stream of liberalism and embraced anthropological monism.[40] Emil Brunner identified body, soul, and spirit as "functions" and asserted that "ontologically man is a unity."[41] Karl Barth characterized the biblical view of the human person as "one whole man" while insisting that the Bible does not explain what men consist of but focuses entirely on human relationships to God.[42] As we saw in our study of God's image, however, pure functionalism is reductionistic and intellectually dissatisfying, for function must be grounded in being and structure. Man's unique capacity to represent God, relate to him, and reign as his servant on earth implies that humans have a nature not possessed by animals.

The Bible does teach that there is a distinction between man's body and soul. The Lord is "the God of the spirits of all flesh" (Num. 16:22; 27:16). God "formeth the spirit of man within him," literally "in his inward parts" (Zech. 12:1). Therefore, spirit is not identical to flesh, but is something

---

37. Erickson, *Systematic Theology*, 479–80.
38. Gundry, *Sōma in Biblical Theology*, 3–8. See Rudolf Bultmann, *Theology of the New Testament, Volume 1*, trans. Kendrick Grobel (New York: Charles Scribner's Sons, 1951), 192–203; and J. A. T. Robinson, *The Body: A Study in Pauline Thought*, Studies in Biblical Theology 5 (London: SCM, 1952). For a summary of the critique of Robinson by James Barr and others, see Erickson, *Systematic Theology*, 483–85.
39. Gundry, *Sōma in Biblical Theology*, 79–80, emphasis original.
40. Erickson, *Systematic Theology*, 481–82.
41. Brunner, *Man in Revolt*, 362–63n1, 373n3.
42. Barth, *Church Dogmatics*, III/2, sec. 46.5 (432–33).

distinctly made by God within man's body. Christ compared gaining the whole world with losing one's "soul" (*psychē*, Matt. 16:26), implying that the soul is something different from bodily health and material prosperity. Christ also contrasted his disciples' willing "spirit" (*pneuma*) with their weak "flesh" (*sarx*), where "flesh" evidently referred to physical weakness because they were falling asleep (Matt. 26:41; Mark 14:38).[43] Paul says that a person's "flesh" can suffer destruction though "the spirit may be saved" (1 Cor. 5:5).

The Bible especially distinguishes between the body and the soul in death.[44] Ecclesiastes 12:7 says, "Then shall the dust return to the earth as it was: and the spirit shall return unto God who gave it." Genesis 35:18 says that when Rachel was in the process of dying, "her soul" was "departing" or "going out" (*yats'a*). Elijah prayed for God to resurrect a dead child, saying, "Let this child's soul come into him again" (1 Kings 17:21)—literally, "return to within him" (*shub 'al qirbbo*). When Christ raised a dead girl to life, "her spirit returned" (Luke 8:55 ESV), implying that her spirit "is seen as distinct from and surviving the death of the physical body."[45] The human spirit animates the body, and "the body without the spirit is dead" (James 2:26). Charles Hodge wrote, "The relation between the two is a vital union, in such a sense as that the soul is the source of life to the body. When the soul leaves the body the latter ceases to live."[46] The Lord Jesus said that people can "kill the body, but are not able to kill the soul" (Matt. 10:28), implying that body and soul are two substances with distinct properties. The godly commit their spirits to God when they are dying (Luke 23:46; Acts 7:59; cf. Ps. 31:5). The Bible speaks of those who have died and gone to heaven as "souls" or "spirits" (Heb. 12:23; Rev. 6:9; 20:4). Hence, Paul speaks of personal existence after death as being "absent from the body" (2 Cor. 5:8).

We conclude that the Holy Scriptures warrant a belief in the functional unity and substantial duality of the human constitution. God has wedded

---

43. On Matt. 26:41, see Gundry, *Sōma in Biblical Theology*, 110–11.

44. Greg Nichols, *Lectures in Systematic Theology, Volume 2: Doctrine of Man* (Seattle: CreateSpace Independent Publishing Platform, 2017), 174–75.

45. Robert H. Stein, *Luke*, The New American Commentary 24 (Nashville: Broadman & Holman, 1992), 263. It might be argued that Luke 8:55 should be translated as "her life revived," for that appears to be the sense of the same Greek phrase, *epistrepsen to pneuma*, in Judg. 15:19 LXX. However, the latter text does not refer to raising the dead but to reviving a man *before* he died. A better parallel, while not using the exact same language, is Elijah's prayer for God to raise a boy from the dead (*epistraphētō . . . hē psyche*, 3 Kingdoms 17:21 LXX [1 Kings 17:21]).

46. Hodge, *Systematic Theology*, 2:45.

together the body and spirit in man in such a way that death unnaturally separates them, and man's destiny will not be complete until body and soul are reunited in the resurrection. Body and spirit interpenetrate and influence each other so profoundly that the biblical terminology for the human constitution overlaps significantly. Human life cannot be compartmentalized. However, the Bible also teaches that man consists of two distinct substances. The body is not identical to the soul, and the spirit cannot be reduced to a function of the body.

Objections to the Duality of the Human Constitution

A number of objections are raised to the view that man consists of a unified functional personality in two substances: body and soul.

1. *Biblical duality is merely functional.* It is objected that Scripture passages contrasting body and soul reflect different functions or dimensions of man's life, but do not indicate that the body and soul are different substances.

In reply, we note that the Bible teaches that man's spirit or soul is not destroyed by physical death, but the person continues in conscious existence, albeit apart from the body until the resurrection.[47] We will demonstrate the immortality of the soul in the next chapter. Here we draw the conclusion that if the soul or spirit of man survives the death of the body and continues in a separate existence for a time, then that soul or spirit must be a distinct entity from the body. Therefore, anthropological monism is false and undermines Christian hope in the glory of the church triumphant in heaven even now. John Calvin rightly said that the soul is "an immortal yet created essence," not just "a force divinely infused into bodies" or "transient energy."[48]

2. *Biblical holism must control the entire doctrine of man.* The popularity of monism among twentieth-century scholars has exerted some sway over Reformed theologians. For example, G. C. Berkouwer said, "It appears clearly, then, that Scripture never pictures man as a dualistic, or pluralistic being, but that in all its varied expressions the whole man comes to the fore."[49] Anthony Hoekema acknowledged the biblical doctrine of the human person's continued existence after death and recognized that

---

47. Pss. 17:15; 31:5; 73:24–26; Isa. 14:9–10; Eccles. 12:7; Matt. 10:28; 17:3; 22:31–32; Luke 16:22–23; 23:43, 46; Acts 7:59; 2 Cor. 5:6, 8; Phil. 1:21–23; Heb. 12:23.
48. Calvin, *Institutes*, 1.15.2.
49. Berkouwer, *Man: The Image of God*, 203. See his chapter "The Whole Man" (194–233).

the Bible can speak of that existence in terms of "souls" and "spirits."[50] However, influenced by biblical scholars such as Robinson and theologians such as Berkouwer, Hoekema rejected "the view that man consists of body and soul" and opted for what he calls "psychosomatic unity."[51]

The position of Berkouwer and Hoekema is very puzzling. First, the fact that the Bible sometimes uses the terms "body" and "soul" in a holistic manner does not require that it always do so, nor that the whole person be their essential meaning. In accord with the Bible, we should teach man's unity as a holistic being, yet also teach that the soul or spirit continues after death. Second, it is difficult to understand how one can deny that man consists of two substances, soul and body, and simultaneously affirm that believers live in Christ's presence after their bodies die. If there is no distinct substance to the human spirit, then the death of the body is the end of the man. Therefore, we judge Berkouwer's and Hoekema's treatments to be confusing. We affirm that the soul is an immaterial substance joined to the body in life but immortal in death.

3. *Duality leads to a divided worldview.* Another objection against human duality as body and soul is that such a doctrine sets up a split worldview that divides human life between the secular (body) and the sacred (soul). Such a mental dichotomy can deter Christians from the application of biblical principles to the so-called secular realm of science, politics, and so forth. It can blind Christians to the impact of physical factors upon our spiritual lives, such as a lack of sleep and proper nutrition. A divided worldview can also leave Christians vulnerable to ungodly ideas promoted in a supposedly objective and neutral field of study.

In response, we recognize that these are real dangers. However, such a divided worldview does not arise from the biblical doctrine of human duality. John Cooper writes, "It is hard to see why there is a causal connection between the two. Why should believing that I will be with Christ from death until bodily resurrection lead me to think that politics or intellectual activity or anything else in life is religiously neutral?"[52] Here it is important to remember that the Bible affirms both duality and unity. The human body and soul are both created by God and therefore are fundamentally good and exist for God's glory. They are organically intertwined

---

50. Hoekema, *Created in God's Image*, 220–22. He cited Matt. 10:28; Heb. 12:23; 1 Pet. 3:18; Rev. 6:9.
51. Hoekema, *Created in God's Image*, 209–10, 216–17.
52. Cooper, *Body, Soul, and Life Everlasting*, 201.

and function as one until separated at death, and this is an unnatural condition remedied by the resurrection. There is no basis here for a secular-sacred dualism.

4. *A combination of unity and duality is not plausible.* Another objection is that it is difficult to understand how humanity can exist in unity and duality without sacrificing one or the other.

Millard Erickson proposes a helpful analogy to human unity and duality in a chemical compound.[53] Let us illustrate with salt consisting of sodium-chloride. Sodium in itself is a metal that reacts violently with water, while chlorine is a poisonous gas. However, salt is not a metal box holding a gas. Rather, salt consists of chlorine and sodium atoms intermingled and bound together to form crystals. Salt has qualities very different from either individual element, qualities that make salt tasty, soluble in water, and useful for life. In popular language, we sometimes refer to salt content simply as "sodium," such as in the phrases "reduced sodium" and "low sodium," even though sodium is only one element in the compound.[54]

Similarly, human nature is not a body holding a soul like a box holds a gas. Rather, body and soul are intermingled and bound together to form one compound person who is neither merely a body nor merely a spirit, but something more. If the body and soul are separated by death, then the body is unstable and quickly breaks down, whereas God sends the soul to another place. However, joined together, the body and soul form a living image of God, a human person with qualities different from both angels and animals. We conclude from this analogy that this doctrine is a plausible concept.

However, we acknowledge that all questions about bodies and souls press against the boundaries of our understanding. Human unity in duality is both a mystery and a necessity. It should not surprise us that men stumble at this amazing doctrine. John Flavel (1628–1691) said, "It is a most astonishing mystery to see heaven and earth married together in one person; the dust of the ground and an immortal spirit clasping each other with such dear embraces and tender love."[55] Yet without this personal unity in duality, mankind would lack the infrastructure of the image of

---

53. Erickson, *Systematic Theology*, 492.

54. Of course, nutritional science teaches us that there are other sources of sodium in food, such as baking soda and monosodium glutamate, but in popular usage "reduced sodium" is roughly the equivalent of "less salt."

55. John Flavel, *Pneumatologia: A Treatise of the Soul of Man*, in *The Works of John Flavel*, 6 vols. (1820; repr., Edinburgh: Banner of Truth, 1968), 2:493.

God on earth, the fundamental capacities to know, choose, and act as is necessary to live as sons of God and royal stewards of the world.

The Human Constitution Contrasted to Those of Angels and Animals

At this point, it will be helpful in our consideration of human nature to contrast it to both heavenly beings and other earthly creatures. This will clarify man's distinct constitution as a combination of flesh and spirit.

First, in some respects, *men and angels* have much in common. Both were created as sons of God.[56] God made both to serve him according to his will, and both are morally accountable to him.[57] Men consist of a compound of body and spirit. Angels are spirits,[58] yet they may manifest themselves in the form of a physical body, even one that can receive food.[59] The spirits of deceased believers join with the angels in the heavenly city (Heb. 12:22–23). When God will raise his people from the dead, in some ways they will be like angels, for the resurrected saints will never die again and will no longer marry (Luke 20:34–36).

However, men and angels are also quite different. Though angels may assume bodies to fulfill temporary missions on earth, such bodies are not essential to their nature, which is entirely spiritual. Flavel said, "They abide in these bodies, as we do in an inn, for a night or short season."[60] However, the human body is essential to our full identity and function. Thysius said, "The nature of the human soul is not like the angels (who are also spirits), because angels are essences that are distinguished from body to such a degree that they do not tend by nature to have a body; but the soul, on the other hand, does have that tendency."[61] It is interesting to note that while the Bible does speak of angels as spirits (Heb. 1:14), it does not appear to ever refer to angels as "souls" (plural Hebrew *nephesh*, Greek *psychē*).

Consequently, angels and humans have distinct natures and destinies. Angels cannot die (Luke 20:36), but men can and do die (Gen. 2:17; Heb. 9:27). God blessed angelic nature with swiftness and power that men do not possess in this age (Ps. 104:4). Man is thus somewhat lower than the angels (Heb. 2:7, 9). However, God blessed human nature with the high-

---

56. Job 1:6; 2:1; 38:7; Luke 3:38.
57. Gen. 2:15–17; Ps. 103:20; Jude 5–6.
58. 1 Kings 22:21; Ps. 104:4; Acts 23:8–9.
59. Gen. 18:1–8, 22; 19:1, 15.
60. Flavel, *Pneumatologia*, in *Works*, 2:511.
61. Polyander, Walaeus, Thysius, and Rivetus, *Synopsis Purioris Theologiae*, 13.17 (1:321).

est honor in the incarnation. Christ did not take on the nature of angels to redeem them from their sins, but he took on human nature to save his covenant people (v. 16). God did not subject the world to come to the angels, but to the incarnate Lord Jesus and the sons and daughters whom he will bring to glory (vv. 5, 9–10). Remarkably, though God made angels superior by nature, in the end God has made them the servants of those whom he saves by grace (Heb. 1:14; cf. 1 Cor. 6:3).

Second, when we compare *men and animals*, we also find many similarities. Both have bodies derived from the earth.[62] Both are male and female, and multiply through sexual reproduction.[63] Both have "spirit" in the sense of "breath" or biological life, and both die.[64] Both animals and men may be called "souls" in that they are living, animate creatures.[65]

However, God created man alone in God's image and gave man dominion over the animals.[66] The Bible attributes properties to human beings that it does not attribute to the animals: rationality, volition, moral agency and accountability, and immortality. Evidently, the soul or spirit of man is of another nature than the soul or spirit of beasts. Each man, woman, or child is worth more than many animals.[67] The human body has a sacred quality to it because of God's image, so that the unlawful destruction of human life is a great crime, whereas men may kill and eat animals (Gen. 9:3–6). God is kind to the animals and provides for their physical needs,[68] but he does not enter into familial relationships with them or call them sons and daughters of God, as he does human beings.[69] The Bible often speaks of judgment day for men and angels, but never for animals. There is no indication in the Bible that individual animals continue to exist after death, but it clearly teaches that man's soul is immortal according to the will of its Creator.

---

62. Gen. 1:24; 2:7; 3:19; Eccles. 12:7.
63. Gen. 1:22, 27–28; 6:19; 7:3, 9, 16; 9:1.
64. Ps. 49:12, 20; Eccles. 3:19–21.
65. Gen. 1:20–21, 24, 30; 2:7, 19; 9:4–5, 10, 12, 15–16. In Aristotelian philosophy, life was categorized as (1) a vegetative soul, such as in plants, which is the vital power of growth and reproduction; (2) a sensitive soul, such as in animals, which adds to the vegetative the power to employ physical senses and to respond to sense perception; and (3) a rational soul, found in men and spirits, which adds to the vegetative and sensitive the power to consider intellectual objects. Aquinas, *Summa Theologica*, Pt. 1, Q. 78, Art. 1. This distinction was adopted by Brakel, *The Christian's Reasonable Service*, 1:310–11. It does not reflect a modern scientific understanding of biological life, for plants do sense their environment and respond to it.
66. Gen. 1:26–28; 9:2–6; Ps. 8:6–8.
67. Matt. 6:26; 10:30; 12:12.
68. Pss. 104:10–30; 145:9; Matt. 6:26.
69. Luke 3:38; John 1:12; Rom. 8:15; 2 Cor. 6:18; Gal. 4:5.

Sing to the Lord

Longing for God with Body and Soul

O Lord of Hosts, how lovely the place where thou dost dwell!
Thy tabernacles holy in pleasantness excel.
My soul is longing, fainting, Jehovah's courts to see;
My heart and flesh are crying, O living God, for thee.

Blest who thy house inhabit, they ever give thee praise;
Blest all whom thou dost strengthen, who love the sacred ways.
So they from strength unwearied go forward unto strength,
Till they appear in Zion before the Lord at length.

O hear, Lord God of Jacob, to me an answer yield;
The face of thine Anointed, behold, O God our shield.
One day excels a thousand if spent thy courts within;
I'll choose thy threshold, rather than dwell in tents of sin.

Our sun and shield, Jehovah, will grace and glory give;
No good will he deny them that uprightly do live.
O God of Hosts, Jehovah, how blest is ev'ry one
Whose confidence reposes on thee, O Lord, alone.

Psalm 84
Tune: Llangloffan
Trinity Hymnal—Baptist Edition, No. 305

Questions for Meditation or Discussion

1. What are some examples in the Bible of how "soul" and "spirit" can refer to physical life?
2. What are some examples in the Bible of how "bone" and "body" can represent the whole person, not just the physical body?
3. What do the authors mean by the "functional unity" of the human constitution?
4. How does the Bible testify to the functional unity of each human person?
5. How does the Bible testify to the substantial duality of the body and soul?
6. Briefly explain the four objections to body-soul duality and how the authors refute them.

7. How does the human constitution compare to and contrast with that of angels?

8. How does the human constitution compare to and contrast with that of animals?

Questions for Deeper Reflection

9. Interact with Robert Gundry's conclusion that the Greek word translated as "body" (*sōma*), while it sometimes can represent the whole person, does not in itself mean "whole person." Is this conclusion warranted by the biblical text and sound reasoning? Why or why not?

10. If the soul had no distinct reality apart from the physical body, then what would that imply about human responsibility? What would it imply about life after death?

11. What implications does the functional unity of the human body and soul have for counseling people who suffer from mental and emotional problems?

13

The Constitution of Man, Part 2

Body and Soul

In the last chapter, we argued that God has revealed in his Word that human beings consist of two substances, body and soul, joined together in personal, vital, and functional unity. In this chapter, we will consider what the Bible teaches about the body and soul. It is important to remember throughout this discussion that God has wedded body and soul together. Though we may discuss them separately, only the unnatural judgment of death actually separates them, and that only for a time until the resurrection. We must view both body and soul not as something that people have but as something that people are.

The Human Body
The visible element of man's compound nature is his body, with all its various tissues, parts, and organs joined together in biological systems. The scientific study of human biology is a glorious task. As theologians, we focus upon three great themes of the Bible relating to the body: the doctrines of creation, sanctification, and glorification. It might be questioned why a systematic theology should pay any attention to the body at all. Greg Allison writes, "The normal state of human existence is an embodied existence."[1] In

---

1. Greg R. Allison, "Toward a Theology of Human Embodiment," *Southern Baptist Journal of Theology* 13, no. 2 (2009): 5 (full article, 4–17).

other words, we cannot escape our bodies in this life or in the age to come, and it is not God's will that we should try. Therefore, we must have a biblical perspective on the human body.

The Goodness of the Body as God's Creation

The human body, though made of elements found in the earth, did not arise by a natural process but by the supernatural work of God (Gen. 2:7). The body is "very good" (1:31). Contrary to some streams of thought, the body is not evil, a hindrance to our spirits, or less glorifying to God than our souls. The body and its natural functions, such as sex in marriage and the enjoyment of food, are to be received as gifts of the Creator (1 Tim. 4:1–3). Paul explained, "For every creature of God is good, and nothing to be refused, if it be received with thanksgiving: for it is sanctified by the word of God and prayer" (vv. 4–5). We should be grateful for our bodies.

David reflects upon the Lord's personal involvement in his life, beginning with his conception in the womb (Ps. 139). He marvels at how God "covered"—literally "knit together" (*sakak*)—his body in the womb (v. 13). The picture is of delicate and skillful artistry (cf. Job 10:11). David then writes, "I will praise thee, for I am fearfully and wonderfully made: marvellous are thy works; and that my soul knoweth right well" (Psalm 139:14). "Fearfully" (*niphal* participle of *yare*) means "inspiring fear or awe." "Wonderfully made" (*niphal* of *palah*) means "set apart or distinguished as special." "Marvellous" (*niphal* of *pala*), a similar-sounding but different word than "wonderfully made," is a term used of miracles—that is, unusual acts of divine power. Man's body is a wonder of God's miraculous creativity. John Calvin said, "The human body shows itself to be a composition so ingenious that its Artificer is rightly judged a wonder-worker."[2] It is no mere machine that we use (or abuse). It is a work of sacred art, a display of God's glory.

The goodness and value of the human body overthrows negative views of our physical life and the activities that sustain it. Proper nutrition and healthy exercise are not a waste of time, but are aspects of wise stewardship that pleases God, who entrusted our bodies to us. Loving sexual intimacy within marriage is not dirty or defiling, but is a beautiful gift of God for delightful companionship, producing children, and guarding us against fornication. Vocations such as construction,

---

2. Calvin, *Institutes*, 1.5.2.

farming, and the skilled trades are just as noble as more academic jobs, such as religious teaching or scientific research.[3] The Reformers and Puritans have much to teach us here, for they understood that God assigns each person a calling or vocation in society (1 Cor. 7:17, 20), and we depend upon each other in community like parts of a body for our shared prosperity.[4]

The Importance of the Body for Holiness

The human body plays a crucial part in the process of sanctification. The battle against sin engages the body. Paul writes, "Let not sin therefore reign in your mortal body, that ye should obey it in the lusts thereof" (Rom. 6:12). The Holy Spirit does not lead us in an otherworldly mystical path, but in the practical sanctification of the way we use our physical bodies. Paul says, "For if ye live after the flesh, ye shall die: but if ye through the Spirit do mortify the deeds of the body, ye shall live" (8:13). The body is to be consecrated to God for his worship in all of life. We read in 12:1, "I beseech you therefore, brethren, by the mercies of God, that ye present your bodies a living sacrifice, holy, acceptable unto God, which is your reasonable service."

Nothing highlights the significance of a believer's body for holiness more than its union with Christ. A Christian's union with Christ is not physical but by the Holy Spirit (1 Cor. 6:17). However, the Spirit does not merely unite our souls to Christ, but "your bodies are the members of Christ" (v. 15). Just as God's Son took a full human nature to himself in the incarnation, including "flesh and blood" (Heb. 2:14, 17), so the Spirit joins both body and soul of his people to Christ. Christ purchased the entire person of the believer with his death so that "your body is the temple of the Holy Ghost. . . . Therefore, glorify God in your body" (1 Cor. 6:19–20). The body is "for the Lord" (v. 13). All things about the body, from arranging our hair to eating our food, should be directed to glorifying God and doing good to others (10:31; 11:14–15).

---

3. Cooper, *Body, Soul, and Life Everlasting*, 203.
4. Ronald S. Wallace, *Calvin's Doctrine of the Christian Life* (Tyler, TX: Geneva Divinity School Press, 1982), 148–56; William Perkins, *A Treatise of the Vocations, or, Callings of Men* (London: John Legat, 1603), 3, 13, 22–23, 28; William Gouge, *Building a Godly Home, Volume 1, A Holy Vision for Family Life*, ed. Scott Brown and Joel R. Beeke (Grand Rapids, MI: Reformation Heritage Books, 2013), 18–19; Richard Steele, *The Tradesman's Calling* (London: for J. D. by Samuel Spring, 1684), 1; and Stephen Innes, *Creating the Commonwealth: The Economic Culture of Puritan New England* (New York: W. W. Norton, 1995), 7.

Union with Christ both honors the body and places it under his headship. We do not find true holiness by a harsh asceticism, but by an experiential communion with Christ in his death (Col. 2:19–23). Appropriating their union with the risen Lord by faith, believers lift their hearts above mere physical gratification to seek heavenly glory with Christ and to put to death every motion of sin as it seeks to misuse and abuse the body (3:1–5). Like athletes pursuing a glorious reward, they strive to bring their bodies "into subjection" to the will of God (1 Cor. 9:27). Yet they do not treat their bodies as enemies, but as God's creations, designed to glorify him.

The Salvation of the Body in Christian Hope

The body is not a cocoon from which the soul must escape to fly higher. The body participates in eternal life. Comparing the body to clothing and a tent, Paul writes, "If so be that being clothed we shall not be found naked. For we that are in this tabernacle do groan, being burdened: not for that we would be unclothed, but clothed upon, that mortality might be swallowed up of life" (2 Cor. 5:3–4). The Christian hope is not to get rid of the body ("be unclothed"), but for the body to be made immortal ("swallowed up of life"; cf. Isa. 25:8).

The bodies of all people have an eternal destiny. Though many have returned to dust, not one will fail to rise at the resurrection, "both of the just and unjust" (Acts 24:15). Christ said, "Marvel not at this: for the hour is coming, in the which all that are in the graves shall hear his voice, and shall come forth; they that have done good, unto the resurrection of life; and they that have done evil, unto the resurrection of damnation" (John 5:28–29). The bodies of the wicked, reunited with their souls, shall receive Christ's sentence of condemnation and be cast into the torments of hell (Matt. 5:29–30; 10:28). However, the righteous have a better hope.

When Christ returns in glory, he will "change our vile body, that it may be fashioned like unto his glorious body, according to the working whereby he is able even to subdue all things unto himself" (Phil. 3:21). The phrase "vile body" may also be translated as "lowly body" (ESV), for it does not denigrate the body as inherently unclean, but literally means "the body of our humiliation" or "low estate" (*to sōma tēs tapeinōseōs hēmōn*). Just as Christ "humbled" (*tapeinoō*) himself but was exalted to glory (2:8–9), so those united to him will be lifted up from their body's present state of humiliation to share in his incarnate glory. Our bond with Christ is the Spirit, and that same Spirit will bring believers into Christ's resurrection life (Rom. 8:11). This transformation will bring us into the full experience of our relationship to God as his sons, for the full glory of our "adoption" includes "the redemption of our body" (v. 23). The Lord will bring our dying or dead bodies from corruption to incorruption, from dishonor to glory, from weakness to power, from natural life to spiritual life (1 Cor. 15:42–44). This glorious Christian hope enables the believer to rejoice: "O death, where is thy sting? O grave, where is thy victory? The sting of death is sin; and the strength of sin is the law. But thanks be to God, which giveth us the victory through our Lord Jesus Christ" (vv. 55–57).

The Human Soul

We cannot directly observe souls or spirits. We have an immediate experience of the function of our own souls through our thoughts and affections. However, we cannot see or tangibly feel the souls of men or detect angelic spirits through scientific instruments. John Flavel quoted Athanasius (c. 297–373) as saying, "Three things are unknown to men according to their essence, viz. God, angels, and the souls of men."[5] This wraps our subject in mystery. Martin Luther admitted, "We are still incapable of giving a definition of the soul."[6]

Theologians have offered helpful explanations of the soul. Calvin said, "The soul is an incorporeal substance . . . set in the body . . . not only that it may animate all its parts . . . but also that it may hold the first place in ruling man's life . . . to arouse him to honor God."[7] Flavel wrote, "The soul of man is a vital, spiritual, and immortal substance, endowed with an understanding, will, and various affections; created with an inclination to the body, and infused therein by the Lord."[8] Wilhelmus à Brakel said, "The soul is a spiritual, incorporeal, invisible, intangible, and immortal personal entity adorned with intellect and will."[9] These definitions are helpful, but they primarily tell us what the soul is *not* and how it *functions*, but not what it *is* in its essence.

---

5. Athanasius, cited in Flavel, *Pneumatologia*, in *Works*, 2:489.
6. Luther, *Lectures on Genesis*, in *LW*, 1:13 (Gen. 1:2).
7. Calvin, *Institutes*, 1.15.6.
8. Flavel, *Pneumatologia*, in *Works*, 2:495.
9. Brakel, *The Christian's Reasonable Service*, 1:310.

We know certain truths about the human soul because God has revealed them in his Word. However, we must approach the subject of the human spirit with a measure of epistemic reserve, not rushing to rationalistic conclusions but clinging to the teaching of the Scriptures.

The Immortality of the Human Soul

The soul of man evidences its distinct existence from the body most clearly in what the Bible teaches about death. Whereas the body is mortal, the soul is immortal. We do not use the word *immortal* here in the sense of absolute immortality by nature, which belongs to God alone (1 Tim. 6:16); in the sense of eternal life in communion with God, which is a gift of grace (2 Tim. 1:10); or to imply that God could not annihilate the soul if he so chose, for nothing is impossible with the Creator (Jer. 32:17). We are not affirming the Greek doctrine of the immortality of the soul, with its belief in the eternal preexistence of the soul and its cycle of reincarnation,[10] for God created man in the beginning (Gen. 1:1, 26; 2:7), and after death comes judgment (Heb. 9:27). We are also not saying that the soul is immune from the experience of death, for it undergoes the process of the body's dying and then its separation from that body at death. Thus, the Bible speaks of people dying, not just their bodies dying. The immortality of the human soul means that though death destroys the body and returns it to dust, physical death does not and cannot destroy the soul.

Christ taught the immortality of the soul when he referred to men as "them which kill the body, but are not able to kill the soul" (Matt. 10:28). The body's life can be extinguished by human means, but no human act can kill the soul. This statement would be nonsense if "soul" (*psychē*) here simply meant "life." The soul is different from the body, and they have different natures. The body is mortal, but the soul is immortal, not subject to death.

Proponents of annihilationism or conditional immortality object that Christ went on to say, "Fear him which is able to destroy both soul and body in hell" (Matt. 10:28). The Greek word translated as "destroy" (*apollymi*) here can mean "to cause to die" (2:13). Therefore, the objector says, the wicked soul will die when God annihilates it in the consuming fires of hell.[11]

---

10. Plato, *Phaedo*, 71–72, 77–78, in *Plato, Volume 1, Euthyphro, Apology, Crito, Phaedo, Phaedrus*, trans. H. N. Fowler, Loeb Classical Library (New York: Macmillan, 1908), 243, 257, 267.

11. Clark Pinnock, "The Conditional View," in *Four Views on Hell*, ed. William Crockett (Grand Rapids, MI: Zondervan, 1992), 146; and Edward William Fudge, "The Case for Conditionalism,"

In response, we would point out, first, that the word "destroy" (*apol-lymi*) can mean "ruin," such as in Matthew 9:17: "Neither do men put new wine into old bottles: else the bottles break, and the wine runneth out, and the bottles perish [*apollymi*]: but they put new wine into new bottles, and both are preserved." The word translated as "bottles" means "wine-skins" (ESV). The pressure of fermenting wine does not completely destroy old wineskins, but it can cause them to tear open so that they become useless for holding wine. Second, other Scripture passages clearly indicate that the fire of hell burns forever (Matt. 18:8; 25:41; Mark 9:43–48), for Christ will sentence the wicked to eternal punishment (Matt. 25:46), where "the smoke of their torment ascendeth up for ever and ever: and they have no rest day nor night" (Rev. 14:11). Therefore, the Bible does not teach that God will annihilate the wicked in hell, but that he will give them over to everlasting ruin. The soul is immortal, surviving physical death and continuing forever.

To deny the immortality of the soul is to fall into an ancient error. Luke identified the error of the Sadducees as their denial of the resurrection and existence of angels or "spirits" (*pneuma*, Acts 23:8). Christ corrected this error by saying that the God of Abraham, Isaac, and Jacob "is not the God of the dead, but of the living" (Matt. 22:32).

Other Scripture passages also indicate that the human spirit departs the body but continues in conscious existence after death. Ecclesiastes 12:7 says, "Then shall the dust return to the earth as it was: and the spirit shall return unto God who gave it." The text alludes to God's punishment of death upon Adam and his race in Genesis 3:19: "For dust thou art, and unto dust shalt thou return." However, the "spirit" (*ruakh*) does not return to the earth or cease, but it returns to the God who first created it and infused it into man's body (Gen. 2:7).

Christ taught us the immortality of the soul. He spoke of the deaths of a rich man and a beggar, the latter of whom "was carried by the angels" to meet Abraham and the former of whom was in torment "in hell," though his body "was buried" in the earth (Luke 16:22–23). In Luke 23:46, the dying Christ prayed the words of Psalm 31:5, saying, "Father, into thy hands I commend my spirit." Shortly before this, Christ had promised the repentant thief dying on the cross beside him, "Verily I say unto thee,

in Edward William Fudge and Robert A. Peterson, *Two Views of Hell: A Biblical and Theological Dialogue* (Downers Grove, IL: InterVarsity Press, 2000), 20–21, 43.

Today shalt thou be with me in paradise" (Luke 23:43). Though Christ's body died and was buried, his spirit went that very day into his Father's presence in heaven—where that thief's spirit and the spirits of all repentant sinners who have died still live with him.

Other New Testament texts indicate the same. As Stephen died, he prayed, "Lord Jesus, receive my spirit" (Acts 7:59). The saints in the heavenly city of God are called "the spirits of just men made perfect" (Heb. 12:23). The wicked men of Noah's generation are now "spirits in prison" (1 Pet. 3:19). These texts indicate that the human spirit does not cease with death, but instead meets its Maker, either to receive blessedness or punishment.

Even when there is no explicit mention of the soul or spirit, the Bible reveals the continuing personal existence of believers apart from the body after death. At times the Scriptures speak as if the body were merely a "tabernacle" in which the person temporarily dwells (2 Cor. 5:1, 4; 2 Pet. 1:13–14). In one such context, the apostle Paul says of death, "We are confident, I say, and willing rather to be absent from the body, and to be present with the Lord" (2 Cor. 5:8). He also writes, "For to me to live is Christ, and to die is gain," for death is "to depart, and to be with Christ; which is far better" (Phil. 1:21, 23).[12] Therefore, it is the Christian view of death that the human person continues in conscious existence after he dies, for his spirit or soul is immortal.

The Immateriality and Spirituality of the Human Soul

As already observed, Matthew 10:28 demonstrates that the human soul is of a different nature from the human body, for the soul cannot be killed by men. This implies that it does not consist of earthly material, for that can be disrupted by material forces. Therefore, the soul of man is not merely an energetic state of matter or one of matter's functions or activities, but a distinct, immaterial substance.

We find confirmation of the immateriality of spirits in a statement by the risen Lord Jesus: "Behold my hands and my feet, that it is I myself: handle me, and see; for a spirit hath not flesh and bones, as ye see me have" (Luke 24:39). Christ was proving his physical, bodily resurrection from the

---

12. It is not clear whether "the souls of them that were slain for the word of God" refers to their spirits or their persons, for "souls" (plural *psychē*) can mean either (Rev. 6:9). However, it is clear that Revelation depicts the martyrs as alive, active, and in communication with God.

dead lest his disciples think that only his spirit had returned. He appealed to the senses of both touch ("handle") and vision ("see"), implying that both Christ and his followers understood that spirits are intangible and invisible by nature. Furthermore, he made this truth explicit when he said, "A spirit hath not flesh and bones."

When we say that the soul is an *immaterial substance*, we immediately run into the problem of terminology. Precisely defining *immaterial* versus *material* is a difficult task philosophically and scientifically. This is especially the case since physicists have discovered that on the subatomic level, particles of "matter" behave like waves of energy fields. For our purposes, we will focus on matter on the macroscopic level, which has the properties of mass, detectability by the senses, and measurable dimensions or quantities, such as volume. This seems to be the commonsense idea of matter that Christ differentiated from "spirit" when he invited the disciples to touch and see his resurrected body. That is not to imply that spirits have no substance, but that they consist of another kind of substance than our bodies. We use the word *substance* here not in a technical, philosophical sense, but as it is commonly used to refer to an entity, something that exists and has real being.[13] What this substance is we do not know.

We can, however, say something about the properties of the human spirit. The continuation of a person apart from the body after death implies that the core of human personality lies in the soul and not the body. Therefore, souls are evidently personal substances with understanding and will. Prior to death, they dwell in or with our bodies; after death, they are with the risen Christ or in a place of torment. Therefore, souls have locations. Furthermore, if the soul is the core of the person, with its thoughts, feelings, and choices, then the soul must be able to interact with the material world in order to direct the body and receive information and impressions from the physical senses.

Locating the core of the human person in the soul has important ethical implications. Personhood does not hinge upon the development or proper functioning of the body. Whether a human being is a tiny embryo in the womb,[14] a child who is mentally disabled, a veteran with a disability, or

---

13. See the definitions of *substance* and *essence* in *Merriam-Webster's Collegiate Dictionary*, 11th ed. (Springfield, MA: Merriam-Webster, 2003).

14. David called what God formed in his mother's womb "me," a personal pronoun indicating that an embryo is not just material that becomes a person, but the person himself in his earliest form (Ps. 139:13–16).

an elderly woman who no longer recognizes her own children, he or she consists of both body and soul, and therefore is a person. Though such a human being may not be able to function with the full expression of personality, he or she remains essentially personal.[15] Therefore, we must treat all human beings with the dignity and justice owed to people.

We should not misunderstand the immateriality of the human spirit to imply that it naturally exists apart from the body and uses the body merely as a house or tool. In this regard, we find Calvin's calling the body the "prison" of the soul to be too harsh.[16] As we saw in our survey of biblical terminology, God closely connects soul or spirit with the life of the body. Antonius Thysius said, "The soul has a natural, constant feeling for and leaning toward the body as toward the other half of a composition. . . . Without the body the soul is not entirely blessed, but it is fully happy only when it is united with the body. This is proof that the resurrection of the body is necessary for mankind's blessedness."[17] Flavel said that God created the soul "with an inclination to the body."[18] Paul can state it as a general principle that "no man ever yet hated his own flesh; but nourisheth and cherisheth it" (Eph. 5:29). Flavel observed that like husband and wife, the body and soul are wedded by God and are one, "not essentially one," for "they have far different natures, but they are personally one."[19]

The Unity of the Human Soul (vs. Trichotomy)

So far, we have used the terms "spirit" and "soul" as virtually interchangeable with regard to the human constitution. However, some theologians hold to a view of human nature known as *trichotomy*, which says that man consists of three parts: his body, soul, and spirit. A key text for this view is 1 Thessalonians 5:23: "And the very God of peace sanctify you wholly; and I pray God your whole spirit and soul and body be preserved

---

15. On functional versus essential definitions of personhood, see Bruce A. Ware, "Human Personhood: An Analysis and Definition," *Southern Baptist Journal of Theology* 13, no. 2 (Summer 2009): 18–31.

16. Calvin, *Institutes*, 1.15.2; 3.3.20; 3.9.4; and *Commentaries*, on 2 Cor. 5:4. Derek Brown criticizes Calvin on this point for being influenced by Platonic philosophy. Derek J. Brown, "Calvin's Theology of the Human Body," in *Reformation Faith: Exegesis and Theology in the Protestant Reformation*, ed. Michael Parsons (Eugene, OR: Wipf and Stock, 2014), 31–37. Calvin explicitly interacts with Plato on the topic of the soul in *Institutes*, 1.15.6. However one may evaluate Calvin's "prison" language, it is clear that his overall view of the body has many positive elements. Furthermore, one must read this language with sympathy for Calvin's painful medical conditions.

17. Polyander, Walaeus, Thysius, and Rivetus, *Synopsis Purioris Theologiae*, 13.24 (1:324–25).

18. Flavel, *Pneumatologia*, in *Works*, 2:495.

19. Flavel, *Pneumatologia*, in *Works*, 2:594.

blameless unto the coming of our Lord Jesus Christ." It is argued that here we have a threefold division that encompasses human nature.

Another text used to support trichotomist anthropology is Hebrews 4:12: "For the word of God is quick, and powerful, and sharper than any twoedged sword, piercing even to the dividing asunder of soul and spirit, and of the joints and marrow, and is a discerner of the thoughts and intents of the heart." The text is said to distinguish "soul and spirit" as two entities.

This interpretation, however, is problematic. If it were carried out consistently, we would conclude from Hebrews 4:12 that there are no less than six distinct parts of human nature: soul, spirit, joints, marrow, thoughts, and intents. If we were to approach other texts using the same hermeneutic, Deuteronomy 6:5 would imply that we consist of three parts: heart, soul, and might. However, in Mark 12:30, where the Lord Jesus quotes this very text, we would discover that we consist of four parts: heart, soul, mind, and strength.[20] This *reductio ad absurdum* argument shows that we cannot assume a list intends to teach us about distinct parts of the human constitution. Rather, such Scripture passages pile up terms in order to emphasize that God calls us to exercise holy love with our whole being.

The Scriptures often use "soul" and "spirit" in a virtually interchangeable manner. Both "soul" and "spirit" are used of animal life.[21] Hannah said that she was "a woman of a sorrowful spirit" and had "poured out my soul before the LORD" (1 Sam. 1:15). Job said, "Therefore I will not refrain my mouth; I will speak in the anguish of my spirit; I will complain in the bitterness of my soul" (Job 7:11). Isaiah prayed, "With my soul have I desired thee in the night; yea, with my spirit within me will I seek thee early" (Isa. 26:9). Mary worshiped God, saying, "My soul doth magnify the Lord, and my spirit hath rejoiced in God my Saviour" (Luke 1:46–47). Similarly, John reported that Christ said, "Now is my soul troubled," and wrote of Jesus, "He was troubled in spirit" (John 12:27; 13:21). Both statements use the same word translated as "troubled" (passive *tarassō*), but one with "soul" and one with "spirit." Such parallel expressions are a typically Hebraic way of stating the same idea in complementary words, implying that both "soul" and "spirit" can be used to refer to the inner person.

20. Cf. Erickson, *Systematic Theology*, 479.
21. Gen. 1:20–21, 24, 30; 2:7, 19; 6:17; 7:15, 22; Eccles. 3:21.

Though the semantic range of "soul" and "spirit" may not be identical, with respect to the immaterial part of man, they refer to the same thing. Therefore, we speak of the human constitution being dualistic, not trichotomistic, in nature.

The Faculties of the Human Soul

The human soul is made by God with the capacity to act in a number of ways. In the Scriptures, the "heart" is the command center of human activity: from the heart flow all the acts of one's life (Prov. 4:23; Mark 7:21–23). A study of the Bible's use of terminology for spirit or soul readily reveals the soul's capacity for acts that we would consider *mental*, such as knowledge (1 Cor. 2:11), understanding (Isa. 29:24), and memory and meditation (Ps. 77:6); *emotional*, such as desire (Isa. 26:9), anguish (Job 7:11), sorrow (Matt. 26:38; Mark 8:12), and joy (Luke 1:47); and *volitional*, such as choices (Ex. 35:21; Ezra 1:1, 5) and inclinations (Matt. 26:41).[22]

Theologians have long distinguished the activities of the soul according to its powers or *faculties*.[23] The term *faculties* (from Latin *facultas*) does not refer to different parts of a compound substance, but to abilities to do something.[24] Girolamo Zanchi (1516–1590) said, "All potencies of the soul are called faculties, i.e. *dynameis* [powers]. And they are called *facultates*, because by them those things happen easily (*facile*) to which they are destined by the Creator."[25]

The faculties of the soul are necessary for human beings to function as persons. As we explained under the doctrine of the Trinity, a "person" must be rational, volitional, and in relationships with other persons, just as the Father, the Son, and the Holy Spirit know and love one another.[26] God created man as a personal creature with the faculties of mind and will so that people can

---

22. Further Scripture references are presented in Nichols, *Lectures in Systematic Theology*, 2:180–81.

23. An excellent introduction to the doctrine of the soul's faculties in Reformed orthodoxy, as well as its earlier roots, may be found in Paul Helm, *Human Nature from Calvin to Edwards* (Grand Rapids, MI: Reformation Heritage Books, 2018).

24. Richard A. Muller, *Dictionary of Latin and Greek Theological Terms: Drawn Principally from Protestant Scholastic Theology*, 2nd ed. (Grand Rapids, MI: Baker Academic, 2017), 118; cf. Thomas Aquinas's statement: "A power [*potentia*] of the soul is nothing else than the proximate principle of the soul's operation." *Summa Theologica*, Part 1, Q. 78, Art 4, Answer.

25. Girolamo Zanchi, *De primi hominis lapsu, de peccato, et de lege Dei*, 1.6.2, in *Reformed Thought on Freedom: The Concept of Free Choice in Early Modern Reformed Theology*, ed. Willem J. van Asselt, J. Martin Bac, and Roelf T. te Velde, Texts and Studies in Reformation and Post-Reformation Thought (Grand Rapids, MI: Baker Academic, 2010), 74.

26. See *RST*, 1:931–33.

relate to him and to each other in a personal manner, each unique individual conscious of himself as "I" and communicating to other persons as "you."[27]

Philosophers and theologians from ancient times to today have engaged in complex analyses of the soul's faculties, their relations to each other, and their relations to the senses, conditions, and motions of the body.[28] Plato said that human life is driven by three factors: reason, physical appetite, and ambition/indignation.[29] Aristotle postulated two basic faculties of the soul behind all human motivation: the intellect and desire.[30] Augustine spoke of "memory," "understanding," and "will," which together are "one life," "one mind," and "one substance."[31] Aquinas identified the intellect and the will as the two key motivating factors in human activity, though they act together in an inseparable manner.[32] As Edward Reynolds (1599–1676) said, "The will alone is a blind faculty," unable to choose the good apart from the understanding's power to inform it of what is good.[33]

It is common today to speak of the soul's activities in terms of the *mind, emotions,* and *will.* Flavel made a threefold distinction in the soul's faculties as "understanding, will, and various affections."[34] He said, "The understanding is a faculty of the reasonable soul by which a man apprehends and judges all intelligible things." He also said, "The will is a faculty of the rational soul, whereby a man either chooseth or refuseth the things which the understanding discerns and knows."[35] The "affections," Flavel said, draw the soul toward what it perceives as true happiness and press it to avoid what it perceives as unhappiness.[36]

However, other Reformed theologians, such as Calvin, William Ames, Thysius, James Ussher, Reynolds, and Jonathan Edwards (1703–1758), adopted an approach that considered the soul to have two basic faculties,

---

27. Nichols, *Lectures in Systematic Theology,* 2:178.

28. See Calvin's references to the analyses of the philosophers in *Institutes,* 1.15.6. It should be noted that these Greek philosophers used "soul" *(psychē)* with meanings different from that of orthodox Christian theology.

29. Plato, *The Republic,* trans. and ed. Desmond Lee, rev. ed., Penguin Classics (London: Penguin, 1974), 4.434d–441c (206–17).

30. Aristotle, *De Anima (On the Soul),* trans. and ed. Hugh Lawson-Tancred, Penguin Classics (London: Penguin, 1986), 3.10 (213–14).

31. Augustine, *On the Trinity,* 10.11.18, in NPNF[1], 3:142.

32. Aquinas, *Summa Theologica,* Part 1, Q. 82, Art. 4. See Brian Davies, *Aquinas,* Outstanding Christian Thinkers (London: Continuum, 2002), 99.

33. Edward Reynolds, *A Treatise on the Passions and Faculties of the Soul,* in *The Whole Works of Right Rev. Edward Reynolds,* 6 vols. (1826; repr., Morgan, PA: Soli Deo Gloria, 1996), 6:317. Henceforth cited as *Passions and Faculties.*

34. Flavel, *Pneumatologia,* in *Works,* 2:495.

35. Flavel, *Pneumatologia,* in *Works,* 2:503, 506.

36. Flavel, *Pneumatologia,* in *Works,* 2:509.

understanding and *will*, with will including the appetites or desires for good.[37] Augustine said, "For the will is in them all [all the affections]; yea, none of them is anything else than will. For what are desire and joy but a volition of consent to the things we wish? And what are fear and sadness but a volition of aversion from the things which we do not wish?"[38] Herman Bavinck said, "The will is not a specific faculty; it is nothing other than the faculty of desiring itself in its highest form. . . . This faculty of desiring . . . includes all sorts of inclinations that it manifests in instinct and desire, in wish and longing, and in this way also in willing."[39]

It may be helpful to consider love as a prime example of the relation of affections to the will. Certainly, love involves the affections (Deut. 21:15–16), but love is also a choice of the will (10:15; 30:19–20). The Holy Scriptures speak much more often of the love of the heart than the choices of the will. Augustine said that the great division within mankind into "two cities" is defined "by two loves: the earthly by the love of self, even to the contempt of God; the heavenly by the love of God, even to the contempt of self. The former, in a word, glories in itself, the latter in the Lord."[40] The greatest duty and delight for which God created our souls is to know and love the Lord (4:35, 39; 6:4–5). We might tentatively propose that the soul's faculties can be best summarized in the capacities to know and to love.

The human soul and its faculties are not morally and spiritually neutral, but always stand in some relation to God and his will. The mind or faculty of understanding may be characterized by darkness and blindness or by light and spiritual perception (Eph. 1:18; 4:17–18; cf. Matt. 6:22–23). The Bible describes the heart as possessing a moral and spiritual character that directs one's actions. Bad hearts produce the bad fruit of evil words and works; good hearts produce good words and works (Luke 6:43–46). Having a good heart is crucial for a right response to God's Word (8:15). Theologians speak of the "disposition" (Latin *habitus*) of the soul's faculties to refer to the prevailing, enduring character that directs

---

37. Calvin, *Institutes*, 1.15.7; *Commentaries*, on Gen. 1:26; Ames, *The Marrow of Theology*, 1.8.73 (106); cf. 1.4.52 (87); Polyander, Walaeus, Thysius, and Rivetus, *Synopsis Purioris Theologiae*, 13.32 (1:327); Ussher, *A Body of Divinity*, 5th head (91); Reynolds, *Passions and Faculties*, in *Works*, 6:278, 329; Edwards, *Religious Affections*, in *WJE*, 2:96.

38. Augustine, *The City of God*, 14.6, in *NPNF*[1], 2:266.

39. Herman Bavinck, *Foundations of Psychology*, trans. Jack Vanden Born, Nelson D. Kloosterman, and John Bolt, in *Bavinck Review* 9 (2018): 232 (full article, 1–244). This work is not a biblical-theological treatise but a psychological-philosophical-historical discussion of the soul and its faculties.

40. Augustine, *The City of God*, 14.28, in *NPNF*[1], 2:282–83.

a person's thoughts, choices, and actions.[41] To give a "new heart" to a sinner (Ezek. 36:26) is not to create a new substance or component in the soul or to empower a new faculty, but to impart a new disposition to the existing faculties, a disposition to trust and love the Lord and keep his commandments.

As we will see, the doctrine of the soul's faculties provides an important infrastructure for theological discussions of sin and salvation. Paul Helm writes that Reformed orthodox theologians "reworked faculty psychology in incorporating into it an Augustinian account of grace as effectual."[42] The Augustinian doctrine of original sin accounts for sin's corruption not only of the desires but also of the mind and will.[43] An aspect of the faculty of understanding that is crucial for spiritual life is the conscience. Flavel said that the conscience is "the judgment of a man upon himself, with respect or relation to the judgment of God." He illustrated this point by saying, "The voice of conscience is the voice of God; for it is his vice-regent and representative."[44] (The conscience and its activity in sinners will be discussed in a later chapter on the topic of the punishment of sin.[45] The free choice of the will, a crucial topic in the doctrines of sin and of salvation, will receive separate treatment in a chapter of its own.[46] Later, in the locus of soteriology, the doctrine of regeneration will be presented in terms of God giving new spiritual dispositions to existing faculties, so that sinners know, trust, and love the Lord.[47])

The classical language of the faculties and the dispositions of the soul remains helpful for theological discourse. However, we use it with the following caveats. First, we recognize that the soul ordinarily exercises its faculties in conjunction with the body. Thus, the soul's intellect, memory, affections, and so on are profoundly shaped by the condition of one's body—though such faculties continue after death (Luke 16:23–26). Second, by using faculty language, we are not endorsing all the logical conclusions that scholastic theologians asserted in connection to the

---

41. Editorial "Glossary of Concepts and Terms," in Polyander, Walaeus, Thysius, and Rivetus, *Synopsis Purioris Theologiae*, 2:665; and Muller, *Dictionary of Latin and Greek Theological Terms*, 146. Aquinas cited Aristotle as saying, "Habit is a disposition whereby that which is disposed is disposed well or ill." *Summa Theologica*, Part 2.1, Q. 49, Art. 1.
42. Helm, *Human Nature from Calvin to Edwards*, 107.
43. See chap. 21.
44. Flavel, *Pneumatologia*, in *Works*, 2:504.
45. See the discussion of the human means of sin's punishment in chap. 24.
46. See chap. 22.
47. See *RST*, vol. 3 (forthcoming).

faculties and dispositions. Third, by speaking of the soul's faculties, we are not dividing the soul into parts or modules, but identifying the one soul's abilities to act. These faculties may be considered distinctly, but they cannot be separated. Who can conceive of thought without any feeling, or choice without any knowledge?[48]

The Origin of the Human Soul

God created man in his full constitution by communicating life to a body formed of the dust so that man was "a living soul" (Gen. 2:7). Man's body had an earthy origin, but the man's life as a soul was "the immediate effect of God's creating power," as Flavel said.[49] The words "living soul" in and of themselves do not specifically refer to the human spirit in distinction from animals (v. 19). However, God's gift of life to the first man implies the creation of his spirit, for the human spirit vivifies and animates the material body (James 2:26). That spirit is a distinct and immaterial substance. It is unreasonable to suppose that the soul arose from mere matter since they are of different natures. Therefore, we infer from Genesis 2:7 and the broader teaching of Scripture that God specially created Adam's soul out of nothing. Job 32:8 says, "But there is a spirit in man: and the inspiration of the Almighty giveth them understanding."

It is quite a different question, however, to ask how the souls of all those who descend from Adam come into existence. Theologians offer three main answers.[50] First, the *preexistent* view of the soul holds that all rational people lived as spirits prior to being implanted into bodies. This belief was taught by Plato[51] and was later held by the Christian theologian Origen.[52] The Latter-Day Saints (Mormon) Church teaches that souls are not created but existed with God in the beginning.[53] However, such views are speculative and have no biblical basis. David said that God made "me" in his mother's womb (Ps. 139:13–15), implying that each person originates with physical conception and did not exist beforehand. Romans

---

48. On the "intertwining" of intellect and will, see Helm, *Human Nature from Calvin to Edwards*, 151–74.

49. Flavel, *Pneumatologia*, in *Works*, 2:492.

50. Berkhof, *Systematic Theology*, 196–97.

51. Plato, *Phaedo*, 71–72, 77–78 (243, 257, 267).

52. Origen, *De Principiis*, 1.7.3–4, in *ANF*, 4:263–64.

53. See Joseph Smith, "The King Follett Sermon," The Church of Jesus Christ of Latter-Day Saints, https://www.lds.org/ensign/1971/05/the-king-follett-sermon?lang=eng&clang=pes; *Doctrine and Covenants*, 93:29, The Church of Jesus Christ of Latter-Day Saints, https://www.lds.org/scriptures/dc-testament/dc/93.29?lang=eng#28.

9:11 indicates that when people are "not yet born" they have not "done any good or evil," but the idea of preexistence suggests that souls existed as moral agents before they were implanted in the body. Only when God made the first man's body and breathed life into him did he become a living soul (Gen. 2:7).[54]

Second, the *traducian* view of the soul—taught by Tertullian,[55] many Lutherans,[56] and some Reformed theologians[57]— holds that human parents generate the soul of a child just as they generate that child's body. Some, like Tertullian, have viewed the soul as a corporeal or material substance; other traducians see it as immaterial, but capable of being generated, formed, or kindled from other souls. Proponents of this view argue that each soul must derive from Adam because God ended his work of creation on the seventh day (Gen. 2:2). Traducianism is also used to explain how each person inherits moral corruption and death from Adam (Rom. 5:12; cf. Ps. 51:5). However, these arguments are not conclusive. God finished his work of creating new *kinds* of creatures in the first six days, but that does not mean he does no further supernatural works.[58] Though original sin is passed down through natural generation, it could be propagated in some other manner rather than by derivation from a parent's soul (Rom. 5:18).[59]

Third, the *creationist* view of the soul is that God makes each individual soul out of nothing at the beginning of each human life. This view has been held by Peter Lombard[60] and Reformed theologians such as Calvin, Johannes Wollebius, Thysius, Francis Turretin, Edwards, and others.[61] Proponents of the creationist view of the soul point to biblical texts that

---

54. Vermigli, *The Peter Martyr Library*, 4:40.

55. Tertullian, *A Treatise on the Soul*, chaps. 4–5, in *ANF*, 3:184–85. Tertullian argued that the soul is "corporeal" in some sense because of its close relation to the body.

56. L'Ubomír Batka, "Luther's Teaching on Sin and Evil," in *The Oxford Handbook of Martin Luther's Theology*, ed. Robert Kolb, Irene Dingel, and L'Ubomír Batka (Oxford: Oxford University Press, 2014), 244–45.

57. Hungarian *Confessio Catholica*, in *Reformed Confessions*, 2:564; and William G. T. Shedd, *Dogmatic Theology*, 2 vols. (New York: Charles Scribner's Sons, 1888), 2:19–94. Traducianism was cautiously favored by Reymond, *A New Systematic Theology of the Christian Faith*, 424–25.

58. Flavel, *Pneumatologia*, in *Works*, 2:514; Turretin, *Institutes*, 5.1311 (1:481); and Brakel, *The Christian's Reasonable Service*, 1:314.

59. Flavel, *Pneumatologia*, in *Works*, 2:519–22. On original sin, see chaps. 19–21.

60. Lombard, *The Sentences*, 2.19.7.2 (2:81).

61. Calvin, *Commentaries*, on Gen. 3:6; Wollebius, *Compendium*, 1.5.(4).ii (57); Polyander, Walaeus, Thysius, and Rivetus, *Synopsis Purioris Theologiae*, 13.53 (1:335, 337); Turretin, *Institutes*, 5.13 (1:477–82); and Jonathan Edwards, "The Great Concern of a Watchman for Souls," in *WJE*, 25:64. Louis Berkhof mistakenly attributed traducianism to Edwards without citation. Berkhof, *Systematic Theology*, 197.

teach that God made the spirits of all men.[62] However, these Scripture passages do not clearly reveal whether God creates each soul out of nothing or out of the souls of the child's parents, just as God employs their bodies to make their child's body (Ps. 139:13–16).

A major reason why theologians have embraced a creationist view of the soul is their belief that the human spirit is a simple spiritual substance. Spiritual substances cannot be produced by the physical matter of the body. Neither can a simple substance, having no parts, be divided or multiply itself. Therefore, they conclude, neither human bodies nor spirits can produce a new soul. It must be directly created by God, which is to say, out of nothing.[63] There are philosophical reasons that suggest the simplicity and indivisibility of the soul,[64] but we do not find these ideas taught in the Scriptures or implied from them by necessary consequence. In reality, we know very little about the ontological properties of the soul. Therefore, we hesitate to accept this logical argument, for it is speculative.

Orthodox theologians have allowed for uncertainty on this question. Augustine was open to both the traducian and the creationist views, but was unsure how to establish biblically and theologically which one was correct.[65] Reynolds presented arguments for creationism, but did so "reserving notwithstanding unto myself and others, the liberty and modesty of Saint Austin's [Augustine's] hesitation."[66] Hodge opposed traducianism, but confessed that "generation, the production of a new individual of the human race, is an inscrutable mystery."[67] Though Bavinck and Louis Berkhof favored creationism, they acknowledged that good arguments could be made for traducianism and creationism.[68] Reynolds believed that the Holy Spirit gave us the liberty to remain uncertain in this matter because

---

62. Isa. 42:5; 57:16; Zech. 12:1; Heb. 12:9.

63. Reynolds, *Passions and Faculties*, in *Works*, 6:246; Flavel, *Pneumatologia*, in *Works*, 2:519; Turretin, *Institutes*, 5.137 (1:480); Brakel, *The Christian's Reasonable Service*, 1:313; and Hodge, *Systematic Theology*, 2:71.

64. "From this attribute of spirituality, flows immediately the next of simplicity, unity, or actuality: for matter is the root of all perfect composition, every compound consisting of two essential parts, matter and form." Reynolds, *Passions and Faculties*, in *Works*, 6:254. Reynolds cited Cicero ("Tully") and built upon the presuppositions of Aristotelian philosophy regarding composition, form, and matter. See Thomas Ainsworth, "Form vs. Matter," in *The Stanford Encyclopedia of Philosophy* (Spring 2016 Edition), https://plato.stanford.edu/archives/spr2016/entries/form-matter/.

65. Augustine, Letter 166, to Jerome, in *NPNF*[1], 1:523–32. See Turretin, *Institutes*, 5.13.1 (1:477).

66. Reynolds, *Passions and Faculties*, in *Works*, 6:245.

67. Hodge, *Systematic Theology*, 2:78.

68. Bavinck, *Reformed Dogmatics*, 2:581; and Berkhof, *Systematic Theology*, 200.

of Ecclesiastes 11:5: "As thou knowest not what is the way of the spirit, nor how the bones do grow in the womb of her that is with child: even so thou knowest not the works of God who maketh all."[69] Here we come up against mystery and may do best to rest content in what God has chosen to reveal or conceal (Deut. 29:29).

In whatever way God may form the soul, it is clear from Scripture that he makes every individual human being in both body and spirit.[70] Therefore, we must acknowledge our dependence upon God and recognize that we owe to him the submission of every motion of our hearts, for he made them. He is sovereign over souls, and they are accountable to him.

The Centrality of the Human Soul for Pleasing God

We observed earlier in this chapter that the human body has an important function in our service to God and the process of sanctification. However, the Holy Scriptures also reveal that just as the soul is the center of the person, so the soul is central in pleasing God. Religion without the devotion of the inner man, or "heart," offends God (Matt. 15:8; citing Isa. 29:13).

The Psalms especially highlight the importance of the inner devotion of the spirit to God. David cried out for God to renew his heart and spirit, for he understood that the worship God desires arises from a spirit broken over sin and contrite in heart (Ps. 51:10, 17). The root of Israel's disobedience against God was that they were "a generation whose heart was not steadfast, whose spirit was not faithful to God" (Ps. 78:8 ESV). Though God made our bodies, he rejoices not in physical greatness but in inward piety. Psalm 147:10–11 says, "He delighteth not in the strength of the horse: he taketh not pleasure in the legs of a man. The Lord taketh pleasure in them that fear him, in those that hope in his mercy." For this reason, God does not merely judge outward conduct, but "the Lord weigheth the spirits" (Prov. 16:2).

Therefore, a principal promise of saving grace is that God will give people "a new heart" and "a new spirit" (Ezek. 36:26; cf. 11:19). The salvation of the soul is crucial for a right relationship with God, for without it men are at best whitewashed tombs full of death. Have you been born again? It is not sufficient to inform your mind with the truth and reform your behavior. Jesus Christ said to one of the most biblically literate and

---

69. Reynolds, *Passions and Faculties*, in *Works*, 6:245.
70. Ps. 139:14–16; Zech. 12:1; cf. Ps. 33:15.

religiously devoted men of the day, "Ye must be born again" (John 3:7). Do you have a new heart and a new spirit that love God?

Spiritual rebirth is only the beginning. Even after regeneration, Christians still need the Lord to work in their spirits a greater spiritual wisdom and love that makes their lives more pleasing to God because they are more fruitful in good works.[71] Though God does care for our physical needs (Matthew 6), our greatest need as believers is "to be strengthened with might by his Spirit in the inner man; that Christ may dwell in your hearts by faith" (Eph. 3:16–17).

In an age when people obsess about eating right, exercising, and lavishing both comforts and cures upon their bodies, our priority must be to "be renewed in the spirit of your mind" so as to put off sin and put on the likeness of Christ (Eph. 4:23). As Paul writes, "For bodily exercise profiteth little: but godliness is profitable unto all things, having promise of the life that now is, and of that which is to come" (1 Tim. 4:8). Where are your priorities? How are you using your time and the means of grace to cultivate your soul? Do not be deceived. The body is precious, but there is more to life than the body and the possessions by which we please the body. No study of the human soul would be complete without soberly weighing Christ's words in Matthew 16:26: "For what is a man profited, if he shall gain the whole world, and lose his own soul?"

Sing to the Lord
Proclaiming God's Peace to One's Own Soul

Be still my soul: the Lord is on thy side;
Bear patiently the cross of grief or pain;
Leave to thy God to order and provide;
In ev'ry change he faithful will remain.
Be still my soul: thy best, thy heav'nly Friend
Through thorny ways leads to a joyful end.

Be still my soul: thy God doth undertake
To guide the future as he has the past.
Thy hope, thy confidence let nothing shake;
All now mysterious shall be bright at last.
Be still my soul: the waves and winds still know
His voice who ruled them while he dwelt below.

---

71. Eph. 1:17–19; Phil. 1:9–11; Col. 1:9–12.

Be still my soul: when dearest friends depart,
And all is darkened in the vale of tears,
Then shalt thou better know his love, his heart,
Who comes to soothe thy sorrow and thy fears.
Be still my soul: thy Jesus can repay
From his own fullness all he takes away.

Be still my soul: the hour is hast'ning on
When we shall be forever with the Lord,
When disappointment, grief, and fear are gone,
Sorrow forgot, love's purest joys restored.
Be still my soul: when change and tears are past,
All safe and blessed we shall meet at last.

Katharina von Schlegel, trans. Jane Borthwick
Tune: Finlandia
Trinity Hymnal—Baptist Edition, No. 579

Questions for Meditation or Discussion

1. Why should systematic theology give attention to the human body?
2. What does God's creation of the human body imply about it? About him?
3. Why are our bodies important for the pursuit of holiness?
4. What will eternal life mean for the Christian's body?
5. What do the authors not mean by the "immortality" of the soul?
6. How would you prove from the Holy Scriptures that the soul is immortal?
7. How do the Scriptures reveal that the soul is immaterial?
8. What are the "faculties" of the soul? Give some examples.
9. What are three views of the origin of each human soul?
10. Why is the soul central to knowing and pleasing God?

Questions for Deeper Reflection

11. What is the view of human nature called "trichotomy"? What arguments are made for this view? Do you agree with it? Why or why not?
12. Which view of the soul's origin has stronger evidence? Why? Is the evidence conclusive enough to make a firm doctrinal stand, or should we leave the matter open? Why?

14

God's Covenant with Adam, Part 1

Biblical Teaching

Robert Rollock (c. 1555–1599) said, "All the word of God appertains to some covenant; for God speaks nothing to man without the covenant."[1] It is no exaggeration to say that biblical history is the history of God's covenants. The Hebrew term translated as "covenant" (*berit*) appears more than 280 times in the Old Testament. The New Testament contains more than thirty uses of the Greek term for "covenant" (*diathēkē*). The major events of biblical history all revolve around God's making and keeping covenants. Jesus Christ's saving work was promised in a covenant, his death established the covenant, his office is to mediate the covenant, his servants are ministers of the covenant, and his people receive the blessings of the covenant.[2] The Bible is a covenantal document.

It has been said, "Reformed theology is covenant theology."[3] Covenant theology sees an essential unity in God's plan of salvation through the ages. This unity is undergirded by the continuity of God's promises in what theologians call "the covenant of grace." The covenant of grace answers the horrible

---

1. Robert Rollock, *A Treatise of God's Effectual Calling*, in *Select Works of Robert Rollock*, 2 vols. (Grand Rapids, MI: Reformation Heritage Books, 2008), 1:33.
2. Isa. 42:6; 49:8; 54:10; 55:3; Jer. 31:31–34; 32:40; Ezek. 37:26; Matt. 26:28; Mark 14:24; Luke 22:20; 1 Cor. 11:25; 2 Cor. 3:6; Gal. 3:15–17, 29; Heb. 7:22; 8:6–13; 9:15; 13:20.
3. Richard L. Pratt Jr., "Reformed Theology Is Covenant Theology," *Reformed Perspectives Magazine* 12, no. 20 (May 16–22, 2010), http://thirdmill.org/articles/ric_pratt/ric_pratt .RTiscovenant.html.

problem caused by man's violation of God's arrangement with Adam in paradise, called "the covenant of works." The doctrine of the covenant of works lays an important foundation for understanding Christ's work of salvation as the representative of his chosen people with respect to God and his law.

Objections to the Doctrine of the Covenant of Works

Theologians from a variety of perspectives, ranging from neoorthodoxy[4] all the way to evangelical dispensationalism,[5] have objected to the concept of a covenant of works with Adam. Even within Reformed circles, where the covenant of grace is a traditional concept, some theologians, such as John Murray and Anthony Hoekema, have rejected this formulation.[6] Therefore, we need to address these objections and make a case for the covenant of works. The following reasons were given by Murray and Hoekema for rejecting the phrase "covenant of works," though both men embraced many elements of the doctrine itself.[7]

1. *The term* covenant *does not appear in Genesis 2.* In fact, *covenant* does not appear until Genesis 6:18, where it refers to God's covenant with Noah. Therefore, to speak of a covenant with Adam is to impose theological categories on the Bible.

In response, we point out that it is fallacy of reasoning to say that a concept cannot be present because a particular word is not used.[8] We speak of the *Trinity* and the *fall of man*, though neither term appears in the Bible. Genesis 2 presents marriage as a covenant, though it is not called one until Malachi 2:14. We will argue below that Genesis 2 contains a covenant in essence, though the word is absent.

2. *No formal oath is sworn between God and Adam in Genesis 2.* An oath is an essential element of a covenant, as seen in the Lord's covenant with Abraham (Genesis 15). The words of Genesis 2:16–17 are not a covenant but a command.

---

4. Barth, *Church Dogmatics*, IV/1, sec. 57.2 (64).

5. John MacArthur and Richard Mayhue, eds., *Biblical Doctrine: A Systematic Summary of Bible Truth* (Wheaton, IL: Crossway, 2017), 870.

6. For a survey of other theologians who reject the covenant of works, see Cornelis Pronk, "The Covenant of Works in Recent Discussion," in *No Other Foundation than Jesus Christ: Pastoral, Historical, and Contemporary Essays* (Mitchell, ON: Free Reformed, 2008), 223–31.

7. All four objections appear briefly in John Murray, "The Adamic Administration," in *Collected Writings of John Murray*, 4 vols. (Edinburgh: Banner of Truth, 1977), 2:49, and with further elaboration in Hoekema, *Created in God's Image*, 119–21.

8. On the answers to this and the next objection, see Justin Taylor, "Was There a Covenant of Works?," in *Covenant Theology: A Baptist Distinctive*, ed. Earl M. Blackburn (Birmingham, AL: Solid Ground, 2013), 137–38 (full chapter, 137–43).

In response, we assert that an explicit oath is not essential to a covenant. Neither a formal oath nor the word *covenant* explicitly appears in God's promise to David (2 Samuel 7), but other texts call that promise a covenant and a sworn oath (2 Sam. 23:5; Ps. 89:3, 34–35).

3. *God's relationship with Adam is not legal and meritorious but fatherly and gracious.* To describe it as a "covenant of works" is thus not wise. The terminology may even suggest that God dealt with man in a cold, legalistic, commercial manner.

In response, we acknowledge the abundant, gracious goodness of God in his dealings with Adam. Adam was the son of God (Luke 3:38). We also do not wish to quarrel about words when theological agreement is present. However, we find in the Scriptures that the term "works," though excluded from the justification of sinners, is a beautiful and sweet word for the obedience of God's children.[9] Genesis depicts God's arrangement with Adam to be contingent upon his works of obedience to God's law. When Paul contrasts Adam to Christ, he does so in terms of "disobedience" and "obedience" (Rom. 5:19).[10] While "covenant of works" does not say everything that God reveals about his first covenant with man, what it does communicate is faithful to Scripture.

4. *In the Bible, a covenant with God always applies to his redemptive dealings with man.* However, God's dealings with Adam in the garden were not redemptive because man had not yet sinned. Therefore, the term should not be applied to matters before the fall.

In reply, we say that this objection begs the question. The Bible nowhere states that all covenants are redemptive. As we will demonstrate, the Scriptures reveal that God's words to Adam before the fall constituted a covenant conditioned upon his obedience, and other Scripture passages confirm that it was indeed a covenant.

Answering objections to the covenant of works is not sufficient to prove that the Scriptures teach the doctrine. That requires a positive demonstration from the text of God's Word. Much of the difficulty in making such a demonstration lies in the question of how to define a covenant. Therefore, before making a case, we will consider that definition.

---

9. Prov. 31:31; Matt. 5:16; Eph. 2:10; 1 Tim. 2:10; 5:10, 25; 6:18; 2 Tim. 3:17; Titus 2:7, 14; 3:8, 14; Heb. 10:24; James 2:14–26; 1 Pet. 2:12; Rev. 14:13.

10. Richard C. Barcellos, *The Covenant of Works: Its Confessional and Scriptural Basis*, Recovering Our Confessional Heritage 3 (Palmdale, CA: Reformed Baptist Academic Press, 2016), 88.

The Essential and Common Elements of Covenants

What is a covenant? The traditional Reformed definition of a covenant is a mutual compact, agreement, or contract between parties.[11] This contractual definition created some formal tension in Reformed theological systems, for God's lordship makes it improper for him to enter into a contract with his creatures[12]—the Lord does not ask for our consent, but decrees his will.[13]

It is better, in our judgment, to start with a more refined and biblical definition of covenant that allows for proper covenants between God and men, to which Scripture attests. Herman Bavinck said that God's covenant "is not really a compact but a pledge," and the response demanded of people is not a condition for entering the covenant so much as the conduct required of the people upon whom God has already lovingly and authoritatively imposed his covenant.[14] A covenant, then, is more in the nature of a pledge, promise, oath, and solemn commitment than a contract. Murray observed that a biblical covenant is better described by "sworn fidelity" than a "mutual contract."[15] Thus, we would tentatively define a covenant

---

11. Joel R. Beeke and Mark Jones, *A Puritan Theology: Doctrine for Life* (Grand Rapids, MI: Reformation Heritage Books, 2012), 219–20. William Perkins said that the "covenant of grace" is "nothing else but a compact made between God and man touching reconciliation and life everlasting. . . . God is the principal, and He promises righteousness and life eternal in Christ. Man again binds himself by God's grace to believe and to rest upon the promise." Perkins, *An Exposition of the Symbol*, in *Works*, 5:94–95. Francis Turretin defined a divine covenant as "the agreement of God with man by which God promises his goods . . . and by man, in turn, duty and worship are engaged. . . . It consists of a mutual obligation of the contracting parties." Turretin, *Institutes*, 8.3.3 (1:574). See also Wollebius, *Compendium*, 1.21.iv–v (118); Ussher, *A Body of Divinity*, 8th head (109–10); Herman Witsius, *The Economy of the Covenants between God and Man*, 2 vols. (1822; repr., Grand Rapids, MI: Reformation Heritage Books, 2010), 1.1.3, 9–12; 2.1.5 (1:43–47, 165); and Hodge, *Systematic Theology*, 2:354–55.

12. Contracts bind their parties to exchange goods according to commutative justice, but God in his covenants sovereignly determines how he will distribute his goods to people, from whom he receives nothing that he does not first give. See the discussion of commutative justice in *RST*, 1:814.

13. Note Turretin's statement that "a covenant of God with man strictly speaking cannot exist." Turretin, *Institutes*, 8.3.1 (1:574). John Gill attempted to solve the problem by teaching that a proper covenant exists only between God the Father and God the Son. Gill, *Body of Divinity*, 216. However, this does not give due weight to God's covenant with Christ *and those in federal union with him by God's decree* (cf. Westminster Larger Catechism, Q. 31). The Bible often testifies that God made covenants with people, not merely with Christ.

14. Bavinck, *Reformed Dogmatics*, 204. Herman Bavinck's words "not really a compact but a pledge" were applied by him specifically to the covenant with Abraham, but he said this principle was reaffirmed "with ever-increasing clarity" in subsequent covenantal dealings with Israel. He noted that the "pledge" nature of a covenant may be the reason why the Septuagint's translators rendered God's *berit* as *diathēkē* ("testament" as a sovereign disposition of rights and goods) and not *synthēkē* ("agreement, contract, treaty"; cf. Dan. 11:6 LXX). Bavinck, *Reformed Dogmatics*, 205. See Vos, *Reformed Dogmatics*, 2:77–78.

15. John Murray, *The Covenant of Grace* (1953; repr., Phillipsburg, NJ: Presbyterian and Reformed, 1988), 10. See also Geerhardus Vos, *Redemptive History and Biblical Interpretation: The Shorter Writings of Geerhardus Vos*, ed. Richard B. Gaffin Jr. (Grand Rapids, MI: Baker, 1980), 167–68.

as *a solemn promise that functions as a verbal, legal instrument to define a relationship of loyalty.* Let us look more closely at this definition.

At the heart of a covenant is *a solemn promise.*[16] Such a promise may be conditional or unconditional. The term "covenant" (*berit*) first appears in the Bible in God's promise to save Noah and never to destroy the earth with a flood again.[17] Many Scripture passages identify God's covenant with his promise or oath.[18] God's law considered as mere law places man under obligation. When God makes a covenant, he also binds himself to others in obligations that he freely chooses and solemnly pledges to fulfill.[19]

A covenant functions as *a verbal, legal instrument to define a relationship of loyalty.* In the Old Testament, covenants are closely associated with a Hebrew term meaning loyalty and faithful, steadfast love (*khesed*). The word is variously translated as "mercy," "kindness," "lovingkindness," "goodness" (KJV), or "steadfast love" (ESV). The Bible often describes the Lord as the God who keeps covenant and faithful love.[20] We find a parallel among human covenants. Abraham and Abimelech swore oaths that they would treat each other with loyalty as defined in their covenant (Gen. 21:22–32). Covenants establish a relationship of binding obligation with the expectation of faithfulness.[21]

Though there is considerable diversity among biblical covenants, there are some common elements that appear in many of them (though not all). These are not essential to a covenant, but help us to identify covenants and understand how they may function.

Covenants often place one party in a position of *subordination to another's lordship*, such as when God took Israel to be his people and asserted himself to be the God whom they must obey (Ex. 6:7; 20:1–17). In all of God's covenants with men, God acts with sovereign lordship, never negotiating the terms or seeking some benefit from men, but announcing

---

16. Calvin, *Institutes*, 4.14.6; Ames, *The Marrow of Theology*, 1.24.11 (150); and Greg Nichols, *Covenant Theology: A Reformed and Baptistic Perspective on God's Covenants* (Birmingham, AL: Solid Ground, 2011), 117, 155.

17. Gen. 6:18; 9:9, 11–13, 15–17; cf. Isa. 54:9–10.

18. Deut. 29:12–13; Josh. 23:14–16; 1 Chron. 16:16; 2 Chron. 21:7; Neh. 9:8; Ps. 105:9; Luke 1:68–73; Rom. 9:4; Gal. 3:15–18; Eph. 2:12; Heb. 8:6; 9:15.

19. O. Palmer Robertson, *The Christ of the Covenants* (Phillipsburg, NJ: Presbyterian and Reformed, 1980), 6–7.

20. Deut. 7:9, 12; 1 Kings 8:23; 2 Chron. 6:14; Neh. 1:5; 9:32; Dan. 9:4; cf. Pss. 25:10; 89:28, 50; 106:45; Isa. 54:10; 55:3.

21. Robert Gonzales defines a covenant as "a formal commitment or obligation that is self-imposed or imposed upon another party or parties." Robert Gonzales Jr., "The Covenantal Context of the Fall: Did God Make a Primeval Covenant with Adam?," *Reformed Baptist Theological Review* 4, no. 2 (2007): 8 (full article, 5–32).

the covenant according to his will for his glory in man's good. William Ames said, "This way of entering into covenant is not between those who are equal before the law but between lord and servant."[22]

Some human covenants also display this theme of subordination. Jonathan and David made a covenant, swearing oaths of steadfast love. This was more than personal friendship; it was also a political alliance in which Jonathan yielded to David as the next king, for he gave David his royal garments and weapons, and he recognized that God would give David victory over all his enemies.[23] Kings and nations made covenants with each other, mutual treaties of loyalty and cooperation, generally with one nation submitting to the protective and ruling authority of another nation.[24]

Covenants may include or be supplemented by *laws to obey*, such as God's covenant with the nation of Israel.[25] God's covenant with Noah (Gen. 9:8–17), though unconditional, was made in the context of God's renewing of mankind's original obligation to be fruitful, multiply, fill the earth, and rule over its creatures (vv. 1–7). God's new covenant consists of promises that God will sovereignly cause his people to be faithful to him, but nevertheless, their faithfulness is at the heart of the covenant.[26]

Whereas a covenant may formally bring one party under the lordship of another party, it may also include the *authorization of the performance of an office* by the subordinate party. When the Lord made the covenant with Israel at Mount Sinai, he made the people "a kingdom of priests, and an holy nation" (Ex. 19:6). God's calling upon the Levitical house of Aaron to serve as priests was also a covenant.[27] God's covenant with David centered upon the promise that his offspring would reign as king forever as a "servant" under God's authority (7:5, 8, 13–14).[28]

Another common, though perhaps not essential, feature of biblical covenants is that the parties entering into covenant often act as *representatives of a larger group in union with them*. God's covenants with Noah, Abraham, Aaron, Phinehas, and David also included their seed or

22. Ames, *The Marrow of Theology*, 1.10.10 (111).
23. 1 Sam. 18:3–4; 20:8–17; 23:16–18.
24. Josh. 9:6–16; 1 Sam. 11:1; 1 Kings 5:12; 15:19; 20:34; Ezek. 17:11–18.
25. Ex. 19:5; Lev. 26:3, 14–15, 44–45; Jer. 31:32, 36–37.
26. Isa. 54:9–10, 13 (cf. John 6:44–45); Jer. 31:31–34; 32:38–40; Heb. 8:10–11.
27. Lev. 24:5; Num. 18:19; 25:12–13; Neh. 13:29; Jer. 33:21; Mal. 2:4–7.
28. In David's prayer of response to God's promise, he repeatedly called himself "thy servant" (2 Sam. 7:19–21, 25–29; cf. 1 Kings 3:6–7; 8:24–26, 66; 11:32–38; 14:8; etc.).

offspring.[29] Similarly, David's covenant with Jonathan bound him to show faithful love to Jonathan's household and offspring (1 Sam. 20:15, 42), resulting in rich blessings to Jonathan's son Mephibosheth (2 Samuel 9). In the covenant between Abraham and Abimelech, Abraham represented his family and hundreds of servants, and Abimelech represented the city of Gerar (Gen. 20:2; 21:22–34). When the Lord made a covenant with Israel, the nation was represented in the formal ceremony by seventy of its elders (Ex. 24:1–2, 9–11).

God often appointed an *observable sign* or "token" (Hebrew *ot*) as a visible reminder of his covenant. The sign of the covenant with Noah was the rainbow (Gen. 9:12–13, 17). God commanded Abraham to circumcise the males of his household and said, "It shall be a token of the covenant betwixt me and you" (17:11; cf. Rom. 4:11). When the Lord commanded Israel to keep the Sabbath holy, their obedience was to be "a sign" that the Lord had set them apart as his holy people (Ex. 31:13, 16–17). However, the Bible does not explicitly identify a "sign" of God's covenant with David. Therefore, signs are not essential to covenants.

In conclusion, we may cautiously define the essence of a covenant as *a solemn, verbal promise that legally defines a relationship of loyalty.* Covenants often involve other elements, such as *submission to another's lordship, laws to obey, authorization of an office, representation of a people,* and *observable signs.*

The Essential Elements of a Covenant in Genesis 2

God's words in Genesis 2:15–17, in their context, fulfill this definition of a covenant. The text says, "And the LORD God took the man, and put him into the garden of Eden to dress it and to keep it. And the LORD God commanded the man, saying, Of every tree of the garden thou mayest freely eat: but of the tree of the knowledge of good and evil, thou shalt not eat of it: for in the day that thou eatest thereof thou shalt surely die."

We find here the essential features of a covenant. God's speech to Adam was a *solemn, legal, verbal revelation.* Though God acts throughout this creation account, these words are his only direct speech to man in Genesis 2. This heightens their significance. Furthermore, the Hebrew syntax repeats the verbs for emphasis; the text may be literally translated, "From every tree of the garden eating you shall eat," but if you eat from the one

---

29. Gen. 9:9; 15:18; 17:7–10; Num. 18:19; 25:13; Ps. 89:28–37.

forbidden tree, then "dying you shall die."[30] The latter construction often appears in a judicial sentence of death.[31] The same syntactical construction with this or another verb may also have "the force of an oath," as Greg Nichols observes.[32] The very word "death" connotes a sober and fearsome consequence to come upon man. Therefore, the words communicate a solemn warning fitting for a law or oath.

God's words in their context contain an *implicit promise*. God authorized Adam to eat of any tree except the forbidden one, including "the tree of life" (Gen. 2:9). He who ate of the latter tree would "live for ever" (3:22). We conclude, then, that the threat of death for violating God's command, combined with the presence of the tree of life, implied a promise of everlasting life for keeping God's command: "Do this and live."[33] There is no hint of merit in this promise, for God had already provided abundant life to Adam before requiring anything from him. The fact that God spoke a command rather than an explicit promise does not exclude his words from functioning as a covenant. The verb translated as "command" (*tsavah*) is quite consistent with a covenant. Psalm 111:9 says, "He hath commanded [*tsavah*] his covenant for ever." Many Scripture passages summarize God's covenants of promise with the word "command," for the Lord God sovereignly imposes his covenants upon man.[34]

God's words define his relationship to Adam in terms of *mutual loyalty and love*. The verb "commanded" stresses the authority with which God spoke and the obligation placed upon man. However, God did not treat man like a slave, for he prefaced the prohibition with a reminder that he had lavishly shown his love for the man in providing him with a beautiful and nurturing home. It was no hard labor that God demanded, but the simplest of tasks that required a morally perfect creature to acknowledge the supremacy of God. Ames said that it was "a covenant of friendship, so to speak, between the Creator and the creature."[35] God

---

30. The construction consists of the same verb appearing first as an infinitive absolute and then as an imperfect.

31. Mathews, *Genesis 1–11:26*, 211. See Gen. 20:7; 26:11; Ex. 19:12; 21:12, 15–17; 22:19; 31:14–15; Lev. 20:2, 9–10, 15; 24:16–17; Num. 15:35; 35:16–18, 21, 31; 1 Sam. 20:31; 22:16; Ezek. 18:13.

32. Nichols, *Covenant Theology*, 353. See Gen. 32:12; 46:4; Num. 26:65 (cf. Ps. 95:11); Judg. 21:5; 1 Sam. 14:39, 44; 1 Kings 2:37, 42.

33. Cf. Lev. 18:5; Ezek. 20:11, 13; Rom. 10:5; Gal. 3:12.

34. Deut. 4:13; 29:1; Josh. 7:11; 23:16; Judg. 2:20; 1 Kings 11:11; 2 Kings 17:35; 18:12; 1 Chron. 16:15; Ps. 105:8; Jer. 11:8.

35. Ames, *The Marrow of Theology*, 1.24.13 (150–51).

and Adam's relationship was truly like that of a generous father and an obedient son in his father's image, united by love for each other (cf. Gen. 5:1–3; Luke 3:38).

It might be objected that no relationship of love would involve such a test. However, we find throughout the Holy Scriptures that God tests his covenant people. William Strong (d. 1654) wrote, "God loves to try the obedience of the best of his creatures, to give them matter and occasion to exercise the graces that he has given them."[36] Such tests benefit God's people by bringing them to maturity, as was the case even for Jesus Christ in his human nature (Heb. 5:8). It was so for Adam. As Nichols points out, the prohibition had positive "educational" value, for it offered Adam the opportunity to learn obedience experientially under temptation, just as a king subjects his son to "rigorous and difficult training" to equip him to rule.[37] Robert Gonzales writes that the knowledge of "good and evil" was "a necessary quality and prerogative of kings (2 Sam. 14:17, 20; 1 Kings 3:9)," and so this tree was designed to test the man in a way that could further equip him with the wisdom needed to serve as God's royal son ruling over the earth.[38]

The eating of fruit is inherently a morally indifferent act, but it became a matter of utmost moral significance when God spoke his command. The test of the tree of knowledge could have strengthened and developed Adam's love for God, and thereby deepened the fellowship of God and man. By refusing the forbidden fruit despite its attractiveness to the senses (Gen. 2:9; 3:6), Adam would have effectively said, "The Lord God is my supreme good. I choose him and his will." Given God's love, we would expect that such loyalty would have resulted in God granting Adam a deeper experiential knowledge of himself and sweeter communion with him, just as Jesus promised to his obedient disciples (John 14:21, 23).

God's word to Adam was a solemn, verbal promise that legally defined a relationship of loyalty. Therefore, we conclude that God made a covenant with Adam.

---

36. William Strong, *A Discourse of the Two Covenants*, Westminster Assembly Project (1678; facsimile repr., Grand Rapids, MI: Reformation Heritage Books, 2011), 4.

37. Nichols, *Covenant Theology*, 345–46. However, we disagree with Nichols when he sets the educational function of the Adamic covenant against its legal, probationary function: "Its design is parental rather than probationary" (344). The two are not mutually exclusive, for man's continuance in the status of God's son was conditional upon his obedience, and mankind lost that privilege when Adam listened to Satan instead of God (cf. John 8:42–44).

38. Gonzales, "The Covenantal Context of the Fall," 28–29.

Other Common Covenantal Elements in Genesis 2

We also find that other elements often observed in biblical covenants appear in this text. The divine person speaking to Adam is identified with a *name of covenantal lordship*. The divine name used here and throughout Genesis 2:4–25 is "the LORD God" (*YHWH Elohim*), as opposed to the simple word "God" (*Elohim*) that appears in Genesis 1:1–2:3. The name "the LORD" had a special covenantal significance, for God manifested the meaning of that name by proving himself to be the sovereign and faithful God who keeps his covenant and brings his people under his lordship (Ex. 3:14–17; 6:2–8).[39] The exact combination "the LORD God" appears several times with respect to God's covenant of the kingdom with David and faithfulness to his royal offspring.[40] And it sometimes appears as another name for "the God of Israel."[41] Therefore, the name suggests that God dealt with Adam as his covenant Lord.

In accordance with his covenantal name, God established his lordship over man through the word of prohibition. Though God created man to rule over the world and the animals that inhabit it,[42] God spoke to this newly created king in a manner that established Adam's subordinate position and communicated his need to remain in loyal obedience to his covenant Lord. As Thomas Watson said, God gave this prohibition "to show his sovereignty" in such a manner as "to bind [Adam] fast to him."[43]

Just as God asserted himself as Adam's covenant Lord, so he also authorized Adam to function in *the office of prophet, priest, and king.*[44] In Israel, these offices were closely connected to the implementation of God's covenant. Likewise, Adam's office arose from God's covenant of works. We must remember that Genesis 1 has already revealed God's creation of man in the image of God. We saw that the image of God implies the capacities to reveal God, worship God, and reign for God.[45] Genesis 2 reveals that God called man to exercise those capacities. Though it does not appear that Adam had to work to survive in the garden, God assigned

---

39. See the discussion in chap. 6 of how the cosmic perspective of creation in Genesis 1 transitions to the covenantal perspective in Genesis 2.

40. 2 Sam. 7:25; 1 Chron. 17:16–17; 28:20; 2 Chron. 1:9; 6:41–42; Pss. 72:18; 80:4, 17–19; 84:8–9, 12.

41. Pss. 59:6; 72:18. The only other uses that we could find occur in Ex. 9:30; 2 Kings 19:19; Jonah 4:6.

42. Gen. 2:15, 19–20; cf. 1:26–28.

43. Watson, *A Body of Divinity*, 128.

44. Liam Goligher, "Adam, Lord of the Garden," in *God, Adam, and You*, 66–70.

45. See chap. 8.

him a vocation (Gen. 2:15). Wolfgang Musculus commented that it was "as if some official duty were assigned to the son of a king" so that his luxury would not make him a sluggard. At the same time, Adam's vocation "would have brought him the greatest pleasure and the fullest opportunity for knowing God's providence and benevolence."[46]

Adam was the righteous king of the world. Where we read, "And the LORD God took the man, and put him into the garden of Eden to dress it and to keep it" (Gen. 2:15), the verb translated as "put" (*niphil* of *nuakh*) means to cause to rest,[47] and is used several times in the Bible of God giving rest to his people in their inheritance, especially in connection to the king's victorious peace.[48] It may suggest Adam's entrance into his royal dominion. Martin Luther said that God "places man into that garden as into a castle and temple" to be his "dwelling place and royal headquarters."[49] When the Lord brought the animals to Adam "to see what he would name them," and Adam "gave names to all" the animals (vv. 19–20), it was as if the Father was introducing his royal son into the first exercise of his authority. Naming is an act of sovereignty.[50]

Adam served God like a holy priest for his glory. Adam's work was literally said to be "to serve" (Hebrew *abad*) and "to guard" (*shamar*) the garden (Gen. 2:15). The job description of the Levites and priests uses the same verbs.[51] This suggests that "there is a spiritual dimension to human work because it is done as service to God," as Richard Belcher writes.[52] The verb "commanded" (*tsavah*), with "the LORD" as its subject, appears only two more times in Genesis (7:5, 16), but many other times in the Pentateuch. It is especially concentrated in Scripture passages concerning the construction of the tabernacle (Exodus 39–40) and consecration of the priests (Leviticus 8–9).[53] Since the garden was like a temple,[54] we see that God called Adam to the work of a consecrated worshiper or priest, ministering to the Lord in his presence and guarding the holiness of his

---

46. Wolfgang Musculus, *In Mosis Genesim* (1554), 63, cited in *RCS/OT*, 1:87.
47. Mathews, *Genesis 1–11:26*, 208.
48. Deut. 25:19; Josh. 1:13, 15; 21:44; 22:4; 23:1; 2 Sam. 7:1, 11; 1 Kings 5:4; 1 Chron. 16:21; 22:9, 18; 23:25; 2 Chron. 14:6–7; 15:15; 20:30; Isa. 14:1; 63:14; Ezek. 37:14.
49. Luther, *Lectures on Genesis*, in *LW*, 1:101 (Gen. 2:15). Antonius Thysius said Adam's placement in the garden was "like a master in his kingly court" (*tamquam Dominum in Basilica sua*). Polyander, Walaeus, Thysius, and Rivetus, *Synopsis Purioris Theologiae*, 13.47 (1:333).
50. Gen. 1:5, 8, 10; 2 Kings 23:34; 24:17.
51. Num. 3:7–8; 8:26; 18:7.
52. Belcher, *Genesis*, 62.
53. Mathews, *Genesis 1–11:26*, 210.
54. See chap. 6.

sacred space. All of man's life is meant to be a living sacrifice to God (Rom. 12:1), and the Lord designated one day in seven for special devotion to the holy work of worship (Gen. 2:1–3). At the heart of Adam's priestly work was obedience to God's command for God's glory (vv. 16–17). Luther discerned that in this text "the church is established without walls and without any pomp," and "the temple is earlier than the home" or "government of the state."[55]

The first priest-king in the world was also a prophet. God spoke directly to Adam in the garden (Gen. 2:16–17). Luther said, "Here the Lord is preaching to Adam and setting the Word before him." Luther argued that since Adam was alone, he had the implicit responsibility of speaking God's word to others, beginning with his wife once God created her and continuing with their children.[56] God's word to mankind was law: "The LORD God commanded the man," a phrase similar to the often-repeated expression in the Pentateuch, "the LORD commanded Moses."[57] Just as Moses received and proclaimed the divine words that would define Israel's covenant relationship with the Lord, so Adam received and proclaimed the divine words that defined mankind's covenant relationship with its Creator.

The Lord God's words and acts toward Adam in Genesis 2 commissioned him to an office that combined the functions of a prophet, priest, and king. Adam was not a mediator of salvation, but he performed those functions as appropriate to the situation before the fall.

God treated Adam as *the representative of his natural descendants*, just as other biblical covenants often included the offspring of one or more parties involved, or the kingdom over which either party ruled. Though the Lord would soon create for Adam a wife with whom he would have children, God's words addressed Adam with the singular "thou" in their permission, prohibition, and penalty (Gen. 2:16–17).[58] Adam represented his family in this legal arrangement. God had threatened Adam with the penalty of death, yet the genealogy of Genesis 5 reports not only the death of Adam but the death of his descendants with the eightfold refrain "and

---

55. Luther, *Lectures on Genesis*, in *LW*, 1:103–4 (Gen. 2:16–17).
56. Luther, *Lectures on Genesis*, in *LW*, 1:105 (Gen. 2:16–17).
57. "The LORD [had] commanded Moses" appears twenty times in Exodus, ten in Leviticus, and twenty-two in Numbers.
58. Although the pronoun is not present in the Hebrew text, the three finite verbs in "thou mayest freely eat," "thou shalt not eat," and "thou shalt surely die" are all in the second person masculine singular form.

he died."[59] God's word of death to Adam brought death to his natural descendants when Adam disobeyed, an indication that he represented them before God in the covenant (Rom. 5:12; 1 Cor. 15:22).

We observe lastly from Genesis 2:16–17 that though the term "sign" does not appear, God's words to Adam revolved around *observable tokens of faithfulness*: not eating of "the tree of the knowledge of good and evil." Like circumcising one's sons or keeping the Sabbath, abstinence from the fruit of that tree served as a visible sign of inward fidelity. Luther commented that God made this tree "so that Adam might have a definite way to express his worship and reverence toward God."[60] Its fruit did not bear any inherent offensiveness or poison, for it was "good for food" and "pleasant to the eyes" (3:6). It was simply forbidden by God. Though eating fruit is inconsequential in itself, Adam's decision to abstain would have represented a humble disposition of the heart to obey God's commandment merely because it was the will of God. John Calvin said that it was "a kind of first lesson in obedience, that man might know he had a Director and Lord of his life," for obedience to God "is the only rule of living well."[61] As Andrew Willet (1562–1621) wrote, following the thoughts of Gregory the Great (c. 540–604), man's turning away from something good would "show his humility to his Creator," yet the ease of refraining from one tree when so many others were available to him would make it plain that eating its fruit arose from sheer "transgression and disobedience."[62]

Why was the tree associated with "the knowledge of good and evil"? Calvin commented that it was not because God denied to man knowledge and wisdom, for that would be inconsistent with the image of God, "but that he might not seek to be wiser than became him, nor by trusting to his own understanding, cast off the yoke of God, and constitute himself an arbiter and judge of good and evil."[63] The tree tested how man would seek knowledge: in submissive dependence upon the word of the Lord God or in proud independence, as if he were his own lord and god (Gen. 3:5–6, 22).[64] He could lead men into a sweet experiential knowledge of God and his good will, or a tragic experiential knowledge of evil and its consequences.

---

59. Gen. 5:5, 8, 11, 14, 17, 20, 27, 31.
60. Luther, *Lectures on Genesis*, in *LW*, 1:94 (Gen. 2:9).
61. Calvin, *Commentaries*, on Gen. 2:16–17.
62. Willet, *Hexapla*, 33, citing Gregory, *Morals in Job*, 35.10, in *RCS/OT*, 1:91.
63. Calvin, *Commentaries*, on Gen. 2:9.
64. See also Huldrych Zwingli, cited in *RCS/OT*, 1:93; and Hamilton, *The Book of Genesis, Chapters 1–17*, 165–66.

The other trees visibly displayed God's love to his human creature and his faithful offer of life upon obedience. We should not view the trees as magical, but as means of faithful communion with the God who reigns over life and death.[65] The tree of life functions in Proverbs as a metaphor for God's blessing on those who receive divine wisdom.[66] John of Damascus wrote that it was as if the Lord had said, "By means of all created things you will be drawn up to me, their Creator, and from them reap the one fruit which is myself, who am the true life."[67]

God made a covenant with Adam. We acknowledge that the term "covenant" does not appear in Genesis 2. However, we observe that God revealed himself as the covenant Lord and gave to Adam a solemn, legal, verbal revelation of his will, with an implicit promise of everlasting life, that defined their mutual relationship as generous Father and obedient son, who was called to serve God as prophet, priest, and king—an authorized officer representing his offspring with visible signs of his faithfulness. Thus, we are entirely justified in calling this arrangement a covenant.

Other Scripture Passages That Reveal the Covenant of Works

We also find references to the covenant of works in other Scripture passages. In *Hosea 6:6–7*, the Lord rebuked Israel: "For I desired mercy, and not sacrifice; and the knowledge of God more than burnt offerings. But they like men have transgressed the covenant: there have they dealt treacherously against me." The key phrase is "like men" (Hebrew *ke-adam*). Some interpreters have identified *adam* with a city of that name (Josh. 3:16) and translated it "at Adam." However, there is no biblical record of Israel sinning against God at that location, and this translation requires emending the Hebrew text, which reads "like," not "at." Another interpretation is to read the text as a comparison of Israel's sin to mankind's universal covenant breaking. If so, we must ask, How did all mankind come to be in a covenant relationship with God? The only explicitly named covenant in the Bible that relates to all mankind is that of Noah, and that covenant is a simple promise never to flood the whole world again. Another interpretation is to read the phrase to mean "like Adam" (KJV mg., ESV). In that case, which seems most likely, Hosea 6:7 indicates that Israel's rebellion against the laws of God's covenant parallels Adam's rebellion against the command of God's original

---

65. Hamilton, *The Book of Genesis, Chapters 1–17*, 163.
66. Prov. 3:18; 11:30; 13:12; 15:4.
67. John of Damascus, *An Exact Exposition of the Orthodox Faith*, 2.11, in *ACCS/OT*, 1:61.

covenant.[68] A reference to Adam's covenant breaking would fit with Hosea's other references to sins committed in early history (2:3; 9:10), including allusions to the book of Genesis (11:8; 12:3–4).[69]

Another significant text regarding the covenant of works is *Isaiah 24:5–6*: "The earth also is defiled under the inhabitants thereof; because they have transgressed the laws, changed the ordinance, broken the everlasting covenant. Therefore hath the curse devoured the earth, and they that dwell therein are desolate: therefore the inhabitants of the earth are burned, and few men left." God will send a "curse" upon the whole world because its people have "broken the everlasting covenant." It might be argued that "earth" (*erets*) should be understood as "land"—that is, the land of Israel. However, the context indicates that all nations are in view. This section of Isaiah (chaps. 24–27) speaks of worldwide judgment and final salvation. It follows a long section of the prophecy in which the Lord pronounces his judgments against various nations (chaps. 13–23). Chapter 24 shows its international scope in its references to "the isles of the sea" ("coastlands of the sea," ESV) and "the kings of the earth" (vv. 15, 21). Therefore, Isaiah 24:5–6 teaches that people of all nations have violated God's covenant and are liable to his curse. The only legal arrangement that Scripture records God making with the whole human race and resulting in a curse upon the earth is God's command to the first man. Edward Young concluded, "The eternal covenant here spoken of designates the fact that God has given His Law and ordinances to Adam, and in Adam to all mankind."[70]

The apostle Paul compared and contrasted Adam and Christ in *Romans 5:12–19*. We will reserve the study of this important text for our discussion of original sin. However, at this point, we note that the immediate consequences of Adam's sin included "condemnation" (*katakrima*) for our race (vv. 16, 18). The word, only here and in Romans 8:1, is an intensified form of "judgment," and the cognate verb (*katakrinō*) means to judge someone to be legally guilty and liable to punishment.[71] Here the punishment is "death" (vv. 12–17), precisely the judgment threatened against Adam by God in the garden. Paul's argument in Romans 5 presupposes that God set up a legal arrangement with Adam so that Adam's

---

68. Robertson, *The Christ of the Covenants*, 22–24.
69. Benjamin B. Warfield, *Selected Shorter Writings*, ed. John E. Meeter (Nutley, NJ: Presbyterian and Reformed, 1970), 1:128.
70. Edward Young, *The Book of Isaiah*, 3 vols. (Grand Rapids, MI: Eerdmans, 1969), 2:158.
71. Matt. 12:41–42; 20:18; 27:3; Mark 10:33; 14:64; 16:16; Luke 11:31–32; John 8:11; Rom. 2:1; 8:3, 34; 14:23; Heb. 11:7; James 5:9; 2 Pet. 2:6.

disobedience would bring mankind under guilt and punishment. In this regard, Adam was a type or shadow of Christ (v. 14). Paul understood Christ's saving work to take place in a covenantal context, in fulfillment of the promise of the ancient covenants.[72] Furthermore, Paul writes of Adam's sin as a "transgression" (v. 14), which implies breaking a "law" (4:15). Paul refers in the context to the "law" given to Israel (5:13, 20), which, of course, was a covenant. Therefore, it is reasonable to conclude that Paul also viewed God's legal arrangement with Adam in a manner similar to God's covenantal relationships with Israel and Christ.

If it were merely a matter of being the first human being to break God's command, then Paul would have traced our condemnation to Eve, not Adam. Laying the fall of mankind at the feet of Adam implies that he held a special legal position among human beings that could be granted only by God. Johannes Polyander (1568–1646) said that Adam is "the head and universal beginning of the whole human race," and though Eve sinned first, Adam's sin plunged the race into ruin, "as he is the chief parent by virtue of the covenant God established with him."[73]

We have seen that Genesis 2 reveals a covenant that promised life and threatened death conditional upon Adam's obedience or disobedience. In Adam, all men are covenant breakers and liable to God's condemnation and curse. Only Christ, who fulfills the promises in the new covenant, delivers sinners from all condemnation (Rom. 8:1). The covenant of works stands as the counterpoint to God's covenant of saving grace in Christ, our last Adam. If we abandon the doctrine of the covenant of works, we lose the legal basis for mankind's fall in Adam and justification in Christ, and we undermine the parallel between Adam and Christ, especially regarding the imputation of sin and righteousness.[74]

The Foundational Position of Covenants in God's Relationships to Man

Since the Lord made a covenant with the first man and all his natural descendants, and he structured all of redemptive history with covenants, we conclude that God wills for covenants to function as the basic framework

---

72. Rom. 9:4–5; 11:27; 1 Cor. 11:25; 2 Cor. 3:6; Gal. 3:15–17; 4:24; Eph. 2:12–13. Note how Paul used the covenantal formula "God of . . ." with regard to Christ (2 Cor. 11:31; Eph. 1:3, 17; cf. John 20:17; 1 Pet. 1:3).

73. Polyander, Walaeus, Thysius, and Rivetus, *Synopsis Purioris Theologiae*, 14.5 (1:339).

74. Belcher, *Genesis*, 68–69.

for all his relationships with human beings. This means that covenant is vital to practical piety. When we read in Scripture of the prayers of the godly, they are frequently addressed to God based on his faithfulness to keep his covenants. Bavinck said, "Covenant is the essence of true religion."[75]

First, consider the infinite gap between the Creator and his creature. On that basis alone, man could know God only as a servant knows his master. There could be no fellowship or friendship between God and man. By means of the covenant, however, the Lord bridges this gap and promises, "I will walk among you, and will be your God, and ye shall be my people" (Lev. 26:12). Bavinck said, "For then God has to come down from his lofty position, condescend to his creatures, impart, reveal, and give himself away to human beings."[76]

Second, the creature by nature cannot have any claims upon the Creator. After serving God for all its existence, mankind could only say, "We are unprofitable servants: we have done that which was our duty to do" (Luke 17:10). The covenantal promises grant to men the right and freedom to draw near to God and expect blessing and life from him when the conditions of the covenant are fulfilled.

Third, in covenant, God treats men as "rational and moral beings," as Bavinck said, not like plants, animals, or inanimate objects, but as people called "to serve him in love, freely and willingly."[77] Mere commandment and law, though well within God's sovereign rights, could never draw forth the glad obedience of men like God's rich promises do.

Therefore, in his wisdom, God made covenant central to his dealings with mankind. From the beginning, God has coupled law with promise in order to demonstrate his abundant goodness and enduring faithfulness, that he might woo people to glorify him and enjoy him forever.

Sing to the Lord
God's Faithfulness to His Covenant Promises

O give the Lord wholehearted praise,
To Him thanksgiving I will bring;
With all His people I will raise
My voice and of His glory sing.

---

75. Bavinck, *Reformed Dogmatics*, 2:569. The following points are summarized from his discussion.
76. Bavinck, *Reformed Dogmatics*, 2:569.
77. Bavinck, *Reformed Dogmatics*, 2:570.

His saints delight to search and trace
·His mighty works and wondrous ways;
Majestic glory, boundless grace,
And righteousness His work displays.

God's promise shall forever stand,
He cares for those who trust His word;
Upon His saints His mighty hand
The wealth of nations has conferred.

From Him His saints' redemption came;
His covenant sure no change can know;
Let all revere His holy Name
In heaven above and earth below.

Psalm 111
Tune: Germany
The Psalter, No. 304
Or Tune: Ossett
Trinity Hymnal—Baptist Edition, No. 767

Questions for Meditation or Discussion

1. What are four objections to the doctrine of the covenant of works? How do the authors answer those objections?
2. How do the authors define a covenant? How would you restate their meaning in your own words?
3. What evidence is there that this definition describes God's arrangement with Adam?
4. What are five common but not essential characteristics of biblical covenants?
5. How are these common covenantal characteristics evident in God's dealings with Adam?
6. What do the following passages of Scripture indicate or imply about the covenant with Adam: (1) Hosea 6:6–7, (2) Isaiah 24:5–6, and (3) Romans 5:12–19?
7. Why are covenants God's basic framework for his relationships with men?
8. How has reading this chapter increased your understanding of God's covenants? What questions has it left you asking?

Questions for Deeper Reflection

9. Critique the authors' definition of a covenant for its strengths and weaknesses, biblically and theologically. Would you change or refine the definition to improve it? How?

10. Select one of the Scripture passages listed under question 6. What arguments can be made to see a reference to the covenant of works in that text? What arguments can be made not to see such a reference there? Which is the best interpretation, and why?

15

God's Covenant with Adam, Part 2

Historical and Systematic Theology

Covenant theology has been woven into the Reformed confessional identity since the seventeenth century.[1] The Westminster Confession of Faith (7.1) says, "The distance between God and the creature is so great, that although reasonable creatures do owe obedience unto Him as their Creator, yet they could never have any fruition of Him as their blessedness and reward, but by some voluntary condescension on God's part, which He hath been pleased to express by way of covenant."[2] Thus, the assembly of divines presented covenant as the great bridge by which God linked heaven and earth and ordered his relationships with men. The confession (7.2) proceeds to say, "The first covenant made with man was a covenant of works (Gal. 3:12), wherein life was promised to Adam; and in him to his posterity (Rom. 10:5; 5:12–20), upon condition of perfect and personal obedience (Gen. 2:17; Gal. 3:10)."[3]

We find the same doctrine in the Westminster Shorter Catechism (Q. 12), which says, "When God had created man, he entered into a covenant of life with him, upon condition of perfect obedience; forbid-

---

1. For an early confessional example of the covenant with Adam, see the Irish Articles (Art. 21). The covenant of works was affirmed on the Continent in the Formula Consensus Helvetica (Canons 7–12). *Reformed Confessions*, 4:93–94, 522–23.
2. *Reformed Confessions*, 4:242.
3. *Reformed Confessions*, 4:242.

ding him to eat of the tree of the knowledge of good and evil, upon the pain of death (Gal. 3:12; Gen. 2:17)."[4] The covenant of works is here called "a covenant of life," but its violation was the ruin of mankind. The Shorter Catechism (Q. 16) explains: "The covenant being made with Adam, not only for himself, but for his posterity; all mankind, descending from him by ordinary generation, sinned in him, and fell with him, in his first transgression (Gen. 2:16–17; Rom. 5:12; 1 Cor. 15:21–22)."[5]

In this chapter, we will consider the historical roots of this doctrine and offer a systematic analysis of its mature formulation in Reformed orthodox theology.

Historical Roots of the Reformed Orthodox Doctrine

It has been claimed that covenant theology is "of comparatively recent development," being "unknown" to the church in ancient and medieval times, and while it is mentioned in the Westminster Confession, it was not fully developed until Johannes Cocceius wrote on the subject in the Netherlands.[6] However, covenant theology has much deeper roots, reaching through the Reformers into the earliest periods of the church.[7]

Patristic, Medieval, and Counter-Reformation Theology

Early Christian theologians understood Adam's condition before the fall in a manner consistent with important elements of the covenant of works. Irenaeus recognized a "legal" covenant that spanned history, grounded in the "natural precepts" of God's unchanging will that he had implanted in human nature so that man might enjoy fellowship with God in glory through obedience.[8] Adam ruined himself and marred God's image by his disobedience, but Christ is the "recapitulation" of Adam in order to save us.[9] Jerome (d. 420) and Cyril of

---

4. *Reformed Confessions*, 4:354.
5. *Reformed Confessions*, 4:355.
6. Charles Fred Lincoln, "The Development of the Covenant Theory," *Bibliotheca Sacra* 100 (1943): 136 (full article, 134–63).
7. Andrew A. Woolsey, *Unity and Continuity in Covenantal Thought: A Study in the Reformed Tradition to the Westminster Assembly*, Reformed Historical-Theological Studies (Grand Rapids, MI: Reformation Heritage Books, 2012); and J. Ligon Duncan III, "The Covenant Idea in Ante-Nicene Theology" (PhD diss., University of Edinburgh, 1995), https://www.era.lib.ed.ac.uk/bit stream/handle/1842/10618/Duncan1995.pdf.
8. Irenaeus, *Against Heresies*, 4.13; 4.14.1; 4.15.1; 4.25.1, 3, in *ANF*, 1:477–79, 496.
9. Irenaeus, *Against Heresies*, 3.18.1–2; 3.21.10; 3.22.3; 3.23.1, in *ANF*, 1:446, 454–55. See also John Chrysostom, Homilies 10 and 12 on Romans, in *NPNF*[1], 11:402–3, 423.

Alexandria (d. 444) interpreted Hosea 6:7 as comparing Israel's sins to Adam's covenant breaking.[10]

The doctrine that God made a covenant with Adam before the fall appears in explicit form as early as Augustine. He said, "For the first covenant, which was made with the first man, is just this: 'In the day ye eat thereof, ye shall surely die'" (Gen. 2:17).[11] If Adam "had willed to continue," he would have gained the reward of divine blessing.[12] The tree of life was a "sacrament" and "sign."[13] Against the Pelagians, Augustine said that Adam represented all mankind, so that all men and children "have . . . broken God's covenant in that one in whom all have sinned"— that is, Adam (cf. Rom. 5:12).[14] Andrew Woolsey writes, "The picture he presented of the divine arrangement with Adam in Eden before the fall contained all the ingredients of such a covenant as later portrayed by the 'covenant theologians.'"[15]

Though the Adamic "covenant" may not have been a theme explicitly treated by medieval theologians, the concept was embedded in the Augustinian tradition. For example, Peter Lombard said that God gave Adam and his posterity temporal life but promised eternal life:

> To preserve what he had given and for the deserving of what he had promised, God added the command of obedience to the natural reason that had been placed in the soul of man at creation, by which he was able to discern between good and evil. By observing this command, man would not lose what he had been given and would obtain what had been promised, so that he might come to his reward through merit.[16]

We also find an Adamic covenant in the teaching of Ambrogio Catarino (or Catharinus) Politi (1484–1553), a Dominican theologian and

---

10. Warfield, *Selected Shorter Writings*, 1:116–17. On Cyril, see *Patrologiae Graeca*, ed. J. P. Migne, 161 vols. (Paris: Imprimerie Catholique, 1864), vol. 71, col. 169–70.

11. Augustine, *The City of God*, 16.27, in NPNF[1], 2:326.

12. Augustine, *On Rebuke and Grace*, chap. 32, in NPNF[1], 5:484.

13. Augustine, *The Literal Meaning of Genesis*, 8.4.8, in *The Works of Saint Augustine: A Translation for the Twenty-First Century, Part I, Volume 13, On Genesis*, intro. and trans. Edmund Hill, ed. John E. Rotelle (Hyde Park, NY: New City Press, 2002), 351. Henceforth cited as *Works*, 1/13.

14. Augustine, *The City of God*, 16.27, in NPNF[1], 2:326; cf. *On Marriage and Concupiscence*, 2.24.11, in NPNF[1], 5:292.

15. Woolsey, *Unity and Continuity in Covenantal Thought*, 173.

16. Lombard, *The Sentences*, 2.20.6 (2:91–92). See also John of Damascus, *An Exact Exposition of the Orthodox Faith*, 2.30, in NPNF[2], 9.2:43–44.

Counter-Reformation polemicist. He said that God made a covenant with Adam as the representative of mankind before the fall in order to open the way to elevate man to eternal life while asserting God's lordship over man.[17] Protestant writers were aware of Catarino's view of Adam and the covenant.[18]

Reformed Theology in the Sixteenth Century

Over the course of the sixteenth century, the Reformed doctrine of God's covenant with Adam progressively developed from seeds of thought already present in the Augustinian tradition.[19] A covenant of works is implicit in the doctrine of law taught by John Calvin and his successor, Theodore Beza (1519–1605). Calvin and Beza viewed God's covenants throughout redemptive history to be one in substance, but they still wrote of a covenant of law that promised eternal life for perfect obedience.[20] Calvin rejected the medieval concept that God's covenant renders good works meritorious, but affirmed rather that "the reward for works depends on the free promise of the law."[21] God's command to Adam in the garden was the prime example of this principle of covenantal law, whereby obedience would have granted Adam eternal life.[22] In fact, Calvin said that the tree of life given to Adam, like the rainbow given to Noah, was a sacrament and seal of God's covenant.[23] Though Calvin and Beza did not call this

---

17. Aaron C. Denlinger, *Omnes in Adam ex Pacto Dei: Ambrogio Catarino's Doctrine of Covenantal Solidarity and Its Influence on Post-Reformation Reformed Theologians* (Göttingen: Vandenhoek and Ruprecht, 2011), 11, 142–43, 157; and William Cunningham, *The Reformers and the Theology of the Reformation* (Edinburgh: T&T Clark, 1866), 377–78.

18. John Salkeld, *A Treatise of Paradise* (London: by Edward Griffin for Nathaniel Butter, 1617), 301.

19. R. Sherman Isbell, "The Origin of the Concept of the Covenant of Works" (ThM thesis, Westminster Theological Seminary, 1976), 14–73; David A. Weir, *The Origins of the Federal Theology in Sixteenth-Century Reformation Thought* (Oxford: Oxford University Press, 1990), 99–152; Rowland S. Ward, *God and Adam: Reformed Theology and the Creation Covenant* (Wantirna, Australia: New Melbourne Press, 2003); Beeke and Jones, *A Puritan Theology*, 217–36; and Woolsey, *Unity and Continuity in Covenantal Thought*, 344–539.

20. Calvin, *Institutes*, 2.9.4; 2.17.5; *Commentaries*, on Jer. 32:40; Rom. 5:19; Theodore Beza, Theodore Beza's Confession (Art. 18, 22), in *Reformed Confessions*, 2:247, 272–73; and *A Booke of Christian Questions and Answers*, trans. Arthur Golding (London: by William How, for Abraham Veale, 1572), 56v. The original was *Quaestionum et responsionum christianarum libellus* (1570). For a modern translation, see Theodore Beza, *A Little Book of Christian Questions and Answers* (Allison Park, PA: Pickwick, 1986), Q. 129, 163–64.

21. Calvin, *Commentaries*, on Rom. 3:20. On medieval concepts of merit, see Heiko Augustinus Oberman, *The Harvest of Medieval Theology: Gabriel Biel and Late Medieval Nominalism* (Durham, NC: Labyrinth, 1983), 166–72; and Peter A. Lillback, *The Binding of God: Calvin's Role in the Development of Covenant Theology*, Texts and Studies in Reformation and Post-Reformation Thought (Grand Rapids, MI: Baker Academic, 2001), 46–50.

22. Calvin, *Commentaries*, on Gen. 2:16–17; 3:19; *Institutes*, 1.15.8; and Beza, *A Booke of Christian Questions and Answers*, 43v.

23. Calvin, *Institutes*, 4.14.18.

arrangement a covenant, we find the concept seminally present in early Genevan theology.[24]

Zacharias Ursinus (1534–1583) may have been the first Reformed theologian to use the language of a "covenant of creation" and "natural covenant" between God and Adam.[25] Ursinus's colleague Caspar Olevianus (1536–1587) also wrote of this covenant, referring to it as a "covenant of creation," "natural covenant," "first covenant," and "law of creation."[26] Franciscus Junius (1545–1602) also referred to the "covenant" made by God the Father in the love of his Son with our first parents, promising life for honoring God but otherwise threatening death.[27]

The earliest known use of the phrase "covenant of works" is attributed to British Reformed theologians. Dudley Fenner (1558–1587) may have been the first theologian to use the phrase in its Latin form (*foedus operum*) in 1585, contrasting it with the "covenant of gracious promise" (*gratuitae promissionis foedus*).[28] He may have learned it from his older friend, Thomas Cartwright (1535–1603), whose posthumous publications contrasted "the covenant of grace, called the gospel" with "the covenant of works, called the law," which "was given to Adam" before sin and the revelation of the gospel.[29] Robert Rollock said in 1596 that the covenant of God with man is "twofold," consisting of "the covenant of nature or

---

24. Woolsey, *Unity and Continuity in Covenantal Thought*, 282. See the extended argument for this conclusion in Lillback, *The Binding of God*, 276–304.

25. Zacharius Ursinus, *The Larger Catechism* (Q. 36), trans. Lyle D. Bierma, Fred Klooster, and John Medendorp, in *An Introduction to the Heidelberg Catechism*, Texts and Studies in Reformation and Post-Reformation Thought (Grand Rapids, MI: Baker Academic, 2005), 168–69. He also said that the "divine law" teaches "the kind of covenant that God established with mankind in creation" (Q. 10, p. 164). On the dating of this work to circa 1562, see Bierma's introduction (137). See also Zacharius Ursinus, *The Summe of the Christian Religion*, trans. Henry Parry (London: James Young, 1645), 517, 617 (Q. 92, 115).

26. Cited in Lyle D. Bierma, *The Covenant Theology of Caspar Olevianus* (Grand Rapids, MI: Reformation Heritage Books, 2005), 112–16; cf. Woolsey, *Unity and Continuity in Covenantal Thought*, 427–29.

27. Franciscus Junius, *Theses Theologicae* (1592), 25.3, in *Opuscula Theologica Selecta*, ed. Abraham Kuyper, Bibliotheca Reformata 1 (Amsterdam: Fredericum Muller cum Soc. Et Joannem Hermannum Kruyt, 1882), 184. On Junius and the covenant with Adam, see William K. B. Stoever, "The Covenant of Works in Puritan Theology: The Antinomian Crisis in New England" (PhD diss., Yale University, 1970), 31–32; and Mark W. Karlberg, *Covenant Theology in Reformed Perspective* (Eugene, OR: Wipf and Stock, 2000), 98.

28. Dudley Fenner, *Sacra Theologia*, 2nd ed. (Apud Eustathium Vignon, 1586), 4.1 (39). The first edition was published in 1585. On Fenner, see Weir, *The Origins of the Federal Theology*, 141–43.

29. Thomas Cartwright, *A Treatise of Christian Religion* (London: Felix Kyngston for Thomas Man, 1616), chaps. 13–14 (80, 74 [irregular pagination; should be 86]). Both Cartwright and Fenner traveled to the European continent, so it is possible that they learned the phrase there. Woolsey, *Unity and Continuity in Covenantal Thought*, 443–45.

works, and the covenant of grace (Gal. 4:24)."[30] The covenant of works promised life forever upon the "condition" of good works.[31] The term *condition* does not mean that man's good works had merit or that some wage was owed to them, for man owed God his good works in thankfulness for the gifts of creation and in order to glorify his Creator.[32] Adam's sin plunged the entire race descending from him into sin and death, both because of our natural relationship to Adam as our first father and because of his God-given role as our covenant representative.[33] William Perkins also taught "the covenant of works," which God "made with condition of perfect obedience and expressed in the moral law."[34] Perkins said, "The law, or covenant of works, propounds the bare justice of God without mercy," and linked it to Adam's original state: "The law was in nature by creation. The gospel is above nature and was revealed after the fall."[35] God required obedience from man in the garden of Eden and tested that obedience by prohibiting him from eating from the tree of the knowledge of good and evil, so that if man "persisted in his obedience" he would enjoy eternal life, but if he transgressed he would suffer "temporal and eternal death."[36]

Therefore, God's covenant with Adam was a doctrine taught explicitly by Augustine; implicitly affirmed by Lombard, Calvin, and Beza; and asserted with growing sophistication by other sixteenth-century Reformed theologians, such as Ursinus, Rollock, and Perkins. It was certainly not the invention of seventeenth-century theologians such as the Westminster divines.

Systematic Analysis of the Reformed Orthodox Doctrine

The covenant of works became a standard part of Reformed orthodox theology. We find it in influential systematic theologies like those by Johannes Wollebius and James Ussher,[37] and in the introduction to the New Testament in the *Statenvertaling* Bible (1637), the Dutch counterpart to the

---

30. "Robert Rollock's Catechism on God's Covenants," trans. and intro. Aaron C. Denlinger, *Mid-America Journal of Theology* 20 (2009): 110 (Q. 2) (full article, 105–29).
31. Rollock, "Catechism," 111 (Q. 7–8).
32. Rollock, *A Treatise of God's Effectual Calling,* in *Select Works,* 1:37; and "Catechism," 111–12 (Q. 12–13).
33. Breno L. Macedo, "The Covenant Theology of Robert Rollock" (ThM thesis, Puritan Reformed Theological Seminary, 2012), 118–20.
34. Perkins, *A Golden Chain,* chap. 19, in *Works,* 6:65.
35. Perkins, *Commentary on Galatians,* on Gal. 4:24–25, in *Works,* 2:302–3.
36. Perkins, *A Golden Chain,* chap. 9, in *Works,* 6:31.
37. Wollebius, *Compendium,* 1.8.(1).2 (64); and Ussher, *A Body of Divinity,* 8th head (111).

Authorized or King James Version.[38] Many significant treatises addressing the covenant of works were written by theologians such as David Dickson, John Ball (1585–1640), Samuel Rutherford (1600–1661), Cocceius, Francis Roberts (1609–1675), William Strong, Anthony Burgess (d. 1664), Francis Turretin, Nehemiah Coxe (fl. 1670, d. 1689), Ezekiel Hopkins (1634–1690), Herman Witsius (1636–1708), Wilhelmus à Brakel, Thomas Boston, John Colquhoun (1748–1827), and Thomas Bell (1733–1802).[39]

These theologians exhibited significant unity in their view of the covenant with Adam, but with some variety regarding specific questions. In the following treatment, we will analyze the Reformed orthodox teachings about the Adamic covenant under several major principles.

Covenants in General

Reformed orthodox theologians recognized the *doctrinal centrality of the covenants* in systematic theology. Error regarding the covenant of works obscures the covenant of grace and produces confusion about the law and Christ's saving work.[40] A right understanding of the Adamic covenant lays the foundation for our practical knowledge of ourselves and God's

---

38. "Inhoudt des Nieuwen Testaments," in *Statenvertaling* (Leiden: Paulus Aertsz van Ravesteyn, 1637), fol. *2r; English translation from "The Argument of the New Testament," *The Dutch Annotations upon the Whole Bible*, trans. Theodore Haak (1657; facsimile repr., Leerdam, The Netherlands: Gereformeerde Bijbelstichting, 2002). See Kersten, *Reformed Dogmatics*, 1:192.

39. David Dickson, *Therapeutica Sacra; Shewing Briefly the Method of Healing of Diseases of Conscience, Concerning Regeneration* (Edinburgh: Evan Tyler, 1664), 71–85; John Ball, *A Treatise of the Covenant of Grace* (London: by G. Miller for Edward Brewster, 1645), 6–14; Samuel Rutherford, *The Covenant of Life Opened: or a Treatise of the Covenant of Grace* (Edinburgh: by Andre Anderson, for Robert Broun, 1655), 3–56; Johannes Cocceius, *The Doctrine of the Covenant and Testament of God*, trans. Casey Carmichael (Grand Rapids, MI: Reformation Heritage Books, 2016), 27–57; Francis Roberts, *Mysterium et Medulla Bibliorum. The Mysterie and Marrow of the Bible: Viz. God's Covenants with Man* (London: by R. W. for George Calvert, 1657), 1.2–2.1 (10–60); Strong, *A Discourse of the Two Covenants*, 1–111; Anthony Burgess, *Vindiciae Legis: or, A Vindication of the Morall Law and the Covenants*, Westminster Assembly Project (1647; facsimile repr., Grand Rapids, MI: Reformation Heritage Books, 2011), 104–40; Turretin, *Institutes*, 8.3–6 (1:574–86); Nehemiah Coxe, *A Discourse of the Covenants that God Made with Men before the Law* (London: J. D. for Nathaniel Ponder and Benjamin Alsop, 1681), 15–45, reprinted in Nehemiah Coxe and John Owen, *Covenant Theology from Adam to Christ*, ed. Ronald D. Miller, James M. Renihan, and Francisco Orozco (Palmdale, CA: Reformed Baptist Academic Press, 2005), 42–58; Ezekiel Hopkins, *The Doctrine of the Two Covenants* (London: Richard Smith, 1712), 59–124; Witsius, *The Economy of the Covenants*, book 1 (1:41–62); Brakel, *The Christian's Reasonable Service*, 1:355–67; Thomas Boston, *A View of the Covenant of Works*, in *Works*, 11:171–339; John Colquhoun, *A Treatise on the Covenant of Works* (Edinburgh: Thomsons Brothers, 1821); and Thomas Bell, *A View of the Covenants of Works and Grace; and a Treatise on the Nature and Effects of Saving Faith. To which Are Added, Several Discourses on the Supreme Deity of Jesus Christ* (Glasgow: by Edward Khull and Co. for W. Somerville et al., 1814), 3–296. Bell was a minister of the Presbytery of Relief who served in Jedburgh and Glasgow.

40. Brakel, *The Christian's Reasonable Service*, 1:355; and Hopkins, *The Doctrine of the Two Covenants*, 1.

redemptive will.[41] Therefore, Witsius said that whoever would study God's covenants must do so with "sacred awe" as a teachable "disciple of the Holy Scriptures."[42]

The Bible reveals a *variety of kinds of covenants.* Reformed orthodox theologians tended to define covenants as mutual agreements between consenting parties. Consequently, they often discussed covenants as if they were legal contracts in which the parties would "sign on" to mutually agreed-upon stipulations. Since God sovereignly imposes covenants upon men, some theologians came to the surprising conclusion that God's dealings with men are not properly covenants.[43] However, these theologians also recognized that a biblical covenant might be a permanent decree, a solemn promise, or a testament (Num. 18:19; Jer. 33:20; Heb. 9:15–17).[44] In that case, a covenant is a unilateral pledge, a "one-sided (*monopleuron*)," to use Turretin's terminology, but more commonly "two-sided (*dipleuron*)."[45] We see here an example of the exegetical sensitivity of Reformed orthodox theologians, who did not aim to proof text "a prefabricated doctrine" but to open up the Holy Scriptures.[46]

The element of voluntary consent that Reformed theology recognized in two-sided covenants, though not essential to God's making a covenant, does show us the *requisite human response* to God's covenants, for consent is man's reverential and grateful duty, and the only means by which he can claim the promises of the covenant.[47] We must not think that man's consent is necessary to bind him to his covenantal duties toward God, for the Lord's covenants are his sovereign injunctions and commands (Heb. 9:20).[48] Since God sovereignly initiates all his covenants, they are all "monopleuric" in essence, but God's covenants create relationships of "mutuality" and "responsibility."[49] Therefore, it is a mistake to play off

---

41. Coxe, *A Discourse of the Covenants,* 2.1 (17).
42. Witsius, *The Economy of the Covenants,* 1.1.1 (1:41–42).
43. Burgess, *Vindiciae Legis,* 124; Roberts, *Mysterium et Medulla Bibliorum,* 2.1.4 (25); Turretin, *Institutes,* 8.3.1 (1:574); and Hopkins, *The Doctrine of the Two Covenants,* 5–8.
44. Ball, *A Treatise of the Covenant of Grace,* 3; and Witsius, *The Economy of the Covenants,* 1.1.3 (1:42–43).
45. Turretin, *Institutes,* 8.3.3 (1:574).
46. J. Mark Beach, "Christ and the Covenant: Francis Turretin's Federal Theology as a Defense of the Doctrine of Grace" (PhD diss., Calvin Theological Seminary, 2005), 92.
47. Coxe, *A Discourse of the Covenants,* 1.2.2; 1.3.5–6 (5, 8–9).
48. Witsius, *The Economy of the Covenants,* 1.1.13 (1:47).
49. Richard A. Muller, "The Covenant of Works and the Stability of Divine Law in Seventeenth-Century Reformed Orthodoxy: A Study in the Theology of Herman Witsius and Wilhelmus à Brakel," *Calvin Theological Journal* 29 (1994): 86–87 (full article, 75–101).

covenant against election, as if they were two divergent streams in Reformed thought instead of complementary truths.

Reformed orthodox theologians often discussed covenants as if they were legal contracts. Ironically, contractual language can obscure the *personal and loving fidelity* that the covenants seal—an important theme in covenant theology.[50] We should also never misunderstand covenant theologians to assert a merely contractual relationship without personal love. The binding formality of the covenant does not negate faithful love but seals it, just as the solemn vows of matrimony seal the love between a bride and groom.[51]

Introduction to the Covenant with Adam

Reformed orthodox theologians said that although Genesis does not explicitly call God's dealings with Adam a covenant, the text contains the *implicit revelation of a covenant with Adam.* The threat of death for violating God's prohibition logically implies the promise of life for observing his law, which is the principle of "do this and live" seen throughout the Scriptures.[52] The tree of life was a visible confirmation of this promise, and the tree of knowledge was a sign of the contrary threat, just as the rainbow was a sign of the covenant with Noah (Genesis 9).[53] This interpretation of Genesis 2 is confirmed by Hosea 6:7, which is best translated as "transgressed the covenant like Adam" (*ke-adam*), as is evident when compared to Job 31:33, "covered my transgressions as Adam" (*ke-adam*; cf. Gen. 3:12).[54]

The teachings of the apostle Paul also indicate a covenant of works with Adam. Paul contrasts the law "of works" and "the law of faith" as two different ways of justification (Rom. 3:27).[55] Paul says, "The commandment . . . was ordained to life" (Rom. 7:10), and as such it must have

---

50. Turretin, *Institutes*, 8.3.2 (1:574).

51. See Theodore Beza, *Sermons upon the Three First Chapters of the Canticle of Canticles*, trans. John Harmar (Oxford: Joseph Barnes, 1587).

52. Lev. 18:5; Deut. 27:26; Ezek. 20:11; Matt. 19:17; Gal. 3:12.

53. On these arguments, see Ball, *A Treatise of the Covenant of Grace*, 6; Burgess, *Vindiciae Legis*, 123; Turretin, *Institutes*, 8.3.7 (1:575–76); Brakel, *The Christian's Reasonable Service*, 1:360–62; Boston, *A View of the Covenant of Works*, in *Works*, 11:182; and Colquhoun, *A Treatise on the Covenant of Works*, 66. See also Won Taek Lim, *The Covenant Theology of Francis Roberts* (Chungnam, South Korea: King and Kingdom, 2002), 70–89.

54. Turretin, *Institutes*, 8.3.8 (1:576); Brakel, *The Christian's Reasonable Service*, 1:365–66; Boston, *A View of the Covenant of Works*, in *Works*, 11:182; and Colquhoun, *A Treatise on the Covenant of Works*, 6–7.

55. Boston, *A View of the Covenant of Works*, in *Works*, 11:182; and Colquhoun, *A Treatise on the Covenant of Works*, 12–13.

been given first to man in his original sinless state.[56] Children are not guilty of their parents' sins, but Adam's sin brought condemnation on mankind (Romans 5), which implies that God made a special legal arrangement with Adam. Paul's parallel between Adam and Christ implies a covenant with the former, just as we are saved by covenant in the latter.[57]

In Galatians 4:21–31, Paul explicitly calls the promise of justification by legal works a covenant when he speaks of "the two covenants" (Gal. 4:24).[58] Paul does not reduce the Mosaic covenant to a law of works, for Moses wrote of the gospel as well, and the old covenant saints hoped in the promise of Christ.[59] The covenant of which Paul writes was a law that demanded perfect obedience with the threat of a curse (Gal. 3:10; 5:3).[60] This law could bring only death to sinners (2 Cor. 3:6). Paul attributes the origin of death to the first Adam and life to the last Adam (Rom. 5:12, 17; 1 Cor. 15:21–22).[61] When we line up Paul's contrast of two covenants with his contrasts of death in Adam versus life in Christ, it is apparent that the covenant Paul has in view was a legal covenant that God made with Adam.[62]

Theologians used *diverse names for the covenant with Adam*. They called it a "covenant of friendship," because the parties were already at peace with each other and needed no reconciliation. They also named it a "covenant of creation" or "covenant of nature," because it stood upon the original integrity of human nature as God created it. Some called it a "covenant of life" because of its implicit promise of life upon condition of obedience. Others called it a "legal covenant" or "covenant of works," because its condition was obedience to God's command.[63] The variety of titles applied to this covenant reminds us not to wax dogmatic over specific terms.

---

56. Colquhoun, *A Treatise on the Covenant of Works*, 13.

57. Burgess, *Vindiciae Legis*, 123–24; Boston, *A View of the Covenant of Works*, in *Works*, 11:183; and Colquhoun, *A Treatise on the Covenant of Works*, 7–10, 18–20.

58. Rollock, "Catechism," 110 (Q. 2); Perkins, *Commentary on Galatians*, on Gal. 4:24–25, in *Works*, 2:302–3; Boston, *A View of the Covenant of Works*, in *Works*, 11:181; and Colquhoun, *A Treatise on the Covenant of Works*, 5–6.

59. Strong, *A Discourse of the Two Covenants*, 22; and Bell, *A View of the Covenants of Works and Grace*, 8.

60. Bell, *A View of the Covenants of Works and Grace*, 90, 93.

61. Bell, *A View of the Covenants of Works and Grace*, 150–52.

62. The preceding arguments are developed and defended exegetically in the previous chapter.

63. Rollock, *A Treatise of God's Effectual Calling*, in *Select Works*, 1:34; Ames, *The Marrow of Theology*, 1.24.13 (150–51); Dickson, *Therapeutica Sacra*, 80–82; Roberts, *Mysterium et Medulla Bibliorum*, 1.2.3; 2.1.4 (17, 24–25); Strong, *A Discourse of the Two Covenants*, 2; Rutherford, *The Covenant of Life Opened*, 18–20; Goodwin, *Of the Creatures*, in *Works*, 7:22–23, 49; *Ephesians*, in *Works*, 1:157; Turretin, *Institutes*, 8.3.4 (1:575); Coxe, *A Discourse of the Covenants*, 1.5; 2.6–7 (12, 28–29); Witsius, *The Economy of the Covenants*, 1.1.15; 1.2.1 (1:49–50); Colquhoun, *A Treatise on the Covenant of Works*, 3; and Gill, *Body of Divinity*, 313.

In accord with Reformed orthodox teachings, we may offer the following *summary of the first covenant* made in history: The Lord God freely made a covenant with Adam as the federal representative of all his natural descendants, in which God threatened death for disobedience but promised eternal life for perfect obedience, according to the visible signs of the tree of the knowledge of good and evil and the tree of life.[64]

The Covenant of Works and the Law

God crystallized the obedience required of man into the law about eating the fruit of the garden's trees. Theologians called this a *positive, symbolic, and sacramental law*. It was positive because it did not arise immediately from either the moral perfection of the divine nature or the human nature made in God's image, but merely from God's will.[65] It was symbolic because it allowed for a more open display of obedience to God's authority.[66] It was sacramental because the trees acted as signs of the covenant to assure Adam that both the promised life and threatened death were certain.[67] The trees had no inherent power to impart life or inflict death, but the cause of life and death was the power of God's word.[68] The tree of knowledge was so named because man's response to God's prohibition would result in new experiential knowledge of good and evil.[69]

Reformed orthodox theologians also taught that the covenant engaged man through *natural moral law*. The positive law of the trees was rooted in man's natural obligation to obey God.[70] The natural law is that law of God grounded in God's nature and inherent in human nature.[71] A classic Scripture passage for natural law is Romans 2:14–15, where the apostle Paul says that "the Gentiles, which have not the law"—that is, they lack the written Word of God—still "by nature" follow some of its precepts

---

64. Witsius, *The Economy of the Covenants*, 1.2.1 (1:50); Strong, *A Discourse of the Two Covenants*, 1; and Colquhoun, *A Treatise on the Covenant of Works*, 5.
65. Burgess, *Vindiciae Legis*, 104; and Colquhoun, *A Treatise on the Covenant of Works*, 47–50.
66. Burgess, *Vindiciae Legis*, 106.
67. Witsius, *The Economy of the Covenants*, 1.6.1 (1:104–5); Colquhoun, *A Treatise on the Covenant of Works*, 112; and Roberts, *Mysterium et Medulla Bibliorum*, 2.1.1; 2.1.4 (22, 25), citing Augustine, *The Literal Meaning of Genesis*, 8.4.8; 8.6.12; 8.13.28–30, in *Works*, 1/13:351, 354, 363.
68. Strong, *A Discourse of the Two Covenants*, 3, citing Luther. See Luther, *Lectures on Genesis*, in *LW*, 1:95–96 (Gen. 2:9).
69. Roberts, *Mysterium et Medulla Bibliorum*, 2.1.4 (31–33); Witsius, *The Economy of the Covenants*, 1.6.18 (1:113–14); Turretin, *Institutes*, 8.4.3–5; 8.5.3 (1:579, 581); Hopkins, *The Doctrine of the Two Covenants*, 66; and Colquhoun, *A Treatise on the Covenant of Works*, 116.
70. Turretin, *Institutes*, 8.4.4 (1:579).
71. Colquhoun, *A Treatise on the Covenant of Works*, 44.

because of "the work of the law written in their hearts, their conscience also bearing witness." Being created by God in his image, mankind has an inner law—not the saving grace promised in Christ (Jer. 31:33), but a universal sense of direction and obligation.[72] Though theologically there is a distinction between the natural law of Adam and the moral law of the Ten Commandments,[73] they contain the same ethical principles, so that Adam had the essence of the Decalogue in his mind and heart.[74] Though we presently associate law with the coercion of sinners (1 Tim. 1:9), sinless Adam would have found the law to be "the perfect law of liberty" (James 1:25).[75]

Roberts identified God's natural or moral law in the heart with the covenant of works, but most theologians distinguished them.[76] Natural law arises from God's absolute authority as Creator, for which obedience is due to him without any promise of a reward. A covenant, however, arises from God's love, for in a covenant, he freely promises to reward obedience.[77] God wrote natural law on the human heart by creation, but he made the covenant by his word and signs. Though in Christ we escape the penalty of the covenant of works and are justified by grace, the natural and moral law remains a rule of life to direct us, for man is always under the authority of God.[78]

The covenant of law placed man under the *requirement of perfect and perpetual obedience.*[79] That obedience was to be perfect in its inward motives (Matt. 7:18), perfect with respect to every part of God's law (Gal. 3:10; James 2:10), perfect in every part of man's existence to the highest degree (Luke 10:27–28), and perpetual until God concluded the trial and bestowed his reward.[80] Most theologians thought that the test would have lasted only

---

72. Burgess, *Vindiciae Legis*, 60–62, 67, 105, 115–18; Coxe, *A Discourse of the Covenants*, 2.2 (18–19); Turretin, *Institutes*, 8.3.12 (1:577); and Boston, *A View of the Covenant of Works*, in *Works*, 11:179, 191.

73. Burgess, *Vindiciae Legis*, 148–49. Burgess noted three distinctions: (1) the moral law contains some positive law, such as the specific day of the Sabbath commandment; (2) the moral law increases obligation by its revelation; (3) the moral law, considered in the context of the whole covenant with Israel, includes the call to faith and repentance.

74. Burgess, *Vindiciae Legis*, 150; and Colquhoun, *A Treatise on the Covenant of Works*, 45. On natural law, see Witsius, *The Economy of the Covenants*, 1.3.2, 8 (1:60, 62).

75. Witsius, *The Economy of the Covenants*, 1.3.5–6 (1:61–62); and Brakel, *The Christian's Reasonable Service*, 1:358.

76. Roberts, *Mysterium et Medulla Bibliorum*, 2.1.1 (20–21).

77. Burgess, *Vindiciae Legis*, 122.

78. Dickson, *Therapeutica Sacra*, 71–72; and Boston, *A View of the Covenant of Works*, in *Works*, 11:191–92.

79. Westminster Larger Catechism (Q. 20), in *Reformed Confessions*, 4:303.

80. Boston, *A View of the Covenant of Works*, in *Works*, 11:194–96; and Colquhoun, *A Treatise on the Covenant of Works*, 54–56, 58–59.

for a limited probationary period, so that God might grant his reward.[81] This test of obedience was not unreasonable, for God created Adam in a state of complete goodness as God's image (Gen. 1:27, 31), with flawless knowledge, righteousness, and holiness (Eph. 4:24; Col. 3:10).[82] Therefore, perfect and perpetual obedience for Adam did not mean striving after an impossible standard, as it does for fallen sinners, but merely continuing to be what God had created him to be, and out of that holiness to produce good works. God well fitted Adam to keep this covenant of obedience.[83]

A violation of this covenant would constitute a *transgression of the whole law*. If Adam disobeyed God's command, he would in effect forsake God as his highest purpose and supreme good, and embrace the lust of the flesh, the lust of the eyes, and the pride of life (1 John 2:16).[84] By that one act of rebellion, our first parents broke, in principle, all of the Ten Commandments. They abandoned their God and made gods out of themselves and the Devil. They did not keep the ordinance God had appointed, by which their obedience would glorify him. They despised the name of God in his attributes of goodness, wisdom, trustworthiness, and so on; profaned the sacramental sign; ignored God's word; and misconstrued his providential works. They made themselves unfit for holy worship on the Sabbath. They overthrew their duties as husband and wife, abandoned their descendants, and did not honor their heavenly Father. They murdered themselves and all mankind. They gave themselves over to sensual desires. They stole what was not their own. They bore false witness against the Lord. They became discontent and covetous. Truly, this one sin contained a world of evils.[85] The single act of eating the fruit made Adam and his race liable to the full penalty threatened in the covenant, just as the Mosaic law threatens a curse upon all who fail to obey every commandment (Gal. 3:10; cf. Deut. 27:26; 28:15).[86]

---

81. Witsius, *The Economy of the Covenants*, 1.2.17; 1.3.25 (1:59, 70); Boston, *An Illustration of the Doctrines of the Christian Religion*, in *Works*, 1:232; and Colquhoun, *A Treatise on the Covenant of Works*, 5, 58. We note, however, that Hopkins thought a limited probationary period was a speculative doctrine, not clearly revealed in the Scriptures. Hopkins, *The Doctrine of the Two Covenants*, 117–18.

82. Witsius, *The Economy of the Covenants*, 1.2.9 (1:54); and Boston, *A View of the Covenant of Works*, in *Works*, 11:184–85.

83. Roberts, *Mysterium et Medulla Bibliorum*, 2.1.5 (34); and Witsius, *The Economy of the Covenants*, 1.3.23 (1:69).

84. Strong, *A Discourse of the Two Covenants*, 14; and Coxe, *A Discourse of the Covenants*, 2.8.3 (31).

85. Polyander, Walaeus, Thysius, and Rivetus, *Synopsis Purioris Theologiae*, 14.7–8 (1:341); Ussher, *A Body of Divinity*, 8th head (119–20); and Boston, *Human Nature in Its Fourfold State*, 132–33.

86. Roberts, *Mysterium et Medulla Bibliorum*, 2.1.4 (30–33); cf. Witsius, *The Economy of the Covenants*, 1.3.24 (1:69–70).

The Human Party of the Covenant of Works

Reformed orthodox theologians said that in the covenant of works, Adam stood as the *federal representative of his natural descendants.*[87] The text of Genesis teaches that Adam was the representative head of mankind. God's word to "be fruitful, and multiply" (Gen. 1:28) was not addressed to Adam alone, but to the race as a whole. The law of marriage (2:18–24) also was not for Adam alone, but Christ said it is God's law to mankind (Matt. 19:5). The death penalty that God threatened upon Adam (Gen. 2:17) has brought death upon all men (Rom. 5:12). Paul's teaching on the opposition of the first Adam and the last Adam (Rom. 5:15–19) as sources of condemnation or justification shows us that Adam legally represented his descendants just as Christ represents God's elect people.[88] Since our natural parents do not represent us before God in this manner, Adam's role must be attributed to more than his natural headship as the father of the race. It presumes a covenant in which God legally appointed him to this weighty position.[89]

Reformed orthodox theologians understood that the covenant of works with Adam holds a crucial place in their polemic against theologies tending toward Pelagianism. Without this covenant, the foundation for the doctrine of original sin is shaken.[90] To those who objected that this arrangement is unfair, it was answered that no one would complain if Adam brought blessing to all mankind. The Lord gave us a sinless and well-equipped representative. Would we have done better than Adam? Furthermore, every sincere believer rejoices in the representative principle when Christ acts as our representative in procuring our salvation. Ultimately, these theologians reminded objectors that God acted with infinite wisdom and sovereign authority, and our minds must rest submissively in his ways.[91]

Although Adam represented mankind in a manner similar to Christ's representation of his people, there is *no mediator of grace* in the covenant

---

87. Strong, *A Discourse of the Two Covenants,* 2, 73–74; Goodwin, *Ephesians,* in *Works,* 1:75; Coxe, *A Discourse of the Covenants,* 2.5 (26–27); Turretin, *Institutes,* 8.3.11; 9.9.11–13 (1:576–77, 616–17); Boston, *A View of the Covenant of Works,* in *Works,* 11:186–88; and Colquhoun, *A Treatise on the Covenant of Works,* 18–20, 33–39.

88. Witsius, *The Economy of the Covenants,* 1.2.14–15 (1:58); and Hopkins, *The Doctrine of the Two Covenants,* 92–94.

89. Hopkins, *The Doctrine of the Two Covenants,* 85–88.

90. Boston, *A View of the Covenant of Works,* in *Works,* 11:180.

91. Witsius, *The Economy of the Covenants,* 1.2.16–18 (1:58–59); and Boston, *A View of the Covenant of Works,* in *Works,* 11:189.

of works, for it was made directly between God and man. No mediator was necessary, for God had created man in his holy image. Therefore, man needed no satisfaction for his sins and no intercessor in God's holy presence.[92] Though the tree of life was a sacramental sign of receiving life from God, it was not a sacrament of Christ as the Mediator of saving grace.[93] This is the great difference between the covenant of works and the covenant of grace. Both covenants demanded the same obedience for justification, but the covenant of works required man to work his own righteousness by the goodness already supplied to him by God, whereas the covenant of grace grants sinners the righteousness of another.[94]

The Consequences of the Covenant of Works

The covenant with Adam contained the *threat of death in the fullest sense.*[95] The death threatened to Adam included separation from life in its widest meaning. In the Bible, death includes the separation of the soul from God (or *spiritual death*; Eph. 2:1, 5; cf. 4:18; 1 Tim. 5:6), the separation of the body from the soul (or *physical death*; John 8:52), the afflictions that result in physical death (Ex. 10:17; 1 Cor. 15:31; 2 Cor. 11:23), and the separation of the sinner from all enjoyment of God's goodness as he suffers punishment in hell (or *eternal death*; Rev. 20:14). When God imposed the death sentence on Adam and Eve, it included all manner of afflictions, such as sorrow, sweating, and toil (Gen. 3:16–19). When Paul writes that "death" came through Adam (Rom. 5:12), that was the full "wages of sin" in contrast to "eternal life" (6:23), including spiritual death (8:6–7). God executed this death upon Adam and his family in stages, with spiritual death coming immediately, afflictions soon following, physical death falling upon each person in God's appointed time, and eternal death ultimately seizing all the unregenerate.[96] The sin of man's representative broke the covenant of works. Its promise of justification and life could no longer offer any hope to mankind. However, the curse of the covenant abides on

---

92. Ball, *A Treatise of the Covenant of Grace*, 9; Dickson, *Therapeutica Sacra*, 77–78; and Roberts, *Mysterium et Medulla Bibliorum*, 2.1.5 (34).
93. Burgess, *Vindiciae Legis*, 136; and Witsius, *The Economy of the Covenants*, 1.6.3, 20 (1:106, 114).
94. Hopkins, *The Doctrine of the Two Covenants*, 78.
95. Coxe, *A Discourse of the Covenants*, 2.2 (20).
96. Roberts, *Mysterium et Medulla Bibliorum*, 2.1.4 (27–30). See also Burgess, *Vindiciae Legis*, 109; Witsius, *The Economy of the Covenants*, 1.5.3–21 (83–93); Boston, *A View of the Covenant of Works*, in *Works*, 11:208–14; and Colquhoun, *A Treatise on the Covenant of Works*, 88–100.

all who are not reconciled to God by Christ's grace (John 3:18; Eph. 2:3). Man's inability to keep the law does not release him from this sentence of death.[97] God does not lose his right to our obedience because we cannot render it to him, especially since that inability is due to our unwillingness.

The covenant of works also promised the *reward of eternal life*. Though the text of Genesis 2:17 does not explicitly include a promise of life with the threat of death, Reformed theologians argued for its implicit presence. First, the threat of death for disobedience implies a promise of life for obedience. Second, the tree of life was a sacramental sign of life without end (3:22; cf. Rev. 2:7). Third, the moral law revealed through Moses, which is essentially the same as the law given to Adam, promises reward and life for obedience.[98] Fourth, people ignorant of the Scriptures commonly believe that God will reward the good, for God has impressed this principle upon human nature in the conscience (Rom. 2:15). Fifth, God put Adam to the test under a law of works, and it is scarcely conceivable that he would not reward obedience rendered under trial.[99]

Reformed theologians agreed that God promised that Adam would live forever in fellowship with God if he obeyed the divine command. This much is evident from the threat of death upon condition of disobedience (Gen. 2:17) and God's explanation that to eat of the tree of life is to live forever (3:22). However, theologians debated the question of whether the promised life entailed a translation of Adam to heavenly glory or his continuance in a perfect but earthly paradise.[100] Thomas Goodwin and John Gill argued that Adam would have enjoyed a blessed and never-ending natural life on earth, but not a supernatural life in glory. The moral law of the Old Testament does not promise heaven, but applies "do this and live" to earthly favors. Paul contrasts Adam's earthly life to Christ's heavenly glory (1 Cor. 15:47–50).[101] Some theologians, such as Roberts, Coxe, Witsius, and Hopkins, while perhaps favoring the reward of heavenly glory, demurred from offering a dogmatic answer to this question since the Scriptures are silent on it.[102] Others, such as Calvin, Turretin, Boston,

---

97. Dickson, *Therapeutica Sacra*, 78–79.
98. Lev. 18:5; Ps. 19:11; Rom. 7:10; 10:5; Gal. 3:11–12.
99. Brakel, *The Christian's Reasonable Service*, 1:360–62; Witsius, *The Economy of the Covenants*, 1.4.2–3, 7 (1:71–72, 74); and Coxe, *A Discourse of the Covenants*, 2.3 (21–25).
100. Beeke and Jones, *A Puritan Theology*, 227–29.
101. Goodwin, *Of the Creatures*, in *Works*, 7:49–53; and Gill, *Body of Divinity*, 314–15.
102. Roberts, *Mysterium et Medulla Bibliorum*, 2.1.4 (26–27); Coxe, *A Discourse of the Covenants*, 2.3.1 (23); Witsius, *The Economy of the Covenants*, 1.4.9 (1:76); and Hopkins, *The Doctrine of the Two Covenants*, 60–64.

and Colquhoun, stated that God would have translated Adam at some point to heavenly glory if he had persevered in obedience. In the New Testament Gospels, God's law promises eternal life in God's kingdom to those who keep it fully (Matt. 19:16–17; Luke 10:28). Paul indicates that this is the same eternal life that Christ obtained by his satisfaction of the law's demands and that we receive by faith.[103] Furthermore, it is reasonable to think that if God threatened eternal death in hell for disobedience, God would have granted Adam eternal life in heaven for obedience.[104] Reformed theologians with various views on this question generally agreed that heaven is sweeter to believers in Christ than it ever would have been to Adam, if for no other reasons than that Christians have tasted the bitterness of sin and they commune with the incarnate Lord Jesus Christ as those redeemed by his precious blood.[105]

Reformed orthodox theologians often emphasized *God's sovereignty in granting a reward* to man's obedience. God did not make a covenant with his equal, but with a creature infinitely below him. God had every right to require obedience without promise of reward, for it is man's duty to the Lord (Luke 17:10). Therefore, God's covenant was an act of love and goodness to man.[106] However, this raises a question: Do God's love and goodness necessarily make him a covenant God, or is the covenant God's free and sovereign choice? Witsius, for one, wrestled with this question. He affirmed that God owes his creatures nothing (Rom. 11:35–36), but in the end he found himself unable to resolve how God could not reward obedience with eternal life, though he bowed before God's incomprehensibility.[107] Turretin went even further, saying that while justice did not bind God to reward man, God's goodness and love "demanded" a covenant that promised eternal reward, for God "could not help loving and rewarding the creature doing his duty."[108] Other theologians, like Coxe and

---

103. Rom. 7:10; 8:3–4; Gal. 3:11–12; 4:5.
104. Calvin, *Commentaries*, on Gen. 2:17; Turretin, *Institutes*, 8.6.4–9 (1:583–85); Boston, *A View of the Covenant of Works*, in *Works*, 11:204; and Colquhoun, *A Treatise on the Covenant of Works*, 68, 73–76.
105. Goodwin, *Of the Creatures*, in *Works*, 7:49–52; Coxe, *A Discourse of the Covenants*, 2.3.1 (23); Hopkins, *The Doctrine of the Two Covenants*, 67–68; Boston, *A View of the Covenant of Works*, in *Works*, 11:205–6; Gill, *Body of Divinity*, 314–15; and Colquhoun, *A Treatise on the Covenant of Works*, 77–78.
106. Roberts, *Mysterium et Medulla Bibliorum*, 2.1.2, 4 (23, 25); Coxe, *A Discourse of the Covenants*, 1.3 (6–7); and Witsius, *The Economy of the Covenants*, 1.4.11–13 (1:76–77).
107. Witsius, *The Economy of the Covenants*, 1.4.10–23 (1:76–82).
108. Turretin, *Institutes*, 8.3.6, 9, 10 (1:575–76). The Latin verb translated as "demanded" is *postulō*, and "could not help" is *non potuit*, the latter being a perfect tense of *posse*. To speak of God in terms of *non posse* is a strong statement of natural divine necessity.

Colquhoun, asserted that God's acts of goodness are always sovereign and free.[109] God could have created people, glorified himself through their obedience, and returned them painlessly to nonexistence without violating his justice or goodness.[110] Goodwin walked a fine line by saying that we may not speak of any "obligation" or "recompense" for God (Rom. 11:35), but we may say God does what is most fitting for him to do (Heb. 2:10).[111]

The Covenant of Works and the Glory of God

God's covenant with Adam made known his glory to man in a marvelous manner. Reformed orthodox theologians taught that it revealed *God's attributes in general*. It demonstrated God's infinite condescension in that he entered a covenant with a mere creature over whom he had absolute sovereignty and authority. It showed his generous goodness in that he dealt with man as a covenant partner and offered a promise of life to one to whom God owed nothing. Its easy command encouraged man to view God's absolute sovereignty as sweet and moderate. The covenant manifested God's wisdom in treating his rational creation in a manner designed to draw out man's free and willing service by a reasonable law and a remarkable reward. God's making man in goodness and holiness and guarding him against temptation by such a sobering law made known God's own goodness and holiness. The terrible threat of the law also prepared the way to demonstrate God's justice in punishing sin. God's righteous retribution was highlighted by the ingratitude of man's sin, for in breaking such a covenant, man despised God's goodness. Its condition of obedience was well suited to display how easily the best creature can change and fall away apart from constant dependence on its Creator. Conversely, its unbreakable words proved God's unchanging faithfulness to do what he promised. Lastly, the covenant of works prepared the way for the revelation of God's grace in Christ according to his eternal purpose to exalt man higher than Adam ever stood, and all for the glory of God.[112]

The Reformed divines also said that the covenant of works displayed *God's goodness in particular*. In making such a covenant, it was as if God rose from his glorious throne and stooped infinitely low to display the

---

109. See Ex. 33:19; Isa. 45:9; Rom. 9:15, 19–21.

110. Coxe, *A Discourse of the Covenants*, 2.4.1 (25); and Colquhoun, *A Treatise on the Covenant of Works*, 80.

111. Goodwin, *Of the Creatures*, in *Works*, 7:23–24.

112. Dickson, *Therapeutica Sacra*, 74–77; Watson, *A Body of Divinity*, 129; and Colquhoun, *A Treatise on the Covenant of Works*, 120–24.

infinite treasures of his goodness. In this arrangement, God sweetly allured man to a closer love and friendship with himself.[113] The covenant was an overflowing fountain of abundant goodness, offering man an unmerited reward that trumpeted the truth that "he is a rewarder of them that diligently seek him" (Heb. 11:6).[114]

The goodness of God in this covenant may be illustrated by an analogy drawn (with some modifications) from Boston.[115] Let us imagine a farmer desires to pass on the family business to his son. The father promises his son that he will receive it upon one condition: managing a particular vineyard as his father commands him. To communicate the seriousness of his intent, the father draws up legal papers to this effect. However, this is no cold, commercial transaction. It is a fatherly act drenched with love. All the son's training and tools are given to him freely by his father. The son owes his obedience to his father already, with or without the promised reward. However, the father's goodness to his son abounds in attaching this rich promise. This is a weak analogy to the infinite goodness of God to his son, Adam, before the fall.

There is so much divine goodness loaded in the first covenant that Reformed orthodox theologians could speak of it in terms of *God's grace to Adam.*[116] Rutherford said, "God then never loved to make any covenant, yea even that of works, without some acts and out-goings of grace."[117] In the garden, we find that "law is honeyed with love."[118] Furthermore, nothing that God gave to man in the garden or promised for man's obedience came by the way of merit, for God cannot be man's debtor, man owes everything to God, and man's obedience can never deserve eternal life.[119] The covenant of works is not a legalistic intruder into biblical theology, but, as Willem van Asselt (1946–2014) said, Reformed theologians have sought to "articulate the permanence of God's original and gracious intention to establish a continuous relationship of fellowship or friendship with human beings."[120]

---

113. Dickson, *Therapeutica Sacra*, 73–74; Burgess, *Vindiciae Legis*, 127–28; Turretin, *Institutes*, 8.2.16 (1:574); and Colquhoun, *A Treatise on the Covenant of Works*, 26, 122–24.
114. Boston, *A View of the Covenant of Works*, in *Works*, 11:184.
115. Boston, *A View of the Covenant of Works*, in *Works*, 11:181.
116. Roberts, *Mysterium et Medulla Bibliorum*, 1.2.3 (17).
117. Rutherford, *The Covenant of Life Opened*, 22.
118. Rutherford, *The Covenant of Life Opened*, 35.
119. Rutherford, *The Covenant of Life Opened*, 23, citing Thomas Bradwardine, *De Causa Dei*, 1.39; Turretin, *Institutes*, 8.4.16–17 (1:578); and Colquhoun, *A Treatise on the Covenant of Works*, 79.
120. Willem J. van Asselt, "Christ, Predestination, and Covenant," in *The Oxford Handbook of Early Modern Theology, 1600–1800*, ed. Ulrich L. Lehner, Richard A. Muller, and A. G. Roeber (Oxford: Oxford University Press, 2016), 223 (full chapter, 213–27).

For all the abundant goodness of God in the covenant of works, we must remember that it is *not the covenant of grace*. God made the covenant of works with Adam as the head of mankind upon condition of perfect obedience. It has no provision of mercy or forgiveness, but says, "Do this and live." God made the covenant of grace with Jesus Christ and God's elect in him upon condition of Christ's work as their surety to fulfill all the requirements of the law. It promises abundant mercy and full forgiveness, and says, "Believe in Christ alone for salvation and live." Though both covenants give an important place to works, Rutherford reminded us that order is important: "The administration of the law-covenant is first habitual holiness of works and then a crown. The administration of grace is first faith and a title to Christ our life and hope of glory, and then habitual holiness, begun here and perfected hereafter."[121]

Sing to the Lord

Adam and the Last Adam

> Adam our father and our head,
> Transgressed and justice doomed us dead;
> The fiery law speaks all despair,
> There's no reprieve nor pardon there.
>
> Call a bright council in the skies;
> Seraphs, the mighty and the wise,
> Speak; are you strong to bear the load,
> The weighty vengeance of a God?
>
> In vain we ask; for all around
> Stand silent through the heavenly ground;
> There's not a glorious mind above
> Has half the strength or half the love.
>
> But O! unmeasurable grace!
> Th' eternal Son takes Adam's place;
> Down to our world the Saviour flies
> Stretches his arms and bleeds and dies.
>
> Amazing work! Look down, ye skies,
> Wonder and gaze with all your eyes;

---

121. Rutherford, *The Covenant of Life Opened*, 47.

Ye saints below and saints above,
All bow to this mysterious love.

Isaac Watts
Tune: any long meter (may be sung to Old Hundredth, the tune to the traditional doxology)
John Rippon, *A Selection of Hymns from the Best Authors* (New York: William Dursell, 1792), No. 38.

Questions for Meditation or Discussion

1. What claim is sometimes made regarding the early church and the development of covenant theology?
2. What evidence is there for the doctrine of the covenant of works, in at least seed form, prior to the Reformation?
3. How did the doctrine of God's covenant with Adam develop in sixteenth-century Reformed theology?
4. Explain the distinction between a *monopleuron* covenant and a *dipleuron* covenant.
5. What are the names that Reformed divines employed for the covenant with Adam?
6. How was God's command to Adam, in the language of Reformed theology, a positive, symbolic, and sacramental law?
7. How did Reformed orthodox theologians believe God's covenant with Adam related to natural law?
8. How did Adam function as a "federal representative" in the covenant? Why was this doctrine significant in the Reformed battle against Pelagianism?
9. How did Reformed divines argue that God's covenant with Adam involved the promise of a reward, namely, eternal life?
10. How does the doctrine of the covenant of works glorify God?
11. What is one thing that you have learned or seen more clearly about God and his covenants by reading this chapter? How should you respond to that truth in faith and love?

Questions for Deeper Reflection

12. Reformed orthodox covenant theology has often used contractual language to describe God's covenants. What is the strength of such language? The weakness?

13. What did Reformed theologians debate concerning the reward of eternal life offered to Adam? What arguments were presented? Which is most biblical? Why?

14. Someone says, "God's covenant with Adam was a covenant of grace." In what sense is this statement true? In what sense is it false? How would you restate it more precisely?

16

God's Covenant with Adam, Part 3

Practical Implications

Reformed theology is experiential and practical theology. While the doctrine of God's covenant with Adam may seem like a theological abstraction from a bygone era, it is rich in implications for us today. Therefore, we conclude our treatment of the covenant of works with some of the practical applications proposed by various theologians.[1] We will integrate these applications with the biblical teachings we explored in previous chapters studying Genesis 2.[2]

The Covenant of Works Reveals the Covenant Lord

In the covenant of works, God made himself known as "the LORD God," the God of the covenant (Gen. 2:4–25). The covenant of works revealed God as the covenant Lord of his people. However, this lordship was not sheer sovereignty, which God already possessed by nature and by virtue of creating man, but was covenant lordship, a familial bond between the divine Father and his earthly sons. In the covenant of works, the Creator pledged himself to Adam to be mankind's all-sufficient Lord and Father forever if Adam would obey him.

---

1. See especially Brakel, *The Christian's Reasonable Service*, 1:367; Boston, *A View of the Covenant of Works*, in *Works*, 11:216–220; and Nichols, *Covenant Theology*, 355–58.
2. See chaps. 6 and 14.

The Lord of Our Life

First, Genesis 2 reveals the God of the covenant as the Lord of our life. He gave man life, and he warned that he would take it away if man sinned. The first words of his covenant were "Of every tree of the garden thou mayest freely eat" (Gen. 2:16). Every breath that man took in the garden testified of God's goodness to him (v. 7). Every sight, smell, and taste from its verdant foliage nurtured by sparkling streams of water sang of God's kindness. The tree of life silently pledged eternal life.

We should, therefore, *admire God's abundant generosity.* When we are tempted to doubt God's goodness in the wilderness of this world, let us remember that he originally put man in paradise. God created man in order to bless him (Gen. 1:28). We should train ourselves to sing, "The LORD is good to all: and his tender mercies are over all his works" (Ps. 145:9).

The covenant also calls us to *fear God's severe justice.* The last words of God's covenant with Adam were "In the day that thou eatest thereof thou shalt surely die" (Gen. 2:17). God's goodness is not unconditional positive regard, a plastic smile that shines mechanically upon men while they commit rebellion and wickedness. He is "the Judge of all the earth" who will surely "do right" (Gen. 18:25). His justice falls upon the sinner like a razor-sharp sword to cut off his life. "The wages of sin is death" (Rom. 6:23).

The Lord of Our Location

Second, the God of the covenant is the Lord of our home and calling in life. The context for God's covenant word was the garden where God put the man and assigned him his work (Gen. 2:15). The very mention of trees in the covenant reminded Adam that his keeping of the covenant would involve doing God's will in his ordinary, day-by-day agricultural work in the place God had provided.

Therefore, the covenant teaches us to *submit to God's providential vocation.* The Lord has set each of us in a particular place and given us a calling to fulfill. Adam's obedience to God's covenant lordship was not an other-worldly spirituality, and neither was it confined to weekly public worship (though he had that also, Gen. 2:1–3). We learn from this to serve God in the course of our ordinary duties according to our place, station, relationships, and vocation. Paul commands us, "Whether therefore ye eat, or drink, or whatsoever ye do, do all to the glory of God" (1 Cor. 10:31).

The location of the covenant also shows us our calling to *persevere under God's fatherly training*. The garden was a beautiful paradise, but it was also a place of trial. There man faced the forbidden tree. There man encountered the Serpent with its temptation. God did not ordain these things out of evil intent, but because man needed to grow to maturity as God's royal son. If the covenant Lord is our Lord through Christ, then we must expect him to train us through trials as well. Our calling as covenantal beings is to persevere in faith and obedience under these trials, trusting that they will lead us deeper into holiness and communion with the Lord (Heb. 12:5–14).

The Lord of Our Law

Third, the covenant of works reveals God to be the Lord of our law. God's covenant was established with a word of authority: "And the LORD God commanded the man" (Gen. 2:16). Man's original state was not as John Dryden (1631–1700) wrote,

> But know, that I alone am king of me.
> I am as free as Nature first made man
> 'Ere the base laws of servitude began
> When wild in woods the noble savage ran.[3]

To the contrary, the covenant of works teaches us that no man has ever been king of himself, but people have lived under the law of God from the beginning.

The covenant teaches us that we must *obey God's authoritative commands*. The seemingly arbitrary prohibition against eating a particular fruit shows us that mankind must follow God's laws simply because of his supreme authority, if for no other reason. God adds the further incentives of his promises and warnings. These make God's laws more desirable than "much fine gold" and "sweeter also than honey," for "by them is thy servant warned: and in keeping of them there is great reward" (Ps. 19:10–11).

The covenant's promises and threats also impose upon us the obligation to *believe God's faithful word*. Our fall into sin and misery took its starting point from the Serpent's incitement to disbelieve God's word: "Ye shall not surely die" (Gen. 3:4). On the contrary, "God is not a man, that he should lie" (Num. 23:19). In all of God's covenants he requires faith

---

3. John Dryden, *The Conquest of Granada by the Spaniards* (London: by T. N. for Henry Herringman, 1672), 7.

in his word, for "without faith it is impossible to please him: for he that cometh to God must believe that he is, and that he is a rewarder of them that diligently seek him" (Heb. 11:6).

The Lord of Our Love

Fourth, the covenant of works reveals God to be the Lord of our love. It is no accident that the record of God's covenantal word immediately proceeds to describe the institution of the marriage covenant (Gen. 2:18–25). The covenant was a word of betrothal, in a manner of speaking, for in it the Lord God offered himself to be wedded forever to man in righteousness and love (cf. Hos. 2:19–20).

Therefore, we should *admire God's loving condescension* in making a covenant with such as us. Thomas Boston drew attention to "the wonderful condescension of God, and of his goodness and grace toward his creature man," saying, "He stooped so low as to enter into a covenant with his own creature, a covenant wherein he shewed himself a most bountiful and gracious God toward man."[4] Did the eternal Lord of glory bind himself to dust and breath? We should say with David, "Who am I, O Lord GOD? And what is my house, that thou hast brought me hitherto?" (2 Sam. 7:18). Adam's violation of this covenant did not nullify God's intention; rather, God wonderfully transposed it into the higher key of the saving grace that he had planned from eternity (Eph. 1:3–5).

We need not admire God's love with mere historical interest now that the covenant of works is broken, but should *embrace God's loving bond* in the covenant of grace. Christ is the Bridegroom (Mark 2:19–20; John 3:29), come to woo and win his bride, that she may wait for him faithfully until their wedding day (2 Cor. 11:2; Rev. 19:7–8). Let us therefore enter the "marriage-covenant with this blessed Husband, the Lord Jesus Christ," which involves, as Edward Pearse (c. 1633–1673) wrote, a free and hearty giving of him to us and ourselves to him, a close and intimate union between us by the Holy Spirit, a rich and lasting friendship, strong and ardent affections, and mutual delight and satisfaction that will never end.[5]

The covenant of works reveals God as the covenant Lord of his people. He is everything to them: their generous Provider, righteous Judge,

4. Boston, *A View of the Covenant of Works*, in *Works*, 11:216.
5. Edward Pearse, *The Best Match, or the Soul's Espousal to Christ* (London: for Jonathan Robinson and Brabazon Aylmer, 1673), 2, 6–22. The book was reprinted with modernized language in 1994 by Soli Deo Gloria.

job-assigning Master, character-training Father, authoritative Lawgiver, and faithful promise keeper, who comes down to their level and proposes nothing less than to be their loving Husband forever. What a God he is! And his glory shines all the brighter in the covenant of grace than it ever did in the covenant of works. Let us, therefore, give ourselves to his praise. As John Newton (1725–1807) said, "Let us love and sing and wonder, let us praise the Saviour's name!"[6]

The Covenant of Works Engages the Covenant Servant

The presence of the covenant Lord implies a covenant servant. We do not use the word *servant* in a demeaning manner, as a synonym for *slave*, but rather in an official manner, as the servant of the great King. Man's creation as God's image implied that Adam was a son of God (Gen. 5:1–3; Luke 3:38), and therefore he served his Father with great dignity. God authorized man to serve him in the three functions of a prophet, a priest, and a king. This teaches us a great deal about who we are as human beings and how we are to conduct ourselves.

The Prophetic Servant

First, God commissioned man to be God's prophetic servant. God made his covenant with Adam by speaking words to him before any other human being existed. The covenant of works, like all of God's covenants, revolved around God's giving his word to man.

We learn from this that God made man to *hear and meditate on God's Word*. The attitude of the faithful covenantal servant is "Speak, Lord; for thy servant heareth" (1 Sam. 3:9). Jeremiah expressed the true prophetic spirit when he said, "Thy words were found, and I did eat them; and thy word was unto me the joy and rejoicing of mine heart: for I am called by thy name, O Lord God of hosts" (Jer. 15:16). Meditation on the Word of God is not the calling merely of preachers (1 Tim. 4:15), but of everyone who desires to walk in the path of God's blessing.[7]

The prophetic dimension of Adam's original office in the covenant also teaches us to *speak God's Word to others*. Since Adam received the covenantal word alone, he had to tell it to his wife and family, just as God

---

6. John Newton, "Praise to the Redeemer," in *Twenty-Six Letters on Religious Subjects . . . To Which Are Added, Hymns, Etc. by Omicron* (London: W. Oliver, 1777), 297.
7. Pss. 1:1–3; 63:6; 119:15, 23, 48, 78, 97, 99, 148.

commanded fathers among his people to do in their households (Deut. 6:6–7). Christians must also be prepared to speak to outsiders (Col. 4:6), communicating with gentleness and reverence the "reason of the hope that is in you" (1 Pet. 3:15).

The Priestly Servant

Second, the covenant of works shows us that God made man to be his priestly servant. The garden was the sacred place of God's special presence, where he met with man. God called man to "serve" (*'abad*) and "guard" (*shamar*) paradise (Gen. 2:15), just as the priests and Levites served and guarded the holy tabernacle and temple.[8] Adam did this in the ordinary labor of the first six days of the week, but in a special manner on the seventh day, which God had set apart for holy rest (vv. 1–3).

The priestly aspect of Adam's covenantal office shows us our duty to *worship the holy Lord*. Whether we are happy or sad, every day should be marked by praises and prayers (James 5:13). We have the duty to glorify God in the public worship of the church on the Lord's Day. God's Word commands us, "Serve the LORD with gladness: come before his presence with singing" (Ps. 100:2). The reference later in the psalm to entering "his gates" and "his courts" makes it clear that public worship is particularly in view (v. 4).

A corollary to this duty is our responsibility to *keep God's worship holy*. God called Adam to keep or guard the garden. Priests had to distinguish "between holy and unholy, and between unclean and clean," so that nothing unclean would pollute God's worship, and men would conduct worship as the Lord commanded.[9] Worship is sacred to God. Mankind has a grave priestly responsibility to honor God's holiness by worshiping according to God's Word.

The Kingly Servant

Third, God's covenant with Adam engaged him to be God's kingly servant. God commanded Adam and Eve to exercise dominion over the earth (Gen. 1:28). In the covenantal context of Genesis 2, we find Adam already beginning that work before Eve's creation when God appointed him to work the garden and brought the animals to him to receive their names.

---

8. Num. 3:7–8; 8:26; 18:7.
9. Lev. 10:10–11; cf. 9:5–7, 10, 21; 10:1–2.

As God's royal covenant servants, we may *use our freedom to enjoy God's world*. God "giveth us richly all things to enjoy" (1 Tim. 6:17). Tasty food, loving sexual intimacy between husband and wife—these are good gifts that God desires for us to enjoy. Paul explained, "For every creature of God is good, and nothing to be refused, if it be received with thanksgiving: for it is sanctified by the word of God and prayer" (4:4–5).

However, we must remember that man is not the supreme king but a servant-king under the Lord of lords. Therefore, we must also *own our responsibility to do God's will*. Human beings are stewards of the earth and their personal resources; God is the owner of all. The Master will call his stewards to account (Luke 12:42–48). We must feel the weight of this responsibility. One of the great lessons of the covenant of works is that human beings are covenant servants to the Lord, and he will judge all of them according to their works (Matt. 16:27).

The Covenant of Works Clarifies the Servant's Apostasy from the Lord

The revelation of God's covenant in Genesis 2 was written not for Adam but for us. It addresses mankind in its fallen condition and sets up a context within which we can properly understand our apostasy from our Creator. We will speak to the historical event of this apostasy and its consequences for humanity under the next major topic of anthropology, the doctrine of sin. Here we summarize some of the practical implications of the first covenant regarding that apostasy.

The Adamic Apostasy

First, the covenant of the garden teaches us to view mankind's falling away from God as corporate or collective apostasy in Adam. We did not fall away from God as individuals. God sovereignly dealt with the human race in the person of our first father and covenant representative. Mankind fell away from God in Adam when Adam sinned (Rom. 5:12–19).

We must learn from that to *acknowledge man's changeability at his best*. Even in a state of perfect righteousness, man could fall into the depths of depravity. Man is a creature, not the eternal, immutable Creator, who cannot sin.[10] Let us set aside all illusions about how strong and stable we

---

10. Nichols, *Covenant Theology*, 356.

are. David remembered with regret, "In my prosperity I said, I shall never be moved" (Ps. 30:6). Experience taught him otherwise. Let us never put our trust in man (Jer. 17:5–8) or in ourselves. If sinless Adam could fall so far so quickly, what shall we think of sinful men today? If we try to find our righteousness in ourselves, we may find ourselves "full of fears and doubts," as Thomas Watson said, for we are not building on a firm foundation.[11]

The covenant thus teaches us to *recognize our solidarity with Adam in sin.* It is true that "all have sinned, and come short of the glory of God" (Rom. 3:23). Recognizing one's sin is a beginning step to becoming a Christian, as well as one we make repeatedly as we walk with God (1 John 1:5–10). However, the covenant of works calls us to go deeper. We must realize that Adam's sin is our sin and his condemnation is our condemnation (Rom. 5:12, 16, 18). John Colquhoun said, "Be persuaded, reader, that this covenant was made with the first Adam, in thy name, or for thee in particular."[12] In Adam, we are all covenant breakers. Recognizing our solidarity with Adam humbles us, but also helps us to see our need for a better covenant head.

The Legal Apostasy

Second, the covenant of works shows us the nature of our apostasy. It is rebellion against God's law and failure to live up to God's righteous commandment. Though this principle has universal application through the natural law in human nature (Rom. 2:14–16), it particularly comes to a head in how we respond to the laws that God has expressly stated, just as Adam's sin was crystallized in his rebellion against God's command.

The covenant of works enables us to *understand man's quest for external legal righteousness.* Though in rebellion against God's law, man's nature and covenantal orientation continually prompt him to pursue righteousness through the law, sometimes with great zeal. Colquhoun said, "Nothing is more natural for us than to do, that we may live; than to think that our performances will entitle us to the favour and enjoyment of God; and that if we do our part, God will do his."[13] We see this quest in the devout but unregenerate Jews of Paul's day (Rom. 10:2–3). Sinners

---

11. Watson, *A Body of Divinity*, 130.
12. Colquhoun, *A Treatise on the Covenant of Works*, 40.
13. Colquhoun, *A Treatise on the Covenant of Works*, 40.

generally seek legal righteousness by replacing God's law with human traditions about external acts, as the Pharisees did (Matthew 23). The result is hypocritical religion (15:1–20). This impulse is not confined to any ethnicity or culture. Fallen men "desire to be under the law" (Gal. 4:21), as William Strong observed, bringing to God external worship without a heart of faith and repentance, just as Cain did (Genesis 4).[14] We should not be surprised to find our own hearts stubbornly seeking righteousness that we hope to attain through what we do.

Reflecting upon the covenant of works calls us to *be humbled under the law's righteous verdict* against us. This was the Lord's purpose in the thunderous words of law from Mount Sinai and the loving words of law from Christ to the self-righteous rich young ruler.[15] To be sure, God's law is hard for sinners to hear. It shows us our sins, unmasks our corrupt hearts, and reveals God's wrath against sinners (Rom. 3:19–20; 4:15; 7:7). By nature, we hate God's law and cannot submit to it (8:7–8). However, the covenant with Adam shows us that the problem is not with the law but with us. God's law was given to us when man was living in perfect purity in paradise. The law is not unfair, but we have become unrighteous. When the law says to us, "You have sinned and are sinful, and deserve the wrath of God in hell forever," we should reply with sorrow, "Yes, Lord, it is true."

The Heinous Apostasy

Third, the covenant of works helps us to see that man's fall was a heinous apostasy from the living God. In other words, it was a crime of cosmic proportions, worthy of the worst of punishments. People may make light of the sin in the garden, asking, "What's the big deal about eating a piece of fruit?" However, the sin of our first parents consisted of gross rebellion against the law of their Creator and flagrant rejection of his goodness despite all he had done for them.

The covenant presses us to *grieve over the gravity of man's ingratitude and treason.* The Lord God had given man his life and existence. He had communed with him in personal fellowship. He had provided him with meaningful work and a home full of delights. He had elevated him to be master of the animals. He had given him a most suitable earthly

---

14. Strong, *A Discourse of the Two Covenants*, 22–23.
15. Dickson, *Therapeutica Sacra*, 85. See Exodus 19–20; Mark 10:17–22.

companion and friend. All that God required for man to show his loyalty and submission was to abstain from one tree, a small price to pay in order to render homage to the supreme Lord of heaven and earth. Man owed God his total allegiance for the simple fact that God is God. By breaking God's law, man treated his lavishly generous Lord as if he were a wicked tyrant and became a traitor, rebel, and enemy of the sovereign God. The horrible weight of this crime should grieve and humble us. It was our crime in Adam (Rom. 5:12), and it is our crime by choice (1:21).

God's covenant of works also calls us to *renounce all false hopes of saving ourselves*. If sinless Adam did not stand, how can we think that sinners like us will stand? We should say, "If thou, LORD, shouldest mark iniquities, O Lord, who shall stand?" (Ps. 130:3). David wisely prayed, "And enter not into judgment with thy servant: for in thy sight shall no man living be justified" (Ps. 143:2).

Ezekiel Hopkins reminded us that those who appeal to the works of the law for their righteousness must face sobering facts about the covenant of works:

1. God's holy law demands full and complete obedience, and it curses those who fail in any one point (Gal. 3:10). Do you think that a few good deeds will justify you?
2. God's holy justice demands satisfaction for every violation of his law. How can you make satisfaction for your sins when all you might do for God is the duty you owe him?
3. God's covenant of "Do this and live" was given to a morally perfect man. How can any man stained with original sin and habitual corruption restore himself to the purity that the law requires?[16]

The holy law of God will not justify sinners; it only shows us our sin and condemnation.

If you have not been converted to repentance and faith in Christ, your fall in Adam, as well as your own violations of God's commandments, ought to convince you of your lost state before God. You are in a dreadful state and predicament. God's avenging justice hangs over you like a sword. You cannot help yourself. You have failed in Adam and you continue to fail every day. The door of death and the gates of hell are wide open to receive you. You are utterly guilty, and so you are subject to the

---

16. Hopkins, *The Doctrine of the Two Covenants*, 118–22.

condemnation of the law of God. Great is your wickedness, and Christ alone can save you from it.

The Covenant of Works Foreshadows the Redeeming Lord and Servant

Paul wrote that Adam was a type of Christ (Rom. 5:14). Though a full exposition of Christ's person and work must wait until we treat the locus of Christology, we may say some things by way of anticipation for the sake of making gospel application of the covenant with Adam. Just as the covenant of works revealed God as the covenant Lord and engaged man as God's covenant servant, so it foreshadowed Christ both as Lord and servant.

The Lord and Servant of Our Life

First, the Lord God gave life to man and provided abundantly for his sustenance and satisfaction. God also gave man a law of obedience by which he might obtain eternal life. The incarnate Christ fulfills both roles.

God's covenant with Adam, seen in light of its typological fulfillment in Christ, calls us to *believe in Christ as the Lord and life giver*. God breathed life into the first man (Gen. 2:7). Christ breathes upon his people the life-giving Holy Spirit (John 20:22). Adam had no life at all before God infused it into him. Christ is the resurrection and the life of spiritually dead sinners (John 11:25; Eph. 2:5–6). God placed Adam by a river of flowing water (Gen. 2:10). Christ grants to sinners streams of living water, even an inward spring of satisfaction overflowing to eternal life (John 4:14; 7:37–39). Trust in Christ, and drink forever.

Christ obtained eternal life for his people by being a faithful covenant servant. Therefore, we must also *believe in Christ as the last and life-giving Adam*. Death came by the first Adam's sin, but resurrection life by Christ's obedience (Rom. 5:17; 1 Cor. 15:21–22). Raised and exalted by the Father for humbling himself and becoming obedient unto death (Phil. 2:8–9), Christ became the bearer of the life-giving Spirit (1 Cor. 15:45). Stop trying to be your own Adam, and rest all your hopes upon the last Adam appointed by God.

The Lord and Servant of Our Location

Second, the garden was not only a place of nurture and pleasure, but also of work and trial, all at the Lord God's appointment. Adam had to serve the Lord and persevere through trial in order to continue in paradise. Christ is both the Lord of our daily work and the persevering servant whom we follow to the heavenly paradise.

God's covenant with Adam reminds us that we must *serve the Lord Christ in our daily vocations.* Paul said, "And whatsoever ye do, do it heartily, as to the Lord, and not unto men; knowing that of the Lord ye shall receive the reward of the inheritance: for ye serve the Lord Christ" (Col. 3:23–24). It is a particular joy of Christians to do their work for the One who died and rose again for them (2 Cor. 5:14–15). Whether you are a student, an engineer, a housewife, a plumber, or a retired person volunteering in some capacity, serve Jesus Christ and anticipate his "Well done" and reward (Matt. 25:14–30).

However, it is our privilege not just to view Christ as the Lord of our service but as the servant of our Lord (Isa. 42:1). Christ, though sinless, grew in his human obedience through the painful trials imposed upon him by the Father (Heb. 4:15; 5:7–8). Christ persevered and finished his earthly race, enduring the shame of the cross "for the joy that was set before him," and ascended to heaven to sit "at the right hand of the throne of God" (12:1–2). We must *follow Christ through the trials of this world.* Drawing strength from his Holy Spirit and with eyes fixed on his humble example (Phil. 1:19–20; 2:5), we, too, can persevere through painful trials until we are with him in the heavenly paradise (Luke 23:43). By the grace of union and communion, Christ's perseverance becomes the perseverance of his redeemed people.

The Lord and Servant of Our Law

Third, the Lord God defined his relationship with man by his commandment. Life and communion with God depended on Adam's obedience to the law of God. In the same way, Christ came both as Lawgiver and as Law-keeper, and we must receive him as both.

Since Jesus is Lord, we must *obey Christ as the Lawgiver.* Just as surely as Adam was obligated to keep the command of the Lord God in the garden, so we are obligated to keep the commands of Jesus Christ. In the Sermon on the Mount, we see Christ speaking as the One greater than Moses, giving the true meaning of God's moral law and piety with the breathtaking authority of "I say unto you."[17] If we do not keep Christ's

---

17. Matt. 5:18, 20, 22, 28, 32, 34, 39, 44; 6:2, 5, 16, 25, 29.

commands, then we do not love him (John 14:15). True discipleship is inseparable from submission to all the word of Christ (Matt. 28:18–19). If we refuse to have Christ reign over us as our King, then he will destroy us (Luke 19:27).

Yet who among us has obeyed Christ as we ought? We must not obey Christ in order to seek to obtain righteousness by keeping his commandments, but must seek the righteousness of God that is by faith (Phil. 3:9). Christ is that righteousness (1 Cor. 1:30), for he alone is the servant who always does what is pleasing to his Father (Matt. 12:18; John 8:29). Where man broke the covenant of law, Christ became the "surety" of the covenant of grace (Heb. 7:22). A surety is a person who has bound himself to fulfill the legal obligations of another and to bear his liabilities.[18] We must *rest in Christ as the surety of his people.* Receive him, and him alone, as your righteousness before God, and God will justify you by faith alone (Rom. 3:24, 28). Flee from the broken covenant of works to the covenant of grace. Be done with any thought of meriting God's favor by your good works. The promise of the covenant of grace is not given to doing but to believing in Christ. Trust him as your all in all. Receive him and be saved.

The Lord and Servant of Our Love

Fourth, the Lord God made a covenant with man as an act of condescending love, binding himself to man through a promise of eternal life if only man would walk with him in holiness. The law of the covenant required man to respond with wholehearted love, choosing God as his life above any visible, earthly thing. The Lord then instituted the covenant of marriage between man and woman, a bond of love that would serve to illustrate the union formed by God's covenant of grace.

If we are believers in Christ, then we should *rejoice in Christ's love as the Husband of his bride.* No husband has demonstrated love for his wife that can compare to Christ's giving of himself to redeem the church from the filth of sin (Eph. 5:25–27). What love is this that not only saves sinners but takes them to be Christ's bride? Benjamin Keach (1640–1704) said, "To kiss the king's hand is a great favour, but it is a far greater token of special love to be made his queen."[19] The Christian can live every day

---

18. Gen. 43:9; 44:32; Prov. 6:1–5.

19. Benjamin Keach, *The Display of Glorious Grace, or, The Covenant of Peace Opened* (London: by S. Bridge, for Mary Fabian, Joseph Collier, and William Marshall, 1698), 228.

"by faith in the Son of God, who loved me and gave himself for me" (Gal. 2:20 ESV).

Union with God's Son makes repentant believers into adopted sons of God (Gal. 3:26–27). Those who are joined to Christ by a Spirit-worked faith may *live in Christian freedom, not under the covenant of works.* Christians are heirs, not slaves (4:7). They should not live as if under a covenant that only keeps sinners in "bondage" (vv. 24–25). They are not justified by the law and are not bound to keep the law in order to be counted righteous, but are free to live by faith, doing works out of love (5:3–6). They increasingly obey the law of God, which is the law of love, by the inward influences of the Holy Spirit (vv. 14, 22). Look to the law for direction but not for righteousness. Wilhelmus à Brakel said, "This exhortation is necessary since even God's children are often inclined to dwell upon their works, and accordingly, are either encouraged or discouraged."[20] The high privilege of the Christian is to live in the freedom of the sons of God, a freedom that will expand into glory when God's Son is revealed.

Sing to the Lord

God's Blessing on the Man Who Keeps His Word

> That man is blest who, fearing God,
> From sin restrains his feet,
> Who will not stand with wicked men,
> Who shuns the scorners' seat.
>
> Yea, blest is he who makes God's law
> His portion and delight,
> And meditates upon that law
> With gladness day and night.
>
> That man is nourished like a tree
> Set by the river's side;
> Its leaf is green, its fruit is sure,
> And thus his works abide.
>
> The wicked like the driven chaff
> Are swept from off the land;

---

20. Brakel, *The Christian's Reasonable Service*, 1:367.

They shall not gather with the just,
Nor in the judgment stand.

The Lord will guard the righteous well,
Their way to Him is known;
The way of sinners, far from God,
Shall surely be o'erthrown.

Psalm 1
Tune: Meditation
The Psalter, No. 1
Or Tune: Irish
Trinity Hymnal—Baptist Edition, No. 446

Questions for Meditation or Discussion

1. How does the revelation of God's lordship over man's life in Genesis 2 motivate us to fear and hope in the Lord?

2. What does the Lord God's assigning Adam his home and vocation imply about our residence and calling in life today?

3. What can we learn about God's authority over us by his giving a law to Adam?

4. How does God's making a wife for Adam and bringing them into covenant with each other foreshadow his relationship with his people?

5. Describe the responsibilities of every human being according to Adam's office as: (1) a prophetic servant of God, (2) a priestly servant of God, and (3) a kingly servant of God.

6. What does Adam's violation of the covenant of works show us about ourselves?

7. How does the covenant of works help us to understand a sinner's bent toward legalism? What is the right way for sinners to listen to God's law as it addresses them as covenant breakers?

8. Why is man's violation of the covenant of works a great and heinous offense against God?

9. How should we glorify Christ as the Lord and Servant to whom the covenant with Adam pointed with regard to the following?

   • Christ as the Lord and Servant of our life
   • Christ as the Lord and Servant of our location

- Christ as the Lord and Servant of our law
- Christ as the Lord and Servant of our love

Questions for Deeper Reflection

10. How can the doctrine of the covenant with Adam help us in evangelism?
11. What practical consequences might there be for the Christian life if we abandon the doctrine of the covenant with Adam?

Section C

The Doctrine of Sin

17

Introduction to the Doctrine of Sin

God created man in a state of pure goodness but put his obedience to the test. Man's response was tragic: "God hath made man upright; but they have sought out many inventions" (Eccles. 7:29), or "schemes" (ESV). The first occurrence of the word "sin" in the Bible depicts it as a wild animal, crouching "at the door" to seize a man and destroy him if he does not repent (Gen. 4:7). Man quickly became the willing slave of sin's ruinous power.

Before we trace the fall of man into sin in Genesis 3 (see chap. 18), we will step back to look at the big picture of what the Holy Scriptures say about sin in general. Understanding the nature of sin is not a matter of speculative philosophy, but of informed repentance and victorious spiritual warfare. G. C. Berkouwer said, "This subject is a matter of the greatest importance. For the man who misconstrues the nature of his sin . . . is engaged in an urgent peril. Sin . . . is a very vicious and mortal enemy, an irascible and persistent power, which must certainly be known in order to be overcome."[1]

One might think that as often as we sin, we must all be experts in the subject. However, sin is amazingly deceitful and blinding in its effects on the human heart.[2] Sin wraps itself in a cloak, spreads abroad dense fog, waits for darkest night, and moves stealthily. Therefore, we must listen carefully to God's Word and pray earnestly that God's Spirit, the Author of that Word, would illuminate our minds and hearts to see sin for what it is.

---

1. G. C. Berkouwer, *Sin*, Studies in Dogmatics (Grand Rapids, MI: Eerdmans, 1971), 234–35.
2. Jer. 17:9; Rom. 1:21; Eph. 4:22; Heb. 3:13.

Foundational Theological Truths about Sin

We begin by framing the doctrine of sin in the broad teachings of the Holy Scriptures so that we may draw general inferences about the nature of sin.

1. *Sin is not an illusion.* It is not merely a human perception, but "a real evil."[3] God, whose perspective on things is always true, sees sin and hates it. Genesis 6:5–7 says, "God saw that the wickedness of man was great in the earth. . . . And the Lord said, I will destroy man whom I have created." It is God's knowledge of the true state of mankind that permits us to say that all people are sinful and corrupt (Ps. 14:2–3).

2. *Sin is not an eternal reality.* We deduce this from monotheism and creation *ex nihilo.*[4] The only eternal Being is the triune God (Gen. 1:1–2; Col. 1:16). We must reject any essential dualism that posits two eternal principles in the world, one good and one evil.[5] Evil angels were not always so, but fell from their original state (2 Pet. 2:4; Jude 6).[6] Sin did not have a place in man at first, but entered the human world by Adam's transgression (Rom. 5:12).

3. *Sin is not a substance.* We deduce this from the second point and from the goodness and universality of God's works of creation.[7] There is only one Creator (Neh. 9:6). God created everything in the world (Ex. 20:11). Everything that God made was very good (Gen. 1:31). Therefore, sin is not a thing, substance, or material, but a deprivation and depravation of God's good creatures—that is, the loss and corruption of what God originally made them to be.[8] Lutheran Christians in the sixteenth century rightly rejected the idea that sin is "something essential . . . that Satan infused into human nature."[9]

We must not, however, take sin to be mere deprivation, but also account for the disordered energy of sin as a power in human existence. Francis Turretin said that though sin has no status as an eternal reality or created substance, and thus is rightly understood as "privation," or loss of original righteousness, that loss is "corrupting" in its infection of man's being. Sin is like a bodily sickness that not only takes away health but also

---

3. Murray, "The Nature of Sin," in *Collected Writings*, 2:77.
4. See chap. 3 on creation *ex nihilo.*
5. See chap. 2 on false theories of origins.
6. On Satan and the demons, see *RST*, 1:1133–57 (chap. 55).
7. See chap. 2 on the universality of creation and the Creator's goodness.
8. Bavinck, *Reformed Dogmatics*, 3:136.
9. Formula of Concord (Epitome, 1.17), in *The Book of Concord*, 490. See Hoekema, *Created in God's Image*, 168.

causes the organs and systems of the body to malfunction in a disorderly, defiling, and destructive manner.[10] Human nature, with all its abilities and energies, is turned away from God and his truth and toward the creature and the Devil's falsehood.[11] Therefore, sin, though deprivative in nature, is powerful in effect.

4. *Sin is not physical evil.* The Lord God threatened death if Adam sinned, imposed suffering upon sinners, and banished them from paradise (Gen. 2:17; 3:14–19, 23–24). Yet these evils were not sins, but the consequences of sin. Sin does not consist in "what is unpleasant," as Geerhardus Vos said, but operates in "the ethical" realm.[12] John Murray said, "It is moral evil. . . . It is a violation of the category of *ought*; it is wrong."[13] Sin is an offense against the Lord as the righteous Judge (13:13; 18:20, 25).

5. *Sin is not merely external action.* Moral evil resides in the inward thoughts (Gen. 6:5). Christ taught us that the manifold pollutions that defile mankind spew out of one source: the human heart (Mark 7:21–23). A bad tree produces bad fruit (Matt. 7:17–19; 12:33). Louis Berkhof wrote, "Sin does not consist only in overt acts, but also in sinful habits and in a sinful condition of the soul."[14]

6. *Sin is not merely hurting other people.* John MacArthur and Richard Mayhue write, "Sin must be understood from a theocentric or God-centered standpoint. At its core, sin is a violation of the Creator-creature relationship. Man only exists because God made him, and man is in every sense obligated to serve his Creator."[15] Thus, Joseph's cry against his temptress was, "How then can I do this great wickedness, and sin against God?" (Gen. 39:9). David confessed his adultery and murder with this contrite prayer to the Lord: "Against thee, thee only, have I sinned, and done this evil in thy sight" (Ps. 51:4).[16] Berkouwer said, "Sin is always against God."[17]

The Biblical Terminology of Sin

The Holy Scriptures contain a rich vocabulary to describe sin, placing a spotlight on man's fallen condition and magnifying God's forgiveness and

---

10. Turretin, *Institutes*, 9.1.5 (1:592).
11. Bavinck, *Reformed Dogmatics*, 3:138–39.
12. Vos, *Reformed Dogmatics*, 2:24.
13. Murray, "The Nature of Sin," in *Collected Writings*, 2:77.
14. Berkhof, *Systematic Theology*, 233.
15. MacArthur and Mayhue, eds., *Biblical Doctrine*, 453.
16. See also Gen. 20:6; Ex. 16:7–8; Lev. 6:2; 26:40; Num. 5:6; 2 Sam. 12:13; Ps. 2:2; Isa. 3:8; Jer. 3:25; Luke 15:18; Acts 4:26; 1 Cor. 8:12; Rom. 8:7.
17. Berkouwer, *Sin*, 242.

transforming grace. Many terms refer to specific sins, such as adultery, or categories of sin, such as foolishness. Our focus here is on the general terminology used in Scripture for sin.

Old Testament Terminology

We may identify more than a dozen terms closely associated with the idea of sin in the Old Testament. The first three are the most common.[18]

1. The Hebrew root represented in the noun "sin" (*khatta'ah*) and the verb "to sin" (*khata'*) appears almost six hundred times in the Hebrew Bible (e.g., Gen. 4:7). Its literal meaning is to fail or miss a mark. This is evident in the statement "Among all this people there were seven hundred chosen men lefthanded; every one could sling stones at an hair breadth, and not miss [*khata'*]" (Judg. 20:16). However, the concept of sin inherent in this term is not a mere mistake, but a willful aiming at the wrong goal.[19]

2. The Hebrew root represented in the noun "transgression" or "rebellion" (*pesha'*) and the verb "to transgress or rebel" (*pasha'*) appears more than 130 times (e.g., Ex. 23:21; 1 Kings 8:50; 12:19). Its central idea is that of defiance of authority (2 Kings 1:1).

3. The noun "iniquity" (*'avon*) is used more than 230 times. It generally functions as a broad term for moral evil (e.g., Gen. 15:16; 1 Kings 8:47).[20] It is associated with the guilt that makes a person liable to punishment unless confession and forgiveness take place (Num. 15:31). Thus, it is sometimes translated as "punishment" (Gen. 4:13; Lam. 4:22).

These three Hebrew roots appear together in several statements that sum up all the sin and guilt of a people.[21] Overlapping in meaning and comprehensive in scope, the three terms function together to teach us that when a person sins, he willfully fails to attain his created purpose and defiantly rebels against the Lord's authority, and consequently incurs guilt and liability to punishment. Yet the Bible also uses them to communicate God's total forgiveness granted to those who turn from sin to trust in his mercy, grace, and love.

There are several other general terms related to sin.

4. The verb "to hear" (*shama'*), sometimes translated as "to obey," plays a significant role in references to sin. God's pronouncement of judg-

---

18. *NIDOTTE*, 2:87–89.
19. Erickson, *Systematic Theology*, 520.
20. *NIDOTTE*, 1:310–12.
21. Ex. 34:7; Lev. 16:21; Job 13:23; Ps. 32:1–2, 5; Isa. 59:12; Jer. 33:8; Ezek. 21:24; Dan. 9:24.

ment against Adam began with a rebuke because he had "hearkened" (*shama'*, Gen. 3:17) or "listened" (ESV) to his wife's voice. In a positive sense, the term is featured in important statements about how God's people must keep covenant by obeying the Lord.[22] Negatively speaking, to "not hear" God's Word is a major way of expressing sin, appearing eighty-eight times in the Old Testament, thirty-six times in Jeremiah alone.[23] To hear God's Word is an act of faith (Isa. 55:2); to refuse to hear it is an expression of unbelief (2 Kings 17:14). Israel's refusal to listen to the Lord constituted the people's breaking of God's covenant and receiving his curse.[24] Not listening is the characteristic of a fool (Prov. 1:7; 10:8; 15:5).

5. A concept of sin closely related to hearing is the description of sinners as deaf or blind to God's Word, spiritually unresponsive because they lack spiritual "ears" (*'oznayim*) or "eyes" (*'enayim*).[25] This same idea is expressed as having a "hard" heart, using terms such as "to be strong" (*khazaq*, Ex. 4:21; Josh. 11:20); "be severe or stubborn" (*qashah*, Ex. 7:3; Deut. 2:30; the adjective *qasheh* with "neck," Ex. 32:9; 33:5; 34:9); or "heavy" (*kabad*, Ex. 10:1; Isa. 6:10).

6. The noun "evil" (*ra'* or *ra'ah*) and the verb "to do evil" (*ra'a'*) stand in contrast to the "good" in which God created the world (Gen. 1:31; 2:17). This root can be used in the sense of natural disaster or physical affliction (Isa. 45:7). When used in a moral sense, it communicates a deviation from God's will that displeases him (1 Kings 11:6; 14:22; etc.).

7. The noun "wickedness" (*rish'ah*) and the verb "to commit wickedness" (*rasha'*) are the opposite of "righteousness" (Prov. 11:5; 13:6; Ezek. 18:20). Thus, they connote a status of guilt before the Lord (Job 10:15; 1 Kings 8:32).

8. Other verbs translated as "to rebel" (*marah* and *marad*) also invoke the idea of defying the authority of a king and disobeying his law (Gen.

22. Gen. 22:18; 26:5; Ex. 19:5; 23:21–22; 24:7; Deut. 4:1, 30; 5:1; 6:3–4; 7:12; 9:1; 11:13, 27; 12:28; 13:4, 18; 15:5; 18:15; 26:17; 27:9–10; 28:1–2, 13; 30:2, 8, 10, 20; 1 Sam. 3:9; 15:22; Isa. 1:10, 19; Jer. 7:23; 11:4.
23. Lev. 26:14, 18, 24, 27; Num. 14:22; Deut. 1:43; 8:20; 9:23; 11:28; 18:19; 28:15, 45, 62; 30:17; Josh. 1:18; 5:6; Judg. 2:2, 17, 20; 6:10; 1 Sam. 12:15; 15:19; 28:18; 1 Kings 20:36; 2 Kings 17:14; 18:12; 21:7; 22:13; 2 Chron. 25:16; 35:22; Neh. 9:16–17, 29; Job 36:9; Pss. 81:11; 106:25; Prov. 5:13; Isa. 28:12; 30:9; 42:24; 48:8; Jer. 3:13, 25; 6:19; 7:13, 24, 26–28; 9:13; 11:3, 8; 12:17; 13:11, 17; 16:12; 17:23, 27; 18:10; 19:15; 22:5, 21; 25:3–4, 7–8; 26:4–5; 29:19; 32:23, 33; 34:14, 17; 35:13–17; 36:31; 40:3; 42:13, 21; 43:4, 7; 44:5, 16, 23; Ezek. 3:7; 20:8, 39; Dan. 9:11, 14; Hos. 9:17; Zeph. 3:2; Zech. 1:4; 7:11, 13; Mal. 2:2.
24. *NIDOTTE*, 4:178–79.
25. Deut. 29:4; Pss. 69:23; 115:5–8; 135:16–18; Isa. 6:9–10; 44:18; Jer. 5:21; Ezek. 12:2.

14:4; Deut. 1:26). Another term (*sarar*) seems to emphasize the sullen, stubborn attitude behind the rebellion (Deut. 21:18; Prov. 7:11).

9. The personal, relational offense of this treachery is emphasized in a term (*ma'al*) used of Israel's sin against God (Lev. 26:40) and of a wife's infidelity to her husband (Num. 5:12, 27).

10. The idea of offense or guilt appears more than a hundred times in the root (*asham*) also translated as "trespass offering" (Lev. 5:5–7, 15–19; cf. Gen. 26:10).

11. Sin is also referred to with the noun for "ignorance" (*shegagah*) and the verb meaning "to go astray or sin unintentionally" (*shegag*). The law of Moses used these terms for sins not committed as flagrant violations of known commandments, yet the law still required atonement for them (Lev. 4:2, 22, 27; Num. 15:24–29).

12. Another Hebrew root, variously translated as "wickedness," "iniquity," or "injustice" (noun '*awel*, verb '*awal*), seems to focus on the wrongfulness of the act (Pss. 7:3; 37:1).

13. A verb often used for "pass" or "pass over" ('*abar*) is used several times for a transgression of a law, an example of rebellion against authority.[26]

14. The verb "to wander" or "to go astray" (*ta'ah*) can be used to describe departure or seduction from what is right.[27] It is used in the metaphor of a straying sheep (Ps. 119:176; Isa. 53:6). Another verb (*shagah*) has a similar meaning (Ps. 119:10; cf. Deut. 27:18).[28]

15. To this list, we may add the concept of uncleanness or defilement (Hebrew roots *tame'* and *niddah*). In the ceremonial law, uncleanness arose from a physical condition, not moral impurity (Leviticus 11–15). However, in some Scripture passages, these terms function metaphorically for sin's contamination that made the sinner incompatible with the holiness of God.[29]

New Testament Terminology

Just as the Hebrew Bible employs three main terms for sin, so also the Greek New Testament also uses three main terms, supported by

---

26. Num. 14:41; Deut. 17:2; 26:13; Josh 7:11, 15; 23:16; Judg. 2:20; 1 Sam. 15:24; 2 Kings 18:12; Est. 3:3; Ps. 148:6; Isa. 24:5; Jer. 34:18; Hos. 6:7; 8:1.
27. 2 Kings 21:9; 2 Chron. 33:9; Pss. 58:3; 95:10; 119:10, 176; Prov. 7:25; 10:17; 12:26; 14:22; 21:16; etc.
28. Erickson, *Systematic Theology*, 518.
29. Ezek. 36:25, 29; Zech. 13:1; cf. Ps. 51:7.

several others. However, the nuances we observed in the Hebrew roots largely disappeared in the Septuagint and the Greek New Testament, for all three Greek word groups function generically and are often interchangeable.

1. The Greek noun "sin" (*hamartia*) frequently renders the Hebrew word "sin" (*khatta'ah*), but also renders "iniquity" ('*avon*) and "transgression" (*pesha'*) in the Septuagint (Ps. 32:1–2; Dan. 9:24). The noun appears more than five hundred times in the Greek Old Testament and more than 170 times in the New Testament, and the corresponding verb (*hamartanō*) more than 250 times and forty times respectively. In secular Greek, like its primary Hebrew counterpart (*khatta'ah*), the noun had the concrete sense of failing or missing the mark. However, in biblical usage, it is an indefinite term and only occasionally manifests that specific nuance (Rom. 3:23).[30]

2. The Greek term for "unrighteousness" (*adikia*) and related words also has a broad meaning in biblical Greek, though its lexical form is directly opposite to righteousness. It appears more than 450 times in the Greek Septuagint, rendering dozens of Hebrew words, including "sin" (*khatta'ah*) and "iniquity" ('*avon*). It appears seventy times in the New Testament.[31] It is used sometimes in a manner nearly synonymous with "sin" (*hamartia*).[32]

3. The Greek term "lawlessness" (*anomia*) is used more than 220 times in the Septuagint and fifteen times in the New Testament. Though the root has a specific meaning of transgressing the law, it often functions as a general term for sin.[33]

4. We find the concepts of badness, harmfulness, or evil, sometimes applied in a moral sense, in Greek words such as *kakia* and *ponēria* (Rom. 1:29). The adjective "evil" (*ponēros*) is used almost eighty times in the New Testament, often for the moral evil of demons or wicked men.

5. The Greek term for "transgression" (*parabasis*) carries the sense of rebellion against the law of God.[34] So does its rarer verbal cognate, "transgress" (*parabainō*).[35] The picture is of stepping over a boundary that should not be crossed.

---

30. *NIDNTTE*, 1:255–56, 258–59.
31. *NIDNTTE*, 1:156–58.
32. Rom. 6:13; Heb. 8:12; 1 John 1:9; 5:17.
33. Matt. 7:23; 13:41; 23:28; 24:12; 2 Cor. 6:14; Titus 2:14; Heb. 1:9; 8:12; 10:17.
34. Rom. 2:23; 4:15; 5:14; Gal. 3:19; 1 Tim. 2:14; Heb. 2:2; 9:15.
35. Matt. 15:2–3; Acts 1:25; 2 John 9.

6. In contrast to "obedience" (*hypakoē*), we find the Greek term for "disobedience" (*parakoē*) in a few New Testament texts.[36] It carries the sense of refusing to listen (cf. *parakouō*, Matt. 18:17). Similar are the words "disobedient" (*apeithēs*, Titus 1:16; 3:3) and "disobey" (Rom. 10:21, *apeitheō*), which in the Septuagint render words for rebellion (Isa. 30:9).[37] The refusal to listen is an act of unbelief toward God's Word (John 3:36; 1 Pet. 2:7). The New Testament affirms the same view of the hardening and blinding effects of sin as the Old.[38] Sin has the tragic effect of leaving people in a state of stubborn foolishness.

7. The noun "error" (*plane*) and the related verb "to go astray" (*planaō*) can refer to mental deception (Matt. 22:29; 24:4–5), but also to moral departure from the right way (Rom. 1:27; Rev. 2:20), as when a sheep wanders (Matt. 18:12; 1 Pet. 2:25).

8. A somewhat similar idea appears in the term "trespass" (*paraptōma*),[39] the root meaning of which is "a culpable moral slip, stumble, or fall" (*parapiptō*).[40]

9. In the New Testament, the concept of "impurity" or "uncleanness" (*akatharsia*) or being "unclean" (*akathartos*) is applied to sin in general as a moral pollution incompatible with the holy service of God (Rom. 6:19; 2 Cor. 6:17). It appears several times with specific reference to sexual sin as a predominant form of moral defilement among the Gentiles.[41]

A Conceptual Summary of the Biblical Terminology for Sin

Based on our study of the Bible's vocabulary for sin, we may make the following observations about the biblical view of sin and connect it to the doctrine of creation. We find three basic streams of thought about sin that together enhance our sense of its horror.

First, sin is *refusing to hear the divine word* and respond with faith and faithfulness. We may call this a covenantal view of sin. The Creator is the speaking God who makes a verbal covenant with man. Sin rejects

---

36. Rom. 5:19; 2 Cor 10:6; Heb. 2:2.
37. *TDNT*, 6:10–11.
38. Mark 4:12; John 9:39–41; 12:37–40; Acts 26:18; 28:26; Rom. 1:21–22; 11:7–10; 2 Cor. 4:4; Eph. 4:17–19.
39. Matt. 6:14–15; Mark 11:25; Rom. 4:24; 5:15–18, 20; 11:11–12; 2 Cor. 5:19; Gal. 6:1; Eph. 1:7; 2:1, 5; Col. 2:13.
40. *TDNT*, 6:170–72.
41. Rom. 1:24; 2 Cor. 12:21; Gal. 5:19; Eph. 4:19; 5:3; Col. 3:5; 1 Thess. 4:7.

the word of the covenant as untrustworthy and the God of the covenant as evil. Instead, sin embraces deceit and the deceiver.

Therefore, sin brings spiritual *hardness* toward God and foolishness. Though the sinner retains his essential faculties as a human being, he loses his spiritual eyes and ears, so to speak, and his inner man becomes dead in disbelief and disobedience. God made man to receive, repeat, and reflect his word, but man became hardened by the deceitfulness of sin. The result is slavery.

Second, sin is *missing the divine mark* and failing to fulfill the purpose of being God's image bearer.[42] We may call this a teleological view of sin. The Creator made all things very good, but sin is evil, a destructive distortion of the Creator's design. To sin is to depart from him, straying from the path of life under God's blessing and pursuing death.

As a result, sin brings moral *pollution* and defilement that exclude the sinner from God's holy presence. This is a sacral view of sin's consequences. The Creator placed man in a sacred place to offer his holy worship to God. Sin is spiritual corruption and filth that so stains man that he must be banished from God's presence. God made man to worship and commune with him, but sin disables man as a worshiper and shuts him out from the presence of the Lord. The consequence is shame.

Third, sin is *rebellion against divine authority* and transgression of God's law. We may call this a political view of sin. The Creator is the owner, and he has the right to order and command his creatures as he sees fit. Sin is treason, a foolish attempt to overthrow the reign of the supreme King and to usurp his place.

Consequently, sin brings *guilt* and liability to punishment upon the sinner. This is a judicial view of sin's consequences, for the Creator is the Judge of all the earth. Sin is criminal injustice, a violation of the Creator's righteous order that demands retribution against the sinner. Rebellion provokes punishment. The result is fear.

Understanding these three aspects of sin enables us to grasp the evil of sin and prepares us to receive God's gifts of wisdom, righteousness, sanctification, and redemption in Christ (1 Cor. 1:30). Hardness (*duritia*) against God's Word is overcome by God's effectual calling (vv. 23–24). Augustine prayed, "A closed heart doth not exclude Thine eye, nor does man's hardness of heart [*duritia*] repulse Thine hand, but Thou dissolvest it when

---

42. Hoekema, *Created in God's Image*, 175.

Thou willest, either in pity or in vengeance."[43] Murray explained that sin involves both "pollution" (Latin *macula*, literally "stain" or "blemish") and "guilt" (*reatus*). The former consists in the unholiness and depravity of man's character and actions so that "man stands in contradiction to the holiness of God." The latter consists of demerit and liability to punishment because of man's lawless rebellion against God's justice.[44] Justification removes the guilt of sin and grants us a righteous status before God, and sanctification removes sin's pollution over time.

Theological Definitions of Sin's Center and Root

The Ten Commandments and various sin lists in the Bible demonstrate the variety of sins that people commit. What do all sins have in common? What is the central thrust of sin that makes it sinful? There are various proposals as to how we may define sin's taproot and core principle. Each definition that we cite below takes up a strand of Augustine's thought.

Sensuality versus Rationality

The Bible closely identifies righteousness with wisdom (Prov. 2:1–9). It commends self-controlled sober-mindedness (Titus 2:2, 5–6). By contrast, the first sin involved grasping for physical gratification in the forbidden fruit (Gen. 3:6). Worldliness is allowing our lusts to reign over us to please our eyes, flesh, and pride (1 John 2:16). Therefore, we might define the core of sin as sensuality as opposed to godly rationality, passion versus wise self-control.

This definition will especially appeal to us if we tend to view the human spirit as closer to God than the human body, a common perspective in ancient Greco-Roman culture. Augustine imbibed this error when he temporarily embraced the dualistic doctrine of Manichaeism. It might be argued that the mature Augustine still tended to identify sin with sensuality in some ways, particularly in his negative view of sexual desire and passion.[45] Peter Lombard perpetuated the Augustinian idea that it is because

---

43. Augustine, *Confessions*, 5.1, in *NPNF*[1], 1:79.
44. Murray, "The Nature of Sin," in *Collected Writings*, 2:80–81. Murray here noted that some theologians had distinguished between "the guilt of sin" (*reatus culpae*) and "liability to punishment" (*reatus poenae*). However, most Reformed orthodox theologians said that this is a false dichotomy, and *reatus culpae* and *reatus poenae* are the same. See Calvin, *Commentaries*, on Gen. 3:19; Ames, *The Marrow of Theology*, 1.12.3 (116); and Turretin, *Institutes*, 9.3.6 (1:595). Turretin said that the distinction was used by Roman Catholic theologians to support the idea of forgiven believers still having to bear temporal punishments for their sins.
45. Augustine, *The City of God*, 14.16–18, in *NPNF*[1], 2:275–77.

of sexual passion that original sin is passed on in reproduction. Lombard seems to have thought that the "kindling for sin" (*fomes peccati*) lies primarily in the desires of the physical flesh.[46]

However, God made both body and soul (Gen. 2:7), and made them very good (1:31). He provided the richest delights for Adam and Eve in the garden (2:9, 16); his prohibition was not a demand for bodily self-denial.[47] The sin of our first parents was not primarily lust for food, but the pursuit of wisdom independently from God (Gen. 3:5–6). Defining sin as sensuality does not adequately explain how many sins, though called "the works of the flesh," are really vices of the soul, not of the body (Gal. 5:19–21),[48] or how spirits such as the Devil are sinful.[49] Augustine acknowledged that his former slavery to sensual desires was a consequence of his proud rebellion against the Lord.[50]

The theme of sensuality reminds us of an important truth about human sinfulness. Sin preoccupies us with this world—what we can experience now by our senses—and deadens us to the invisible heavenly glory of God. Christ warns against living for "treasures upon earth" and calls people to pursue "treasures in heaven," for "no man can serve two masters" (Matt. 6:19–24). The message of God's kingdom is often choked out and made unfruitful in people's hearts by "the care of this world, and the deceitfulness of riches" (13:22). We must not be like the man with the "muck-rake" in John Bunyan's (1628–1688) allegory, whose attention is so consumed with raking up sticks and dirt that he cannot look up to see the heavenly crown offered to him.[51] Instead, we must "seek those things which are above, where Christ sitteth on the right hand of God" (Col. 3:1). The pull of sin toward this world manifests sin's character as unbelief, which we will examine below.

Pride versus Humility

The Scriptures speak strongly against pride: "God opposes the proud but gives grace to the humble" (James 4:6; 1 Pet. 5:5 ESV). The bait with which Satan lured Adam and Eve to their deaths was "Ye shall be as gods" (Gen. 3:5), or even "like God" (ESV). It is pride that lifts up a person against God

---

46. Lombard, *The Sentences*, 2.30.7–9 (2:148–49). For a critique, see Calvin, *Institutes*, 2.1.9.
47. Calvin, *Institutes*, 2.1.4.
48. Augustine, *The City of God*, 14.3, in NPNF[1], 2:263.
49. Vos, *Reformed Dogmatics*, 2:22.
50. Augustine, *Confessions*, 2.2.2; 7.7.11, in NPNF[1], 1:55, 107.
51. John Bunyan, *The Pilgrim's Progress, The Second Part*, in *The Works of John Bunyan*, ed. George Offor, 3 vols. (1854; repr., Edinburgh: Banner of Truth, 1991), 3:184–85.

(Ps. 10:4) and brings him low in humiliation and destruction (Prov. 11:2; 16:18; 18:12). The day of the Lord is against everything "proud and lofty" (Isa. 2:12). Conversely, the beginning and essence of wisdom is the fear of the Lord (Job 28:28; Prov. 9:10). Christ taught that the only way into God's kingdom was through the low door of inward poverty and humility (Matt. 5:3; 18:3–4). Therefore, we might identify the root of sin to be pride.

This definition also has an ancient pedigree. The Wisdom of Sirach, an ancient Jewish writing that was well respected by early Christians, says, "The beginning of pride is when one departeth from God, and his heart is turned away from his Maker. For pride is the beginning of sin" (Sir. 10:12–13). Theologians from Augustine to Gregory the Great to Peter Lombard cited this statement as an explanation of sin's root in the heart.[52] John Calvin affirmed that Augustine spoke rightly on this point, though Calvin sought an explanation deeper than pride.[53]

Pride fits well with the Bible's emphasis on sin as rebellion, especially when we see that pride implies loving self to the exclusion of loving God.

Selfishness versus Love

Another definition of sin builds on Christ's summary of the law in the two great commandments: "Thou shalt love the Lord thy God with all thy heart, and with all thy soul, and with all thy mind" and "Thou shalt love thy neighbour as thyself" (Matt. 22:37, 39). The second presumes that sinners already love themselves. Paul condemns sinners as "lovers of their own selves" (2 Tim. 3:2) and complains that "all seek their own" interests (Phil. 2:21), whereas true love does not seek its own (1 Cor. 13:5). Therefore, we might propose a definition of sin as mere self-love stripped of love for God and our neighbors. This is very close to identifying the core of sin as pride. Augustine said that another word for the proud is "self-pleasers," and added that the godly are guided by "love of God," but the ungodly by "love of self."[54]

The understanding of sin as unbounded self-love was taught by Jonathan Edwards, who learned it from his grandfather Solomon Stoddard (1643–1729).[55] Edwards said, "The ruin which the Fall brought upon

---

52. Augustine, *The City of God*, 12.6; 14.13, in *NPNF*[1], 2:229, 273; and Lombard, *The Sentences*, 2.43.7–8 (2:210–11). Lombard cited Gregory, *Moralia*, 31.45.87.

53. Calvin, *Institutes*, 2.1.4.

54. Augustine, *The City of God*, 14.13, in *NPNF*[1], 2:273.

55. Edwards, *Miscellanies* no. 301, "Sin and Original Sin," in *WJE*, 13:387.

the soul of man consists very much in that he lost his nobler and more extensive principles, and fell wholly under the government of self-love."[56]

There is much to commend this definition, for it ties our understanding of sin to the core content of God's law. It also helps us to understand how sin can have such energy and yet consist of a deprivation and depravation of human nature, not the addition of any new substance or structure. However, we do not find the definitions of sin as pride or self-love, as insightful as they are, to be sufficient. Exegetically, the emphasis of God's Word does not fall on the pride or selfishness of sin, but on its rebellion and treason against God. Vos wrote, "Sin, in the strict sense, is only conceivable as sin against God" (cf. Ps. 51:5).[57] Berkhof said, "Sin always has relation to God and his will."[58] Theologically, these definitions run the risk of becoming man-centered rather than God-centered, for they define sin in terms of us. Experientially, defining sin as pride or selfishness does not explain why people would expend, abase, or even destroy themselves in the service of a false god or for the sake of an inordinate love for a creature.[59] Wayne Grudem says that such definitions also fail to account for the fact that "much self-interest is good and approved by Scripture, as when Jesus commands us to 'lay up for yourselves treasures in heaven' (Matt. 6:20)."[60] Practically, such definitions leave it unclear how we are to determine which attitudes and activities are wrong. We have seen in our relativistic culture how easy it is to use "love" as a justification for all kinds of violations of God's commandments.

Idolatry versus the Worship of God

Paul's great epistle to the Romans begins its exposition of the doctrine of sin with man's refusal to glorify his Creator and foolish choice to give his worship to images of created things (Rom. 1:19–23). This is the great offense against which God's anger burns (v. 18). The flood of sins that inundate the Gentile world is the judicial consequence of man's worshiping the creature instead of the Creator (vv. 24–32). Therefore, we might define sin as idolatry as opposed to glorifying God, where idolatry is glorifying a creature instead of God. It could be argued that this was the heart of

---

56. Edwards, *Charity and Its Fruits*, in *WJE*, 8:252.
57. Vos, *Reformed Dogmatics*, 2:23.
58. Berkhof, *Systematic Theology*, 232.
59. Vos, *Reformed Dogmatics*, 2:22–23; and Erickson, *Systematic Theology*, 530.
60. Grudem, *Systematic Theology*, 491.

Adam and Eve's fall, for they chose creatures (the tree, the Serpent, and themselves) above God.

Augustine recognized how closely intertwined the themes of pride, self-love, and vainglory are. The question of glory stood at the center of his contrast between the city of man and the city of God, the two societies into which mankind is divided. Augustine said,

> Accordingly, two cities have been formed by two loves: the earthly by the love of self, even to the contempt of God; the heavenly by the love of God, even to the contempt of self. The former, in a word, glories in itself, the latter in the Lord. For the one seeks glory from men; but the greatest glory of the other is God, the witness of conscience. The one lifts up its head in its own glory; the other says to its God, "Thou art my glory, and the lifter up of mine head" [Ps. 3:3].[61]

Augustine proceeded to quote Romans 1:21–25, tying together the theme of glory with the contrast between those who worship creatures and those who worship the true God.

Our deepest motivations spring from what we aim to glorify. The Westminster Shorter Catechism (Q. 1) offers some support for this idea in its opening statement: "Man's chief end is to glorify God and to enjoy him forever."[62] In recent times, writers in the biblical counseling movement have explored how specific sins are rooted in inordinately large desires or fears, such that we effectively turn created things into idols.[63]

Here again, we encounter a legitimate insight into the nature of sin. The Scriptures encourage us to view even covetousness and the love of money as matters of false worship (Matt. 6:24; Col. 3:5). However, when God summarized the moral law in the Ten Commandments, he devoted the second commandment to forbidding idols, but the rest to other matters. We do not find that the Bible uses idolatry as a master category for all sin or that it employs idolatry of the heart as the diagnostic key to spiritual growth. Therefore, we hesitate to define sin strictly as idolatry lest we lose biblical balance in our ethics and doctrine of sanctification. This approach to sin focuses on inordinate desires, but sin also arises from a refusal to trust and obey God.

---

61. Augustine, *The City of God*, 14.28, in *NPNF*[1], 2:282–83.
62. *Reformed Confessions*, 4:353.
63. David Powlison, "Idols of the Heart and 'Vanity Fair,'" *Journal of Biblical Counseling* 13, no. 2 (1995): 35–38, https://www.ccef.org/resources/blog/idols-heart-and-vanity-fair; and Elyse M. Fitzpatrick, *Idols of the Heart: Learning to Long for God Alone*, rev. ed. (Phillipsburg, NJ: P&R, 2016).

Unbelief versus Faith in God's Word

Another possible approach to formulating a definition for sin is to seek its center in unbelief. The temptation in the garden, which we will explore in the next chapter, hinged on whether Adam and Eve would believe God's word when the Serpent contradicted it (Gen. 3:4). The great failure of the people of Israel in the wilderness was that "they believed not his word" (Ps. 106:24). The writer to the Hebrews asserted that "without faith it is impossible to please him" (Heb. 11:6), citing examples of how faith motivated God's people to obey him. Faith is essential to worship, for by faith we give "glory to God," believing that "what he had promised, he was able also to perform" (Rom. 4:20–21). Faith is also essential to all good works, "for whatsoever is not of faith is sin" (14:23).

We also find this strand of thought in Augustine, for he said that unbelief "is the sin wherein all sins are included."[64] The Reformers, with their emphasis on faith as the instrument by which God saves sinners by grace, likewise highlighted the centrality of unbelief. Martin Luther said, "Unbelief is the root, sap, and chief power of all sin."[65] He also said that unbelief is the supreme act of hatred toward God and the basis for idolatry: "What greater rebellion against God, what greater wickedness, what greater contempt of God is there than not believing in his promise? . . . Does not a man who does this deny God and set himself up as an idol in his heart?"[66] Calvin said, "First the woman is led away from the word of God by the wiles of Satan, through unbelief. . . . Men then revolted from God, when, having forsaken his word, they lent their ears to the falsehoods of Satan." He went on to say, "Unbelief was the root of defection; just as faith alone unites us to God. Hence flowed ambition and pride."[67] Calvin saw the first sin as a compound of disobedience, irreverence, pride, and ambition, but he considered unbelief to be at the bottom of it all, for "Adam would never have dared oppose God's authority unless he had disbelieved in God's Word."[68]

Unbelief, then, has been a definitive factor in all sin from the fall to today. However, if we define sin as unbelief, we must not understand unbelief in a merely negative way, as a lack of faith, but as actual opposition

---

64. Augustine, *Lectures or Tractates on the Gospel According to St. John*, 89.1, in *NPNF*[1], 7:358.

65. Luther, *Preface to the Epistle of St. Paul to the Romans*, in *LW*, 35:369.

66. Luther, *The Freedom of a Christian*, in *LW*, 31:350.

67. Calvin, *Commentaries*, on Gen. 3:6.

68. Calvin, *Institutes*, 2.1.4.

to God, or we will not sufficiently account for the perverse energy of sin. Hatred against God cannot be separated from unbelief toward his word,[69] just as faith goes hand in hand with love for God.[70] This leads us to consider a central theme observed in the Bible's vocabulary of sin: rebellion.

Rebellion against God's Law versus Obedience

John writes, "Sin is the transgression of the law" (1 John 3:4), or, "Sin is lawlessness" (ESV). Though the word translated as "lawlessness" (*anomia*) can be a generic term for sin, it has a more precise nuance of rebellion against God's law, which must obtain in this text or the verse becomes a tautology: "sin is sin." Therefore, John offers us a concise definition of sin as "lawlessness" in contrast to doing righteousness (vv. 7, 10). The apostle Paul explains that the law gives "the knowledge of sin" (Rom. 3:20), but "where no law is, there is no transgression" (4:15), and "sin is not imputed when there is no law" (5:13). Sin, then, viewed not merely as an act but as a mindset, "is enmity against God," which results in an adamant refusal to be "subject to the law of God" (8:7).

Augustine said, "Sin, then, is any transgression in deed, or word, or desire, of the eternal law. And the eternal law is the divine order or will of God."[71] Thomas Aquinas later cited Augustine's statement with approval.[72] The idea was influential in Reformed orthodoxy, as we see in the writings of William Perkins and William Ames.[73] The Westminster Shorter Catechism (Q. 14) says, "What is sin? Sin is any want of conformity unto, or transgression of, the law of God,"[74] and cited 1 John 3:4 in support of this definition. Such a view of sin corresponds to the Reformation doctrine that good works must be "performed according to the law of God," as the Heidelberg Catechism (LD 33, Q. 91) says.[75]

Defining sin as contrariety to God's law has many strengths. It focuses attention on sin's relation to God, and not its relation to ourselves. It preserves the biblical emphasis on sin as rebellion against God and transgression of his commandments. It reflects the nature of man's first sin, which was a violation of God's spoken prohibition. It undergirds the doctrine of

---

69. John 3:18–20; 5:38, 42; 8:40–45.
70. John 16:27; Gal. 5:6; 1 Pet. 1:8; 1 John 2:3.
71. Augustine, *Reply to Faustus the Manichaean*, 22.27, in NPNF[1], 4:283.
72. Aquinas, *Summa Theologica*, Pt. 2.1, Q. 71, Art. 6.
73. Perkins, *An Exposition of the Symbol*, in *Works*, 5:82; and Ames, *The Marrow of Theology*, 1.11.4; 1.13.2; 1.14.2 (114, 120–21).
74. *Reformed Confessions*, 4:355.
75. *The Three Forms of Unity*, 99–100.

God's retributive justice against sinners. It paves the way for the gospel, in which Christ redeemed man from sin by satisfying both the precept and penalty of God's law.

However, Turretin observed that Augustine's definition of sin in terms of "desire, word, and deed contrary to the law of God" strictly applies only to "actual sin (and indeed sins of commission)." Turretin offered his own expanded definition of sin: "an inclination, action, or omission at variance with the law of God," where "law" includes the "natural" law implanted in man's conscience and the written law of God's Word.[76] Berkhof said, "Sin may be defined as a lack of conformity to the moral law of God, either in act, disposition, or state."[77] Grudem says, "Sin is any failure to conform to the moral law of God in act, attitude, or nature."[78]

If we define the core of sin as violation of divine law, then we must make it clear that God's law cannot be separated from God. Berkhof notes that "lack of conformity to the law of God" is a "correct formal definition of sin," but since the "material content" of the law is love for God, sin is "opposition to God."[79] God's law reflects God's righteous nature (Ps. 119:137), man's creation in God's righteous image (Eph. 4:24), and God's requirement that man love God totally (Deut. 6:5). Therefore, sin is an offense against who God is and a deadly distortion of who God made man to be. To reject God's law is to hate God (Rom. 8:7). When people break God's law, they "walk contrary" to God (Lev. 26:21–28, 40–41), for they "despise" and "abhor" his commandments (vv. 15, 43). Thomas Watson commented, "Sin strikes at the very Deity. . . . Sin would not only unthrone God, but un-God him."[80] God's judgment of lawbreakers is his vindication of his holiness and Word (Isa. 5:16, 24–25).

A Reflection on the Complex Meaning of Sin

Defining sin is a difficult matter, but we will attempt to draw together the various lines of thought that this chapter has uncovered. Sin is real but has no independent existence or substance. Rather, sin arose in history as an ethical and moral distortion of God's personal creatures, a distortion seated in their innermost beings. At the core of sin is hatred against God

---

76. Turretin, *Institutes*, 9.1.3–4 (1:591–92).
77. Berkhof, *Systematic Theology*, 233.
78. Grudem, *Systematic Theology*, 490.
79. Berkhof, *Systematic Theology*, 232; cf. 222. See also Vos, *Reformed Dogmatics*, 2:25.
80. Watson, *A Body of Divinity*, 133–34.

as our Creator and Lawgiver. Human hostility to God takes a form that distorts our creation in his image and, thus, our relation to him as sons to the Father. Sin rejects this relationship and replaces humble, filial love with proud independence, so that natural self-love descends into the pit of self-deification. The image of God and the covenant with Adam engage man as God's covenant servant according to the threefold office of prophet, priest, and king. Sin twists man into a false prophet who refuses to receive God's Word by faith and speaks lies; an unholy priest who pollutes God's worship and seeks after created idols; and a rebellious king who transgresses God's laws and incurs liability to his sovereign retribution.

The multidimensional notion of man's identity and calling helps us to understand why it is difficult to reduce sin to a single focal point. Sin corrupts each aspect of the threefold office of God's covenant servant, whether sin is considered as "unbelief" (prophet), "idolatry" (priest), or "rebellion" (king). Man's original identity as God's image-bearing, created son draws attention to sin's inherent pride and selfishness. Just as we could not define the image of God in a single phrase, so we cannot adequately define sin in a single statement.

Reformed orthodoxy recognized the complexity of the matter. Johannes Polyander, Johannes Wollebius, Turretin, and Wilhelmus à Brakel all defined sin as "lawlessness" or a violation of God's law (1 John 3:4), but they also identified sin's first motion as unbelief toward God's word (Gen. 3:1–5).[81] Perhaps we might say that sin's definitive act is rebellion against God's law, its defiling desire is turning from God's glory to creatures, and its deepest root is unbelief toward God's revelation—all expressing its damnable character as enmity against God.

An Experiential Application of Sin's Definition: What Have I Done?

It would be great wickedness to consider the meaning of sin in an abstract manner without reflecting upon what it implies for us. Do you confess that you have sinned? If you do not, then you deceive yourself and call God a liar, for his Word declares that all have sinned (1 John 1:8, 10). You must acknowledge that you—that is, your soul, mind, and heart—are sinful and

---

81. Polyander, Walaeus, Thysius, and Rivetus, *Synopsis Purioris Theologiae*, 14.1, 7, 12–18; Wollebius, *Compendium*, 1.9.(1).3; 1.9.(2).v; 1.11.(1) (66–67, 71); Turretin, *Institutes*, 9.1.3; 9.6.6 (1:591, 605); and Brakel, *The Christian's Reasonable Service*, 1:373, 382.

that you commit sin. However, you must not stop there. If you confess your sin, do you understand what you are confessing?

Consider the implications of what we have studied in this chapter. Sin is not just the foolish mistakes you have made or the way you have brought trouble to your life or that of others. When you confess sin, you are admitting that you have lifted yourself up against God. You are acknowledging that you have refused to listen when he has spoken to you in his Word. You have turned away from the very purpose and meaning of your life—to glorify God—and have sought your glory in mere people and things. You have rebelled against the King of kings and have attempted to overthrow his reign. You have been hard-hearted, stubborn, polluted, defiled, guilty, and worthy of punishment.

In short, *you have hated God*. John Owen (1616–1683) reminded us that since sin is "enmity against God" (Rom. 8:7), every sin is hatred toward the Lord and rebellion against his authority. Whether or not we are believers, the least degree of sin is hostility against God, just as "every drop of poison is poison, and will infect, and every spark of fire is fire, and will burn."[82] Think of it: the smallest motion of sin in your heart is a criminal act of hostility to God.

Surely, even a faint realization of what sin is should lead us to humble ourselves before God and cry out in horror, "What am I, and what have I done?"

Sing to the Lord

Contrition over Sin

> Before thee, God, who knowest all,
> With grief and shame I prostrate fall.
> I see my sins against thee, Lord,
> The sins of thought, of deed, and word.
> They press me sore; I cry to thee:
> O God, be merciful to me!
>
> O Lord, my God, to thee I pray:
> O cast me not in wrath away!
> Let thy good Spirit ne'er depart,

---

82. John Owen, *The Nature, Power, Deceit, and Prevalency of the Remainders of Indwelling Sin in Believers*, in *The Works of John Owen*, ed. William H. Goold, 16 vols. (1850–1853; repr., Edinburgh: Banner of Truth, 1965–1968), 6:177.

But let him draw to thee my heart
That truly penitent I be:
O God, be merciful to me!

O Jesus, let thy precious blood
Be to my soul a cleansing flood.
Turn not, O Lord, thy guest away,
But grant that justified I may
Go to my house at peace with thee:
O God, be merciful to me!

Magnus B. Landstad, trans. Carl Döving
Tune: The Lord's Prayer
Trinity Hymnal—Baptist Edition, No. 409

Questions for Meditation or Discussion

1. What are six important truths about what sin is *not*? For each, state what positive truth can be said about what sin is.
2. What are the three most common general words for sin in the Hebrew Old Testament? What does each mean?
3. What are the three most common general words for sin in the Greek New Testament?
4. What definition of sin identifies it closely with the body? Why is this definition faulty?
5. What biblical support can be given for the idea that the root of all sin is pride?
6. What definition of sin is based on Matthew 22:37–39?
7. What are the strengths and weaknesses of defining sin as idolatry?
8. What biblical support can be given to show that all sin is rooted in unbelief?
9. What are the strengths and weaknesses of defining sin as lawlessness?
10. How can we bring together these diverse biblical conceptions of sin?
11. How has studying the meaning of sin affected your view of your own sin?

Questions for Deeper Reflection

12. How do the authors summarize the biblical terminology for sin? Is this threefold summary an accurate description of sin? Why or why not?

13. In a discussion with other Christians, one person is arguing that all sin is selfishness, whereas another makes a case that the root of all sin is pride. How would you respond? Is either position an adequate definition of sin? Why or why not?

18

The Fall of Man into Sin and Misery

Sin is not a mere principle or idea, but a real evil that appeared in history at a specific time. While there is a great deal of mystery about the origin of moral evil, the Bible records the entrance of sin into this world in Genesis 3. The first part of that text especially reveals the sin of God's creatures against him, and the second part reveals God's righteous acts toward them.

Genesis 3 presents the history of man's fall. As emphasized earlier, it is crucial for the Christian faith that we view the early chapters of Genesis not as myths but as historical narratives about real people and events.[1] The account of Genesis 3 is not an allegory for everyone's loss of innocence or a primitive story explaining why people fear snakes, wear clothing, and so on. The text represents itself as an account of what actually took place with the first man and woman, and we should receive it as historical truth, for it is the Word of God.

Our familiarity with the narrative of the fall can dull our ability to seriously contemplate its message to us. Genesis 3 is real history, yet it is also theological history. It not only records events but also teaches truths.

The Transgression of Creatures against Their God

Whereas the first chapter of Genesis describes creation from a cosmic perspective and the second chapter from a covenantal perspective, the third chapter speaks of the breaking of God's covenant by man at the instigation of Satan.

---

1. See the first half of chap. 3.

The Rebellion of the Devil and His Angels

The first enemy of God appeared in the garden as "the serpent" (Gen. 3:1). In some respects, the text describes the Serpent as an ordinary snake: it is compared to other animals, moved on its belly through the dust, and struck at the feet of human beings (vv. 1, 14–15). However, this Scripture passage indicates that either through a real serpent or by assuming its form, a greater power was at work. The Serpent was very "crafty" (ESV), which translates a term (*'arum*) that can mean "prudent,"[2] but that also can carry the sense of an evil schemer (Job 5:12; 15:5). Its conversation with the woman and deceitful manipulation to turn her against God displayed a superhuman evil intelligence. God had made the animals good and subordinated them to man.[3] In the form of a serpent, an evil power had intruded into paradise.

The original Israelite audience would have recognized the Serpent as an evil spirit, for in the ancient Near Eastern cultures, snakes symbolized the powers of life and death in the spirit world, such as the cobra that adorned the headdress of the pharaoh.[4] The term translated "serpent" (*nakhash*) can refer to great reptiles, such as Rahab, a symbol for the power of Egypt (Ps. 89:10; Isa. 51:9), or Leviathan, a sea monster that can represent the power of evil (Isa. 27:1). The New Testament confirms the interpretation of the Serpent as an evil spirit when we read of "that old serpent, called the Devil, and Satan, which deceiveth the whole world" (Rev. 12:9).

The focus of Genesis is on mankind, not the history of demonic powers. The testimony of the Holy Scriptures in general is that Satan and the demons were created by God as angels (Matt. 25:41; Col. 1:16), but fell into rebellion against God and malevolence toward the human race (1 Pet. 5:8; 2 Pet. 2:4).[5] It is clear from Genesis 3 that Satan was operating as an enemy of God and his people in the garden.[6]

Satan's Deceit regarding God's Word

Satan's temptation of Adam and Eve shows us that the core of sin is rebellion against God rooted in unbelief toward his revelation.[7] God made his

---

2. Prov. 12:16, 23; 13:16; 14:8, 15, 18; 22:3; 27:12.
3. Gen. 1:25–26, 28; 2:19–20.
4. *NIDOTTE*, 3:85; and Vos, *Biblical Theology*, 34.
5. Calvin, *Commentaries*, on Gen. 3:1–3.
6. On Satan and the demons, see *RST*, 1:1133–57 (chap. 55).
7. See the previous chapter on the meaning of sin.

covenant with man through his word, and Satan attacked man's relationship with God by undermining God's word. This chapter is of much practical importance because Satan's devices have not significantly changed.

Whereas the Lord God always addressed the man first in the garden (Gen. 2:16–17; 3:9), the Tempter addressed the woman and ignored the man (3:1–2). The Serpent used the plural form ("Ye shall not eat . . . ?," v. 1), drawing out the woman to speak as the representative of the family, and she answered in the plural ("We may eat . . . ," v. 2). The Devil avoided a frontal confrontation with the head of the household and inverted God's order of leadership (1 Tim. 2:11–14).

Satan began by insinuating *doubt about God's word*. The Serpent said to the woman, "Yea, hath God said, Ye shall not eat of every tree of the garden?" (Gen. 3:1). The text may be translated, "Did God actually say . . . ?" (ESV), for the phrase translated "actually" (*aph ki*) can function as a marker for emphasis.[8] Satan raised questions about God's word, subtly suggesting that Eve might take the place of a judge to critically evaluate what God had said.[9] John Calvin said that Satan aimed to "indirectly weaken their confidence in the word."[10] It should not surprise us that the theological and spiritual battles that the church must wage so often revolve around the authority of the Holy Scriptures. Furthermore, Satan's question nudged his listener to question the goodness of God, as if the Creator were stingy in his prohibitions. The very use of "God" in a context that consistently uses the name "the LORD God" shifts attention away from God's covenantal kindness to mankind and may suggest a more distant cosmic Creator.

Satan led the woman into a *distortion of God's word*. She replied, "We may eat of the fruit of the trees of the garden: but of the fruit of the tree which is in the midst of the garden, God hath said, Ye shall not eat of it, neither shall ye touch it, lest ye die" (Gen. 3:2–3). Her response was largely faithful, but it suggested that she was beginning to underestimate God's kindness. God's words were emphatic in their rich provision: "Of *every* tree of the garden thou mayest *freely* eat" (2:16) or "surely eat" (ESV), but Eve merely said, "We *may* eat of the fruit of the trees." Her sense of

---

8. Bruce Waltke and M. O'Connor, *An Introduction to Biblical Hebrew Syntax* (Winona Lake, IN: Eisenbrauns, 1990), 39.3.4d (663). See Hamilton, *The Book of Genesis, Chapters 1–17*, 186n1.

9. Kidner, *Genesis*, 67.

10. Calvin, *Commentaries*, on Gen. 3:1–3.

God's lavish goodness to man was somewhat diminished. Eve also exaggerated God's restriction, as we see by her adding "neither shall ye touch it," as if God were harsh.[11] We should be warned by this that if we lose our gratitude for God's provision and start to view him as overly authoritarian or restrictive, then we are on very dangerous ground. Furthermore, Eve was not properly assessing the certainty and weight of God's warning, for he had said, "thou shalt surely die" (v. 17), but she simply said, "lest you die." These are subtle changes, but they reflect a decline in godly fear of God and confidence in his word.[12]

The Devil proceeded to make a bold *denial of God's word*. He said, "Ye shall not surely die" (Gen. 3:4), using the same emphatic form to negate God's word that the Lord God had used in affirming it. The first contradiction of God's word consisted of a denial that God would judge sinners.[13] This may have been one reason why Paul warns the churches not to let anyone deceive them by denying that God will punish the wicked.[14] Satan went on to say, "For God doth know that in the day ye eat thereof, then your eyes shall be opened, and ye shall be as gods, knowing good and evil" (v. 5). The Tempter attacked God's justice, truthfulness, and love. He asserted that God did not speak the truth, but used his law only to hold people back from glory and wisdom. Satan also sought to deceive Eve concerning the nature of man, promising that man could become a god unto himself, independent in his wisdom, instead of a servant who depended on his Lord. Tragically, sin did not elevate man to a superhuman level, but degraded him as an image bearer of God. Man cast off his faith in the Lord God only to realize that faith in God was the cable by which God held man up in his lofty position.

By this strategy of cultivating unbelief in God's word while proposing his own promise, Satan aimed to dethrone God in man's heart and take his place. Consequently, man's compliance made human beings into children of the Devil (John 8:42–47; 1 John 3:8, 10) and made Satan into the "prince" and "god" of this world (John 12:31; 2 Cor. 4:4). Martin Luther said, "The source of all sin truly is unbelief and doubt and abandonment of the Word. Because the world is full of these, it remains in idolatry, denies the truth of God, and invents a new god."[15]

---

11. Vos, *Biblical Theology*, 35.
12. Cf. Luther, *Lectures on Genesis*, in *LW*, 1:155; Calvin, *Commentaries*, on Gen. 3:1–3.
13. Kidner, *Genesis*, 68.
14. 1 Cor. 6:9; Gal. 6:7; Eph. 5:6.
15. Luther, *Lectures on Genesis*, in *LW*, 1:149.

Man's Defiance of God's Word

When man embraced the Devil's lies, unbelief quickly set in motion corrupt desires that produced disobedience (James 1:14–15). Genesis 3:6 says, "And when the woman saw that the tree was good for food, and that it was pleasant to the eyes, and a tree to be desired to make one wise, she took of the fruit thereof, and did eat, and gave also unto her husband with her; and he did eat."

In the brief scope of this verse, we have an anatomy of sin as it corrupts the whole person. Sin begins with false perceptions based upon unbelief: "the woman saw." The tree was the same, but now she viewed it in a different light because she had cast off faith in the word of the Lord and accepted Satan's lie. Sin develops through corrupt desires based on this false perception. The three desires mentioned here—the desire to satisfy the body, the desire to possess beautiful things, and the desire to be wise, which in context means to be like God—line up with Satan's temptation of Christ and John's analysis of the love of the world. From these desires came the outward act of disobedience and rebellion against God's law. We may illustrate the threefold deceitful desire of sin in the following table:

Desire	Genesis 3:6	Luke 4:1–13	1 John 2:16
Physical Satisfaction	"good for food"	"command this stone that it be made bread"	"lust of the flesh"
Beautiful Possessions	"pleasant to the eyes"	"shewed unto him all the kingdoms of the world"	"lust of the eyes"
Godlike Greatness	"to make one wise"	"pinnacle of the temple"	"pride of life"

Table 18.1. The Threefold Pattern of Sinful Desire

Here we have a lens through which to see the basic dimensions of all human sin. Unbelief in God's revelation and trust in Satan's lies darken the human mind so that it no longer perceives matters rightly. Through this self-deceit, the desires of the body and soul become depraved, leading sinners to commit outward acts of transgression against God. Genesis 3:6 bears witness to the depravity of man's entire nature and life. It also teaches us that faith in God's word is "the best guardian" of our hearts, as Calvin observed.[16]

---

16. Calvin, *Commentaries*, on Gen. 3:6.

The great irony of Genesis 3:6 is that man already possessed every good thing needed to satisfy all his desires, and he would have enjoyed them fully had he obeyed God's command. He was created in God's image, surrounded by the paradise of pleasure and beauty, and commissioned to subdue and rule the entire world. Yet man's acceptance of Satan's deceit made God's gifts seem hollow and awakened deceitful desires that disrupted man's joy and led him to disobedience. Consequently, he lost the very things that he thought he was gaining.

Man became a covenant breaker. Many minimize Adam's sin as a small transgression, just eating a piece of fruit, but as William Perkins said, this one sin contained many sins: "unbelief . . . of the truth of God's word," "contempt of God," "pride and ambition," ingratitude for God's good gifts, craving to be wiser than God, the blasphemies of charging God "with lying and envy," the "murder" of themselves and their descendants, and discontent with their high status—in short, "the breach of the whole law of God."[17]

The Righteousness of God toward Sinners

Throughout Genesis, God remains the main character, the great agent who is active in accomplishing his good will. It would be a mistake to focus entirely upon the Serpent, Adam, and Eve in Genesis 3, for the text also reveals much about the Lord God.

God's Silence during the Temptation

Genesis 1:1–2:3 resonates with a steady drumbeat of the words and acts of "God." Likewise, throughout Genesis 2:4–25, "the LORD God" is constantly working and speaking. In Genesis 3:9–24, we hear God's voice in the garden questioning and judging, and we read of his actions of mercy and punishment. However, in the account of the temptation and its immediate consequences, God is silent (vv. 1–8). There is no recorded word or deed from the Lord. In a text full of divine activity, this silence is thunderous and pregnant with meaning.

The Lord God left the man to himself to test him. We find a parallel in God's dealings with Hezekiah: "God left him, to try him, that he might know all that was in his heart" (2 Chron. 32:31). That is not to say that God abandoned Adam and Eve or withdrew any good gifts

---

17. Perkins, *An Exposition of the Symbol*, in *Works*, 5:87–88.

from them. Neither was this an act of judgment. Rather, it was an act of God's sovereign freedom not to add any further gifts to confirm man in holiness.[18] In this covenant, man had to stand against the Tempter by making good use of all that the Lord had given and taught him. The Lord God had provided man with everything he needed for happiness, holiness, and eternal life. Now the man must act in faith and obedience or fall under judgment.

However, we should not misinterpret the Lord God's silence as an interruption of his sovereign providence (Ps. 135:6). In the mystery of God's eternal decree, the fall had its place.[19] God has no pleasure in sin and cannot be the cause of any sin, but he did ordain sin for the sake of his good and holy purposes.[20] Genesis itself teaches this. In the last chapter of the book, Joseph cautions us against thinking that injustice takes place apart from God's sovereign will. Joseph said to his brothers, "But as for you, ye thought evil against me; but God meant it unto good" (Gen. 50:20). In the same way, what the sinners in the garden meant for evil, God had planned before time began for good, in order that he might glorify his grace and justice through Jesus Christ (Rom. 9:21–23; 2 Tim. 1:9).[21]

God's Secret Judgments upon Sinners

The Lord God had warned that Adam would surely die if he transgressed the covenant (Gen. 2:17). As we will discuss more fully later in this chapter, death has tentacles that grasp every part of human existence now and forever. We see God's secret judgments falling upon Adam and Eve even before God openly confronted them.

First, they experienced *bitter shame*. Satan had promised, "Your eyes shall be opened" (Gen. 3:5), and indeed, "the eyes of them both were opened" (v. 7), but not with the happy results they anticipated. In their righteousness, they had been "naked" but "not ashamed"; now, in their sin, "they knew they were naked," and, in their shame, sought to cover themselves. Sin immediately estranged them from God and from each other. Horatius Bonar (1808–1889) said, "Unfallen man needed no covering, and asked for none; but fallen man, under the bitter consciousness of the unworthy and unseemly condition to which sin has reduced him,

---

18. Willard, *A Compleat Body of Divinity*, 179.
19. On God's decree, election, and reprobation, see *RST*, 1:957–1057 (chaps. 48–51).
20. Calvin, *Commentaries*, on Gen. 3:1–3.
21. Perkins, *An Exposition of the Symbol*, in *Works*, 5:86.

as unfit for God, or angels, or man to look upon, cries out for covering—covering such as will hide his shame even from the eye of God."[22] Wolfgang Capito (c. 1478–1541) said that Adam, having lost communion with God and embraced the devilish intruder, "was tormented by the disgrace of sin, an avoidance of God and a hatred for truth."[23]

Mankind's attempts to cover their shame are pitiful. Adam and Eve tried "fig leaves." Leaves pulled from a tree quickly wither and break apart. These were real fig leaves, but they function in the text of Genesis as the first example of a pattern that runs through human history. In the Bible, a leaf can represent the weakest and most flimsy of things (Lev. 26:36; Job 13:25). Clothing can symbolize a person's righteousness and public vindication.[24] Whether people attempt to cover their shame with good works and religious activities or by plunging themselves into sin and celebrating the sins of others, all their efforts fail.

Second, Adam and Eve experienced *guilt and fear in God's presence.* When they heard God coming to them, they "hid themselves from the presence of the Lord God amongst the trees of the garden" (Gen. 3:8). They were "afraid" (v. 10). Their sin had poisoned the fellowship that they once enjoyed with God (2:15–25), and they fled his presence. The trees, once tangible reminders of his goodness to them, became the instruments by which they sought to hide from God (3:8). Their response to God shows that they had a keen sense that they deserved divine punishment. They were guilty in God's eyes and knew it.

Our first parents did not run to the Lord seeking forgiveness and reconciliation. Instead, their response demonstrated fear rooted in stubborn hostility. This, too, reveals how fallen mankind responds to God, even when God comes clothed in the gospel of Christ. John 3:19–20 says, "And this is the condemnation, that light is come into the world, and men loved darkness rather than light, because their deeds were evil. For every one that doeth evil hateth the light, neither cometh to the light, lest his deeds should be reproved." Though sinners may stride confidently through life, when God exposes them to the light of Christ, they recoil in guilty fear and seek a hiding place in the darkness—unless changed by God's grace (vv. 3, 21).

---

22. Horatius Bonar, *Earth's Morning: or Thoughts on Genesis* (New York: Robert Carter and Brothers, 1875), 99.
23. Wolfgang Capito, *Hexemeron* (1539), 285r–86r, in *RCS/OT*, 1:143.
24. Job 29:14; Ps. 132:9; Isa. 61:3, 10; Zech. 3:3–4.

God's Patient Confrontation of Sinners

The Lord God did not withdraw from the garden after Adam and Eve sinned, but manifested himself to them in righteousness and mercy. This was an inevitable confrontation because of who God is in his authority, righteousness, omniscience, faithfulness to his covenant, and love.

God came asking questions, a mark of his patience and desire for sinners to examine themselves (cf. Jonah 4:4, 9–11). God addressed Adam first, which was fitting for his responsibility as the head of the family. God's first question, "Where art thou?" displayed not a lack of knowledge, but a loving invitation for Adam to come to him in confession of sin (Gen. 3:9).[25] It could have provoked the man to reflect on why he was hiding from God, the "where" not of location but of condition: "Where are you spiritually?"[26] Adam's response was superficial and avoided the problem. God then asked more pointedly, "Who told thee . . . ?" (v. 11), a question that should have led Adam to acknowledge the influence of the Tempter.

God then asked directly, "Hast thou eaten of the tree, whereof I commanded thee that thou shouldest not eat?" (Gen. 3:11). Man's response was shocking, for rather than confessing his sin, he displayed his selfishness and hatred (v. 12). Adam blamed his wife; he who once loved her as "flesh of my flesh" (2:23) now effectively said, "Kill her and not me." Here we see the roots of masculine domestic abuse, when men try to avoid their own shame and guilt by verbally or physically attacking their wives. Deeper still, Adam blamed God, calling Eve "the woman whom thou gavest to be with me." God's questions had unmasked the heart of disobedience: man's hatred for God and for his neighbor (Rom. 8:7; Titus 3:3). Calvin said, "Adam . . . had set himself, as a rebel, against God."[27] There was no point in further questions: the man was bent upon blame-shifting and accusing, not confessing. God then questioned the woman and received a similarly evasive answer: "The serpent beguiled [or "deceived," ESV] me, and I did eat" (Gen. 3:13). Sinners see themselves as victims even as they attack God and each other.[28]

God's Spoken Judgments on Sinners

God pronounced his judgment on each of the three sinners in the garden. First, *God spoke his supreme curse on Satan*. We will examine the

---

25. Willet, *Hexapla* (1608), 51, in *RCS/OT*, 1:145.
26. Ambrose, *Paradise*, 14.70, cited in *ACCS/OT*, 1:84.
27. Calvin, *Commentaries*, on Gen. 3:12.
28. Hamilton, *The Book of Genesis, Chapters 1–17*, 194.

gracious implications of these words for mankind later in this chapter; here we focus on their meaning for the Tempter. God asked Satan no questions. There was no sign of mercy here, but only "Thou art cursed" (Gen. 3:14). To be "cursed" reverses the creation pattern of God blessing his creatures (1:22, 28). If Satan used a real serpent in the temptation, it is possible that God humbled the animal as a sign of his displeasure against sin. However, the thrust of God's curse was aimed at Satan (Rom. 16:20). Licking the dust like a serpent is a biblical idiom for the total defeat of an enemy.[29] Going on one's belly is a mark of an unclean creature, an abomination (Lev. 11:42).[30] Therefore, God told Satan that he would completely humiliate him, making him a detestable thing (cf. Ezek. 28:11–19). Satan had successfully deceived the woman and would have his cursed "seed" or spiritual offspring among mankind. However, through the woman, God would raise up a "seed" who would crush the Serpent's head (Gen. 3:15). In the fullness of time, a mighty Savior would destroy the Devil and all his works, and deliver God's people from all of Satan's power.

Second, *God afflicted the woman in her domestic relationships.* Her joy in bearing children would be mingled with great pain (Gen. 3:16). Many women since the fall have died in childbirth, as Rachel did (35:17–19). The woman's relationship with her husband would be marred by conflict as she would seek unsuccessfully to control him (cf. 4:7).[31] Richard Belcher comments, "Marriage becomes a battlefield over who will control the relationship."[32] God's punishments implicitly affirm the distinction of roles between men and women in the home. The Lord's intention was for those roles to be a blessing, but he judicially gave sinners over to the distortion of those relationships by the lawlessness and selfishness of sin.

Third, *God punished the man with hard labor and death.* The Lord God attributed the violation of his covenant prohibition to the man (Gen. 3:17). God then declared, "Cursed is the ground for thy sake," which meant that it would produce "thorns" and "thistles," and only with the "sweat" of hard work would the man get the food he needed to live. When God's steward-king over the earth fell, God's curse fell on his earthly

---

29. Ps. 72:9; Isa. 49:23; Mic. 7:17.
30. *NIDOTTE*, 3:86.
31. See the exegesis of Gen. 3:16 in chap. 11, under the discussion of man's role as authoritative leader and woman's role as empowering helper.
32. Belcher, *Genesis*, 75.

dominion (1:28). Whereas the woman's punishment reflected her orientation toward her husband and children, the man's affliction reflected his orientation toward his vocation and work.[33] Consequently, every area of blessing granted to man in paradise, including work and family (2:15, 18), was subjected to pain and futility, and all creation began to groan with mankind in misery (Rom. 8:20–22).

Man's earthly sorrows for sin culminate when he returns to the dust: "In the sweat of thy face shalt thou eat bread, till thou return unto the ground; for out of it wast thou taken: for dust thou art, and unto dust shalt thou return" (Gen. 3:19).[34] God's judgment was a reversal of his act of creation (2:7). Other Scripture passages allude to this penalty of returning to dust as the doom of mankind.[35] Adam's fall as our covenant head and representative was real, historical, and fraught with dire universal implications (Rom. 5:12; 1 Cor. 15:21–22).

Long before Adam succumbed to physical death, the Lord God banished him from paradise (Gen. 3:22–24). God repeated the Serpent's promise of divinity with searing irony, for man's quest to become a god had cost him everything. Man lost access to the tree of life, by which he could have lived forever (v. 22). The entrance of the garden, the temple of God's presence on earth, was now blocked by fearsome cherubim and a "flaming sword" (v. 24). Cherubim are supernatural angelic creatures that guard the honor of God's holy places and serve as his royal attendants when he goes forth from heaven.[36] Sin alienated man from the very hosts of heaven. Estranged from the Creator, man became the enemy of heaven and earth.

For all the sorrows inflicted upon men and women by the fall, it is remarkable that God did not curse humanity as he cursed the Serpent. Even as God punished mankind, he also revealed that they would not physically die at that moment, but would continue to pursue their creation mandate to be fruitful, multiply, fill the earth, and exercise dominion over its creatures (Gen. 1:28; 9:1–3). God's restraining of the full execution of his curse upon the entire race shows his marvelous patience and mercy,

---

33. Hamilton, *The Book of Genesis, Chapters 1–17*, 203.

34. "The conjunction 'till' is not simply chronological, as though the words could mean: 'thou wilt have to endure hard labour up till the moment of death.' The force is climactic: 'thy hard labour will finally slay thee.' In man's struggle with the soil, the soil will finally conquer and claim him." Vos, *Biblical Theology*, 37.

35. Job 34:15; Ps. 104:29; Eccles. 3:20; 12:7.

36. Ex. 25:18–22; 26:1, 31; 1 Sam. 4:4; 2 Sam. 22:11; 1 Kings 6:23–35; 2 Chron. 3:7–14; Pss. 18:10; 80:1; 99:1; Isa. 37:16; Ezek. 10 (cf. chap. 1); 28:14, 16.

by which mankind may repent and hope in his faithful love. The Savior would come to wear the thorns Adam earned and bear the curse of sin (Matt. 27:29).[37]

The Severity and Goodness of God

Having studied Genesis 3, it is fitting that we reflect on God's dealings with our fallen race. This Scripture passage reveals to us God's severity in imposing death upon sinners and his goodness in promising salvation for sinners who repent and believe.

God's Sanction of Threefold Death for Sin

The Lord God had added this sanction to his covenant with Adam: "In the day that thou eatest thereof thou shalt surely die" (Gen. 2:17). The exegesis of Genesis 3 supports the interpretation of this death as a three-fold penalty.

First, the immediate effect of Adam's sin was *spiritual death*. Man's rebellion against God's word ruptured his relationship with God, tearing open an immense chasm of hatred against God that expressed itself in shame, guilt, fear, and an unwillingness to accept personal responsibility (Gen. 3:7–13). The depth of human depravity after the fall is shocking; it was a total lapse from spiritual life to spiritual death. This death was separation and alienation from life-giving fellowship with God (Eph. 2:1–3; 4:18). It involved the destruction of the core content of God's image in man: spiritual knowledge, righteousness, and holiness (v. 24).

Adam's immediate descendants manifested their spiritual state by worshiping in a way that was displeasing to God, by murdering, by committing sexual sin, and by refusing to repent but rather glorying in sin (Genesis 4). Genesis summarizes the human condition apart from God's saving grace with these words: "The LORD saw that the wickedness of man was great in the earth, and that every intention of the thoughts of his heart was only evil continually" (6:5). Once "very good" (1:31), man's heart was now completely corrupted. The loss of God's moral image did not leave a vacuum, but inward perversity. This condition was so pervasive that God killed every human being on earth by the flood, with the sole exception of Noah and his family. It remains pervasive today (Rom. 3:10–18).

---

37. Tertullian, *On the Crown*, 14.3, in *ACCS/OT*, 1:95.

Second, God sentenced man to *physical death*. Mankind's mortality would soon show itself in bodily weariness and pain (Gen. 3:16, 19). In due time, it would claim each man's life, and he would die (5:5, 8, 11; etc.). The spirit departs and the body, once so full of life and beauty, decays horribly into earth (3:19). "Then shall the dust return to the earth as it was: and the spirit shall return unto God who gave it" (Eccles. 12:7). God's image bearer on earth was subjected to futility. Mortality seized mankind in the garden and began to execute God's sentence of death on every human being at the time of God's choosing (Job 14:5, 14; Heb. 9:27).

Third, man became subject to *eternal death*—the ultimate manifestation of death. Though the full doctrine of hell is not revealed in the account of the fall, we do find it foreshadowed there. God banished man from the earthly paradise where eternal life was promised and available, then armed his holy angels against man (Gen. 3:24). Earth rose up against man to frustrate his labors and finally take his life (vv. 17–18). Where shall man go, if both heaven and earth reject him? He must go to an accursed place of divine wrath.

Sin incurs God's curse (Gen. 3:14; Gal. 3:10). This curse has not yet come in all its fullness, for God continues to grant humanity many blessings in this world. He did not pronounce the first man and woman "cursed" like the Devil. However, God's curse does fall upon unrepentant sinners (Gen. 4:11; 9:25; 12:3), for they are the spiritual offspring of the Devil (1 John 3:10–12). That curse will manifest itself fully in the last day, when Christ will say to the wicked, "Depart from me, ye cursed, into everlasting fire, prepared for the devil and his angels" (Matt. 25:41). The very thought of hell should make us tremble. Yet this is the culmination of the death that Adam brought upon the human race.

God's Seed-Promise of the Victor

In the midst of the darkest chapter in the Bible, we find the radiant light of God's goodness shining in the promise of Christ. Genesis 3:15 contains the *protoevangelium*, the "first gospel," in which God revealed salvation both in its accomplishment and application. It is a signal display of God's grace that when he pronounced the curse on the Devil, even before he declared the punishment coming on the woman and the man, he made known the grace of Christ. The Lord God said to the Serpent, "And I will put enmity between thee and the woman, and between thy seed and her seed; it [or he][38] shall bruise thy head, and thou shalt bruise his heel."

The Hebrew term translated here as "seed" (*zera'*) often means off-spring or children. It is a crucial term in the covenants God made with Noah, Abraham, Aaron, Phinehas, and David, and their "seed."[39] The word appears in Genesis almost forty times in connection with God's promises to the patriarchs. This usage of "seed" suggests that the promise expresses the divine covenant of grace, which was further revealed pro-gressively in subsequent historical covenants.

The word "seed," though singular, bears both an individual and a corporate sense (cf. Gen. 4:25; 15:5), and both senses appear in this text regarding Satan and his people on the one hand, and Christ and his people on the other.[40] Thomas Goodwin argued that "seed" must focus upon Christ personally, for he alone is the captain who wins this victory over Satan (Heb. 2:14), given that all humanity has become captive to Satan and powerless in themselves to overcome him. Yet the "seed" must include God's people corporately, for it is set in opposition to Satan's "seed," the wicked among mankind, such as Cain (1 John 3:8, 12). The New Testa-ment promises that the church, not simply Christ alone, will crush Satan under its feet (Luke 10:19; Rom. 16:20).[41]

God promised *the application of salvation* in Genesis 3:15. Satan had tempted the woman to turn away from God and toward the Devil, but God said that he would put "enmity," or hatred (*'eybah*, cf. Num. 35:21–22), between them to shatter their unholy alliance. These words imply that God by his sovereign grace would turn the woman and her seed back to himself in repentance and faith.

God extended this gracious enmity by promising to divide "thy seed and her seed." The seed of the Serpent are not his demonic host, but those among humanity who, through Satan's wicked influence, live their lives in imitation of him, as his spiritual children.[42] Comparably, the seed of the woman are her spiritual offspring by sovereign grace, those who walk in her footsteps of faith and repentance (cf. Rom. 4:12). We find the two

---

38. The Hebrew pronoun (*hu'*) is masculine. For some reason, the reading "she" (*ipsa*) came into the Latin Vulgate rendering of Gen. 3:15 instead of the masculine "he" (*ipse*), leading some medieval and Roman Catholic writers to take it as a reference to the virgin Mary.

39. Gen. 9:9; 17:7–8; 22:15–18; Num. 18:19; 25:13; 2 Sam. 7:12; Ps. 89:3–4; Jer. 33:21–22.

40. Anonymous [Westminster Divines], *Annotations upon All of the Books of the Old and New Testament* (London: Evan Tyler, 1657), on Gen. 3:15.

41. Goodwin, *Of Christ the Mediator*, in *Works*, 5:310–15.

42. Luke 3:7; John 8:42–44; 1 John 3:10, 12; cf. Matt. 13:38–39.

seeds contrasted in the line of Cain, infamous for its wickedness (Genesis 4), and the line of Seth, renowned for its godliness (Genesis 5).

God's sovereign grace fomented a spiritual war between two peoples on earth. Though mankind had rebelled against God and followed Satan, the Lord would effectually call a people back. Geerhardus Vos said, "Man in sinning had sided with the serpent and placed himself in opposition to God. Now the attitude towards the serpent becomes one of hostility; this must carry with it a corresponding change in man's attitude towards God."[43]

God also promised *the accomplishment of salvation.* Although the promise expanded in its first part to encompass two peoples, it contracted in its second part to focus upon a climactic battle between the Serpent and the great Seed of the woman, both of whom are spoken of in the singular, thus indicating two individuals.[44] O. Palmer Robertson writes,

> The struggle in this last instance is not between "seed" and "seed," as in the previous phrase. Satan himself as an individual has been reintroduced into the conflict. As the prince of his people, he stands as representative of their cause. To correspond to the narrowing from "seed" to "Satan" on one side of the enmity, it would appear quite appropriate to expect a similar narrowing from a multiple "seed" of the woman to a singular "he" who would champion the cause of God's enmity against Satan.[45]

Paul taught that the singular "seed" can have both an individual sense and a collective sense for those in union with that individual (Gal. 3:16, 29). Genesis had already proposed in Adam the idea of a single person to represent others in God's covenant. The Seed of the woman is the last Adam, sent by God to undo what the first Adam did by his fall.

God granted to Satan power to "bruise" the "heel" of the Seed of the woman, but promised that the Seed would "bruise" the Serpent's "head."[46] To tread upon an enemy with one's foot denotes absolute

---

43. Vos, *Biblical Theology*, 42.
44. Belcher, *Genesis*, 77. The Septuagint translated "he" as the masculine singular pronoun (*autos*). C. John Collins argues that when the Hebrew term for "seed" (*zera'*) is collective, it always takes a plural pronoun, but a singular pronoun indicates a reference to an individual (2 Sam. 7:13). C. John Collins, "A Syntactical Note (Genesis 3:15): Is the Woman's Seed Singular or Plural?," *Tyndale Bulletin* 48, no. 1 (1997): 139–47.
45. Robertson, *The Christ of the Covenants*, 99.
46. The same word "bruise" (*shuph*) is used for the actions of both the seed and the Serpent. It appears only here and in Job 9:17 (although there may be a similar root in Ps. 139:11), and its

victory: "You will tread on the lion and the adder; the young lion and the serpent you will trample underfoot" (Ps. 91:13 ESV).[47] In the decisive battle of this spiritual war, both Satan and the last Adam would hurt each other, but the last Adam would crush the Serpent's head under his foot. Here we find the pattern of messianic suffering leading to glory that Christ said pervades the Old Testament in its witness to him (Luke 24:26–27). The Lord's words in Genesis 3:15 foreshadowed both the cross and empty tomb of Jesus Christ.

John's apocalyptic visions allude to this conflict, for he writes that Satan, "that old serpent . . . which deceiveth the whole world," lies in wait to devour the male child born of the woman, but the child is exalted to reign in heaven (Rev. 12:4–5, 9). The Devil can wage war only with the woman's "seed, which keep the commandments of God, and have the testimony of Jesus Christ" (v. 17).[48] In John's words, we see the Serpent, the woman, and her seed—both the individual Christ and the corporate church—described in eschatological imagery.

Last, God promised *the agent of salvation*. As the Seed of the woman, he must be a human being (cf. Gen. 4:25), born of a woman (Gal. 4:4). He must be capable of suffering, for Satan would "bruise his heel" (Gen. 3:15). However, he must also be of great excellence so as to conquer the evil demonic power that came in the guise of the Serpent. Such a conquest required a supernatural person, and the Lord God hints at his personal plurality in this context ("us," v. 22). Therefore, God promised that the salvation he was already applying to sinners would be accomplished by one who is both a mortal man and a divine person. While we should be cautious not to draw a fully developed Christology from this text, it does hint at the coming of the incarnate Lord.

The Savior came to glorify God against his enemy. Michael Barrett says, "Rather than being directed to humankind, this first declaration of the gospel is part of the curse against the serpent, Satan himself. People would certainly benefit, but God's glory was the issue. The serpent's defeat and people's salvation were the means of declaring that glory."[49]

---

meaning is somewhat uncertain. In Romans 16:20, Paul seems to interpret it with a word meaning "bruise, break, crush" (*syntribō*).

47. See also Pss. 7:5; 44:5; 60:12; 108:13; Isa. 10:6; 14:25; Mic. 7:10; Mal. 4:4.

48. On the allusions in Revelation 12 to Gen. 3:15, see John (Giovanni) Diodati, *Pious and Learned Annotations upon the Holy Bible*, 3rd ed. (London: by James Flesher, for Nicholas Fussell, 1651), on Gen. 3:15; and Goodwin, *Of Christ the Mediator*, in *Works*, 5:315–16.

49. Michael P. V. Barrett, *Beginning at Moses: A Guide for Finding Christ in the Old Testament*, rev. ed. (Grand Rapids, MI: Reformation Heritage Books, 2018), 112.

The Lord God provided a type of Christ's work when he clothed Adam and Eve's nakedness with the skins of animals (Gen. 3:21). God was giving them a remedy for the shame that had fallen upon them because of their sin (2:25; 3:7). This act anticipated the animal sacrifices that later foreshadowed Christ's substitutionary atonement (cf. 4:4; 8:20; 22:13). God was showing our first parents that though they deserved death, through the death of a substitute their shame would be covered with honor once again. They must abandon the fig leaves of their own works and depend upon God's provision.[50]

Genesis 3 contains evidence that Adam received God's promise with faith. We read in verse 20, "Adam called his wife's name Eve; because she was the mother of all living." Previously, he had called her "Woman" (2:23). Although it is not surprising that Adam would name his wife according to her motherhood of the human race, it is surprising that he chose the name "Eve" (*khavvah*), which sounds like "live" (*khavah*) and "living" (*kkay*), for God had just pronounced a death sentence on them all (3:19). Adam renamed Eve with an eye on God's promise that she would be the mother of the Seed who would overcome death and restore life.[51]

If God's grace could impart faith to Adam with such a small promise, how much more should we, equipped with the whole Bible, hope entirely in Jesus Christ? We have the divine testimony that Christ has come in the flesh, died for our sins, and risen again from the dead. Furthermore, Christ is coming again. God promises the people in union with Christ that he will "bruise Satan under your feet shortly" (Rom. 16:20). However, this promise belongs only to those who receive Christ and all his benefits by faith.

Consider the alternative. Adam's sin has plunged you into sin, guilt, alienation from God, and alienation from other people. Apart from Christ, you are in a state of spiritual death and subject to the Devil's power. Physical death is already at work in your body and one day will kill you. After this comes eternal death, unceasing torment for your sins.

Thanks be to God for Jesus Christ our Lord! In Christ, believers have victory over the Devil, sin, death, and hell itself. Grasp hold of Christ by faith, and you will discover that he has grasped hold of you. Follow him to the end, and he will welcome you into paradise.

---

50. Belcher, *Genesis*, 76.
51. Luther, *Lectures on Genesis*, in *LW*, 1:220.

Sing to the Lord

Victory over the Serpent

Praise the Saviour now and ever;
Praise him, all beneath the skies;
Prostrate lying, suff'ring, dying
On the cross, a sacrifice.
Vict'ry gaining, life obtaining,
Now in glory he doth rise.

Man's work faileth, Christ's availeth;
He is all our righteousness;
He, our Saviour, has forever
Set us free from dire distress.
Through his merit we inherit
Light and peace and happiness.

Sin's bonds severed; we're delivered;
Christ has bruised the serpent's head;
Death no longer is the stronger;
Hell itself is captive led.
Christ has risen from death's prison;
O'er the tomb he light has shed.

For his favor, praise forever
Unto God the Father sing;
Praise the Saviour, praise him ever,
Son of God, our Lord and King.
Praise the Spirit; through Christ's merit,
He doth us salvation bring.

Venantius H. C. Fortunatus, trans. Augustus Nelson
Tune: Upp Min Tunga
Trinity Hymnal—Baptist Edition, No. 174

Questions for Meditation or Discussion

1. Who is the Serpent (or behind the Serpent) in Genesis 3? What arguments can be made for this interpretation?
2. What strategy did Satan use to tempt the sinless man and woman in the garden?

3. How did succumbing to Satan's lies change the woman's perception of the forbidden fruit?
4. What lessons can we learn from God's silence during the temptation?
5. What immediate consequences fell upon the first two sinners in the human race?
6. How did the Lord show his patience with these sinners when he confronted them?
7. What judgments did the Lord send upon the man and woman?
8. What "threefold death" came upon mankind for our fall in Adam? How would you prove from Scripture that both spiritual death and eternal death are included?
9. How does Genesis 3:15 reveal both the application and accomplishment of salvation?
10. How have you seen the Adamic pattern of temptation, sin, and its consequences played out in your own life as one fallen in Adam?

Questions for Deeper Reflection

11. What threefold pattern about sin do the authors observe in Genesis 3, Christ's temptation, and 1 John 2? How helpful is their analysis of this pattern? Why?
12. What arguments can be made for and against the interpretation that the promise of Genesis 3:15 refers to Christ and his people? What is the proper interpretation of this text? Why?

19

The State of Sin, Part 1

Historical Theology of Original Sin

The New England Primer taught generations of children to learn the letter "A" by the rhyme "In Adam's fall, we sinned all."[1] Likewise, the doctrine of original sin is part of the ABCs of biblical Christianity. The term *original sin* does not refer specifically to the first sin, but to the state of sin that plagues all of Adam's natural descendants and is the origin of all other sins (Rom. 5:12). A related doctrine is called *total depravity*. "Depravity" means a state of corruption or distortion (Latin *depravatio*). "Total" does not refer to the intensity of sin, as if everyone were as bad as they possibly could be, but to the extent of corruption, for sin corrupts every part of the human person and stains everything that we do. Christianity is not a religion for people who are basically good yet sometimes do wrong; it is the good news of salvation for people whose hearts are profoundly corrupted by enmity against God.

Although original sin is basic to biblical Christianity, it is also a highly controversial doctrine. This should not surprise us. The Devil always attacks most fiercely those truths that are most important to the faith. Furthermore, false teachers who flatter the "itching ears" of the self-righteous always find plenty of eager listeners (2 Tim. 4:3–4). If we are honest, we all would prefer an easier message than one so humbling and grievous to

---

1. Ford, ed., *The New England Primer*, 64.

our proud souls. Yet God has revealed it in the Word for his glory in our good, and we dare not neglect it.

The doctrine of original sin developed over Christian history in close connection to the doctrine of predestination. Under the doctrine of God, we traced various views of predestination from the early church through the Pelagian controversy and all the way to Reformed orthodoxy.[2] In this chapter, we will build upon that previous study to look more closely at the historical development of the doctrine of sin.

The Early and Medieval Church

The church tends to focus its theological endeavors on the areas where it is most challenged by false teaching. In the early centuries of Christianity, the greatest attacks came against doctrines concerning the Trinity and Christ's person. Consequently, the doctrine of sin did not receive as much attention until Pelagianism arose at the end of the fourth and beginning of the fifth centuries.[3]

The Early Church on Original Sin

The tension between the fall of man in Adam and human responsibility appears very early among biblical interpreters. In an apocryphal Jewish writing dating from the late first century or early second century, we read, "O thou Adam, what hast thou done? For though it was thou that sinned, thou art not fallen alone, but we all that come of thee" (2 Esdras 7:48). In the narrative, an angel replies that man must "fight" and "get the victory," and reminds the speaker that Moses said, "Choose thee life, that thou mayest live" (vv. 57–59).[4]

In the early church, we find scattered statements that affirm mankind's fall into sin and misery through Adam.[5] At the same time, they testified to man's free moral agency.[6] They did not systematically integrate the two ideas; they asserted human responsibility in order to

---

2. On the historical theology of predestination, see *RST*, 1:1000–1030 (chap. 50).

3. William Cunningham, *Historical Theology*, 2 vols. (Edinburgh: T&T Clark, 1863), 1:179–80.

4. See Peter Sanlon, "Original Sin in Patristic Theology," in *Adam, the Fall, and Original Sin*, ed. Madueme and Reeves, 90.

5. Justin Martyr, *Dialogue with Trypho*, chap. 88, in *ANF*, 1:243; Irenaeus, *Against Heresies*, 3.18.1–2; 5.16.3, in *ANF*, 1:446, 544; Athanasius, *On the Incarnation of the Word*, secs. 4, 6, in *NPNF²*, 4:38–39; *Against the Heathen*, sec. 3, in *NPNF²*, 4:5; *Against the Arians*, 1.51, in *NPNF²*, 1:336. See J. N. D. Kelly, *Early Christian Doctrines*, 5th ed. (London: Bloomsbury, 1977), 167, 170–71, 346–48.

6. Tertullian, *Exhortation to Chastity*, chap. 2, in *ANF*, 4:50–51.

avoid philosophical fatalism and to press people to repentance and faith.[7]

Pelagius and his follower Celestius (fl. 400–430) exploited this lack of theological integration when they asserted human freedom in an imbalanced manner that overthrew the doctrine of man's fall.[8] The Pelagians taught that Adam's sin did not bring condemnation or moral corruption upon the entire race. Rather, sinfulness arises by poor choices that develop into bad habits. By nature, man always has the ability to sin or not to sin, and it is theoretically possible for a person to never sin.[9] Adam's sin did not introduce into humanity "any intrinsic bias in favour of wrong-doing," but only encouraged sin "by custom and example," as J. N. D. Kelly summarized.[10] Celestius said, "Sin is not born with man, but is committed afterwards by man. It is not the fault of nature, but of free will."[11] Pelagianism, however, was not a variation within Christianity, but apostasy to a pagan belief in man's self-made virtue.[12]

Pelagianism clashes with a biblical view of grace as the necessary divine endowment to restore the human heart to holy intentions to obey God (Eph. 2:5, 10; Phil. 2:13). Pelagius was especially provoked by Augustine's prayer for grace: "Give what Thou commandest, and command what Thou wilt."[13] Augustine said that an essential part of the Christian faith is the contrast between Adam and Christ, "the two men by one of whom we are sold under sin, by the other redeemed from sins—by the one have been precipitated into death, by the other are liberated unto life; the former of whom has ruined us in himself, by doing his own will instead of His who created him; the latter has saved us in Himself, by not doing His own will, but the will of Him who sent Him."[14] Adam's sin brings sin to all the world by "natural descent," not "imitation," and "even if there were in men nothing but original

---

7. Calvin, *Institutes*, 2.2.4, 9; and Cunningham, *Historical Theology*, 1:181.

8. Bavinck, *Reformed Dogmatics*, 3:85–86.

9. Pelagius, *The Christian Life and Other Essays*, trans. Ford Lewis Battles (Pittsburgh: s.n., 1972), 55–56, 61, 64.

10. Kelly, *Early Christian Doctrines*, 358.

11. Cited in G. F. Wiggers, *An Historical Presentation of Augustinism and Pelagianism from the Original Sources*, trans. and ed. Ralph Emerson (Andover: Gould, Newman, and Saxton, 1840), 83.

12. Benjamin B. Warfield, "Augustine and the Pelagian Controversy," in *Two Studies in the History of Doctrine* (New York: Christian Literature Co., 1897), 5; and Bavinck, *Reformed Dogmatics*, 3:86–87.

13. Augustine, *Confessions*, 10.29, in NPNF[1], 1:153. Augustine mentioned the conflict in *A Treatise on the Gift of Perseverance*, chap. 53, in NPNF[1], 5:547.

14. Augustine, *On Original Sin*, 2.28.24, in NPNF[1], 5:246–47.

sin, it would be sufficient for their condemnation."[15] Augustine held to a realistic view of sin's transmission—that is, sin and guilt come to Adam's descendants through sexual generation.[16] Augustine insisted that he was not inventing a new doctrine, but reasserting the catholic Christian faith.[17] He quoted Ambrose (d. 397), who said, "All of us human beings are born under the power of sin, and our very origin lies in guilt."[18] Augustine said that "original sin" is both "sin" and "itself also the punishment of sin," implying that our corruption is punishment for the guilt of Adam's sin.[19]

The churches responded to the Pelagian crisis with a spectrum of views, with many theologians taking positions that might be called semi-Augustinianism or semi-Pelagianism. The Council of Carthage (418) affirmed that infants are born with "original sin" through Adam (Rom. 5:12) and condemned Pelagianism as contrary to the teaching of catholic Christianity.[20] However, some theologians rejected Augustine's doctrine of predestination and total human inability. John Cassian (c. 360–c. 433) said that Adam's fall had weakened human free will so that it needs God's grace, but it still must cooperate with grace for God to save the soul. Sin has wounded man, but has not cast him into spiritual death. The Council of Orange (or Aurasiacum, 529) opposed semi-Pelagianism by asserting that grace must prompt every good motion of man's heart, but the council also rejected the doctrine of sovereign reprobation to damnation.[21] The decrees of Orange were omitted from the medieval compilation of conciliar documents most commonly used from the tenth century onward and had limited subsequent influence until their publication in 1538.[22]

---

15. Augustine, *On the Merits and Remission of Sins, and on the Baptism of Infants*, 1.9.9; 1.15.12, in *NPNF*[1], 5:18, 20.

16. J. V. Fesko, *Death in Adam, Life in Christ: The Doctrine of Imputation*, Reformed, Exegetical and Doctrinal Studies (Fearn, Ross-shire, Scotland: Christian Focus, 2016), 38–39.

17. Bavinck, *Reformed Dogmatics*, 3:85.

18. Cited in Augustine, *Answer to Julian*, 2.3.5, in *Works*, 1/24:307. See Ambrose, *Penance*, 1.3.13, in *NPNF*[2], 10:331.

19. Augustine, *Answer to the Pelagians, III: Unfinished Work in Answer to Julian*, 1.47, in *Works*, 1/25:73–74.

20. Wiggers, *An Historical Presentation of Augustinism and Pelagianism*, 171–73; and Sanlon, "Original Sin in Patristic Theology," in *Adam, the Fall, and Original Sin*, ed. Madueme and Reeves, 86–88.

21. Kelly, *Early Christian Doctrines*, 371–72; and Reinhold Seeberg, *Text-Book of the History of Doctrines*, trans. Charles E. Hay (Philadelphia: Lutheran Publication Society, 1905), 1:370–71, 380–82.

22. A. N. S. Lane, introduction to John Calvin, *The Bondage and Liberation of the Will*, ed. A. N. S. Lane, trans. G. I. Davies, Texts and Studies in Reformation and Post-Reformation Thought (Grand Rapids, MI: Baker, 1996), xxviin94.

The Medieval Church on Original Sin

The Augustinian and semi-Augustinian views of original sin continued in medieval catholic Christianity, with an emphasis on our realistic union with Adam through the physical body or a shared human nature. Anselm of Canterbury (c. 1033–1109) said that God in his goodness granted to Adam the privilege of passing down to future generations a human nature in "justice and happiness," but instead he passed on a fallen nature still obligated to perfect righteousness but corrupted by sin and obligated to make satisfaction for sin.[23] This condition is communicated to them because they are produced from Adam by natural human power and will, unlike Christ in his virgin birth.[24] Anselm did not believe, however, that "the sin of Adam descends to infants in such a way that they ought to be punished for it, as if they themselves had committed it personally."[25] Original sin is not a personal offense, but an offense of human nature against God.[26]

Peter Lombard followed Augustine in teaching that Adam's offspring derive their sinfulness from their first father by natural propagation, not imitation.[27] Lombard viewed propagation in a very physical manner, speaking of each person's derivation from Adam's body.[28] He said that since sexual generation inevitably involves irrational lust, it produces an infant whose body is polluted and whose soul is corrupted as soon as it is infused into the body.[29] Original sin is a fault and makes one liable to God's judgment and wrath, since it consists of "concupiscence," an inward "attraction to pleasure" that is "the tyrant" in the body.[30]

Thomas Aquinas also taught original sin. Citing Romans 5:12, he said, "The first sin of the first man is transmitted to his descendants, by way of origin." He explained, "All men born of Adam may be considered as one man, inasmuch as they have one common nature, which they receive from their first parents."[31] Unlike the relationship between ordinary

---

23. Anselm, *The Virgin Conception and Original Sin*, chap. 2, in *A Scholastic Miscellany: Anselm to Ockham*, ed. and trans. Eugene R. Fairweather, Library of Christian Classics, Ichthus Edition (Philadelphia: Westminster, 1956), 185.
24. Anselm, *The Virgin Conception and Original Sin*, chap. 23, in *A Scholastic Miscellany*, ed. Fairweather, 195.
25. Anselm, *The Virgin Conception and Original Sin*, chap. 22, in *A Scholastic Miscellany*, ed. Fairweather, 194.
26. Anselm, *The Virgin Conception and Original Sin*, chap. 23, in *A Scholastic Miscellany*, ed. Fairweather, 197.
27. Lombard, *The Sentences*, 2.30.4 (2:146–47).
28. Lombard, *The Sentences*, 2.30.14 (2:152).
29. Lombard, *The Sentences*, 2.31.4 (2:154).
30. Lombard, *The Sentences*, 2.30.7–8 (2:148–49).
31. Aquinas, *Summa Theologica*, Pt. 2.1, Q. 81, Art. 1.

parents and children, Adam's descendants "share in his guilt."[32] Adam's sin robbed human nature of its original righteousness, and hence all his descendants are prone to sin, for "the first sin infects human nature with a corruption pertaining to nature."[33] Original sin is not merely the absence of righteousness, but a "habit" or "disposition" toward sin, which is "concupiscence."[34]

However, some Franciscan theologians began compromising this doctrine, prompting Thomas Bradwardine (d. 1349) to complain, "Many are blindly rushing into Pelagianism."[35] William of Ockham (d. 1347) and Gabriel Biel (d. 1495) taught that the unregenerate could attain "congruent merit" by doing their best in their fallen condition, so that God would reward them with grace. Nominalist theology swerved into Pelagianism by granting to unconverted people the ability to do, by nature, a pure act of love to God, to which God promised infused spiritual grace.[36]

Reformation Churches

Given the Reformers' emphasis on salvation by grace alone, it is not surprising that the doctrine of original sin rose to a position of prominence in Reformation polemics.

The Lutheran Churches on Original Sin

Martin Luther received and taught the Augustinian view of original sin, the corruption of all mankind into bad trees that can bear only bad fruit.[37] He asserted in the Heidelberg Disputation (1518) that free choice in fallen man can do nothing but commit mortal sin.[38] Original sin is more than "lack of original righteousness," but is also "a propensity toward evil," a "nausea toward the good, a loathing of light and wisdom, and a delight in error and darkness."[39] Luther said that Adam begot Seth in his own image

---

32. Aquinas, *Summa Theologica*, Pt. 2.1, Q. 81, Art. 1, Reply Obj. 1.
33. Aquinas, *Summa Theologica*, Pt. 2.1, Q. 81, Art. 2, Answer and Reply Obj. 3.
34. Aquinas, *Summa Theologica*, Pt. 2.1, Q. 82, Art. 1, 3.
35. Cited in Heiko A. Oberman, *The Dawn of the Reformation: Essays in Late Medieval and Early Reformation Thought* (Edinburgh: T&T Clark, 1986), 213; cf. Calvin, *Institutes*, 3.11.15.
36. Alister E. McGrath, *Iustitia Dei: A History of the Christian Doctrine of Justification*, 3rd ed. (Cambridge: Cambridge University Press, 2005), 146; and Oberman, *The Harvest of Medieval Theology*, 132–33.
37. Ľubomir Batka, "Martin Luther's Teaching on Sin," December 2016, *Oxford Research Encyclopedias: Religion*, http://religion.oxfordre.com/view/10.1093/acrefore/9780199340378.001 .0001/acrefore-9780199340378-e-373.
38. Luther, *Heidelberg Disputation*, in *LW*, 31:40, 48–49.
39. Luther, *Lectures on Romans*, in *LW*, 25:299 (Rom. 5:12).

(Gen. 5:3), which includes "original sin and the punishment of eternal death, which was inflicted on Adam on account of his sin."[40] Thus, Adam's sin brought both condemnation and corruption on his descendants.

Desiderius Erasmus (1466–1536), a Renaissance scholar and Roman Catholic theologian, attacked Luther's view of human depravity in his *Diatribe or Sermon Concerning Free Will* (1524). He argued that the Holy Scriptures often confirm "the power of the human will whereby man can apply to or turn away from that which leads unto eternal salvation."[41] Like the semi-Pelagians, Erasmus said that sin has wounded but not destroyed man's free will.[42] Though the fall of Adam enslaved the human will to sin, God's universal grace has restored the will, giving everyone the opportunity to find further grace if they will strive for it.[43] God's commands imply human ability to do what God commanded.[44] People must add their efforts to God's grace so that it may attain its goal, for "it is in our power to turn away from offered grace."[45] Erasmus sought to avoid Pelagianism by attributing salvation mostly to grace, but he also attempted to attribute a small contribution to human free will as God's universal grace mitigates the effects of the fall.[46] Consequently, his approach was semi-Pelagian.

Luther's response, *The Bondage of the Will* (1525), is a wide-ranging book that delves not only into human sin and freedom, but also into divine predestination and providence.[47] The great thrust of Luther's book may be summarized, "Let God be God!"[48] Luther was concerned that people would misinterpret it as asserting fatalism or stating that God is the author of sin—which Luther denied.[49] Luther said that all men are under God's wrath (Rom. 1:18) and without any spiritual goodness (3:9–20).[50] Scripture teaches "the constant bent and energy of the will

---

40. Luther, *Lectures on Genesis*, in *LW*, 1:340 (Gen. 5:3).
41. Desiderius Erasmus, *A Diatribe or Sermon Concerning Free Will*, in *Discourse on Free Will*, trans. and ed. Ernst F. Winter (New York: Continuum, 1989), 20.
42. Erasmus, *Diatribe*, in *Discourse on Free Will*, 26.
43. Erasmus, *Diatribe*, in *Discourse on Free Will*, 22–23, 29.
44. Erasmus, *Diatribe*, in *Discourse on Free Will*, 32.
45. Erasmus, *Diatribe*, in *Discourse on Free Will*, 43–44; cf. 60, 71, 77.
46. Erasmus, *Diatribe*, in *Discourse on Free Will*, 92–93.
47. See Robert Kolb, *Bound Choice, Election, and Wittenberg Theological Method*, Lutheran Quarterly Books, ed. Paul Rorem (Grand Rapids, MI: Eerdmans, 2005); and Joel R. Beeke, *Debated Issues in Sovereign Predestination: Early Lutheran Predestination, Calvinian Reprobation, and Variations in Genevan Lapsarianism* (Göttingen: Vandenhoek and Ruprecht, 2017), 13–24. See also *LW*, 25:385–94; 33:199, 272.
48. Kolb, *Bound Choice*, 32.
49. Luther, *Lectures on Genesis*, in *LW*, 5:50; and *Bondage of the Will*, in *LW*, 33:175, 178–79.
50. Martin Luther, *The Bondage of the Will*, trans. James I. Packer and O. R. Johnston (Grand Rapids, MI: Baker, 1957), 273–84. The translators correlate these references to the Weimar edition of Luther's *Works* (*WA*), 18:756–64.

to evil" (cf. Gen. 6:5).[51] God's laws do not reveal man's ability, for that would imply that every man has the ability to keep God's will perfectly. On the contrary, God's commands demonstrate the inability of sinners to do what they ought to do, in order to drive them to Christ.[52]

The Lutheran Church declared in the Augsburg Confession (1530), "Since the fall of Adam all human beings who are propagated according to nature are born with sin, that is, without fear of God, without trust in God, and with concupiscence," which "damns and brings eternal death to those who are not born again."[53] Men retain the freedom of will to do external acts of righteousness by which civil society is maintained, but they have no power to produce "spiritual righteousness" in the heart apart from the saving influence of the Spirit through the Word.[54]

Later, in the Formula of Concord (1577), Lutherans made it clear that original sin is not human nature per se (for sin is not a substance), but the deep and pervasive corruption of human nature.[55] The human will is entirely opposed to God (Rom. 8:7) and unable to change itself, for it is dead in sin (Eph. 2:5). However, when the Holy Spirit has begun his work and offered grace through the Word, the will of man is able "to help and cooperate."[56] In this early stage of grace, man must not resist God's grace, "for those who persistently resist the Holy Spirit and stubbornly struggle against what is recognized truth . . . will not be converted."[57] Yet such nonresistance itself is possible only by the grace of the Spirit, for conversion is entirely his gift.[58]

The Early Reformed Churches on Original Sin

The doctrine of original sin featured prominently in Reformed theology from its inception. In the First Helvetic Confession (Arts. 8–9), Heinrich Bullinger (1504–1575) and other Swiss theologians declared that original sin is the "pestiferous infection . . . spread through the entire human race." While people still have "free will," nevertheless "we are not able

---

51. Luther, *The Bondage of the Will*, 242 (*WA*, 18:736).
52. Luther, *The Bondage of the Will*, 152–58 (*WA*, 18:673–80).
53. Augsburg Confession (Art. 2), in *The Book of Concord*, 39.
54. Augsburg Confession (Art. 18), in *The Book of Concord*, 51.
55. Formula of Concord (Epitome, Art. 1), in *The Book of Concord*, 487–91.
56. Formula of Concord (Epitome, 2.3, 11), in *The Book of Concord*, 492–93; cf. Formula of Concord (Solid Declaration, 2.7–14), in *The Book of Concord*, 544–46.
57. Formula of Concord (Solid Declaration, 2.60), in *The Book of Concord*, 555. See also Formula of Concord (Epitome, 11.12; Solid Declaration, 11.40), in *The Book of Concord*, 518, 647.
58. Formula of Concord (Solid Declaration, 2.89), in *The Book of Concord*, 561.

to embrace and follow good (except as we are illuminated by the grace of Christ and moved by His Spirit)."[59]

John Calvin called original sin our "inherited corruption" and "inborn defect" from Adam.[60] Calvin denied that men became sinners by mere imitation of Adam, for then Paul could not parallel Adam with Christ (Rom. 5:17). Rather, Adam was "the root of human nature," and plunged that nature into ruin. This is not simply a matter of shared guilt, but of the infection of human nature with corruption and depravity.[61] It is not "liability for another's transgression"; rather, Adam's sin condemns us by involving us in the same corruption even before we commit any actual sin.[62] The spread of Adam's sin to his descendants is not through "the substance of the flesh or soul," but "because it had been so ordained by God."[63]

Calvin gave this definition of original sin: "a hereditary depravity and corruption of our nature, diffused into all parts of the soul, which first makes us liable to God's wrath, then also brings forth in us those works which Scripture calls 'works of the flesh' [Gal. 5:19]."[64] His emphasis on the corruption of every part of human nature stands opposed to medieval theologians such as Lombard, who located corruption mainly in the body.[65] The human will was not destroyed by the fall "because it is inseparable from man's nature," but it "was so bound to wicked desires that it cannot strive after the right" and "can beget nothing but evil."[66]

Just as Erasmus attacked Luther, so Calvin's doctrines of predestination and original sin were opposed by Albertus Pighius (c. 1490–1542), Jerome Bolsec (c. 1510–1584), Jean Trolliet (fl. 1550), and Sebastian Castellio (1515–1563). Against Pighius, Calvin wrote his *Defense of the Sound and Orthodox Doctrine of the Bondage and Liberation of Human Choice* (1543).[67] When discussing the freedom of the will, Calvin distinguished between freedom from coercion and freedom from necessity. The former he allowed, for he believed that man's will, even in his fallen condition, acts without being "forcibly moved by an external impulse." A coerced willingness is a contradiction in terms. The latter,

59. *Reformed Confessions*, 1:344–45.
60. Calvin, *Institutes*, 2.1.5. He cited Rom. 5:12; Ps. 51:5.
61. Calvin, *Institutes*, 2.1.6.
62. Calvin, *Institutes*, 2.1.8. Cf. *Commentaries*, on Rom. 5:15, 17.
63. Calvin, *Institutes*, 2.1.7.
64. Calvin, *Institutes*, 2.1.8.
65. Calvin, *Institutes*, 2.1.9.
66. Calvin, *Institutes*, 2.2.12, 26.
67. Lane, introduction to Calvin, *The Bondage and Liberation of the Will*, xiv.

however, he rejected, for man's will "is of necessity driven to what is evil and cannot seek anything but evil," not by any external compulsion, but "because of its corruptness." For this reason, Calvin did not favor the term "freedom" of the will, for it suggests that people can choose God apart from grace.[68]

Reformed Christianity incorporated the doctrine of original sin into its major early confessional statements.[69] The Belgic Confession (Art. 15) says,

> We believe that through the disobedience of Adam original sin is extended to all mankind, which is a corruption of the whole nature and an hereditary disease, wherewith infants themselves are infected even in their mother's womb, and which produceth in man all sorts of sin, being in him as a root thereof; and therefore is so vile and abominable in the sight of God that it is sufficient to condemn all mankind.[70]

The Heidelberg Catechism (Q. 7–8) says that the "depravity of human nature" comes "from the fall and disobedience of our first parents, Adam and Eve, in Paradise; hence our nature has become so corrupt, that we are all conceived and born in sin" and are "so corrupt that we are wholly incapable of doing any good, and inclined to all wickedness."[71]

Tridentine and Modern Roman Catholicism on Original Sin

The Roman Catholic Church declared at the Council of Trent that Adam's transgression in paradise deprived his posterity of man's original righteousness and put them under the power of sin, death, and God's wrath. Original sin is transmitted not by imitation, but by propagation. Human power or merit cannot take it away, but only the grace of Christ.[72] However, the council also said that baptism completely removes the guilt and stain of original sin, and remaining concupiscence in the baptized is not properly called sin, but is merely an inclination

---

68. Calvin, *The Bondage and Liberation of the Will*, 68–69.
69. First Confession of Basel (Art. 2); First Helvetic Confession (Art. 8); French Confession (Art. 10–11); Thirty-Nine Articles (Art. 9); Second Helvetic Confession (chap. 8), in *Reformed Confessions*, 1:288, 345; 2:144–45, 757, 820–22.
70. *The Three Forms of Unity*, 32.
71. *The Three Forms of Unity*, 70.
72. The Canons and Decrees of the Council of Trent, Session 5, Art. 1–3, in *The Creeds of Christendom*, ed. Schaff, 2:84–85. An exception is made for "the blessed and immaculate Virgin Mary" (Art. 5, 2:88).

to sin.[73] In this last point, the Roman church rejected the Reformation stance.

According to traditional Roman Catholicism, original righteousness is a supernatural grace added to human nature. Original sin centers upon the loss of this grace, not the corruption of man's whole nature. Concupiscence arises because man's spirit is no longer empowered to rule over the body with its earthly desires.[74] Gregg Allison says, "The Catholic position minimizes the devastating effect of sin on human reason or intellect."[75] Roman Catholic theologians oppose both Pelagians and the Protestant Reformers, the latter of whom, according to Rome, "taught that original sin has radically perverted man and destroyed his freedom."[76] We should note that some modern Roman Catholic theologians have reinterpreted Genesis and the traditional doctrine in a mythological manner to represent not a historical fall but an allegory of the universal experience of moral and spiritual failure.[77]

Other Streams of Sixteenth-Century Thought

In the sixteenth century, an anti-Trinitarian, rationalistic movement known as Socinianism arose among dissenters against the Romanist religion. Faustus Socinus (1539–1604) denied the doctrine of original sin.[78] His views became influential in Poland. The Racovian Catechism (1605, rev. 1680) asserted, "By the fall of Adam the nature of man is by no means so deprived of the liberty and power of obeying or not obeying God in those things which he requires of him under threat of punishment or promise of reward." It added, "The fall of Adam, as it was but one act, could not have power to deprave his own nature, much less that of his posterity." A disposition to sinning is formed by a habit of committing actual sins.[79] John Biddle (1615–1662), an English Socinian, denied that "the sin of our first parents" did bring upon "their posterity the guilt

---

73. The Canons and Decrees of the Council of Trent, Session 5, Art. 5, in *The Creeds of Christendom*, ed. Schaff, 2:87–88.

74. *Catechism of the Catholic Church* (New York: Doubleday, 1995), secs. 399–400, 405. The catechism is also available online at http://www.vatican.va/archive/ENG0015/_INDEX.HTM.

75. Gregg R. Allison, *Roman Catholic Theology and Practice: An Evangelical Assessment* (Wheaton, IL: Crossway, 2014), 128.

76. *Catechism of the Catholic Church*, sec. 406.

77. Roger Haight, "Sin and Grace," in *Systematic Theology: Roman Catholic Perspectives*, ed. Francis Schüssler Fiorenza and John P. Galvin (Minneapolis: Fortress, 1991), 2:93–94.

78. David Munro Corey, *Faustus Socinus* (1932; repr., Eugene, OR: Wipf and Stock, 2009), 108.

79. *The Racovian Catechism*, trans. and introduction Thomas Rees (London: Longman, Hurst, Rees, Orme, and Brown, 1818), 325–26.

of hell-fire, deface the image of God in them, darken their understanding, enslave their will, deprive them of the power to do good, and cause mortality."[80] This complete denial of original sin has passed into modern Unitarianism.

The Anabaptists were a diverse movement, and some apparently denied or minimized original sin,[81] but at least some of their theologians affirmed it, albeit with their own distinctive nuances. Balthasar Hubmaier (c. 1480–1528) said that Adam's fall caused human flesh to lose its ability to do anything other than sin and put the soul in a position of helplessness until healed by the Word of God; however, in Hubmaier's anthropology, the spirit remained pure.[82] Menno Simons (1496–1561) taught that Adam's fall corrupted him and all his offspring, and brought them under God's just condemnation.[83]

Post-Reformation Churches

In the late-sixteenth and seventeenth centuries, the Reformed doctrine of original sin was subjected to systematic challenges, fortified by theological defenses, and compromised by modifications.

Arminianism on Original Sin

Jacob Arminius taught that Adam's sin brought upon his natural descendants both a liability to death under God's wrath and the loss of original righteousness.[84] It is notable that Arminius considered original sin to consist only of the "absence of original righteousness," not privation of righteousness plus the presence of corruption.[85] This aligned Arminius more closely with the Roman view.

Arminius said, "In this state, the free will of man toward the True Good is not only wounded, maimed, infirm, bent, and weakened; but it is also imprisoned, destroyed, and lost . . . it has no powers whatever except such as are excited by divine grace."[86] This is the Reformed doctrine of in-

---

80. John Biddle, *A Twofold Catechism* (London: J. Cottret, for Ri. Moone, 1654), 24–25. See Owen, *Vindiciae Evangelicae*, in *Works*, 12:144.
81. Bavinck, *Reformed Dogmatics*, 3:87, 90.
82. Chankyu Kim, *Balthasar Hubmaier's Doctrine of Salvation in Dynamic and Relational Perspective* (Eugene, OR: Pickwick, 2013), 47–50.
83. Menno Simons, *A Clear, Incontrovertible Confession and Demonstration . . . and Solution of the Principal Points of the Defense of John A'Lasco against Us*, in *The Complete Works of Menno Simons*, 2 parts in 1 vol. (Elkhart, IN: John F. Funk and Brother, 1871), 2:155–56.
84. Arminius, *Public Disputations*, 7.15–16, in *Works*, 2:156–57.
85. Arminius, *Private Disputations*, 31.10, in *Works*, 2:375.
86. Arminius, *Public Disputations*, 9.7, in *Works*, 2:192.

ability insofar as the statement goes, but the fulcrum on which these words turn is the meaning of "grace." Arminius taught a doctrine of prevenient grace, which man must not resist so that he can receive more grace and so be saved. Grace is necessary, but man's will is decisive for the outcome.[87] Arminius, at this point, moved toward semi-Pelagianism, thereby stepping away from Reformed theology.

After Arminius, some Arminians went further. Philipp van Limborch said that Adam's sin brought mortality to mankind, but did not directly communicate corruption or guilt to his descendants, much less plunge them into spiritual or eternal death. Limborch said, "Infants are born in a less degree of purity than Adam was created, and have a certain inclination to sin, which they derived not from Adam but from their next immediate parents."[88] For Limborch, sin is always a personal and voluntary action, not a corruption of nature.[89]

Reformed Orthodoxy on Original Sin

The Reformed churches responded to the teachings of Arminius's followers at the Synod of Dort (1618–1619). The Canons of Dort (Head 3/4, Art. 1–2) teach that with the sole exception of Christ, all men "have derived corruption from their original parent," which includes "blindness of mind, horrible darkness, vanity and perverseness of judgment," so that man has become "wicked, rebellious, and obdurate in heart and will, and impure in his affections."[90] The "unregenerate man" is "utterly dead in sin" and "destitute of all powers unto spiritual good."[91] Original sin "by itself suffices to condemn the whole human race."[92] When some people reject the gospel, "the fault lies in themselves," but when others hear the gospel and are converted, it "is not to be ascribed to the proper exercise of free will, whereby one distinguishes himself above others, equally furnished with grace sufficient for faith . . . but it must be wholly ascribed to God, who . . . has chosen His own from eternity in Christ."[93]

---

87. Arminius, *Declaration of Sentiments*, in *Works*, 1:664; *Apology*, Art. 17, in *Works*, 2:20; and *Certain Articles*, 17.13, 17, in *Works*, 2:722.
88. Van Limborch, *Compleat System*, 1:192.
89. John Mark Hicks, "The Theology of Grace in the Thought of Jacobus Arminius and Philip van Limborch: A Study in the Development of Seventeenth-Century Dutch Arminianism" (PhD diss., Westminster Theological Seminary, 1985), 67–73, http://evangelicalarminians.org/wp-content/uploads/2013/07/Hicks.-The-Theology-of-Grace-in-the-Thought-of-Arminius-and-Limborch.pdf.
90. *The Three Forms of Unity*, 140.
91. Canons of Dort (Head 3/4, Rej. 4), in *The Three Forms of Unity*, 149.
92. Canons of Dort (Head 3/4, Rej. 1), in *The Three Forms of Unity*, 148.
93. Canons of Dort (Head 3/4, Art. 9–10), in *The Three Forms of Unity*, 143.

Conversion is a "resurrection from the dead" and is not in the power of man to take or reject.[94]

The Westminster Confession of Faith (6.2–4) likewise says that Adam and Eve, by their disobedience to God's prohibition, "fell from their original righteousness and communion, with God, and so became dead in sin, and wholly defiled in all the faculties and parts of soul and body." Consequently, "they being the root of all mankind, the guilt of this sin was imputed; and the same death in sin, and corrupted nature, conveyed to all their posterity descending from them by ordinary generation." These words presuppose that Adam's headship over mankind is both natural ("root . . . generation") and legal ("guilt . . . imputed").[95] The Westminster divines said, "From this original corruption, whereby we are utterly indisposed, disabled, and made opposite to all good, and wholly inclined to all evil, do proceed all actual transgressions."[96] Adam's sin "brought mankind into an estate of sin a misery" because "the covenant being made with Adam, not only for himself but for his posterity, all mankind, descending from him by ordinary generation, sinned in him, and fell with him, in his first transgression."[97]

The Formula Consensus Helvetica (Canon 10) says,

> The sin of Adam is imputed by the mysterious and just judgment of God to all his posterity. For the Apostle testifies that "in Adam all sinned, by one man's disobedience many were made sinners" (Rom 5:12, 19) and "in Adam all die" (1 Cor 15:21–22). But there appears no way in which hereditary corruption could fall, as a spiritual death, upon the whole human race by the just judgment of God, unless some sin of that race preceded, incurring the penalty of that death. For God, the most supreme Judge of all the earth, punishes none but the guilty.[98]

Reformed orthodoxy and British Puritanism continued to maintain the doctrine of original sin, both in its polemical force and practical implications. Anthony Burgess wrote a 555-page treatise titled *The Doctrine of Original Sin, Asserted and Vindicated against the Old and*

---

94. Canons of Dort (Head 3/4, Art. 12), in *The Three Forms of Unity*, 145. See 3/4.r8 (152).

95. See Westminster Shorter Catechism (Q. 16), in *Reformed Confessions*, 4:355. On the debate in nineteenth-century American Presbyterianism over the nature of Adam's headship, see George P. Hutchinson, *The Problem of Original Sin in American Presbyterian Theology* (Nutley, NJ: Presbyterian and Reformed, 1972).

96. Westminster Confession of Faith (6.4), in *Reformed Confessions*, 4:241–42.

97. Westminster Shorter Catechism (Q. 16–17), in *Reformed Confessions*, 4:355.

98. *Reformed Confessions*, 4:523. This is an explanation of "in consequence of the just judgment of God" in the Canons of Dort (Head 3/4, Art. 2), in *Reformed Confessions*, 4:135.

New Adversaries Thereof, Both Socinians, Papists, Arminians, and Anabaptists. And Practically Improved for the Benefit of the Meanest Capacities [lowest level of education].[99] Thomas Goodwin wrote a treatise of similar size, *An Unregenerate Man's Guiltiness before God, in Respect of Sin and Punishment*, a large part of which dealt with the imputation of Adam's guilt and communication of his corruption to mankind.[100]

Two notable features of the Reformed doctrine of original sin are total depravity and total inability. We defined total depravity at the beginning of this chapter. Goodwin summarized it when he said, "Sin is nothing else but a disorder and confusion of all the powers of our souls, whereby they are turned rebels, and will not be subject to God (Rom. 8:7)."[101] Total inability does not mean that fallen men can do nothing useful for society, but rather that they can do nothing pleasing to God or take the first step of willing the good that God requires, without regenerating grace. Burgess said, "As it denotes that our power to good is lost by this original sin, so also is our will and desire. . . . We must not then conceive of man, as indeed miserably polluted, and such as cannot help himself, but is very willing, and heartily desireth to be freed from all bondage." Instead, man's original sin includes "an unwillingness, and an averseness" to God's law and gospel; the will is totally against God.[102]

In 1720, Thomas Boston published *Human Nature in Its Fourfold State: Of Primitive Integrity, Entire Depravation, Begun Recovery, and Consummate Happiness or Misery*, a book that became a classic in Scottish Reformed practical divinity.[103] The second part of the book, on "the state of nature," treats man's sinfulness, misery under God's wrath, and inability to save himself. Boston's book has been judged one of the finest on this topic.

---

99. Anthony Burgess, *The Doctrine of Original Sin, Asserted and Vindicated against the Old and New Adversaries Thereof, Both Socinians, Papists, Arminians, and Anabaptists. And Practically Improved for the Benefit of the Meanest Capacities* (London: by Abraham Miller for Thomas Underhill, 1658).
100. Goodwin, *An Unregenerate Man's Guiltiness before God, in Respect of Sin and Punishment*, in *Works*, 10:1–567.
101. Goodwin, *An Unregenerate Man's Guiltiness*, in *Works*, 10:125.
102. Burgess, *The Doctrine of Original Sin*, 97–98.
103. Thomas Boston, *Human Nature in Its Fourfold State: Of Primitive Integrity, Entire Depravation, Begun Recovery, and Consummate Happiness or Misery* (Edinburgh: James McEuen and Co., 1720). When we cite this book elsewhere, we refer to the 1964 Banner of Truth reprint cited earlier.

Modern Attacks on the Doctrine of Original Sin

The doctrine came under public attack again within the professing Christian church when John Taylor (1694–1761) published *The Scripture-Doctrine of Original Sin Proposed to Free and Candid Examination.*[104] Taylor professed faith in the Scriptures, but he said that no interpretation of Scripture may be accepted that is "contradictory to the common sense and understanding of mankind."[105] Therefore, he begged the question, for he started his investigation of original sin presuming that the fall brought no significant corruption to human reason. It is no surprise that he concluded that Adam's sin was merely personal and brought nothing upon his offspring except mortality.[106] Taylor's book was popular and influential, going through three editions in two decades and a fourth in 1767 after the author had died.[107]

Taylor's anthropological heresy provoked vigorous replies in England, including those of Isaac Watts (1764–1748), David Jennings (1691–1762), and John Wesley (1703–1791).[108] Wesley's book leaned heavily on "long extracts from others' work, especially that of Watts."[109] Wesley agreed with the Westminster divines that "the fall brought mankind into an estate of sin and misery."[110] He said, "Our nature is deeply corrupted, inclined to evil, and disinclined to all that is spiritual good, so that without supernatural grace, we can neither will nor do what is pleasing to God."[111] However, like Arminius, Wesley added the doctrine of universal and prevenient grace: "Whatever they were by nature, the grace of God was more or less given to all. Though they were wholly inclined to all evil by nature, yet by grace they might recover all goodness."[112] Wesley

---

104. John Taylor, *The Scripture-Doctrine of Original Sin Proposed to Free and Candid Examination* (London: for the author, by J. Wilson, 1740).

105. Taylor, *The Scripture-Doctrine of Original Sin*, 3.

106. Taylor, *The Scripture-Doctrine of Original Sin*, 13, 19, 23, 25, 35.

107. G. T. Eddy, *Dr. Taylor of Norwich: Wesley's Arch-Heretic* (Eugene, OR: Wipf and Stock, 2003), 51. Eddy notes that in a subsequent work, Taylor denied substitutionary atonement (53).

108. Isaac Watts, *The Ruin and Recovery of Mankind: or, an Attempt to Vindicate the Scriptural Account of These Great Events upon the Plain Principles of Reason* (London: R. Hett and J. Brackstone, 1740); David Jennings, *A Vindication of the Scripture-Doctrine of Original Sin, from Mr Taylor's Free and Candid Examination of It* (London: R. Hett and J Oswald, 1740); and John Wesley, *The Doctrine of Original Sin According to Scripture, Reason, and Experience* (Bristol: E. Farley, 1757).

109. Eddy, *Dr. Taylor of Norwich*, 103.

110. Wesley, *The Doctrine of Original Sin*, 135.

111. Wesley, *The Doctrine of Original Sin*, 154.

112. Wesley, *The Doctrine of Original Sin*, 139; cf. 154. The first sentence in the original was part of a rhetorical question: "Why not, if whatever they were by nature, the grace of God was more or less given to all?"

concluded his treatise with a sixty-page excerpt from Boston's *Fourfold State*.[113]

Across the Atlantic, Jonathan Edwards also replied to Taylor.[114] He said that the Scriptures represent all men as guilty of sin and unable to be justified by works, so all are condemned by the law to suffer God's punishment.[115] This, he argued, shows that all people are subject to a powerful and prevailing tendency toward moral evil.[116] The depravity of man's nature also has a tendency to put people in a condition of spiritual "folly and stupidity," so that they choose idols over the true God despite God's revelation of himself in creation and the Word.[117] Taylor had attempted to interpret the "death" that Paul said came upon man because of Adam's disobedience as merely physical death (Romans 5), but Edwards pointed out that Taylor had failed to account for Paul's usage of "death" throughout Romans, which entailed much more than the death of the body.[118] Edwards's treatise went through six printings in the eighteenth century and six more in the first four decades of the nineteenth.[119]

Beginning in the nineteenth century, liberal modernism has denied the fall into original sin and has asserted false optimism about human goodness. Friedrich Schleiermacher rejected the historical veracity of Genesis.[120] He defined godliness as a "feeling of absolute dependence" that is "a universal element of life," found not merely in certain individuals but in the "general nature of man."[121] Though "feeble and suppressed," this godliness is "already present in human nature," waiting to be "stimulated" by Christ's influence.[122] Albrecht Ritschl (1822–1889) denied that sin has any origin outside of each individual's choice, though he acknowledged that sinners influence each other.[123] Accordingly, liberal modernists of the early twentieth century taught a form of Pelagianism in which man is basically

---

113. Wesley, *The Doctrine of Original Sin*, 463–522.
114. Jonathan Edwards, *The Great Christian Doctrine of Original Sin Defended . . . A Reply to the Objections and Arguings of Dr. John Taylor* (Boston: S. Kneeland, 1758).
115. Edwards, *Original Sin*, in *WJE*, 3:114–15. He cites 1 Kings 8:46; Job 9:2–3; Ps. 143:2; Eccles. 7:20; Rom. 3:19; Gal. 2:16; 3:10; 2 Cor. 3:6–9; 1 John 1:7–10.
116. Edwards, *Original Sin*, in *WJE*, 3:120.
117. Edwards, *Original Sin*, in *WJE*, 3:148–49, 152. Edwards refers to Ps. 115:4–8; Jer. 2:12–13; and the latter half of Romans 1.
118. Edwards, *Original Sin*, in *WJE*, 3:305–8.
119. Clyde A. Holbrook, introduction to Edwards, *Original Sin*, in *WJE*, 3:93.
120. Schleiermacher, *The Christian Faith*, 40 (1:151).
121. Schleiermacher, *The Christian Faith*, 33 (1:134).
122. Schleiermacher, *The Christian Faith*, 106 (2:476).
123. Cited in Bavinck, *Reformed Dogmatics*, 3:45–46, 88.

good.[124] Coupled with the doctrine of human evolution, theological liberalism tends to view mankind as improving through external means such as education and social justice.[125]

Neoorthodox theologians, awakened by the wars and atrocities of the first half of the twentieth century, returned to a more realistic view of human sin than their liberal modernist teachers and colleagues. However, neoorthodox theologians failed to root universal sin in the sin of Adam. Karl Barth denied the historical fall of man in Adam, but instead interpreted "Adam" as a symbol of everyone's pride.[126] Emil Brunner acknowledged that, according to the apostle Paul, "sin now dominates man and humanity as a whole," but denied that Genesis teaches the fall of man or that it is a major theme for Paul: "The condemnation of all is not directly attributed to the fall of Adam but to the sin of all."[127] Both the scientific reconstruction of history and human responsibility, Brunner said, force us to abandon original sin.[128]

Both liberal modernism and neoorthodoxy deny original sin based upon a skeptical view of the historical accounts of the Holy Scriptures.[129] In so doing, they must radically reconstruct the Christian doctrine of salvation. Paul's theology hinges upon Adam's fall and its parallel to Christ's saving work (Romans 5). If we set aside the doctrine of the historical sin of Adam and its imputation to his natural descendants, then we have forsaken the biblical diagnosis of mankind's misery and hence also the biblical remedy, which is the gospel of Christ.

Summary Reflection on the Historical Doctrine of Original Sin

Since its earliest days, biblical Christianity has recognized the devastating effects of Adam's sin upon the human race. Far from a merely personal transgression, Adam's violation of God's commandment precipitated the fall of mankind into a state of spiritual corruption and death. However, the church through the ages has also affirmed human moral agency and responsibility. The intersection of these two doctrines has proven difficult to navigate.

---

124. J. Gresham Machen, *Christianity and Liberalism* (1923; repr., Grand Rapids, MI: Eerdmans, 1992), 64.
125. Bavinck, *Reformed Dogmatics*, 3:46–47.
126. Barth, *The Epistle to the Romans*, 181; and Barth, *Christ and Adam*, 78–79.
127. Brunner, *Man in Revolt*, 119–20n.
128. Brunner, *Man in Revolt*, 120–21.
129. On the liberal and neorthodox views of special revelation, see *RST*, 1:287–95, 304–9.

Pelagianism seeks to solve the problem by jettisoning the doctrine of original sin and affirming the power of the human will to choose good apart from internal regenerating grace. Orthodox Christianity rejects that solution as contrary to the biblical teaching that all people, since Adam's fall, are sinful, enslaved, and condemned (Rom. 3:10–20; 5:12–19; 6:17). Nevertheless, the Pelagian view of man periodically resurfaces among professing Christians.

The Augustinian tradition, reaffirmed and clarified by Luther, Calvin, and the Reformed churches, teaches that man's sinful condition can be remedied only by the transforming power of sovereign grace. Humanity is universally enslaved to sin (total inability, Rom. 8:7–8) in every aspect of human nature (total depravity, Titus 3:3). Men remain morally responsible for sin, but spiritually dead until God saves them through the grace of Jesus Christ (Eph. 2:1–10).

Through the ages, however, many theologians have attempted to craft a middle road between Augustinianism and Pelagianism. It proposes that God's grace partially heals man from original sin so that people have the ability to embrace further grace. Though this solution seeks to ascribe the glory of salvation entirely to God, at a practical level it gives man ultimate veto power over his salvation, logically requiring that man must credit himself, along with God, for his redemption. After all, God could not save him without his making himself willing to cooperate with grace. Ultimately, this view supports the medieval formula that God saves the person who tries his best. If embraced in its full implications, such a doctrine destroys the gospel of salvation by grace alone and replaces it with a law that cannot save.

What does the Bible teach about original sin? How does it relate to the question of free will? We will address these questions in the next three chapters.

Sing to the Lord

The Only Hope of Sinners

Lord, I deserve Thy deepest wrath,
Ungrateful, faithless I have been;
No terrors have my soul deterred,
Nor goodness wooed me from my sin.

My heart is vile, my mind depraved,
My flesh rebels against Thy will;

I am polluted in Thy sight,
Yet, Lord, have mercy on me still!

Without defense, to Thee I look,
To Thee, the only Savior, fly;
Without a hope, without a friend,
In deep distress to Thee I cry.

Speak peace to me, my sins forgive,
Dwell Thou within my heart, O God,
The guilt and power of sin remove,
And fit me for Thy blest abode.

Basil Manly Jr.
Tune: any long meter (may be sung to Rockingham Old, the tune used for
"'Twas on That Night When Doomed to Know")
The Baptist Psalmody: A Selection of Hymns for the Worship of God,
ed. Basil Manly and Basil Manly Jr. (New York: Sheldon & Co., 1850),
No. 445

Questions for Meditation or Discussion

1. Define the following terms: (1) original sin and (2) total depravity.
2. What tension existed in the doctrine of man's spiritual condition as taught by the Christian theologians of the first few centuries?
3. Briefly describe the teaching of the following theologians regarding original sin and grace: (1) Pelagius, (2) Augustine, (3) John Cassian, (4) Anselm of Canterbury, (5) Thomas Aquinas, and (6) William of Ockham.
4. What have the Lutheran churches affirmed about original sin and saving grace in the Augsburg Confession and the Formula of Concord?
5. How would you summarize the Reformed stance on original sin as stated in the First Helvetic Confession, the Belgic Confession, and the Heidelberg Catechism?
6. How did the Roman Catholic Church address this doctrine at the Council of Trent?
7. What was the teaching of Jacob Arminius regarding original sin? What about later Arminians, such as Philipp van Limborch?

8. How do the Canons of Dort explain how people respond to the gospel in a manner according to the doctrine of original sin? How should this affect how we view our own response to the gospel?

Questions for Deeper Reflection

9. How did theologians such as Cassian and John Wesley modify the doctrine of original sin by teaching universal grace? What effect does this have upon our view of lost sinners?

10. John Taylor said that our doctrine of original sin cannot contradict human common sense and understanding. Is this a valid approach? Why or why not?

20

The State of Sin, Part 2

Universal Sin, Imputed Guilt, and Lack of Righteousness

Original sin is not a popular concept. It is much more common to find sentiments like those of Jean-Jacques Rousseau, who said, "The fundamental principle of morality about which I have reasoned in all my writings . . . is that man is a naturally good being, loving justice and order; that there is no original perversity in the human heart, and that the first movements of nature are always right."[1] Like many today, Rousseau blamed man's sins on the inequalities of society.[2] We live in a culture of victimhood. The biblical doctrine about human corruption and condemnation, by contrast, is often seen by modern people as unduly negative, unloving, and inhumane.

Though the doctrine of original sin is controversial, the reality of sin is overwhelming and irrefutable. Its poison begins in the cradle and raises its ugly head in childish lies and playground cruelty. Sin distorts our relationships, dirties our business dealings, defiles our sexuality, and damages our world. Its ruinous effects range from broken marriages to genocidal wars.

---

1. Jean-Jacques Rousseau, *Letter to Beaumont* (1763), in *The Collected Writings of Rousseau, Volume 9, Letter to Beaumont, Letters Written from the Mountain, and Related Writings*, trans. Christopher Kelly and Judith R. Bush, ed. Christopher Kelly and Eve Grace (Hanover, NH: University Press of New England, 2001), 28.

2. Tatha Wiley, *Original Sin: Origins, Developments, Contemporary Meanings* (New York: Paulist, 2002), 112–13.

Sin clings to our last breath, and there is no more horrifying end than to die in one's sins.

God's Word is like a mirror that reflects our sins back to us so that we may repent, trust in Christ for salvation, and walk in the liberty of increasing obedience (James 1:21–25). Therefore, we must listen to what God has revealed to us about this dark doctrine of sin, not because it is easy to hear, but because it is necessary.

The Universal State of Sin

The state of sin is the universal condition of man regardless of ethnic or religious background, as Paul demonstrates from various Old Testament Scripture passages (Rom. 3:9–18). John Murray commented, "The apostle has selected a series of indictments drawn from the Old Testament and covering the wide range of human character and activity to show that, from whatever aspect men may be viewed, the verdict of Scripture is one of universal and total depravity."[3] Edward Reynolds said, "All men, and every part of man, [are] shut up under the guilt and power of sin."[4] For example, Paul says, "There is none righteous, no, not one: there is none that understandeth, there is none that seeketh after God. They are all gone out of the way, they are together become unprofitable; there is none that doeth good, no, not one" (vv. 10–12). He writes of the corruption of their words (vv. 13–14), actions (vv. 15–17), and minds (v. 18).

This is the witness of the whole Bible. Biblical history from Genesis 3 onward is the history of sin. Israel's history is a chronicle of rebellion and unbelief against the Lord.[5] Solomon testified, "There is no man that sinneth not" (1 Kings 8:46). The nations around Israel wallowed in idolatry, immorality, and injustice.[6] The wise confess, "Who can say, I have made my heart clean, I am pure from my sin?" (Prov. 20:9). "There is not a just man upon earth, that doeth good, and sinneth not" (Eccles. 7:20). Kings and nations rage against the Lord (Ps. 2:1–2). The religious honor God with their lips while their hearts are far from him, and the wisdom of the wise perishes (Isa. 29:13–14). Thomas Goodwin said that sin is a "universal flood that covers the face of the earth."[7]

---

3. Murray, *The Epistle to the Romans*, 1:102.
4. Reynolds, *The Sinfulness of Sin*, in *Works*, 1:121.
5. Ex. 16:28; 32:7, 9; Deut. 29:4; 31:6, 29; 2 Kings 17:7–23; Neh. 9:16–17, 26–30, 33–35; Psalms 78; 106; Dan. 9:5–15.
6. Isa. 44:9–20; Jer. 10:1–16; Amos 1; cf. Eph. 4:17–19; 1 Thess. 4:5.
7. Goodwin, *An Unregenerate Man's Guiltiness before God*, in *Works*, 10:6.

Children are not exempt from this spiritual plague. The motion of man's heart "is evil from his youth" (Gen. 8:21). David confessed that from the moment of his conception in the womb, he was "in iniquity" and "in sin" (Ps. 51:5). He did not call his condition a potential for sin or a tendency toward sin, but said it was sin. Though children have a kind of innocence in comparison to adults (Isa. 7:16), still the experience of parents and teachers confirms that "the wicked are estranged from the womb: they go astray as soon as they be born, speaking lies" (Ps. 58:3).[8] Sadly, we do not need to teach children to sin, but must train them not to sin, for "foolishness is bound in the heart of a child" (Prov. 22:15). Here, foolishness does not refer to mental simplicity, but to destructive moral waywardness (5:23; 17:12).

The New Testament likewise declares the universal sinfulness of mankind. Peter echoes the words of Isaiah: "Ye were as sheep going astray" (1 Pet. 2:25; cf. Isa. 53:6). It is "the will of the Gentiles" to live in sexual lust and idolatry (1 Pet. 4:3). John warns, "If we say that we have no sin, we deceive ourselves, and the truth is not in us. . . . If we say that we have not sinned, we make him a liar, and his word is not in us" (1 John 1:8, 10). James says, "We all stumble in many ways" (James 3:2 ESV). Paul writes, "For all have sinned, and come short of the glory of God" (Rom. 3:23). When God's law calls fallen men to account, not one person will be justified in God's sight for his deeds, but the whole world is "guilty before God" (vv. 19–20).

Each of us must personally appropriate this doctrine and then acknowledge, "My nation is sinful. My family is sinful. I have sinned against God. I am a guilty sinner by nature. Apart from the grace of God, my heart is a factory of idols and a fountain of impurity. I have nothing in which to boast before God, and no cause to look down upon anyone in self-righteousness. If God were to judge me for what I deserve, he would rightly damn me to hell."

The Deadly Dimensions of Original Sin

The Scriptures trace the root of this pervasive corruption to one source: "by one man sin entered into the world, and death by sin" (Rom. 5:12). Adam's sin cast all his natural descendants into a moral and spiritual pit. His sin was propagated to his offspring, making them sinners, in a twofold manner: imputation of guilt and transmission of sin.[9] This is *original sin*: our sin before we commit actual sin. Wilhelmus à Brakel wrote, "Original

---

8. Bavinck, *Reformed Dogmatics*, 3:89.
9. Ames, *A Sketch of the Christian's Catechism*, 17–18. See Watson, *A Body of Divinity*, 143.

sin consists of imputed guilt and inherent pollution."[10] These contrast to the saving graces of justification and sanctification.

The *imputation of sin* brings legal guilt and condemnation, resulting in the punishment of death. To impute means to count, credit, or blame (cf. Rom. 4:8). Charles Hodge said, "In the judicial and theological sense of the word, to impute is to attribute anything to a person or persons, upon adequate grounds, as the judicial or meritorious reason of reward or punishment."[11] Theologians speak of the imputation of Adam's sin to mankind, for "by the offence of one judgment came upon all men to condemnation" (5:18).

The imputation of sin is accompanied by the *transmission of sin* as an inherent deprivation and corruption of human nature. Herman Bavinck said, "In the case of Adam and all his descendants, a sinful state followed the sinful deed."[12] Sinful Adam produced offspring in his sinful likeness (Gen. 5:3). His natural descendants have a twofold problem with the condition of their souls: they lack the original righteousness that was inherent in the image of God and they have a ruling propensity to evil (6:5).

The Westminster Shorter Catechism (Q. 18) says, "The sinfulness of that estate whereinto man fell, consists in the guilt of Adam's first sin, the want of original righteousness, and the corruption of his whole nature, which is commonly called Original Sin; together with all actual transgressions which proceed from it."[13]

In the remainder of this chapter, we will examine the guilt of Adam's first sin and the lack of original righteousness. In the next, we will consider the corruption of man's whole nature with its two tragic corollaries: total depravity and inability.

The Imputation of Sin: The Guilt of Adam's First Sin

Adam did not sin merely as a private individual, but his first sin transgressed the covenant in which he represented all mankind.[14] Though God's

---

10. Brakel, *The Christian's Reasonable Service*, 1:382. See Berkhof, *Systematic Theology*, 245–46; and Matthew Barrett, *Salvation by Grace: The Case for Effectual Calling and Regeneration* (Phillipsburg, NJ: P&R, 2013), 38. Some Reformed theologians, while teaching the imputation of Adam's sin, do not consider it to be an aspect of original sin, which they restrict to the inherent corruption of man. Thus, Turretin, *Institutes*, 9.10.2 (1:629–30). The difference is a matter of terminology and not doctrinal content. See Hodge, *Outlines of Theology*, 325.
11. Hodge, *Systematic Theology*, 1:194.
12. Bavinck, *Reformed Dogmatics*, 3:106–7.
13. *Reformed Confessions*, 4:355.
14. See chaps. 14–15.

words "in the day that thou eatest thereof thou shalt surely die" (Gen. 2:17) were addressed specifically to Adam in the singular, death came to all Adam's descendants after the fall (Genesis 5). God's subsequent destruction of all mankind outside of Noah's family in the flood included many children who had committed no actual, conscious acts of disobedience against God's law (7:21–23). Since death is the penalty for sin, this implies that Adam's guilt rested upon the entire human race.[15] Reynolds said, "We were all one in Adam, and with him; in him legally, in regard of the stipulation and covenant between God and him . . . and in him naturally, and therefore unavoidably subject to all that bondage and burden which the human nature contracted in his fall."[16]

The Apostle Paul's Doctrine of Adam and Christ

The apostle Paul reflects upon the effects of Adam's sin when he contrasts man's fall in Adam with the saving work of Jesus Christ. Paul writes, "For since by man came death, by man came also the resurrection of the dead. For as in Adam all die, even so in Christ shall all be made alive" (1 Cor. 15:21–22). Paul regards death as the penalty for sin (v. 3; cf. Rom. 6:23). "In Adam all die" refers to the death penalty specifically threatened against Adam for disobedience to God's covenant (Gen. 2:17).[17] Therefore, God is punishing mankind for the sin of their first father and covenant representative.

The reason for this punishment becomes clear in Paul's teaching on the imputation of Adam's sin in Romans 5. There he writes, "Wherefore, as by one man sin entered into the world, and death by sin; and so death passed upon all men, for that all have sinned" (v. 12). The Greek phrase (*eph hō*) linking "death passed upon all men" and "all have sinned" has been the subject of various interpretations.[18] Here we consider three major lines of interpretation: local, consecutive, and causal.

1. "In whom all sinned": this *local* meaning refers back to Adam, as in the Latin Vulgate (*in quo*).[19] This would imply that all men are counted

---

15. John Brown of Haddington, *Systematic Theology: A Compendious View of Natural and Revealed Religion* (1817; repr., Grand Rapids, MI: Reformation Heritage Books, 2015), 210.

16. Reynolds, *The Sinfulness of Sin*, in *Works*, 1:118.

17. Goodwin, *An Unregenerate Man's Guiltiness*, in *Works*, 10:13, 15.

18. The preposition *epi* is flexible in meaning. With the dative case, it can refer to location (on, in, upon, or above), authority (over), basis, cause, purpose, result, manner, or time (at the time of, during). Joseph Fitzmyer lists eleven interpretations of *eph hō*. *Romans: A New Translation with Introduction and Commentary*, The Anchor Bible 33 (New York: Doubleday, 1993), 413–16.

19. Cf. the local sense in Josh. 5:15; 2 Kings 19:10 (LXX); Mark 2:4 (majority Greek text reading); Acts 7:33.

as having transgressed in the garden in solidarity with Adam. The local interpretation is grammatically and theologically possible, but exegetes raise two objections to its likelihood: "one man" is quite far away in the sentence from this phrase in order to be its antecedent (twenty-one words in the Greek text) and Paul favors another preposition, "in" (*en*), to describe being "in" Christ or "in" Adam (1 Cor. 15:22).[20]

2. "With the result that all sinned": this *consecutive* reading sees actual sin as the consequence of spiritual death coming upon all men.[21] However, though spiritual death does produce actual sin, in this context, Paul emphasizes that sin produces death, not vice versa.[22]

3. "Because all sinned": most English translations and modern commentators tend to take the phrase in a *causal* sense (cf. 2 Cor. 5:4), referring to the reason for the coming of death to all people.[23] If the sense is causal, then we must ask when "all sinned." It might be proposed that Adam's sin corrupted mankind so that they, too, committed sin and consequently were subjected to death. This is the idea of mediate imputation.[24] Or it may be said that Paul "ascribed death to two causes," Adam's first sin (v. 12a) and the actual sins of all people (v. 12b).[25]

However, it is best to understand Paul as teaching here the *immediate imputation* of Adam's sin to mankind.[26] Paul does not write that "all became sinful" or "all were sinning," but "all sinned." Furthermore, Paul goes on to say that death reigned "even over them that had not sinned" like Adam (Rom. 5:14). In other words, death did not come to all because of their personal, actual sins.[27] Why then do all die? Paul says, "By one man's offense death reigned by one" (v. 17). Therefore, "because all

20. Fitzmyer, *Romans*, 414; and Schreiner, *Romans*, 273–74.

21. Schreiner, *Romans*, 276.

22. Rom. 5:17, 21; 6:23; 7:5; 8:10. Note also Paul's words in Rom. 5:12, literally, "on account of sin, death." On this basis, Schreiner changed his view of *eph hō*, which he set forth in his commentary on Romans, and embraced the causal view: "because all sinned." Thomas R. Schreiner, "Original Sin and Original Death: Romans 5:12–19," in *Adam, the Fall, and Original Sin*, ed. Madueme and Reeves, 274.

23. S. Lewis Johnson Jr., "Romans 5:12—An Exercise in Exegesis and Theology," in *New Dimensions in New Testament Study*, ed. Richard N. Longenecker and Merrill C. Tenney (Grand Rapids, MI: Zondervan, 1974), 305. "Because" is the translation of the English Standard Version, New International Version, Holman Christian Standard Bible, New Revised Standard Version, and New King James Version. The New American Standard Bible (1995) reads "inasmuch as," probably in the causal sense of "since." The KJV's "for that" also appears to have a causal meaning (John 12:18; Acts 4:16).

24. See the discussion and rebuttal in Berkhof, *Systematic Theology*, 239, 243.

25. Fitzmyer, *Romans*, 416. This is called a consecutive reading, but it is very close to causal in interpretation.

26. Fesko, *Death in Adam, Life in Christ*, 213; and Johnson, "Romans 5:12," in *New Dimensions in New Testament Study*, ed. Longenecker and Tenney, 312–16.

27. Murray, *The Epistle to the Romans*, 1:183.

sinned" indicates that Adam's sin was counted as their sin, his guilt was their guilt, and the death that he merited became their death. Romans 5:12 begins and ends with the same thought: Adam's sin brought death to all, and all die because all sinned in Adam.[28]

The doctrine of the immediate imputation of Adam's sin is confirmed by Paul's teaching that the sin of one man is the basis for all mankind's "condemnation" (Rom. 5:16, 18). "Condemnation" (*katakrima*) is a legal and judicial term, coupled with "judgment" (*krima*; cf. 2:2–3; 13:2).[29] Goodwin said, "God could not condemn them for that act, unless he did in justice judge them guilty of it."[30] Murray wrote, "Condemnation is . . . the judicial sentence which pronounces us to be unrighteous. . . . All men are under the condemnation of God because of the one sin of the one man."[31] Death did not come to man merely as a natural consequence of descent from a mortal man. Death came by God's legal verdict of condemnation upon all men because of Adam's sin. Paul contrasts this condemnation to the justification of sinners gained by Christ (cf. 8:33–34). Just as Christ's obedience unto death makes believers to be counted as righteous apart from their works (5:19; cf. 3:24–25, 28; 4:3, 6), so Adam's disobedience made all in him to be counted as condemned sinners. Although our sinful acts increase our condemnation, our guilty status does not begin with personal sins but with Adam's sin.

God's Justice and Man's Guilt regarding Adam

Upon what basis does God justly reckon Adam's guilt and condemnation to mankind? The imputation of Adam's sin rests upon our natural and federal unions with him.[32] Adam is the father and natural root of the entire human race. The Scriptures teach "a law of solidarity" by which the children receive good or suffering according to the conduct of their parents (Ex. 20:5; Heb. 7:9–10),[33] but solidarity in suffering "is not the same

---

28. Fesko, *Death in Adam, Life in Christ*, 209.
29. See the use of the verb *katakrinō* in Mark 14:64; James 5:9.
30. Goodwin, *An Unregenerate Man's Guiltiness*, in *Works*, 10:11.
31. Murray, *The Epistle to the Romans*, 1:195.
32. On the attempt by some theologians, such as William G. T. Shedd, to ground imputation entirely on a natural or realistic relationship with Adam, see John Murray, *The Imputation of Adam's Sin* (Grand Rapids, MI: Eerdmans, 1959), 22–41; and Hutchinson, *The Problem of Original Sin in American Presbyterian Theology*, 36–59.
33. Johnson notes that the interpretation of Heb. 7:9–10 must take into account the role of typology in the author's argument, which may prevent us from drawing general conclusions about human solidarity with our forefathers. Johnson, "Romans 5:12," in *New Dimensions in New Testament Study*, ed. Longenecker and Tenney, 314–15.

as to be punished for the sin of another," as Bavinck said.[34] Each person is culpable for his sins, not the sins of his fathers (Ezek. 18:1–4). It does not help to say that in Adam generic human nature sinned and became guilty, for an abstract nature does not incur guilt, but persons do, and the persons of Adam's descendants did not yet exist when Adam sinned.[35] Therefore, Paul must have in view a special legal relationship between Adam and his natural descendants such that Adam's sin was counted against them. This legal relationship was established by God's covenant.[36] James Ussher wrote, "In the covenant, the sin of the first Adam . . . is reckoned to all the posterity that descend from him by carnal generation, because they were in him, and of him, and one with him." Consequently, "we all are become subject to the imputation of Adam's fall, both for the transgression and guiltiness."[37]

The strongest objection against this doctrine of the imputation of Adam's sin arises from the charge of injustice. God's own law prohibited punishing children for their parents' sins: "The fathers shall not be put to death for the children, neither shall the children be put to death for the fathers: every man shall be put to death for his own sin" (Deut. 24:16; cf. 2 Kings 14:6). Ezekiel 18:20 says, "The soul that sinneth, it shall die. The son shall not bear the iniquity of the father, neither shall the father bear the iniquity of the son: the righteousness of the righteous shall be upon him, and the wickedness of the wicked shall be upon him." Therefore, the objector concludes, God's justice would never condemn a person for the sin of another.[38]

In reply, we acknowledge that God does not impute sin to a person merely because one of his ancestors sinned. Adam stood in special relation to mankind. Though the Genesis account seems to indicate that Eve was the first human being to sin, it was Adam's transgression that brought sin, condemnation, and death to the whole race (Rom. 5:12–19). God's covenant in paradise constituted Adam as the federal head or covenant representative of us all. Therefore, the imputation of Adam's sin does not contradict the principle that the soul that sins shall die, for in God's economy "all sinned" when Adam sinned.

---

34. Bavinck, *Reformed Dogmatics*, 3:105.
35. Johnson, "Romans 5:12," in *New Dimensions in New Testament Study*, ed. Longenecker and Tenney, 309.
36. Gill, *Body of Divinity*, 330.
37. Ussher, *A Body of Divinity*, 9th head (126–27).
38. McCall, *Against God and Nature*, 165.

If the objector insists that this is not fair, then we would respond:

1. It is not for the creature to dictate to the Creator what is just and what it unjust. Who are we to argue with God?
2. Adam was the natural root of human nature, for all humanity, even Eve, sprang from him. This helps us to see the reasonableness of God entering into a covenant with Adam as the representative of his family.[39]
3. God provided mankind with an excellent representative, fully good and sinless in every way, able to keep God's law, and tested only with the easiest of prohibitions in a place of happiness and plenty. Does not this show God's goodness to us?
4. If it were not just for God to impute Adam's sin to those whom he represented, then it would not be just for God to impute Christ's righteousness to those whom he represented. This is precisely the parallel that Paul makes in Romans 5. To reject as unjust the imputation of one man's action to others undermines the structure of the gospel of Christ acting on our behalf as the second Adam.
5. If God made each human being his own "Adam," so to speak, standing or falling on his own independently of any representive outside of himself, then there would be no possibility of salvation for those who sinned. This is the position of Satan and the demons—do we want to share in it?
6. Everyone in Adam shares his corruption from the first moment of existence and confirms Adam's rebellion as soon as he can commit actual sin. On judgment day, no one will be able to plead innocent and argue that his condemnation is unjust, for his own works will condemn him.

We must feel the weight of Adam's guilt. Adam's transgression was grave, for it involved defiance against the authority of the great God and Lawgiver, despising God as our supreme good, treating God like a liar, slandering God as unloving and malicious, and challenging the sovereign Lord as if we could be independent of him.[40] How great is our condemnation for the sin of Adam! Recall the magnitude of our first father's transgression in the garden, and charge it to your account in your conscience. Adam's sin contained "pride, ambition, rebellion, infidelity, ingratitude, idolatry, con-

---

39. Cf. the Westminster Confession of Faith (6.3), in *Reformed Confessions*, 4:242.
40. Goodwin, *An Unregenerate Man's Guiltiness*, in *Works*, 10:28–30.

cupiscence, theft, apostasy, unnatural affection, violation of covenant, and an universal renunciation of God's mercy promised."[41] Here is the "efficient cause" of the sin and misery of innumerable people across the generations.[42] Let us marvel at the horrendous weight of Adam's one act of disobedience. Woe unto mankind for the guilt of our fall!

The Absence of Life: The Lack of Original Righteousness

When Adam sinned, he destroyed his spiritual legacy to his children. The Lord created man in his image (Gen. 1:28). At the heart of that image is to be alive unto God in knowledge, righteousness, and holiness (Eph. 4:24; Col. 3:10; cf. Rom. 6:12).[43] When God threatened death upon disobedience (Gen. 2:17), one aspect of that death was the immediate loss of spiritual life in fellowship with God.[44] Man's spiritual goodness was not merely lessened by the fall, but extinguished. As a result, none of fallen man's thoughts are good (6:5).

If it is objected that Genesis never explicitly ties man's lack of righteousness to Adam's transgression, we answer with James Hamilton that Genesis traces the consequences of the fall according to the book's genre—not as a theological treatise but as narrative: "The reader goes from 'very good' in Genesis 1:31 to 'only evil continually' in 6:5, and in between is Adam's sin in 3:1–7. . . . The narrator does not have to *tell* his audience that the transition point was the sin of Adam. He has *shown* them."[45] In the plotline of Genesis, the sin of Genesis 3 is the fulcrum on which is hinged the rise of sin and the fall of man.

The Scriptures do not tell us how Adam's sin is transmitted to the race. Certainly, God does not produce sin in anyone or entice them to sin (James 1:13). Some theologians, holding to a traducian view of the soul's origin, argue that each person derives his sinfulness from the sinfulness of his parents because he gets his soul from them.[46] Others, holding a creationist view of each soul's origin, say that the souls of Adam's descendants are immediately created in the womb without original righteousness as a judicial consequence of Adam's sin and that they are further corrupted by

---

41. Reynolds, *The Sinfulness of Sin*, in *Works*, 1:118.
42. Polyander, Walaeus, Thysius, and Rivetus, *Synopsis Purioris Theologiae*, 15.11 (1:359).
43. See chaps. 8–10 on the image of God.
44. See chap. 18 on the threefold death involved in God's sanction against covenant breakers.
45. James M. Hamilton, "Original Sin in Biblical Theology," in *Adam, the Fall, and Original Sin*, ed. Madueme and Reeves, 193, emphasis original.
46. See chap. 13 on the origin of the soul.

their union with their fallen bodies.[47] The question is muddled when we approach it as if the soul existed for even a moment apart from the body. We deal not with an abstract soul, but with the conception of a whole human person, a son or daughter of Adam who shares in the guilt of his covenant breaking.[48] This is a puzzling question, and it is best not to be dogmatic about it, for the origin of the soul is a great mystery to us. As David Clarkson (1622–1686) said, if we find a man in a pit, we do not stand and wonder exactly how he fell in so much as give our attention to how to get him out.[49] The important point about original sin is not *how* it comes to us, but *what* it is, so that we might know our need for a Savior.

Original sin means that human nature has become destitute of spiritual good. Paul writes, "I know that in me (that is, in my flesh), dwelleth no good thing" (Rom. 7:18). "Flesh" in this context refers to man in his fallen state of enmity against God (v. 5; 8:5–8). As a believer who delights in God's law (7:22), Paul qualifies his statement: there is "no good thing" in him only with respect to his "flesh" or remnants of the old man in him. What then would Paul say of the person who still exists "in the flesh" and not "in the Spirit" (8:9)? Adam's fall has left no good thing until the Spirit regenerates us. "There is none that doeth good, no, not one" (3:12).

The Bible depicts righteousness and truth as light, but says that before salvation, "you were darkness" (Eph. 5:8 ESV). It is not merely that unbelievers are *in* darkness, though that is true (Isa. 9:2; 1 Pet. 2:9), but that they *are* darkness. Darkness and deceit fill their minds and hearts (Rom. 1:21; Eph. 4:18). Darkness covers their daily activities (1 John 1:6). They are ruled by Satan's kingdom, the spiritual power of darkness.[50]

Mankind is not merely weakened by sin but "dead in trespasses and sins" (Eph. 2:1; cf. Rom. 8:6; Col. 2:13). A person can be religious but spiritually dead (Rev. 3:1). God compared Israel to a valley full of "dry bones"—not just deceased but utterly without hope of resuscitation apart from God's supernatural Spirit (Ezek. 37:1–14). Salvation is a passage "from death unto life" in one's present spiritual state; a change from

---

47. Perkins, *An Exposition of the Symbol*, in Works, 5:90; Flavel, *Pneumatologia*, in Works, 2:519–22; and Turretin, *Institutes*, 9.12.8–19. For a slightly different view, see Reynolds, *Passions and Faculties*, in Works, 6:247–49.

48. Brakel, *The Christian's Reasonable Service*, 1:393; and Gill, *Body of Divinity*, 335–37.

49. David Clarkson, "Of Original Sin," in *The Works of David Clarkson*, 3 vols. (Edinburgh: Banner of Truth, 1988), 1:5.

50. Acts 26:18; cf. Luke 22:53; 2 Cor. 6:14; Eph. 6:12; Col. 1:13.

hatred to Christian love (1 John 3:13–14). Jesus described the prodigal son's conversion by saying he "was dead, and is alive again" (Luke 15:24, 32). The self-indulgent are dead even while they live (1 Tim. 5:6). Christ said, "He that heareth my word, and believeth on him that sent me . . . is passed from death unto life." He ascribed this change to his omnipotent power to raise the dead (John 5:24–25).

Apart from saving grace, human beings exist in the total absence of spiritual life. Though they may engage in some religious activities such as fasting and prayer, and civic virtues such as friendship and parenting, they are morally evil and displeasing to God (Matt. 5:46–47; 6:5; 7:11). And Christ said that this is the state of the vast majority of people (7:13–14). To those who think that they keep God's commandments, the Lord Jesus says, "There is none good but one, that is, God" (19:17). Therefore, salvation is "impossible" by man's efforts and only possible by God's omnipotence (v. 26). God must plant godliness as a new creation in the heart, and though religion may flourish in many people in various ways, Christ said that "every plant, which my heavenly Father hath not planted, shall be rooted up" (15:13).

Therefore, let us take account of our spiritual portfolio by nature. God made us wealthy in holiness, but Adam made beggars of us all. When David sorrowed over his sin, he traced his adultery and murder back to his infant corruption (Ps. 51:5). Rather than excusing his sin, this accentuated his humiliation. Just as original sin is the root of our actual sins, so original sin should be the deepest ground of our contrition.[51] We should begin grieving over sin with the absence of original righteousness. Clarkson said, "Man's soul is left like a ruined castle; the bare ragged walls, the remaining faculties, may help you to guess what it has been; but all the ornaments and precious furniture is gone."[52]

Christ's distinguishing marks of the true members of God's kingdom start with inward poverty (Matt. 5:3). Christ's disciples recognize that they do bad things because of the badness of their hearts. Repentance is not merely cleaning up bad behaviors, but grieving over our fallen nature's emptiness of all spiritual good and turning to Christ to give us the righteousness for which his grace has made us hunger (v. 6). So long as we think that we are spiritually rich, we will say that we "have need of

---

51. Clarkson, "Of Original Sin," in *Works*, 1:4.
52. Clarkson, "Of Original Sin," in *Works*, 1:6.

nothing" from Christ. Only when we know that we are "wretched, and miserable, and poor, and blind, and naked" are we ready to receive the riches of Christ (Rev. 3:17–18). Do you see yourself as impoverished by nature, with nothing to offer to God unless Christ comes by faith and dwells in you? Or are you "rich" in self-righteousness? If so, ask God to show you your poverty.

Sing to the Lord

Lamenting Mankind's Sinfulness

The God Who sits enthroned on high
The foolish in their heart deny;
No one does good; corrupt in thought,
Unrighteous works their hands have wrought.

From heav'n the Lord with searching eye
Looked down the sons of men to try,
To see if any understood
And sought for God, the only good.

From righteousness they all depart,
Corrupt are all, and vile in heart;
Yea, ev'ry man has evil done;
Not one does good, not even one.

Thy lowly servant they despise,
Because he on the Lord relies;
But they shall tremble yet in fear,
For to the righteous God is near.

Psalm 14
Tune: Blackburn
The Psalter, No. 23
Or Tune: Eisenach
Trinity Hymnal—Baptist Edition, No. 474 (missing the first stanza)

Questions for Meditation or Discussion

1. Why is the doctrine of sin so difficult, even offensive, for people to hear?
2. How do the Holy Scriptures testify that all people on earth are sinners?

3. Explain the meaning of the following aspects of original sin: (1) imputation of sin and (2) transmission of sin.

4. How does Romans 5 teach the immediate imputation of Adam's sin to mankind?

5. How can God count all of Adam's natural descendants guilty for his sin?

6. Why is this not a violation of justice, given that a child should not be punished for the sin of its father?

7. What Scripture passages show us that all in Adam enter this world without any spiritual good or spiritual life in them?

8. David Clarkson said, "Man's soul is left like a ruined castle." What does this illustration suggest about mankind in the state of sin?

9. How does knowing our lack of original righteousness help us to become poor in spirit?

10. How aware are you of your lack of righteousness apart from Christ? How does that awareness affect you? How should it affect you?

Questions for Deeper Reflection

11. What are the three main interpretations of "for that" (*eph hō*) in Romans 5:12? Which is the best interpretation? Why? What implications does that have for the doctrine of original sin?

12. A non-Christian says to you, "The problem with you Reformed Christians is that you have such a negative view of people—original sin and all that. It's no wonder that Christians have been so hateful, bigoted, and violent through history. If you only had a positive view of people's goodness, you would learn to love." How do you respond?

21

The State of Sin, Part 3

Total Depravity and Inability

The corruption of sin is an iron fist, and we cannot deliver ourselves from its vise-like grip. In the Bible, sin is not merely a bad choice, but an evil power that rules and destroys—and even when its reign is broken, it still wages war. Perhaps worst of all, sin numbs the soul and blinds the eyes of the heart, so that sinners often perish while being quite pleased with themselves. Some of the worst sinners in history have been the most religious. As Andreas Rivetus (1573–1651) said, sin is "the disease which Satan tries to make incurable by hiding it."[1]

We must unmask sin and reckon with its force. We do not seek a knowledge of sin in a salacious manner, for it is shameful to speak of the things that men do in darkness. Rather, we expose evil by bringing it into the light of God's Word. The Christian approach to sin is a combination of contrition and combat. Sin is the great enemy, and it is within us all. Yet God has conquered sin through the death and resurrection of Jesus Christ. Christ came to save his people from their sin and to destroy the works of the Devil. Therefore, we may—indeed, we must—study sin with evangelical repentance and hope.

Total Depravity: The Corruption of Man's Whole Nature

Johannes Wollebius said, "Original sin consists not only of . . . the loss of the good originally given, but also the addition of the corresponding

---

1. Polyander, Walaeus, Thysius, and Rivetus, *Synopsis Purioris Theologiae*, 15.5 (1:353).

evil."[2] The spiritually dead walk under the influence of this world and its demonic ruler, seeking after whatever their rebellious minds and bodies desire (Eph. 2:1–3). Sinners are not just without fellowship with God, but are "alienated from the life of God" (4:18). This is "the old man," mankind in Adam, "which is corrupt according to the deceitful lusts" (v. 22). Man bears within himself the secret death of "enmity against God" (Rom. 8:7; cf. James 4:4). Human beings are enemies of God, his gospel, and godly people.[3] This depravity or corruption is total—that is, it poisons all human nature. William Perkins thus defined original sin as "a disorder or evil disposition in all the faculties and inclinations of man, whereby they are all carried inordinately against the law."[4] The Westminster Shorter Catechism (Q. 18) speaks of the "corruption of [man's] whole nature" to communicate the pervasive influence of sin throughout human life.[5]

The Depravity of the Heart

The stronghold of reigning sin is in the heart. We read in Genesis 6:5 that God perceived in man that "every imagination of the thoughts of his heart was only evil continually." Man's heart generates nothing but moral evil at all times. Thomas Boston commented, "All their wicked practices are here traced to the fountain and spring-head: a corrupt heart was the source of all. The soul, which was made upright in all its faculties, is now wholly disordered. The heart that was made according to God's own heart, is now the reverse of it, a forge of evil," so that "every inward motion" is "only evil."[6]

Jeremiah said, "The sin of Judah is written with a pen of iron, and with the point of a diamond: it is graven upon the table of their heart, and upon the horns of your altars" (Jer. 17:1). In contrast to the Ten Commandments, which were engraved in stone, sin and false worship are deeply etched into the human heart. John Mackay writes that Jeremiah's language "points to the deep-seated, incorrigible wickedness of the human heart."[7] Engraving in stone implies permanence: sin cannot be erased and replaced

---

2. Wollebius, *Compendium*, 1.10.(1).viii (70).
3. Rom. 5:8; 11:28; Phil. 3:18; Col. 1:21.
4. Perkins, *An Exposition of the Symbol*, in *Works*, 5:89. See Ames, *The Marrow of Theology*, 1.13.2 (120).
5. *Reformed Confessions*, 4:355.
6. Boston, *Human Nature in Its Fourfold State*, 61.
7. John L. Mackay, *Jeremiah: An Introduction and Commentary, Volume 1, Chapters 1–20*, Mentor Commentary (Fearn, Ross-shire, Scotland: Christian Focus, 2004), 508.

with covenant fidelity without a supernatural work of God (31:33). Eze-kiel said that people have a "whoring heart" that departs from the Lord and pursues idols (Ezek. 6:9 ESV).

It is common for people to think of sin in terms of wrongful actions, but the heart of sin is sin in the heart. The Lord wisely made the last of the Ten Commandments a prohibition not of criminal actions, but of evil desires (Ex. 20:17). It might be objected that sin is only sin when it involves a clear choice and an act of the will. Temptation presents us with choices, but it is not identical to sin, for our Lord Jesus was tempted by Satan, but never sinned (Matt. 4:1; Heb. 4:15). However, "all the motions" of our inward corruption, as the Westminster Confession (6.5) says, "are truly and properly sin (Rom. 7:5, 7–8, 25; Gal. 5:17)."[8] An evil desire or thought may engage our wills and thus be voluntary, even without a conscious decision on our part.[9] In Romans 7, the apostle Paul wrote of sin as an evil force that dwelt within him. David Clarkson analyzed Paul's words to identify indwelling sin as a forbidden evil (v. 7); a perverse evil and a fruitful evil (v. 8); a deceitful evil (v. 11); a debasing evil (v. 14); an unreasonable evil (v. 15); a positive evil; an intimate, inherent evil; and a permanent evil (v. 17); a watchful evil (v. 21); an imperious evil; a tyran-nical evil; and a rebellious, conflicting, warlike evil (v. 23); a powerful evil; a complete evil; a deadly evil; and a miserable evil (v. 24).[10]

Religious hypocrites focus on externals while neglecting the sins of the heart (Matt. 23:23–28). Christ said, "That which cometh out of the man, that defileth the man. For from within, out of the heart of men, proceed evil thoughts, adulteries, fornications, murders, thefts, covetousness, wick-edness, deceit, lasciviousness, an evil eye, blasphemy, pride, foolishness: all these evil things come from within, and defile the man" (Mark 7:20–23). Man's root problem is not his biological disorders, his parents, his friends, or his society, but his corrupt heart.

The Depravity of the Entire Life

The inner defilement of the heart contaminates the sinner's whole life. Job 14:4 queries, "Who can bring a clean thing out of an unclean? Not one." Consequently, we read in 15:14, "What is man, that he should be

8. *Reformed Confessions*, 4:242. See Turretin, *Institutes*, 9.2 (1:593–94).
9. Turretin, *Institutes*, 9.2.2 (1:593).
10. Clarkson, "Of Original Sin," in *Works*, 1:4. These are Clarkson's words, but selected and rearranged.

clean? And he which is born of a woman, that he should be righteous?" Fallen man is "abominable and filthy," and "drinketh iniquity like water" (v. 16).[11]

Sin corrupts men's speech, actions, relationships, purposes, and mindsets (Ps. 36:1–4; Rom. 3:13–18). Their desires have become evil lusts (James 4:1–4; 1 Pet. 2:11). Even the "conscience is defiled" (Titus 1:15). Mankind is "in the flesh," the fallen state of man without God's Spirit (Rom. 7:5–6; 8:9), and from this inherent corruption arise all actual sins that we commit, for they are "the works of the flesh" (Gal. 5:19–21). Although "flesh" can refer to the corruption of the body (2 Cor. 7:1; cf. Rom. 6:12; 8:12–13), it does not refer to the body alone, for man's mind and wisdom can be "fleshly" (2 Cor. 1:12; Col. 2:18), and the works of the flesh include mental sins such as anger and envy (Gal. 5:19–21).[12]

A wound to the soul might affect only part of its faculties, but the spiritual death of the soul entirely disables its every function in regard to God (Rom. 8:6–8). John Brown of Haddington (1722–1787) said, "All the powers of the accursed soul are dead while it liveth. The eyes of the understanding are shut, and, as it were glazed in a ghastly manner; the speech of cordial prayer and praise is laid [down]; the right pulse of affections towards God is stopped; every spiritual sense is locked up, and all within cold and stiff as a stone."[13]

The devastating effect of sin upon the mind is especially appalling. Since mankind rejected God, our thinking has become futile or worthless in spiritual matters (Rom. 1:21; Eph. 4:17). The most intelligent men are caught in spiritual stupidity as they ignore the Lord and worship idols (Ps. 92:5–6; Jer. 10:7–8, 14). Man cannot know God by his own wisdom (1 Cor. 1:21). Religious leaders may be highly trained in the Holy Scriptures, but if they lack God's grace, then they are blind guides.[14] The gospel message is foolish nonsense to sinners, even to the wise men of this world (vv. 18–20). In the state of fallen nature, "man receiveth not the things of the Spirit of God: for they are foolishness unto him" (2:14). We cannot trust in man, for that is to depart from the Lord (Jer. 17:5). We cannot follow our hearts, for they lead us into spiritual prostitution (Num. 15:39). Man, created to rule the animals, has become more foolish

---

11. On sin as the sinner's preferred food, see Prov. 9:17; 19:28; 20:17; Isa. 44:20.
12. Goodwin, *An Unregenerate Man's Guiltiness*, in *Works*, 10:43, 127–28.
13. Brown, *Systematic Theology*, 216.
14. Matt. 15:14; 23:16, 17, 19, 24, 26; Luke 6:39; cf. John 3:1–3, 10–12.

than the beasts.[15] Jeremiah said, "The heart is deceitful above all things, and desperately wicked: who can know it?" (Jer. 17:9). The mind of man was made to be his guiding light: "If therefore the light that is in thee be darkness, how great is that darkness!" (Matt. 6:23).

The doctrine of total depravity does not mean that every person is sinful to the greatest degree he could be (2 Tim. 3:13);[16] that people have no conscience and awareness of sin (Rom. 1:32; 2:14–15); that sinners lack all appreciation for moral and compassionate behavior (Acts 2:47); or that every sinner approves of every kind of sin (1 Cor. 5:1).[17] Total depravity means that corruption infects the whole person and stains every act he performs. Paul says that corruption infects the reasoning, the willing, and the feeling of man: "For we ourselves also were sometimes foolish, disobedient, deceived, serving divers lusts and pleasures, living in malice and envy, hateful, and hating one another" (Titus 3:3). Paul includes himself, though he had been a law-abiding Pharisee (Phil. 3:6).[18] Edward Reynolds illustrated this truth by saying that just as there is saltiness "in every drop of the sea . . . so is there sin in every faculty of man."[19] In the unbeliever, this pervasive depravity reigns (Rom. 5:21; cf. 6:14). Everything unbelievers do is sin (3:12–18), though their sins are of different kinds and different measures of heinousness (John 19:11). Some people are criminals and others are decent citizens, but still Isaiah 64:6 describes their sad condition: "All our righteousnesses are as filthy rags." Even the prayers and worship of an unrepentant sinner are abominations to God (Prov. 15:8; 28:9).

In light of this biblical teaching, we must reject the error of so-called "positive thinking" or the self-esteem gospel. Robert Schuller (1926–2015) redefined original sin as a lack of self-esteem: "We feel too unworthy. . . . By nature we are fearful, not bad. Original sin is not a mean streak; it is a nontrusting inclination."[20] Schuller apparently did not recognize that not trusting God is an insult to his veracity; unbelief is rebellion. A shift in the definition of sin brings a corresponding shift in the definition of

---

15. Prov. 6:6–8; Isa. 1:3; Jer. 8:7. See Boston, *Human Nature in Its Fourfold State*, 67.

16. Clark Pinnock evinces confusion at this point when he writes, "Does the Bible generally not leave us with the impression that one can progress in sin as in holiness, and that how total one's depravity is varies from person to person and is not a constant?" Clark H. Pinnock, "From Augustine to Arminius: A Pilgrimage to Theology," in Clark H. Pinnock, ed., *The Grace of God and the Will of Man* (Minneapolis: Bethany House, 1989), 22.

17. Berkhof, *Systematic Theology*, 246; and Barrett, *Salvation by Grace*, 40.

18. Boston, *Human Nature in Its Fourfold State*, 84.

19. Reynolds, *The Sinfulness of Sin*, in *Works*, 1:122.

20. Robert H. Schuller, *Self-Esteem: The New Reformation* (Waco, TX: Word, 1982), 67. See Reymond, *A New Systematic Theology of the Christian Faith*, 455.

salvation. Schuller wrote, "If the deepest curse of sin is what it does to our self-esteem, then the atoning power of the Cross is what it does to redeem our discarded self-worth."[21] Schuller said, "To be born again means that we must be changed from a negative to a positive self-image—from inferiority to self-esteem, from fear to love, from doubt to trust."[22] Here is a sad example of a classic doctrine reinterpreted to fit a popular but ill-conceived idea from modern culture. Against this false diagnosis of man's condition and false gospel, we must maintain the biblical truth that sin is rebellion against God, and this rebellion has so permeated human nature that our whole person is both disobedient and disorderly.

Spiritual death is worse than the absence of life; it is the presence of decay and disgusting defilement, the spiritual equivalent of a rotting corpse. Though our actual sins further provoke God's wrath (Eph. 5:6), it is our original sin that makes us by nature the objects of his fury (2:3). As Clarkson pointed out, actual sins violate specific commands of God's law at particular times, but original sin "is a violation of all God's commands at once," containing the roots and essence of all sin constantly in our very person.[23] As a result, John Calvin said, "no matter how splendid we may appear before men . . . God loathes us; we are damned and lost before him; the angels abhor us . . . and all things demand vengeance on us, because we defile them."[24]

Depravity still stains the total being of the believer, though God has given him a new inward principle of spiritual life that produces good works. The believer's best works are mixtures of righteousness and remaining sin that defiles the motives if not the acts themselves. Never in all his earthly days has he loved God with all his heart, soul, and might, but this is what God's law requires (Deut. 6:5). Even godly Isaiah had to cry out in the presence of the Holy One, "Woe is me! For I am undone; because I am a man of unclean lips, and I dwell in the midst of a people of unclean lips: for mine eyes have seen the King, the LORD of hosts" (Isa. 6:5). Therefore, even the believer's praises and good works must be offered up through Christ the Mediator, and by his perfect righteousness they are pleasing to God (Heb. 13:15–16).

---

21. Schuller, *Self-Esteem*, 101.
22. Schuller, *Self-Esteem*, 68.
23. Clarkson, "Of Original Sin," in *Works*, 1:8.
24. John Calvin, *Sermons on the Epistle to the Ephesians* (Edinburgh: Banner of Truth, 1973), 129.

Total Inability: The Dominion of Sin

Sin rules sinners with complete dominion. Christ gave this ominous warning to those with a superficial faith in him: "Verily, verily, I say unto you, Whosoever committeth sin is the servant of sin" (John 8:34). Though they might be physical descendants of Abraham, if the doing of sin characterized their lives, then they were not sons like Isaac, but slaves like Ishmael, who would be expelled from God's house (v. 35). The word translated in verse 34 as "servant" (*doulos*) may be translated as "slave" (ESV), the opposite of one who is "free" (v. 36). However, Christ did not speak of slavery against one's will here, but enslavement of the will. He said, "Ye are of your father the devil, and the lusts of your father ye will do," literally, "you choose to do" (*thelete poiein*, v. 44). Though these people were not consciously following Satan—they were, after all, outwardly pious, monotheistic Jews—nevertheless they chose to follow satanic ways by rejecting Christ's word, hating God's messengers, and loving Satan's lies. Voluntary slavery is the most terrifying bondage, for how can such slaves be set free? Christopher Love (1618–1651) said, "Unless the Son make you free, you are slaves indeed, slaves to sin, slaves to your lusts, slaves to the creatures, and slaves to the devil by whom you are taken captive at his will."[25]

When Adam first sinned, he turned from listening to God's word to listening to Satan's lies. Since then, man has been in bondage to the Devil (Heb. 2:14–15). Satan is "the ruler of this world" (John 12:31; 14:30; 16:11 ESV)—yes, even "the god of this world" (2 Cor. 4:4). Sinners are "of the devil," even "children of the devil" (1 John 3:8, 10). Human beings are in "the snare of the devil," and only God can deliver them by the gift of repentance (2 Tim. 2:25–26). The world is the Devil's kingdom, and he rules it with such power that men cannot escape unless one stronger than the Devil, the Son of God, defeats him (Luke 11:18–22; Col. 1:13).

In his epistle to the Romans, Paul describes sin as a power that reigns over those not yet saved through the death and resurrection of Christ. Paul writes of "both Jews and Gentiles, that they are all under sin" (Rom. 3:9; cf. Gal. 3:22). John Murray commented, "To be 'under sin' is to be under the dominion of sin."[26] Believers may rejoice to hear that "sin shall

---

25. Christopher Love, *The Naturall Mans Case Stated: or, an Exact Mapp of the Little World Man, Considered in Both His Capacities, Either in the State of Nature, or Grace* (London: by E. Cotes, for George Eversden, 1652), 61–62; modernized version: Christopher Love, *The Natural Man's Condition*, ed. Don Kistler (Orlando, FL: Northampton Press, 2012), 37.

26. Murray, *The Epistle to the Romans*, 1:102.

not have dominion over you," but those outside of Christ have no such freedom (Rom. 6:14, 17). Sin is their lord and master. They are "free from righteousness" (6:20), not that they have no moral obligation to obey God, but that righteousness has no effective influence in ruling their lives. Even the effect of God's law is only to provoke them to more sin (7:5, 7–13).

Therefore, we must reject Pelagianism and its proposal that people can deliver themselves from sin because of the power of their free will. Sadly, this error has infected some branches of evangelicalism. Charles Finney said, "The human will is free, therefore men have power or ability to do all their duty."[27] This is an astonishing claim, for it means that every person has the power to love God with all his heart, soul, and strength, and never to sin. Here we find unmixed Pelagianism of a kind that Jacob Arminius would have rejected. Finney said that "moral depravity" consists of "choice" and denied that depravity or sin is found in a state of nature or mind that lies behind choice.[28] Such a doctrine distorts our view of salvation. Finney said that once the Holy Spirit gives a sinner knowledge of the truth, the sinner is the active agent in regeneration, and so "regeneration consists in the sinner changing his ultimate choice."[29] Against this error, we must acknowledge that the Scriptures teach both man's free moral agency and man's enslavement to the ruling power of sin. Regeneration is a mighty work of deliverance by the triune God, not a mere choice or decision that a human being makes (Titus 3:3–6).

In light of man's spiritual death and enslavement to sin, theologians speak of fallen mankind's *total inability* to do good until God saves them through Christ. Ames said, "The bondage of sin consists in man's being so captivated by sin that he has no power to rise out of it," for "this bondage destroys . . . the power to perform acts spiritually good and acceptable."[30] The Holy Scriptures contain several statements that deny that a sinner "is able" (*dynatai*) to serve God. Unregenerate sinners are

---

27. Charles G. Finney, *Lectures on Systematic Theology: Embracing Ability, (Natural, Moral, and Gracious,) Repentance, Impenitence, Faith and Unbelief, Justification, Sanctification, Election, Reprobation, Divine Purposes, Divine Sovereignty, and Perseverance* (Oberlin, OH: James M. Fitch, 1847), 17.

28. Charles G. Finney, *Lectures on Systematic Theology: Embracing Lectures on Moral Government, Together with Atonement, Moral and Physical Depravity, Regeneration, Philosophical Theories, and Evidences of Regeneration* (Oberlin, OH: James M. Fitch, 1846), 450. Cited henceforth as Finney, *Lectures on Systematic Theology* (1846).

29. Finney, *Lectures on Systematic Theology* (1846), 497, 500. On Finney's view of sin and regeneration, see R. C. Sproul, *Willing to Believe: The Controversy over Free Will* (Grand Rapids, MI: Baker, 1997), 181–85.

30. Ames, *The Marrow of Theology*, 1.12.43–44 (119).

- *unable to speak what God counts as good.* Matthew 12:34, 37 says, "O generation of vipers, how can ye, being evil, speak good things? For out of the abundance of the heart the mouth speaketh. . . . By thy words thou shalt be condemned."
- *unable to obey God's law and please God.* Romans 8:7–8 says, "The carnal mind is enmity against God: for it is not subject to the law of God, neither indeed can be. So then they that are in the flesh cannot please God."
- *unable to be saved.* Matthew 19:25–26 says, "When his disciples heard it, they were exceedingly amazed, saying, Who then can be saved? But Jesus beheld them, and said unto them, With men this is impossible; but with God all things are possible."
- *unable to spiritually perceive or enter God's kingdom.* John 3:3, 5 says, "Except a man be born again, he cannot see the kingdom of God. . . . Except a man be born of water and of the Spirit, he cannot enter into the kingdom of God."
- *unable to listen to God's Word with an open mind.* John 8:43 says, "Why do ye not understand my speech? Even because ye cannot hear my word" (cf. Jer. 6:10).
- *unable to receive truth revealed by God's Spirit.* First Corinthians 2:14 says, "But the natural man receiveth not the things of the Spirit of God: for they are foolishness unto him: neither can he know them, because they are spiritually discerned."
- *unable to come to Christ in faith.* John 6:65 says, "No man can come unto me, except it were given unto him of my Father" (cf. v. 44).
- *unable to believe in Christ for salvation.* John 12:39–40 says, "Therefore they could not believe, because that Esaias said again, He hath blinded their eyes, and hardened their heart; that they should not see with their eyes, nor understand with their heart, and be converted, and I should heal them."
- *unable to confess from the heart that Jesus is Lord.* First Corinthians 12:3 says, "No man can say that Jesus is the Lord, but by the Holy Ghost."
- *unable to receive the Holy Spirit.* John 14:17 says, "Even the Spirit of truth; whom the world cannot receive, because it seeth him not, neither knoweth him: but ye know him; for he dwelleth with you, and shall be in you."

• *unable to bear good fruit that glorifies God.* John 15:5 says, "I am the vine, ye are the branches: he that abideth in me, and I in him, the same bringeth forth much fruit: for without me ye can do nothing."

Fallen man is so ruled by sin that he is unable to respond rightly to God's law or the gospel. Though sinners have eyes, they are blind to God's greatness and goodness; though they have ears, they are deaf to his Word.[31] Like Samson, they have "fallen into the hands of our grand adversary," and he has put out the eyes of their hearts.[32] This is God's judgment upon mankind for turning away from him (Rom. 11:7–10): their hearts are unresponsive and their eyes blind.[33] Reynolds observed that this does not prevent sinners from understanding the "grammatical construction" of the Bible's sentences, but it does blind them to "the spiritual light and beauty of the Word."[34] They will remain in this state until God gives them new hearts with new spiritual perception and new love for him (Deut. 29:4; 30:6).

The doctrine of total inability contradicts the teaching that unsaved men have the ability to choose God when assisted by his grace. Arminians say that the human will always stands in a position of indifference, so it can will either good or evil. Arminius wrote, "Herein consisteth the liberty of the will, that all things required to enable it to will any thing being accomplished, it still remains indifferent to will or not."[35] Here Arminius used the definition posited by Roman Catholic philosopher Luis de Molina (1535–1600)[36] and adopted by Molina's fellow Jesuit theologians.[37] Arminius affirmed the semi-Pelagian principle that God's grace seeks a willing response from all men and grants further

---

31. Deut. 28:28–29; Pss. 58:4; 115:4–8; 135:15–18; Isa. 42:18–19; 43:8; 56:10; 59:9–13; Matt. 15:14; 23:16–17, 19, 24, 26; Luke 4:18; 6:39; John 9:39; Rom. 11:7; 2 Cor. 3:14; 4:4; 1 John 2:11; Rev. 3:17.

32. Boston, *Human Nature in Its Fourfold State*, 79.

33. Isa. 6:9–10, cited in Matt. 13:14–15; Mark 4:12; Luke 8:10; John 12:37–41; Acts 28:26–27.

34. Reynolds, *The Sinfulness of Sin*, in *Works*, 1:103.

35. "Libertas arbitrii consistit in eo, quod homo positis omnibus requisitis ad volendum vel nolendum, indifferens tamen sit ad volendum vel nolendum." Jacobus Arminius, *Articuli nonnulli diligenti examine perpendi* (c. 1620), 11, available at https://reader.digitale-sammlungen.de/resolve/display/bsb10945232.html; English translation in John Owen, *A Display of Arminianism*, in *Works*, 10:117. See Arminius, *Certain Articles*, 6.9, in *Works*, 2:487.

36. Luis de Molina, *Concordia*, 1.2.3, cited in Alexander Aichele, "The Real Possibility of Freedom," in *A Companion to Luis de Molina*, ed. Matthias Kaufmann and Alexander Aichele (Leiden: Brill, 2014), 5.

37. See Gisbertus Voetius, *Disputatio philosophico-theologica, continens quaestiones duas, de Distinctione Attributorum divinorum, et Libertate Voluntatis*, in *Reformed Thought on Freedom*, 148–50.

grace "to those who do what is in them," as taught by medieval nominalist theologian Gabriel Biel.[38] In such a view, the freedom of the will includes the "power of resisting the Holy Spirit" and nullifying his saving call.[39]

Since such a view of the human will grants it the power to stop God's will, Martin Luther said that theologians who teach it are "attributing divinity to free choice."[40] After God has done all that he can, man remains in control of the outcome. This contradicts the teaching of our Lord, who said, "All that the Father giveth me shall come to me," and, "No man can come to me, except the Father which hath sent me draw him" (John 6:37, 44). John Owen accused the Arminians of making an "idol" out of free will by granting it supremacy over the Holy Spirit.[41]

Some theologians, such as Jonathan Edwards, distinguished between natural ability and moral ability, saying that fallen man has natural ability because he retains the faculties of the soul, but lacks moral ability because of sin's corruption.[42] This distinction was found previously in the modified Reformed theology of John Cameron (1580–1625) and Moise Amyraut (1596–1664). However, most Reformed theologians have not favored it. Natural and moral ability are not opposites; our inability is both natural and moral. "Natural inability" is fitting because "by nature" all men are, from birth, in a state of sin (Eph. 2:3), not by their choices, experiences, or habits developed over time. If we say that man retains natural ability, then we may be suggesting that man has power in himself to believe the gospel and love God without a regeneration of human nature. Though Edwards did not intend to communicate this error, his choice of words is confusing. We do better to teach *total inability*, while also teaching that aspects of God's image remain in fallen human nature.[43] Man still has a will that

38. Richard A. Muller, "Grace, Elections, and Contingent Choice: Arminius's Gambit and the Reformed Response," in *The Grace of God, the Bondage of the Will*, ed. Thomas R. Schreiner and Bruce A. Ware, 2 vols. (Grand Rapids, MI: Baker, 1995), 2:261.

39. Arminius, cited in Owen, *A Display of Arminianism*, in *Works*, 10:117. See Arminius, *Certain Articles*, 17.5, in *Works*, 2:497.

40. Luther, *The Bondage of the Will*, in *LW*, 33:106–7, cited in Matthew Barrett, "The Bondage and Liberation of the Will," in *Reformation Theology: A Systematic Summary*, ed. Matthew Barrett (Wheaton, IL: Crossway, 2017), 459.

41. Owen, *A Display of Arminianism*, in *Works*, 10:115–17.

42. Edwards, *The Freedom of the Will*, in *WJE*, 1:159.

43. Bavinck, *Reformed Dogmatics*, 3:121–22; Hodge, *Systematic Theology*, 2:260–67; Hodge, *Outlines of Theology*, 340–42; Vos, *Reformed Dogmatics*, 58–60; and Berkhof, *Systematic Theology*, 247–48.

freely chooses—a point that we will examine in more detail in the next chapter. However, that will is so corrupt that it is unable to do anything that seeks, trusts, obeys, or pleases God.

The Canons of Dort (Head 3/4, Art. 3) summarize mankind's enslavement to sin: "All men are conceived in sin, and by nature children of wrath, incapable of saving good, prone to evil, dead in sin, and in bondage thereto, and without the regenerating grace of the Holy Spirit, they are neither able nor willing to return to God, to reform the depravity of their nature, or to dispose themselves to reformation."[44]

It might be objected that if man has no ability to turn to God or to do good, then he has no free will, and God would not be just to command and judge sinners. According to this view of freedom, "An agent is free when he could have chosen to do otherwise than he did."[45] If God does not at least supply what each person needs to be saved if he so chooses, then God is unjust.[46] This is an old Pelagian argument.[47]

In reply, we note that the Word of God teaches both human responsibility and human inability to please God apart from saving grace. Furthermore, Reformed theologians make a distinction regarding freedom. Wollebius wrote, "The will remains free from coercion, but not free to choose between good and evil. The will has been made so evil that it is better described as enslaved than as free."[48] People are morally accountable because they do as they choose and choose as they please, but they are so corrupt that only sin pleases them.[49]

God's law does not teach us about our ability, but about our obligation. It does not say, "You can," but, "You should." God wrote his law upon the human conscience when he created man in righteousness, and it suited man perfectly (Eccles. 7:29; Rom. 2:14–15). Though man has changed for the worse, God's law has not changed. Though unconverted sinners cannot obey the law, it still serves to show them their sin (Rom. 3:20).

---

44. *The Three Forms of Unity*, 141.
45. Bruce R. Reichenbach, "Freedom, Justice, and Moral Responsibility," in *The Grace of God and the Will of Man*, ed. Pinnock, 285.
46. Reichenbach, "Freedom, Justice, and Moral Responsibility," in *The Grace of God and the Will of Man*, ed. Pinnock, 289. Reichenbach argues on the basis of his concept of distributive justice, which he distinguishes from retributive justice. Essentially, he views God as bound by justice to exercise a prescribed level of goodness to all sinners.
47. Robert F. Evans, *Pelagius: Inquiries and Reappraisals* (New York: Seabury, 1968), 100–101, 104; and Karen C. Huber, "The Pelagian Heresy: Observations on Its Social Context" (PhD diss., Oklahoma State University, 1979), 59–60.
48. Wollebius, *Compendium*, 1.10.(1).xix–xx (71).
49. On the topic of free will, see the next chapter.

It might also be objected that human beings still do much good to each other and engage in noble acts of courage and compassion. In reply, we recognize that there is a kind of love that remains in humanity, an extension of self-love to others who are like us or who treat us well, but Christ taught that this love is common among sinners and does not please God: "For if ye love them which love you, what thank have ye? For sinners also love those that love them. And if ye do good to them which do good to you, what thank have ye? For sinners also do even the same. And if ye lend to them of whom ye hope to receive, what thank have ye? For sinners also lend to sinners, to receive as much again" (Luke 6:32–34). The Canons of Dort (Head 3/4, Art. 4) explain the domestic and civic virtues of the wicked as follows:

> There remain, however, in man since the fall, the glimmerings of natural light, whereby he retains some knowledge of God, of natural things, and of the differences between good and evil, and discovers some regard for virtue, good order in society, and for maintaining an orderly external deportment. But so far is this light of nature from being sufficient to bring him to a saving knowledge of God and to true conversion, that he is incapable of using it aright even in things natural and civil. Nay, further, this light, such as it is, man in various ways renders wholly polluted and holds it in unrighteousness, by doing which he becomes inexcusable before God.[50]

When Christians speak of total depravity and total inability, we do not speak on the level of common ethical behavior, but the holy standard of God's law.[51] Boston pointed out that the assertion of fallen man's goodness would shatter if people had their eyes opened to the spiritual demands of the moral law, as in Christ's Sermon on the Mount. Natural man's piety, morality, and self-discipline cannot approach true righteousness (Matt. 5:20). When the Spirit powerfully applies God's law to the heart to expose inward corruptions—such as malicious anger, sexual lust, the abuse of religion to seek the honor of man instead of God, and the love of earthly treasures instead of heavenly ones—men sense their need for God's sovereign grace to take the chains of sin off their free will.[52]

---

50. *The Three Forms of Unity*, 141.
51. Bavinck, *Reformed Dogmatics*, 3:122–23.
52. Boston, *Human Nature in Its Fourfold State*, 97.

Therefore, man in the state of sin, though he may be outwardly civilized, is a slave of sin and an enemy of God. Though he still has all the faculties of human nature that God gave him at creation, he is so empty of spiritual goodness and so corrupted by sin that he is unable to serve God acceptably. Furthermore, he does not regret this or grieve over his sins, except insofar as they bring him trouble. If God were to come down from heaven and teach man about righteousness, sin, and salvation, man would do everything in his power to destroy God. We see this nowhere more clearly than in the crucifixion of Jesus Christ.

The Amazing Patience and Mercy of God to Sinners

Though people's acts of charity and decency do not lessen their depravity, inability, and offensiveness to God, the Lord still treats the wicked with amazing patience and mercy. God hates them with great anger for their sins (Ps. 5:5; Rom. 1:18), but out of the wealth of his goodness, he showers kindness upon them to lead them to repentance (Acts 14:15–17; Rom. 2:4). Even as Christ anticipated that the people of Jerusalem would murder him cruelly on the cross, he cried out in compassion, "How often would I have gathered thy children together, even as a hen gathereth her chickens under her wings, and ye would not!" (Matt. 23:37).

The doctrine of sin's dominion should deeply affect us and stir us to seek Christ. Perkins said, "We must never be at rest till we have some assurance in conscience that in Christ we have freedom from this bondage, and can . . . give thanks that we are delivered from the power of darkness, and translated into the kingdom of Christ." This is the only reasonable response, for "the spiritual thralldom under sin is of all miseries most loathsome and burdensome."[53]

How Christians should pity the nations! Though guilty and culpable, they are also miserable and helpless. We should hate their sins and oppose their acts of injustice, but let us also be like Jesus, who "was moved with compassion on them, because they fainted, and were scattered abroad, as sheep having no shepherd" (Matt. 9:36). Let us who are saved by grace remember that we were once just as the lost are now: dead in sin, driven along by satanic lies and selfish ambition, damned under God's wrath, and

---

53. Perkins, *An Exposition of the Symbol*, in *Works*, 5:94.

distant from the Savior and any hope of salvation (Eph. 2:1–3, 12). Let us pour out our fervent prayers for God to send them gospel preachers and open their eyes (Matt. 9:37–38; Acts 26:16–18). And, as much as God providentially allows us according to our gifts and callings, let us speak the truth in love to them, for God's Word is God's means of giving life to the dead.

Most of all, we should praise God for saving sinners from this horrible state of sin. The doctrine of sin provides the dark background for "the praise of the glory of his grace" (Eph. 1:6). For when God's elect were "dead in sins," he made them alive with Christ because he is "rich in mercy" and loved them with "his great love" (2:4–5). Without the doctrine of original sin, we will presume upon God's love, for we view ourselves as lovable. Humbled under the weight of our disobedience and defilement, however, we Christians will marvel that God loved us and saved us through his Son.

Sing to the Lord

Confessing Original and Actual Sin

God be merciful to me,
On Thy grace I rest my plea;
Plenteous in compassion Thou,
Blot out my transgressions now;
Wash me, make me pure within,
Cleanse, O cleanse me from my sin.

My transgression I confess,
Grief and guilt my soul oppress;
I have sinned against Thy grace
And provoked Thee to Thy face;
I confess Thy judgment just,
Speechless, I Thy mercy trust.

I am evil, born in sin;
Thou desirest truth within.
Thou alone my Saviour art,
Teach Thy wisdom to my heart;
Make me pure, Thy grace bestow,
Wash me whiter than the snow.

Broken, humbled to the dust
By Thy wrath and judgment just,
Let my contrite heart rejoice
And in gladness hear Thy voice;
From my sins O hide Thy face,
Blot them out in boundless grace.

Psalm 51
Tune: Ajalon
The Psalter, No. 140
Trinity Hymnal—Baptist Edition, No. 415

Questions for Meditation or Discussion

1. What Scripture passages testify that the human heart is corrupted by sin?
2. Why is the corruption of the heart so significant for our spiritual state?
3. How would you demonstrate from the Bible that sin has corrupted man's entire nature?
4. How did Robert Schuller redefine sin? What implications does his view have?
5. How do the Holy Scriptures reveal that fallen man is enslaved to the Devil?
6. What is the doctrine of total inability? Prove it from the Bible.
7. How can we answer the objection that the doctrine of total inability contradicts the free will of all mankind and thus implies that God cannot justly judge men for their sins?
8. How can we answer the objection that the doctrine of total inability fails to account for the many good deeds that unconverted people perform?
9. How do the doctrines of total depravity and total inability highlight the marvelous goodness, patience, and mercy of God?
10. When you consider your own depravity and inability by nature, how are you moved to give thanks and praise to God?

Questions for Deeper Reflection

11. What does it mean to say that sin is an "evil disposition" or a "habitual deviation" of human nature? Why is it important to assert

this rather than saying that human nature itself is sin or that sin is a substance in human nature?

12. How has sin affected man's mind and thinking? What implications does this have for teaching and preaching the truth of God? How should this motivate us to pray? How much do you pray for God's grace to empower the ministry of the Word?

22

The Free Choice of the Will

Sin's dominion raises questions about man's liberty, will, moral agency, and responsibility. The freedom of the will properly pertains to the doctrine of man, but we have chosen to treat it under the doctrine of sin because our great questions regarding human liberty pertain to man's present state as an unregenerate sinner or as a redeemed but imperfect saint.

The doctrine of free will is a difficult horse to ride because it is easy to fall off to the right or to the left. On the one hand, we can slip into a complete denial of free moral agency. Since ancient times, some philosophers have argued that our freedom and responsibility are illusions in a fatalistic world. In the modern world, many secular scientists are inclined to attribute all human activity to the chemical processes of the brain, thus denying that human beings have souls and free will. As a result, modern secular society finds itself caught on the horns of a dilemma: it thinks there is no basis to believe in freedom, but such notions are necessary if people are to function responsibly in society.[1] Against such deterministic or fatalistic notions, the orthodox Christian faith has historically affirmed that human beings have wills, make real choices, and are morally accountable to God for them.

On the other hand, we can fall off the horse on the other side by attributing a kind of divinity to the human will so that man is his own lord. No matter what God may decree or how sinful a person may become, some argue that man retains an equal power to choose good or evil, and

---

1. Stephen Cave, "There's No Such Thing as Free Will: But We're Better Off Believing in It Anyway," *The Atlantic* (June 2016), https://www.theatlantic.com/magazine/archive/2016/06/theres-no-such-thing-as-free-will/480750/.

thus has the ability to conquer sin or to thwart God's will. Against this libertarian error, the orthodox Christian faith affirms that human beings are always under the sovereignty of God. Furthermore, man's moral state is never one of absolute liberty, but each person is either a slave to sin or a servant of God.

The Terminology and Concept of Free Will

When we consider this matter, we need to examine our philosophical assumptions by God's Word, lest we read into the Holy Scriptures teachings not actually found there. What does the Bible actually say about freedom and will? What does "free will" mean in the theological tradition of the Christian church?

The Biblical Terminology of Freedom and Will

The Bible often speaks of the act of choosing and has various words to express this: to "choose" (Hebrew *bakhar*, Greek *eklegomai*), to "will" or "desire" (Hebrew *abah*, Greek *thelō*), and related verbs for desire, delight, intention, and purpose. There can be no doubt that human beings engage in volitional acts and make real choices. However, the New Testament does not frequently speak of the human "will" (Greek *thelēma*), and when it does, it refers to a concrete choice, desire, or act of the will, not an abstract faculty of the soul.[2] We see the same emphasis on concrete choices or desires where this Greek term is used in the Septuagint version of the Old Testament to render Hebrew terms such as "pleasure" (*khephets*; e.g., Isa. 44:28) and "desire" (*ratson*; e.g., Ps. 145:19).

The Bible does not attribute the source of human decisions to an abstract will so much as to the "heart," which is the center of human life, the seat of our thoughts, desires, and intentions, and the source of our words and deeds (Prov. 4:23; Mark 7:21). People who act voluntarily do so out of "a willing heart" (*nedib leb*, Ex. 35:5, 22; 2 Chron. 29:31). Sinners "devise" or "plan" (*kharash*) evil in their hearts (Prov. 6:14, 18).[3] This verb means to fabricate,[4] suggesting that the heart is like an industrial center that manufactures sin.[5]

---

2. Matt. 21:31; Luke 12:47; 22:42; 23:25; John 1:13; 1 Cor. 7:37; 16:12; Eph. 2:3; 2 Pet. 1:21.
3. Cf. 1 Sam. 23:9; Prov. 3:29; 12:20; 14:22.
4. Gen. 4:22; 1 Kings 7:14; Jer. 17:1; cf. the cognate noun "craftsman" in Ex. 28:11; Deut. 27:15; 1 Sam. 13:19; 2 Sam. 5:11; Isa. 44:11–13; etc.
5. Goodwin, *The Vanity of Thoughts*, in *Works*, 3:511.

All human beings have a responsibility to direct their hearts to the Lord and his revelation.[6] Since man's thoughts and choices flow out of his heart, this responsibility implies that the heart has a kind of self-direction, and thus responsibility. Man's moral accountability to God is expressed as the Lord's searching and trying of the heart.[7] The Scriptures never represent the human heart as suspended in moral indifference between good and evil, but as inherently inclined to wickedness or righteousness (Gen. 6:5; Pss. 73:1; 125:4). Christ said, "A good man out of the good treasure of the heart bringeth forth good things: and an evil man out of the evil treasure bringeth forth evil things" (Matt. 12:35).

We must also consider how the biblical writers used terms for freedom and liberty. Hebrew terms for freedom operate in the conceptual realms of prosperity and political-legal liberty, not what modern writers think of as the freedom of the will. One root means to "release" (*khaphash*) from bondage or the obligation of servitude.[8] Another word (*deror*) means "liberty" in the sense of release from slavery, as in the year of jubilee.[9] The references to "freewill offerings" (Lev. 22:18; etc.) do not involve any Hebrew word for "free," but translate a single word meaning "willingness, voluntariness" (*nedabah*; cf. Ps. 110.3, Hos. 14:4).[10] There is no explicit reference in the Old Testament to the freedom of the will.

The New Testament employs a Greek word group (*eleutheros, eleutheria, eleutheroō*) that can refer to liberty from legal obligation or slavery.[11] The same word group also refers to the spiritual liberty of the Christian (Gal. 5:1). Christian freedom consists of release from the obligation to keep the old covenant ceremonial laws (1 Cor. 9:19; Gal. 2:4; 5:1) and deliverance from bondage to the reigning power of sin so that the Christian may serve God in righteousness.[12] Thus, the New Testament takes the Old Testament concept of liberty from bondage and translates it into the realm of spiritual redemption from bondage to sin.[13] This inward spiritual

---

6. 1 Sam. 7:3; 2 Chron. 12:14; 19:3; 20:33; 30:19; Ezra 7:10; Job 11:13; Pss. 57:7; 78:8; 90:12; 108:1; 112:7; Prov. 22:17; 23:12.

7. 1 Chron. 28:9; 29:17; Pss. 7:9; 44:21; Jer. 11:20; 17:10; 20:12; Rev. 2:23.

8. Ex. 21:2; Lev. 19:20; Deut. 15:12; Isa. 58:6; Jer. 34:9–16.

9. Lev. 25:10; Isa. 61:1; Jer. 34:8, 15, 17; Ezek. 46:17.

10. The term translated as "liberty" (*rakhab*) in Ps. 119:45 refers to a broad or spacious place as opposed to the confinement of distress.

11. Matt. 17:26; Rom. 7:3; 1 Cor. 7:21–22; 12:13; Eph. 6:8; Col. 3:11; Rev. 6:15; 13:16.

12. John 8:31–36; Rom. 6:18, 20, 22; 8:2; 2 Cor. 3:17–18.

13. D. A. Carson, *The Gospel According to John*, The Pillar New Testament Commentary (Grand Rapids, MI: Eerdmans, 1991), 350.

freedom is a privilege of God's sons.[14] However, it is not the absolute power of independent self-determination, but the power to choose and do good as a faithful son of God who lives by God's Spirit.

We conclude that the Scriptures do not focus on the will as the center of human self-direction and do not use the language of "freedom" to describe the power of the will to choose good or evil. Instead, the biblical writers focus on the heart as the control center of a man and use "freedom" to describe release from bondage, whether to civil law or to spiritual enslavement. We must be careful not to read concepts of the liberty of the will into biblical statements about will or freedom that pertain to legal or spiritual freedom. Furthermore, if Christians do not embrace the term "free will," no one should accuse them of being unbiblical or heretical,[15] so long as they acknowledge the biblical truths that human beings act voluntarily from their hearts according to their own perceptions and desires; people are responsible and morally accountable to God; and preachers should address them with exhortations, promises, appeals, and warnings, and not treat them like passive blocks of stone.

Talking of free will easily leads to misunderstanding. If we affirm it without qualification, then we may lead people into Pelagianism and undermine the truth of salvation by grace alone. John Calvin did not wish to quarrel about words, but warned, "How few men are there, I ask, who when they hear free will attributed to man do not immediately conceive him to be master of both his own mind and will, able of his own power to turn himself toward either good or evil?"[16] If, on the other hand, we deny free will without qualification, then we may encourage fatalism and antinomianism, and undermine the doctrine of human responsibility to God. However, since the term "free will" is embedded in modern culture and the theological traditions of Christendom, we cannot avoid it. We must define it and explain it biblically.

The Philosophical and Theological Concept of Free Will

Philosophers have debated the meaning of human choice and freedom since ancient times. The Greeks used the term *autexousia* (self-authority or

---

14. John 8:35–36; Rom. 8:2, 14–15, 21; Gal. 4:7, 30–31.
15. Martin Luther seemed to deny the freedom of the will categorically. Luther, *The Bondage of the Will*, 104, 148–49 (*WA*, 18:635–36, 670–71). However, he probably intended to do so only with respect to spiritual righteousness, not civic righteousness and public decency. See the Augsburg Confession (Art. 18), in *The Book of Concord*, 51.
16. Calvin, *Institutes*, 2.2.7.

self-determination) and the Romans *liberum arbitrium* (free judgment or free choice) and *voluntas* (will, intention, or desire). Some Greek philosophers, such as the Stoics, taught determinism or fatalism, the belief that all things that happen do so necessarily and cannot be otherwise. Aristotle's view is disputed, but it appears that he did not teach determinism, but gave place to contingency in his philosophy.[17]

Aristotle also discussed what it means to have a will. He said that "choice" is "a deliberate appetition of things that lie in our power."[18] In other words, the will of man involves both the reasoning to consider possible goals and deliberate about which is best, and the appetite or desire for what is perceived as good, for every purpose and aim seeks after some good.[19] When rational judgment and desire coincide, a choice has been made. Aristotle's definition of the will influenced Christian theologians such as Thomas Aquinas, Calvin, and Francis Turretin.[20]

Though the words *free will* are not expressly used in the Bible, the idea of free will does have an important place in the Christian theological tradition and can be useful, as Turretin said, if rightly defined.[21] Augustine used the language of free will but clarified it when he wrote, "There is . . . always within us a free will—but it is not always good."[22] R. C. Sproul explained, "We can have a good free will or an evil free will."[23] How can we speak of free will without contradicting the biblical view that unregenerate sinners are in bondage to sin, and spiritual freedom in Christ consists of the ability to serve God with a willing heart?

It may surprise people to know that the Reformed tradition has often affirmed the freedom of the will. Calvin said, "If freedom is opposed to coercion, I both acknowledge and consistently maintain that choice is free, and I hold anyone who thinks otherwise to be a heretic."[24] Heinrich Bullinger wrote in the Second Helvetic Confession (chap. 9), "But in outward things, no man denies but that both the regenerate and unregenerate have their free will. . . . So he may speak or keep silence; go out of his house or

---

17. Richard A. Muller, *Divine Will and Human Choice: Freedom, Contingency, and Necessity in Early Modern Reformed Thought* (Grand Rapids, MI: Baker Academic, 2017), 87–103.
18. Aristotle, *Ethics*, 3.3 (120); cf. 6.2 (205–6).
19. Aristotle, *Ethics*, 1.1 (63).
20. Aquinas, *Summa Theologica*, Pt. 2.1, Q. 13, Art. 1; Calvin, *Institutes*, 1.15.7; and Turretin, *Institutes*, 10.1.4; 10.2.7 (1:660, 663).
21. Turretin, *Institutes*, 10.1.3 (1:660).
22. Augustine, *On Grace and Free Will*, 31.15, in *NPNF*[1], 5:456.
23. Sproul, *Willing to Believe*, 62.
24. Calvin, *The Bondage and Liberation of the Will*, 68.

abide within."[25] Girolamo Zanchi said, "Man after the Fall, although he is made both slave of sin, and bound to many miseries, still has not lost altogether all freedom of choice, but he always retains one that is natural for him."[26] William Ames wrote that "the freedom of the will [is] essential to man's nature," even in the "bondage" of sin.[27] John Owen said, "We grant man, in the substance of all his actions, as much power, liberty, and freedom as a mere created nature is capable of. We grant him to be free in his choice of all outward coaction [compulsion], or inward natural necessity, to work according to election [choice] and deliberation, spontaneously embracing what seemeth good unto him."[28] Turretin insisted, "We establish free will far more truly than our opponents."[29]

The Westminster Confession of Faith (9.1) says, "God hath endued the will of man with that natural liberty, that it is neither forced, nor, by any absolute necessity of nature, determined to good, or evil (Matt. 17:12; James 1:14; Deut. 30:19)."[30] There is a kind of liberty built into human nature ("natural liberty") without which man ceases to be a rational agent—that is, ceases to be man.[31] Human beings make real choices and should be exhorted to make right choices.

The Westminster Confession also avoids determinism, in which a person's choices are completely preset "by any absolute necessity of nature." In other words, what a man wills is not the mere consequence of his nature, experiences, and circumstances, as if he were a machine or robot, or the consequence of a natural instinct like that of an animal. Calvin said, "We do not, with the Stoics, contrive a necessity out of the perpetual connection and intimately related series of causes, which is contained in nature."[32] Rather, the choices of the will arise spontaneously from within the heart after the person has perceived the situation and made a judgment about what is good.[33]

What Reformed theologians do not say, however, is that the will of man is independent of God's will and can frustrate the will of God, for the Bible

25. *Reformed Confessions*, 2:824.
26. Zanchi, *De primi hominis lapsu*, 1.6.1, in *Reformed Thought on Freedom*, 64.
27. Ames, *The Marrow of Theology*, 1.12.44 (119).
28. Owen, *A Display of Arminianism*, in *Works*, 10:116.
29. Turretin, *Institutes*, 10.1.3 (1:660).
30. *Reformed Confessions*, 4:246.
31. Turretin, *Institutes*, 10.3.11 (1:667).
32. Calvin, *Institutes*, 1.16.8.
33. Turretin, *Institutes*, 10.2.5; 10.3.10 (1:662, 667). See Cunningham, *The Reformers and the Theology of the Reformation*, 499–500.

teaches the opposite (Ps. 33:10–11; Prov. 21:1). The Reformed doctrine of free choice is all the more striking when seen in combination with the Reformed doctrine of God's sovereignty.[34] The Westminster Confession (3.1) states that God decreed "whatsoever comes to pass: yet so, as thereby neither is God the author of sin, nor is violence offered to the will of the creatures; nor is the liberty or contingency of second causes taken away, but rather established."[35] God's decree and providence determine what will come to pass, but this necessity does not force men to make particular choices contrary to their preferences any more than God is forced to be good, though he is necessarily good.[36] God's providence operates with omnipotent power in a manner consistent with human will and incomprehensible to human understanding. The Westminster Confession (5.2) says that God's providence ensures that God's decree will "come to pass immutably, and infallibly (Acts 2:23)," yet through "second causes" that may be free or contingent in themselves.[37] Indeed, Reformed theologians insist that man's free will is not only compatible with God's sovereign will but completely dependent on it, for God is the Creator and man the creature.[38] Only God has absolute freedom of will (Ps. 115:3); man's liberty of will is a finite image of God's.

What then is human free will? We may define it as the soul's capacity to choose what it judges to be good, without external compulsion or internal necessity.[39] No one forces it, and it is not mechanical or automatic, but it is a personal ability to will what a man perceives in his heart to be good.

Free Will in the Fourfold State of Man

Augustine's teaching that our will is always free but not always good points to an important factor in considering this doctrine: the changing

---

34. On the doctrines of God's decree and providence, see *RST*, 1:957–1105 (chaps. 48–53).

35. *Reformed Confessions*, 4:238.

36. John Bradford, *A Treatise of Election and Free-Will*, in *The Writings of John Bradford, Volume 1, Sermons, Meditations, Examinations, Etc.*, ed. Aubrey Townsend for the Parker Society (Cambridge: Cambridge University Press, 1848), 213. See also Paul Helm, *John Calvin's Ideas* (Oxford: Oxford University Press, 2004), 151–52.

37. *Reformed Confessions*, 4:240.

38. Zanchi, *De primi hominis lapsu*, 1.6.1, in *Reformed Thought on Freedom*, 65.

39. Cf. Girolamo Zanchi, *De operibus Dei intra spatium sex dierum creatis* (1591), 3.3.3, in *Reformed Thought on Freedom*, 55; *De primi hominis lapsu*, 1.6.1, in *Reformed Thought on Freedom*, 73; Franciscus Junius, *Theses Theologicae* (Leyden, 1592), 22.17, in *Reformed Thought on Freedom*, 100; Owen, *A Display of Arminianism*, in *Works*, 10:119; and Turretin, *Institutes*, 10.1.2 (1:660).

state of man through redemptive history.[40] Augustinian theologians developed the idea of a fourfold state of man.[41] Zanchi said, "Since there are four states of man: before the Fall, after the Fall, under grace, and in glory; so it is customary to dispute on his free choice in a fourfold way."[42] Thomas Boston went so far as to say these four states are "things very necessary to be known by all that would see heaven."[43]

1. The State of Innocence: Changeable Ability to Choose God

Our consideration of man's states begins with his creation. The Westminster Confession (9.2) says, "Man, in his state of innocency, had freedom and power to will and to do that which was good and well pleasing to God (Eccles. 7:29; Gen. 1:26); but yet, mutably, so that he might fall from it (Gen. 2:16–17; 3:6),"[44] Although the Genesis account of man's creation and fall does not mention the "will," it does have significant implications for it. The covenant with Adam presented either life or death to man, contingent upon his obedience or disobedience. Calvin said, "In this integrity man by free will had the power, if he so willed, to attain eternal life." Adam was responsible for his sin: "he fell solely by his own will."[45]

Man was "very good" in this state, for "God created man in his own image" (Gen. 1:27, 31). This image included knowledge, righteousness, and holiness (Eph. 4:24; Col. 3:10), so that man was morally "upright" (Eccles. 7:29).[46] God created man in such a state that man was righteous and could do righteousness. His will, as one faculty of his righteous soul, "was disposed," according to Boston, "by its original make, to follow the Creator's will." It was not a will of indifference, but a good will. Boston wrote, "It was not left in an equal balance to good and evil: for at that rate he had not been upright, nor habitually conformed to the law; which in no moment can allow the creature not to be inclined towards God as his chief end, any more than it can allow man to be a god to himself."[47]

---

40. Augustine, *On Grace and Free Will*, 31.15, in NPNF[1], 5:456.
41. Lombard, *The Sentences*, 2.25.5–6 (2:118); Wollebius, *Compendium*, 1.8.xii (65); and Turretin, *Institutes*, 8.1.9 (1:571). This concept was introduced in chap. 1 in the discussion of how the Christian faith approaches anthropology in a redemptive-historical manner.
42. Zanchi, *De operibus Dei*, 3.3.3, in *Reformed Thought on Freedom*, 53 (cf. 58).
43. Boston, *Human Nature in Its Fourfold State*, 37.
44. *Reformed Confessions*, 4:246.
45. Calvin, *Institutes*, 1.15.8.
46. See chaps. 8–10 on the image of God.
47. Boston, *Human Nature in Its Fourfold State*, 41.

However, God's prohibition and man's fall show that man was not so confirmed in righteousness that he was unable to sin. Augustine said, "The first freedom of will which man received when he was created upright consisted in an ability not to sin, but also in an ability to sin."[48] Strictly speaking, "an ability to sin" is not power, but a limitation of power. True power in the inner man consists of self-control, the strength to repulse temptation like a city with walls (Prov. 16:32; 25:28). Man had the power to do right, but his power was not infinite or immutable—it could be abused and lost.

2. The State of Sin: Inability to Choose God

Adam's sin removed man from his original state and plunged him into a state of sin and misery. The Westminster Confession (9.3) says, "Man, by his fall into a state of sin, hath wholly lost all ability of will to any spiritual good accompanying salvation (Rom. 5:6; 8:7; John 15:5): so as, a natural man, being altogether averse from that good (Rom. 3:10, 12), and dead in sin (Eph. 2:1, 5; Col. 2:13), is not able, by his own strength, to convert himself, or to prepare himself thereunto (John 6:44, 65; Eph. 2:2–5; 1 Cor. 2:14; Titus 3:3–5)."[49] Mankind is corrupted by sin, so that he is unable to seek God or please him apart from saving grace.[50]

The unrenewed human will is enslaved to evil and disabled from turning to God or any true spiritual good. Calvin said, "We are all sinners by nature; therefore we are held under the yoke of sin. But if the whole man lies under the power of sin, surely it is necessary that the will, which is its chief seat, be restrained by the stoutest bonds."[51] No temporal affliction or rational persuasion is sufficient to turn the will to spiritual good.[52] David Clarkson said of the enslaving strength of original sin, "All the cords of love, all the bonds of afflictions, cannot restrain this." He added, "Nothing but an infinite power can conquer it; none but the almighty arm of God can restrain it."[53] For this reason, when God saw man's powerlessness under sin, the Lord came himself (Isa. 59:16–21) to save those "without strength" (Rom. 5:6).

However, man in the state of sin still has a will, and it retains a shadow of its former liberty. Calvin said "that man has choice and

---

48. Augustine, *The City of God*, 22.30, in *NPNF*[1], 2:510.
49. *Reformed Confessions*, 4:246.
50. See chap. 21.
51. Calvin, *Institutes*, 2.2.27.
52. 2 Kings 17:13–14; Prov. 27:22; Jer. 5:3.
53. Clarkson, "Of Original Sin," in *Works*, 1:12.

that it is self-determined, so that if he does anything evil, it should be imputed to him and to his own voluntary choosing."[54] Franciscus Junius said, "Some traces of the freedom of choice of man are still visible, although they are totally corrupt."[55] The same was affirmed by the Westminster divines. The Scripture passages that the confession cites in its affirmation of the "natural liberty" of the will all pertain to humanity *after* the fall.[56]

The Scriptures tell us that wicked men make choices in all kinds of earthly matters. They choose whom they will marry (Gen. 6:2), what preacher they want to hear (John 5:35), and which man will rule them as king (1 Sam. 8:18). Of their own will, people file lawsuits and seek loans (Matt. 5:40, 42). Military commanders choose how to distribute their troops in various places (1 Sam. 13:2; 2 Sam. 10:9; 17:1). Craftsmen choose which materials will best serve the object that they intend to make (Isa. 40:20). In all such matters, they have liberty of will.

The wicked also freely choose wickedness. Sinners choose to do what God hates (Isa. 65:12; 66:3). They choose which false gods and idols they will worship (Judg. 10:14; Isa. 1:29; 41:24). Of their own will, they put God to the test (Matt. 12:38). Proud men choose the best means of honoring themselves, such as taking the privileged seats at banquets (Luke 14:7). Enemies of Christ choose wicked sinners and reject the Lord of glory (Matt. 27:21). Those with power over the righteous abuse them however they will (17:12). Those who hear the gospel call of Christ are not willing to come to him (23:37; John 5:40).

Augustine said, "The free will taken captive does not avail, except for sin; but for righteousness, unless divinely set free and aided, it does not avail."[57] Bullinger wrote in the Second Helvetic Confession (chap. 9), "Therefore, as touching evil or sin, man does evil, not compelled either by God or the devil, but of his own accord; and in this respect he has a most free will."[58] Augustine said of the unconverted, "This will, which is free in evil things because it takes pleasure in evil, is not free in good things, for the reason that it has not been made free. Nor can a man will any good thing unless he is aided by Him who

---

54. Calvin, *The Bondage and Liberation of the Will*, 69.
55. Junius, *Theses Theologicae*, 22.43, in *Reformed Thought on Freedom*, 104.
56. Deut. 30:19; Matt. 17:12; James 1:14. See *Reformed Confessions*, 4:246.
57. Augustine, *Against Two Letters of the Pelagians*, 3.24.8, in NPNF¹, 5:414.
58. *Reformed Confessions*, 2:823. See Zanchi, *De primi hominis lapsu*, 1.6.1, in *Reformed Thought on Freedom*, 67.

cannot will evil, that is, by the grace of God through Jesus Christ our Lord."[59]

There is an obvious tension in the words "free will taken captive" so that it is "free in evil" but unable to do good. It is the same tension we observed between the biblical truth that God's image in man was destroyed in some respects but continues in others. Man has not ceased to be man, but he has ceased to be what he once was. Augustine said,

> For it was by the evil use of his free-will that man destroyed both it and himself. For, as a man who kills himself must, of course, be alive when he kills himself, but after he has killed himself ceases to live, and cannot restore himself to life; so, when man by his own free-will sinned, then sin being victorious over him, the freedom of his will was lost. . . . What kind of liberty, I ask, can the bond-slave possess, except when it pleases him to sin? For he is freely in bondage who does with pleasure the will of his master. Accordingly, he who is the servant of sin is free to sin.[60]

In the state of sin, man dwells in a paradox of liberty and bondage. Boston said, "Sin is the natural man's element; he is as unwilling to part with it as fish are to come out of the water on to dry land. . . . He is a captive, a prisoner, and a slave, but he loves his conqueror, his jailor, and master."[61] Corrupt liberty and culpable bondage intertwine and reinforce each other, so that the fallen free will itself is man's fetter. Clarkson said that unregenerate sinners are "both unable, and unwilling to be able, and unable to be willing."[62]

Unrepentant sinners are still responsible to choose God and his ways, and are culpable for their refusal to do so. Though the pharaoh of the exodus represented the nadir of hard-heartedness, the Lord still rebuked him: "How long wilt thou refuse to humble thyself before me? Let my people go, that they may serve me" (Ex. 10:3). Elijah rebuked unfaithful Israel for wavering between two opinions, and said, "If the LORD be God, follow him: but if Baal, then follow him" (1 Kings 18:21). God's Wisdom reprimands fools who "hated knowledge, and did not choose the fear of the LORD" (Prov. 1:29).

---

59. Augustine, *Against Two Letters of the Pelagians*, 1.7.3, in NPNF[1], 5:379.
60. Augustine, *Enchiridion*, chap. 30, in NPNF[1], 3:247.
61. Boston, *Human Nature in Its Fourfold State*, 99.
62. Clarkson, "Man's Insufficiency to Do Anything of Himself," in *Works*, 2:104.

It might be asked how these exercises of will by the wicked can be called freedom. Biblically, spiritual freedom is the ability to do good and reject evil (John 8:32–36; Rom. 6:18, 22) in a manner that perceives and reflects God's glory in Christ (2 Cor. 3:17–18). The answer is that, just as we may speak of a defiled remnant of the image of God in the ruins of fallen human nature, so we may speak of a twisted fragment of human freedom to choose good. Sinners still choose what seems good to their minds and pleases their wills (cf. Gen. 3:6). In that regard, they somewhat reflect God's willing of good and abhorrence of evil (cf. Rom. 12:2, 9). Here it is helpful to remember that "good" can refer to what is beneficial and helpful for the body, personal advancement, and human society.[63] Sustained in existence by God's common grace, the wicked often choose many good things in this limited sense and reject what they perceive to be harmful to themselves and their environment.

However, sinners have rejected God and made themselves fools, and the Lord has given them over to a "debased mind to do what ought not to be done" (Rom. 1:28 ESV). Their perception and love of good is corrupted, so that they act according to their illusions of what is good, but apart from submission to the God whom they hate. Consequently, of them it is said, "Woe unto them that call evil good, and good evil; that put darkness for light, and light for darkness; that put bitter for sweet, and sweet for bitter!" (Isa. 5:20). Their minds are darkened and their wills depraved, so that theirs is a falsely thinking, freely willing, culpable bondage to sin.

3. The State of Grace: Renewed but Imperfect Ability to Choose God

The application of salvation to a person initiates the process of giving him spiritual freedom. Paul says, "Where the Spirit of the Lord is, there is liberty" (2 Cor. 3:17). The Westminster Confession (9.4) says, "When God converts a sinner, and translates him into the state of grace, He freeth him from his natural bondage under sin (Col. 1:13; John 8:34, 36); and, by His grace alone, enables him freely to will and to do that which is spiritually good (Phil. 2:13; Rom. 6:18, 22); yet so, as that by reason of his remaining corruption, he doth not perfectly, nor only, will that which is good, but doth also will that which is evil (Gal. 5:17; Rom. 7:15, 18–19, 21, 23)."[64]

---

63. Brakel, *The Christian's Reasonable Service*, 1:410.
64. *Reformed Confessions*, 4:246.

Conversion is the transition from slavery to freedom, yet freedom under a new Master. Paul writes in Romans 6:17–18, "But God be thanked, that ye were the servants of sin, but ye have obeyed from the heart that form of doctrine which was delivered you. Being then made free from sin, ye became the servants of righteousness." Augustine said, "He will not be free to do right, until, being freed from sin, he shall begin to be the servant of righteousness. And this is true liberty, for he has pleasure in the righteous deed; and it is at the same time a holy bondage, for he is obedient to the will of God."[65]

No longer is sin engraved on the heart with a pen of iron while God's law testifies against it on tablets of stone. Now God's Word is written on the tablets of the heart with the indelible ink of the Holy Spirit (2 Cor. 3:3; Heb. 8:10). The sinner is given a "new heart" (Ezek. 36:26), an "honest and good heart" that receives God's Word and bears fruit with perseverance (Luke 8:15). Regeneration is not a new choice of the will, but a new creation of the heart, the supernatural gift of a new vital disposition toward God that reorients all the faculties, including the will.

Free will is no longer an empty shadow, but a living, vibrant reality. Consequently, the regenerate have a new willingness that is worked in them by God: "For it is God which worketh in you both to will and to do of his good pleasure" (Phil. 2:13). The Holy Spirit dwells in them, but does not take them over like mindless robots. Boston said, "Regenerating grace is powerful and efficacious, and gives the will a new turn. It does not indeed force it, but sweetly, yet powerfully draws it, so that His people are willing in the day of His power (Ps. 110:3)."[66] They choose God's house over the life of the wicked (84:10). They choose God's way and God's Word (119:30, 173). With illuminated minds, they choose what is best, indeed the only thing necessary: to be a disciple who hears Christ's word (Luke 10:42).

These Spirit-worked desires and choices are met with bitter opposition from the indwelling sin that remains in believers, producing frustration and heartache over remaining sin and imperfect obedience (Rom. 7:15–24; Gal. 5:17). Yet God will faithfully complete what he has begun, unto the perfect sanctification of the whole person (Phil. 1:6; 1 Thess. 5:23–24).[67]

---

65. Augustine, *Enchiridion*, chap. 30, in *NPNF*[1], 3:247.
66. Boston, *Human Nature in Its Fourfold State*, 213.
67. The doctrines of effectual calling, sanctification, and perseverance are treated under the topic of soteriology. See *RST*, vol. 3 (forthcoming).

4. The State of Glory: Perfect and Unchangeable Ability to Choose God

Believers attain the promised perfection only in the final state of God's elect. The Westminster Confession (9.5) says, "The will of man is made perfectly and immutably free to good alone in the state of glory only."[68] Only in heaven do we find "the spirits of the righteous made perfect" (Heb. 12:23 ESV). When Christ returns in the visible glory of God and raises the dead to life, the image of God will be fully perfected in the children of God (1 John 3:2). They will return to the paradise of God, where there will be no Serpent or tree of the knowledge of good and evil to test them, but only the tree of life—"and they shall reign for ever and ever" (Rev. 22:1–5).

Then they will attain the highest level of freedom that creatures can possess: "the glorious liberty of the children of God" (Rom. 8:21). This immutable freedom is the ideal human image of God's infinite and eternal freedom, for God's free will is so good that he cannot sin (James 1:13). Augustine explained,

> Neither are we to suppose that because sin shall have no power to delight them, free will must be withdrawn. It will, on the contrary, be all the more truly free, because set free from delight in sinning to take unfailing delight in not sinning. For the first freedom of will which man received when he was created upright consisted in an ability not to sin, but also in an ability to sin; whereas this last freedom of will shall be superior, inasmuch as it shall not be able to sin.[69]

Therefore, the freedom of the will is not the will's neutrality between good and evil, but the power to rationally choose what is truly good, especially the supreme good. This is why turning away from God is such a horrendous abuse and corruption of free will. Jeremiah 2:12–13 says, "Be astonished, O ye heavens, at this, and be horribly afraid, be ye very desolate, saith the LORD. For my people have committed two evils; they have forsaken me the fountain of living waters, and hewed them out cisterns, broken cisterns, that can hold no water."

Man's freedom was initiated in a sinless but limited manner in the garden. The fall shattered our freedom, though fragments remained. God restores spiritual freedom at regeneration and completes it at the resurrec-

---

68. *Reformed Confessions*, 4:246.
69. Augustine, *The City of God*, 22.30, in *NPNF*[1], 2:510.

tion to life. If anyone objects that we cannot be truly free if we have an inability to choose sin, consider what Augustine said: "Are we to say that God Himself is not free because He cannot sin?"[70] True freedom consists in our likeness to God, for that is what we were made to be.

Practical Implications of the Will's Freedom and Bondage

Though the doctrine of human free will is a flashpoint for controversy, it is a very practical doctrine. This is especially the case with respect to the church's evangelism of lost sinners. Therefore, we conclude with some practical applications drawn from Isaiah 55, God's evangelistic call based upon the redeeming work of Christ (Isaiah 53) and the church's fruitful union with him (Isaiah 54).

1. *Offer Christ as the sufficient Savior for sinners.* "Ho, every one that thirsteth, come ye to the waters, and he that hath no money; come ye, buy, and eat; yea, come, buy wine and milk without money and without price. Wherefore do ye spend money for that which is not bread? And your labour for that which satisfieth not? Hearken diligently unto me, and eat ye that which is good, and let your soul delight itself in fatness" (Isa. 55:1–2). Do not fret about whom God has chosen, but call people to come to Christ. Promise them that in him God has prepared a spiritual feast that will fully satisfy all who come by faith.

2. *Point sinners to the faithfulness of God in his covenant through Christ.* "Incline your ear, and come unto me: hear, and your soul shall live; and I will make an everlasting covenant with you, even the sure mercies of David" (Isa. 55:3). We are not saved by trusting in our own freedom and power, but by trusting in the covenant faithfulness of the God and Father of our Lord Jesus Christ. Tell people to rest their trust upon God's promises in Christ.

3. *Rely on God to gather sinners to their glorified Prophet and King.* "Behold, I have given him for a witness to the people, a leader and commander to the people. Behold, thou shalt call a nation that thou knowest not, and nations that knew not thee shall run unto thee because of the Lord thy God, and for the Holy One of Israel; for he hath glorified thee" (Isa. 55:4–5). Though the Christian church must testify to people about Christ, Christ alone has the divine power to call the enslaved nations to himself so that they run willingly and eagerly to him.

---

70. Augustine, *The City of God*, 22.30, in *NPNF*[1], 2:510.

4. *Call sinners as responsible moral agents to turn to God and righteousness.* "Seek ye the Lord while he may be found, call ye upon him while he is near: let the wicked forsake his way, and the unrighteous man his thoughts: and let him return unto the Lord, and he will have mercy upon him; and to our God, for he will abundantly pardon" (Isa. 55:6–7). Though slaves of sin, the unregenerate are still human beings with minds and wills—and the responsibility to use them rightly. Therefore, we must not shrink from addressing them as God does in his Word—with commands, exhortations, warnings, rebukes, promises, and encouragements.

5. *Submit to God's Word in those matters that you do not understand.* "For my thoughts are not your thoughts, neither are your ways my ways, saith the Lord. For as the heavens are higher than the earth, so are my ways higher than your ways, and my thoughts than your thoughts" (Isa. 55:8–9). As limited creatures and corrupted sinners, there is much about God and his ways that we do not comprehend. Rather than quarrelling with God about sin and salvation, we must bow before him as the Lord whose mind is infinitely wiser and holier than ours.

6. *Have confidence in God's Word as the sovereign instrument of new life.* "For as the rain cometh down, and the snow from heaven, and returneth not thither, but watereth the earth, and maketh it bring forth and bud, that it may give seed to the sower, and bread to the eater: so shall my word be that goeth forth out of my mouth: it shall not return unto me void, but it shall accomplish that which I please, and it shall prosper in the thing whereto I sent it" (Isa. 55:10–11). Though sinners are dead, God's Word is not in vain, for through the Word God gives life and fruitfulness to a barren world—according to his sovereign will.

7. *Hope in the freedom and eternal glory of Christ.* "For ye shall go out with joy, and be led forth with peace: the mountains and the hills shall break forth before you into singing, and all the trees of the field shall clap their hands. Instead of the thorn shall come up the fir tree, and instead of the brier shall come up the myrtle tree: and it shall be to the Lord for a name, for an everlasting sign that shall not be cut off" (Isa. 55:12–13). We must believe with all our hearts that Christ sets his people free and will give them the eternal happiness that will fill the new heaven and new earth. Then we will know free will indeed for the glory of God alone.

Sing to the Lord

Choosing God's Way and Persevering in It, All by Grace

My grieving soul revive, O Lord,
According to Thy word;
To Thee my ways I have declared,
And Thou my prayer hast heard.

Teach me to know Thy holy way
And think upon Thy deeds;
In grief I ask for promised grace
According to my needs.

Keep me from falsehood, let Thy law
With me in grace abide;
The way of faithfulness I choose,
Thy precepts are my guide.

I cleave unto Thy truth, O Lord;
From shame deliver me;
In glad obedience I will live
Through strength bestowed by Thee.

Psalm 119:25–32
Tune: Northrepps
The Psalter, No. 324

Questions for Meditation or Discussion

1. Why is it difficult to talk about the free choice of the human will without falling into error?
2. What do the authors observe about the Bible's use of terms for (1) the human will, (2) the human heart, and (3) freedom or liberty?
3. What did early Reformed theologians, such as John Calvin and Francis Turretin, say about the free choice of the will?
4. How do the authors define the free will of man?
5. Describe the condition of man and his will in each of the following states: (1) innocence, (2) sin, (3) grace, and (4) glory.
6. How can perishing sinners still have the free choice of the will if they are slaves of sin?

7. How does the biblical and Reformed doctrine of the will encourage zealous, humble, and hopeful evangelism?

8. Of the practical implications listed at the end of this chapter, which seems most helpful to you right now? Why? What do you need to do about it?

Questions for Deeper Reflection

9. Why might people be surprised to hear that Reformed theologians believe in the free choice of the will, though by nature that choice always fall short of genuine spiritual good? How would you explain the classic Reformed doctrine of the free choice of the will to help them see its coherence with Reformed theology as a whole?

10. In your own church tradition, how have people typically viewed the free choice of the will? How would you critique this view's strengths and weaknesses according to the Holy Scriptures?

23

Actual Sins

The Diverse, Poisonous
Fruit of Original Sin

Sinful hearts produce sinful acts. When the Bible speaks of "sin," it sometimes refers to the corruption that dwells within fallen human beings (Rom. 7:5, 17). In this sense, sin is an evil power that rules the unbeliever and continues to attack the believer from within (6:12, 17; cf. Gal. 5:17; 1 Pet. 2:11). However, the Scriptures also use the term "sin" to refer to human actions.[1] Christ said, "A corrupt tree bringeth forth evil fruit" (Matt. 7:17). This fruit of original sin is called *actual sin.*

Man's rebellion against God works itself out in a complex variety of actual sins. Scripture testifies to this complexity in its various commandments and in its lists of sins, some of which are quite extensive.[2] To give a systematic exposition of actual sins would require a full treatise on ethics.[3] In this chapter, we will outline only some basic features of various actual sins.

---

1. Note the verb to "sin" (*hamartanō*) in Matt. 18:15, 19; Luke 15:18; etc., and the phrase "commit sin" (*poieō hamartian*) in John 8:34; James 5:15; 1 John 3:4, 8–9.
2. Prov. 6:16–19; Matt. 15:19; Mark 7:21–22; Rom. 1:29–31; 13:13; 1 Cor. 5:9–11; 6:9–10; 2 Cor. 12:20–21; Gal. 5:19–21; Eph. 4:25–29, 31; 5:3–6; Col. 3:5, 8–9; 1 Tim. 1:9–10; 2 Tim. 3:2–5; Titus 3:3; 1 Pet. 2:1; 4:3, 15; Rev. 21:8; 22:15.
3. A fulsome discussion of Christian ethics from a Reformed experiential perspective may be found in Brakel, *The Christian's Reasonable Service*, vols. 3–4. A brief exposition of God's law and Christian character will be presented in *RST*, vol. 3 (forthcoming).

Dimensions of Actual Sin

Sinners tend to neglect some categories of sin so that they might justify themselves. A full-orbed perspective on sin, in its different dimensions, helps us to repent and trust in Christ alone.

Sins against God and One's Neighbor

People often excuse sin by saying that it is a private, personal affair and is no one else's business. This is a lie. All sin is a violation of the duty that we owe to others, especially our duty to the personal God who made us and rules over us.

Our Lord said, "The first of all the commandments is, Hear, O Israel; the Lord our God is one Lord: and thou shalt love the Lord thy God with all thy heart, and with all thy soul, and with all thy mind, and with all thy strength: this is the first commandment. And the second is like, namely this, Thou shalt love thy neighbour as thyself. There is none other commandment greater than these" (Mark 12:29–31; cf. Deut. 6:4–5; Lev. 19:18). Our neighbors include people who are ethnically and culturally different from us (Lev. 19:34; Luke 10:29–37).

In a parallel text in Matthew 22:40, Christ added, "On these two commandments hang all the law and the prophets." The word translated as "hang" (*kremannymi*) means to suspend from something so that it holds up a person's or object's weight.[4] If we refuse to love God wholeheartedly or to love people as ourselves, then our obedience to the whole law falls to the ground.

The law of God has a marvelous simplicity. We may summarize it in one word: *love*. Samuel Willard said, "The whole law is nothing else but a rule of love."[5] The apostle Paul writes, "Owe no man any thing, but to love one another: for he that loveth another hath fulfilled the law," and after quoting five of the Ten Commandments, says that every commandment "is briefly comprehended in this saying, namely, Thou shalt love thy neighbour as thyself. Love worketh no ill to his neighbour: therefore love is the fulfilling of the law" (Rom. 13:8–10). Sin, then, is enmity against God and his image bearers.

We should not set up a false dichotomy between sins against God and sins against man. Our duty of love to God is absolute and all-

---

4. Matt. 18:6; Luke 23:39; Acts 5:30; 10:39; 28:4; Gal. 3:13.
5. Willard, *A Compleat Body of Divinity*, 582.

encompassing, demanding "all thy heart"; our duty of love to people is subordinate, an important aspect of loving God. All sins are against God, even sins such as murder or adultery that directly strike at human beings (Gen. 39:7–9; Ps. 51:4). Every sin against a human being is also a sin against God because God created man in his image (Gen. 9:6; James 3:9–12). Willard explained, "God and our neighbor do not stand upon even ground, so as that these must divide our love," but "God stands as the ultimate object, and highest end and center of all our love," and man, his creature, should receive our love as it passes on to God, like a river that waters its shores but does not stop until it reaches the ocean.[6]

Sin, then, always involves a failure to love God. Since all sin is against God, we should learn to weigh the seriousness of sin according to the gravity of offending such a glorious Lord. John Owen said, "He that hath slight thoughts of sin had never great thoughts of God. Indeed, men's undervaluing of sin ariseth merely from their contempt of God."[7]

When we sin against God in matters of worship and holiness, we also sin indirectly against our neighbor because we fail to be right images of God, set a bad example, and give people cause to slander God's name and Word.[8] We contribute to the corruption and death of our world. We rob people of the good that might have radiated from our good works when instead we pour our affections, time, and strength into the black hole of sin.

For every wrong we commit, we should say, "I have sinned against God and against man" (cf. Luke 15:18).

Sins of Omission and Commission

The Scriptures broaden our understanding of sin even further by recognizing that we sin by not doing what God has required us to do (sins of omission) as well as by doing what God has forbidden us to do (sins of commission).

Sins of commission are easily illustrated by the "Thou shalt not" commandments. As to sins of omission, we bear a responsibility to actively pursue God's revealed will. Christ compared it to a master-servant relationship

---

6. Willard, *A Compleat Body of Divinity*, 583.
7. Owen, *A Practical Exposition upon Psalm CXXX*, in *Works*, 6:394.
8. 2 Sam. 12:14; Rom. 2:23–24; Titus 2:1–10.

and said, "And that servant, which knew his lord's will, and prepared not himself, neither did according to his will, shall be beaten with many stripes. . . . For unto whomsoever much is given, of him shall be much required: and to whom men have committed much, of him they will ask the more" (Luke 12:47–48). Wilhelmus à Brakel said of any sin of omission, "Although many neither give heed to this nor are disturbed hereby, it is a great sin, for it proceeds from unwillingness and lovelessness in relation to the will of God."[9]

James concisely enunciated the principle behind sins of omission: "Therefore to him that knoweth to do good, and doeth it not, to him it is sin" (James 4:17). This does not obligate every person to do every possible good, for only God has unlimited power and is present in all places. James taught us to live submissively under the limitations of God's providence, recognizing that we can live and act only "if the Lord will" (v. 15). The "good" we must do refers to our biblically defined duties toward God and people in our circumstances.

The greatest omission man commits is his failure to obey the greatest commandment. Who can say that he has loved the Lord with all his heart, all his soul, all his mind, and all his strength? Every day, every minute, we transgress this law, and in so doing transgress the whole law that hangs upon it. If we did nothing else wrong, just for this alone we would need the death of God's Son to redeem us from God's everlasting curse.

Though the distinction between omission and commission illuminates an important and often neglected aspect of sin, we should recognize that every sin of omission implies a sin of commission, and vice versa. Geerhardus Vos said, "If I love God less and forget God, then it is because something else has taken the place of God in my heart."[10]

Sins in Thought, Word, and Deed

Actual sins involve both inward and outward acts, and so are commonly defined as any failure to conform to God's law in thought, word, or deed.[11] Moses said in Deuteronomy 10:12, "And now, Israel, what doth the LORD thy God require of thee, but to fear the LORD thy God, to walk in all his

---

9. Brakel, *The Christian's Reasonable Service*, 1:394.
10. Vos, *Reformed Dogmatics*, 2:70.
11. Cf. Augustine, *Reply to Faustus the Manichaean*, 22.27, in NPNF[1], 4:283. See chap. 17.

ways, and to love him, and to serve the LORD thy God with all thy heart and with all thy soul."

External acts of praise and worship do not please God when the heart is far from him (Isa. 29:13), for this is the essence of hypocrisy (Matt. 15:8–9). God desires faithfulness and wisdom in "the inward parts" and has no pleasure in religious worship unless it is accompanied by "a broken and contrite heart" (Ps. 51:6, 16–17). Though many Old Testament laws focused upon outward actions, because the covenant governed the civil life of national Israel, they also revealed God's will for the inner man. Willard said, "They greatly err, who think these commands to require only the outward behavior of men, for the sufficient observing of them. Men's laws can reach no further, but God is Lord of the conscience, and Judge of that; and he observes, not only what we do, but with what heart."[12]

The Lord Jesus made it clear that the law is spiritual and demands righteousness from the inside out. Unjust anger in the heart breaks God's command against murder even if it is not expressed (Matt. 5:21–22). The law against adultery prohibits looking at a person to lust after him or her in one's heart (vv. 27–28). The evil motive of desiring to get praise from men poisons pious acts such as charitable giving, prayer, and fasting (6:1–2, 5, 16). Moral darkness and rebellion against God fill the mind that loves material wealth and seeks treasures on earth (vv. 19–24). Therefore, if we would have a place in God's kingdom, we must have a righteousness that exceeds that of religious hypocrites with their external rules (5:20). We must be "poor in spirit" and "pure in heart" (vv. 3, 8)— that is, we must be humbled and have clean motives through an inward repentance (4:17).

Yet God does not focus exclusively upon the interior life. He demands that the words of a man's tongue be good and the actions of his hands be clean (Pss. 15:3; 24:4). Sin in any part of the human constitution provokes God's wrath. Solomon said, "These six things doth the LORD hate: yea, seven are an abomination unto him: a proud look, a lying tongue, and hands that shed innocent blood, an heart that deviseth wicked imaginations, feet that be swift in running to mischief, a false witness that speaketh lies, and he that soweth discord among brethren" (Prov. 6:16–19). A sinner can do wrong even with his gestures (vv. 12–13).

---

12. Willard, *A Compleat Body of Divinity*, 580. He cited 2 Chron. 25:2; Prov. 23:26; Matt. 5:28; Heb. 4:12.

Domains of Actual Sin

In addition to the two great commandments, God revealed the nature of sin in the Ten Commandments, where he summarized his moral law.[13] In the first four commandments, we see the vertical dimension of our duty to love God, and in the last six, the horizontal dimension of our responsibility to love our neighbor. Each commandment reveals one domain in which sin violates God's will.

1. *Sins regarding God's unique glory.* "Thou shalt have no other gods before me" (Ex. 20:3). People sin whenever they attribute divine attributes, theoretically or practically, to anyone or anything other than the true God. They owe to God and him alone their divine worship, knowing that they always live in his holy presence ("before me").

2. *Sins regarding God's prescribed worship.* "Thou shalt not make unto thee any graven image, or any likeness of any thing. . . . Thou shalt not bow down thyself to them, nor serve them" (Ex. 20:4–5). People defile God's worship and insult his holiness when they add humanly invented images or forms of worship to what God told us to do in worship.

3. *Sins regarding God's awesome name.* "Thou shalt not take the name of the LORD thy God in vain" (Ex. 20:7). Human beings treat God as if his glory were an empty thing ("vain") when they treat anything associated with God's glory in a casual or flippant manner. How much more do they insult him when they profane his name in curses and blasphemy!

4. *Sins regarding God's holy day.* "Remember the sabbath day, to keep it holy" (Ex. 20:8). God has reserved one day in seven as a day for us to rest from the works of our ordinary vocations and to devote ourselves to public and private worship. However, in breaking this commandment, mankind defies God's lordship over their time. People sin against God when they work on his day apart from labors of piety, necessity, or mercy, or refuse to seek his face with his assembled church.

5. *Sins regarding proper human authority.* "Honour thy father and thy mother" (Ex. 20:12). Human rebellion against God manifests itself in contempt and rebellion against people in authority over us in the home, the church, the workplace, and the civil government. Likewise, people sin when they abuse their authority so as to dishonor an office that God instituted.

---

13. Westminster Shorter Catechism (Q. 41), in *Reformed Confessions*, 4:359. On the moral law and the Ten Commandments, see chap. 34.

6. *Sins regarding sacred human life.* "Thou shalt not kill" (Ex. 20:13). Mankind's hatred for God spills over into attacks upon his image, such as violence against the human body, hateful speech toward a human person, inward malice, and callous neglect.

7. *Sins regarding faithful human sexuality.* "Thou shalt not commit adultery" (Ex. 20:14). All attempts to pursue sexual pleasure outside of God's ordained means of a loving marriage between one man and one woman are spiritually unclean in God's sight.

8. *Sins regarding rightful human property.* "Thou shalt not steal" (Ex. 20:15). Human lawlessness rears its ugly head in all disregard for the rights of people to possess and rightly enjoy their property. This includes theft, destruction of others' property, and laziness at work.

9. *Sins regarding true human testimony.* "Thou shalt not bear false witness against thy neighbour" (Ex. 20:16). Knowledge of the truth is precious, and sinners rob each other of this treasure and defy the God of truth by their perjuries, lies, deceptions, and gossip.

10. *Sins regarding submissive human contentment.* "Thou shalt not covet . . . any thing that is thy neighbour's" (Ex. 20:17). Like Adam and Eve in the garden, people show their malicious distrust of God's good providence as they greedily desire what God has given to others instead of them. In this, too, they sin against each other, because love for one's neighbor cannot coexist with bitter envy for what they have.

The scope of sin is as wide as human existence. Its hostility against God knows no bounds, and it invades every aspect of human culture. Man is against God in all dimensions of God's holy worship. Man is against man, the image of God, with respect to authority, life, sexuality, property, testimony, and contentment. If we were to draw out the implications of the Ten Commandments, as the Westminster Larger Catechism (Q. 91–152) does, we would find a comprehensive catalog of sin that rebels against man's whole moral duty.[14] Thus, we see in our actual sins that man is a rebel and traitor with his whole being.

Diverse Circumstances of Actual Sin

Though circumstances cannot make sin into righteousness—we do not believe in situational ethics—circumstances can profoundly affect the impact of sin on ourselves and others.

---

14. *Reformed Confessions*, 4:319–39.

Sins in Public and Secret

Some sins are public. Peter openly denied that he was a disciple of Christ (Matt. 26:69–75). Pontius Pilate unjustly sentenced Jesus Christ to death by crucifixion before a crowd of people (Luke 23:4, 13–25). Such sins are obvious even before judgment day (1 Tim. 5:24). When public sins do not receive speedy recompense, they tend to embolden other sinners (Eccles. 8:11).

Other sins are hidden, such as when Achan hid forbidden treasure from Jericho (Josh. 7:1, 21) or when David committed adultery with Bathsheba (2 Sam. 12:12; cf. Prov. 9:17). Sinners like to hide in the darkness (Job 24:13–17; John 3:19), flattering themselves that no one will discover them (Ps. 36:2). Yet God's curse will find out the secret sin of a man and punish him for it (Deut. 27:15, 24; Ps. 101:5; Gal. 6:7). The curse of the Lord, like a guided missile, will unerringly find the sinner to destroy him (Zech. 5:1–4). Though wicked fools may boast, "The LORD shall not see," he who formed the eye certainly can see their injustice and will punish them (Ps. 94:7–9, 23). We should fear God in all that we do, "for God shall bring every work into judgment, with every secret thing, whether it be good, or whether it be evil" (Eccles. 12:14).

It is possible for sin to be hidden, in some sense, from the sinner who commits it because of the culpable darkness of his mind (Eph. 4:18–19). The conscience may be seared (1 Tim. 4:2). The godly themselves do not perceive the fullness of their iniquity. Yet this does not excuse sin. Herman Bavinck said, "The standard of sin is not the consciousness of guilt but the law of God."[15] Whether it breaks the heart or causes smirks and laughter (Prov. 10:23), sin is evil. David leads us to pray, "Who can understand his errors? Cleanse thou me from secret faults" (Ps. 19:12).

Sins of Individuals and Societies

The Bible teaches individual responsibility and accountability. God does not punish people for the sins of others, but "the soul that sinneth, it shall die" (Ezek. 18:4). On judgment day, the Lord will examine each person for his own deeds. Paul says, "For we must all appear before the judgment seat of Christ; that every one may receive the things done in his body, according to that he hath done, whether it be good or bad" (2 Cor. 5:10).

---

15. Bavinck, *Reformed Dogmatics*, 3:150.

However, in the Holy Scriptures, God also addresses groups of people for their sins. In the Old Testament, God moved the prophets to denounce entire nations for specific iniquities (Isaiah 13–23; Amos 1–2). Such sins may bring down God's temporal judgments upon the whole nation unless there is widespread repentance among the people (Jonah 3). Christ similarly denounced entire towns for rejecting the gospel and sealing their own damnation (Luke 10:12–15), though some people in those towns had repented, believed, and been saved (Luke 4:31, 38; John 1:44).

An ethnic group with a definite culture often has characteristic sins, as we see when Paul wrote to Titus in Crete: "One of the Cretans, a prophet of their own, said, 'Cretans are always liars, evil beasts, lazy gluttons.' This testimony is true. Therefore rebuke them sharply, that they may be sound in the faith" (Titus 1:12–13 ESV). Paul's instructions to Titus, to choose men of godly integrity in every city to serve as elders, plainly imply that these moral flaws did not apply to everyone from Crete, but were generalizations (vv. 5–9).

Sinful societies exercise powerful means to conform people to their corrupt expectations (Rom. 12:2). Willem Teellinck (1579–1629) compared the world to a monster with three horns· (1) wicked traditions and customs (Matt. 15:1–9; Col. 2:8), (2) sinful celebrities and false models of success (Ps. 73:1–15), and (3) a corrupt cultural system that uses promises of reward and threats of punishment to promote evil (Num. 22:7; 1 Sam. 22:7–8). With these horns, societies drive sinners along in worldliness and attack the righteous.[16]

Churches, as societies of God's people, also have prevailing sins. Christ addressed whole churches, giving commendation or rebuke according to the character of each congregation (Revelation 2–3). Failure to repent could bring divine correction to the church as a body (2:5), even if the congregation's fault lies mainly in tolerating a sinner in its midst instead of disciplining that person (v. 20). Like Israel with Achan, the sins of one person can bring affliction upon the group (Joshua 7). This does not mean that the Lord lumps people together in shared guilt by association, for he distinguished those who did not participate in the sins he rebuked (Rev. 2:24; 3:4). When God admonishes a group, each person must respond individually (2:20). Thus, Christ ends his message to each church with a

---

16. Willem Teellinck, *The Path of True Godliness*, trans. Annemie Godbehere, ed. Joel R. Beeke, Classics of Reformed Spirituality (Grand Rapids, MI: Reformation Heritage Books, 2003), 63–68.

word to the singular "he that hath an ear" (*ho echōn ous*), and his promises also are directed to individuals, "he that overcometh" (*ho nikōn*).

Sins of Oppressors and Victims

The Lord takes the oppression of the poor and weak very seriously. The Israelites were to treat a foreigner among them according to the same principle that guided how they treated each other: "You shall love him as yourself" (Lev. 19:33–34 ESV). God said to Israel, "You shall not wrong a sojourner or oppress him, for you were sojourners in the land of Egypt. You shall not mistreat any widow or fatherless child. If you do mistreat them, and they cry out to me, I will surely hear their cry, and my wrath will burn, and I will kill you with the sword, and your wives shall become widows and your children fatherless" (Ex. 22:21–24 ESV). If you have oppressed someone under your power and not repented of it, you may be sure that you have offended God and provoked his righteous outrage. God's law considers sins against vulnerable people—in ancient cultures, these were the widows, fatherless, foreigners, and poor (Zech. 7:10)—to be especially grievous. True religion that pleases God shows itself by caring for the needy (James 1:27) and serving brothers in Christ who suffer hardship, persecution, and need (Matt. 25:31–46).

However, the Bible does not teach liberation theology, the belief that God preferentially favors the poor and oppressed regardless of their spiritual state. Such theology is not based on the Bible as God's inerrant self-revelation, but on a Marxist reading of history.[17] God's law prohibited favoritism to the rich, but also prohibited favoritism to the poor (Ex. 23:2–3; Lev. 19:15). In a disordered society, everyone can be an oppressor, even a proud child (Isa. 3:5). God does not grant a righteous status to the poor and weak per se, but calls all people to become poor in spirit so that they might receive his blessing (Hos. 14:3; Matt. 5:3).

God's justice does not discriminate. Government officials and others in Judah perpetrated injustice against the fatherless and the widow, and God rebuked them for it (Isa. 1:17, 23; 10:1–2). God's judgment would fall upon the nation because of their oppression.[18] Yet God said, "The

---

17. D. D. Webster, "Liberation Theology," in *Evangelical Dictionary of Theology*, 635–38. A seminal text for liberation theology is Gustavo Gutiérrez, *A Theology of Liberation* (Maryknoll, NY: Orbis, 1973). This form of theology has many branches, but it is especially prominent among Roman Catholics in Latin America.

18. Jer. 5:28–29; 7:6–7; 22:3–5; Ezek. 22:1, 7; Mal. 3:5.

LORD shall have no joy in their young men, neither shall have mercy on their fatherless and widows: for every one is an hypocrite and an evildoer, and every mouth speaketh folly. For all this his anger is not turned away, but his hand is stretched out still" (Isa. 9:17). We certainly may not look down upon the oppressed as if they are worse sinners than others, but we also must not self-righteously condemn the rich either. We all must repent, lest we perish for our sins (Luke 13:1–5).

Degrees of Actual Sin

In a world of sin, we must discern the seriousness of various sins so that we can deal with them wisely without overreacting or underreacting, whether in our personal sanctification or in the pursuit of accountability for our families, friends, churches, and societies under civil governments.[19]

The Roman Catholic Church defines some categories of sin, such as adultery or murder, as mortal ("deadly" to the soul) and other sins as venial (from the Latin *venialis*, "pardonable").[20] In Rome's view, mortal sins put a person out of a state of grace, placing him or her back under eternal condemnation, whereas venial sins are not as serious and, thus, are judged as consistent with being in a state of grace. The Reformers recognized this distinction as an error.[21] John Calvin said, "All sin is mortal. For it is rebellion against the will of God, which of necessity provokes God's wrath, and it is a violation of the law, upon which God's judgment is pronounced without exception."[22] As Paul says, "The wages of sin is death" (Rom. 6:23), regardless of what sin is committed. The violation of any command is an offense against the whole law (James 2:10–11). The law pronounces its curse against anyone who does not abide in the keeping of everything commanded (Gal. 3:10). Christ taught that mere words spoken in malicious anger make a person liable to the fires of hell (Matt. 5:22). Furthermore, David committed adultery and murder, but there is no indication that he left a state of grace—though his Lord disciplined him severely for his sins (2 Samuel 11–12).

However, it is also an error to consider all sins to be of equal weight. The Lord showed Ezekiel some sins of the people, but said that he would see "greater abominations" (Ezek. 8:6, 13, 15). One nation can be more

---

19. Grudem, *Systematic Theology*, 504.
20. *Catechism of the Catholic Church*, secs. 1854–1863, 2268.
21. Bavinck, *Reformed Dogmatics*, 3:153–55.
22. Calvin, *Institutes*, 2.8.59.

corrupt than others (16:47–52). One generation of sinners can do "worse" than a previous generation (Jer. 7:26; 16:12).[23] Christ said that the person who had handed him over to Pilate had committed a "greater sin" than Pilate had (John 19:11). Christ also compared some sins to a "speck" but others to a "log" (Matt. 7:3 ESV). It is possible for the wicked to grow "worse and worse" in the sins they commit (2 Tim. 3:13).

Degrees of sin are evidenced in degrees of judgment (Luke 12:47–48). Christ warned cities that refused his gospel that "it shall be more tolerable for the land of Sodom in the day of judgment, than for thee" (Matt. 11:24; cf. 10:15). He also said that some sinners, such as hypocritical religious teachers, would "receive greater damnation" (Mark 12:40; Luke 20:47). This frightening truth should restrain sinners, for the worse their sins are, the more painful their hell.

What makes some sins more heinous than others? The Bible reveals multiple factors that aggravate sin. The following factors are mostly adapted from the extensive treatment of this question in the Westminster Larger Catechism (Q. 151).[24]

- *The person of the sinner.* Sin may be aggravated by privileges enjoyed by the sinner, such as knowledge of God's Word (Matt. 11:21–24; Luke 12:47–48) or a position from which to teach and influence others (Gal. 2:11–14; James 3:1). We should fear to be a stumbling block to others swayed by our example (Matt. 18:6–7).
- *The person against whom one sins.* Sins are more heinous when committed in direct contempt against God himself (2 Kings 19:4, 16, 22) or against a person to whom God has given authority (Prov. 30:17). Likewise, sins of injustice against the weak and vulnerable are great in God's sight (Amos 5:11–12) and, as we have seen, especially call down God's wrath upon oppressors (Ex. 22:21–24).
- *The extent of sin's action.* Sin's motion in the heart is a grave matter, but it becomes even more serious when it erupts into physical acts of wickedness (James 1:14–15). We see this when Cain's anger led him to murder his brother (Gen. 4:5–12).
- *The perversity of the sinner's reason.* Sin that aims to meet real needs in unlawful ways, such as a hungry man stealing food, is not

---

23. Thomas Watson, *The Ten Commandments* (Edinburgh: Banner of Truth, 1965), 189.
24. *Reformed Confessions*, 4:338–39.

as great an offense as sin that needlessly destroys people, relationships, and dignity, such as a lustful man committing adultery with his neighbor's wife (Prov. 6:30–35).

- *The height of the sinner's defiance.* If people persist in sinning after God has sent judgments upon them or they have witnessed it falling on others, then they aggravate their guilt (Jer. 5:3; Dan. 5:18–23). Sins committed in a bold, shameless, and brazen manner provoke God to greater anger (Num. 15:30; Jer. 3:3; 6:15).
- *The depth of sin's abnormality.* Scripture speaks with special outrage against sins committed "against nature" (Rom. 1:26). Similarly, the Word sharply rebukes sins that violate the common decency of man (1 Cor. 5:1; 1 Tim. 5:8).
- *The holiness of the sinner's situation.* Gross sins committed in sacred acts of worship are greatly aggravated, such as hypocrisy in giving to the church's ministry to the poor (Acts 5:1–11) and disorder at the Lord's Supper (1 Cor. 12:17–30). Officers in the church must walk in the fear of God, lest they profane God's holy things by corrupt leadership or teaching (1 Sam. 2:12–17; Mal. 2:1–9).

These factors that aggravate sin should give us pause. If the least sin deserves the fire of hell, then how much more do aggravated sins provoke God to send judgment? If you recognize that you are presently guilty of a particularly heinous sin, you must repent immediately. Do not mistake a lack of affliction for indifference or weakness on God's part. The worst judgment in this world is God's giving a sinner over to a hard heart so that he slips blindly into hell.[25]

Sing to the Lord

Overcoming Sin by Christ's Power

> Teach me, O Lord, thy holy way,
> And give me an obedient mind;
> That in thy service I may find
> My soul's delight from day to day.
>
> Guide me, O Saviour, with thy hand,
> And so control my thoughts and deeds,

---

25. On the sin against the Holy Spirit, see *RST*, vol. 3 (forthcoming).

That I may tread the path which leads
Right onward to the blessed land.

Help me, O Saviour, here to trace
The sacred footsteps thou hast trod;
And, meekly walking with my God,
To grow in goodness, truth, and grace.

Guard me, O Lord, that I may ne'er
Forsake the right, or do the wrong:
Against temptation make me strong,
And round me spread thy shelt'ring care.

Bless me in ev'ry task, O Lord,
Begun, continued, done for thee:
Fulfill thy perfect work in me;
And thine abounding grace afford.

William Matson
Tune: Penitence
Trinity Hymnal—Baptist Edition, No. 456

Questions for Meditation or Discussion

1. What is "actual sin"? How is it different from "original sin"?
2. Why is all sin an offense against God? Why is all sin also a wronging of our neighbor?
3. What are "sins of commission" and "sins of omission"? Show from Scripture that sins of omission are violations of God's law.
4. How does the Bible reveal that we can sin in the thoughts and attitudes of our hearts?
5. Briefly describe the ten domains in which we can sin according to the Ten Commandments.
6. What are some of the diverse circumstances of actual sin?
7. What does the "heinousness" of a sin mean? What factors aggravate a sin's heinousness? For each factor, give some biblical basis for seeing it as an aggravation of sin.
8. Examine yourself. Do you hear God's declarations against sin with humility and brokenness? Do you seek God's grace in Jesus Christ for the forgiveness of sin and victory over its dominion? Are you

striving against sin by faith in Christ's cross, as the Spirit strives against sin within you?

9. Is there a particular sin for which God is convicting you? How are you striving to repent of it by grace?

10. How can you make use of the teaching in this chapter to cultivate a greater hatred for sin?

Questions for Deeper Reflection

11. A friend says, "Once I believed that some sins are mortal and venial, but now I see that all sins are the same in God's sight." How do you respond?

12. Two friends are arguing. One says, "Poor, exploited, oppressed people can't be blamed for committing crimes because they have suffered so much wrong." The other says, "Oppressed people are just as much to blame for their sins as oppressors." What do you say?

24

The Punishment of Sin by God

Just as God is blessed and the source of all happiness, so sin is accursed and the root of all misery. God's Word teaches us that sin is a Pandora's box that, once opened, unleashes a flood of evil upon the world: "In the day that thou eatest thereof thou shalt surely die" (Gen. 2:17). This was true of Adam's sin, and it is true of the original sin in all of us and every one of our actual sins. These consequences flow not merely as a natural result of sin, but by God's punishment of sinners. The Holy Scriptures teach the doctrine of divine punishment (from Latin *poena*, "penalty" or "pain").[1] Therefore, "by the fear of the LORD men depart from evil" (Prov. 16:6).

Thinking about the punishment of sin is not pleasant, but it is necessary. The Heidelberg Catechism (LD 1, Q. 2) teaches us that we must know the greatness of our "sins and miseries" in order to "live and die happily" in Christ.[2] The Westminster Shorter Catechism (Q. 19) outlines those miseries when it asks, "What is the misery of that estate whereinto man fell?" and answers, "All mankind by their fall lost communion with God (Gen. 3:8, 10, 24), are under his wrath and curse (Eph. 2:2–3; Gal. 3:10), and so made liable to all miseries in this life, to death itself, and to the pains of hell for ever (Lam. 3:39; Rom. 6:23; Matt. 25:41, 46)."[3]

---

1. Berkhof, *Systematic Theology*, 256. He cites as examples Ex. 32:33; Lev. 26:21; Num. 15:31; 1 Chron. 10:13; Pss. 11:6; 75:8; Isa. 1:24, 28; Matt. 3:10; 24:51. See also Erickson, *Christian Theology*, 554–56.
2. *The Three Forms of Unity*, 68.
3. *Reformed Confessions*, 4:355.

At this point, the doctrine of sin touches upon other major doctrinal loci, such as the doctrines of God's justice and providence, the church, and last things. A fuller treatment of those topics is found in the appropriate places in this systematic theology; our treatment here will be brief, but will address important points for a full-orbed view of sin.

The Two Aspects of Sin's Punishment

Sin is punished because it is against God. He is the ultimate reason for the punishment of sin. That punishment is distinguished into two aspects: the loss of communion with God and the infliction of pain under God's wrath. The former appears in God's expulsion of our fallen first parents from the garden where he had met with them (Gen. 3:23–24). The latter appears in his judgments of suffering and death upon them (vv. 16–20).

The traditional theological distinction used here is the punishment of loss versus the punishment of sense. Thomas Aquinas said, "In so far as sin consists in turning away from God, its corresponding punishment is the pain of loss [*poena damni*]. . . . But in so far as sin turns inordinately (to the mutable good), its corresponding punishment is the pain of sense [*poena sensus*]."[4] In medieval theology, this distinction was employed to explain the twofold punishment of sinners in hell: the loss of the beatific vision of God and the infliction of the pains of hellfire. The distinction was also received by Reformed theologians. Antonius Walaeus (1572–1639) said, "The punishment that is owed for sin is twofold, being either the pain of loss [*poena damni*], or the pain of sense [*poena sensus*]."[5]

Sin Breaks Communion with God

God and sin oppose each other in an absolute antithesis.[6] John writes, "This then is the message which we have heard of him, and declare unto you, that God is light, and in him is no darkness at all" (1 John 1:5). If we claim to walk with God as his friends but conduct ourselves in a habit of unrepentant sin, we are liars and hypocrites (v. 6; cf. Amos 3:3). There can never be peace between God and sin. Paul exclaims, "What fellowship hath righteousness with unrighteousness? And what communion hath light with darkness?" (2 Cor. 6:14).

---

4. Aquinas, *Summa Theologica*, Pt. 2.1, Q. 87, Art. 4.
5. Polyander, Walaeus, Thysius, and Rivetus, *Synopsis Purioris Theologiae*, 16.25 (1:395).
6. On God's righteousness and justice, see *RST*, 1:810–26.

Therefore, sin has broken man's communion with God, destroying our friendship and fellowship with him (Isa. 59:2). This is the greatest loss conceivable, for all human happiness is bound up in God (Pss. 36:9; 63:3; 73:25–26).[7] "Man lost God," Thomas Boston said. "Had the sun been forever darkened in the heavens, it had been no such loss as this. God is the cause and fountain of all good; and the loss of him must be the loss of everything that is good and excellent."[8] To be "without God" is to have "no hope" (Eph. 2:12).

Sinners may be reconciled to God (2 Cor. 5:18–21), but sin can never be reconciled to him, for sin is enmity against God (Rom. 8:7). John Owen said, "Enemies may be reconciled, but enmity cannot; yea, the only way to reconcile enemies is to destroy the enmity."[9] Christ came to save sinners not *in* their sins, but *from* their sins (Matt. 1:21), yes, to *destroy* their sins (1 John 3:8). The Holy Spirit dwelling in believers engages in continual militant conflict with sin (Gal. 5:17; cf. 1 Pet. 2:11).

Oh that God would give us eyes to see that every sin wars against God, and God wars against every sin! All of God's attributes are against sin: his omnipresence exposes it, his knowledge judges it, his love abhors it, his righteousness condemns it, his compassion grieves over it, his wisdom plots against it, his majesty looms over it, and his power punishes it.

Sin Provokes God's Wrath

The Bible describes God's attitude toward sin as anger, wrath, indignation, and fury.[10] God hates sin and consequently hates unrepentant and unforgiven sinners (Ps. 5:4–5). We should not conceive of God's wrath as an uncontrolled passion or as an impersonal process, but as wise and righteous divine anger against moral wrong.[11] As Boston wrote, God's wrath is not like sinful human rage; it is not mixed with inward disturbance or agitation, but is righteous displeasure: "a holy fire of anger."[12]

Someone may object that God is love and has no animosity toward anyone, but unconditionally accepts all people. Therefore, it is wrong to

---

7. Willard, *A Compleat Body of Divinity*, 216–17.
8. Boston, *An Illustration of the Doctrines of the Christian Religion*, in *Works*, 1:295.
9. Owen, *The Nature . . . of Indwelling Sin in Believers*, in *Works*, 6:176.
10. On God's wrath, see *RST*, 1:852–61.
11. Against the notion of God's wrath as an impersonal process caused by the sinner, see Berkouwer, *Sin*, 378–80.
12. Boston, *An Illustration of the Doctrines of the Christian Religion*, in *Works*, 1:296.

speak of him as having personal anger toward sinners. People may reject God, we are told, but God never rejects people.

In reply, we joyfully confess that the Lord is "merciful and gracious, longsuffering, and abundant in goodness and truth" (Ex. 34:6). However, the Lord also said that he "will by no means clear the guilty" (v. 7). G. C. Berkouwer noted, "An unbiased study of Scripture can only impress upon us the number and frequency of the biblical allusions to God's wrath."[13] He added, "In our analysis of the scriptural data, we have no right to choose for *either* the love *or* the wrath of God."[14] We must believe both.

God's wrath is not cruelty, but zealous justice against "sin, which is committed against the most high majesty of God."[15] Samuel Willard said, "It is a very righteous wrath; it is nothing else but what sinners justly deserve for their sin."[16] John Brown of Haddington queried, "Doth God take pleasure in the misery of man?" and answered, "He takes no pleasure in it as distressing to man; but he takes pleasure in it as the just punishment of man's sin."[17]

Therefore, God's righteousness causes him not only to break fellowship with guilty sinners, but to execute his curse upon them (Matt. 25:41; Gal. 3.10) with punishments that inflict grievous torments upon them fitting for their sins (Rom. 2:6–9).

The Temporal Operations of Sin's Punishment

God's wrath is active to punish sin in this world. "God is angry with the wicked every day" (Ps. 7:11). When Paul writes, "The wrath of God is revealed from heaven" (Rom. 1:18), he uses the present tense. John Murray commented, "The wrath of God is dynamically, effectively operative in the world of men."[18] Therefore, God's punishment of sinners not saved by faith in Christ has both a temporal aspect and an eternal aspect. Sin not only dooms them to hell, but also makes them "liable to all miseries

---

13. Berkouwer, *Sin*, 356.
14. Berkouwer, *Sin*, 380. He added, "Attempts to tone down the wrath of God are powerless in the face of the strong and frequent biblical words of threat and judgment" (384).
15. The Heidelberg Catechism (LD 5, Q. 11), in *The Three Forms of Unity*, 71.
16. Willard, *A Compleat Body of Divinity*, 218.
17. John Brown of Haddington, *Questions and Answers on the Shorter Catechism* (1846; repr., Grand Rapids, MI: Reformation Heritage Books, 2006), 82. The original title was *An Help for the Ignorant: or, an Essay toward an Easy, Plain, Practical, and Extensive Explication of the Assembly's Shorter Catechism* (1761).
18. Murray, *The Epistle to the Romans*, 1:35.

in this life."[19] God warned that sin would bring death (Gen. 2:17). Willard said, "There is something of death in every misery. Man begins to die as soon as he begins to live."[20]

On this basis, theologians distinguish between temporal punishment in this life and eternal punishment in hell. Full justice awaits judgment day, but God cannot fail to do justice in all his providential works. God exercises his judgment with sovereign freedom; he may apply, delay, or restrain his punishments as he sees fit, but justice will be done. We further distinguish between inward punishments aimed primarily at the soul and outward punishments upon both the body and our circumstances.[21] Here we are not considering the general effects of Adam's sin, namely, the universality of original sin and the curse upon the world. Rather, we are considering the specific judgments God sends against particular individuals or groups for their sins.

Sin Is Punished through Judgments on the Soul

Judgments against the outer man are more sensible and plain, but judgments directly against the heart and soul are more terrible in their effects.

Inward punishments include *judicial abandonment to sin* (Acts 7:42). Paul's exposition of the wrath of God in Romans 1 does not feature outward judgments so much as inward ones through the repeated statement that God "gave them up" or "gave them over" (*paradidōmi*, Rom. 1:24, 26, 28). The verb, a common term meaning to deliver or hand over, can refer to delivering someone over to judicial punishment, such as imprisonment, whipping, or execution.[22] This is Paul's meaning here. God judicially gives people over to sexual sin, homosexuality, and a debased mindset to punish them for their idolatry and refusal to glorify or thank their Creator (vv. 19–23, 25, 28). Similarly, God gives some people over to the power of "strong delusion" so that they believe Satan's lies and follow anti-Christian religion—a judgment for not loving the truth of the gospel (2 Thess. 2:9–12).

Another form of inward punishment is *judicial hardening in unbelief.* The classic biblical example of hardening is the pharaoh of the exodus (Rom. 9:17–18; cf. Exodus 4–14). The Lord gives sinners over to hardness

---

19. The Westminster Shorter Catechism (Q. 19), in *Reformed Confessions*, 4:355.

20. Willard, *A Compleat Body of Divinity*, 223.

21. For these two distinctions, see Brakel, *The Christian's Reasonable Service*, 1:412; and Gill, *Body of Divinity*, 341–42.

22. Matt. 4:12; 5:25; 10:17, 19, 21; 18:34; 27:2, 26; Acts 8:3; 12:4; 22:4; 2 Pet. 2:4.

of heart as punishment for their sins so that they are utterly unresponsive to the Word of God (Isa. 6:9–10; Rom. 11:7–10). As a result, sinners become stubbornly foolish, as when Pharaoh pursued Israel to the Red Sea though he had experienced God's plagues (Ex. 14:4).

We should never conceive of judicial abandonment or hardening in such a manner that would implicate God in sin, as if he infused or encouraged moral evil in the soul. God cannot be tempted to sin and cannot tempt others, but is the giver of every good gift (James 1:13, 17). The Lord does not abandon or harden sinners by the addition of evil, but by the subtraction of good. He reduces the proper operations of intelligence, affection, and conscience that many unbelievers still enjoy by his providence so that men grow more blind and obstinate.[23] God withdraws a measure of his common grace, and men rush forward into sin to their own harm. When God gives them over to hardness of heart, their hardness is still sin for which they are responsible (Ex. 9:34–10:3). Peter Lombard said, "Some sin is both sin and a punishment for sin."[24]

Sin Is Punished through Judgments on the Body

We cannot attribute every affliction to the personal sin of the sufferer; sometimes the sorrow has nothing to do with punishment for the sufferer, but serves a larger purpose (Job 1–2; John 9:1–3). However, many specific troubles come upon sinners as judgments from God.[25] Since every area of life is under God's sovereignty and every aspect of human activity is corrupted by sin, God's judgment may strike in innumerable ways. The covenant curses of God's law to Israel are a study in such afflictions, as are the writings of the prophets.

God can bring famine to a region by infestation or drought (Lev. 26:19–20; Deut. 28:22–24, 38–39). God can attack the basis of a nation's wealth, leading to economic disaster (Isa. 19:5–10). God can cause a people to suffer military defeat and conquest (Deut. 28:25–26; Isa. 13:17–19). He can destroy their public works, places of worship, and infrastructure (Lev. 26:30–32; Ezek. 26:4). He can subjugate people under tyranny and oppression (Lev. 26:16–17; Isa. 19:4). He can scatter people as exiles far from their homes (Lev. 26:33; Isa. 20:4).

---

23. 2 Sam. 17:14; 1 Kings 12:15; Job 12:17; Isa. 19:12–14.
24. Lombard, *The Sentences*, 2.36.1 (2:181).
25. Pss. 7:11–13; 37:10, 35; 64:7; 73:18–19; 92:7–9.

God can open the door for violent crime and injustice to increase (Deut. 28:29–31). The Lord can send wasting and disabling illness (Lev. 26:16; Rev. 2:22). He can put people into financial bondage through debt (Deut. 28:44). God might cause wild animals to maul and kill people (Lev. 26:22; 2 Kings 17:25). He can devastate a sinner's family by giving his spouse and children over to gross wickedness and great sorrow (Amos 7:17). The Lord can inflict insanity to punish the wicked (Deut. 28:28, 34), as he did to King Nebuchadnezzar for a time (Dan. 4:28–33). Or God might send people through trauma that leaves them in a condition of irrational fear when nothing outwardly threatens them (Lev. 26:36–37). This, however, is not to assign all or even most cases of mental illness to a moral cause any more than outward physical afflictions.[26]

If sinners do not repent, the Lord can simply kill them (Acts 12:20–23; Rev. 2:23). Death is the fate of Adam's descendants (1 Cor. 15:22). It is God who executes this final temporal judgment upon mankind: "the LORD killeth" (1 Sam. 2:6).

Temporal judgments serve to restrain sin. Even if sinners do not repent, God's hand of judgment reduces or removes their ability to do evil. The flood removed an entire world of sin and violence (Genesis 6). God's judgment on the Tower of Babel frustrated man's ambition to exalt himself (Genesis 11). God breaks the teeth of the wicked, as it were, so that they cannot devour God's people like lions (Ps. 58:6). The death of Herod the Great made it possible for the family of Jesus Christ to return to the land of Israel (Matt. 2:20). The death of Herod Agrippa I slew a wicked persecutor of the church (Acts 12).

We should recognize the evidence around us that God's wrath is revealed from heaven. Though affliction does not necessarily indicate the punishment of a particular sin, when judgment falls on notorious sinners, let us acknowledge the justice of God. The world ascribes such afflictions to blind nature or idols that do not exist, and it conceals the depravity of its leaders and celebrities when they suffer the consequences of evil conduct. However, when God strikes the wicked, we should fear him, declare his work, wisely consider his actions, rejoice in him, and trust in him (Ps. 64:7–10). Our response should not be to gloat self-righteously over afflicted sinners, but to proclaim the gospel of saving grace and the coming

---

26. For a sympathetic discussion of depression, see Archibald Alexander, *Thoughts on Religious Experience* (1844; repr., Edinburgh: Banner of Truth, 1967), 32–50; and Murray, *Christians Get Depressed Too.*

judgment, and to repent of our own sins, lest we likewise perish under God's wrath (Luke 13:1–5).

The Human Means of Sin's Punishment

God's providence in this age generally works through means, and God uses human means to punish sin. To some extent, these human means restrain and avenge sin in this world. John Calvin noted that God has set up "a twofold government in man," one "spiritual" through the conscience in "the inner mind," and the other "political" to regulate only "outward behavior."[27] Through both means, God manifests his righteous judgment against sinners.

Sin Is Inwardly Judged by the Conscience

God's judgment against sin appears in his restraint of sin through common decency and a sense of shame. This is not a consequence of man's goodness, but the result of a sense of God's righteous judgment that the Bible calls the *conscience*.[28] William Ames said, "The conscience of man . . . is a man's judgment of himself, according to the judgment of God of him."[29] Conscience is not a choice or act of the will, but "an act of practical judgment, proceeding from the understanding."[30] The conscience is bound by what a person understands God's will to be.[31]

We find an example of the conscience's activity in Abimelech, pagan king of Gerar. When God revealed to Abimelech that he had taken the wife of Abraham, the pagan showed a concern for "integrity" (Gen. 20:5). God told him, "Yes, I know that you have done this in the integrity of your heart, and it was I who kept you from sinning against me. Therefore I did not let you touch her" (v. 6 ESV). The verb translated as "kept" (*khasak*) means to hold back or restrain.[32] Perhaps God exercised this restraint on Abimelech by a medical condition, for the text speaks later of God healing

---

27. Calvin, *Institutes*, 3.19.15.

28. John 8:9; Acts 23:1; 24:16; Rom. 2:15; 9:1; 13:5; 1 Cor. 8:7, 10, 12; 10:25, 27–29; 2 Cor. 1:12; 4:2; 5:11; 1 Tim. 1:5, 19; 3:9; 4:2; 2 Tim. 1:3; Titus 1:15; Heb. 9:9, 14; 10:2, 22; 13:18; 1 Pet. 2:19; 3:16, 21.

29. William Ames, *Conscience, with the Power and Cases Thereof*, 1.1, in *The Works of the Reverend and Faithfull Minister of Christ William Ames*, 2 books in 1 vol. (London: John Rothwell, 1643), 1:2.

30. Ames, *Conscience, with the Power and Cases Thereof*, 1.1.6, in *Works*, 1:3.

31. Ames, *Conscience, with the Power and Cases Thereof*, 1.3.2, in *Works*, 1:6. Ames demonstrated the binding authority of the conscience by citing Acts 4:20; 20:22; Rom. 1:14; 1 Cor. 9:16; 2 Cor. 5:14.

32. Gen. 22:12, 16; 39:9; 2 Sam. 18:16; Job 7:11; Prov. 10:19.

him of a problem related to infertility (vv. 17–18).[33] However, Abimelech did have a sincere concern for morality and justice, for he publicly rebuked Abraham for doing wrong and sought to remedy the situation in an honorable manner (vv. 8–16). The people feared God's punishment (vv. 7–8, 11). Therefore, the account reveals both an outward physical restraint and an inward psychological restraint of evil.

The New Testament teaches that in the moral shambles of the unbelieving world there remains a sense of right and wrong that produces a degree of self-control. Even in a sexually immoral culture, there were some norms that people generally did not violate (1 Cor. 5:1). The wicked often provide for their own families (1 Tim. 5:8), demonstrating some likeness to God (Matt. 7:11). The people of the world punish a murderer or thief (1 Pet. 4:15). A common sense of decency is implied in Paul's command, "Repay no one evil for evil, but give thought to do what is honorable [*kalos*] in the sight of all" (Rom. 12:17 ESV; cf. 2 Cor. 8:21).[34]

God sustains in mankind a sense of moral accountability to his law and liability to his wrath. Paul explains that "the Gentiles, which have not the law, do by nature the things contained in the law" (Rom. 2:14). In light of his indictment of all men in that context, he cannot mean that Gentiles live righteous lives that please God (cf. 1:18–32; 3:9–18). Paul evidently has in mind domestic and civil virtues that some non-Christians exercise. Literally, they "do the things of the law" (*ta tou nomou poiōsin*)—that is, they engage in behaviors that follow universal moral principles.[35]

How do we explain these moral virtues among those in whom sin reigns? Paul explains that they have "the work of the law written in their hearts, their conscience also bearing witness, and their thoughts the mean while accusing or else excusing one another" (Rom. 2:15). Paul does not refer here to the gracious writing of the law on the heart in the new covenant (Jer. 31:33; 2 Cor. 3:3), which produces an inward holy desire to do God's will (Ps. 40:8). Rather, the Gentiles have the "work of the law" (Rom. 2:15), which is the knowledge of sin and of God's wrath against sinners (3:20; 4:15). This is the function of the "conscience," which is "bearing witness" or legal testimony. The activity of the conscience anticipates

---

33. "The king could not engage in sexual relations." Mathews, *Genesis 11:27–50:26*, 260.

34. On the interpretation of Rom. 12:17, see Douglas Moo, *The Epistle to the Romans*, The New International Commentary on the New Testament (Grand Rapids, MI: Eerdmans, 1996), 785.

35. Moo, *The Epistle to the Romans*, 150; and Hoekema, *Created in God's Image*, 197.

judgment day, "the day of wrath" (2:5), "when God shall judge the secrets of men" (v. 16). When men sin, they may experience a small foretaste of divine wrath in their guilt, shame, and fear.

Through the conscience, God manifests his righteous judgment to man. Calvin said, "When they have a sense of divine judgment, as a witness joined to them, which does not allow them to hide their sins from being accused before the Judge's tribunal, this sense is called 'conscience.' For it is a certain mean between God and man, because it does not allow man to suppress within himself what he knows, but pursues him to the point of convicting him."[36]

Therefore, the voice of conscience in unregenerate man is not a spark of remaining goodness, but a flickering beam of hellfire reflecting off God's broken image. It does not motivate men out of an inward love for righteousness, for they are enslaved to hatred against God and his holy law (Rom. 8:7). Insofar as it restrains outward eruptions of sin and prompts acts of virtue, it does so through fear of punishment and craving for self-righteousness.

Although conscience exercises a real check upon behavior, we should not overestimate its influence. Paul says that sinners know "the judgment of God, that they which commit such things are worthy of death," but they "not only do the same, but have pleasure in them that do them" (Rom. 1:32). Conscience is often powerless over the practical judgment, affections, and actions of sinners, for "there is no fear of God before their eyes" (3:18). God's law, though holy, righteous, and good, provokes the rebellious hearts of sinners to more sin (7:7–12).

Sin Is Outwardly Judged by the Civil Government

God reinforces the inward work of the conscience through the outward work of the civil magistrate in punishing sin. After the flood had destroyed a world full of violence (Gen. 6:11–13), the Lord instituted capital punishment so that men would inflict the death penalty upon anyone who willfully murdered another human being (9:5–6). God's personal demand ("I require it") and the basis of this penalty in the murderer's assault upon God's image make it clear that the death penalty implemented the judgment of God.[37] Since God condemns personal revenge (Lev. 19:18), this

---

36. Calvin, *Institutes*, 3.19.15.
37. Mathews, *Genesis 1–11:26*, 403.

command to Noah suggests a civil process overseen by authorities acting according to law, which, later, God explicitly instructed the Israelites to do (Deut. 19:15–21).

The execution of civil justice restrains sin in a society. God repeatedly told the people of Israel that if they would punish the evildoer, the people "shall hear, and fear," and consequently be restrained from committing wickedness.[38] Conversely, "because sentence against an evil work is not executed speedily, therefore the heart of the sons of men is fully set in them to do evil" (Eccles. 8:11). And, of course, the death penalty removes an evildoer from society so that he can do no more harm, which is a blessing to the vulnerable and persecuted (Ps. 94:3–6, 21–23). Civil law can prevent or mitigate persecution against believers.[39] Government officials may persecute believers due to the influence of Satan over this world (Revelation 13), but as Tom Schreiner says, "Even the most oppressive governments . . . hold evil in check to some extent, preventing society from collapsing into complete anarchy."[40]

However, though criminal punishment benefits society and the church, the primary purpose of the judicial system is justice.[41] Herman Bavinck noted how modern society has "viewed criminals as victims" and turned "crime into a disease and punishment into a means of cure."[42] However, "punishment is imposed, in the first place, not because it is useful, but because justice requires it."[43] God has ordained "the powers that be" to praise and bless those who do good, but "to execute wrath upon him that doeth evil" (Rom. 13:1, 4; cf. 1 Pet. 2:13–14). The civil government is not to judge inward beliefs or affections, but "works," whether good or evil (Rom. 13:3). The civil authorities are the servants of the sovereign Lord, who equips them with deadly force ("the sword") to punish criminals. When the government carries out its divine vocation of justice, it helps people to set aside their desires for personal revenge and to leave justice to the "wrath" of God (12:19). Criminal justice is a manifestation of God's wrath against sin insofar as officials act as agents of true justice (cf. Deut. 21:22–23).[44]

---

38. Deut. 13:11; 17:13; 19:20; 21:21.
39. Esther 8–10; Isa. 45:1–4, 13; Acts 16:35–38; 22:24–29; 23:11–35; 1 Tim. 2:2.
40. Thomas R. Schreiner, *1, 2 Peter, Jude*, The New American Commentary 37 (Nashville: Broadman & Holman, 2003), 129.
41. Berkhof, *Systematic Theology*, 258.
42. Bavinck, *Reformed Dogmatics*, 3:164–65.
43. Bavinck, *Reformed Dogmatics*, 3:167.
44. Murray, *The Epistle to the Romans*, 2:151–53.

The apostolic teaching on civil government does not present the magistrate as a means of saving grace, but rather as a means of justice and wrath in a fallen world. In this respect, the function of civil government differs markedly from parenting and church discipline. Whereas God gives "the sword" to civil officials, he gives "the rod" to parents, and its spiritual equivalent to church elders (1 Cor. 4:21). Fathers and mothers should apply corporal punishment to their children out of a loving desire that they will be delivered from their inherent moral foolishness and its deadly effects—not to display God's wrath or to do harm.[45] The reproofs of the church should aim at winning back the member straying into sin.[46] Even when a church must excommunicate a member for unrepentant sin and obstinacy in the face of repeated warnings, it does so with redemptive hope that this discipline will be a means of awakening and salvation (1 Cor. 5:5). God has entrusted to the church "the ministry of reconciliation" (2 Cor. 5:18), but appointed the civil official as "the minister of God, a revenger to execute wrath upon him that doeth evil" (Rom. 13:4). Civil government, parenting, and pastoral ministry are all noble callings but of a very different nature, designed to complement each other in advancing God's righteous purposes in the world.

The Eternal Fulfillment of Sin's Punishment

All forms of temporal punishment fall short of the glorious justice that God will display in the eternal damnation of sinners. Despite all human attempts to exalt ourselves and debase God, "the mighty man shall be humbled, and the eyes of the lofty shall be humbled: but the LORD of hosts shall be exalted in judgment, and God that is holy shall be sanctified in righteousness" (Isa. 5:15–16).

Sin Is Fully Punished after Death and Especially after the Resurrection

The eternal punishment of sin begins for the soul upon death. The Westminster Larger Catechism (Q. 86) says, "The souls of the wicked are at their death cast into hell, where they remain in torments and utter darkness, and their bodies kept in their graves, as in their prisons, till the resurrection and judgement of the great day (Luke 16:23–24; Acts 1:25; Jude 6–7)."[47]

---

45. Prov. 13:24; 22:15; 23:13–14; 29:15.
46. Matt. 18:12, 15; Luke 17:3; James 5:19–20.
47. *Reformed Confessions*, 4:317.

Christ described one man's fate: after he died in the midst of great wealth and luxury, he found himself being tormented in flame. He had feasted sumptuously every day while neglecting the beggar at his gate, but after death he thirsted and could not have a drop of water (Luke 16:22–25). Ralph Venning (c. 1622–1674) wrote, "Wicked men are called the men of this world (Ps. 17:14). They have their portion and consolation in this life (Luke 6:24; 16:25). . . . But when they come to be damned, neither riches, nor honors, nor pleasures will descend with them."[48]

Eternal punishment will come to its fullness at the resurrection, when "they that have done evil" will be raised unto "damnation" (John 5:29). At that time, "the Son of man shall come in the glory of his Father with his angels; and then he shall reward every man according to his works" (Matt. 16:27). The King will "sit upon the throne of his glory" and summon all mankind to appear before him (25:31–32). William Perkins said that Christ's appearance "in endless glory and majesty" will be so "terrible and dreadful" that wicked men "shall desire the mountains to fall upon them and the hills to cover them."[49] He will manifest to them their sins. They will be taken away "into everlasting punishment" (v. 46). God's holy angels will "cast them into the furnace of fire: there shall be wailing and gnashing of teeth" (13:50).

Sin Is Fully Punished through Sorrows of Loss and Sense

The two aspects of sin's punishment will both be manifested in eternity. Johannes Wollebius said, "This state [of the damned] consists of the loss of the highest good and the undergoing of the highest evil."[50] We see both in Christ's words of judgment: "Depart from me, ye cursed, into everlasting fire, prepared for the devil and his angels" (Matt. 25:41). Here we see the punishment of loss ("depart from me") and the punishment of sense ("into everlasting fire").[51]

The eternal *punishment of loss* consists of the removal of the wicked from the enjoyment of all favor and mercy from God. Willard explained, "This consists in a total privation of all the happiness [they were] made

---

48. Ralph Venning, *Sin, the Plague of Plagues; or, Sinful Sin the Worst of Evils* (London: John Hancock, 1669), 70; modernized version: *The Sinfulness of Sin*, Puritan Paperbacks (Edinburgh: Banner of Truth, 1965).
49. Perkins, *An Exposition of the Symbol*, in *Works*, 5:294.
50. Wollebius, *Compendium*, 1.12.(1).viii (74).
51. Venning, *Sin, the Plague of Plagues*, 67.

capable of."[52] The Lord will reject them forever. He will exclude them from all beauty, pleasure, and comfort. He will separate them from the sweet company of the saints and angels. Christ pictured this aspect of judgment as being shut out of a feast and cast into the outer darkness (Matt. 8:11–12; 22:13; cf. 25:10).

The eternal *punishment of sense* consists of the infliction of horrible pain upon the wicked by the wrath of God. As a consequence of their choosing to rebel against him, the Lord will subject them to sorrows in body and soul forever. He will imprison them in sadness and torment with the Devil, the demons, and wicked human beings. Christ pictured this aspect of judgment as being cast into a furnace of flaming fire.[53] Venning said, "To pluck out a right eye, to cut off a right hand, were a pleasure and recreation in comparison of being damned in hell (Matt. 5:30)."[54]

Sin Is Fully Punished with Absolute Righteous Wrath

The wicked will experience the unmixed wrath of God (Rev. 14:10). He will give them "judgment without mercy" (James 2:13). God will "make his power known" upon "the vessels of wrath fitted to destruction" (Rom. 9:22). The eternal punishment of the wicked will display the glory and power of the Lord God (Rev. 19:1–4).

It will not be a case of might makes right. God will not simply overpower them like a cosmic bully. The image of opened books in the vision of Revelation implies that God will make his justice plain and manifest in every case (Rev. 20:12). Human hypocrisy will fail, "for there is nothing covered, that shall not be revealed; neither hid, that shall not be known" (Luke 12:2). God will reveal sin not only in its event, but also in its violation of his law, "that every mouth may be stopped, and all the world may become guilty before God" (Rom. 3:19). The law will testify against sinners (John 5:45), as will their own consciences (Rom. 2:15–16). Perkins said that when God opens the book of each man's conscience, then "his very conscience shall be as good as a thousand witnesses; whereupon he shall accuse and condemn himself."[55] God "will render to every man according to his deeds" (v. 6). Sin will then be demonstrated to be the ugliest corruption, darkest treason, and foulest ingratitude against God.

---

52. Willard, *A Compleat Body of Divinity*, 238.
53. Matt. 5:22; 7:19; 13:42, 50; 18:8–9; 25:41; Mark 9:43–49; John 15:6.
54. Venning, *Sin, the Plague of Plagues*, 79.
55. Perkins, *An Exposition of the Symbol*, in *Works*, 5:297.

Consider what the Holy Scriptures teach about the properties of the wrath of God.[56] God's wrath against sinners is *irresistible in its force.* Nahum said, "Who can stand before his indignation? And who can abide in the fierceness of his anger? His fury is poured out like fire, and the rocks are thrown down by him" (Nah. 1:6). God's wrath is *inconceivable in its power.* Moses exclaimed, "Who knoweth the power of thine anger?" (Ps. 90:11). His wrath is *unbearable in its effects.* Isaiah wrote, "The sinners in Zion are afraid; fearfulness hath surprised the hypocrites. Who among us shall dwell with the devouring fire? Who among us shall dwell with everlasting burnings?" (Isa. 33:14). His wrath is *infinite in its reach.* The Lord said, "For a fire is kindled in mine anger, and shall burn unto the lowest hell, and shall consume the earth with her increase, and set on fire the foundations of the mountains" (Deut. 32:22). His wrath is *unavoidable in its punishment.* The New Testament warns those who hear the gospel, "How shall we escape, if we neglect so great salvation?" (Heb. 2:3; cf. Heb. 12:25). His wrath is *constant in its exercise and eternal in its duration.* "And the smoke of their torment ascendeth up for ever and ever: and they have no rest day nor night" (Rev. 14:11). And no one will be able to accuse God of injustice, for his wrath is *righteous in its judgment,* as we will see on "the day of wrath and revelation of the righteous judgment of God" (Rom. 2:5).

Oh, the dreadful weight of sin! Boston said, "See here the great evil of sin. Many reckon it but a small matter to transgress God's holy and righteous law. . . . But if they would consider the dreadful effects of sin, they would be of another mind. Sin is the worst of evils."[57] Venning said, "Is not sin exceedingly sinful that separates him from all good, past, present, and to come?"[58] The doctrine of the punishment of sin should strongly motivate us to fear God (Matt. 10:28).

Willard said, "Let this be a word of solemn awakening to convince sinners of the present misery that is upon them. It may be, for the present, you are under the patience of God, and the miseries which are the portion of sinners are not fallen, in their full weight, upon you, and you begin to bless yourselves, and say, The bitterness of death is over." However, you must not fool yourself to think you are safe in an unconverted state

---

56. Some of the following are adapted from Brown, *Questions and Answers on the Shorter Catechism,* 83.

57. Boston, *An Illustration of the Doctrines of the Christian Religion,* in *Works,* 1:300.

58. Venning, *Sin, the Plague of Plagues,* 77.

toward God. Willard continued, "You have no fellowship with him; you are far from him, at an everlasting distance. You are the subjects of his wrath, and stand just in the way of the floods of his indignation."[59] What madness it is to stay in that dangerous position! Will you be so insane as to play in the place of death and to joke at the entrance to hell? Get right with God through faith in Christ. "Let this consideration make Christ precious to you," as Willard said.[60] His blood is the only refuge from the wrath of God.

Sing to the Lord

God's Judgment on the Wicked and Vindication of the Righteous

Hear, Lord, the voice of my complaint,
Preserve my life from fear,
Hide me from plotting enemies
And evil crowding near.
The workers of iniquity
Their deadly shafts prepare;
They aim at me their treacherous words;
O save me from their snare.

The wicked in their base designs
Grow arrogant and bold;
Conspiring secretly they think
That God will not behold;
They search out more iniquity,
Their thoughts and plans are deep,
God will smite, for He is near
His saints to guard and keep.

The wicked, by their sins o'ercome,
Shall soon be brought to shame;
The hand of God shall yet appear,
And all shall fear His Name.
The just shall triumph in the Lord,
Their trust shall be secure,
And endless glory then shall crown
The upright and the pure.

---

59. Willard, *A Compleat Body of Divinity*, 219–20.
60. Willard, *A Compleat Body of Divinity*, 220.

Psalm 64
Tune: Monora
The Psalter, No. 165
Trinity Hymnal—Baptist Edition, No. 753

Questions for Meditation or Discussion

1. What are the "pain of loss" and the "pain of sense"?
2. Why must sin break our fellowship with and enjoyment of God?
3. Why must sin bring down God's wrath?
4. What judgments might God send against a sinner's soul as punishment for sin?
5. What judgments might God send against a sinner's body or possessions as punishment for sin?
6. How does God employ the conscience to judge sin internally?
7. How does God make use of civil government to judge sin externally?
8. When will God fully punish sinners?
9. How will sinners experience eternal divine punishment in both "loss" and "sense"?
10. What eight qualities make God's wrath a terrifying thing to face?
11. Do you deserve to experience God's wrath forever? If so, how will you escape it? How can a just and holy God not send you to hell?

Questions for Deeper Reflection

12. How can someone discern whether his sufferings in this life are judgments sent as punishment of his sins by an angry God?
13. Someone argues that unrepentant sinners lose the joy of fellowshipping with God, but he does not inflict suffering on anyone, for God is love. Why is that idea inadequate, both biblically and theologically?

25

Sin and the Believer

Nothing reveals more about a person than how he relates to his sins. All people have consciences that accuse them of wrong when they go against what they perceive as God's will. Many people feel remorse. However, only those to whom God has granted new hearts hate sin as sin and turn from it to the true God. Yet even they are mixtures of sin and righteousness in this life. They are regenerated and are being sanctified, but have not yet been glorified.

This chapter is not an exposition of the doctrines of regeneration, conversion, and sanctification—such are the domain of soteriology.[1] Rather, it is an experiential consideration of how the believer in Christ relates to sin in his life. It is a painful subject, yet one that evidences God's grace and gives hope to the people of God.

The Believer's Humble Response to Sin

To encounter God is to have one's sins exposed. Christ said that part of the Spirit's work of bearing witness was that he would "reprove the world of sin" (John 16:8). When God converts a sinner, conviction becomes contrition, a deep inward brokenness over sin. David said, "The LORD is nigh [near] unto them that are of a broken heart; and saveth such as be of a contrite spirit" (Ps. 34:18). God is not pleased with merely external worship, but "the sacrifices of God are a broken spirit: a broken and a

---

1. See the chapters on effectual calling, regeneration, and especially repentance and faith in *RST*, vol. 3 (forthcoming).

contrite heart, O God, thou wilt not despise" (51:17). The Holy Spirit moved Isaiah to write, "For thus saith the high and lofty One that inhabiteth eternity, whose name is Holy; I dwell in the high and holy place, with him also that is of a contrite and humble spirit, to revive the spirit of the humble, and to revive the heart of the contrite ones" (Isa. 57:15). God cares little about ornate buildings; his favored temple is the person who is humbled and broken under his Word (66:1–2).

We must not prescribe rules to the Holy Spirit about how he leads sinners to conversion and then manifests the new life within them. There is a mystery about the new birth that we cannot penetrate (John 3:8). Archibald Alexander (1772–1851) said, "There are, doubtless, great diversities in the appearances of the motions and actings of spiritual life in its incipient stages."[2]

However, by whatever route God may bring sinners to his Son, all true members of God's kingdom have this in common: they are "poor in spirit" (Matt. 5:3). Christ said, "The Spirit of the Lord is upon me, because he hath anointed me to preach the gospel to the poor; he hath sent me to heal the brokenhearted, to preach deliverance to the captives, and recovering of sight to the blind, to set at liberty them that are bruised" (Luke 4:18; citing Isa. 61:1). Christ's church is not a proud people, but "a bruised reed" that Christ tenderly nurtures by the Holy Spirit as he brings justice to the nations (Matt. 12:18–20; citing Isa. 42:1–3).

Therefore, we may summarize the believer's response to sin as *humility*. Wilhelmus à Brakel said, "Humility issues forth from a right judgment of one's self. The humble acknowledge . . . that they have sinned and come short of the glory of God. . . . They are worthy of having been cast into hell long ago."[3] He added, "The essence of humility consists in lowliness of heart." It opposes both pride that puffs up the heart in arrogance and despondency that casts it down in despair.[4] As Charles Bridges (1794–1869) said, pride lifts up the heart against God and fights against him for supremacy.[5] By contrast, humility motivates dependent and persevering action along the pathway of confession, repentance, faith, prayer, watchfulness, combat, and thanksgiving.

---

2. Alexander, *Thoughts on Religious Experience*, 23.
3. Brakel, *The Christian's Reasonable Service*, 4:70.
4. Brakel, *The Christian's Reasonable Service*, 4:69.
5. Charles Bridges, *A Commentary on Proverbs*, Geneva Series of Commentaries (1846; repr., Edinburgh: Banner of Truth, 1968), 228.

Confession of Sin

When God brings a sinner to a saving encounter with himself, the spiritual sight of God's holiness elicits a confession of sin. Christ depicted the kind of man whom God justifies and exalts as one who humbly grieves over his wrongs and prays, "God be merciful to me a sinner" (Luke 18:13–14). Confession of sin continues to characterize the believer after conversion. David wrote of his bitter experience of backsliding into sin and said, "I acknowledge my sin unto thee, and mine iniquity have I not hid. I said, I will confess my transgressions unto the LORD; and thou forgavest the iniquity of my sin" (Ps. 32:5). David had tried to hide his sins from God and man (v. 3), but he came to call God "my hiding place" (v. 7). Murray Brett says that we "need to change our hiding place"; rather than covering our sins and hiding in deceit, we must confess our sins and hide in God's mercy.[6] David presented his case as an example of how the godly seek the Lord in their prayers (v. 6) and a model for all to follow by faith (vv. 8–10). This believing, willing confession of sins "belongs in common to all the children of God."[7]

The children of God walk in the light, while this world walks in the darkness and has no fellowship with God (1 John 1:5–6). Walking in the light means conducting oneself in obedience to God's commands, especially the command to love one another (2:8–11). However, walking in the light does not mean living without sin, but confessing one's sins when the light of God's Word exposes them. John says, "If we say that we have no sin, we deceive ourselves, and the truth is not in us. If we confess our sins, he is faithful and just to forgive us our sins, and to cleanse us from all unrighteousness" (1:8–9). Healthy Christian living requires regularly confessing sin to God and asking for his forgiveness (Matt. 6:12). An unwillingness to confess sin except when outwardly compelled may indicate that a person is still a slave of sin.

Repentance toward God

A humble response to sin goes beyond confession to include a heartfelt repentance of sin. The gospel message demands repentance for salvation (Mark 1:15). Saving repentance is not just a change of beliefs or a religious

---

6. Murray G. Brett, *Growing Up in Grace: The Use of Means for Communion with God* (Grand Rapids, MI: Reformation Heritage Books, 2009), 54.
7. Calvin, *Commentaries*, on Ps. 32:6.

decision, but a complete reorientation of a person by grace. The Westminster Larger Catechism (Q. 76) explains the meaning of repentance in a manner that we can analyze according to its source, motives, and acts:

> *The Divine Source of Repentance*: "Repentance unto life is a saving grace (2 Tim. 2:25), wrought in the heart of a sinner by the Spirit (Zech. 12:10) and word of God (Acts 11:18, 20–21) . . ."

> *The Motives of Repentance*: (1) "whereby, out of the sight and sense, not only of the danger (Ezek. 18:28, 30, 32; Luke 15:17–18; Hos. 2:6–7), but also of the filthiness and odiousness of his sins (Ezek. 36:31; Isa. 30:22), and" (2) "upon the apprehension of God's mercy in Christ to such as are penitent (Joel 2:12–13) . . ."

> *The Essential Acts of Repentance*: "he so grieves for (Jer. 31:18–19) and hates his sins (2 Cor. 7:11), as that he turns from them all to God (Acts 26:18; Ezek. 14:6; 1 Kings 8:47–48), purposing and endeavouring constantly to walk with him in all the ways of new obedience (Ps. 119:6, 59, 128; Luke 1:6; 2 Kings 23:25)."[8]

Repentance marks the beginning of the Christian life and characterizes it all the way through to the end. God's Spirit leads God's children to put their sins to death (Rom. 8:12–14). Thus, repentance does not display a lack of spirituality, but demonstrates real spirituality. Continued repentance also constitutes an essential aspect of church growth. Christ calls churches to repent of their sins and lack of love (Rev. 2:4–5; 3:3).

Christian repentance engages the whole person: the actions of the "hands," the thoughts and motives of the "heart," and the emotions of the inner man: "be afflicted, and mourn, and weep" (James 4:8–9). No cold-hearted or superficial dealing with sin will suffice. The God of grace and mercy calls us to tear our hearts and grieve over sin (Joel 2:12–13). The blessing of his kingdom rests upon those who mourn over sin, treat others with meekness instead of arrogance, and hunger and thirst for righteousness (Matt. 5:4–6).

God has given his people means to facilitate their growth in repentance. We must make good use of them. Sit regularly under a preaching ministry that exposits God's Word and searches men's hearts. Meditate on God's law in its applications to thought, word, and deed in order to expose your sins.

---

8. *Reformed Confessions*, 4:314.

Set your mind on the promises of the gospel, that the goodness of God in Christ may woo you away from sin back to your loving Father. Cultivate friendships with godly people and invite them to correct your transgressions. Take regular time to confess your sins to God and pray for forgiveness and sanctifying grace. You may need to begin by confessing your lack of confession and the deceitful hardness that is starting to numb your soul.

Faith in Christ

Faith is the empty hand by which we receive Christ with his saving benefits (John 1:12). Paul says, "We have believed in Jesus Christ, that we might be justified" (Gal. 2:16). Christians also believe in Christ in order to be sanctified. Faith looks to Christ as the One who came to "save his people from their sins" (Matt. 1:21). Faith calls upon Christ as the Redeemer who gave himself to make his people zealous to serve God (Titus 2:14). Arthur Pink (1886–1952) said, "They who do not yearn after holiness of heart and righteousness of life are only deceiving themselves when they suppose they desire to be saved by Christ. The plain fact is, all that is wanted by so many today is merely a soothing of their conscience, which will enable them to go on comfortably in a course of self-pleasing . . . without fear of eternal punishment."[9]

God has taught the Christian to say, "In the LORD have I righteousness and strength" (Isa. 45:24). Believers must look to Christ daily as their justifying righteousness. John counsels believers, "My little children, these things write I unto you, that ye sin not. And if any man sin, we have an advocate with the Father, Jesus Christ the righteous: and he is the propitiation for our sins: and not for ours only, but also for the sins of the whole world" (1 John 2:1–2). Christ's wrath-appeasing sacrifice and heavenly intercession lay the only foundation for our confidence that God forgives and accepts us.

Believers must also rely upon the Lord for their sanctifying strength. Paul's first instruction regarding spiritual warfare is "Be strong in the Lord, and in the power of his might" (Eph. 6:10). With these words, Paul points Christians to the divine power operating in the risen Lord Jesus (1:19–20).[10] To put sin to death, they must set their hearts on things above, "where Christ sitteth on the right hand of God," for Christ "is our life" (Col. 3:1–4).

---

9. Arthur W. Pink, *Practical Christianity* (Grand Rapids, MI: Guardian, 1974), 26.

10. Compare "in the power of his might" (*en tō kratei tēs ischuous*, Eph. 6:10) with the very similar phrase translated as "of his mighty power" (*tou kratous tēs ischuous*, 1:19).

It is by faith in Christ that God's children overcome the world (1 John 5:4–5). There is more power in the death of Christ to conquer sin and Satan than in all the intelligence and self-denial of man (Col. 2:20–23). John Owen said, "Set faith at work on Christ for the killing of thy sin. His blood is the great sovereign remedy for sin-sick souls. Live in this, and thou wilt die a conqueror; yea, thou wilt, through the good providence of God, live to see thy lust dead at thy feet."[11] Faith is everything; without it, nothing else mentioned in this chapter will bear any spiritual good, for faith unites us to Christ, and Christ is all.

Prayer for the Spirit's Grace

Faith breathes out prayer, and faith in Christ for justifying and sanctifying grace expresses itself in prayers for the same. The Lord Jesus taught us to pray, "And lead us not into temptation, but deliver us from evil" (Matt. 6:13). To enter "into temptation" refers to a situation of severe testing in which our weaknesses are exposed to Satan's assaults (26:41). "Evil" in this context refers to moral evil or sin.[12] It may specifically refer to Satan, for the adjective is articular and singular: "the evil one" (*ho ponēros*).[13] Therefore, just as we should pray daily for our physical needs ("our daily bread," 6:11), so we should ask each day for God's protection against and deliverance from sin.

There may be times when the saints entangle themselves in sin, injure their souls, and weaken their love for righteousness. While their hearts are set on sin, any prayers they offer are deeply irreverent (Ps. 66:18). Neither should they confess sins to God to gain forgiveness without the intention to forsake sin (Prov. 28:13). They must go to God in repentance with the intent of fighting sin, or at least with hearts breaking over the weakness of their repentance.[14]

The Psalms teach the godly to pray for God to empower them to overcome sin. David said, "Keep back thy servant also from presumptuous sins; let them not have dominion over me: then shall I be upright, and I shall be innocent from the great transgression" (Ps. 19:13).

In another psalm, we read a prayer for God to illuminate the believer to understand the Word (Ps. 119:33–34). This is followed by a prayer that

---

11. Owen, *Of the Mortification of Sin in Believers; the Necessity, Nature, and Means of It*, in *Works*, 6:79.
12. Matt. 5:11, 37, 39, 45; 6:23; 7:11, 17–18.
13. Thus, Matt. 13:38–39, and possibly 5:37, but the expression refers to a man in Matt. 5:39.
14. Brakel, *The Christian's Reasonable Service*, 3:454.

God will lead his child in the pathway of obedience and grant him growing repentance to turn away from sin: "Make me to go in the path of thy commandments; for therein do I delight. Incline my heart unto thy testimonies, and not to covetousness. Turn away mine eyes from beholding vanity; and quicken thou me ["give me life," ESV] in thy way" (Ps. 119:35–37).

We should pray likewise for each other. Christ taught us to pray "*Our Father . . . deliver us,*" implying that we should pray for the sanctification of the whole family of God. Paul commands intercession for other saints (Eph. 6:18) and models it in his written prayers for the spiritual growth of believers.[15]

Watchfulness against Temptation

The New Testament frequently commands Christians to "watch" (*grēgoreō*), a verb meaning to stay awake and alert. The Scriptures often frame the call to watchfulness with an eschatological outlook that anticipates Christ's sudden return at a time no man can predict.[16] The Bible couples this perspective of hope with an awareness that a spiritual battle rages in these last days (cf. Heb. 1:2; 1 John 2:18). Thus, when Paul told the Thessalonian believers to "watch and be sober" (1 Thess. 5:6), he did so both in the context of waiting for the dawning of the day of the Lord (vv. 1–5) and engaging in spiritual warfare against sin as we wait (vv. 7–10). The Lord Jesus modeled watchfulness against temptation in his climactic battle in the garden of Gethsemane and called his disciples to do the same: "Watch and pray" (Matt. 26:38–41; Mark 14:34–38).

Brakel said, "Spiritual watchfulness consists in watching over our soul in a careful and circumspect manner in order that no evil may befall her."[17] Proverbs counsels us, "Keep thy heart with all diligence" (Prov. 4:23). The opposite of watchfulness is spiritual lethargy, inattention, and laziness. Brakel warned, "We are by nature very drowsy," but "the enemies are wakeful and are tireless in the execution of their assaults."[18] Therefore, we must guard our hearts, which, as John Flavel said, requires "the diligent and constant use . . . of all holy means and duties, to preserve the soul from sin, and maintain its sweet and free communion with God."[19]

---

15. For example, see Eph. 1:15–20; 3:14–21; Phil. 1:9–11; Col. 1:9–14; 1 Thess. 3:11–13; 2 Thess. 1:11–12.
16. Matt. 24:42–43; 25:13; Mark 13:34–37; Luke 12:36–40; Rev. 16:15.
17. Brakel, *The Christian's Reasonable Service*, 4:11.
18. Brakel, *The Christian's Reasonable Service*, 4:11, 13.
19. Flavel, *A Saint Indeed*, in *Works*, 5:423.

Christians must adopt the attitude of sentinels who never know when the next attack will come. Carelessness kills. Elders must keep watch for false teachers, even in their own midst (Acts 20:30–31). Believers must exercise a wise alertness and manly courage as they stand firm in their faith (1 Cor. 16:13). Like his Master, Paul joins watchfulness with petition: "Continue in prayer, and watch in the same with thanksgiving" (Col. 4:2). Peter accentuates the need for spiritual sobriety and guardedness by comparing Satan to "a roaring lion . . . seeking whom he may devour" (1 Pet. 5:8).

Combat against Sin and Satan

The saints must do more than watch and pray—they must fight. The Holy Spirit who dwells within them produces holy desires contrary to the lusts of their flesh (Gal. 5:17). They must "walk in the Spirit," exerting continual effort to move in the right direction against the headwind of sin (v. 16). Paul says, "If we live in the Spirit, let us also walk in the Spirit" (v. 25). Here he is using another verb (*stoicheō*) that means to march or keep in step, indicating that we must follow the Spirit's leadership, which he exercises through the Word (6:16). Christians must deny themselves, put their sinful passions to death, and serve one another in love (5:13, 19–24).

Each Christian has the personal responsibility to fight against sin and Satan. It is true that we can fight only in "the whole armour of God" (Eph. 6:11). Pink said, "It is called 'the armour of God' because He both provides and bestows it, for we have none of our own; and yet, while this armour is of God's providing and bestowing, we have to put it on!" This means we must put into action the graces God has given us in Christ.[20] We must exert the spiritual muscles of love, joy, peace, patience, kindness, goodness, faithfulness, gentleness, and self-control.

We must destroy each of the works of the flesh and cultivate all the fruit of the Spirit. This is one reason why God gave us the multiplicity of his commandments and exhortations. If holiness came effortlessly from abiding in Christ by faith, then we would need no lists of sins to avoid and virtues to embrace. Faith in Christ draws down heavenly power to obey specific commandments and put down particular sins.

Sanctification is not easy. We must endure "a great fight of afflictions" (Heb. 10:32). We must "flee" from evil desires, "follow after righteousness," "fight the good fight of faith," and "lay hold on eternal life" (1 Tim. 6:11–12).

---

20. Pink, *Practical Christianity*, 124.

We must stand our ground against the onslaught of many powerful, invisible enemies (Eph. 6:10–12). We must "earnestly contend for the faith which was once delivered unto the saints" (Jude 3). We must "strive to enter in at the strait gate" (Luke 13:24). And we must be "struggling" in our prayers for each other (Col. 4:12 ESV). Alexander wrote, "The Christian is a soldier and must expect to encounter enemies, and to engage in many a severe conflict."[21]

Thanksgiving to the Father

Though believers must still grieve over sin and fight for obedience, they may do so with joyful confidence in their Savior. Grace evokes gratitude. Paul writes, "But God be thanked, that ye were the servants of sin, but ye have obeyed from the heart that form of doctrine which was delivered you" (Rom. 6:17). Therefore, Christians should regularly thank God for the grace that set them free from sin's enslaving power and made them obedient to God.

Christians should remember that their salvation was nothing less than rescue from the kingdom of Satan and admission into Christ's kingdom. Paul prayed for the saints at Colossae, that they would be increasingly "giving thanks unto the Father, which hath made us meet to be partakers of the inheritance of the saints in light: who hath delivered us from the power of darkness, and hath translated us into the kingdom of his dear Son: in whom we have redemption through his blood, even the forgiveness of sins" (Col. 1:12–14).

Let us declare the praises of our Savior. Let every believer say, "I love the LORD, because he hath heard my voice and my supplications" (Ps. 116:1). Everyone saved by grace can say, "He brought me up also out of an horrible pit, out of the miry clay, and set my feet upon a rock" (40:2). In the midst of the battle against indwelling sin, we should frequently give glory to God, apart from whom we would not fight sin at all. Though remaining sin makes us "wretched," let us say, "I thank God through Jesus Christ our Lord" that the victory is ours (Rom. 7:24–25).

The Believer's Paradoxical Experience of Sin

Christian experience contains many tensions. It is important to maintain a balanced perspective on saints and their sins so that we grow neither discouraged nor overconfident.

---

21. Alexander, *Thoughts on Religious Experience*, 130.

Forgiveness of Guilt, but with Appropriate Shame

God grants believers forgiveness for "all trespasses," having satisfied the debt of their sins and cancelled their liability to punishment at the cross (Col. 2:13–14). He is not stingy with mercy, but grants them "the forgiveness of sins, according to the riches of his grace" (Eph. 1:7). They are free from all condemnation (Rom. 8:1). However, at the same time, they remember their past sins, sense their remaining corruption, and see their continuing acts of sin. This grieves them and makes them feel ashamed, precisely because they now serve God from their hearts.

The Lord promised Israel, "I will establish my covenant with thee; and thou shalt know that I am the Lord: that thou mayest remember, and be confounded, and never open thy mouth any more because of thy shame, when I am pacified toward thee for all that thou hast done, saith the Lord God" (Ezek. 16:62–63). On the one hand, God promised to reconcile them to himself in a covenant relationship. He would be "pacified" (*kaphar*), which meant that his anger would be removed by the atonement of their guilt. On the other hand, they would still feel shame and disgrace for their previous unfaithfulness, and rightly so. As William Greenhill (1598–1671) commented, God's forgiveness teaches sinners to say, "Ah, what have we done! How have we sinned against a God of love, against mercy, against grace! We will do it no more."[22]

This then is not a shame that includes a fear of rejection, but a shame mingled with the freedom of security a believer experiences because his sins are forgiven. We see both shame and freedom in Paul's words: "What fruit had ye then in those things whereof ye are now ashamed? For the end of those things is death. But now being made free from sin, and become servants to God, ye have your fruit unto holiness, and the end everlasting life. For the wages of sin is death; but the gift of God is eternal life through Jesus Christ our Lord" (Rom. 6:21–23). Believers are on a new path, the road of holiness leading to eternal life by the free grace of God, but still they "are ashamed of their past life," as John Murray said.[23]

Deliverance from Sin's Dominion, but with Remaining Corruption

By their vital union with Christ, believers share in his death and resurrection so that they are "dead to sin" and "walk in newness of life" (Rom.

---

22. William Greenhill, *An Exposition of the Prophet Ezekiel*, ed. James Sherman (Edinburgh: James Nichol, 1864), 411.
23. Murray, *The Epistle to the Romans*, 1:236.

6:2, 4). They are no longer under sin but "under grace," so that sin cannot rule them as their master any more (v. 14). God's law could never have set them free, but only provoked sin (7:5). However, they are now "married" to the risen Christ by the bond of the Holy Spirit so that they bear fruit for God (vv. 4, 6). They experience this new reality in the holy motions of their hearts toward God in faith and love. Their mindset toward the Lord is no longer one of sheer enmity, but they desire to please him, and they are able to do so by the life-giving Spirit of Christ within them (8:6–10).

Yet in their hearts they also experience great conflict and disappointment with themselves. They "delight in the law of God after the inward man" (Rom. 7:22), and "with the mind . . . serve the law of God" (v. 25). However, they find "evil is present" in them (v. 21), a principle of sin that wars against their holy desires, hinders them from obeying God as they desire, and stirs them to do the very things that they hate (vv. 19, 23).[24] Brakel wrote, "Indwelling corruption greatly torments and grieves believers."[25]

This conflict can cause great searchings of heart among the children of God. Brakel said, "The converted detect much of the old Adam within themselves. They observe how they frequently fall—indeed, even continue in sin, being captured and captivated by sin. By this their faith easily falters, fearing that sin still has dominion over them."[26] However, Brakel sought to assure true believers that "sin has no dominion when there is a union with Christ by faith," and "this union results in lively, spiritual exercises" in love and good works. Such union with Christ "brings forth internal opposition and hatred towards all that is sin," resulting in "strife against sin" and "a delight, a love for, and a desire to do whatever pleases the Lord."[27]

Christians live in the painful paradox of salvation begun but not completed. They love God and his righteous law, for he has set them free from the reign of sin, but they still find sin and evil in themselves as they wait for their full redemption and glorification. Indwelling sin would not hurt them so much if they did not truly love God. This can be a comfort to them, for the inward battle between holy love and sin evidences a true conversion. Yet believers cannot be satisfied until they love the Lord with all their hearts, all their souls, and all their strength.

---

24. On Romans 7 and the identity of the wretched man as a regenerate believer walking with God, see the chapters on sanctification in *RST*, vol. 3 (forthcoming).

25. Brakel, *The Christian's Reasonable Service*, 4:251.

26. Brakel, *The Christian's Reasonable Service*, 1:398.

27. Brakel, *The Christian's Reasonable Service*, 1:398–99.

Assurance of Salvation, but with Fear of the Lord

When God's children walk with him, they ordinarily (though not necessarily) experience assurance of their salvation and acceptance with God. The Spirit who leads them is "the Spirit of adoption," who "beareth witness with our spirit, that we are the children of God" (Rom. 8:14–16). God has given them precious promises that he will dwell with them as their covenant God and their loving Father (2 Cor. 6:16–18). However, these very promises of God's presence with them motivate them to purify themselves and pursue holiness "in the fear of God" (7:1). True assurance does not make careless, casual Christians, but fosters reverence for the Father.

Assurance and fear appear to be opposites, but Peter gives three reasons why they go together. First, assurance brings sobering fear because of *the holiness of our Father.* Peter says, "But as he which hath called you is holy, so be ye holy in all manner of conversation; because it is written, Be ye holy; for I am holy. And if ye call on the Father, who without respect of persons judgeth according to every man's work, pass the time of your sojourning here in fear" (1 Pet. 1:15–17). The more we stand assured that the holy God is our Father, the more our hearts will fear him with childlike reverence mingled with love for his holy majesty. Brakel said, "Reverence for God engenders in God's children a careful guarding against displeasing God by disobedience and the commission of sins, and a being active to please Him in all things."[28]

Second, assurance brings grateful fear because of *the price of our redemption.* Peter continues, "Ye know that ye were not redeemed with corruptible things, as silver and gold, from your vain conversation [conduct] received by tradition from your fathers; but with the precious blood of Christ, as of a lamb without blemish and without spot" (1 Pet. 1:18–19). As the Spirit increases our confidence that Christ redeemed us and we are his, he will likewise increase a weighty sense of awe over the terrible cost Christ paid to save us.

Third, assurance brings a careful fear because of *the condition of our assurance.* Peter exhorts those saved by faith in God's promises to increase their faith, virtue, knowledge, self-control, patience, godliness, brotherly affection, and love in order "to make your calling and election sure," for the one who is lacking in such virtues grows nearsighted and can no longer see his cleansing from sin (2 Pet. 1:5–10). We cannot lose our salvation,

---

28. Brakel, *The Christian's Reasonable Service*, 3:295.

but we can lose our assurance. While we are saved only by faith in Christ (v. 1), we enjoy assurance of salvation by walking in growing holiness. Anthony Burgess said, "Assurance makes a man walk with much tenderness against sin, for such evil would put him out of the heaven of experiencing how sweet the Lord is."[29] He does not want to lose the heaven on earth of God's manifest favor.

Such considerations mean little to the self-satisfied, but to those who, like the Galilean fisherman, have confessed, "I am a sinful man" (Luke 5:8), the very truths that uphold assurance also ignite the flame of godly fear. Alexander wrote, "The brighter his discoveries of the divine glory, and the stronger his love, the deeper are his views of the turpitude of sin. The more he is elevated in affection and assured hope, the deeper is he depressed in humility and self-abasement. . . . When his tears flow in copious showers, he would be at a loss to tell whether he was weeping for joy or for sorrow. He might say, for both."[30]

The Believer's Fervent Hope for Complete Purity from Sin

Sin shall not have the last word in the believer's life. God elected his people to be his holy sons and daughters in Christ (Eph. 1:4–5). He predestined them "to be conformed to the image of his Son" (Rom. 8:29). God's sovereign purpose of grace cannot fail. His people will be pure.

Christ did not come to reduce sin, but to destroy it (1 John 3:8). That work will be fully applied when Christ returns. John says, "Beloved, now are we the sons of God, and it doth not yet appear what we shall be: but we know that, when he shall appear, we shall be like him; for we shall see him as he is" (v. 2). On that day, Christ will present believers "to himself a glorious church, not having spot, or wrinkle, or any such thing; but . . . holy and without blemish" (Eph. 5:27). William Cowper (1731–1800) expressed this hope when he wrote,

> Dear dying Lamb, thy precious blood
> Shall never lose its power,
> Till all the ransomed church of God
> Be saved, to sin no more.[31]

---

29. Anthony Burgess, *Faith Seeking Assurance*, ed. Joel R. Beeke, Puritan Treasures for Today (Grand Rapids, MI: Reformation Heritage Books, 2015), 70.

30. Alexander, *Thoughts on Religious Experience*, 77.

31. William Cowper, "There Is a Fountain Filled with Blood" (1771), in *Trinity Hymnal—Baptist Edition*, no. 188.

This hope motivates Christians to pursue holiness in this age, for "every man that hath this hope in him purifieth himself, even as he is pure" (1 John 3:3). Revelation 19:6–8 makes it a matter of joyful praise: "Alleluia: for the Lord God omnipotent reigneth. Let us be glad and rejoice, and give honour to him: for the marriage of the Lamb is come, and his wife hath made herself ready. And to her was granted that she should be arrayed in fine linen, clean and white: for the fine linen is the righteousness of saints."

Amen! Come quickly, Lord Jesus.

Sing to the Lord

Meditating on Sin and Christ's Cross

> Stricken, smitten, and afflicted, see him dying on the tree!
> 'Tis the Christ by man rejected; yes, my soul, 'tis he, 'tis he!
> 'Tis the long-expected Prophet, David's Son, yet David's Lord;
> By his Son God now has spoken: 'tis the true and faithful Word.
>
> Tell me, ye who hear him groaning, was there ever grief like his?
> Friends through fear his cause disowning, foes insulting his distress;
> Many hands were raised to wound him, none would interpose to
>   save;
> But the deepest stroke that pierced him was the stroke that Justice
>   gave.
>
> Ye who think of sin but lightly nor suppose the evil great
> Here may view its nature rightly, here its guilt may estimate.
> Mark the Sacrifice appointed, see who bears the awful load;
> 'Tis the Word, the Lord's Anointed, Son of Man and Son of God.
>
> Here we have a firm foundation, here the refuge of the lost;
> Christ's the Rock of our salvation, his the name of which we boast.
> Lamb of God, for sinners wounded, Sacrifice to cancel guilt!
> None shall ever be confounded who on him their hope have built.

Thomas Kelly
Tune: O Mein Jesu, Ich Muss Sterben
Trinity Hymnal—Baptist Edition, No. 192

Questions for Meditation or Discussion

1. Why is a believer's fundamental response to sin humility?

2. How do the Holy Scriptures make it plain that confession of sin is not merely something done at conversion, but a regular part of a healthy Christian life?

3. What does the Westminster Larger Catechism (Q. 76) teach about repentance regarding its (1) divine source, (2) motives, and (3) essential acts?

4. Why must a believer repeatedly exercise faith in Christ in order to triumph over sin?

5. What are some helpful prayers the Bible teaches us to pray when facing temptation and sin?

6. Why is it necessary for a Christian to constantly maintain spiritual watchfulness?

7. When talking to another Christian, you discover that he believes he need not actively fight to put sin to death and put on righteousness because Christ has already won the battle. How would you help him to see in the Holy Scriptures his duty and need to battle for holiness?

8. What reasons does every believer have to give thanks to God, even when facing his sins?

9. What is the Christian's ultimate hope regarding his sin? Quote specific promises of God.

Questions for Deeper Reflection

10. Should a forgiven child of God feel shame for his sins? Why or why not? If so, what kind of shame is appropriate for a Christian, and what kind of shame is not appropriate?

11. Why should a Christian who is assured of his salvation still fear the Lord? How is such fear compatible with full assurance?

26

Suffering and the Believer

Christians suffer and should expect to suffer as long as they remain in this world.[1] The apostolic admonition to new converts is "We must through much tribulation enter into the kingdom of God" (Acts 14:22). The narrative of Job's trials reveals that God-fearing saints may suffer financial ruin, bereavement of family members, and loss of health (Job 1:13–19; 2:7). From Joseph through Jeremiah to Jesus Christ, the history of God's servants is watered with tears. We do not know all the specific reasons why many afflictions fall upon God's children, but experience confirms that "man that is born of a woman is of few days and full of trouble" (14:1).

The suffering of the saints raises theological questions,[2] pressing upon us perplexing practical challenges to faith and godliness. All suffering is ultimately traceable to our tragic fall in Adam. Yet the Scriptures also teach that all affliction is sent to Christians by a wise, fatherly God. Romans 8:28 says, "And we know that all things work together for good to them that love God, to them who are the called according to his purpose." The "all things" of this verse includes "tribulation, or distress, or persecution, or famine, or nakedness, or peril, or sword" (v. 35). The important thing is not the amount of affliction we receive, but how we respond to that affliction.

---

1. Portions of this chapter are adapted from Joel R. Beeke, *How Should We Consider Christ in Affliction?* (Grand Rapids, MI: Reformation Heritage Books, 2018); "How Afflictions Work for Good," in *The Banner of Sovereign Grace Truth* 18, no. 3 (March 2010): 72–73. Used by permission. The former is a letter by Joel Beeke that he has often shared in other formats.

2. For a gospel-centered response to the problem of evil, see *RST*, 1:1091–97.

Here lie the Christian's deepest questions about trials. They want to respond to affliction in a God-glorifying manner (Phil. 1:20), but they feel that they often fall short and fear they may lose their grip in the heat of affliction. To prepare for affliction before it comes is hard; to look back on it with gratitude after it is over is harder; but to live like Christ in affliction is hardest. Hence, believers ask themselves, How may I grow in grace while suffering affliction? The answer to that question will serve as a fitting conclusion to our treatment of anthropology, for what is more characteristic of all men's condition in this world than affliction?

The Saints' Participation in the Afflictions of a Fallen World

Much of the affliction experienced by the saints consists of *suffering in solidarity with their fallen race.* Christians must remember that though they are redeemed and regenerated, they still live in a world cursed because of Adam's sin (Gen. 3:17). They suffer in domestic relationships and in vocational labor because of our first parents' disobedience (vv. 16, 19). Though the Spirit is life to them because of Christ's righteousness, their bodies are still mortal and subject to death until the resurrection (Rom. 8:10–11).

Pain tends to produce mental tunnel vision so that our awareness shrinks to our own sad situation, but we need to remember the bigger picture. Suffering and death characterize the whole world in this age (Rom. 5:12). Creation "was made subject to vanity" and "the bondage of corruption," so that "the whole creation groaneth and travaileth in pain" (8:20–22). The Spirit of God does not remove this groaning, but accentuates it in believers through their sharp longing for the glorious realization of their redemption and adoption (vv. 21, 23). Let us also remember, as John Murray said, "These groans and travails are not death pangs but birth pangs."[3]

The sorrows of the saints also may consist of *suffering God's judgments against their nation.* Jeremiah exclaimed, "Oh that my head were waters, and mine eyes a fountain of tears, that I might weep day and night for the slain of the daughter of my people!" (Jer. 9:1). The prophet experienced the traumatic destruction of Jerusalem, the holy city, for its sins against the Lord. Several centuries later, the Lord Jesus warned his disciples in Judea to "flee to the mountains" when Gentile armies would

---

3. Murray, *The Epistle to the Romans,* 1:305.

again attack Jerusalem (as they did in AD 70), for "there shall be great distress in the land" (Luke 21:20–23). In such times, when God is plucking up a nation, the godly should not marvel at their sufferings or stumble at their disappointed personal ambitions, but be grateful if God preserves their lives (Jer. 45:1–5). Should we expect to personally prosper when God's church is scattered, the nation is desolated, and many people die?[4]

When God's people suffer because of divine judgments upon their land, they can remember that God said, "I will shake the heavens, and the earth, and the sea, and the dry land; and I will shake all nations" (Hag. 2:6–7). However, the church need not fear, for God's Spirit abides with his people (v. 5). Furthermore, the awesome God who shakes all things is bestowing upon them a kingdom that cannot be shaken, so they should serve him with reverent fear (Heb. 12:26–29).

God's Fatherly Purposes for Affliction upon His Saints

Though believers suffer as a consequence of mankind's sin, they should not think that God afflicts them to satisfy his divine justice according to the covenant of works. They are no longer "under the law" with its curse (Rom. 3:19; Gal. 4:5; cf. 3:10). God does not punish his children according to the justice that their sins deserve (Ps. 103:10). United to Christ, they stand in a state of "no condemnation" (Rom. 8:1). However, believers in Christ still suffer many a "fiery trial" in this world (1 Pet. 4:12). God has not abandoned them, but the Holy Spirit rests upon them, for they are "partakers of Christ's sufferings" (vv. 13–14).

Saints do not suffer by collateral damage as God targets the wicked with his wrath. On the contrary, God has loving and wise purposes for everything that happens to his children. He cares for every hair on their heads (Matt. 10:30). The Father "chastens," or "disciplines" (*paideuō*), his people (Heb. 12:5–11), a term that includes painful correction (v. 11; cf. 1 Cor. 11:32) that trains a child to bring him to wise maturity (Acts 7:22; 22:3; Titus 2:12).[5]

Ezekiel Hopkins said, "Hence therefore with what calmness and sweet peace may a true Christian look upon all his afflictions? Though they be sore and heavy, and seem to carry much wrath in them, yet they have nothing of the curse." Hopkins added, "If I have an interest in the righ-

---

4. Calvin, *Commentaries*, on Jer. 45:5.
5. See *paideuō* and *paideia* in Prov. 1:2, 7–8; 3:11–12; 4:1, 13; 15:5; 23:12–13; etc. LXX.

teousness of Christ, justice is already satisfied, the curse removed, and all the sorrows and afflictions I suffer, are but the corrections of a gracious Father, not the revenge of an angry God."[6] Poverty, loss of family members or friends, pain, disease, and death itself are no curses to believers, but the loving methods God uses to cleanse them from sin and carry them to heaven.

Afflictions can be very heavy and difficult to bear. If you are a Christian, your faith can help you understand some of the rich benefits that affliction brings under the hand of the Father. Though bitter to body and soul, afflictions serve as strong medicine for you in the hands of your great physician.

First, through affliction, *God humbles believers deeply*, showing us that, apart from divine grace, we are nothing but sin and corruption. He teaches Christians the same lesson he taught Israel in the wilderness: "To humble thee, and to prove thee, to know what was in thine heart, whether thou wouldest keep his commandments, or no." He shows us our dependence on God and his Word, the manna of the soul, "that he might make thee know that man doth not live by bread only, but by every word that proceedeth out of the mouth of the LORD doth man live" (Deut. 8:2–3). In the wilderness, God reveals our inadequacy and his absolute sufficiency.

One of the most humbling aspects of trials is that we often do not understand the specific reasons why they come upon us. Yet it is precisely when we do not comprehend the Father's ways that we can learn submissive trust in his will. When God revealed himself to Job, the Lord did not explain why the trials had come, but instead revealed his incomprehensible majesty (Job 38–41). Job responded by praising God and repenting of questioning his ways (42:1–6). We learn in trials to trust God to do what is right and not to allow our finite outlook on life to challenge God's holiness. Edward Payson (1783–1827) was asked if he understood the reason for the great pain and weakness that afflicted his body as he slowly died. He said, "No, but I am as well satisfied as if I could see ten thousand. God's will is the very perfection of all reasons."[7]

Second, through affliction, *God exposes believers' sins*. As the saying goes, *schola crucis, schola lucis* (The school of the cross is a school

---

6. Hopkins, *The Doctrine of the Two Covenants*, 82–83.
7. Cited in Asa Cummings, *A Memoir of the Rev. Edward Payson*, 3rd ed. (Boston: Crocker and Brewster, 1830), 353.

of light).[8] In the bright light of sorrow, Christians come to see that sin dishonors God, defiles the soul, and damns the unrepentant. When our hearts turn blind eyes to their sin, God's hand comes heavily upon us until we recognize and acknowledge the evil that we have done (Ps. 32:3–4). Through affliction we learn, as Thomas Watson said, "Sin unrepented of ends in a tragedy. It has the devil for its father, shame for its companion, and death for its wages (Rom. 6:23). What is there in sin, then, that men should continue in it? Say not it is sweet. Who would desire the pleasure which kills?"[9] This insight is not the natural effect of sorrow, for the blindness of man stupefies him to the evil of his sins even in affliction (Isa. 1:2–9). However, God's grace sharpens the edge of suffering to pierce the conscience and make the heart bleed wholesome drops of repentance.

In hard and fearful times, God brought the sons of Jacob to remember their sins against their brother Joseph (Gen. 42:21–22). In affliction, the Holy Spirit searches our souls for sins, drags them out of their hiding places in the heart, and sets them in the light of God's holy and all-searching eye (Ps. 90:8). Though we hide behind our fig leaves, God comes asking, "Where art thou?" (Gen. 3:9). William Bridge (1600–1671) said, "Suffering times are sin-discovering times. . . . You see how it is in winter, when the leaves are off the hedges, you can see where the birds' nests were; when the leaves were on in summer time, you could not see those nests." The sins we cannot see in the summer of prosperity are more visible in the winter of affliction.[10]

Third, through affliction, *God purges believers' corruption.* "Before I was afflicted I went astray," the psalmist confessed, "but now have I kept thy word" (Ps. 119:67). The Holy Spirit uses affliction as a medicine to destroy the deadly disease of sin in us so that we may bring forth healthy and godly fruit. When sin makes us backslide from our Savior, he, as the Good Shepherd, sends the rod of affliction to set us straight. Sanctified affliction cures sin.

It is as good for us to be chastised with affliction as it is for a tree to be pruned so that it bears more fruit (John 15:2). John Bunyan wrote, "It is said that in some countries trees will grow, but will bear no fruit, because

---

8. William Bridge, "Sermons on Faith," sermon 5, in *The Works of the Rev. William Bridge,* 5 vols. (London: Thomas Tegg, 1845), 2:372. The saying is also cited by other Puritans and is sometimes attributed to Martin Luther.

9. Watson, *The Ten Commandments,* 209.

10. Bridge, "Sermons on Faith," sermon 5, in *Works,* 2:372.

there is no winter there."[11] The Christian needs the winter of affliction if he is to experience the spring of blossoming, the summer of growing, and the autumn of harvesting.

God arranges the seasons of sorrow and prosperity in our lives according to his wise design to meet our spiritual needs. James R. Miller (1840–1912) said,

> The Master adds some new touch of loveliness to the picture he is bringing out in our souls. Afflictions, sanctified, soften the asperities of life. They tame the wildness of nature. They temper human ambitions. They burn out the dross of selfishness and worldliness. They humble pride. They quell fierce passions. They reveal to men their own hearts, their own weaknesses, faults, blemishes and perils. They teach patience and submission. They disciple unruly spirits. They deepen and enrich our experiences. Ploughing the hard soil and cutting long and deep furrows in the heart, the heavenly Sower follows, and fruits of righteousness spring up. . . . Thus viewed from any side, affliction appears as a messenger of God sent to minister to us in the truest way.[12]

Fourth, through affliction, *God draws believers near to him.* The Lord uses affliction to make us seek him, to bring us back into communion with himself, and to keep us close by his side. The Lord said of Israel, "In their affliction they will seek me early" (Hos. 5:15). Affliction drove a woman of Canaan to the Son of David (Matt. 15:22) and a dying thief to a dying Savior (Luke 23:42). Not Manasseh's crown but his chains brought him to acknowledge that the Lord is God (2 Chron. 33:11–13).

When people wander from God to pursue their idols, God may strike their idols to bring them back. As a Husband, he is jealous over the affections of his own (1 Cor. 10:22). The Lord said of Israel, "Therefore, behold, I will hedge up thy way with thorns, and make a wall, that she shall not find her paths. And she shall follow after her lovers, but she shall not overtake them; and she shall seek them, but shall not find them: then shall she say, I will go and return to my first husband; for then was it better with me than now" (Hos. 2:6–7). George Swinnock (c. 1627–1673)

---

11. Bunyan, *Seasonable Counsel: or, Advice to Sufferers*, in *Works*, 2:694. Modern botanists refer to this phenomenon as the "chilling requirement" for a fruit tree to blossom.

12. J. R. Miller, *Week-Day Religion* (Philadelphia: Presbyterian Board of Publication, 1880), 90–92.

wrote, "Affliction, saith Chrysostom, is the shepherd's dog, which takes the lamb into its mouth when it goeth astray; not to bite it, but to bring it home."[13]

Fifth, through affliction, *God conforms believers to Christ.* Christians are called to "put on the new man," the "image" of God, in which "Christ is all" (Col. 3:10–11). The Lord uses afflictions to conform us to Christ, "that we might be partakers of his holiness" (Heb. 12:10). Thomas Watson said, "God's rod is a pencil to draw Christ's image more lively upon us."[14]

God's Son had to suffer in order to perfect his obedience and save his people (Heb. 2:10, 18; 5:8–9). If we would inherit God's kingdom as sons, then we must suffer with the Son (Rom. 8:17). Through the way of suffering, we become followers of the Lamb of God. All our paths of affliction have already been traveled, overcome, and sanctified by our Shepherd, whose substitutionary blood is our sure pledge that no affliction is able to separate us from the love of God in Christ Jesus (vv. 32, 39).

Sixth, through affliction, *God expands believers' joy.* Afflictions work for good because the Lord balances them with comfort and joy. David wrote, "For his anger endureth but a moment; in his favour is life: weeping may endure for a night, but joy cometh in the morning" (Ps. 30:5). Resurrection follows crucifixion. Christ told his disciples, "Your sorrow shall be turned into joy" (John 16:20). The Lord brings his people into the wilderness to speak comfortably to them (Hos. 2:14). Where godly suffering abounds, consolation also abounds (2 Cor. 1:4–5).

The apostle Paul sang songs in prison, knowing that sweet would follow the bitter. In the cellar of affliction, we find the Lord's choicest wines. Samuel Rutherford exclaimed, "How blind are my adversaries, who sent me to a banqueting-house, to a house of wine, to the lovely feasts of my lovely Lord Jesus, and not to a prison, or place of exile!"[15] In affliction, God's pilgrim people sometimes experience sweet raptures of divine joy that lead them to the very borders of heavenly Canaan. They discover, as Watson said, "God's rod hath honey at the end of it."[16] At such mo-

---

13. George Swinnock, *The Christian Man's Calling*, in *The Works of George Swinnock*, 5 vols. (Edinburgh: James Nichol, 1868), 2:131.

14. Thomas Watson, *A Divine Cordial; or, the Transcendent Priviledge* [sic] *of Those That Love God, and Are Savingly Called* (London: Thomas Parkhurst, 1663), 28; modernized version: *All Things for Good*, Puritan Paperbacks (Edinburgh: Banner of Truth, 1986).

15. Samuel Rutherford, *Letters of Samuel Rutherford*, ed. Andrew A. Bonar (repr., Edinburgh: Banner of Truth, 1984), 162.

16. Watson, *A Divine Cordial*, 30. For the biblical allusion, see 1 Sam. 14:27.

ments, they can confess, "Behold, happy is the man whom God correcteth: therefore despise not thou the chastening of the Almighty: for he maketh sore, and bindeth up: he woundeth, and his hands make whole. He shall deliver thee in six troubles: yea, in seven there shall no evil touch thee" (Job 5:17–19).

Seventh, through affliction, *God increases believers' faith*. Affliction works for good by helping us walk by faith and not by sight (2 Cor. 5:7). James said, "The trying of your faith worketh patience" (James 1:3). In prosperity, we talk about living by faith yet often darken counsel by words without knowledge; but in adversity, we come to the experiential knowledge of what it means to live and endure by faith. Here we see the great difference between the effect of affliction on the wicked and its effect on God's children. Thomas Manton (1620–1677) said, "The fruit of punishment is despair and murmuring, but of trial, patience and sweet submission."[17]

Only in the fire does faith prove itself more precious than gold (1 Pet. 1:7). The purest gold will not pass into the age to come, but John Brown of Edinburgh (1784–1858) noted that faith is far superior: "Purified and strengthened by the trials it is exposed to under the influence of the Holy Spirit, faith, with all the graces which grow out of it, survives the wreck of all material things, and, at the revelation of Jesus Christ, is found to praise, and honor, and glory."[18]

Eighth, through affliction, *God weans believers from this world*. Christ told his disciples, "If ye were of the world, the world would love his own: but because ye are not of the world, but I have chosen you out of the world, therefore the world hateth you" (John 15:19). A dog does not usually bite those who live in its home, but only strangers. Likewise, the world's bite reminds us that we are not at home, but "strangers and pilgrims on the earth" (Heb. 11:13).

God's temporal judgment teaches us to say, "Although the fig tree shall not blossom, neither shall fruit be in the vines; the labour of the olive shall fail, and the fields shall yield no meat; the flock shall be cut off from the fold, and there shall be no herd in the stalls: yet I will rejoice in the LORD, I will joy in the God of my salvation" (Hab.

---

17. Thomas Manton, *A Practical Commentary, or An Exposition with Notes on the Epistle of James*, in *The Complete Works of Thomas Manton*, 22 vols. (London: James Nisbet, 1871), 4:28.
18. John Brown, *Expository Discourses on the First Epistle of the Apostle Peter* (New York: Robert Carter, 1855), 68.

3:17–18). This enables us to hold the world loosely, but also encourages us to cling to Christ with all our might. Watson said, "God would have the world hang as a loose tooth which, being twitched away, doth not much trouble us."[19]

Ninth, through affliction, *God prepares believers for their heavenly inheritance.* Affliction elevates our soul heavenward, so that we look for "a city which hath foundations, whose builder and maker is God" (Heb. 11:10). Affliction paves the way to glory. "For our light affliction, which is but for a moment, worketh for us a far more exceeding and eternal weight of glory" (2 Cor. 4:17). We are children of the King on our way to reign with him in eternal glory. John Trapp (1601–1669) wrote, "He that rides to be crowned will not think much of a rainy day."[20]

Child of God, do you believe that affliction is for your spiritual good? Do you trust that God will provide everything necessary or good for you, both in this age and the age to come? Then do what Paul calls you to do in 1 Thessalonians 5:18: "In *every thing* give thanks: for this is the will of God in Christ Jesus concerning you."

Let us therefore trace all our sorrows back to the tender love of the heavenly Father. He proved his love at the cross. Paul said, "If God be for us, who can be against us? He that spared not his own Son, but delivered him up for us all, how shall he not with him also freely give us all things" (Rom. 8:31–32). Robert Leighton (1611–1684) said, "If the children of God consider their trials, not in their natural bitterness, but in the sweet love whence they spring, and the sweet fruits that spring from them, that we are our Lord's gold, and that he tries us in the furnace to purify us . . . this may beget not only patience, but gladness even in the sufferings."[21]

The Saints' Communion with Christ in Affliction

Although Christians suffer with all creation, in a special sense we are "joint-heirs with Christ" and "suffer with him, that we may be also glorified together" (Rom. 8:17). The saints have fellowship with Christ in his crucifixion (Phil. 3:10) so that "the sufferings of Christ abound in us"

---

19. Watson, *A Divine Cordial*, 30.
20. John Trapp, *A Commentary on the Old and New Testaments*, ed. Hugh Martin, 5 vols. (London: Richard D. Dickinson, 1867–1868), on Gen. 24:61 (1:92).
21. Robert Leighton, *A Commentary upon the First Epistle of Peter*, on 1 Pet. 4:12–13, in *The Whole Works of Robert Leighton* (New York: Robert Carter and Brothers, 1859), 316.

(2 Cor. 1:5). Therefore, earthly sorrow is an opportunity for communion with Christ.

The most effective means for living as a Christian in affliction is to consider Christ, the fountainhead of all vital Christianity (Heb. 3:1). Isaac Ambrose (1604–1664) said, "In this knowledge of Christ, there is an excellency above all other knowledge in the world; there is nothing more pleasing and comfortable, more animating and enlivening, more ravishing and soul contenting."[22] This necessitates a Spirit-worked faith enabling us to look to him, to feast on him, to depend on him. In the locus of Christology later in this volume, we will study the wonders of Christ's person and work, but it is good to present an appetizer for the soul to encourage you to consider Christ in affliction.

First, consider the *piety of Christ*. His life was God-centered. He loved the Lord his God with all his heart, all his soul, and all his strength, and his neighbor as himself. The Father delighted in him as God's sinless servant and perfect Son (Isa. 42:1; Matt. 3:17). Holy from his conception in the virgin's womb (Luke 1:35), he exercised a growing human obedience under the athletic training of his afflictions (Heb. 5:8). He lived to do his Father's will, to sanctify his church through his death (10.7–10).

As we "run with patience the race that is set before us," we can move forward only by "looking unto Jesus the author and finisher of our faith" (Heb. 12:1–2). Christ's enduring obedience, even to death on the cross, is the model for our humility (Phil. 2:5–8), the merit for our righteousness before God (3:9), and the mighty power by which God works obedience in us now (2:11–13). Christ is not a dead example but the living Lord, through whom the same Spirit of holiness who raised him from the dead now raises up the nations to walk in the obedience of faith (Rom. 1:4–5; 6:4).

Second, consider the *perseverance of Christ*. The Lord directs our hearts into "the patience of Christ" (2 Thess. 3:5 KJV mg.) so that his endurance may be ours. This is the pathway that all God's sons must walk. William Dyer (d. 1696) said, "God hath one Son without sin but no son without sorrow; he had one Son without corruption, but no son without correction."[23]

---

22. Isaac Ambrose, *Looking unto Jesus: A View of the Everlasting Gospel; or, the Soul's Eyeing of Jesus, as Carrying on the Great Work of Man's Salvation, from First to Last* (Philadelphia: J. B. Lippincott and Co., 1856), 17.

23. William Dyer, *Christ's Famous Titles, and a Believer's Golden Chain* (London: n.p., 1663), 140.

We need endurance both for great trials and for the small ones that we face again and again. The latter can affect us like the torture that drips water at intervals on the forehead of a prisoner, resulting in growing agitation and even insanity. Repeated trials over long periods of time can make us to cry out, "How long?" (Ps. 13:1–2). Christ provides us the strength to bear one more drop, take one more step, live one more day, even in the severest of sorrows. He earned that provision for us by enduring his sufferings to their end. From Gethsemane to Golgotha, he confirmed that "having loved his own which were in the world, he loved them unto the end" (John 13:1). Drop by drop of blood, for six long hours he poured out his life and never answered his mockers a word. Jesus "endured the cross" (Heb. 12:2). Look more to Christ. Rest more in his perseverance, for your perseverance rests in his. He is "the breaker" to go before his flock in opening all our paths (Mic. 2:13). He was tempted in all points as we are, yet without sin (Heb. 4:15). Jesus not only knows our affliction, he has identified himself with it. He has borne it. And he will sanctify it.

Third, consider the *power of Christ*. Being the infinite God-man, Jesus received power on earth to bear unspeakable sufferings on our behalf. And through the merit of these sufferings, he now receives royal power in heaven from his Father to rule and strengthen us in our sufferings (Matt. 28:18). Christ shepherds his people "in the strength of the LORD, in the majesty of the name of the LORD his God" (Mic. 5:4). If he desires to weigh us down with affliction—yes, heavy, staggering affliction—we must not be alarmed, but look to him for strength.

Let us not be ashamed of our weakness under trial. Fear not, for God will not overburden us: "There hath no temptation taken you but such as is common to man: but God is faithful, who will not suffer you to be tempted above that ye are able; but will with the temptation also make a way to escape, that ye may be able to bear it" (1 Cor. 10:13). John Downame (1571–1652) said, "The Lord doth not measure out our afflictions according to our faults but according to our strength, and looketh not at what we have deserved, but at what we are able to bear."[24] God's grace is sufficient for us, and his strength is made perfect in our weakness (2 Cor. 12:9).

---

24. John Downame, *The Christian Warfare against the Devill, World and Flesh: Wherein Is Described Their Nature, the Maner of Their Fight and Meanes to Obtaine Victorye* (London: William Stansby, 1634), 867.

Fourth, consider the *prayers of Christ*. He often set time apart on earth to pray to his Father, especially in hours of need.[25] He continually prays in heaven for all his church (Heb. 7:25; 1 John 2:1). His prayers are effectual (John 11:42). No condemnation can come upon God's children while he who died for their sins intercedes for them (Rom. 8:34). If it encourages us to know that a dear saint on earth prays for us, how much more should it embolden our souls that God's Son intercedes for us at the right hand of God!

We, too, ought to make more use of prayer, especially in combating spiritual depression under afflictions. Knowing that we have a sympathetic High Priest in heaven, let us pray with boldness for the mercy and grace that we need (Heb. 4:15–16). A prayerless affliction is like an open sore, ripe for infection; a prayerful affliction is like a sore soothed with the balm of Gilead—the healing ointment of Jesus's blood.

Fifth, consider the *presence of Christ*. He is at no time absent from us, even when our faith does not actively grasp him (Matt. 28:20; Heb. 13:5). Even in our darkest hours, he is close beside us. "Who is among you that feareth the LORD, that obeyeth the voice of his servant, that walketh in darkness, and hath no light? Let him trust in the name of the LORD, and stay upon his God" (Isa. 50:10). Only of him can it be declared, "The darkness and the light are both alike to thee" (Ps. 139:12).

In the hands of our Prophet, Priest, and King, all our afflictions are sanctified for God's glory and our good. John Flavel said, "Behold, then, a sanctified affliction is a cup, whereinto Jesus hath wrung and pressed the juice and virtue of all his mediatorial offices. Surely, that must be a cup of generous, royal wine, like that in the supper, a cup of blessing to the people of God."[26] Oh, what tender love! You are never forgotten by Jesus Christ, despite your negligence toward him. Take heart. The Jesus who never failed you in yesterday's afflictions is still present to give you strength today (Matt. 6:34). Wait on your ever-present Savior (Ps. 46:1). He will not let you down; indeed, he cannot let you down, for he is the same yesterday, today, and forever (Heb. 13:8).

Sixth, consider the *plan of Christ*. The Lord Jesus persevered because of the joy set before him (Heb. 12:2). Having suffered, he entered his glory, just as God had foreordained and foretold (Luke 24:25–26). At his name,

---

25. Matt. 14:23; 19:13; Mark 1:35; Luke 5:16; 6:12; 9:18, 28–29; 11:1; 22:32, 40–46; John 17.
26. Flavel, *Navigation Spiritualized*, in *Works*, 5:252.

every knee shall bow, to the glory of God the Father (Phil. 2:10–11). The eternal plan behind all his affliction was eternal glory.

Christ pursued eternal glory—not only for himself, but also for us, the children of God. He departed from earth to "prepare a place for you" in the Father's house (John 14:2–3). With his eyes upon his impending crucifixion and resurrection, he prayed, "Father, I will that they also, whom thou hast given me, be with me where I am; that they may behold my glory" (17:24). When he returns, "then shall the righteous shine forth as the sun in the kingdom of their Father" (Matt. 13:43). If we would be more submissive under affliction and learn to praise God in trial, we must think more about God's plan for our eternal glory. Your sad days on earth are nearly over. Don't overestimate them. Think more of your coming crown and your eternal communion with the triune God, his saints, and the holy angels. Remember the order of God's plan:

> Light after darkness,
> Gain after loss,
> Strength after weakness,
> Crown after cross.[27]

Consider Christ. Seek grace to live in him and like him today through your afflictions, and you will discover with the apostle, "For me to live is Christ, and to die is gain" (Phil. 1:21). Hope in the Lord and his redemption (Ps. 130:7). "Wait on the LORD: be of good courage, and he shall strengthen thine heart: wait, I say, on the LORD" (27:14).

Sing to the Lord

Comfort in Sorrow

> When peace, like a river, attendeth my way,
> When sorrows like sea-billows roll;
> Whatever my lot, thou hast taught me to say,
> It is well, it is well with my soul.
> It is well with my soul; it is well, it is well with my soul.

> Though Satan should buffet, though trials should come,
> Let this blest assurance control,
> That Christ has regarded my helpless estate,

---

27. Frances R. Havergal, *Under the Surface*, 3rd ed. (London: J. Nisbet and Co., 1876), 175.

And has shed his own blood for my soul.
It is well with my soul; it is well, it is well with my soul.

My sin—O the bliss of this glorious thought!—
My sin, not in part, but the whole,
Is nailed to the cross and I bear it no more;
Praise the Lord, praise the Lord, O my soul!
It is well with my soul; it is well, it is well with my soul.

O Lord, haste the day when the faith shall be sight,
The clouds be rolled back as a scroll,
The trump shall resound and the Lord shall descend:
"Even so"—it is well with my soul.
It is well with my soul; it is well, it is well with my soul.

Horatio Spafford
Tune: It Is Well
Trinity Hymnal—Baptist Edition, No. 580

Questions for Meditation or Discussion

1. Why do God's saints suffer simply by being part of this world and of their nation?
2. How does God the Father use affliction to deal with the sins of his children?
3. In what ways do sorrows serve to deepen the relationship between Christians and God?
4. How can affliction mingled with divine grace increase joy and faith?
5. How do sorrows help believers to let go of this world and embrace God's kingdom?
6. What encouragement can Christians find in Christ's piety?
7. How can Christ's patient endurance and perseverance help saints on the journey?
8. Why does meditation on Christ's death, resurrection, and exaltation to God's right hand strengthen believers in their trials?
9. What does Christ's presence with his people as their Prophet, Priest, and King offer them as they endure affliction?
10. What unfailing plan does Christ pursue with his people? Why do you need to remember that?

Questions for Deeper Reflection

11. Why does extreme or extended sorrow pose such a spiritual challenge to the Christian? How does sorrow specifically assault the Christian's beliefs, emotions, and activity?

12. Consider a Christian you know who is experiencing great trials. Based on something you learned from this chapter, write him or her a letter of encouragement—and send it.

PART 4

CHRISTOLOGY:
THE DOCTRINE OF CHRIST

Analytical Outline: Christology

Section A: The Doctrine of the Covenant of Grace

I. Introduction to the Covenant of Grace
  A. Why Study the Covenant of Grace?
    1. The Covenant Stands in the Closest Relation to Christ
    2. The Covenant Structures Redemptive History
    3. The Covenant Supports God-Centered Faith
    4. The Covenant Shapes Spiritual Experience
    5. The Covenant Directs the Church's Practice
    6. The Covenant Glorifies God in His Attributes
  B. The Meaning of "Covenant" Reviewed
    1. A Solemn Promise That Functions as a Legal Instrument to Define a Relationship of Loyalty
    2. Common Elements: Lord, Laws, Office, Representative, Sign
  C. Basic Theses of Reformed Covenant Theology
    1. The Perpetual Continuity of God's Gospel
    2. The Covenant of Works
    3. The Covenant with God's Son and Those in Union with Him
    4. The Diverse Administrations of God's Covenant of Grace
    5. The Essential Unity of God's Covenant of Grace
    6. The Abiding Duty to Obey God's Moral Law
    7. The Church's Union with Her Covenant God through Faith
II. Historical Perspectives on Divine Covenants
  A. The Early and Medieval Church
    1. Marcion
    2. Irenaeus

D. His Particular Names of Office
   1. Names of Divine Revelation
      a. Prophet
      b. Word
      c. Truth
      d. Image of God
      e. Faithful Witness
      f. Amen
      g. Rabbi, Master, and Teacher
      h. Apostle
      i. Light
      j. Star
      k. Dayspring
      l. Sun of Righteousness
   2. Names of Divine Reconciliation
      a. Priest, High Priest
      b. Advocate
      c. Forerunner
      d. Surety
      e. Lamb
      f. Temple
      g. Cornerstone
      h. Way
      i. Door
      j. Peace
   3. Names of Divine Reign
      a. King, King of the Jews, King of Kings
      b. Son of Man
      c. Firstborn
      d. Head
      e. Prince, Prince of Life, Captain of Their Salvation
      f. Breaker
      g. Life, Bread of Life, the Resurrection and the Life
      h. Bridegroom
      i. Judge
      j. Son of David
      k. David
      l. Branch
      m. Root

3. The Two Dimensions of Christ's Obedience: Passive and Active
   a. The Distinction between Christ's Passive and Active Obedience
   b. Christ's Passive Obedience to the Father's Decretive Will
   c. Christ's Active Obedience to the Father's Preceptive Will
   d. Objections to the Doctrine of Christ's Active Obedience
      i. Already Owed to God
      ii. Only a Prerequisite to His Atoning Death
      iii. Promotes Antinomianism
   e. Christ's Active and Passive Obedience United in His Life and Death
4. Christ's Climactic Obedience in His Passion
   a. Christ's Obedience at Gethsemane
   b. Christ's Obedience at Gabbatha
   c. Christ's Obedience at Golgotha
5. Practical Implications of Christ's Sacrificial Obedience
   a. Recognize that God Will Glorify His Law
   b. Rely on Christ to Deliver You from Your Punishment
   c. Rest on Christ's Obedience as Your Righteousness
   d. Resist the Temptation to Perfectionism
   e. Reckon the High Value of Obedience to God
   f. Run the Race of Obedience in Imitation of Christ
   g. Remain Patient through Suffering unto Death
D. The Perfections of Christ's Sacrificial Accomplishment
   1. The Sufficiency of Christ's Perfect Sacrifice
   2. The Finality of Christ's Perfect Sacrifice
   3. The Efficacy of Christ's Perfect Sacrifice
   4. The Universality of Christ's Perfect Sacrifice
   5. The Particularity of Christ's Perfect Sacrifice
      a. The Scriptural Evidence for Particular Redemption
      b. Objections to Particular Redemption
         i. It Contradicts Christ's Sacrifice for the "World" and "All"
         ii. It Fails to Account for the Perishing of Some of the Redeemed
         iii. It Limits the Value of What Christ Has Done
         iv. It Discourages Evangelism and Missions
         v. It Is Inconsistent with God's Sincere Gospel Call

C. Supremacy: To Live Is Christ
    1. The Supremacy of Christ
    2. The Challenges of Nihilism and Existentialism
    3. The Answer of Living unto the Lord

Section A

The Doctrine of the Covenant of Grace

27

Introduction to the
Covenant of Grace

The Westminster Shorter Catechism (Q. 20) asks, "Did God leave all mankind to perish in the estate of sin and misery?" Left unanswered, that is a terrifying question. It reminds us that God could have damned the entire human race to the hell we all deserved. However, the catechism's answer is full of hope: "God having, out of his mere good pleasure, from all eternity, elected some to everlasting life, did enter into a covenant of grace, to deliver them out of the estate of sin and misery, and to bring them into an estate of salvation by a Redeemer."[1]

The Westminster divines perceived that the doctrine of redemption revolves around three foci: election, the covenant of grace, and Jesus Christ the Redeemer. We presented the doctrine of election in the first volume of this work.[2] In the second half of this second volume, we will study the doctrines of the covenant of grace and the person and work of Jesus Christ. By "the covenant of grace," we refer to the great covenant rooted in eternity, spanning history, and consisting of the solemn promises that undergird all of God's historical covenants and are fulfilled in the new covenant by Christ. A synonym for "covenantal" is "federal" (from the Latin *foedus*, "covenant"), and covenant theology is sometimes called federal theology.

---

1. *Reformed Confessions*, 4:355–56.
2. On election, see *RST*, 1:979–1057 (chaps. 49–51).

In the Westminster Standards, the doctrine of the covenant of grace stands with one foot in the gospel of Christ[3] and the other in the sacraments of the church.[4] We will treat the covenant of grace with respect to the gospel here in the locus of Christology, and with respect to the church and the sacraments in the locus of ecclesiology in a later volume.[5]

Why Study the Covenant of Grace?

The doctrine of the covenant of grace is beautiful to contemplate; the covenant is like a gold ring that clasps the diamond of our Lord Jesus. It is also unspeakably sweet to the believing soul, for the covenant presents Christ to us as silver dishes serve up a sumptuous feast. However, someone might find it strange to begin a consideration of the doctrine of Christ with several chapters on the covenant of grace. Why spend all this time on a seemingly arcane aspect of biblical theology? Why not skip the covenant and immediately consider the person of Christ? There are several reasons why we should spend time on this doctrine:

1. *The covenant stands in the closest relation to Christ.* God said that he would give his Servant "for a covenant of the people" (Isa. 42:6). Edward Young said, "To say that the servant is a covenant is to say that all the blessings of the covenant are embodied in, have their root and origin in, and are dispensed by him. At the same time he is himself at the center of all these blessings, and to receive them is to receive him, for without him there can be no blessings."[6] The Holy Scriptures repeatedly link the work of the Lord Jesus to God's covenant.[7] Therefore, to know Christ in his riches we must know the biblical doctrine of the covenant.

2. *The covenant structures redemptive history.* The key figures of that history—Abraham, Moses, David, and ultimately Jesus Christ—each stand in intimate relation to God's historical covenants, which progressively unfold God's eternal covenant of grace. God's redemptive dealings with the nation of Israel grew out the root of his covenant with Abraham.[8]

---

3. Westminster Confession of Faith (7.1–6; 14.2; 17.2); Westminster Larger Catechism (Q. 30–36, 57, 79); and Westminster Shorter Catechism (Q. 20), in *Reformed Confessions*, 4:242–43, 250, 253, 304–6, 310, 315, 355–56.
4. Westminster Confession of Faith (27.1, 5; 28.1); Westminster Larger Catechism (Q. 162–66, 174, 176); and Westminster Shorter Catechism (Q. 92, 94), in *Reformed Confessions*, 4:265–66, 342–43, 345–46, 366.
5. On the doctrine of the church or ecclesiology, see *RST*, vol. 4 (forthcoming).
6. Young, *The Book of Isaiah*, 3:120–21.
7. For example, see Matt. 26:28; Acts 3:25–26; Rom. 11:26–27; Gal. 3:16–17; Eph. 2:12–13.
8. Gen. 15:18; 17:1–14; Ex. 6:2–8; Neh. 9:8; Isa. 51:1–2.

God's redemption of Israel from Egypt culminated in God's coming down in glory on Mount Sinai to make a covenant with his people to bless or curse them according to their obedience.[9] The pinnacle of Israel's national blessing was the kingdom of David and his descendants, which the Lord established by "an everlasting covenant" on which the godly rested their hope.[10] The Lord fulfilled his promises to Abraham, Moses, and David in Jesus Christ, who perfectly obeyed the law of Moses and suffered its curse in order to establish the "new" covenant in his blood.[11] Sinclair Ferguson says that the theme of "covenant" is "the architectonic principle" of the Bible: "Indeed it is the framework within which God sets the scene for the coming of Christ and for the bringing in of his kingdom."[12]

3. *The covenant supports God-centered faith.* In the promises of his covenant, the Lord reveals himself so that people may trust in him with all their hearts. When the walls and gates of Jerusalem lay in ruins, Nehemiah was able to call on him whose faithfulness can never be broken, the "LORD God of heaven, the great and terrible God, that keepeth covenant and mercy for them that love him and observe his commandments" (Neh. 1:5; cf. Ps. 103:17–18). Though centuries have elapsed since God made his promises, his people can bank on the fact that he will remember his covenant forever.[13]

4. *The covenant shapes spiritual experience.* David says, "The secret of the LORD is with them that fear him; and he will shew them his covenant" (Ps. 25:14). God grants an inward knowledge of his covenant ways to those whose sins he forgives. He guides them in the way of his goodness, righteousness, mercy, and truth (vv. 8–13). God promises in his covenant the twofold gift of his Word and Holy Spirit to abide with his people forever (Isa. 59:21). "Through the blood of the everlasting covenant," God works in his people what pleases him through Jesus Christ so that they do many good works (Heb. 13:20–21). If we desire to understand true Christian experience, then we must learn about the covenant of grace.

5. *The covenant directs the church's practice.* God's covenant defines the identity, membership, privileges, and obligations of "my people" (Lev. 26:12; cf. Ex. 6:7). The church is a covenantal people, the assembly of

---

9. Ex. 19:5; 24:7; 34:28; Lev. 26:9, 15.
10. 2 Sam. 7:12–16; 23:5; Ps. 89:3, 39.
11. Ezek. 37:24–27; Luke 1:68–73; 22:20; Gal. 3:13; 4:4–5.
12. Sinclair B. Ferguson, foreword to Cornelis P. Venema, *Christ and Covenant Theology: Essays on Election, Republicationism, and the Covenants* (Phillipsburg, NJ: P&R, 2017), x.
13. Ex. 6:5; Lev. 26:42, 45; Pss. 105:8–10; 111:5, 9; Ezek. 16:60.

believing Jews and those Gentiles who were formerly "strangers from the covenants of promise," but who now, by Christ's blood, have been made "fellow citizens with the saints" (Eph. 2:12–13, 19). The relation of adults and their children to the church is defined by God's covenant. The Lord's Supper is explicitly called a covenantal ordinance.[14] We must ground our view of the church's life, work, and witness in the Bible's teaching concerning the covenant.

6. *The covenant glorifies God in his attributes.* He is "the faithful God, which keepeth covenant and mercy with them that love him" (Deut. 7:9). When God's people reflect upon God's covenant ways, they sing of God's faithful love (Ps. 89:1–2) and declare, "Thou art righteous" (Neh. 9:8). God's eternity shines in his covenant, which endures "to a thousand generations" (Ps. 105:8) and will outlast the mountains (Isa. 54:10). His mighty works of redemption display his fidelity to the covenant (Ex. 6:2–6; Ps. 111:9). Do you want to know more of who and what God is? Then reverently study and faithfully keep his covenant.

The Meaning of "Covenant" Reviewed

The Bible presents a diversity of covenants between God and sinners. O. Palmer Robertson notes that God made a "covenant of preservation" with Noah, mankind, and all living creatures (Genesis 9). In subsequent history, God made the "covenant of promise" with Abraham (Genesis 12–22), the "covenant of law" with Israel (Exodus 19–24), the "covenant of the kingdom" with David (2 Samuel 7), and the new covenant or "covenant of consummation" in Christ (Hebrews 8).[15]

What is a covenant? What do we mean by God's covenants with man? We have already proposed that a covenant may be defined as *a solemn promise that functions as a legal instrument to define a relationship of loyalty.*[16] In John Murray's terse phrase, it is a promise of "sworn fidelity."[17] The solemnity of the promise may be expressed in an oath or a ceremony. The relationship of loyalty is often summed up in the Hebrew word *khesed*, variously translated as "mercy," "kindness," "lovingkindness," "goodness" (KJV), or "steadfast love" (ESV). Although there is diversity

---

14. Matt. 26:28; Mark 14:24; Luke 22:20; 1 Cor. 11:25.

15. Robertson, *The Christ of the Covenants*, 61. Robertson notes, "This phrase 'covenant of law' must not be confused with the traditional terminology which speaks of a 'covenant of works'" (173).

16. See chap. 14.

17. Murray, *The Covenant of Grace*, 10.

in the biblical covenants, some elements that often appear in covenants (though not in all of them) are the honoring of one party in the covenant as *lord* over the other party; *laws* that define obedience to the covenant lord; the authorization of the covenant servant to perform a specified *office*; an individual who acts as the *representative* of a larger group of people in the covenant; and a visible *sign*, such as the rainbow for Noah (Gen. 9:8–17) and circumcision for Abraham (17:7–11).

For example, in Psalm 89, the psalmist celebrates the Lord's unfailing "mercy" (*khesed*), for God had declared, "I have made a covenant with my chosen, I have sworn unto David my servant, thy seed will I establish for ever, and build up thy throne to all generations" (Ps. 89:2–4). God promises never to break his covenant with David's "seed," but says he will discipline them "if they break my statutes, and keep not my commandments" (vv. 29–34). Here we have God's faithful love, his sworn oath, David's representation of his offspring, God's lordship, the kingly office of David and his seed, and their obligation to keep God's laws.

Basic Theses of Reformed Covenant Theology

Since God's revelation has unfolded progressively over history, we look to the New Testament to teach us how to properly interpret the covenants of the Bible. In the New Testament, few books have as much to say about God's covenants as Paul's epistle to the Galatians, especially the third and fourth chapters. Here we find a concentration of the key terms "covenant," "Abraham," "promise," "seed," "son," "heir," and "law."[18] Paul gives extensive attention in this passage to the relationship between God's promises to Abraham, his laws given to Israel through Moses, and his saving grace to those in Christ today. Therefore, we will look to Galatians, one of Paul's greatest expositions of justification by faith alone (Gal. 2:16), for the basic outline of truths that we will develop more fully from the whole of the Bible in later chapters.

The Perpetual Continuity of God's Gospel

Paul rebuked the Galatians for beginning to turn aside from the gospel of faith in Christ alone and looking to their works to complete them (Gal.

---

18. See "covenant" (Gal. 3:15, 17; 4:24), "Abraham" (3:6–9, 14, 16, 18, 29; 4:22), "promise" (3:14, 16–18, 21–22, 29; 4:23, 28), "seed" (3:16, 19, 29), "son," sometimes translated as "children" (3:7, 26; 4:4, 6–7, 22, 30), "heir" (3:29; 4:1, 7), and "law" (3:2, 5, 10–13, 17–19, 21, 23–24; 4:4–5, 21).

3:1–5). He then shows from the history of God's people that justification by faith alone is not something new, but the ancient promise by which God has saved his people in all ages. Salvation comes to people not by works of the law, but "by the hearing of faith" (vv. 2, 5), "even as Abraham believed God, and it was accounted to him for righteousness" (v. 6; cf. Gen. 15:6).

Paul's choice of Abraham as an example is strategic for a number of reasons. Abraham, of course, was the father of the Jewish nation. The covenant with Abraham was the root from which all of God's dealings with Israel and Christ grew. Furthermore, the Jews commonly viewed Abraham as a man who gained God's blessing by his obedience to God's commands. The ancient Jewish book of Jubilees says, "Abraham was perfect in all his deeds with the Lord, and well-pleasing in righteousness all the days of his life."[19] Paul rejects such a view of Abraham, teaching that he was justified as one who "believeth on him that justifieth the ungodly" (Rom. 4:1–5). Justification by faith is "the gospel" that God preached to Abraham, not just for him but for the blessing of "all nations" (Gal. 3:8–9).

Covenant theology upholds the principle that there is one Mediator between God and man. Whatever else we may say about God's covenants, we must be clear that there is only one gospel, the gospel of justification by grace through faith, not by works. James Fergusson (1621–1667) commented, "The godly under the Old Testament, and the godly under the New, are justified one and the same way. . . . The gospel therefore is no new doctrine, but the same in substance with that which was taught to Abraham, and to the church under the Old Testament."[20]

The Covenant of Works

Having established that the gospel of grace is God's message of salvation in all ages, Paul next introduces another principle that operates quite differently from the gospel: the principle of law (Gal. 3:10–14). Whereas the gospel says, "The just shall live by faith" (v. 11; cf. Hab. 2:4), the law says, "The man that doeth them shall live in them" (Gal. 3:12; cf. Lev. 18:5). The law pronounces God's "curse" against everyone who does not

---

19. Jubilees 23:10, in *The Apocrypha and Pseudepigrapha of the Old Testament*, ed. R. H. Charles, 2 vols. (Oxford: Oxford University Press, 1913), 2:48.

20. James Fergusson, *A Brief Exposition of the Epistles of Paul to the Galatians, Ephesians, Philippians, Colossians, and Thessalonians* (1841; repr., Edinburgh: Banner of Truth, 1978), on Gal. 3:6 (48).

do everything commanded (Gal. 3:10). Consequently, those who desire to be righteous before God by their works must keep the whole law of Moses, "all things which are written in the book of the law" (v. 10; 5:3; cf. James 2:10).

Paul aims in this passage to overthrow the soul-damning error of joining faith in Christ with righteousness by our works. When it comes to justification, faith and works mix no better than fire and water: they are two contradictory principles.[21] God does not justify people by making them morally better. Neither does God justify people by merely releasing them from the Mosaic ceremonial laws so that they can become members of God's people by allegiance to Christ the Lord. God justifies people, Paul explains, by placing the curse of his law upon Christ (Gal. 3:13). Christ was born "under the law" and kept all of its precepts to "redeem them that were under the law" (4:4–5). Consequently, those who have faith in Christ are released from the curse and receive the blessing of Christ's Spirit by faith in the gospel (3:1–2, 14).

Paul says that these two principles of law and gospel are "two covenants" (Gal. 4:24). William Perkins commented that Paul teaches "the covenant of works and the covenant of grace, one promising life eternal to him that does all the things contained in the law, and the other to him that turns and believes in Christ. . . . The law, or covenant of works, propounds the bare justice of God without mercy. The covenant of grace, or the gospel, reveals both the justice and mercy of God."[22]

Paul invokes the covenant of works when he addresses people "that desire to be under the law [*hypo nomon*]" (Gal. 4:21). It might be objected that all of ancient Israel was under the law. There is a sense in which believers in the old covenant era were under the law, for they lived as minor children in bondage "under [*hypo*] tutors and governors" (v. 2), and the many Mosaic regulations were a heavy "yoke" upon them (Acts 15:10), though they were justified by faith apart from their works (Rom. 4:4–8). In a similar way, Paul could speak of living "as under the law" (*hōs hypo nomon*) when he willingly subjected himself to the bondage of Jewish ceremonies to "gain the Jews" for the gospel of Christ (1 Cor. 9:20).

However, in Galatians 4:21, Paul addresses those who "desire to be under the law" in the sense of seeking justification by works of the law.

---

21. Calvin, *Commentaries*, on Gal. 3:12.
22. Perkins, *Commentary on Galatians*, on Gal. 4:24, in *Works*, 2:302.

They are "under the law" in its strict demands for perfect righteousness, condemnation for sin, and incarceration under sin's power (3:22–23; cf. 5:3–4). This is not the position of believers during the old covenant, but of unbelievers distorting the law of Moses into a covenant of works to attain their own righteousness (Rom. 10:3). In this strong sense, "under the law" means accursed bondage to sin in sharp antithesis to the reigning influence of God's saving grace (6:14). This is not because of any evil in the law itself (7:12), but because the law has no power to deliver from the guilt and power of sin, but only aggravates them (4:15; 7:7–11).[23] All forms of bondage to the law, both in its ceremonies and its condemnation, are removed in the liberty that God's sons now enjoy in the Spirit (Gal. 3:23–26; 4:5–6, 21–31; 5:18).

Paul associates the covenant of works with Mount Sinai and the slave Hagar (Gal. 4:24–25). God magnified the law in the Mosaic covenant revealed at Sinai in order to give Israel a deeper experience of its bondage to sin and guilt before Christ came (3:22–24). The law, considered as moral precepts engraved on tablets of stone and not as living principles written by the Spirit on the heart, can only kill and condemn (2 Cor. 3:3, 6–7). The ceremonies of the law were but shadows of Christ (Col. 2:16–17). However, just as Abraham and Sarah wrongfully involved Hagar to pursue an heir by the "flesh" instead of by faith in the "promise" (Gal. 4:28–29), so unbelievers abused the law of Moses to pursue righteousness by their own works instead of by faith in God's promise. Thus, Hagar corresponds to "Jerusalem which now is" (v. 25), where the unbelieving Jews and Judaizers in the church twisted God's law into an opportunity for hypocritical, legalistic self-righteousness (Matt. 23:2–4; Gal. 2:12).[24]

The covenant of works is not the Mosaic covenant per se, for Paul demonstrates that old covenant believers after Moses, such as David and Habakkuk, knew the gospel of justification by faith (Rom. 1:17; 4:6–8).[25] The covenant of works and the covenant of grace both came before Moses, for Paul illustrates the two covenants in Abraham's two sons, Ishmael and Isaac (Gal. 4:22–23). Though Paul speaks of the covenants by way of allegorical comparison to the circumstances of the sons' birth, Paul regards

---

23. Murray, *The Epistle to the Romans*, 1:229.
24. We are indebted to Stephen Myers for this understanding of Hagar's role in Galatians 4.
25. The relation of the Mosaic law covenant and the covenant of works will be further examined in chap. 31.

Isaac, not Ishmael, to be a child of God (Rom. 9:7–9). Paul also contrasts the two sons in terms of "flesh" versus "Spirit" (Gal. 4:29), where "flesh" represents man's corruption and inability to keep God's law,[26] the state of mankind since the fall of Adam, whose disobedience brought sin and condemnation to all his natural descendants (Rom. 5:12–19). Speaking of God's law, Paul says, "The scripture hath concluded all under sin," not merely Jews but Gentiles, too (Gal. 3:22). "All the world" outside of Christ is "under the law"[27] and thus "guilty before God" (Rom. 3:19). Therefore, the covenant of works is not the Mosaic covenant of law but a covenant first given by God to all mankind in its first father, Adam—who violated it.

Therefore, the structure of covenant theology consists of two covenants: a covenant of works in Adam and a covenant of grace in Christ. This distinction is crucial for spiritual experience: people must discern whether they are relating to God through the covenant of works or the covenant of grace, for the former approach may produce religious people, but they will live under bondage, persecute God's children, and suffer God's rejection (Gal. 4:24, 29–30).

The Covenant with God's Son and Those in Union with Him

After contrasting works and faith, Paul turns his attention to the unbreakable "covenant" consisting of God's "promises" to Abraham (Gal. 3:15–17). Paul argues, "Now to Abraham and his seed were the promises made. He saith not, And to seeds, as of many; but as of one, And to thy seed, which is Christ" (v. 16). Paul does not deny that the singular "seed" has a corporate sense referring to the people of God (v. 29; cf. Rom. 9:7–8). Rather, he treats the singular form as a divine revelation that the promise of "seed" is particularly made to one person, Jesus Christ. When Abraham trusted in the promise of a "seed," his faith rested in Jesus Christ as God's Mediator of blessing (cf. John 8:56).

God's faithfulness to his promise is guaranteed not only by the nature of a covenant, which even among men is inviolable (Gal. 3:15), but also by the fact that God made the covenant with his Son. God's covenant people

---

26. Rom. 7:5–6; 8:3–9, 12–13; Gal. 3:3; 5:16–17, 19–24; 6:8.

27. In Rom. 3:19, "under the law" translates a different Greek phrase (*en tō nomō*, cf. Rom. 2:12) than that rendered "under the law" (*hypo nomon*) in other texts (Rom. 6:14–15; 1 Cor. 9:20; Gal. 3:23; 4:4–5, 21; 5:18). Yet the meaning seems similar: in the domain or under the dominion of the law. In Rom. 2:12, Paul contrasts *anomōs* with *en nomō*, just as in 1 Cor. 9:21 he contrasts *anomos theō* with *ennomos Christō*.

are adopted "sons," but Christ is the "Son" (4:4–6). They will receive the promised inheritance because Christ is God's rightful heir. They are covenant sons because they have "faith in Christ Jesus" and "have put on Christ"; in union with Christ, they are "Abraham's seed, and heirs according to promise" (3:26–29).

Covenant theology teaches us to regard the covenant of grace as first and foremost a covenant between God the Father and God the Son. As we will see later in this book, this implies that the covenant of grace is rooted in the eternal counsel of the triune God. Christ is not only the Mediator of the covenant, but also the heir of the covenant blessings. He dispenses to God's people the blessings that he himself received from God. This comforts God's people, who know that they are unworthy of receiving God's covenantal blessing. Perkins said, "Be not discouraged. You must not receive the promise immediately [directly] of God, but Christ must do it for you. Though you are unworthy, yet there is dignity and worthiness sufficient in Him."[28]

The Diverse Administrations of God's Covenant of Grace

So far, Paul's treatment of the covenant in Galatians 3 has emphasized the continuity of God's promises and grace throughout time. However, he also teaches that God administers his promises in different ways in different periods of history, especially with respect to "the law" (Gal. 3:17–24). God "added" the law to his promises "till the seed should come to whom the promise was made"—that is, Christ (v. 19). Abraham knew God's righteous laws long before God gave the Ten Commandments on Mount Sinai (Gen. 18:19; 26:5). However, the law of Moses brought God's people under a distinctive administration that continued until Christ fulfilled his redemptive work.

Earlier, we considered the law as the covenant of works, a contrary principle to God's promises of grace by faith (Gal. 3:10–12). However, here Paul speaks of the law as an addition, not a replacement to the covenant; the law does not nullify the promise or militate against it as the only way to eternal life (vv. 17, 21). Nevertheless, the addition of the law until Christ came shows that God's manner of administering his promises does change. The people of God came under a strict legal system that accentuated their sense of guilt ("transgressions," v. 19) and bondage ("con-

---

28. Perkins, *Commentary on Galatians*, on Gal. 3:16, in *Works*, 2:190.

cluded," or literally, "imprisoned" under sin, v. 22). God imposed these regulations not to encourage legalism, but to press people to take hold of "the promise by faith of Jesus Christ" (v. 22).

The Mosaic law was a "schoolmaster" (*paidagōgos*) for Israel (Gal. 3:24–25), a term that does not refer to a teacher but a "guardian" (ESV) who supervised a boy until he grew into maturity.[29] The word suggests restraint, moral accountability, and subjection to rules suited to an immature son (cf. 4:1–2). When Christ came and accomplished redemption, God's people left behind their minority under that guardian and entered the newly inaugurated privileges of God's adopted sons (4:4–7). The old covenant as a distinct historical administration of God's promises passed away and the new covenant began (cf. Heb. 8:13).

Because God administers his covenant differently in different periods of redemptive history, we must beware of flattening the varied topography of the covenants. Rather, we must make good use of biblical theology to trace the progressive unfolding of God's covenant of grace.

The Essential Unity of God's Covenant of Grace

Though diverse in administration, God's covenant with his people has an essential core that remains the same through all the ages. This unity is evident in the principles we have already elucidated. Abraham had the same gospel as Paul (Gal. 3:6). The law "was added" to the covenant, not to replace the promise as the basis for the inheritance, but to regulate the life of Israel until Christ came (vv. 17–19). Therefore, the Lord continued to keep his covenant with Abraham after making the covenant of law with Israel at Mount Sinai. Herman Bavinck said that the covenant with Abraham "is the foundation and core" of the covenant with Israel through Moses (cf. Ex. 2:24; Deut. 7:8).[30]

God's covenant with Abraham is fulfilled today with his Son and those in union with him in the new covenant. Christ himself is the preeminent "seed" of Abraham (Gal. 3:16), and God's covenant with Abraham was a covenant with Christ, who came in the fullness of time (4:4). Just as Abraham was counted righteous by faith, so justified believers in Christ "are the children of Abraham," who receive "the blessing of Abraham" (3:7, 14). Paul says, "And if ye be Christ's, then are ye Abraham's seed,

---

29. Richard N. Longenecker, *Galatians*, Word Biblical Commentary 41 (Dallas, TX: Word, 1990), 146–48.
30. Bavinck, *Reformed Dogmatics*, 3:220.

and heirs according to the promise" (v. 29). In the Holy Scriptures, the people of Israel are the "seed" of Abraham,[31] and Abraham is the nation's "father."[32] In effect, Paul says that believers in Jesus Christ are the true Israel. That is not to deny the Jewish people a place in God's future purposes of salvation by Christ (Rom. 1:16; 11:27–28), but it shows that the only way for Jews and Gentiles to enjoy the promised blessing of Abraham is to trust in Jesus Christ. In Christ alone is the true circumcision, that of the heart by God's Spirit.[33]

Therefore, covenant theology asserts that there is one covenant of grace, administered in various historical covenants through the ages. God has not nullified his covenants, and he does not fulfill them in some manner apart from the church of Christ. Rather, each covenant builds on those previous to it and advances the same divine purposes of redemption and revelation in Christ. Reformed covenant theologians call the revealed purpose that forms this overarching unity the covenant of grace, for it is a promise sealed with God's oath. God's great promises in all his historical covenants are fulfilled in Jesus Christ to the glory of God (2 Cor. 1:20). John Gill wrote, "The covenant of grace is but one and the same in all ages, of which Christ is the substance. . . . For though the covenant is but one, there are different administrations of it; particularly two, one before the coming of Christ, and the other after it."[34]

The Abiding Duty to Obey God's Moral Law

After reading Paul's teaching that Christ came "to redeem them that were under the law" (Gal. 4:5), one might conclude that believers are no longer bound to keep God's commandments. However, Paul goes on in Galatians 5 to teach that the life directed by God's Spirit is a life of obedience to God's laws. He warns us against using our "liberty" in Christ as an opportunity for "the flesh," but calls us to serve one another in love, "for all the law is fulfilled in one word, even in this; Thou shalt love thy neighbor as thyself" (vv. 13–14). Here Paul quotes the Mosaic law of love (Lev. 19:18), indicating the Christian's duty to obey the moral precepts revealed in the covenant of law. Such love moves the Christian to fulfill the precepts

---

31. Josh. 24:3; Ps. 105:6; Isa. 41:8; Jer. 33:26; 2 Cor. 11:22.
32. Ex. 3:6; Josh. 24:3; Isa. 51:2; Matt. 3:9; Luke 1:73; 3:8; 16:24, 30; John 8:39, 53, 56; Acts 7:2.
33. Rom. 2:28–29; Phil. 3:3; Col. 2:11.
34. Gill, *Body of Divinity*, 345.

of the Ten Commandments that regulate our conduct toward our neighbor (Rom. 13:8–10).

The relation of believers to God's commandments must be seen in light of the historical transition of God's people from a state of minority to the privileges of sonship (Gal. 4:4–7). On the one hand, the law of Moses no longer acts as their guardian (3:25), binding them with its many regulations. On the other hand, it is the very nature of true sons to obey their Father's holy commandments (2 Cor. 6:17–18) as his righteous image bearers (Rom. 8:29).

Paul's teaching on the Christian life affirms that it is a life of obeying God's moral law. Paul firmly opposes placing Christians under the obligation of circumcision and other ceremonial duties connected with it (Gal. 2:3; 4:10–11; 5:2–3). He asserts, "For in Jesus Christ neither circumcision availeth any thing, nor uncircumcision; but faith which worketh by love" (v. 6). Such love must not be set against obedience to God's moral law, as Paul makes clear in a parallel statement: "Circumcision is nothing, and uncircumcision is nothing, but the keeping of the commandments of God" (1 Cor. 7:19). A natural interpretation of "commandments" (plural *entolē*) is the moral law summarized in the Ten Commandments, elucidated by apostolic teaching (1 Cor. 14:37).[35] Paul says that the Old Testament was written "for our admonition" so that Christians might learn to avoid the sins of lust, idolatry, fornication, impiety, and discontent that entangled Israel (10:6–11). Believers can do so because they are a new creation (Gal. 6:15), "created in Christ Jesus unto good works" (Eph. 2:10).

The Christian is led by the Spirit and is "not under the law" (Gal. 5:18). John Calvin explained that since God accepts the good works of a believer in Christ despite their "defects," the law no longer afflicts the conscience and "will act only in the capacity of a kind adviser."[36] However, the Christian must still put to death "the works of the flesh," which include "idolatry," "murders," and "adultery," violations of the second, sixth, and seventh commandments (vv. 19–21). Paul commends "the fruit of the Spirit" (v. 22) and "he that soweth to the Spirit" (6:8), agricultural

---

35. The New Testament uses the term "commandment" (*entolē*) to refer to one or more of the Ten Commandments in Matt. 15:3–4; 19:17–19; Luke 23:56; Rom. 7:7–13; 13:9; Eph. 6:2. Paul's immediate concern here is sexual purity and proper conduct in marriage (1 Cor. 6:12–7:40), which pertains to the seventh commandment (Ex. 20:14).

36. Calvin, *Commentaries*, on Gal. 5:18.

metaphors rooted in Old Testament language about Israel's responsibility to do righteousness in obedience to God's law (Isa. 5:1–7; Hos. 10:12). Regarding the fruit of the Spirit, Paul comments, "Against such there is no law" (Gal. 5:23), an understatement that highlights the beautiful manner in which Spirit-worked graces fulfill God's commandments.

Therefore, covenant theology teaches us that the continuity of God's covenantal ways is found in both the gospel promises and the moral laws of God. Whether in the days of Abraham, Moses, David, Paul, or us, one's fundamental obligations toward God and man remain the same. Those obligations take the form of commandments that we must obey. The grace of the Holy Spirit does not replace the moral law, but gives us the will and strength to keep it.

The Church's Union with Her Covenant God through Faith

From first to last, God's covenant of grace calls for the answer of man's faith to embrace the promises and receive salvation (Gal. 3:6–14, 22–26). Such faith is not a bare mental belief, but a reception of the Holy Spirit (vv. 2, 14), who dwells mightily in believers, crying, "Abba, Father" (4:6). Saving faith, exhibited outwardly in the sign of baptism, unites people to Jesus Christ (3:26–27) and unites believers in Christ to each other (v. 28).

Therefore, the covenant of grace is a living word by which God creates vital union and experiential communion between himself and his people. The aim of redemption and the heart of the covenant relationship is God's dwelling with his people (Ex. 29:45–46). The Lord promised Israel that if the nation kept his covenant, "I will set my tabernacle among you: and my soul shall not abhor you. And I will walk among you, and will be your God, and ye shall be my people" (Lev. 26:11–12). Remarkably, Paul quotes these old covenant words and applies them to the new covenant church, declaring, "Ye are the temple of the living God" (2 Cor. 6:16).

Christians are the people who "have known God," and better yet, "are known of God" (Gal. 4:9). They are thus his new covenant people, of whom God promises, "They shall all know me" (Jer. 31:34). Many in ancient Israel did not know the Lord, even though their nation was under his covenant.[37] However, the mutual knowledge of God and his people has always been at the heart of the covenant of grace. By this knowledge, the

---

37. Judg. 2:10; 1 Sam. 2:12; Jer. 9:3, 6; Hos. 4:1; 5:4; 1 Cor. 10:5.

Lord joins individuals to himself in the bond of faith. David says, "And they that know thy name will put their trust in thee: for thou, LORD, hast not forsaken them that seek thee" (Ps. 9:10). Nahum writes, "The LORD is good, a stronghold in the day of trouble; and he knoweth them that trust in him" (Nah. 1:7).

Covenant theology is experiential theology. It is not merely a form of biblical interpretation, an exercise of systematic thinking, or an argument for Reformed distinctives. True covenant theology is knowing God and being known by him—a relationship forged with faith in Christ by the Holy Spirit. Covenant theology trains the soul to cry out to the Lord as "my rock, and my fortress, and my deliverer; my God, my strength, in whom I will trust" (Ps. 18:2).

In summary, we present the following basic theses of covenant theology:

1. The Perpetual Continuity of God's Gospel
2. The Covenant of Works
3. The Covenant with God's Son and Those in Union with Him
4. The Diverse Administrations of God's Covenant of Grace
5. The Essential Unity of God's Covenant of Grace
6. The Abiding Duty to Obey God's Moral Law
7. The Church's Union with Her Covenant God through Faith

We will develop each of these theses in greater detail in future chapters, except for the doctrine of the covenant of works, which we taught earlier in this volume.[38]

Before we proceed, however, you should pause to consider the application of these truths to yourself. Can you say, "The Lord is my God, and I am one of his people"? Are you personally in covenant with God? Do you know God, and are you known by him? Have you trusted in Jesus Christ to save you from the guilt of your sins and make you a child of God? Have you received the Holy Spirit so that you are growing to be more like your Father?

The remainder of this volume will say much about God's covenant and Christ. Yet you must not rest content to view these topics as a spectator to God's covenant ways. You must be a traveler with God's people on their journey to the city of God with the covenant of grace as your map. This is possible only by the grace of Jesus Christ, received by faith. Christ is the essence of the

---

38. On the covenant of works, see chaps. 14–16.

covenant. Do you have him, know him, and treasure him as your Savior, Lord, and covenant Head? Take time to examine yourself, seek the Lord's mercy in prayer, and commit yourself to honoring the God of the covenant.

Sing to the Lord

God's Covenant Love

The tender love a father has
For all his children dear,
Such love the Lord bestows on them
Who worship Him in fear.

The Lord remembers we are dust,
And all our frailty knows;
Man's days are like the tender grass,
And as the flow'r he grows.

The flow'r is withered by the wind
That smites with blighting breath;
So man is quickly swept away
Before the blast of death.

Unchanging is the love of God,
From age to age the same,
Displayed to all who do His will
And reverence His Name.

Those who His gracious cov'nant keep
The Lord will ever bless;
Their children's children shall rejoice
To see His righteousness.

Psalm 103
Tune: Avondale
The Psalter, No. 278

Questions for Meditation or Discussion

1. Someone says to you, "I have no interest in studying the covenant of grace. I simply want to know God and Christ." How do you respond?

2. Why is the doctrine of the covenant important for understanding the history of God's redemptive works?

3. How does the doctrine of the covenant influence faith and spiritual experience?

4. What is the authors' basic definition of a "covenant"? What common elements do they identify in many biblical covenants?

5. How would you show from the Holy Scriptures that God has saved people by the same gospel through the ages?

6. How does Paul interpret the fact that God made his covenant with Abraham "and his seed" (Gal. 3:16)? What does this imply about God's covenant of grace?

7. What evidence is there that God has administered his covenant relationship with his people in diverse ways in different periods of history?

8. What arguments do the authors make for the essential unity of the one covenant of grace through the ages?

9. How do the authors argue that although Christians are not "under the law," they still have an obligation to avoid the sins prohibited in God's moral law and to practice the duties required by it?

10. Is the Lord your covenant God? How do you know?

Questions for Deeper Reflection

11. The authors argue that of the "two covenants" Paul speaks of in Galatians 4:24, the covenant of bondage is not the Mosaic law per se but the covenant of works with all mankind in Adam. Do you agree with this interpretation? Why or why not?

12. What are the implications of God's making the covenant of grace primarily with his Son and then with those in union with him?

13. What does Paul mean when he says that "the law . . . was added because of transgressions" (Gal. 3:19)? Make sure your answer addresses the significance of both "added" and "transgressions."

28

Historical Perspectives
on God's Covenants

There is a complexity to God's covenant ways that defies simplistic sum-
maries. The Holy Scriptures present us with several covenants made with
God's people at different points in history. Some aspects of what God has
required of his people have changed over time. Yet the Scriptures also declare the basic continuity of God's promises and demands, for God never
changes. It is no easy matter to fit together this continuity and discontinuity into a systematic approach that is biblically faithful and logically
coherent.

In this chapter, we offer a historical survey of various proposals about
the doctrine of God's covenants. This review will reveal both the differences of opinion among theologians and the significant unity in the
teachings of orthodox Christianity on this matter, especially within the
Augustinian and Reformed traditions.[1] It is not our purpose to argue for
or against specific points of exegesis or doctrine here, but to accurately
present the different views and set the stage for more detailed theological
discussions in chapters to come.

The Early and Medieval Church

Very early in its history, the Christian church faced the challenge of a
heretical solution to the relationship of the biblical covenants. Marcion

---

1. See Woolsey, *Unity and Continuity in Covenantal Thought*.

of Pontus (fl. 145) taught that the Creator of the physical world and the God of the Jews was an evil being, whereas Jesus Christ revealed a god of absolute love and spirituality, and abolished the law.[2] To sustain his heresy, Marcion rejected all of the Scriptures except fragments of Luke's Gospel and much of Paul's epistles.[3] The Old Testament is so interwoven with the New Testament that he could rip out the Old only by mutilating the New. The leaders of the early church opposed Marcionism, believing that the Old Testament, being inspired by the Holy Spirit, finds its prophetic fulfillment in Jesus Christ.[4] Justin Martyr said, "I am entirely convinced that no Scripture contradicts another."[5] Irenaeus said that "the two covenants" are "of one and the same substance, that is, from one and the same God. . . . For there is one salvation and one God."[6] He added that Abraham's faith was the same as ours, for Abraham trusted in the future accomplishment of things promised by God.[7] Though there was a bondage in the multitude of old covenant regulations, Irenaeus said that Christ did not overthrow the moral principles revealed to Moses; rather, his teaching was "a fulfilling and an extension of them," for the Ten Commandments are "natural precepts" implanted in human nature, and he who does not observe them is not saved by God's grace.[8]

Augustine taught that God established a covenant with Adam that promised blessing and threatened death depending on man's obedience, and Adam's sin made all mankind into covenant breakers.[9] When Adam violated the first covenant, God immediately revealed the gospel of Jesus Christ.[10] The voice of Christ spoke through Moses and Elijah, and so we read the Old Testament in order to listen to God's Son (cf. Matt. 17:3, 5).[11] Law and promise assisted each other in God's economy of salvation: "The law was therefore given, in order that grace might be sought; grace was

---

2. Marcion, *Antitheses*, as cited in Adolf Harnack, *Marcion: The Gospel of the Alien God*, trans. John E. Steely and Lyle D. Bierma (Durham, NC: Labyrinth, 1990), 60–62; cf. Justin Martyr, *First Apology*, chap. 26, in *ANF*, 1:171; and Tertullian, *Against Marcion*, 1.2, 19, in *ANF*, 3:272, 285.

3. Irenaeus, *Against Heresies*, 1.27.2, in *ANF*, 1:352; cf. Harnack, *Marcion*, 25–51.

4. Justin Martyr, *First Apology*, chap. 31, in *ANF*, 1:173.

5. Justin Martyr, *Dialogue with Trypho the Jew*, chap. 65, in *ANF*, 1:230.

6. Irenaeus, *Against Heresies*, 4.9.1, 3, in *ANF*, 1:472–73.

7. Irenaeus, *Against Heresies*, 4.21.1, in *ANF*, 1:492.

8. Irenaeus, *Against Heresies*, 4.13.1; 4.15.1; 4.16.4, in *ANF*, 1:477, 479, 482.

9. Augustine, *The City of God*, 16.27, in *NPNF*[1], 2:326; *On Rebuke and Grace*, chap. 32, in *NPNF*[1], 2:326; and *The Literal Meaning of Genesis*, 8.4.8, in *Works*, 1/13:351. For further discussion of Augustine's teachings of the covenant of works, see chap. 15.

10. Augustine, *On Nature and Grace*, chap. 23, in *NPNF*[1], 5:128.

11. Augustine, Sermon 78, cited in A. D. R. Polman, *The Word of God According to St. Augustine*, trans. A. J. Pomerans (Grand Rapids, MI: Eerdmans, 1961), 84.

given, in order that the law might be fulfilled."[12] God brought his people through "different stages of history," but "none, even of the just men of old, could find salvation apart from the faith of Christ."[13] Augustine said that as he read the Old Testament, "everywhere Christ meets me and refreshes me."[14] The stages of history can be called different covenants, and the "old" is cancelled by the "new" (Jeremiah 31). However, the covenant made with Abraham does not pass away (Ps. 105:8), for it is "the covenant, namely, of justification and an eternal inheritance, which God hath promised to faith" (cf. Rom. 4:10–11).[15] Thus, we find that the new covenant was hidden inside of the old, both concealed and revealed by the types and shadows of the old covenant.[16]

In the medieval period, Thomas Aquinas distinguished between the old and new covenants, calling them the Old Law and the New Law. He taught that the laws given to Israel contained moral, ceremonial, and judicial precepts. The ceremonies and judicial regulations bound old covenant Israel, but the moral law binds all mankind, reflecting as it does the natural law embedded in the mind of man as God created him.[17] Aquinas taught that all the saved through history have been redeemed through faith in Jesus Christ, and thus "at all times there have been some persons belonging to the New Testament,"[18] for the Holy Spirit produced in them love and faith in the "eternal promises,"[19] and they "were not justified except through faith in Christ, who is the Author of the New Testament."[20] Thus, in all the prophets, we hear the same Christ speaking. As Thomas Weinandy writes, for Aquinas, "All other 'words,' spoken at various times . . . are but manifestations of that one eternal Word," the Son of God.[21] However, there are

---

12. Augustine, *On the Spirit and the Letter*, chap. 34, in *NPNF*[1], 5:97.

13. Augustine, *The Enchiridion on Faith, Hope, and Love*, trans. J. B. Shaw (Washington, DC: Regnery, 1961), 137.

14. Augustine, *Against Faustus*, 12.27, cited in Michael Cameron, "The Christological Substructure of Augustine's Figurative Exegesis," in *Augustine and the Bible*, ed. and trans. Pamela Bright (Notre Dame, IN: University of Notre Dame Press, 1999), 94.

15. Augustine, *Expositions on the Book of Psalms*, trans. H. M. Wilkins, 6 vols. (Oxford: John Henry Parker, 1847–1857), 105.7 (5:152).

16. Polman, *The Word of God According to St. Augustine*, 104. For examples of Augustine's typology, see Matthew Levering, *The Theology of Augustine: An Introductory Guide to His Most Important Works* (Grand Rapids, MI: Baker Academic, 2013), 29.

17. Aquinas, *Summa Theologica*, Part 2.1, Q. 98, Art. 5; Q. 99, Art. 2–5.

18. Aquinas, *Summa Theologica*, Part 2.1, Q. 106, Art. 1, Reply 3; Art. 2, Reply Obj. 2.

19. Aquinas, *Summa Theologica*, Part 2.1, Q. 107, Art. 1, Reply Obj. 2.

20. Aquinas, *Summa Theologica*, Part 2.1, Q. 107, Art. 1, Reply Obj. 3.

21. Thomas G. Weinandy, "The Supremacy of Christ: Aquinas' *Commentary on Hebrews*," in *Aquinas on Scripture*, ed. Thomas G. Weinandy, Daniel A. Keating, and John P. Yocum (London: T&T Clark, 2005), 226.

distinctions between the old and new covenants, for in the new covenant we have the accomplished fact of redemption, which, for the old covenant saints, was the promised future. Therefore, the new covenant saints enjoy a greater abundance of the Holy Spirit and more perfect revelation.[22] The new covenant is in the old covenant just as the tree is in the seed.[23]

Reformation Theologians

In his defense of justification by faith alone, Martin Luther made a strong contrast between law and gospel, the old covenant and the new covenant.[24] The old makes conditional promises of physical blessings based on obedience; the new makes unconditional promises, granting "the forgiveness of sins, grace, righteousness, and eternal life freely, for Christ's sake." The old covenant produced a physical people for God who were spiritually enslaved, but the new covenant grants freedom in the Holy Spirit.[25] However, Luther also taught that God revealed the promise of Christ as early as Genesis 3:15, and Luther even called it "the spiritual covenant"—that is, "the promise of the Seed who would crush the head of the serpent."[26] The Old Testament saints were justified by faith, not by works of the law, and their faith, like ours, was in Christ.[27] Luther saw two covenants operating in God's dealings with Abraham and his offspring: "the material one involving the land of Canaan and the spiritual one involving the eternal blessing."[28] Luther also affirmed the law's continuing importance to direct the lives of Christians.[29] Luther's absolute, categorical law-gospel dichotomy served to defend the gospel against Rome's teaching of justification by works, but when writing against antinomianism, Luther emphasized the importance of obeying God's law.[30] Luther said, "Christ, the truth, has come, not to destroy the Law," but to make us into "friends of the Law."[31] Luther wrote that Christ makes us "doers of the Law," first

22. Aquinas, *Summa Theologica*, Part 2.1, Q. 106, Art. 3–4; Q. 107, Art. 1–2.

23. Aquinas, *Summa Theologica*, Part 2.1, Q. 107, Art. 3.

24. Luther, *Lectures on Galatians, 1535*, in *LW*, 26:301.

25. Luther, *Lectures on Galatians, 1535*, in *LW*, 26:437–39.

26. Luther, *Lectures on Genesis*, in *LW*, 2:71.

27. Luther, *Lectures on Galatians, 1535*, in *LW*, 26:85, 239.

28. Luther, *Lectures on Genesis*, in *LW*, 3:111; cf. 3:115–16.

29. See Martin Luther's exposition of the Ten Commandments for Christians in the Small Catechism and Large Catechism, in *The Book of Concord*, 351–54, 386–431.

30. Bernhard Lohse, *Martin Luther's Theology: Its Historical and Systematic Development*, trans. and ed. Roy A. Harrisville (Minneapolis: Fortress, 1999), 181.

31. Cited in Edward A. Engelbrecht, *Friends of the Law: Luther's Use of the Law for the Christian Life* (St. Louis, MO: Concordia, 2011), 166, 178–79.

by the "imputation of righteousness" through faith in Christ, and second by "the Holy Spirit, who creates a new life and new impulses in us, so that we may keep the Law."[32]

Ulrich Zwingli (1484–1531) is often regarded as the initiator of Reformed covenant theology.[33] Zwingli argued that "the Christian people also stand in the gracious covenant with God in which Abraham stood with him." He saw parallels between "the earlier covenant" of Genesis 17 and "our covenant": God is our God, and we must walk uprightly before him; he is the God of our seed, and the covenant sign (circumcision then, baptism now) is given to adults and young children.[34] In fact, Zwingli saw Christians as participating in a covenant that predates Abraham, reaching all the way back to Adam and Noah.[35] Zwingli acknowledged that in some respects "the Old Testament has passed away but the New is everlasting."[36] He did recognize differences with regard to ceremonies and other regulations, such as the physical particulars of circumcision and food regulations,[37] but stressed the unity of the eternal covenant confirmed by Christ's blood and appropriated by faith in Christ.[38]

Zwingli's successor, Heinrich Bullinger, published *The One and Eternal Testament or Covenant of God*, a milestone in Reformed covenant theology.[39] Like Zwingli, Bullinger found the substance of God's eternal covenant in Christ in Genesis 17. Circumcision was a sign of "the eternal covenant of God."[40] The covenant is summarized in the promise

32. Luther, *Lectures on Galatians, 1535*, in LW, 26:260.

33. Lillback, *The Binding of God*, 311. Heinrich Bullinger commended Ulrich Zwingli for being God's instrument to clarify "as no one has done for a thousand years, the chief point of his religion," namely, "his one eternal covenant." Cited in Lillback, *The Binding of God*, 98.

34. Cited in Lillback, *The Binding of God*, 95–96. See Ulrich Zwingli, *Petition of Certain Preachers of Switzerland to the Most Reverend Lord Hugo, Bishop of Constance, That He Will . . . Allow the Priests to Marry*, in *The Latin Works and the Correspondence of Huldreich Zwingli Together with Selections from His German Works, Volume 1*, ed. Samuel M. Jackson, trans. Henry Prebel, Walter Lichtenstein, and Lawrence A. McLouth (New York: G. P. Putnam's Sons, 1912), 154; *Of Baptism*, trans. G. W. Bromily, in *Zwingli and Bullinger*, The Library of Christian Classics XXIV (Philadelphia: Westminster, 1953), 131, 138; and *Regarding Original Sin*, in *The Latin Works of Huldreich Zwingli, Volume 2*, ed. William J. Hinke (Philadelphia: Heidelberg Press, 1922), 21. See also W. P. Stephen, *The Theology of Huldrych Zwingli* (Oxford: Clarendon, 1986), 206.

35. Woolsey, *Unity and Continuity in Covenantal Thought*, 224.

36. Zwingli, *Concerning Choice and Liberty Respecting Food*, in *Works*, 1:111.

37. Zwingli, *Concerning Choice and Liberty Respecting Food*, in *Works*, 1:73, 77, 97.

38. Zwingli, *Regarding Original Sin*, in *Works*, 2:30; and Woolsey, *Unity and Continuity in Covenantal Thought*, 218–19.

39. Heinrich Bullinger, *De Testamento Seu Foedere Dei Unico et Aeterno*. An English translation is found in Charles S. McCoy and J. Wayne Baker, *Fountainhead of Federalism: Heinrich Bullinger and the Covenantal Tradition* (Louisville: Westminster/John Knox, 1991), 99–138.

40. Heinrich Bullinger, *The Decades of Henry Bullinger*, ed. Thomas Harding, trans. H. I., 4 vols. in 2 (1849–1852; repr., Grand Rapids, MI: Reformation Heritage Books, 2004), 1.2:168.

"I am the all-sufficient God" and the command "Walk before Me in integrity."[41] The promise reveals that the covenant stands not on any human merit, but only on the sheer grace of God.[42] The covenant includes the children of Christians, even the children of hypocritical and wicked parents in the church, as it did with Israel (Deut. 1:39), and so they should be baptized.[43] Like Zwingli, Bullinger's covenantal vision was to reform Zurich according to the patterns of Old Testament Israel, with church and state as distinct yet inseparable aspects of one righteous community under God.[44] The law of this community would be God's unchanging moral law, the Ten Commandments, which is "the very absolute and everlasting rule of true righteousness and all virtues, set down for all places, men, and ages, to frame themselves by."[45] Those who fail to cling to God by faith and to walk in holiness will be "excluded, disinherited, and rejected from the covenant."[46] Bullinger's conditional covenant is not a synergistic partnership between God and man, for man's faith is the gift of God.[47] Bullinger said that circumcision signified that God, of his mere grace, made an unbreakable promise to cut away by the Spirit whatever would hinder the covenant and friendship between him and his people.[48] It is a covenant of grace.[49]

John Calvin emphasized the unity of God's covenant through the ages. He said, "All men adopted by God into the company of his people since the beginning of the world were covenanted to him by the same law and by the bond of the same doctrine as obtains among us."[50] He

---

41. Bullinger, *De Testamento*, in *Fountainhead of Federalism*, 112.
42. Bullinger, *De Testamento*, in *Fountainhead of Federalism*, 104–5.
43. Bullinger, *De Testamento*, in *Fountainhead of Federalism*, 108.
44. J. Wayne Baker, *Heinrich Bullinger and the Covenant: The Other Reformed Tradition* (Athens, OH: Ohio University Press, 1980), 107; Bruce Gordon and Emidio Campi, eds., *Architect of Reformation: An Introduction to Heinrich Bullinger, 1504–1575*, Texts and Studies in Reformation and Post-Reformation Thought (Grand Rapids, MI: Baker Academic, 2004), 198, 256–57; and Bullinger, *De Testamento*, in *Fountainhead of Federalism*, 113.
45. Bullinger, *The Decades*, 1.1:210–11.
46. Bullinger, *De Testamento*, in *Fountainhead of Federalism*, 111.
47. Richard Muller, *Christ and the Decree: Christology and Predestination in Reformed Theology from Calvin to Perkins* (Durham, NC: Labyrinth, 1986), 41, 43, 44; and Bierma, *The Covenant Theology of Caspar Olevianus*, 38.
48. Bullinger, *The Decades*, 1.2:174.
49. Contra those scholars who posit two distinct streams within the Reformed tradition, one focused on unconditional election by grace alone and the other on the covenant conditioned upon obedience. Thus, Baker, *Heinrich Bullinger and the Covenant*, xxii–xxiii; and Leonard J. Trinterud, "The Origins of Puritanism," *Church History* 20, no. 1 (March, 1951): 45 (full article, 37–57). For a critical response, see Cornelis P. Venema, *Heinrich Bullinger and the Doctrine of Predestination: Author of "the Other Reformed Tradition"?*, Texts and Studies in Reformation and Post-Reformation Thought (Grand Rapids, MI: Baker Academic, 2002), 27–32.
50. Calvin, *Institutes*, 2.10.1.

wrote, "The covenant made with all the patriarchs is so much like ours in substance and reality that the two are actually one and the same. Yet they differ in the mode of dispensation."[51] Calvin explained that the Lord administered his covenant according to an "orderly plan," such that when he first revealed salvation to Adam, "it glowed like a feeble spark," but then, over history, "the light grew in fullness" until "Christ, the Sun of Righteousness, fully illumined the whole earth."[52] Yet the bright light of the new covenant promises "nothing new"; the new covenant refers to "a renewal and confirmation of the covenant," which was not made void by the exile of the Jews.[53] The moral law of God also remains the same, for it was engraved in the human spirit when God made man in his image and was reaffirmed in the Ten Commandments.[54] The differences in "the manner of dispensation" consist in the Old Testament's focus on earthly benefits, physical ceremonies, outward obedience to the law, bondage through fear of judgment, and the nation of Israel—not to the exclusion of eternal, spiritual, and internal realities, but as types of those blessings displayed more openly in the New Testament church of all nations.[55]

Calvin's teaching on the covenant was closely tied to his view of the sacraments as the signs of the mutual pledge of covenant faithfulness between God and man.[56] Salvation, however, is not bound to the sacraments, but is a gift of God's sovereign grace to whom he chooses: "God's election alone rules as of free right."[57] Yet election does not negate the privileges of the covenant. The offspring of Christians are holy to the thousandth generation, unless they prove themselves to be unclean and thus exclude themselves (Ex. 20:6; 1 Cor. 7:14–15).[58] This means that children may be baptized even if their parents are wicked, so long as they had a godly ancestor in the past and a believer sponsors them.[59] Elec-

---

51. Calvin, *Institutes*, 2.10.2.
52. Calvin, *Institutes*, 2.10.20.
53. Calvin, *Commentaries*, on Isa. 55:3.
54. Calvin, *Institutes*, 2.8.1, 51; 4.20.16.
55. Calvin, *Institutes*, 2.11.1–12. See Woolsey, *Unity and Continuity in Covenantal Thought*, 268–75.
56. Calvin, *Institutes*, 4.16.1; 4.19.2.
57. Calvin, *Institutes*, 4.16.15.
58. Calvin, *Institutes*, 4.16.14–15.
59. John Calvin, letter of Nov. 7, 1559, to John Knox, in *Letters of John Calvin*, ed. Jules Bonnet, trans. Marcus R. Gilchrist, 4 vols. (Philadelphia: Presbyterian Board of Publication, 1858), 4:74–75. See Robert Letham, "Baptism in the Writings of the Reformers," *The Scottish Bulletin of Evangelical Theology* 7, no. 1 (Spring 1989): 40 (full article, 21–44), available at http://www.biblicalstudies.org.uk/articles_sbet-01.php.

tion also does not nullify the obligation between God and his people, but undergirds it.[60] Calvin said, "We must now consider how the covenant is rightly kept . . . for as God binds himself to keep the promise he has given to us; so the consent of faith and of obedience is demanded of us."[61] Though "the covenant of grace is common to hypocrites and true believers," God's sovereign grace effectually produces this "internal renovation" only in "the elect."[62]

Reformed and Presbyterian Orthodoxy

Though every theologian brings his own nuances to the doctrine of the covenant of grace, the basic ideas of Reformed covenant theology that we find in Zwingli, Bullinger, and Calvin continued in later theologians, such as Theodore Beza in Geneva,[63] the Heidelberg theologians Zacharias Ursinus[64] and Caspar Olevianus,[65] Robert Rollock in Scotland,[66] and William Perkins in England.[67] In the period of Reformed orthodoxy, covenant theology was developed with greater sophistication as a central motif of Reformed theology in contrast to Roman, Lutheran, and Arminian theologies.[68] Many seventeenth-century Reformed divines produced treatises on the covenant of works and the covenant of grace.[69]

---

60. Calvin, *Commentaries*, on Zech. 9:11; Rom. 9:4; 1 Cor. 1:13, cited in Woolsey, *Unity and Continuity in Covenantal Thought*, 307.

61. Calvin, *Commentaries*, on Gen. 17:9.

62. Calvin, *Commentaries*, on Deut. 32:6.

63. Theodore Beza's Confession (Art. 18, 22, 23, 48), in *Reformed Confessions*, 2:247, 273–75, 293–94.

64. Ursinus, *The Summe of the Christian Religion*, 124–30, 417–19, 435 (Q. 18–19, 74, 77).

65. Caspar Olevianus, *An Exposition of the Apostles' Creed*, trans. Lyle D. Bierma, intro. R. Scott Clark (Grand Rapids, MI: Reformation Heritage Books, 2009), 9–14; and Bierma, *The Covenant Theology of Caspar Olevianus*, 81–82.

66. Rollock, *A Treatise of God's Effectual Calling*, in *Select Works*, 1:33–52; and "Catechism," 109–29 (Q. 1–102).

67. Perkins, *A Golden Chain*, chaps. 31, 33, in *Works*, 6:153–55, 161–65; and *An Exposition of the Symbol*, in *Works*, 5:94–97.

68. For a study of how the covenantal theme progressively declined in a rationalistic direction in the theologies of Jacob Arminius, Simon Episcopius, and Philipp van Limborch, see Richard A. Muller, "The Federal Motif in Seventeenth Century Arminian Theology," *Nederlands archief voor kerkgeschiedenis* (*Dutch Review of Church History*) Nieuwe Serie 62, no. 1 (1982): 102–22.

69. Ball, *A Treatise of the Covenant of Grace*; Thomas Blake, *Vindiciae Foederis, or, A Treatise of the Covenant of God Entered with Man-Kinde* (London: for Abel Roper, 1653); William Bridge, *Christ and the Covenant* (London: for Thomas Parkhurst, 1667); Peter Bulkeley, *The Gospel-Covenant or the Covenant of Grace Opened* (London: by M. S. for Benjamin Allen, 1646); Burgess, *Vindiciae Legis*; Edmund Calamy, *Two Solemne Covenants Made Between God and Man: viz. The Covenant of Workes, and the Covenant of Grace* (London: for Thomas Banks, 1647); Cocceius, *The Doctrine of the Covenant and Testament of God*; Patrick Gillespie, *The Ark of the Testament Opened* (London: by R. C., 1661); *The Ark of the Covenant Opened, or, A Treatise of the Covenant of Redemption between God and Christ* (London: for Tho. Parkhurst, 1677); Robert Harris, *A Brief Discourse of Mans Estate in the First and Second Adam* (London: by J. Flesher for John Bartlet, the elder, and John Bartlet, the younger, 1653);

The theme of the covenants took an important place in Reformed systematic theology.[70]

The Westminster Confession of Faith (chap. 7) makes the following points that well summarize classic Reformed and Presbyterian covenant theology regarding God's law and gospel. God's covenants express his "voluntary condescension" to meet his creatures on their level so that they can enjoy him. His first covenant with man was the "covenant of works," promising life to Adam and his offspring "upon condition of perfect and personal obedience." God made "the covenant of grace" to address the needs of fallen man, offering life in Christ, requiring faith in Christ, and promising the Spirit of Christ to convert the elect. The Bible calls the covenant of grace "a testament" because it grants an eternal inheritance by the death of Christ. God administered the covenant in different ways under the law (a time of promises and types to foreshadow Christ) and the gospel (when Christ has come). These are not "two covenants of grace, different in substance, but one and the same, under various dispensations."[71] That last statement is almost a quotation of Calvin.[72] Though early Reformed theologians debated the nature and function of the Mosaic covenant, they were unified in regarding God's dealings with his old covenant people as being under the covenant of grace.[73]

We will illustrate the covenant theology of Reformed orthodoxy by presenting the doctrine of law and gospel set forth by one of its premier exponents, Thomas Boston.[74] Proper understanding of the two covenants is necessary because of their role in man's salvation, Boston said. The first covenant shows our lost estate in Adam, and the second offers the remedy in Jesus Christ. Boston asserted the doctrine of a covenant of works not only against Arminians on the Continent, but also against the denial of

---

Samuel Petto, *The Great Mystery of the Covenant of Grace: or the Difference between the Old and New Covenant Stated and Explained* (Stoke-on-Trent, England: Tentmaker, 2007); John Preston, *The New Covenant, or, the Saints Portion: A Treatise Unfolding the All-Sufficiencie of God, and Mans Uprightnes, and the Covenant of Grace* (London: by J. D. for Nicolas Bourne, 1629); Roberts, *Mysterium et Medulla Bibliorum*; Rutherford, *The Covenant of Life Opened*; Obadiah Sedgwick, *The Bowels of Tender Mercy Sealed in the Everlasting Covenant* (London: by Edward Mottershed, for Adoniram Byfield, 1660); Strong, *A Discourse of Two Covenants*; and Witsius, *The Economy of the Covenants.*

70. For example, see Turretin, *Institutes*, 8.3–6; 12.1–9 (1:574–86; 2:169–247).

71. *Reformed Confessions*, 4:242–43. See the Westminster Larger Catechism (Q. 20, 22, 30–35), in *Reformed Confessions*, 4:303–5.

72. Calvin, *Institutes*, 2.10.2.

73. For various views of the Puritans on the Mosaic covenant, see Beeke and Jones, *A Puritan Theology*, 279–303.

74. The material that follows is adapted from Joel R. Beeke and Randall J. Pederson, introduction to Boston, *Works*, 1:I-10–I-14.

it by at least one colleague in the Church of Scotland, John Simson (c. 1668–1740), professor of divinity in the College of Glasgow.[75] Boston argued that God made a covenant of works with the first man, for Genesis 2 presents the elements of a covenant; Galatians 4:24–26 contrasts a covenant of legal bondage to a covenant of Spirit-given freedom; Hosea 6:7 alludes to Adam's covenant breaking; Romans 3:27 contrasts the law of works to the law of faith that is the covenant of grace; and Romans 5:12–19 teaches the imputation of Adam's sin to mankind, presupposing that he was their federal head.[76]

The covenant of grace was established in eternity, Boston said, in the counsel of the Trinity. Boston used the terms "covenant of redemption" and "covenant of grace" to name the eternal and temporal sides of the covenant. He wrote, "The covenant of redemption and the covenant of grace, are not two distinct covenants, but one and the same covenant. I know that many divines do express themselves otherwise in this matter; and that upon very different views, some of which are no ways injurious to the doctrine of free grace."[77] As with the covenant of works, there are two parties to this covenant: God the Father, representing the offended party, and Christ, the second (or last) Adam, representing the elect. Boston saw this as consistent with the Westminster Larger Catechism (Q. 31): "The covenant of grace was made with Christ as the second Adam, and in him with all the elect as his seed."[78] He based the doctrine on Galatians 3:16: "Now to Abraham and his seed were the promises made. He saith not, And to seeds, as of many; but as of one, and to thy seed, which is Christ."[79] Just as Adam was the "representative" for "the persons of all his natural seed" in God's covenant, so the Lord Jesus Christ is the "representative . . . of all his spiritual seed," the "last Adam," who took human nature and fulfilled God's covenant by offering up "perfect obedience" and suffering "the penalty" for sin as his people's substitute.[80]

Therefore, Boston said, the efficacy of the covenant rests in Christ's role, which he fulfilled. He wrote, "The covenant of grace is absolute, and not conditional to us. For being made with Christ as representative

---

75. Boston, *A View of the Covenant of Works from the Sacred Records*, in *Works*, 11:180.
76. Boston, *A View of the Covenant of Works*, in *Works*, 11:181–83; cf. Boston, *An Illustration of the Doctrines of the Christian Religion*, in *Works*, 1:230–33.
77. Boston, *A View of the Covenant of Grace from the Sacred Records*, in *Works*, 8:396–97.
78. *Reformed Confessions*, 4:305.
79. Boston, *A View of the Covenant of Grace*, in *Works*, 8:396.
80. Boston, *An Illustration of the Doctrines of the Christian Religion*, in *Works*, 1:320.

of his seed, all the conditions of it were laid on him, and he has fulfilled the same."[81] Boston said it is "sinful and dangerous" to act toward God as if we were "parties contractors and undertakers" in the covenant. He explained that if people regard their faith, repentance, and obedience as the conditions of the covenant, then they will claim "life and salvation, as having done their part." However, "this quite overturns the nature of the covenant of grace (Rom. 4:4; 11:6)" and puts people in Christ's place. "The true way of covenanting is, to take up the covenant of grace as a free promise of life and salvation, upon condition of Christ's obedience and death performed already."[82] If part of the conditions of the covenant rested on us, then the glory of salvation would be divided between God and man.[83]

Boston was careful, however, to guard the unconditional nature of the covenant from being twisted into a denial of the crucial part that faith and obedience have in Christianity. Faith is not our righteousness, but is the instrument by which we are united with and married to Christ, and receive his imputed righteousness.[84] Our holiness is not our fulfillment of the requirements of the covenant, but is the result of voluntary union with Christ. True believers have surrendered themselves to Christ "to be ruled by him, as well as to be saved by him."[85] There is "an infallible connection between godliness and the glorious life in heaven established by promise in the covenant of grace" (cf. 1 Tim. 4:8), but the condition of eternal life and hope of the Christian is "the obedience and satisfaction of Christ apprehended by faith, and not our godliness."[86]

The writings of Reformed orthodox theologians such as Boston exhibit a peculiar tendency that is both a strength and a weakness: their treatment of the covenant revolved around the accomplishment and application of salvation, not the historical process of revelation.[87] Reformed covenant theology generally focused on the gospel so much that it did not chart the unfolding of the covenant of grace in its progressive revelation over the course of history. That is the task of Reformed biblical theology.

---

81. Boston, *An Illustration of the Doctrines of the Christian Religion*, in *Works*, 1:334.
82. Boston, *An Illustration of the Doctrines of the Christian Religion*, in *Works*, 1:335–36.
83. Boston, *An Illustration of the Doctrines of the Christian Religion*, in *Works*, 1:339.
84. Boston, *An Illustration of the Doctrines of the Christian Religion*, in *Works*, 1:598.
85. Boston, *A View of the Covenant of Grace*, in *Works*, 8:569.
86. Boston's notes in Edward Fisher, *The Marrow of Modern Divinity*, intro. Philip Graham Ryken and William VanDoodewaard (Fearn, Ross-shire, Scotland: Christian Focus, 2009), 129.
87. For example, William Strong's *A Discourse of the Two Covenants* is a massive treatise on salvation.

This study was not utterly neglected in earlier centuries. We find significant forays into this redemptive-historical investigation in the writings of John Owen,[88] Johannes Cocceius,[89] Herman Witsius,[90] and Jonathan Edwards.[91] However, Reformed biblical theology as a distinct discipline did not flower until the early twentieth century through the teachings of Geerhardus Vos.[92]

Unlike some "biblical theology," which is dominated by a skeptical and evolutionary perspective, Vos's biblical theology is a legitimate outgrowth and refinement of Reformed covenant theology.[93] Vos wrote, "Reformed theology . . . has from the beginning shown itself possessed of a true historic sense in the apprehension of the progressive character of the deliverance of truth." It "may justly be considered the precursor of what is at present called biblical theology," but not in a degeneration into "a relativity of truth," for the history of developing biblical truth "remains a history of revelation"—revelation that always agrees "with the sum of truth as it lies in the eternal mind and purpose of God."[94] With these convictions, Reformed biblical theology can be a great asset to covenant theology in elucidating how each of God's acts in biblical history relates to his historical covenants with his people.[95]

Particular Baptist Theologians

In seventeenth-century England, a number of Baptist divines found most principles of Reformed orthodoxy to be congenial to their understanding of the Scriptures, yet they formulated a distinct doctrine of the covenant of grace that suited their view of the New Testament church. They were

---

88. John Owen, *Theologoumena Pantodapa: Sive de Natura, Ortu, Progressu, et Studio Verae Theologiae* (Oxford: Henry Hall, 1661). An English translation is available in John Owen, *Biblical Theology: The History of Theology from Adam to Christ*, trans. Stephen P. Westscott (Orlando, FL: Soli Deo Gloria, 1994).

89. Cocceius, *The Doctrine of the Covenant and Testament of God.*

90. Witsius, *The Economy of the Covenants*, book 4 (2:108–464).

91. Edwards, *A History of the Work of Redemption*, in *WJE*, vol. 9.

92. See especially Vos, *Biblical Theology*. Richard Gaffin writes that Vos's approach is strikingly original and "largely without direct antecedents." Gaffin, introduction to Vos, *Redemptive History and Biblical Interpretation*, xii.

93. For Vos's critique of the rationalistic "biblical theology" of Johann P. Gabler, see Vos, *Biblical Theology*, 9. See also Vern S. Poythress, "Kinds of Biblical Theology," *Westminster Theological Journal* 70, no. 1 (Spring 2008): 129–42.

94. Vos, *Redemptive History and Biblical Interpretation*, 232–33.

95. Other questions regarding Reformed covenant theology, such as the controversy over presumptive regeneration and various ways that Reformed theologians and churches have taught parents to view their young children in relation to the covenant, will be treated under the locus of ecclesiology in *RST*, vol. 4 (forthcoming).

known as "Particular Baptists" because of their view that Christ's death redeemed a particular people, in contrast to the "General Baptists," who believed that Christ's death made all people redeemable if they so choose. In the Second London Baptist Confession (7.3), written in 1677 and reaffirmed in 1689, the Particular Baptists said,

> This covenant is revealed in the gospel; first of all to Adam in the promise of salvation by the seed of the woman (Gen. 3:15), and afterwards by farther steps, until the full discovery thereof was completed in the New Testament (Heb. 1:1); and it is founded in that eternal covenant transaction that was between the Father and the Son about the redemption of the elect (2 Tim. 1:9; Titus 1:2); and it is alone by the grace of this covenant that all the posterity of fallen Adam that ever were saved did obtain life and a blessed immortality, man being now utterly incapable of acceptance with God upon those terms on which Adam stood in his state of innocency (Heb. 11:6, 13; Rom. 4:1–2ff.; Acts 4:12; John 8:56).[96]

Like the Presbyterian Westminster Confession, the Second London Baptist Confession affirms that God saves all his people throughout history by one covenant of grace rooted in the "eternal covenant transaction" between God the Father and God the Son. However, the Baptist Confession does not state that the old covenant and the new covenant are two administrations of the one covenant of grace—the doctrine of Westminster. Instead, it speaks of the progressive revelation of the gospel that culminates in the new covenant, leaving the relation of the old and new covenants undefined.

Many if not all of the early subscribers to the Second London Baptist Confession held a distinctly Particular Baptist view of the covenants,[97] a view that some theologians now call "1689 Federalism."[98] Nehemiah Coxe and Benjamin Keach taught that God's dealings with Abraham involved two covenants, just as Abraham had physical offspring (ethnic Israel) and

---

96. *Reformed Confessions*, 4:541. See *A Confession of Faith, Put Forth by the Elders and Brethren of Many Congregations of Christians, (Baptized upon Profession of Their Faith) in London and the Country. With an Appendix Concerning Baptism* (London: for John Harris, 1688), 7.3 (27).

97. Pascal Denault, *The Distinctiveness of Baptist Covenant Theology: A Comparison between Seventeenth-Century Particular Baptist and Paedobaptist Federalism* (Birmingham, AL: Solid Ground, 2013).

98. Richard C. Barcellos, ed., *Recovering a Covenantal Heritage: Essays in Baptist Covenant Theology* (Palmdale, CA: Reformed Baptist Academic Press, 2014). See also the articles at http://www.1689federalism.com/.

spiritual offspring (believers in Christ, Gal. 3:7).[99] At this point, their views were closer to those of Luther than to Reformed theology.[100] The covenant with Abraham's physical seed, "the covenant of circumcision" (Acts 7:8), was a covenant of works demanding obedience to God's commands (Gen. 17:1, 9), which "were fully stated in by the law of Moses, which was a covenant of works, and its condition or terms, 'Do this and live.'"[101] However, Coxe said, the covenant with Abraham's "carnal seed" did not negate or diminish "the covenant of grace" given to believers, but "was added, and made subservient to the great ends thereof" by the external and typical features of the old covenant.[102] As Keach explained, the Mosaic covenant of law served to show man his inability to attain righteousness by his works.[103] The law did not save anyone, but "all believers, who lived under the Old Testament, were saved by the covenant of grace [that] Christ was to establish."[104] According to Keach, the Bible speaks of plural "covenants of promise" (Eph. 2:12) because they were "divers revelations" of the one covenant of grace in Christ.[105] God made the covenant of grace with Christ in eternity and revealed it to man immediately after the fall, but did not ratify it and execute its outward dispensation until Christ came as a man, died for our sins, and rose from the dead.[106] The covenant of grace during the old covenant was a promise; it was not a fully ratified covenant until the new covenant.

Early Baptist theologians held a variety of views on the covenant. The Second London Baptist Confession does not specifically teach the doctrine of Coxe and Keach, but leaves open or undefined the relation of the covenant of grace to the Abrahamic and Mosaic covenants. It allows for diversity among those who subscribe to it. Other "Calvinistic" Baptists,

---

99. Coxe, *A Discourse of the Covenants That God Made with Men before the Law*, 4.3–4 (71–73); available in modern reprint in Miller, Renihan, and Orozco, eds., *Covenant Theology from Adam to Christ*, 72–73; and Benjamin Keach, *The Ax Laid to the Root: or, One Blow More at the Foundation of Infant Baptism, and Church-Membership . . . Part I* (London: for the Author, 1693), 3. See D. B. Riker, *A Catholic Reformed Theologian: Federalism and Baptism in the Thought of Benjamin Keach, 1640–1704*, Studies in Baptist History and Thought (Eugene, OR: Wipf and Stock, 2009), 134–41; and Denault, *The Distinctiveness of Baptist Covenant Theology*, 117–29.

100. Luther, *Lectures on Genesis*, in *LW*, 2:71; 3:111, 115–16, as discussed above.

101. Coxe, *A Discourse of the Covenants*, 5.7 (104); also in Miller, Renihan, and Orozco, eds., *Covenant Theology from Adam to Christ*, 90–91. See also Keach, *The Ax Laid to the Root*, 12.

102. Coxe, *A Discourse of the Covenants*, 5.8 (106–9); also in Miller, Renihan, and Orozco, eds., *Covenant Theology from Adam to Christ*, 91–93. See Keach, *The Display of Glorious Grace*, 181.

103. Keach, *The Display of Glorious Grace*, 15.

104. Keach, *The Display of Glorious Grace*, 113–14.

105. Keach, *The Display of Glorious Grace*, 181.

106. Benjamin Keach, *The Everlasting Covenant, a Sweet Cordial for a Drooping Soul: or, the Excellent Nature of the Covenant of Grace Opened* (London: for H. Barnard, 1692), 17.

such as Robert Purnell (1606–1666), John Bunyan, and, in the eighteenth century, John Gill, held to a view of the covenants closer to classic Reformed theology in affirming that the one covenant of grace had different administrations in different eras in history.[107] Yet the seminal idea of Coxe and Keach did continue in the writings of some later Baptist theologians, such as R. B. C. Howell (1801–1868), who taught that the old covenant and new covenant are not two forms of the same covenant, but two different covenants. The gospel has always been the same, being rooted in the eternal covenant of redemption between the persons of the triune God, but the new covenant entered its visible administration only with the completion of Christ's work.[108]

Liberal Modernism and Neoorthodoxy

As the unbelieving historical criticism of the Enlightenment swept into the church to produce liberal modernism, its skepticism withered faith in the Old Testament.[109] Friedrich Schleiermacher regarded the Jewish faith as a weak form of monotheism, holding that the law of Moses relates to Christianity on the same level as paganism does.[110] Further, the Old Testament lacks the spirituality and inspiration of the New.[111] Albrecht Ritschl regarded the Old Testament as significant only insofar as it historically prepared for the New Testament, having no authority in itself.[112] Adolf Harnack (1851–1930) said that the Old Testament contains comfort and wisdom for God's people, but much of it teaches "a religion and a morality other than Christian," which, if taken as "authoritative," continually endangers the freedom and spirituality of Christianity.[113]

---

107. Robert Purnell, *A Little Cabinet Richly Stored with All Sorts of Heavenly Varieties, and Soul-Reviving Influences* (London: by R. W. for Thomas Brewster, 1657), 35; John Bunyan, *Doctrine of the Law and Grace Unfolded* (London: for M. Wright, 1659), 139–40; cf. Bunyan, *Works*, 1:524; and Gill, *A Body of Divinity*, 345. Gill notes that "the law of Moses . . . was not delivered as a pure covenant of works, though the self-righteous Jews turned it into one, and sought for light and righteousness by it . . . nor a pure covenant of grace. . . . But it was a part and branch of the typical covenant, under which the covenant of grace was administered under the former dispensation" (269).

108. Robert Boyte C. Howell, *The Covenants* (Charleston, NC: Southern Baptist Publication Society, 1855), 101, 115.

109. On liberal modernism, see the discussion of the Bible's subordination to human reason in *RST*, 1:287–95.

110. Schleiermacher, *The Christian Faith*, 8.4, 12.1–2 (1:37–38, 60–62).

111. Schleiermacher, *The Christian Faith*, 132.2 (2:608–9).

112. J. H. W. Stuckenberg, "The Theology of Albrecht Ritschl," *The American Journal of Theology* 2, no. 2 (April 1898): 277 (full article, 268–92).

113. Adolf Harnack, *What Is Christianity? Lectures Delivered in the University of Berlin During the Winter-Term 1899–1900*, trans. Thomas Bailey Saunders, rev. 2nd ed. (New York: G. P. Putnam's Sons, 1902), 200–201.

Liberalism's dim view of the Old Testament, combined with its reduction of the New Testament to a message of love, fostered an approach to the Bible not far from Marcionism. It concluded that the Old Testament is sub-Christian in its ethic and that the redeeming works of God are myths.[114] Harnack said that the "gospel" of Christ, though springing out of the Old Testament, is "a new religion" of love.[115]

Furthermore, just as we found with Marcion, liberal attempts to reconstruct the Christian message apart from a biblical and covenantal context mutilated New Testament Christianity. The great doctrines of Christ's apostles became code words for a modern philosophy or political agenda—or were discarded on the trash heap of ancient legends. For example, existentialist theologian Paul Tillich (1886–1965) interpreted Christ's resurrection to be a symbol, perhaps one with no "objective reality" as a historical event, but meaningful as an affirmation of victory over "existential estrangement" and "the power of the New Being." But the matter of Christ's bodily resurrection, which the apostle Paul regards as central to the gospel (1 Cor. 15:1–5), was judged by Tillich to be an "absurd question" bordering on "blasphemy."[116]

In his reaction against liberalism, Karl Barth did not return to Reformed covenant theology so much as subject it to criticism, take up some of its elements, and forge his own unique way. Barth affirmed, "The covenant is a covenant of grace." By this he meant that God determines and establishes his covenant in freedom with undeserving man, grants to man God's blessing and "powerful Yes" to bring him into fellowship with God as man's divine "companion," and engages man in the necessary response of "gratitude."[117] However, Barth objected to the classic conception of the covenant of works and covenant of grace because they rest upon an abstract divine righteousness that Christ must satisfy before God can be merciful to sinners. Barth also rejected the covenant of works because it usurped the primacy of the covenant of grace and introduced dualism into God's covenant dealings.[118] Barth's rejection of a covenant of works established on God's

---

114. See Bavinck, *Reformed Dogmatics*, 3:211–12.
115. Adolf Harnack, *History of Dogma*, trans. Neil Buchanan, 7 vols. (Boston: Roberts Brothers, 1895–1900), 1:41–42.
116. Paul Tillich, *Systematic Theology*, 3 vols. (Chicago: University of Chicago Press, 1957), 2:154–56.
117. Barth, *Church Dogmatics*, IV/1, sec. 57.2 (38–42).
118. Barth, *Church Dogmatics*, IV/1, sec. 57.2 (63–66).

justice corresponded to his ultimate identification of law with gospel. G. C. Berkouwer explained, "There is therefore also no room in Barth's conception for the view that man was placed under the law of the good Creator before the fall into sin and unrighteousness. . . . Law is the form of the gospel."[119]

Barth linked the covenant not merely with redemption but with God's universal love for all creation. He said, "The inner basis of the covenant is simply the free love of God, or more precisely the eternal covenant which God has decreed in Himself as the covenant of the Father with His Son as the Lord and Bearer of human nature, and to that extent the Representative of all creation."[120] The covenant of grace is not with some individuals whom God elected, redeemed, and regenerated. The covenant is with man as man: "Real man lives with God as His covenant-partner." This is so through Jesus Christ, who is "man for man, for other men, His fellows."[121] Jan van Genderen and Willem Velema write, "According to Barth, the covenant is not established with particular people—neither with believers and their children, nor only with the elect portion of humanity—but with all people."[122] Barth's intertwining of covenant and creation undermines both the doctrines of man's fall and God's deliverance of man from wrath into a state of grace. Berkouwer noted that Barth excluded from his theology "a transition from wrath to grace in history."[123] Consequently, the covenant of grace is not an instrument of redemption, but an announcement that man is already in covenant with the Creator through Jesus Christ. As Emil Brunner said critically of Barth's view, mankind is like the crew of a shipwrecked vessel who do not know they are "in shallow water in which they cannot drown."[124]

Classic and Revised Dispensationalism

Far different from liberal modernism and neoorthodoxy, evangelical dispensationalism is a system that is built on faith in the Bible as the inerrant

---

119. G. C. Berkouwer, *The Triumph of Grace in the Theology of Karl Barth*, trans. Harry R. Boer (Grand Rapids, MI: Eerdmans, 1956), 324.

120. Barth, *Church Dogmatics*, III/1, sec. 41.2 (97).

121. Barth, *Church Dogmatics*, III/2, sec. 45.1 (242).

122. J. van Genderen and W. H. Velema, *Concise Reformed Dogmatics*, trans. Gerrit Bilkes and Ed M. van der Maas (Phillipsburg, NJ: P&R, 2008), 544.

123. Berkouwer, *The Triumph of Grace in the Theology of Karl Barth*, 253.

124. Cited in Berkouwer, *The Triumph of Grace in the Theology of Karl Barth*, 264.

Word of God. However, it interprets the covenants of the Holy Scriptures according to an absolute distinction between Israel and the Christian church. The term *dispensationalism* can be misleading, for Reformed covenant theologians have long spoken of God's different administrations of the covenant of grace as "dispensations."[125] According to the dispensationalist system, however, God's promises to Israel are not fulfilled in the church of Jesus Christ, but await a future fulfillment in the millennium after Christ returns to reign on earth in open glory.

Though the belief in a literal millennium when Christ will reign on earth after his glorious return ("premillennialism") had advocates in the early church,[126] the strong Israel-church distinction of dispensationalism was popularized by John Nelson Darby (1800–1882), a leader of the Plymouth Brethren movement that broke away from the Church of England. Darby made an absolute distinction between God's earthly people, Israel, and God's heavenly people in union with Christ, the church. This distinction led him to interpret biblical promises directed to Israel as exclusively theirs, fulfilled not in the church but in a future era.[127]

The origins of this doctrine have been traced to the Roman Catholic writers Manuel Lacunza (1731–1801) and Bernard Lambert (1738–1813), both of whose writings were available to Darby. Lambert asserted a two-stage return of Christ, the first to gather his saints and the second to start the millennium.[128] Lacunza's book, *La venida del Mesías en gloria y majestad* (*The Coming of the Messiah in Glory and Majesty*), was translated into English by Edward Irving (1792–1834), a zealous advocate of the restoration of the Spirit's revelatory gifts of prophecy and tongues.[129] Lacunza's book, as translated by Irving,

---

125. See the Westminster Confession of Faith (7.6), in *Reformed Confessions*, 4:243.

126. Papias, cited in *ANF*, 1:154; and Irenaeus, *Against Heresies*, 5.30.4, in *ANF*, 1:560. Irenaeus called the millennium the "seventh day," corresponding to the Sabbath in the week of creation. Irenaeus, *Against Heresies*, 5.28.3, in *ANF*, 1:557. Unlike dispensationalists, Irenaeus taught that the godly of all ages (Israel and the Christian church) will be raised from the dead together at Christ's coming. Irenaeus, *Against Heresies*, 5.22.2, in *ANF*, 1:494.

127. Vern S. Poythress, *Understanding Dispensationalists*, 2nd ed. (Phillipsburg, NJ: P&R, 1994), 14–18.

128. Timothy C. F. Stunt, "Influences in the Early Development of J. N. Darby," in *Prisoners of Hope? Aspects of Evangelical Millenialism in Britain and Ireland, 1800–1880*, ed. Crawford Gribben and Timothy C. F. Stunt, Studies in Evangelical History and Thought (Eugene, OR: Wipf and Stock, 2004), 63–65; and Crawford Gribben, *Evangelical Millennialism in the Trans-Atlantic World, 1500–2000* (New York: Palgrave Macmillan, 2011), 83–84.

129. Juan Josafat Ben-Ezra (Manuel Lacunza), *The Coming of the Messiah in Glory and Majesty*, trans. Edward Irving, 2 vols. (London: L. B. Seeley and Son, 1827). On Irving, see Arnold Dallimore, *Forerunner of the Charismatic Movement: The Life of Edward Irving* (Chicago: Moody, 1983).

presents the essential outline of dispensationalism: after God gathers a church from the Gentiles and it falls into spiritual decline, God will bring the Jews to himself and then Christ will return to reign in his kingdom.[130] A large gap stands between the coming of the Lord to raise his people from the dead and the final day of general resurrection and judgment.[131] Between these great events stands the millennium of Revelation 20,[132] when the Jews will be restored to their land and Jerusalem will be the capital of the whole earth.[133]

Other elements of dispensationalism also appeared among the Irvingites. Irving's "Preliminary Discourse" to Lacunza's work repeatedly used the term "dispensation" to describe distinct eras in the history of redemption.[134] An article in the Irvingite magazine *The Morning Watch* taught that the seven churches of Revelation 2–3 represented seven epochs of church history, the sixth of which is the time of the church, which will conclude when it is caught up to meet the Lord in the sky, and the seventh of which is the "period of the great tribulation" between the rapture and Christ's coming to reign in Zion.[135] Samuel Prideaux Tregelles (1813–1875) said, "I am not aware that there was any definite teaching that there would be a secret rapture of the Church at a secret coming, until this was given forth as an utterance in Mr. Irving's church, from what was there received as being the voice of the Spirit."[136]

After Darby popularized his doctrine, classic dispensationalism arose in the United States outside of Plymouth Brethren circles primarily through the influence of C. I. Scofield (1843–1921), who edited *The Scofield Reference Bible*, and his student Lewis Sperry Chafer (1871–1952), who wrote the first dispensational systematic theology.

Chafer divided history into seven dispensations: innocence in Eden, conscience after the fall, human government after the flood, promise after

---

130. Ben-Ezra (Lacunza), *The Coming of the Messiah in Glory and Majesty*, 2:151.

131. Ben-Ezra (Lacunza), *The Coming of the Messiah in Glory and Majesty*, 1:57–58.

132. Ben-Ezra (Lacunza), *The Coming of the Messiah in Glory and Majesty*, 1:89, 92. Lacunza said that the "thousand years" may represent an indefinitely long period of time.

133. Ben-Ezra (Lacunza), *The Coming of the Messiah in Glory and Majesty*, 1:316–18, 321–22; 2:285, 288.

134. For example, note Irving's contrast between "our present spiritual dispensation and church" and "the earthly dispensation, which had begun with Moses." Irving, "Preliminary Discourse," in Ben-Ezra (Lacunza), *The Coming of the Messiah in Glory and Majesty*, xciv.

135. Fidus, "Commentary on the Epistles to the Seven Churches in the Apocalypse," *The Morning Watch; or Quarterly Journal on Prophecy, and Theological Review* 2 (1830): 510–18.

136. S. P. Tregelles, *The Hope of Christ's Second Coming: How Is It Taught in Scripture? And Why?* (London: Houlston & Wright, 1864), 26.

the covenant with Abraham, law after Moses, grace in the new covenant for the church, and kingdom in the new covenant with Israel.[137] Given the rigid distinction between Israel and the church, promises made to Israel cannot be fulfilled in the church, and so there are two new covenants. The church and its union with Christ come into existence in "a hitherto unannounced age" after Israel rejected its King and kingdom.[138] The church age is a "parenthesis" in God's plan,[139] or, to use Chafer's preferred term, an "intercalation" or insertion with no relation to God's previous or subsequent dealings with Israel.[140] Christ's throne in heaven is not the throne promised to the Son of David, which Christ will occupy only when he returns to earth.[141]

Classic dispensationalists made alarming statements that gave the impression that salvation was by works under the Old Testament. *The Scofield Reference Bible* says, "Law is connected with Moses and works; grace with Christ and faith (John 1:17; Rom. 10:4-10). Law blesses the good; grace saves the bad (Ex. 19:5; Eph. 2:1-9). Law demands that blessings be earned; grace is a gift (Deut. 28:1-6; Eph. 2:8; Rom. 4:4-5)." The note continues, "As a dispensation, grace begins with the death and resurrection of Christ (Rom. 3:24-25; 4:24-25). The point of testing is no longer legal obedience as the condition of salvation, but acceptance or rejection of Christ, with good works as the fruit of salvation (John 1:12-13; 3:16; etc.)."[142] However, in another place, Scofield commented, "Law neither justifies a sinner nor sanctifies a believer (Gal. 2:16; 3:2-3, 11-12)."[143] When pressed on the issue, Chafer and Scofield denied that anyone was ever saved by obedience to the law; salvation is always by grace—though their statements on this matter are not easy to reconcile.[144]

In the mid-twentieth century, dispensational theologians such as John Walvoord (1910-2002), Dwight Pentecost (1915-2014), and Charles

---

137. Lewis Sperry Chafer, *Systematic Theology*, 8 vols. (Dallas, TX: Dallas Seminary Press, 1947), 1:40-43.
138. Chafer, *Systematic Theology*, 1:xvi.
139. Note Darby's reference to "the Gentile parenthesis" in Israel's history. John Nelson Darby, *The Collected Writings*, ed. William Kelly (repr., Oak Park, IL: Bible Truth Publishers, 1962), 2:35, cited in Poythress, *Understanding Dispensationalists*, 17. See H. A. Ironside, *The Great Parenthesis* (Grand Rapids, MI: Zondervan, 1943).
140. Chafer, *Systematic Theology*, 4:41.
141. Chafer, *Systematic Theology*, 1:xxxv.
142. *The Scofield Reference Bible*, on John 1:16 (1115).
143. *The Scofield Reference Bible*, on Gal. 3:24 (1245).
144. Charles Ryrie, *Dispensationalism*, rev. ed. (Chicago: Moody, 1995), 107-9.

Ryrie (1925–2016) revised the dispensational stance to make it more consistent with the gospel of salvation by grace alone and other biblical teachings.[145] This revision, however, raised the question of what defines dispensationalism as a distinct theological system. Ryrie said that "the absolutely indispensable part" of this perspective is that "a dispensationalist keeps Israel and the church distinct"—God is working out "two distinct purposes" through "two peoples."[146] Thus, Ryrie said, the new covenant given to Israel (Jeremiah 31) is "not being fulfilled today."[147] This key distinction is guarded, Ryrie taught, by the consistently "literal" interpretation of Scripture.[148] However, dispensationalists regularly interpret the Bible according to figures of speech, typology, and spiritual application. They insist on literal interpretation specifically when dealing with Old Testament prophecies for Israel.[149] Dispensationalism, with its distinction between God's earthly and heavenly people, also tends toward a two-level doctrine of sanctification ("carnal" versus "victorious" Christianity), though not all dispensationalists subscribe to that view.[150]

Recent Evangelical Proposals for Covenantal Models

In the latter part of the twentieth century and the beginning of the twenty-first century, a number of new ideas have been proposed to explain the relationships among God's redemptive-historical covenants, especially among evangelical theologians seeking an alternative to classic or revised dispensationalism on the one hand and covenant theology on the other.[151]

Some theologians propose progressive dispensationalism, so called to reflect their understanding of God's progressive revelation of his grace over the course of redemptive history.[152] In this perspective, God's covenants

---

145. See the comparison between classic and revised dispensationalism in Craig A. Blaising and Darrell L. Bock, *Progressive Dispensationalism: An Up-to-Date Handbook of Contemporary Dispensational Thought* (Wheaton, IL: Victor, 1993), 23–46. The new view is reflected in *The New Scofield Reference Bible* (New York: Oxford University Press, 1967).

146. Ryrie, *Dispensationalism*, 38–39.

147. Ryrie, *Dispensationalism*, 171.

148. Ryrie, *Dispensationalism*, 40, 80, 82.

149. Poythress, *Understanding Dispensationalists*, 24–25. For example, Poythress notes Scofield's interpretation of the promise of "rain" as both physical precipitation and "a mighty effusion of the Spirit." *The Scofield Reference Bible*, on Zech. 10:1 (974).

150. On two-level or higher-life views of sanctification, see the treatment of controversies about sanctification in *RST*, vol. 3 (forthcoming).

151. One such proposal that is generally sympathetic to covenant theology but with a unique distinction between promissory covenants and administrative covenants is found in Thomas Edward McComiskey, *The Covenants of Promise: A Theology of the Old Testament Covenants* (Grand Rapids, MI: Baker, 1985).

152. Blaising and Bock, *Progressive Dispensationalism*, 48.

with Abraham and David find their fulfillment in the first coming of Jesus Christ, though the actual reign of Christ awaits his second coming.[153] The new covenant promised in Jeremiah 31 is fulfilled in Christ's finished work, and its spiritual blessings are being applied presently to Gentiles in Christ, but its complete fulfillment will take place when the kingdom is restored to the nation of Israel.[154] It is not entirely clear whether progressive dispensationalism fits the category of dispensationalism.[155] It does not seem to sustain the distinguishing mark of the teachings of Darby, Scofield, Chafer, and Ryrie, namely, the absolute separation of Israel from the church in God's promises and plan.

Other theologians advocate what they call new covenant theology.[156] Tom Wells and Fred Zaspel affirm strong links between Israel and the church: the church is indeed one "olive tree" with the patriarchs (Rom. 11:16–24).[157] John Reisinger writes, "The whole of the history of redemption revolves around 'Abraham and his seed.'"[158] However, while Wells and Zaspel acknowledge a "unity of God's purpose through the ages," they regard it a "mistake" to call this unifying purpose "the covenant of grace" because the New Testament emphasizes the discontinuity between the old and new covenants.[159] The implication for ethics is that no command of the Old Testament can inform us of our duty before God unless the same command is explicitly taught in the New Testament.[160] It is as though the Father had said, "From now on, listen to my Son. Even Moses and the Prophets must stand mute in his presence."[161] Thus, Wells and Zaspel teach

---

153. Robert L. Saucy, *The Case for Progressive Dispensationalism* (Grand Rapids, MI: Zondervan, 1993), 48–49, 66, 74–75.

154. Saucy, *The Case for Progressive Dispensationalism*, 126–27, 134.

155. Saucy characterizes "non-dispensationalists" as those who believe "no real distinction remains for national Israel subsequent to the founding of the New Testament church." Saucy, *The Case for Progressive Dispensationalism*, 143. However, many theologians outside of dispensationalism teach that God still has purposes to fulfill with ethnic Israel, including nondispensational premillennialists, who locate that fulfillment in a future kingdom on earth.

156. Fred G. Zaspel, "A Brief Explanation of 'New Covenant Theology'" (unpublished paper); and Dennis M. Swanson, "Introduction to New Covenant Theology," *The Master's Seminary Journal* 18, no. 1 (Fall 2007): 152–53 (full article, 149–63). For a Reformed Baptist critique of new covenant theology, see Richard C. Barcellos, *In Defense of the Decalogue: A Critique of New Covenant Theology* (Enumclaw, WA: Winepress, 2001); and *Getting the Garden Right: Adam's Work and God's Rest in Light of Christ* (Cape Coral, FL: Founders, 2017).

157. Tom Wells and Fred Zaspel, *New Covenant Theology* (Frederick, MD: New Covenant Media, 2002), 59–65.

158. John G. Reisinger, *Abraham's Four Seeds: A Biblical Examination of the Presuppositions of Covenant Theology and Dispensationalism* (Frederick, MD: New Covenant Media, 1998), 2.

159. Wells and Zaspel, *New Covenant Theology*, 45.

160. Wells and Zaspel, *New Covenant Theology*, 1–2, 7–14. Wells calls this the "logical priority" of the New Testament.

161. Wells and Zaspel, *New Covenant Theology*, 17.

that we cannot distinguish the moral, ceremonial, and judicial dimensions of God's old covenant law and apply the moral law to the Christian today, and neither are the Ten Commandments "a compact summary of all moral law."[162] The Sabbath is merely a type of our new covenant spiritual rest in Christ, and the fourth commandment no longer binds believers to a special day of rest and worship, for "every day is a Sabbath."[163]

Another proposal is called progressive covenantalism, developed exegetically by Tom Schreiner and Peter Gentry and systematically by Stephen Wellum.[164] This perspective, too, attempts to construct a via media between dispensationalism and Reformed covenant theology based on a fresh exegesis of the Holy Scriptures.[165] In contrast with some advocates of new covenant theology, progressive covenantalism teaches that there was a covenant of creation in which Adam stood as the representative head of the human race.[166] Israel's identity and promises are not fulfilled in a future political entity (contra dispensationalism), but in Jesus Christ, the true. Israel, by union with whom God's people in all eras receive justification and sanctification.[167] At this point, these theologians agree with Reformed covenant theology.

Progressive covenantalists also teach that the church participates in this reality only "in union with Christ through faith," and therefore "does not have the same essential nature as O[ld] T[estament] Israel," for the new covenant people of God consist of a new spiritual community regenerated by the Spirit.[168] Furthermore, progressive covenantalists argue that the Ten Commandments must be interpreted in their covenantal context and applied to us today as they are fulfilled in Christ.[169] A major consequence of this approach is that the Sabbath is not seen as a universal moral law, but a foreshadowing of the Christian's spiritual rest in Christ. However,

---

162. Wells and Zaspel, *New Covenant Theology*, 74–75.

163. Wells and Zaspel, *New Covenant Theology*, 234–36.

164. Peter J. Gentry and Stephen J. Wellum, *Kingdom through Covenant: A Biblical-Theological Understanding of the Covenants* (Wheaton, IL: Crossway, 2012), 24; and Stephen J. Wellum and Brent E. Parker, introduction to *Progressive Covenantalism: Charting a Course between Dispensational and Covenant Theologies*, ed. Stephen J. Wellum and Brent E. Parker (Nashville: B&H Academic, 2016), 3.

165. Gentry and Wellum, *Kingdom through Covenant*, 23.

166. Wellum and Parker, introduction to *Progressive Covenantalism*, ed. Wellum and Parker, 3; and Gentry and Wellum, *Kingdom through Covenant*, 611–23.

167. Jason S. DeRouchie, "Father of a Multitude of Nations: New Covenant Ecclesiology in OT Perspective," in *Progressive Covenantalism*, ed. Wellum and Parker, 27–33.

168. Brent E. Parker, "The Israel-Christ-Church Relationship," in *Progressive Covenantalism*, ed. Wellum and Parker, 44–45.

169. Stephen J. Wellum, "Progressive Covenantalism and the Doing of Ethics," in *Progressive Covenantalism*, ed. Wellum and Parker, 222–23.

progressive covenantalism does promote a practice of the Lord's Day that is often similar to that of people believing that the fourth commandment mandates the Christian Sabbath.[170]

Comparative Conclusions

As we wrap up our historical survey of various views of God's covenant, it will be helpful to compare them to the theses of covenant theology set forth in the previous chapter. We do so in three summary conclusions.

First, Reformed covenant theology teaches *the perpetual continuity of God's gospel* and the contrast of that gospel to *the covenant of works* that God made with Adam. Both Marcion and many liberal modernists have considered the Old Testament as another religion than that of Jesus Christ. Classic dispensationalists also made some statements suggesting that Old Testament saints were not saved by grace through faith in Christ. However, the mainstream Christian tradition through the centuries has affirmed Christ as the Mediator of all salvation. As to the Adamic covenant, the doctrine appears as early as Augustine and has been affirmed by Particular Baptists and progressive covenantalists. Other evangelical traditions may not teach a formal covenant of works, but do distinguish between the law and the gospel, the former saying, "Do this and live."

Second, Reformed covenant theology affirms God's covenant of grace to be a *covenant with God's Son and those in union with him*, so that God's saved people of all ages have enjoyed *union with their covenant God by faith*. In other words, God makes his saving covenant with his Son and the particular people he has chosen to bring to himself. Progressive covenantalism agrees that union with Christ is the only way of salvation and the great promise of all covenants. Barth grossly distorted this principle into universalism and confused the redemptive covenant in Christ with God's goodness to all creation. Classic and revised dispensationalism, on the other hand, reserve spiritual union with Christ to the New Testament church, making God's covenantal dealings with Israel a matter of an earthly kingdom.

Third, Reformed covenant theology recognizes *the diverse administrations and essential unity of God's covenant of grace*, a unity that includes *the abiding duty to obey God's moral law* as summarized for

---

170. Thomas R. Schreiner, "Goodbye and Hello: The Sabbath Command for New Covenant Believers," in *Progressive Covenantalism*, ed. Wellum and Parker, 159–88.

Israel in the Ten Commandments. Luther and the Particular Baptists Coxe and Keach affirmed that God revealed the gracious covenant of salvation from the fall onward and gave the Ten Commandments as a summary of his universal moral law. However, they made a much stronger distinction between the old covenant and the new than Reformed theologians, to the point of finding two covenants in God's dealings with Abraham. Dispensationalists and new covenant theologians do not see the historical covenants as administrations of the covenant of grace and teach that Christians have no moral obligations to obey the Ten Commandments, except insofar as the commandments are restated in the New Testament. Progressive covenantalists believe that the historical covenants reveal and administer God's eternal plan (which is somewhat similar to the Reformed concept of the covenant of grace). Progressive covenantalism calls people to obey the Ten Commandments (and all of the Old Testament), but only in light of a biblical theology encompassing all of Scripture and culminating in Christ's fulfillment of the law in a greater revelation of righteousness and wisdom.

While the full case for Reformed covenant theology has yet to be made, the issues should now be more clear, as well as what is at stake in them for the law, the gospel, and the church. The question to which we will turn in the following chapters is "What does Scripture say?"

Sing to the Lord

Rejoicing in Covenant Blessings

Jehovah's Cov'nant shall endure,
All ordered, everlasting, sure!
O child of God, rejoice to trace
Thy portion in its glorious grace.

'Tis thine, for Christ is giv'n to be
The Covenant of God to thee;
In Him, God's golden scroll of light,
The darkest truths are clear and bright.

O sorrowing sinner, well He knew,
Ere time began, what He would do!
Then rest thy hope within the veil;
His covenant mercies shall not fail!

O doubting one, th' Eternal Three
Are pledged in faithfulness for thee;
Claim every promise, sweet and sure,
By covenant oath of God secure.

O Love that chose, O Love that died,
O Love that sealed and sanctified!
All glory, glory, glory be,
O covenant Triune God, to Thee!

Frances Ridley Havergal
Tune: Old One Hundredth (Doxology)
The Poetical Works of Frances Ridley Havergal (New York: E. P. Dutton & Co., 1888), 235.

Questions for Meditation or Discussion

1. What was the teaching of Marcion? How did the early church respond to it?
2. Describe the teachings of the following theologians regarding God's covenants: (1) Augustine, (2) Aquinas, and (3) Luther.
3. Imagine that you have been asked to give a three-minute presentation on the covenant theology of early Reformed theologians (Zwingli, Bullinger, and Calvin). How would you outline what you would say?
4. What does the Westminster Confession of Faith state regarding the covenant of grace, the law, and the gospel?
5. What do the authors say is both a strength and weakness of Reformed covenant theology as it is commonly taught? How does Reformed biblical theology help this weakness?
6. What is the Particular Baptist doctrine of the covenant of grace as found in (1) the 1689 Second London Baptist Confession and (2) the writings of Coxe and Keach?
7. How have liberal modernists generally viewed the Old Testament?
8. What is Barth's unique approach to God's covenant?
9. According to Ryrie, what is the essential idea of dispensationalism? How does this idea affect how dispensationalists interpret the Bible?
10. Briefly describe the following new evangelical approaches to the covenants: (1) progressive dispensationalism, (2) new covenant theology, and (3) progressive covenantalism.

Questions for Deeper Reflection

11. Of the various views of God's covenants surveyed in this chapter, which do you find most convincing? Give one or two of the most significant reasons why.

12. Why have Christians as diverse as Lutherans, Reformed, and Baptists looked to the Ten Commandments given to Israel at Mount Sinai as a summary of how we should live? If the Ten Commandments are a summary of a Christian's duties, what does that imply about God's covenant of grace?

29

The Perpetual Continuity
of God's Gospel

The central feature of God's covenant of grace is the gospel of Jesus Christ. The gospel towers like a mountain over the landscape of covenant theology—all eyes are drawn to it and all streams of grace flow down from it, no matter where one stands in time and space. We recognize that the term *gospel* especially pertains to the work of the incarnate Christ (Mark 1:1), for with Christ's coming in the flesh the "Sun of righteousness" has risen upon the world (Mal. 4:2) and the Lord has "brought life and immortality to light through the gospel" (2 Tim. 1:10).[1] However, the basic truths of the gospel were revealed from ancient times (Rom. 16:25–26), so that the New Testament gospel differs from the Old Testament doctrine of salvation "only in clarity of presentation," as John Calvin said.[2]

This is an important point of doctrine. The continuity of the gospel through time shows us that God's people are united by a common salvation and belong to the same spiritual family, whether we are talking about Enoch, Isaac, Ruth, Isaiah, Mary, Paul, or Augustine. Furthermore, the continuity of the gospel through the epochs of history assures us that there is always only one way of salvation. This truth energizes the church for its evangelistic mission.

---

1. Calvin, *Institutes*, 2.9.1–2.
2. Calvin, *Institutes*, 2.9.4.

Salvation Always through the One Mediator

Is salvation always by grace through faith in Christ? Yes, for only Christ can save us from our sins. The doctrine that Christ alone (*solus Christus*) is the Mediator between God and man stands or falls with the uniqueness of Christ's person and work, and the glory given to him on account of it. William Perkins said, "Christ stands alone in the work of redemption, without colleague or partner, without deputy, or substitute, whether we respect the whole work of redemption, or the least part of it."[3] A full proof of this truth would fill this whole volume, for it stands upon mankind's need for salvation, Christ's incarnation, and his saving work as the Prophet, Priest, and King of his people. We will only sketch the doctrine here.

The uniqueness of Christ's saving work can be appreciated only when it is seen against the dark backdrop of humanity's desperate state since Adam's fall. Man stands under God's condemnation because of the guilt and shame of our sins. Though created by God in perfect goodness, mankind lost its original righteousness. We are so pervasively corrupted by rebellion against God that we have no resources in ourselves to take the least step toward him. Man is blind and dead in sin. Truly, the salvation of sinners requires an extraordinary Redeemer.

Who is Jesus that he can save us? Christ is not merely one of God's servants, not even the greatest of them; he is the eternal Son of God. The Gospel of John highlights Christ's unique glory by introducing him as the eternal Word who "was with God" and "was God" (John 1:1).[4] Whereas John the Baptist was only a "witness" to God's light, Christ is "the true Light" who illuminates the world (vv. 7–9). People become children of God by a new birth, faith, and adoption (vv. 12–13), but Christ is "the only begotten of the Father" (v. 14).

Christ is the only revealer of God. John says, "No man hath seen God at any time; the only begotten Son, which is in the bosom of the Father, he hath declared him" (v. 18). Jesus says, "No man knoweth who the Son is, but the Father; and who the Father is, but the Son, and he to whom the Son will reveal him" (Luke 10:22).

Christ is the only way to God. Jesus says, "I am the way, the truth, and the life: no man cometh unto the Father, but by me" (John 14:6). "The way" cannot refer to a path to traverse a physical distance; rather, it is the

---

3. Perkins, *Commentary on Galatians*, on Gal. 4:8–11, in *Works*, 2:272.
4. On the deity of the Son of God as attested by this text and others, see *RST*, 1:886–88.

path for overcoming the relational distance that personally separates us from God, implying "that man is now estranged from the Lord and in a wandering condition," as John Brown of Wamphray (c. 1610–1679) said.[5] Only Christ can reconcile us to God and restore our friendship with the Father. Therefore, our future hinges upon whether we have Christ: "He that hath the Son hath life; and he that hath not the Son of God hath not life" (1 John 5:10–12).

Christ alone can save sinners, whether they are Jews or Gentiles. Peter says that though the Jewish religious leaders rejected Christ, God has made him the cornerstone of God's temple on earth (Acts 4:11), just as was prophesied (Ps. 118:22). We cannot be part of God's people without resting upon him, as Peter explains: "Neither is there salvation in any other: for there is none other name under heaven given among men, whereby we must be saved" (Acts 4:12). God emphatically declares here that there is no other Savior in all the world.

Paul ties the uniqueness of Christ to the uniqueness of God: "For there is one God, and one mediator between God and men, the man Christ Jesus; who gave himself a ransom for all" (1 Tim. 2:5–6). Just as there is only one God and all other gods are false, so there is only one Mediator who can reconcile men to God, and all other mediators are not to be trusted. The reason for this follows: Christ alone died as the "ransom" for sinners (v. 6)—that is, he gave his life as the substitute to pay their redemption price in their place (cf. Mark 10:45). This world has known many religious teachers and leaders of spiritual movements, but only one has died for our sins and risen again from the dead. That is the core of the apostolic gospel message (1 Cor. 15:3–5) and the center of all truly Christian thinking.

Therefore, we conclude that whomever God has saved since the fall of man has received salvation through faith in Jesus Christ. Caspar Olevianus said, "All the elect are granted the same faith, by which from the beginning they were engrafted into the Son of God."[6] As Perkins said, this is one reason why Christians confess in the Apostles' Creed that the church is "catholic"— that is, "general or universal," for "the church has had a being in all times and ages, ever since the giving of the promise to our first parents in paradise."[7]

---

5. John Brown of Wamphray, *Christ the Way, the Truth, and the Life* (Grand Rapids, MI: Soli Deo Gloria, 2016), 17.

6. Olevianus, *An Exposition of the Apostles' Creed*, 132.

7. Perkins, *An Exposition of the Symbol*, in *Works*, 5:386. The doctrine of the church will be examined in *RST*, vol. 4 (forthcoming).

Salvation by Faith in Christ through All Ages

How can God have saved people through Christ before Christ came? God revealed Christ in his Word from the beginning. The entire Old Testament is a revelation of Christ, his suffering, and his glory (Luke 24:25–27, 44–47). In Christ's death and resurrection, God was fulfilling what he had spoken "by the mouth of all his prophets," specifically mentioning "Abraham," "Moses," and "Samuel and those that follow after, as many as have spoken" (Acts 3:18, 22, 24–25).[8]

It is a tenet of confessional Reformed Christianity that God revealed the gospel from the beginning of redemptive history. The Heidelberg Catechism (LD 7, Q. 19) says that we know of the Mediator, Jesus Christ, "from the holy gospel, which God Himself first revealed in Paradise; and afterwards published by the patriarchs and prophets, and represented by the sacrifices and other ceremonies of the law; and lastly, has fulfilled . . . by His only begotten Son."[9]

Although Christ's coming brought salvation to light with greater glory, power, and clarity, the gospel preached by Paul is the same gospel that God revealed through his ancient prophets and recorded in the Old Testament Scriptures (Rom. 1:1–4; 3:21; 16:25–26). In what follows, we do not attempt to explore the features of each historical covenant (a study we reserve for later), but aim to trace the gospel through the history of God's redemptive revelation.[10]

Faith in Christ and the First Promise of Salvation

As soon as man fell into sin, God revealed the promise of salvation in delivering his judgment on the Tempter: "And I will put enmity between thee and the woman, and between thy seed and her seed; it shall bruise thy head, and thou shalt bruise his heel" (Gen. 3:15). The Belgic Confession (Art. 17) says that here we see "our most gracious God" drawing near "to seek and comfort" man after he had "thrown himself into temporal and spiritual death, and made himself wholly miserable."[11] We examined this

---

8. On the revelation of Christ in the Old Testament, see Barrett, *Beginning at Moses*; and David Murray, *Jesus on Every Page: Ten Simple Ways to Seek and Find Christ in the Old Testament* (Nashville: Thomas Nelson, 2013). See also Dennis E. Johnson, *Him We Proclaim: Preaching Christ from All the Scriptures* (Phillipsburg, NJ: P&R, 2007).

9. *The Three Forms of Unity*, 73. See also the Second Helvetic Confession (chap. 13) and the Westminster Confession of Faith (7.3, 8.6), in *Reformed Confessions*, 2:833; 4:242–43, 245.

10. For an exploration of the historical covenants, see chaps. 31–32.

11. *The Three Forms of Unity*, 34.

promise in some detail in our study of the fall of man.[12] Here we summarize our findings as we trace the revelation of the gospel through history.

In these words to the Serpent, God announced the accomplishment and application of salvation for God's glory over his enemy. Regarding application, God said he would turn some of fallen humanity against the Devil and, by implication, back to himself. This work of sovereign grace would create an enduring conflict between two kinds of people in the world: the wicked seed of the Devil and the saved seed of the woman. Regarding accomplishment, God foretold a great conflict between Satan and a coming Redeemer descended from Eve, in which Satan would attack the Redeemer, but the Redeemer would have complete victory over Satan for the sake of his people.[13] Announced in words of judgment against the Serpent, this promise centered on God's glory through both judgment and salvation. Herman Bavinck said, "Genesis 3:15 already contains the entire covenant in a nutshell and all the benefits of grace."[14]

Salvation through the promised Redeemer began with our first parents. God explicitly promised to turn the woman against Satan (Gen. 3:15), though she had just chosen to follow Satan against God. Her subsequent words at the birth of her children show her faith in the Lord, particularly her faith in the promise of the "seed" (4:1, 25). Genesis also implies that Adam embraced this promise by faith, for he renamed his wife "Eve," meaning "life," though God had just pronounced against them the sentence of death (3:19–20).

It is also evident that Adam and Eve raised their descendants to know the Lord and his grace. Abel was a righteous man (Matt. 23:35; 1 John 3:12) who lived by faith in God and worshiped him acceptably (Gen. 4:4; Heb. 11:4). In the days of Seth and his children, men began "to call upon the name of the LORD" (Gen. 4:26), a reference to prayer, most likely in the context of public worship.[15] Among Adam's godly descendants, Enoch's deathless translation to heaven after walking with God on earth implied the hope of victory over sin and death (5:23). Enoch was also a prophet who foretold the second coming of Christ to judge the wicked

---

12. See the last part of chap. 18.

13. *The Dutch Annotations upon the Whole Bible*, on Gen. 3:15.

14. Bavinck, *Reformed Dogmatics*, 3:221.

15. Other references to calling on God's name in Genesis take place in the context of an altar or other sacred location, suggesting something more formal than private prayer (Gen. 12:8; 13:4; 21:33; 26:25); cf. 1 Kings 18:24; 2 Kings 5:11; 1 Chron. 16:8; Pss. 99:6; 105:1; 116:4, 13, 17; Isa. 12:4; Lam. 3:55; Joel 2:32; Zeph. 3:9; Zech. 13:9.

(Jude 14–15). Noah also lived by faith in God's promises and was an heir "of the righteousness which is by faith" (Heb. 11:5–7). This is the imputed righteousness of justification through Christ: "the just shall live by faith" (10:38). Therefore, Noah "had a special eye to Christ by faith," for, as Francis Roberts said, "none can inherit Christ's righteousness, but by faith in Christ."[16]

How was it possible for believers such as Abel, Enoch, and Noah to trust in Christ? First, they had the seed-promise of Christ (Gen. 3:15). There is good reason to believe that Adam and Eve passed this promise down to subsequent generations. As we have noted, Eve expressed hope in the coming seed when, at the birth of Seth, she said, "God . . . hath appointed me another seed instead of Abel, whom Cain slew" (4:25). Lamech named his son "Noah" (*noakh*), meaning "rest" (*nuakh*), in hope that one would come to redeem people from the curse, saying, "This same shall comfort us concerning our work and toil of our hands, because of the ground which the LORD hath cursed" (5:29). Here again we find the hope of the promised seed who would bring salvation from sin and misery.

Second, it was possible for primeval believers to trust in Christ because of the types of Christ given to them by God. As we explained earlier, a "type" is a historical person, event, or institution designed by God to foreshadow Christ and his kingdom in a way that is imperfect and yet illuminating.[17]

One type of Christ that God gave to the primeval believers was animal sacrifice. Such sacrifices were anticipated by God's provision of clothing for the shamed couple through the death of animals (Gen. 3:21), a sign that, given in conjunction with the seed-promise, taught them that the coming Redeemer must suffer as their substitute in order to cover their shame. The actual offering of animal sacrifices to God by subsequent generations (4:4; 8:20–21) suggests that these ancient believers understood the principle of atonement by substitution. The Holy Scriptures do not tell us the historical origin of sacrifices, but it is not reasonable to think that godly people would have thought that the killing and burning of God's good creatures would please him unless he had revealed it to be so, especially before the flood, when man was not yet authorized to eat the animals (9:3; cf. 1:29). The sacrifice of animals to appease God's wrath by substituting

---

16. Roberts, *The Mysterie and Marrow of the Bible*, 264–65.
17. See chap. 7 on Adam as a type of Christ.

the sacrifice for the sinner was practiced in ancient societies of all kinds, albeit with much superstition, which suggests an institution early in human history. Certainly the Israelites for whom Genesis was written would have understood animal sacrifices to be for atonement (Lev. 1:4; 17:11). Therefore, we conclude that in some manner the Lord instituted animal sacrifices as a type of Christ in order to nurture the faith of believers.

The Lord also shaped the faith of his people by giving them a type of judgment and salvation in the flood. The waters of the flood destroyed mankind because the human heart was universally corrupted by sin (Gen. 6:5–7). However, God provided one way of salvation, the ark, constructed by the obedience of one righteous man (6:9, 22; 7:5). After the flood, Noah and his family were like a new humanity sent out to be fruitful and multiply God's image in a renewed creation (9:1, 6–7; cf. 1:27–28). Their future safety from the curse of another flood arose from God's pleasure in Noah's sacrificial burnt offerings (8:20–22). God established the security of this arrangement by a covenant of preservation with Noah and all creatures linked to him by their salvation in the ark (9:8–11). God designed Noah's flood to teach his people about the coming judgment (Matt. 24:37–38) and the covenant of peace (Isa. 54:9), in which God saves sinners by union with the one man who obeyed God and offered a pleasing sacrifice. This, too, contributed to the developing faith of the godly in the coming Redeemer.

No doubt, there was much that these believers did not understand about Christ and his work, although we cannot assume their knowledge was limited to what Genesis reveals to us. The book of Genesis was not written for Adam or Noah, but by Moses for Israel from a perspective many centuries after the patriarchs, and therefore may not contain all the revelations given to people in earlier times for their own use. However, it is clear that from the earliest ages of history, God saved people by sovereign grace through faith in the promised Redeemer.

Faith in Christ among the Hebrew Patriarchs

From the line of Noah's son Shem came Terah and his sons Abraham, Nahor, and Haran (Gen. 11:10–26). Theirs was a mixed heritage. On the one hand, the family had become spiritually corrupt with idolatry (Josh. 24:2). On the other hand, we would expect the preservation of core traditions, such as the account of man's creation and fall, the seed-promise of redemption, the genealogies from Adam to Abraham, and the story of the flood—traditions later written down by Moses in Genesis 1–11. The words of God's call to Abraham in Genesis 12:1–3 provide a more brilliant revelation of God's saving plan that shaped the faith not only of the patriarchs, but of every believer since then. The promises in that text are organized under two imperatives: "Get thee out of thy country" and "Thou shalt be a blessing."[18]

The first imperative is a call for Abraham to live by faith—that is, to trust God's word practically by leaving his home and people to go to an unknown land (Heb. 11:8). With this calling came the promises of multiplication into "a great nation," enrichment by God's blessing, and glorification with a great "name" or honor (Gen. 12:2). The broader biblical context links these promises not only to earthly benefits, but also to salvation and participation in God's kingdom.

Abraham's quest for the "land" (Gen. 12:1)[19] answers to mankind's expulsion from the garden of Eden (3:24). Abraham died without inheriting the land of Canaan, but the Lord remained his covenant God (26:24; 28:13; cf. Matt. 22:31–32), showing that the promise transcended earthly property to reach to the heavenly city of God (Heb. 11:13–16; cf. 12:22). Calvin said of the patriarchs, "They would have been more stupid than blocks of wood to keep on pursuing the promises when no hope of these appeared on earth, unless they expected them to be fulfilled elsewhere."[20]

God promised to make Abraham into a "great nation" (Gen. 12:2), his "seed" (v. 7).[21] God granted Abraham and Sarah physical offspring by supernatural intervention in that barren old couple's lives,[22] some of whom were true sons of Abraham by God's sovereign, electing grace, and some of whom were not (Rom. 9:6–13). However, God also promised to make Abraham the "father of many nations" (Gen. 17:5) by their sharing Abraham's faith in God's grace (Rom. 4:16–17). God said he would make Abraham and his seed to "be fruitful" and "multiply,"[23] words that echo God's original blessing on those created "in the image of God" (Gen. 1:26–28; cf. 9:1–7). The true descendants of Abraham

---

18. The other Hebrew verbs used in God's speech in Gen. 12:1–3 are imperfect ("I will") or the *vav* plus perfect, also known as *veqatal* ("shall . . . be blessed").

19. For the promise of "land," see also Gen. 12:7; 13:15, 17; 15:7, 18; 17:8; 24:7; 26:4; 28:13; 35:12; 50:24.

20. Calvin, *Institutes*, 2.10.13.

21. For the promise of "seed" as numerous as dust, stars, or sand, see Gen. 13:16; 15:5; 28:14; 32:12.

22. Gen. 18:10–14; 21:1–2; Rom. 4:19–21.

23. Gen. 17:2, 6; 22:17; 26:4, 24; 28:3; 35:11; 48:4; cf. 47:27; Ex. 1:7.

bear the good fruit of faith, repentance, and obedience.[24] Therefore, these promises offered the hope that God would fill his land with a people bearing his likeness.

The Lord said he would "bless" (*barak*) Abraham (Gen. 12:2), a verb that means "to confer abundant and effective life."[25] Blessing for Abraham included material wealth (24:1, 35), but was far grander in scope. John Gill commented that God promised to bless Abraham, "not only with temporal blessings, but principally with spiritual ones, since Abram in person had no share of the land of Canaan; even with . . . friendship with God."[26] In Genesis, the promise "I will bless thee" (12:2) comes after God's blessing on his created image bearers (1:27–28; 5:1–2) was eclipsed by the curse due to man's fall away from God.[27] The core of God's blessing is the restoration of sinners to his favor and presence (Num. 6:22–27; Pss. 5:12; 67:1). Paul identifies the Abrahamic blessing with the graces of justification in Christ and sanctification by the Spirit (Gal. 3:8, 14). Those who trust in Christ are "blessed along with Abraham, the man of faith" (v. 9 ESV). Abraham's justification by faith was the same imputation of righteousness enjoyed by believers in Christ today (v. 6; cf. Rom. 4:1–5).

God's pledge to "make thy name great" (Gen. 12:2) meant that he would grant Abraham the honor and glory of a king (cf. 17:6, 16), as the Lord said to Abraham's descendant David: "I . . . have made thee a great name, like unto the name of the great men that are in the earth" (2 Sam. 7:9). These promises were fulfilled in the house of David (Ps. 72:17), from which sprang "Jesus Christ, the son of David, the son of Abraham" (Matt. 1:1).[28] The promise of glory recalls God's creation of man in his image with the royal honor of ruling the world (Gen. 1:26). Fallen mankind seeks self-glorification independent of God, as seen at the Tower of Babel, where men said, "Let us make us a name" (11:4). God frustrated this proud aim, but his purpose to exalt man with "glory and honour" over creation came to fruition in Christ, who died and rose again to bring "many sons unto glory"—that is, to save "the seed of Abraham" (Heb. 2:5–10, 16; cf. Ps. 8:4–6).

---

24. Luke 3:8–9; 19:8–9; John 8:39–40; cf. 1 Pet. 3:6.

25. Currid, *A Study Commentary on Genesis: Genesis 1:1–25:18*, 252.

26. John Gill, *Gill's Commentary*, 6 vols. (1852–1854; repr., Grand Rapids, MI: Baker, 1980), on Gen. 12:2 (1:74). On Abraham as the "friend" of God, see 2 Chron. 20:7; Isa. 41:8; James 2:23.

27. On the curse, see Gen. 3:17; 4:11; 5:29; 8:21; 9:25.

28. Mathews, *Genesis 11:27–50:26*, 114–15.

In summary, this first portion of God's promises to Abraham gave to the patriarchs the hope of eternal glory by God's justifying and sanctifying grace given to an elect people. To be sure, the initial fulfillment of those promises revolved around Abraham's physical progeny through Isaac. However, we cannot limit these promises to the earthly kingdom of physical Israel without ripping them out of their redemptive-historical context in Genesis or denying their proper interpretation in the New Testament.

The second imperative in Genesis 12:1–3, "Thou shalt be a blessing," both commanded and empowered Abraham to become a channel of blessing to others.[29] The two promises that accompany it demonstrate both the specificity and breadth of God's redemptive plan.

God's blessing was spiritually discriminating. He said, "I will bless them that bless thee, and curse him that curseth thee" (Gen. 12:3). These words echoed the division of mankind, in God's first promise, between the seed of the cursed Serpent and the seed of the woman (3:14–15).[30] In the promise to Abraham, the blessed were defined by their love for Abraham, the friend of God, and the cursed by their hatred against the people of God. God's blessing would give the former victory over the latter (Gen. 22:17; Num. 24:8–9). Christ said God's true people would be marked by their love for each other (John 13:35). The Lord would review the practical fruit of love on judgment day as evidence to distinguish those whom he will bless from those he will curse (Matt. 25:31–46).

God's blessing is ethnically universal. The Lord said, "In thee shall all families of the earth be blessed" (Gen. 12:3).[31] The word translated as "families" (plural *mishpakhah*) refers to a clan, a people sharing a common ancestor, often larger than an individual household (Num. 26:5–9) but smaller than a tribe (1 Sam. 9:21). Whereas God divided sinful humanity into families, languages, and nations at Babel (Gen. 11:1–9),[32] his redeeming purpose in Abraham was to unite a new humanity under his blessing in Christ (Acts 3:25–26). Thus, in this promise, God "preached the gospel beforehand to Abraham" (Gal. 3:8 ESV). All believers, regard-

---

29. In Genesis, words of blessing are sometimes presented as imperatives (Gen. 1:22, 28; 24:60; 27:29). As such, they are both mandates and invocations of God's empowerment to fulfill those mandates.

30. Currid, *A Study Commentary on Genesis: Genesis 1:1–25:18*, 253.

31. Here the KJV follows the passive rendering "be blessed." On the alternative translation, "will bless themselves," see Mathews, *Genesis 11:27–50:26*, 116–17. The New Testament "understands it as passive (Acts 3:25; Gal. 3:8)." Kidner, *Genesis*, 125.

32. Note the repeated use of "family" (*mishpakhah*) in the table of nations preceding the account of Babel (Gen. 10:5, 18, 20, 31, 32).

less of ethnicity, social status, or gender, are "one in Christ Jesus," and all are "Abraham's seed, and heirs according to the promise" (vv. 28–29).

When God called Abraham to follow him by faith, he promised nothing less than the blessing of salvation for a fallen world through Jesus Christ. In God's promises of blessing to Abraham and all the world through him, we find "an understood antithesis between Adam and Christ," as Calvin said, for "from the time of the first man's alienation from God, we are all born accursed," but here "a new remedy is offered unto us."[33]

This gospel engendered the same justifying faith in Christ within the patriarchs as it does in Christians today. Abraham "believed in the LORD; and he counted it to him for righteousness" (Gen. 15:6). Abraham's faith rested in God's promise of "seed," which can refer to an individual heir (vv. 3–4) and a multiplied people (v. 5). Abraham and those after him would have seen this promise of seed as an elaboration of the first seed-promise of a redeemed people and their Redeemer (3:15), just as Moses linked that promise to later covenants by the prominent use of terms such as "seed" and "generations" in Genesis.[34] Abraham, then, would have seen the promise of his future seed as a further revelation of God's pledge of salvation in the garden through Christ. Just as in the first gospel promise, the individual and corporate sides of "seed" allow for the promise to point to both a people and a particular Redeemer (cf. Gal. 3:16, 29).

There is evidence that Abraham had faith in the Redeemer's death. God taught Abraham the principle of sacrificial substitution when, at Mount Moriah, the Lord provided a ram to die in the place of Isaac, who was the entire covenantal seed of Abraham at the time.[35] Abraham responded to this substitution by naming the place of the sacrifice "The LORD will provide," which was more than a general affirmation of providence, for it became a saying: "On the mount of the LORD it shall be provided" (Gen. 22:13–14 ESV). Giovanni Diodati (1576–1649) said, "The common proverb that was taken from thence signified, that in the greatest extremities of the church, God would miraculously provide for the safety of it; and especially that there should, by pure miracle of grace,

---

33. Calvin, *Commentaries*, on Gen. 12:3.

34. On the formulaic use of "generations" for key figures in God's covenants, see Gen. 2:4; 5:1; 6:9; 10:1; 11:10, 27; 25:12–13, 19; 36:1, 9; 37:2. "Generations" (*toledot*) is related to the verb translated to "bear" or "beget" (*yalad*) a child (4:25–5:5).

35. See Sidney Greidanus, *Preaching Christ from Genesis: Foundations for Expository Sermons* (Grand Rapids, MI: Eerdmans, 2007), 203.

be provided the true Lamb that was to be slain for men, namely, Jesus Christ."[36] Solomon built the temple on this "mount" (2 Chron. 3:1), and Christ died at this location. It seems likely that Abraham's words "The LORD will provide" expressed faith that God would one day provide a sacrifice to die as the substitute for Abraham's seed so that they would live.

There is also evidence for Abraham's hope in the resurrection. Abraham's willingness to sacrifice Isaac arose from his faith in God's ability to raise the dead (Heb. 11:17–19). Abraham said as he departed with Isaac, "I and the lad will go yonder and worship, and [we will] come again to you" (Gen. 22:5).[37] At the very least, this indicates that Abraham trusted in God's supernatural, life-giving power.[38] It seems likely that Abraham also believed that God would use this power to raise his people from the dead, for he "died in faith," still waiting for the inheritance (Heb. 11:13–16). Paul says that Abraham's faith in God's power to give the old barren couple a child was trust in God "who gives life to the dead" (ESV), setting forth Abraham's faith as the prototype of the Christian's faith in Christ crucified and risen again (Rom. 4:17, 23–25). The patriarchs hoped in the resurrection from the dead (cf. Job 19:25–27).

This is the gospel according to Abraham, so to speak. Abraham's faith was not as well informed as ours is today, but it was faith in Christ. The epistle to the Hebrews moves fluidly from saving faith in Christ under the new covenant (Heb. 10:19–22, 38–39) to the faith of Abraham, Sarah, Isaac, Jacob, Joseph (11:8, 11, 20–22), and other old covenant saints, and back to perseverance in faith "looking unto Jesus" (12:1–2). When speaking of his eternal deity as "I am," Christ said, "Your father Abraham rejoiced to see my day: and he saw it, and was glad" (John 8:56, 58). Whether Christ implied that God granted to Abraham a prophetic vision of the future, as some ancient Jews had speculated,[39] or more likely referred to the patriarch's faith in God's promises and types of Christ,[40] the point remains that Christ was the object of Abraham's faith, joy, and hope, just as he is ours today.

---

36. Diodati, *Pious and Learned Annotations upon the Holy Bible*, on Gen. 22:14.
37. The Hebrew verb is first person plural, including Isaac in those who will "come again."
38. Vos, *Biblical Theology*, 85–86.
39. Gerald L. Borchert, *John 1–11*, The New American Commentary 25A (Nashville: Broadman & Holman, 1996), 308; cf. Abraham's visionary experience in Gen. 15:12, 17.
40. Poole, *Annotations upon the Holy Bible*, 3:325, on John 8:56.

Faith in Christ under the Law of Moses

The ministry of Moses was epic and extraordinary. Never before and never again in that era did any man enjoy such "face-to-face" intimacy with God or work such "signs" and "wonders" (Deut. 34:10–12). Moses was God's instrument to redeem his people from political and social bondage (Ex. 3:9–10), his chosen mediator of the divine word (19:3, 7; Deut. 5:24–31), and the effective intercessor for his mercy (Ex. 8:12–13; 32:11–14). However, Moses foretold that God would raise up a Prophet like him, and the people's salvation or destruction would hinge upon whether they listened to that Prophet (Deut. 18:15–19; Acts 3:22–23). The ministry of Moses was not final, but anticipatory of a greater work to come after Israel had experienced God's blessing and curse, when the Lord would give his people an inward circumcision (Deut. 30:1–10).

The Lord revealed the gospel with greater clarity through Moses. Israel's redemption was a grand type of salvation in Christ. God redeemed his people not because of their obedience (Deut. 9:6–7; Josh. 24:14), but in order that they should be his special people who would obey him (Ex. 19:4–5; Deut. 7:6–8). Though it was redemption by great acts of power (Ex. 6:6), it was also redemption through the blood of the Passover lamb that turned God's judgment away from Israel (12:12–13). Thus, the grace of Israel's exodus presented a physical, national picture of salvation in Jesus Christ (1 Cor. 5:7; Titus 2:14).

God's law for Israel set up a system of sacrifices for sin as another type of Christ.[41] Spiritually discerning Israelites understood that such sacrifices could not accomplish atonement beyond an external cleansing, for God built glaring deficiencies into the system (Heb. 10:1–4). The sacrifices were mere animals; rituals with their blood could never be a substitute in God's eyes for man's obedience (1 Sam. 15:22; Ps. 40:6–8). Therefore, men of spiritual wisdom and faith celebrated the rituals by looking ahead to "the true Sacrifice," as Augustine said.[42] The priests who made atonement for Israel's sin needed atonement for their own sins (Lev. 16:11). The work of atonement had to be repeated year after year (16:29–30), so that the priests could never say, "It is finished." Consequently, the old covenant system in itself could not relieve people of their "conscience of sins" (Heb. 10:2), for the conscience can be cleansed only by the blood of Christ (9:14; 10:19, 22).

---

41. Ex. 29:36; 30:10; Lev. 1:4; 4:20, 26, 30, 35; 16:15–6; etc.
42. Augustine, *Expositions on the Book of Psalms*, 40.12, in NPNF¹, 8:123.

Therefore, the Lord designed the sacrificial system to point beyond itself to direct Israel's faith to the perfect Priest and his once-for-all sacrifice. John Owen said that the theology revealed to Moses was "nothing else but a more clear annunciation of the first evangelical promise," for the Mosaic institutions and rituals "confirm, prefigure, and expound the promised Mediator, His coming redemptive work, and the eternal salvation which would, in time, be won through His shed blood."[43] However, there remained an "obscurity" to this typical revelation, Herman Witsius observed, like a veil that concealed the deeper truth (2 Cor. 3:13–16), so that most Israelites "did not penetrate into the spiritual mysteries . . . with the eyes of understanding and faith."[44] The teachings of the New Testament are therefore more plain than the Old.

Though Israel's sacrifices could not atone for sin, believers in old covenant Israel could still enjoy the assurance of complete forgiveness on the basis of God's promises in Christ. David says, "Blessed is he whose transgression is forgiven, whose sin is covered. Blessed is the man unto whom the LORD imputeth not iniquity, and in whose spirit there is no guile" (Ps. 32:1–2). David here describes imputed righteousness by faith apart from works of the law (Rom. 4:4–8). He celebrates the Lord "who forgiveth all thine iniquities," for "as far as the east is from the west, so far hath he removed our transgressions from us" (Ps. 103:3, 12; cf. Mic. 7:18–19). Francis Turretin concluded that "justification and remission of sins was granted to them," which "the clear promises of God given to them concerning it plainly prove."[45] Paul also cites the words of the prophet Habakkuk, "The just shall live by faith," as testimony to justification by faith in Christ.[46] Isaiah revealed the object of justifying faith, declaring that God's "righteous servant" would "justify many; for he will bear their iniquities" (Isa. 53:11).

The old covenant saints were not only justified by faith in the promised Christ, but also sanctified by the Spirit's grace. The Holy Spirit was present with Israel from the day the nation came out of Egypt (Isa. 63:11; Hag. 2:5). The good Spirit of God instructed the people through Moses (Neh. 9:20). To be sure, many Israelites resisted the Holy Spirit and grieved him so that the Lord became their enemy (Isa. 63:10; Acts 7:51). However,

---

43. Owen, *Biblical Theology*, 4.2 (375–76).
44. Witsius, *The Economy of the Covenants*, 4.13.5–6 (2:364–65).
45. Turretin, *Institutes*, 12.10.12 (2:250).
46. Rom. 1:17; Gal. 3:11; citing Hab. 2:4; cf. Heb. 10:38.

some Israelites were transformed by God's grace through faith in Christ. Moses counted "the reproach of Christ"—that is, what "he must suffer for the expectation of Christ, and after the example of Christ"[47]—to be "greater riches than the treasures of Egypt" (Heb. 11:26). Pious Israelites confessed with the psalmist, "O how love I thy law! It is my meditation all the day" (Ps. 119:97). They depended upon the leading of the Holy Spirit to obey God's Word, praying, "Teach me to do thy will; for thou art my God: thy spirit is good; lead me into the land of uprightness" (143:10). They also prayed for forgiveness of sins and inward cleansing (51:9–10). And they sought God's grace to illuminate their minds and turn their hearts to keep God's commandments (119:18, 36).

It is true that God's dealings with Israel involved earthly matters of nation, kingdom, land, ceremonies, and external laws of justice. However, godly Israelites looked beyond these things to set their hope on eternal glory with the Lord (Pss. 23:6; 73:24–26). The reality of their hope was exemplified in the translation of Elijah to heaven without seeing death (2 Kings 2:11). The old covenant saints trusted in the promise of God's salvation, love, and blessing even after the heavens and the earth would pass away (Ps. 102:25–28; Isa. 51:6).[48]

The revelation of Christ under the old covenant especially flourished with the rise of David's monarchy. Israel's hope of salvation became even more clearly focused on a particular person, the Son of David, in whom God's covenant promises would be fulfilled. God also revealed to David that God's Son would reign over all nations (Psalm 2) upon a heavenly throne as the Priest-King (Psalm 110). David's psalms foreshadowed both Christ's sufferings (Ps. 22:1, 18; Matt. 27:35, 46) and resurrection (Ps. 16:10; Acts 2:30–31). The later prophets declared the coming salvation in Christ with increasingly detailed promises.[49]

In conclusion, from the garden to the later Hebrew prophets, God spoke the gospel of his Son (Rom. 1:1–3). The Spirit of Christ testified to the ancient prophets of "the sufferings of Christ, and the glory that should follow," and they diligently searched his word (1 Pet. 1:10–11). To Israel was "the gospel preached" as it is to us today, and if it did not benefit them

---

47. *The Dutch Annotations upon the Whole Bible*, on Heb. 11:26.
48. Calvin, *Institutes*, 2.10.15.
49. For example, see Isa. 7:14; 9:6–7; 11:1–5; 16:5; 32:1–2; 33:17; 42:1–9; 49:1–12; 50:4–9; 52:13–53:12; 55:3–4; 61:1–3; 63:1–6; Jer. 23:5–6; 30:9; 33:15–16; Ezek. 34:23–24; 37:24–25; Dan. 7:13–14; Hos. 3:5; Amos 9:11–12; Mic. 5:2–4; Zech. 6:12–13; 9:9; 12:7–10.

it was due to the people's lack of faith (Heb. 4:2). The two great benefits of Christ, the double grace of justification and sanctification, were granted to old covenant believers (Ps. 19:12–13).[50] The hope of God's ancient people looked to the resurrection of the dead (Acts 24:14–15; 26:6–8).

We must neither dismiss the Old Testament as lacking the gospel nor overestimate the revelation it contains. Bavinck said, "It would be foolish to think that the benefits of forgiveness and sanctification, of regeneration and eternal life, were therefore objectively nonexistent in the days of the Old Testament. They were definitely granted then as well by Christ, who is eternally the same." However, Bavinck noted, "The consciousness and enjoyment of those benefits were far from being as rich in the Old Testament as in the time of the New Testament. . . . The spiritual and eternal clothed itself in the form of the natural and temporal."[51]

The first and most fundamental thesis of covenant theology is the continuity of God's gospel. The gospel of Jesus Christ is the unbreakable cable that holds together all of God's covenantal dealings. The whole Bible, not just the New Testament, is the Word of Christ. Yet God's revelation of Christ is progressive, increasing over time. Calvin said, "At the beginning when the first promise of salvation was given to Adam it glowed like a feeble spark. Then, as it was added to, the light grew in fullness, breaking forth increasingly and shedding its radiance more widely. At last—when all the clouds were dispersed—Christ, the Sun of righteousness, fully illumined the whole earth."[52]

Practical Applications of the Continuity of the Gospel

The principle that Christ alone (*solus Christus*) is the Mediator of salvation has several important applications to the Christian life:

1. *We should trust in Christ alone for salvation.* From beginning to end, God has saved sinners only by faith in Christ. Do you think that you will be saved in a manner different from Abraham, David, or Peter? Submit to God's righteousness, which is found in his Son Jesus Christ. Do not seek to add to it. Look not to your good works, the church's ceremonies, or the intercession of the saints. Rest your hope for salvation on Christ crucified and risen from the dead. Christ is the all-sufficient Savior for all people who would draw near to God.

---

50. On the meaning of Ps. 19:12–13, see *RST*, 1:191.
51. Bavinck, *Reformed Dogmatics*, 3:221.
52. Calvin, *Institutes*, 2.10.20.

2. *We should read the whole Bible to know Christ.* Since God has been revealing the same gospel from Genesis to Revelation, we should read all of Scripture, and do so with an expectation that it is about Christ. Read it with the constant prayer that the Holy Spirit will reveal Christ to you. Seek to understand how Christ manifested himself in each era of redemptive history through personal appearances, promises, and types. While you should not read Christ into texts in an artificial manner, you should strive to grow in your understanding of how each part of the Bible, interpreted in light of the whole Word of God, points us to Christ and our need for him.

3. *We should preach Christ from all Scripture.* If God has called you to preach the Word, then do so with the dual convictions that all Scripture is profitable and that all Scripture aims to make us wise unto salvation by faith in Christ. Preach with the absolute confidence that God's Son is sufficient for all our spiritual and eternal needs. Preach with a sensitivity to the breadth and diversity of Christ's ministry as our Prophet, Priest, and King. Read the rest of this volume with the holy resolution to know Christ better so that you can preach Christ more faithfully.

4. *We should trust in the faithfulness of the God and Father of Jesus Christ.* God has consistently operated according to the same plan of salvation for thousands of years. What a demonstration of his faithfulness! The Father is faithful to his Son and to his children adopted in his Son. Rest your confidence on the reliability of this unchanging God. Take your stand on his promises, knowing that all the promises are fulfilled in Christ.

5. *We should count as one family believers in Christ from all times and places.* The one gospel of God has saved people from immensely different cultures and peoples. Adam was the fallen king of the world. Abraham was a nomadic sheik from Mesopotamia. Moses was a powerful and highly educated man in the royal courts of Pharaoh in Egypt. Rahab was a prostitute in an ancient pagan city. When the gospel went forth into the Roman Empire, God saved Jews and Gentiles, slaves and freemen, Greeks and barbarians. If you are a Christian, this is your family. Cherish your heritage and love God's people, despite all the differences among us.

6. *We should send the gospel of Christ to all nations.* The gospel has been God's means of salvation throughout history, so it is certainly the only means of salvation today. Beware of the false teaching that there are many ways to God. The Bible knows of only one. For the sake of Christ's name, do what you can to spread the good news to all people. Tell those

in your circles of influence as God opens doors. Give your money, prayers, and efforts in cooperation with Christ's church to send out gospel preachers to the nations. If God calls you to do so, be willing to go or to send your child as a messenger of the gospel.

7. *We should anticipate the international joy of the eternal city of God.* When the kingdom of glory comes, believers from all over the world will join with Abraham, Isaac, Jacob, and the saints of all ages in glorifying God and enjoying him forever. We will serve God together as one people redeemed by the blood of the Lamb. There Joshua will be your brother, and Mary your sister. What a day that will be! All the rich diversity of the nations will be united to shine with God's glory. And it will all be to the glory of Jesus Christ. Set your hope upon that heavenly promise, and you will have a light to guide you in your darkest days on earth.

Sing to the Lord

The Gospel of the Old Testament

How blest is he whose trespass hath freely been forgiv'n,
Whose sin is wholly covered before the sight of heav'n.
Blest he to whom Jehovah imputeth not his sin,
Who hath a guileless spirit, whose heart is true within.

While I kept guilty silence my strength was spent with grief,
Thy hand was heavy on me, my soul found not relief;
But when I owned my trespass, my sin hid not from Thee,
When I confessed transgression, then Thou forgavest me.

So let the godly seek Thee in times when Thou art near;
No whelming floods shall reach them, nor cause their hearts to fear.
In Thee, O Lord, I hide me, Thou savest me from ill,
And songs of Thy salvation my heart with rapture thrill.

The sorrows of the wicked in number shall abound,
But those that trust Jehovah, His mercy shall surround;
Then in the Lord be joyful, in song lift up your voice;
Be glad in God, ye righteous, rejoice, ye saints, rejoice.

Psalm 32
Tune: Rutherford ("The Sands of Time Are Sinking")
The Psalter, Nos. 83–84

Or Tune: Prysgol
Trinity Hymnal—Baptist Edition, No. 462

Questions for Meditation or Discussion

1. What is the doctrine of *solus Christus*?
2. List some key Scripture passages asserting the doctrine of *solus Christus* and briefly describe what each means.
3. What are the two main ways that the saints before Abraham knew the gospel of Christ? Give examples of each.
4. What reasons are there to think that God's promise to Abraham, "I will bless thee" (Gen. 12:2), referred to more than mere physical blessings?
5. How does the New Testament understand God's promise to Abraham, "In thee shall all families of the earth be blessed" (Gen. 12:3)? (Cite specific Scripture passages.)
6. How did God design the sacrificial system under the law of Moses to point beyond itself to Christ?
7. How would you prove from Scripture that the old covenant saints were (1) justified by faith, (2) sanctified by grace, and (3) hoping in eternal glory?
8. A friend says to you, "I have been reading the Bible for a long time, but lately I've decided not to bother reading the Old Testament. I just want to read about Christ." How do you respond?
9. How is your family tree a source of honor for you? How is it a source of shame? How does it affect you to know that if you are a believer in Christ, then your spiritual family tree includes Abraham, Moses, and all true believers through the ages?

Questions for Deeper Reflection

10. What gospel truths are clearly revealed in Genesis 3:15? What gospel truths were not clearly revealed until later?
11. What arguments do the authors offer that saints such as Noah and Abraham knew and believed the promise of Genesis 3:15? Do you agree with their position? Why or why not?
12. What difference would it make for us if Abraham was saved by his sincerity and good works, but not by the grace of Christ? What if he was saved by a general faith in God but was completely ignorant of Christ?

30

The Eternal Covenant with God's Son and Those in Union with Him

As we defined it earlier, a covenant is a solemn promise that functions as a legal instrument to define a relationship of loyalty.[1] Promises and relationships require more than one party. Who are the parties of the covenant of grace? The Westminster Larger Catechism (Q. 31) says, "The covenant of grace was made with Christ as the second Adam, and in him with all the elect as his seed."[2] On one side of the covenant bond stands God, and on the other side stand Jesus Christ and his people in union with him.

Christ is an eternal person, for he is God the Son, the second person of the Trinity. Therefore, to say that the covenant was made between God and Christ implies that the covenant of grace is an eternal arrangement, not merely the promises revealed to humanity at various points in time. However, as the Larger Catechism reminds us, God also made the promises of the covenant of grace to those in union with Christ. This implies that the covenant of grace is revealed in history and calls forth a personal and practical response from God's people, for in it God "freely offereth unto sinners life and salvation by Jesus Christ; requiring of them faith in Him, that they may be saved."[3]

Some theologians refer to the eternal mode of the covenant of grace as "the counsel of peace" (Zech. 6:13). The same arrangement is called

---

1. This definition of a covenant was presented in chap. 14 and reaffirmed in chap. 27.
2. *Reformed Confessions*, 4:305.
3. Westminster Confession of Faith (7.3), in *Reformed Confessions*, 4:243.

the "covenant of redemption" and the *pactum salutis* (Latin for "covenant of salvation").[4] In this chapter, we will examine the biblical basis for this doctrine, its historical development, theological implications, and practical applications.

Biblical Teaching on the Counsel of Peace

While it is plain in the Bible that God made covenants with his people, it may not be immediately obvious that God the Father made a covenant with his Son. However, this doctrine arises from the clear teaching of the Holy Scriptures regarding the mission of Christ to save sinners. We will explore several lines of biblical testimony to the counsel of peace.

The Predestination of the Mediator

Michael Horton writes, "The doctrines of the Trinity and predestination (or God's decree) converge at the point of the eternal covenant of redemption (*pactum salutis*) between the persons of the Godhead."[5] God's eternal predestination of people to salvation centers upon his Son, Jesus Christ (Eph. 1:3–4; 2 Tim. 1:9).[6] Christ is the Elect of God (Isa 42:1; cf. Matt. 12:18). Rejected by men, Christ is "elect" and "precious" to God (1 Pet. 2:6). Christ is the "lamb without blemish" who was "foreordained before the foundation of the world" to redeem God's people from their sins (1:18–20). This foreordaining—literally, "foreknowledge"—is "an act of God in eternity past whereby he determined that his Son would come as the Saviour of mankind."[7] In the purposes of God, he is "the Lamb slain from the foundation of the world" (Rev. 13:8).

The person of whom we speak, however, is not one who came into being at a point in history and thus was subject to God's decree, but a person who was already existing "in the beginning," the Word who "was with God" and "was God" (John 1:1). He is not merely God's Servant, but the only begotten Son of the Father who participates in all his Father's glory, wisdom, and ways (John 1:14, 18; 5:19–20).[8] Therefore, Christ is not merely the object of God's election, but the electing God himself (15:16,

4. Muller, *Dictionary of Latin and Greek Theological Terms*, 252.

5. Michael Horton, *The Christian Faith: A Systematic Theology for Pilgrims on the Way* (Grand Rapids, MI: Zondervan, 2011), 309.

6. On the doctrine of election, see *RST*, 1:979–1057 (chaps. 49–51).

7. Wayne A. Grudem, *1 Peter: An Introduction and Commentary*, Tyndale New Testament Commentaries 17 (Downers Grove, IL: InterVarsity Press, 1988), 90.

8. On the deity of the Son and his relation to the Father in the Trinity, see *RST*, 1:882–97.

18). This implies that when the Father elected the Son, the Son consented and agreed with the Father in the unity of the divine will.

This eternal, intra-Trinitarian counsel is the basis of Christ's mission, as revealed in the Gospel of John. Christ was "sent" by God "into the world" to save sinners (John 3:17; 10:36). The Father has granted to the Son the authority to administer both eternal life and judgment according to "the will of the Father which hath sent" him (5:20–30). This grant includes specific people whom the Father gives to the Son so that he will save them to the end (6:37–39; 10:27–29). The Son must lay down his life for them, of which Christ said, "This commandment have I received of my Father" (10:11, 15, 18). As Christ's earthly life drew to a close, he prayed, "I have glorified thee on the earth: I have finished the work which thou gavest me to do. And now, O Father, glorify thou me with thine own self with the glory which I had with thee before the world was" (17:4–5). Before time began, the Father gave Christ a great work and a people to save by it (v. 6), with the expectation that God would then glorify his Son with the "glory, which thou hast given me: for thou lovest me before the foundation of the world" (v. 24).[9]

The Divine Oath to the Priest-King

Another line of evidence for the counsel of peace arises from God's oath concerning David's "Lord": "The LORD said unto my Lord, Sit thou at my right hand, until I make thine enemies thy footstool. . . . The LORD hath sworn, and will not repent, Thou art a priest for ever after the order of Melchizedek" (Ps. 110:1, 4). The Father directly addresses the Son in this oath ("thou"), not merely swearing about him but swearing a promise to him. This promise reveals a covenant between God and Christ, just as God's covenant with David was a sworn promise (89:3).[10] The covenant pertains to Christ's office to serve God like Melchizedek, a king-priest who blessed God's people for God's glory (Gen. 14:18–20). By this oath "was Jesus made a surety of a better testament" (Heb. 7:22)—that is, he undertook to pay his people's covenantal obligations to God.[11]

When did God make this covenant with Christ? It can be argued that God made this covenant with Christ at his heavenly coronation at God's

---

9. Nichols, *Covenant Theology*, 306–9.
10. See also Gen. 21:31–32; Deut. 4:31; 7:8–9, 12; 8:18; 31:20; Josh. 9:15; Judg. 2:1; 2 Kings 11:4; Ezek. 16:8.
11. J. V. Fesko, *The Trinity and the Covenant of Redemption* (Fearn, Ross-shire, Scotland: Christian Focus, 2016), 101.

right hand (Ps. 110:1).[12] However, the covenant cannot have been ratified for the first time when Christ ascended into heaven, for Christ's priestly office rests upon this oath (Heb. 5:4–6). The sons of Aaron were made priests "without an oath," but by this oath "was Jesus made surety" (7:21–22). Therefore, the sworn covenant of God with Christ must have preceded his death, resurrection, and ascension, for it was as the "high priest" of his people that he "offered up himself" once for all on the cross (vv. 26–27). His death was not merely to save those under the New Testament, but was also "for the redemption of the transgressions that were under the first testament," so that "they which are called might receive the promise of eternal inheritance" (9:15). Christ functioned as a priest from the fall of man so that by his intercession his people could know God's justifying grace (cf. Ps. 32:1–2).[13] Matthew Henry (1662–1714) commented, "He was designed for a priest, in God's eternal counsels; he was a priest to the Old Testament saints, and will be a priest for all believers to the end of time."[14] Therefore, it is best to regard this oath as one long established when David penned these words a thousand years before Christ came in the flesh. Since other Scripture passages reveal Christ's predestination before the world existed to die as a sacrifice for sins, as we saw, we conclude that the Father made an eternal covenant with his Son to be the Priest of his people.

The Covenant Servant of the Lord

The Lord further revealed Christ and his work through the prophecies granted to Isaiah concerning God's "servant."[15] We find a remarkable oracle in Isaiah 49:1–12, where the Servant recounts the Lord's promises to him, "a declaration of consolation and strength which will sustain the servant in the task that lies ahead of him," as Edward Young commented.[16] God promised his Servant that God "will be glorified" in him (v. 3). The Servant will "be glorious in the eyes of the LORD" (v. 5) and will be honored by kings (v. 7). The Lord will make his Servant to be God's

12. Nichols, *Covenant Theology*, 281–82, 288. On the fulfillment of Ps. 110:1 at Christ's resurrection and ascension, see Acts 2:32–34; Eph. 1:20.

13. For examples of Christ's priestly intercession prior to his ascension, see Zech. 1:12–13; 3:1–5; Luke 22:31–32; John 17.

14. *Matthew Henry's Commentary on the Whole Bible*, on Ps. 110:4 (904).

15. For confirmation that the "Servant" is Christ, note the citations of Isaiah's prophecies in Matt. 8:17; 12:17–20; Luke 22:37; John 12:37–38; Acts 8:32–35; 1 Pet. 2:22. Though the Servant is called "Israel" (Isa. 49:3), this must be taken in the sense that he acts as the ideal Israel to fulfill God's purposes for his people; but the Servant is not the nation of Israel, for Isaiah writes that the Servant will restore Israel to God (vv. 5–6).

16. Young, *The Book of Isaiah*, 3:269.

"salvation unto the end of the earth," bringing Jews and Gentiles to him (v. 6). As the conquering King, he will release "the prisoners" and those "in darkness," and will bring them from all lands to a place of safety and satisfaction (vv. 9–12).

Though these promises obviously have great significance for the redeemed, the Lord spoke them directly to his Servant. The Servant recounts this divine revelation as taking place in the midst of his humiliation and trials (Isa. 49:4). This passage reads as if we are transported ahead of Isaiah's time into the earthly ministry of Christ. However, the divine persons giving and receiving these promises were alive and present when Isaiah wrote them down seven centuries before Christ was born (cf. John 12:41). Therefore, they reveal the commitments that God the Father had already made to his Son before his earthly ministry.

God's promises to his Servant revolve around his covenant in their fruit and root. The fruit of his promises is covenantal: "I will preserve thee, and give thee for a covenant of the people" (Isa. 49:8; cf. 42:6; 54:10; 55:3). God's covenant of grace with his people has deep roots in his promises to his "servant," a covenantal term associated with Jacob and especially David, of whom the Lord said, "I have made a covenant with my chosen, I have sworn unto David my servant" (Ps. 89:3).[17] The sure fulfillment of this saving purpose is sealed by God's oath, another covenantal form of expression (Isa. 45:22–23; cf. Phil. 2:9–11).

The Covenant Seed of God's Servant

It might be objected that God consistently makes his covenants in Scripture with a person and his seed,[18] but this is not the case with Christ, who has no physical offspring. In reply, we note that Isaiah names Christ the "everlasting Father" of his people (Isa. 9:6). God's covenant Servant has spiritual "seed." Isaiah 53:10–11 says, "Yet it pleased the LORD to bruise him; he hath put him to grief: when thou shalt make his soul an offering for sin ["when his soul shall make an offering," mg.], he shall see his seed, he shall prolong his days, and the pleasure of the LORD shall prosper in his hand. He shall see of the travail of his soul, and shall be satisfied: by

---

17. On Jacob as God's servant, see Isa. 41:8; 44:1–2, 21; 45:4; 48:20; Jer. 30:10; 46:27–28; Ezek. 28:25; 37:25. On David as God's servant, see 2 Sam. 3:18; 7:5, 8, 20, 26; 24:10; 1 Kings 3:6; 8:24–26; 11:13, 32, 34, 36, 38; 14:8; 19:34; 20:6; Ps. 132:10; Isa. 37:35; Jer. 33:21–22, 26; Ezek. 34:23–24; 37:24–25.

18. Gen. 9:9; 17:7; Num. 18:19; 25:13; 2 Sam. 7:12; Neh. 9:8; cf. Isa. 59:21.

his knowledge shall my righteous servant justify many; for he shall bear their iniquities." We hear echoes in this prophecy of the Priest-King already revealed by God's oath in Psalm 110.

This text makes a logical connection: the Servant's offering of himself for the sins of his people results in God giving him life, seed, and success in carrying out God's will.[19] Since he bore his people's sins (Isa. 53:11), "therefore," God will reward him with royal glory (v. 12; cf. Phil. 2:9).[20] The "seed" promised to God's Servant is not physical sons and daughters, but the people counted righteous for his sake: "my righteous servant [shall] justify many" (Isa. 53:11). This justified seed is the true Israel: "In the LORD shall all the seed of Israel be justified, and shall glory" (45:25).

Therefore, as God promised elect seed to Abraham (Isa. 41:8), so he promised elect seed to Christ. Abraham's seed was given through a physically barren woman; Christ's seed arises from a spiritually barren people reconciled to God (54:1). When Christ came, though many rejected him (53:3), he was able to lean upon God's promise that if he gave his life as a sacrifice for sin, he would be highly exalted (52:13) and enjoy life with the spiritual family justified by his righteousness. This is the covenant of redemption.

The Counsel of Peace with the Messianic Branch

We find another reference to the Lord's covenant with Christ when God commanded Zechariah to perform the symbolic action of crowning the priest Joshua with "silver and gold" and declared, "Behold the man whose name is The BRANCH; and he shall grow up out of his place, and he shall build the temple of the LORD: even he shall build the temple of the LORD; and he shall bear the glory, and shall sit and rule upon his throne; and he shall be a priest upon his throne: and the counsel of peace shall be between them both" (Zech. 6:11–13).

The title "Branch" refers to God's special "servant" (Zech. 3:8), the messianic King whom God would raise up out of the house of David (Jer. 23:5–6; 33:15; cf. Isa. 11:1–2). The placing of the crown upon the priest's head symbolized the union of the two offices in one man. This had never been permitted in Israel before (2 Chron. 26:16–21). This unusual

---

19. In Isa. 53:10, the word translated as "when" (*'im*) is more often rendered "if" (cf. 58:9, 13). It sometimes means "though," but a concessive sense is unlikely here because the text does not oppose his death to his fulfilling of God's will, but joins them: "It pleased the LORD to bruise him." Even if it is best understood as "when" (KJV, ESV), the idea is still one of consequence.

20. Young, *The Book of Isaiah*, 3:358.

circumstance has led some commentators to argue that the text reveals a "diarchy," or joint rule, between the priest and the king. However, as George Klein says, "One must take liberties with the text to defend the notion of a diarchy, a concept that neither biblical nor historical sources support."[21] It is better to interpret the text to predict the coming of one who is both Priest and King, just as David prophesied (Ps. 110:1, 4).[22]

The oracle concludes, "And the counsel of peace shall be between them both" (Zech. 6:13). The word translated as "counsel" (*'etsah*) is a term for wisdom; here it refers to God's eternal plan.[23] John Mackay comments, "'Counsel' is not used in Hebrew to refer to a relationship between two parties, as if priest and king will be able to get on well together. . . . 'Counsel of peace' here is that deliberate policy which procures peace."[24] "Peace" (*shalom*) is the well-being experienced when people relate to God and one another with harmony and justice (8:16). Zechariah foretold that the King would come humbly to bring a universal kingdom of "peace" (9:9–10). Such peace is possible only by "the blood of thy covenant," the sacrifice for sins necessary to deliver sinners from divine judgment and bring them into peace with God (v. 11). God promised that through "my servant the BRANCH," God would "remove the iniquity of that land in one day" (3:8–9), a declaration of perfect atonement on account of which guilt would be thrown away like dirty clothes exchanged for garments of beauty (vv. 3–5). Therefore, the "counsel of peace" is God's sovereign decree to bring peace through the Branch, who serves as God's covenantal Priest and King. Zechariah's prophecy has strong covenantal overtones, forecasting the fulfillment of God's covenant with David's seed to "build the temple of the LORD" (6:12–13).[25] The phrase "counsel of peace" also fits a covenant, for "taking counsel" (*ya'ats*) with other people can result in a "covenant" (Ps. 83:5),[26] and "counsel of peace" may be compared to "covenant of peace" (Isa. 54:10; Ezek. 34:25; 37:26).[27]

---

21. George L. Klein, *Zechariah*, The New American Commentary 21B (Nashville: B&H, 2008), 204. See Fesko, *The Trinity and the Covenant of Redemption*, 67–69.

22. John L. Mackay, *Haggai, Zechariah, Malachi: God's Restored People*, Focus on the Bible (Fearn, Ross-shire, Scotland: Christian Focus, 2003), 137.

23. Isa. 25:1; 28:29; 44:26; 46:9–10; Jer. 49:20; 50:45; Mic. 4:12.

24. Mackay, *Haggai, Zechariah, Malachi*, 140.

25. Meredith G. Kline, *Glory in Our Midst: A Biblical-Theological Reading of Zechariah's Night Visions* (Eugene, OR: Wipf and Stock, 2001), 222.

26. Psalm 83:5 may be literally translated, "For they took counsel with one heart; against Thee they cut a covenant."

27. Kline, *Glory in Our Midst*, 226–27; Fesko, *The Trinity and the Covenant of Redemption*, 73.

When Zechariah writes, "The counsel of peace shall be between them both," to whom does he refer? It cannot be the priest and the king, because in this text they are one person. Neither does the text speak of two offices in a substantive fashion. It must refer to the Lord and the Branch.[28] Counsel "between" these two appears to refer to a plan that they formed together, probably with the implication of an alliance or covenant that binds them together to perform their plan.[29] God needs no counsel from others (Isa. 40:13–14), yet amazingly here the Branch shares in God's counsel-making, which implies that he also is God. Therefore, this text bears testimony to "the mutual will of the Father and the Son," as Herman Witsius said,[30] for the purpose of bringing God's people into peace through the exercise of Christ's kingly and priestly offices. As linked to the covenant with David and God's oath regarding the Priest-King in Psalm 110:4, the "counsel of peace" constitutes a further revelation of God's covenant of redemption with his Son.[31]

The Covenant Grant of the Kingdom

The Lord Jesus Christ said to his disciples, "I appoint unto you a kingdom, as my Father hath appointed unto me; that ye may eat and drink at my table in my kingdom, and sit on thrones judging the twelve tribes of Israel" (Luke 22:29–30). The verb twice translated as "appoint" (*diatithēmi*) is a cognate to the word rendered as "testament" or "covenant" (*diathēkē*). The verb can mean "arrange" or "dispose" in Greek,[32] but its common use in the Greek Bible (more than seventy times) is for making a covenant.[33] Leon Morris commented, "Jesus speaks of all this in the language of covenant," for the verb is "the usual biblical word for the making of a covenant."[34]

The context confirms that this statement is covenantal. Christ has just said, "This cup is the new testament [*diathēkē*] in my blood, which is shed

---

28. Brakel, *The Christian's Reasonable Service*, 2:254–55.
29. The combination of "counsel" (*'etsah*) and "between" (*beyn*) in Zech. 6:13 is unique in the Hebrew Bible. There are several instances, however, of speaking of a "covenant" that is "between" (*beyn*) two parties (Gen. 9:12–17; 17:2, 7, 10–11; 26:28; 1 Kings 15:19; 2 Kings 11:17; 2 Chron. 16:3; 23:16).
30. Witsius, *The Economy of the Covenants*, 2.2.7 (1:169).
31. Kline, *Glory in Our Midst*, 227.
32. Henry George Liddell, Robert Scott, et al., *A Greek-English Lexicon* (Oxford: Clarendon, 1996), 415.
33. In the LXX, see Gen. 9:17; 15:18; 21:27, 32; 26:28; 31:44; Ex. 24:8; Deut. 4:23; 5:2–3; 7:2; 9:9; 29:1, 12, 14, 25; 31:16; etc. In the New Testament, see Acts 3:25; Heb. 8:10; 9:16–17; 10:16.
34. Leon Morris, *Luke: An Introduction and Commentary*, Tyndale New Testament Commentaries 3 (Downers Grove, IL: InterVarsity Press, 1988), 327.

for you" (Luke 22:20).[35] It is legitimate to interpret Christ's kingdom saying in verses 29–30 in light of the Lord's Supper because Christ links the two by speaking of eating and drinking at his table in the future kingdom feast (v. 30; cf. Matt. 26:29). Therefore, both the scriptural use of the word (*diatithēmi*) and the context lead us to conclude that Luke 22:29 may be literally translated, "I make a covenant with you, just as my Father made a covenant with me, for a kingdom."[36]

Of what covenant with his Father does Christ speak? Christ's reference to "my kingdom" and "thrones" alludes to God's covenant with David (2 Sam. 7:12–14; cf. 2 Chron. 7:18; Ps. 122:5). However, elements of Christ's teaching transcend the Davidic covenant. Christ attaches greatness in his kingdom to humble servanthood toward others as opposed to earthly glory (Luke 22:25–27). He links his servanthood to giving up his body and blood to a violent death (vv. 19–22; cf. Mark 10:45) to ratify the new covenant promised to Israel for inner transformation and atonement of sins (Luke 22:20; cf. Jer. 31:31–34). Therefore, this covenant is larger in scope than the promises of the Davidic covenant and the new covenant, though it includes them and links them to Christ's mission. The Father made a covenant with his Son that required Christ to give up his life for others and promised him the kingdom of grace and glory.

Christ's literal words "I make a covenant with you, just as my Father made a covenant with me" could be interpreted to refer to two covenants, with the latter grounded upon the former. However, the promise of both is essentially the same: "a kingdom . . . my kingdom" (Luke 22:29–30). His disciples will "eat and drink" not at their own table, Christ says, but "at my table" (v. 30). Therefore, it seems best to view this as one covenant, established by the Father with the Son and his faithful disciples, who enjoy its blessings with Christ through his mediation.

The Parallel of Adam and Christ

Another biblical theme pointing us in the direction of a covenant between God and his Son is found in those Scripture passages that compare and contrast Christ and Adam. Adam is a "figure" or type of Christ (Rom. 5:14). This analogy is significant for covenant theology because, as we

---

35. Stein, *Luke*, 550.

36. Thus, Theodore Beza translated *diatithēmi* as the Latin *paciscor*, "make a pact." J. V. Fesko, *The Covenant of Redemption: Origins, Development, and Reception* (Göttingen: Vandenhoek & Ruprecht, 2016), 39. See also Diodati, *Pious and Learned Annotations*, on Luke 22:29.

have argued, the Bible presents God's dealings with Adam before the fall as a covenant that inflicted death upon all of Adam's natural descendants as a punishment for his disobedience.[37]

Adam was God's "son" who was tested by temptation in the garden; Christ is God's "Son" who was tested by temptation in the wilderness (Luke 3:22, 38; 4:1–2). Paul writes, "For as in Adam all die, even so in Christ shall all be made alive" (1 Cor. 15:22). The "one man's disobedience" resulted in all of mankind falling into a state in which they are counted as "sinners" under God's "condemnation"; the "obedience of one" brought those in Christ into a state in which they are counted as "righteous" by God's "justification" (Rom. 5:16, 19).

Adam's disobedience had this effect by virtue of the covenant that God made with him and his seed. This implies that God made a similar arrangement with his Son, so that he is the federal representative of those in union with him. Geerhardus Vos said, "There are two alternatives: one must either deny the covenantal arrangement as a general rule for obtaining eternal life, or, by granting the latter, he must also regard the gaining of eternal life by the Mediator as a covenant arrangement and place the establishing of a covenant in back of it."[38]

The Covenant God of Jesus Christ and the Elect

The Father is the covenant God of the Son. Christ spoke of his Father as "my God" (Mark 15:34; John 20:17). Though the Son is fully God (20:28), he stands in a covenantal relationship with the Father. This is not the covenantal relationship shared by all pious Jews, but a special relationship, as implied in Paul's words: "Blessed be the God and Father of our Lord Jesus Christ, who hath blessed us with all spiritual blessings in heavenly places in Christ" (Eph. 1:3).[39] God the Father is "the God . . . of our Lord Jesus Christ" (so also v. 17). This is a covenantal formula, similar to the divine title "God of Abraham."[40] "Blessed" and "blessings" allude to the Abrahamic covenant (Gen. 12:2). The words "Father" and "bless" also allude to the covenant of the kingdom made with David (2 Sam. 7:14, 29); the Lord was known as "the God of David."[41]

---

37. On the covenant of works, see chaps. 14–16.
38. Vos, *Redemptive History and Biblical Interpretation*, 245.
39. We touched on this point in *RST*, 1:982–83.
40. Gen. 26:24; 28:13; 31:42, 53; Ex. 3:6, 15–16; 4:5; 1 Kings 18:36; 1 Chron. 29:18; 2 Chron. 30:6; Ps. 47:9; Matt. 22:32; Mark 12:26; Luke 20:37; Acts 3:13; 7:32.
41. 2 Kings 20:5; 2 Chron. 21:12; 34:3; Isa. 38:5; cf. 1 Chron. 28:9.

Christ, the son of Abraham and son of David, relates to God and his people in a manner foreshadowed by Abraham and David. The Lord made a historical covenant with Abraham and his seed to be their God (Gen. 17:7). He promised deliverance to David's anointed seed (Pss. 18:50; 89:29–37). We conclude that these promises reflect a greater covenant that God made with Christ so that he and his seed would receive deliverance and enjoy God as their God. As Paul goes on to explain, this covenantal relationship in Christ was not established in history but in eternity in the counsel of God's electing will (Eph. 1:4, 11).

God's covenant with Christ transcends the covenants with Abraham and David, yet the latter covenants must be regarded as historical administrations of the former. They are "the covenants of promise" of which all in Christ are beneficiaries (Eph. 2:12, 19). Their participation in the covenant of grace in Jesus Christ does not bypass the ancient covenants, but fulfills them and makes believers heirs of their blessings (Luke 1:68–73). Therefore, the covenants of promise granted to Abraham and David are manifestations in history of God's eternal covenant of grace in Christ. This is an unspeakable blessing to believers in Christ, for "the God and Father of our Lord Jesus Christ" is now to them "the Father of mercies and God of all comfort," for they know that in Christ "all the promises of God find their Yes" (2 Cor. 1:3, 20 ESV).

The Eternal Promise of Life for the Elect

The last line of biblical evidence that we present are Paul's words in Titus 1:2: "hope of eternal life, which God, that cannot lie, promised before the world began"—literally, "before times everlasting" (*pro chronōn aiōniōn*). The last phrase locates the giving of this promise in God's eternal decree of salvation in Christ (2 Tim. 1:9), which God decided before the creation of the world (1 Cor. 2:7; Eph. 1:4).[42]

To whom did God make this promise? The New Testament often speaks of God's ancient promises to the patriarchs,[43] but no one existed before time began except God. Given that Paul has just written of "God" and "Jesus Christ" (Titus 1:1), both of whom are the source of "grace, mercy, and peace" (v. 4), this promise refers to God's commitment to his Son that the elect would obtain eternal life through faith in him. This is

---

42. George W. Knight III, *The Pastoral Epistles: A Commentary on the Greek Text*, The New International Greek Testament Commentary (Grand Rapids, MI: Eerdmans, 1992), 284–85.
43. Acts 7:5, 17; 13:32; 26:6; Rom. 4:21; Gal. 3:19; Heb. 6:13; 11:11.

"the promise of life which is in Christ Jesus"; it is in him in the sense that it was first given to him in eternity and it is now openly revealed through him in his death and resurrection (2 Tim. 1:1, 9–10). Thomas Goodwin said, "All the promises that now are revealed are but the manifestation of that grand promise; but copies, as it were, of that which was made to Christ. . . . As all promises are made in him, so all promises were made to him, and to us as one with him."[44]

In summary, the Holy Scriptures reveal that God predestined his Son before the world to accomplish the redemption of his elect people (1 Pet. 1:19–20). In making this decree, the persons of the Trinity entered into a solemn commitment that the Son would become the everlasting Priest-King (Ps. 110:4) to save from Israel and the nations the spiritual seed justified by his sacrificial death (Isa. 49:1–12; 53:10–11). This commitment is called "the counsel of peace" between the Lord and the Priest-King (Zech. 6:13). The Son brings his people into his covenant with the Father to share his kingdom with them (Luke 22:29–30). As Adam represented his offspring before God in the covenant of works, Christ represents his people before God in the covenant of grace (Rom. 5:14–19). As in the covenant with Abraham and his seed, God made a covenant of blessing with Christ and those in him (Eph. 1:3–4). God promised his Son before time began that they would receive eternal life (Titus 1:2).

Historical Development of the Doctrine of the Counsel of Peace

Early in Reformed theology, one finds the seeds of the doctrine of the counsel of peace or covenant of redemption. Contrary to the theory of Wilhelm Gass (1818–1889), the concept was not invented by Johannes Cocceius in the mid-seventeenth century.[45] Johannes Oecolampadius (1482–1531) identified the "eternal covenant" (Isa. 55:3) with God's entering into a "covenant with his Son" (*pactum cum filio suo*).[46] John Calvin also wrote of God's "covenant, which he has made with Christ and with all his members,"[47] but it does not appear that Calvin developed the idea of the

---

44. Goodwin, *Of Christ the Mediator*, in *Works*, 5:29.
45. Richard A. Muller, "Toward the *Pactum Salutis*: Locating the Origins of a Concept," *Mid-America Journal of Theology* 18 (2007): 11 (full article, 11–65). See Cocceius, *The Doctrine of the Covenant and Testament of God*, 5.88–89 (85–89).
46. Johannes Oecolampadius, *In Iesaiam Prophetam Hypomnematon* (Basle: n.p., 1525), 268r. See Beeke and Jones, *A Puritan Theology*, 239.
47. Calvin, *Commentaries*, on Jer. 22:29–30.

eternal covenant of redemption in his theology.[48] Caspar Olevianus developed this concept of an eternal arrangement between the Father and the Son in relation to Christ's office as the surety of his people.[49] A statement of a "covenant" between God and Christ as the High Priest of his people is also found in the writings of Jacob Arminius.[50]

The doctrine of an eternal covenant between the Father and the Son was conceived in the theological matrix of the Trinity and nurtured by the Reformed teaching that Christ is the Mediator according to both his natures, human and divine.[51] William Perkins said that Christ was "called of his Father from all eternity to perform the office of the Mediator, that in Him all those which should be saved might be chosen."[52] Christ as the Mediator "was first of all predestinated as He was to be our Head . . . and we secondly predestinated in Him."[53] Yet as God, Christ also "together with the Father decreed all things," and thus gives voluntary consent to this purpose.[54] For "as He is God He does design and set Himself apart to the same work." Yet it is God the Father, the first person in the order of the Trinity, who especially chose Christ for this mission (John 6:27).[55] Perkins recognized that actual union with Christ is covenantal[56] and that believers access God's covenantal promises only in Christ (Gal. 3:15–17), "for the office of Christ to which he is set apart is to receive the promises of God for us and to apply it unto us."[57] However, to our knowledge, Perkins did not explicitly teach an eternal intra-Trinitarian covenant.

In the early seventeenth century, the doctrine of an intra-Trinitarian covenant of redemption began to flower, as seen in the theological writ-

---

48. Lillback, *The Binding of God*, 212–14.

49. Bierma, *The Covenant Theology of Caspar Olevianus*, 107–12.

50. Arminius, *Oration on the Priesthood of Christ*, in *Works*, 1:31–32. See Raymond A. Blacketer, "Arminius' Concept of Covenant in Its Historical Context," *Nederlands archief voor kerkgeschiedenis* (*Dutch Review of Church History*) 80, no. 2 (2000): 211–12 (full article, 193–220).

51. Carl R. Trueman, "The Harvest of Reformation Mythology? Patrick Gillespie and the Covenant of Redemption," in *Scholasticism Reformed: Essays in Honour of Willem J. Van Asselt*, ed. Maarten Wisse, Willemien Otten, and Marcel Sarot (Leiden: Brill, 2010), 197–98.

52. Perkins, *A Golden Chain*, chap. 15, in *Works*, 6:47.

53. Perkins, *An Exposition of the Symbol*, in *Works*, 5:334.

54. Perkins, *A Golden Chain*, chap. 15, in *Works*, 6:48.

55. Perkins, *An Exposition of the Symbol*, in *Works*, 5:103–4; cf. Johannes Polyander, Antonius Walaeus, Antonius Thysius, and Andreas Rivetus, *Synopsis Purioris Theologiae, Synopsis of a Purer Theology: Latin Text and English Translation, Volume 2, Disputations 24–42*, trans. Riemer A. Faber, ed. Henk van den Belt (Leiden: Brill, 2016), 26.16 (107).

56. Perkins, *An Exposition of the Symbol*, in *Works*, 5:367.

57. Perkins, *Commentary on Galatians*, on Gal. 3:16, in *Works*, 2:189–90.

ings of Paul Bayne (c. 1573–1617) and Thomas Hooker (1586–1657).[58] We find a succinct statement of the doctrine in the writings of William Ames, who said that by God's calling of Christ to his mediatorial office, "he bound his Son to this office through a special covenant," expressed in Isaiah 53:10: "If he should make himself an offering for sin then he would see his offspring, would prolong his days, and the delight of the Lord would prosper through him." This covenant involved God "choosing, foreordaining, and sending" his Son.[59] Ames said, "The agreement between God and Christ was a kind of advance application of our redemption and deliverance of us to our surety and our surety to us."[60]

It appears that David Dickson (c. 1583–1662) was the first person to use the term *covenant of redemption* for the counsel of peace, saying in 1638, "The covenant of salvation betwixt God and man is one thing, and the covenant of redemption betwixt God and Christ is another thing."[61] From this point onward, many Reformed theologians began making a distinction between the covenant of redemption and the covenant of grace, including Patrick Gillespie (1617–1675), Obadiah Sedgwick (c. 1600–1658), Samuel Rutherford, John Owen, Thomas Brooks, John Flavel, Samuel Willard, Witsius, Wilhelmus à Brakel, Wilhelmus Schortinghuis (1700–1750), Charles Hodge, and Vos.[62]

---

58. Paul Bayne[s], *An Entire Commentary upon the Whole Epistle of St Paul to the Ephesians* (1866; repr., Stoke-on-Trent, England: Tentmaker, 2007), 17, 22; *A Commentarie upon the First and Second Chapters of Saint Paul to the Colossians* (London: by Richard Badger, for Nicholas Bourne, 1634), 105; and Thomas Hooker, *The Soules Exaltation* (London: by Iohn Haviland, for Andrew Crooke, 1638), 170.

59. Ames, *The Marrow of Theology*, 1.19.4–6 (132). Here we follow Ames's version of Isa. 53:10. "Covenant" translates the Latin *pactum*. William Ames, *Medulla Theologica*, new ed. (Amsterdam: Ioannem Iansonium, 1634), 1.19.3 (80).

60. Ames, *The Marrow of Theology*, 1.24.3 (149). "Agreement" translates the Latin *transactio*. Ames, *Medulla Theologica*, 1.24.3 (105).

61. Cited in Muller, "Toward the *Pactum Salutis*," 17. See also "The Sum of Saving Knowledge," 2.1–3, in *Westminster Confession of Faith* (Glasgow: Free Presbyterian Publications, 1994), 324. The "Sum" is attributed to David Dickson and James Durham. On Dickson's doctrine in its historical theological context, see Carol A. Williams, "The Decree of Redemption Is in Effect a Covenant: David Dickson and the Covenant of Redemption" (PhD diss., Calvin Theological Seminary, 2005).

62. Gillespie, *The Ark of the Covenant Opened*, 1; Sedgwick, *The Bowels of Tender Mercy*, 4; Rutherford, *The Covenant of Life Opened*, 326; John Owen, *An Exposition of the Epistle to the Hebrews*, 7 vols. (repr., Edinburgh: Banner of Truth, 1991), 2:78; Brooks, *Paradise Opened*, in *Works*, 5:350; Flavel, *The Fountain of Life*, in *Works*, 1:36; Samuel Willard, *The Doctrine of the Covenant of Redemption* (Boston: Benj. Harris, 1693), 42, 94; Witsius, *The Economy of the Covenants*, 2.2.1; 3.1.1 (1:165, 281); Brakel, *The Christian's Reasonable Service*, 1:262; Wilhelmus Schortinghuis, *Essential Truths in the Heart of a Christian*, trans. Harry Boonstra and Gerrit W. Sheeres, ed. James A. De Jong (Grand Rapids, MI: Reformation Heritage Books, 2009), 65; Hodge, *Systematic Theology*, 2:357–58; Vos, *Reformed Dogmatics*, 83–84, 92–93.

However, many other Reformed theologians have held the view that the covenant of redemption and the covenant of grace constitute one covenant, with some promises made to Christ as the last Adam and other promises made to those in union with him as his seed. Theologians who have espoused this view include John Preston (1587–1628), Francis Roberts, Robert Purnell, William Strong, Samuel Petto (c. 1624–1711), John Bunyan, Benjamin Keach, Thomas Boston, Jonathan Edwards, John Brown of Haddington, John Gill, Archibald Alexander Hodge, James Boyce (1827–1888), Herman Bavinck, and William Shedd (1820–1894).[63]

The Reformed doctrine of the counsel of peace is Trinitarian and Christ-centered. Edward Reynolds, commenting on Psalm 110:4, said that the Holy Scriptures reveal "the consent of the whole Trinity" in Christ's office and work. The counsel engaged "the Father's consent in his act of ordination" (cf. John 6:27), the Son's voluntary pledge to do God's saving will as "a sacrifice for sin" (cf. Heb. 10:9), and "the consent of the Holy Ghost, which did hereunto anoint him" and by whom Christ "was consecrated, warranted, and enabled unto this great function."[64]

Reformed divines did not treat this doctrine as a matter of metaphysical speculation but as the foundation of the gospel of Christ crucified to be the atoning substitute for our sins.[65] Brown said, "From eternity God foresaw our ruined case; and, before we fell, had settled the whole method of our redemption, in a covenant of grace. Here indeed every divine person engaged to bear his share of the work; but the agreement was formally between the Father . . . and his eternal Son . . . representing the whole number of men that were chosen to everlasting life."[66]

---

63. John Preston, *The New Covenant, or the Saints Portion. A Treatise Unfolding the All-Sufficiencie of God, Mans Uprightness, and the Covenant of Grace* (London, by I. D. for Nicolas Bourne, 1630), 387; Roberts, *The Mysterie and Marrow of the Bible*, 69, 71, 73, 76; Purnell, *A Little Cabinet Richly Stored*, 25–28; Strong, *A Discourse of the Two Covenants*, 124, 126, 137–38; Samuel Petto, *The Difference between the Old and New Covenant Stated and Explained: with an Exposition of the Covenant of Grace in the Principal Concernments of It* (London: Eliz. Calvert, 1674), 18–35; Bunyan, *The Doctrine of the Law and Grace Unfolded*, in *Works*, 1:522–23; Keach, *The Everlasting Covenant*, 4–21; Boston, *A View of the Covenant of Grace from the Sacred Records*, in *Works*, 8:396–97; Edwards, "Miscellanies," no. 2, in *WJE*, 13:198; Brown, *Questions and Answers on the Shorter Catechism*, 88; Gill, *Body of Divinity*, 217; Hodge, *Outlines of Theology*, 370–72; James P. Boyce, *Abstract of Systematic Theology* (1887; repr., Cape Coral, FL: Founders, 2006), 235; Bavinck, *Reformed Dogmatics*, 3:215; and Shedd, *Dogmatic Theology*, 2:360–61.
64. Reynolds, *An Exposition of the Hundred and Tenth Psalm*, in *Works*, 2:347.
65. Fisher, *The Marrow of Modern Divinity*, 64. See also Goodwin, *Of Christ the Mediator*, in *Works*, 5:12. Goodwin called the transaction "a covenant" (5:27).
66. John Brown of Haddington, *A Dictionary of the Holy Bible*, 3rd ed., 2 vols. (Edinburgh: W. Anderson and J. Fairbairn, 1789), 1:320.

Theological Implications of the Counsel of Peace

The doctrine of God's covenant of redemption with his Son has significant implications for other Christian doctrines, such as the Trinity, the atonement of Christ, the eternity and conditions of the covenant of grace, and the relationship between the covenant of grace and the gospel.

The Counsel of Peace and the Trinity

Karl Barth objected to the doctrine of the covenant of redemption because he believed it undermined the unity of the Trinity.[67] Barth said, "Can we really think of the first and second persons of the triune Godhead as two divine subjects and therefore as two legal subjects who can have dealings and enter into obligations one with another? This is mythology, for which there is no place in a right understanding of the doctrine of the Trinity as the doctrine of the three modes of being of the one God."[68]

In reply, we would argue that it is appropriate for us to use the language of "counsel" and "covenant" for the eternal plan of the triune God, because, though God has one will, his will is related to the perspective of each divine person.[69] To be sure, God's decree "is properly an essential act, or belongs to all of the three persons in common, as they are one in the essence," as Willard wrote. However, God's one divine will engages each divine person according to the "order" among the persons of the Trinity, so that each person has a distinct "appropriation" of God's purpose, particularly with regard to how that purpose is worked out. This arrangement is "called a covenant only by way of analogy, as it is accommodated to our understanding."[70]

If we deny that this is possible, then we run the risk of denying that the Father, the Son, and the Holy Spirit are distinct persons who know each other and love each other. God is love in his undivided, simple essence (1 John 4:8), but the statements "the Father loveth the Son" (John 3:35) and "I [the Son] love the Father (14:31) express distinct personal relations in that love, as Gill noted.[71] Vos warned that to insist so strongly on God's unity that the three divine persons cannot enter into a covenant with each other would lead to the heresy of modalism and "undermine

---

67. On the doctrine of the Trinity, see *RST*, 1:876–953 (chaps. 45–47).
68. Barth, *Church Dogmatics*, IV/1, sec. 57.2 (65).
69. Brakel, *The Christian's Reasonable Service*, 1:252.
70. Willard, *The Doctrine of the Covenant of Redemption*, 21–26.
71. Gill, *Body of Divinity*, 218.

the reality of the entire economy of redemption with its person to person relationships."[72] The counsel of peace, far from undermining the doctrine of the Trinity, guards and expresses the distinct personhood of each member of the Trinity.[73] Just as God designed the most intimate and loving of human relationships to be covenantal, so the counsel of peace reveals "the relationship and life of the three persons in the Divine Being as a covenantal life," as Bavinck said. This is evidenced in our redemption, for "it is the triune God alone, Father, Son, and Spirit, who together conceive, determine, carry out, and complete the entire work of salvation."[74]

The Counsel of Peace and the Atonement

The Holy Scriptures reveal that Christ offered himself freely and voluntarily, though in obedience to his Father's will. Christ says, "Therefore doth my Father love me, because I lay down my life, that I might take it again. No man taketh it from me, but I lay it down of myself. I have power to lay it down, and I have power to take it again. This commandment have I received of my Father" (John 10:17–18). The cross was a revelation of the Son's love for sinners (Gal. 2:20; Eph. 5:2, 25).

One objection against the doctrine of substitutionary atonement is that God would engage in gross injustice if he required a righteous person to suffer for the sins of others. In reply, we note that the doctrine of the counsel of peace reveals that God the Son, equal in majesty and glory with his Father, willingly agreed to this purpose in the eternal covenant.

Owen wrote, "These things proceeded from and were founded in the will of the Son of God; and it was an act of perfect liberty in him to engage in his peculiar concernments in this covenant. What he did, he did by choice, in a way of condescension and love." This doctrine is crucial, Owen noted, to establish that Christ's sufferings as a righteous man "were just and equal," for they were not imposed upon him from above, but he "voluntarily consented" to them in the eternal counsel of peace.[75]

Therefore, Christ's atoning death for his people's sins was not a miscarriage of justice, but a revelation of the love of each person in the Trinity for lost sinners. The Father, the Son, and the Spirit joyfully concurred in forming this eternal plan at divine expense for God's glory.

---

72. Vos, *Redemptive History and Biblical Interpretation*, 246.
73. See Horton, *The Christian Faith*, 303.
74. Bavinck, *Reformed Dogmatics*, 3:214–15.
75. Owen, *An Exposition of the Epistle to the Hebrews*, 2:87.

The Counsel of Peace and the Eternity of the Covenant of Grace

God's covenantal love for his people is "from everlasting to everlasting" (Ps. 103:17–18). Saving grace was "given us in Christ Jesus before the world began" (2 Tim. 1:9). Eternal life was "promised before the world began" by "God, that cannot lie" (Titus 1:2). Yet how can this covenant be eternal when the promises were not revealed to mankind until after the fall? The doctrine of the counsel of peace shows us that God's covenant was actually initiated in eternity between the persons of the Trinity.

It might be objected that the eternal covenant of redemption is not the same as the covenant of grace made with sinners in human history. As we saw, a number of sound Reformed divines distinguished them as two covenants. They argued that the covenant of redemption and the covenant of grace have different covenanting parties (the Father and Christ versus God and elect sinners) engaged with different covenantal terms (the Father's promise to exalt Christ upon his accomplishment of redemption versus God's promise to give eternal life to all who believe). The covenant of redemption requires that Christ suffer for our sins, but the covenant of grace requires that we believe in Christ.[76]

In reply, we say that God did not make a covenant with Christ as considered by himself, but as the Surety of the elect, and he did not make a covenant with people considered by themselves, but as in Christ the Mediator (Heb. 7:21–22; 8:6). When God made covenants with people in time, such as David, those covenants were primarily with Christ, of whom David was a type (Ps. 89:20–27). In the counsel of peace, God promised to his Son the grace and glory that will be granted both to him and those in union with him (Ps. 110:1–4)—the grace and glory promised in the covenant of grace. The covenant of grace, with its promise of salvation by grace apart from our works, stands upon God's eternal counsel of Christ's redeeming work.[77] Therefore, it is best to consider God's eternal arrangement with his Son and God's covenant of grace with his people to be "two modes"—eternal and temporal—of "the one evangelical covenant of mercy," as Shedd said.[78] The requirement placed upon Christ to live and die as the Surety and the requirement placed upon people to trust

---

76. Brooks, *Paradise Opened*, in *Works*, 5:350–51; and Van Genderen and Velema, *Concise Reformed Dogmatics*, 556–57.

77. For these answers to objections, see Keach, *The Everlasting Covenant*, 10–19.

78. Shedd, *Dogmatic Theology*, 2:360.

in Christ are not mutually exclusive, but fit together in one covenant. The first requirement pertains to the legal necessity of satisfying God's justice; the second requirement pertains to the instrument of receiving Christ and his salvation.

The Bible does not speak of three covenants, but of two: the covenant of works and the covenant of grace (Gal. 4:24). God made one covenant with Adam and his seed, and another covenant with the last Adam and his seed (Rom. 5:12–19).

In the covenant of grace, God made some promises specifically to Christ regarding his exaltation and seed (Isa. 53:10–11) and some promises to the people in union with Christ (54:1–17). However, two sets of promises can cohere in one covenant, for God's covenant with Abraham included promises specifically for Abraham (Gen. 17:4–6) and other promises that Abraham shared with his seed (vv. 7–8). God made the eternal covenant of grace with his Son as both Heir and Mediator of the inheritance gained by his death (Heb. 1:2; 9:15). Christ's people receive this inheritance only by union with him (Rom. 8:17). God promised this inheritance in his covenant with Christ, for "through the blood of the everlasting covenant," God raised Christ from the dead (Heb. 13:20). Yet the same covenant engages God's people, for it is "the blood of thy covenant" (Zech. 9:11), where "thy" refers to God's people, not Christ.[79] Therefore, there is one covenant of grace made with Christ and his seed in different respects, all of which hinge upon Christ's redeeming blood and issue forth into glory for God's Son and his people.[80]

In arguing for one covenant of grace as opposed to distinct covenants with Christ and his people, we are not suggesting that Reformed theologians who differ with us have departed from orthodoxy. The Reformed confessions do not address this question. Though we believe that it is more scriptural to speak of one covenant of grace with two dimensions, it is possible for godly Christians to distinguish between the covenant of redemption and the covenant of grace while still holding to sound doctrine regarding Christ, his redeeming work, and its application.[81]

---

79. "Thy" (Zech. 9:11) translates a feminine Hebrew suffix, referring corporately to the "daughter of Zion" (v. 9).

80. For these arguments, see Petto, *The Difference between the Old and New Covenant Stated and Explained*, 19–30; Keach, *The Everlasting Covenant*, 6–10; and Boston, *A View of the Covenant of Grace from the Sacred Records*, in *Works*, 8:397.

81. Note the moderate statements made concerning this debate in Turretin, *Institutes*, 12.2.12 (2:177); Boston, *An Illustration of the Doctrines of the Christian Religion*, in *Works*, 1:333; and Hodge, *Outlines of Theology*, 369.

Furthermore, both perspectives may be abused to the detriment of the gospel. Theologians holding to one covenant of grace with Christ and his seed may be more prone to diminish human responsibility, break the link between election on the one hand and conversion on the other (cf. Rom. 8:30; 1 Thess. 1:3–5), fall into the error that God already counts as righteous the elect in Christ even though they do not yet believe (eternal justification, contra Gal. 2:16), and perhaps even think that God's elect will be saved regardless of whether they have a living faith that produces works of obedience to God's law (antinomianism).[82] Those who affirm one covenant of grace, as we do, must carefully protect the distinction between God's promises to Christ and his promises to us—the latter of which require faith and repentance for salvation and commend good works as evidence of regeneration. On the other hand, those who distinguish between God's covenant of redemption with Christ and his covenant of grace with his people may be more prone to find our righteousness in our faith and obedience instead of Christ alone (legalism).[83] Those who affirm distinct covenants with Christ and men must carefully preserve the doctrine that Christ alone is the basis for God's promises to us; our faith saves us only by uniting us with him, and his righteousness is our only ground for justification with God (Rom. 5:19; Phil. 3:9). They must also sustain the essential unity of the covenant of redemption and the covenant of grace in regard to their beneficiaries, lest they fall into the error that God covenanted with Christ to die for mankind as a whole and then takes specific people to himself through the covenant of grace. God's counsel of peace with the Mediator is for the redemption of the elect, and this same purpose is executed in history through the revealed covenant of grace.[84]

The Counsel of Peace and the Conditions of the Covenant of Grace

Is the covenant of grace conditional or unconditional?[85] In other words, when God promises eternal life in the covenant, does he require conditions that must be fulfilled in order for him to grant life?

---

82. Beeke and Jones, *A Puritan Theology*, 257.
83. Keach, *The Everlasting Covenant*, 15; and Boston, *An Illustration of the Doctrines of the Christian Religion*, in *Works*, 1:335.
84. Kersten, *Reformed Dogmatics*, 1:233–37.
85. On the historical discussion among the Puritans of covenantal conditions, see Joel R. Beeke, "The Assurance Debate: Six Key Questions," in *Drawn into Controversie: Reformed Theological Diversity and Debates within Seventeenth-Century British Puritanism*, ed. Michael A. G. Haykin and Mark Jones, Reformed Historical Theology 17 (Göttingen: Vandenhoeck & Ruprecht, 2011), 267–70.

How we answer that question depends on how we are using the term *condition*.[86] If by the word we simply mean something that must come to pass for God's promise of life to be realized, then certainly God's covenant of grace has conditions for us. We must have faith in Christ to be justified (Gal. 2:16) and have eternal life (John 3:16). We must have holiness to see the Lord (Heb. 12:14), beginning with the cleansing of the heart that faith works (Matt. 5:8; Acts 15:9). In this regard, some theologians speak of faith in Christ as a condition of the covenant.[87]

However, if by *condition* we refer to something we do that fulfills God's covenant requirements so that we have a right to the promise of life, then God's covenant of grace is unconditional for us. Our justification is in no way a reward of debt, but a gift of grace (Rom. 4:4–5). Faith is merely the instrument of justification and adoption, the empty hand by which we receive Christ (John 1:12). Holiness is not the price of eternal life, but the way to arrive there (Matt. 7:13–14, 21). For all that God's people believe and do, they can never say, "I did my part, now God owes it to me to do his." All is of grace.[88]

On the other hand, God's covenant does have a condition for his Son: Christ must fulfill his office as Prophet, Priest, and King to save his people. His obedience unto death fulfills God's law both in its requirements and penalty (Gal. 3:12–14; 4:4). Christ is our wisdom, righteousness, sanctification, and redemption (1 Cor. 1:30). Just as the two sides of this covenantal arrangement are called the covenant of redemption and the covenant of grace, so God requires the price of redemption from Christ and grants the gift of grace to us.[89] Bunyan said, "The condition was made with one, and also accomplished by him alone . . . even by one man Jesus Christ, as it is clear from Romans 5:15–17."[90]

Robert Traill (1642–1716) said, "The Son of God's taking on him man's nature, and offering it in sacrifice, was the strict condition of all the glory and reward promised to Christ and his seed (Isa. 53:10–11)." Faith

---

86. See the distinctions between kinds of conditions in Turretin, *Institutes*, 12.3 (2:184–89); Hodge, *Systematic Theology*, 2:364–65; and Vos, *Reformed Dogmatics*, 2:112–15.

87. Rollock, *A Treatise of God's Effectual Calling*, in *Select Works*, 1:39–42; and Bulkeley, *The Gospel-Covenant*, 321–25.

88. On faith being not properly a condition of justification, see Robert Shaw, *An Exposition of the Confession of Faith*, 2nd ed. (Edinburgh: John Johnstone, 1846), 131 (on Westminster Confession of Faith, 11.2–3); and Joel R. Beeke, "The Relation of Faith to Justification," in *Justification by Faith Alone*, ed. Don Kistler (Morgan, PA: Soli Deo Gloria, 1995), 62–68.

89. Boston, *A View of the Covenant of Grace from the Sacred Records*, in *Works*, 8:396–97.

90. Bunyan, *The Doctrine of the Law and Grace Unfolded*, in *Works*, 1:522.

is "a mere instrument receiving that imputed righteousness of Christ" and "is neither condition nor qualification, nor our gospel-righteousness, but in its very act a renouncing of all such pretences." Consequently, "We proclaim the market of grace to be free (Isa. 55:1–3)."[91]

Furthermore, the risen Christ mediates to us saving grace so that we repent and receive forgiveness of our sins (Acts 5:31). Faith itself is God's gift through Christ by the Holy Spirit (1 Cor. 12:3). Therefore, anything that might be considered a condition, even in the broadest sense, of the covenant is a gift of unconditional grace (Jer. 31:31–34). Ames concluded that the covenant of grace "requires no properly called or prior condition" on our part, for all that is necessary to obtain eternal life is "given by grace as a means to grace."[92]

We may sum up with the words of G. H. Kersten: "All the conditions of the covenant are perfectly fulfilled by Christ, and by Him alone, for all the elect. Can a fallen man fulfill one condition to enter into covenant with God?" He noted, "Christ not only acquired, but also applies the benefits of the covenant, included among which are certainly faith and obedience." God has revealed in his Word "a conditional form for obtaining salvation," to teach us "that faith and repentance are necessary to salvation." But "the work of man" does not establish the covenant.[93]

Practical Applications of the Counsel of Peace

The covenant formed between the members of the Trinity in God's eternal counsels transcends our comprehension. Who can grasp what it means for the Father and the Son to enter into covenant with each other with the full consent of the Holy Spirit for our salvation? Nevertheless, this doctrine, like all biblical teachings, has application for life:

1. *We should trust in Christ alone.* Brakel said, "The elect neither need to accomplish nor merit salvation, nor add anything to the acquisition thereof, for by this covenant all the weighty conditions were laid upon Christ."[94] Let us go to Christ with empty hands, poor in spirit, knowing that all our riches must come from him. Let us cast off all our own righteousness as dung and long to be clothed in Christ as our righteousness

---

91. Robert Traill, *A Vindication of the Protestant Doctrine Concerning Justification, and of Its Preachers and Professors, from the Unjust Charge of Antinomianism*, in *The Works of the Late Reverend Robert Traill*, 4 vols. (Edinburgh: J. Ogle et al., 1810), 1:277.

92. Ames, *The Marrow of Theology*, 1.24.19 (151).

93. Kersten, *Reformed Dogmatics*, 1:239–40.

94. Brakel, *The Christian's Reasonable Service*, 1:262.

before God. Edwards wrote, "As the condition of the first covenant was Adam's standing, so the condition of the second covenant is Christ's standing. . . . We are to do nothing but only to receive Christ and what he has done already. Salvation is not offered to us upon any condition, but freely and for nothing."[95]

2. *We should marvel at God's eternal love.* In God's infinite love for his Son, he eternally covenanted with him to bring his people to glory (John 17:23–24). Brakel said,

> This covenant reveals a love which is unparalleled, exceeding all comprehension. How blessed and what a wonder it is to have been considered and known in this covenant . . . to have been the object of the eternal, mutual delight of the Father and the Son to save you! . . . Oh, how blessed is he who is incorporated in this covenant and, being enveloped and irradiated by this eternal love, is stirred up to love in return, exclaiming, "We love Him, because He first loved us" (1 John 4:19).[96]

3. *We should examine ourselves to see if we are in Christ* (2 Cor. 13:5). All our hope is bound up in being united to Christ (Col. 1:27); apart from him, we are without God and hopeless (Eph. 2:12). Since all of salvation is bound up in the eternal covenant between the Father and the Son in the Spirit, the application of salvation can take place only "because of and in union with Christ," as Vos said.[97]

4. *We should contemplate the loyalty inherent in love.* It is amazing to think that God freely chose to manifest the Father's love for the Son in the Spirit by means of an eternal covenant in the Deity. Love need not be sealed in covenant promises to be true love, but by God's will the strongest bonds of love are covenantal. This reveals something to us about God's love, especially his loyal or steadfast love (*khesed*).[98] Love does good to all, but especially delights to bind itself in commitments that express union with and partnership with the beloved.

5. *We should honor our covenant commitments*, especially the duties laid on us in the covenant of grace. God did not regard it as demeaning to his glory to enter into a covenant from eternity. Indeed, he counted the

---

95. Edwards, "Miscellanies," no. 2, in *WJE*, 13:198.
96. Brakel, *The Christian's Reasonable Service*, 1:263.
97. Vos, *Redemptive History and Biblical Interpretation*, 248.
98. See the discussion of God's love (*khesed*) in *RST*, 1:788.

bonds of a covenant a fit means of glorifying the love shared among the Father, the Son, and the Holy Spirit. Therefore, we should not regard our covenants as hindrances, but as holy engagements well suited to enable us to live out the highest love. This has much to say to us about how we honor our wedding vows and love our spouses. It has even more to say about the fidelity with which we should keep covenant with God and obey his commandments.

6. *We should rest confidently in our hope* that if we are in Christ, God will save us to the end. God has not only promised salvation to us, but he has promised our salvation to Christ. Strong said, "It is one of the greatest grounds of faith that is in the Word of God, that Christ is engaged by covenant, as well as unto us; and therefore he being the Son, will be faithful to his Father. And also that God is engaged unto Christ as well as unto us, and therefore will be faithful to him also, and will not break with the Son."[99]

7. *We should glorify God for his covenant in Christ.* When the covenant of grace is viewed merely from the perspective of God's dealings with man in history, it has a tendency to become man-centered in its orientation. Vos said, "By the outworking of the doctrine of the counsel of peace this danger was averted and the center placed in God." The covenant of redemption grounds all of God's saving works in the will of the eternal, triune God. Vos wrote, "Here it is God who issues the requirement of redemption as God the Father. Again, it is God who for the fulfillment of that requirement becomes the guarantor as God the Son. Once again, it is God to whom belongs the application of redemption as God the Holy Spirit."[100]

Sing to the Lord

Glorying in God's Covenant with His Son

The Lord unto His Christ hath said,
Sit Thou at My right hand
Until I make Thy enemies
Submit to Thy command.
A scepter prospered by the Lord
Thy mighty hand shall wield;

99. Strong, *A Discourse of the Two Covenants*, 130.
100. Vos, *Redemptive History and Biblical Interpretation*, 247.

From Zion Thou shalt rule the world,
And all Thy foes shall yield.

Thy people will be gladly Thine
When Thou shalt come in might
Like dawning day, like hopeful youth,
With holy beauty bright.
A priesthood that shall never end
The Lord hath given Thee;
This He hath sworn, and evermore
Fulfilled His word shall be.

Thou shalt subdue the kings of earth
With God at Thy right hand;
The nations Thou shalt rule in might
And judge in ev'ry land.
The Christ, refreshed by living streams,
Shall neither faint nor fall,
And He shall be the glorious Head,
Exalted over all.

Psalm 110
Tune: All Saints New
The Psalter, No. 303

Questions for Meditation or Discussion

1. What are three terms used for the eternal agreement within the Trinity to redeem sinners?
2. How would you prove from Scripture that God predestined Christ to be the Mediator?
3. What does Psalm 110:4 reveal about the basis of Christ's priesthood?
4. What does God promise to his Servant in the prophecy of Isaiah?
5. What is the "counsel of peace" in Zechariah 6:13?
6. How does Ephesians 1:3–4 contribute to the doctrine of the covenant of redemption?
7. What other evidence is there in the New Testament that God made a covenant with his Son for the salvation of his people?
8. Why might someone object against the counsel of peace because of the doctrine of the Trinity? How can this objection be answered?

9. How does the doctrine of the counsel of peace help us to defend the doctrine of substitutionary atonement?
10. Of the practical applications listed at the end of the chapter, which seems most important for you to implement right now? Why? How will you do this?

Questions for Deeper Reflection

11. What are the different views of Reformed theologians regarding the relationship of the covenant of redemption to the covenant of grace? What position do the authors take? Do you agree or disagree with them? Why?
12. How would you answer this question: "Is the covenant of grace conditional or unconditional?" Explain and clarify your answer in light of the discussion in this chapter.

31

The Diverse Administrations of God's Covenant of Grace, Part 1

Noah, Abraham, and Moses

When Christians read the Old Testament, they often feel both distant from and near to ancient believers. On the one hand, they sense how foreign the Old Testament world is to them. Whether reading God's command that Abraham circumcise all the males in his household or the instructions on how to pour or sprinkle the blood of sacrifices, Christians discover many things they do not believe they are obligated to perform—though those Scriptures are the Word of God and are therefore profitable to believers today. On the other hand, Christians can identify with the faith and spiritual experience of the Old Testament saints. They read of David's trust in God as his rock and refuge, and of his communion with the Lord, and their hearts rejoice.

There is both diversity and continuity in God's covenants with men through the ages. There are two transcendent covenants, the covenant of works and the covenant of grace, but the Bible also reveals several historical covenants that God made at different stages of history. Morton Smith (1923–2017) said, "The Bible presents a series of covenants that may be described as gracious in character. They are all a part of the progressive revelation of the ultimate Covenant of Grace."[1]

---

1. Morton H. Smith, *Systematic Theology*, 2 vols. (Greenville, SC: Greenville Seminary Press, 1994), 1:333.

General Observations about the Ancient Covenants

The gospel reveals the core of the covenant of grace: the accomplishment and application of salvation through Christ. God revealed the gospel just after the fall of man in the promise of the "seed" of a woman (Gen. 3:15),[2] which has covenantal significance in Genesis, where God makes covenants with individuals and their seed.[3] We may therefore view it as the first revelation of the covenant of grace, though it is not expressly covenantal in form.

Later in the Bible after Genesis 3:15, we read of the explicit covenants God made with men. God's covenant with Noah was universal in scope, including all humanity and "every living creature" (Gen. 9:8–10), but God made subsequent covenants with his particular people that concerned their redemption, culminating in the new covenant when Christ came in the flesh, died for our sins, and rose again. We can summarize the relationship between the past redemptive-historical covenants and the grace of Christ as follows: *every redemptive-historical covenant is at its core the covenant of grace, but dispenses God's grace through a temporary external administration that points typologically ahead to Christ.*

Balance is required here in our theology. If we focus on the spiritual promises and moral instructions of these covenants, then we see that they are truly one covenant of grace. If, however, we focus on the external administrations ordained for Abraham, Israel, and David, much of which foreshadowed the spiritual realities of Christ, then we see that they are distinct historical covenants. We must maintain both covenantal multiplicity and unity in balance in our covenant theology in order to do justice to the Holy Scriptures.

In this chapter and the next, we will walk through the Bible's teaching on the redemptive-historical covenants with an emphasis on their diversity and the progressive development of God's covenantal revelation through the ages. We must constantly remember, however, that this multiplicity of administration is grounded upon the one covenant of grace. We will present biblical and theological arguments for the unity of the covenant of grace in a subsequent chapter.

We begin our study of the redemptive-historical covenants in Ephesians 2, where Paul explains the relationship between the redemptive-historical

---

2. We discussed Gen. 3:15 at the end of chap. 18 and touched on it again in chap. 29.
3. Gen. 9:9; 15:18; 17:7; 22:16–18; 26:3–4, 24; 28:13–14.

covenants and the grace of Christ. We may express that relationship with the terms "temporary administrations" and "typological revelations." Here we reflect the language of the Westminster Confession of Faith (7.5–6), which says that the covenant of grace "was differently administered in the time of the law, and in the time of the gospel," the former including "promises" and "types" of Christ, and the latter the exhibition of "Christ, the substance."[4]

First, the redemptive-historical covenants made prior to the incarnation of Jesus Christ implemented *temporary administrations* of Christ's grace. Paul called them "the covenants of promise" (Eph. 2:12). The plural "covenants" (also in Rom. 9:4) authorizes us to speak of them as distinct historical covenants, though they are manifestations of the one covenant of grace made in Christ eternally and revealed in "the promise."[5] Matthew Poole commented, "The covenants were several, as that with Abraham, and that by Moses, and differ in some accidents, but the promise in them was one and the same, which was the substance of each."[6] The Gentile nations outside of these covenants were "without Christ . . . having no hope, and without God in the world" (Eph. 2:12), implying that by contrast, the covenants of promise united believing Israelites to God through Christ.

We call these covenants "administrations" because through them, God administered, or dispensed, his mercies to his people through specific promises, commands, offices, and forms of worship (cf. Rom. 9:4). God's execution of his purpose in history is his "dispensation" (*oikonomia*, Eph. 1:10), his wise administration, management, or stewardship of resources (cf. Luke 16:2–4) to develop his Son's kingdom over the course of history.[7] John Brown of Haddington said, "Under the Old Testament, this covenant of grace was externally administered by promises, prophecies, sacrifices, circumcision, and the passover, and other types and ordinances. Under the New, it is administered in the preaching of the gospel, baptism, and the Lord's Supper; in which grace and salvation are held forth in more fullness, evidence, and efficacy, to all nations."[8]

---

4. *Reformed Confessions*, 4:243.

5. "The covenants of promise" literally reads "of *the* promise" (Eph. 2:12), referring to God's promise of blessing to Abraham, a blessing that involves the gospel of salvation. See 1:13; 3:6; cf. Gal. 3:14, 15–18, 21–22, 29.

6. Poole, *Annotations upon the Holy Bible*, 3:668, on Eph. 2:12.

7. Poole, *Annotations upon the Holy Bible*, 3:663–64, on Eph. 1:10. Paul elsewhere compares the old covenant laws to temporary stewards or administrators (*oikonomos*) that God set over his children in their minority (Gal. 4:2).

8. Brown, *A Dictionary of the Holy Bible*, 1:321.

Although the historical covenants implemented administrations of Christ's grace, these administrations were temporary, for Paul contrasts the situation of the Gentiles "at that time" to "now in Christ Jesus," because "the blood of Christ" has brought about a new redemptive-historical situation (Eph. 2:12–13). The very term "covenants of promise" reflects the arrival of greater, promised blessing. In Christ Jesus, God has "abolished . . . the law of commandments" (v. 15). Gentiles were once outsiders to the covenants because they did not receive circumcision (v. 11), but God has now made Gentiles who are in Christ fellow citizens with the saints (v. 19). This indicates that the external requirements of the covenants with Abraham and Israel were temporary.

Second, the covenants prior to Christ's coming served as *typological revelations* of his saving grace. By "typological," we mean that these covenants involved many people, institutions, and events divinely designed to foreshadow Christ and his kingdom.[9] The "circumcision in the flesh made by hands" (Eph. 2:11) foreshadowed "the circumcision made without hands"—that is, "the circumcision of Christ" (Col. 2:11; cf. Rom. 2:29). Christ and his people are being fitted together as a "holy temple in the Lord" (Eph. 2:21), implying that the temple "made with hands"[10] was a physical type of a spiritual reality. The types both revealed Christ to believers and veiled him to unbelievers, as many people without saving faith or grace participated in the temporal redemptions (such as the exodus from Egypt and restoration from exile) and external rites provided in the covenants.

Thomas Boston called the historical covenants "typical of the covenant of grace." Their salvation was typical, such as Noah's salvation from the waters of the flood, which was a type of salvation from God's eternal wrath. Their ceremonies were typical, such as the animal sacrifices. Their parties were typical, for Noah, Abraham, and David each stood "as representative of his seed," which was a shadow of "Jesus Christ representing his spiritual seed in the covenant of grace."[11]

Therefore, we should read the Old Testament from a twofold perspective. On the one hand, Christians today can profoundly identify with the

---

9. For a discussion of biblical typology, see Witsius, *The Economy of the Covenants*, 4.6 (2:188–243).

10. Mark 14:58; Acts 7:48; Heb. 9:11, 24. See Francis Foulkes, *Ephesians: An Introduction and Commentary*, Tyndale New Testament Commentaries 10 (Downers Grove, IL: InterVarsity Press, 1989), 86–87.

11. Boston, *An Illustration of the Doctrines of the Christian Religion*, in *Works*, 1:328; cf. *A View of the Covenant of Grace*, in *Works*, 8:390.

faith and spiritual experience of the Old Testament saints, for they participated in the same saving grace as we do today. On the other hand, modern believers should recognize that some things in the Old Testament were but temporary administrations that no longer bind us in a literal sense, especially the types that Christ has fulfilled. We must learn from the New Testament how to recognize, interpret, and apply those types.

The Covenant of Preservation with Noah and His Seed

The first covenant explicitly mentioned in the Bible is the covenant with Noah. Though this covenant is more directly connected to creation than redemption, through it God provided a foundation of common grace necessary for the progress of redemptive history in a fallen world.

Biblical Exposition of the Covenant of Preservation

After commanding Noah to build the ark to escape the worldwide flood, the Lord said, "Every thing that is in the earth shall die. But with thee will I establish my covenant; and thou shalt come into the ark, thou, and thy sons, and thy wife, and thy sons' wives with thee" (Gen. 6:17–18). God made this covenant primarily with Noah, a righteous man saved by grace (vv. 8–9). The covenant separated Noah and his family from those God would destroy for their sins.[12] The mention of "the ark" implicitly attached a condition to this promise: Noah had to obediently build the means of his deliverance. Yet Noah's faith rested upon God's promise alone (Heb. 11:7), which was "like a wall of iron, against all the terrors of death," as John Calvin said.[13]

The subsequent narrative emphasizes the mutual covenant fidelity of the Lord and Noah. Noah built, loaded, and boarded the ark with his family, just as God "commanded" him (Gen. 6:22; 7:5, 9, 16). But ultimately, the safety of Noah and those with him was the work of God and not man: "the LORD shut him in" (v. 16). They alone of all breathing creatures were saved from the deadly waters of the flood (vv. 21–24). At the center of the flood narrative is the statement that "God remembered Noah, and every living thing, and all the cattle that was with him in the ark" (8:1). The verb translated as "remembered" (*zakar*) is associated with keeping

---

12. Nichols, *Covenant Theology*, 146–47.
13. Calvin, *Commentaries*, on Gen. 6:18.

a covenant,[14] which suggests that God had already entered a special covenant bond with Noah through the promise of deliverance from judgment to come.[15]

When the waters receded and Noah emerged from the ark at God's command, the patriarch offered burnt offerings on an altar. Pleased by this sacrifice, God promised, "While the earth remaineth, seedtime and harvest, and cold and heat, and summer and winter, and day and night shall not cease" (Gen. 8:20–22). God renewed his creation mandate in a purged but still fallen world (9:1–7). Then God addressed Noah and his sons: "I establish my covenant with you, and with your seed after you; and with every living creature that is with you. . . . I will establish my covenant with you; neither shall all flesh be cut off any more by the waters of a flood; neither shall there any more be a flood to destroy the earth" (vv. 9–11). This covenant secured the promise God had already made to Noah in response to his sacrifice. God appointed the rainbow to be the sign of the covenant (vv. 12–17).

Theological Reflection on the Covenant of Preservation

God used Noah to save the human race from destruction. God's covenant with Noah is not a temporal administration of *saving* grace to God's particular people, but rather an administration of God's *common* grace to all mankind until heaven and earth pass away.[16]

However, this historical covenant was vitally related to the covenant of grace, for it restrained God's wrath against mankind's sin and preserved God's created order until his saving purposes were fulfilled through the promised Seed of the woman (3:15), a promise God could not break.[17] Therefore, this arrangement may be called the covenant of preservation.[18] Through this covenant, God struck a heavy blow at the seed of the Serpent and preserved the seed of the woman from being overwhelmed by sinful men so that the great Seed might be sent into the world in due time.[19] The covenant of preservation demonstrates God's faithfulness to

---

14. Gen. 9:15–16; Ex. 2:24; 6:5; Lev. 26:42, 45; 1 Chron. 16:15; Pss. 105:8; 106:45; 111:5; Ezek. 16:60.

15. Meredith G. Kline, *Kingdom Prologue: Genesis Foundations for a Covenantal Worldview* (Overland Park, KS: Two Age Press, 2000), 230–32.

16. Cf. Calvin, *Commentaries*, on Gen. 9:8–9. For the doctrine of common grace, see *RST*, vol. 3 (forthcoming).

17. Barrett, *Beginning at Moses*, 115.

18. Robertson, *The Christ of the Covenants*, 114–15.

19. Robertson, *The Christ of the Covenants*, 109.

his seed-promise. God's dealings with Noah show that "the Lord knoweth how to deliver the godly out of temptations, and to reserve the unjust unto the day of judgment to be punished" (2 Pet. 2:9).[20]

Salvation from the flood in the ark is a magnificent type of eternal judgment and redemption through Christ. Both the flood and the coming of the Son of Man bring sudden destruction on the world (Matt. 24:37–39). Just as God once destroyed the wicked world by water, so he will ultimately destroy it by fire (2 Pet. 2:5–7). The salvation of eight people through water is a picture of the salvation of sinners by Christ's death, resurrection, ascension, and session at God's right hand—a salvation applied inwardly by faith and sealed outwardly by the waters of baptism (1 Pet. 3:18–22; cf. Heb. 11:7). We see much of Christ in God's provision through Noah of only one way for salvation by the obedience of one man, so that the people united with him (his "seed") entered a renewed creation and experienced a stable hope on the basis of that man's sacrifice. God compares the covenant of preservation to his unbreakable "covenant of peace": "For this is as the waters of Noah unto me: for as I have sworn that the waters of Noah should no more go over the earth; so have I sworn that I would not be wroth [angry] with thee, nor rebuke thee. For the mountains shall depart, and the hills be removed; but my kindness shall not depart from thee, neither shall the covenant of my peace be removed, saith the LORD that hath mercy on thee" (Isa. 54:9–10).

Therefore, the covenant with Noah reveals both God's severity and mercy in a manner that calls sinners to repent of sin (Rom. 2:4–5) and seek salvation in the greater Noah, Christ.[21] After studying this covenant, we must ask ourselves whether we are safe in Christ's "ark." If God's judgment were to fall upon our world today, would we be prepared? Ask yourself, "Am I trusting in the obedience of God's righteous Son? Am I part of his family?" There is no other way to escape the judgment that will one day destroy our world. Do not fool yourself into thinking that you will prepare yourself when the time comes. Just as with the flood, people will go on with their ordinary lives until suddenly judgment falls—and it is too late to repent.

The Covenant of Promise with Abraham and His Seed

The historical covenant out of which develop all of God's subsequent dealings with his people is his covenant with Abraham and his seed. If the cove-

---

20. Roberts, *The Mysterie and Marrow of the Bible*, 255.
21. Roberts, *The Mysterie and Marrow of the Bible*, 251–52.

nant with Noah secured the stability of this fallen world to allow for God's subsequent saving works, then the covenant with Abraham is the living root from which those works grow. Whereas the covenant with Noah brought temporal preservation to the entire human race, the covenant with Abraham promised eternal blessing for a people taken from every clan on earth.

Biblical Exposition of the Covenant of Promise

God unfolded his covenant with Abraham in a complex and progressive manner, beginning with the promises by which God called him to go up from Ur of the Chaldees to an unknown land (Gen. 12:1–3). Though Abraham had no children at the time, the Lord pledged to give the land to him and his offspring, whom God would greatly multiply (vv. 1–3, 7; 13:14–17). The promise of land and offspring echoes the creation mandate (1:28). The blessing of Abraham was the redemptive reversal of the curse that came because of man's fall (3:14, 17)—saving grace.[22] Paul teaches that the singular "seed" points particularly to one son of Abraham, Jesus Christ, and collectively to those in union with him, both Jews and Gentiles (Gal. 3:16, 28–29; cf. Acts 3:25–26). However, in another sense, all the Israelites are "children . . . of the covenant" because they are Abraham's physical descendants (Acts 3:25; cf. Rom. 9:4; 11:1).

Later God renewed his promise of offspring, stirring Abraham to the exercise of justifying faith (Gen. 15:4–6). The Lord then formally "made a covenant" with Abraham so that he might know with certainty that God would give the land to his seed (vv. 8, 13, 18). God instructed Abraham to kill sacrificial animals and lay their pieces on the ground, where they were exposed to scavengers (vv. 9–11)—a sign that covenant breakers would die under God's curse.[23] However, God rendered Abraham passive before his awesome presence (v. 12), and the Lord alone passed between the sacrificial pieces (v. 17). Thus, God himself took the oath to fulfill the covenant requirements, even including bearing the curse. The covenant is, in John Murray's words, "divinely unilateral."[24] God promised to save Abraham's seed after four centuries of oppression in a foreign land and to bring them back to the Promised Land (vv. 13–16, 18–21).

---

22. See the study of Gen. 12:1–3 and its relation to the gospel in chap. 29.

23. Deut. 28:15, 26; 1 Sam. 17:43–46; Jer. 34:18–20. For examples from other Scripture passages and other ancient Near Eastern cultures, see Meredith G. Kline, *By Oath Consigned: A Reinterpretation of the Covenant Signs of Circumcision and Baptism* (Grand Rapids, MI: Eerdmans, 1968), 17; and Robertson, *The Christ of the Covenants*, 130–37.

24. Murray, *The Covenant of Grace*, 17.

After some years had passed, the Lord appeared again to Abraham when he was ninety-nine years old to further reveal his covenant (Gen. 17:1). God called Abraham to walk before him in righteous integrity, and again promised to multiply his offspring and give them the land (vv. 1–2, 7–8). Changing his name from "Abram" to "Abraham," God also gave more specific promises—he would be "a father of many nations" (v. 5) and the father of "kings" (v. 6; cf. 49:10). The word translated as "covenant" (*berit*) appears thirteen times in Genesis 17, more frequently than in any other chapter in the Bible.[25]

This covenant engaged God to give himself to his covenant people as "their God" (Gen. 17:7–8). Calvin said, "Whenever God declares that he will be our God, he offers to us his paternal favour."[26] To Abraham's physical offspring, this commitment entailed their redemption from physical enemies and God's special presence among them on earth (26:24; 28:13, 15). However, Calvin noted that this promise signified "that this was a spiritual covenant, not confirmed in reference to the present life only. . . . For those whom God adopts to himself . . . he also constitutes heirs of celestial life."[27] Those who have the Lord as their God have favor and communion with him (Lev. 26:11–12; 2 Cor. 6:16). Francis Roberts said, "God hath all good in him; God brings all good with him. If God be theirs by covenant, all's theirs by covenant also. Behold what manner of promise this is. Is there a greater, or more eminent promise in all the Bible?"[28] Abraham's status was that of God's "servant," which speaks of his privileged position as the recipient of God's grace.[29] Abraham is even called God's "friend."[30]

The covenant with Abraham is also called the "covenant of circumcision" (Acts 7:8). The Lord demanded that Abraham and his seed "keep my covenant" by circumcising every male child (including children of slaves) born in Abraham's household as a sign of the covenant (Gen. 17:9–14). Circumcision was essential to this covenant: "any uncircumcised male . . . has broken my covenant" (v. 14 ESV).[31] Whereas the rainbow was

---

25. Gen. 17:2, 4, 7, 9, 10, 11, 13, 14, 19, 21.
26. Calvin, *Commentaries*, on Jer. 31:33.
27. Calvin, *Commentaries*, on Gen. 17:7–8. The theme of divine adoption latent in the promise of the Lord being "their God" (cf. Rev. 21:7) comes out explicitly in the covenants of law (Ex. 4:22; Deut. 14:1; Isa. 63:16; 64:8; Jer. 31:9; Hos. 1:10; 11:1) and kingdom (2 Sam. 7:14; Ps. 89:26).
28. Roberts, *The Mysterie and Marrow of the Bible*, 406.
29. Gen. 26:24; Ex. 32:13; Deut. 9:27; Ps. 105:6, 42.
30. 2 Chron. 20:7; Isa. 41:8; James 2:32.
31. On the absolute requirement of circumcision, see also Ex. 4:24–26; 12:43–44, 48; Josh. 5:2–9. For an argument that the censure of Gen. 17:14 applied to men who, not being circumcised

an objective sign of the covenant with Noah, something external to him, circumcision was applied to the covenant people—the Lord said "my covenant shall be in your flesh" (v. 13)—as a sign of God's relationship with them as their God and his promises regarding the future "seed" (v. 7).

God's covenant was a means of executing his sovereign election. The covenant was not with Ishmael, the son of Hagar, but with Isaac, the son to be born of Sarah, "and with his seed after him" (Gen. 17:18–21). Thus, this covenant was not universal, but was granted according to God's election (Neh. 9:7–8). In Abraham's blessed and circumcised "seed," there are two seeds (Gen. 21:12–13), one elected and the other rejected with respect to the covenant of grace, though sharing in some of its privileges (Rom. 9:4–13).

After the birth of Isaac, the Lord tested Abraham's obedience by commanding him to sacrifice his son and then stopping him from doing so at the last moment (Genesis 22). The Lord swore an oath to bless Abraham, multiply his seed, give them victory, and bless all the world through them (vv. 17–18). The oath communicated the unchangeable nature of God's purpose to give "strong consolation" to those who hope in him (Heb. 6:13–18). Peter later identified these words as a "covenant" (Acts 3:25).

The Lord expressed the gracious bond of his covenant relationship to Abraham by saying, "I know him" (Gen. 18:19). Although this was a relationship created by sovereign grace, human obedience played a crucial part as the way in which God brought his people into the promised blessings. Abraham had to pass on God's word to his offspring, "and they shall keep the way of the LORD, to do justice and judgment; that the LORD may bring upon Abraham that which he hath spoken of him" (v. 19). When Abraham proved himself willing to offer Isaac by faith in God's promise (Heb. 11:17), God promised blessing "because thou hast done this thing, and hast not withheld thy son, thine only son . . . because thou hast obeyed my voice" (Gen. 22:16, 18). Abraham was a man justified by faith alone (15:6), but the Lord could say, "Abraham obeyed my voice, and kept my charge, my commandments, my statutes, and my laws," and "because" of that obedience, "shall all the nations of the earth be blessed" (26:4–5). Abraham's obedience had no merit in which he could glory (Rom. 4:2), but it was an important means by which God fulfilled his promises.[32]

in infancy, refused circumcision in their adulthood as well, see Witsius, *The Economy of the Covenants*, 4.8.12 (2:249–50).

32. Here we disagree with Meredith Kline's choice of words when he said that Abraham's "faithful performance of his covenantal duty" sustained "a causal relationship to the blessing

Theological Reflection on the Covenant of Promise

We may visualize the seed of Abraham as two overlapping circles, one representing his physical offspring through Isaac and Jacob by ordinary generation, and the other his spiritual offspring by promise and faith. The area where the circles overlap represents the Israelites who are saved by faith in Christ. At the center of that overlap is Christ himself, the great Seed who is both physical Israel and spiritual Israel in the highest sense (Isa. 49:3).

Given the two seeds of Abraham, some theologians have proposed that God made two distinct covenants with him.[33] Thus, they distinguish God's promises of grace to Abraham from the "covenant of circumcision" (Acts 7:8) linked to keeping the law (Gal. 5:3). However, it is best to understand the Scriptures as revealing not two covenants with Abraham, but one. The Bible speaks of God's "covenant" with Abraham in the singular, never the plural.[34] The promises of Genesis 15 and 17 both refer to God's granting the Promised Land to Abraham's seed (15:18; 17:8), showing that they are not two covenants, but one.[35]

We can better understand how God's one covenant with Abraham can pertain to two seeds when we consider the covenant as a temporary administration and typological revelation of Christ's saving grace. As a *temporary administration* of the covenant of grace, the historical covenant of promise was God's means to dispense saving grace to true believers,

---

of Isaac and Israel," for "it had a meritorious character that procured the reward enjoyed by others." Kline qualified this statement by distinguishing between Christ's meriting the eternal kingdom and Abraham's works, to which God granted "an analogous kind of value" to merit Canaan. Kline, *Kingdom Prologue*, 325. Similarly, Kline saw in the Mosaic covenant "a principle of meritorious works, operating not as a way of eternal salvation but as the principle governing Israel's retention of its provisional, typological inheritance." Meredith G. Kline, "Gospel until the Law: Rom 5:13–14 and the Old Covenant," *Journal of the Evangelical Theological Society* 34, no. 4 (December 1991): 434 (full article, 433–46). However, it is best to avoid the term "merit" with regard to a believer's works, for historically the term has denoted worthiness to receive God's reward because of one's perfect fulfillment of God's covenantal standard, in contrast to the gift of grace (cf. Gen. 32:10; Rom. 4:4–5). See the Westminster Larger Catechism (Q. 193), *Reformed Confessions*, 4:350.

33. Luther, *Lectures on Genesis*, in *LW*, 2:71; 3:111, 115–16; Coxe, *A Discourse of the Covenants*, 4.3–4, 5.7 (71–73, 104); also in Miller, Renihan, and Orozco, eds., *Covenant Theology from Adam to Christ*, 72–73, 90–91; Benjamin Keach, *The Ax Laid to the Root*, 3, 12; Charles Hodge, *Discussions in Church Polity*, ed. William Durant, pref. Archibald Alexander Hodge (New York: Charles Scribner's Sons, 1878), 66; McComiskey, *The Covenants of Promise*, 146; and Paul R. Williamson, *Sealed with an Oath: Covenant in God's Unfolding Purpose*, New Studies in Biblical Theology (Downers Grove, IL: InterVarsity Press, 2007), 89–90.

34. Ex. 2:24; 6:3–4; Lev. 26:42; 2 Kings 13:23; 1 Chron. 16:15–16; Neh. 9:7–8; Ps. 105:8–9; Luke 1:72–73; Acts 3:25; 7:8.

35. Peter J. Gentry and Stephen J. Wellum, *Kingdom through Covenant: A Biblical-Theological Understanding of the Covenants*, 2nd ed. (Wheaton, IL: Crossway, 2018), 312–18 (cf. 1st ed., 275–80).

Abraham and his spiritual seed in Israel. Their justifying faith came by hearing the promises of God, just as ours does today (Gen. 15:5–6). God's word nurtured their hope in the coming of Christ, the great "Seed" of the covenant (Gal. 3:16), the royal "son of Abraham" (Matt. 1:1).

It is a mistake to view the blessings promised to Abraham as merely physical; the covenant of promise centers on salvation from sin. Micah rejoiced in this truth: "Who is a God like unto thee, that pardoneth iniquity, and passeth by the transgression of the remnant of his heritage? He retaineth not his anger for ever, because he delighteth in mercy. He will turn again, he will have compassion upon us; he will subdue our iniquities; and thou wilt cast all their sins into the depths of the sea. Thou wilt perform the truth to Jacob, and the mercy to Abraham, which thou hast sworn unto our fathers from the days of old" (Mic. 7:18–20).

In this temporary covenantal administration, circumcision was a sign of the covenant. Circumcision's immediate, plain significance in Genesis 17 is the Lord's commitment to be the God of Abraham and his future "seed" (vv. 7–9). The covenantal bond confirmed the imputation of righteousness to Abraham by faith (15:6); "the sign of circumcision" functioned for Abraham as "a seal of the righteousness of the faith which he had yet being uncircumcised" (Rom. 4:11).[36] Circumcision was not a seal of justification for all of Abraham's offspring, for many of them lacked the patriarch's faith (v. 12). However, it did signify that Abraham's household was the clan whose father was accepted by God and enjoyed special access to him—later revealed as God's priestly people (Ex. 19:6).[37] Thus, though only applied to males, circumcision had corporate significance for the whole people. The cutting of the foreskin from the male sexual member pictures both judgment and offspring. Calvin said, "It is probable that the Lord commanded circumcision for two reasons; first, to show that whatever is born of man is polluted; then, that salvation would proceed from the blessed seed of Abraham."[38]

Later in redemptive history, God used circumcision to remind the people of Israel of their duty to "circumcise . . . the foreskin of your heart"—

---

36. Murray, *The Epistle to the Romans*, 1:138.

37. Some scholars propose that the background of Abrahamic circumcision was the partial circumcision required of Egyptian kings and priests, who were considered sons of the gods. See John D. Meade, "The Meaning of Circumcision in Israel: A Proposal for a Transfer of Rite from Egypt to Israel," *Southern Baptist Journal of Theology* 20, no. 1 (2016): 35–54. This proposal resonates with Israel's covenantal status as God's firstborn "son," "a kingdom of priests, and an holy nation" (Ex. 4:22; 19:6). However, the interpretation of Egyptian circumcision is not entirely certain, and the Bible does not associate circumcision directly with priestly status.

38. Calvin, *Commentaries*, on Gen. 17:11.

that is, to repent of sin, love God, and keep his commandments in covenant fidelity (Deut. 10:16; cf. Jer. 4:4). Circumcision was not a sign of an internally sanctified people, however, for many men bearing external circumcision lacked internal grace (Rom. 2:25–26). The merely physical seed of Abraham were part of the wicked seed of the Serpent (John 8:39, 44). Yet circumcision demarcated the people to whom God had given his word (Rom. 3:1–2). Though some other nations, such as Egypt, practiced a kind of circumcision for various reasons (Jer. 9:25–26), this procedure marked Abraham's offspring as a distinct people, especially among the uncircumcised Canaanites (Judg. 14:3).

God's covenant with Abraham also served as a *typological revelation* of Christ and his future work. God's covenant relation as the God of Abraham was a type of the covenant of grace in which he is "the God and Father of our Lord Jesus Christ" from the foundation of the world (Eph. 1:3–4). The promised redemption from a land of slavery (Gen. 15:14) was a type of salvation from the tyranny of sin (Titus 2:14). The land of Canaan was the temporary home for the patriarchs as pilgrims on their way to the city of God (Heb. 11:13–16), for the land was a type of the true "rest" that even Joshua could not give Israel, but which belongs to those who receive the promise by faith (4:1–11), "the promise of eternal inheritance" (9:15).

Circumcision was also a type of salvation in Christ. Although we do not know how much Abraham understood of this typology, Moses opened the typological significance of circumcision when he promised God's future work of heart circumcision for the people (Deut. 30:6), to take place after Israel experienced "the blessing and the curse," suffered exile "among all the nations," and returned to the land (vv. 1, 3–4). The New Testament proclaims the circumcision of the heart as a now present reality by the work of the Holy Spirit (Rom. 2:25–29), through whom believers are "sealed" in Christ (Eph. 1:13; 2 Cor. 1:22). This circumcision takes place by union with Christ—"in him also you were circumcised"—and the "circumcision of Christ" consists of the double grace of "putting off the body of the sins of the flesh" and being "forgiven" of "all trespasses" by Christ's death, foreshadowed in the bloody cutting of the ancient rite (Col. 2:11, 13 ESV).[39] Though individuals among Abraham's ancient descendants already

---

39. Paul links spiritual circumcision to Christ's burial and resurrection (Col. 2:11–12). Kline argues that "the circumcision of Christ" refers to Christ's death as a violent divine judgment against sin (cf. Rom. 8:3). Kline, *By Oath Consigned*, 46–47.

enjoyed these graces (Pss. 32:1; 37:31; 143:10), the nation as a whole was characterized as "uncircumcised" in the heart, for they were ruled by law breaking and were under God's wrath.[40] Yet God's covenant of circumcision would not fail, for it looked forward to the coming of Christ.

How exceptionally precious is spiritual circumcision! It is the essence of a true covenantal relationship with God. It is an absolute requisite to be a son or daughter of Abraham. Have you received this gift of God by the Holy Spirit? Do not rely on any outward rite, such as physical circumcision or baptism. Instead, examine yourself for a true likeness to Abraham: inward faith in the gospel of Christ and visible works of obedience to God's Word (John 8:39; Rom. 4:12).

When the promised spiritual circumcision in Christ arrived with the outpoured Spirit, physical circumcision passed away as a divine mandate, for the type was fulfilled in the "new creation" of the church (Gal. 6:15 ESV).[41] Yet the covenant with Abraham, insofar as it is an outcropping into time of the eternal covenant of grace, continues today in Christ (Luke 1:72–73). Both Jewish and Gentile believers in Christ are the spiritual seed of Abraham and the heirs of God's covenant promise to Abraham (Gal. 3:26, 29). They are circumcised in a manner that transcends human performance or praise (Rom. 2:29). Therefore, though the Abrahamic covenant has passed away as an external administration (the law of circumcision being abrogated), its great promises remain in effect "to a thousand generations" (Ps. 105:8). All believers in Christ may regard Abraham as "our father" (Rom. 4:12; cf. v. 16). With Abraham, they are heirs not just of the land of Canaan but "of the world" (v. 13). They can rejoice, "We are the circumcision, which worship God in the spirit, and rejoice in Christ Jesus, and have no confidence in the flesh" (Phil. 3:3). Is this true of you?

The Covenant of Law with Israel through Moses

After Abraham, Isaac, and Jacob died, their offspring found themselves enslaved in Egypt. God raised up a deliverer, Moses, to whom he appeared at Mount Sinai. Through Moses, the Lord confronted Pharaoh with words of authority and works of power. God redeemed Israel from Egypt and led them, now a nation of many thousands of people, into the wilderness to worship him at the same mountain. There the Lord made a covenant

---

40. Lev. 26:41; Jer. 6:10; 9:26; Ezek. 44:7, 9; Acts 7:51.
41. Acts 15:1, 5, 11, 19–20; 1 Cor. 7:18–19; Col. 3:11.

that defined his relationship with the nation of Israel, a covenant growing from the root of his promises to Abraham and preparing for the coming of his Son, Jesus Christ.

Biblical Exposition of the Covenant of Law

The documents of God's covenant with Israel through Moses are very extensive, consisting its initial establishment at Mount Sinai, recorded in Exodus 19–40 and the entire book of Leviticus, with additional teachings in parts of the book of Numbers,[42] and the covenant's renewal on the border of the Promised Land, recorded in the book of Deuteronomy. These covenantal documents constitute a system of regulations by which God governed Israel as his graciously redeemed theocratic society on earth. Though the Abrahamic, Davidic, and new covenants all engage God's people to obey the Lord, the Mosaic covenant is preeminently the covenant of law.

The combination of grace and law is evident in God's first declaration of the covenant on Mount Sinai: "Ye have seen what I did unto the Egyptians, and how I bare you on eagles' wings, and brought you unto myself. Now therefore, if ye will obey my voice indeed, and keep my covenant, then ye shall be a peculiar treasure unto me above all people: for all the earth is mine: and ye shall be unto me a kingdom of priests, and an holy nation" (Ex. 19:4–6). The Lord reminded his people that the covenant rested upon a gracious foundation, for he had saved them and preserved them with the tenderness and power of a mother eagle caring for her young (Deut. 32:9–12).[43] He promised them remarkable blessings. They would be God's "peculiar treasure" (*segullah*), a term for a king's silver and gold (1 Chron. 29:3; Eccl. 2:8), for he had chosen them to be the people he would especially cherish as a free act of his fatherly love.[44] They would enjoy access to the sacred presence of the King dwelling among them (Lev. 26:11–12). Willem VanGemeren explains, "The words 'kingdom' and 'nation' are parallel, as are 'priests' and 'holy.' The Lord thus promises to take Israel as his consecrated nation, set apart to himself and privileged to serve

---

42. See Numbers 3–6, 9, 15, 18–19, 27–30, 35–36.

43. On the imagery of God's "wings" for his powerful compassion, see Pss. 17:8; 36:7; 57:1; 61:4; 63:7; 91:4.

44. Deut. 7:6–8; 14:1–2; 26:18–19; Mal. 3:17. A cognate term to *segullah* is used in other ancient Near Eastern literature of a king who is the beloved servant of his god, and also of a vassal king who is the servant of the suzerain. Gentry and Wellum, *Kingdom through Covenant*, 1st ed., 317.

the great King as a visible manifestation of God's kingdom on earth."[45] God made the enjoyment of these blessings conditional upon the obedience of the nation: "if ye will obey . . . then ye shall be . . ." A holy status with access to the holy Lord required holy living (11:44–45). This conditional promise pertained to the nation as a whole community.[46]

The Lord proceeded to display his glory on the mountain (Ex. 19:16–18) and reveal the law of the covenant, beginning with the broad principles of the Ten Commandments (20:1–17) and the many specific regulations that applied these principles to Israel's national life (chaps. 21–23). The Ten Commandments were called "the words of the covenant" (34:28), and the regulations "the book of the covenant" (24:7). In a formal covenant-cutting ceremony, Moses led the people in making a solemn promise to keep God's commands, then sprinkled sacrificial blood on an altar (representing God) and on the people (vv. 4–8). Moses and representative leaders of Israel then ascended partway up the mountain and ate a meal in the presence of God's manifest glory (vv. 9–11)—a symbolic act of fellowship between God and his priestly people. Afterward, God instructed Moses in how to construct the means of that fellowship: the earthly tabernacle where God dwelt and received the sacrificial ministry of his appointed priests (described in Exodus 25–31; implemented in Exodus 35–Leviticus 9).

The covenant of law instituted a system of covenantal officers through whom God cared for the Israelites and held them accountable. The prototype for these officers was Moses, who functioned as a "mediator" (Gal. 3:19) of God's external blessings. Like Abraham, Moses was the "servant" of the Lord.[47] Moses functioned as a prophet who brought God's word,[48] a priest of sacrifice and intercession who consecrated the Aaronic priesthood,[49] and a king who delivered God's people and judged their enemies, judged the people according to the law, and constructed the tabernacle.[50] God raised up prophets, priests, and judges/kings after Moses

---

45. Willem A. VanGemeren, *The Progress of Redemption: The Story of Salvation from Creation to the New Jerusalem* (Grand Rapids, MI: Baker, 1988), 148.

46. Nichols, *Covenant Theology*, 210–11.

47. Ex. 14:31; Num. 11:11; 12:7–8; Deut. 34:5; Josh. 1:1, 2, 7, 13, 15; 8:31, 33; 9:24; 11:12, 15; 12:6; 13:8; 14:7; 18:7; 22:2, 4, 5; 1 Kings 8:53, 56; 2 Kings 18:12; 21:8; 1 Chron. 6:49; 2 Chron. 1:3; 24:6, 9; Neh. 1:7, 8; 9:14; 10:29; Ps. 105:26; Dan. 9:11; Mal. 4:4; Heb. 3:5; Rev. 15:3.

48. Ex. 4:12; 19:3, 7; Deut. 5:23–31.

49. Ex. 24:6–8; chaps. 28–29; 32:11–13; 39:43; Leviticus 8–9; Num. 6:22–27; 14:13–19; Deut. 33:1.

50. Ex. 14:21–27; 18:13–16; 40:16–33. On judges and kings, see Ex. 18:21–22; Deut. 17:9, 12, 14–20.

to fill these covenantal offices, as we will see in more detail when we study the offices of Christ.

The Sabbath was the sign that the Lord had sanctified Israel (Ex. 31:13; cf. Ezek. 20:12, 20). The Sabbath was an institution established at creation (Gen. 2:1–3) and expanded for Israel to include the Sabbath year, one year out of every seven when the land could rest from agriculture (Lev. 25:1–7).

God's law manifests God's righteous requirement of obedience and his just severity and wrath against sin (Rom. 4:15). Accordingly, the covenant of law mandated the death penalty for many crimes.[51] The confirmation of the covenant climaxed in the declaration of blessings and curses. If the people kept God's commandments, God promised to bless them with rain, abundant food, offspring, peace, safety, victory, and communion with God (Lev. 26:1–13; Deut. 28:1–14). However, if Israel would not obey God's laws and refused to repent, then God would curse the people with disease, defeat, oppression, fear, drought, famine, danger, death, desolation, and dispersion among the nations (Lev. 26:14–39; Deut. 28:15–68).

The covenant of law pressed Israel to choose between life in communion with God and death under his judgment. Moses exhorted the people, "I have set before you life and death, blessing and cursing: therefore choose life, that both thou and thy seed may live: that thou mayest love the LORD thy God . . . for he is thy life" (Deut. 30:19–20). Sadly, Israel's subsequent history proved that the nation chose poorly. God was not surprised. The Lord told Moses that after his death, "this people will rise up, and go a whoring after the gods of the strangers of the land, whither they go to be among them, and will forsake me, and break my covenant which I have made with them" (Deut. 31:16).

Theological Reflection on the Covenant of Law

God's covenant with Israel made the Lord's blessings conditional on the people's obedience to his holy and gracious law (Ex. 19:5–6). The Lord said, "Cursed be the man that obeyeth not the words of this covenant, which I commanded your fathers in the day that I brought them forth out

---

51. Capital crimes under the law of Moses included murder (Ex. 21:12), striking or cursing one's parents (v. 15), kidnapping and selling victims as slaves (v. 16), gross negligence resulting in someone's death (v. 29), bestiality (22:19), Sabbath-breaking (31:14–15; 35:2), child sacrifice (Lev. 20:2), adultery (v. 10), incest (vv. 11–12), male-with-male sexual relations (v. 13), sorcery (v. 27), blaspheming God's name (24:16), entering God's holy places without divine authorization (Num. 1:51; 3:10, 38; 18:7), and encouraging others to worship any god besides the Lord (Deuteronomy 13).

of the land of Egypt, from the iron furnace, saying, Obey my voice, and do them, according to all which I command you: so shall ye be my people, and I will be your God: that I may perform the oath which I have sworn unto your fathers, to give them a land flowing with milk and honey, as it is this day" (Jer. 11:3–5; cf. 7:23).

The question arises whether the covenant of law is a covenant of works, offering eternal life and threatening damnation based on one's obedience to God's commandments. When Paul opposes those seeking justification by their works, he points out that "Moses describeth the righteousness which is of the law, That the man which doeth those things shall live by them" (Rom. 10:5). The law abstracted as a principle of justification is the equivalent of a covenant of works, as Paul says, "for as many as are of the works of the law are under the curse: for it is written, Cursed is every one that continueth not in all things which are written in the book of the law to do them. . . . And the law is not of faith: but, The man that doeth them shall live in them" (Gal. 3:10, 12; cf. Deut. 27:26; Lev. 18:5; Ezek. 20:11).

Furthermore, the law of Moses was a "yoke of bondage" (Gal. 5:1) for both the wicked (4:24–25) and godly Jews (Acts 15:10). One aspect of this bondage was the fearful display of God's wrath at Mount Sinai (Ex. 20:18–21; Heb. 12:18–21), showing the inaccessibility of his holiness as contrasted to the open access enjoyed in Christ (10:19–22; 12:22–24). The combination of law and wrath displayed the broken covenant of works and the danger of sinners under the law.[52] The people did not enjoy the liberty of God's sons, but were weighed down with the multitude of ceremonies that God had imposed on them like "tutors and governors" for minor children (Gal. 4:1–3). The sacrifices were a burden to the people economically, and especially because they constantly impressed the guilt of sin upon the conscience (Heb. 10:1–3).[53]

However, while the Mosaic covenant contained a potent reminder of the covenant of works, it was another *temporary administration* of the covenant of grace. To appreciate this, we must distinguish between God's law as an absolute demand for righteousness in the covenant of works and God's law as embedded in his gracious covenant with Israel. Calvin noted that the word "law" can refer to either the "precepts, rewards, and punishments" that are especially prominent in the Mosaic administration,

---

52. John Colquhoun, *A Treatise on the Law and the Gospel*, intro. Joel R. Beeke, ed. Don Kistler (Grand Rapids, MI: Soli Deo Gloria, 2009), 56–57.

53. Calvin, *Institutes*, 2.11.9.

or to "the whole of what has been taught by Moses," including both com-mandments and gospel promises.[54] The law's absolute demand in relation to righteousness offers life to the perfectly obedient (Matt. 19:16–19). However, the Holy Scriptures depict God's holistic law-covenant with Israel as an administration of the covenant of grace, for the law did not nullify the promise given to Abraham (Gal. 3:15–17) or present an alterna-tive means of gaining life—the law is certainly not "against the promises of God" (v. 21). Smith said, "Paul is teaching that the Mosaic economy was an extension, an enlargement or an expansion on the Abrahamic, not a contradiction to it in any way."[55]

The Mosaic covenant was primarily national in its orientation, dealing with Israel as a society. The Lord said, "If ye [plural] will obey . . . ye [plu-ral] shall be . . . an holy nation" (Ex. 19:5–6). Most of the blessings and curses of the covenant of law pertain to external, physical, and national prosperity, not internal, spiritual, and eternal salvation (Leviticus 26; Deuteronomy 28). Brown said, "God made with the Hebrews a national covenant, importing [signifying], that he affirmed them for his peculiar people, and gave them the peaceable and happy enjoyment of Canaan, on condition of their obedience to his laws."[56]

The Lord was not dealing with the people of Israel in a strictly legal manner, but in a way of mercy. Consider the following points:

- Israel did not become his people by obeying the law, but were already counted by God as "my people" before the exodus (Ex. 3:7, 10; 5:1).
- God redeemed Israel as an act of compassion and faithfulness to his covenant with Abraham (Ex. 2:24–25; 6:5–6).
- The Lord gave the law to Israel as to his covenant people who had already received his covenantal mercy and national redemption (Ex. 20:2).
- When God revealed the Ten Commandments, he called himself "the LORD thy God" five times by virtue of his gracious covenant with Abraham (Ex. 20:2, 5, 7, 10, 12).
- The law itself was a gift of love, for it revealed wisdom and righ-teousness that would exalt an obedient people (Deut. 4:5–8).

---

54. Calvin, *Commentaries*, on Rom. 10:5.
55. Smith, *Systematic Theology*, 1:338.
56. Brown, *A Dictionary of the Holy Bible*, 1:318.

- God did not give them the Promised Land because of any righteousness in them, but in order to keep his covenant promise to the patriarchs (Deut. 9:4–6).
- The covenantal curses would fall only if the nation persistently refused to repent: "And if ye will not yet for all this hearken unto me, then I will punish you. . . . And if ye will not be reformed by me by these things . . . then will I . . ." (Lev. 26:18, 23–24).
- God did not banish the nation from the land upon its first transgression (as he banished Adam from the garden), but patiently called it to repentance for centuries before sending it into exile (2 Kings 17:13–14, 18; 2 Chron. 36:15–16).
- Even when Israel broke God's covenant and was sent into exile, God promised not to utterly reject them, but to remember his covenant (Lev. 26:44–45).

Furthermore, the covenant of law served as a temporary administration of Christ's saving grace to individuals. It sharply warned of God's wrath against individual covenant breakers who deceived themselves by thinking they did not need to repent.[57] God's judgments against the nation were painful reminders of the necessity of turning back to the Lord and finding forgiveness.[58] The covenant of law threatened death against sinners—"the soul that sinneth, it shall die" (Ezek. 18:4). However, the covenant did not require perfect obedience, but persevering evangelical obedience that included repentance from sins (vv. 26–28). The Lord said to the "house of Israel" that all of the people should "repent, and turn yourselves from all your transgressions. . . . Cast away from you all your transgressions. . . . Turn yourselves, and live" (vv. 30–32). Those individuals who kept God's covenant by repentance and faith received God's blessing (Ps. 25:8–11).[59] Thus, while God's law considered in an absolute sense demands nothing less than perfect obedience, God embedded that law in a gracious covenant.

Therefore, individuals in Israel under the historical covenant of law experienced a complex relation to God's transcendent covenants of works and of grace. Unbelievers were corporately under the national covenant and received many temporal benefits of the covenant of grace, but they

---

57. Deut. 27:15–26; 29:18–21; Jer. 11:3.
58. 1 Kings 8:33–36; cf. 17:1; 18:30–46; Deut. 28:23–25.
59. Nichols, *Covenant Theology*, 224.

remained personally under the broken covenant of works in Adam. Believers were also corporately under the same national covenant and suffered temporal afflictions under the outward display of the covenant of works against sin, but they were individually saved by Christ through the covenant of grace.[60]

God used the covenant of law to further administer his redemptive-historical purposes in the world. The "law of commandments" built a "wall" that divided or separated the Jews from the Gentiles (Eph. 2:14–15). For example, the regulations about clean and unclean things (Leviticus 11–15) made it very difficult for Jews to eat with Gentiles (Acts 10:28; Gal. 2:12). Just as the covenant with Noah created a stable world environment, so the Mosaic covenant created a national/cultural environment in which God preserved the seed of Abraham in the land, especially his spiritual seed who clung to his word (Ps. 78:5–7).[61] Paul compared the law to a confinement or guardian for God's people that aggravated both God's wrath and man's sin, revealing the need for saving grace in Christ.[62] Tragically, many Israelites resisted God's purpose in the law and perverted it into an occasion for hypocritical ethnic pride (Rom. 2:1–3, 17–24) and legalistic self-righteousness (9:31–32). However, this also served God's administration of his saving purposes, for Israel's rejection of Christ became the occasion of the gospel mission to the Gentiles, which set the stage for the reconciliation of "all Israel" to its Redeemer (11:11–12, 25–26).

In the covenant of law, God dramatically expanded his *typological revelation* of Christ's saving grace. The redemption and exodus of Israel, the Passover lamb, the Aaronic priesthood, the tabernacle, and the prophetic ministry of Moses were all types pointing to Christ.[63] The Sabbath days and years foreshadowed the eternal rest into which Christ will lead his people (Ps. 95:11; Heb. 3:7–4:11). Regulations requiring Israelites to discern between clean and unclean to avoid offending God's holiness foreshadowed a sanctified people who, empowered by God's promises, labor to cleanse themselves "from all filthiness of the flesh and spirit, perfecting holiness in the fear of God," knowing that Christ has made them "the temple of the living God" (2 Cor. 6:16; 7:1). All these "types and ordi-

---

60. Colquhoun, *A Treatise on the Law and the Gospel*, 55, 63–64.
61. On God's word and the distinctiveness of the Jews, see Deut. 4:8; Ps. 147:19–20; John 4:22; Rom. 3:1–2.
62. Rom. 4:15; 5:20; 7:8; Gal. 3:19, 22–25; 4:1–4.
63. On these types, see the discussion in chap. 29 of faith in Christ under the law of Moses.

nances" served "to instruct and build up the elect in faith in the promised Messiah, by whom they had full remission of sins, and eternal salvation."[64]

The national covenant presented a picture of man's plight in Adam and God's promise in Christ.[65] In Israel, we see God's "son," his "first-born" (Ex. 4:22), given a blessed place to dwell in God's presence and a holy law to keep, yet proving disobedient and suffering banishment and death—like Adam (Gen. 2:4–3:24; 5:1–5). In this respect, we find an echo of the covenant of works in the covenant of law—not bringing Israel into a covenant of works, but showing the absolute necessity of justification and sanctification in Jesus Christ.[66] Yet types look forward to Christ, not backward to Adam. Israel was a type of Christ, God's Son, who was brought out of Egypt and suffered temptation in the wilderness (Matt. 2:15; 4:1). However, whereas Israel failed and fell because of its corruption in Adam, Christ stood and succeeded as the last Adam.

Abraham's physical offspring abused the external, typological quality of the law to their own harm: "with many of them God was not well pleased" (1 Cor. 10:5). They gloried in outward religion without inner piety.[67] Moses looked ahead to the promise of inner circumcision (Deut 30:6), but lamented, "The LORD hath not given you an heart to perceive, and eyes to see, and ears to hear" (29:4). Given to a people who, for the most part, lacked the Spirit of God, the old covenant was a ministry of "death" and "condemnation" (2 Cor. 3:7, 9).[68] Until Christ came, the spiritual seed of Abraham waited in expectation for the day when God's people would be called "the city of righteousness, the faithful city" (Isa. 1:26; cf. Heb. 12:22).

When Paul looked back to Israel at the Red Sea and in the wilderness of Sinai, he said, "Now these things were our examples, to the intent that we should not lust after evil things, as they also lusted. . . . They are written for our admonition" (1 Cor. 10:6, 11). Christians must learn from Israel's experiences not to presume that outward participation in God's ordinances means that we please God and hence are safe from his judgment. The Israelites received remarkable benefits from God's covenant (vv. 1–4), but most of them proved to be idolaters, immoral sinners, and unbelieving grumblers

---

64. Westminster Confession of Faith (7.5), in *Reformed Confessions*, 4:243.
65. Calvin, *Institutes*, 2.11.3; and Nichols, *Covenant Theology*, 233.
66. Witsius, *The Economy of the Covenants*, 4.4.49 (2:183–84).
67. Isa. 1:10–20; Jer. 7:1–8, 11. The last verse is cited in Luke 19:46.
68. Witsius, *The Economy of the Covenants*, 4.4.47; 4.13.22 (2:183, 372).

(vv. 7–10). Today, many people who participate in Christian worship and even partake of the Lord's Supper may still provoke God's wrath (vv. 16, 22). The failures of Israel under the covenant of law should stir us to watchfulness and self-examination: "Therefore let anyone who thinks that he stands take heed lest he fall" (v. 12 ESV). Do not make the church into a hiding place for hypocrites. Rather, "flee from idolatry" (v. 14).

The Mosaic covenant also reminds us that since the fall of man, God sends his law to us wrapped in grace. Moses shattered the stone tables of the Ten Commandments when Israel broke the covenant (Ex. 32:15–20). God wrote them afresh on new tablets when he revealed his grace (34:1–8, 28), and later they were placed in the ark in the tabernacle, where the priests atoned for sin by sacrificial blood. John Colquhoun said, "This signified that as the ark with the mercy seat was an eminent type of Christ, so the law is *in Christ* to believers, and in His hand is issued forth as from the mercy seat to them."[69] Be comforted, dear believer. The law now comes to you in the hands of Christ. While his yoke is full of authority, it is not a burden, but true liberty and rest (Matt. 11:28–29).[70]

Sing to the Lord

Praising the God of Abraham

> Unto the Lord lift thankful voices,
> Come, worship while your soul rejoices;
> Make known His doings far and near
> That peoples all His Name may fear,
> And tell, in many a joyful lay
> Of all His wonders day by day.
>
> Ye seed from Abraham descended,
> To whom His favors are extended,
> And Jacob's children, whom the Lord
> Has chosen, hearken to His word.
> He is the Lord, our Judge divine;
> In all the earth His glories shine.
>
> Jehovah's truth will stand forever,
> His covenant-bonds He will not sever;

---

69. Colquhoun, *A Treatise on the Law and the Gospel*, 51, emphasis added.
70. Boston's notes in Fisher, *The Marrow of Modern Divinity*, 50.

The word of grace which He commands
To thousand generations stands;
The covenant made in days of old
With Abraham He doth uphold.

Psalm 105
Tune: Pierre
The Psalter, No. 425
Or Tune: Thankful Voices
Trinity Hymnal—Baptist Edition, No. 763

Questions for Meditation or Discussion

1. What two principles do the authors draw from Ephesians 2 regarding "the covenants of promise"? What does each principle mean?

2. List the key Scripture texts for the following covenants: (1) the covenant with Noah, (2) the covenant with Abraham, and (3) the covenant with Israel.

3. What titles do the authors use for these three covenants? Why?

4. What is the outward sign of each of these covenants?

5. How does the covenant with Noah undergird our world with common grace?

6. How does the covenant with Noah point to Christ?

7. A friend of yours says, "God's promises to Abraham were all about physical, temporal benefits such as children and land." How do you respond?

8. How is circumcision a type of Christ's saving work?

9. Your friend also says, "Moses only taught law and works; God revealed grace through Christ." How do you respond?

10. According to Paul, what warning do we learn from the history of Old Testament Israel (1 Cor. 10)? How would you evaluate your life based on that warning?

Questions for Deeper Reflection

11. Did God make one or two covenants with Abraham? Present a biblical-theological argument for your position.

12. On what basis might someone say that the Mosaic covenant is a covenant of works? Do you agree or disagree? Why?

13. The authors distinguish between historical covenants and the eternal covenant of grace, and they analyze the historical covenants before Christ in terms of a distinction between a temporary administration of grace and a typological revelation of grace. Critique these distinctions. How are they helpful and illuminating? How might they overlook or distort aspects of the Bible's teaching on the covenant(s)?

32

The Diverse Administrations of God's Covenant of Grace, Part 2

David and the New Covenant

Although God's redemptive dealings with mankind have progressively revealed his one, eternal covenant of grace, God manifested that covenant in distinct historical covenants. These covenants prior to Christ's coming functioned as temporary administrations of God's grace and typological revelations of Christ. In the previous chapter, we surveyed God's covenant of preservation with Noah and his seed, God's covenant of promise with Abraham and his seed, and God's covenant of law with Israel. In this chapter, we continue our survey by examining the covenant with David and his seed, and the new covenant in Christ.

The Covenant of Kingdom with David and His Seed

Both the Abrahamic and Mosaic covenants anticipated that God would raise up kings for his people (Gen. 17:6; Deut. 17:14–20). After Joshua led the people to inherit the Promised Land, God raised up judges to deliver Israel from its enemies. Israel's first king, Saul, proved to be an object lesson in backsliding until the Lord rejected him (1 Sam. 15:22–23). Saul died in apostasy and disgrace (28:7; 31:4). Despite this tragedy, the Lord had already provided for himself another king, "a man after his own heart,"

David, the son of Jesse, of the tribe of Judah, whom he anointed with the Spirit of the Lord (13:14; 16:1, 13). After many years and much conflict, David secured his kingdom over all Israel and established his throne in Jerusalem (2 Sam. 5:1–10). With him, God made "an everlasting covenant" (2 Sam. 23:5).

Biblical Exposition of the Covenant of Kingdom

The major references to God's covenant or sworn oath to David appear in the Psalms (89:3–4, 19–51; 132:11–18), reflecting on historical accounts that do not explicitly call God's promises to David a covenant (2 Samuel 7; 1 Chronicles 17). The historical background was that the Lord "had given him rest" (*hiphil* of *nuakh*)—that is, dominance over his enemies so that they no longer disturbed the peace of his kingdom (2 Sam. 7:1). Moses had foretold that after Israel inherited the land, "and when he giveth you rest [*hiphil* of *nuakh*] from all your enemies round about, so that ye dwell in safety; then there shall be a place which the LORD your God shall choose to cause his name to dwell there" (Deut. 12:10–11).[1] David evidently recognized the fulfillment of this promise and proposed to Nathan the prophet the construction of a more permanent home for "the ark of God," the golden symbol of God's throne with Israel in the tabernacle (2 Sam. 7:2).

However, the Lord told David that he would *not* build the temple. God reminded David that he had not commanded anyone to build him a house (2 Sam. 7:5–7)—a significant fact, because man is not authorized to worship God in any way except as he commands. The Lord also reminded David that all of his victories had come by God's sovereign grace (vv. 8–9). God did affirm that he had given Israel rest from its enemies, implying that the time to build the temple was near. But though David had aspired to build a house for God, God turned the tables and promised to build David a "house"—that is, a royal dynasty (v. 11). After David died, God would establish forever the kingdom of David's "seed" (v. 12). This royal son would build the "house for my name," the Lord said (v. 13). Later history records the initial fulfillment of this promise in Solomon.[2] In contrast to pagan deities who supposedly rewarded their servants for building

---

1. To "give rest" (*hiphil* of *nuakh*), though often used as a general expression for "to put, set, lay," is used as a special term for God's settling the people to enjoy the Promised Land in peace (Ex. 33:14; Deut. 3:20; 12:10; 25:19; Josh. 1:13, 15; 21:44; 22:4; 23:1; 2 Sam. 7:1, 11; 1 Kings 5:4; 1 Chron. 22:9, 18; 23:25; 2 Chron. 14:6–7; Isa. 63:14). There may be an echo of Eden here, where God "put"—literally, "caused to rest" (*hiphil* of *nuakh*)—the newly created Adam (Gen. 2:15).

2. 1 Kings 3:2; 5:3–5; 8:16–20; 1 Chron. 22:9–10; 28:6.

magnificent temples for them, the Lord does all for his servants out of his sovereign grace, and his temple was constructed not by human merit but in fulfillment of divine promises.[3]

In the midst of these promises, the Lord also promised to have a special relationship with David's royal seed. God said, "I will be his father, and he shall be my son. If he commit iniquity, I will chasten him with the rod of men, and with the stripes of the children of men: but my mercy shall not depart away from him, as I took it from Saul, whom I put away before thee" (2 Sam. 7:14–15). The statement "I will be his father, and he shall be my son" is similar to the formula "[I] will be your God, and ye shall be my people" (Lev. 26:12), implying a covenant between the divine Father and the Davidic son, the King and his king.[4] God thereby made the king the covenant representative of Israel, God's firstborn son (Ex. 4:22). This act of adoption also exalted the Davidic king to supreme authority, "higher than the kings of the earth" (Ps. 89:27; cf. 2:7–8). Best of all, this adoption granted to the kings of the house of David an everlasting place in God's love that their sins could not take away. Though the Father would discipline them, he would not reject David's house forever (89:34; Jer. 33:20–21). Sin can bring disaster upon an individual king who disobeys God, but it could not destroy the Davidic line or kingdom.[5] Dale Davis writes of the covenant of the kingdom in 2 Samuel 7, "Death cannot annul it (vv. 12–13), sin cannot destroy it (vv. 14–15), time will not exhaust it (v. 16)."[6]

Two key words appear repeatedly in God's promise to David and David's response: "servant" (twelve times)[7] and "house" (fourteen times).[8] We have already noted the designation of Abraham and Moses as God's covenantal servants. "Servant" here refers to David in relation to God,[9] whom David addresses six times as "Lord God" or "Master Jehovah" (*Adonai YHWH*).[10] The covenant of the kingdom defined a Lord-servant

---

3. Dale Ralph Davis, *2 Samuel: Out of Every Adversity*, Focus on the Bible (Fearn, Ross-shire, Scotland: Christian Focus, 1999), 74–75.

4. The language of the Davidic covenant corresponds to examples in the ancient Near East when a suzerain "father" king made a covenant with a vassal "son" king. Ronald F. Youngblood, "2 Samuel," in *The Expositor's Bible Commentary, Revised Edition*, ed. Tremper Longman III and David E. Garland, 13 vols. (Grand Rapids, MI: Zondervan, 2006–2012), 3:389.

5. Davis, *2 Samuel*, 78.

6. Davis, *2 Samuel*, 77. We have slightly altered the original formatting and punctuation.

7. 2 Sam. 7:5, 8, 19, 20, 21, 25, 26, 27 (2x), 28, 29 (2x).

8. 2 Sam. 7:1, 2, 5, 6, 7, 11, 13, 16, 18, 19, 25, 26, 27, 29.

9. On God's frequent references to David as "my servant," see 2 Sam. 3:18; 1 Kings 11:13, 32, 34, 36, 38; 14:8; 2 Kings 19:34; 20:6; Ps. 89:3, 20; Isa. 37:15; Jer. 33:21, 22, 26; Ezek. 34:23, 24; 37:24, 25.

10. 2 Sam. 7:18, 19 (2x), 20, 28, 29.

relationship between God and the house of David. The Lord authorized David's "house" to rule God's people as his servant-king for the construction and preservation of God's "house" with his worshipers. The future of the monarchy and temple was tied to the obedience of God's servant, the royal son of David, as the representative and leader of God's people (1 Kings 6:11–13; 9:4–9). The books of Kings and Chronicles trace the rise, decline, renewal, and exile of the royal "house of David."

Theological Reflection on the Covenant of Kingdom

The four decades of Solomon's kingship (1 Kings 11:42) brought unprecedented peace and prosperity to Israel (1 Kings 9–10; 2 Chronicles 9). Truly did outsiders observe that the Lord made Solomon king because God loved Israel (2 Chron. 2:11; 9:8). However, God did not grant the covenant of kingdom to encourage Jews (or Christians) to long for the Messiah to bring a golden age of dominion and wealth for his saints in this fallen world (Matt. 6:19–20, 28–32).[11] Rather, as we have seen with regard to the covenants with Abraham and Israel, this covenant served as a temporary administration and a typological revelation of Christ's grace.

The Lord used the Davidic covenant to implement a *temporary administration* of the covenant of grace to provide for his people. Through David and his seed, the Lord gave Israel:

- *national salvation from enemies*,[12] to guard godly Israelites from being crushed under pagan oppression and assimilated into pagan culture;
- *justice in society*,[13] to protect the righteous poor in Israel and foster their hope in the kingdom of perfect righteousness;[14]
- *stability under God's love*,[15] so that though the people tended to degenerate to the level of Sodom,[16] national destruction was delayed for four centuries;[17]

---

11. The doctrine of the millennium will be discussed under the locus of eschatology in *RST*, vol. 4 (forthcoming).

12. 1 Samuel 17; 2 Sam. 8:1–14; 2 Chron. 14:8–12; 16:7–10.

13. 2 Sam. 8:15; 23:3–5; 1 Kings 10:9; 1 Chron. 18:14; 2 Chron. 9:8.

14. Ps. 72:1–2; Isa. 9:7; Jer. 23:5; 33:15.

15. 2 Sam. 7:15; 23:5; Ps. 89:28–34.

16. Compare the sordid tale of Judges 19 with the events at Sodom recorded in Genesis 19. In the end, Israel became worse than Sodom, and only God's mercy preserved it from a similar doom (Isa. 1:9–10; Ezek. 16:48).

17. 1 Kings 11:13, 32, 34, 36; 15:4; 2 Kings 8:19; 19:34; 20:6; 2 Chron. 7:18; 13:5; 21:7.

- *greater revelation of true spirituality*, in the treasury of experiential devotion found in David's psalms and the wisdom of practical godliness in Solomon's proverbs; and
- *God's special presence secured in God's "house,"* the place God had "chosen,"[18] where God's "name" dwelt and people sought God's forgiveness and help.[19]

The covenant of kingdom was a *typological revelation* of the spiritual and eternal kingdom of Jesus Christ. When believers went to the house of the Lord and observed the rituals, they saw not only the building, priests, and sacrifices visible to the eyes, but by faith they saw God's beauty, power, and glory; found spiritual satisfaction in his goodness and holiness; and perceived the coming judgment.[20] This also was a way in which God administered his saving grace to his elect. Yet the typological quality of the covenant meant that it was only a temporary administration, and both the temple and David's throne fell under God's judgment.

The fulfillment of the kingdom-type would not take place apart from the physical line of David, as promised. For this reason, the covenant continued after God humbled the Davidic throne, shattered its dominion by the hand of Babylon, exiled the royal seed, and returned the people to the land without restoring the monarchy.[21] At points, it appeared that the Lord had rejected the line of David (Ps. 89:38–51). The Lord went so far as to tell King Jeconiah that if he were a "signet" ring upon the Lord's hand, God would pull him off and throw him away, for none of his "seed" would rule upon David's throne (Jer. 22:24, 30). However, the Lord later told Jeconiah's descendant Zerubbabel (1 Chron. 3:10–19; Matt. 1:12) that he was God's chosen servant, taken by the Lord as his "signet" (Hag. 2:23). God empowered Zerubbabel by the Spirit to rebuild the temple (Zech. 4:6–10). The covenant continued for the house of David, but the earthly monarchy had passed, so Zerubbabel never reigned as king in Judah, but only as a governor in the Persian Empire (Hag. 2:21). John Calvin said, "The temporal kingdom, therefore, which involved the house of David, was only a type, so that the substance and ultimate reality of what is constrained in this prophecy cannot be found in it."[22]

---

18. 1 Kings 11:13, 32, 36; 2 Kings 21:7; 23:27; 2 Chron. 6:6; 12:13; 33:7; Zech. 3:2.

19. 1 Kings 8:1, 10–11, 29–50; 9:3.

20. Pss. 27:4; 63:2; 65:4; 73:17–19; 84:1–2. See Witsius, *The Economy of the Covenants*, 4.6.3 (2:189).

21. Robertson, *The Christ of the Covenants*, 249.

22. John Calvin, *Sermons on 2 Samuel, Chapters 1–13*, trans. Douglas Kelly (Edinburgh: Banner of Truth, 1992), 325.

In the historical covenant with David, the Lord chose Mount Zion, the hill on which Jerusalem stands, as the location of his special presence (Ps. 132:11–14). Christ teaches us that this administration of God's presence passed away with his coming (John 4:20–21). Christ himself is now the focus of God's special presence (1:14; 2:19–21), and his throne is in the heavenly Jerusalem (Rev. 21:10; 22:1). However, even in the abolition of the earthly Davidic administration, God continues to keep his covenantal promise to David, who looked forward to Christ's resurrection and session at God's right hand in heaven (Acts 2:30–36).

David, as a real man in history, was a type of Christ in his humiliation under unjust persecution and his exaltation to the throne. The throne of David and Solomon was called "the throne of the LORD" (1 Chron. 29:23) in anticipation of Christ's exaltation to the right hand of God (Ps. 110:1).[23] Therefore, the Messiah is more than the Son of David; he is the Son of God enthroned as David's Lord at his Father's right hand in glory (Matt. 22:41–45). The covenant with David referred immediately to David's merely human offspring Solomon, whom God adopted as his "son," but it referred typologically to God's eternal Son and those in union with him, whether or not they were physical descendants of David.[24]

Other aspects of divine revelation associated with the covenant of kingdom were also typological. David's psalms are full of Christ (Luke 24:44; cf. Ps. 41:9; John 13:18), even in those cases when they may more immediately refer to David's own experience (note Ps. 41:4). The temple was an outward emblem of "Immanuel" (Isa. 7:14), God dwelling with us in the incarnate Lord (John 1:14; 2:19–21), and consequently of the church (Eph. 2:20–22). Just as God used Solomon to build his house, so God's Son said, "I will build my church" (Matt. 16:18). The binding together of God's "house" and David's "house" in the covenant (2 Sam. 7:5–7, 11, 13, 16) anticipated the day when God's temple would be the spiritual seed of the Son of David. The "rest" enjoyed by Israel through the king's victories foreshadowed the eternal rest in Christ.

The typological quality of the Davidic covenant had different effects on the two seeds of Abraham. Abraham's merely physical offspring enjoyed

---

23. Robertson, *The Christ of the Covenants*, 250–51.
24. The promise "I will be his father, and he shall be my son" (2 Sam. 7:14; 1 Chron. 17:13) was applied immediately to Solomon (22:9–10; 28:6), but applied typologically in the New Testament to Christ as God's eternal Son (Heb. 1:2–3, 5) and to the church as God's adopted sons and daughters (2 Cor. 6:18). On the immediate and typological referents of God's promises to David, see Youngblood, "2 Samuel," in *The Expositor's Bible Commentary, Revised Edition*, ed. Longman and Garland, 3:390.

the covenant's physical and political blessings while their hearts remained unconverted. Yet their merely external worship was rebuked by the psalms of David, which demanded nothing less than integrity and piety in the heart (Pss. 15:1–5; 24:3–4), and instructed sinners to seek forgiveness and cleansing by grace (25:4–14; 32:1–2; 51:1–19). The prophets called them to turn from their sins back to the Lord and to receive by faith the free grace of the coming kingdom (Isa. 55:1–7), for the Lord promised, "I will make an everlasting covenant with you, even the sure mercies of David" (v. 3).[25] For the spiritual offspring of Abraham, the covenant of kingdom and its fruits encouraged their hope in great David's greater Son, the Son of God. The Lord promised to send "my servant David" to be the shepherd-king of his people (Ezek. 34:23–24; 37:24–25), a promise fulfilled in the Good Shepherd (John 10:11).

Are you hoping in a future kingdom of righteousness and peace? The only way to attain this kingdom is by trusting in the King of righteousness and Prince of Peace. Christ alone can bring you to the kingdom of God, for he is the Son of David.

The New Covenant through Our Lord Jesus Christ

We come now to the climax of God's historical covenants, the fullest and final revelation of his covenant of grace that we will receive in this age: the new covenant. Reformed theologians have sometimes used the term "new covenant" as a synonym for the covenant of grace, but in the Bible, the "new covenant" is a distinct historical administration of God's gracious purposes that follows the covenants with Abraham, Israel, and David. Morton Smith said, "The plan of salvation is successively revealed by a series of gracious covenants culminating in the New Covenant."[26] The new covenant was formally ratified by the death of Christ and hence is a "testament," or sovereign disposition, of Christ's inheritance after his death (Luke 22:20; Heb. 9:15–16).[27]

Biblical Exposition of the New Covenant

The later Hebrew prophets looked ahead to another historical covenant that God promised to make with his people, called a "covenant of peace"

---

25. In Isa. 55:3, the phrase "everlasting covenant" (*berit 'olam*) alludes to 2 Sam. 23:5, and the word "mercies" (*khesed*) alludes to 2 Sam. 7:15. See also Ps. 89:1–3, 28.

26. Smith, *Systematic Theology*, 1:336.

27. Owen, *An Exposition of the Epistle to the Hebrews*, 6:64, 74. See the Canons of Dort (Head 2, Rej. 2), in *The Three Forms of Unity*, 137–38.

and an "everlasting covenant."[28] Once it is called a "new covenant" (Jer. 31:31), a phrase later picked up by the Gospels and Epistles, especially the epistle to the Hebrews.[29] This covenant promised salvation for God's people by God's Christ in the midst of God's judgment on Israel and its royal line, as threatened in the Mosaic and Davidic covenants. The Lord promised to send his Spirit-anointed Servant to be "for a covenant of the people, for a light of the Gentiles" (Isa. 42:1, 6). God's Servant, the embodiment of "the covenant of the people," would not only save Israel, but also bring God's "salvation unto the end of the earth" (49:6, 8). This is spiritual salvation, in which God's people are honored as "priests of the LORD" who are clothed in "the garments of salvation" and "the robe of righteousness" (61:6–11), for the Lord "will make an everlasting covenant with them" (v. 8). The kingdom of David's son would be boundless (9:6–7), so that the nations would seek the Lord and his Word, and learn his peace and justice (2:1–4) until, by the grace of the Spirit-empowered King, "the earth shall be full of the knowledge of the LORD, as the waters cover the sea" (11:1–9).

God promised, "As for me, this is my covenant with them, saith the LORD; my spirit that is upon thee, and my words which I have put in thy mouth, shall not depart out of thy mouth, nor out of the mouth of thy seed, nor out of the mouth of thy seed's seed, saith the LORD, from henceforth and for ever" (Isa. 59:21; cf. Rom. 11:26–27). This promise could be interpreted as a corporate reference to Zion or Israel, and "seed" as the members of the covenant community (cf. Isa. 54:1–3). However, it is better understood as a reference to God's Servant. God's covenant with his people revolves around an individual ("thee") who is anointed by the Spirit and given the prophetic word to speak—the Christ.[30] The promise of the covenant consists in the everlasting gift of

---

28. This terminology is not limited to any one covenant. "Covenant of peace" is used of the new covenant (Isa. 54:10; Ezek. 34:25; 37:26) and the priestly covenant with Phinehas (Num. 25:12; cf. Mal. 2:5). "Everlasting covenant" is used of the new covenant (Isa. 61:8; Jer. 32:40; 50:5; Ezek. 16:60; 37:26) and a variety of other covenants and their signs (Gen. 17:7, 13, 19; Ex. 31:16; Lev. 24:8; Num. 25:13; 2 Sam. 23:5; 1 Chron. 16:17; Ps. 105:10). A similar expression for a perpetual covenant is a "covenant of salt" (Num. 18:19; 2 Chron. 13:5; cf. Lev. 2:13).

29. Matt. 26:28; Mark 14:24; Luke 22:20; 1 Cor. 11:25; 2 Cor. 3:6; Heb. 8:8, 13; 9:15; 12:24. There are textual variants in the texts of Matthew and Mark, some of which omit "new." The KJV often renders it "new testament."

30. Isa. 11:2, 4; 42:1; 49:2; 51:16. J. Alec Motyer, *Isaiah: An Introduction and Commentary*, Tyndale Old Testament Commentaries 20 (Downers Grove, IL: InterVarsity Press, 1999), 419; cf. Gary Smith, *Isaiah 40–66*, The New American Commentary 15B (Nashville: Broadman & Holman, 2009), 604–6.

the Spirit and the word to Christ's "seed," those whom he would redeem and justify by his death (53:10–11). In context, his "seed" is not defined by physical descent but by spiritual allegiance: "them that turn from transgression in Jacob" and those who "fear the name of the LORD from the west, and his glory from the rising of the sun" (59:19–20). They are Israel's "children" by union with the Lord, for they are effectually "taught of the LORD" and are beyond the reach of condemnation, for "their righteousness is of me, saith the LORD" (54:13, 17; cf. John 6:45). By union with the greater Joshua, they will forever keep God's word in their "mouth" as Joshua did by continual meditation, and the Lord will be with them (Josh. 1:8).[31]

The prophets portray the new covenant as God's renewal of a failed marriage by making everlasting vows (Isa. 54:4–10) and transforming an adulterous woman into a repentant wife (Ezek. 16:1–8, 59–63). This renewed marriage would redefine Zion: formerly the "city" that was a "harlot," it would be purged and redeemed to be "the city of righteousness, the faithful city" (Isa. 1:21–27). The prophecy of Hosea extensively develops this marriage metaphor as an image of the new covenant, vividly illustrated by Hosea's experiences with his own unfaithful wife. The Lord said, "And I will betroth thee unto me for ever; yea, I will betroth thee unto me in righteousness, and in judgment, and in lovingkindness, and in mercies. I will even betroth thee unto me in faithfulness: and thou shalt know the LORD" (Hos. 2:19–20). As in Ezekiel, the background of this commitment was Israel's whoring after things, people, and idols (vv. 2–13). Nevertheless, God made an everlasting covenantal commitment, for a betrothal in the ancient world was a solemn pledge to be married that legally bound the couple as husband and wife even before they lived together.[32] Gary Smith comments, "God will create an unconditional, everlasting, and unending connection between himself and his covenant people."[33] His covenant would be "defined by" his attributes of righteousness, justice, faithful love, and mercy.[34] In fact, the same Hebrew syntax can be used for

31. Young, *The Book of Isaiah*, 3:441.
32. Ex. 22:16; Deut. 20:7; 22:23–30; Matt. 1:18; Luke 1:27. See Thomas E. McComiskey, "Hosea," in *The Minor Prophets: An Exegetical and Expository Commentary*, ed. Thomas E. McComiskey, 3 vols. (Grand Rapids, MI: Baker, 1992–1998), 1:45.
33. Gary V. Smith, *Hosea, Amos, Micah*, The NIV Application Commentary (Grand Rapids, MI: Zondervan, 2001), 63.
34. McComiskey, "Hosea," in *The Minor Prophets*, 1:45. He says the preposition "by" in this passage "denotes the sphere of the action of the verb. Yahweh's efforts to woo Israel will be in the sphere of, and thus limited and defined by, the following attributes."

the groom paying the bride price (2 Sam. 3:14).[35] God, not his people, was the One who would pay the price to enter into a new covenant between himself and his disgraced bride. Though the law requires God's people to fulfill the demands of righteousness and justice, God would fulfill the law's requirements for them. Yet they would also be transformed into faithful covenant partners: "thou shalt know the LORD" (Hos. 2:20), not merely in the mind, but with faithful love and covenant keeping (4:1–3, 6; 6:6–7).[36] Though spoken immediately to Israel, this covenant included the Gentiles as well (Rom. 9:25–26, citing Hos. 1:10; 2:1).[37]

Prophecies of the new covenant also employed the metaphor of a shepherd and his sheep to foretell the coming of the King. The "shepherds of Israel" had exploited and neglected the sheep (Ezek. 34:1–8). The Lord declared that he would seek after his lost sheep, save them, judge the wicked among them, and put them in good pastures (vv. 11–22). God promised that "my servant David"—that is, Christ the Son of David—would shepherd them as their King, and "I the LORD will be their God. . . . And I will make with them a covenant of peace" (vv. 23–25). They would enjoy safety and abundance in the land, "showers of blessing" that would make the earth fruitful (vv. 26–28), a promise that was partially fulfilled when the exiles returned but that would not find complete fulfillment until the home of God's people became "like the garden of Eden" (36:35; cf. Isa. 51:3). Though the people were like wandering sheep, God would reassert his authority over them as their Shepherd and "bring [them] into the bond of the covenant" (Ezek. 20:37).[38] By his grace, his "lost sheep" would gladly say, "Come, and let us join ourselves to the LORD in a perpetual covenant that shall not be forgotten" (Jer. 50:5–6). The "covenant of peace" would be "an everlasting covenant with them" (Ezek. 37:26), in which God promised that he would cleanse them from their sins, "David my servant" would reign over them, they would obey his commandments, they would dwell safely in the land, and he would set his holy presence with them forever (vv. 23–28).

The most significant Old Testament revelation of the new covenant took place in Jeremiah's "book of consolation" (chaps. 30–33). The Lord told the people of Israel that he would restore them to the land, release

---

35. Duane A. Garrett, *Hosea, Joel*, The New American Commentary 19A (Nashville: Broadman & Holman, 1997), 93.

36. Garrett, *Hosea, Joel*, 93–94.

37. McComiskey, "Hosea," in *The Minor Prophets*, 1:45.

38. The figurative statement "I will cause you to pass under the rod" (Ezek. 20:37) invokes the picture of a shepherd counting his sheep (Lev. 27:32).

them from their bondage (Jer. 30:1–8), and grant that they "shall serve the LORD their God, and David their king, whom I will raise up unto them" (v. 9). This was a promise not merely of a restored Davidic monarchy, but of the coming Messiah already mentioned in Jeremiah's prophecy (23:5).[39] The Lord renewed his covenant promise that he would be their God and they would be his people (30:22), for he had loved them with "an everlasting love" (31:1, 3). On his side, he was Israel's loving Father; on their side, Israel repented of sin (vv. 9, 18–20).

God would "make a new covenant" with Israel and Judah, "not according to the covenant" he made when he saved them from Egypt, which they broke (Jer. 31:31–32). It could be called "new"[40] not only in contrast to the previous covenantal administrations, but also in connection with the theme of salvation as a "new" creation:[41] "the LORD hath created a new thing" (v. 22).[42] The new covenant contains the following promises (vv. 33–34), which, in contrast to the "if ye will" of the Mosaic covenant (Ex. 19:5; cf. Jer. 11:3–4), stand on God's unilateral "I will":

- *Inward covenant faithfulness:* "I will put my law in their inward parts, and write it in their hearts." The Lord wrote the Ten

---

39. John L. Mackay, *Jeremiah: An Introduction and Commentary, Volume 2: Chapters 21–52,* Mentor Commentary (Fearn, Ross-shire, Scotland: Christian Focus, 2004), 190.

40. Though it is sometimes argued that the Hebrew adjective translated as "new" (*khadash*) means "renewed," the lexical support for this argument is not convincing. Though the verbal form (*piel* of *khadash*) means "renew" (1 Sam. 11:14; Pss. 51:22; 104:30), the adjective translated as "new" (*khadash*) in Jer. 31:31 often means "recently made or obtained," as in a "new king" (Ex. 1:8), new food as opposed to old food from a previous harvest (Lev. 26:10), a "new" or recently built house (Deut. 20:5; 22:8), a "new wife," one just married (Deut. 24:5), "new gods" as opposed to the Lord, whom they had known (Deut. 32:17; Judg. 5:8), or newly made objects such as containers, tools, clothing, or carts (Josh. 9:13; Judg. 15:13; 16:11–12; 1 Sam. 6:7; 2 Sam. 6:3; 21:16; 1 Kings 11:29–30; 2 Kings 2:20; 1 Chron. 13:7; Job 32:19; Isa. 41:15). See *NIDOTTE*, 2:30–32. Texts that *might* support the meaning of "renewed" or "repaired" are "the new court" (2 Chron. 20:5); "my glory [life] was fresh [renewed] in me" (Job 29:20); and "the new gate" (Jer. 26:10; 36:10). It is also sometimes argued that the Greek word used of the "new" (*kainos*) covenant (Heb. 8:8, 13; 9:15) means "renewed" as opposed to another term (*neos*) that means "new in time." However, *kainos* is used of "new bottles" or wineskins (Matt. 9:17), "new" treasures versus "old" (Matt. 13:52), "new" cloth versus "old" (Mark 2:21), and a "new" tomb where no one has yet been buried (John 19:41). Furthermore, though Hebrews 8–9 uses *kainos* of the new covenant, the same epistle also uses *neos* of the same covenant (Heb. 12:24). *Kainos* and *neos* appear together as apparent synonyms in contrast to "old" (Luke 5:36–39; compare Eph. 4:22–24 with Col. 3:9–10). Therefore, the proposed linguistic distinction fails.

41. On the theme of God's "new" work or creation, see Ps. 51:10; Isa. 42:9–10; 43:18–21; 48:6–7; 62:2; 65:17–18; 66:22; Ezek. 11:19; 18:31; 36:26.

42. The verb translated as "created" (*bara'*) in Jer. 31:22 is consistently used of divine acts of creation. The subsequent phrase, "A woman shall compass a man," is difficult to interpret, but may mean that Israel, pictured in this context as a "virgin" and "daughter" (vv. 21–22), though weak and suffering in itself (30:6), will "besiege" (*sabab*, cf. Josh. 7:9) her enemy, though he be like a "mighty man" (*geber*, cf. Jer. 41:16). See Calvin, *Commentaries*, on Jer. 31:22. For other interpretations, see Mackay, *Jeremiah*, 2:226–27.

Commandments on tablets of stone (Ex. 31:18), but now God creates a holy desire to do his will (Ps. 40:8). Though individuals in Israel had this inward grace (37:30–31; Isa. 51:7), many had sin deeply engraved in their hearts (Jer. 17:1). God promised to give his whole people a new heart with new springs of motivation to obey (Ezek. 11:19; 36:26–27). Prosper of Aquitaine (c. 390–c. 455) said, "He infuses his will into the hearts of those who are called . . . [and] with the pen of the Holy Spirit the Truth mercifully rewrites on the pages of their souls all that the devil enviously falsified."[43]

- *Covenantal union and communion*: "[I] will be their God, and they shall be my people. And they shall teach no more every man his neighbour, and every man his brother, saying, Know the Lord: for they shall all know me, from the least of them unto the greatest of them, saith the Lord." Though individuals such as Josiah knew the Lord in a practical, righteous manner (Jer. 22:15–16), the nation was characterized by a refusal to know the Lord (2:8; 9:3, 6) and his good ways (4:22), and thus was like the Gentiles under God's wrath (10:25). From this willful spiritual ignorance God would save them, creating a people defined by the experiential knowledge of God.[44] God promised to do this by the gift of a new heart (24:7). God would join himself to them in mutual love and fellowship (Lev. 26:11–12; Ezek. 37:27). He would be theirs; they would be his. Augustine said, "God has promised us himself as our reward."[45]

- *Permanent atonement for sin's guilt*: "For I will forgive their iniquity, and I will remember their sin no more." To "remember" sin is to reject sinners and punish them (Jer. 14:10; Hos. 8:13).[46] The opposite implies the complete atonement of guilt so that the offender is utterly forgiven (cf. Jer. 33:8). The word "for" indicates that this forgiveness was the foundation upon which the previous promises rested. God would provide perfect, once-for-all atonement in a manner that the old covenant sacrifices could only foreshadow. Therefore, the new covenant implied the abolition of the ceremonial law with its sacrifices (Heb. 10:14–18) and the replacement of the Aaronic priesthood with another, perfect Priest (7:11–28; cf. Ps. 110:4).

---

43. Prosper of Aquitaine, *The Call of All Nations*, 1.8, in *ACCS/OT*, 12:219.
44. Hos. 2:20; John 10:14; 17:2–3; Gal. 4:8–9; Phil. 3:8; 2 Pet. 1:3; 1 John 2:13–14, 27; 5:20.
45. Augustine, Sermon 331.4, in *Works*, 3/9:192, cited in *ACCS/OT*, 12:216.
46. See also Pss. 25:7; 109:14; Isa. 43:25; Hos. 9:9.

Jeremiah 31:31–34 is the longest Old Testament text quoted in the New Testament and a central text for the argument in the book of Hebrews for the superiority and sufficiency of Christ (Heb. 8:8–12; cf. 10:16–17). The author of Hebrews says that Christ "obtained a more excellent ministry" than the Aaronic priests because "he is the mediator of a better covenant, which was established upon better promises" (8:6). In contrast to the conditional promises of the old covenant, which Israel broke (v. 9), the new covenant has unconditional promises that God will make his people to be forgiven covenant breakers transformed into covenant keepers (vv. 10–12). Promises of spiritual and eternal blessing require a Mediator who can convey such blessings; Jeremiah's "new covenant" requires the coming of Christ (cf. Jer. 23:5–6; 31:9; 33:15–16).

Calvin commented, "God made a new covenant, when he accomplished through his Son whatever had been shadowed forth under the Law." For example, the animal sacrifices could not make propitiation for sin, but Christ accomplished redemption. "But," Calvin said, "the coming of Christ would not have been sufficient, had not regeneration by the Holy Spirit been added. It was, then, in some respects, a new thing, that God regenerated the faithful by his Spirit, so that it became not only a doctrine as to the letter, but also efficacious, which not only strikes the ear, but penetrates into the heart, and really forms us for the service of God."[47] Whereas "many aspects of the Mosaic covenant were external," John Mackay observes, now God promised a covenant that he would write internally to produce "genuine spiritual change."[48]

The covenantal promise "they shall be my people" would be fulfilled when God gave them a new heart "that they may fear me for ever . . . I will put my fear in their hearts, that they shall not depart from me";[49] the promise "I will be their God" would find its consummation in the divine resolve: "I will make an everlasting covenant with them, that I will not turn away from them, to do them good. . . . Yea, I will rejoice over them to do them good" (Jer. 32:38–41). The Lord declared in Jeremiah's book of consolation his intention to both "cleanse" and "pardon" his people, all for the praise of his name among all the nations (33:8–9).

---

47. Calvin, *Commentaries*, on Jer. 31:31–32.
48. Mackay, *Jeremiah*, 2:236–37.
49. On the fear of the Lord as the essence of a proper response to God and his Word, see Deut. 4:10; 5:29; 6:1–2; 10:12; 28:58; Eccl. 12:13; Jer. 5:20–24; 10:7.

The last promises of the Old Testament regarding this covenant centered upon Christ. He is "the messenger of the covenant," who would come "like a refiner's fire, and like fullers' soap" to cleanse God's people so that their worship would please the Lord (Mal. 3:1–4). The "King" would come humbly to Jerusalem, riding on a donkey, but bringing a worldwide kingdom of peace (Zech. 9:9–10), and, "By the blood of thy covenant I have sent forth thy prisoners out of the pit wherein is no water" (v. 11). God had ratified the covenant of law by "the blood of the covenant" (Ex. 24:8), but the law could not deliver Israel from its curses upon their sins (Zech. 5:1–4): the old covenant was broken (11:10). This, then, was a promise of another covenant that would release the prisoners from a hopeless death and make them "prisoners of hope" (9:12). Whose blood would ratify this covenant? Zechariah's prophecies suggested that it would be the blood of the shepherd sold for thirty pieces of silver (11:12–13), against whom God would send the "sword" of divine judgment (13:7; cf. Matt. 26:15, 31).

In the New Testament, there is a reference to the new covenant in Christ's institution of the Lord's Supper,[50] several in Hebrews,[51] and a few others.[52] Although the Holy Scriptures do not explicitly identify a "sign" for the new covenant, Christ's words "This cup . . . is the new covenant" (Luke 22:20 ESV) are similar to God's statement "This is my covenant" regarding circumcision (Gen. 17:10). The Lord's Supper, then, is the sign of the new covenant. Christ's instructions for the Supper link the new covenant to his blood shed for the forgiveness of sins (Matt. 26:28). The new covenant feast is not a remembrance of national deliverance from Egypt, as was the Passover, but a remembrance of eternal salvation from sin by the body and blood of Christ offered up in his death (1 Cor. 11:23–26). Jesus is the "surety" of the new covenant (Heb. 7:22), the Priest whose once-for-all sacrifice and continual intercession as the Righteous One guarantees the salvation of his people (vv. 25–27). Christ is the Mediator of all the graces involved in the covenant's "better promises" (8:6–12): his priestly ministry establishes the foundational promise of complete atonement for sins; his kingly ministry fulfills the promise of writing the law upon the heart; and

---

50. Matt. 26:28; Mark 14:24; Luke 22:20; 1 Cor. 11:25.
51. Heb. 7:22; 8:6–10, 13; 9:15–17; 10:16, 29; 12:24; 13:20.
52. Rom. 11:27; 2 Cor. 3:6. See also the covenant grant of the kingdom in Luke 22:29 (Greek), as discussed in chap. 30. Galatians 4:24 appears to refer to the covenant of grace that spans redemptive history.

his prophetic ministry causes his people to know the Lord. Christ applies these blessings by the ministry of the Holy Spirit (2 Cor. 3:3–6).

The life and soul of the new covenant is our Lord Jesus Christ. This explains the relative scarcity of explicit references to the covenant in the New Testament books of the Bible. Christ himself has arrived, and his person and work fill the pages of the Gospels and Epistles.

Theological Reflection on the New Covenant

The new covenant is the historical administration of Christ's saving grace to which the types of previous covenants pointed. Christ is the Mediator of the new covenant, for his blood redeemed sinners from their transgressions, including those committed under the law of Moses (Heb. 9:15). In this sense, the grace of the new covenant reaches back to the previous historical covenants and binds them together as one covenant of grace, for no one can be saved apart from Christ.

However, as a distinct historical covenant, the new covenant has the character of a "testament" that was not ratified in a formal sense until "the death of the testator" (Heb. 9:16–17). In that sense, the new covenant had a beginning in time ("the days come . . . when I will make a new covenant," 8:8), though the covenant of grace was conceived in eternity. Isaac Ambrose said, "As Christ, so the covenant of grace (which applies Christ to us), was first promised and then promulgated [legally executed]. . . . The covenant promulgated, or new covenant . . . is that covenant which God makes with all believers since the coming of Christ."[53] Furthermore, since Christ's death accomplished redemption "once for all" (10:10; cf. 7:27; 9:12), the new covenant is not a temporary administration of the covenant of grace, but an "everlasting covenant" (13:20). Its glory will not fade away like the old covenant (8:13; cf. 2 Cor. 3:7–11), but will shine with even greater brightness when Christ returns.

Jeremiah's new covenant was explicitly made "with the house of Israel, and with the house of Judah" (Jer. 31:31). God's promises to "the seed of Israel" cannot fail (vv. 35–37). What then of the Gentile nations? Jeremiah prophesied God's judgment upon them, but offered glimmers of hope.[54] Other prophets foretold the gathering of Gentiles into God's

---

53. Ambrose, *Looking unto Jesus*, 90. We have slightly adjusted the punctuation to fit modern standards.

54. Jeremiah 46–51 contains oracles of judgment on the nations, but these include some promises of restoration from captivity (46:26; 48:47; 49:6, 39) and an invitation for the fatherless and widows to trust in the Lord (49:11).

salvation.[55] In the prophecy of Zechariah, the Lord applied to the Gentiles the "their God, my people" promise central to the new covenant: "Many nations shall be joined to the LORD in that day, and shall be my people" (Zech. 2:11). O. Palmer Robertson says, "Now the essence of the covenantal relationship explicitly is being extended to the inclusion of Gentiles."[56]

The new covenant defines membership in God's new covenant community according to inward law-keeping and knowledge of God, not outward ritual or genealogical descent from Abraham (Jer. 31:33–34). The "one heart, and one way" that unifies new covenant Israel is the fear of the Lord that makes people alive and responsive to his Word (32:39–40; cf. Ezek. 11:19).[57] This was the circumcision of the heart promised by Moses (Deut. 30:6). Though not explicit in these texts, the spiritual essence of the new covenant opens the way for the inclusion of the Gentiles. Physical Israelites who did not participate in the spiritual circumcision would be cut off from the covenant people, whereas Gentile outsiders to whom God gave saving grace would be grafted into the people of God (Rom. 2:25–29; 11:17–24). Yet the new covenant does not abandon the physical offspring of Abraham, for it centers upon Jesus Christ, the Seed of Abraham (Gal. 3:16); it was first executed with the apostles and the community gathered with them, who were all Jews; and it is being fulfilled in the world by the gospel, which is for the Jew first and also for the Gentile (Rom. 1:16).

How should we compare the old covenant and the new covenant? Before we answer that question, we must clarify what we mean by "old covenant." Only once do the Holy Scriptures speak explicitly of the "old" covenant (2 Cor. 3:14), where Paul refers to the writings and ministry of Moses (vv. 7, 13) in contrast to the "new" covenant ministry of the apostles by the Spirit (v. 6).[58] In a handful of texts in Hebrews, we read of the "first" covenant, in contrast to the covenant that is "better," "second,"

---

55. Ps. 22:27; Isa. 2:2–3; 11:9; 19:25; 42:1–7; 49:6–7; 56:7; 65:1; Zeph. 3:9–10; Mal. 1:11; Luke 24:45–47.

56. Robertson, *The Christ of the Covenants*, 48.

57. For "one heart" as an expression of unity among people, see 1 Chron. 12:38; 2 Chron. 30:12; Acts 4:32. See Gerald L. Keown, Pamela J. Scalise, and Thomas G. Smothers, *Jeremiah 26–52*, Word Biblical Commentary 27 (Nashville: Thomas Nelson, 1995), 160–61. Alternatively, "one heart, and one way" could be interpreted as integrity and holistic devotion to the Lord as opposed to double-mindedness. See Mackay, *Jeremiah*, 2:263.

58. The "reading" of the "old testament" implies that writings are in view (2 Cor. 3:14). See also Heb. 8:13, where "made . . . old" translates a verb (perfect *palaioō*) related to the adjective translated as "old" (*palaios*). The same verb also appears later in this verse, where it is translated

and "new" (Heb. 8:6–8).[59] The language clearly indicates that two distinct historical covenants are in view. The first covenant consists of "the covenant that I made with their fathers in the day when I took them by the hand to lead them out of the land of Egypt" (v. 9). Narrowly speaking, then, the "old covenant" is the covenant of law made with Israel through Moses. However, the Lord brought Israel out of Egypt as a fulfillment of his covenant with Abraham before he made the covenant of law at Mount Sinai (Ex. 6:2–8).[60] Therefore, the old or first covenant broadly includes all of what we today call the "Old Testament."

There are several differences between the old covenant and the new covenant.[61] These differences spring from Christ's coming in the flesh to accomplish redemption. Christ is the embodiment of the new covenant (Isa. 42:6).[62] Therefore, the new covenant brings the following:

- *A greater revelation of God's saving grace* (John 1:14, 17). Instead of the "letter" of the law, it brings "the ministry of the Spirit" to God's people (2 Cor. 3:6, 8 ESV).[63] Instead of "the ministry of condemnation" to a nation of unbelievers, it gives "the ministry of righteousness" in the justification of a church of believers (v. 9 ESV).

- *The substance of the outward shadows given under the old covenant* (Col. 2:16–17; Heb. 10:1). The ministry of Melchizedek, the promise of Canaan to the patriarchs, the Aaronic priesthood, and the holy places in Jerusalem built by the son of David all give way to the new covenant's focus on Christ and the Holy Spirit.[64]

- *Boldness to draw near to God* (Heb. 4:14–15; 10:19, 22). Though God remains "a consuming fire" requiring godly reverence (12:28–29), the new covenant welcomes believers to approach him with liberty, not the terror of the Israelites at Mount Sinai (vv. 18–24).

- *A transformed people who enjoy a real spiritual union and communion with God.* Though there are still false brethren in the church

---

as "decayeth" (present *palaioō*) and is parallel to "waxeth old" (*geraskō*). The emphasis in Heb. 8:13 is on the first covenant's passing away.

59. On the "first" covenant, see Heb. 8:7, 13; 9:1, 15, 18; cf. "first tabernacle" (9:6, 8) and "first" referring to "sacrifices and offering," with "second" referring to God's "will" for Christ's death (10:9).

60. Robertson, *The Christ of the Covenants*, 281.

61. Calvin, *Institutes*, 2.11; and Leigh, *A Treatise of the Divine Promises*, 74–76.

62. See Witsius, *The Economy of the Covenants*, 4.15.1–19 (2:405–13).

63. On the "spirit" versus the "letter," see also Rom. 2:29; 7:6.

64. See the typological interpretations in Heb. 7:1–10; 9:1–28; 11:8–10, 13–16; 12:22–24; 13:9–16.

(Gal. 2:4), the covenant promise is "all shall know me, from the least to the greatest" (Heb. 8:11). Instead of a nation of covenant breakers (Hos. 6:6–7), the new covenant people of God are "saints" sanctified by Christ and the indwelling Spirit (1 Cor. 1:2; 6:11, 19–20).

- *God's saving grace sent out to all nations.* The old covenant limited God's grace to Israel and those Gentiles whom the Lord attracted to his people and temple (1 Kings 8:41–42). In Christ, God's salvation goes out to the world (Isa. 49:6; Acts 13:47) to bless all nations, as God promised Abraham (Gen. 12:3; 22:18).

The ancient covenants with Abraham, Israel, and David were temporary administrations of God's grace in Christ, but the new covenant is an "eternal covenant" because it stands upon Christ's accomplishment of an "eternal redemption" through the "eternal Spirit" so that his people will receive an "eternal inheritance" (Heb. 9:12, 14–15; 13:20 ESV). These things are not typological revelations of saving grace, such as those found in the earlier covenants that "made nothing perfect" (7:19; cf. 9:9; 10:1; 11:40). The new covenant promises that very grace by which Christ has "perfected" his people (10:14) so that they enter the heavenly Jerusalem as "the spirits of just men made perfect" (12:22–23) and await the resurrection (6:2; 11:35). However, as we will argue in the next chapter, the new covenant fulfills all God's covenants, which together are one covenant of grace. This is because the sum and center of every divine covenant is Jesus Christ.

We should not consider the new covenant without hungering and praying for its promises to be fulfilled in our lives. Without the grace promised in this covenant, God's laws will do nothing but condemn us, for they are not written in our hearts and we are blind to Christ (2 Cor. 3:1–4:6). We must know the Lord, for there is no greater treasure, wisdom, or power (Jer. 9:24–25). Therefore, let us earnestly pray with Calvin:

Grant, Almighty God, that as thou hast favoured us with so singular a benefit as to make through thy Son a covenant which has been ratified for our salvation—O grant, that we may become partakers of it, and know that thou so speakest with us, that thou not only shewest us by thy Word what is right, but speakest also to us inwardly by thy Spirit, and thus renderest us teachable and obedient, that there may be an evidence of our adoption, and a proof that thou wilt govern and rule us, until we shall at length be really and fully united to thee through Christ our Lord. Amen.[65]

As we lift up these desires to God, let us look to God's only begotten Son, Jesus Christ. The new covenant is the covenant ratified in his blood. None of its promises can come to fruition in your life apart from the One who was crucified for our sins and rose again. Over the course of our study of the diverse administrations of God's covenant of grace, we have repeatedly called you to examine yourself. Such self-examination boils down to this: Do you know Christ? Do you have him? God's covenantal testimony on this point is plain and simple: "God hath given to us eternal life, and this life is in his Son. He that hath the Son hath life; and he that hath not the Son of God hath not life" (1 John 5:11–12).

Sing to the Lord

Praise God for the Son of David

Christ shall have dominion over land and sea,
Earth's remotest regions shall His empire be;
They that wilds inhabit shall their worship bring,
Kings shall render tribute, nations serve our King.

Refrain:
Christ shall have dominion over land and sea,
Earth's remotest regions shall His empire be.

When the needy seek Him, He will mercy show;
Yea, the weak and helpless shall His pity know;
He will surely save them from oppression's might,
For their lives are precious in His holy sight.

Ever and forever shall His Name endure,
Long as suns continue it shall stand secure;
And in Him forever all men shall be blest,
And all nations hail Him King of kings confessed.

Unto God Almighty joyful Zion sings;
He alone is glorious, doing wondrous things.

---

65. Calvin, *Commentaries*, on Jer. 31:33.

Evermore, ye people, bless His glorious Name,
His eternal glory thro' the earth proclaim.

Psalm 72
Tune: St. Gertrude (same as "Onward, Christian Soldiers")
The Psalter, No. 200
Trinity Hymnal—Baptist Edition, No. 678

Questions for Meditation or Discussion

1. What are the major texts in the Bible regarding God's covenant with David?
2. What did God promise to David concerning his "seed"?
3. What two key words appear repeatedly in God's promises to David? What is the significance of these words in the covenant?
4. What were five major benefits of God's covenant with David for Israel at the time?
5. What are some other titles given to the "new covenant"?
6. What promises did Isaiah record regarding this covenant?
7. How is the new covenant portrayed like a renewed marriage?
8. What specific promises did the Lord give in Jeremiah 31:31–34?
9. To what does the Bible refer when it speaks of the "old covenant"? Prove it from Scripture.
10. In what five ways does the new covenant excel the old covenant?
11. Can you claim the promises of the new covenant as your own? Why or why not?

Questions for Deeper Reflection

12. The authors point to Psalm 41 as an example of a psalm that refers directly to David but typologically to Christ. Do you agree with their interpretation? Why or why not?
13. In what sense is the new covenant in Jeremiah 31 "new"?
14. How does the new covenant promised in the prophets relate to the eternal covenant of grace? Are the two identical or distinct in some way? Explain and defend your answer.

33

The Essential Unity of God's Covenant of Grace

Behind the historical covenants God made with his people stands one covenant of grace.[1] John Calvin said, "The covenant made with all the patriarchs is so much like ours in substance and reality that the two are actually one and the same. Yet they differ in the mode of dispensation."[2] John Gill agreed, writing, "The covenant of grace is but one and the same in all ages, of which Christ is the substance," though "there are different administrations of it."[3]

The belief in one covenant of grace that spans history marks a theological watershed dividing Reformed covenant theology and other theological systems. Dispensationalism, at least as presented by Lewis Sperry Chafer and Charles Ryrie, teaches that God aims to fulfill two distinct purposes for two distinct peoples, Israel and the church.[4] Similarly, progressive covenantalism affirms "the unity of God's plan-promise culminating in the new covenant," but not one covenant of grace.[5] Therefore, in the face of controversy, we must present a biblical-theological argument for the covenant of grace.

---

1. Our references to the "historical covenants" in this chapter exclude the covenant with Noah. As we noted in chap. 31, the Noahic covenant was an administration of common grace, not saving grace in Christ, though it was foundational to the subsequent covenants in sustaining a stable world where God's saving grace could operate.
2. Calvin, *Institutes*, 2.10.2.
3. Gill, *Body of Divinity*, 345.
4. Ryrie, *Dispensationalism*, 39.
5. Wellum and Parker, introduction to *Progressive Covenantalism*, 2.

The Argument Outlined for One Covenant of Grace

In previous chapters, we began to lay out an argument for the doctrine of the covenant of grace. First, we argued that God has been saving sinners by the same gospel since the fall of man. God embedded this gospel in his covenants with Abraham, Israel, and David, and brought its full revelation with the arrival of Jesus Christ and the inauguration of the new covenant. Since there is one gospel, God has one people saved by one Mediator through one faith, albeit a faith revealed with increasing clarity through the ages.[6]

Second, God promised the gift of salvation in Christ in a covenant made before time began. In the counsel of peace, the persons of the Trinity committed themselves to execute the plan of salvation for God's chosen people through the mediation of Christ. Therefore, there is an overarching covenant that binds all of God's gracious dealings with man into one. Every promise of salvation draws from this one counsel.[7]

Third, the ancient covenants of promise, law, and kingdom all served a twofold function: to implement temporary administrations of God's saving grace and to give typological revelations of that grace, culminating in the new covenant ratified in Christ's blood. Though they were distinct administrations, they functioned as a unified, progressively unfolding plan to bring the grace of Christ to God's people in every era. Since Christ's grace flows from the Father's eternal covenant with the Son, the historical covenants, or the "covenants of promise" (Eph. 2:12), administered one covenant.[8]

Fourth, we add a polemical argument that dispensationalism breaks the repeated promise-fulfillment pattern where the New Testament cites the Old. Peter argues from God's promise that David's descendant would reign on David's throne to its fulfillment in Christ's resurrection, ascension, and session at God's right hand (Acts 2:30–36). He also applies to the church titles and promises given to Israel (1 Pet. 2:9). James says that the gathering of the Gentiles into the church by the preaching of the gospel fulfills the prophecy of Amos concerning David's house (Acts 15:13–17). The New Testament Epistles apply the new covenant promised to Israel (Jer. 31:31–34) to the church (2 Cor. 3:3, 6; Heb. 8:6–13), based

---

6. On the perpetuity of the gospel, see chap. 29.
7. On the covenant of redemption or counsel of peace, see chap. 30.
8. On the covenants of promise as temporary administrations and typological revelations of Christ's grace, see chaps. 31–32.

on Christ's atoning death (1 Cor. 11:25). Paul says, "And if ye be Christ's, then are ye Abraham's seed, and heirs according to promise" (Gal. 3:29). Christ teaches that the Old Testament revealed his death and resurrection, as well as the preaching of the gospel to all nations by the power of the Holy Spirit—the mission of the church (Luke 24:44–49). This pattern contradicts the dispensational principle that God has two purposes for two peoples, and these two must be kept separate in biblical interpretation. Instead, we see that God's covenants with Abraham, Israel, and David are all fulfilled in the new covenant.

Simply based on these arguments, we believe that we have theological warrant to speak of one covenant of grace.

Here we face an objection. Ryrie said, "The all-embracing covenants of covenant theology are not in the Bible. The whole covenant system is based on deduction and not on the results of an inductive study of Scripture."[9] Stephen Wellum and Peter Gentry say, "We cannot speak of 'the covenant' in the way the theologians of classic covenant theology do, because this language is never found in the Bible. Instead, we can speak only of the covenants (plural)."[10]

In reply, we note that all four of the above arguments are derived from the study of the Holy Scriptures. Furthermore, every doctrine of Christianity is derived from a mixture of induction and deduction—unless we simply repeat the words of Scripture without presenting their meaning and application. If these criticisms mean that a doctrine must be precisely stated in the Bible in order to be true, then dispensationalism and progressive covenantalism would fail the test, for the Bible never explicitly says God has two purposes for two peoples or that his one plan for his kingdom is unfolded through the progression of his covenants.

We do recognize the importance of grounding our doctrine upon what the Holy Scriptures say or what may be directly inferred from them. It is perilous to build a doctrine upon a series of logical deductions several steps removed from the explicit words of Scripture. Therefore, to confirm the basis for our doctrine, in this chapter we will argue that a careful reading of the historical covenants of promise reveals one covenant of grace in Christ. We will proceed along three main lines to present a fifth, a sixth, and a seventh argument (in addition to the four above). They are as follows.

---

9. Ryrie, *Dispensationalism*, 193; cf. MacArthur and Mayhue, eds., *Biblical Doctrine*, 870.
10. Peter J. Gentry and Stephen J. Wellum, *God's Kingdom through God's Covenants: A Concise Biblical Theology* (Wheaton, IL: Crossway, 2015), 234.

Fifth, there is at least one promise central to all of the redemptive covenants, one core promise that they all share in common. A covenant is a solemn promise that functions as a legal instrument to define a relationship of loyalty.[11] Therefore, the promise that spans all the covenants constitutes an overarching covenant uniting them all—the covenant of grace.

Sixth, an examination of each covenant shows that it is rooted in any covenants previous to it, sustains their basic commitments, and advances their fulfillment. Though distinct historical covenants, they develop organically from each other to form one covenant. This point will occupy much of this chapter because it requires us to return to each covenant in Scripture.

Seventh, though the Bible sometimes uses the plural "covenants," it also can use the singular "covenant" or "oath" to refer to more than one historical covenant. Therefore, we have biblical warrant to speak of one covenant of grace. This will be the final point of this chapter before we consider practical implications of this doctrine.

The Core Promise: Their God, His People

Although the covenants that God made with his people share much in common, one promise stands out as central to them all. The Lord says again and again, *You shall be my people, and I will be your God.*[12] God promised Abraham, "I will establish my covenant between me and thee and thy seed after thee in their generations for an everlasting covenant, to be a God unto thee, and to thy seed after thee. . . . I will be their God" (Gen. 17:7–8). Derek Kidner identifies this as "the essence of the covenant" with Abraham.[13]

The Lord repeated this promise when he announced that he would redeem Israel from Egypt (Ex. 6:7) and after making a covenant with them at Mount Sinai (29:45–46). The promise stood at the heart of the covenant of law, for if Israel kept God's commandments, the Lord said, "I will walk among you, and will be your God, and ye shall be my people" (Lev.

---

11. On the definition of a covenant, see chap. 14.

12. References to the covenant people as God's people and to him as their God pervade the Scriptures. For some prominent examples, see Gen. 17:7–8; Ex. 6:7; 29:45; Lev. 26:12, 45; Deut. 4:20; 7:6; 14:2, 21; 26:17–19; 27:9; 28:9; 29:13; 2 Sam. 7:24; 1 Chron. 17:22; 2 Chron. 35:3; Ps. 50:7; Isa. 40:1; 51:22; Jer. 7:23; 11:4; 24:7; 30:22; 31:33; 32:38; Ezek. 11:20; 14:11; 34:30; 36:28; 37:23, 27; Dan. 9:19–20; Hos. 1:9–10; 2:23; Joel 2:17; 2:27; Zech. 8:8; 9:16; 13:9; John 20:17; 2 Cor. 6:16, 18; Heb. 11:16; Rev. 21:3, 7. See also the more than four hundred references in the Holy Scriptures to "the LORD thy God," "the LORD your God," or "the LORD their God."

13. Kidner, *Genesis*, 140.

26:12). John Murray said, "The spirituality of relationship which is the center of the Abrahamic covenant is also at the center of the Mosaic . . . namely, union and communion with God."[14]

The promise took on a particularly focused form in the covenant with David. God said of David's royal seed, "I will be his father, and he shall be my son" (2 Sam. 7:14). The God-people relationship was thus centered on an individual as part of a Father-son relationship. This secured God's relationship with the nation. Afterward, David confessed, "Thou hast confirmed to thyself thy people Israel to be a people unto thee for ever: and thou, LORD, art become their God" (v. 24).

At the center of God's new covenant is his pledge: "[I] will be their God, and they shall be my people" (Jer. 31:33). These words are fulfilled by the double grace of God's complete acceptance of his people and their persevering reverence for him and his Word (vv. 33–34; 32:38–40). Paul applies the same promise to God's new covenant people (2 Cor. 6:16). The promise appears among the last chapters of the Bible: "They shall be his people, and God . . . [will] be their God. . . . He that overcometh shall inherit all things; and I will be his God, and he shall be my son" (Rev. 21:3, 7).

Calvin, therefore, rightly called this "the very formula of the covenant," saying, "The Lord always covenanted with his servants thus: 'I will be your God, and you shall be my people.' The prophets also commonly explained that life and the whole of blessedness are embraced in these words." In connection with this assertion, Calvin cited Psalm 33:12: "Blessed is the nation whose God is the LORD; and the people whom he hath chosen for his own inheritance."[15] This blessing belongs to those that fear the Lord and hope in his faithful love (v. 18).

Running through all of God's historical covenants with his chosen people is one great promise that he will bind himself to them and them to him. This promise is not incidental to the covenants, but stands at their very heart. Therefore, God's ancient covenants with Abraham, Israel, and David, and his new covenant in the incarnate Christ, are one covenant in substance.

This conclusion becomes even more evident when we consider the meaning of God's promise. For a people to have the Lord as "their God"

---

14. Murray, *The Covenant of Grace*, 20–21; cf. Jeong Koo Jeon, *Covenant Theology: John Murray's and Meredith G. Kline's Response to the Historical Development of Federal Theology in Reformed Thought* (Lanham, MD: University Press of America, 1999), 131.

15. Calvin, *Institutes*, 2.10.8. He also cited Lev. 26:11–12; Ps. 144:15; Hab. 1:12.

indicates their adoption by God and his giving himself to them as their Father. The "God of Abraham" counted Israel to be his "son," and consequently delivered him from slavery in Egypt.[16] After the Lord made the covenant of law with Israel, he regarded the nation corporately as his "children," placing them under special obligation to honor and obey him,[17] and individually regarded as his beloved sons and daughters those who feared him and kept his covenant.[18] As we have already noted, God especially took the offspring of David as his adopted son.[19] The new covenant applies the promise of adoption to those who trust in God's Son and walk in his ways,[20] and links their adoption to promises in previous covenants.[21] Although the New Testament emphasizes the doctrine of adoption much more than the Old Testament, the theme runs like a golden thread through all the historical covenants in which the Lord is the God of his people.

When the Lord pledged himself to be the God of his people, he promised his special presence with them. The Lord was "with" the patriarchs.[22] God's special presence with Israel was the purpose for which he redeemed them, the distinguishing mark of his people among all nations, the reward of their obedience to his covenant, and their hope in the face of judgment and exile.[23] The Lord was with David and Solomon in a special way to give them success, and he reminded David of it when making his covenant with him.[24] Whereas God had met with Abraham at his altars and had manifested his glory in the tabernacle ordained through Moses, he now established his presence with his people in the enduring structure of the temple (1 Kings 8:12–13, 57). God's promise of presence found its greatest fulfillment in him who was named "Immanuel"—that is, "God with us" (Isa. 7:14; Matt. 1:23). Christ said, "I am with you always, to the end of the age" (Matt. 28:20 ESV). God's people are now the temple in which he dwells (Eph. 2:18–22). Paul applies the promise of God's presence to his living temple in the new covenant by quoting the very words of Leviticus

16. Ex. 4:5, 22–26; Isa. 63:16; 64:8; Hos. 11:1.
17. Deut. 14:1–2; Isa. 1:2; 30:1; Mal. 1:6; 2:10.
18. Ps. 103:17–18; Jer. 31:9, 18–20; Mal. 3:17.
19. 2 Sam. 7:14; 1 Chron. 17:13; Ps. 89:26–27.
20. John 1:12; Rom. 8:14–16; Gal. 4:5; Eph. 1:4–5; 1 John 3:1–2, 10.
21. Note the allusions to the covenants with Abraham, Israel, and David in Gal. 3:26–29; 2 Cor. 6:16–18; Rev. 21:7.
22. Gen. 21:22; 26:24, 28; 28:13–15; 31:3.
23. Ex. 29:45–46; 33:12–16; Lev. 26:11–12; Isa. 41:10; 43:2, 5; Jer. 30:11; 46:28.
24. 1 Sam. 16:18; 18:12, 14; 2 Sam. 7:3, 9; 1 Chron. 17:2, 8; 28:20.

26:11–12, showing that their meaning had not fundamentally changed (2 Cor. 6:16). The ultimate hope of God's people is that God will dwell with them as their God (Rev. 21:3).

Therefore, when we consider God's promise that *you shall be my people, and I will be your God*, it is not the bare words that unite the covenants, but the promise's essential meaning. Though there were differences in how God administered this promise over the course of history, the promise remains the same. God is taking a people into union with himself so that he and they will dwell together in vital communion. This promise is the one covenant of grace.

The Organic Unity of the Covenants

Another biblical argument for the doctrine of one covenant of grace is the vital interconnection among the historical covenants. The Holy Scriptures do not present them as isolated dispensations in history, but so weave them together that to pull them apart would unravel them all. The historical covenants are as the roots, trunk, branches, and fruit of one tree. Each covenant grows organically out of those that preceded it and advances their promises.

The Law of Moses Expanded and Advanced the Covenant with Abraham

When the Lord saved Israel from Egypt, made the covenant of law with the nation at Mount Sinai, and brought the people to the Promised Land, he did not abrogate the covenant with Abraham; rather, he was beginning to fulfill it. The Lord had compassion on Israel in Egypt because "God remembered his covenant with Abraham, with Isaac, and with Jacob" (Ex. 2:24). The Lord revealed himself to Israel as "the LORD God of your fathers, the God of Abraham, the God of Isaac, and the God of Jacob" (3:15; cf. 4:5). He redeemed his people and led them to the land of Canaan because he was keeping his oath to the patriarchs (6:2–8).[25] Murray said, "The only interpretation of this is that the deliverance of Israel from Egypt and the bringing of them into the land of promise is in fulfillment of the covenant promise to Abraham."[26]

---

25. Moses emphasized this point to underline that Israel's inheritance was a gift of grace. See Deut. 1:8; 6:10; 7:8; 9:5.

26. Murray, *The Covenant of Grace*, 20.

God's covenant of law at Mount Sinai did not replace his covenant of promise with Abraham (Gal. 3:15–17), but rested upon it and reiterated its promised blessings: enjoyment of God's blessings in the land, multiplication of offspring, and the enjoyment of God.[27] Law was not foreign to God's covenant with Abraham, which had obligated him and his seed to obedience.[28] Moses called the Israelites to "enter into covenant with the LORD thy God, and into his oath, which the LORD thy God maketh with thee this day: that he may establish thee to day for a people unto himself, and that he may be unto thee a God, as he hath said unto thee, and as he hath sworn unto thy fathers, to Abraham, to Isaac, and to Jacob" (Deut. 29:12–13; cf. 30:20). Eugene Merrill comments, "The present covenant rises out of the ancient promises of the Lord to the patriarchal ancestors of the nation."[29]

God's patience with Israel's covenant breaking was the direct consequence of his faithfulness to his promise to Abraham, Isaac, and Jacob (Ex. 32:13; Deut. 9:27). Though the Lord foresaw that Israel would later fall under the covenant curses and go into exile, he promised to "remember my covenant with Jacob," "Isaac," and "Abraham" and not "destroy them utterly" and "break my covenant with them" (Lev. 26:42, 44). God's covenant with Abraham was still in effect under the covenant of law, and the latter developed the former.

The Covenant with David Expanded and Advanced the Covenants with Abraham and Israel

In the covenants of promise and law, God said he would raise up kings for Israel and regulated their selection and conduct.[30] Therefore, when God made David the king of Israel, he was fulfilling his ancient covenants. The Lord who made "an everlasting covenant" with David was "the God of Israel" and "the Rock of Israel" (2 Sam. 23:3, 5), allusions to the covenant of law.[31]

The covenant with David (2 Samuel 7) is packed with allusions to promises fulfilled. Through David's victories over his enemies, God had given

---

27. Lev. 26:3–13, 42–45; Deut. 29:12–13; cf. Gen. 12:1–3; 17:1–8.

28. Gen. 17:1; 18:19; 22:16–18; 26:5.

29. Eugene H. Merrill, *Deuteronomy*, The New American Commentary 4 (Nashville: Broadman & Holman, 1994), 380.

30. Gen. 17:6, 16; 35:11; 49:10; Deut. 17:14–20.

31. David's use of "rock" (*tsur*), "just" (*tsadiq*), "grass" or "herb" (*deshe'*), and "rain" (*matar*, 2 Sam. 23:3–4) alludes to Deut. 32:1–3, suggesting that God made the covenant with David to fulfill his covenant with Israel.

"rest" to his people in the land and prepared the way for a lasting home for his special presence, just as Moses had foretold.[32] David had experienced God's presence "with" him, victory over his enemies, the gift of "a great name," and the establishment of Israel in the land (vv. 9–10)—the blessings granted to Abraham in the covenant of promise.[33] Like Abraham, David received a promise of a special "seed" (v. 12). The building of a "house" for the Lord (v. 13) was anticipated by Jacob's dream and exclamation: "This is none other but the house of God, and this is the gate of heaven" (Gen. 28:17).

The covenant with David partially fulfilled and significantly advanced his covenant with Israel. God's promises to David moved the king to pray, "What one nation in the earth is like thy people, even like Israel . . . which thou redeemedst to thee from Egypt, from the nations and their gods? For thou hast confirmed to thyself thy people Israel to be a people unto thee for ever: and thou, Lord, art become their God. . . . The Lord of hosts is the God over Israel: and let the house of thy servant David be established before thee" (2 Sam. 7:22–26).[34]

God's covenant of kingdom depended upon keeping the covenant of law. David exhorted his son Solomon, "Keep the charge of the Lord thy God, to walk in his ways, to keep his statutes, and his commandments, and his judgments, and his testimonies, as it is written in the law of Moses, that thou mayest prosper in all that thou doest, and whithersoever thou turnest thyself: that the Lord may continue his word which he spake concerning me" (1 Kings 2:3–4).[35]

The covenant with David did alter some aspects of the law of Moses. God had revealed the design for the tabernacle, but it was now replaced by the pattern of the temple that God revealed to David (1 Chron. 28:11–12, 19). The transition to the temple required a restructuring of the Levites' duties (1 Chronicles 23–26). However, these changes did not affect the substance of the covenant in its promise, the Ten Commandments, or most of its regulations.

When Solomon built the temple, he led the people to celebrate the covenant faithfulness of "the Lord God of Israel" (1 Kings 8:15, 17, 20,

---

32. Ex. 33:14; Deut. 3:20; 12:1–11; 25:19; 2 Sam. 7:1, 11; 1 Kings 5:2–4.
33. Gen. 12:1–3, 7; 15:18; 17:6; 22:17–18; 26:3; 28:15.
34. David's words reinforce the link between God's covenant with Israel and his covenant with David. Cf. "over Israel" (*'al Yisrael*, 2 Sam. 7:8, 26; cf. 5:3, 12, 17, etc.), "establish," "stablish," or "confirm" (*kun*, 7:12–13, 16, 24), and "for ever" (*'ad 'olam*, vv. 13, 16, 25–26). Cf. Davis, *2 Samuel*, 103.
35. Robertson, *The Christ of the Covenants*, 31–32.

23, 25). In the innermost chamber of the temple stood the ark, containing "the covenant of the LORD, which he made with our fathers, when he brought them out of the land of Egypt" (v. 21; cf. vv. 51, 53). Though the temple's construction immediately fulfilled God's promise to David, Solomon said, "There hath not failed one word of all his good promise, which he promised by the hand of Moses his servant" (v. 56). Neither did the covenant with David replace the law, but Solomon asked God to incline the people's hearts "to keep his commandments . . . which he commanded our fathers" (v. 58).

Though the covenants with Abraham, Israel, and David were distinct historical covenants, they did not abolish each other. O. Palmer Robertson says, "Instead of 'wiping clean the slate' and beginning anew, each successive covenant with Abraham's descendants advanced the original purposes of God to a higher level of realization."[36] Neither do these covenants run parallel to and independently of one another, but they are organically intertwined. The ancient covenants were in fact one covenant that God progressively developed in stages.

The New Covenant Continues and Fulfills the Ancient Covenants

The new covenant inaugurated a new era with the coming of Christ in the flesh and his complete accomplishment of redemption. The new covenant is a glorious advance over the previous historical covenants. This everlasting covenant of peace brings a greater revelation of God's grace, the substance of the types given in the old covenant, liberty to draw near to the holy God, a regenerated people who know the Lord, and the sending of God's saving grace to all nations.[37] The new covenant is "a better covenant, which was established on better promises" (Heb. 8:6). Consequently, with Christ's death, the "first" covenant became "old" and "ready to vanish away" (v. 13), a truth visibly manifested when the veil of the temple was torn in two even as Christ breathed his last (Mark 15:38). Christians are not under the old covenant, and we should not judge others based upon its shadows, for the substance, Christ, has arrived (Col. 2:16–17).

However, when we examine the New Testament, we discover that God has not abandoned his previous covenants, but is fulfilling them. The first

---

36. Robertson, *The Christ of the Covenants*, 29. The "slate" refers to a chalkboard on which messages could be written and easily erased to start again.

37. On these points, see the discussion of the new covenant in the previous chapter.

words in the New Testament are "The book of the generation of Jesus Christ, the son of David, the son of Abraham" (Matt. 1:1). In Christ, God is keeping the promises of the ancient covenants. Christ said, "Think not that I am come to destroy the law, or the prophets: I am not come to destroy, but to fulfil" (5:17).

Similarly, the Gospel of Luke opens with a revelation that God was sending a messenger who would turn "many of the children of Israel . . . to the Lord their God" (Luke 1:16). This was a promise of covenantal renewal. That messenger was the forerunner to the King who would sit on "the throne of his father David" (v. 32). The virgin mother of that King rejoiced that God "has helped his servant Israel, in remembrance of his mercy, as he spoke to our fathers, to Abraham and to his offspring forever" (vv. 54–55 ESV). Leon Morris said, "God's action in the Messiah is . . . a continuation of his mercy to Abraham."[38] Greg Nichols speaks of "the messianic fulfilment of the Abrahamic covenant."[39] God revealed that he was raising up salvation "in the house of his servant David," for he remembered "his holy covenant; the oath which he sware to our father Abraham" (vv. 69, 72–73). Christ came to keep the ancient covenants and bring their promises to fruition. Robert Stein comments, "Although the term 'fulfilled' is not found in the account, the entire context and vocabulary come from the O[ld] T[estament] and speak of God's keeping his covenantal promises and visiting his people in his Son's coming."[40]

There is complexity to the way in which the new covenant relates to the ancient covenants. We see this in Jeremiah 31:31–34. On the one hand, it is a "new" covenant, "not according to the covenant" that God made with Israel, which the people broke. This "breaking" of the covenant consisted of refusing to listen to God's words, but instead worshiping other gods.[41] The new covenant promises salvation from covenant breaking by the graces of heart transformation, experiential knowledge of God, and complete forgiveness.

On the other hand, the new covenant of Jeremiah 31:31–34 renews the great concerns of the ancient covenants. God did not reject the offspring of Abraham, but made this covenant with "the house of Israel" and "the house

---

38. Morris, *Luke*, 94.
39. Nichols, *Covenant Theology*, 258.
40. Stein, *Luke*, 94–95.
41. On "breaking" (*parar*) the covenant, see Lev. 26:15; Deut. 31:16, 20; Jer. 11:10; Ezek. 16:59.

of Judah," though it would include others.[42] God said he would write "my law" in the hearts of his people, implying that God had not abandoned the great teachings of the covenant of law, but was applying them in a more effectual mode.[43] The central promise of the Abrahamic covenant, that God would be "their God" and they would be his people, triumphed in the new covenant—for the people of God "shall all know me," which was the aim of the ancient covenants.[44] To sum up, the new covenant fulfills the central concerns of the ancient covenants in both law and gospel, but in a new way that effectively saves the covenant people, and not merely a remnant of individuals among them. The new covenant is the covenant of grace historically accomplished by Christ and effectually applied through the Spirit of Christ.

When the Lord promised to "make an everlasting covenant" that would include the gift of a new heart to fear him, he identified himself as "the God of Israel" (Jer. 32:36–40), a title referring to his covenant with Israel at Mount Sinai (7:21–23; 11:3–4; 34:13), which required that very fear.[45] When presenting the new covenant, Jeremiah recorded God's promise to "cause the Branch of righteousness to grow up unto David; and he shall execute judgment and righteousness in the land," for the salvation of Judah (33:15–16). The Lord asserted in the strongest terms that his covenants with David and the Levitical priesthood would endure as long as the heavens and earth (vv. 17–26). The seed of David and the Levites would multiply "as the host of heaven" and "the sand of the sea" (v. 22), an allusion to God's promise to Abraham regarding his seed (Gen. 15:5; 22:17). The new covenant does not nullify the covenants with Abraham, Israel, and David, but fulfills them in Christ the King-Priest and advances them beyond their initially revealed scope so that all the blessed seed are kings and priests in Christ.[46] Matthew Henry commented, "Three of God's covenants . . . with David and his seed . . . with Aaron and his seed, and . . . with Abraham and his seed, seemed to be all broken and lost while the captivity lasted; but it is here promised that . . . they shall all three take place again, and the true intents and meaning of them all shall be abundantly answered in the New Testament blessings."[47]

---

42. On the inclusion of the Gentiles in the new covenant, see the last part of the previous chapter.

43. See the next chapter on God's moral law and the Christian.

44. Ex. 6:7; 31:13; 1 Kings 18:37; 2 Kings 19:19; Prov. 2:5; Ezek. 16:62; 20:12, 26, 38, 42, 44; 36:23; etc.

45. Jer. 5:24; 44:10; cf. Deut. 4:10; 5:29; 6:2, 13, 24; 8:6; 10:12, 20; etc.

46. Isa. 61:6; 66:20–21; 1 Pet. 2:5–9; Rev. 1:5–6; 5:10. See F. B. Huey, *Jeremiah, Lamentations,* The New American Commentary 16 (Nashville: Broadman & Holman, 1993), 301–2.

47. *Matthew Henry's Commentary on the Whole Bible,* on Jer. 33:17–26 (1296).

Therefore, when Paul confronted false teachers who were leading people into legalism among the Galatian churches, he did not tell the Galatian brethren to ignore the Old Testament. Instead, Paul affirmed the ancient covenants and taught Christians to view them as they are fulfilled in Christ (Gal. 3:15–17). Although the requirement of circumcision has passed away (5:2–3, 6), the promise given to Abraham endures today among all united to Christ by faith and the Spirit (3:6–9, 14). Genealogical descent no longer defines the blessed seed, but union with Christ (vv. 27–28): "And if ye be Christ's, then are ye Abraham's seed, and heirs according to the promise" (v. 29). The application of the title "Abraham's seed" to Jewish and Gentile believers in Christ reveals both the continuation of the covenant with Abraham and its expansion in Christ.

The Holy Scriptures reveal over and over again that God's acts of mercy from ancient times to the new covenant era all spring from the promises revealed in his covenant with Abraham and progressively manifested with greater detail and clarity through redemptive history.[48] The continuity of the Abrahamic promises into the new covenant should not surprise us, for God revealed that he will keep his covenant with the patriarchs "to a thousand generations" of those who "love him and keep his commandments" (Deut. 7:9; cf. Ps. 105:8–9).[49]

What of God's covenantal promises to Abraham's physical offspring, the Jews?[50] After citing a promise of the new covenant (Rom. 11:27), Paul says of Jews who do not yet believe in Christ, "As concerning the gospel, they are enemies for your sakes: but as touching the election, they are beloved for the fathers' sakes" (v. 28). On the one hand, individual unbelievers of any ethnicity are enemies of Christ's gospel and church. This has grave implications for unbelieving Israel.[51] On the other hand, the physical seed of Abraham, Isaac, and Jacob remains the corporate object of God's electing love as expressed in the covenant with Abraham.[52] Though many unbelieving "branches" of the Abrahamic

---

48. Reymond, *A New Systematic Theology of the Christian Faith*, 512–18. Reymond cites and comments on Gen. 17:19; 26:3–4; 28:13–15; 35:12; Ex. 2:24; 4:5; 32:12–14; 33:1; Lev. 26:42; Deut. 1:8; 4:31; 7:8; 9:27; 29:12–13; Josh. 21:44; 24:3–4; 2 Kings 13:23; 1 Chron. 16:15–17; Neh. 9:7–8; Ps. 105:8–10, 42–43; Mic. 7:20; Matt. 1:1; 8:11; Luke 1:54–55, 68–73; John 8:56; Acts 3:25–26; Rom. 4:11–12; 15:8–9; Gal. 3:9, 13–14, 16–17, 29.

49. Robertson, *The Christ of the Covenants*, 37–39.

50. On the eschatological future of ethnic Israel, see *RST*, vol. 4 (forthcoming).

51. Amos 3:2; Rom. 2:9; 1 Thess. 2:14–16.

52. Paul's reference to national Israel being "beloved" according to divine "election" pertains to the corporate election of Israel (Deut. 7:8; 10:15), not individual election. On corporate election, individual election, and Israel in Paul's teaching in Romans 9, see *RST*, 1:1041–45.

tree have been broken off, "God has the power to graft them in again" (v. 23 ESV) and one day will bring in Israel's "fulness" (v. 12 KJV, cf. ESV mg.). Therefore, the unity of the covenant of grace does not posit the "replacement" of Israel by the church,[53] but the expansion of spiritual Israel from an elect remnant in national Israel (9:6; 11:5) to include elect Jews and Gentiles from all nations, who together are now fellow citizens in God's spiritual Israel (Eph. 2:19), his "holy nation" by union with Christ (Ex. 19:4–6; 1 Pet. 2:9). Michael Horton says, "Just as the New Testament church is complete only as it grows out of the Old Testament church, the Israel of God attains its eschatological form only with the inclusion of the nations. . . . The church does not replace Israel; it fulfills the promise God made to Abraham that in him and his seed all the nations would be blessed."[54] God is still lovingly gathering Jews to their Messiah, for "the gospel . . . is the power of God unto salvation to every one that believeth; to the Jew first, and also to the Greek" (Rom. 1:16).

In the end, the unity of God's covenants as one covenant of grace derives from the unity of God's promises in one Lord Jesus Christ. Christ did not come to discard God's promises to the patriarchs, but "to confirm the promises" in order to glorify God's faithfulness (Rom. 15:8). Paul says, "For the Son of God, Jesus Christ . . . was not yea and nay, but in him was yea. For all the promises of God in him are yea, and in him Amen, unto the glory of God by us" (2 Cor. 1:19–20). Christ is the substance of the covenants, and therefore, in substance they are one.

The Singular "Covenant" in Biblical Usage

Someone might object that though the Scriptures reveal the unity of the covenants, they do not speak of them as a singular "covenant," and therefore we should not use the terminology of the covenant of grace. Rather, this objection proposes, it would be more biblical to speak of one divine purpose or plan.

In reply, we question the logic of the objection. Recall that so far we have presented six lines of argument that there is one covenant of grace. These may be summarized as follows:

---

53. For the charge that covenant theology is "replacement theology," see Paul P. Enns, *The Moody Handbook of Theology*, rev. ed. (Chicago: Moody, 2008), 537. Some covenant theologians have used replacement language, such as Bavinck, *Reformed Dogmatics*, 4:667.

54. Horton, *The Christian Faith*, 730.

1. The same gospel of Christ is embedded in all the historical covenants.
2. Salvation was promised in an eternal covenant between the Father and the Son.
3. The ancient covenants temporarily administered Christ's grace through types of Christ.
4. A pattern of promise and fulfillment closely links the New Testament to the Old.
5. The essence of each covenant remained the same: the "their God, my people" promise.
6. Each covenant grew organically out of those that preceded it to fulfill their promises.

It is plain that the covenants are stages of development in one progressively unfolding promise that unites God and his people in mutual fidelity through Christ. Recall, too, that a covenant is a solemn promise that legally defines a relationship of faithful love. Therefore, we rightly conclude that the distinct historical covenants are one eternal covenant of grace in Christ.

Furthermore, we add a seventh line of argument that directly challenges the premise of the objection. The Bible *does* use singular terminology to refer to multiple historical covenants. The plural "covenants" appears only three times in the Bible for divine arrangements.[55] Far more common is the singular "covenant" or "oath." Though the singular often refers to a particular historical covenant, at times it refers to multiple covenants. Let us present some examples.

Leviticus 26 is a key text for the covenant of law, setting forth the covenantal blessings and curses tied to obedience and disobedience. After looking ahead to the future judgment and exile of the disobedient nation, the Lord said, "And yet for all that, when they be in the land of their enemies, I will not cast them away, neither will I abhor them, to destroy them utterly, and to break my covenant with them: for I am the LORD their God" (v. 44). To which covenant did the Lord refer here? The answer may seem obvious, for the chapter speaks several times of the "covenant" of law that God made with Israel after the exodus (vv. 9, 15, 25, 45) and concludes, "These are the statutes and judgments and laws, which the LORD made between him and the children of Israel in mount Sinai by the hand of Moses"

---

55. Rom. 9:4; Gal. 4:24; Eph. 2:12.

(v. 46). However, shortly before promising not to "break my covenant" (v. 44), the Lord had said, "Then will I remember my covenant with Jacob, and also my covenant with Isaac, and also my covenant with Abraham will I remember" (v. 42). Furthermore, the blessings of obedience repeat the promises of God's covenant with the patriarchs.[56] Therefore, the singular "covenant" that God will not break is *both* the covenant of promise with Abraham and the covenant of law with Israel his seed.

The book of Deuteronomy is full of references to the "covenant,"[57] identified in several texts with the Ten Commandments written by God on the tablets of stone.[58] However, Israel's obedience to his commandments positioned them to receive the mercies of the God who swore his "covenant" with their "fathers,"[59] which refers to the patriarchs Abraham, Isaac, and Jacob.[60] When Moses called the Israelites to "enter into covenant with the LORD thy God," they did so to be his people and have him as their God, "as he hath sworn unto thy fathers, to Abraham, to Isaac, and to Jacob" (Deut. 29:12–13). Therefore, the singular "covenant" in Deuteronomy consists of both the promises to Abraham and the law of Moses.

The book of Psalms contains many references to the "covenant," always in the singular. Some of these texts refer to the covenant of kingdom with David and his seed,[61] some especially to the covenant of law,[62] and some to the covenant with Abraham.[63] However, other references to God's singular "covenant" look back to the covenant with Abraham while including the law of Moses. Psalm 106 recounts God's gracious dealings with his people from their time in Egypt through at least the period of the judges in Canaan (vv. 39–43), and possibly the exile and the postexilic period (vv. 46–47).[64] Though spanning the covenants of promise and law, God's compassion for his afflicted people is expressed: "He remembered for them his covenant" (v. 45). Similarly, Psalm 111 twice speaks of "his covenant"

---

56. Note being fruitful and multiplying (Lev. 26:9; cf. Gen. 17:6; 28:3; 35:11; 48:4) and walking with God and having him as one's God (Lev. 26:12; cf. Gen. 17:1, 7–8).

57. "Covenant" (*berit*) appears twenty-six times in Deuteronomy.

58. Deut. 4:13; 5:1–22; 9:9, 11, 15.

59. Deut. 4:31; 7:9, 12; 8:18; 29:25; 31:20.

60. Deut. 1:8, 10–11; 4:37; 6:10; 7:8; 9:5; 10:15–16, 22; 29:13; 30:20.

61. Pss. 89:3, 28, 34, 39; 132:12.

62. Note the references to "covenant" in the context of God's law, testimonies, statutes, or commandments in Pss. 25:10, 14; 50:5, 16; 78:10, 37; 103:18.

63. Ps. 105:6, 8, 9, 10, 42. However, the psalm ends with a reference to the law of Moses (v. 45).

64. On the historical setting, see Derek Kidner, *Psalms 73–150: An Introduction and Commentary*, Tyndale Old Testament Commentaries (Downers Grove, IL: InterVarsity Press, 1975), 415–16.

without further qualification (vv. 5, 9), though referring to God's Abrahamic grant of the inheritance (v. 6), his Mosaic commandments (v. 7), and his "redemption" (v. 9). These are further examples of a biblical manner of speaking of multiple covenants under the singular "covenant."

After Israel went into exile and then returned to the land, the Levites led the people to praise the Lord for his faithfulness through history (Neh. 9:4–38). In a long but beautiful prayer, they spoke of creation (v. 6), the election of Abraham and God's "covenant" to give the land of Canaan to his seed (vv. 7–8), the exodus and the giving of God's law at Mount Sinai (vv. 9–14), his grace in the wilderness and the inheritance of the land (vv. 15–25), Israel's rebellion against "thy law" (vv. 26, 29, 34), and the rebellion and judgment of "our kings" and other leaders (vv. 33–34), resulting in the loss of the "kingdom" and the subjugation of God's people to foreign "kings" (vv. 36–37). The prayer climaxes in an appeal to "our God . . . who keepest covenant" (v. 32). The singular "covenant" encompasses the covenant of promise, the covenant of law, and the covenant of kingdom. From the perspective of the postexilic period, they are one covenant.

The emphasis of the Holy Scriptures regarding the new covenant falls upon its distinctive superiority over the ancient covenants, for Christ has come and accomplished redemption. However, we find texts that use the singular "covenant" in a manner inclusive of old and new. The covenant of peace promised in Isaiah 54:9–10 is clearly the future new covenant, for it promises the end of God's wrath against his people.[65] However, Isaiah 55:3 promises, "I will make an everlasting covenant with you, even the sure mercies of David." The one "covenant" is evidently both the new covenant and the covenant with David.[66]

The new covenant summarizes and fulfills the ancient covenants. Isaiah 59:20–21 promises the permanent grant of God's Spirit to his people according to "my covenant." This is a reference to the new covenant blessing of the Spirit, yet it also draws in the Abrahamic covenant ("thy seed"), the Mosaic covenant ("them that turn from transgression in Jacob"), and the Davidic covenant ("Zion").[67] Isaiah 61:8 says, "I will make an everlasting

---

65. Note also how Christ quotes Isa. 54:13 and alludes to Isa. 55:1 (John 6:44–45; 7:37).

66. The "sure [*niphal* of *aman*] mercies [plural *khesed*] of David" (Isa. 55:3) alludes to Psalm 89:28: "My mercy [*khesed*] will I keep for him [David] for evermore, and my covenant shall stand fast [*niphal* of *aman*] with him."

67. On Jacob's transgression as a violation of the Mosaic law, see Isa. 58:1–2. "Zion" represents the kingdom of David, for it is the hill on which Jerusalem is built (62:1), "the city of the LORD" (60:14), on account of the covenant with David, for David established his throne there and Solomon built God's "house" there (2:3).

covenant with them," in the context of Christ's future ministry (v. 1; cf. Luke 4:18), yet speaks of "Zion" (v. 3), the restoration of Israel's honor and prosperity in the land (vv. 4–5), and "the seed which the LORD hath blessed" (v. 9), the latter a clear allusion to the covenant with Abraham. The singular "covenant" is the new covenant, but it includes the covenants with Abraham, Israel, and David.

The Davidic covenant is a bridge unifying the Abrahamic, Mosaic, and new covenants, for the great Son of David is the pinnacle of the ancient promises, the fulfiller of the ancient law, and the center of the new covenant. God said, "I the LORD will be their God, and my servant David a prince among them. . . . I will make with them a covenant of peace" (Ezek. 34:24–25). In a sense, the new covenant is the Davidic covenant brought to its glorious fulfillment. Later in the same prophecy (37:24–26), we read of the following:

- *The fruition of the Davidic covenant*: "David my servant shall be king over them; and they all shall have one shepherd."
- *The fruition of the Mosaic covenant*: "they shall also walk in my judgments, and observe my statutes, and do them."
- *The fruition of the Abrahamic covenant*: "they shall dwell in the land that I have given unto Jacob my servant, wherein your fathers have dwelt."
- *The fruition of all these through the one new covenant*: "I will make a covenant of peace with them; it shall be an everlasting covenant with them."[68]

The Scriptures also describe God's covenants as his swearing of an oath.[69] The epistle to the Hebrews makes much of this, citing God's oath to bless and multiply Abraham (Gen. 22:17) as proof that God intended to give believers "strong consolation" (Heb. 6:13–18). Most relevant to our purpose is that the writer of Hebrews immediately proceeds to say that this oath sets our hope upon "Jesus, made an high priest for ever after the order of Melchizedek" (vv. 19–20). He virtually quotes Psalm 110:4, which also describes a divine oath: "The LORD hath sworn, and will not repent, Thou art a priest." The writer of Hebrews effectively joins the two oaths as one. In the next chapter of Hebrews, the author speaks of this oath in more detail to argue for the superiority of Christ's priesthood over

---

68. Robertson, *The Christ of the Covenants*, 42.
69. For example, see Luke 1:73 (to Abraham); Acts 2:30 (to David); and Acts 7:17 (to Abraham).

that of Aaron's (Heb. 7:20–22, 28). Here also we find a connection, for just as God's oath to Abraham revealed "the immutability [*ametathetos*] of his counsel," so God's oath to Christ grants him "an unchangeable [*aparabatos*] priesthood" (6:17; 7:24). Yet his oath to Christ is the basis of the new covenant (7:21–22). The covenant with Abraham and the new covenant both stand upon one divine oath. Since a divine oath of grace to his people is a covenant (Pss. 89:3; 105:8–9), this one oath is one eternal covenant transcending all the covenants. This, as we saw elsewhere, is the covenant of redemption or counsel of peace.[70]

In summary, the Scriptures employ the singular "covenant" to describe the integrated system of the Abrahamic, Mosaic, and Davidic covenants. They also speak of the singular new "covenant," though it gathers together the promises of all the ancient covenants and fulfills them. The new covenant may even be called "the sure mercies of David" (Isa. 55:3), and it is founded upon the divine oath that God revealed to Abraham (Heb. 6:13–18; 7:20–22). We conclude that the historical covenants that God made with his people are one covenant of grace, God's eternal counsel in Christ, which comes to its full expression in the new covenant. While we must not minimize the progress of revelation, the distinctions among the historical covenants, or the superiority of the new covenant over the ancient covenants, we may rightly speak of the singular covenant of grace that is revealed and executed in them all.

The Practical Significance of the Unity of God's Covenant of Grace

God revealed the doctrine of the one covenant of grace for his glory and the good of his people. Therefore, we must not only understand, believe, and defend the doctrine, but we must apply it to our lives in practical godliness. This doctrine has many practical implications for personal godliness, several of which we have presented in previous chapters, such as our ability to depend upon God's immutability and faithfulness to his promises, though they were given thousands of years ago.[71] Here we focus on seven implications for how we approach the Word of God. Since the Bible is our means of receiving spiritual life (John 6:63) and the light to guide our way (Ps. 119:105), approaching the Bible rightly is crucial for our spiritual well-being.

---

70. On the covenant of grace as the eternal counsel of peace, see chap. 30.
71. See the concluding sections of chaps. 29 and 30.

1. A Christ-Centered Method of Interpreting the Bible

The doctrine of the covenant of grace teaches us that the Bible is governed by a pattern of promise and fulfillment. Christ is the center of history. All of the Old Testament looks forward to him, and the New Testament reveals how he fulfilled the ancient promises and applies them by the Holy Spirit. Therefore, whatever portion of the Holy Scriptures we are reading, we should view it as part of a great wheel of truth where all the spokes converge on Christ. Though not every sentence is specifically about Christ, we should always ask, "How does this text help to reveal our need of Christ and Christ's sufficiency to save us to the glory of God?"

2. The Careful Use of Typology

One way in which the promise-fulfillment pattern operates in Scripture is through the use of types, shadows of Christ and his kingdom that appear in the Old Testament. Types have a real existence in history as people, events, and institutions, and must be understood in their historical settings. Typology is no excuse for wild allegorizing of the text. However, when someone or something in the Old Testament connects to a theme that spans the Bible and points to the fulfillment of ancient promises in Christ, we may rightly see it as a type of Christ. Our best guide for faithful biblical typology is the New Testament's use of the Old Testament.

3. The Profit of Studying All Scripture

The doctrine of the covenant of grace helps us to combat our unbelieving tendency to consign portions of the Bible to oblivion, especially parts of the Old Testament that seem irrelevant, boring, or offensive. The whole Bible is God's covenantal document, and therefore it all is profitable for our study and spiritual life, for it is able to lead us into the wisdom of Christ. This principle encourages us to prayerfully pay attention to the most difficult passages with the expectation that they, too, will help us to live unto God through Christ.

4. The Importance of Knowing the Bible as a Whole

If each part of the Bible reveals an aspect of the one covenant of grace, then we must not approach the Scriptures in an atomistic manner. If we seize upon favorite verses and treat them as isolated promises, then at best we miss the big picture of what God is doing, and at worst we may completely misinterpret those texts. We must learn to see the Bible as a whole. In order to do this, it is helpful to read through the entire Bible on a regular basis. This is also one reason why preaching through books of the Bible benefits churches.

5. The Necessity of Reading Each Text in Its Covenantal Context

The whole Bible reveals one covenant of grace, but that covenant was revealed and implemented in several historical covenants. Therefore, we must not flatten the complex topography of the Bible and read it as though God revealed it all in a single day. Instead, when we approach a particular text of Scripture, we should ask, "What is the specific covenantal context of this text? What covenants preceded it and frame it? How is its teaching developed in later covenants and fulfilled in the new covenant?"

6. The Application of Each Text according to Our Present Covenantal Context

We must never ask *whether* a Scripture passage applies to us, but *how* it applies to us. All of the Bible is God's Word to us, calling us to a faithful response. At the same time, we do not live under the old covenant. The meaning of God's Word remains the same throughout time, but its application to God's people changes according to the historical covenant or administration under which they live. Though we may be reading a text about Abraham, Aaron, Solomon, or Isaiah, we read it as those under the new covenant. Christ has revealed the moral law in greater clarity and beauty, fulfilled the ancient types, accomplished the promised redemption, inaugurated the messianic kingdom from his heavenly throne, and sent the Holy Spirit in his fullness. In the next chapter, we will discuss how that should affect how Christians make use of the Old Testament law.

7. The Indispensability of Faith and Obedience

A covenant is a solemn promise that functions as a legal instrument defining a relationship of loyalty. If the whole Bible is one covenant of grace, then it constantly aims at establishing and perfecting a relationship of loyalty between God and people so that he is theirs and they are his in Christ. At its core, the Bible is God's promise calling us to a living faith in Christ. Therefore, we abuse the Bible and rebel against God if we treat the Holy Scriptures merely as an object to study and master intellectually. To read the Bible covenantally is to read it as a call to relationship with God and his people. We have not done our duty toward any Scripture passage until we respond with faith and obedience toward Christ. Only then does the Bible function as intended: not merely as a book of literature but as a bond of love.

Sing to the Lord

God's Faithfulness to His Covenant Promises

My song forever shall record
The tender mercies of the Lord;
Thy faithfulness will I proclaim,
And ev'ry age shall know Thy name.

I sing of mercies that endure,
Forever builded firm and sure,
Of faithfulness that never dies,
Established changeless in the skies.

Behold God's truth and grace displayed,
For He has faithful covenant made,
And He has sworn that David's son
Shall ever sit upon his throne.

The heav'ns shall join in glad accord
To praise Thy wondrous works, O Lord;
Thy faithfulness shall praise command
Where holy ones assembled stand.

Psalm 89
Tune: Maryton
The Psalter, No. 241
Trinity Hymnal—Baptist Edition, No. 101

Questions for Meditation or Discussion

1. The authors say, "Behind the historical covenants God made with his people stands one covenant of grace." What do they mean by "historical covenants"? By "one covenant of grace"?

2. What are the seven lines of argument that the authors advance to show that there is one covenant of grace?

3. What core promise is found in all of the covenants from Abraham to the end of the Bible? Give a sampling of Scripture passages where the promise is found across these covenants.

4. What do the authors mean by "the organic unity of the covenants"?

5. Show from the Holy Scriptures that (1) the law of Moses expanded and advanced the covenant with Abraham, (2) the covenant with David expanded and advanced the previous covenants, and (3) the new covenant continues and fulfills the ancient covenants.

6. What are some Scripture passages that use the singular "covenant" for multiple covenants?

7. What does the use of the singular "covenant" for multiple covenants imply?

8. Of the seven implications of the covenant's unity, which do you find most interesting? Why? How can that principle help you to profit more from the Bible? How could you help others?

Questions for Deeper Reflection

9. After reading this chapter, how would you describe your view of the biblical covenants in comparison to covenant theology, dispensationalism, and other views (see chap. 28)? How has reading this chapter affected your theology?

10. What are some effects that could come from denying the unity of God's covenant of grace? Consider both theological and practical effects.

11. What are some dangers of the doctrine of the one covenant of grace? Insofar as they address these issues in this chapter, have the authors avoided these dangers? Why or why not?

34

The Abiding Duty to Obey
God's Moral Law

Biblical spirituality is centered on union with Christ, empowered by the Holy Spirit, and directed by the law of God. We must not neglect that last point. The psalmist exults, "Blessed are those whose way is blameless, who walk in the law of the LORD!" (Ps. 119:1 ESV). Our Lord Jesus Christ says, "If ye love me, keep my commandments. . . . He that hath my commandments, and keepeth them, he it is that loveth me" (John 14:15, 21). Therefore, we need God's laws to direct our love for the Lord, and our obedience to his laws is the proof that we love him.

The Bible's approach to law is covenantal. God gave his commandments in the context of solemn promises that defined relationships of faithfulness. The Lord multiplied Abraham's seed because, he said, "Abraham obeyed my voice, and kept my charge, my commandments, my statutes, and my laws" (Gen. 26:3–5). Moses prefaced his recital of the Ten Commandments by saying, "The LORD our God made a covenant with us in Horeb," and the commandments begin, "I am the LORD thy God" (Deut. 5:2, 6). Therefore, our study of God's covenant brings us to consider the doctrine of divine law. Through all the covenants runs a common stream of moral instruction springing from God's very nature as God and our nature as his image bearers.

Biblical Terminology for God's Law

The Bible uses a rich variety of terms to refer to God's revealed, preceptive will for mankind.[1] Psalm 119 uses eleven Hebrew words: "law" (*torah*, v. 1), "testimonies" (*'edah*, v. 2), "ways" (*derek*, v. 3), "precepts" (*piqqud*, v. 4), "statutes" (*khoq*, v. 5), "commandments" (*mitsvah*, v. 6), "judgments" (*mishpat*, v. 7), "word" (*dabar*, v. 9), "word" (*'imrah*, v. 11), "ways" (*'orakh*, v. 15), and "statutes" (*khuqqah*, v. 16), each repeated many times though the psalm. A twelfth word for law in the Old Testament is "charge" (*mishmeret*, Deut. 11:1). Such language appears richly in the revelation of God's law in Deuteronomy.[2]

Of these dozen words, six stand out. The most common is that rendered as "law" (*torah*, 220 times), which means "teaching, instruction,"[3] though in a morally binding sense, whether the instruction of parents to children (Prov. 1:8; 3:1) or the covenant Lord to his people (Deut. 27:26; 28:58). "Commandment" (*mitsvah*) is also very common (181 times); it refers to an authoritative order as from a king.[4] The two words translated as "statute" or "ordinance" (*khoq* and *khuqqah*), when either is used by itself, almost always refer to ceremonial laws.[5] The term rendered as "judgment" (*mishpat*) speaks of the activity and decisions of judges[6] or judicial laws,[7] but also a "manner," "fashion," or pattern that one must follow in ritual worship.[8] With regard to "word" (*dabar*), the "ten commandments" (Ex. 34:28; Deut. 4:13; 10:4) are literally "ten words." Hence, they are called the Decalogue (from Greek *deka*, "ten," and *logos*, "word").

In the New Testament, we often find the Greek words translated as "law" (*nomos*, 197 times) and "commandment" (*entolē*, seventy-one times), which in the Greek Septuagint commonly render *torah* and *mitsvah*

---

1. On the distinctions between God's preceptive and decretive will, see *RST*, 1:764–67.

2. Of the twelve terms noted above, seven (*torah*, *'edah*, *derek*, *khoq*, *mitsvah*, *mishpat*, *dabar*) appear together in Deuteronomy 4–5 for divine law. See Deut. 4:1–13, 40, 44–45; 5:1, 10, 22, 31, 33. Three others appear elsewhere in Deuteronomy for God's law: "word" (*'imrah*, 32:2; 33:9), "statutes" (*khuqqah*, 6:2; 8:11; 10:13; 11:1; etc.), and "charge" (*mishmeret*, 11:1). The exceptions are "precepts" (*piqqud*) and "ways" (*'orakh*).

3. Cf. 2 Chron. 17:9. Compare the apparently related verb "teach" (*yarah*, Ex. 35:34; Deut. 33:10; Prov. 4:4).

4. 1 Kings 2:43; 2 Kings 18:36; 2 Chron. 8:15; 24:21; 29:15, 29; 30:6, 12; 35:10, 15, 16; etc.

5. *Khoq*: Ex. 12:24; 29:28; 30:21; Lev. 6:18, 22; 7:34; 10:10–11, 13–15; 24:9; Num. 18:8, 11, 19; Deut. 16:12; for an exception, see Num. 30:16. *Khuqqah*: Ex. 12:14, 17, 43; 13:10; 27:41; 28:43; 29:9; Lev. 3:17; 7:36; 10:9; 16:29, 31, 34; 17:7 (note context); 19:19; 23:14, 21, 31, 41; 24:3; Num. 9:3, 12, 14; 10:8; 15:15; 18:23; 19:2, 10, 21; 31:21; for an exception, see Lev. 20:8.

6. Lev. 19:15; Deut. 1:17; 10:18; 16:18–19; 17:8–9, 11; 25:1.

7. Ex. 21:1, 31; Lev. 24:22; Num. 35:24.

8. Ex. 26:30; Lev. 5:10; 9:16; Num. 9:3, 14; 15:24; 29:6, 18, 21, 24, 27, 30, 33, 37.

respectively. Sometimes the two Greek words are roughly equivalent, as in Romans 7:12: "Wherefore the law is holy, and the commandment holy, and just, and good." We also find rarer words translated as "ordinance" or "righteousness" (*dikaiōma*, Luke 1:6; Rom. 2:26; Heb. 9:1, 10), "ordinance" (*dogma*, Eph. 2:15; Col. 2:14), and "charge" or "commandment" (*parangelia*, 1 Thess. 4:2; 1 Tim. 1:5).

In summary, the vocabulary of the Bible with respect to the law speaks of God's authoritative verbal communication to humanity to instruct and direct us in how we are morally obligated to serve him and treat each other with justice. Now we turn from the diction of the law to its theological meaning and functions.

Law and Gospel: Distinct but Complementary

The Bible's teaching may be summarized as law and gospel.[9] We must not confuse law and gospel, lest we lose both. Paul says that "the gospel" is the promise of justification "through faith," but "the law is not of faith" (Gal. 3:8, 12). On the other hand, Paul says, "Is the law then against the promises of God? God forbid" (v. 21). We must distinguish law and gospel, but recognize that both reflect God's character and serve the purposes of his wise covenantal plan.

Richard Greenham (c. 1542–1594) defined the law as "that part of the Word that commandeth all good, and forbiddeth all evil." The gospel, he said, is "that part of the Word which containeth the free promises of God, made unto us in Jesus Christ, without any respect of our deservings."[10] Greenham explained that though the law and gospel differ in many things, they are "both of God."[11] Greenham said, "God hath two hands; in one he holdeth a hammer to break the proud . . . in the other hand he hath a horn, to pour God's blessing upon the humble."[12]

God gave his law to reveal *the moral duty of man*. Its commandments tell us what God requires of us (Deut. 10:12–13). The prophet Micah said, "He hath shewed thee, O man, what is good; and what doth the LORD

---

9. Theodore Beza's Confession (Art. 22), in *Reformed Confessions*, 2:273.

10. Richard Greenham, *A Short Forme of Catechising*, in *The Workes of the Reverend and Faithfull Servant of Jesus Christ M. Richard Greenham*, ed. H. H., 5th ed. (London: William Welby, 1612), 72.

11. Greenham, *A Short Forme of Catechising*, in *Workes*, 88.

12. Greenham, *Grave Counsels or Divine Aphorismes*, in *Workes*, 50. See Greenham's allusions to Jer. 23:29 in *Godly Instructions for the Due Examination and Direction of Al* [sic] *Men, to the Attainment and Retaining of Faith and a Good Conscience*, 36.2, 78.14, in *Workes*, 709, 826.

require of thee" (Mic. 6:8). Here the word translated as "require" (*darash*) can also mean "seek." In other words, God has communicated in his law what he desires and expects of us.

God gave his gospel to reveal *the message of salvation.* The term "gospel" means "good news" (Isa. 40:9–11; 52:7; 61:1 ESV). The message about Christ's person and work as the incarnate "Son of God" is "the gospel" (Mark 1:1). Therefore, the gospel is not a timeless principle, but the news of God's intervention in human history through his Son (1 Cor. 15:3–5). Whereas the law reveals our duty, the gospel promises salvation, righteousness, and glory by Christ's grace (Rom. 1:16–17; 2 Thess. 2:14). Salvation comes by calling upon the name of the Lord Jesus. Therefore, God's means of salvation is the preaching of the gospel (Rom. 10:13–15).

The Holy Scriptures contrast law and gospel in the starkest of terms when considering our justification.[13] Apart from Christ, God's law can only make known our sin and God's wrath against us (Rom. 3:19–20; 4:15; 7:7). The saving "righteousness of God" by which sinners are "justified" is manifested "without the law" and only "by faith" in Christ and "his blood" (3:21–25). Paul insists, "A man is justified by faith without the deeds of the law" (v. 28). Paul does not thereby nullify the law, but says rather that "we establish the law" (v. 31) when we recognize that its righteous demands and just penalty can be answered for us only by Christ.

Therefore, Paul sets law and gospel in absolute antithesis with regard to our justification. The law demands our works; the gospel requires faith in Christ (Gal. 3:11–12). If we seek to be righteous by doing the works of the law, then the law curses us; by faith in Christ alone, we receive salvation from the curse and enjoy the blessing of God (vv. 10, 13–14). We must maintain this antithesis in our minds and in our preaching. If we mingle our works of the law with our justification, then we nullify God's grace, "for if righteousness come by the law, then Christ is dead in vain" (2:21). The Lord Jesus warned that God will not justify the person who approaches God trusting in his righteousness, but God will justify the sinner who comes humbly crying out for God to make propitiation for his sins (Luke 18:9–14).

---

13. The doctrines of justification and sanctification will be treated more thoroughly in *RST*, vol. 3 (forthcoming).

The gospel, however, does not end with justification, but also reveals the grace of sanctification (2 Thess. 2:14). Believers in Christ are no longer "under law"—that is, in the position of an enslaved sinner with no power to fulfill God's commands or escape their curse (Rom. 6:14–18). Having died with Christ, they have died to the law and are united to the risen Christ to bear fruit from God (7:4). Their union with Christ gives them a new relation to the Lawgiver: that of sons and daughters led by the Spirit of adoption (8:14–15). Christ suffered God's condemnation in their place, "that the righteousness of the law might be fulfilled in us, who walk not after the flesh, but after the Spirit" (v. 4). Whether circumcised or uncircumcised in the flesh, they have the inward circumcision by the Spirit, and so "keep the precepts of the law" (2:26–29 ESV).[14] The love that the Spirit of Christ produces in them gives them the inner motivation by which they can keep the law, for "love is the fulfilling of the law" (13:9–10).

The same union with Christ that liberates believers from the law's condemnation also transforms them into those who obey the law—what John Calvin called the "double grace" granted by union with Christ.[15] The law is an antithesis to the gospel in justification, but, Calvin wrote, no one should "infer from this that the law is superfluous for believers, since it does not stop teaching and exhorting and urging them to do good, even though before God's judgment seat it has no place in their consciences." Calvin reminded us, "The whole life of Christians ought to be a sort of practice of godliness, for which we have been called to sanctification. Hence it was the function of the law, by warning men of their duty, to arouse them to a zeal for holiness and innocence."[16]

Those who by grace have come to love God can confess, "His commandments are not grievous" (1 John 5:3). Though "evil is present" in them still to resist God's will, they "delight in the law of God after the inward man" (Rom. 7:21–22). God's grace in Christ has made them "servants of sin" no more, but "servants of righteousness" (6:17–18), and "the law is holy, and the commandment holy, and just, and good" (7:12). God's law refreshes, informs, and warns them, and they count it more desirable

---

14. The word *dikaiōmata* in Rom. 2:26, translated as "righteousness" (KJV) or "precepts" (ESV), was used in the LXX to translate "statutes" (plural *khoq*), and that appears to be its meaning here. See Deut. 4:1, 5, 6, 8, 14, 40, 45; etc.

15. Calvin, *Institutes*, 3.11.1; cf. 3.11.6.

16. Calvin, *Institutes*, 3.19.2; cf. 2.7.12.

"than much fine gold" and "sweeter also than honey" (Ps. 19:7–11). The godly person loves God's law (119:97, 113, 163, 165).

Therefore, the Word of God teaches us to distinguish law and gospel, but also to recognize that both come from God for our good. In your thinking and teaching, maintain an absolute antithesis between our works of obedience to the law and our justification by faith in Christ alone. With regard to sanctification, never forget that knowing the law has no power to make us holy. However, as a believer united to Christ, receive God's law as a dear friend and cherished advisor, for it is a mirror in which you can see God's moral beauty.

The Moral, Ceremonial, and Judicial Law of Moses

In addition to distinguishing the law from the gospel, we must make distinctions within the law of God, especially as it was given to Israel through Moses. To be sure, law did not begin with Moses. "The work of the law" has been written in human nature, particularly man's conscience, from creation (Rom. 2:14–15). The Lord God "commanded" Adam that he could eat of all the trees of the garden, but not the tree of the knowledge of good and evil (Gen. 2:16–17). God called Abraham to walk blamelessly before him in subjection to his commandments and statutes, and to teach his offspring to do the same (17:1; 18:19; 26:5). However, God greatly expanded the revelation of his law in the Mosaic covenant, so much so that it was called "the law of Moses" (Josh. 8:31–32; 23:6).

Many Christians have made distinctions within the Mosaic law between the moral, ceremonial, and judicial law. "Moral" refers to unchanging principles of righteousness that apply to all mankind. "Ceremonial" pertains to ordinances of external worship that foreshadowed Christ. "Judicial" laws are directions for criminal and civil justice in Israel's ancient theocratic society.[17] The doctrine of threefold law has ancient roots. Irenaeus distinguished between the Ten Commandments and the larger Mosaic legislation, teaching that the former expressed "natural precepts, which from the beginning He had implanted in mankind," and the latter included laws that were "typical" and "temporal" but pointed to things that are "real" and "eternal," plus other laws instituted by God for Israel because of the hardness of their hearts.[18] Augustine observed the difference between "moral"

---

17. Calvin, *Institutes*, 4.20.15.
18. Irenaeus, *Against Heresies*, 4.14.3; 4.15.1–2, in *ANF*, 1:479–80.

and "symbolical" laws, also noting civil regulations that were "suitable to the times of the Old Testament" but were "fulfilled by Christ."[19] Thomas Aquinas formulated his doctrine of the Mosaic law according to the distinction between "moral," "ceremonial," and "judicial precepts."[20] Calvin commended "that common division of the whole law of God published by Moses into moral, ceremonial, and judicial laws."[21] The Westminster Confession of Faith (19.2–5) affirmed the same distinction: the "moral law" binds all people to obedience by "the authority of God the Creator"; the "ceremonial laws" were "typical ordinances" that are "now abrogated, under the new testament"; and the "judicial laws" were given to Israel as a "body politic," but have "expired" and no longer bind any nation "further than the general equity thereof may require."[22]

The Old Testament Doctrine of the Threefold Law

The Mosaic law does not come neatly packaged in separate bodies of text labeled "moral," "ceremonial," and "judicial." Often these laws are mingled together. For example, the first part of Leviticus 19 contains instructions for the peace offering (vv. 5–8), a command to leave a portion of the harvest in the field so that the poor of the land may glean it (vv. 9–10), and prohibitions against stealing, lying, false oaths, and fraud (vv. 11–13).

However, this threefold distinction in the law is not a theological imposition upon the biblical text, but a truth that arises out of the Scriptures. To begin with, the Lord revealed the law at Mount Sinai with an immediately obvious distinction between the Ten Commandments (Ex. 20:1–17) and the larger system of statutes that Moses wrote in a "book," or scroll (24:4, 7), culminating in the completion of Deuteronomy as the "book of the law" (Deut. 29:21; 30:10; 31:24–26). Therefore, God distinguished between the Decalogue and the book of the law.[23]

The Lord set apart the Ten Commandments from the book of the law in a number of ways.[24] First, God spoke these commandments, and only them, with his own voice directly to the people (Ex. 20:1, 19). Moses emphasized this point as a mark of distinction when he said, "These words

19. Augustine, *Reply to Faustus the Manichaean*, 4.2, 6.2, 19.18–19, in *NPNF*[1], 4:161, 167, 246. On the Ten Commandments and natural law, see Augustine, *Expositions on the Book of Psalms*, 57.1 (3:97).

20. Aquinas, *Summa Theologica*, Pt. 2.1, Q. 99, Art. 2–4.

21. Calvin, *Institutes*, 4.20.14.

22. *Reformed Confessions*, 4:255–56.

23. Nichols, *Covenant Theology*, 211–14.

24. Deut. 4:12–13; 5:22; 9:10; 10:1–4.

the LORD spake . . . and he added no more" (Deut. 5:22). Second, God gave these laws with an extraordinary display of his holy majesty, with thunder, lightning, and the sound of a trumpet (Ex. 20:18). Third, God wrote these commandments on tablets of stone by his own power (31:18; 32:16; 34:28), whereas Moses wrote the others on scrolls. Fourth, God called these commandments the "covenant," implying that they summarized his will for his people (34:28; Deut. 4:13). Fifth, the Lord ordered Moses to keep the tablets of the Ten Commandments in the ark of the covenant, God's symbolic throne in the holy tabernacle.[25] Sixth, Moses repeated them again before Israel entered the land (Deut. 5:6–21).

Why are the Ten Commandments unique in God's covenantal law? The Decalogue alludes to God's nature as "the LORD" and his creation of heaven and earth (Ex. 20:2, 4–6, 11). The Ten Commandments express God's nature as reflected in man and the created order. Consequently, theologians have often linked the Decalogue to the law of nature, the moral precepts engraved upon the human mind and conscience by the Creator (Rom. 2:14–15).[26] Consider how each commandment reflects truth that Moses recorded in Genesis 1–2:

1. No other gods: God alone is the Creator of all things outside of himself.
2. No idols: The glorious God must not be confused with his visible creation.
3. Reverence: The Creator is powerful and wise, worthy of all honor.
4. Sabbath: God made the world in six days and set apart the seventh as holy.
5. Honoring parents: God is like a Father to mankind and instituted the family.
6. No murder: Human life is sacred, for God created man uniquely in his image.
7. No adultery: God ordained marriage for one man and one woman to be one flesh.
8. No theft: God gave man authority over the world and thus the right to own property.

---

25. Ex. 25:16, 21–22; 31:18; 40:20. On the ark as God's throne, see 1 Sam. 4:4; Ps. 99:1.
26. Irenaeus, *Against Heresies*, 4.15.1, in *ANF*, 1:479–80; Tertullian, *Against the Jews*, chap. 2, in *ANF*, 3:152; Augustine, *Expositions on the Book of Psalms*, 57.1 (3:97); Aquinas, *Summa Theologica*, Pt. 2.1, Q. 90, Art. 2; Q. 99, Art. 2, Reply Obj. 1; Calvin, *Institutes*, 4.20.16; and Westminster Confession of Faith (19:1–2), in *Reformed Confessions*, 4:255.

9. No perjury: God speaks truth and reality, and man is created to be his image.

10. No coveting: God richly provided for man in the garden; he should be content.[27]

The Ten Commandments are "the base and foundation" of the other laws revealed through Moses, as Francis Roberts said.[28] This distinction is borne out in the structure of Deuteronomy, which begins with a historical introduction (chaps. 1–4) and transitions to "the testimonies, and the statutes, and the judgments" (4:45), set forth in a block of exhortations to faithfully love the Lord (chaps. 5–11), beginning with the Ten Commandments, and then a larger block of specific regulations (chaps. 12–26), which begins, "These are the statutes and judgments" (12:1).[29]

We see this distinction between the Ten Commandments and other laws in Moses's own words: "He declared unto you his covenant, which he commanded you to perform, even ten commandments [plural *dabar*]; and he wrote them upon two tables of stone. And the LORD commanded me at that time to teach you statutes and judgments, that ye might do them in the land whither ye go over to possess it" (Deut. 4:13–14).[30]

In subsequent revelation God taught that some laws were ceremonial and distinguished their observance from moral obedience.[31] Samuel

---

27. On these points, see *The Reformation Heritage KJV Study Bible*, ed. Beeke, Barrett, Bilkes, and Smalley, on Ex. 20:1–17 (117–18).

28. Roberts, *The Mysterie and Marrow of the Bible*, 662.

29. Meredith G. Kline, *Treaty of the Great King: The Covenantal Structure of Deuteronomy* (Eugene, OR: Wipf and Stock, 1963), 61–62.

30. Is a further distinction present in Deuteronomy 4:13–14? Some theologians have thought so, taking "statutes" to refer to the ceremonial law and "judgments" to the judicial. Thus, Aquinas, *Summa Theologica*, Pt. 2.1, Q. 99, Art. 3–4; Roberts, *The Mysterie and Marrow of the Bible*, 661; Poole, *Annotations upon the Holy Bible*, 1:346, on Deut. 4:13–14; and Colquhoun, *A Treatise on the Law and the Gospel*, 65. There is some basis for this interpretation, since, as we noted earlier, the term "statute" (*khoq* or *khuqqah*) often refers to ceremonial regulations, and "judgment" (*mishpat*) is associated with the decisions of judges. Other threefold patterns include "commandments" (plural *mitsvah*), "statutes," and "judgments" (Lev. 26:15; Deut. 5:31; 6:1; 7:11; 8:11; 26:17; 30:16; 1 Kings 6:12; 8:58; Neh. 1:7; 10:29); and the similar "testimonies," "statutes," and "judgments" (Deut. 4:45; 6:20). However, it is not entirely clear that these threefold patterns of terms indicate a distinction between "statutes and judgments" as ceremonial and judicial laws. The combination could function in Deuteronomy as a hendiadys for God's entire law (Deut. 4:1, 5, 8, 14, 45; 5:1, 31; 6:1, 20; 7:11; 11:32; 12:1; 26:16–17). "Judgment" (*mishpat*) is strongly associated with judicial matters, but the word can refer to a required pattern of ceremonial observance. We also find some combinations that do not fit into the threefold pattern. Deuteronomy 6:17 speaks of "commandments," "testimonies," and "statutes." Note also the fourfold clusters of legal terms in Deut. 11:1; 2 Chron. 19:10; Neh. 9:13.

31. Jonathan F. Bayes, *The Threefold Division of the Law*, Salt and Light Series (Newcastle upon Tyne, England: The Christian Institute, 2017), 10–12, https://www.christian.org.uk/wp-content/uploads/the-threefold-division-of-the-law.pdf.

rebuked Saul, saying, "To obey is better than sacrifice, and to hearken than the fat of rams" (1 Sam. 15:22). When David and his men needed food, the priest gave them the "shewbread," though the law said that only the priests could eat of it (1 Sam. 21:6; Mark 2:25–26). David elevated doing God's will from the heart above offering sacrifices (Ps. 40:6–8) and identified true sacrifices as humility and repentance (51:17). Through Jeremiah, the Lord reminded the people of Israel that when he brought them out of Egypt, he commanded them to obey, not to offer sacrifices (Jer. 7:21–23). The Lord said, "I desired mercy, and not sacrifice" (Hos. 6:6; cf. Matt. 12:7). Is it conceivable that God would reverse the order: "I desire sacrifice, not mercy"? Scripture passages such as these taught Israel to distinguish the ceremonial law from other precepts.[32] However, we cannot divorce the ceremonial entirely from the moral, for the ceremonial law gave specific forms to Israel by which it fulfilled its general moral obligation to glorify God as defined in the first four of the Ten Commandments.

God presented the nonceremonial regulations in two forms: simple imperatives, also known as apodictic law ("Thou shalt" or "Ye shall") and case law (often preceded by "if," "when," or "whoever"). The "book of the covenant" that God revealed after speaking the Ten Commandments (Ex. 24:4, 7) consists of large blocks of case law concerning civil and criminal matters (chaps. 21–22). These two forms of law reflect two forms of wisdom, for the law imparts wisdom to people,[33] especially civil leaders.[34] Simple commands and prohibitions of the law resemble moral admonitions in Wisdom Literature; case laws resemble proverbial aphorisms.[35] Case law applied moral principles with divine wisdom to specific situations under God's theocratic rule over Israel. Given the complexity of life, case law did not explain exactly how to handle every situation, but illustrated the application of moral principles, required the exercise of wisdom for specific cases, and may even have allowed for modifications of the letter of the law for special situations so that the principles of justice would be preserved.[36]

---

32. Irenaeus, *Against Heresies*, 4.17.1, 3, 4, in *ANF*, 1:482–84.

33. Deut. 4:6; Ezra 7:14, 25; Pss. 19:7; 37:30–31; 119:98; Prov. 7:1–4; 28:7; cf. 2 Tim. 3:15–16.

34. Deut. 1:13, 15; 16:19; cf. 1 Kings 3:12, 28; Prov. 8:15–16.

35. Leo G. Perdue, *Proverbs*, Interpretation: A Bible Commentary for Teaching and Preaching (Louisville: John Knox, 1989), 26; and Joseph Blenkinsopp, *Wisdom and Law in the Old Testament: The Ordering of Life in Israel and Early Judaism* (Oxford: Oxford University Press, 1995), 92–93, 151. Compare the simple prohibition of Deut. 19:14 with the admonition of Prov. 22:28.

36. For example, consider the complex case of the daughters of Zelophehad (Num. 27:1–11; 36:1–4). The complexity of applying judicial law required a hierarchical system of judges (Deut. 1:15–18).

Therefore, the law of Moses contained some inherent distinctions (see Table 34.1) requiring differentiating between the Ten Commandments and the "book of the law"; within the latter, between ceremonial laws and other regulations; and among the last, between simple moral imperatives and case laws for judicial wisdom.

The Ten Commandments		

The Book of the Law		
	Other Regulations	
Ceremonial Laws	Simple Imperatives: Often Moral Principles	Case Law: Judicial Wisdom

Table 34.1. Distinctions Inherent in the Mosaic Law

Christ's Doctrine of the Threefold Law

The Lord Jesus Christ said, "Think not that I am come to destroy the law, or the prophets: I am not come to destroy, but to fulfil. For verily I say unto you, Till heaven and earth pass, one jot or one tittle shall in no wise pass from the law, till all be fulfilled" (Matt. 5:17–18). In the context of the Sermon on the Mount, Christ was referring here to the fulfillment of the law not in his priestly work of atonement, but in his prophetic work of revealing God's will. He proceeded to base our entrance into the kingdom of heaven and relative greatness in it upon obedience to God's "commandments" (vv. 19–20).

What are the commandments of Christ's kingdom? They are the moral law. None of the commandments he went on to cite in Matthew 5 pertains to ceremonial laws, but only to moral precepts, whether the Ten Commandments (vv. 21, 27) or other regulations (vv. 21, 31, 33, 38, 43). Even when quoting a judicial law, such as the punishment for murder, Christ focused on its moral principle and implication for those repenting of sin to seek his kingdom and escape hell (vv. 21–22). When the Lord Jesus said, "Ye have heard that it was said . . . but I say . . ." (vv. 21–22), he was contrasting the true meaning of the moral law to the traditions of "the scribes and Pharisees" (v. 20). Johannes Wollebius said, "Christ did not correct an imperfect law, nor did he decree a new one like a second Moses, but he upheld the law against the corruptions of the Pharisees."[37]

It might be objected that Christ internalized the law, thereby transforming it. However, the law did not prohibit only murder, but also hatred (Lev. 19:17). The law was always about loving one's neighbor (v. 18), even foreigners (v. 34), as oneself. Jewish rabbis of Jesus's time identified love to be the essence of the law (Luke 10:25–28),[38] as did Christ (Matt. 22:37–40) and the apostle Paul (Rom. 13:9). The great Mosaic confession of God's oneness and uniqueness is immediately followed by the command to love God with all one's powers of mind, heart, and body (Deut. 6:4–5), which Christ identified as "the first of all the commandments" (Mark 12:29–30). The law of Moses was always a law of love. John Murray wrote, "Love renders to the requirements enunciated in the law the full measure of the obedience demanded. If we may use the metaphor, love fills to the brim the cup which the law puts into our hands."[39]

Whereas the Pharisees criticized Christ and his disciples for breaking their Sabbath traditions (Matt. 12:1–13), Christ did not negate the fourth commandment, but claimed it as his own, "for the Son of man is Lord even of the sabbath day" (v. 8). Christ explained that keeping the Sabbath holy is consistent with works of necessity (vv. 1–5), piety (v. 5), and mercy (vv. 11–12). Christ treated the Sabbath just as he treated other moral aspects of the Mosaic law: he did not abolish it, but revealed its true intent and practice as a law of love (v. 7).

In contrast to his treatment of the moral law, Christ fulfilled the ceremonial law by performing the priestly work that it foreshadowed and by teaching that its instructions no longer bind people to literal observance of the rituals, but now serve to reveal principles of Christ's spiritual kingdom. The Pharisees accused his disciples of doing wrong when they did not wash their hands before a meal, as prescribed by "the tradition of the elders" (Matt. 15:1–2). Christ first blasted the Pharisees for their hypocrisy in using human traditions to nullify "the commandment of God" to honor one's parents, quoting from the Ten Commandments and the book of the

---

37. Wollebius, *Compendium*, 1.13.(1).ix (76).

38. Rabbi Hillel said, "That which is hateful to you do not do to another; that is the entire Torah, and the rest is its interpretation." Shabbat 31a, https://www.sefaria.org/Shabbat.31a?lang=bi. Rabbi Akiva said that loving your neighbor as yourself (Lev. 19:18) is the fundamental truth of the law. Jerusalem Talmud, Nedarim 30b, https://www.sefaria.org/Jerusalem_Talmud_Nedarim.30b?lang=en.

39. John Murray, *Principles of Conduct: Aspects of Biblical Ethics* (Grand Rapids, MI: Eerdmans, 1957), 23.

law (vv. 3–9). Here again we see that Christ taught us that we must keep the moral teachings of God's law. Second, Christ taught the crowds that despite the ceremonial law regarding uncleanness, a person is not made unclean by what he eats, but only by what comes out of his heart, "for out of the heart proceed evil thoughts, murders, adulteries," and other sins (vv. 10–20). Remarkably, though a law-abiding Jew (Gal. 4:4), Jesus Christ "declared all foods clean" (Mark 7:19 ESV; cf. Acts 10:14–15). Donald English comments on Mark 7:19, "The effect . . . is the abrogation of the rules on food and diet contained in law, as well as the 'tradition' linked to them. By implication all the ritual regulations and their social implications go with them."[40]

How did Christ view the civil jurisprudence in the law of Moses? On the one hand, he distinguished judicial laws from purely moral laws. The Pharisees challenged Christ's doctrine of divorce by citing the Mosaic law that regulated divorce (Matt. 19:7; cf. Deut. 24:1). Christ said that Moses allowed divorce for a variety of reasons "because of the hardness of your hearts . . . but from the beginning it was not so" (Matt. 19:8). The civil law was in some ways an accommodation to God's theocratic rule over a largely sinful people; though it did not contradict God's righteous requirements, neither did it fully enforce them. At such points, the judicial law was an incomplete revelation of God's will "at the beginning"—that is, when God created humanity (v. 4).

On the other hand, Christ did not discard the judicial law, but drew from it principles of righteous wisdom, because the judicial law applies the moral law to specific cases. For example, he quoted the Old Testament law requiring that judicial verdicts, especially regarding crimes worthy of the death penalty, rest upon testimony from two or three witnesses.[41] However, Christ did not apply this principle to civil law, but to the process of church discipline, which terminates not in death but excommunication (Matt. 18:15–17; cf. 2 Cor. 13:1).

In summary, Christ applied the law of Moses to his disciples in a manner revealing a threefold distinction. He took the Ten Commandments and aspects of other laws and gave further revelation concerning their unchanging moral principles. He taught that ceremonial laws did not literally express God's moral law, but were types of spiritual realities, such

---

40. Donald English, *The Message of Mark: The Mystery of Faith*, The Bible Speaks Today (Leicester, England: Inter-Varsity Press; Downers Grove, IL: InterVarsity Press, 1992), 145.
41. Num. 35:30; Deut. 17:6; 19:15; Heb. 10:28.

as inner uncleanness. Lastly, he distinguished the judicial law from the moral law, but drew principles of righteousness and wisdom from it that continue to guide our lives. Christ applied all of the law of Moses to his disciples, but in a manner well described by the distinction between the moral, ceremonial, and judicial law.

The Apostolic Doctrine of the Threefold Law

Paul is a good disciple of his Master, and we find Paul's teaching on the law in full agreement with Christ's. Paul quotes one of the Ten Commandments and applies it directly to children in the church: "Honour thy father and mother" (Eph. 6:2). However, Paul also warns Christians not to let anyone judge them according to Old Testament ceremonies, for they are "a shadow" of Christ (Col. 2:16–17). He distinguishes between ceremonial law and our obligation as Christians to God's moral law when he says, "Circumcision is nothing, and uncircumcision is nothing, but the keeping of the commandments of God" (1 Cor. 7:19). Furthermore, Paul can quote a law requiring the death penalty, "Purge the evil from your midst,"[42] but apply it as a principle calling for church discipline (5:13). Here are three different ways of applying the law of Moses that correspond to the categories of moral, ceremonial, and judicial.

Three great doctrines of the New Testament undergird this distinction in the law. First, Christ came as our great High Priest, offered himself as the perfect sacrifice, and now intercedes in God's heavenly presence (Heb. 7:27–8:1). This necessitated "a change also of the law" (7:12)—that is, the abolition of "the law of a carnal commandment" pertaining to earthly holy places and physical rituals (v. 16). The ceremonial aspects of the law had to pass away.

Second, the promised Son of David has been enthroned at God's right hand in heavenly glory and has poured out the Holy Spirit (Acts 2:30–35). This necessitated a change in how God administered his theocratic kingdom among his people. The judicial laws, which so wisely applied God's moral principles to Israel's national life in Canaan, could not function literally as God's binding directives to his new covenant people congregating in churches among all nations and united by the Word and Spirit.

Third, Christ ratified the new covenant in his blood (1 Cor. 11:25). In the new covenant, God promised, "I will put my laws into their mind, and

---

42. Deut. 13:5; 17:7; 19:19; 21:21; 22:24; 24:7 ESV.

write them in their hearts" (Heb. 8:10; cf. Jer. 31:33). "My law" appears elsewhere in Jeremiah for the law of Moses, especially with respect to its moral precepts.[43] Calvin said, "God does not say here, 'I will give you another Law,' but *I will write my Law*, that is, the same Law, which had formerly been delivered to the Fathers. He then does not promise anything different as to the essence of the doctrine, but he makes the difference to be in the form only."[44] The divine writing of the law on the heart alludes specifically to God's writing of the Ten Commandments on the tablets of stone (cf. Jer. 17:1; 2 Cor. 3:3). Hence, God gives the inner motivation to keep the moral law summarized in the Ten Commandments, and those commandments continue to direct the covenant people of God in paths of righteousness for his name's sake.

The Doctrine Clarified: Three Dimensions of the Mosaic Law

When we speak of the moral, ceremonial, and judicial law, we refer to three dimensions, or aspects, of the one Mosaic law. These dimensions are vitally related to each other, though each dimension is more prominent in certain laws. Ceremonial laws stand upon the moral obligation to worship God and define that obligation with specific forms. Judicial laws apply moral principles to Israel's national situation and so reveal divine wisdom.[45]

Recognizing this truth cautions against applying the Mosaic law in a simplistic fashion. For example, we cannot ignore the judicial regulations when seeking for moral guidance. Christ's teaching about one's obligation to care for one's parents (Matt. 15:3–7) drew upon the commandment to honor one's father and mother (Ex. 20:12), as well as a judicial regulation, "He that curseth his father, or his mother, shall surely be put to death" (21:17). Christ's teaching did not deal specifically with cursing or the death penalty, but he cited the latter regulation to support his argument that neglecting one's parents on a religious pretext is hypocrisy. Similarly, the ceremonial law regarding cleanliness and uncleanliness reveals the moral duty to separate oneself from whatever God says violates his holiness—typologically pointing to spiritual cleansing (2 Cor. 6:17–7:1).

---

43. Jer. 6:19; 9:13; 16:11; 26:4; 44:10; cf. 32:23 ("thy law"); 44:23 ("his law"). We say "especially with respect to its moral precepts" because the Lord rebukes Israel for performing its ceremonies at the temple while rejecting "my law" (6:19–20; 26:1–4), and in some texts specifies their violation of "my law" as worshiping false gods (9:13–14; 16:11; 44:3, 8, 10). By contrast, note Ezekiel's use of "my law" for ceremonial regulations (Ezek. 22:26).

44. Calvin, *Commentaries*, on Jer. 31:33, emphasis original.

45. On the grounding of ceremonial and judicial law upon moral law, see Calvin, *Institutes*, 4.20.14.

Even the Ten Commandments contain elements in addition to the unchanging moral law. For example, Francis Turretin said that the fourth commandment is "mixed"—that is, "partly moral, partly ceremonial."[46] The obligation to set apart regular days of rest for the purpose of sacred worship is moral, universal, and perpetual; the selection of a particular day is ceremonial and changeable by God. There were also other aspects of the Sabbath under the Mosaic covenant that were ceremonial and temporary, such as the other Sabbaths besides the weekly day of rest (Lev. 16:31), the Sabbath years (25:1–7), the prohibition against kindling a fire on the Sabbath, and the imposition of the death penalty for Sabbath breaking (Ex. 35:2–3). Such Mosaic aspects of the Sabbath passed away with the old covenant and do not bind us today in Christ (Col. 2:16–17). God changed the particular day from the seventh to the first, "the Lord's day" (Rev. 1:10).

Turretin said, "The decalogue is not only a compendium of the moral law, but in it is given the foundation of the whole Mosaic law."[47] Therefore, elements of the Ten Commandments reflect that covenant. The preface to the Ten Commandments sets them in the context of Israel's national redemption from Egypt, which applies to Christians today as a type fulfilled in their eternal redemption in Christ. The fourth commandment addresses the head of each household as the one who determines the work days of children and servants, raising the question of how the Sabbath applies to a man who lives in a different cultural situation, such as in predominantly Muslim nations, where virtually all employers demand work on the Lord's Day. The fifth commandment promises long life "in the land which the LORD thy God giveth thee" (Deut. 5:16), referring to the covenantal blessings in Canaan,[48] but today its promise broadens to a principle that honoring parental authority tends to promote health and happiness wherever we live on "the earth" (Eph. 6:3).

Therefore, we must take a balanced approach to the law of Moses. On the one hand, we must interpret each text in the law with sensitivity to its content, context, and culmination in the New Testament. Any given law may have moral, ceremonial, and judicial dimensions. On the other hand, we must teach the law to our families and churches, and do so with the threefold distinction in mind. The Ten Commandments are the preeminent

---

46. Turretin, *Institutes*, 11.13.19 (2:84). He regarded this as "the opinion of the orthodox."
47. Turretin, *Institutes*, 11.13.22 (2:85).
48. Deut. 4:26, 40; 5:33; 6:2; 11:9; 17:20; 22:7; 25:15; 30:18; 32:47.

summary of the moral law. Therefore, make good use of historical catechisms that build their moral instruction upon the Decalogue, summarized
in the two great commandments. Teach the ceremonial law to point people
to Jesus Christ as the glorious reality anticipated by all the shadows. As
to other regulations, recognize their moral dimension and press it upon
people's consciences as Christ did. When it comes to the judicial dimension
exemplified in Israel's criminal and civil case law, receive it not as modern
legislation but as God's wisdom for righteous living in a complex world.

The Three Uses of the Moral Law

Just as God's law can be distinguished in its moral, ceremonial, and judicial
dimensions, so the moral law has three uses or modes of application. The
doctrine of the three uses of the law was embraced by the Reformation
churches, both Lutheran and Reformed.[49]

The Civil Use to Restrain Sin

The law functions in society to restrain sinful conduct and to guide authorities in making just laws for their people. Israel was a theocracy, and
its laws concerning religion and blasphemy should not be applied to the
civil laws of modern nations. However, the law's moral principles of justice among men should direct the laws of all societies, such as when the
Ten Commandments prohibit rebellion against proper authority, unjust
destruction of human life, adultery, theft, and perjury. Coupled with the
implementation of civil justice by the magistrate, the moral law places
some restraint on sinful behaviors by demanding the punishment of evil-
doers (Rom. 13:1–7) and deterring others from criminal acts.[50] Righteousness is essential to any good civil government.[51] Its laws and judicial rulings
will be effective only insofar as they resonate with clear moral principles
in the consciences of the public.

The law can also serve to rebuke and restrain sinners apart from government enforcement, resulting in a measure of "civil" or behavioral righteousness. This appears to be Paul's point when he says, "The law is not
made for a righteous man, but for the lawless and disobedient, for the

---

49. Formula of Concord (Epitome, 6.1), in *The Book of Concord*, 502; and Calvin, *Institutes*,
2.7.6–13; 4.20.15–16. See Joel R. Beeke, *Puritan Reformed Spirituality* (Darlington, England:
Evangelical Press, 2006), 101–10.
50. On deterrence, see Deut. 13:11; 17:13; 19:20; 21:21; Prov. 19:25; 21:11; Eccl. 8:11.
51. Prov. 8:15; 16:12; 20:8; 29:4, 14; 31:4–5, 9.

ungodly and for sinners, for unholy and profane, for murderers of fathers and murderers of mothers, for manslayers, for whoremongers, for them that defile themselves with mankind, for menstealers, for liars, for perjured persons" (1 Tim. 1:9–10). George Knight comments, "The law's intention is to indicate to the lawless and rebellious that they should avoid sins."[52] It is not difficult, in the last half of Paul's list, to trace the fifth, sixth, seventh, eighth, and ninth commandments. The Ten Commandments rebuke flagrant violators of God's moral principles and may move them to regret and reform their behavior.

However, the moral law is powerless to save from sin; only Christ can save by his Spirit (Rom. 8:3–4). Apart from God's Spirit, the mindset of fallen mankind is "enmity against God"; it cannot willingly be "subject to the law of God" (v. 7). The law can actually aggravate indwelling sin by provoking impenitent sinners to greater rebellion against God's revealed will (7:7–11). Finally, sinners may distort God's law by their hypocrisy so that they can judge others but remain unrepentant and wicked themselves (2:1–5, 17–24).

The Evangelical Use to Convict Sinners

Paul explains that whatever the law says, it says "that every mouth may be stopped, and all the world may become guilty before God . . . for by the law is the knowledge of sin" (Rom. 3:19–20). In context, Paul is using the testimony of the law to lead people to consider the gospel of salvation and righteousness by grace. The law shows us that "by the deeds of the law there shall no flesh be justified in his sight" (v. 20).[53] We must know the reality and evil of our sin in order to believe the gospel, for who will trust in God to justify him from the guilt of sin if he does not see his sin or its guilt? The law assists the conscience in this matter, as Paul says: "I had not known sin, but by the law" (7:7). The Heidelberg Catechism (LD 2, Q. 3) says, "Whence knowest thou thy misery? Out of the law of God."[54]

Christ made use of the law in this manner when he said, "Except your righteousness shall exceed the righteousness of the scribes and Pharisees, ye shall in no case enter into the kingdom of heaven" (Matt. 5:20). Jesus proceeded to declare that the law's moral principles

---

52. Knight, *The Pastoral Epistles*, 83.
53. Murray, *The Epistle to the Romans*, 1:107.
54. *The Three Forms of Unity*, 69.

condemn sins of the heart as worthy of damnation and hell (vv. 21–22, 27–31). Christ's message culminated in the warning that only "he that doeth the will of my Father" will "enter into the kingdom of heaven"; to the rest, he will say, "I never knew you: depart from me, ye that work iniquity" (7:21, 23). The Sermon on the Mount, while providing encouragement and moral guidance for those who love God and belong to his kingdom, also strips away self-righteousness and hypocrisy to show sinners their need of saving grace. When the Holy Spirit fills the preaching of the Word with power, it pierces the souls of sinners like a double-edged sword and causes them to cry out for the mercy that only the gospel offers (Acts 2:36–38). It makes them feel as if they stand naked before the living God (Heb. 4:12), who will judge them guilty and condemn them to hell eternally if they do not find a better righteousness in another, even Jesus Christ, who knew no sin, but was made "sin for us . . . that we might be made the righteousness of God in him" (2 Cor. 5:21).

Furthermore, the law continues to convict God's saved people of their sins, repeatedly driving them back to Christ for a fresh application of his cleansing blood to their consciences (Heb. 9:13–14; 1 John 1:7, 9). The Westminster Confession of Faith (19.6) says that though the law can neither justify us nor condemn believers in Christ, it does serve to uncover "the sinful pollutions of their nature, hearts, and lives; so as, examining themselves thereby, they may come to further conviction of, humiliation for, and hatred against sin, together with a clearer sight of the need they have of Christ, and the perfection of His obedience."[55]

The Didactic Use to Direct Saints

Believers are no longer "under the law" in a state of helpless corruption and condemnation, for they are "under grace" (Rom. 6:14). Grace reigns in their lives (5:21), so that they are no longer "servants of sin," but "have obeyed from the heart" God's Word (6:17). Their response to God's amazing grace must be to offer themselves as living sacrifices set apart as "holy" (*hagios*) to God, seeking to know his "good" (*agathos*) will (12:1–2) and walking in kingdom "righteousness" (*dikaiosunē*) by the Holy Spirit (14:17). These are the very properties of God's moral law:

---

55. *Reformed Confessions*, 4:256; cf. the Heidelberg Catechism (LD 44, Q. 115), in *The Three Forms of Unity*, 109.

"the commandment [is] holy [*hagios*], and just [or "righteous," *dikaios*], and good [*agathos*]" (7:12). Therefore, God's law continues to provide ethical direction for Christians, though it no longer condemns them in their state before God, for they are righteous in Christ Jesus (8:1).

If not for the law, Christians would not know what pleases the Lord (Eph. 5:17) and would become enslaved to human opinions and traditions (Col. 2:8, 20–23). The Heidelberg Catechism (LD 33, Q. 91) says that "good works" are "only those which proceed from a true faith, are performed according to the law of God, and to His glory; and not such as are founded on our imaginations or the institutions of men."[56]

It might be objected that though Christians may do things that correspond to the law (Gal. 5:22–24), they do so simply as motivated by love, not by any regard to obey God's commandments. The Christian life is a spiritual life, not a legal life. The only thing that drives the Christian life, it might be said, is "faith which worketh by love" (v. 6). Believers in Christ must merely "love one another: for he that loveth another hath fulfilled the law" (Rom. 13:8).

In reply, the New Testament abounds with specific ethical commands, not merely general exhortations to walk in the Spirit of love. The New Testament also invokes the Ten Commandments as binding moral principles for the disciples of Jesus Christ.[57] It often restates the same moral principles as the Ten Commandments in other words (e.g. Eph. 4:25–5:6). Furthermore, Christ denies that his disciples walk by an ethic of mere love apart from obedience to his laws; to the contrary, he says, "If ye love me, keep my commandments" (John 14:15; cf. 1 John 5:3). Revelation defines God's people as those who "keep the commandments of God" (Rev. 12:17; 14:12; cf. 22:14). In contrast, it characterizes the damned as murderers, sorcerers, fornicators, thieves, idolaters, and liars—that is, as transgressors of the law (9:21; 21:8; 22:15). While ceremonies such as circumcision do not bind us now, what remains crucial is "the keeping of the commandments of God" (1 Cor. 7:19). If someone further objects that Paul means here only his own "commandments" (14:37), we reply that his first epistle to the Corinthians includes warnings against idolatry, sexual immorality, theft, and covetousness (5:11; 6:9–10), which obviously express the prohibitions of the moral law of the Ten Commandments.

---

56. *The Three Forms of Unity*, 99–100.
57. Matt. 5:21–22, 27–28; Mark 2:23–3:5; 7:9–10; 10:19; Rom. 7:7; 13:9; Eph. 6:2; James 2:11–12.

Conclusion

Make good use of the law in your own life. Do not be so foolish as to say that you do not need God's commandments. They are a light to your path. Would you walk through a land full of pits and precipices in utter darkness? To be sure, the law's light painfully exposes our sins. However, in the great Physician's hands, the law serves to lead us to the cure, not to condemnation. It shows us why we must trust in Christ alone. It shows us how we must repent—in particular detail—so that we can grow in Christ.

The moral law is like a stick. In the hands of people in general, the moral law is a measuring rod or ruler by which we see how certain conduct measures up to righteousness and justice. As such, it is a set of principles to inform our conscience and to guide civil leaders. In the hands of an evangelistic preacher, the law is a stick that beats us out of the bushes where we hide from God and drives us to seek refuge in Christ lest we suffer God's wrath forever. However, once we are saved, the law becomes like a walking stick or cane that Christ puts in our hands, so that we can lean upon his law for direction and wisdom while we walk with God by grace. Samuel Bolton (1606–1654) said, "The law sends us to the gospel that we may be justified; the gospel sends us to the law to frame our way of life. . . . As the law was given with evangelical purposes, so it is now kept from evangelical principles, principles of faith, love, and delight."[58]

Therefore, study God's law. Meditate upon his commandments day and night. Consider it to be your great responsibility to obey God's law in every respect with your entire soul, mind, and strength (Josh. 1:7–8).

Most of all, use the law as a mirror to see Christ. Marvel at Christ's perfect obedience to God's law in its every stipulation. Glorify God's Son as the perfect law-keeper on behalf of his people. Trust him as your only righteousness. And follow him, even if you are stumbling as you go, down the path of obedience so that your good works may please and glorify God.

Sing to the Lord

Glorifying the Lord for His Law

Jehovah's perfect law restores the soul again;
His testimony sure gives wisdom unto men;

---

58. Samuel Bolton, *The True Bounds of Christian Freedom*, Puritan Paperbacks (Edinburgh: Banner of Truth, 1964), 72–73.

The precepts of the Lord are right
And fill the heart with great delight.

The Lord's commands are pure, they light and joy restore;
Jehovah's fear is clean, enduring evermore;
His statutes, let the world confess,
Are wholly truth and righteousness.

They are to be desired above the finest gold;
Than honey from the comb more sweetness far they hold
With warnings they Thy servant guard,
In keeping them is great reward.

When Thou dost search my life, may all my thoughts within
And all the words I speak Thy full approval win.
O Lord, Thou art a rock to me,
And my Redeemer Thou shalt be.

Psalm 19
Tune: Haddam
The Psalter, No. 38
Trinity Hymnal—Baptist Edition, No. 448

Questions for Meditation or Discussion

1. What are the six most significant words used in the Old Testament for God's law?
2. How would you explain the difference between the law and the gospel, and how they work together for God's glory?
3. Briefly define and give an example of each of the following: (1) the moral law, (2) the ceremonial law, and (3) the judicial law.
4. How did the Lord set apart the Ten Commandments from the rest of the Mosaic law?
5. What Old Testament Scripture passages show that ceremonial laws differ from other laws?
6. What is "case law"? Give some examples of case laws that are judicial.
7. How does the Lord Jesus Christ apply the moral principles of the Mosaic law?
8. What does Christ teach concerning the ceremonial law of cleanliness and uncleanliness?

9. Give two examples of Christ's teaching about judicial laws. How did he apply them?

10. How would you explain and prove to a group of high school students the civil, evangelical, and didactic uses of the law?

Questions for Deeper Reflection

11. How does judicial case law relate to wisdom? Illustrate your answer with specific texts.

12. What do the authors mean when they say that moral, ceremonial, and judicial are "dimensions" of the law, and that one law may involve more than one dimension?

13. How would you build an argument that Christians should still obey the moral law as revealed to Moses, but can do so in grace and not legalism?

35

The Church's Union with Her Covenant God through Faith

God's covenant of grace is his solemn promise that defines a relationship of faithful love between him and his people in Christ. Although that relationship has a legal dimension in its promises and commandments, it transcends mere legal commitments. The covenant finds its fruition in the union and communion between God and his people.

The relationship stands upon God's sovereign commitment to love us and show us grace. Paul says, "If God be for us, who can be against us?" (Rom. 8:31). J. I. Packer says, "The words 'for us' declare God's covenant commitment. The goal of grace . . . is to create a love relationship between God and us who believe . . . and the bond of fellowship by which God binds Himself to us is His covenant. . . . This covenant relationship is the basis of all biblical religion."[1]

Therefore, the covenant of grace is not merely a theological topic to study but a call to know God personally. We know God by faith in his covenant Word, for the Word reveals Christ. Through faith, the Holy Spirit moves us to call upon the Lord in prayer and to rejoice in him in praise. Faith binds us to God through Christ so that we know his love for us and respond with love for him. The spiritual dynamic of faith and love shapes our entire lives into an exercise of walking with God.

---

1. J. I. Packer, *Knowing God* (Downers Grove, IL: InterVarsity Press, 1973), 237–38.

Understanding the Covenant's Aim to Create and Strengthen Faith

The core of the covenant is God's promise. William Ames said, "It is called a covenant because it is a firm promise."[2] A promise calls forth faith. When God makes a promise to people, he gives them both the warrant and obligation to trust him. Hebrew 10:23 exhorts us to "hold fast the profession of our faith without wavering" and gives the reason why we should: "for he is faithful that promised." Therefore, the immediate aim of the covenant promise is faith.

Abraham is our example, for "he staggered not at the promise of God through unbelief; but was strong in faith, giving glory to God; and being fully persuaded that, what he had promised, he was able also to perform" (Rom. 4:20–21). Similarly, Sarah received the strength to conceive the blessed seed "through faith," for "she judged him faithful who had promised" (Heb. 11:11). By contrast, many in Israel, though they were Abraham and Sarah's physical descendants, did not personally profit from God's promise because they lacked faith (4:1–2). Only those who have "faith in Christ Jesus" are "Abraham's seed, and heirs according to the promise" (Gal. 3:26, 29).

God's covenant of salvation is a covenant of grace. Therefore, God brings us into covenant relation to himself by faith in Christ, not by our works. Caspar Olevianus said, "This covenant between God and us is a gracious one and does not rest upon any condition of our own worthiness or merit, but exists through faith alone."[3] Christ is the essence of the covenant (Isa. 42:6); to partake in the covenant, we must receive him. John Brown of Haddington said, "Christ graciously brings us into the bond of the covenant by uniting himself to us. . . . And we dutifully enter into the bond of it, by faith."[4]

Hear the voice of God calling to you in the promises of his covenant. Do not harden your heart through unbelief and turn away from the living God (Heb. 3:7–12). He summons you and commands you through his covenant to trust him. Do not resist his Word; allow it to pierce you and reveal the unbelief and sins that God has never failed to see (4:11–13). Respond to God's promise by coming to him through Jesus Christ, the

---

2. Ames, *The Marrow of Theology*, 1.24.11 (150).
3. Olevianus, *An Exposition of the Apostles' Creed*, 14.
4. Brown, *Systematic Theology*, 252.

kind and sympathetic Savior, and you will find that God welcomes you to "the throne of grace" (vv. 14–16).

God's covenant not only calls us to trust him, but its very form as a solemn promise gives us strong confidence. God first entered into a formal covenant with Abraham when the patriarch asked, "O Lord GOD, how am I to know that I shall possess it [the inheritance]?" (Gen. 15:8 ESV). The Lord said, "Know for certain . . . ," and then "made a covenant with Abram" (vv. 13, 18 ESV). Later God sealed the covenant in an explicit oath. He said, "By myself have I sworn . . . I will bless thee . . . and in thy seed shall all the nations of the earth be blessed" (22:16–18). The New Testament reflects upon that oath: "God, willing more abundantly to shew unto the heirs of promise the immutability of his counsel, confirmed it by an oath: that by two immutable things, in which it was impossible for God to lie, we might have a strong consolation" (Heb. 6:17–18). Since it is impossible for God to lie and inconceivable for him to break an oath, Christians have a hope that is "an anchor of the soul, both sure and stedfast," a hope that grasps Christ, our High Priest, as he intercedes for us (vv. 19–20).

Therefore, God made the covenant of grace with the intention of providing his people with the ground for absolute confidence and unshakable faith in him. If we persist in trusting in man and human resources, then we turn away from the Lord and fall under his curse; if we trust in the Lord, then we receive his blessing, and he sustains us in the most difficult of circumstances (Jer. 17:5–8). The more we trust him—and we all should trust him far more than we do—the more we will be able to face trials and tears with courageous godliness (Pss. 27:1–3; 56:3–10).

Entering the Covenant Relationship by Faith in Christ

God calls us to enter the spiritual relationship promised in the covenant of grace and receive its saving benefits.[5] William Strong said, "It's our duty to enter our covenant with the Lord; and this is the great end of the publishing of the gospel, to bring men into the bond of the covenant."[6]

When we speak of "entering" the covenant relationship, we should avoid any concept that God proposes the covenant but ratifies it only when we give

---

5. Of course, the covenant of grace has many nonsaving benefits for those externally associated with Christ's church. Such relationships to the covenant in Reformed theology will be discussed under the locus of ecclesiology in *RST*, vol. 4 (forthcoming). Here we focus upon receiving the saving benefits in Christ through a vital, spiritual, internal covenant relationship to God.

6. Strong, *A Discourse of the Two Covenants*, 165.

our consent. The covenant of grace consists of God's sovereign promises, such as his eternal oath to Christ (Ps. 110:4), the free offer of the gospel to all who repent and believe in Christ (2:10–12; John 3:16), and the absolute promises of effectual grace in the new covenant (Jer. 31:31–34). God applies those promises in time according to his free and eternal election of whom he will save in Christ (Eph. 1:3–4).[7] God's will alone has determined the promises of the covenant and the parties included in those promises.

However, the covenant defines a living relationship between God and his people, and that relationship begins with each individual at a certain point in time (Gal. 1:15; Eph. 2:4–5). Until the elect have faith in Christ, they have no vital union with him; they are not God's people. but are "children of wrath, even as others" (Eph. 2:3).[8] They are outsiders to the covenant's saving benefits and have no claim on its promises (Gal. 4:21–31; Eph. 2:12), for Christ is the Mediator of the new covenant (Heb. 8:6). Therefore, we must enter the covenant relationship by believing God's promises and receiving Christ with all the grace that is in him. At that point, God, who grants us saving faith as his gift (Eph. 2:8), establishes a vital covenantal relationship between us and him. Then we can say, "O my God, I trust in thee" (Ps. 25:2).

Reasons Why Many Do Not Enter the Covenant Relationship

The call to enter God's covenant goes out as an invitation to a free banquet (Isa. 55:1–3).[9] Who would be so foolish as to refuse such an invitation? Yet, for various reasons, many are not willing to come,[10] as our Lord taught in his parable of the wedding feast (Matt. 22:1–14).

First, *they do not believe in the riches of God's free grace.* In the parable, the king sent out this message: "I have prepared my dinner: my oxen and my fatlings[11] are killed, and all things are ready: come unto the mar-

---

7. John Gill said, "It is a notion that commonly obtains, that God makes a covenant of grace with men when they believe, repent, etc. but it is no such thing; the covenant of grace does not then begin to be made, only to be manifest; it then openly takes place, its blessings are bestowed, its promises applied, its grace wrought in the hearts of men, when God puts his fear there, gives a new heart, and a new spirit, and puts his own Spirit there, to work faith, repentance, and every other grace; but then the covenant is not new made, but all this is done in virtue and in consequence of the covenant of grace made in eternity." *Body of Divinity*, 247–48.

8. Keach, *The Display of Glorious Grace*, 245–46.

9. For a survey of the covenantal significance of meals, see Walter T. McCree, "The Covenant Meal in the Old Testament," *Journal of Biblical Literature* 45, no. 1/2 (1926): 120–28.

10. The last clause of Matt. 22:3 can be literally translated, "They were not willing to come" (*ouk ēthelon elthein*).

11. The word translated as "fatlings" (*sitistos*) is rare, a *hapax legomenon* in the New Testament. It means "animals especially fed and thus in prime condition." Leon Morris, *The Gospel according to*

riage" (Matt. 22:4). However, the people "made light of it" (*ameleō*, v. 5)—that is, they did not care and neglected the invitation (cf. Heb. 2:3). Astonishingly, they turned up their noses at the glory of the king and the wealth of his hospitality. In the same way, many people do not come to the feast of God's covenant because they do not perceive the immense goodness of God and despise the offer of his gospel.

This rejection of grace may take the form of practical atheism. In men's proud minds, God has little practical significance. A subtler form of unbelief may come wrapped in false humility. People may claim that they are simply too sinful for God to accept them and that they cannot pay the price of admission to his banquet—a misunderstanding of and insult to God's free grace. Or people may not explicitly reject God's grace so much as wallow in spiritual laziness. Wilhelmus à Brakel said, "They perceive something of this matter and are desirous of being partakers thereof. This desire is, however, the desire of a sluggard who does not wish to make an effort."[12] The glorious riches of God's covenant are not, in their eyes, worthy of their wholehearted pursuit.

Second, people will not enter a covenant relationship with God because *they love this world as their treasure.* Christ said that those who were invited "went their ways, one to his farm, another to his merchandise" (Matt. 22:5; cf. Luke 14:18–20). People despise God's covenant because their hearts are preoccupied with the riches and relationships of this world (cf. 8:14). Thomas Manton said, "Excusing is refusing. . . . They care not for these things, being biased and prepossessed with other affections."[13] Perhaps God's warnings of judgment frighten them, but they push such thoughts away and focus on their pursuit of worldly gain and pleasing people, as Felix did when Paul spoke to him (Acts 24:24–27).

Third, people may despise the covenant because *they violently hate God's Son and servants.* In Christ's parable of the king's feast, he says that after some went away to their farms and businesses, "the rest seized his servants, treated them shamefully, and killed them" (Matt. 22:6 ESV). Given that the king made the banquet for the marriage of "his son" (v. 2), this shows that some people refuse to enter the covenant because they hate Christ. God's Son is the Lord and heir of God's kingdom, and those

---

Matthew, The Pillar New Testament Commentary (Grand Rapids, MI: Eerdmans; Leicester, England: Inter-Varsity Press, 1992), 548. The emphasis falls on the excellent quality of the food.

12. Brakel, *The Christian's Reasonable Service*, 1:447.

13. Manton, *A Sermon Preached on Matthew XXII. 11–13*, in *Works*, 16:12.

who crave to be lords and masters resent him with envy and murderous hatred (21:38; 27:18). Even if they cannot get their hands on Christ, they abuse his servants verbally and physically. Martin Luther said, "They are the high, wise and prudent, the exalted spirits; they not only despise but martyr and destroy the servants in order to retain their own honor and praise, yea, in order to be something."[14]

Fourth, people may fail to enter a covenant relationship with God because *they profess religion but lack saving grace.* In the parable of the wedding feast, the king discovers a guest at the banquet who is not clothed in "a wedding garment," and has him thrown out into the "outer darkness," where there is "weeping and gnashing of teeth" (Matt. 22:11–13). The wedding garment symbolizes salvation, as the prophet said: "He hath clothed me with the garments of salvation, he hath covered me with the robe of righteousness, as a bridegroom decketh himself with ornaments, and as a bride adorneth herself with her jewels" (Isa. 61:10). Manton said, "Those who come to the wedding feast without a wedding garment" are those "who take up a bare profession of the gospel without newness of heart and life."[15] Christ explained, "For many are called, but few are chosen" (Matt. 22:14). Therefore, Christ's parable teaches us that some people respond superficially to the invitation to the covenantal feast, but the King knows that they are not his elect, for they lack salvation and are religious hypocrites.

Brakel said, "Many are knowledgeable concerning the truth, view it as glorious and desirable, and esteem those to be very blessed who are partakers of the covenant. They go to church, are outwardly religious, and refrain themselves from being involved in the gross pollution of the world. Thus they consider themselves partakers of the covenant." However, "they do not know the truth internally, do not perceive the spiritual dimension of these matters, and in their hearts neither esteem the Surety of this covenant as precious, nor have a desire for Him alone."[16]

Let us beware lest these evil motives detain us from entering a saving relationship to God through his covenant of grace. God mercifully holds out his promise to us, but the opportunity will not last forever. He will close the door to the feast of grace. Then all the riches, status, and pleasures of

---

14. *Sermons of Martin Luther*, ed. and trans. John Nicholas Lenker, 8 vols. (Grand Rapids, MI: Baker, 1989), 5:229. We have slightly modernized the punctuation.

15. Manton, *A Sermon Preached on Matthew XXII. 11–13*, in *Works*, 16:16.

16. Brakel, *The Christian's Reasonable Service*, 1:448.

this world will pass away. Human self-righteousness will be exposed for the filthy rags that it is. The Lord will unmask hypocrisy and openly reveal and condemn fallen mankind's hatred for Christ. Woe to those who are found outside of the covenant of grace on the day of judgment!

Exhortation to Enter the Covenant Relationship by Faith

Hear the voice of Christ calling. The Lord says, "Ho, every one that thirsteth, come ye to the waters, and he that hath no money; come ye, buy, and eat; yea, come, buy wine and milk without money and without price" (Isa. 55:1). He gently asks, "Wherefore do ye spend money for that which is not bread? And your labour for that which satisfieth not?" (v. 2). Christ promises, "I am the bread of life: he that cometh to me shall never hunger; and he that believeth on me shall never thirst" (John 6:35). He lovingly pleads, "If any man thirst, let him come unto me, and drink" (7:37). God invites, "Let the one who is thirsty come; let the one who desires take the water of life without price" (Rev. 22:17 ESV).

Christ will never reject anyone who comes to him in faith (John 6:37). Brakel said, "The Lord shall turn no one away who in truth comes unto Him through Christ—even if for so many years you have been disobedient to this friendly offer; even if until now your entire life has been nothing but sin; and even if until now you have done abominable things, are a murderer, an adulterer and fornicator, a thief, a slanderer, and a liar."[17]

If you have not yet come to Christ by faith, then consider who it is that calls you. He is the Son of God, the Mediator of the new covenant. He has all the promises of the covenant in his hand. He can write the law on your heart by the Spirit so that you delight to do God's will. Christ can give you the knowledge of God, so that the Lord becomes your God and you become one of his people. Christ died for sinners, and he can take away the guilt of your sins so that God will never give you what you deserve or remember your guilt against you. Christ needs nothing from you, but he offers you everything in the covenant of grace. Will you receive this Christ?

Consider, too, what will happen to those who neglect this great salvation. You are already a covenant breaker in Adam, and if you refuse to trust in Christ after hearing the gospel, you also make yourself a covenant despiser, one who tramples on Christ and treats his blood as if it were worthless. Though perhaps you live comfortably now, death will snatch

---

17. Brakel, *The Christian's Reasonable Service*, 1:450.

you away from all your comforts. God will one day summon you to his fiery throne of judgment. Then it will be too late, and God's burning indignation will terrify and devour you forever. Both the covenant of works and the covenant of grace will testify against you. Your conscience will make you groan with shame even as your body burns in the torments of hell. Brakel said, "Outside of this covenant there is nothing but misery."[18]

Sinner, flee from the wrath that is to come! The promises of the covenant hold out grace to the worst of sinners, grace sufficient to save all who trust in the covenant God of Jesus Christ. Turn from sin, trust in Christ, and embrace the covenant of grace.

Repentant saint, marvel and rejoice that you are in the covenant of grace! You have Christ as your Mediator, all the promises of the covenant as your inheritance, and God himself as your eternal portion. Meditate upon how this covenant reveals God's glory. Give him the praise he deserves. Brown said, "Now, O my soul, think what astonishing displays of Jehovah's perfections appear in this covenant! Behold how infinite mercy, grace, and love excite [arise to action]! How infinite wisdom plans! Infinite persons engage! How all infinite perfections work for the redemption of sinful men—of sinful *me*!"[19]

Exercising Faith by Prayer to the Covenant God

Calling upon the Lord is not merely the entrance into the covenant, but it is the way of the covenant through all our earthly pilgrimage. Prayer is the life breath of the covenant, a vital link between the covenant people and their covenant God.

The covenant shapes the language of prayer: "Save us, O Lord our God" (Ps. 106:47). The psalmists frequently take the covenantal address of "our God" and make it intensely personal as "my God" (more than fifty times). In the New Testament, the apostle Paul uses the same covenantal language: "I thank my God upon every remembrance of you" (Phil. 1:3; cf. 1 Cor. 1:4). Do you know the intimacy of saying to God, "Thou art my God"? This is the inestimable privilege of his children.

The covenant reveals God's compassionate and enduring love, stirring his people's hope that he will hear and answer them (Ps. 103:13–17). God's nature as the faithful, covenant-keeping God is the special ground of their

---

18. Brakel, *The Christian's Reasonable Service*, 1:449.
19. Brown, *Systematic Theology*, 255, emphasis original.

confidence in prayer. At the darkest points in Israel's history, believers were enabled to pray with confidence because they could address the Lord as the God who keeps covenant and mercy (Neh. 1:5; 9:32; Dan. 9:4).

God's covenant stands in the background of the effectual prayers of his servants. James encourages us, "The effectual fervent prayer of a righteous man availeth much," and uses Elijah as an example: "He prayed earnestly that it might not rain: and it rained not on the earth by the space of three years and six months. And he prayed again, and the heaven gave rain, and the earth brought forth her fruit" (James 5:16–18; cf. 1 Kings 17–18). Elijah obtained the faith to pray such great things from God's covenant. The Lord had said in the Mosaic covenant that if the people of Israel broke his law, he would send drought and famine, but if they repented and obeyed, he would bless the land with rain (Lev. 26:4, 19–20; 1 Kings 8:35–36). Elijah observed Israel's apostasy and prayed for God to keep his covenant word. When the people turned from Baal to declare the Lord to be God, Elijah again called upon God to keep his covenant promise.

In the new covenant, we find a similar example of prayer in Paul, who, upon hearing of evidences of new covenant grace in the Ephesian saints, thanked God and addressed his petitions to the covenant Lord, "the God of our Lord Jesus Christ" (Eph. 1:15–17). This is God's "covenant name," as S. M. Baugh says; he is not merely the God of Abraham or the God of Israel, but is the God of our Lord Jesus Christ and all in union with him (cf. v. 3).[20] Paul called upon God to produce by the Spirit an increasing knowledge of God among the Ephesian believers (vv. 15–19; cf. Col. 1:9–11). Paul was praying the promises of the covenant (Isa. 59:21; Jer. 31:34).

Effective prayer lifts up God's covenant promises to him and calls upon him to keep his word. William Gurnall (1616–1679) said, "Prayer is nothing but the promise reversed, or God's word framed into an argument, and retorted by faith upon God again."[21] Manton said, "Show him his own handwriting; God is tender of his word."[22]

When we draw near to God through believing prayer, we enjoy communion with the triune God as our God. Paul says, "For through him we both have access by one Spirit unto the Father" (Eph. 2:18). We begin to

---

20. S. M. Baugh, *Ephesians*, Evangelical Exegetical Commentary (Bellingham, WA: Lexham Press, 2015), 116.

21. William Gurnall, *The Christian in Complete Armour*, 2 vols. in 1 (1662–1665; repr., Edinburgh: Banner of Truth, 2002), 2:88.

22. Manton, *Sermons upon Psalm CXIX*, on Ps. 119:26, in *Works*, 6:242. Manton refers to Monica's prayers for Augustine. See Augustine, *Confessions*, 5.9.17, in *NPNF*[1], 1:85.

experience, though only as a foretaste, the spiritual realities promised to us in Christ. John Calvin said that prayer is "a communion of men with God by which, having entered the heavenly sanctuary, they appeal to him in person concerning his promises in order to experience . . . that what they believed was not vain, though he had promised it in word alone."[23] Having taken hold of God's covenant of peace, the war between God and us has ceased, and "free and open trade to heaven" is opened along the "navigable river" of the Holy Spirit, as Benjamin Keach said. This is the spiritual "traffic" between heaven and earth by which God generously enriches our souls with his free grace in answer to our prayers, and he graciously accepts us and our service as we offer ourselves to him through Jesus Christ.[24]

You will find that as God's covenantal Word increasingly guides your prayers, your requests will be more focused on eternal and spiritual matters. Furthermore, God's Spirit will lead you through his Word to give more time and energy to adoration, confession, and thanksgiving—not just asking God for what you want. While prayer will always include petitions for our needs and desires, the covenant of grace will teach us increasingly that what we need and desire most is God himself (Pss. 43:4; 63:1–2).

Engaging in the Love Relationship with the Covenant God

The great aim of the covenant is that God's people would know his love and love him (Deut. 6:4–5; 7:6–9). The Bible closely associates covenants with "faithful love" (*khesed*), for covenants create a bond of loyalty where affection and kindness can flourish.[25] This is the spiritual meaning of the central promise of the covenant: that God is our God and we are his people in mutual loyalty and love.[26]

Far from being a mere contract such as men form with each other for commercial interests, God's covenant of grace creates a relationship of love that Scripture describes in terms of adoption and marriage. Keach said that God becomes our God in the covenant not merely by being our Creator or having a legal or formal connection to us, but by creating a special relationship with us as a father relates to his children and as a husband relates to the woman he marries and loves with his dearest affections.[27]

---

23. Calvin, *Institutes*, 3.20.2.
24. Keach, *The Display of Glorious Grace*, 260–61.
25. On covenants and loyal love (*khesed*), see the definition of a covenant in chap. 14.
26. See the discussion of this core promise that pervades the covenant of grace in chap. 33.
27. Keach, *The Display of Glorious Grace*, 226–27.

The Covenant as Our Adoption by God

Adoption by God is one of the great themes and doctrines of the Bible.[28] God's covenant of grace progressively revealed his adoption of his people under the covenant with Abraham,[29] the Mosaic covenant,[30] the covenant with David,[31] and the new covenant,[32] in which Christ and his apostles taught believers to view God as "our Father."[33] Olevianus said, "The name *Father* reminds us of the firmest of covenants between God and us in Christ His only begotten Son, and of His unchangeable love toward us."[34] By adoption, God commits himself to a relationship of tender love and compassion with his people.[35]

Although all the persons of the Trinity participate in our spiritual adoption (Gal. 4:4–6), adoption especially orients us toward God the Father as "our Father" in Christ (Matt. 6:9).[36] The adoptive relationship is covenantal and grounded upon Christ, who said to his disciples, whom he called "my brethren," that "I ascend unto my Father, and your Father; and to my God, and your God" (John 20:17). The phrase "my God" implies that Christ performed his saving work as the person designated by divine covenant for that labor and subsequent glory (cf. 17:1–5). On the basis of Christ's death, resurrection, and exaltation to glory in fulfillment of that covenant, Christ's disciples share in the status and privileges pertaining to sonship ("your Father").

This covenantal adoption brings Christians into the most intimate relation with the Father's love by union with Christ (John 17:22–23). Jesus Christ addressed God as "Abba" in the garden of Gethsemane (Mark 14:36), using the Aramaic term that a Jewish child would have employed with reverence and familiarity to address his father. James Edwards comments, "Only in Mark does Jesus call God 'Abba,' a term of intimacy, trust, and affection. . . . 'Abba' recollects Jesus' original Aramaic . . .

---

28. The doctrine of adoption is explored in more detail under the locus of soteriology in *RST*, vol. 3 (forthcoming).

29. Ex. 4:22–26; Isa. 63:16; 64:8; Hos. 11:1.

30. Deut. 14:1–2; Ps. 103:17–18; Isa. 1:2; 30:1; Jer. 31:9, 18–20; Mal. 1:6; 2:10; 3:17.

31. 2 Sam. 7:14; 1 Chron. 17:13; Ps. 89:26–27.

32. John 1:12; Rom. 8:14–16; 2 Cor. 6:18; Gal. 3:26; 4:5; Eph. 1:4–5; 1 John 3:1–2, 10; Rev. 21:7.

33. Matt. 6:9; Luke 11:2; Rom. 1:7; 1 Cor. 1:3; 2 Cor. 1:2; Gal. 1:4; Eph. 1:2; Phil. 1:2; 4:20; Col. 1:2; 1 Thess. 1:1, 3; 3:11, 13; 2 Thess. 1:1, 2; 2:16; 1 Tim. 1:2. Note also "your Father" in Matt. 5:16, 45, 48; 6:1, 8, 15; 7:11; 10:20, 29; 18:14; Luke 6:36; 12:30, 32.

34. Olevianus, *An Exposition of the Apostles' Creed*, 40.

35. Ps. 103:13; Jer. 31:20; Hos. 11:1; Mal. 3:17.

36. Perkins, *An Exposition of the Lord's Prayer*, in *Works*, 5:430.

displaying an intimacy, boldness, and simplicity in address to God that was not characteristic of Jewish prayers. Seldom, if ever, did rabbis presume such intimacy with God."[37] As those redeemed by Christ, adopted by God, and indwelt by the Spirit of God's Son, we, too, may address God as "Abba, Father" (Rom. 8:15; Gal. 4:4–6). We may approach God with the boldness and freedom of a child with the perfect father (Eph. 2:18; 3:12). God's pleasure in and friendship with the believer who obeys Christ's commandments is expressed by Christ in the words "my Father will love him" (John 14:23).[38]

How much do you trust in the Father's love for you, child of God? He loved you before you did any good thing. He loved you before Christ died for your sins, and his love is at the bottom of all Christ did for you. Do you receive his love and revel in it? You can be confident that the Father is pleased with you because of Jesus Christ and takes pleasure in your good works by his Spirit. When you confess your sins with repentance, you can still say, "God is my Father, and he loves me yet."

God's love for us aims to awaken in us love for him so that we may glorify and enjoy him forever. Do you return his love with an answering love from your heart? Your acts of Christian obedience and service should be full of love for this loving Father. Are you a joyful child of God living under your Father's blessing? "Behold, what manner of love the Father hath bestowed upon us, that we should be called the sons of God" (1 John 3:1).

The Covenant as Our Marriage to God

Another biblical metaphor for the church's covenant relationship to God is marriage. The Lord is the Bridegroom of his people, and they are his bride.[39] The Lord said of Israel, when it was "the time of love," that "I sware unto thee, and entered into a covenant with thee, saith the Lord GOD, and thou becamest mine" (Ezek. 16:8). Like adoption, this spiritual marriage springs from God's sovereign election and eternal love, and brings to God a people made holy by union with Christ to the praise of his glorious grace (Eph. 1:3–6; 5:25–27).

---

37. James R. Edwards, *The Gospel according to Mark*, The Pillar New Testament Commentary (Grand Rapids, MI: Eerdmans, 2002), 433–34.

38. Owen, *Communion with God*, in *Works*, 2:19–21.

39. Isa. 54:5; 62:5; Jer. 2:2; 3:14; 31:32; Ezek. 16:8; Hos. 2:7, 19–20; Matt. 9:15; 25:1–13; Mark 2:19–20; Luke 5:34–35; John 3:29; 2 Cor. 11:2; Eph. 5:22–32; Rev. 19:7; 21:2, 9; 22:17.

The Lord comes for his church like a victorious warrior to embrace his bride: "As the bridegroom rejoiceth over the bride, so shall thy God rejoice over thee" (Isa. 62:5). "The LORD thy God in the midst of thee is mighty; he will save, he will rejoice over thee with joy; he will rest in his love, he will joy over thee with singing" (Zeph. 3:17).[40] This is an extraordinary revelation of God's love for his bride, for it describes the Lord as if he were a man overwhelmed with the happiness of being with his beloved. God, of course, does not need us, and we do not add to his joy. Yet God's infinite joy in himself bursts out in songs of love for his people, for it is God's delight to love us with an unspeakably great love. Calvin commented, "This feeling is indeed ascribed to God with no strict correctness; for we know that he can instantly accomplish whatever it pleases him: but he assumes the character of men; for except he thus speaks familiarly with us, he cannot fully show how much he loves us."[41]

Just as adoption particularly relates Christians to the Father, so spiritual marriage relates them especially to God the Son. He is the Bridegroom for whom they long (Mark 2:19–20). Jesus Christ has entered a particularly intimate relation with his people because he shares their human nature and experiences in a fallen world (Heb. 2:14–18). He is united to them more closely than a husband is to his wife, for they are "one spirit" with him (1 Cor. 6:17), and he is their life (Col. 3:4). He is the King whom they find supremely beautiful (Ps. 45:2), and though they have not yet seen him except by faith, they love him and rejoice in him as they wait for his coming (1 Pet. 1:7–8).

Owen said that this spiritual marriage results in "a conjugal relation" between Christ and his people that "is attended with suitable conjugal affections."[42] Christ and his bride willingly give themselves to each other in faithful love. Just as Hosea said to his poor, unfaithful bride, "Thou shalt abide for me many days; thou shalt not play the harlot, and thou shalt not be for another man: so will I also be for thee" (Hos. 3:3), so Christ takes his bride to himself, saying, "I will be for thee, and thou shalt be for me, and not another."[43] Christ receives us with delight, treasuring us with a heart full of compassion and generosity. The church receives Christ with

---

40. Though marital language is not explicitly used in Zeph. 3:17, Israel is addressed in the feminine, implying that God is delighting in his bride. John L. Mackay, *Jonah, Micah, Nahum, Habakkuk and Zephaniah*, Focus on the Bible (Fearn, Ross-shire, Scotland: Christian Focus, 1998), 401.
41. Calvin, *Commentaries*, on Zeph. 3:17.
42. Owen, *Communion with God*, in *Works*, 2:54.
43. Owen, *Communion with God*, in *Works*, 2:56.

joy, treasuring him with a heart of single-minded devotion and submission.[44] Obedient believers are not merely Christ's servants; they are Christ's friends to whom he opens his heart (John 15:15).[45] Strong said, "This is a matrimonial covenant, and it is a covenant of friendship."[46]

If you are not yet a Christian, then please allow us to plead with you to enter what Edward Pearse called "the best match."[47] Do you want a match who has honor and greatness? He is God and man, the brightness of his Father's glory, the King of kings and Lord of lords. Do you want riches and treasures? Christ's riches are the best, for they last forever, are infinitely great, and will satisfy all your desires. Are you looking for a generous heart in a spouse? Jesus Christ is willing to lay out his riches for his spouse so that her joy may be full. Do you want wisdom and knowledge? The infinite wisdom of God shines in him; he is Wisdom itself, and knows perfectly how to glorify himself and do good to those who love him. Are you looking for beauty? He is altogether lovely, more than all the beauty of human beings and angels combined. Are you seeking someone who will truly love you? Christ is love itself, love that is higher than the heavens and deeper than the seas. Do you want a husband who is honored and esteemed? This Husband is adored by the saints and angels. Everyone whose opinion really matters treasures him, and God the Father delights in him. Do you seek a match who will never die and leave you a widow? Christ is the King immortal and eternal; he is the resurrection and the life. Do not delay; do not be distracted. Receive Jesus Christ now as your Lord and Savior. You will never regret it. But if you refuse him, you will regret it forever.[48]

Christian, do you live by faith in the Son of God, who loved you and gave himself for you? He is your beloved and your friend. His love took him to the cross and tomb for your sake. Do your affections stream out toward him in holy love? Do you long for his appearing? You should aim in all your Christian service to be a friend of the Bridegroom who does not just draw people to yourself, but preeminently helps people love him more even as you decrease (John 3:28–30). The great essential for all service to Christ is a heart burning with love for the Lord (21:15–17).

---

44. Owen, *Communion with God*, in *Works*, 2:118.

45. Owen, *Communion with God*, in *Works*, 2:119.

46. Strong, *A Discourse of the Two Covenants*, 167.

47. Edward Pearse, *The Best Match: The Soul's Espousal to Christ*, ed. Don Kistler (Grand Rapids, MI: Soli Deo Gloria, 1994), 56–70.

48. This paragraph adapted from Joel R. Beeke, *Revelation*, The Lectio Continua Expository Commentary on the New Testament (Grand Rapids, MI: Reformation Heritage Books, 2016), 480. Used by permission.

How can we cultivate greater love for God? Love is an active principle, and we must fan its affections into flame and put it into practical action. At the same time, our love must draw its vitality from a root outside of ourselves. John says, "We love him, because he first loved us" (1 John 4:19). God's love for us is revealed supremely in the gospel of Christ crucified for our sins (v. 10). And that gospel is embedded in the covenant of grace, the promises of which are sure, being confirmed with an oath by the God who cannot lie. Therefore, meditate upon the covenant and its specific promises in Christ, exercise your faith to trust in them more, pray for God to fulfill his promises increasingly in you, stir up your affections of love toward this loving and lovely Savior, put your love into action with good works, and persevere in faithful love in imitation of the God who keeps covenant and mercy to a thousand generations. This is the fruit that grows from the covenant of grace.

Sing to the Lord

Resting in the Covenant of Grace

A debtor to mercy alone,
Of covenant mercy I sing;
Nor fear with thy righteousness on,
My person and off'ring to bring.
The terrors of law and of God
With me can have nothing to do;
My Saviour's obedience and blood
Hide all my transgressions from view.

The work which his goodness began,
The arm of his strength will complete;
His promise is Yea and Amen,
And never was forfeited yet.
Things future, nor things that are now,
Nor all things below or above,
Can make him his purpose forgo,
Or sever my soul from his love.

My name from the palms of his hands
Eternity will not erase;
Impressed on his heart it remains,

In marks of indelible grace.
Yes, I to the end shall endure,
As sure as the earnest is giv'n;
More happy, but not more secure,
The glorified spirits in heav'n.

Augustus M. Toplady
Tune: Lllangristiolus
Trinity Hymnal—Baptist Edition, No. 99

Questions for Meditation or Discussion

1. What about the covenant of grace calls forth our faith in God?
2. If God sovereignly establishes his covenant as he wills, then why does each person need to enter into a covenant relationship with God personally?
3. What are four reasons why people hear the gospel but do not enter into a covenant relationship with God?
4. How would you exhort a friend to enter the covenant relationship by faith in Christ? What arguments would you lovingly and gently press upon him?
5. How does the covenant of grace shape the language of prayer?
6. How does the covenant of grace enable believers to pray according to God's revealed will with great faith?
7. What covenantal relation do Christians especially have toward God the Father? God the Son?
8. What does "Abba" mean? What is its significance for the Christian life (Rom. 8:15; Gal. 4:6)?
9. Why is love for Jesus Christ essential to the Christian life? For Christian service?
10. Have you entered a covenant relationship with the true God? If so, how? If not, why not?

Questions for Deeper Reflection

11. What are some promises of God's covenant that are precious to you? How can you turn those promises into fervent and effectual prayers?
12. Prepare a detailed outline for a lesson you would teach to high school students about how Christians can grow in their love for God as their covenant God. Make it scriptural and practical.

13. Reformed and Puritan theologians such as John Owen made much of how the Song of Solomon pictures the love relationship between Christ and his people. Is this a legitimate interpretation of that book of the Bible? Why or why not? How might a Christian benefit from meditating on the Song in a Christ-centered manner?

Section B

The Doctrine of the Person of Christ

36

Introduction to the Study of Christ's Person and Work

The Christian life is a long and difficult race, and we must run it "looking unto Jesus" (Heb. 12:2). We cannot endure as Christians merely by observing a list of rules, embracing a philosophy of life, or pursuing a series of experiences. The Christian must have Christ. Jesus Christ, the Son of God, is everything to the believer. This is true not only for our conversion and justification, but also for our spiritual growth. Therefore, it is our great duty, necessity, and delight to know him in an ever-increasing way. John Flavel said, "A saving, though an immethodical knowledge of Christ, will bring us to heaven (John 17:2), but a regular and methodical, as well as saving knowledge of him, will bring heaven into us (Col. 2:2–3)."[1]

In our pragmatic age, people often chase after earthly success. Christians sometimes aim no higher. Even our prayers can revolve around getting things we want and avoiding things we fear. However, when Jesus Christ poured out his heart in prayer shortly before his betrayal and crucifixion, he asked that his people might "be with me where I am; that they may behold my glory" (John 17:24). This should also be our fervent desire. John Owen said, "One of the greatest privileges and advancements of believers, both in this world and unto eternity, consists in their beholding the glory of Christ."[2] Therefore, let us press on to know the Lord Jesus.

---

1. Flavel, *The Fountain of Life*, in *Works*, 1:21.
2. Owen, *Meditations and Discourses on the Glory of Christ, in His Person, Office, and Grace: with the Differences between Faith and Sight*, in *Works*, 1:286. Henceforth cited as *The Glory of Christ*, in *Works*.

The Value of Studying Christology

Nothing is more valuable than knowing Christ, and God in Christ. Such knowledge is our very life (John 17:3). Paul reveled in "the excellency of the knowledge of Christ Jesus my Lord," compared to which he counted all things only "loss" and "dung" (Phil. 3:8). To understand why, we have to unpack the doctrines of Christ's person and work. Here, let us simply whet our appetite for feasting on the Bread of Life—a feast that will continue forever and for which this book is only an introduction.

First, Christology is a *central* subject. At the core of Christianity is the gospel, and at the core of the gospel is Jesus Christ himself.[3] Paul said that we are saved by "the gospel," or the good news of Christ: "For I delivered unto you first of all that which I also received, how that Christ died for our sins according to the scriptures; and that he was buried, and that he rose again the third day according to the scriptures" (1 Cor. 15:1–4). Thus, Paul was determined to preach "Jesus Christ, and him crucified" (2:2). The Lord Jesus informed us that he is the great theme of the Bible, including all the parts of the Old Testament (Luke 24:25–26, 44).[4] Christ is central by divine design, for the Father has arranged all of creation and all of redemption around his Son so that "in all things he might have the preeminence" (Col. 1:16–18). In short, "the Father loveth the Son, and hath given all things into his hand" (John 3:35). Bartel Elshout says, "These words tell us why God the Father was moved to give His Son to be the Savior of a fallen world: because He loves His Son! . . . This is the fountain from which all theology flows."[5]

Second, Christology is a *polemical* subject. The Devil sought to destroy Jesus from the moment of his birth (Rev. 12:4). Though Christ's exaltation to glory puts him completely out of Satan's reach (v. 5), the evil one now wars against those who bear "the testimony of Jesus" (v. 17). The Devil's servants in the church pose as ministers of righteousness but labor to draw people away from devotion to Christ by preaching "another Jesus" (2 Cor. 11:3–4, 13–15). From ancient times to the modern world, the church has repeatedly faced attacks upon the doctrine of Christ.

Third, Christology is a *necessary* subject. Though all doctrinal error has harmful consequences, there are many errors that people can embrace

---

3. Donald G. Bloesch, *Jesus Christ: Savior and Lord*, Christian Foundations (Downers Grove, IL: InterVarsity Press, 1997), 15.
4. On the gospel message as revealed through the ages, see chap. 29.
5. Bartel Elshout, "The Father's Love for His Son," in *The Beauty and Glory of the Father*, ed. Joel R. Beeke (Grand Rapids, MI: Reformation Heritage Books, 2013), 3.

without destroying their souls. This is not the case regarding the fundamental truths of Christ's person and work. The New Testament warns, "Whosoever denieth the Son, the same hath not the Father" (1 John 2:23). Any religious teacher who denies the incarnation of our Lord "is not of God," but "of antichrist" (4:3). Therefore, the efficacy of the church's evangelism, its selection of faithful pastors and teachers, and indeed its eternal salvation all hinge upon its holding to a sound doctrine of Christ.

Fourth, Christology is an *awakening* subject. The preaching of Christ is often used by God to rouse people from spiritual slumber and revive true religion. The Lord Jesus sends the Holy Spirit to convict sinners and bring believers to a deeper experiential knowledge of the things of God (John 16:7–15). Christ said of the Spirit, "He shall glorify me" (v. 14). Therefore, when we study and proclaim the doctrine of Christ, we cooperate in the Spirit's great enterprise of testifying to Christ (15:26–27). When the Spirit illuminates sinners regarding Christ, they come to life: "Awake thou that sleepest, and arise from the dead, and Christ shall give thee light" (Eph. 5:14).

Fifth, Christology is a *captivating* subject. The study of Christ enthralls the heart because no human being is as lovely as Christ (Ps. 45:2). He is "altogether lovely" (Song 5:16). All the fullness of deity dwells in him, in personal union with a perfect and exalted human nature (Col. 2:9–10). We find the best of heaven and earth in Jesus Christ. Thus, it is the hope of God's people that they will "see the king in his beauty" (Isa. 33:17). Each Christian's greatest need is to set his mind on Christ as he is seated at God's right hand (Col. 3:1–2).

Sixth, Christology is a *glorious* subject. In Christ we find the "riches" of God's "glory" (Phil. 4:19; Col. 1:27). Paul writes of "the unsearchable riches of Christ" (Eph. 3:8). Christ's love surpasses knowledge (v. 19). God has hidden in his Son "all the treasures of wisdom and knowledge" (Col. 2:3). Too often, Christians rest in a shallow understanding of the Lord Jesus, failing to explore the depths. Flavel said, "All other sciences are but shadows; this is a boundless, bottomless ocean."[6] Therefore, let us give our lives to pursuing the knowledge of Christ.

The Theological Method of Biblical Christology

We know Jesus Christ through the written Word of God. Though the rationalistic skepticism of the last few centuries has spawned a host of attempts

---

6. Flavel, *The Fountain of Life*, in *Works*, 1:36.

to reconstruct our view of Jesus, our knowledge of him does not stand upon the uncertain ground of human historical studies.[7] Neither is faith in Christ a mystical leap into the unknown or an unbiblical subjective encounter with the holy. Rather, faith in Christ is confident trust in what God declares concerning his Son (1 John 5:10). John says of the "signs" recorded in his gospel, "These are written, that ye might believe that Jesus is the Christ, the Son of God; and that believing ye might have life though his name" (John 20:31). Our Christology must be biblical, for apart from the Holy Scriptures, we have no access to Christ, either as a historical figure or as the heavenly Lord. The question, then, is how the Bible reveals Christ and teaches us to seek the knowledge of him.

Christology "From Above" or "From Below"

Wolfhart Pannenberg (1928–2014) spoke of two methods of Christology: "For Christology that begins 'from above,' from the divinity of Jesus, the concept of the incarnation stands at the center. A Christology 'from below,' rising from the historical man Jesus to the recognition of his divinity, is concerned first of all with Jesus' message and fate and arrives only at the end at the concept of the incarnation."[8] The latter reflects Pannenberg's limitation of divine revelation to historical events, not the words of Scripture.[9] As Robert Letham points out, Pannenberg taught that in Christ's resurrection his deity was not only revealed but made real: "Jesus's identity depends on the resurrection."[10] We find a similar affirmation of Christology from below in Jürgen Moltmann, who speaks of "anthropological Christology" and says, "The centre of this christology is the human being Jesus of Nazareth, not the exalted or pre-existent Christ."[11]

The method of the early and medieval orthodox Christian church, according to this scheme, was Christology "from above." However, some modern theologians, such as Emil Brunner and Rudolf Bultmann, have undertaken their own kinds of Christology "from above," which tend to detach Christ from the historical Jesus in a manner contrary to the ortho-

---

7. On the so-called quest for the historical Jesus, see the discussion of whether orthodox Christology is ahistorical in chap. 42.

8. Wolfhart Pannenberg, *Jesus—God and Man*, trans. Lewis L. Wilkins and Duane A. Priebe, 2nd ed. (Philadelphia: Westminster, 1977), 33.

9. See the discussion of special revelation confined to historical events in *RST*, 1:309–13.

10. Letham, *Systematic Theology*, 543. He notes the implication for the doctrine of God: "God becomes part of the cosmic process, in some ways interdependent—codependent—with the world, as dependent on it as it is dependent on him. This is panentheism" (542).

11. Jürgen Moltmann, *The Way of Jesus Christ: Christology in Messianic Dimensions*, trans. Margaret Kohl (San Francisco: HarperCollins, 1990), 55.

dox tradition.[12] The resulting figure is sometimes called the "kerygmatic Christ"—that is, the exalted Christ of the apostolic "preaching" (Greek *kerygma*).[13] Pannenberg criticized the "from above" method for its presumption of Christ's deity and its neglect of the real, historical individual Jesus of Nazareth. Such an approach, Pannenberg argued, "is closed to us," because "one would have to stand in the position of God himself in order to follow the way of God's Son into the world."[14] Likewise, Moltmann argues that this shift in Christology is necessitated by the shift from the medieval God-centered worldview to the modern human-centered worldview.[15]

Pannenberg advocated Christology "from below" because "Christology must begin with the man Jesus," though always with respect to "his relationship with God." This approach follows the same trajectory as theological liberalism, which views Jesus as the man supremely dependent upon God.[16] Friedrich Schleiermacher said, "The Redeemer, then, is like all men in virtue of the identity of human nature, but distinguished from them all by the constant potency of His God-consciousness."[17] Christology "from below" is accompanied by a measure of skepticism toward the historical reliability of the Scriptures, requiring the theologian to sift through legendary materials and determine by critical reasoning their true historical core.[18]

What are we to make of these categories "from above" and "from below"? First, when taken to its extremes, this distinction rests on a false dichotomy. Christ, as we shall see, is both God and man joined in one person (John 1:1, 14). This false dichotomy of "above" and "below" reflects the modern dichotomy between faith and feeling on the one hand and reason and historical facts on the other. An exclusively "from above" approach removes faith from the real acts of God in history; an entirely "from below" approach undercuts faith by grounding our knowledge of Christ on the tentative arguments of human scholarship. Neither extreme is wise or healthy.[19]

---

12. Erickson, *Christian Theology*, 608–9. On Christian faith in Christ as set against full confidence in the facts of the Gospel narratives, see Emil Brunner, *The Mediator: A Study of the Central Doctrine of the Christian Faith*, trans. Olive Wyon (Philadelphia: Westminster, 1947), 167–68.

13. On Rudolf Bultmann's doctrine of the kerygmatic Christ, see Alister E. McGrath, *The Making of Modern German Christology* (Oxford: Basil Blackwell, 1986), 127–43.

14. Pannenberg, *Jesus—God and Man*, 34–35.

15. Moltmann, *The Way of Jesus Christ*, 55–58.

16. Pannenberg, *Jesus—God and Man*, 36.

17. Schleiermacher, *The Christian Faith*, 94 (2:385). On Schleiermacher's Christology, see Moltmann, *The Way of Jesus Christ*, 59–60.

18. See the discussion of the historicity of Christ's resurrection in Pannenberg, *Jesus–God and Man*, 88–106.

19. Erickson, *Christian Theology*, 612–15.

Second, it is not accurate to use the label "from above" to lump the Christology of historical Christian orthodoxy together with the views of theologians such as Brunner and Bultmann, who treat the Holy Scriptures as faulty human documents, not the Word of God. Their attempts to construct a Christology "from above" are not grounded in the historical life of Jesus, which they regard as relatively uncertain in comparison to the proclaimed message (*kerygma*) about Christ's spiritual meaning for us. Only orthodox Christology is truly "from above," for it stands upon the doctrines revealed by the One who "came down from heaven" (John 3:11–13; 6:38). Stephen Wellum points out that if Scripture is not the sufficient ground for Christology, then we will be able to say nothing about Christ with certainty.[20]

Third, the insistence of some modern theologians upon Christology "from below" contradicts a fundamental theme of grace: revelation and redemption always proceed from God to man, not the other way around.[21] We find this principle of divine initiation in God's sending his Son into the world (John 3:16; Gal. 4:4). Furthermore, since God initiates revelation in Christ, we can know truths about Christ that would otherwise remain beyond the reach of human knowledge. Therefore, Christology "from above" must have priority over "from below," for Christ the Revealer is "of the Father" (John 1:14, 18).

Fourth, Wellum points out that there is "an ontological priority" to Christ's deity, for "Christ was the divine Son before he was the incarnate Son." Furthermore, Wellum says, his deity has an "epistemological priority," for to start with his humanity in an age saturated with pluralistic and relativistic assumptions tends to strip Christ not only of his deity, but also of his authority as the One supernaturally enabled by the Spirit to speak as God's perfect representative and to act as his great agent. Such Christology "from below" does not start with a biblical view of man, but with a secular view of man. Not surprisingly, it discovers a Jesus whose mindset is essentially the same as that of modern and postmodern secular people today.[22]

---

20. Stephen J. Wellum, *God the Son Incarnate: The Doctrine of Christ*, Foundations of Evangelical Theology (Wheaton, IL: Crossway, 2016), 87. Wellum argues that Christology "from above" should be defined not by the doctrine of Christ's deity but by the doctrine of special verbal revelation (86n15). His proposal is intriguing, but the terminology of "from above" and "from below" seems to be already fixed in theological discourse.

21. Thomas Torrance, *Incarnation: The Person and Life of Christ*, ed. Robert T. Walker (Downers Grove, IL: InterVarsity Press, 2008), 9–10.

22. Wellum, *God the Son Incarnate*, 190. See also David F. Wells, *The Person of Christ: A Biblical and Historical Analysis of the Incarnation*, Foundations for Faith: An Introduction to Christian Doctrine (Alliance, OH: Bible Scholar Books, 1984), 172–75.

The Biblical Approach

When we examine the Holy Scriptures, we find that they reveal both the deity and humanity of Christ, but in a manner that emphasizes that God the Son has come to us. In the Old Testament, the prophets foretold the birth of a child who would be called "Wonderful, Counsellor, the mighty God, the everlasting Father, the Prince of Peace" (Isa. 9:6). This child is "Immanuel," God with us (7:14). The King would be born in lowly Bethlehem, but his "goings forth have been from of old, from everlasting," and he would shepherd his people "in the strength of the LORD, in the majesty of the name of the LORD his God" (Mic. 5:2, 4). He is the righteous King, and he would be named "THE LORD OUR RIGHTEOUSNESS" (Jer. 23:6).

The Gospel of John exemplifies Christology "from above," for it opens with Christ "in the beginning," sharing the divine nature and participating in the divine work of creation (John 1:1–3). It is this eternal "Word" who "was made flesh" in the person of "Jesus Christ" (vv. 14, 17). Christ is the One whom the Father sent into the world to accomplish his saving will (6:37–40). The Synoptic Gospels, though beginning with Christ's birth or baptism, have a no less exalted view of Christ, for he is the uniquely beloved "Son of God," whose sandals a great prophet is unworthy to carry (Mark 1:1, 7, 11). Christ commands demons and disease to depart, and they do (vv. 27, 42). Christ's deity does not gradually appear in the storyline; "the reader, in his very first encounter with Jesus, is left in no doubt as to his being from above."[23]

Paul's epistles do not dwell on the story of Christ's earthly life, but declare him to be God's "Son Jesus Christ our Lord, which was made of the seed of David according to the flesh" (Rom. 1:3). Paul says, "When the fulness of the time was come, God sent forth his Son, made of a woman, made under the law, to redeem them that were under the law, that we might receive the adoption of sons" (Gal. 4:4–5). To Paul, Jesus Christ is not merely a prophet, teacher, or healer, but the Lord by whom all things, visible and invisible, were made and for whom they exist (Col. 1:16).

The epistle to the Hebrews likewise opens with a glorious view of the "Son," who is the Creator, the glory of the Father, the King of righteousness, and the object of the angels' worship (Heb. 1:2–3, 6, 8–12). Rather

---

23. Donald Macleod, *The Person of Christ*, Contours of Christian Theology (Downers Grove, IL: InterVarsity Press, 1998), 25.

than starting with the gentle Galilean and rising up "from below" to consider his special relationship to God, Hebrews starts with the brightness of divine glory and then says that this great person took human "flesh and blood" to deliver God's covenant people by his priestly sacrifice and merciful assistance (2:14–18).

We find the same approach in the other New Testament writings. James, though the brother of Jesus, regards himself as merely a "servant" of "the Lord Jesus Christ," for he is "the Lord of glory" (James 1:1; 2:1). John writes of Christ as "the Word of life," lately seen and touched by the apostles, but who "was from the beginning" (1 John 1:1–2). In Revelation, Christ is the glorious one, "the first and the last" (Rev. 1:17; 22:13), a title that Isaiah ascribes to the eternal Lord Jehovah, and him alone (Isa. 41:4; 44:6).

Nowhere does the Bible encourage us to start our Christology "from below." Rather, it exults in the truth that the Most High has lowered himself to meet us where we are and save us. Whether we encounter Jesus of Nazareth lying in the manger or enthroned at God's right hand, we soon discover that he is Lord and Christ (Luke 2:11; Acts 2:36). Christ appears to us in the Word with divine authority, requiring us to trust in him (John 14:1), just as the Father said: "This is my beloved Son, with whom I am well pleased; listen to him" (Matt. 17:5 ESV).

Therefore, our Christology must be done in faith and obedience. We do not approach Jesus as another figure in ancient historical documents, but as the Lord revealing himself in the Word. Christ demands that we build our lives upon his words and warns that if we do not, then we are foolish and will suffer ultimate loss (Matt. 7:24–27). On the one hand, Christ demands everything of us, even our supreme love (10:38). On the other hand, Christ offers us nothing less than true rest (11:28–30) and endless satisfaction (John 4:14). Our response must be to receive him by faith (1:12; 6:35). This does not negate the use of our reason; on the contrary, it liberates reason to function as God's noble servant: listening to his words, meditating upon them for deepening understanding, and directing all of life by the clear light of what God has said.

A Paradigm for Christology

How can we approach the study of the doctrine of Christology in a manner that duly honors Christ as one sent "from above," but who served God as a man here "below"? We find one valid paradigm in Paul's proclamation of Christ in Philippians 2:6–11. In that text, Paul sets forth the gospel of Christ in a manner designed to promote unity, humility, and mutual service in the church by calling people to adopt Christ's mindset and attitude (vv. 1–5).[24] Therefore, this Christological paradigm is experiential, practical, and doxological in its aim.[25]

First, Paul writes of *Christ's eternal deity*: "Who, being in the form of God, thought it not robbery to be equal with God" (Phil. 2:6). The word translated as "form" (*morphē*)[26] has as its basic meaning the outward appearance or shape of something. However, God does not have a visible shape. It is not helpful in this context to identify "form" with "glory," "appearance," or "image," for the same term appears in "the form of a servant" (v. 7). Neither is "the form of God" a reference to Adam as the "image of God."[27] The "form" word group can refer to inner character or nature,[28] and the term itself was used by philosophers for the distinctive character of a thing or concept.[29] J. B. Lightfoot (1828–1889) concluded that "form" implies "essential attributes."[30] Moisés Silva, while questioning Lightfoot's identification of "form" with philosophical ideas of essence, agrees that in this text it refers to "true divine nature" in contrast to "human nature."[31] Gordon Fee says it means "that which truly characterizes a given reality."[32] For Christ to exist in the form of God is "to possess the whole fullness of attributes which make God God," as B. B. Warfield

---

24. The verb translated as "let this mind be" (*phroneō*) is very common in Philippians (1:7; 2:2, 5; 3:15, 19; 4:2, 10). It refers not just to intellectual activity but also to one's attitude and intent.

25. In our discussion of Philippians 2:6–11, we are indebted to Peter T. O'Brien, *The Epistle to the Philippians*, The New International Greek Testament Commentary (Grand Rapids, MI: Eerdmans, 1991), 205–68.

26. "Form" (*morphē*) is found only in Mark 16:12 and Phil. 2:6, 7 in the New Testament. See Judg. 8:18; Job 4:16; Isa. 44:13; Dan. 3:19 LXX.

27. Contra James D. G. Dunn, *Christology in the Making: A New Testament Inquiry into the Origins of the Doctrine of the Incarnation*, 2nd ed. (Grand Rapids, MI: Eerdmans, 1989), 15.1 (115). Cognates of *morphē* can be used of God's conforming his people to the image of Christ (Rom. 8:29; 2 Cor. 3:18). However, *morphē* is never used in the LXX or New Testament for Adam or the "image" of God. Gordon Fee notes, "There is no linguistic tie to the Genesis narrative." *Pauline Christology: An Exegetical-Theological Study* (Peabody, MA: Hendrickson, 2007), 383. Furthermore, if Paul depicts Christ merely as the last Adam in Phil. 2:6, then it seems very strange that he would speak of him "being made in the likeness of men" (v. 7), which implies he was formerly not human. For a critique of Dunn's exegesis of Phil. 2:6–11, see Fee, *Pauline Christology*, 390–93.

28. Rom. 12:2; 2 Cor. 3:18; Gal. 4:19.

29. *TDNT*, 4:744–45.

30. J. B. Lightfoot, *Saint Paul's Epistle to the Philippians* (London: Macmillan and Co., 1903), 110, 132.

31. Moisés Silva, *Philippians*, 2nd ed., Baker Exegetical Commentary on the New Testament (Grand Rapids, MI: Baker Academic, 2005), 101.

32. Fee, *Pauline Christology*, 378.

(1851–1921) said.[33] The Greek present participle translated as "being" implies that this always has been and always will be true of Christ.[34] Thus, "being in the form of God" means Christ is eternally "equal with God," as Paul explains.[35]

Christ did not regard his divine equality as "robbery" (*harpagmos*), which appears to be an idiomatic expression for something one possesses but chooses not to exploit.[36] Perhaps more precisely, it means that Christ regarded his deity as consisting not of getting but of giving.[37] As John put it, "God is love," manifested especially in the gift of the Son (1 John 4:8–9). Similarly, though at an infinitely lower level, we should view whatever goods and abilities we have not as things to exploit for mere self-aggrandizement, but as a platform to serve others, for that is at the heart of our bearing God's image and imitation of Christ.

Second, Paul writes of *Christ's assumed humanity*: Christ "made himself of no reputation, and took upon him the form of a servant, and was made in the likeness of men" (Phil. 2:7). The verb translated as "made . . . of no reputation," also rendered as "emptied" (ESV), does not imply that Christ divested himself of his divine attributes or equality with God, but that he "took" to himself a human nature and thus made himself weak and subject to futility.[38] Christ's incarnation did not involve the subtraction of his deity, but the addition of humanity.[39] He assumed to himself "the form of a servant," or "slave" (*doulos*), the essential characteristics of one under the lordship of another. Christ, without ceasing to be God, became truly human. If the Lord Christ was willing to become as we are, then we should be willing to be what we are: God's servants who exist to do his will.

---

33. Benjamin B. Warfield, "The Person of Christ according to the New Testament," in *The Person and Work of Christ*, ed. Samuel G. Craig (Philadelphia: Presbyterian and Reformed, 1950), 39.

34. Fee, *Pauline Christology*, 376.

35. On "equal with God" as a further explanation of "in the form of God," see G. Walter Hansen, *The Letter to the Philippians*, The Pillar New Testament Commentary (Grand Rapids, MI: Eerdmans, 2009), 145.

36. Roy W. Hoover, "The Harpagmos Enigma: A Philological Solution," *Harvard Theological Review* 64 (1971): 95–119.

37. "*Harpagmos* means neither something not yet possessed but desirable (to be snatched at, *res rapienda*), nor something already possessed (*res rapta*) and to be clung to (*retinenda*), but rather the act of snatching (*raptus*). . . . That deity means not, as is popularly supposed, getting, but, paradoxically, giving is, indeed, the heart of the revelation in Christ Jesus." C. F. D. Moule, "Further Reflections on Philippians 2:5–11," in *Apostolic History and the Gospel: Biblical and Historical Essays Presented to F. F. Bruce on His 60th Birthday*, ed. W. Ward Gasque and Ralph P. Martin (Grand Rapids, MI: Eerdmans, 1970), 271, 276 (full chapter, 264–76). See Fee, *Pauline Christology*, 381–83.

38. "Took" (*labōn*) is a participle, modifying "made himself of no reputation" (*kenoō*) by explaining how he did so. For examples of *kenoō* as "make weak or futile," see Jer. 14:2; 15:9 LXX; Rom. 4:14; 1 Cor. 1:17; 9:15; 2 Cor. 9:3.

39. On the error of kenotic theology, see chap. 42.

Third, Paul writes of *Christ's incarnate states*: "And being found in fashion as a man, he humbled himself. . . . Wherefore God also hath highly exalted him" (Phil. 2:8–9). Christ voluntarily took upon himself a state of humiliation. He embraced a position lower than others so that he might serve them, just as we should (vv. 3–4). This self-humbling culminated in the "cross," an excruciating humiliation offensive to both Jews and Gentiles, the lowest position possible in ancient society (1 Cor. 1:21–23).

The shift from verses 6–8 to verses 9–11 is marked, signaling a definitive new state.[40] God "superexalted" Christ,[41] making him the "most high" over all creation.[42] Whereas the Roman imperial cult asserted that the gods had made Caesar the "Lord" (*kyrios*), the gospel announces that the one true God made the crucified Christ to be Lord, and not merely an earthly emperor, but the Lord of heaven and earth.[43] By the Father's decree, all rational creatures will bow and confess that Jesus is Lord (v. 10). Paul's statement that "every knee should bow" to Christ and "every tongue should confess" him alludes to ancient prophecy concerning the Lord God (Isa. 45:22–23), implying that receiving such worship is the unique right of Jehovah, the only God. In Christ's state of exaltation, the person who has always been God is honored as God, though he is now also a man. Christians tend to focus on Christ's humiliation, especially his cross, but the Scriptures also call us to set our minds on Christ seated at God's right hand in glory (Col. 3:1–2). Wilhelmus à Brakel said, "That is the beginning of heaven, where the beholding of Christ in His glory will be the eternal joy and occupation of the elect."[44]

Fourth, Paul intertwines his description of these states with *Christ's mediatorial work*: "He humbled himself, and became obedient unto death, even the death of the cross. Wherefore God also hath highly exalted him . . . that every tongue should confess that Jesus Christ is Lord, to the glory of God the Father" (Phil. 2:8–11). Though "servant" (*doulos*) and "Lord" (*kyrios*) reveal Christ's humanity and deity, they also highlight his

---

40. On topical, grammatical, and syntactical differences between: Phil. 2:6–8 and vv. 9–11, see R. P. Martin, *Carmen Christi: Philippians ii.5–11 in Recent Interpretation and in the Setting of Early Christian Worship*, Society for New Testament Studies Monograph Series 4 (Cambridge: Cambridge University Press, 1967), 229.

41. Richard R. Melick, *Philippians, Colossians, Philemon*, The New American Commentary 32 (Nashville: Broadman & Holman, 1991), 105.

42. The verb translated as "highly exalted" (*hyperypsoō*) in Phil. 2:9 appears in the Septuagint's rendering of Ps. 97:9: "For thou, Lord, art high above all the earth; thou art exalted far above all gods."

43. Hansen, *The Letter to the Philippians*, 163.

44. Brakel, *The Christian's Reasonable Service*, 1:653.

functions as God's appointed Mediator. Key leaders under God's ancient covenants were called the Lord's servants, including Abraham, Moses, Joshua, and David.[45] Christ is God's great "servant" (*doulos*), in whom God is glorified by the salvation of his international covenant people (Isa. 49:3–8 LXX). At the heart of Christ's mediatorial work is his obedience, even to the point of suffering God's curse on the cross (Deut. 21:23). Death for us is inevitable in a fallen world, but for Christ it was voluntary obedience to the Father, another indication that Christ is the eternal God,[46] who embraced death to fulfill his mission of salvation.

God the Father blessed Christ for his extreme obedience by greatly honoring him, which is also for our sake, that we may be lifted from humiliation to glory (Phil. 3:21). As "Lord" (*kyrios*), Christ still serves as the divine Mediator to save God's people and punish his enemies (Psalm 110 LXX; Acts 2:32–36). Thus, God's "servant" was "exalted . . . very high" so that "the pleasure of the LORD shall prosper in his hand" (Isa. 52:13; 53:10). The result of Christ's active lordship will be "the glory of God the Father" for all eternity. Therefore, we must trust in Christ, both in his past work as God's lowly servant and his present work as the exalted Lord, to save us from our sins for the glory and praise of the triune God.

In the scope of this short text, Paul lays out a beautiful paradigm for Christology. We begin with Christ's deity, consider his incarnation as a man, reflect upon his two incarnate states of humiliation and exaltation, and finally study his mediatorial office and work as prophet, priest, and king in the light of those two states.[47] Therefore, after an examination of Christ's names and titles, we will follow this method for the pursuit of a biblical, God-honoring, and soul-enriching Christology.

The Spiritual Dynamics of Christology

Since the Lord Jesus Christ can be properly known only as an object of our faith, submission, and adoration, the study of Christology is not only a theological endeavor but a spiritual exercise. This is true of all theology, but in a special manner regarding Christology.[48] As we see in the Pharisees,

---

45. For a few examples among many, see Gen. 26:24; Josh. 1:2; 24:29; 2 Sam. 7:5. The covenantal servant theme is traced in chaps. 31–32.

46. Ralph P. Martin, *Philippians: An Introduction and Commentary*, Tyndale New Testament Commentaries 11 (Downers Grove, IL: InterVarsity Press, 1987), 111.

47. These are the same topics addressed in the Westminster Shorter Catechism (Q. 21–28), though the catechism addresses Christ's two states after his mediatorial office. *Reformed Confessions*, 4:356–57.

48. On the spiritual dynamic of theology in general, see *RST*, 1:145–58 (chap. 8).

it is entirely possible to be well versed in the Holy Scriptures but ignorant of Christ, and consequently to miss eternal life (John 5:39). In Paul's treatment of the ministry of the Word in 2 Corinthians 3–4, we find a series of principles to guide us in our study of spiritual Christology.

The Necessity of the Spirit

Paul taught that though his fellow Jews regularly heard the reading of the Scriptures, in many cases a veil covered their hearts and their minds were hardened (2 Cor. 3:14–16).[49] Charles Hodge commented, "They neither understood nor felt the power of the truth."[50] However, "where the Spirit of the Lord is, there is liberty" (v. 17). In this context, "liberty" refers to righteousness and life in contrast to condemnation and death (vv. 6, 9). Such liberty is possible because "with the Spirit of the living God," Christ writes the word "not in tables of stone, but in fleshy tables of the heart" (v. 3). Philip Hughes (1915–1990) said, "We are warned, therefore, of the terrible possibility of intellectual hardening when face to face with the glorious revelation of divine truth."[51] To avoid this hardening, you need the Spirit. Therefore, let us pray for the Father to grant us the Spirit so that we may feed on Christ (Luke 11:13; Eph. 1:17–20).

The Transforming Glory

The Holy Spirit reveals Christ in a way that makes us like him. Paul says, "We all, with unveiled face, beholding the glory of the Lord, are being transformed into the same image from one degree of glory to another. For this comes from the Lord who is the Spirit" (2 Cor. 3:18 ESV). Believers, in contrast to unbelievers, are "beholding" God as he reveals himself in Christ.[52] When the Spirit pulls aside the veil of our hardness, what we see in the Word is "glory"; not just truth, but true majesty and splendid beauty in Jesus Christ—the very "glory of God" (4:6). As a result, we experience a process of transformation into "glory," not deification into demigods,

---

49. The word translated as "blinded" (*pōroō*) in the KJV actually means "hardened" (cf. Mark 6:52; 8:17; John 12:40).

50. Charles Hodge, *A Commentary on 1 & 2 Corinthians* (Edinburgh: Banner of Truth, 1974), 445.

51. Philip E. Hughes, *Paul's Second Epistle to the Corinthians*, The New International Commentary on the New Testament (Grand Rapids, MI: Eerdmans, 1962), 111.

52. On the translation of *katoptrizomenoi* as "beholding" or "beholding as in a glass [mirror]," see Hughes, *Paul's Second Epistle to the Corinthians*, 118–19n19; David E. Garland, *2 Corinthians*, The New American Commentary 29 (Nashville: Broadman & Holman, 1999), 199–200; and George H. Guthrie, *2 Corinthians*, Baker Exegetical Commentary on the New Testament (Grand Rapids, MI: Baker Academic, 2015), 227.

but sanctification into the image of God by conformity to Christ (v. 4). We must approach Christology with this twofold desire: to see God's glory in Christ (Ps. 27:4) and to become conformed to his image in knowledge, righteousness, and holiness (Eph. 4:24; Col. 3:10). Do you pant after the glory of Christ like a deer pants for water (Ps. 42:1)? Do you long to be more like Jesus in his moral perfection and meek love?

The Clear Truth

We have the undeserved privilege of communicating the gospel to men, women, and children—the gospel that the Spirit uses to bring divine glory to earth. Therefore, "we do not lose heart" (2 Cor. 4:1 ESV). Hughes commented, "The Apostle is making no arrogant claim to self-sufficiency (cf. 3:5). . . . It is not an achievement of human ability but a consequence of divine mercy."[53] At the same time, Paul says, the merciful revelation of God's glory in the doctrine of Christ strikes a death blow to all deceitful tactics that people may use to promote themselves and their party. Instead, "by manifestation of the truth," the faithful servants of God are "commending ourselves to every man's conscience in the sight of God" (2 Cor. 4:2). Our goal must be to simply and clearly display the truth that God revealed, knowing that God is watching and will hold both speaker and listener (and writer and reader) accountable. God is jealous over his Son's glory and will judge us if we distort the truth. We speak "in the sight of God" (2:17). Let us pray for boldness (Eph. 6:19–20) and set our faces like flint, as Christ himself did when facing his foes (Isa. 50:7).

The Satanic Blindness

The study and teaching of Christology is a struggle, but it is primarily a struggle against demonic forces, not against people. The gospel is "hid to them that are lost," because "the god of this world hath blinded the minds of them which believe not" (2 Cor. 4:3–4). Specifically, Satan blinds unbelievers to "the light of the gospel of the glory of Christ" (v. 4 ESV). It may be that they can learn the words and even explain the theological formulas, but they are utterly insensible to the divine glory in Christ. The word of Christ does not evoke their trust, love, and worship. We must be

---

53. Hughes, *Paul's Second Epistle to the Corinthians*, 121–22.

realistic about how people will respond to our attempts to teach Christology. Do we think that our talking about Christ will dispel the darkness that Christ's incarnate presence did not? We do not have the power to bring a single soul to Christ.

The Demands of Self-Denial

When the world's hardness confronts us, it tests our motives in ministry. How will we respond to rejection? Are we doing Christology for our sake or for Christ? Paul says, "For we preach not ourselves, but Christ Jesus the Lord; and ourselves your servants for Jesus' sake" (2 Cor. 4:5). Hodge commented, "To preach one's self is to make self the end of preaching; that is, preaching with the design to attract to ourselves the admiration, the confidence or homage of men."[54] We must deny our inherent selfishness that screams for recognition. The selfish desire for the praise of men is nothing less than treason against Christ, for if indulged it would set us up as Lord, though we are nothing more than servants of the people around us. There is no Christology without taking up your cross. Make it your byword: "He must increase, but I must decrease" (John 3:30). Furthermore, beware of secret bitterness over your sacrifices for the gospel. You are not losing; you are gaining by serving Christ and his gospel.

The Omnipotent Illumination

Despite man's unbelief and Satan's blinding influence, some people do see the glory of God in the doctrines of Christology. This is entirely by the power of God. Paul says, "For God, who commanded the light to shine out of darkness, hath shined in our hearts, to give the light of the knowledge of the glory of God in the face of Jesus Christ" (2 Cor. 4:6). Paul here alludes to God's sovereign act when he spoke into the primeval darkness, "Let there be light," with the result that "there was light" (Gen. 1:3).[55] In the same way, inward saving illumination is a supernatural act of omnipotent

---

54. Hodge, *A Commentary on 1 & 2 Corinthians*, 463.

55. Some scholars propose that 2 Cor. 4:6 does not allude to Gen. 1:3 but to Isa. 9:2 (9:1 LXX), "The people that walked in darkness [*skotos*] have seen a great light: they that dwell in the land of the shadow of death, upon them hath the light shined [*phōs lampsei*]." Garland, *2 Corinthians*, 217. However, Paul speaks of God commanding light to shine, which does not appear in Isaiah 9, but in Genesis 1. Isaiah 9 speaks of light breaking into "Galilee," a prophecy of Christ's public ministry (Matt. 4:12–17), whereas 2 Corinthians 4 is about the dawning of light in the heart. Paul alludes to Gen. 1 in this context by the phrase "the image of God" (v. 4). Shortly afterward, Paul speaks of salvation as a new creation (5:17). So it is best to see 4:6 as an allusion to creation.

power to effect a new creation. John Owen said, "The act of God working faith in us is a creating act: 'We are his workmanship, created in Christ Jesus' (Eph. 2:10)."[56] This truth should deepen our humility as we study and teach this subject. We need help that only God can give. At the same time, knowing this should increase our hope and expectation. God has the power to cause Christ's glory to irradiate the hearts of sinners, and God has determined to use that power in the lives of countless elect individuals among all nations.

The Earthen Vessels

Even while exulting in the wonder of God's grace, Paul pauses to recognize the lowliness of God's servants: "But we have this treasure in earthen vessels" (2 Cor. 4:7). God has chosen to keep the "treasure" of Christ's glory not in strong and ornate chests as in a king's palace, but in easily broken clay jars such as people once used for common tasks (cf. 2 Tim. 2:20).[57] That is what we are. Yet there is a wise divine purpose behind this paradox: "that the excellency of the power may be of God, and not of us" (2 Cor. 4:7). As people observe our weakness, distress, and persecution, they see that the gospel's glory comes from no mere man, but from the God who raised Jesus from the dead (vv. 8–14). It is God's way to lay the death of Jesus upon those who proclaim his glory (v. 10).

The spiritual dynamic of Christology is ever accompanied by humiliation. We should be thankful for this. Our weakness protects us and others from glorying in flesh and pushes us to glory in the Lord alone (1 Cor. 1:30–31). Furthermore, suffering with Christ prepares us to share in his glory (Rom. 8:17). In God's providence, our sorrows cooperate with the study of Christology so that we deeply identify with Jesus and experience our union with him in both suffering and resurrection (Phil. 3:10). Take heart, dear believer, as you grieve over your sins and suffer distress from the world. Your tears will water the seed of this doctrine so that it bears much fruit in your life.

---

56. Owen, *Discourse Concerning the Holy Spirit*, in *Works*, 3:321. See Joel R. Beeke, "The Illumination of the Spirit," in *The Holy Spirit and Reformed Spirituality: A Tribute to Geoffrey Thomas*, ed. Joel R. Beeke and Derek W. H. Thomas (Grand Rapids, MI: Reformation Heritage Books, 2013), 52–69.

57. "Clay jars were unexceptional, affordable, disposable, and put to a wide variety of uses in the ancient world. As mass-produced, throwaway containers for the general population, they were both fragile and expendable. Paul's emphasis, however, seems to rest on the idea of fragility . . . and perhaps the unassuming 'ordinariness' of clay containers, rather than suggesting that the human minister is of little value or disposable." Guthrie, *2 Corinthians*, 253.

Sing to the Lord

Desiring to See the Beauty of the Lord in Troubled Times

Jehovah is my light,
And my salvation near;
Who shall my soul affright,
Or cause my heart to fear?
While God my strength, my life sustains,
Secure from fear my soul remains.

My one request has been,
And still this prayer I raise,
That I may dwell within
God's house through all my days,
Jehovah's beauty to admire,
And in His temple to inquire.

When troubles round me swell,
When fears and dangers throng,
Securely I will dwell
In His pavilion strong;
Within the covert of His tent
He hides me till the storm is spent.

Uplifted on a rock
Above my foes around,
Amid the battle shock
My song shall still resound;
Then joyful off'rings I will bring,
Jehovah's praise my heart shall sing.

Psalm 27
Tune: Millennium
The Psalter, No. 71

Questions for Meditation or Discussion

1. How does Christ's prayer in John 17:24 reveal his deep desire?
   How should it direct our desires and prayers?
2. Explain the value of studying Christology, in that it is
   • a central subject
   • a polemical subject

- a necessary subject
- an awakening subject
- a captivating subject
- a glorious subject

3. What do some theologians mean by Christology "from above" versus "from below"?

4. What response do the authors offer to the "from above" and "from below" distinction?

5. What pattern can we observe about how the Bible teaches us Christology?

6. What paradigm for Christology can be derived from Philippians 2:6–11?

7. What spiritual dynamics of Christology do we find revealed in the following texts from 2 Corinthians: (1) 3:14–17, (2) 3:18, (3) 4:1–2, (4) 4:3–4, (5) 4:5, (6) 4:6, and (7) 4:7?

8. Which aspects of the spiritual dynamics of Christology do you find most humbling? Which aspects are most encouraging to you?

Questions for Deeper Reflection

9. Why do the authors object to grouping the Christologies of classic orthodox Christianity, Emil Brunner, and Rudolf Bultmann together under the label "Christology 'from above'"? Is their objection valid? Why or why not? What does this objection reveal about how careful we must be in creating categories for theological views?

10. Based on 2 Corinthians 3:14–4:7, what are some specific prayer requests you can lift up to God for your study of Christology as you read this book? What are some requests you can pray to God about your own ministry? After you list these requests, pray them.

37

The Names of Christ

In the Bible, names matter. They can express a cry of despair (1 Sam. 4:21) or fly as banners of hope. Adam named his wife "Eve," or "life," after hearing that though his sin had merited death, God would raise up the Seed of the woman and bring salvation (Gen. 3:15–20). Lamech named his son "Noah," or "rest," in the hope that God would give people rest from the curse (5:29). The Lord changed Abram's name to "Abraham" and Sarai's to "Sarah" as reminders of his promises to them (17:5, 15). And their son was "Isaac," or "laughter," both to mark their incredulity at the promise (vv. 17–19) and to celebrate their joy when it came true (21:3, 6).

When people name their children, sometimes they simply choose the name of a favored relative in the family (Luke 1:60–61). However, when God named his Son, he revealed his Son's unique glory. The Son is God, and God's "names" manifest his glory, grace, power, and presence (Pss. 75:1; 91:14; 99:3).[1] Christ's names also reveal who he is and what he has done. God makes known his Son's names to us and evokes our faith in those names so that we may receive Christ himself and have him dwelling in us (John 1:12).

God revealed many names for his Son.[2] Each of them, like a sparkling facet on a diamond, is a revelation of the gospel for our faith. None of them is able to exhaust all that Christ is for us. Studying them serves as

---

1. On the glory of the divine "name," see *RST*, 1:520–21.
2. In this chapter, we use the word *name* in a manner that includes not just personal names, but also titles. For example, it appears that the "name" granted to Christ in Phil. 2:9 is "Lord" (v. 11), and in Heb. 1:4–5, the "name" is "Son."

a doorway into the riches of our Savior. As we consider these names, we will follow the order set by the Apostles' Creed in its confession of belief in "Jesus Christ, [the Father's] only begotten Son, our Lord."[3] Hence, we will address his human name ("Jesus"), his names of office (such as "Christ"), and his names of deity ("Son," "Lord," and so on).

His Human Name: Jesus

Our Lord bears the human name *Jesus* (Greek *Iēsous*). Joseph and Mary did not choose this name; it was commanded from heaven (Matt. 1:21; Luke 1:31). That is not to say that the name was unique, for there were other men named "Jesus" (Col. 4:11). It was a common name among Jews through the beginning of the second century AD.[4] For this reason, people spoke of "Jesus of Nazareth" in order to distinguish him from others with the same name.[5] Therefore, the name "Jesus" testifies to Christ's humanity—it is the name of a man.

Why did God ordain through angels that this name would be given to his incarnate Son? The answer to this question comes from both the name's historical background and its etymological meaning. Historically, "Jesus" was the Greek form of "Joshua" (Hebrew *Yehoshu'a*),[6] as appears from the use of "Jesus" in the Septuagint and New Testament for that great Israelite leader Joshua, the son of Nun.[7] Joshua's parents named him "Oshea," or "Hoshea" (ESV),[8] but the prophet Moses renamed him "Joshua" (Num. 13:16 ESV), perhaps in conjunction with Joshua's faith that the Lord would give the Israelites victory over their enemies so that they could inherit the land of Canaan (14:6–9). Joshua succeeded Moses as the servant of the Lord (Josh. 1:1–2; 24:29) and brought Israel into the Promised Land just as God had sworn to Abraham (21:43–45; 23:14). The land of Canaan was a type of the saints' eternal rest in their glorious inheritance, the kingdom of God (Heb. 4:7–9; 11:13–16).[9]

---

3. *The Three Forms of Unity*, 5.
4. *TDNT*, 3:285.
5. Matt. 26:71; Mark 1:24; 10:47; 14:67; 16:6; Luke 4:34; 18:37; 24:19; John 1:45; 18:5, 7; 19:19; Acts 2:22; 6:14; 10:38; 22:8; 26:9; cf. Matt. 21:11; Acts 3:6; 4:10.
6. After the exile, the Hebrew name *Yehoshu'a* was shortened to *Yeshu'a*, which was then transliterated into Greek as *Iēsou* or *Iēsous* (Ezra 2:2; Neh. 8:17). In Latin, it became *Jesus* (pronounced Yay-soos).
7. Ex. 17:9–10; 1 Kings 16:34; etc. LXX; Acts 7:45; Heb. 4:8.
8. This is the same name given to the prophet "Hosea" (Hebrew *Hoshe'a*).
9. It may be that "Jesus" also alludes to another Joshua, son of Josedech, the high priest who served the returned exiles alongside Zerubbabel and foreshadowed the coming Priest-King (Hag. 1:1, 13, 14; 2:2, 4; Zech. 3:1–10; 6:11–13). See Vos, *Reformed Dogmatics*, 3:8.

Etymologically, the name "Jesus" or "Joshua" derives from Hebrew roots meaning "the LORD is salvation."[10] The Scriptures couple God's name and salvation to communicate that the Lord, and he alone, saves his people from evil by his sovereign grace.[11] We ordinarily must exercise caution in deriving the meaning of words from their etymology instead of looking to their usage, but the Scriptures explicitly state, "Thou shalt call his name JESUS: for he shall save his people from their sins" (Matt. 1:21). Hence, his name "Jesus" means that he is the Savior, as John of Damascus observed.[12] Unlike Joshua, Jesus does not merely rescue his people from physical dangers, but gives them victory over the spiritual evil that alienates them from God.

The Greek phrase "he shall save" in Matthew 1:21 emphasizes "he" (*autos*): he and he alone will do this.[13] The Heidelberg Catechism (LD 11, Q. 29) says, "Why is the Son of God called Jesus, that is, a Savior? Because He saveth us, and delivereth us from our sins; and likewise, because we ought not to seek, neither can find salvation in any other."[14] William Perkins said, "He is both a perfect and absolute Savior, as also the alone Savior of man, because the work of salvation is wholly and only wrought by Him, and no part thereof is reserved to any creature in heaven or in earth."[15]

Therefore, the name "Jesus" identifies Christ as God's human servant who alone saves people and brings them into their eternal inheritance. However, "the name speaks to us of the divine omnipotence of salvation," as Geerhardus Vos said.[16] Though "Jesus" is a human name, its meaning suggests that in this man, God has come to us, for God says, "I, even I, am the LORD; and beside me there is no saviour" (Isa. 43:11; cf. 45:21).[17]

The name "Jesus" is a sober warning to those careless about their sins, for how can they embrace this "Savior" if they do not believe they

---

10. Vos, *Reformed Dogmatics*, 3:6. "Joshua" (*Yehoshu'a*) derives from "the LORD" (*YHWH* or its shortened form, *Yah*) and the verb translated as "rescue, save" (*yasha'*). Compare "Elisha" (*Elisha'*), meaning "God is salvation."

11. Ex. 14:13, 30; 15:2; 1 Sam. 17:47; 2 Chron. 20:17; Ps. 3:8; Lam. 3:26; Jonah 2:9.

12. John of Damascus, *An Exact Exposition of the Orthodox Faith*, 3.2, in NPNF², 9.2:46.

13. Morris, *The Gospel according to Matthew*, 29–30.

14. *The Three Forms of Unity*, 77.

15. Perkins, *An Exposition of the Symbol*, in *Works*, 5:98. Perkins was not excluding the other persons of the Trinity, but clarified that the Father saves through the Son, and the Spirit saves by applying the work of the Son (99).

16. Vos, *Reformed Dogmatics*, 3:7.

17. Herman Witsius, *Sacred Dissertations on the Apostles' Creed*, trans. Donald Fraser, 2 vols. (1823; repr., Grand Rapids, MI: Reformation Heritage Books, 2010), 9.12 (1:237).

are sinners in need of salvation? Perkins reminded us that before we can acknowledge the Savior, we must believe and feel the offense of our sins against God. To receive Jesus, we must know that without him we will perish forever, for lost people are the only ones that Jesus came to save (Matt. 18:11; Luke 19:10).[18]

The name "Jesus" also contains a sweet promise to believers. Caspar Olevianus said, "Since God, who cannot lie, commanded from heaven that His Son manifested in the flesh be given this name Jesus, that is, 'Savior,' I know for certain and have the assurance that He fully and perfectly saves me, body and soul. . . . Faithful is He who bears that splendid name Jesus. He will do what He promised."[19]

His Official Name: Christ

Jesus is *the Christ*. Though we call him "Jesus Christ," the word "Christ" is not a family name, like Smith or Garcia, but a title reflecting the office to which God appointed him. Thus, he is also called "Christ Jesus" (Rom. 3:24; 8:1; etc.). The title "Christ" transliterates a Greek word meaning "anointed" (*christos*). In the Septuagint, this word renders the Hebrew word "Messiah" (*mashiakh*), which carries the same meaning (cf. John 1:41). To "anoint" (*mashakh*) a person's head with oil could be a general sign of festivity or honor (Amos 6:6; Dan. 10:3), but it often functioned to designate a person called to sacred office by God's appointment. Thus, the king of Israel was called "the LORD's anointed."[20] Anointing with oil also represented the Spirit's empowerment for service.[21] Vos affirmed this "twofold" significance of anointing for an individual: it was "a declarative, explanatory act," as "the proof that he is authorized to exercise a certain office," and "an equipping act whereby the gifts of the office are granted . . . by the power of the Holy Spirit."[22] Thus, anointing involved both appointment to and qualification for the office. Someone who was appointed without qualification would lack needed giftedness or the competence to perform the office. Someone who was qualified without appointment would lack the needed authority, the right to perform the office.

18. Perkins, *An Exposition of the Symbol*, in *Works*, 5:100.
19. Olevianus, *An Exposition of the Apostles' Creed*, 54. We omit a Scripture reference that Olevianus cited.
20. 1 Sam. 16:6; 24:6, 10; 26:9, 11, 16, 23; 2 Sam. 1:14, 16; 19:21.
21. 1 Sam. 16:13; Isa. 61:1; cf. 11:2; 42:1.
22. Vos, *Reformed Dogmatics*, 3:10.

In the Old Testament, anointing was the means by which people were ordained to one of the three offices of God's covenantal servants. Moses anointed Aaron and his sons in their consecration to serve God as holy priests (Ex. 28:41; 29:9). Samuel anointed Saul to be God's appointed king over Israel (1 Sam. 10:1; 15:1). Elijah anointed Elisha to succeed him as the Lord's prophet (1 King 19:16). Thus, the messianic title "anointed" was used of Spirit-empowered prophets (Ps. 105:15), priests (Lev. 4:3, 5), and kings (1 Sam. 2:10; Ps. 18:50).

However, "Christ" was particularly applied to the unique individual who would reign by God's decree over the entire world (Ps. 2:2, 7–8).[23] The Lord promised to grant the Holy Spirit to the One who would reign in divine power and righteousness (Isa. 11:2–5), and reveal the good news that sets mourning sinners free (61:1–3). "The Lord's Christ" is nothing less than God's "salvation" and "revelation" for "all peoples" (Luke 2:26–35). Thus, by the time of Jesus's birth and earthly ministry, there was a common expectation among the Jews and Samaritans that God would send an anointed ruler and revealer to save his people and dwell with them forever. The role of king was especially prominent in the messianic hopes of the day.[24]

Simon Peter's confession that Jesus is "the Christ" (Mark 8:29) communicates a unique glory, for in that context the title surpasses what might be said about God's prophets, even great servants of God such as the miracle-working Elijah (vv. 27–28). Though Peter's mind was still clouded by falsehoods about the Messiah (vv. 31–33), his confession of Christ declared truth of such divine character that it could be known only by saving revelation from God (Matt. 16:17). It requires supernatural faith to perceive that the humble Jesus of Nazareth is the Christ, the Lord with sovereign authority over the church and power to build it though all hell oppose him (v. 18).

Therefore, the Christ exercises sovereign authority and power to save his people by the Holy Spirit. Jesus points out that though "Christ" is the son of David, he is also David's Lord, who sits at God's right hand (Mark 12:35–37; cf. Ps. 110:1). This Christ transcends all other anointed servants of God as the heavens are above the earth. He supremely is "the Christ of

23. For the application of Psalm 2 to Jesus Christ, see Acts 4:25–26; 13:33; Heb. 1:5; 5:5; Rev. 2:26–27; 12:5; 19:15.
24. Matt. 2:1–4; 22:42; Mark 15:32; Luke 23:2, 35–39; John 4:25, 29, 42; 7:26–27, 31, 42; 12:34.

God" (Luke 9:20), the One anointed by God to do what God sent him to do (John 17:3, 7). His authority and power are given to him by God (v. 2; Matt. 28:18). As Olevianus said, we can trust that Christ was "sent with a mandate from the Father."[25]

To confess that Jesus is the Christ in the full sense of the term is to acknowledge him as the divinely authorized, Spirit-anointed Mediator of God's covenant of grace—the Prophet, Priest, and King upon whom our salvation hangs.[26] No one prior to Christ was anointed to all three offices, showing Christ's unique position in history.

Other General Names of His Saving Office

There are many other names that God's Word gives to Christ to communicate what he is for his people. Some of these refer to his work in general.

Christ is the *Mediator* between God and man,[27] in the sense of a middleman chosen to establish a relationship between two parties and to intercede with the greater for his blessings on the lesser.[28] His mediation revolves around the covenant established by his redeeming death (1 Tim. 2:5–6; Heb. 9:15), for the relationship between God and man is broken by sin. Christ's office as Mediator shows us "the abominable nature of sin," and yet calls us to "admire the love of God, in sending such a blessed Mediator to make peace for us," as Benjamin Keach said.[29]

He is God's *Servant*, the obedient agent by whom God's Spirit accomplishes God's saving will.[30] God gave this title to key leaders through whom he established and implemented his covenant, such as Moses and David.[31] Preeminently, Christ is God's Servant, the mighty "arm of the LORD" who came as a "man of sorrows" and yet was "exalted" because he accomplished his work as God's "righteous servant" (Isa. 52:13; 53:1, 3, 11).

---

25. Olevianus, *An Exposition of the Apostles' Creed*, 56.

26. Heidelberg Catechism (LD 12, Q. 31), in *The Three Forms of Unity*, 78.

27. Mediator: 1 Tim. 2:5; Heb. 8:6; 9:15; 12:24; cf. Job 9:33 LXX.

28. *TDNT*, 4:601–2 (sense 3). For a secular example, see Flavius Josephus, *Antiquities*, 16.2.24, in *The Works of Josephus*, trans. William Whiston (Peabody, MA: Hendrickson, 1987), 427. On the Mediator's intercession to God for sinners, see the Belgic Confession (Art. 26), in *The Three Forms of Unity*, 44.

29. Benjamin Keach, *Preaching from the Types and Metaphors of the Bible* (1855; repr., Grand Rapids, MI: Kregel, 1972), 318.

30. Servant: Isa. 42:1; 49:3, 6; 52:13; 53:11; Ezek. 34:23–24; 37:24–25; Zech. 3:8; Matt. 12:8. It is likely that the references to Jesus as God's "Son" or "child" (*pais*) in Acts 3:13, 25; 4:27, 30 should also be understood as "servant" (4:25; cf. Isa. 42:1; 49:6; 52:13 LXX).

31. The covenantal servant theme is touched upon in several places in chaps. 31–32.

He is called the *Savior*,[32] which means someone who rescues those who are in great trouble. This title can be used of a human "deliverer" raised up by God to rescue his people from their enemies (Judg. 3:9, 15 LXX), but it often refers to God in the Septuagint, and in the New Testament, it always refers to Christ or God.[33]

Other general names for Christ's office include the following. He is the *Messenger* or *Angel* (Hebrew *mal'ak*) of the Lord,[34] not a created spirit, but the One who is God and is sent by God (Ex. 23:20–23). "The Lord" comes to "his temple" as "the messenger [*mal'ak*] of the covenant" (Mal. 3:1). He is the *Last Adam* (1 Cor. 15:45), for just as Adam's disobedience brought condemnation and death to all in him, so Christ's obedience unto death brought justification and life to all in him (v. 22; Rom. 5:14). He is the *Son of Abraham* (Matt. 1:1)—not just another descendant of Abraham, but Abraham's great seed (Gal. 3:16), in whom the promises of blessing are fulfilled for Israel and all nations (Gen. 22:18; Acts 3:25–26).

The Lord's names and titles offer us salvation in a manner that we can lay hold of. Proverbs 18:10 says, "The name of the Lord is a strong tower: the righteous runneth into it, and is safe." This promise does not encourage a magical invocation of the Lord's name, as if repeating syllables has power (Acts 19:13–17). Rather, God promises that we can hide ourselves in him by trusting in who he is, what he has done, and what he will do for us. This "strong tower" is entered only by the one who "runneth" there in humility, need, and trust. Charles Bridges said, "Every man is as his trust. A trust in God communicates a divine and lofty spirit. We feel that we are surrounded with God, and dwelling on high with him. Oh, the sweet security of the weakest believer, shut up in an impregnable fortress!"[35]

His Particular Names of Office

We may also consider names of Christ that proclaim particular aspects of his mission. We classify them according to Christ's threefold office.

---

32. Savior: Luke 2:11; John 4:42; 5:31; 13:23; Eph. 5:23; Phil. 3:20; 2 Tim. 1:10; Titus 1:4; 2:13; 3:6; 1 John 4:14.

33. On God as "Savior" (*sōtēr*), see also Deut. 32:15; 1 Sam. 10:19; Ps. 23[24]:5; 24[25]:5; 26[27]:1, 9; 61:3, 7 [62:2, 6]; 64:6 [65:5]; 78:9 [79:9]; 94:1 [95:1]; Isa. 12:2; 17:10; 45:15, 21; 62:11; Mic. 7:7; Hab. 3:18 LXX; Luke 1:47; 1 Tim. 1:1; 2:3; 4:10; Titus 1:3; 2:10; 3:4; Jude 25.

34. Angel of the Lord: Gen. 16:7–14; 22:11–18; Ex. 3:2–6; Num. 22:22–35; etc.

35. Bridges, *A Commentary on Proverbs*, 288.

Names of Divine Revelation

Jesus is the great and final *Prophet* who declares God's word,[36] and he himself is the living and eternal *Word*.[37] The latter indicates not only divine revelation but creative action (John 1:1–3; cf. Ps. 33:6). Christ both reveals the truth and is the *Truth* (John 14:6; cf. 1 John 5:20). He is the *Image of God* who infinitely transcends Adam, being the Creator of all, yet who became for us the last Adam, revealing God's glory and restoring that glory to us.[38] Christ is the *Faithful Witness* who testifies God's truth to a hostile world (Rev. 1:5; 3:14), and the *Amen* whose words are absolutely trustworthy and in whom God's promises all come true (v. 14; cf. 2 Cor. 1:20). He is the *Rabbi, Master*, and *Teacher* whose disciples we must be if we would learn the truth and be like him.[39] Though he sent out the apostles, he is the great *Apostle*, or one sent out from God.[40]

As the revealer, Christ is the *Light* who illuminates men's darkness,[41] including the *Star* that brightens their night and anticipates the morning (Num. 24:17; Rev. 2:28; 22:16); the *Dayspring* or dawn that brings hope and direction to the despairing (Luke 1:78–79); and the *Sun of Righteousness*, who rises "with healing in his wings" (Mal. 4:2; cf. Ps. 84:11). James Large said, "Take away the sun from our system, and all would be darkness and death. . . . So man without a Saviour is a ruin, and his soul without a spiritual sun to enlighten it, a desolation."[42]

Names of Divine Reconciliation

Jesus is the *Priest*,[43] even the *High Priest*,[44] who made atonement for sins and intercedes for God's blessing on his people. As the interceding Priest,

---

36. Prophet: Deut. 18:15; Luke 7:16; Acts 3:22; 7:37; cf. Matt. 17:5.
37. Word: John 1:1, 14; 1 John 1:1; Rev. 19:13.
38. Image of God: 2 Cor. 4:4; Col. 1:15–17; cf. Rom. 8:29; 1 Cor. 15:49.
39. The following terms are used of Christ. Rabbi (transliterated from Greek *rabbi*, derived from a Hebrew word meaning "great one"): Matt. 23:8; 26:25, 49; Mark 9:5; 11:21; 14:45; John 1:38, 49; 3:2; 4:31; 6:25; 9:2; 11:8; cf. *rabboni* in Mark 10:51; John 20:16. Master/teacher (*didaskalos*): Matt. 10:24–25; Luke 18:18; John 1:38; and many other texts in the Gospels. Master (*epistatēs*): Luke 5:5; 8:24, 45; 9:33, 49; 17:13. Master/instructor (*kathēgētēs*): Matt. 23:8, 10.
40. Apostle: Heb. 13:1; cf. John 17:18; 20:21.
41. Light: Isa. 42:6; 49:6; 61:1; Matt. 4:16; Luke 2:32; John 1:5, 9; 3:19; 8:12; 9:5; 11:9–10; 12:35–36, 46; cf. Rev. 21:23.
42. James Large, *Sunday Readings for a Year: or, Two Hundred and Eighty Scripture Titles and Symbols of Christ* (London: Hodder and Stoughton, 1879), 248.
43. Priest: Ps. 110:4; Zech. 6:13; Heb. 5:6; 7:1, 3, 11, 15, 17, 21; 8:4; 10:21.
44. High Priest: Heb. 2:17; 3:1; 4:14–15; 5:1, 5, 10; 6:20; 7:26–28; 8:1, 3; 9:7, 11, 25.

Christ is the heavenly *Advocate* before the Father (1 John 2:1). He has gone ahead of his people as their priestly *Forerunner* into God's holy presence in heaven to open the way for them (Heb. 6:20; cf. 12:1–2). In all this, he functions as the *Surety* of the covenant (Heb. 7:22), someone who pledges himself to take on the legal obligations of another, whether paying his debts or suffering his punishment.[45] He does so as the perfect *Lamb* sacrificed in the place of his people to redeem them from their sins.[46]

Christ is not only the Priest and the Lamb, but also the *Temple* where God's glory meets his reconciled people (John 2:19–21; cf. 1:14). Christ is the *Cornerstone* on which believers are built together to live as God's spiritual temple and holy priesthood through Christ's finished work.[47] The leaders of Israel rejected this Stone, but God made it the foundation of his church and kingdom, and those who stumble over it will be destroyed.[48]

Christ is the only *Way* to God (John 14:6), the sole road that bridges the relational gap between the righteous God and unrighteous men. He is the *Door* through which we must pass if we are to enter into abundant and eternal life (10:7–10), which consists of fellowship with the living God (5:26; 17:3). By his shed blood for sinners, Christ is the *Peace* of

---

45. On the term translated as "surety" (*enguos*), which is *hapax legomenon* in the New Testament, see *enguaō* in Prov. 6:1, 3; 17:18 LXX; and *enguēs* in Prov. 22:26 LXX. Here the Septuagint renders forms of the Hebrew root *'arab*, used of Judah's acting as a surety for Benjamin, even unto offering to suffer in his place (Gen. 43:9; 44:32).

46. Lamb: John 1:29, 36; 1 Pet. 1:19; Rev. 5:6–13; 7:14; 12:11; and many other texts in Revelation.

47. Christ is called the "cornerstone" (*akrogōniaios*, Eph. 2:20; 1 Pet. 2:6). He is also portrayed as "the head of the corner" (*kephalē gōnias*), an expression used once in the Old Testament (Ps. 117[118]:22 LXX) and elsewhere only in its New Testament citations (Matt. 21:42; Mark 12:10; Luke 20:17; Acts 4:11; 1 Pet. 2:7). Scholars are divided as to whether these terms should be interpreted as "cornerstone" or "capstone," the former being part of a foundation and the latter the last stone added at the top of a structure. See Andrew T. Lincoln, *Ephesians*, Word Biblical Commentary 42 (Dallas, TX: Word, 1990), 154–56. Joachim Jeremias advocates for "capstone." *TDNT*, 1:792–93. However, "cornerstone" is a far better fit with the biblical usage. The phrase *kephalē gōnias* is connected with stumbling or falling on a stone (1 Pet. 2:7–8; cf. Rom. 9:33), and one cannot trip over a capstone once it is set in place, as Christ has already been exalted. The only use of *akrogōniaios* in the Septuagint identifies Christ as the cornerstone in the foundation of God's building in Zion (Isa. 28:16 LXX). A similar expression, "corner stone" (*lithos gōniaios*), is used for the "foundation" or base of the earth (Job 38:6). Evidence for "capstone" is later than the New Testament. Furthermore, it is unlikely that Paul would have described Christ as the capstone (the last stone added) in a metaphor in which the temple is still growing and being built (Eph. 2:20–22). Thus, R. J. McKelvey, "Christ the Cornerstone," *New Testament Studies* 8 (1962): 352–59; and H. Krämer, in *Exegetical Dictionary of the New Testament*, ed. Horst Robert Balz and Gerhard Schneider, 3 vols. (Grand Rapids, MI: Eerdmans, 1990), 1:268.

48. Rejected Stone: Ps. 118:22; Isa. 8:14–15; Matt. 21:42–44; Mark 12:10; Luke 20:17–18; Acts 4:11; Rom. 9:33; 2 Pet. 2:7–8.

believers, whether Jews or Gentiles, so that they are brought near to God
(Eph. 2:13–14; cf. Judg. 6:24).

Names of Divine Reign

Jesus is the *King*,[49] specifically "the King of the Jews,"[50] and universally
"the King of kings," the latter a title given to human emperors for their
dominion over many kingdoms, but applied to Christ as the supreme Lord
of all.[51] Jesus often used the enigmatic name *Son of Man* for himself, which
can simply mean a "man,"[52] but also designates the man who receives
universal dominion from God (Dan. 7:13–14).[53]

The preeminence of this King is reflected in the name *Firstborn*,[54] which
does not speak of Christ's origin but his supremacy, for he possesses all the
rights of a firstborn son (Job 18:13; Ps. 89:27). He is the *Head*,[55] a name of
authority that denotes Christ both as sovereign Lord over all things (Eph.
1:22; Col. 2:10) and as the loving Lord who nurtures his body, the church
(Eph. 4:15; Col. 2:19). The New Testament also calls him the *Prince*, using
a term referring to a founding father, pioneer, or leader but applied spiritually in titles such as "the Prince of life" (Acts 3:15) or "the captain of their
salvation" (Heb. 2:10).[56] He uses his royal power as the *Breaker* who goes
ahead of his people and opens a way for them through all obstacles (Mic.
2:13; cf. Ps. 107:16).

Christ is the *Life* of God's people.[57] Jesus called himself the "bread of
life" (John 6:35), for receiving him nourishes and satisfies us forever, and
"the resurrection and the life" (11:25), for he conquers death and gives

---

49. King: Isa. 32:1; Jer. 23:5; Ezek. 37:24; Zech. 9:9; Matt. 21:5; 25:34, 40; Luke 19:38; John
12:15; 18:36–37.
50. King of the Jews: Matt. 2:2; 27:11, 29, 37; Mark 15:2, 9, 12, 18, 26; Luke 22:3, 37, 38; John
18:33, 39; 19:3, 19, 21. See also "the King of Israel" in Matt. 27:42; Mark 15:32; John 1:49; 12:13.
51. King of kings: 1 Tim. 6:15; Rev. 17:14; 19:16. For the use of the title for human emperors,
see Ezra 7:12; Ezek. 26:7; Dan. 2:37. See also the reference to Christ as "the prince [*archōn*] of the
kings of the earth" (Rev. 1:5).
52. Son of man as "man": Num. 23:19; Job 25:6; Ps. 8:4; Ezek. 2:1; and often in Ezekiel's
prophecy.
53. For a sampling of Christ's theologically freighted "Son of man" sayings, see Matt. 9:6; 12:8;
13:37, 41; 16:27; 17:22; 18:11; 19:28; 20:28; 24:27, 30; 25:31; 26:2, 64. See also B. B. Warfield,
*The Lord of Glory: A Study of the Designations of Our Lord in the New Testament with Especial
Reference to His Deity* (1907; repr., Grand Rapids, MI: Zondervan, n.d.), 84–88.
54. Firstborn: Rom. 8:29; Col. 1:15; 1:18; Heb. 1:6.
55. Head: 1 Cor. 11:3; Eph. 1:22; 4:15; 5:23; Col. 1:18; 2:10, 19.
56. The term *archēgos* is translated as "prince" (Acts 3:15; 5:21), "captain" (Heb. 2:10), and
"author" (12:2). In the Septuagint, it often refers to a familial, civil, or military authority (Ex. 6:14;
Num. 10:4; 1 Chron. 5:24; 12:21; 26:26; etc. LXX). On the sense of "author" or "founder," see
TDNT, 1:487–88.
57. Life: John 14:6; Col. 3:4; 1 John 1:2.

the powerful vitality of grace and glory. His inexpressible beauty and love appear in the name *Bridegroom*.[58] In our union of spiritual marriage to him, we "bring forth fruit unto God" (Rom. 7:4). This King brings not only life and love, but also retributive justice, being the coming *Judge* of all mankind, living and dead.[59]

The Scriptures use names to link Christ's reign to the covenant with David. God's Word calls Jesus the *Son of David*,[60] a messianic title that particularly points to Solomon,[61] whose construction of God's house and kingdom of peace and glory foreshadowed Christ's work. In other texts, he is simply called *David* in a prophetic and typological sense.[62] Picturing David's house as a tree cut off by divine judgment, the prophets call Christ the *Branch* that will spring up in weakness but grow and flourish in righteousness (Isa. 11:1).[63] Similarly, he is called the *Root* of Jesse or David.[64] Indeed, he is the *Vine* (John 15:1–8)—all that God called Israel to be in producing the fruit of righteousness and justice—so that if we abide in him like branches we bear much fruit, but apart from him we can do nothing.[65] Another Davidic image is the conquering *Lion of the Tribe of Judah* (Rev. 5:5; cf. Gen. 49:9).

Four of the most beloved of Christ's names appear together in the prophecy of the *Wonderful Counselor, Mighty God, Everlasting Father*, and *Prince of Peace*, who will reign forever "upon the throne of David" (Isa. 9:6–7). These four names portray the coming King as the Mediator of supernatural wisdom, divine power, eternal compassion, and sovereign peace.

Perhaps most prized of all by the saints is the designation of Christ as our loving *Shepherd*.[66] This name draws upon strands of Old Testament

---

58. Bridegroom: Matt. 9:15; 25:1–10; Mark 2:19–20; Luke 5:34–35; John 3:29; cf. Psalm 45; Isa. 62:5.

59. Judge: Acts 10:42; 2 Tim. 4:8; James 5:8–9.

60. Son of David: Matt. 1:1; 9:27; 12:23; 15:22; 20:30–31; 21:9, 15; 22:42; Mark 10:47–48; 12:35; Luke 18:38–39; 20:41. Compare Paul's phrase "of the seed of David" (Rom. 1:3; 2 Tim. 2:8).

61. 1 Chron. 29:22; 2 Chron. 1:1; 13:6; 30:26; 35:3; Prov. 1:1; but note 2 Sam. 13:1; 2 Chron. 11:18.

62. David: Jer. 30:9; Ezek. 34:23–24; 37:24–25; Hos. 3:5.

63. The same idea expressed with a different Hebrew word for "branch" appears in Isa. 4:2; Jer. 23:5; 33:15; Zech. 3:8; 6:12. On the metaphor of a tree stump, see Job 14:7–8; Isa. 6:13; Dan. 4:14–15, 23, 26. For a study of the messianic "Branch" in his humiliation, deity, righteousness, and reign, see Barrett, *Beginning at Moses*, 161–68.

64. Root: Isa. 11:10; Rom. 15:12; Rev. 5:5; 22:16.

65. On Israel as God's vine or vineyard, see Ps. 80:8–19 (note the reference to the Davidic king in v. 17); Isa. 5:1–7; 27:2–6; Ezek. 15:1–8; 17:1–10 (applied to the king, vv. 11–21); 19:10–14; Hos. 10:1; 14:4–7; Matt. 21:33–45; Mark 12:1–12; Luke 20:9–19.

66. Shepherd: Zech. 13:7; Matt. 9:36; 25:32; 26:31; Mark 14:27; John 10:2, 11–12, 14, 16; Heb. 13:20; 1 Pet. 2:25; 5:4; cf. Luke 15:1–7. For a series of devotional and theological meditations on the Lord as our Shepherd in Psalm 23, see Joel R. Beeke, *The Lord Shepherding His Sheep* (Welwyn Garden City, England: Evangelical Press, 2015).

thought regarding both David and the Lord God, weaving them together as one potent metaphor.[67]

After such an overwhelming parade of names (and there are more), it is not surprising to read that Christ is our *All* (Col. 3:11), the fullness of God's grace and glory given to fill all the needs and desires of all God's people from all nations for all eternity (John 1:14; Col. 2:9–10). As Philip Henry (1631–1696) said, Christ is our all in election, creation, providence, redemption, conversion, justification, consolation, preservation, teaching, strength, death, judgment, and eternity.[68] Therefore, if you have Christ, you can rejoice even if every other support or resource fails, for in him you have the God of your salvation (Hab. 3:17–18).

We must draw near to God in prayer with conscious dependence on and explicit appeal to the name of Christ. The church is defined as "all that in every place call upon the name of Jesus Christ our Lord" (1 Cor. 1:2). How rich our prayers could become if we salted them with the names and titles we are surveying in this chapter!

His Names of Deity

Jesus Christ is the *Son of God* (Mark 1:1). Twice God announced, "This is my beloved Son" (v. 11; 9:7). While there was some precedent for this title in God's adoption of the human offspring of David's royal line (1 Chron. 28:6), its usage in the New Testament points to a person far greater than any man (cf. Matt. 22:41–46). The Son of God is the special object of the Father's love, his Beloved.[69] He has the power to turn stones into bread and to calm a raging storm (4:3; 14:33). He has a unique relationship to God the Father, for Jesus says, "No man knoweth the Son, but the Father; neither knoweth any man the Father, save the Son, and he to whomsoever the Son will reveal him" (11:27). B. B. Warfield commented, "The Son can be known only by the Father in all that He is, as if His being were infinite and as such inscrutable to the finite intelligence; and His knowledge alone—again as if He were infinite in His attributes—is competent to compass the depths of the Father's infinite being."[70]

---

67. On David as the shepherd of the people, see 2 Sam. 5:2; 1 Chron. 11:2; Ps. 78:70–72. On the Lord as their Shepherd, see Gen. 49:24; Pss. 23:1; 28:9; 80:1; Eccl. 12:11; Isa. 40:11. On God and the Davidic heir converging in one Shepherd-King, see Ezek. 34:11–24; Mic. 5:2–4; Zech. 12:8.

68. Philip Henry, *Christ All in All: What Christ Is Made to Believers* (Grand Rapids, MI: Soli Deo Gloria, 2016), 351–54.

69. Matt. 3:17; 12:18; 17:5; Mark 1:11; 9:7; Luke 3:22; 9:35; 20:13; John 3:35; 5:20; 10:17; 15:9; 17:24; Eph. 1:6; Col. 1:13; 2 Pet. 1:17.

70. Warfield, *The Lord of Glory*, 82–83.

The title "Son of God" both reveals Christ's deity and underscores his unique personality in distinction from the Father. While "Son" implies that in some sense he is "of the Father," it also implies that he has the same nature as the Father, sharing the divine "glory," and that "in the beginning" (John 1:1, 14).[71] The Father shares with the Son one divine activity, knowledge, power, life, and will (5:17–30).[72] Christ is the Son not merely in his temporal mission, but as to the eternal identity of his person. He was not adopted at his baptism, but was already God's Son before he was sent into the world (Matt. 2:15; Luke 1:35; cf. 2:49). Warfield said,

> The force of a passage like [John] 3:16 (cf. 3:35; 5:20)—"God so loved the world that He gave His only begotten Son"—seems to turn on the intimacy of the relation expressed by the term "only begotten Son" having been already existent before the giving: otherwise how is the greatness of the love expressed in the giving to be measured? Similarly in a passage like 3:17 there seems an indication of the Sonship as underlying the mission: He was sent on this mission because He was Son—He did not become Son by being sent.[73]

Hence, Christ's sonship preceded his mission and is the foundation of it. He lived in a relationship of love with his "Father" even "before the foundation of the world" (John 17:24).

The Bible not only calls Jesus the Son of God, but also names him *God* (Hebrew *El* or *Elohim*, Greek *theos*). Isaiah prophesied that the child to be born to us would be "the mighty God" (Isa. 9:6), a title of the Lord God, Jehovah (10:20–21; cf. Jer. 32:18). The psalmist addresses Christ as "God" when attributing to him an eternal dominion (Ps. 45:6), which the New Testament cites to prove Christ is superior to the angels (Heb. 1:7–9). John writes, "In the beginning was the Word, and the Word was with God, and the Word was God" (John 1:1).[74] Thomas reverently addressed the risen Christ as "My LORD and my God" (20:28). There are

---

71. On the eternal generation of the Son from the Father, see *RST*, 1:933–40. Athanasius noted that it is the eternal generation of the Son that constitutes them "Father" and "Son." If Christ were coeternal with God without eternal generation, then the two persons might be called "brothers." Athanasius, *Four Discourses against the Arians*, 1.4.14, in *NPNF²*, 4:314.

72. On the essential oneness of the Son with the Father as set forth in John 5 and other texts, see *RST*, 1:893–98.

73. Warfield, *The Lord of Glory*, 198–99.

74. For a brief refutation of the gross mistranslation of *theos* in John 1:1 as "a god," see *RST*, 1:886. Others interpret *theos* to mean "divine" or "godlike," but this is not the meaning of the word as exhibited in its New Testament usage, and it does not fit the context in John 1:1–3, where the person described is the eternal Creator with the Father. See Greg Nichols, *Lectures in Systematic*

other Scripture passages that, when analyzed in the Greek text, also appear to use "God" for Christ.[75]

The New Testament often calls Christ the *Lord*. Sometimes "Lord" (*kyrios*) may mean "master" or "sir" (Matt. 10:24; 13:27). However, Christ is "the Lord of glory" (1 Cor. 2:8), the "Lord of lords" (1 Tim. 6:15; Rev. 17:14; 19:16), and the "Lord of all" (Acts 10:36). These are titles of deity.[76] The centurion of Capernaum addressed Christ as "Lord" when the soldier said he was not worthy for Christ to enter his house, but Jesus could heal his sick servant merely by speaking the word (Luke 7:6–7). Christ was already Lord at his birth, was still Lord on the cross, and was manifestly Lord on the third day after that, when it was proclaimed, "The Lord is risen indeed" (2:11; 23:42; 24:34). "Lord" is the term used to translate the divine name Jehovah (*YHWH*) from the Old Testament. When the New Testament quotes Old Testament statements about Jehovah and applies them to Jesus as "Lord," it is clear that God's Word is calling Jesus "Jehovah."[77]

Other names attributed to Christ also reveal his deity. He is *Immanuel* (Isa. 7:14), which means "God with us" (Matt. 1:23).[78] Charles Spurgeon (1834–1892) said, "Believer, he is God with thee, to protect thee; thou art not alone." Especially, Spurgeon said, Christ is God with us "by the influence of the Holy Spirit" to illuminate, convict, convert, and comfort us.[79] He is called *The LORD Our Righteousness* (Jer. 23:6), a name that combines the divine name (*YHWH*) with the promise of a Davidic king who would reign in justice and righteousness (v. 5). Jesus says, "Before Abraham was, I am [*egō eimi*]" (John 8:58). The striking use of the present tense for Christ's existence in the distant past identifies him as *I AM*, the

---

Theology, Volume 3: Doctrine of Christ (Seattle: CreateSpace Independent Publishing Platform, 2018), 479–80.

75. Rom. 9:5; Titus 2:13; 2 Pet. 1:1. The latter two texts employ a structure in which two singular nouns are joined by "and" and placed under one singular article, resulting in the translation "our great God and Savior Jesus Christ" and "our God and Savior Jesus Christ" (ESV). The same construction appears in 2 Pet. 1:11; 2:20; 3:18 in the phrase "Lord and Saviour Jesus Christ," where the words "Lord" and "Saviour" both refer to Christ.

76. The title "Lord of lords" is used of God alone in the Old Testament, and that in parallel with "God of gods" (Deut. 10:17; Ps. 136:2–3). The other two titles are unique, but compare "Lord of glory" to "God of glory" (Ps. 29:3; Acts 7:2), and "Lord of all" to "Lord of all the earth" (Josh. 3:11, 13).

77. Rom. 10:9, 13; 14:9–12; Phil. 2:10–11; 1 Thess. 1:8–9; Heb. 1:10–12. Note James's reference to the "Lord of sabaoth" (a reference to "the LORD of hosts") in the context of "the coming of the Lord" (James 5:4, 7, 8).

78. The difference in spelling between "Immanuel" (Isa. 7:14) and "Emmanuel" (Matt. 1:23) reflects the latter's Greek transliteration *Emmanouēl* of the original Hebrew *'Immanu-El*.

79. C. H. Spurgeon, *Sermons on Christ's Names and Titles*, ed. Chas. T. Cook (Greenwood, SC: Attic Press, 1961), 16–17.

One who revealed himself to Moses, saying, "I AM THAT I AM" (*egō eimi ho ōn*, Ex. 3:14 LXX), the God of Abraham, Isaac, and Jacob (v. 15).[80]

Christ is the *Alpha and Omega, the Beginning and the End, the First and the Last* (Rev. 22:13; cf. 1:17; 2:8), the titles of the Almighty (1:8), the only God (Isa. 44:6). By claiming the first and last letters in the Greek alphabet, Christ asserted himself to be the Creator who made all things, the One whom all things will ultimately glorify, and the Lord who calls into existence every generation in between in an orderly manner (41:4).[81]

It is a tremendous comfort to know that Jesus is our Lord and our God, Immanuel, the Alpha and Omega. In him perfect majesty and meekness meet for our benefit. Godefridus Udemans (c. 1581–1649) said, "If we believe in Christ as Lord, He is also our friend and brother (John 15:15; 20:17)."[82] What a friend we have in Jesus!

The experiential knowledge of the Lord's names ignites saving faith in our hearts. Psalm 9:10 says, "They that know thy name will put their trust in thee: for thou, LORD, hast not forsaken them that seek thee." Psalm 91:14 says, "Because he hath set his love upon me, therefore will I deliver him: I will set him on high, because he hath known my name." Therefore, use Christ's names like windows in which you can see the face of your Savior, so to speak. Trust him to be what he says he is and love him supremely for the sake of his name.

Treasuring and Honoring the Names of Christ

Knowing Christ's names is good, but what are we to do with them? We must go beyond head knowledge and engage our hearts to know him by his names, take his names on our lips in prayer and praise, and learn to do all things for the glory of his name. Perhaps you are overwhelmed by the many names listed in this chapter. If so, select a few of Christ's names that have especially impressed you, memorize them, and meditate on them in the passages of the Holy Scriptures in which they appear. Consider how

---

80. See also the Lord's use of *egō eimi* in Isa. 41:4; 43:10, 25; 45:18–19; 48:12 LXX. On Christ as the eternal "I Am," see *RST*, 1:562.

81. The same word translated as "beginning" (*archē*) in the phrase "the beginning and the end" (Rev. 21:6; cf. 1:8; 22:13) also appears in the phrase "the beginning of the creation of God" (3:14), and evidently has the same meaning of "source" or "Creator." Alternatively, the term can mean "principality" or "ruler" (Eph. 1:21).

82. Godefridus Udemans, *The Practice of Faith, Hope, and Love*, trans. Annemie Godbehere, ed. Joel R. Beeke, Classics of Reformed Spirituality (Grand Rapids, MI: Reformation Heritage Books, 2012), 63.

they reveal God's glory in Christ and Christ's sufficiency for your needs. Handle the names of Christ like gold coins or gemstones of great value that you dare not lose or damage.

We begin by treasuring his names. The names of the Lord are exceedingly precious to his people. Indeed, they are precious to the Lord, who says, "Thou shalt not take the name of the LORD thy God in vain; for the LORD will not hold him guiltless that taketh his name in vain" (Ex. 20:7). God insists that his name be honored and not treated as a common thing. Instead, let us "give unto the LORD the glory due unto his name" (Pss. 29:2; 96:8).

To be sure, God's "name" in Scripture is more than the names and titles he takes to himself, but includes the full breadth of his self-revelation—his manifest glory (Ex. 33:19; 34:5, 14). Nevertheless, his names are radiant beams of that glory, and we must receive them with faith and reverence for his honor and our good.

The names and titles of Jesus Christ our Lord are revealed so that we may honor and glorify God. This is God's purpose that will be fulfilled universally on the day of Christ, for the Father gave him the "name that is above every name" so that every rational creature will "confess that Jesus Christ is Lord, to the glory of God the Father" (Phil. 2:9–11).

However, we do not need to wait for that day to begin living for his name. The Word of God commands us here and now, "Whatsoever ye do in word or deed, do all in the name of the Lord Jesus, giving thanks to God and the Father by him" (Col. 3:17). We do that by filling our lives with "the word of Christ," individually and communally (v. 16), constantly exercising faith in the risen Lord who is our life (vv. 1–4), so that we put sin to death (vv. 5–9), put on God's renewed image in Christ (vv. 10–11), and imitate him in humble love (vv. 12–15). Christians often end their prayers by saying, "In Jesus's name." Let Jesus's name fly like a banner over your entire life.

Sing to the Lord

The Glorious Names of Jesus Christ

Join all the glorious names of wisdom, love, and pow'r,
That mortals ever knew, that ever angels bore:
All are too poor to speak his worth,
Too poor to set my Savior forth.

Great Prophet of my God, my tongue would bless thy name:
By thee the joyful news of our salvation came,
The joyful news of sins forgiv'n,
Of hell subdued and peace with heav'n.

Jesus, my great High Priest, offered his blood and died;
My guilty conscience seeks no sacrifice beside:
His pow'rful blood did once atone
And now it pleads before the throne.

Thou art my Counselor, my pattern, and my Guide,
And thou my Shepherd art; O keep me near thy side;
Nor let my feet e'er turn astray
To wander in the crooked way.

My Savior and my Lord, my Conqu'ror and my King,
Thy scepter and thy sword, thy reigning grace, I sing:
Thine is the pow'r; behold I sit
In willing bonds beneath thy feet.

Isaac Watts

Tune: Darwall

Trinity Psalter Hymnal (Willow Grove, PA: The Committee on Christian Education of the Orthodox Presbyterian Church and The Psalter Hymnal Committee of the United Reformed Churches in North America, 2018), No. 377

Questions for Meditation or Discussion

As you answer the questions below, give a Scripture reference pertinent to the meaning of each of Christ's names that you mention.

1. What does the name "Jesus" mean? What is its Old Testament background?
2. What does the title "Christ" mean?
3. What are other general names of Christ's office?
4. What names does the Bible give to Christ that pertain to illumination?
5. What other names of Christ pertain especially to divine revelation?
6. What are the names of Christ that pertain to divine reconciliation?

7. What four especially precious names of Christ appear in the early prophecies of Isaiah?

8. In what other names and titles is Christ magnified with respect to divine reign?

9. How would you prove Christ's deity simply by the names of deity ascribed to him?

10. How should we treasure and honor the names of our Lord Jesus Christ? What is one practical use that you should make of his names to strengthen your spiritual life? Which names in particular do you need to lay hold of now?

Questions for Deeper Reflection

11. You are assigned the task of giving a fifteen-minute devotional to a group of high school students on the meaning of the name "Jesus Christ." Write an outline of what you would say, and do not forget to make practical applications.

12. You are debating the deity of Christ with someone who says, "When Jesus is called the Son of God in the Bible, it does not mean that he is God, just that he is David's offspring, whom God adopted as his child as he promised" (2 Sam. 7:14). How do you respond?

13. Select one of the names or titles of Christ from this chapter that is especially meaningful to you. How does this name and its meaning strengthen your faith? Inflame your love?

38

The Deity of Christ

Christians confess the deity of Christ, that he is fully and eternally God.[1] The deity of Jesus Christ is more than a doctrine to understand and believe; it is his glory that shines through the Holy Scriptures and captivates people to serve him. Franciscus Junius told how, as a young man, he departed from the godliness of his father and plunged into atheism. His father, seeking to woo him gently to the Christian faith, set out a copy of the New Testament in their home in the hope that his son would read it. Junius recounted,

> I opened the New Testament which was divinely offered. As I did that, the book displayed to me at first glance that very majestic chapter of the evangelist and apostle John, "In the beginning was the Word, etc." I read part of the chapter, and I was so moved as I read that immediately I perceived that the divinity of the argument and the grandeur and authority of the writing surpassed by a great margin all streams of human eloquence. My body shuddered, [and] my mind was dumbfounded.[2]

---

1. For some other contemporary sources on the deity of Christ, see Wellum, *God the Son Incarnate*; Macleod, *The Person of Christ*; Wells, *The Person of Christ*; Millard J. Erickson, *The Word Became Flesh: A Contemporary Incarnational Christology* (Grand Rapids, MI: Baker, 1991); Fee, *Pauline Christology*; Robert M. Bowman Jr. and J. Ed Komoscewski, *Putting Jesus in His Place: The Case for the Deity of Christ* (Grand Rapids, MI: Kregel, 2007); and Robert Letham, *The Message of the Person of Christ*, The Bible Speaks Today, Bible Themes (Nottingham, England: InterVarsity Press, 2013). For an analysis of New Testament Christology in the context of ancient Judaic monotheism, see Richard Bauckham, *Jesus and the God of Israel: God Crucified and Other Studies on the New Testament's Christology of Divine Identity* (Grand Rapids, MI: Eerdmans, 2008).

2. Franciscus Junius, "The Life of Franciscus Junius," in *A Treatise on True Theology: With the Life of Franciscus Junius*, trans. David C. Noe (Grand Rapids, MI: Reformation Heritage Books, 2014), 34.

Junius went on to read the Bible several times and became a committed Christian. Later in life, he flourished as one of the premier Reformed theologians of the late sixteenth century. He rejoiced that God had entrusted all revealed truth to his Son, the "God-man," for "he is without doubt the only Immanuel, the Word made flesh, and God made manifest in the flesh, in whom are hidden all the treasures of wisdom and knowledge."[3]

Since Christ's deity is so glorious and precious to the church's faith, we must defend it against all attacks. This doctrine has been virulently assaulted through the centuries. In our study of the doctrine of the Trinity, we noted various kinds of error by which Satan has drawn people away from the truth about Christ's deity: modalism (Christ is not a distinct person but one form in which God appears), essential subordinationism (Christ is inferior to the Father in essence), tritheism (the Father, the Son, and the Spirit are three gods), and panentheism (in Jesus, the divine Spirit that lives in us all finds one of its highest expressions).[4]

The doctrine of biblical, orthodox Christianity is that Jesus Christ is the Son of God, a person distinct from the Father and the Spirit, but himself fully God, sharing the one divine nature with the Father and the Spirit in all the glory of deity. As Francis Turretin pointed out, the question is not whether Christ is God's Son or divine in some sense of the words, for many say so, but "whether he is true and eternal God, coessential with the Father."[5]

The Crucial Importance of Christ's Deity for Christianity

Someone might object that we should not quarrel about words with people who love Jesus and desire to live by his teaching, but accept their faith regardless of whether they agree with a confessional statement about his deity. In reply, we answer that when people say that they love Jesus, we must ask, "Which Jesus—the real Christ or one of their imagination?" It is not pride but humility to submit to what God has revealed in the Holy Scriptures concerning his Son.

First, Christ's deity is indispensable for *faith in Christ*. Saving faith in Christ requires us to trust in him as we trust in God the Father (John 14:1), for only God can save us from all sin and misery (Isa. 45:22). Our

---

3. Junius, *A Treatise on True Theology*, 124, 126.
4. On these heretical views of Christ and God, see *RST*, 1:904–6, 910, 913, 918, 923–24, 926.
5. Turretin, *Institutes*, 3.28.3 (1:282).

faith in God is categorically different from our faith in men or any other creature, for we depend upon his infinite lordship and love (Ps. 31:14–19). God curses those who give that kind of trust to mere men; it is an act of treason against him (Jer. 17:5–6). The denial of Christ's deity leads people away from wholehearted dependence upon Christ and into self-reliance.

Second, Christ's deity is indispensable for *divine self-revelation*. Christ is "the Word" who is "God" (John 1:1). He makes known the invisible God (John 1:18; 14:9; Col. 1:15). That is not to say that all revelation of God depends upon the incarnate Lord, but only by God's coming to us in Christ does divine revelation bring into effect a personal, experiential knowledge of God. Since Christ is God, he is indeed "revelation of God," for "Jesus Christ is the Son of the Father, and as such he is the revelation he brings."[6]

Third, Christ's deity is indispensable for *effectual salvation*. If Christ is not God, then he cannot save his people from their sins.[7] The Savior had to accomplish "everlasting righteousness" for his people (Dan. 9:24), even "the righteousness of God" (Rom. 3:21–22; cf. Isa. 51:5–8). He had to bear the burden and pay the price for the countless sins of the "many" in whose place he died (Mark 10:45). He had to sovereignly lay down his life and take it up again in obedience to his Father (John 10:17–18). Having accomplished salvation, he must apply it to individuals who call upon him all over the world (Rom. 10:12; 1 Cor. 1:2) to the end of the age, when his church's mission will be complete (Matt. 28:20). Only God can do these things. Athanasius said that "such grace" required "the Word of God, which had also at the beginning made everything out of nought. . . . For being the Word of the Father, and above all, He alone of natural fitness was both able to recreate everything, and worthy to suffer on behalf of all and to be ambassador for all with the Father."[8] If we abandon Christ's deity, then we lose the gospel.

Fourth, Christ's deity is indispensable for *God's kingdom among men*. Stephen Wellum says, "The only one who can bring God's kingdom into reality is God himself," for "the rule of God, the obedience of his people, and the judgment of his enemies . . . require the presence and power of

---

6. Torrance, *Incarnation*, 188; cf. Douglas F. Kelly, *Systematic Theology: Grounded in Holy Scripture and Understood in the Light of the Church, Volume 2, The Beauty of Christ: A Trinitarian Vision* (Fearn, Ross-shire, Scotland: Christian Focus, 2014), 2:192.

7. Perkins, *An Exposition of the Symbol*, in *Works*, 5:112–13; and Westminster Larger Catechism (Q. 38), in *Reformed Confessions*, 4:306.

8. Athanasius, *On the Incarnation of the Word*, sec. 7, in *NPNF*[2], 4:40.

the divine king."[9] Yet Jesus claimed to meet all the expectations of the kingdom in himself and his work.[10] Therefore, it is both "the kingdom of God" (Mark 1:14–15) and Christ's kingdom.[11] Because of the divine Christ, we may say to God's people, "The king of Israel, even the LORD, is in the midst of thee" (Zeph. 3:15).

Fifth, Christ's deity is indispensable for *evangelical reverence*, the childlike, joyful fear of God by faith in the gospel (Mal. 3:16–17; 1 Pet. 1:14–19). Only by the gospel of the God-man can we be awestruck at the Son's sovereign glory, aware of his terrifying wrath, and hidden safely in his grace, so that we "rejoice with trembling" (Ps. 2:10–12). Wilhelmus à Brakel said, "If the Lord Jesus is God, meditation upon Him as such will generate great reverence in our hearts." However, the deity of Christ also comforts us, for "He is almighty to deliver, keep, and comfort the soul, as well as usher him into eternal felicity. How blessed is such a soul which may have the Lord Jesus as his Savior!"[12]

Sixth, Christ's deity is indispensable for *Christian discipleship*. Those who claim to be disciples of Jesus but reject his full divinity do not understand the claims that Jesus laid on his followers. He said, "He that loveth father or mother more than me is not worthy of me: and he that loveth son or daughter more than me is not worthy of me" (Matt. 10:37). Charles John Brown (1806–1884) said, "Behold here a teacher who, utterly unlike all that had come from God before him, claims for himself the supreme affection of his disciples; claims, not for another, but for himself, the very throne of their hearts."[13] This is right and good only if Christ is the God who rightly demands the total love of our whole being (Deut. 6:4–5).

Seventh, Christ's deity is indispensable for *Trinitarian spirituality*.[14] Christian prayer and public worship are profoundly shaped by the doctrine of the Trinity. Christians enjoy access to the Father in the Spirit through the Son (Eph. 2:18), whose mediatorial work of salvation depends upon his deity. The saints have distinct communion with God the Son (1 John 1:3), from whom they receive divine grace and to whom they direct their worship (Rev. 1:4–5; 5:9). Remove the deity of Christ, and we negate all that is distinctly Christian about our faith, worship, and living.

---

9. Wellum, *God the Son Incarnate*, 198.
10. Wellum, *God the Son Incarnate*, 156–57.
11. Matt. 13:41; 16:28; Luke 22:30; Eph. 5:5; 2 Tim. 4:1.
12. Brakel, *The Christian's Reasonable Service*, 1:512.
13. Charles J. Brown, *The Divine Glory of Christ* (Edinburgh: Banner of Truth, 1982), 13.
14. On Trinitarian spirituality, see *RST*, 1:944–52.

Eighth, Christ's deity is indispensable for *balanced ecclesiology*. Christ said, "I will build my church; and the gates of hell shall not prevail against it" (Matt. 16:18). Christ is not merely the church's founding father, he is its Lord and owner ("my church"). Consequently, no mere man (or group of men) has the right to assert absolute authority over the church, but possesses delegated authority only insofar as he obeys (or they obey) Christ's Word. At the same time, the church can move ahead in her work with great confidence, for all the powers of darkness cannot destroy her because the Lord of heaven and earth is with her (28:20).

Ninth, Christ's deity is indispensable for *evangelistic love*. Those who deny Christ's deity may be zealous in proselytizing for their religious party, but their zeal may be stained by hypocritical pride (Matt. 23:5, 15). Indeed, if we deny that Christ is God, then there is little that distinguishes Christianity from other religions. John Hick (1922–2012) believed that Jesus is merely one of many ways that the divine reality reaches out to mankind.[15] However, Hick recognized, "if Jesus was literally God incarnate, and if it is by his death alone that men can be saved, and by their response to him alone that they can appropriate that salvation, then the only doorway to eternal life is Christian faith."[16] Truly Christian zeal for missions springs from the dual conviction that "whosoever shall call upon the name of the Lord shall be saved" (Rom. 10:13) and that this "Lord" is specifically "the Lord Jesus" (v. 9).

Tenth, Christ's deity is indispensable for *biblical fidelity*. This is not a secondary doctrine in the Holy Scriptures, but a great theme revealed in the Old Testament and pervasive in the New Testament. Those who fail to see the divine glory of Christ read the Bible with a veil over their hearts (2 Cor. 3:14–15; 4:4). If we would be faithful students of the Word of God, then we must accept this doctrine and allow it to transform our lives.

The Clear Revelation of Christ's Deity in the Bible

God's Word testifies to the deity of his Son. The evidence for this doctrine is so clear in its presentation and overwhelming in its scope that faith in Christ as the incarnate God has stood as common ground for many diverse denominations of professing Christians through the centuries.

---

15. On religious pluralism, including the view of John Hick, see *RST*, 1:299–304.

16. John Hick, "Jesus and the World Religions," in *The Myth of God Incarnate*, ed. John Hick (London: SCM, 1977), 180.

An Outline of Biblical Evidence for Christ's Deity

The Holy Scriptures demonstrate that Christ is God in many ways. We may summarize the lines of evidence for the deity of Jesus Christ as follows.

1. The *preexistence of deity*: indications that Christ was living and active before his entrance into this world as a human being (discussed below).

2. The *prophecies of deity*: promises of God's coming to his people fulfilled in Jesus,[17] particularly promises that God would come as the divine Messiah.[18]

3. The *names of deity*: the names and titles given to Christ, such as God (John 1:1), the Son of God (Matt. 16:16), Lord (Phil. 2:11), Lord of lords (Rev. 17:14), and God with us (Matt. 1:23).[19]

4. The *attributes of deity*: traits such as holiness (Acts 3:14), eternity (John 8:58), sovereign power (Matt. 8:26), infinite knowledge (John 16:30), omnipresence (Matt. 28:20), self-existence (John 5:26), and immutability (Heb. 1:10–12).[20] When we examine these divine attributes of Christ, we are led to confess with Paul, "In him dwelleth all the fulness of the Godhead bodily" (Col. 2:9). Wellum comments, "The entire fullness and sum total of deity inhabits the Son, who has added to himself a human nature."[21]

5. The *relations of deity*: Christ is the only begotten Son of the Father (John 3:16), and the Holy Spirit is the Spirit of the Son (Gal. 4:6). In the relations of the Trinity, Christ shares in the fullness of the divine life and activity with the Father and the Spirit.[22]

6. The *actions of deity*: Christ does what only God does as Creator, Lord, and Redeemer (see below).

7. The *honors of deity*: Christ hears prayer and receives worship (see below).[23]

---

17. Isa. 40:3, 5, 9–10; Mal. 3:1–6. Note the fulfillment of these prophecies in the coming of Jesus (Mark 1:1–9).

18. Pss. 45:6–7; 110:1; Isa. 9:6; Mic. 5:2. On the divine Messiah, see *RST*, 1:883–84.

19. See the section on Christ's names of deity in the previous chapter. See also *RST*, 1:561–63, 886–87.

20. On Christ's divine attributes, see *RST*, 1:887–88. In particular, see Christ's holiness (1:573, 579), vitality (1:618–19), simplicity (1:626), infinity (1:641), aseity (1:645–46), omnipresence (1:656), eternity (1:665–66), immutability (1:696–97), omniscience (1:725–26, 730–31), wisdom (1:733), foreknowledge (1:739, 748), authority (1:768–69), power (1:771–72), love (1:798), truth (1:809), righteousness (1:813), and joy (1:844–45).

21. Wellum, *God the Son Incarnate*, 192.

22. On the Son's relationship to the Father and the Spirit, see *RST*, 1:889–98.

23. This is an expansion upon the traditional method of proving Christ's deity by his divine names, attributes, works, and worship. See Perkins, *An Exposition of the Symbol*, in *Works*,

In summary, since the Bible reveals Christ's activity long before he became a man; foretells the coming of Christ as the coming of God; calls him by the names of God; ascribes to him the attributes, relations, and actions of God; and gives him the honors of God, then Christ is God.

We must remember that these truths do not stand in the context of polytheism, where God is regarded as the best among many divinities and powers, but in the context of biblical monotheism, where God stands as the unique one with no others to whom we can compare him (Deut. 4:39; Isa. 40:18, 25). Brown said, "Near to *Him* in the scale of being? The thing is an impossibility. . . . The instant the unity of Jehovah has been grasped as importing such an aloneness of unapproached being, majesty, glory, as has been described, the immediate and unavoidable conclusion is, that Jesus Christ, by himself and his apostles, claims to be Jehovah."[24]

In this outline, points 2–5 have already been presented in other sections of this work, as the footnotes show. Therefore, we proceed to the evidence for points 1, 6, and 7.

Preexistence of Deity

If Christ is God, then he must always have been God, for God is eternal. If he was a mere man, then he did not exist before his conception in Mary's womb. Therefore, an important line of argumentation for Christ's deity is the Bible's revelation of his preexistence.

The Old Testament tells us of a mysterious figure called the "angel of the LORD," who was both sent by the Lord ("angel" means messenger) and yet spoke and acted as the Lord.[25] He was called "the LORD," "God," the "God of Abraham," and "Lord" (*Adonai*).[26] He bore God's "name" and authority (Ex. 23:21); brought Israel into the Promised Land, destroying its enemies (v. 23); and told the prophet the word of God that he must speak (Num. 22:35, 38). He was the covenant Lord of Israel (Judg. 2:1–5). He said that his name was "wonderful" or beyond human understanding, and to meet him was to see God (13:18, 22 ESV). He could massacre an

---

5:109–10; Ames, *The Marrow of Theology*, 1.5.17–21 (89–91); Wollebius, *Compendium*, 1.2.(2).v (42–43); Polyander, Walaeus, Thysius, and Rivetus, *Synopsis Purioris Theologiae*, 8.24–30 (1:219–25); and Westminster Larger Catechism (Q. 11), in *Reformed Confessions*, 4:301.

24. Brown, *The Divine Glory of Christ*, 28, emphasis original.

25. Gen. 16:7–14; 22:11–18; Ex. 3:1–6; 23:20–23; Num. 22:22, 35, 38; Judg. 2:1–5; 6:11–24; 13:1–22; 2 Kings 19:34–35; Zech. 1:12; 3:1–5.

26. Gen. 16:13; 22:12; Ex. 3:4–6; Judg. 6:12, 14–15.

entire army in a night—an act of God (2 Kings 19:34–35). This was no angel in the sense of a created spirit sent from heaven, but the Lord himself, the preincarnate Son of God sent by the Father.[27]

Micah prophesied of Christ's preexistence, saying, "But thou, Bethlehem Ephratah, though thou be little among the thousands of Judah, yet out of thee shall he come forth unto me that is to be ruler in Israel; whose goings forth have been from of old, from everlasting" (Mic. 5:2). The "goings forth" could be interpreted either as the ancient origin of this ruler in the line of David,[28] as his eternal generation by the Father,[29] or as his activity as a preexistent person long before his birth in Bethlehem.[30] The last interpretation is more likely, for the prophecy could be paraphrased, "In stark contrast to the lowly status of David's family and origin in Bethlehem, from that same city will arise the supernatural King who has been active from ancient times."[31]

The preexistence of Christ was taught by Christ himself. James Dunn disagrees, saying, "There is no indication that Jesus thought or spoke of himself as having pre-existed with God prior to his birth or appearance on earth."[32] However, Dunn acknowledges that the Gospel of John as-

---

27. Calvin, *Institutes*, 1.13.10; Bavinck, *Reformed Dogmatics*, 1:329; and Ron Rhodes, *Christ before the Manger: The Life and Times of the Preincarnate Christ* (Grand Rapids, MI: Baker, 1992), 79–102. See *RST*, 1:273.

28. Thus, Kenneth L. Barker, *Micah, Nahum, Habakkuk, Zephaniah*, The New American Commentary 20 (Nashville: Broadman & Holman, 1999), 97–98. "From of old" (*miqqedem*) and "everlasting," literally "days of eternity" (*yemey 'olam*), can refer to ancient times such as those of Moses or David from the perspective of the later prophets (Deut. 32:7; Neh. 12:46; Pss. 77:5, 11; 143:5; Isa. 45:21; 63:9, 11; Amos 9:11; Mic. 7:14; Mal. 3:4).

29. Thus, Poole, *Annotations upon the Holy Bible*, 2:948, on Mic. 5:2. "From of old" (*miqqedem*) can be applied to the eternity of God himself: "Art thou not from everlasting, O Lord my God, mine Holy One?" (Hab. 1:12).

30. Thus, Barrett, *Beginning at Moses*, 133. "From of old" (*miqqedem*) can be used of God's activity as King: "For God is my King of old, working salvation in the midst of the earth" (Ps. 74:12).

31. Several factors make this interpretation of Mic. 5:2 most likely. First, the word translated as "goings forth" (plural *motsa'ah*) most aptly refers not to the ruler's origin in time or eternity (which would be singular), but to his various activities from ancient times. The Hebrew term favors a dynamic sense of motion or activity. The word appears only once elsewhere, where it refers to a latrine in a very literal sense of "goings forth" (2 Kings 10:27). The closely related term "going forth" (*motsa'*) denotes the motion of people (Num. 33:2; 2 Sam. 3:25; 1 Kings 10:28; 2 Chron. 1:16) or things (Num. 30:12; Deut. 8:3; 23:23; 2 Kings 2:21; 2 Chron. 32:30; Ps. 19:6; Hos 6:3). It can, however, occasionally have a more static sense of origin, such as "a vein for the silver" found in a mine (Job 28:1). Second, the "goings forth . . . from of old, from everlasting" makes an emphatic contrast to the insignificance of the little town of Bethlehem in the first part of the verse, which would hardly be merited by merely identifying the child as a son of David (whose royal line was not glorious in Micah's time), but makes good sense if it announces the supernatural King. Third, the prophecy's intention to reveal a supernatural figure is confirmed two verses later, for the coming King will reign "in the strength of the Lord, in the majesty of the name of the Lord his God" (v. 4). Fourth, Micah had prophesied earlier that God himself would come (1:3), using the same verb translated as "come forth" (*yatsa'*). Therefore, Micah taught that the coming Messiah had been active from ancient times, for he would be the incarnation of the one eternal God and Savior.

32. Dunn, *Christology in the Making*, 32.2 (254).

cribes sayings to Jesus that explicitly assert his divine preexistence—sayings Dunn must discount as inauthentic to maintain his thesis.[33] The Son of God said, "I came down from heaven, not to do mine own will, but the will of him that sent me" (John 6:38; cf. 3:13, 31). Christ claimed, "I am from above" and "I proceeded forth and came from God" (8:23, 42; cf. v. 38; 16:28). Jesus astonished his hearers by saying, "Verily, verily, I say unto you, Before Abraham was, I am" (8:58). The Son was with the Father in his glory and love before the foundation of the world (17:5, 24).

The other Gospels imply Christ's preexistence by his statements about his coming for the purpose of his divine mission. Christ said, "I have come" to fulfill the law and the prophets (Matt. 5:17 ESV); "I came not to call the righteous, but sinners to repentance" (Luke 5:32); and he had "come" to bring divine judgment ("fire") and division among men (12:49, 51). Christ was not speaking of his purpose in coming to a particular place, but the purpose of his entire life. This implies the intentional movement of his person from outside this world into it to fulfill a mission. Simon Gathercole points out that this is not the language used by prophets of their prophetic mission, but it is language used by heavenly beings sent on missions to earth.[34]

We find the same theme in more of Christ's statements: "The Son of man came to seek and to save the lost" (Luke 19:10 ESV) and "The Son of man came not to be ministered unto, but to minister, and to give his life a ransom for many" (Mark 10:45). Christ's self-identification as "the Son of man" alludes to a heavenly King (Dan. 7:13–14). Jesus's teaching that he came to save sinners "transports the mind back into the pretemporal, heavenly existence of the Son of Man and conveys the idea of His voluntary descent to earth," as B. B. Warfield wrote.[35] The sense that these "coming" texts announce the arrival of a heavenly figure on earth is heightened by other texts. The demons said to Jesus, "Art thou come to destroy us? I know thee who thou art, the Holy One of God" (Mark 1:24;

---

33. Dunn, *Christology in the Making*, 4.4, 6.5 (29–32, 56–59). See the response in Macleod, *The Person of Christ*, 47–52. On the historical reliability of the Gospel of John, see Craig L. Blomberg, *The Historical Reliability of John's Gospel: Issues and Commentary* (Downers Grove, IL: InterVarsity Press, 2001).

34. Simon J. Gathercole, *The Preexistent Son: Recovering the Christologies of Matthew, Mark, and Luke* (Grand Rapids, MI: Eerdmans, 2006), 84–85, 95–99, 102–6, 119–20. See Dan. 9:22–23; 10:12, 14, 20.

35. B. B. Warfield, "Jesus' Mission, According to His Own Testimony," *Princeton Theology Review* 13, no. 4 (October 1915): 568 (full article, 513–86). See 1 Enoch 48:2–6, in *The Apocrypha and Pseudepigrapha of the Old Testament*, ed. Charles, 2:216.

cf. Matt. 8:29). Christ is "the dayspring from on high" that has visited us in our darkness (Luke 1:78).[36]

The apostolic witness to Christ confirms that he indeed is the preexistent Son of God. John says, "In the beginning was the Word" (John 1:1). It was Christ whom Israel encountered in the wilderness (1 Cor. 10:4). Paul implies that the Son existed before he became a man, writing, "When the fulness of the time was come, God sent forth his Son, made of a woman" (Gal. 4:4; cf. Rom. 8:3) and "Christ Jesus came into the world to save sinners" (1 Tim. 1:15). Christ was already "being in the form of God" prior to taking upon himself "the form of a servant" (Phil. 2:6–7). As Paul writes elsewhere, "For ye know the grace of our Lord Jesus Christ, that, though he was rich, yet for your sakes he became poor, that ye through his poverty might be rich" (2 Cor. 8:9). When was Christ rich, if not in heaven before he was born into the lowly household of a carpenter?[37] There are also the several texts we will examine in the next section that reveal Christ's work of creation.

The man who was born in Bethlehem, preached in Galilee, and was crucified outside of Jerusalem is far more than a man. He is the eternal Lord, living and active from the first moment of history, and hence rightly named "Alpha and Omega, the beginning and the end, the first and the last" (Rev. 22:13). His resurrection did not give him a new kind of life that he never before possessed, but manifested through his risen humanity the eternal life that was always his (John 11:25).

Actions of Deity

The Lord Jesus Christ performs divine acts, thereby showing that he is God, the second person of the Trinity. This conclusion cannot be avoided by claiming that God appointed him to function in a divine role, for these actions require a being with divine attributes to perform them.

The act of *election* to salvation, holiness, and glory is generally ascribed to God the Father, who "hath chosen us in him [Christ] before the foundation of the world" (Eph. 1:4). However, Christ could say that he, too, is the author of election: "Ye have not chosen me, but I have chosen you, and ordained you, that ye should go and bring forth fruit, and that your fruit should remain: that whatsoever ye shall ask of the Father in my name,

---

36. Gathercole, *The Preexistent Son*, 150–53, 238–41.
37. Macleod, *The Person of Christ*, 56.

he may give it you. . . . I have chosen you out of the world, therefore the world hateth you" (John 15:16, 19). To choose who will be separated from this sinful world and bear fruit for God is an act of absolute sovereignty.

The work of *creation* is the work of God alone (Isa. 44:24); however, creation was not accomplished by the Father alone, but by the Father, the Son, and the Holy Spirit cooperating as the triune God.[38] John alludes to Genesis 1:1 when he writes, "In the beginning was the Word. . . . All things were made by him; and without him was not any thing made that was made" (John 1:1, 3). Augustine said, "From which it appears clearly, that he himself was not made, by whom all things were made."[39] Though the Father made the world "by" the Son (Heb. 1:2), Christ was not merely an instrument of God's work, but was himself the Creator, for Hebrews says of the Son, "Thou, Lord, in the beginning hast laid the foundation of the earth; and the heavens are the works of thine hands" (v. 10; citing Ps. 102:25). The extent of Christ's creative work is universal: "For by him were all things created, that are in heaven, and that are in earth, visible and invisible, whether they be thrones, or dominions, or principalities, or powers: all things were created by him, and for him" (Col. 1:16). Thomas Manton said that all things were created by him "as an equal co-operating cause, or co-worker with God the Father (John 5:19)."[40] Far from being a created angel, Christ is the Creator of the angelic "powers," just as he is the Creator of all things. This implies "the glory and majesty of the Redeemer," Manton wrote, for the angels "excel in strength" (Ps. 103:20), but all their power is from Christ their Creator, and they are "infinitely inferior to our Redeemer, by whom and for whom they were made."[41]

Christ's role in creation is central to Christian monotheism. Paul says, "To us there is but one God, the Father, of whom are all things, and we in him; and one Lord Jesus Christ, by whom are all things, and we by him" (1 Cor. 8:6). The phrases "of whom are all things" and "by whom are all things" both refer to the Creator.[42] Paul affirms the monotheistic Jewish *Shema*, "Hear, O Israel: The LORD our God is one LORD" (Deut. 6:4), and

---

38. On the uniqueness and Trinity of the Creator, see chap. 2.

39. Augustine, *On the Trinity*, 1.6.9, in *NPNF*[1], 3:21.

40. Manton, *Christ's Eternal Existence and the Dignity of His Person Asserted and Proved, in Opposition to the Doctrine of the Socinians*, in *Works*, 1:435.

41. Manton, *Christ's Eternal Existence*, in *Works*, 1:439.

42. Compare *tou theou panta kai tō theō* in Josephus, *Wars of the Jews*, 5.218, in *Flavia Josephi Opera*, ed. Benedictus Niese (Berolini: Weidmannos, 1888), 6:464. The phrase in 1 Cor. 8:6 translated as "by [or through] whom are all things" (*di hou ta panta*) is used of God in Heb. 2:10, and therefore does not connote mere instrumentality, but the divine agency by which all things exist.

yet applies it to both the Father and the Son, who are both the Creator God.[43] Richard Bauckham writes that Paul is "maintaining monotheism" and yet "including Jesus in the unique identity of the one God affirmed in the Shema," for "the term 'Lord,' applied here to Jesus as the 'one Lord,' is taken from the Shema itself." Bauckham explains, "He maintains monotheism not by adding Jesus to but by including Jesus in his Jewish understanding of the divine uniqueness."[44]

Christ also engages in the divine work of *providence*, sustaining and directing all things according to God's decree. "By him all things consist" or continue in existence (Col. 1:17). Christ is "upholding all things by the word of his power"—that is, carrying them along toward their appointed goal (Heb. 1:3).[45] The Lamb of God opens the seals of God's scroll, executing the divine decree as various troubles come on the earth (Rev. 5:9; 6:1). Christ exercises divine control over not only the general course of events, but also specifics. Jesus said that the time when one of his disciples would die was dependent upon his sovereign "If I will" (John 21:22).

Athanasius said of all things, "The holy Word of the Father . . . holds them together and binds them to Himself, having left nothing void of His own power, but on the contrary quickening and sustaining all things everywhere, each severally and all collectively. . . . He produces as the result a marvelous and truly divine harmony."[46] This reign over the entire creation requires that Christ be omnipotent, omnipresent, and perfectly wise. John Calvin said, "To govern the universe with providence and power, and to regulate all things by the command of his own power . . . is the function of the Creator alone."[47]

The Lord Jesus demonstrates his deity by working *miracles by a mere word*. The centurion recognized Christ's sovereignty, and so told him that he need not come to his house, but, "speak the word only, and my servant shall be healed. For I am a man under authority, having soldiers under me: and I say to this man, Go, and he goeth; and to another, Come, and he cometh; and to my servant, Do this, and he doeth it" (Matt. 8:8–9). Similarly, Jesus "cast out the spirits with his word" (v. 16; cf. vv. 31–32). When a storm at sea threatened to drown him and his disciples, he "rebuked

---

43. See *RST*, 1:881–82.
44. Bauckham, *Jesus and the God of Israel*, 28, 30. Bauckham calls this "Christological monotheism."
45. On these texts and the Trinitarian work of providence, see *RST*, 1:1064–65, 1076–78.
46. Athanasius, *Against the Heathen*, sec. 42, in *NPNF*[2], 4:26.
47. Calvin, *Institutes*, 1.13.12.

the wind and the sea; and there was a great calm," so that his disciples exclaimed, "What manner of man is this, that even the winds and the sea obey him!" (vv. 26–27). The answer to their question is that this person is God, of whom the psalmist said, "He sent his word, and healed them, and delivered them from their destructions. . . . He maketh the storm a calm, so that the waves thereof are still" (Ps. 107:20, 29).

It might be objected that the prophets and apostles also worked miracles even though they were mere servants of God. In reply, we acknowledge that as God's incarnate Son, Christ worked miracles in submission to his Father by God's Spirit.[48] However, Christ's miracles indicate that Christ is the inaugurator of the kingdom by the Spirit (Matt. 12:28).[49] Turretin said, "The apostles deny that they wrought miracles by their own power, but in the name of Christ (Acts 4:7, 10, i.e., by his power and authority)."[50] Christ used his miracles to reveal himself as the King of the kingdom, who rules creation at his mere word of command. These works reveal his essential union with the Father so that we may believe that he is the Son of God (John 10:30, 36–38; 14:10–11).

Christ asserts his divine authority to give *forgiveness of sins*, saying, "Thy sins be forgiven thee. . . . The Son of man hath power on earth to forgive sins" (Mark 2:5, 10). This shocked his hearers, who thought, "Why doth this man thus speak blasphemies? Who can forgive sins but God only?" (v. 7). They had good reasons to raise this question, for all sin is against God, and God alone has the right to grant forgiveness.[51] Christ did not correct their theology or their understanding of what he claimed, but validated his authority to forgive sin by healing a paralyzed man by his mere command (vv. 10–12)—another sign of his deity. In the process, he exercised his divine attribute of omniscience to know their very thoughts (v. 8).[52]

Perhaps the greatest miracle Christ performs in this age is *spiritual resurrection of the dead*. God's Son says, "He that heareth my word, and believeth on him that sent me, hath everlasting life, and shall not come into condemnation; but is passed from death unto life. . . . The hour is coming, and now is, when the dead shall hear the voice of the Son of God: and

---

48. Luke 4:14; John 5:36; 10:25; Acts 10:38.
49. Wellum, *God the Son Incarnate*, 197–98.
50. Turretin, *Institutes*, 3.28.23 (1:288).
51. Pss. 32:1–2, 5; 51:1–4; Isa. 43:25; Mic. 7:18.
52. Edwards, *The Gospel according to Mark*, 77–79.

they that hear shall live" (John 5:24–25). Christ's voice, as the expression of his sovereign will, is sufficient to call sinners out of spiritual death into the life of faith in his word. He can do this because he is the only begotten Son of God the Father: "For as the Father hath life in himself; so hath he given to the Son to have life in himself" (v. 26).[53]

Christ pours out the *gift of the promised Spirit* upon the church.[54] In the Old Testament, God promised to "pour out" (*ekcheō*) the Spirit upon all his people (Joel 3:1–2[2:28–29] LXX), as Peter declared on Pentecost (Acts 2:16–18). This is the work of the only God, by which he saves his people who call upon his name and makes them faithful to him.[55] However, Peter went on to say that Jesus, "being by the right hand of God exalted, and having received of the Father the promise of the Holy Ghost, he hath shed forth [*ekcheō*] this, which ye now see and hear" (v. 33), for he is "Lord" (v. 36), and forgiveness and the Spirit are received "in the name of Jesus Christ" (v. 38). Without denying that the Father gives the Spirit to his people,[56] the New Testament also teaches that Christ sends and gives the Spirit.[57] The Spirit is God;[58] he who gives God to man must himself be God. Christ received the Spirit in his humanity as the Mediator, but his ability to give the Spirit to his people throughout the world depends on his deity. Augustine said, "He received as man, and shed forth as God."[59]

Christ guards those whom he regenerates in the divine work of *spiritual preservation in the faith*. Despite all the efforts of Satan and this corrupt world, allied with the remaining unbelief and corruption that plagues the saints' hearts, Christ will keep them to the end. He says, "I give unto them eternal life; and they shall never perish, neither shall any man pluck them out of my hand. My Father, which gave them me, is greater than all; and no man is able to pluck them out of my Father's hand" (John 10:28–29). In this exercise of saving grace, Christ's power and the Father's power are one divine and effectual power, for Christ next said, "I and my Father are one" (v. 30). Heinrich Bullinger explained, "One . . . not in concord or agreement, but in [identity] and

---

53. On John 5:26 and its implications for the Trinity, see *RST*, 1:896, 911, 937–38.
54. Turretin, *Institutes*, 3.28.24 (1:288); and Wellum, *God the Son Incarnate*, 198.
55. Isa. 44:3–6; Ezek. 36:27; Joel 2:27, 32.
56. Luke 11:13; John 14:16, 26; Gal. 4:6; Titus 3:5–6.
57. Mark 3:8; Luke 24:49; John 4:10, 14; 7:37–39; 15:26; 16:7; 20:22.
58. On the deity and personality of the Holy Spirit, see *RST*, 1:888–90.
59. Augustine, *On the Trinity*, 15.25.46, in *NPNF¹*, 3:225.

being; for in that place the power and majesty of God are handled. . . . To give life everlasting doth belong to the power of God: to preserve, and so to preserve that none may be able to pluck them out of his hands, belongeth to the same power."[60]

Most spectacular, however, will be Christ's work of *physical resurrection of the dead* on the last day. Jesus says of the Son of Man, "The hour is coming, in the which all that are in the graves shall hear his voice, and shall come forth; they that have done good, unto the resurrection of life; and they that have done evil, unto the resurrection of damnation" (John 5:28–29). To raise "all that are in the graves," the bodies of billions of people, some of which turned to dust thousands of years ago, is a task calling for omnipotence and omniscience.

The deity of Christ will be openly displayed in his work of *final judgment*, for the Father "hath given him to execute judgment" (John 5:27). Jesus Christ will search the hearts and lives of all men, judge them according to their works, and send them into either eternal life or eternal punishment.[61] Then there will be no doubt concerning his divine power, knowledge, and righteousness. All will then bow the knee and confess that Jesus Christ is Lord (Phil. 2:10–11). Furthermore, Christ will judge not merely as an administrator of God's justice, but as the sovereign Lord, calling men to account as "his own servants" for what they did with "his goods," the "talents" that he gave to them, and rewarding them with his "joy" (Matt. 25:14–30). Such a judgment reveals Christ's divine authority over all things, all people, and all blessing.[62]

When we encounter a person who chose who would be saved, created the universe, upholds and directs it, works miracles by his mere command, forgives sins, raises people from spiritual death to life, will resurrect the bodies of all those who have died, and will render divine judgment over each of their lives, who can this be except God? Wellum says, "In the Bible's presentation of Christ, he is in an entirely different category than any created thing. Jesus alone is identified with the Creator-Covenant Lord in all his actions, character, and work."[63]

---

60. Bullinger, *The Decades*, 2.1:244–45, 248. The original reads "selfsameness and being," translating the Latin phrase *identitate et essentia*.
61. Isa. 11:1–5; Matt. 16:27; 25:31–46; Acts 10:42; Rom. 2:16; 14:9–10; 2 Cor. 5:10; 2 Tim. 4:1; Rev. 2:23.
62. Brown, *The Divine Glory of Christ*, 20–21.
63. Stephen J. Wellum, *Christ Alone: The Uniqueness of Jesus as Savior: What the Reformers Taught . . . and Why It Still Matters*, The Five Solas Series (Grand Rapids, MI: Zondervan, 2017), 56.

Honors of Deity

Deity is not an abstract quality, but the nature of the One whom we must love and glorify with all our heart, soul, and strength (Deut. 6:4–5). The Lord is jealous over his glory and will not share it with another (Ex. 20:5; Isa. 42:8). Therefore, one of the most telling lines of evidence that Christ is God arises from divine honors rightly given to him by his creatures.

God's Word commends to us *calling upon Christ in prayer,* even to the point of making it essential for our salvation. While Christ directs us to pray to God "our Father" (Matt. 6:9), Jesus also answers prayer (John 14:13–14). Just as saving faith moves believers to confess "the Lord Jesus," so it also breathes forth prayers, for "whosoever shall call upon the name of the Lord shall be saved" (Rom. 10:9, 13). God's people are "all that in every place call upon the name of Jesus Christ our Lord" (1 Cor. 1:2). With their dying breath, they can pray with Stephen, "Lord Jesus, receive my spirit" (Acts 7:59). Prayer is a divine honor because it expresses absolute dependence upon another person for one's greatest needs (Pss. 121:1–2; 124:4). Prayer assumes that the person we address can hear us wherever we are and has the power to help us (1 Kings 8:38–40). Therefore, God's people renounce prayer to all others and call upon God alone to save them (Ps. 20:7–9; Hos. 14:3). Their calling upon the name of Jesus honors him as God.

The Bible also commends *worshiping Christ in adoration.* It is the Father's will that "all men should honour the Son, even as they honour the Father" (John 5:23), and therefore, the Father has given the Son the supreme honors of judging and giving life (vv. 22, 24). Both men and angels worshiped Christ when he came into the world (Matt. 2:1–12; Heb. 1:6). Christ willingly received the worship of men and women during his earthly life.[64] While some of this might have entailed only a respectful bowing to him, when he walked on water and calmed the wind, "they that were in the ship came and worshipped him, saying, Of a truth thou art the Son of God" (Matt. 14:33). After Christ rose, he again was worshiped (28:9, 17; Luke 24:52). The visions of Revelation portray the worship of Christ in heaven (Rev. 5:9, 12), using the same language as that employed in the worship of the Creator (4:11); indeed, God and the Lamb are worshiped together with the same worship by all

---

64. Matt. 8:2; 9:18; 15:25; 18:26; 20:20.

creation (5:13). We may not rightly give our worship to any creature, not even to an apostle or angel, but should worship God alone.[65] Therefore, Christ is fully God, equally worthy of our worship and adoration with the Father.

Do you worship Christ? Do you humble yourself before him in awe and wonder, and say, "Thou art the Son of God"? Do you regard him as the One in whom the fullness of deity dwells? Is Christ divinely glorious in your eyes? It is one thing to acknowledge his deity as a doctrine, but another thing to see his glory with the eyes of your heart. Meditate on Christ and pray for the Holy Spirit to show you the glory of God in him.

Objections to Christ's Deity

Opponents of Christ's deity raise a number of objections to this doctrine, from the Arian trajectory of seeing Christ as a superhuman being created by God to the Socinian/Unitarian trajectory of seeing him as a man greatly exalted by God.[66] Some of these objections we have already addressed.[67] As we consider others, let us remember that we cannot force God to conform to what seems reasonable to our finite and fallen human minds, but must humbly receive what he says and bow before his incomprehensible mystery (Ps. 145:3; Rom. 11:33).

First, some, especially those who deny the divine authority and trustworthiness of the Holy Scriptures,[68] object that the earliest Jewish disciples of Jesus viewed him simply as a human teacher, but later Christians, influenced by Hellenistic thought, divinized him into the Lord.

In response, Millard Erickson says, "The evolutionary view of Christology . . . must fail because of the lack of time. Paul wrote his earliest epistles within about twenty years of the end of Christ's life and the events of Pentecost."[69] Larry Hurtado writes, "Devotion to Jesus as divine erupted suddenly and quickly, not gradually and late, among first-century circles of followers. More specifically, the origins lie in Jewish Christian circles of the earliest years. Only a certain wishful thinking continues to attribute

---

65. Matt. 4:9–10; Acts 10:25–26; Rev. 19:10; 22:8–9.

66. On the heresies of Arius, Socinus, and others, see chap. 41. See also *RST*, 1:905, 910, 918, 923–26.

67. Against the assertion that John 1:1 should be translated "The Word was a god," see *RST*, 1:886. Against the objection that the doctrine of the Trinity is a logical contradiction, see *RST*, 1:930–31.

68. For a historical survey of and response to theological liberalism, see *RST*, 1:287–95.

69. Erickson, *The Word Became Flesh*, 465.

the reverence of Jesus as divine decisively to the influence of pagan religion and the influx of Gentile converts."[70]

Second, opponents of Christ's deity object that the name "Son" implies that Christ is a lesser being than the Father and had a beginning. Arius (d. 336) reportedly said, "If the Father begat the Son, he that was begotten had a beginning of existence: and from this it is evident, that there was a time when the Son was not."[71]

In response, we observe that the Son did not have a beginning in time, but already existed "in the beginning," at which point he was "God" (John 1:1). Before time began, "before the foundation of the world," the Son lived with the Father in a relationship of infinite love and perfect oneness (17:22, 24). Consequently, Christ's being "the only begotten Son" (1:18; 3:16) does not indicate that he was created by God, but that he eternally relates to the Father as the Son from the Father (1:18), who shares with him in the whole divine nature (5:26; 14:9; 16:15). The biblical teaching on Christ's sonship does not imply inferiority, but eternal equality.[72]

Third, some object that the Son's authority over the world is "given" to him (Matt. 28:18; John 17:2). This implies that he is not God, for God does not receive authority from anyone, but possesses all majesty and sovereignty in himself (1 Chron. 29:11). Thus, the man Jesus is not Lord by nature, but the Father grants him by the Spirit to share partially in God's sovereignty.[73]

In response, Athanasius said that when we read in the Holy Scriptures that certain prerogatives were "given" to Christ or "received" by him, "we must say that our Lord, being Word and Son of God, bore a body, and became Son of Man, that, having become Mediator between God and men, He might minister the things of God to us, and ours to God. . . . These are gifts given from God to us through Him. For the Word was never in want."[74] Thus, the grant of supreme authority pertains to the states of Christ as the incarnate Mediator, the God-man, not simply his divine na-

---

70. Larry W. Hurtado, *Lord Jesus Christ: Devotion to Jesus in Earliest Christianity* (Grand Rapids, MI: Eerdmans, 2003), 650.
71. Cited in Socrates Scholasticus, *Ecclesiastical History*, 1.5, in NPNF², 2:3. See also the response of Athanasius, *Four Discourses against the Arians*, 1.4.11–1.9.34, in NPNF², 4:312–26.
72. On the eternal generation of the Son, see *RST*, 1:933–40.
73. *The Racovian Catechism*, 57–58; and James D. G. Dunn, *The Theology of Paul the Apostle* (Grand Rapids, MI: Eerdmans, 1998), 10.5 (254–55).
74. Athanasius, *Four Discourses against the Arians*, 4.6, in NPNF², 4:435.

ture as God (Phil. 2:6–11).[75] As God, he possessed divine authority even in his state of humiliation, for he was already Lord.[76] The Father glorified Christ's humanity and placed the Mediator into a state of exaltation to give eternal life to his people (John 17:2) through the ministry of the church (Matt. 28:18–20). It would be inappropriate and impossible for Christ to exercise universal sovereignty unless he were God.

Fourth, some object that the Son cannot be equal to the Father, for Christ said, "If ye loved me, ye would rejoice, because I said, I go unto the Father: for my Father is greater than I" (John 14:28). Therefore, Christ must be subordinate and inferior to the Father, who alone is God.[77]

In reply, we note that Christ spoke of his coming transition from humiliation to exaltation, saying, "I go unto the Father." James Fisher (1697–1775) wrote, "He does not speak in that place of his nature, as God, but of his office, as Mediator; in which respect he is the Father's servant (Isa. 42:1)."[78] As God, the Son is equal to the Father and one with him in his divine power and will (John 1:1; 5:17–18, 23; 10:30). As man, and especially as man in a state of humiliation, it is entirely appropriate for Christ to say, "My Father is greater than I."[79]

Fifth, objectors note that Jesus said, "Why callest thou me good? There is none good but one, that is, God" (Mark 10:18). Christ clearly put God in a unique category and excluded himself and all others from it, they argue.[80]

In reply, we note that if this line of reasoning is valid, then Christ also denied his own goodness. Is Christ evil? No, Jesus is God's "beloved Son," in whom he is "well pleased" (Mark 1:11). The solution is to see that Christ was not teaching about his identity, but challenging the assumptions of the man who said, "Good Master [teacher], what shall I do that I may inherit eternal life?" (10:17). Christ's words rebuked the man's assumption that he could find goodness in a merely human teacher or in his own works of obedience to the law (vv. 19–20). Jesus pressed the man to consider his sinfulness and Christ's worthiness to be followed even at

---

75. On Christ's states of humiliation and exaltation, see the paradigm for Christology in chap. 36.

76. Luke 2:11; 4:32, 36; 5:24; 7:6–8.

77. *The Racovian Catechism*, 59–60.

78. James Fisher et al., *The Assembly's Shorter Catechism Explained* (Stoke-on-Trent, England: Berith, 1998), 6.35 (53).

79. Perkins, *An Exposition of the Symbol*, in *Works*, 5:110–11.

80. On the Arian use of Mark 10:18, see Hilary of Poitiers, *On the Trinity*, 9.2, in *NPNF²*, 9.1:155.

the cost of all his earthly riches (v. 21). If the man had reflected rightly on Christ's words, he would have realized that the person speaking to him was both good and God.[81]

Sixth, some object that Christ spoke of the Father as "my God" (Matt. 27:46; John 20:17). Therefore, they argue, Christ is not God, but a worshiper of God.[82]

In reply, we observe that Christ's humanity indeed makes him a worshiper of the Father (Heb. 2:12). Yet this is a nature and posture that Christ took to himself for our salvation (vv. 14–16), whereas the Son dwelt eternally in the radiance of God's divine nature, by which he created the world (1:2–3). Scripture passages describing the Father as the God of Jesus Christ (Eph. 1:3, 17) do not communicate the Father's essential superiority to the Son, but his covenant relationship with the Son according to the eternal counsel of peace made between them for the salvation of the elect by the work of Christ the incarnate Mediator.[83]

Seventh, some object that Jesus is a man (John 19:5; 1 Tim. 2:5), depicted in the Gospels as limited in strength, knowledge, and life. However, God is infinite and immortal. Therefore, they conclude, Jesus cannot be God: "Two substances endued with opposite and discordant properties, such as are God and man, cannot be ascribed to one and the same individual."[84]

In reply, we affirm that Jesus is fully human, having become like us in every way though without sin (Heb. 2:17; 4:15). However, the Holy Scriptures also affirm that he is fully God, as demonstrated by the seven lines of biblical evidence that we listed earlier. Faithfulness to God's Word demands that we believe in both Christ's deity and humanity. Hilary of Poitiers (c. 315–368) said that we must not "forget our Lord Jesus Christ is being treated of as a person of two natures, since he, who was abiding in the form of God, took the form of a servant. . . . The same person is in the form of a servant and in the form of God."[85]

The testimony of the Holy Scriptures is that Jesus is God. However, God's Word frames Christ's deity in the doctrine of the Trinity, so that we learn to say Jesus is God the Son, lest we neglect the deity and distinct

---

81. Hilary of Poitiers, *On the Trinity*, 9.15–17, in *NPNF²*, 9.1:160.
82. *The Racovian Catechism*, 60.
83. See the section on the covenant God of Jesus Christ and the elect in chap. 30.
84. *The Racovian Catechism*, 56.
85. Hilary of Poitiers, *On the Trinity*, 9.14, in *NPNF²*, 9.1:159. We have lowercased some words in accordance with modern usage.

personality of the Father and the Holy Spirit, and the relations among the divine persons. Furthermore, Jesus is Christ's human name, reflecting the incarnation of God the Son in history and his continuing existence as a truly human being. Wellum wisely says, "To preserve Trinitarian relations and the reality of the incarnation, it is better to say that Jesus is God the Son incarnate."[86] The Westminster Confession of Faith (8.2) says, "The Son of God, the second person in the Trinity, being very and eternal God, of one substance and equal with the Father, did, when the fulness of time was come, take upon Him man's nature. . . . Which person is very God, and very man, yet one Christ, the only Mediator between God and man."[87]

Consequently, we may join with Christians since the early centuries of the church in addressing Christ with the words of the "greater doxology," or *Gloria in excelsis*: "Lord God, Lamb of God, Son of the Father who takes away the sin of the world, have mercy on us."[88] This Christ we adore, and this Christ we honor with our absolute faith and reliance.

The Climactic Significance of Christ's Deity for the Christian Life

If Christ were not God, there would be no Christianity. As we saw at the beginning of this chapter, his deity is crucial for our faith. The doctrine of Christ's full divinity also has massive practical significance for the Christian life. Here we offer some spiritual directions to help you apply this truth to your life:

1. *Recognize the horrible evil of your sins.* William Perkins said, "No man could save our souls, no, not all the angels of heaven, unless the King of heaven and earth, the only Son of God, had come down from heaven and suffered for us, bearing our punishment. Now the consideration of this must humble us and make us to cast down ourselves under the hand of God for our sins . . . that some tears of sorrow and repentance might gush out for this our woeful misery."[89]

2. *Trust Christ's sufficiency for complete salvation.* Petrus van Mastricht (1630–1706) said that the doctrine of Christ's deity "commends to us the sufficiency and perfection of our Mediator, from which it is said that

---

86. Wellum, *God the Son Incarnate*, 208. See his discussion on this matter (206–8).

87. *Reformed Confessions*, 4:244.

88. On the ancient origins of the *Gloria in excelsis* and its use in Lutheran and Reformed worship, see *The New Schaff-Herzog Encyclopedia of Religious Knowledge*, ed. Samuel Macauley Jackson, 12 vols. (New York; London: Funk & Wagnalls, 1908–1914), 3:51; 5:501–2.

89. Perkins, *An Exposition of the Symbol*, in *Works*, 5:115.

all fullness dwells in him (Col. 1:19), and he fills all in all (Eph. 1:23), so that from his fullness we can draw grace upon grace (John 1:16); indeed, in him we are made complete (Col. 2:10)."[90] In giving Christ for sinners, God has given all of himself. Surely, then, you can rest upon Christ as all that you need for salvation and eternal life. You are foolish, but in Christ is all wisdom (v. 3). You by nature are dead in sin, but in Christ is resurrection from the dead (v. 13). You are guilty of many transgressions, but in Christ is complete forgiveness, the cancelling of all our debts (vv. 13–14). Brown said, "He who died on the accursed tree, 'the just for the unjust,' is none other than the 'I Am,'" and therefore, "who shall set any limits to the efficacy of His atoning blood and vicarious righteousness?"[91] You have been a slave of Satan and his demonic forces, but in Christ is total victory against all the powers of darkness (v. 15). In a word, you are empty of all spiritual good, but "ye are complete in him" (v. 10) if you trust him and receive him (vv. 6–7).

3. *Find comfort in Christ's sonship and your adoption in him.* If you rejoice that Jesus is the Son of God, then you may also rejoice that you are an adopted son or daughter of God by union with him (Gal. 4:4–5; Eph. 1:5). Perkins said, "Whereas Christ Jesus is the Son of God, it serves as a means to make miserable and wretched sinners, that are by nature the children of wrath and damnation, to be sons of God by adoption. . . . Let all such as fear God enter into a serious consideration of the unspeakable goodness of God, comforting themselves in this, that God the Father has vouchsafed by His own Son to make them of the vassals of Satan to be His own dear children."[92]

4. *Bow the knee to Christ in holy awe.* The glory of Christ's deity calls you to go beyond a consideration of your own salvation and to contemplate the Savior. He does not exist for you, but you and all things exist "for him" (Col. 1:16). Thomas Goodwin said, "God's chief end was not to bring Christ into the world for us, but us for Christ. He is worth all creatures. And God contrived all things that do fall out, and even redemption itself, for the setting forth of Christ's glory, more than our salvation."[93] Therefore, "be swallowed up with profound awe and self-abasement" be-

---

90. Petrus van Mastricht, *Theoretical-Practical Theology*, trans. Todd M. Rester, ed. Joel R. Beeke, 7 vols. (Grand Rapids, MI: Reformation Heritage Books, 2018–), 1.2.26.22 (2:563).

91. Brown, *The Divine Glory of Christ*, 90.

92. Perkins, *An Exposition of the Symbol*, in *Works*, 5:114.

93. Goodwin, *Ephesians*, in *Works*, 1:100.

fore the glory of Christ, as Brown said, because when you gaze upon him, you stand in the presence of the holy, holy, holy Lord.[94]

5. *Think often and warmly of Christ.* Since Christ is God, you should be thinking about him all the time, together with the Father and the Holy Spirit. This is the taproot of Christian spirituality: to set your mind and desires upon Christ (Col. 3:1–2). John Owen said, "The principal actings of the life of faith consist in the frequency of our thoughts concerning him; for hereby Christ liveth in us. . . . A great rebuke it ought to be unto us, when Christ has at any time in a day been long out of our minds." And when we do think of Christ, Owen said, "all our thoughts concerning Christ and his glory should be accompanied with admiration, adoration, and thanksgiving."[95]

6. *Live unto the Lord Christ.* Direct your life and death at him as your great goal and holy ambition (Phil. 1:20–21; 3:8–12). He died and rose again so that his people no longer live for themselves, but for him (Rom. 14:8–9; 2 Cor. 5:14–15). Brown said, "*To live to* any Being is the highest worship that can possibly be rendered to him. We are commanded to *live to Christ*, taking his will as our highest law, and himself as our highest end of existence." The great tragedy of fallen humanity is that we live to ourselves. Brown exclaimed, "Oh the frightful guilt of this, as seen in the light of the absolute soleness of Jehovah's glory, that infinite chasm which subsists between him and all creatures whatsoever! . . . We transfer from God to ourselves the esteem, the confidence, the fear, the love, the service, which are due only to him."[96] Repent, therefore, of living unto yourself, and live unto Christ.

7. *Offer yourself to God in gratitude for his Son.* God's gift of his Son to us displays the infinite depths of his love (John 3:16). Paul says, "He that spared not his own Son, but delivered him up for us all, how shall he not with him also freely give us all things?" (Rom. 8:32). Your only fitting response is to give yourself to God (Rom. 12:1). Perkins said, "Whereas God the Father of Christ gave His only Son to be our Savior, as we must be thankful to God for all things, so especially for this great and unspeakable benefit. . . . We should give unto God both body and soul in token of our thankfulness for this wonderful blessing that He has given His only Son to be our Savior."[97] Give yourself to God for Christ's sake, today and

---

94. Brown, *The Divine Glory of Christ*, 93.
95. Owen, *The Glory of Christ*, in *Works*, 1:319–20.
96. Brown, *The Divine Glory of Christ*, 83–85, emphasis original.
97. Perkins, *An Exposition of the Symbol*, in *Works*, 5:115.

every day of your life, until you see him face-to-face and are liberated to live wholly and solely for his glory.

Sing to the Lord

Christ Our God and the Son of God

> My heart doth overflow,
> A goodly theme is mine;
> My eager tongue with joyful song
> Doth praise the King Divine.
>
> Supremely fair Thou art,
> Thy lips with grace o'erflow;
> His richest blessings evermore
> Doth God on Thee bestow.
>
> Triumphantly ride forth
> For meekness, truth, and right;
> Thy arm shall gain the victory
> In wondrous deeds of might.
>
> Thy royal throne, O God,
> For evermore shall stand;
> Eternal truth and justice wield
> The scepter in Thy hand.
>
> Since Thou art sinless found,
> The Lord, Thy God confessed,
> Anointeth Thee with perfect joy,
> Thou art supremely blest.

Psalm 45
Tune: Mornington
The Psalter, No. 124
Or Tune: Leominster
Trinity Hymnal—Baptist Edition, No. 125

Questions for Meditation or Discussion

1. Why is Christ's deity crucial for the following aspects of the Christian faith?

- faith in Christ
- God's revelation of himself
- salvation
- God's kingdom
- childlike reverence
- being a disciple of Jesus
- Trinitarian spirituality
- balanced authority in the church
- zealous love to evangelize the lost
- faithfulness to the Bible

2. What are the seven lines of evidence for Christ's deity?

3. Give examples of how Christ's deity can be proven from his names and attributes.

4. What do the authors mean by Christ's "preexistence"? How does the Bible testify to this doctrine?

5. How does the Bible show us that Christ is the Creator and Lord of the universe?

6. How do Christ's works of saving sinners demonstrate his deity?

7. How will Christ's deity be evident by his actions when he returns?

8. Imagine that someone says, "Just because people pray to Jesus and worship him does not mean he is God, just that they recognize the divinity that is in him—the divinity in us all." How do you respond?

9. When a person learns that you belong to a church that teaches the Trinity, she says, "Jesus said that he is the Son of God the Father. That proves that God is greater than Jesus, which Jesus said himself." How do you answer her?

10. After you read the closing applications of Christ's deity for the Christian life, which affected you the most? Why? What do you need to do in response?

Questions for Deeper Reflection

11. How would you explain how Christ was "given" authority over all things if he was already God (Matt. 28:18; John 17:2)? How can Christ both possess inherent authority as God and receive delegated authority from God?

12. How might the statement "Jesus is God" be misunderstood by the following people?

- a pantheist who thinks all things are one
- a panentheist who believes that God dwells in us all
- a polytheist who believes in many gods and powerful spirits
- a modern Arian who believes the Father created Christ as a godlike spirit
- a monotheistic modalist who believes Jesus is the Father incarnate
- a modern Socinian who thinks God gave the man Jesus a semidivine status as Lord

13. How would you expand the statement "Jesus is God" so that it rules out these false understandings and explicitly states the orthodox Christian view of Christ Jesus?

39

Christ's Incarnation, Part 1

The Coming of the Incarnate Son

For thousands of years, God's people hung their hope on the promise of a coming Savior—the Seed of the woman who would conquer the Tempter who overcame us (Gen. 3:15). The prophets eagerly received God's revelations concerning this Christ and searched them diligently concerning his sufferings and glory (1 Pet. 1:10–12). He would be the light (Isa. 42:6), even the radiant glory of the Lord (60:1). Yet, mysteriously, he would also be the suffering Servant of Jehovah (52:13–53:12). The messianic hope of Israel centered upon the coming of God himself: "I come, and I will dwell in the midst of thee, saith the LORD" (Zech. 2:10). His coming, Herman Witsius said, is "the foundation of our hope, and the source of all our joy."[1]

Graced with the Holy Spirit, godly Jews looked to Christ's arrival as the coming of salvation, light, glory, and redemption, and yet also suffering and division (Luke 2:25–38). When he was born of Mary, they rejoiced with great joy, for their Savior and Lord had come. The promise of incarnation was fulfilled.

The person of Jesus Christ is unique in who he is and what he means to us. Though "being in the form of God," he "took upon him the form of a servant, and was made in the likeness of men" in order to carry out

---

1. Witsius, *Sacred Dissertations on the Apostles' Creed*, 14.1 (2:2).

his mission from the Father (Phil. 2:6–8).[2] The Heidelberg Catechism (LD 14, Q. 35) summarizes the doctrine of the incarnation well: "God's eternal Son, who is, and continueth true and eternal God, took upon Him the very nature of man, of the flesh and blood of the Virgin Mary, by the operation of the Holy Ghost; that He might also be the true seed of David, like unto His brethren in all things, sin excepted."[3]

The Incarnate Lord's Unique Identity

The word *incarnation* means "being or becoming in flesh" (Latin *en*, "in," plus *carne*, a form of *caro*, "flesh"). The term is based on John 1:14: "And the Word was made flesh,[4] and dwelt among us, (and we beheld his glory, the glory as of the only begotten of the Father,) full of grace and truth." Though John had said, "The Word was God" (v. 1), he did not write, "God became flesh," for that might suggest that the divine nature was changed into flesh, or that the Father or the entire Trinity was made flesh. Instead, he specified the incarnation of one divine person, "the Word"—that is, "Jesus Christ," the "Son" of God (vv. 17–18, 34). It was not the divine nature but one divine person that became incarnate as man.[5] Richard Sibbes (1577–1635) quipped that all three divine persons acted in the incarnation like three sisters making a garment that only one of them wore.[6]

The Word Became Flesh

The verb translated as "was made" (*ginomai*) or "became" (ESV) is used in John 1:14 of "the Word" for the first time in this Gospel. Previously, John wrote that the Word simply "was" (imperfect *eimi*, vv. 1–2), whereas "all things" in the created universe were "made" (*ginomai*), or came into being, through him (vv. 3, 10). Now John changes verbs to describe the entrance of the eternal Word into the created order.

The Word became "flesh" (*sarx*, John 1:14), a term that can refer specifically to the body (6:54), but that more generally means "humanity" (17:2).[7] "Flesh" connotes man's weakness, futility, and inability to produce

---

2. On the interpretation of Phil. 2:6–8, see the paradigm for Christology in chap. 36.
3. *The Three Forms of Unity*, 79.
4. Latin Vulgate: *Et Verbum caro factum est.*
5. Perkins, *An Exposition of the Symbol*, in *Works*, 5:119; Witsius, *Sacred Dissertations on the Apostles' Creed*, 14.4 (2:4); and Bavinck, *Reformed Dogmatics*, 3:275–77.
6. Richard Sibbes, *The Fountain Opened*, in *The Works of Richard Sibbes*, ed. Alexander Grosart, 7 vols. (repr., Edinburgh: Banner of Truth, 1973), 5:479; and Gill, *Body of Divinity*, 383.
7. On *sarx* as a term for humanity, see Matt. 16:17; 24:22; Luke 3:6; Acts 2:17; Rom. 3:20; 1 Cor. 1:29.

the life of God's kingdom (1:13; 3:6; 6:63).[8] John Calvin commented, "He intended to show to what a mean and despicable condition the Son of God, on our account, descended from the height of his heavenly glory," for "the word *flesh* is not taken here for corrupt nature . . . but for mortal man," marking "his frail and perishing nature."[9] The divine Savior clothed himself in the very human nature that desperately needs salvation. Therefore, John's statement is surprising, even shocking, for he brings together the eternal and omnipotent Word with frail and mortal humanity. Yet John insists in his epistles that true, saving faith necessarily affirms that "Jesus Christ is come in the flesh" (1 John 4:2–3; 2 John 7).

We must view the doctrine of Christ's incarnation in the light of biblical, Trinitarian monotheism, not other views of God. In pantheism, all things are God, and the divine appears in many avatars. From the perspective of materialistic atheism, Christ's incarnation would be seen as another step in the evolution of biological life. For the panentheist, God is already incarnate in the universe as a soul indwells a body, and Christ is just one embodiment of the world soul. In polytheism, Christ would be one among many gods and spirits. However, biblical monotheism sharply distinguishes the one God from his creation. The incarnation of the divine Word is nothing less than the union of two categorically different natures in one person. Ignatius (d. c. 108) said that we have "one Physician" who is "both made and not made; God existing in flesh."[10] Irenaeus said, "He took up man into Himself, the invisible becoming visible, the incomprehensible being made comprehensible, the impassible becoming capable of suffering."[11]

Christ's incarnation reflects the Trinitarian mission of salvation. This theme figures prominently in John's writings, in which the Father "sent" his Son into the world with the Holy Spirit.[12] We also learn from Paul that at the time of God's appointing, the Father "sent forth his Son," so that he was "made of a woman, made under the law, to redeem them that were

---

8. On the weakness and mortality of man as *sarx*, see Pss. 55:5[56:4]; 77[78]:39; Isa. 31:3; 40:6; Jer. 17:5 LXX; Rom. 8:3; 1 Cor. 15:50. See also the discussion of terms for the human constitution in chap. 12.

9. Calvin, *Commentaries*, on John 1:14.

10. Ignatius, *Epistle to the Ephesians*, chap. 7, in ANF, 1:52.

11. Irenaeus, *Against Heresies*, 3.16.6, in ANF, 1:443.

12. See the Christological use of *apostellō* in John 3:17, 34; 5:36, 38; 6:29, 57; 7:29; 8:42; 10:36; 11:42; 17:3, 8, 18, 21, 23, 25; 20:21; 1 John 4:9, 10, 14; and *pempō* in John 4:34; 5:23, 24, 30, 37; 6:38–40, 44; 7:16, 18, 28, 33; 8:16, 18, 26, 29; 9:4; 12:44, 45, 49; 13:20; 14:24; 15:21; 16:5.

under the law, that we might receive the adoption of sons" and experience that adoption by "the Spirit of his Son" (Gal. 4:4–6). The divine preexistence of the Son is implied by his being "sent" in parallel to the sending of the divine Spirit, the Son's coming into the world by being "born of a woman," and Paul's use of the Greek verb meaning "became" (*ginomai*) instead of the usual word for "born" (*gennaō*).[13] Furthermore, Paul did not write, "through a woman," as if Mary were merely an instrument, but "of" or "out of" (*ek*) a woman, indicating that the preexistent Son took his human nature from the substance of his earthly mother.[14]

In order to save the family that the Father gave him (Heb. 2:11–13), the Son "took part" (*metechō*), or shared, their "flesh and blood" (v. 14). He was "made like unto his brethren" so that as their High Priest he could make propitiation for their sins and help them in their temptations (vv. 17–18). Thus, Christ is the incarnate Lord, Redeemer, and Helper of his people,[15] for "he took not . . . angels; but he took . . . the seed of Abraham" (v. 16).[16] The verb translated as "took" (*epilambanomai*) means to seize, grasp, or take hold of. "Helps" (ESV) may reflect the purpose of such grasping, but it is not the meaning of the word. Hebrews 2:16 might refer to Christ taking hold of Abraham's seed to redeem them from bondage and bring them to their inheritance (vv. 10, 14–15), as in Israel's exodus,[17] for mankind, not "angels," will rule the new creation (v. 5). Many modern commentators interpret verse 16 as a statement of salvation, without reference to the incarnation.[18] However, the immediate context speaks of Christ's taking flesh and blood (v. 14) in order to serve as his people's atoning and assisting Priest (vv. 17–18). Traditionally, verse 16 has been interpreted to refer to Christ's assumption of human nature.[19] Christ took hold of "the seed of Abraham," assuming to himself human

13. Fee, *Pauline Christology*, 213–16.

14. Wellum, *God the Son Incarnate*, 212.

15. Compare Heb. 2:14–18 with the language of Isa. 41:8–10 LXX.

16. In Heb. 2:16, "on him the nature of" and "on him" are not in the Greek text, but were supplied by the translators.

17. That interpretation can appeal to the only use of *epilambanomai* in the canonical LXX with respect to God and his people, where he brings them out of Egypt (Jer. 38:32[31:32] LXX; cited in Heb. 8:9). However, the parallel is not exact, for Jeremiah speaks of taking the people "by the hand," which is not the expression in Heb. 2:16.

18. David L. Allen, *Hebrews*, The New American Commentary (Nashville: Broadman & Holman, 2010), 222–23.

19. John Chrysostom, *Homilies on the Epistle to the Hebrews*, 5.1, in NPNF¹, 14:388; Owen, *An Exposition of the Epistle to the Hebrews*, 3:454–61; Poole, *Annotations upon the Holy Bible*, on Heb. 2:16 (3:818); Turretin, *Institutes*, 13.5.7–8 (2:308); and Philip E. Hughes, *A Commentary on the Epistle to the Hebrews* (Grand Rapids, MI: Eerdmans, 1977), 115–18.

flesh and blood descended from the patriarchs, in order to bring the covenant people to enjoy his glory as sons united to the incarnate Son.[20] The Lord's descent to Mount Sinai (Ex. 19:11, 18; Neh. 9:13) and then to the tabernacle (cf. Num. 12:5) to bring Israel to its inheritance was only a type of the incarnation (Eph. 4:8–10), for the Son of God was made "lower than the angels" in order to bring "many sons unto glory" (Heb. 2:9–10).

Leo the Great (c. 400–461) said,

> Therefore the Word of God, Himself God, the Son of God who "in the beginning was with God," through whom "all things were made" and "without" whom "was nothing made" [John 1:1–3] with the purpose of delivering man from eternal death, became man: so bending Himself to take on Him our humility without decrease in His own majesty, that remaining what He was and assuming what He was not, He might unite the true form of a slave to that form in which He is equal to God the Father [Phil. 2:6–7].[21]

God Dwelt among Us

In becoming flesh, the Word "dwelt among us"—literally "made his tabernacle" or "pitched his tent" (*skēnoō*) in our midst (John 1:14).[22] In combination with the word translated as "glory" (*doxa*), this identifies Christ as the true tabernacle in which God's glory dwells with his people.[23] Just as the Lord directed Moses to construct the tabernacle with plain materials on the outside, but to use gold within where the divine glory would appear (Exodus 25–26), so Christ's humble humanity concealed the unspeakable majesty of his deity, except for his brief transfiguration (Matt. 17:1–9). This should astonish us, for the glory of God overwhelms human nature and cannot be contained in any created temple (1 Kings 8:11, 27; Isa. 66:1–2), but in Christ all the infinite glory of God dwells in harmonious personal union with one finite man (Col. 2:9; Heb. 1:3). John Owen said that Christ alone is the "true, substantial tabernacle, where God dwelleth personally" as "our God in the covenant of grace." Thus, Christ "is the

---

20. Cf. Sirach 4:11, "Wisdom exalteth her children, and layeth hold [*epilambanomai*] of them that seek her," which refers not so much to Wisdom helping her devotees as bringing them close to participate in her life, joy, and glory—indeed, to receive her as their inheritance (vv. 12–16).

21. Leo the Great, *Sermons*, "On the Feast of the Nativity," 1.2, in *NPNF*², 12:129.

22. Gen. 13:12 LXX. See *aposkēnoō* in v. 18. See also Rev. 21:3.

23. On the "glory" (*doxa*) in the "tabernacle" (*skēnē*), see Ex. 40:34–35; Lev. 9:23; Num. 14:10; 16:19 LXX. See also the reference to Christ's "glory" and his body being the "temple" in John 2:11, 21.

only way and means of our approach unto God in holy worship, as the tabernacle was of old."[24]

Therefore, though the Word became flesh, he remains fully God, for in his flesh his divine "glory" was manifested to his disciples (John 1:14).[25] The glory of Christ was his own divine glory as the Son, "glory as of the only begotten of the Father" (v. 14), his eternal greatness and majesty with the Father (17:5). Concealed in his assumed humanity, this "glory" consisted in the reality of his deity visible to the eyes of faith as he worked miracles, taught, and died on the cross.[26] If he had not remained God when he became man, then he would have had no glory to show them. Yet he did come with glory, full of "grace and truth" (1:14), which may be John's way of expressing God's "steadfast love and faithfulness" (Ex. 34:6 ESV).[27] God's saving, covenantal mercies came to us with all their divine fullness in the incarnate Son as never before (John 1:16–17).[28]

Paul says of Jesus Christ that "God was manifest in the flesh" (1 Tim. 3:16).[29] Witsius said, "On account of the very intimate union of that human nature with God the Son, the actions performed by it might be no less the actions of God than the creation or government of the universe, and it might be justly said of him when exhibited to view, 'Lo! This is our God, we have waited for him, and he will save us; this is Jehovah, we have waited for him, we will be glad and rejoice in his salvation' [Isa. 25:9]."[30] Theodorus VanderGroe (1705–1784) wrote, "As poor, sinful men, we lost

---

24. Owen, *An Exposition of the Epistle to the Hebrews*, 6:19. See Kelly, *Systematic Theology*, 2:154–55.

25. Murray, "The Person of Christ," in *Collected Writings*, 2:136.

26. See the use of *doxa* and *doxazō* in John 2:11; 11:4, 40; 12:23–24, 27–28; 13:31–32; 17:8–10, 22.

27. Kelly, *Systematic Theology*, 2:158; and George E. Ladd, *A Theology of the New Testament*, rev. ed. (Grand Rapids, MI: Eerdmans, 1993), 302. The pair *khesed* and *emet* is often rendered by a form of "mercy" (*eleos*) and "truth" (*alētheia*) in the LXX.

28. "Grace" (*charis*) rarely appears with "truth" (*alētheia*) in the LXX. There is a parallel to the triad of glory, grace, and truth in John 1:14 in *hoti eleon kai alētheian agapa kyrios ho theos, charin kai doxan dōsei* (Ps. 83:12[84:11] LXX), which may be translated, "For the Lord God loves mercy and truth; he will give grace and glory."

29. Though many translations omit "God" (*theos*) from 1 Tim. 3:16, the reading appears in the majority of manuscripts and has early attestation in Gregory of Nyssa, *Against Eunomius*, 2.1, 4.1, 4, in NPNF[2], 5:101, 155, 188; and Chrysostom, *Homilies on Timothy*, Homily 11, in NPNF[1], 13:442. In uncial Greek manuscripts, *theos* was abbreviated to its first and last letters in a manner that could easily be misread as *hos*, "who." See John William Burgon, *The Revision Revised* (London: John Murray, 1883), 98–105, 424–501; and James R. White, *The King James Only Controversy: Can You Trust the Modern Translations?* (Minneapolis: Bethany House, 1995), 207–9, both of whom favor the reading "God was manifest." Even if it were the case that "God" did not appear in the original text, Paul's statement clearly asserts the revelation of a being "in the flesh" who stands at the center of godliness, and that can only be God himself. Thus, Nichols, *Lectures in Systematic Theology*, 3:488–89.

30. Witsius, *Sacred Dissertations on the Apostles' Creed*, 14.10 (2:8–9).

all true knowledge of God in Adam. . . . Behold, however, this most high God in his infinite mercy is pleased to manifest Himself in the flesh unto us," and that as the supremely wise, almighty, and true God of infinite holiness, justice, love, mercy, and grace.[31]

We conclude that Christ is the God-man (Greek *Theanthrōpos*, Latin *Deus homo*).[32] The incarnation was not an act of subtraction in which the Son cast off his deity, but one of addition in which he embraced our humanity. Augustine said, "God's Son, assuming humanity without destroying His divinity, established and founded this faith, that there might be a way for man to man's God through a God-man."[33]

When we see the divine majesty of Christ, as when he walked on water, we may be tempted to cry out, "It is a spirit," and think that he only appeared to be human (Matt. 14:26). But the Lord assures us that we need not fear, for though he is God, even "I Am,"[34] it is "Jesus" who reaches out his human hand to us (vv. 27, 31). Augustine paraphrased Christ as saying, "Though I walk upon the sea, though I have under my feet the elation and the pride of this world, as the raging waves, yet have I appeared as very man, yet does my gospel proclaim the very truth concerning me, that I was born of a virgin, that I am the Word made flesh."[35]

God the Son became human in all our weakness and mortality without ceasing to be God (John 1:14), so that his glory, grace, and truth have become the salvation of those who receive him by faith (v. 12). Indeed, this doctrine illuminates what it means to receive him, for we must receive him as he is, God the Son incarnate. John's Gospel was "written, that ye might believe that Jesus is the Christ, the Son of God; and that believing ye might have life through his name" (20:31). John shows what this means both at the beginning of his Gospel—"The Word was God. . . . And the Word was made flesh" (1:1, 14)—and at its end, where Thomas says to Jesus, "My

---

31. Theodorus VanderGroe, *The Christian's Only Comfort in Life and Death: An Exposition of the Heidelberg Catechism*, trans. Bartel Elshout, ed. Joel R. Beeke, 2 vols. (Grand Rapids, MI: Reformation Heritage Books, 2016), 1:296–98.

32. Polyander, Walaeus, Thysius, and Rivetus, *Synopsis Purioris Theologiae*, 25.26 (2:80–81). See Ames, *The Marrow of Theology*, 1.18.17, 28 (130–31); and Wollebius, *Compendium*, 1.16. (1).2 (86).

33. Augustine, *The City of God*, 11.2, in NPNF[1], 2:206. On Christ as the "God-man," see also Augustine, *Enchiridion*, chap. 108, in NPNF[1], 3:272; *Reply to Faustus the Manichaean*, 13.8, in NPNF[1], 4:203; and Anselm, *Why God Became Man* (*Cur Deus Homo*), 2.6–8, in *A Scholastic Miscellany*, ed. Fairweather, 150–54.

34. Christ's "it is I" (Matt. 14:27) is literally "I am" (*egō eimi*), which in the context of his walking on water is likely a reference to the divine name of Jehovah, for it is he who walks upon the sea (Job 9:8; Ps. 77:19; Hab. 3:15).

35. Augustine, *Sermons*, 75.7.8, in NPNF[1], 6:339.

LORD and my God," which Christ identifies as a confession of true saving faith (20:28–29). If we would become children of God, then we, too, must trust Christ as the incarnate God and Lord.

The Incarnate Lord's Unique Birth

God honored his Son by decreeing the unique character of his birth, a birth somewhat similar to the miraculous birth of Isaac to old Abraham and barren Sarah, but far more amazing.

The Promise of the Virgin Birth

God announced the unique birth of his Son through a promise given seven centuries before Christ arrived. Though wicked King Ahaz refused to trust the Lord, even when offered the opportunity to ask God for a sign, Isaiah prophesied that the Lord would give his people[36] a "sign"—namely, "Behold, a virgin shall conceive, and bear a son, and shall call his name Immanuel" (Isa. 7:14). The child would be a sign of grace, for "Immanuel" means "God with us."

The word translated as "virgin" (*'almah*) refers to a young woman who is not married, and thus in ancient Israel presumably not sexually active. The birth of a child to a young woman who had had sexual relations with a man would scarcely have qualified as a sign to Israel.[37] The Septuagint renders the term *parthenos*, which explicitly speaks of sexual virginity.[38] Isaiah's wife had already born him a child (Isa. 7:3), and so this prophecy does not refer to any child of his. Rather, God promised the birth of a far greater child, one who would be "God with us," for "unto us a child is born," and he will be called "the mighty God" (9:6).

This Hebrew term for "virgin" (*'almah*) is also used of Rebekah (Gen. 24:43) when she was a young woman of marriageable age who had never had sexual relations with a man (v. 16).[39] The promise of Immanuel may allude directly to Rebekah and Isaac, for he was the first recipient of God's explicit promise to be "with thee" (26:3, 24). In Christ, God's covenant with Abraham, Isaac, and Jacob would come to fruition (Isa. 41:8–10).

---

36. In Isa. 7:14, the "you" in "shall give you a sign" is plural, referring to the Lord's people, not Ahaz.

37. Letham, *The Message of the Person of Christ*, 53–54.

38. Lev. 21:13–14 LXX; cf. the metaphorical use in 2 Cor. 11:2; Rev. 14:4.

39. See J. Alec Motyer, *The Prophecy of Isaiah* (Downers Grove, IL: InterVarsity Press, 1993), 84–85. Another term sometimes translated as "virgin" (*betulah*) can refer to a married woman (Joel 1:8).

The Event of the Virgin Birth

Centuries after Isaiah recorded his prophecies, the angel Gabriel came to Mary, a "virgin" (*parthenos*) betrothed to Joseph, and said, "Behold, thou shalt conceive in thy womb, and bring forth a son, and shalt call his name Jesus" (Luke 1:27, 31). His words echo the Immanuel promise of Isaiah.[40] The Gospel of Matthew identifies Jesus as the promised Immanuel (Matt. 1:22–23) after twice asserting that he was not born by the union of Joseph and Mary, but conceived "of the Holy Ghost" (vv. 18, 20)—that is, from the Spirit's causal activity.[41] It is fitting that the Holy Spirit acted as the efficient cause in forming Christ's human nature, for the Father anointed Jesus as the reservoir of all the graces of the Spirit to men.[42] This does not make the Holy Spirit the Father of Jesus, for Christ's conception took place not of the Spirit's substance or by his generation, but by the Spirit's power and activity.[43]

Though the Spirit is the cause of Christ's conception, the word translated as "conceive" in Luke 1:31 is the same used of ordinary human conception (v. 36).[44] Jesus was not implanted in Mary's womb, but was formed of her flesh by the Spirit.[45] Speaking by inspiration of the Holy Spirit, Elizabeth said to Mary that Jesus was "the fruit of thy womb" and that Mary was "the mother of my Lord" (vv. 42–43). Hence, Jesus was conceived by the supernatural work of the Holy Spirit upon Mary's body, then experienced the natural processes of gestation and birth.[46] Greg Nichols writes, "Thus, Mary contributed everything that any human mother contributes to the conception of her son. She was in every sense Jesus' biological mother."[47] However, Joseph had no biological relation to Jesus (Matt. 1:25).[48]

---

40. Compare *idou hē parthenos en gastri hexei kai texetai huion, kai kaleseis to onoma autou Emmanouēl* (Isa. 7:14 LXX) to *idou syllēpsē en gastri kai texē huion, kai kaleseis to onoma outou Iēsoun* (Luke 1:31).

41. The preposition in the phrase translated as "of the Holy Ghost" (Matt. 1:18, 20) is *ek*, denoting origin, cause, or agency. Verse 20 literally says he was "begotten/born from" (*gennēthen ek*) the Spirit, and the same language can be used of the person or activity that causes the conception of a child (v. 16; John 8:41; cf. 1:13; 3:6).

42. Ames, *A Sketch of the Christian's Catechism*, 77. See Isa. 11:2; Luke 3:22; 4:18; Acts 2:33; Eph. 1:3.

43. Perkins, *An Exposition of the Symbol*, in *Works*, 5:125–26.

44. On *syllambanō* as referring to the conception of a child, see Gen. 4:1, 17, 25; 16:4; 19:36; 21:2; 29:32, 34, 35; 30:5, 7, 8, 10, 12, 17, 19, 23; 38:3, 4; 1 Sam. 1:20; Hos. 1:3, 6, 8; etc. LXX.

45. In scholastic terminology, the Holy Spirit was the efficient cause of Christ's conception, and Mary's body the material cause. See Wollebius, *Compendium*, 1.16.(2).i–ii (89).

46. Polyander, Walaeus, Thysius, and Rivetus, *Synopsis Purioris Theologiae*, 25.19–22 (2:77–79).

47. Nichols, *Lectures in Systematic Theology*, 3:523. See Murray, "The Person of Christ," in *Collected Writings*, 3:134.

48. In this regard, note the peculiar expression in Mark 6:3, where Jesus is not called the son of Joseph, but "the son of Mary." See Torrance, *Incarnation*, 89.

Thus, the virgin conception and birth confirm Christ's true humanity and link him to the ancient promises of Abraham's seed. That Christ became a man physically descended from Abraham, Isaac, Jacob, Judah, and David was crucial for the fulfilment of God's covenant. Herman Bavinck said, "Jesus became human—'flesh'; he came into the flesh (John 1:14; 1 John 4:2–3) from the loins of the patriarchs according to the flesh (Rom. 9:5); he is Abraham's offspring (Gal. 3:16), from the tribe of Judah (Heb. 7:14), a descendant of David (Rom. 1:3)."[49]

Christ's virgin birth shows that in Christ God accomplishes supernatural salvation. The Savior was born by miraculous conception. The angel concludes, "For with God nothing shall be impossible" (Luke 1:37; cf. 18:26–27). Do we believe this? Skeptics do not, but that is just the outworking of their prior rejection of the supernatural God. J. Gresham Machen (1881–1937) said, "The overwhelming majority of those who reject the Virgin Birth reject also the supernatural content of the New Testament. . . . It really concerns all miracles. And the question concerning all miracles is simply the question of the acceptance or rejection of the Saviour that the New Testament presents."[50] In particular, do we believe that salvation is a supernatural work of God? Wayne Grudem writes, "The virgin birth of Christ is an unmistakable reminder that salvation can never come through human effort, but must be the work of God himself."[51] The angel's words echo God's promise regarding the miraculous birth of Isaac to aged Abraham and Sarah (Gen. 18:14), and thereby remind us that God creates and multiplies his people by his supernatural power in the virgin-born Christ.

The Explanation of the Virgin Birth

Mary believed the angel (Luke 1:45), but she sought a deeper understanding, asking, "How shall this be, seeing I know not a man?" (v. 34). The angel's answer in verse 35 further highlighted the supernatural wonder of the virgin birth and the child born, while avoiding any hint of a sexual encounter. First, he said, "The Holy Ghost shall come upon thee," a promise of divine empowerment (Acts 1:8) that alludes to Isaiah's promise of the

---

49. Bavinck, *Reformed Dogmatics*, 3:252. Paul indicates Christ's physical descent from David: "of the seed of David according to the flesh" (Rom. 1:3). Peter says that God promised David that Christ would be "of the fruit of his loins, according to the flesh" (Acts 2:30). This implies that Mary was a physical descendant of David, and Jesus a physical descendant of Mary.

50. Machen, *Christianity and Liberalism*, 108–9. On this topic, see J. Gresham Machen, *The Virgin Birth of Christ* (New York: Harper, 1930).

51. Grudem, *Systematic Theology*, 530.

Spirit's renewal of creation in righteousness and peace (Isa. 32:15–17).[52] Second, he said, "The power of the Highest shall overshadow thee," which alludes to the cloud of glory that came upon the tabernacle (Ex. 40:35).[53] The phrase "power of the Highest," a circumlocution for God,[54] emphasizes that God came to dwell with his people with his infinite power to save them. Third, the child begotten by the "Holy Ghost" would also be "holy," separated from sin and set apart for God's sacred purposes. This confirms Christ's preservation from original sin, which is propagated by ordinary generation (Ps. 51:5; John 3:6). Fourth, he was "the Son of God," which in the larger context means he was no mere man, but the Lord come in the flesh (Luke 2:11).[55]

Therefore, the virgin birth was a sign that the Son born to Mary is more than a mere man, but the inaugurator of the new creation by the Spirit, the glory of God come to tabernacle among men, the sinless Holy One who accomplishes God's will, and the Son of God, the Lord of heaven and earth. Truly, he is Immanuel, God with us, just as Isaiah prophesied.[56] William Perkins noted that God's presence in Jesus Christ infinitely transcends his general omnipresence with all things, his gracious presence in believers, and even his glorious presence in heaven, for "the Godhead of the Son is present and dwells with and in the manhood," so that it participates in his very person and belongs uniquely to him. As a result, Christ's manhood "is thereby perfected and enriched with unspeakable dignity."[57] He is the incomparable King before whom all previous kings in the line of David were mere shadows, for he alone brings God's living temple and, by his perfect obedience, establishes God's kingdom with men forever.

When we consider the alternatives, as Grudem points out, we can see that the virgin birth was a very wise means by which to signal the entrance of the incarnate Son into the world. If God had created the human nature

---

52. The verb translated as "come upon" (*eperchomai*) in Luke 1:35 also appears in Isaiah's prophecy, "until the Spirit comes upon you from on high" (*heōs an epelthē eph' hymas pneuma aph' hypsēlou*, Isa. 32:15 LXX).

53. The verb translated as "overshadow" (*episkiazō*) in Luke 1:35 is used of the glory cloud in Ex. 40:35 LXX; Luke 9:34. See also the use of *skiazō* for the same in Num. 9:18, 22; 10:36; Isa. 4:5 LXX.

54. Matt. 26:64; Luke 22:69.

55. In Luke's Gospel, the "Son" uniquely knows and pleases his Father, speaks to men with absolute authority, terrifies the demons, controls creation with his mere word, is the heir of God the Father, will sit at God's right hand in glory, and will reign over his people forever. Luke 1:32–33; 3:22; 4:3, 41; 8:28; 9:35; 10:22; 20:13–14; 22:69–70. On the meaning of the title "Son of God," see the section on Christ's names of deity in chap. 37.

56. See Wellum, *God the Son Incarnate*, 238.

57. Perkins, *An Exposition of the Symbol*, in *Works*, 5:128–29.

of Jesus without him being conceived and born of a human mother, then it would be more difficult for us to believe that Christ is truly human. If God had brought forth Jesus by the ordinary union of a man and woman, then it would be more difficult for us to believe that Christ is truly God—he would seem merely human. However, Jesus's virgin birth from a human mother illustrates both his deity and his humanity.[58]

The doctrine of the virgin birth, though challenged by modern rationalists, has been the belief of the church since its earliest centuries. It was proclaimed by Ignatius at the close of the first century.[59] Justin Martyr wrote of it, as did Irenaeus, who included the virgin birth in his summary of the apostolic faith confessed by Christians in all places.[60] It was part of the ancient Apostles' Creed and the Nicene Creed,[61] and reaffirmed in the Reformed confessions.[62]

The virgin birth calls us to submit our minds and hearts to God's Word, regardless of how difficult it may be to accept.[63] Mary and Joseph are our examples in this matter, for despite the potential scandal of her pregnancy,[64] they believed God's word and submitted to his will (Matt. 1:24–25; Luke 1:38). In the same way, we must trust in the supernatural power and faithfulness of the God who revealed his Son in this manner. If God cannot be trusted with this, then how can we trust him to save us from hell and raise us from the dead to reign with Christ forever?

The Incarnate Lord's Unique Person

Christ is fully God and fully man. Since the beginning of the incarnation, he is both at the same time: one person existing in two natures. By "person," we mean "someone who is unique, rational, volitional, and in relationships with other persons."[65] Charles Hodge noted, "The Son of

---

58. Grudem, *Systematic Theology*, 530.

59. Ignatius, *Epistle to the Ephesians*, chaps. 18–19; and *Epistle to the Smyrnaeans*, chap. 1, in *ANF*, 1:57, 86.

60. Justin Martyr, *First Apology*, chaps. 22, 31–33, 46, in *ANF*, 1:170, 173–74, 178; and Irenaeus, *Against Heresies*, 1.10.1; 3.4.2; 3.19.1–3; 3.21.1, 4–10, in *ANF*, 1:330, 417, 448–49, 451–54.

61. *The Three Forms of Unity*, 5, 7.

62. Belgic Confession (Art. 18); and Heidelberg Confession (LD 14, Q. 35), in *The Three Forms of Unity*, 34–35, 79; and French Confession (Art. 14); Thirty-Nine Articles (Art. 2); and Westminster Confession of Faith (18.2), in *Reformed Confessions*, 2:145–46, 754; 4:244.

63. This is not to say that the doctrine of the virgin birth is irrational nonsense. There are reasonable answers to objections against it. See Macleod, *The Person of Christ*, 28–36; and Wellum, *God the Son Incarnate*, 240–45.

64. Perhaps the Jews insinuated that Jesus was an illegitimate child of a Samaritan in John 8:41, 48.

65. We arrived at this description of a "person" when exploring the doctrine of the Trinity in *RST*, 1:931–33.

God never addresses the Son of Man as a different person from Himself. The Scriptures reveal but one Christ."[66]

Theologians refer to the unity of Christ's constitution as the "hypostatic union," for God the Son took a human nature into union with his person (*hypostasis*).[67] The hypostatic union of the incarnation is not a union of essence, such as the oneness of the Trinity, in which all three persons share one divine nature; a union of grace, such as the oneness of Christ and his people; a union of relationship, such as the union between two friends; or a temporary, instrumental union, such as a man wearing clothing or angels assuming temporary physical form. The hypostatic union is a personal union, such that two natures are joined in one person without change, separation, or confusion.[68]

We may understand that this union exists in Christ, but we cannot fully comprehend it or explain it.[69] That should not surprise us, for the incarnation is unique, without parallel in history. Furthermore, we do not even completely understand our own souls and their union with our bodies, much less the essence and acts of the incomprehensible God. The union of the human soul and body can serve as a distant analogy; the similarity lies in the conjunction of two substances with different properties in one person so that they act together, each according to its properties.[70] However, the soul and body are both finite and created, whereas in Christ, a person with an infinite and eternal divine nature took to himself a finite and temporal human nature. Furthermore, a human being has only one consciousness, residing in the soul, whereas in Christ there coexist in one person an omniscient divine consciousness and a limited human consciousness.

The Holy Scriptures present the deity and humanity of this unique person in the most extraordinary combinations. The prophets foretold that the one Messiah would be both the eternal God and God's anointed covenant Servant (Ps. 45:6–7),[71] both a child and the mighty God (Isa. 9:6),

---

66. Hodge, *Systematic Theology*, 2:382; cf. Vos, *Reformed Dogmatics*, 3:46.

67. Wollebius, *Compendium*, 1.16.(4) (90–91). On *hypostasis* for a divine person, see *RST*, 1:904n14, 913, 919, 931.

68. Perkins, *An Exposition of the Symbol*, in *Works*, 5:127; Wollebius, *Compendium*, 1.16.(4). iii (91); and Turretin, *Institutes*, 13.6.3 (2:311).

69. Ames, *The Marrow of Theology*, 1.18.18, 20 (130); and *A Sketch of the Christian's Catechism*, 35.

70. On the body-soul analogy to the incarnation, see Calvin, *Institutes*, 2.14.1; Hodge, *Systematic Theology*, 2:378–80; and Vos, *Reformed Dogmatics*, 3:52–55.

71. On the interpretation of "God" in Ps. 45:6–7, see *RST*, 1:883–84.

both born in lowly Bethlehem and yet eternal and omnipotent (Mic. 5:2, 4),[72] both the son of David and the Lord (Ps. 110:1; Jer. 23:5–6). The Gospels tell us that Jesus received baptism in a river and experienced hunger and temptation, but called men to leave everything to follow him, spoke with absolute authority, and hung men's eternal destinies on whether they obeyed his words.[73] He slept deeply from the fatigue of his labors, but calmed the wind and the sea with a mere command; he suffered and died, but is the Son of God; he rose from the dead with feet that people could touch, yet has all authority, shares one name with the Father and the Spirit, and is present with all his people in all nations at all times.[74] Likewise the New Testament Epistles tell us that Jesus is God's Son and the son of David according to the flesh; the human last Adam who died, was buried, and rose again, and the Lord who gives all spiritual grace and gifts; the person in whom all the fullness of deity dwells, but a person with a body, flesh and blood, who was crucified on the cross for our redemption.[75]

Therefore, the Holy Scriptures reveal that in the incarnation God the Son took to himself humanity so that he is both God and man in one person. Gregory of Nazianzus said, "What He was He continued to be; what He was not He took to himself."[76] The divine person who is God the Son also became a man, his two natures united but not confused. Calvin said, "We affirm his divinity so joined and united with his humanity that each retains its distinctive nature unimpaired, and yet these two natures constitute one Christ."[77]

This doctrine protects us from falling into various errors concerning the Son of God that would seek to resolve the tension between his deity and humanity. For example, Christ did not pass through phases in which he was first God, then ceased being God and became man. Instead, he is eternally God, and since his conception in Mary's womb, he is the God-man, both in his state of humiliation and in his state of exaltation.[78] It is inconceivable that God the Son should cease to be God, for his divine nature is immutable (Heb. 1:12), and his divine person constantly upholds

---

72. On the interpretation of Mic. 5:2, see the previous chapter.
73. Matt. 3:13–15; 4:1–2, 19–22; 5:22, 28; 7:24, 26, 29.
74. Matt. 8:23–27; 16:16, 21; 28:9, 18–20.
75. Rom. 1:1, 3; 1 Cor. 1:3; 12:3–6; 15:3–4, 21, 45; Col. 1:19–20, 22; 2:9.
76. Gregory of Nazianzus, *Third Theological Oration: On the Son*, sec. 19, in *NPNF*[2], 7:308.
77. Calvin, *Institutes*, 2.14.1.
78. See the exposition of Phil. 2:6–11 in chap. 36.

the universe (v. 3). Athanasius said, "For he was not, as might be imagined, circumscribed in the body, nor while present in the body, was He absent elsewhere; nor, while He moved the body, was the universe left void of his working and providence. . . . Even while present in a human body and Himself quickening it, He was, without inconsistency, quickening the universe as well, and was in every process of nature."[79]

Neither should we think that in Christ's exaltation he left behind his humanity to become simply God again in heaven. God the Son will be incarnate as a man forever. After his resurrection, he remained a man with a human body (Luke 24:39). When he ascended, his human body and soul went up into the sky and then passed into the highest heaven (Acts 1:9). At God's right hand, Christ remains fully human, able to sympathize in his human heart with his suffering people on earth (Heb. 4:15). He will return in the same way as he ascended, as a physical man (Acts 1:11), coming with great glory but still "the Son of man" (Mark 13:26). Forever he will dwell with his bride in the new heaven and new earth as "the Lamb" who was slain for them (Rev. 21:22–23; 22:1, 3). As the Westminster Shorter Catechism (Q. 21) says, Christ "was, and continueth to be, God and man in two distinct natures, and one person, for ever."[80]

Neither did Christ's incarnation change God into a man or mix God and man together into something semihuman and semidivine. Such an idea is inconceivable in light of the biblical doctrine of God, whose nature is infinitely exalted above his creatures. God the Son incarnate displays all the attributes of God in his divine nature and all the attributes of man in his human nature. William Ames explained, "The distinction between the two natures holds because they remain absolutely the same in essence and essential properties as they were before they were joined."[81]

This doctrine also guards against the error of viewing the Son of God and Jesus the man as two distinct persons. As Irenaeus said, the Bible never indicates that "Jesus was merely a receptacle of Christ, upon whom the Christ, as a dove, descended from above."[82] Rather, Jesus is the Christ, the Son of God (Matt. 16:16). Christ came in the flesh (1 John 4:2–3). As John writes, it was the "only begotten Son" whom God sent to be "the

---

79. Athanasius, *On the Incarnation of the Word*, sec. 17, in NPNF², 4:45.
80. *Reformed Confessions*, 4:356. See Murray, "The Redeemer of God's Elect," in *Collected Writings*, 1:34–35.
81. Ames, *The Marrow of Theology*, 1.18.14 (129).
82. Irenaeus, *Against Heresies*, 3.16.1, in ANF, 1:440.

propitiation for our sins" (1 John 4:9–10). It was "Christ" who suffered.[83]
At Golgotha, they "crucified the Lord of glory" (1 Cor. 2:8). The redeemed
are "the church of God, which he hath purchased with his own blood"
(Acts 20:28).[84] These texts do indeed create tension in our minds. God is
spirit, infinite, eternal, and unchangeable. Can God bleed? Can God be
nailed to a cross of wood? No, but Christ's distinct deity and humanity are
joined together in his one person, so that the person who died on the cross
is also the divine Lord. Calvin said, "Let this, then, be our key to right
understanding: those things which apply to the office of the Mediator are
not spoken simply either of the divine nature or of the human."[85] His work
as Mediator requires both deity and humanity in one person.

Hodge said that one consequence of the incarnation is "the *koinōnia
idiōmatōn,* or communion of attributes." He explained, "By this is not
meant that the one nature participates in the attributes of the other, but
simply that the person is the *koinōnos,* or partaker of the attributes of
both natures; so that whatever may be affirmed of either nature may be
affirmed of the person."[86] This is the wonder of God the Son incarnate.[87]

The unique person of the God-man is not a matter for mere curiosity
and theological debate, for he is the living Lord who commands the total
allegiance of our faith. This is not incidental to Christianity, but its very
essence. We must trust in Jesus Christ as God the Son incarnate, for no
one else can "save his people from their sins" (Matt. 1:21). Furthermore,
all the comfort and hope of believers rests in him. It is who he is that
qualifies him as the perfect Savior and the eternal life of the church. If we
have him, and he has us, then we have everything. Thus, the Heidelberg
Catechism (LD 1, Q. 1) says that all our "comfort in life and death"
hinges on this: "That I with body and soul, both in life and death, am
not my own, but belong unto my faithful Savior Jesus Christ."[88] Nothing
more is necessary.

---

83. Luke 24:26, 46; Acts 3:18; 17:3; 26:23; 1 Pet. 1:11; 2:21; 3:18; 4:1; 5:1.

84. It is sometimes objected that the phrase in Acts 20:28 translated as "his own blood" (*tou
haimatos tou idiou*) should be rendered "the blood of his own," as in "his own Son." However,
idios often functions adjectivally as a simple possessive (1:7, 19; 2:6, 8; 3:12; 13:36; 25:19; 28:30).
This reflects its common use in the Septuagint to translate the pronominal suffix. See *Exegetical
Dictionary of the New Testament,* 2:171. We find the same syntactical construction as Acts 20:28
with a simple possessive meaning in Acts 1:25, "his own place" (*ton topon ton idion*), not "the
place of his own."

85. Calvin, *Institutes,* 2.14.3.

86. Hodge, *Systematic Theology,* 2:392.

87. We return to the topic of the *communicatio idiomatum* in chap. 42.

88. *The Three Forms of Unity,* 68.

The Incarnate Lord's Unique Necessity

Christ came into this world for a purpose: "For the Son of man is come to seek and to save that which was lost" (Luke 19:10). He was sent to do his Father's will, saying, "For I came down from heaven, not to do mine own will, but the will of him that sent me" (John 6:38). However, was his incarnation necessary to save sinners, or merely a means that God chose to employ?[89] It seems that there was some necessity for the incarnation, for Paul says, "If righteousness come by the law, then Christ is dead in vain" (Gal. 2:21). Francis Turretin said, "Who can believe that the Father would have wished to send down from heaven his most beloved Son . . . unnecessarily to put on our flesh and expose him to a thousand trials and at last to a most excruciating death for us?"[90] It must have been necessary. But why?

The full answer to this question would require an exposition of Christ's entire saving work, which is the task of the next section of this book.[91] However, we find an answer outlined in the epistle to the Hebrews. Christ is God's Son, the radiance of the Father's glory, the One worshiped by angels, the everlasting King, the immutable Creator.[92] Through Christ, God aims to exalt human beings to reign over creation for his glory (Psalm 8),[93] a status man once held, but from which he fell and no longer enjoys (Heb. 2:6–8). To accomplish this exaltation, God the Son entered man's condition "lower than the angels" and experienced suffering and death for us (v. 9).

The author then says, "For it became him, for whom are all things, and by whom are all things, in bringing many sons unto glory, to make the captain of their salvation perfect through sufferings" (Heb. 2:10). The verb translated as "became" (*prepō*) means to be suitable, proper, or fitting (cf. Matt. 3:15; Eph. 5:3). Philip Hughes said, "To the unregenerate mind, for the divine Redeemer to be humbled by incarnation, and much more so by the shame of dying on a cross, seemed totally inappropriate.

---

89. It is sheer speculation to discuss whether the Son would have become incarnate if man had not sinned. Turretin said, "No other end of the advent of Christ and of his incarnation is ever proposed (whether in the Old or in the New Testament) than that he might save his people from sin." Turretin, *Institutes*, 13.3.4 (2:300).

90. Turretin, *Institutes*, 13.3.17 (2:302).

91. See chap. 43 and following. For a summary statement of the incarnation's necessity with respect to Christ's threefold office as Prophet, Priest, and King, see Brown, *Systematic Theology*, 267–69.

92. Heb. 1:2–3, 6, 8, 10–12.

93. See the discussion of man's creation as God's reigning image bearer in chaps. 6, 8, and 10.

... The purpose of this and the following verses is to show how *fitting* this method of salvation is and, by implication, how totally inappropriate any other notion must be."[94] Christ's sufferings seem to contradict the glory of God, "for whom are all things," and the sovereignty of God, "by whom are all things" (Heb. 2:10). Therefore, there must be some reason why it was very glorifying to the Lord and Creator that his Son should endure the cross. Augustine said that there was no way "more appropriate for curing our misery" than the incarnation, suffering, death, and resurrection of God's Son.[95]

Why was it fitting for God's eternal Son to suffer and die? Christ's people are his "brethren," the "children" God gave him (Heb. 2:11–13). The familial language of "brother" and "child" points to the union of the Son with his people: they are "all of one" (v. 11). Caspar Olevianus said, "It was necessary for the Mediator of the eternal covenant to deal with us in a brotherly way and thus truly to be and eternally remain our Brother, with all the properties of a true brother."[96] To save them, he had to unite himself to their misery and unite them to his glory (vv. 9–10). Calvin said, "Who could have done this had not the self-same Son of God become the Son of man, and had not so taken what was ours as to impart what was his to us?"[97]

Irenaeus said that the incarnation was needed to save us by union with Christ:

> For it was for this end that the Word of God was made man, and He who was the Son of God became the Son of man, that man, having been taken into the Word, and receiving the adoption, might become the son of God. For by no other means could we have attained to incorruptibility and immortality, unless we had been united to incorruptibility and immortality. But how could we be joined to incorruptibility and immortality, unless, first, incorruptibility and immortality had become that which we also are, so that the corruptible might be swallowed up by incorruptibility, and the mortal by immortality, that we might receive the adoption of sons?[98]

---

94. Hughes, *A Commentary on the Epistle to the Hebrews*, 97–98, emphasis original.

95. Augustine, *On the Trinity*, 13.10.13, in NPNF[1], 3:174. As we explain below, we go further than Augustine and say that Christ's incarnation and death were not only fitting but necessary for our salvation.

96. Olevianus, *An Exposition of the Apostles' Creed*, 69.

97. Calvin, *Institutes*, 2.12.2.

98. Irenaeus, *Against Heresies*, 3.19.1, in ANF, 1:448–49.

The logical conclusion, according to Hebrews, is the necessity of the incarnation: "Forasmuch then ["since therefore," ESV] as the children are partakers of flesh and blood, he also himself likewise took part of the same" (Heb. 2:14). The Son took on human flesh so that "through . . . death" he could save the covenant people from death and the Devil (vv. 15–16). The defeat of Satanic power implies that he must be more than a man, yet the Victor had to be a man in union with men who could die their death. The argument continues, "Wherefore in all things it behoved him to be made like unto his brethren" so that he might serve as their atoning and sympathizing "high priest" (vv. 17–18). The verb translated as "behoved" (*opheilō*, "he had to," ESV) means to owe a debt or be under obligation (Matt. 18:28). The priestly work of sacrifice and intercession required God's Son to become a flesh-and-blood man.[99] Hence, as Turretin said, the Mediator had to be the "God-man": "man to suffer, God to overcome; man to receive the punishment we deserved, God to endure and drink it to the dregs; man to acquire salvation for us by dying, God to apply it to us by overcoming; man to become ours by the assumption of flesh, God to make us like himself by the bestowal of the Spirit."[100] This was the only way for Christ to act as God's Priest, the basis of the covenant of salvation (Heb. 7:20–22; 8:6–12).[101]

Later in the same epistle, the author writes that Christ had no "need," unlike the Aaronic priests, to offer a sacrifice for his own sins (Heb. 7:27). However, it was "necessary" that the ceremonial, earthly tabernacle be purified by sacrifice and that heavenly realities be purified by something greater than animal sacrifice (9:23).[102] "Need" and "necessary" translate the same Greek word (*anankē*), which elsewhere in this epistle refers to a legal necessity, something that must take place to avoid violating principles of law and justice.[103]

The reason for this necessity is that "under the law almost everything[104] is purified with blood, and without the shedding of blood there

---

99. Wellum, *God the Son Incarnate*, 223–24.

100. Turretin, *Institutes*, 13.3.19 (2:302–3).

101. Olevianus, *An Exposition of the Apostles' Creed*, 68.

102. It is puzzling what the author means by the purification of "heavenly things" (Heb. 9:23). The best interpretation seems to be that the text does not refer to a cleansing or consecration of heaven itself, but the cleansing of God's people and their consciences (v. 14). These matters are "heavenly" because they involve the human spirit as opposed to fleshly rites (vv. 10, 13), and the citizens of God's city as opposed to worldly people (12:22).

103. Heb. 7:12; 9:16; cf. Luke 23:17; Rom. 13:5. The word *anankē* can also refer to inward compulsion or a condition of need and distress.

104. For exceptions permitting ceremonial purification without blood, see Lev. 5:11–13; Num. 31:22–23.

is no forgiveness of sins" (Heb. 9:22 ESV).[105] This law, though revealed in the earthly tabernacle, is not arbitrary but reflects heavenly, divine, eternal realities (8:5; 9:11, 24). Therefore, the Redeemer had to offer himself as a sacrifice for our sins, which required that he take a human body (10:4–10). By Christ's incarnate work in our flesh and blood, believers may now "draw near" to God and dwell in his holy presence as citizens of the heavenly city rather than face his terrifying wrath (10:19–31; 12:22–24).

Therefore, the incarnation was necessary for our salvation because God's holiness and righteousness demanded that satisfaction be made for sin by blood sacrifice. Anselm of Canterbury said that satisfaction is necessary for salvation, and "no one save God can make it, and no one save man ought to make it, [so] it is necessary for a God-Man to make it."[106] The Heidelberg Catechism (LD 5–6, Q. 15–17) states that the Mediator had to be both a perfectly righteous man, "because the justice of God requires that the same human nature which hath sinned, should likewise make satisfaction for sin; and one, who is himself a sinner, cannot satisfy for others," and true God, "that he might by the power of His Godhead sustain in his human nature, the burden of God's wrath; and might obtain for, and restore to us, righteousness and life."[107]

With these biblical teachings in view, we return to the question of whether Christ's incarnation was necessary. Our answer is twofold. With regard to God, we may not say that his incarnation was absolutely necessary, but only fitting and appropriate for the manifestation of his glory. Calvin said, "If someone asks why this is necessary, there has been no simple . . . or absolute necessity. Rather, it has stemmed from a heavenly decree, on which man's salvation depended."[108] But with regard to Christ's saving work, the incarnation and sacrifice of Christ were necessary. In other words, there was no necessity placed upon God to send his Son, but if God were to save sinful men, then God's Son had to offer the sacrifice required by God's law for their sins and bring them to God's glory. We may refer to this as "consequent absolute necessity," as John Murray said, for it was not absolutely necessary that God save sinners, but consequent upon

---

105. On purification and forgiveness by sacrificial blood, see Lev. 17:11; Eph. 1:7; 1 John 1:7; Rev. 1:5; 7:14.

106. Anselm, *Why God Became Man* (*Cur Deus Homo*), 2.6, in *A Scholastic Miscellany*, ed. Fairweather, 151.

107. *The Three Forms of Unity*, 72. See the Canons of Dort (Head 2, Art.1), in *The Three Forms of Unity*, 134.

108. Calvin, *Institutes*, 2.12.1; cf. Turretin, *Institutes*, 13.3.14 (2:301).

his willing to save them, it was absolutely necessary that the Son become incarnate and die.[109]

The consequent absolute necessity of Christ's incarnation and saving work highlights the centrality of union and communion with Christ for our salvation. Calvin said,

> This is the wonderful exchange which, out of his measureless benevolence, he has made with us; that,
>
> - becoming Son of man with us, he has made us sons of God with him;
> - by his descent to earth, he has prepared an ascent to heaven for us;
> - by taking on our mortality, he has conferred his immortality upon us;
> - accepting our weakness, he has strengthened us by his power;
> - receiving our poverty unto himself, he has transferred his wealth to us;
> - taking the weight of our iniquity upon himself (which oppressed us), he has clothed us with his righteousness.[110]

In this way, the necessity of the incarnation highlights the wonder of God's grace to us in Christ. Truly, this is one of our greatest causes to praise the Lord, for we need nothing as much as we need Jesus.

Sing to the Lord

Celebrating the Incarnation of Our Lord

Hark the herald angels sing,
"Glory to the newborn King;
Peace on earth, and mercy mild,
God and sinners reconciled!"
Joyful, all ye nations, rise,
Join the triumph of the skies;
With th'angelic host proclaim,
"Christ is born in Bethlehem!"
Hark! the herald angels sing,
"Glory to the newborn King."

---

109. John Murray, *Redemption Accomplished and Applied* (Grand Rapids, MI: Eerdmans, 1955), 11–18.

110. Calvin, *Institutes*, 4.17.2. We have added bullet points and removed the repetition of "that."

Christ, by highest heav'n adored,
Christ, the Everlasting Lord!
Late in time behold him come,
Offspring of the Virgin's womb.
Veiled in flesh the Godhead see;
Hail th' Incarnate Deity,
Pleased as man with men to dwell,
Jesus, our Emmanuel.
Hark! the herald angels sing,
"Glory to the newborn King."

Hail, the heav'n-born Prince of Peace!
Hail, the Sun of Righteousness!
Light and life to all he brings,
Ris'n with healing in his wings.
Mild he lays his glory by,
Born that man no more may die,
Born to raise the sons of earth,
Born to give them second birth.
Hark! the herald angels sing,
"Glory to the newborn King."

Charles Wesley
Tune: Mendelssohn
Trinity Hymnal—Baptist Edition, No. 168

Questions for Meditation or Discussion

1. According to John 1:14, who exactly became flesh? Why is it important to be precise in this?

2. What does John 1:14 means when it says this person "was made flesh"?

3. What is the Old Testament allusion behind the phrase in John 1:14 that he "dwelt among us" and "we beheld his glory"? What is the theological significance of this allusion?

4. What does the phrase "God-man" mean when used of Jesus Christ by biblical Christians? How would you prove from various Scripture passages that Jesus is the God-man?

5. What difference should it make to a person's faith in Jesus that he is the God-man? What difference does it actually make to your faith? How do you need to change?

6. What arguments can be made that Isaiah 7:14 predicted the virgin birth?

7. According to Luke 1–2, in what sense was Jesus's human origin supernatural? Natural?

8. What can we learn from Luke 1:35 about Christ?

9. What evidence does the Bible supply that in Christ, God and man are united in one person?

10. Against what errors does this doctrine protect us?

11. How has reading this chapter shown you more of the glory of Christ? How does this call you to respond?

Questions for Deeper Reflection

12. You have been asked to present a thirty-minute teaching on John 1:14, with several practical applications. How would you present your teaching plan in a detailed outline?

13. What are the practical and theological implications of denying the virgin birth of Jesus Christ? Is this doctrine worth fighting over if denied by a minister in your church or association? Why or why not?

14. What does the "consequent absolute necessity" of the incarnation mean? Is this doctrine true? Why or why not?

40

Christ's Incarnation, Part 2

Humanity and Relations

Our Lord Jesus posed the greatest of questions when he asked, "Who do you say that I am?" (Luke 9:20 ESV). Peter's answer, "The Christ of God," is the great confession of the Christian church throughout the ages and the vital core of our faith. Herman Bavinck said, "The doctrine of Christ is not the starting point, but it certainly is the central point of the whole system of dogmatics. . . . In it, as the heart of dogmatics, pulses the whole of the religious-ethical life of Christianity." Hence, the incarnation is central to the Christian faith. Since "Christ is the incarnate Word," Bavinck said, "the incarnation is the central fact of the entire history of the world"; indeed, "it must have been prepared from before the ages and have its effects throughout eternity."[1]

In the last chapter, we argued that the person born of the virgin Mary is the God-man, God the Son incarnate. We previously demonstrated that Christ's deity involves the attributes and acts of God.[2] In this chapter, we will examine in more detail the human attributes of Jesus and the special relations into which his incarnation brought him.

---

1. Bavinck, *Reformed Dogmatics*, 3:274.
2. See chap. 38 and the materials referenced there.

The Incarnate Lord's Human Constitution

There is no one else in all the universe like Christ, for he is one person with two natures. He is truly God. The person who "gave himself for us" is "our great God and Savior Jesus Christ" (Titus 2:13–14 ESV). Also, he is truly human. We are saved by God's grace that abounds to us "by one man, Jesus Christ" (Rom. 5:15). The "one mediator between God and men" is "the man Christ Jesus" (1 Tim. 2:5). His humanity entails both his body and soul.

Christ's Human Body

Although the Bible gives us no physical descriptions of Christ's human appearance, it clearly states that he has a human body. His body is *real*. This is certainly implied in "the Word was made flesh" (John 1:14). The Gospels frequently tell us that Jesus has a head, hands, fingers, and feet.[3] During his earthly life, Jesus broke bread, ate and drank, spat, wept tears, washed people's feet with water and dried them with a towel, and slept.[4]

Christ's body is *tangible*. The references to his hands noted earlier often pertain to him touching people. Jesus is not a spirit that merely appears human, but has flesh and bones that can be grasped and felt (Luke 24:39). The apostles could testify that "the Word of life" was not a heavenly vision, but an earthly person "which we have heard, which we have seen with our eyes, which we have looked upon, and our hands have handled" (1 John 1:1).

His body is *local*. It is in one place at a time. We read of Jesus "walking by the sea of Galilee" and "walking in the temple" (Matt. 4:18; Mark 11:27). He traveled from one geographic location to another.[5] After he rose from the dead, the angel told the women who visited his tomb, "He is not here. . . . He goeth before you into Galilee" (Matt. 28:6–7). When Christ ascended into heaven, "he was taken up" into the clouds until his disciples could see him no more, and he will come back from heaven in the same manner (Acts 1:9–11).

---

3. Jesus's head: Matt. 8:20; 26:7; 27:29–30; Mark 14:3; 15:19; Luke 7:46; 9:58; John 19:2, 30; 20:7. Hands: Matt. 8:3; 9:18; 12:49; 14:31; 27:29; Mark 1:41; 7:32; 8:23; Luke 5:13; 24:39–40. Fingers: Mark 7:33; John 8:6. Feet: Matt. 15:30; 28:9; Mark 5:22; 7:25; Luke 7:38, 44–46; 8:35, 41; 10:39; 17:16; 24:39–40; John 11:2, 32; 12:3.

4. Jesus breaking bread: Matt. 14:19; 15:36; 26:26; Mark 8:6, 19; 14:22; Luke 22:19; 24:30. Eating and drinking: Matt. 11:19; 26:29; 27:34; Mark 2:16; 14:15, 24; Luke 5:30; 7:34, 36; 15:2; 22:11, 15, 16, 18; 24:41–43; John 4:7. Spitting: Mark 7:33; 8:23; John 9:6. Weeping: Luke 19:41; John 11:35; Heb. 5:7. Washing people's feet: John 13:5. Sleeping: Matt. 8:24; Mark 4:38.

5. Matt. 19:1; Luke 9:51; 17:11; John 4:3–4.

Our Lord's body was *developmental* in its progress from infancy to adulthood. He did not enter this world in a state of full physical maturity, but as a child conceived inside his mother's womb (Luke 1:31). When he was born, he was a "babe wrapped in swaddling clothes" (2:12), just like other babies in ancient Israel (Ezek. 16:4). When the magi visited, he was a "young child" (Matt. 2:11). Over time, he "increased" in "stature" (Luke 2:52).

The body of Jesus was *susceptible* to various pains and troubles during his state of humiliation (Isa. 53:2). He felt hunger (Matt. 4:2; 21:18) and thirst (John 19:28). When in the wilderness, "angels ministered unto him," perhaps to protect his body from harm from prolonged fasting from food and the dangers of wild animals (Mark 1:13). After a long journey, Jesus was weary and sat down to rest (John 4:6). In the garden of Gethsemane, he felt such anguish that "his sweat was as it were great drops of blood falling to the ground" (Luke 22:43–44)—probably because of the rupture of capillaries in the skin due to extreme stress.[6] Jesus could be struck, injured, and wounded, and suffered horrible physical abuse by men (Matt. 27:26, 29–30).

Christ's body was *mortal.* In his state of humiliation, he was physically able to die, and he did die on the cross (Mark 15:37), though as God's Son he could not die until he sovereignly dismissed his own life (John 10:17–18). God preserved his body from decay (Ps. 16:10; Acts 2:31; 13:35), but it lay dead and inanimate in the tomb from Friday evening until the first day of the week (Mark 15:42–47). Only after his resurrection is it said, "Christ being raised from the dead dieth no more; death hath no more dominion over him" (Rom. 6:9).

When we survey the biblical teaching on Christ's human body, it is striking how very ordinary Jesus was among men. He lived a fully embodied human existence, just as we do. There was nothing spectacular about his appearance that drew men to him. When he taught in his hometown, his neighbors scoffed, "Is not this the carpenter, the son of Mary?" (Mark 6:3). It is only now, in his state of exaltation, that Christ's human body is "glorious" (Phil. 3:21). It is "raised in incorruption," "raised in glory," and "raised in power" (1 Cor. 15:42–43), but it remains a

---

6. This rare condition is called *hematohidrosis* or *hematidrosis*, from the Greek words for "blood" (*haima*) and "sweat" (*hidrōs*). See "Hematohidrosis," October 31, 2016, National Institutes of Health: Genetic and Rare Diseases Information Center, https://rarediseases.info.nih.gov /diseases/13131/hematohidrosis.

human body, the body of the "last Adam" who gives life to his people (vv. 21–22, 45).

Christ's Human Spirit

Christ's humanity extends beyond his body to include a fully human "soul" or "spirit."[7] One of the most encouraging truths about our Lord's incarnation is that he shares with us in a fully human inner life and experience, while remaining fully God in all his divine attributes.

The incarnate Son has a *limited human mind*. When Jesus was a baby, in his human nature he thought like a baby (Isa. 7:14, 16). The infant Christ "grew, and waxed strong in spirit, filled with wisdom: and the grace of God was upon him" (Luke 2:40). As a child, Jesus learned from other people. Though at age twelve he exhibited unusual understanding of divine truths, still he went to the Jewish teachers and was "asking them questions" (vv. 46–47); over time he "increased in wisdom" (v. 52). Ambrose said, "Jesus advanced in age and in wisdom. . . . For what advances, surely is changed for the better, but what is divine is not changed. So, what is changed is surely not divine," but is "human."[8] He who taught others was himself taught by God (Isa. 50:4–5). Mark Jones says, "Jesus came to a growing understanding of his Messianic calling by reading the Scriptures. He had to learn the Bible just as we must."[9]

To be sure, Christ displayed elements of supernatural knowledge that could have come only from God,[10] but that does not imply human omniscience.[11] As possessed in his human nature, such knowledge was like the supernatural revelations of the Spirit granted to the prophets (2 Kings 6:8–12; Eph. 3:4–5). Jesus foretold many things about his future coming in glory. However, he said, "Of that day and that hour knoweth no man, no, not the angels which are in heaven, neither the Son, but the Father" (Mark 13:32). God vastly expanded Christ's human mind when he glorified him

---

7. Matt. 27:50; Mark 2:8; Luke 23:46; John 11:33, 38; 12:27; 13:21; 19:30. On the human soul and its relation to the body, see chaps. 12 and 13.

8. Ambrose, *The Sacrament of the Incarnation of Our Lord*, 7.72, in *Saint Ambrose: Theological and Dogmatic Works*, trans. Roy J. Deferrari, Fathers of the Church 44 (Washington, DC: The Catholic University of America Press, 1963), 247.

9. Mark Jones, *A Christian's Pocket Guide to Jesus Christ: An Introduction to Christology* (Fearn, Ross-shire, Scotland, Christian Focus, 2012), 32.

10. Matt. 9:4; 12:25; 16:21; John 1:47–48; 4:18; 6:61, 64, 71; 11:14; 13:11.

11. Macleod, *The Person of Christ*, 166. There are some biblical statements that imply Christ's omniscience (John 2:24–25; 16:30; 21:17; Rev. 2:23), but these are properly attributed to his divine nature.

to mediate eternal life to all his people (John 17:1–2),[12] but it is still the mind of a man, "so that it is certain that the knowledge of Christ's human nature is not and can never be the infinite wisdom of God itself," as B. B. Warfield said.[13]

It might be objected that Christ's wisdom could not increase, for he was "full of grace and truth" by virtue of his incarnation (John 1:14). Even as an infant, he was "filled with wisdom" (Luke 2:40).[14] Statements about his ignorance are interpreted to mean that his human mind derived its complete knowledge from his divine nature or that he revealed his perfect knowledge progressively, but his human mind was not truly ignorant of anything.[15]

In reply, we say that John 1:14 describes the "glory" and fullness of the only begotten Son, not the condition of his "flesh" or human nature per se. William Ames said, "There were in Christ two kinds of understanding: a divine understanding whereby he knew all things (John 21:17), and a human, whereby he did not yet know some things (Mark 13:32)."[16] As Bavinck said, "Christ on earth was a pilgrim, not a comprehensive knower . . . he walked by faith and hope, not by sight."[17]

As to the texts in Luke, the Greek word translated as "filled" (*plēroumenon*) in Luke 2:40 is a present participle and better describes a process of being filled or increasing in wisdom, not a state of absolute fullness.[18] Luke 2:52 says that the young Jesus "increased in wisdom and stature, and in favour with God and man." Christ was as full of wisdom at each point of his life as was appropriate for that stage of his human development, just as a young tree may be full of healthy fruit, but can produce even more after it grows larger and more mature. The union of the divine nature and human nature, "instead of impeding or disturbing human development has rather sustained and guided it. His deity did not communicate more knowledge and power to His humanity than was in accord with its age," as Geerhardus Vos said.[19]

12. See Goodwin, *The Heart of Christ in Heaven unto Sinners on Earth*, in *Works*, 4:121.

13. Warfield, *Selected Shorter Writings*, 1:162.

14. Lombard, *The Sentences*, 3.13 (3:50–54); and Aquinas, *Summa Theologica*, Part 3, Q. 7, Art. 12; Q. 15, Art. 3.

15. Gregory the Great, *Epistles*, no. 39, "To Eulogius," in *NPNF²*, 13:48.

16. Ames, *The Marrow of Theology*, 1.18.27 (131).

17. Bavinck, *Reformed Dogmatics*, 3:312. "Not by sight" excludes the "beatific vision" from Christ's human experience until his exaltation.

18. "*plēroumenon*: present participle, not = *plenus*, Vulg., full, but in course of being filled with wisdom—mind as well as body subject to the law of growth." Alexander Balmain Bruce, "The Synoptic Gospels," in *The Expositor's Greek Testament*, ed. W. Robertson Nicholl (New York: George H. Doran, n.d.), on Luke 2:40 (1:478).

19. Vos, *Reformed Dogmatics*, 3:28.

Furthermore, attempts to explain away Christ's admission of ignorance in Mark 13:32 are neither exegetically convincing nor necessary to defend his deity. Athanasius said, "He made this as those other declarations as man by reason of the flesh. For this as before is not the Word's deficiency, but of that human nature whose property it is to be ignorant. . . . He had put on flesh that was ignorant."[20] Christ's human limitations did not necessitate error in his teachings, just as we humans can speak and write true statements, and often do. Christ was anointed by the Holy Spirit to act as the supreme Prophet of his people, so that he "speaketh the words of God," and we must receive his testimony because "God is true" (John 3:33–34). God granted all his prophets infallibility and inerrancy in speaking and writing his word, though they were human with limited and fallible minds (1 Kings 17:24; Ps. 12:6).[21] Christ's limited human mind was united to the person of the Son, who perfectly knew all things in his divine nature, and shared with his human nature all it needed by the Holy Spirit to perform the Father's will flawlessly but in a truly human way, with finite understanding.

The soul of Jesus has *changeable human emotions*. Warfield said, "It belongs to the truth of our Lord's humanity, that he was subject to all sinless human emotions."[22] He was angry and grieved at the hardness of men's hearts (Mark 3:5). He rejoiced at the Father's sovereign granting of salvation to whom he pleased (Luke 10:21). He "marvelled" at the great faith of the centurion (Matt. 8:10) and at the unbelief of his hometown (Mark 6:6). He had "compassion" on the people in their desperate need for a spiritual shepherd (v. 34). When the Pharisees tested him, asking for a miracle, "he sighed deeply in his spirit" (8:12). Holy "zeal" burned within him when he made a whip and drove the merchants out of the temple courts (John 2:14–17). Thomas Goodwin wrote, "Christ having a human nature, the same for substance that ours is, consisting both of soul and body . . . therefore he must needs have affections . . . even affections proper to man's nature, and truly human."[23]

Christ's emotional life was especially displayed in his passion and reaffirmed after his resurrection. In the garden of Gethsemane, he said, "My

---

20. Athanasius, *Against the Arians*, 3.28.43, 45, in *NPNF*[2], 4:417–18.

21. On the inerrancy of the Holy Scriptures, see *RST*, 1:371–94 (chaps. 20–21). On the objection that a fallible human cannot produce an infallible text, see in particular *RST*, 1:384.

22. Benjamin B. Warfield, "The Emotional Life of our Lord," in *The Person and Work of Christ*, 93. See also Stephen Voorwinde, *Jesus' Emotions in the Gospels* (London: T&T Clark, 2011).

23. Goodwin, *The Heart of Christ in Heaven unto Sinners on Earth*, in *Works*, 4:140.

soul is exceeding sorrowful, even unto death" (Matt. 26:38). Ambrose said that these words show Christ had taken "the affection of a human nature."[24] On the cross, he felt the horror of God-forsakenness (27:46). Even now, exalted to God's right hand in heaven, he remembers the full range of sorrows he experienced on earth and sympathizes with us deeply (Heb. 4:15). Yet in his exaltation, he exchanged his sorrows for unsurpassed fullness of joy (Pss. 16:11; 45:7).[25]

Christ has a *freely choosing human will*. Jesus exercised his power and mercy willingly (Matt. 8:3; 15:32). He appointed as apostles those men whom he chose (Mark 3:13). His human will is distinct from the divine will, yet fully submitted to it. He said, "I seek not mine own will, but the will of the Father which hath sent me" (John 5:30; cf. 6:38). His prayers to the Father expressed the desires of his will (17:24). He longed for life and loathed the death of the accursed cross, and yet chose to pray, "Not my will, but thine, be done" (Luke 22:42). His human life consists of constant voluntary obedience to God.

The incarnate Son of God relates to God in *faithful human worship*. Joseph and Mary brought him to the temple as an infant in accordance with the law of Moses and raised him to be a faithful Israelite who worshiped at the temple (Luke 2:21–24, 41–42). As an adult, he was zealous for his Father's house, that it should be a house of prayer (19:45–46; John 2:12–17). The Gospels abundantly testify to Christ's prayer life as he constantly depended upon the Father and gave thanks to him.[26] At least once, Jesus spend a whole night in prayer (Luke 6:12). He addressed God not only as "my Father" but also as "my God" (Mark 15:34; John 20:17). Rightly are the words of Psalm 22:22 applied to him: "I will declare thy name unto my brethren, in the midst of the church will I sing praise unto thee" (Heb. 2:12). Whereas we rebelled against God and sought to stand independently of him for our own glory, Christ's prayerfulness exemplifies dependence on the Father for the glory of God alone—covenant faithfulness.[27]

As a man in a state of humiliation, Jesus had *vulnerable human relationships*. He not only preached and healed, but built relationships, appointing the apostles "that they should be with him" (Mark 3:14).

---

24. Ambrose, *The Sacrament of the Incarnation of Our Lord*, 7.63, in *Saint Ambrose*, 243.

25. On the application of Psalms 16 and 45 to Christ, see Acts 2:25–33; Heb. 1:8–9.

26. Matt. 11:25–26; 14:23; 15:36; 19:13; 26:27, 36–44; Mark 1:35; 6:46; 8:6; 14:23, 32–39; Luke 3:21; 5:16; 6:12; 9:18, 28–29; 10:21; 11:1; 22:17, 19, 32, 41–45; John 6:11, 23; 11:41–42; 12:28; 17:1–26; cf. Heb. 5:7.

27. Torrance, *Incarnation*, 117–18.

He gathered the twelve in the upper room in Jerusalem and said, "With desire I have desired to eat this Passover with you before I suffer" (Luke 22:15)—the repetition being an idiom for emphasis: "I have earnestly desired" (ESV). Of the twelve, he became closest to three in particular, Peter, James, and John (Mark 5:37; 9:2; 13:3; 14:33). It was them he took with him in the garden, telling them of the great sorrow of his soul and asking them, "Tarry ye here, and watch with me" (Matt. 26:38). When they fell asleep, we sense Christ's disappointment when he said to Peter, "What, could ye not watch with me one hour?" (v. 40). The poignant "with me" in both these statements reveals the Savior's deep desire for the comfort of his friends' companionship and his disappointment at their failure.[28] The cross was the pinnacle of Christ's devastating loneliness. Psalm 69:20, a foreshadowing of Christ's passion, says, "Reproach hath broken my heart; and I am full of heaviness: and I looked for some to take pity, but there was none; and for comforters, but I found none."[29]

We conclude that "in all things" Christ became "like unto his brethren" (Heb. 2:17), with the exception that he alone was "without sin" (4:15). His assumption of the entire human nature was necessary for our entire salvation, for he is the last Adam (1 Cor. 15:45). Gregory of Nazianzus (330–389) said, "For that which He has not assumed He has not healed. . . . If only half Adam fell, then that which Christ assumes and saves may be half also; but if the whole of his nature fell, it must be united to the whole nature of Him that was begotten, and so be saved as a whole."[30]

When we survey the biblical testimony to Christ's human body and soul, it especially impresses us that he was "a man of sorrows" (Isa. 53:3). It should amaze us that Christ condescended to become human, especially in our fallen world. As God the Son, he has never experienced the least pain, shame, or grief, but dwells in infinite glory and joy. Every spark of sorrow that touched him was something he willingly embraced by becoming one of us. And he did it all for you, child of God. By Christ's becoming human and suffering for our sins, God demonstrated his love for people with unsurpassed glory.[31] Praise be to his name!

---

28. In both Matt. 26:38 and 40, the words translated as "with me" (*met' emou*) fall at the very end of the sentence, perhaps for emphasis.

29. The very next verse, Ps. 69:21, is fulfilled at the cross of Christ (Matt. 27:34, 48). See also allusions and quotations of this psalm in Mark 15:23, 36; Luke 23:36; John 2:17; 15:25; 19:29; Acts 1:20; Rom. 15:3.

30. Gregory of Nazianzus, *Epistles*, no. 101, in NPNF[2], 7:440. See also John of Damascus, *An Exact Exposition of the Orthodox Faith*, 3.6, in NPNF[2], 9.2:50.

31. Rom. 5:8; Gal. 2:20; Eph. 5:2, 25; 1 John 4:9–10.

The Incarnate Lord's Mediatorial Relations

The Son of God enjoys unique divine relations to the Father and the Holy Spirit in the eternal Trinity.[32] In taking to himself a human nature, God the Son has also taken to himself a new set of unique mediatorial relations for the sake of his people.

Relation to God the Father: Sinlessness

God the Son incarnate now also relates to the Father as a sinless human being, a man perfectly obedient to all of God's commandments. As we noted earlier, the human being conceived in the womb of the virgin was "holy" (Luke 1:35), despite the fact that his mother and all his ancestors were stained and corrupted by original sin, and were saved only by grace (v. 30).[33] The Holy Scriptures do not explain how Christ's supernatural conception relates to his infant holiness—and we do best to avoid speculation—but we can say that Christ's humanity "partook of the essential character of all that God creates: it was very good" (cf. Gen. 1:31).[34] The incarnate Son of God is all that Adam was meant to be, and far more (Luke 3:22, 38).

Christ is God's delightful Son and righteous Servant (Isa. 42:1; 53:11; Mark 1:11). Jesus could make the astounding claim, "I do always those things that please him" (John 8:29). He boldly challenged those who hated him, "Which one of you convicts me of sin?" (v. 46 ESV). Of him it was written in the highest sense, "They hated me without a cause" (15:25, citing Ps. 35:19). Satan is "the prince of this world," but Jesus said that he "hath nothing in me" (John 14:30).

Though absolutely pure from the beginning, Christ's human holiness developed (Luke 2:52) over the course of his obedience through various trials and temptations, which he always overcame (Matt. 4:1–11). Christ's temptations were not in every sense identical to ours, for he lacked any of the inward impulses toward sin that plague fallen mankind; he was tempted to use his omnipotence to avoid the sufferings of his human humiliation; and he was tested far more severely than any other man because he was called to drink the cup of divine wrath and bear the sins of his people as their Mediator.[35] However, his temptations were real and painful (Heb. 2:18). Just as

---

32. On the personal relations in the Trinity, see *RST*, 1:889–99, 933–44.
33. On the doctrine of original sin, see chaps. 19–21.
34. Macleod, *The Person of Christ*, 40–41.
35. Wellum, *God the Son Incarnate*, 459–60.

an athlete in perfect health develops his strength and skill through strenuous exercise and practice, so the sinless Jesus developed the power and maturity of his human righteousness through his trials, culminating in his passion and death. "Though he were a Son, yet learned he obedience by the things which he suffered; and being made perfect, he became the author of eternal salvation unto all them that obey him" (5:8–9).

Simply being among sinners such as we are was a trial for him, prompting the perfectly patient Christ to exclaim, "O faithless and perverse generation, how long shall I be with you? How long shall I suffer you?" (Matt. 17:17). Sinclair Ferguson and Derek Thomas compare his situation to that of a nonsmoker surrounded by smokers, filling his eyes and nostrils with their noxious fumes: "When the Word became flesh this world must have been almost unbearable for him."[36]

The question may be raised, "Was it possible for Jesus Christ to have sinned?" In other words, was Christ "peccable" (able to sin) or "impeccable" (not able to sin). In answering this question, we must make some distinctions based upon what we have already seen from the Scriptures about Christ.[37] First, the human nature of Christ did have the ability to sin during his humiliation.[38] The Lord Jesus experienced true and painful temptation, and had to resist that temptation as a man by the grace of the Spirit. As we have seen, he has a complete human nature, body and soul, including a human mind and freely choosing will. He entered this world in a state of humiliation, vulnerable and changeable. His human nature, considered abstractly, had the capacity to sin (peccability) until confirmed in unchangeable righteousness when he was glorified.

Second, however, the person of Jesus Christ cannot sin. Christ is not two persons, but one person, the Son who eternally exists as God and took to himself a human nature. Neither is Jesus Christ a human nature considered abstractly from his person and divine nature. When we speak of someone sinning, we do not speak of a nature but of a person, for only a person is a morally accountable agent in relationship to God and others. Therefore, if Christ had sinned as a man, the person of the Son would have committed that sin. This is inconceivable, since that person is not only human but also the righ-

---

36. Sinclair B. Ferguson and Derek W. H. Thomas, *Ichthus: Jesus Christ, God's Son, the Saviour* (Edinburgh: Banner of Truth, 2015), 13–14.

37. See Lombard, *The Sentences*, 3.12.3 (3:48–49).

38. On this point, see "Theology Night with Sinclair Ferguson and R. C. Sproul," January 20, 2012, Ligonier Ministries, video recording beginning at 57:16, https://www.ligonier.org/learn /conferences/live-qa-events/jan_20_2012/#, also available at https://youtu.be/CtLK7jFlSyU?t=3436.

teous and unchanging God, who cannot be tempted to sin (Heb. 13:8; James 1:13, 17). Not only Christ's unity, but the very unity of the Trinity, would have been threatened. Therefore, we hold to this mystery in the incarnation: Jesus Christ was (1) able to be tempted in his human nature, (2) able to sin in his humanity considered abstractly, (3) able not to sin due to his human purity, but (4) impeccable as a person because of the union of his humanity with his deity. He could experience temptation but could not be conquered by it.[39]

If it is objected that Christ's impeccability violates his human freedom, then we reply that God preserves his saints from fully and finally falling away without violating their freedom, and he will so glorify his saints in holiness that by grace they will never again choose to sin, yet they will be freer than ever before. God communicated to Christ's human nature by the Holy Spirit all the graces necessary so that, though for a time he suffered real temptation, he never sinned. If it is further objected that an impeccable Christ would never have experienced the spiritual battle of temptation, then we answer that he was not tempted in his omnipotent divine nature, but in his dependent human nature, which must fight temptation by the assistance of the Spirit. Furthermore, since Christ never gave in to temptation, he experienced the force of temptation more strongly and consistently than we who capitulate to it ever have.[40] Satan need not do his utmost to lead us into sin, but with Christ the forces of hell exerted all their furious might precisely because he was sinless—and, thanks be to God, they could not overcome him.[41]

The personal righteousness of Christ is at the center of the apostolic gospel, proclaimed explicitly by a variety of witnesses.[42] John says, "He was manifested to take away our sins; and in him is no sin" (1 John 3:5). The writer to the Hebrews says Christ experienced our trials and temptations but is "without sin" (Heb. 4:15). Now exalted to heaven, he is "holy, harmless, undefiled, separate from sinners" (7:26). Paul writes that though Christ came "in the likeness of sinful flesh" (Rom. 8:3), he "knew no sin," remaining completely free of its corruption (2 Cor. 5:21). John Murray said, "He came into the closest relation to sinful humanity that it was possible for him to come without thereby becoming himself sinful."[43]

39. Hugh Martin, "The Dogmatic Element in Ullman's 'Sinlessness of Jesus,'" in *Christ's Presence in the Gospel History*, 2nd ed. (Edinburgh: John MacLaren, 1865), 321–26; F. W. Kremer, "The Impeccability of the Lord Jesus Christ," *The Reformed Theological Review* 26 (April 1879): 258–77; and Bavinck, *Reformed Dogmatics*, 3:313–15.
40. Grudem, *Systematic Theology*, 539.
41. Macleod, *The Person of Christ*, 227–28.
42. Acts 3:14; 7:52; 22:14; 1 Pet. 1:19; 2:22; Heb. 9:14; 1 John 2:1.
43. Murray, "The Person of Christ," in *Collected Writings*, 2:133.

Therefore, the sinlessness of Christ should teach us the fear of the Lord, for our Savior and Judge is the Righteous One who loves righteousness. Yet it is also the basis of the Christian's hope, for by faith he is united to the Son who is our righteousness. Jesus Christ relates to the Father as the last and perfect Adam, whose sinless obedience pleases the Father completely and fully satisfies the demands of his holy law on behalf of his people.

Relation to God the Spirit: Fullness

Christ's humanity depended upon the Holy Spirit from its conception (Matt. 1:18, 20; Luke 1:35). The Holy Spirit came upon him at his baptism and filled him to face Satan's temptations and preach the word (3:22; 4:1, 14, 18). Christ cast out demons "by the Spirit of God," showing that the kingdom of God was arriving (Matt. 12:28). His personal possession of the Spirit is "without measure" (John 3:34 ESV), for he is the One anointed by the Spirit in his sevenfold fullness (Isa. 11:2). Since he is the Son, his human nature is adorned and empowered with the gifts and fruit of the Spirit far above any other creature.[44] The Spirit always acts from the Father and the Son (John 16:13–15), so that the graces of the Spirit involve the Father's blessing and the Son's personal assumption of his manhood. Thus, this fullness of blessing in Jesus is Trinitarian, involving the Father, the Son, and the Spirit.[45]

Christ's humiliation and crucifixion redeemed his people from God's curse so that God would give them the blessing of the Spirit (Gal. 3:13–14). With the exaltation of Christ to God's right hand, he received an even greater bestowment of the Spirit so that he could pour out the Spirit upon all his people (Acts 2:17–18, 33). Here again, we remember that Christ's reception of the Spirit pertains not to his deity, but to his humanity and mediatorial work. It is only when Jesus Christ is "glorified" that the Spirit is poured out like "rivers of living water" (John 7:37–39; cf. Isa. 44:3). Christ is the spring of the water of life for us—by which we are unified like wheat moistened and compacted into dough, vivified like dry ground receiving rain, and made fruitful like dry trees after rainfall, as Irenaeus said.[46]

---

44. On the *communicatio charismatum sive gratiarum* ("communication of gifts or graces") to Christ's human nature, see Vos, *Reformed Dogmatics*, 3:56–57; and Berkhof, *Systematic Theology*, 324.

45. Wellum, *God the Son Incarnate*, 326–28. On the work of the Spirit in Christ, Wellum cites Owen, *Pneumatologia*, in *Works*, 3:168; and *Christologia*, in *Works*, 1:93.

46. Irenaeus, *Against Heresies*, 3.17.2, in *ANF*, 1:444–45.

Therefore, the Spirit's coming in his fullness to the church overflows from Christ's incarnation, humiliation, and glorification. The Holy Spirit now fills Christians because he first filled Christ. It is not only the doctrine of the Trinity that links the Spirit to the Son, but also the incarnation. The Holy Spirit is "the Spirit of Christ" (Rom. 8:9; 1 Pet. 1:11), even "the Spirit of Jesus Christ" (Phil. 1:19). The Spirit is the living, personal bond between Christ and believers (1 Cor. 6:17), and we receive the Spirit through Christ (Titus 3:5–6).

Relation to God's People: Brotherliness

Christ's incarnation brings him into the closest familial relation with his people, for he has taken their very nature to himself. This is not merely a physical unity, such as that shared by him and Mary by virtue of his conception in her womb, but a far more significant relation of mutual covenantal faithfulness (Luke 8:21; 11:27–28). The risen Lord called his disciples "my brethren" and said, "I ascend unto my Father, and your Father" (John 20:17; cf. Matt. 28:10). He said that those for whom he died and who do his will are his "friends" (John 15:13–15).

Though this relationship is covenantal, its fruition is grounded in Christ's incarnation to share in our nature. "He is not ashamed to call them brethren"—that is, those whom God has "given" him (Heb. 2:11, 13). He partook of the same "flesh and blood" as they do (v. 14). Christ leads them in the worship of God, saying, "I will declare thy name unto my brethren" (v. 12, citing Ps. 22:22). He lowered himself to become their brother so that he might lift up "many sons unto glory" (Heb. 2:10). The incarnation serves God's eternal purpose to predestine his beloved people "to be conformed to the image of his Son, that he might be the firstborn among many brethren" (Rom. 8:29).

Christ truly has entered into human experience. Here the human development of Jesus through every stage of maturity becomes exceedingly precious to us, because, as Irenaeus said, Christ passed through each developmental stage of human life in order to sanctify people at every stage.[47] Therefore, Christ truly understands us. Warfield commented, "It was not merely the mind of a man that was in him, but the heart of a man as well."[48]

This is the wonder of the incarnation, that God the Son has become "God with us" (Matt. 1:23). For all eternity, God has bound himself to

47. Irenaeus, *Against Heresies*, 2.22.4, in *ANF*, 1:391.
48. Warfield, *Selected Shorter Writings*, 1.161.

his people by entering their world and taking their very nature to himself. A closer union of man to God is inconceivable. Charles Octavius Boothe (1845–1924) observed, "We do not understand this mystery . . . but there are two things that we do understand," namely, that a person with "the divine nature" has "appeared in human nature," and second that he is "the crying need" of mankind.[49]

Sing to the Lord

The Passion of Our Incarnate Lord, Foreshadowed in the Psalms

Save me, O God, because the floods
Come in upon my soul;
I sink in depth where none can stand,
Deep waters o'er me roll.

My constant calling wearies me,
My throat is parched and dried;
My eyes grow dim while for my God
Still waiting I abide.

It is for Thee I am reproached,
For Thee I suffer shame,
Until my brethren know me not,
And hated is my name.

It is my zeal for Thy abode
That has consumed my life;
Reproached by those reproaching Thee,
I suffer in the strife.

In full assurance of Thy grace
To Thee my prayers ascend;
In Thy abounding love and truth,
O God, salvation send.

Psalm 69
Tune: Ella
The Psalter, No. 184 (last stanza from No. 185)

---

49. Charles Octavius Boothe, *Plain Theology for Plain People*, intro. Walter R. Strickland II (Bellingham, WA: Lexham Press, 2017), 45.

Questions for Meditation or Discussion

1. What Scripture passages show us that Christ's body was the following: (1) real, (2) tangible, (3) local, (4) developmental, (5) susceptible, and (6) mortal?

2. How do the Holy Scriptures indicate that Christ has a limited human mind?

3. What human emotions does the Bible ascribe to Jesus Christ? List Scripture references for each of them.

4. Why is it important to recognize that Jesus has a human will in our interpretation of Matthew 26:39?

5. Did Jesus experience human longings for companionship and support from his friends? Was Jesus vulnerable to other people in relationship to him? Ground your answers in Scripture.

6. How does knowing that Jesus Christ is truly human in body and soul affect you? What difference does it make in your faith and love toward him?

7. What evidence do we have in the New Testament that Christ is righteous and sinless?

8. How has the Holy Spirit been involved in Christ's life as a human being?

9. How could you use the doctrine that Jesus Christ counts God's people as his brothers and sisters to encourage someone feeling profoundly alone and abandoned?

Questions for Deeper Reflection

10. What arguments are raised against the doctrine that the incarnate Lord Jesus has a limited human mind? Why is that doctrine difficult to receive? Are the arguments against it valid? Why or why not?

11. Someone tells you, "Jesus can't be God, for he prays to God and worships him." How do you respond? Frame your answer according to the doctrines of the Trinity and the incarnation.

12. A Christian reads Hebrew 5:8 and is quite puzzled, asking, "How could Christ have 'learned obedience by the things which he suffered' if he was already sinless?" How do you answer?

41

Christ's Incarnation, Part 3

Historical Development of
Orthodox Christology

The doctrine of the incarnation developed historically alongside the doctrine of the Trinity.[1] During the centuries after the apostles died, the church passed through a series of theological conflicts that forced it to consider who Jesus Christ is. In this furnace of controversy, the Holy Spirit forged the orthodox confession of Christ's person based on God's Word.

If someone asks why we should bother with these controversies and theological terms, we reply with two words: *gospel* and *glory*. The church fathers understood that our salvation rests entirely upon the person of Christ. If we misstep here, then we slip away from the gospel. Furthermore, God the Father has designed all things for his Son. To fail to receive the revelation of Christ's identity is to dishonor the Father's beloved Son, whereas to believe in Christ as he truly is is to glorify him. We have much to learn from the history of this doctrine, both in order to refute false teaching and to understand and appreciate the glory of our Savior.

Christological Errors Faced by the Church

Even in the first century, Paul had to warn against preachers of "another Jesus" (2 Cor. 11:4). John said, "Whosoever denieth the Son, the same hath

---

1. On the historical development of the doctrine of the Trinity, see *RST*, 1:902–28 (chap. 46).

not the Father" (1 John 2:23). False views of Christ arose primarily from three factors: unbiblical Judaistic concepts of the Messiah; Greek polytheistic dualism that radically separated divine spirit from the material world, resulting in various movements known as Gnosticism;[2] and rationalistic attempts to embrace part of the biblical doctrine concerning the person of Christ while denying other aspects of what the Bible says. The early church confronted a variety of errors in Christology, some of which coincided so that multiple errors were taught by the same false teachers. (For a summary of these Christological errors, see Table 41.1, "Early Christological Errors," on p. 830.)

Errors regarding Christ's Person in Relationship to the Father

Given the biblical teaching about the divinity of the Son, it is not surprising that errors arose concerning his unity with and distinction from God the Father.

1. *Christ is another god than the Father.* In the second century AD, the Gnostic teacher Valentinus said that Christ is one divine spirit-being (*aiōn*) among the many emanated by the incomprehensible Father or "Depth" (*Bythos*).[3] In this system, the Creator of the world is yet another being, the platonic "maker" (*dēmiourgos*).[4] A different assertion of multiple divine beings appeared among professing Syrian Christians in the sixth century, initiated by John Ascoutzanges of Apatamea (fl. 557) and philosophically defended by John Philoponos (d. c. 570). They asserted that each person of the Trinity has a distinct essence and nature.[5] This error is called *Tritheism* (Greek *tri-*, "three," and *theoi*, "gods"). A form of Tritheism is taught today by the Church of Jesus Christ of Latter-Day Saints (Mormonism).[6] It contradicts the biblical truths that there is only one God (Deut. 4:39; Isa. 45:22) and that the Father and the Son are one in essence and power (John 10:29–30).[7]

2. *Christ is the same person as the Father.* At the beginning of the third century, Praxeas and Sabellius taught that in Jesus, the Father himself had

---

2. The term *Gnosticism* (from Greek *gnosis*, "knowledge") was coined in the modern era. A number of Gnostic manuscripts, including the Gospel of Truth and the Gospel of Thomas, were discovered in Nag Hammadi, Egypt, in 1945. See Kelly, *Systematic Theology*, 2:212–14, 252–57.

3. Irenaeus, *Against Heresies*, 1.1–2, in *ANF*, 1:316–18.

4. Irenaeus, *Against Heresies*, 1.5.1–2, in *ANF*, 1:322. See *RST*, 1:640.

5. Ry Ebied, A. van Roey, and L. R. Wickham, *Peter of Callinicum: Anti-Tritheist Dossier* (Leuven, Belgium: Departement Oriëntalistiek, 1981), 20–24, 28. To some extent, this error arose from the identification of *physis* and *hypostasis* among the monophysites (see below).

6. See *RST*, 1:923–24. Mormonism goes so far as to teach that men can become gods, thus opening the possibility of there being many deities, not just three (1:610).

7. On the oneness of God, see *RST*, 1:880–82. On the oneness of the persons in the Trinity, see *RST*, 1:893–98.

come and suffered for us. Christ is another mode in which God appears and works.[8] This error is called *Modalistic Monarchianism*. Monarchianism means "only one rule" (Greek *monē archia*), the doctrine of God's absolute personal oneness as opposed to the Trinity of divine persons.[9] A modalistic view of God was also taught by Michael Servetus (1511–1553) and is taught by modern oneness Pentecostalism.[10] The Scriptures show the falsehood of this doctrine by revealing the personal distinction and relationship between the Father and the Son (Matt. 3:17; 14:23).[11] Novatian (fl. 250) said, "What can be so evident proof that this is not the Father, but the Son, as that He is set forth as being obedient to God the Father?"[12] Central to the gospel is the Son's obedience to the Father, even unto the death of the cross (Phil. 2:8)—which requires that they be distinct persons.

Errors regarding the Deity and Humanity of Christ's Person

Although Christians today are accustomed to speaking of Christ's two natures in one person, this formulation of the doctrine was achieved through conflict with false teachings that in various ways denied that the one Christ is both God and man.

3. *Christ is one person, merely a man.* The Ebionites were Judaizers who believed in one Creator God, practiced circumcision and the Mosaic law, and rejected Paul's epistles. They viewed Jesus as a righteous man anointed by God, but not himself God, and some of them denied his virgin birth.[13] To some degree, Islam holds a similar view of Christ.[14] Classic theological liberalism also perpetuates the view that Jesus was a man who

---

8. Tertullian, *Against Praxeas*, chap. 1, in *ANF*, 3:597; and Novatian, *Concerning the Trinity*, chaps. 12, 23, 26, in *ANF*, 5:621–22, 634, 636. On the modalistic error, see *RST*, 1:904.

9. Tertullian, *Against Praxeas*, chaps. 4, 10, in *ANF*, 3:599, 604.

10. On Michael Servetus and oneness Pentecostalism, see *RST*, 1:918, 924.

11. On the personal distinction between the Father and the Son, see *RST*, 1:889.

12. Novatian, *Concerning the Trinity*, chap. 26, in *ANF*, 5:637.

13. Irenaeus, *Against Heresies*, 1.26.1–2; 3.21.1; 4.33.4; 5.1.3, in *ANF*, 1:351–52, 451, 507, 527; Tertullian, *On the Flesh of Christ*, chaps. 14, 18, in *ANF*, 3:534, 537; and Eusebius, *Church History*, 3.27.3, in *NPNF*², 1:159. "Ebionite" likely derives from the Hebrew term translated as "poor" or "needy" ('*ebyon*; cf. Ps. 69:33; 70:5). See editorial note in Eusebius, *Church History*, 3.27.1–2, in *NPNF*², 1:159n2.

14. According to the Qur'an, Jesus, the son of the virgin Mary, is the Messiah. He is God's messenger to Israel, a true prophet who worked miracles (Qur'an 3:45–49; 5:110; 19:30). He foretold the coming of another prophet (61:6), which is interpreted to refer to Muhammed. However, according to Islam's sacred book, Christ is not God and did not know the depths of God. Those who identify Christ as God or believe in the Trinity will not go to paradise but to hell, for Christ is just God's messenger. God is too exalted to have a Son (4:171; 5:72–73, 75, 116; 9:30–31). Furthermore, Christ did not die on the cross (4:157), either because he was not crucified or, on another Muslim interpretation, because he was crucified but recovered. F. P. Cotterell, "The Christology of Islam," in *Christ the Lord: Studies in Christology Presented to Donald Guthrie*, ed. Harold H. Rowdon (Downers Grove, IL: InterVarsity Press, 1982), 289–94.

knew God and revealed God in a unique way, but was not himself God.[15] This error is refuted by the weighty biblical evidence that Christ is God (John 1:1).[16] An early Christian preacher said, "Brethren, it is fitting that you should think of Jesus Christ as of God—as the Judge of the living and the dead. And it does not become us to think lightly of our salvation; for if we think little of Him, we shall also hope but to obtain little."[17] The Father could not have decreed that all men and angels will glorify Jesus as Lord, the name above all names, if he were a mere man (Phil. 2:9–11).

4. *Christ is one divine person, but not human.* The announcement that the divine "Word was made flesh" (John 1:14) was scandalous to dualistic Greek thought. John warned, "Every spirit that confesseth not that Jesus Christ is come in the flesh is not of God: and this is that spirit of antichrist, whereof ye have heard that it should come; and even now already is it in the world" (1 John 4:3). In the Gnostic error of *Docetism* (from Greek *dokeō*, to "think," "seem," or "have an appearance"), taught by people such as Marcion, Christ was said to appear human but to actually be a spirit-being that neither had a body nor experienced suffering.[18] The Scriptures teach clearly that Christ is a true man (1 Tim. 2:5).[19] Ignatius insisted that Christ "was truly born, and did eat and drink. He was truly persecuted under Pontius Pilate; He was truly crucified, and died. . . . He was also truly raised from the dead . . . even as after the same manner His Father will so raise up us who believe in Him by Christ Jesus, apart from whom we do not possess the true life."[20] How glorious is the God-man, for his humanity constitutes him as the perfect Savior for perishing human beings!

5. *Jesus and Christ are two persons: one human, one divine.* In the late first and early second centuries, the Gnostic teachers Valentinus and Cerinthus said that Jesus was a man and that the Christ was the spirit-being that descended upon him at his baptism and departed from him

---

15. Harnack, *What Is Christianity?*, 138, 154–57; and Hick, "Jesus and the World Religions," in *The Myth of God Incarnate*, ed. Hick, 172–73. See *RST*, 1:291–92, 537.

16. For several lines of biblical evidence for Christ's deity, see chap. 38.

17. *Second Epistle of Clement*, chap. 1, in *ANF*, 9:251. Scholars regard this work not as an epistle of Clement of Rome, but as an early Christian sermon, perhaps dating from around the beginning of the second century AD.

18. Irenaeus, *Against Heresies*, 1.22.1, 3; 1.24.2, in *ANF*, 1:348–49; Tertullian, *Against Marcion*, 3.8–11, in *ANF*, 3:327–30; and *On the Flesh of Christ*, chap. 5, in *ANF*, 3:525.

19. On Christ's humanity, see the previous chapter.

20. Ignatius, *Epistle to the Trallians*, chap. 9, in *ANF*, 1:70.

before his crucifixion.[21] On the contrary, the Bible teaches that Jesus has been "Christ the Lord" from his birth (Luke 2:11) and that "Christ died for our sins" (1 Cor. 15:3).[22] The concept of Christ as a divine spirit that dwelt in Jesus continues today in attempts to enfold Christ into pantheism or panentheism.[23] We find it in the teachings of Mary Baker Eddy (1821–1910), founder of Christian Science.[24] Against all such errors, Irenaeus said, "Jesus who suffered for us, and who dwelt among us, is Himself the Word of God. . . . The Word of the Father who descended is the same also that ascended. He, namely, the Only-begotten Son of the only God . . . became flesh for the sake of men."[25] We glorify God by confessing that the Father sent his Son in our flesh to die for our sins (1 John 4:2, 9–10), and now we live for him who died for us (2 Cor. 5:15).

6. *Christ is one person, a man adopted and glorified by God.* Artemon, Theodotus of Byzantium (both in the second century), and Paul of Samosata (fl. 260) taught that Jesus Christ was not the incarnation of the heavenly Son of God, but a human being adopted by God at his baptism and exalted to divine lordship at his resurrection.[26] This error is called *Adoptionism* or *Dynamic Monarchianism*.[27] It reappeared in the fourth century in the teaching of Photinus, during the eighth century in Spain, and in the sixteenth century among Socinians, and it still can be found today.[28] It is refuted by the biblical teaching of Christ's eternal divine preexistence (John 1:1; 8:58).[29] Athanasius said, "God the Word himself is Christ from Mary, God and man; not some other Christ but one and the same; he before ages from the Father, he too in the last times from the Virgin; invisible before

---

21. Irenaeus, *Against Heresies*, 1.1–2; 1.7.2; 1.26.1, in *ANF*, 1:316–18, 325, 351–52; and Hippolytus, *The Refutation of All Heresies*, 6.30; 7.21, in *ANF*, 5:89, 114. Cerinthus included in his doctrine the Ebionite denial of the virgin birth.

22. For the biblical teaching that Jesus Christ is one person, God and man, see chap. 39. On the distinct personalities of God the Son and of God the Holy Spirit, see *RST*, 1:889–91.

23. On the definitions and various forms of pantheism and panentheism, see *RST*, 1:590–98.

24. Mary Baker Eddy, *Miscellaneous Writings, 1883–1896* (Boston: Allison V. Stewart, 1917), 84; cf. 161–68, 180.

25. Irenaeus, *Against Heresies*, 1.9.3, in *ANF*, 1:329.

26. Hippolytus, *The Refutation of All Heresies*, 7.23, in *ANF*, 5:114; Athanasius, *Four Discourses against the Arians*, 4.30–32, 35, in *NPNF²*, 4:445–47; *De Synodis*, sec. 26, in *NPNF²*, 4:463; and Eusebius, *Church History*, 5.28.1–6; 7.28.1–2; 7.30.11, in *NPNF²*, 1:246–47; 312, 315. See the editorial prolegomena, 2.3.2, in *NPNF²*, 4:xxvii.

27. "Dynamic" probably refers to God's gift of "power" (*dynamis*) to Jesus to work "miracles" (*dynameis*).

28. On Photinus, see Socrates Scholasticus, *Ecclesiastical History*, 2.29, in *NPNF²*, 2:56; and Hilary of Poitiers, *De Synodis*, secs. 39, 61, in *NPNF²*, 9:16, 20. On Spanish Adoptionism, see Douglas Dales, *Alcuin: Theology and Thought* (Cambridge: James Clarke and Co., 2013), 63–65. For a Socinian example, see *The Racovian Catechism*, 51–56. For a modern example, see Dunn, *The Theology of Paul the Apostle*, 10.5 (254–55).

29. On Christ's preexistence as God the Son, see chap. 38.

. . . visible now . . . through the human body and whole man, which he has renewed by its appropriation to himself."[30] Christ is not merely a glorified man, but God the Son, worthy of our worship and absolute trust.

7. *Christ is one person, the supernatural Son created by the Father.* Arius, perhaps as he learned from Lucian of Antioch (c. 240–312), taught that Christ is not the eternal and almighty God, but a Son created by God before the creation of the world, and through whom he made the world.[31] Consequently, the Son is a person of great majesty, but does not share in the same deity as God the Father. The Jehovah's Witnesses teach this doctrine today.[32] It is contradicted by the Bible's ascription of God's names, attributes, and actions to Christ (Heb. 1:10–12).[33] Augustine pointed out that Arianism is implicit polytheism: the Arians admit that our Lord Jesus Christ is God, but in refusing to say he is the true God and one God with the Father, they present us with two gods who are unequal in nature.[34] This anti-Trinitarian heresy divides the glory of the one God between two beings, but there is only one God and Savior, and he says, "I will not give my glory unto another" (Isa. 45:21–22; 48:11).

8. *Jesus and the Son are two persons: one human, one divine.* This is the error of Nestorianism, because Nestorius (fl. 428) objected against calling Mary the "God-bearer" (*theotokos*)[35] and was rebuked by Cyril of Alexandria for purportedly dividing Christ in two.[36] Scholars today debate whether Nestorius considered the divine and human in Christ to be two persons.[37] In any case, the Scriptures represent Christ as one person, God

---

30. Athanasius, *Four Discourses against the Arians*, 4.36, in *NPNF²*, 4:447. In some quotations in this chapter, we have put some capitalized words in lower case to conform with modern style.

31. Arius, "Thalia," and letter to Alexander, in Athanasius, *De Synodis*, secs. 15–16, in *NPNF²*, 4:457–58. On Arius, see Theodoret, *Ecclesiastical History*, 1.1, in *NPNF²*, 3:34–40; and Socrates Scholasticus, *Ecclesiastical History*, 1.5, in *NPNF²*, 2:3. On Lucian as the teacher of Arius and his sympathizer, Eusebius of Nicomedia, see Theorodet, *Ecclesiastical History*, 1.4, in *NPNF²*, 3:41; and the editorial prolegomena, sec. 5, in *NPNF²*, 1:11.

32. See *RST*, 1:886, 924.

33. For biblical evidence for Christ's deity, see chap. 38.

34. Augustine, *Answer to the Arian Sermon*, 1.1, in *Works*, 1/18:141.

35. On Mary as *theotokos*, see the mutual "Anathematisms" of Cyril of Alexandria and Nestorius, *NPNF²*, 14:206. It is theologically correct to call Mary the "God-bearer" or mother of our Lord (Luke 1:43), for the person born of her was truly God, albeit born according to his humanity. However, such terminology might suggest that Mary is a divine person, worthy of prayer and adoration. Muslims have mistakenly thought that Christians teach a Trinity of the Father, Mary, and Jesus (Qur'an 5:116). Therefore, it is wise to find other ways of express the truth that God the Son and man are united as one person, our Lord Jesus Christ. See Macleod, *The Person of Christ*, 187–88.

36. Cyril of Alexandria, Epistle to Nestorius, in Acts of the Council of Ephesus (AD 431), in *NPNF²*, 14:197–98.

37. Nestorius seemingly affirmed two persons in Christ, saying, "The Holy Spirit . . . formed out of the Virgin a temple for God the Logos [Word], a temple in which he dwelt. Moreover, the incarnate God did not die; he raised up the one in whom he was incarnate. . . . Since God is within the one who was assumed, the one who was assumed is styled God because of the one who assumed him." Nestorius,

and man, who is addressed in the singular, personal "thou" (Mark 1:11).[38] Fulgentius of Ruspe (c. 467–532) said, "God the Word, having become flesh, has one person of his divinity and his flesh. . . . God the Word did not receive the person of a human being but the nature."[39] The person whom Thomas glorified as "my LORD and my God" had nail-scarred hands (John 20:25–28). Christ's singular personhood is crucial because there is "one mediator between God and men" (1 Tim. 2:5), who stands as the one Surety who legally represents his people (Heb. 7:22).[40]

9. *Christ is one person with one divine-human nature.* In an overreaction to Nestorianism, Eutyches (d. 454) taught that Christ's human nature was deified in union with his deity.[41] This error is called *Monophysitism* for its assertion that Christ has "only one nature" (Greek *monē physis*). The human mingles with the divine in Christ as a drop of honey is dissolved into the vast sea. The many Scripture passages attesting to the human attributes of his body and soul (Luke 2:52; etc.) show that the Monophysite doctrine is false.[42] It might seem to honor Christ if we dilute his humanity into one nature with his deity, but in so doing we subtract an essential aspect of our salvation: Christ as man has obeyed and overcome in our place. Leo the Great said in his *Tome*, or letter to Flavian (d. 449), "For we could not have overcome the author of sin and of death, unless he who could neither be contaminated by sin, nor detained by death, had taken upon himself our nature, and made it his own. . . . For each of the natures retains its proper character without defect; and as the form of God does not take away the form of a servant, so the form of a servant does not impair the form of God."[43]

Errors regarding Christ's Human Body and Soul

Another way in which theologians can go astray in Christology is to compromise Christ's full humanity with regard to his body and soul.

First Sermon against the Theotokos, in *The Christological Controversy*, ed. and trans. Richard A. Norris Jr., Sources in Early Christian Thought (Philadelphia: Fortress, 1980), 125, 130. However, some scholars argue that a recently discovered work indicates that Nestorius affirmed orthodoxy, at least at some point in the controversy. See Nestorius, *The Bazaar of Heracleides*, trans. and ed. G. R. Driver and Leonard Hodgson (Oxford: Oxford University Press, 1925); and J. F. Bethune-Baker, *Nestorius and His Teaching: A Fresh Examination of the Evidence* (Cambridge: Cambridge University Press, 1908).

38. See the section on the incarnate Lord's unique person in chap. 39.

39. Fulgentius of Ruspe, *Letter to Peter on the Faith*, 17.60, in Fulgentius, *Selected Works*, trans. Robert B. Eno, Fathers of the Church 95 (Washington, DC: The Catholic University of America Press, 1997), 96.

40. Vos, *Reformed Dogmatics*, 3:40–41.

41. Leo the Great, *Tome*, in NPNF², 14:257–58.

42. On Christ's human nature, see chap. 40.

43. Leo the Great, *Tome*, in NPNF², 14:254–55.

10. *Christ's human body was not earthly but heavenly in origin.* In the second century, Valentinus and another Gnostic teacher named Apelles taught that the body of Jesus, though human, was formed by God out of a heavenly substance and passed through Mary as water through a pipe.[44] In the sixteenth century, Anabaptist leader Menno Simons similarly taught that Christ did not take human flesh from Mary, but instead brought his flesh from heaven.[45] However, the Holy Scriptures teach that Mary conceived Jesus in such a manner that she was truly his mother, and he was the fruit of her womb and a physical descendant of David (Luke 1:27, 31–32, 42–43).[46] Gregory of Nazianzus condemned the doctrine that Christ "passed through the Virgin as through a channel, and was not at once divinely and humanly formed in her (divinely, because without the intervention of a man; humanly, because in accordance with the laws of gestation)."[47] As Tertullian observed, "Christ, however, having been sent to die, had necessarily to be also born, that he might be capable of death," having taken not a heavenly nature better suited for angels but our "mortal" nature, "for One who was to be truly man, even unto death, it was necessary that He should be clothed with that flesh to which death belongs."[48]

11. *Christ has no human soul but is the divine Word in a body.* The Arian bishop Eudoxius of Antioch (fl. 360) said that the Son "became flesh, but not man. For he took no human soul . . . he was no complete man, but God in the flesh instead of a soul."[49] A similar view was taught by Apollinarius (or Apollinaris) of Laodicea (fl. c. 360), who affirmed the deity of the Word against Arianism, but taught that the incarnation consisted of the union of the Word and human flesh, with the Word acting in the place of a human mind.[50] This view has reappeared at various times even in the

---

44. Irenaeus, *Against Heresies*, 1.7.1–2, in *ANF*, 1:325; and Tertullian, *On the Flesh of Christ*, chaps. 6, 15, in *ANF*, 3:526, 534.

45. Simons, *Reply to Gellius Faber*, in *Works*, 2:99; and *Reply to John A'Lasco*, in *Works*, 2:147–59.

46. On the origin of Christ's flesh, see the section on the event of the virgin birth in chap. 39.

47. Gregory of Nazianzus, *Epistles*, no. 101, in *NPNF*[2], 7:439.

48. Tertullian, *On the Flesh of Christ*, chap. 6, in *ANF*, 3:526–27.

49. Cited in Aloys Grillmeier, *Christ in the Christian Tradition, Volume 1: From the Apostolic Age to Chalcedon (451)*, trans. John Bowden, 2nd ed. (Atlanta: John Knox, 1975), 244. See the anti-Arian statements in Gregory of Nyssa, *Against Eunomius*, 2.13, in *NPNF*[2], 5:127; and Gregory of Nazianzus, *Epistles*, no. 101, in *NPNF*[2], 7:440. For an argument that such may not be the view of Arius himself, see William P. Haugaard, "Arius: Twice a Heretic? Arius and the Human Soul of Christ," *Church History* 29, no. 3 (September 1960): 251–63.

50. Apollinaris of Laodicea, *On the Union in Christ of the Body with the Godhead*, sec. 12; Fragment 25, in *The Christological Controversy*, ed. Norris, 106, 108. See Gregory of Nazianzus, *Epistles*, no. 101, in *NPNF*[2], 7:439–43.

modern era.[51] The result is a form of Monophysitism. Apollinarius said, "He is one nature since He is a simple, undivided Person," teaching that there is "one incarnate nature of the divine Word."[52] This error is refuted by the biblical witness to Christ's complete humanity, including his soul.[53] This error also undermines Christ's ability to save the whole person, for he did not face temptation as one like us (Heb. 2:17–18; 4:15). As Gregory of Nazianzus said, "That which He has not assumed He has not healed."[54] Athanasius said, "In Him the human race is perfectly and wholly delivered from sin and quickened from the dead. . . . The Saviour had not a body without a soul, nor without sense or intelligence . . . nor was the salvation effected in the Word Himself a salvation of body only, but of soul also."[55] This error diminishes the glory of the perfect Savior.

12. *Christ is God and man in one person but has no human will.* Sergius of Constantinople (d. 638), seeking a compromise with Monophysitism, taught that Christ has only one will, the divine will. This error is called *Monothelitism* (from the Greek *monos*, "only one," and *thelēma*, "will"). It contradicts the Bible's teaching that Christ has a human will that must submit to the divine will.[56] Maximus the Confessor (c. 580–662) opposed this teaching, writing, "The double nature of the Lord Jesus manifests itself naturally and logically by a double will and a double energy. Possessing human nature, the incarnate Word also possesses in it a will, because human nature cannot exist without a will. . . . In so far as he was man, the Saviour possessed a human will by nature, which his divine will governed, [that] his human will never opposed."[57] It is important for the gospel that Christ has not only a divine will but also a human will, for we are saved by the voluntary, human obedience of Jesus Christ, the Surety of his people.

---

51. Some proponents of the kenotic view in the nineteenth century held to Apollinarian views that the Word divested himself of glory to become the human spirit of Jesus. See A. B. Bruce, *The Humiliation of Christ*, 5th ed. (Edinburgh: T&T Clark, 1900), 394–410. A recently proposed Apollinarian model of the incarnation appears in J. P. Moreland and William Lane Craig, *Philosophical Foundations for a Christian Worldview*, 2nd ed. (Downers Grove, IL: InterVarsity Press, 2017), 605–9. They argue that "the Logos was the rational soul of Jesus" (605), with his divine omniscience limited to his "subconscious" mind, "at least during his state of humiliation" (608). See Wellum, *God the Son Incarnate*, 388–93, 412–14.
52. Cited in Kelly, *Early Christian Doctrines*, 293.
53. On Christ's soul and inner human life, see chap. 40.
54. Gregory of Nazianzus, *Epistles*, no. 101, in NPNF², 7:440.
55. Athanasius, *Letter to the Church of Antioch*, sec. 7, in NPNF², 4:485.
56. On the biblical teaching regarding Christ's human will, see the section on Christ's human soul in chap. 40.
57. Maximus the Confessor, *Peri Energeiōn kai Thelēmatōn*, chap. 51, in *Opuscula Theologica et Polemica ad Marinum*, in *Patrologiae Graeca*, ed. Migne, 91:45–48, cited in Kelly, *Systematic Theology*, 2:247.

Errors regarding Christ's Person in Relationship to the Father		
Error	*Examples*	*View of Jesus*
1	Valentinus (Gnosticism), John Philoponus (Tritheism)	A distinct god from the Father, one among several divine beings
2	Praxeas, Sabellius (Modalistic Monarchianism)	God the Father incarnate, not a distinct person

Errors regarding the Deity and Humanity of Christ's Person						
Error	*Examples*	*God?*	*Man?*	*Persons*	*Natures*	*View of Jesus*
3	Ebionites	No	Yes	1	1	Godly Jewish man
4	Marcion (Docetism)	Yes	No	1	1	Only appeared human
5	Valentinus, Cerinthus	Yes	Yes	2	2	Man anointed by Christ-Spirit
6	Paul of Samosata, Photinus (Adoptionism, Dynamic Monarchianism)	No	Yes	1	1	Man adopted and deified by God
7	Arius (Arianism)	No	No	1	1	Powerful Son created by Father
8	Nestorianism	Yes	Yes	2	2	Two persons united
9	Eutyches (Monophysitism)	Yes	Yes	1	1	One nature, divine and human mingled

Errors regarding Christ's Human Body and Soul	
Error	*Examples*	*View of Jesus's Humanity*
10	Valentinus, Apelles	Body made of heavenly flesh, not of Mary
11	Arians, Apollinarius	No human soul; body animated by the Word
12	Sergius of Constantinople (Monothelitism)	No human will; only a divine will directing Jesus

Table 41.1. Early Christological Errors

The Great Conciliar Confessions of Christ

Confronted by this swarm of errors, how did the early church respond? It dug deeply into the Holy Scriptures and wrestled with how to express biblical teaching about Jesus Christ in a clear and coherent manner. Church leaders gathered in councils (also called synods) to hammer out confessions of faith to assert their Christian beliefs, show their unity with other orthodox Christians, and distinguish themselves from heretics. Though many synods were held during this time, the six considered in this section had a profound influence on catholic and orthodox Christology. Bruce Shelley notes that these early councils asserted, "In Jesus Christ, true deity (against Arius) and full humanity (against Apollinaris) are indivisibly united in one person (against Nestorius) without being confused (against Eutyches)."[58] (For a summary of the actions of the councils discussed below, see Table 41.2, "The Catholic Orthodox Christology of the Councils," on p. 838.)

At the core of the councils' doctrinal pronouncements stood *the Apostles' Creed*. Very early in the church's history, Christian leaders began confessing doctrines essential to Christianity in the creed or rule of faith.[59] Relative to Christ's person, the creed states, "I believe . . . in Jesus Christ, [God the Father's] only begotten Son, our Lord; who was conceived by the Holy Ghost, born of the Virgin Mary; suffered . . . was crucified . . . [and] rose from the dead."[60] The creed thus affirms that the same person who is God's only Son and our Lord is Mary's human son, who suffered, died, and rose again for our salvation. Thus, it implies that the incarnate Son has two natures in one person. Tertullian was perhaps the first Christian to use such language, saying that Christ is "God and man, differing no doubt according to each substance in its own especial property, inasmuch as the Word is nothing else but God, and the flesh nothing else but man." Christ, then, is not a blend of divinity and humanity as gold and silver mix to make electrum, but "twofold," such that deity and humanity are not "confounded, but conjoined in one person—Jesus, God and man."[61]

As we noted earlier, Arius argued that Christ is God's Son in the sense of being an exalted being created by God the Father and therefore a lesser divinity. Bishops from various locations gathered at the *First Council of*

---

58. Bruce Shelley, *Church History in Plain Language*, rev. R. L. Hatchett, 4th ed. (Nashville: Thomas Nelson, 2013), 123.
59. On the rule of faith and the Apostles' Creed, see *RST*, 1:62, 85–86, 903.
60. *The Three Forms of Unity*, 5.
61. Tertullian, *Against Praxeas*, chap. 27, in *ANF*, 3:624.

Nicaea (325) to discuss the Arian doctrine and defend the true doctrine of Christ.[62] They expanded the Apostles' Creed to clarify that God's Son eternally possessed the same divine nature as the Father, confessing, "the Son of God, the only-begotten of his Father, of the substance of the Father, God of God, Light of Light, very God of very God, begotten, not made, being of one substance (*homoousion*) with the Father." They condemned the teaching that "there was a time when the Son of God was not."[63] The word *homoousion* indicates that the Father and the Son share the same divine nature, and since God is one, the Father and the Son are one God. After the council, this doctrine found strong advocates in Athanasius, Hilary of Poitiers, and the Cappadocian fathers—Basil, Gregory of Nyssa, and Gregory of Nazianzus.

What we today call "the Nicene Creed" was fully formulated at the *First Council of Constantinople* (381), where theologians supplemented the Nicaean confession to more clearly affirm the deity of the Holy Spirit.[64] Furthermore, in addition to condemning the false teachings of the Arians, the canons of this council named as heresy both Sabellianism and Apollinarianism.[65] Thus, the council affirmed that orthodox Christianity teaches both the personal distinction between the Father and the Son, and the Son's incarnation as a complete human being with a human body and human soul, while remaining one substance with the Father as God.

The *First Council of Ephesus* (431) assembled under the leadership of Cyril of Alexandria to address the false teaching attributed to Nestorius. The theologians there condemned Nestorius and approved Cyril's letter, which states that Mary is rightly called the God-bearer, "not as if the nature of the Word or his divinity had its beginning from the holy Virgin, but because of her was born that holy body with a rational soul, to which the Word being personally united is said to be born according to the flesh."[66] Christ is one person, though both divine and human.

The Council of Ephesus was rejected by the Persian or Assyrian churches because of objections to its procedure and differences between Greek and Syriac (a form of Aramaic) theological terminology. It does not

---

62. On the Council of Nicaea, the *homoousion*, and the conflict over the Trinity, see *RST*, 1:905–7.
63. The Creed of Nicaea, in *NPNF*[2], 14:3.
64. On the Council of Constantinople and the Holy Spirit, see *RST*, 1:907.
65. Canons of the First Council of Constantinople (AD 381), canon 1, in *NPNF*[2], 14:172.
66. Acts of the Council of Ephesus (AD 431), in *NPNF*[2], 14:198.

appear to be accurate to label the Church of the East as Nestorian in the sense of two-person Christology.[67]

When confronted with the opposite error of Eutyches, which fused Christ's deity and humanity into one nature, bishops met in the *Council of Chalcedon* (451). There they approved the teaching of Leo, who said, "Accordingly, while the distinctness of both natures and substances was preserved, and both met in one person, lowliness was assumed by majesty, weakness by power, mortality by eternity; and, in order to pay the debt of our condition, the inviolable nature was united to the passible."[68] The "Definition" of Chalcedon gathered together the Christology of the earlier creeds with such completeness that we quote it at length:

> Following the holy Fathers we teach with one voice that the Son and our Lord Jesus Christ is to be confessed as one and the same, that he is perfect in Godhead and perfect in manhood, very God and very man, of a reasonable soul and body consisting, consubstantial [*homoousion*] with the Father as touching his Godhead, and consubstantial [*homoousion*] with us as touching his manhood; made in all things like unto us, sin only excepted; begotten of his Father before the worlds according to his Godhead; but in these last days for us men and for our salvation born of the virgin Mary, the mother of God according to his manhood.
>
> This one and the same Jesus Christ, the only-begotten Son must be confessed to be in two natures, unconfusedly, immutably, indivisibly, inseparably, and that without the distinction of natures being taken away by such union, but rather the peculiar property of each nature being preserved and being united in one person and subsistence, not separated or divided into two persons, but one and the same Son and only-begotten, God the Word, our Lord Jesus Christ, as the prophets of old time have spoken concerning him, and as the Lord Jesus Christ hath taught us, and as the Creed of the Fathers hath delivered to us.[69]

---

67. Sebastian P. Brock, "The 'Nestorian' Church: A Lamentable Misnomer," in *Fire from Heaven: Studies in Syriac Theology and Liturgy* (Aldershot, England: Ashgate, 2006), I.1–14; and Wilhelm Baum and Dietmar W. Winkler, *The Church of the East: A Concise History*, trans. Miranda G. Henry (London: RoutledgeCurzon, 2003), 27–32, 39, http://www.peshitta.org/pdf/CoEHistory.pdf. See John Paul II and Dinkha IV, *Common Christological Declaration between the Catholic Church and the Assyrian Church of the East*, November 11, 1994, http://www.vatican.va/roman_curia/pontifical_councils/chrstuni/documents/rc_pc_chrstuni_doc_11111994_assyrian-church_en.html.

68. Leo the Great, *Tome*, in *NPNF²*, 14:255. Leo's *Tome* may also be found in *NPNF²*, 12:38–43.

69. Acts of the Council of Chalcedon (AD 451), in *NPNF²*, 14:264–65. We break the statement into two paragraphs at the period for the ease of the reader.

The Chalcedonian Definition fences the doctrine of Christ against many heresies.[70] It applies the term "consubstantial" (*homoousion*), or "of the same essence," to both Christ's divine nature in relation to the Father and his human nature in relation to mankind. Like the anti-Arian Creed of Nicaea, it reaffirms that Christ possesses the same deity as God the Father, not as a lesser god or godlike being, but as the one true God. Against Monarchian Modalism, it distinguishes "the Son" from "the Father," and against Adoptionism, it states that Christ is "begotten of his Father before the worlds." To the great truth of the Son's deity, the council added a clear confession that Christ possesses a true human nature just as we do, contrary to Docetism; he is not merely a humanlike being, but is truly and fully man, "of a reasonable soul and body," which opposes Apollinarianism.

The words "two natures, unconfusedly, immutably, indivisibly, inseparably"[71] guard the doctrine of Christ from both Monophysitism and Nestorianism. Jesus Christ shares in the divine nature and human nature in a manner that does not mix their attributes ("unconfusedly") and does not change deity into humanity or humanity into deity ("immutably"). Yet Christ holds those natures together in the unity of his one person, so that the Mediator's acts engage both his natures, his saving works bear the twofold character of the God-man, and he will never lose his full deity or full humanity for all eternity ("indivisibly" and "inseparably").[72]

The Chalcedonian doctrine of Christ's person became a confessional standard in the Western Catholic Church and the Eastern Orthodox Church. The Definition of Chalcedon was rejected by Oriental Orthodox Churches.[73] However, these churches claim to teach not the monophysite view of Eutychus, but the more nuanced "miaphysite" doctrine of Cyril of Alexandria, which says that the Son's deity and humanity unite as "one nature" (*mia physis*), for Christ is one entity, just as body and soul unite in one human being while remaining distinct in properties.[74]

---

70. Wellum, *God the Son Incarnate*, 305.

71. "Unconfusedly, immutably, indivisibly, inseparably" translates the Greek words *asynchytōs, atreptōs, adiairetōs, achōristōs*. The last two terms are close in meaning.

72. *The Creeds of Christendom*, ed. Schaff, 2:62, 65; and Kelly, *Systematic Theology*, 2:203–4.

73. The Oriental Orthodox Churches include the Coptic Orthodox Church in Egypt and several churches in Syria, Armenia, Eritrea, and Ethiopia. These bodies are not to be confused with the Eastern Orthodox Church.

74. On the miaphysite Christology of Cyril of Alexandria, see Thomas Weinandy, "The Soul/Body Analogy and the Incarnation: Cyril of Alexandria," *Coptic Church Review* 17, no. 3 (Fall 1996): 63–66 (full article, 59–66).

We find Chalcedonian Christology expressed in the so-called Athanasian Creed,[75] which says that Christ is "God and man," "God of the substance of the Father, begotten before the worlds; and man of substance of His mother, born in the world . . . of a reasonable soul and human flesh subsisting." However, though Christ is "God and man, yet He is not two, but one Christ. One, not by conversion of the Godhead into flesh, but by taking of that manhood into God. One altogether, not by confusion of substance, but by unity of person."[76]

The Council of Chalcedon set forth the doctrine of Christ's two natures in one person but left an unanswered question: If Christ is only one person (*hypostasis*), and that person is eternally divine, what shall we say about the human person Jesus? This question was addressed in the *Second Council of Constantinople* (553), which stated that we must not view the incarnation as the conjunction of two persons, as if God the Word was with the human person Jesus, indwelt him, or was united to him, but that there was never more than one person involved, because God the Word personally assumed a human body and soul in the hypostatic union.[77] Every other human being is a person in himself, but the man Jesus never existed apart from the divine person of God's Son. Though Christ's humanity is fully personal, the incarnation is not the merging of two persons, but the taking of human nature by an already existing eternal person.

Later theologians have explained the doctrine of the Second Council of Constantinople with the terms "anhypostatic" (Greek *anhypostatos*) and "enhypostatic" (*enhypostatos*).[78] In the theological discourse at the time of the council and the preceding two centuries, these terms meant "without substance, without independent existence, unreal" and "substantial, having independent existence, real," respectively, and thus did not speak directly to the issue of Christ's singular person.[79] However, John of Damascus later

---

75. On the Athanasian Creed, see *RST*, 1:87–88.

76. *The Three Forms of Unity*, 10–11.

77. Capitula of the Second Council of Constantinople (AD 553), capitula 3–5, in *NPNF²*, 14:312–13.

78. Muller, *Dictionary of Latin and Greek Theological Terms*, 27, 106. Technically, the Greek adjectives should be transliterated as *anypostatos* and *enypostatos*, but we retain the *h* in keeping with common theological usage and to make clear the connection to *hypostasis*.

79. G. W. H. Lampe, ed., *A Patristic Greek Lexicon* (Oxford: Oxford University Press, 1961), 164, 485–86; Aloys Grillmeier with Theresia Hainthaler, *Christ in the Christian Tradition, Volume 2: From the Council of Chalcedon (451) to Gregory the Great (590–604), Part 2: The Church of Constantinople in the Sixth Century*, trans. Pauline Allen and John Cawte (Louisville: Westminster John Knox, 1995), 61–64, 193–98, 283–86; F. LeRon Shults, "A Dubious Christological Formula: From Leontius of Byzantium to Karl Barth," *Journal of Theological Studies* 57 (1996): 431–46; and U. M. Lang, "Anhypostatos-Enhypostatos: Church Fathers, Protestant Orthodoxy and Karl

invested "enhypostatic" with a technical sense to communicate that the human nature of God the Son did not exist independently, but its subsistence was "in" another, namely, the eternal person of God the Son. John of Damascus said, "The nature which has been assumed by another hypostasis and has its existence in this is called *enhypostaton*. For this reason also the flesh of the Lord which does not subsist by itself, not even for an instant, is not a hypostasis, but rather *enhypostatos*."[80] He wrote,

> For the flesh of God the Word did not subsist as an independent subsistence [*idiosystatōs*], nor did there arise another subsistence [*hypostasis*] besides that of God the Word, but as it existed in that it became rather a subsistence which subsisted in another [*en autē hypostasa enhypostatos*], than one which was an independent subsistence. Wherefore, neither does it lack subsistence altogether [*anhypostatos*], nor yet is there thus introduced into the Trinity another subsistence.[81]

Thus, the term "enhypostatic" took on special meaning in orthodox Christology. Thomas Aquinas employed the Damascene's terminology in his discussion of the Son's taking human nature to subsist in his own person.[82] Later, Francis Turretin and Lutheran theologian Johannes Quenstedt (1617–1688) spoke of Christ's human nature as "without subsistence" (*anhypostatos*) in itself but "subsisting in" (*enhypostatos*) the Word.[83] However, several other Reformed divines, while teaching the same doctrine, did not use these terms.[84] These variations of terminology in ancient and Protestant orthodoxy caution us against speaking of "a doctrine unan-

---

Barth," *Journal of Theological Studies* NS 49, pt. 2 (October 1998): 631, 634–35, 643–44 (full article, 630–57). On the sense of *hypostasis* as "reality," see *RST*, 1:887, 904n14. The conclusions of Grillmeier, Shults, and Lang regarding the use of *enhypostatos* contradict the earlier conclusions of Friedrich A. Loofs (1858–1928), who misunderstood Leontius of Byzantium to have pioneered the theological use of *enhypostatos* to mean "subsist in," whereas he, like others of the sixth century, used it in the sense of "real, having concrete existence."

80. John of Damascus, *Dialectica*, 45:17–22, cited in Lang, "Anhypostatos-Enhypostatos," 649.

81. John of Damascus, *An Exact Exposition of the Orthodox Faith*, 3.9, in NPNF[2], 9.2:53. See the Greek text in Lang, "Anhypostatos-Enhypostatos," 650. See Vos, *Reformed Dogmatics*, 3:43.

82. Aquinas, *Summa Theologica*, Part 3, Q. 4, Art. 2.

83. Turretin, *Institutes*, 13.6.5 (2:311–12); J. A. Quenstedt, *Theologia Didacto-Polemica, sive Systema Theologicum*, 3.3.1.1.13, cited in Lang, "Anhypostatos-Enhypostatos," 656.

84. Perkins, *An Exposition of the Symbol*, in *Works*, 5:128; *A Golden Chain*, chap. 16, in *Works*, 6:50–51; Ames, *The Marrow of Theology*, 1.18.15 (129–30); Wollebius, *Compendium*, 1.16.(4).i (90–91); John Arrowsmith, *Theanthropos; or, God-Man: Being an Exposition upon the First Eighteen Verses of the First Chapter of the Gospel According to St John* (London: for Humphrey Moseley and William Wilson, 1660), 207; and Goodwin, *Of Christ the Mediator*, in *Works*, 5:51–54. The Christological use of *anhypostatos* but not *enhypostatos* appears in Polyander, Walaeus, Thysius, and Rivetus, *Synopsis Purioris Theologiae*, 25.24 (2:79); and Owen, *Christologia*, in *Works*, 1:233.

imously sponsored by early theology in its entirety, that of the *anhypostasis* and *enhypostasis* of the human nature of Christ," as Karl Barth asserted.[85] It is better to say that the orthodox doctrine affirmed in the Second Council of Constantinople teaches that God the Son did not take to himself a human person, but took a human nature to his person.

This teaching does not justify speaking of Christ's human nature as "impersonal," which poorly describes Christ's perfect humanity,[86] and does not accurately translate *anhypostatos*.[87] Rather, it teaches us that the person of Jesus Christ is one and the same as the person of the eternal Son. Douglas Kelly says, "This cuts out any form of adoptionism of a previously existing human person."[88] Since a person is a unique "someone" in relationships with others, a relationship with Jesus Christ is a relationship "with God himself."[89]

Since Christ is one person, it may appear that he has one will, which is the doctrine of Monothelitism. The *Third Council of Constantinople* (680–681) rejected monothelitist teaching that represents Christ's human "soul as devoid of will or operation." The council reaffirmed the doctrine of the Council of Chalcedon and added that "in him are two natural wills and two natural operations indivisibly, inconvertibly, inseparably, inconfusedly, according to the teaching of the holy Fathers. And these two natural wills are not contrary the one to the other . . . but his human will follows and that not as resisting and reluctant, but rather as subject to his divine and omnipotent will."[90] Hence, Christ offered a truly human obedience to God for his people.

The doctrine of Christ codified by these councils was received in mainstream Christianity as catholic orthodoxy—that is, the true doctrine of the universal church. Medieval theologians worked to preserve its truths and elaborated philosophical arguments to support it.[91]

85. Barth, *Church Dogmatics*, I/2, sec. 15.2.iii (163); cf. IV/1, sec. 64.2.ii (91).

86. Vos, *Reformed Dogmatics*, 3:42.

87. As used by Patristic and Reformed orthodox divines, *anhypostatos* does not denote a lack of consciousness, mind, affection, will, etc., which is the present connotation of "impersonal." Instead, *anhypostatos* is the negation of *hypostasis*, which in these contexts means a particular, distinct, individual subsistence. John of Damascus, *An Exact Exposition of the Orthodox Faith*, 3.6, in NPNF², 9.2:50; and Owen, *Christologia*, in *Works*, 1:233.

88. Kelly, *Systematic Theology*, 2:235; cf. Strong, *Systematic Theology*, 2:679.

89. Dumitru Staniloae, cited in Kelly, *Systematic Theology*, 2:236. On our description of a "person," which leans on Richard of St. Victor, see RST, 1:912–13, 931–33.

90. Definition of Faith of the Third Council of Constantinople (AD 680–681), in NPNF², 14:344–45.

91. See John of Damascus, *An Exposition of the Orthodox Faith*, 3.1–4.8, in NPNF², 9.2:45–77; Lombard, *The Sentences*, 3.1–17 (3:1–72); and Aquinas, *Summa Theologica*, Part 3, Q. 1–19.

Year	Council	Contribution to Confessional Christology
325	Nicaea	The Son has the same divine nature as the Father, the two being one God.
381	Constantinople (1)	The Son is a distinct person from the Father and is incarnate, with a human body and soul.
431	Ephesus	Christ is God and man in one person.
451	Chalcedon	Christ is one person, but with two unmixed natures.
553	Constantinople (2)	The Son did not take a human person, but took a full human nature to his already existing divine person.
680–681	Constantinople (3)	Christ has two distinct but harmonious wills as God and man.

Table 41.2. The Catholic, Orthodox Christology of the Councils

The Reformed Confessional Statements on Christ's Person

The Reformed churches of the sixteenth century embraced the Christology of the ancient councils.[92] John Calvin likewise followed the Christological teachings of the councils because they aptly express biblical truth.[93] He and other Reformers did not view councils as possessing divine and infallible authority, but neither did they despise them. Calvin said, "Although we hold that the Word of God alone lies beyond the sphere of our judgment, and that fathers and councils are of authority only in so far as they accord with the rule of the Word, we still give to councils and fathers such rank and honour as it is meet for them to hold, under Christ."[94]

The Reformed churches of the seventeenth century continued to stand by classic orthodox Christology. The Westminster Confession of Faith (8.2) echoes the Definition of Chalcedon:

> The Son of God, the second person in the Trinity, being very and eternal God, of one substance and equal with the Father, did, when the

---

On the theological and philosophical issues discussed in the thirteenth century, see Richard Cross, *The Metaphysics of the Incarnation: Thomas Aquinas to Duns Scotus* (Oxford: Oxford University Press, 2002); and Kelly, *Systematic Theology*, 2:219–21.

92. Second Helvetic Confession (chap. 11), in *Reformed Confessions*, 2:827–28, 831; Belgic Confession (Arts. 9–10, 18), in *The Three Forms of Unity*, 25, 34–35.

93. Calvin, *Institutes*, 2.14.1, 4; 2.16.12.

94. John Calvin, *Reply to Sadoleto*, in *Tracts Relating to the Reformation*, trans. Henry Beveridge, 3 vols. (Edinburgh: Calvin Translation Society, 1844–1851), 1:66. See also the Westminster Confession of Faith (31.3–4), in *Reformed Confessions*, 4:270.

fulness of time was come, take upon Him man's nature, with all the essential properties, and common infirmities thereof, yet without sin; being conceived by the power of the Holy Ghost, in the womb of the virgin Mary, of her substance. So that two whole, perfect, and distinct natures, the Godhead and the manhood, were separately joined together in one person, without conversion, composition, or confusion. Which person is very God, and very man, yet one Christ, the only Mediator between God and man.[95]

Like the church fathers before them, Reformed divines treasured the doctrine of the person of Christ because it reveals the Mediator, apart from whom we have no salvation. Only the God-man is the way, the truth, and the life (John 14:6). This is the splendor of the Mediator, that he is both fully God and fully man in one person. John Owen said, "This is that glory whose beams are so illustrious, as that the blind world cannot bear the light and beauty of them."[96] However, though the world scoffs at the incarnation, Christ is the light and life of believers. Owen wrote that the person of Christ "is the highest, the best, the most useful object of our thoughts and affections."[97] As Owen said of Christ's incarnation, "This is the glory of the Christian religion—the basis and foundation that bears the whole superstructure—the root whereon it grows. This is its life and soul."[98] The great works of revelation and salvation could never succeed if they did not come through God the Son incarnate. All the believer's life and joy in God's glory spring from him. It will be our great joy one day to "see the king in his beauty" (Isa. 33:17). Even now, let us bend our thoughts, focus our attention, inflame our affections, and pour out our praises upon the Son, who is the brightness of the Father's glory (Heb. 1:3), for it is in contemplating the divine glory of Christ Jesus that God's image both appears to our sight and is formed in our souls (2 Cor. 3:18; 4:4–6). Owen said, "The faith of this mystery ennobles the mind wherein it is—rendering it spiritual and heavenly, transforming it into the image of God."[99] Therefore, by his Spirit's grace, rest your faith in this Christ in whom the human nature unites to divine nature in one person, and know him in your heart and life as Immanuel.

---

95. *Reformed Confessions*, 4:244.
96. Owen, *The Glory of Christ*, in *Works*, 1:310.
97. Owen, *The Glory of Christ*, in *Works*, 1:314.
98. Owen, *Christologia*, in *Works*, 1:48.
99. Owen, *Christologia*, in *Works*, 1:50.

Sing to the Lord

The Call to Adore God's Incarnate Son

(Note the quotations of the Nicene Creed in the second stanza.)

O come, all ye faithful, joyful and triumphant,
O come ye, O come ye to Bethlehem;
Come and behold him born the King of angels;
O come let us adore him, [three times]
Christ the Lord.

God of God, Light of Light;
Lo, he abhors not the Virgin's womb:
Very God, begotten not created;
O come let us adore him, [three times]
Christ the Lord.

Sing, choirs of angels; sing in exultation,
Sing, all ye citizens of heav'n above;
Glory to God in the highest;
O come let us adore him, [three times]
Christ the Lord.

Yea, Lord we greet thee, born this happy morning:
Jesus, to thee be glory giv'n;
Word of the Father, late in flesh appearing;
O come let us adore him, [three times]
Christ the Lord.

Latin text anonymous, trans. Frederick Oakley
Tune: Adeste Fidelis
Trinity Hymnal—Baptist Edition, No. 151

Questions for Meditation or Discussion

1. Why is it important for us to understand the errors about Christ's person that the church has historically rejected and how the councils have guarded the truth of Christ?
2. What are two ways in which people can misunderstand the Son's relationship to the Father?
3. Briefly define the following errors and state a harmful consequence of each: (1) Ebionism, (2) Docetism, (3) Valentinianism/Cerinthian-

ism, (4) Dynamic Monarchianism, (5) Arianism, (6) Nestorianism, and (7) Monophysitism.

4. What error did some Gnostics and Anabaptists make regarding Christ's human body? Is this important to our faith? Why or why not?

5. What error did Apollinarius teach? Why does it matter?

6. What was the doctrinal core of the Christology of the early councils?

7. What was the major contribution of each of these councils to the doctrine of Christ?

   - The First Council of Nicaea (325)
   - The First Council of Constantinople (381)
   - The First Council of Ephesus (431)
   - The Council of Chalcedon (451)
   - The Second Council of Constantinople (553)
   - The Third Council of Constantinople (680–681)

8. Have you personally encountered doctrinal error regarding the person of Christ? Who was teaching the error? What was he or she teaching? How would you classify it according to the terms defined in this chapter? Why is it important to know and believe the truth on that matter?

Questions for Deeper Reflection

9. How did the Council of Chalcedon affirm the oneness of Christ's two natures without compromising their distinction? How does this formulation avoid the error of Nestorianism on the one hand and Monophysitism on the other?

10. Someone says, "I believe that instead of using the Greek terms of the ancient councils, we should simply affirm what the Bible says about Jesus Christ." How do you respond?

42

Christ's Incarnation, Part 4

Theological Questions and Practical Applications

Paul introduces the doctrine of the incarnate Lord and his works by saying, "Great is the mystery of godliness" (1 Tim. 3:16). On the one hand, the incarnation is a "mystery" that we could not know apart from divine revelation and cannot fully comprehend. On the other hand, it is "the mystery of godliness," revealed truth that produces holy love and reverential fear toward God. Therefore, we must contemplate this truth and assimilate it into our hearts until it shapes us into the image of Christ.

In the course of our study on Christ's incarnation, we have considered the Bible's testimony to the event of the incarnation, the person of the incarnate Lord, and the church's historical assertions of Christ's person against various errors. In this last chapter on this doctrine, we discuss some questions of systematic theology and present several practical applications.

Theological Questions about the Incarnation

We need not fear asking questions about the incarnation, so long as we do so submitting to God's Word, for faith seeks a deeper understanding that it might offer higher praise.

Is Orthodox Christology Incoherent?

In the previous chapter, we discussed the Definition of Chalcedon, which states, "Christ is to be confessed as one and the same, that he is perfect in Godhead and perfect in manhood, very God and very man . . . in two natures, unconfusedly, immutably, indivisibly, inseparably, and that without the distinction of natures being taken away by such union, but rather the peculiar property of each nature being preserved and being united in one person and subsistence."[1] While Chalcedon has become a banner of Christian orthodoxy, it has also become the object of criticism by some who say that its doctrine is irrational and illogical.[2]

Friedrich Schleiermacher rejected the two-nature formula of Chalcedon, saying, "How can the unity of life coexist with the duality of natures, unless one gives way to the other?"[3] For example, one person cannot be simultaneously infinite and finite. Schleiermacher is not the only critic to raise this objection.[4] Schleiermacher further argued, "If Christ has two wills, then the unity of the person is no more than apparent," and "if we try to conserve it by saying that the two wills always will the same thing," then "one or the other will is always simply a superfluous accompaniment of the other."[5] While Schleiermacher's view of Christ is unbiblical,[6] his accusation of a contradiction in Chalcedon must be addressed, for if it is true, then the orthodox definition is unstable and tends to degenerate into either Nestorianism or Monophysitism.[7]

In response to this objection, we answer that there is no logical contradiction involved in orthodox Christology, though the incarnation surpasses our understanding. We must remember that we know God not as God knows himself, but as his created image bearers (Gen. 1:26; Isa. 40:28).[8] If we demand comprehensive understanding of God and his ways,

---

1. Acts of the Council of Chalcedon (AD 451), in *NPNF²*, 14:264–65.
2. On this objection and responses to it, see Wellum, *God the Son Incarnate*, 446–55; and Mark Nestlehutt, "Chalcedonian Christology: Modern Criticism and Contemporary Ecumenism," *Journal of Ecumenical Studies* 35, no. 2 (Spring 1998): 175–96.
3. Schleiermacher, *The Christian Faith*, 96 (1:393).
4. Hick, "Jesus and the World Religions," in *The Myth of God Incarnate*, ed. Hick, 178; and A. N. S. Lane, "Christology beyond Chalcedon," in *Christ the Lord*, ed. Rowdon, 270–72.
5. Schleiermacher, *The Christian Faith*, 96 (2:394).
6. Schleiermacher sought to resolve the problem by saying that Christ was a human being with a unique consciousness of God. Thus, Christ reveals the presence of the divinity that indwells us all. Schleiermacher, *The Christian Faith*, 94 (2:385). See the discussion of Christology "from below" and the biblical approach in chap. 36.
7. Jacqueline Mariña, "Christology and Anthropology in Friedrich Schleiermacher," in *The Cambridge Companion to Friedrich Schleiermacher*, ed. Jacqueline Mariña (Cambridge: Cambridge University Press, 2005), 152–54.
8. On our limited, analogical knowledge of God, see *RST*, 1:68–72, 534–36.

then we deny that he is God, the incomprehensible one.[9] There is a mystery to the incarnation but not irrationality; it is an infinite depth of divine rationality that we cannot plumb, yet can receive by faith.

As to specific points made above, first, orthodox Christianity does not argue that Christ has a "unity of life," as Schleiermacher objected, but a unity of person. The Lord Jesus has an absolute, independent, eternal divine life as the Son of the Father (John 5:26),[10] and a contingent, dependent human life that he laid down on the cross and took up in the resurrection (10:17–18). Chalcedon recognized that both of these kinds of life belong to one person, so that we may say that the Son of God is the divine, unconquerable life *and* that the Son of God died. Stephen Wellum says, "All the actions of Christ are actions of the person. He is the agent of all the actions; speaker of all the words; and subject of all the experiences."[11]

Second, in response to the claim that one person cannot have contradictory attributes, we reply that Trinitarian Christian orthodoxy distinguishes between person and nature. The nature is the "what" and the person is the "who." The divine nature is the one being or essence of God in all his divine attributes.[12] The person of the Son is the unique "someone," the particular, rational, volitional subject in relationships with others.[13] The person of the Son shares in the one divine nature with the Father and the Spirit through all eternity. The triune God created Adam such that he and all who came from him would share a common human nature. In the incarnation, the Son of God took to himself human nature without ceasing to subsist in the divine nature. Consequently, he has two natures with vastly diverse sets of attributes united as one person, but they remain distinct as two natures, divine and human. While the incarnation is a supernatural mystery, it is not a logical contradiction, for it says that Christ is infinite and finite in different respects. This doctrine is necessary to explain the Bible's testimony that Christ both suffered hunger and had the power to turn stones into bread; that he slept deeply and yet silenced a storm with a word (Matt. 4:2–3; 8:23–27).[14] The incarnation is God's message to us, and we must believe it though it staggers the imagination and confounds the intellect with Christ's glory.

---

9. On God's incomprehensibility, see *RST*, 1:641–45.
10. On God's vitality and aseity, see *RST*, 1:617–19, 645–46.
11. Wellum, *God the Son Incarnate*, 310.
12. On the divine nature, see *RST*, 1:520–23.
13. On the meaning of "person," see *RST*, 1:931–33.
14. See the section on the incarnate Lord's unique person in chap. 39.

Third, in reply to Schleiermacher's objection against the doctrine of Christ's two wills, we acknowledge that he touches here on one of the most difficult aspects of the incarnation: Christ's twofold rationality. On the one hand, Christ has perfect knowledge of the Father and gives salvation to whomever he chooses (Matt. 11:27; John 5:20–21), evidencing God's omniscience and sovereign will. On the other hand, Christ admitted his ignorance of the day when he will return and submitted his human will to God's will regarding the cross (Mark 13:32; 14:36). He is both the eternal Word by whom all the universe was made (John 1:1–3) and the man who increased in knowledge as time went on (Luke 2:52). Here again, the Scriptures press us to acknowledge that Christ has two natures, that he is both true God and true man. The one person of the incarnate Son exercises two modes of thinking and willing: the one infinite, eternal, simple, and unchangeable; and the other finite, temporal, complex, and changing. The divine wisdom and will function in a manner beyond our comprehension. Therefore, it should not surprise us that it is likewise incomprehensible how the incarnate Son exists and acts on both a divine level and a human level. However, we deny the claim that this makes Christ's human mind and will "superfluous," for it is crucial for our salvation that the Son relates to his Father and to us in a truly human manner. Our High Priest must do so in order to be our covenantal representative before God and our comforting helper in temptation.

Chalcedon remains the best way to express this revealed mystery. Herman Bavinck said, "Whatever the objections that have been advanced in earlier and later times against the two-natures doctrine, it has the advantage that it does not neglect any of the scriptural data, maintains the name of Christ as the only mediator between God and humankind, and in addition still offers the plainest and clearest understanding of the mystery of the incarnation."[15]

Is Orthodox Christology Ahistorical?

Another theological question arises from the objection that the Christology of the ancient creeds is a philosophical abstraction detached from the historical person Jesus of Nazareth. It is said that the language of person and natures is the imposition of Greek philosophy on the message

---

15. Bavinck, *Reformed Dogmatics*, 3:304.

of Christ.[16] This claim is particularly popular among those who reject the overall worldview of traditional Christianity and seek to replace it with another worldview.

This objection resulted in what Albert Schweitzer (1875–1965) called "the quest of the historical Jesus,"[17] really a series of "quests" from the eighteenth century through today.[18] Employing the methods of historical criticism and presupposing that the Holy Scriptures are not God's Word,[19] scholars who undertook this quest claimed to peel away layers of mythology to find the kernel of historical truth. However, their approach to the Bible proved so subjective that each scholar's quest discovered a "Jesus" whose teachings remarkably resembled the philosophy of the scholar himself.[20] One consistent theme in such quests was the refusal to accept the supernatural Christ, the eternal Son of God become man to redeem sinners. The acids of skeptical unbelief so consumed the knowledge of Christ that Rudolf Bultmann said, "I do indeed think that we can now know almost nothing concerning the life and personality of Jesus."[21]

In the relativistic and pluralistic postmodern perspectives that arose in the latter half of the twentieth century, any claim to know the truth about Jesus is greeted with suspicion, and Christ becomes only a mirror in which we see our own spiritual experience.[22] In this respect, postmodernism has arrived at a destination not so far from its modernist point of departure. As Schweitzer said, "Not the historical Jesus, but the spirit which goes forth from Him and in the spirits of men strives for new influence and rule, is that which overcomes the world."[23]

It is highly ironic that the impulse to discover the historical Jesus encouraged people to disbelieve the New Testament, the most reliable and complete source of historical information about Jesus of Nazareth that we have. Based on the testimony of "eyewitnesses" to Christ, the Gospels

---

16. On the Hellenization view of early Christian orthodoxy, see *RST*, 1:536–39.

17. Albert Schweitzer, *The Quest of the Historical Jesus: A Critical Study of Its Progress from Reimarus to Wrede*, trans. W. Montgomery (London: Adam and Charles Black, 1910).

18. Colin Brown, "Historical Jesus, Quest of," in *Dictionary of Jesus and the Gospels*, ed. Joel B. Green, Scot McKnight, and I. Howard Marshall (Downers Grove, IL: InterVarsity Press, 1992), 326–41.

19. On the subjugation of God's special revelation to human reasoning, see *RST*, 1:287–95.

20. Bavinck, *Reformed Dogmatics*, 3:269; and Brown, "Historical Jesus, Quest of," in *Dictionary of Jesus and the Gospels*, 341.

21. Cited in H. D. McDonald, "The Kerygmatic Christology of Bultmann," in *Christ the Lord*, ed. Rowdon, 317.

22. Wellum, *God the Son Incarnate*, 72–76.

23. Schweitzer, *The Quest of the Historical Jesus*, 399.

give us "certainty" in knowing our Lord and his message (Luke 1:1–4). Rather than construct a Jesus out of our own imaginations according to a philosophy foreign to the apostolic writings, we should give "the more earnest heed" to the message that was "spoken by the Lord, and was confirmed unto us by them that heard him; God also bearing them witness, both with signs and wonders, and with divers miracles" (Heb. 2:1–4). We must receive this testimony with faith.

Although the church fathers expressed their concepts of Christ in the Greek and Latin forms of their day, they did not force an alien Christology upon the New Testament, but instead systematized the biblical revelation concerning God and the incarnate Lord. When the fathers wrestled with how to express who Christ was, they turned again and again to the Holy Scriptures to find answers concerning the person and natures of God's Son. Their answers to heretics were not primarily drawn from metaphysical arguments, but from the interpretation of God's Word.[24]

Furthermore, New Testament Christology did not arise from the idle speculations of Christ's disciples. Rather, Jesus Christ repeatedly pressed his followers to consider his identity, both by his actions—his disciples asked, "What manner of man is this, that even the wind and the sea obey him?"—and by his words—he asked them, "Whom say ye that I am?" (Mark 4:41; 8:29). Orthodox Christology is preeminently historical because it is the church's response to Jesus Christ as people saw him with their eyes, touched him with their hands, and heard him with their ears (1 John 1:1–2).

Do the Divine Energies Deify Christ's Humanity?

Chalcedonian Christology presents to us a Christ of two natures, divine and human, in one person. This formulation raises the question of how the natures relate to each other. In classic orthodoxy, God's immutability implies that the assumption of a human nature cannot change the divine nature.[25] However, theologians have wrestled with how the divine nature affects Christ's human nature. To what extent and in what manner does his humanity share in the divine glory? The answers to such questions are

---

24. The Scriptures themselves speak of a "nature" that is not divine (Gal. 4:8) and of the "Godhead" or "divine nature" (Acts 17:29; Rom. 1:20; Col. 2:9), though not in a technical, philosophical sense. See *RST*, 1:521–22.

25. Aquinas, *Summa Theologica*, Part 3, Q. 2, Art. 1, Answer; and Formula of Concord (Solid Declaration, 8.49), in *The Book of Concord*, 624.

bound up in the *communicatio idiomatum* in Christ, which means the sharing or imparting of distinctive properties, divine and human, in his one person.

The communion of properties is personal—that is, the divine nature with all its properties is united as one person with the human nature with all its properties. Hence, the one Christ Jesus displays divine attributes and performs divine acts, and likewise displays human attributes and performs human acts. Thomas Aquinas, following in the footsteps of Cyril of Alexandria and John of Damascus,[26] pointed out that this personal union shapes how we may speak of our incarnate Lord. We may not say that the divine nature is human nature, for we speak abstractly of two distinct natures. We may say of him that "God is man," for we use God concretely for the second person of the Trinity who took human nature to himself. We may also say, "This man is God," for here "man" refers concretely to the person of the Son according to his human nature, and that person is also God.[27] Furthermore, we may say things of the Son of God that pertain to his human nature, such as "the Son of God died," because "Son of God" refers to the person who assumed to himself a mortal nature in addition to his immortal deity. We may say things of the Son of man that pertain to his divine nature, such as "the Son of man gives life," because the subject of that sentence refers to a specific person who is the Lord and eternal life of his people.[28] However, we may not attribute to one nature of our Lord Jesus what pertains to his other nature, such as saying "the deity can suffer" or "the human nature is omnipotent," for then we would be speaking abstractly of natures and not of the person of the incarnate Son.[29] Finally, we should avoid statements that technically are correct but could be misunderstood as promoting heresy, such as "Christ is a creature," which sounds like Arianism.[30] These principles were accepted by Reformed theologians.[31]

Ancient and medieval theologians also taught the doctrine of deification (*theōsis* or *theiōsis*), not that man becomes God, but that man is brought into union with God so that man participates in the divine

---

26. Cyril of Alexandria, Epistle to Nestorius, in Acts of the Council of Ephesus (AD 431), in *NPNF²*, 14:197–98; and John of Damascus, *An Exact Exposition of the Orthodox Faith*, 3.3–4, in *NPNF²*, 9.2:48–49.

27. Aquinas, *Summa Theologica*, Part 3, Q. 16, Art. 1–2.

28. Aquinas, *Summa Theologica*, Part 3, Q. 16, Art. 4.

29. Aquinas, *Summa Theologica*, Part 3, Q. 16, Art. 5.

30. Aquinas, *Summa Theologica*, Part 3, Q. 16, Art. 8.

31. Wollebius, *Compendium*, 1.16.(4).v–vii (91–92); and Turretin, *Institutes*, 13.6.20–21 (2:316).

energies, especially in the incarnation of Christ. John of Damascus said, "The flesh of the Lord received the riches of the divine energies through the purest union with the Word, that is to say, the union in subsistence, without entailing the loss of any of its natural attributes . . . it manifests divine energy." The deification of Christ's humanity is often compared to iron placed in a fire until it is glowing hot: humanity placed in union with deity is glorified with divine energies.[32] "Energy" here means activity or operation.[33] Hot iron can be rightly used to illustrate the distinctly divine and human operations of the one Christ according to his two natures.[34] However, the illustration becomes problematic when pressed to communicate that Christ's human nature performs works that belong properly to the divine nature. John of Damascus said that this deification caused Christ's human flesh to be "life-giving" and empowered him "to cause at his will the cleansing of the leper."[35]

Another example of a tendency to deify Christ's humanity appears in the objection of John of Damascus, Peter Lombard, and Aquinas to the biblical doctrine of Christ's limited human mind; instead, they taught that he has possessed a supernatural fullness of wisdom from the time of his conception in Mary.[36] Aquinas made it clear that Christ's human fullness was still finite, but Lombard went so far as to say that "the soul of Christ . . . knows all things which God knows," though not "as clearly and sharply as God does."[37] As we argued in a previous chapter, these views undermine Christ's true humanity and contradict the biblical testimony that Christ has a finite human mind that developed over time and that even in his adulthood does not know all things (Luke 2:52; Mark 13:32).[38]

---

32. John of Damascus, *An Exact Exposition of the Orthodox Faith*, 3.17, in NPNF[2], 9.2:65. On deification, see also Aquinas, *Summa Theologica*, Part 3, Q. 2, Art. 1, Obj. 3, and Reply Obj. 3; Q. 16, Art. 3, Answer; Q. 16, Art. 5, Reply Obj. 2. On the Christological analogy of heating iron, see Origen, *De Principiis*, 2.6.6, in ANF, 4:283; and Cyril of Alexandria, *A Commentary upon the Gospel According to S. Luke, Part 2*, trans. R. Payne Smith (Oxford: Oxford University Press, 1859), 667. In ancient and medieval science, fire was considered an element along with earth, water, and air. Thus, hot iron was an example of two elements united in one object.

33. Just as Christ's human "mind also performs its natural energies, thinking and knowing . . . and remembering." John of Damascus, *An Exact Exposition of the Orthodox Faith*, 3.19, in NPNF[2], 9.2:68.

34. John of Damascus, *An Exact Exposition of the Orthodox Faith*, 3.15, in NPNF[2], 9.2:62; and Wollebius, *Compendium*, 1.16.(4).xviii (93–94).

35. John of Damascus, *An Exact Exposition of the Orthodox Faith*, 3.17, in NPNF[2], 9.2:66.

36. John of Damascus, *An Exact Exposition of the Orthodox Faith*, 3.22, in NPNF[2], 9.2:69; Lombard, *The Sentences*, 3.13 (3:50–54); and Aquinas, *Summa Theologica*, Part 3, Q. 7, Art. 12; Q. 15, Art. 3.

37. Lombard, *The Sentences*, 3.14.1.3 (3:55).

38. See the discussion of Christ's limited human mind in chap. 40.

Glory and power radiate from Christ's human nature, for the Lord Jesus is the supreme revelation of God to God's creatures and the supreme ruler of God's universal kingdom.[39] However, the divine revelation and reign that radiate from the glorified man Jesus take place on a finite, creaturely level so that men and angels can receive them. God's infinite glory is unapproachable to creatures (1 Tim. 6:16). Therefore, we should not think of the *communicatio idiomatum* as deifying Christ's humanity. Not only is the term *deification* confusing, but it swerves dangerously near the pagan concept of the oneness of God and man.[40] It may be more precise to speak of the *communio idiomatum* (fellowship of properties) as opposed to the *communicatio idiomatum* (impartation of properties), as John Murray said.[41]

God works in Christ for our sake. Paul prayed that the saints would know "what is the exceeding greatness of his power to us-ward [toward us] who believe, according to the working [*energeia*] of his mighty power, which he wrought [*energeō*] in Christ, when he raised him from the dead, and set him at his own right hand in the heavenly places" (Eph. 1:19–20). The same divine energy by which God exalted Christ from the grave to the highest place also works in believers by their union with the risen Christ (cf. 3:20). Christ's glorification is not deification, but the restoration of redeemed humanity to its intended reign over creation (1:22; citing Ps. 8:6). Similarly, Paul writes of Christ's "working [*energeia*] whereby he is able even to subdue all things unto himself," surely an instance of divine power, but here again this divine power works to conform our lowly bodies to "his glorious body" (Phil. 3:21). Just as God raised Christ from the dead by the Spirit, so God will raise us up by the same Spirit (Rom. 8:11), for Christ is the "last Adam," and his human nature is the pattern for all who are united to him by the Spirit (1 Cor. 15:22, 45, 49). Therefore, the divine operations in Christ's human nature are not categorically unique to his incarnate person, but the fountain of effectual grace for all his people.

Does Christ's Humanity Receive Divine Attributes?

Lutheran theology goes beyond previous formulations of Christ's *communicatio idiomatum*. The Lutheran churches confess that Christ's natures

---

39. 2 Cor. 4:4–6; Col. 1:15; Heb. 1:2–3; Rev. 21:22–23; cf. Christ's transfiguration in Matt. 17:1–8; 2 Pet. 1:16–18.
40. Bavinck, *Reformed Dogmatics*, 3:255; and Vos, *Reformed Dogmatics*, 3:37.
41. Murray, "The Person of Christ," in *Collected Writings*, 2:140.

are not "blended," but each retains its "own essential characteristics."[42] However, Lutheran theologians also say that the incarnation lifted up Christ's humanity into the majesty of God so that in his exaltation "he knows everything, is able to do everything, is present for all his creatures . . . not only as God but also as human creature."[43] In classic Lutheran doctrine, Christ's human nature is not "an infinite essence," but neither are the capacities granted to it finite; instead, some of the divine nature's infinite attributes are granted to the human nature.[44] Though Christ's humanity is not made divine in its essential characteristics, there is a real impartation (*realis communicatio*) of some divine attributes to the human nature above and beyond its human properties.[45] Christ's human nature has received "gifts truly infinite and divine," including the power to give life, the power to execute judgment, omnipotence, omniscience, and omnipresence.[46] Christ's human presence in all places explains how his body and blood are with us in the Lord's Supper, as Martin Luther said, thus guarding his interpretation of Christ's words, "This is my body" (Mark 14:22).[47]

Our initial response is that this is a plain contradiction. Lutheran theology teaches that Christ's human nature is both finite and infinite. While we have a deep appreciation for mystery in the Christian faith, to teach logical contradictions is to promote confusion, not truth.

Lutheran theologians attempt to show the reasonableness of their view of Christ's humanity by appealing to the ancient illustration of fire and iron: when combined, each retains its natural attributes, but iron shines and burns with fiery properties.[48] However, nothing except

---

42. Formula of Concord (Epitome, 8.6), in *The Book of Concord*, 510.
43. Formula of Concord (Epitome, 8.16), in *The Book of Concord*, 511. In Lutheran orthodoxy, the principle that infinite divine majesty is communicated to Christ's humanity is called the *genus majesticum*. Heinrich Schmid, *The Doctrinal Theology of the Evangelical Lutheran Church, Verified from the Original Sources*, trans. Charles A. Hay and Henry E. Jacobs, 2nd ed. (Philadelphia: Lutheran Publication Society, 1889), 321–22, 333–41. For an early twentieth-century statement of this doctrine, see Adolf Hoenecke, *Evangelical Lutheran Dogmatics*, trans. James Langebartels, 4 vols. (Milwaukee, WI: Northwestern Publishing House, 1999–2009), 3:82–99.
44. Formula of Concord (Epitome, 8.27–28, 34–36; Solid Declaration, 8.19, 28–29), in *The Book of Concord*, 512–13, 619, 621; and Martin Chemnitz, *The Two Natures in Christ*, trans. J. A. O. Preus (St. Louis, MO: Concordia, 1971), 241–46.
45. Formula of Concord (Solid Declaration, 8.61–63), in *The Book of Concord*, 627–28; and Chemnitz, *The Two Natures in Christ*, 262
46. Johann Gerhard, *Theological Commonplaces*, 4.209–29, in *On the Person and Office of Christ*, trans. Richard J. Dinda, ed. Benjamin T. G. Mayes (St. Louis, MO: Concordia, 2009), 217–43.
47. Luther, *The Sacrament of the Body and Blood of Christ—Against the Fanatics*, in *LW*, 36:342.
48. Chemnitz, *The Two Natures in Christ*, 263, 289–91; and Formula of Concord (Solid Declaration, 8.66), in *The Book of Concord*, 628–29.

the divine nature can possess or exercise divine attributes.[49] God's attributes are not creaturely attributes increased manifold (like raising the temperature of iron), but a kind of life in a category by itself. In the divine simplicity, God's attributes are not powers he has so much as his very essence.[50] To have one divine attribute is to have all, in which case Christ's human nature must also be eternal and uncreated.[51] If divine attributes could be communicated to a creature, then the Son's divine attributes and acts would not prove that he is God, only that he is in union with the Father—which would shake the very doctrine of the Trinity. The doctrine of God militates against granting God's attributes to human nature.[52]

Therefore, we conclude that the Lutheran doctrine entails a contradiction by ascribing contradictory attributes to the same nature. With Reformed theology, we affirm a "real" fellowship between the divine and the human in Christ—not a real impartation of attributes from the divine nature to the human nature, but a real communion of attributes of both natures "with respect to the person, which consists of two natures really unified and claims the properties of both for itself," as Turretin said.[53] The *communicatio* is in his person, not between his natures.

Lutheran theologians claim that the Word of God teaches this contradiction and, therefore, we must receive it as a paradox of the faith.[54] First, they argue that the Scriptures teach Christ's exaltation to a position of "all power" (Matt. 28:18) in order to "fill all things" (Eph. 4:10). This cannot be said of his divine nature, which already possessed omnipotence, omniscience, omnipresence, and infinite majesty; therefore, it must pertain to his human nature in the state of exaltation.[55] Second, they argue that Christ is granted power to give life and judge people as the "Son of man" (Dan. 7:13–14; John 5:27; 6:27)—that is,

---

49. The only alternative is to abandon the Creator-creature distinction and embrace a worldview in which all things are divine or potentially so. Philip Schaff said that Lutheran orthodoxy, in contrast to Martin Luther himself, carried Christology "to the very verge of pantheism, which obliterates the distinction between the divine and the human." *Christ and Christianity* (New York: Charles Scribner's Sons, 1885), 73.

50. On God's attributes as descriptions of his unique nature, see *RST*, 1:518–23. On God's vitality whereby he is a pure act of life, see *RST*, 1:617–19. On God's simplicity, see *RST*, 1:624–37 (chap. 33). An affirmation of God's simplicity ("one divine essence . . . indivisible") appears in the Augsburg Confession (Art. 1), in *The Book of Concord*, 37.

51. On these points, see Turretin, *Institutes*, 13.8.9, 11 (2:323–24).

52. Vos, *Reformed Dogmatics*, 3:70.

53. Turretin, *Institutes*, 13.8.4 (2:322).

54. Chemnitz, *The Two Natures in Christ*, 288.

55. Formula of Concord (Epitome, 8.16), in *The Book of Concord*, 511.

as a human being. Third, they argue that Christ's "flesh" and "blood" are said in the Scriptures to have the power to cleanse from sin and give eternal life (John 6:48–58; 1 John 1:7). This, they say, "refers not only to the merit achieved on the cross once for all," but to the flesh and blood of his human nature.[56]

In response, first, we acknowledge that Christ's exaltation did involve the glorification of his human nature (Luke 24:26) so that all creatures will one day rightly confess that "Jesus Christ is Lord" (Phil. 2:11). However, Christ's exercise of "all authority in heaven and on earth" (Matt. 28:18 ESV) concerns his mediatorial reign in order to glorify God by giving eternal life to his elect people (John 17:1–2). Christ's work as Mediator engages both his natures according to their distinct properties, human as human and divine as divine.

Christ works to "fill all things" (Eph. 4:10), but he does so by the ministry of the Word (vv. 11–13) as he fills his people with the Holy Spirit (3:16–19; 5:18). Jesus Christ is not omnipresent according to his humanity, for the Scriptures say that we no longer have his physical presence (Matt. 9:15; 26:11; Heb. 8:1, 4) because he has left this world and gone to heaven (Luke 24:51; John 16:28; 17:11) until he returns (Acts 3:21; 1 Thess. 4:16).[57] Though he has gone away from us, he has sent the Holy Spirit so that the whole Christ has communion with his people through the Spirit.[58] The Son himself is present with us (Matt. 18:20; 28:19–20), for with the Father he is the omnipresent God who dwells with his people (John 14:23). Therefore, Christ is present with us in a twofold manner: in the omnipresence of his divine nature as the second person of the Trinity and in the spiritual communion his humanity has with us in the bond of the Holy Spirit.

Second, the title "Son of Man," while indicating that Christ is truly human, does not indicate that Christ's human nature has all the capacities required to give eternal life and judge the world (Dan. 7:13–14; John 5:27; 6:27). Rather, this title refers to the person of Christ, who acts according to his two natures as God and man. If we use titles to attribute certain experiences and actions to a particular nature of Christ, then we must say that the deity suffered and died, for Paul says that wicked people "crucified the Lord of glory" (1 Cor. 2:8). The Bible can use a

---

56. Formula of Concord (Solid Declaration, 8.55, 58, 59), in *The Book of Concord*, 626.
57. Turretin, *Institutes*, 13.8.15 (2:326).
58. John 14:12, 16–19; 16:7, 13–15; Rom. 8:9–10; 1 Cor. 6:15–20; Eph. 3:16–17.

title that highlights one of Christ's natures to refer to the person who bears both.

Third, in the Holy Scriptures "blood" need not refer to blood in the body, such as Christ's exalted flesh, but often functions as a figure of speech (metonymy) for death and its consequences, such as the act and guilt of violent bloodshed.[59] Biblical references to Christ's cleansing and saving "blood" do not refer to his glorified human nature, but the reconciliation and redemption accomplished by Christ's sacrificial death—it is "the blood of his cross" (Col. 1:20).[60] Similarly, Christ's reference to "my flesh, which I will give for the life of the world" (John 6:51) has to do with his voluntary death, not his glorified body.

Therefore, we conclude that the Holy Scriptures do not give us the warrant to embrace the Lutheran doctrine that Christ's human nature is omnipotent, omniscient, and omnipresent by virtue of its union with his divine nature. Rather, the person of Christ is omnipotent, omniscient, and omnipresent in his deity while remaining finite in his humanity. The supernatural majesty, ability, and activity granted to Christ's human nature has always been the grace of the Holy Spirit, both in his state of humiliation and state of exaltation.[61] Lutherans object that "in this way there would be no difference between Christ according to his human nature and other holy people."[62] We answer that Christ's humanity is as ours will be—it must be so in order to save us and bring us to glory (Heb. 2:14–18; 4:15). Christ's uniqueness consists not in the divinization of his humanity, but in his unique person in two distinct natures without confusion. It is a distinctive characteristic of Reformed Christology that Christ's humanity is like ours in every respect except that he never sinned, and so he is truly "our Brother and Head."[63]

It might be objected that the Reformed doctrine disengages Christ's human nature from his divine nature, as if the Son were passive with respect to his humanity because the Spirit alone worked in him. However, the Spirit is never disengaged from the Son. The Father, the Son, and the Holy Spirit always act as one, for the external works of the Trinity are

---

59. Gen. 4:10–11; Matt. 23:30; 27:24; Acts 5:28; Heb. 12:4, 24.
60. Eph. 1:7; 2:13; Col. 1:14; 1 Pet. 1:2, 19; Rev. 5:9; etc.
61. Isa. 11:2; 42:1; 61:1; Matt. 3:16; 12:18, 28; Luke 4:1, 14, 18; John 1:33; 3:34; 6:63; 7:37–39; 16:7–15; 20:22; Acts 2:33–36; 10:38; Rom. 1:4; 8:9; 1 Cor. 15:44–45; Gal. 4:6; Titus 3:5–6; Rev. 5:6.
62. Formula of Concord (Solid Declaration, 8.69), in *The Book of Concord*, 629.
63. Bruce, *The Humiliation of Christ*, 128.

undivided.[64] The Son acts in his divine nature upon his human nature by the Spirit, through his human nature by the Spirit, and beyond his human nature by the Spirit.

Therefore, we affirm what Lutheran theologians called the *extra calvinisticum*, the doctrine that Christ's divine nature acts "beyond" or "outside" (Latin *extra*) the capacities of his human nature,[65] such as his cosmic providential work of "upholding all things by the word of his power" (Heb. 1:3). John Calvin said, "For even if the Word in his immeasurable essence united with the nature of man into one person, we do not imagine that he was confined therein. Here is something marvelous: the Son of God descended from heaven in such a way that, without leaving heaven, he willed to be borne in the virgin's womb, to go about the earth, and to hang upon the cross; yet he continuously filled the world even as he had done from the beginning!"[66] Calvin held this view in common with church fathers such as Athanasius.[67]

Did Christ Set Aside His Divine Attributes?

The Lutheran Formula of Concord says of Christ's human nature, "According to the personal union he always possessed this majesty, and yet dispensed with it in the state of humiliation."[68] This statement suggests that Christ divested himself of his divine attributes in the first stage of his incarnate life, or, more likely, refrained from the use of those attributes. In the early seventeenth century, Lutheran theologians debated the nature of this self-limitation, with some arguing that Christ ceased from the public use of these attributes but continued to exercise them in a hidden manner, whereas most Lutherans believed that Christ did not exercise his omnipotence, omniscience, and omnipresence at all during his humiliation except in isolated miracles, but retained them only as latent, potential abilities until his exaltation.[69]

Furthermore, if Christ's deity to some extent divinized his humanity by the addition of divine attributes, then it might be that Christ's human

---

64. On the one divine activity of the Trinity, see *RST*, 1:893–95.
65. The Heidelberg Catechism (LD 17, Q. 47–48), in *The Three Forms of Unity*, 82–83.
66. Calvin, *Institutes*, 2.13.4.
67. Athanasius, *On the Incarnation of the Word*, sec. 17, in *NPNF²*, 4:45. These words of Athanasius are quoted in chap. 39.
68. Formula of Concord (Epitome, 8.16), in *The Book of Concord*, 511.
69. On the controversy between the Tübingen and Giessen theologians, see Bavinck, *Reformed Dogmatics*, 3:258. See also Joar Haga, *Was There a Lutheran Metaphysic? The Interpretation of Communicatio Idiomatum in Early Modern Lutheranism* (Göttingen: Vandenhoek & Ruprecht, 2012), 213–69.

nature humanized his deity in some respects, at least for a time. Evidence for such an idea has sometimes been found in Paul's statement that Christ "emptied himself" (*ekenōsen*) when he took the "form of a servant" (Phil. 2:7 ESV). In the "kenosis" theory (from the Greek word *kenōsis*, "emptying," "depletion"), Christ emptied himself of his omnipotence, omniscience, and omnipresence to live as a man.

Kenotic doctrine was proposed by Nikolaus von Zinzendorf (1700–1760),[70] was systematically developed by Gottfried Thomasius (1802–1875), and was widely promoted in various forms in the nineteenth century in Germany and then Britain.[71] As P. T. Forsyth (1848–1921) explained this idea, the "omni" attributes are not essential to the deity; only Christ's love is essential, so he was able to engage in voluntary self-limitation. Hence, it may be best not to speak so much of natures and attributes as modes of being. God the Son laid aside his divine mode of being, voluntarily contracting his divinity into mere potential, in order to live under the limitations of a human mode of being. In Christ's exaltation, his divinity expanded again into the exercise of all its powers.[72] Kenotic doctrine has some proponents today.[73]

Although offered as a solution to difficulties in Christology, this doctrine has serious problems. Against kenotic theories, we raise the following objections.[74]

First, kenotic theories misinterpret Philippians 2:7, which says that the Son "emptied himself, by taking the form of a servant, being born in the likeness of men" (ESV). The verb translated as "emptied" (*kenoō*) indicates that Christ embraced our human weakness and futility.[75] The manner in which he "emptied himself" is explained by the modifying participle "taking" (*labōn*), namely, "taking the form of a servant." God the Son, who eternally exists in the "form of God," assumed to himself the human

---

70. Bavinck, *Reformed Dogmatics*, 3:303. The influence of Nikolaus Zinzendorf appears in Charles Wesley's hymn "And Can It Be That I Should Gain," which says that Christ "emptied himself of all but love."

71. Thomas R. Thompson, "Nineteenth-Century Kenotic Christology: The Waxing, Waning, and Weighing of a Quest for a Coherent Orthodoxy," in *Exploring Kenotic Christology: The Self-Emptying of God*, ed. C. Stephen Evans (Oxford: Oxford University Press, 2006), 74–95. See also Bruce, *The Humiliation of Christ*, 136–63; and Wellum, *God the Son Incarnate*, 356–64.

72. P. T. Forsyth, *The Person and Place of Jesus Christ* (1909; repr., Grand Rapids, MI: Eerdmans, 1964), 307–11.

73. Wellum, *God the Son Incarnate*, 374–93. We noted William Lane Craig and J. P. Moreland's kenotic Apollinarianism in the previous chapter (see the eleventh error).

74. See Nichols, *Lectures in Systematic Theology*, 3:540–42, 548–59.

75. On *kenoō* as "become weak or futile," see Jer. 14:2; 15:9 LXX; Rom. 4:14; 1 Cor. 1:17; 9:15; 2 Cor. 9:3.

"form of a servant." The incarnation was not by subtraction of divine attributes, but by the addition of a human nature.

Second, kenotic theories deny that Christ was truly God during his humiliation. Francis Hall (1857–1932) said, "Was he God or not? If he possessed the fulness of the Godhead—i.e. all divine attributes—he was God. But, if he was lacking in any of these attributes, he certainly was not God."[76] However, Christ claimed to possess the full divine nature even in his state of humiliation. For instance, he had divine sovereignty: "I lay down my life, that I might take it again. No man taketh it from me, but I lay it down of myself. I have power to lay it down, and I have power to take it again" (John 10:17–18). Similarly, he had divine knowledge: "No man knoweth the Son, but the Father; neither knoweth any man the Father, save the Son" (Matt. 11:27).

Third, kenotic theories deny that Christ performed the works of God during his state of humiliation. However, the Scriptures indicate that the Son continually exercised divine omnipotence and omniscience in the providential work of upholding the universe (Col. 1:16; Heb. 1:3). Furthermore, Christ's earthly ministry involved miracles that not only pointed to the working of his Father (John 14:10) and his Spirit (Matt. 12:28), but caused people to reflect upon the Son's divine nature (8:27; 14:33).[77]

Fourth, kenotic theories substantially alter the orthodox doctrine of God.[78] The idea that God can engage in self-limitation compromises his essential omnipotence, omniscience, and omnipresence; reduces his essence to will or love; and destroys his immutability and simplicity. In a word, kenotic theories reduce the infinite God to the level of a creature who may or may not have divine powers. But the Lord says, "Hast thou not known? Hast thou not heard, that the everlasting God, the LORD, the Creator of the ends of the earth, fainteth not, neither is weary? There is no searching of his understanding" (Isa. 40:28).

Fifth, kenotic theories engage in rationalistic speculation instead of respecting the mystery of biblical truth. Admittedly, there is an incomprehensible glory to Christ's incarnation. Chalcedonian Christology fences the mystery by guarding us from various errors, but it cannot plumb the depths of the God-man. The kenotic approach to the incarnation

76. Francis J. Hall, *The Kenotic Theory: Considered with Particular Reference to Its Anglican Forms and Arguments* (New York: Longmans, Green, and Co., 1898), 221–22.
77. Wellum, *God the Son Incarnate*, 406–7.
78. Wellum, *God the Son Incarnate*, 396–99.

attempts to solve this problem by human reasoning, but it can do so only by compromising the biblical doctrines of God and Christ. The Old Testament, Gospels, and Epistles all testify to the incarnate Son as fully God in all the divine attributes and fully man in the essential attributes of human nature.

Rather than postulating a divine self-limitation or "emptying" (*kenōsis*), it is more biblical to speak of a divine self-concealment or "hiddenness" (*krypsis*) during Christ's humiliation. Calvin said that Christ "did not renounce his divinity, but he kept it concealed for a time."[79] The Word became flesh and was present with us, and his glory was manifest to those who had the faith to see it, but most people, even in Israel, did not know him or receive him (John 1:10–11, 14). Christ is the wisdom and power of God, but he came in apparent weakness and foolishness, especially when he died on the cross (1 Cor. 1:22–25). The gospel of Christ incarnate and crucified communicates "a secret and hidden wisdom of God" (2:7 ESV)—"hidden" not just in God's eternal counsels, but in Christ, so that wicked men unwittingly "crucified the Lord of glory" (v. 8). Hence, Isaiah prophesied, "To whom is the arm of the LORD revealed? . . . He is despised and rejected of men; a man of sorrows" (Isa. 53:1, 3). Though Christ is a mighty weapon for God's glory, he came to us as one hidden (49:2). William Perkins said that Christ's "Godhead was abased, not as is considered in itself, for so it admits no alteration or change, but in respect of the flesh or manhood assumed, under the which, as under a veil, the Godhead lay hid from the first moment of the incarnation to the time of His resurrection, without any great manifestation of His power and majesty therein."[80]

Conclusion to Theological Questions

When we consider the tendency to deify Christ's humanity by divine energies or attributes, or to humanize God by divine kenosis, we realize how precious it is to have a Mediator who is truly God and truly man in two distinct natures. B. B. Warfield said, "The glory of the Incarnation is that it presents to our adoring gaze, not a humanized God or a deified man, but a true God-man—one who is all that God is and at the same time all that man is: on whose almighty arm we can rest, and to whose human

---

79. Calvin, *Commentaries*, on Phil. 2:7, cited in Letham, *Systematic Theology*, 538n109.
80. Perkins, *An Exposition of the Symbol*, in *Works*, 5:137.

sympathy we can appeal. We cannot afford to lose either the God in the man or the man in the God; our hearts cry out for the complete God-man whom the Scriptures offer us."[81]

Practical Applications of the Incarnation

The incarnation of Christ is an unrepeatable event, just as surely as the incarnate Lord is a unique person. We cannot become incarnate, and the Christian life and ministry are not "incarnational," as if we replicate or approximate what Christ did by entering into the life and cultures of other people.[82] That is not to deny the value of understanding the perspective of other individuals and peoples, but to avoid the confusion introduced by referring to our mission as a kind of incarnation.

However, the incarnation of God the Son as Jesus of Nazareth has great practical implications for life. We list several here, each of which is worthy of more meditation and pursuit by God's grace.

1. *Seek after Christ through the gospel.* Christ became incarnate in order to seek after sinners; therefore, we, like Zacchaeus, should seek after him (Luke 19:3, 10). Perkins said, "He came near unto us by taking our nature upon Him, that we again, whatsoever we are, might come near unto Him."[83] Thomas Watson said, "So look unto him, as to believe in him, that so Christ may not only be united to our nature, but to our persons."[84] We do this by attending to the gospel.

2. *Receive Christ as the only Mediator.* Recognizing that the Lord Jesus is God the Son incarnate, the God-man, helps us to appreciate why he said, "I am the way, the truth, and the life: no man cometh unto the Father, but by me" (John 14:6). Thomas Goodwin urged, "Is Christ every way so fit a Saviour? Then choose him, and rest in him alone. It is necessary that a Saviour you should have, for otherwise you perish. And it is as necessary that you should have Jesus Christ, or else you must have none. For there is, there can be, no other."[85]

---

81. Warfield, *Selected Shorter Writings*, 1:166.

82. See John Starke, "The Incarnation Is about a Person, Not a Mission," The Gospel Coalition, May 16, 2011, https://www.thegospelcoalition.org/article/the-incarnation-is-about-a-person-not-a-mission/; and J. Todd Billings, "The Problem with 'Incarnational Ministry," *Christianity Today* (July/August 2012): 58–63, also available at http://jtoddbillings.com/2012/12/the-problem-with-incarnational-ministry/.

83. Perkins, *An Exposition of the Symbol*, in *Works*, 5:122.

84. Watson, *A Body of Divinity*, 165.

85. Goodwin, *Of Christ the Mediator*, in *Works*, 5:63. We have modernized capitalization and punctuation.

3. *Magnify God's love for giving us his Son.* The incarnate Son is the gift of the Father: "For God so loved the world, that he gave his only begotten Son, that whosoever believeth in him should not perish, but have everlasting life" (John 3:16). John Boys (1571–1625) said that God's works of creation and providence reveal "his greatness and goodness," but his work of redemption is "a work of greater might and mercy than all the rest: for in the creation he made man like himself; but in the redemption he made himself like man."[86] Goodwin said, "For him to be made a creature is more than for us to become nothing, or for an angel to become a worm."[87] Furthermore, trust that the God who gave his Son will rule your daily life with the same love. Goodwin said, "Hence learn and be assured, that that love which thus fitted thee with a Saviour, will much more fit thee with all things thou hast need of. Thou shalt have the fittest condition, the fittest calling, the fittest yoke-fellow, the fittest estate, 'food convenient,' as Agar speaks [Prov. 30:8]."[88]

4. *Marvel at Christ as the supernatural Savior.* Christ not only worked miracles; he is a living miracle who provokes men's wonder (Matt. 8:27; 9:8, 33). In Jesus, heaven has come to earth and the divine glory dwells with mankind. Marvel at your salvation in Christ that required the incarnation. Samuel Rutherford said, "When I look to my guiltiness, I see that my salvation is one of our Saviour's greatest miracles, either in heaven or earth."[89] Yet every miracle of personal salvation rests upon the person of Christ, who is the miracle of miracles. John Owen said that Christ's incarnation "is above all miracles, nor can be designed by that name. A mystery it is, so far above the order of all creating or providential operations, that it wholly transcends the sphere of them that are most miraculous."[90]

5. *Love Christ as your Kinsman-Redeemer.* Perkins said, "Job to comfort himself in his afflictions says, 'I know that my redeemer liveth' [Job 19:25]. Now the word which he uses to signify his Redeemer by is very emphatical, for it signifies a kinsman nearly allied onto him of his own flesh that will restore him to life."[91] The Hebrew word "redeemer" (*goel*), as Herman Witsius pointed out, referred to a person's kinsman or close

---

86. John Boys, *An Exposition of the Several Offices Adapted for Various Occasions of Public Worship* (New York: Stanford and Swords, 1851), 46.
87. Goodwin, *Of Christ the Mediator*, in *Works*, 5:65.
88. Goodwin, *Of Christ the Mediator*, in *Works*, 5:62.
89. Rutherford, Letter 170, *Letters of Samuel Rutherford*, 320.
90. Owen, *Christologia*, in *Works*, 1:45–46.
91. Perkins, *An Exposition of the Symbol*, in *Works*, 5:123.

relative that bore responsibility to redeem lost property, purchase freedom from slavery or captivity, avenge murder, and marry a widow to raise up offspring.[92] The wonder of the incarnation is that God the Son became our kinsman to redeem us. He restored our lost inheritance, rescued us from captivity and bondage, took vengeance on the murderer of our souls, and joined himself to us in a covenant of spiritual marriage.[93] When we consider the depth to which Christ came in order to redeem us and the heights to which he exalts us, we should exclaim with Witsius, "O compassion! O almost incredible vehemence of love! O how far doth this love exceed the tenderness of a brother's or a father's affection! With what emotions of gratitude wilt thou be acknowledged! With what return of love wilt thou be recompensed! What heart is so cold and frozen as not to be dissolved, warmed, and kindled into flames, by the ardours of so boundless a love!"[94]

6. *Relate to Christ as your elder brother.* With respect to those whom he saves, Christ "is not ashamed to call them brethren" (Heb. 2:11; cf. John 20:17). Wilhelmus à Brakel wrote, "Since He has become our brother, we may and must have fellowship with Him as such. . . . This yields boldness and familiarity to bring all our needs before Him, who, being man Himself, understands man's frame of mind when he suffers pain and is troubled in both soul and body. He can and does have compassion with them."[95]

7. *Follow Christ as the pattern, root, and motive of holiness.* God has destined his saints "to be conformed to the image of his Son, that he might be the firstborn among many brethren" (Rom. 8:29). Thus, imitation of Christ and relationship with Christ are at the center of our spiritual growth. Goodwin said, "In that he took upon himself such a human nature as should be every way fit for the business of mediation that he was to perform for us, let us endeavor to fit ourselves all that we can, for communion and fellowship with him." We fit ourselves for communion with Christ by pursuing holiness by his grace. Goodwin added, "As he took our nature, let us take his; labour we [let us labor] to be changed into his image, being made partakers of the divine nature [2 Pet. 1:4]. . . . In his power and prerogative indeed we cannot; they are as incommunicable to us, as our

---

92. Witsius, *Sacred Dissertations on the Apostles' Creed*, 14.34 (2:25). See Lev. 25:25–26, 47–49; Num. 35:12, 19, 21, 24–25, 27; Deut. 19:6, 12; Ruth 2:20; 3:9, 12–13; 4:1–8, 14; cf. Deut. 25:5. The term is used of the Lord's relationship to his people: Gen. 48:16; Job 19:25; Isa. 41:14; 43:14; 44:6; etc.

93. Witsius, *Sacred Dissertations on the Apostles' Creed*, 14.37 (2:27).

94. Witsius, *Sacred Dissertations on the Apostles' Creed*, 14.44 (2:34).

95. Brakel, *The Christian's Reasonable Service*, 1:516.

sin was to him; but in graces and in holiness we may."[96] Indeed, likeness to Christ in holiness is an essential aspect of our salvation. Witsius said,

> If we wish to have a solid foundation for our joy in the incarnation of Christ, it is necessary that the same person who was once fashioned in the womb of the Virgin after the likeness of a man, be formed also in our hearts. . . . Since he was conceived by the power of the Holy Ghost, it is not for us to pretend to be his brethren, unless we give evidence by a holy course of life, that we are renewed by the same Spirit after the image of God.[97]

8. *Imitate Christ in humility toward others.* We must embrace "lowliness of mind" and a servant mindset toward other people because we embrace the gospel of Christ who "took upon him the form of a servant" (Phil. 2:3–7). Perkins said, "Christ's incarnation must be a pattern unto us of a most wonderful and strange humility. . . . And that shall we do, when we begin to cast off that high opinion which every man by nature conceives of himself and become vile and base in our own eyes."[98] He added, "He was content to lie in the manger, that we might rest in heaven. This serves to teach us to be content to bear any mean [lowly] condition that the Lord shall send upon us; for this is the very estate of the Son of God Himself."[99] Greg Nichols says, "If we have his mentality, we too will act unselfishly with submissiveness to God's will. . . . We will consider what is best for all God's people, not only what is best for ourselves. We will not look down on other Christians with condescending contempt."[100]

9. *Become like Christ by giving generously to others.* Paul urges Christians to give liberally to meet the needs of other people, especially the saints, saying, "For ye know the grace of our Lord Jesus Christ, that, though he was rich, yet for your sakes he became poor, that ye through his poverty might be rich" (2 Cor. 8:9). Charles Octavius Boothe wrote, "God forbids empty-handed service. We can see why. First, lip service costs nothing, and hence it does not prove the heart. Second, it does nothing to deny and crucify self. The giving of our wealth, if it be true giving, is the

---

96. Goodwin, *Of Christ the Mediator*, in *Works*, 5:66–67.
97. Witsius, *Sacred Dissertations on the Apostles' Creed*, 14.45 (2:34).
98. Perkins, *An Exposition of the Symbol*, in *Works*, 5:122.
99. Perkins, *An Exposition of the Symbol*, in *Works*, 5:132.
100. Nichols, *Lectures in Systematic Theology*, 3:550.

giving of ourselves. . . . It should never be forgotten that we are not our own—we are the Lord's. . . . He has redeemed us from death and hell, having given himself a ransom for us."[101]

10. *Defend the doctrine of Christ against errors.* Those who deny the incarnation do not have God (2 John 7–9). Therefore, we must stand for the truth of the incarnation, and Christian pastors and teachers must defend it against heresy. Olevianus said that Christ's two natures in one person are the foundation and life of the covenant of grace. He warned, "That is why Satan has always tried, and is still trying, with his devices, either to deny or at least to weaken one of the natures in the Mediator of the covenant. When the root of a tree is damaged, the branches wither and there can be no hope for fruit."[102]

11. *Rejoice in Christ as the pioneer of our future glory.* The incarnation is great cause to rejoice (Luke 2:10–11). Brakel said, "If our soul should rejoice in anything, it ought to rejoice in this great and wondrous work of God."[103] One reason to rejoice is that Christ has unspeakably exalted our human nature by taking it unto himself so that his death and glorification are "bringing many sons unto glory" (Heb. 2:6–10). Goodwin said, "We should consider our privilege by having our nature so advanced. . . . What a prerogative is it that our nature should be in him made higher in court than any queen can be in the court of any king; and thus it is, seeing he is one in person with God, not in conjugal relations only, and the rest of his brethren are advanced to be his queen, and the angels to be but his and her guard and servants."[104]

12. *Glorify the incarnate Son.* The citizens of heaven worship and adore Christ as the conquering Lion of Judah and the slain Lamb of God (Rev. 5:5–10). We should, too, for he is worthy. Witsius said, "Hosanna, blessed Jesus, thou true and eternal God, thou true and holy man! In the unity of thy person, we recognize both natures, each possessing its own distinct properties. Thee we acknowledge. Thee we worship. From thy hand alone we expect salvation. May the whole world of thine elect unite in knowing, acknowledging, and adoring thee, and thus be saved through thy blessed name! Amen."[105]

---

101. Boothe, *Plain Theology for Plain People*, 90.
102. Olevianus, *An Exposition of the Apostles' Creed*, 68.
103. Brakel, *The Christian's Reasonable Service*, 1:514.
104. Goodwin, *Of Christ the Mediator*, in *Works*, 5:66.
105. Witsius, *Sacred Dissertations on the Apostles' Creed*, 14.46 (2:35).

Sing to the Lord

The Prayerful Resolve of the Incarnate Son (cf. Heb. 10:5–7)

The off'ring on the altar burned
Gives no delight to Thee;
The hearing ear, the willing heart,
Thou givest unto me.

Then, O my God, I come, I come,
Thy purpose to fulfill;
Thy law is written in my heart,
'Tis joy to do Thy will.

Before Thy people I will now
Thy righteousness proclaim;
Thou knowest, Lord, I will not cease
To praise Thy holy Name.

I never have within my heart
Thy faithfulness concealed,
But Thy salvation and Thy truth
To men I have revealed.

Psalm 40:6–10
Tune: Belmont
The Psalter, No. 109

Questions for Meditation or Discussion

1. How do some theologians argue that the classic doctrine of Christ is self-contradictory?
2. What answer can be given to the charge of contradiction?
3. What is the "quest of the historical Jesus"? What assumptions have driven it?
4. Why is classic orthodoxy firmly rooted in history in its doctrine of Christ?
5. How have some theological traditions deified Christ's humanity?
6. What does the Bible reveal about God's "energies" at work in Christ's human nature?
7. What is the Lutheran teaching regarding the attributes of Christ's human nature?

8. Why should we reject the Lutheran view of Christ's humanity?
9. What is the kenosis view of Christ's incarnation and humiliation?
10. What objections show the falsehood of the kenotic theories?
11. Of the applications listed for the doctrine of the incarnation, select two or three that are especially relevant to you. How can you implement each of these practically?

Questions for Deeper Reflection

12. A friend says to you, "If Christ's human nature does not share in the divine attributes and acts, then there is nothing unique about Jesus. He is just a man like us." How do you respond?
13. You have been invited to speak for thirty minutes to the senior class of a Christian high school on the topic "What is the classic doctrine of the incarnation, and why does it matter to our lives today?" Prepare a detailed outline of what you intend to say.

Section C

The Doctrine of the Work of Christ

43

The Threefold Office of the One Mediator

When Saul of Tarsus traveled to Damascus to arrest Christians, Jesus Christ arrested Saul. Cast down and blinded by Christ's glory, Saul finally saw the truth that the eyes of his heart had formerly been unable to see. After receiving healing and baptism through Ananias, Saul wasted no time in taking up his new calling. To everyone's astonishment, immediately "he preached Christ in the synagogues, that he is the Son of God" (Acts 9:20). Luke recorded the content of a later sermon by Saul, also called Paul, in which he preached Jesus Christ as the promised King from the line of David, the Son of God whose sandals we are not worthy to untie, the Savior who died on the cross, was raised from the dead, and now gives forgiveness of sins and justification to all who believe in him (13:16–41).

The person and work of Christ are the core of the gospel (1 Cor. 2:2). Just as the person of the incarnate Lord is the foundation of our salvation, so his work is the accomplishment and application of our salvation. In the counsel of peace, God entrusted into Christ's hands the entire work of redemption. The kingdom of God rests entirely "upon his shoulder" (Isa. 9:6).

Therefore, having studied the wondrous doctrine of Christ's person, we enter now into the study of his saving work. We must do so with the doctrine of the incarnation always in the background, for only the God-man could do this great work. Christ's person and work are inseparable. John Calvin said, "Now it was of the greatest importance for us that he who was to be our Mediator be both true God and true man."[1] Robert Letham says, "He became incarnate for a particular task. He completed his task successfully because of who he is."[2]

Inadequate Approaches to Christ's Work

How shall we approach this glorious topic? There is a richness to Christ's work that defies comprehension and makes categorization difficult. We face the danger of focusing on one aspect of Christ's mission to such a degree that we neglect others. For example, consider some common images of Christ, each of which contains part of the truth, but when granted a monopoly over this doctrine, results in a distorted and imbalanced approach.

Some people see Christ primarily as a *wise teacher*. Justin Martyr said that Christ is "our Teacher" sent from the Father,[3] who delivers the only philosophy that is "safe and profitable," for his words are powerful to inspire fear in those straying from righteousness and comfort for those who diligently obey.[4] Adolf Harnack went so far as to say that Jesus is merely a man, albeit a man who "knows God in a way in which no one ever knew Him before,"[5] and so Christ "desired no other belief in his person and no other attachment to it than is contained in the keeping of his commandments."[6] Certainly Christ gave much time to teaching and requires obedience to his commandments (Matt. 7:24; 28:19; John 14:15). However, he calls us to view him not merely as our guide to life, but as our life (11:25; 14:6).

Others have seen Jesus Christ as a *terrifying king*. In the apses of ancient and medieval houses of worship, Christ is portrayed in "the majesty of the Lord" (*maiestas domini*)—often with one hand raised and another holding a book, flanked by holy angels—based on the visions of Isaiah, Ezekiel, and John.[7] Such a concept of the Lord left young Martin Luther "stupefied and terror-stricken," asking himself, "Who am I, that I should lift up mine eyes or raise my hands to the divine Majesty?"[8] Today, some

---

1. Calvin, *Institutes*, 2.12.1.
2. Robert Letham, *The Work of Christ*, Contours of Christian Theology (Downers Grove, IL: InterVarsity Press, 1993), 29.
3. Justin Martyr, *First Apology*, chaps. 5–6, 12–17, 21, in *ANF*, 1:164, 166–68, 170.
4. Justin Martyr, *Dialogue with Trypho*, chap. 8, in *ANF*, 1:198.
5. Harnack, *What Is Christianity?*, 138.
6. Harnack, *What Is Christianity?*, 135.
7. James Snyder, "Meaning of the 'Maiestas Domini' in Hosios David," *Byzantion* 37 (1967): 143–52.
8. Cited in Roland Bainton, *Here I Stand: A Life of Martin Luther* (New York: Abingdon, 1950), 41.

evangelical circles so emphasize the last days that they inspire people to fear the judgments Christ will unleash upon the world. Given the casual approach that many take to Jesus Christ today, we do well to remember that King Jesus will judge all mankind (Matt. 25:31–46). However, he is also the tender evangelist who calls the weary and burdened to come to him and find rest, for he is meek and humble (11:28–30).

On the other end of the spectrum is the view of Christ as a *crucified sacrifice*. This image appears artistically in the crucifix, a sculpture portraying Jesus suffering upon the cross.[9] In popular evangelical Christianity today, attention on Christ's saving work centers almost exclusively on his death as an atoning sacrifice for our sins. Christ's death is most surely central to the gospel, but so is his resurrection (1 Cor. 15:3–5). He is not merely the crucified Savior, but also the living Lord at work in the world today (Acts 5:30–31).

Among those who give attention to Christ's present activity, he may be considered to be a *spiritual power*. That is, Christ is primarily viewed according to his ethical influence to make us loving and holy, and his equipping to make us effective in ministry. "Christ in you" becomes the focal point of a higher Christian life, with the promise of victory over sin, happiness, and continual spiritual success.[10] Christ does indeed dwell in his people (Col. 1:27), communicating spiritual life to them (John 14:18–19; Gal. 2:20). However, his kingdom has not yet come in glory and he has not yet brought his people from humiliation to exaltation (1 Cor. 4:8–13). Christians must still strive against sin (1 Cor. 9:24–27), experience great disappointment and sorrow, and struggle against despair in this sin-cursed world (2 Cor. 1:8–9; 4:8–12).

In an alternative view, Christ is portrayed as a *mystical lover*. Such a view might stem from Neoplatonic influences on medieval Christian mysticism, which saw God as the unknowable abyss of goodness and Christ as the spiritual lover who draws the soul into marriage with himself by visions.[11] Or

---

9. All images of Christ are rejected by historic Reformed Christianity, but crucifixes are used in Roman Catholicism and Lutheranism. See "Frequently Asked Questions—Worship & Congregational Life," The Lutheran Church, Missouri Synod, https://www.lcms.org/about/beliefs/faqs/worship-and-congregational-life#crucifixes.

10. Robert Pearsall Smith, *"Walk in the Light." Words of Counsel to Those Who Have Entered into "the Rest of Faith"* (London: Morgan and Scott, n.d.), 146–49. On the higher life movement, see the chapter on controversies regarding sanctification in *RST*, vol. 3 (forthcoming). See also Henry A. Boardman, *The "Higher Life" Doctrine of Sanctification, Tried by the Word of God* (Philadelphia: Presbyterian Board of Publication, 1877), 81–97.

11. *Theologia Germanica*, chap. 53, in *Late Medieval Mysticism*, ed. Ray C. Petry, The Library of Christian Classics 13 (Philadelphia: Westminster, 1957), 347–49; and Teresa of Avila, *The Inte-*

one might encounter this approach to the work of Christ in traditions that overemphasize spiritual experience. Here, too, there is an element of truth, for Christ is not merely a historical or heavenly figure detached from our lives, but a person with whom we have communion (1 John 1:3) according to the mighty working of God's Spirit to manifest his love (Eph. 3:16–19). However, this truth does not encourage a mysticism of essential union with God or ecstatic visions; rather, it grounds spiritual experience upon faith in Christ's objective work (Rom. 5:5–8).

There is also the view of Christ as the *sympathetic sufferer*. Such a view of Christ could be built upon finite theism, in which a personal deity lacks the power to rule over all things but offers moral guidance and emotional support to people.[12] Or it might grow out of panentheism, in which God is the spirit of all the world. Such a Christ is not able to save people from evil, but helps them to cope with it by joining in their pain (what Jürgen Moltmann calls "the *pathos* of God"[13]) and guiding them in creative, responsive, and sympathetic love.[14] It is true that Christ suffered and remains profoundly sympathetic for all who draw near to God through him (Heb. 2:18; 4:15). His comforts overflow in believers' lives so that they can comfort others (2 Cor. 1:3–5). However, Christ is not a victim, but the sovereign Victor (Eph. 1:20–21).

According to liberation theology, Christ is a *revolutionary liberator*. Christ's message, we are told, was that God preferentially identifies with the poor and marginalized because the rich oppress them. Jesus brings a kingdom of justice, love, and peace that requires the transformation of society.[15] Truly, Christ came to bring a kingdom of righteousness and peace (Isa. 9:7), and the knowledge of God motivates men to bring justice to the oppressed (Jer. 22:16). However, the Lord Jesus brought

---

rior Castle, 7.2, in *The Collected Works of St. Teresa of Avila*, trans. Kieran Kavanaugh and Otilio Rodriguez (Washington, DC: ICS Publications, 1980), 2:432–37. See Evelyn Underhill, *Mysticism: A Study in the Nature and Development of Man's Spiritual Consciousness*, 12th ed. (London: Methuen & Co., 1930), 344.

12. On finite theism and a god of sympathy, see *RST*, 1:598–99.

13. Jürgen Moltmann, *The Crucified God: The Cross of Christ as the Foundation and Criticism of Christian Theology* (New York: Harper & Row, 1974), 270.

14. John B. Cobb Jr. and David Ray Griffin, *Process Theology: An Introductory Exposition* (Philadelphia: Westminster, 1976), 96–106. As Cobb and Griffin explain process theology, "Christ" refers not so much to the man Jesus as to the divine energy or force active throughout the world.

15. Emilio A. Núñez C., *Liberation Theology*, trans. Paul E. Sywulka (Chicago: Moody, 1985), 228. See Leonardo Boff, *Jesus Christ Liberator: A Critical Christology for Our Time*, trans. Patrick Hughes (Maryknoll, NY: Orbis, 1978); and Jon Sobrino, *Jesus the Liberator: A Historical-Theological Reading of Jesus of Nazareth*, trans. Paul Burns and Francis McDonagh (Maryknoll, NY: Orbis, 1993).

a kingdom far more lasting than earthly wealth and political structures can build—a kingdom of glory that will never be shaken (Heb.
12:22–24, 28).

The Covenantal Office of the One Mediator

How are we to bring together the various facets of Christ's work in a biblically balanced manner? Reformed orthodoxy offers a solution in a relatively simple form: there is *one Mediator* who performs his incarnate work
in *two states* according to his *threefold office*. The Westminster Larger
Catechism (Q. 36, 42) says, "The only Mediator of the covenant of grace
is the Lord Jesus Christ. . . . Our Mediator was called Christ, because he
was anointed . . . to execute the offices of prophet, priest, and king of his
church, in the estate both of his humiliation and exaltation."[16] In the next
chapter, we will study Christ's two states of humiliation and exaltation.
Here, we consider Christ's office as one Mediator in his threefold function
to reveal God to man, reconcile God and man in a right relationship, and
reign over an everlasting kingdom.

Reformed theology finds its starting point regarding the saving work of
our Lord Jesus in his title "Christ." The Greek word translated as "Christ"
(*christos*) means "anointed" (*chriō*), with the idea of appointment and empowerment to some authorized function as God's servant (Acts 4:26–27;
10:36, 38, 42).[17] As we discussed in an earlier chapter, the biblical term
"Christ," or "Anointed One," designates Jesus as the divinely authorized,
Spirit-anointed Mediator of God's covenant of grace—the Prophet, Priest,
and King upon whom our salvation hangs.[18] Thus, "Christ" is a title of
divinely appointed office.

The act of anointing involves elements of selection, authorization, and
equipping (1 Sam. 16:1–13). Christ's anointing involved his appointment
by the Father to the office of the Mediator in eternity (1 Pet. 1:20); his specific calling to its required labors (Isa. 42:6; 49:1; Heb. 5:4, 5, 10); and his

---

16. *Reformed Confessions*, 4:306–7.

17. The Greek term *pais*, translated as "son" (Acts 3:13, 26) or "child" (4:27, 30), has the
primary meaning of "young child," but a secondary meaning of "servant" (Luke 1:54, 69; 7:7;
12:45; 15:26; John 4:51), just as in Hebrew a man's servants are called "his young men" (Gen.
22:3; Ruth 2:15; 2 Sam. 4:12). The background for the word *pais* as used of Jesus in Acts 4:27
is most likely David, the "servant" (*pais*) of God (v. 25). See also the references to the messianic
"Servant" (*pais*) of the Lord (Isa. 42:1; 49:6; 52:13 LXX; Matt. 12:18). Therefore, the use of
pais in Acts 3–4 indicates Christ's office as God's "Servant," not his eternal sonship in relation
to the Father.

18. See the discussion of the official name "Christ" in chap. 37.

empowerment by the Holy Spirit to perform his mission as the incarnate Word (Isa. 42:1; Luke 1:35; 4:18; John 4:34–35).[19] Hence, the name "Christ" shows us the engagement of the whole Trinity in our salvation.

The term *office* refers to a special trust or commission laid upon a person to perform functions defined by the will of an authority. It is more than a professional vocation or trade, such as electrician or college instructor. Herman Bavinck said, "'Office' is the word that must be used with respect to Christ. For he did not assume the dignity of the mediator himself: God chose, called, and appointed him (Pss. 2:7; 89:19–21; 110:1–4; 132:17; Isa. 42:1; Heb. 5:4–6). The name 'Christ' is not a professional name but the name of an office, a title."[20]

The Only Mediator

Christ's office may be summarized in the word *mediator*. Paul says, "There is one God, and one mediator between God and men, the man Christ Jesus" (1 Tim. 2:5). The term translated as "mediator" (*mesitēs*) refers to a "middleman" selected to establish a relationship between two parties.[21] John Brown of Haddington said that Christ has both "a mediatorial constitution of person, that, having the nature of both parties, he might be a middle person between God and men," and "a mediatorial office, authorizing and qualifying him to manage for us toward God . . . every thing necessary to make up the breach."[22] John Flavel also observed that the need for a mediator implies "a most dreadful breach" or broken relationship between God and man, for on account of sin "the wrath of the Lord was kindled against man" (cf. Ps. 5:5) and "man was filled with unnatural enmity against his God" (cf. Rom. 1:30).[23] Christ's willing undertaking of this task implies "the ardent love and large pity that filled his heart towards poor sinners."[24]

God the Son created the world and rules it in providence because of his divine nature,[25] but the purpose of the Mediator's office is specifically to save men and bring them to God.[26] "Christ Jesus came into the world to save

---

19. Brown, *Systematic Theology*, 280–81.
20. Bavinck, *Reformed Dogmatics*, 3:365.
21. On the word *mediator*, see the discussion of Christ's other official names in chap. 37. See also Bavinck, *Reformed Dogmatics*, 3:363.
22. Brown, *Systematic Theology*, 256.
23. Flavel, *The Fountain of Life*, in *Works*, 1:110.
24. Flavel, *The Fountain of Life*, in *Works*, 1:112.
25. John 5:19–20; 1 Cor. 8:6; Col. 1:16–17; Heb. 1:2–3.
26. In the execution of his kingly office, Christ exercises universal power over all creation, but he does so for the purpose of giving eternal life to God's elect (John 17:2). See chap. 54.

sinners" (1 Tim. 1:15). He was sent by "God our Saviour; who will have all men to be saved, and to come unto the knowledge of the truth" (2:3–4). Hence, when Paul speaks of Christ as "the mediator," he immediately adds, "who gave himself a ransom for all" (vv. 5–6). Christ's mediation revolves around his payment of the redemption price for sinners (cf. Mark 10:45).

Paul's emphatic repetition of "*one* God" and "*one* mediator" (1 Tim. 2:5)[27] indicates that just as surely as God's Word insists that the Lord is the only God, so it insists that Christ is the only Mediator to reunite sinners with God. Other men, such as Moses, have functioned as temporary intermediaries of external blessings between God and his people (Ex. 20:18–21; Deut. 5:5), but they could not mediate salvation. No religion, spirituality, or philosophy can bring people to God except the gospel of Jesus Christ. "He that believeth on him is not condemned: but he that believeth not is condemned already" (John 3:18). The Lord Jesus says,

- "I am the door: by me if any man enter in, he shall be saved" (10:9).
- "I am the way . . . no man cometh unto the Father, but by me" (14:6).
- "I am the vine, ye are the branches . . . without me ye can do nothing" (15:5).

The apostolic testimony is, "Neither is there salvation in any other: for there is none other name under heaven given among men, whereby we must be saved" (Acts 4:12). Flavel said, "He, and no other, is revealed to us by God."[28] Only by having the Son can we have the Father; without the Son, we have no life (1 John 2:23; 5:10–12). Apart from Christ, there is no hope and no access to God (Eph. 2:12, 18). Yet the message of "one mediator" is good news, for God the Savior sent his Son for people of all nations and social statuses (1 Tim. 2:1–5).

Christ's mediation pertains to the ratification and administration of God's covenantal promises, for Christ is "the mediator of the new covenant" (Heb. 12:24; cf. 8:6; 9:15). No one makes himself a mediator between God and men, for God establishes his covenants according to his will. God the Father appointed his Son to this position in his counsel of peace or eternal covenant, in which God swore an oath that Christ would function as Mediator forever (Ps. 110:4; Heb. 5:4–6).[29] Hence, all saving grace throughout

---

27. The Greek word translated as "one" (*heis*) stands at the front of each clause in 1 Tim. 2:5.
28. Flavel, *The Fountain of Life*, in *Works*, 1:112.
29. Ames, *The Marrow of Theology*, 1.19.4–6 (132). On God's counsel or covenant with his Son, see chap. 30.

history, including under the old covenant, came through Jesus Christ and by his blood (9:15). His mediatorial work gathers together all the saving promises of God and gives them to those who are in Christ (2 Cor. 1:20).

The Divine-Human Mediator

Why did Paul refer to the Mediator as "the *man* Christ Jesus" (1 Tim. 2:5)? Some theologians have argued that Christ is Mediator only in his human nature. Augustine said, "As man He was Mediator; but as the Word He was not between [*medius*], because equal to God."[30] Peter Lombard affirmed the same: "He is called mediator according to his humanity, not according to his divinity."[31] Thomas Aquinas deduced that Christ is Mediator only as man, being like us in nature but like God in grace and glory.[32]

However, there are weighty reasons to speak of Christ as Mediator according to both his natures, divine and human.[33] First, Christ's human nature by itself is insufficient to mediate salvation, for the Mediator must be able to both accomplish and apply the promises of the covenant, such as writing God's law upon the heart and atoning for the guilt of sin (Jer. 31:33–34), and that for countless people among all nations (Rev. 7:9).[34] Thus, mediation of salvation requires the divine nature. If we restrict Christ's mediation to his human nature, we must either grant divine attributes to his humanity or open the door for other human beings to act as mediators. Second, a mediator is not a nature, but a person; Scripture repeatedly ascribes the works of salvation to the person Jesus Christ, who is both human and divine.[35] Third, if Christ is the Mediator only according to his humanity, then how was anyone saved before Christ came in the flesh?[36] Fourth, it is appropriate to speak of Christ as the Mediator in both natures because, as William Perkins said, "being both God and man, he doth participate with both extremes."[37] Fifth, as the Son begotten by the Father in the Trinity, Christ is the fitting means by which we have access to the Father in the Spirit (Eph. 2:18).[38] The incarnate second person of

---

30. Augustine, *Confessions*, 10.43.68, in *NPNF¹*, 1:162. See also Augustine, *The City of God*, 11.2, in *NPNF¹*, 2:206.
31. Lombard, *The Sentences*, 3.19.7 (3:82).
32. Aquinas, *Summa Theologica*, Part 3, Q. 26, Art. 2.
33. On the controversy between John Calvin and Francesco Stancaro on this matter, see Stephen Edmondson, *Calvin's Christology* (Cambridge: Cambridge University Press, 2004), 14–39.
34. Wollebius, *Compendium*, 1.17.(1).iv (96–97); and Turretin, *Institutes*, 14.2.1–7 (2:379–81).
35. Bavinck, *Reformed Dogmatics*, 3:364.
36. Hodge, *Outlines of Theology*, 392–93.
37. Perkins, *A Golden Chain*, chap. 18, in *Works*, 6:55.
38. Perkins, *A Golden Chain*, chap. 18, in *Works*, 6:55.

the Trinity is our Mediator particularly to the first person of the Trinity, God the Father (1 John 2:1).[39]

Why, then, "the *man* Christ Jesus" (1 Tim. 2:5)? It may be that Paul's reference to the Mediator as "man" does not exclude his deity but points to Christ's covenantal office as the last Adam (cf. vv. 13–14), whose obedience unto death overcame the consequences of the first Adam's sin and brought overflowing grace for all in Christ so that they rise with him to bear his image.[40] This does indeed highlight Christ's humanity, but it also involves his deity, for the last Adam is the life-giving Spirit who renews countless sinners (1 Cor. 15:45).

The Mediator and the Church's Evangelistic Prayers

Knowing Christ as the one Mediator should drive us to pray for the spread and success of the gospel. There is no other way for people to be saved. In the context in which Paul taught this doctrine, he said, "I exhort therefore, that, first of all, supplications, prayers, intercessions, and giving of thanks, be made for all men. . . . For this is good and acceptable in the sight of God our Saviour; who will have all men to be saved, and to come unto the knowledge of the truth" (1 Tim. 2:1, 3–4). We should pray regularly and fervently for the conversion of all kinds of people, including "for kings, and for all that are in authority" (v. 2).

The unique mediation of Christ should especially motivate us to participate in prayer meetings. Paul says, "I desire then that in every place the men should pray, lifting holy hands without anger or quarreling" (1 Tim. 2:8 ESV). Our churches should be characterized by well-attended, fervent prayer meetings, pleading that the gospel of the only Mediator will go forth with divine power to every nation.

Christ's Threefold Covenantal Office

Although Christ's office as Mediator is one, theologians speak of Christ's "threefold office" (*munus triplex*).[41] Christ was sent by the Father to serve

---

39. Perkins, *An Exposition of the Symbol*, in *Works*, 5:273.

40. Thomas D. Lea and Hayne P. Griffin, *1, 2 Timothy, Titus*, The New American Commentary 34 (Nashville: Broadman & Holman, 1992), 91. See the adamic use of "man" (*anthrōpos*) in Rom. 5:12, 15, 19; 1 Cor. 15:21, 45, 47; as well as references to "old man" and "new man" in Rom. 6:6; Eph. 4:22, 24; Col. 3:9.

41. The Latin term *munus* (office) refers to Christ's official position as the Mediator, and *officium* (service, duty) to his appointed function or work to fulfill that position. The threefold office is known as the *munus triplex*, but *munus* and *officium* are sometimes used interchangeably. See Muller, *Dictionary of Latin and Greek Theological Terms*, 225–26, 240. For *munus*, see Calvin,

as the Prophet, Priest, and King of his chosen people. This threefold office was revealed and functioned from the beginning in the shadows of the Old Testament and was brought to glorious fulfilment in the incarnate ministry of Jesus Christ.

The threefold office can be expressed in various orders without significantly affecting the doctrine.[42] The most common order, as reflected in the Heidelberg Catechism and Westminster Confession and Catechisms, is prophet, priest, and king.[43] This order reflects the emphases of different periods of Christ's public ministry (teaching, dying for our sins, rising to reign) and the application of salvation to an individual (hearing and understanding the word of Christ, believing in Christ for justification, living for Christ by the Spirit's power).[44]

Christ's threefold office perfectly matches the needs created by sin. First, sin is refusal to hear the divine word and respond with faith and faithfulness, with the consequence of foolishness and spiritual hardness toward God. This Christ heals by his prophetic work. Second, sin is rebellion against divine authority and transgression of his law, with the consequence of guilt and liability to punishment upon the sinner. This Christ expiates by his priestly work. Third, sin is missing the divine mark and failing to fulfill the purpose of one's being as God's image bearer, with the consequence of moral pollution that excludes the sinner from serving in God's holy presence. This Christ overcomes by his kingly work.[45]

Christ's Threefold Office in the Old Testament

The doctrine of Christ's office grows out of rich biblical soil. Divinely appointed office is embedded in the divinely ordained covenant. Stephen Wellum writes, "The threefold office comes from the covenantal-typological

---

Institutes, 2.15.1–2, 6; 2.16.1; 3.1.2. For *officium*, see Calvin, *Institutes*, 2.12 (title); 2.14.3, 4; 2.15.1 ("task").

42. In addition to the order prophet, king, and priest in Calvin, *Institutes*, 2.15.1, we find king, priest, and prophet in Calvin's Catechism of 1545 (Q. 34), in *Reformed Confessions*, 1:473; Olevianus, *An Exposition of the Apostles' Creed*, 56; and Perkins, *An Exposition of the Creed*, in *Works*, 5:103. James Ussher introduced the office in terms of prophet, priest, and king, but treated them as priest, prophet, and king. *A Body of Divinity*, 12th–14th heads (149–62). Christ's priestly sacrifice is foundational to all his other official works. Vos, *Reformed Dogmatics*, 3:89. Hence, it could be treated first.

43. Heidelberg Catechism (LD 12, Q. 31), in *The Three Forms of Unity*, 78; and Westminster Confession of Faith (8.1), Larger Catechism (Q. 42), and Shorter Catechism (Q. 23), in *Reformed Confessions*, 4:243, 307, 356.

44. Ames, *The Marrow of Theology*, 1.19.12–13 (132); and Vos, *Reformed Dogmatics*, 3:91.

45. See the conceptual summary of biblical terminology for sin in chap. 17.

development of the biblical storyline to demonstrate how Christ functions as our covenantal mediator."[46]

As we noted earlier, a common though not essential feature of biblical covenants is the appointment of one party to perform an important office as the other party's "servant," or covenantal officer (2 Sam. 7:5, 8; Ps. 89:2–4). God's original covenant with Adam constituted him to function as a ruling king, worshiping priest, and revelatory prophet in the garden of Eden (Gen. 2:15–17), a threefold office rooted in his capacities as God's image bearer (1:26–28).[47] Adam's sin broke the covenant of paradise, corrupted the image of God, and caused man to fall from his high office. Christ is the last Adam (1 Cor. 15:45) and the Image of God (Col. 1:15); the threefold office reaches its consummation in him.

Christ has been exercising his mediatorial functions to save his people since the first promise of victory.[48] Bavinck said, "Already under the Old Testament, he was active as prophet, priest, and king."[49] With the announcement of the first gospel revelation after the fall of man, Christ began to execute the commission given to him in eternity past (2 Tim. 1:9). Jonathan Edwards wrote, "'Tis manifest that Christ began to exercise the office of mediator between God and man as soon as man fell because mercy began to be exercised towards man immediately. . . . From this day forward Christ took on him the care of the church of the elect, he took here the care of fallen man in the execution of all his offices."[50]

The preexistent Christ appeared to the patriarchs and their offspring as the angel of the Lord.[51] The title "angel" designates him as one sent by the Lord to do his will. The divine angel is the Lord of the prophets, revealing God's redemption to Moses (Ex. 3:1–6), compelling Balaam to speak only God's word (Num. 22:35), and caring for Elijah and directing him (1 Kings 19:7; 2 Kings 1:3, 15). No one has ever received a revelation of God except through his Son (John 1:18). It was Christ who was with Israel in the wilderness (1 Cor. 10:4).[52]

---

46. Wellum, *Christ Alone*, 128.
47. On the image of God and the common covenantal elements exhibited in Gen. 2, see chaps. 8 and 14. On the threefold office in Gen. 1–2, see also Richard P. Belcher Jr., *Prophet, Priest, and King: The Roles of Christ in the Bible and Our Roles Today* (Phillipsburg, NJ: P&R, 2016), 5–11.
48. See chap. 29.
49. Bavinck, *Reformed Dogmatics*, 3:365.
50. Edwards, *A History of the Work of Redemption*, in *WJE*, 9:130.
51. See the discussion of Christ's preexistence and the angel of the Lord in chap. 38.
52. Calvin, *Commentaries*, on Ex. 3:2.

The angel of the Lord is the Warrior-King who accompanied Israel in its conquest of the Promised Land. God said to Moses, "Behold, I send an Angel before thee, to keep thee in the way, and to bring thee into the place which I have prepared. Beware of him, and obey his voice, provoke him not; for he will not pardon your transgressions: for my name is in him. But if thou shalt indeed obey his voice, and do all that I speak; then I will be an enemy unto thine enemies, and an adversary unto thine adversaries" (Ex. 23:20–22). He appeared to Joshua on the boundaries of Canaan as a man holding a sword, the "captain of the host of the LORD," in whose holy presence Joshua worshiped (Josh. 5:14–15). This angel is none other than the Lord of the covenant (Judg. 2:1–5) and the destroyer of Israel's enemies (2 Kings 19:34–35).

Most surprisingly, the divine angel acted as the interceding Priest. He called upon the name of the Lord to show mercy to Israel in its exile (Zech. 1:12). In a symbolic vision, when Satan accused the high priest, Israel's representative before a holy God, it was the angel of the Lord who commanded that the priest's filthy clothes be exchanged for clean garments (3:1–5). Michael Barrett writes, "It is His constant 'standing by' as the representative and the advocate for His people that assures their continuing acceptance before the Lord."[53]

The title "Christ," or "Anointed,"[54] specifically links his office to the prophets, priests, and kings.[55] They functioned as God's covenant officers in the Mosaic and Davidic covenants.[56] They, too, were "anointed," whether ceremonially by oil, spiritually by the Holy Spirit, or both.[57] God appointed them to reveal his covenant to the people of Israel for their faith and obedience, to ceremonially reconcile the people to himself despite the uncleanness of their sins, and to reign over them as his theocratic nation. They are rightly regarded as officers of the covenant, for God selected, commissioned, and empowered them to execute his covenantal Word.

These covenant officers not only represented God to Israel but also represented Israel before God. The "covenant" of God pertained not only to the "people" in general, but specifically to the "kings," "princes,"

---

53. Barrett, *Beginning at Moses*, 142.

54. See the discussion of the name "Christ" in chap. 37.

55. Calvin, *Institutes*, 2.15.2; and Olevianus, *An Exposition of the Apostles' Creed*, 56.

56. There are brief references to prophets under the Abrahamic covenant (Gen. 20:7; Ps. 105:15), but this office received little explicit attention until Moses.

57. Ex. 28:41; 29:9; Lev. 4:3, 5; 1 Sam. 2:10; 10:1, 6; 15:1; 16:6, 13; 24:6, 10; 26:9, 11, 16, 23; 2 Sam. 1:14, 16; 19:21; 1 King 19:16; Pss. 18:50; 105:15.

"priests," and "prophets," whose sins broke the covenant (Neh. 9:32–33). Jeremiah often brought the charge of covenant breaking specifically against kings/princes, priests, and prophets.[58] The failure of Israel was concentrated in the failure of these office bearers, calling for the greater office bearer.

The ancient prophets foretold that Christ would fulfill the threefold covenantal office when he came in the flesh. Moses was inspired by the Holy Spirit to declare that God would raise up a "prophet" like him (Deut. 18:15).[59] God made known to David that his Lord was set apart by divine oath to serve as "priest" forever (Ps. 110:4). The Psalms celebrate God's Son, who would be enthroned as "king" and inherit the nations (2:6–8). The promised messianic "Branch" would combine the priesthood and kingship in one person (Zech. 6:11–13).[60] Hence, the coming of this Davidic Messiah would fulfill the promises of the ancient covenants in the new "covenant of peace," an "everlasting covenant" (Ezek. 37:23–27).

God's old covenant revelation prepared Israel for the coming Christ. Though the three offices had never before converged, the Jewish people sensed that they would come together in a perfect leader. The Testament of Levi, a Jewish document dated to the second century BC, foretold that a king would arise in Judah who would be as a priest to the Gentiles and a prophet of God.[61] Philo of Alexandria (d. c. AD 50) spoke of Moses, "the most perfect man that ever lived," as "a king and a lawgiver, and a high priest and a prophet."[62] Flavius Josephus (AD 37–c. 100) extolled John Hyrcanus (d. 104 BC), a ruler of the Jews during the Maccabean period, as one granted by God the highest privileges, namely, "the government of his nation, the dignity of the high priesthood, and prophecy."[63]

Christ's Threefold Office in the New Testament

The New Testament indicates that Christ came in the flesh as his people's Prophet, Priest, and King. In this section, we sketch themes we will develop

---

58. Jer. 2:26; 4:9; 8:1; 26:11, 16; 32:32.
59. On the interpretation of Deut. 18:15–19, see chap. 45.
60. On Zech. 6:11–13, see the discussion of the counsel of peace with the messianic Branch in chap. 30.
61. Testament of Levi 8.14–15; 18:1–14, in *The Apocrypha and Pseudepigrapha of the Old Testament*, ed. Charles, 2:309, 314–15.
62. Philo, *On the Life of Moses*, 1.1; 2.3, in *The Works of Philo: Complete and Unabridged*, ed. Charles Duke Yonge (Peabody, MA: Hendrickson, 1995), 491. This is not a passing remark, but structures Philo's treatment of Moses.
63. Josephus, *Antiquities*, 13.10.7 (299), in *Works*, 355. See Josephus, *The Wars of the Jews*, 1.2.8 (68), in *Works*, 548.

in later chapters in order to demonstrate that the New Testament warrants the doctrine of Christ's threefold office.

Jesus occasionally referred to himself as a "prophet," particularly with regard to his rejection.[64] The Father testified that his Son was the great Prophet whom Moses and Elijah foreshadowed when they appeared with Jesus and God said, "This is my beloved Son, in whom I am well pleased; hear ye him" (Matt. 17:1–5). Christ called himself a "master" (*didaskalos*),[65] literally, a "teacher," and he was often so addressed in the Gospels. Jesus taught with authority and worked supernatural miracles so that many people recognized him as a prophet, though sometimes with little grasp of his true greatness as the Christ.[66] The Lord Jesus claimed to be nothing less than the light of the world, the perfect revelation of God (John 8:12; 14:9).

The risen Christ taught his apostles many things through the Holy Spirit prior to his ascension (Acts 1:1–8). He continues to teach the church through the Spirit by the apostolic Word (John 16:13; 2 Cor. 13:3–4). The apostles preached that Christ is the great "prophet" foretold by Moses and all the prophets, and declared to Israel, "Unto you first God, having raised up his Son Jesus, sent him to bless you, in turning away every one of you from his iniquities" (Acts 3:22–26; cf. 7:37).

Jesus revealed his priesthood subtly but clearly during his earthly ministry. Christ identified Psalm 110 as a prophecy of himself (Matt. 22:41–45), and it declares that the Christ is "a priest for ever after the order of Melchizedek" (Ps. 110:4). As a priest on earth, he interceded for his people's salvation (Luke 22:32; John 17). He taught that he would voluntarily give his life for the sake of others (Mark 10:45; John 10:11, 18). In the institution of the Lord's Supper, Christ explained the purpose of his death by saying his "blood" would be "shed for many for the remission of sins" (Matt. 26:28), using the very language of the sin offering presented by the old covenant priests for the forgiveness of sins (Leviticus 4).[67]

Though Christ's priestly sacrifice was completed on the cross, his priestly activity entered a more glorious stage upon his exaltation

---

64. Mark 6:4; Luke 4:24; 13:33; John 4:44.

65. Matt. 10:24–25; 26:18; John 13:13–14.

66. Matt. 16:14; 21:11, 46; Mark 6:15; 8:28; Luke 7:16; 9:8, 19; 24:19; John 4:19; 6:14; 7:40; 9:17.

67. We read of the "blood" (*haima*) that a priest "sheds" or "pours out" (*ekcheō*) in Lev. 4:7, 18, 25, 30, 34 LXX. The term translated as "remission" (*aphesis*) or "forgiveness" (Matt. 26:28) is cognate to "forgive" (*aphiēmi*), used in "The priest shall make atonement . . . and it shall be forgiven" (Lev. 4:20, 26, 31, 35 LXX).

(1 John 2:1–2). The last act of the risen Lord on earth was that "he lifted up his hands, and blessed them" (Luke 24:50), just as Aaron the high priest lifted his hands and blessed Israel (Lev. 9:22). Christ told his disciples that after he returned to heaven, he would enter a ministry of intercession with the Father to obtain for them the graces of the Holy Spirit (John 14:16–17). His priestly intercession at God's right hand guarantees that he will save all his people to the end (Rom. 8:34; Heb. 7:25–26; 8:1). The book of Hebrews repeatedly calls Christ our "priest" and "high priest."[68]

When Gabriel revealed Christ's conception and birth to Mary, the angel announced Jesus as the promised King of the line of David (Luke 1:32–33). The wise men came from the east, seeking him as "King of the Jews" (Matt. 2:2). Though his kingship was veiled in his humiliation, Christ still built his church, selecting its officers and giving them "the keys of the kingdom of heaven" (16:18–19), a figure of speech for authority delegated to a royal official (Isa. 22:20–22). When Christ rode a donkey into Jerusalem, he intentionally fulfilled ancient prophecy in order to declare himself to be Zion's King (Zech. 9:9; Matt. 21:5). He accepted the praise of the crowds, "Blessed be the King that cometh in the name of the Lord," saying that if the crowds did not say it, the stones would shout it (Luke 19:38–40). The paradox of Christ's redeeming kingship appears most poignantly in the sign placed upon his cross, "King of the Jews" (23:38), suggesting that his greatest victory was won by his death.

When the Jewish high priest asked Jesus if he was "the Christ, the Son of the Blessed," Christ revealed his anticipation of his glorious reign as King by saying, "I am: and ye shall see the Son of man sitting on the right hand of power, and coming in the clouds of heaven" (Mark 14:61–62). The Lord Jesus had taught his disciples that "the Son of man shall come in his glory" and will "sit upon the throne of his glory," for he is "the King" (Matt. 25:31, 34). When Christ poured out the Holy Spirit upon the church at Pentecost, the Spirit filled Peter to declare that the ancient prophecy of the resurrection and enthronement of the royal Son of David had found its fulfillment in Christ, who was sitting at God's right hand (Acts 2:25–36). Later, Christ granted apocalyptic visions to John in which Jesus revealed himself as "King of kings" (Rev. 17:14, 19:16).

---

68. "Priest" (*hiereus*): Heb. 5:6; 7:11, 15, 17, 21; 8:4; 10:21. "High priest" (*archiereus*): Heb. 2:17; 3:1; 4:14–15; 5:5, 10; 6:20; 7:26; 8:1; 9:11. The references to Christ as "priest" (*hiereus*) derive from the Septuagint's rendering of Ps. 110:4.

The teaching of Jesus Christ and his apostles shows us that Christ acted as the Prophet, Priest, and King of his people, both during his humiliation and in his exaltation. Through his performance of this office, Christ fulfilled the ancient promises. He is the Mediator of the new covenant to the elect among all nations.

The Historical Development of the Doctrine of the Threefold Office

The doctrine of the threefold office has deep historical roots, though its full development did not take place until the middle of the sixteenth century. Up until then, it was common for theologians to say that Christ is the King and Priest of his people.[69] Even early Reformed theologians, such as Heinrich Bullinger and John Hooper (c. 1495–1555), taught a twofold office in which Christ's priesthood included teaching.[70]

The concept of a threefold office appeared in seed form in early and medieval Christianity. Eusebius of Caesarea said that the priests, kings, and prophets anointed with oil were types of Christ, "so that all these have reference to the true Christ, the divinely inspired and heavenly Word, who is the only high priest of all, and the only King of every creature, and the Father's only supreme prophet of prophets."[71] Mentions of the threefold office appear in the writings of John Chrysostom, Peter Chrysologus (fl. 433), Joachim of Fiore (d. 1202), and John of la Rochelle (c. 1200–1245).[72] Aquinas said, "Other men have this or that grace bestowed on this or that one: but Christ, as being the Head of all, has the perfection of all graces. Wherefore, as to others, one is a lawgiver, another is a priest, another is a king; but all these concur in Christ, as the fount of all grace."[73]

---

69. Justin Martyr, *Dialogue with Trypho*, chaps. 34, 36, in *ANF*, 1:211–12; Rufinus, *A Commentary on the Apostles' Creed*, in *NPNF²*, 3:545; Cyril of Jerusalem, *Catechetical Lectures*, 10.4, 10, in *NPNF²*, 7:58, 60; Augustine, *Harmony of the Gospels*, 1.4.3, in *NPNF¹*, 6:79; *On the Psalms* (Ps. 45:6), in *NPNF¹*, 8:150; and Luther, *The Freedom of a Christian*, in *LW*, 31:353–54.

70. Bullinger, *The Decades*, 2.1:273–89. See the Second Helvetic Confession (chap. 11), in *Reformed Confessions*, 2:831; and John Hooper, *Declaration of Christ and of His Office* (1547), chap. 3, in *Early Writings*, ed. Samuel Carr (Cambridge: Cambridge University Press, 1843), 19.

71. Eusebius, *Church History*, 1.3.7–8, in *NPNF²*, 1:86. Note, too, the threefold function of offering, teaching, and powerful restoring in Athanasius, *On the Incarnation of the Word of God*, sec. 10, in *NPNF²*, 4:41.

72. John Chrysostom and Peter Chrysologus, cited in Geoffrey Wainwright, *For Our Salvation: Two Approaches to the Work of Christ* (Grand Rapids, MI: Eerdmans, 1997), 110–11; Joachim of Fiore, the "Dragon Figure," in *Book of Figures*, cited in Bernard McGinn, *Anti-Christ: Two Thousand Years of the Human Fascination with Evil* (San Francisco: HarperCollins, 1994), 138; and John of la Rochelle, "Introduction to the Four Gospels," in *Franciscan Christology: Selected Texts, Translations, and Introductory Essays*, ed. Damian McElrath (St. Bonaventure, NY: Franciscan Institute of St. Bonaventure University, 1980), 46–58; cf. Edmondson, *Calvin's Christology*, 33n51.

73. Aquinas, *Summa Theologica*, Part 3, Q. 22, Art. 1, Reply Obj. 3; cf. Q. 26, Art. 1, Reply Obj. 1.

This doctrine developed and blossomed in Reformed Christianity, primarily through the influence of Calvin.[74] He referred to Christ in a twofold manner as King and Priest in his earlier writings,[75] and may have learned the threefold office from Martin Bucer (1491–1551).[76] By 1545, Calvin had incorporated it into his catechism.[77] He wrote, "Therefore, in order that faith may find a firm basis for salvation in Christ, and thus rest in him, this principle must be laid down: the office enjoined upon Christ by the Father consists of three parts. For he was given to be prophet, king, and priest."[78]

The same doctrine was taken up in the Heidelberg Catechism (LD 12, Q. 31), which says,

> Q. Why is He called Christ, that is, anointed?
> A. Because He is ordained of God the Father, and anointed with the Holy Ghost, to be our chief Prophet and Teacher, who has fully revealed to us the secret counsel and will of God concerning our redemption; and to be our only High Priest, who by the one sacrifice of His body, has redeemed us, and makes continual intercession with the Father for us; and also to be our eternal King, who governs us by His Word and Spirit, and who defends and preserves us in (the enjoyment of) that salvation, He has purchased for us.[79]

Objections to the Doctrine of the Threefold Office

Despite the biblical basis and historical pedigree of this doctrine, it still is subject to criticism. We here consider representative objections and offer responses.[80]

1. *Anointing was not required for the prophetic office.* Therefore, the title "Christ," or "Anointed," does not identify a person as a prophet.

---

74. Muller, *Christ and the Decree*, 31.

75. John Calvin, *Institutes of the Christian Religion: 1536 Edition*, trans. and ed. Ford Lewis Battles, rev. ed. (Grand Rapids, MI: H. H. Meeter Center for Calvin Studies/Eerdmans, 1986), 54, 56; and Calvin's Catechisms of 1537 and 1538 (Art. 20 in both), in *Reformed Confessions*, 1:372, 425.

76. Martin Bucer, *In Sacra Quatuor Evangelia, Enarrationes Perpetua* (Basel, 1536), 9, 606–7, cited in Wainwright, *For Our Salvation*, 104. See Mark D. Thompson, "Calvin on the Mediator," in *Engaging with Calvin*, ed. Mark D. Thompson (Nottingham, England: Apollos, 2009), 116.

77. Calvin's Catechism of 1545 (Q. 34–45), in *Reformed Confessions*, 1:473–74.

78. Calvin, *Institutes*, 2.15.1.

79. *The Three Forms of Unity*, 78.

80. Critiques of the doctrine of the threefold office may be found in Johannes Augustus Ernesti, *De Officio Christi Triplici*, in *Opuscula Theologica* (Leipzig: Caspar Fritsch, 1773), 413–38; Albrecht Ritschl, *The Christian Doctrine of Justification and Reconciliation*, ed. H. R. Mackintosh and A. B. Macaulay, 2nd ed. (Edinburgh: T&T Clark, 1902), 3:417–34 (sec. 46); and Pannenberg, *Jesus—God and Man*, 212–25. For a summary and response, see Berkhof, *Systematic Theology*, 356–57.

Furthermore, Jesus did not say, "Thus saith the LORD," which shows that he was not acting as a prophet.[81]

In reply, we note that Psalm 105:15, "Touch not mine anointed, and do my prophets no harm," closely associates prophecy with anointing, probably as a figure of speech for the patriarchs' covenantal consecration and prophetic gifting by the Holy Spirit.[82] Furthermore, the great Prophet of salvation is unveiled in Isaiah 61:1: "The Spirit of the Lord GOD is upon me; because the LORD hath anointed me to preach good tidings." Therefore, the title "Christ" is legitimately connected to the prophetic office.[83] As to Christ's not saying "Thus saith the LORD," neither did Daniel or Habakkuk, each of whom is called a "prophet" by the New Testament (Mark 13:14; Acts 13:40–41). It may be that Christ avoided this prophetic formula to accentuate his superiority over merely human prophets, for he is the incarnate Son who uniquely reveals the Father and brought divine revelation to its climax in this age (Matt. 11:27; Heb. 1:1–2).

2. *The title "King" did not belong to Jesus until his resurrection, when he was exalted as Lord.* Prior to that, he was not a king and did not seek to be one.[84]

In reply, we would argue that prior to his ascension into heaven, Jesus avoided portraying himself as a king so as not to cater to the popular conception of a messianic king (John 6:15) and provoke the charge of subversive political activity.[85] When Pilate asked Jesus if he was a king, the Lord replied, "My kingdom is not of this world: if my kingdom were of this world, then would my servants fight" (John 18:36). However, the trusting centurion recognized that Jesus was the sovereign Lord whose word controlled all things (Matt. 8:8–9). Christ showed his sovereignty when he delivered people from disaster, demons, disease, and death (Luke 8:22–56). "The kingdom of God" was already present in Christ's supernatural assault against the kingdom of Satan by the Holy Spirit (Matt. 12:28). Furthermore, Christ truly was King on the cross, for there he dealt the death blow to Satan and his kingdom (John 12:31; 16:11; 19:19).

---

81. Pannenberg, *Jesus—God and Man*, 214–16.
82. Poole, *Annotations upon the Whole Bible*, 2:162–63, on Ps. 105:15.
83. Calvin, *Institutes*, 2.15.2.
84. Pannenberg, *Jesus—God and Man*, 217–19. Pannenberg also denies that we can speak of Christ's deity prior to the resurrection: "Jesus appeared at the beginning not as a God-man but as a man. . . . Jesus was the bearer of an office from God first as simply man." Only at his resurrection is Christ manifestly active as God (223).
85. Luke 23:2; John 19:12; Acts 17:7.

3. *Jesus did not speak of himself as a "priest" or of his death as an "offering" or "sacrifice."* This terminology arose only in later Christian writings, such as the epistle to the Hebrews. Therefore, to ascribe to Christ the office of a priest is to distort his teaching.[86]

In reply, we note that the Lord Jesus taught that he sovereignly laid down his life to save many people so that by his blood they would receive forgiveness of their sins.[87] Thus, he viewed his death as the fulfillment of the sin offering. Christ cited part of Isaiah 53:12, "He was reckoned among the transgressors," as a prophecy fulfilled in himself (Luke 22:37). Isaiah's prophecy also says, "He bare the sin of many, and made intercession for the transgressors" (Isa. 53:12), and he will "sprinkle many nations" (52:15), which is a priestly/sacrificial act.[88] Furthermore, Christ waited until after his resurrection to teach "many things" to his apostles by his Spirit (John 16:12–13), and we should regard their epistles also as the doctrine of Christ (1 Cor. 14:37; 2 John 9).

4. *The threefold office unnaturally divides Christ's works into artificial categories rather than recognizing their seamless unity.* One might better say that Christ is simply the King, though his kingly work has prophetic and priestly aspects.[89]

In reply, we acknowledge that it is true that Christ's work has great unity, being the work of one person, the only Mediator. Bavinck said, "No single activity of Christ can be exclusively restricted to one office. . . . He does not just perform prophetic, priestly, and kingly activities but is himself, in his whole person, prophet, priest, and king. And everything he is, says, and does manifests that threefold dignity."[90] Letham says, "Christ is prophet, priest, and king simultaneously and continuously."[91] Furthermore, even in the ancient types of Christ's office, there were some areas of overlap, for an old covenant priest ruled over the administration of the temple and taught God's law to the people, which may have foreshadowed

---

86. Pannenberg, *Jesus—God and Man*, 220–21.

87. Matt. 26:28; Mark 10:45; John 10:11, 18. Pannenberg acknowledged, "If Jesus as God-man knew beforehand the course of his life, then his passion too becomes an act and the exercise of an office, in the sense of the passion predictions of the Gospels. Thus the uniform treatment of Jesus' passion as the priestly office emerges alongside the prophetic and royal offices." *Jesus—God and Man*, 223.

88. Ex. 29:21; Lev. 4:6, 17; 5:9; 6:27; 8:11, 30; 14:7, 16, 27, 51; 16:14, 15, 19; Num. 8:7; 19:4, 18, 19, 21.

89. Ritschl, *The Christian Doctrine of Justification and Reconciliation*, 3:427–28. Ritschl leaned here upon Ernesti.

90. Bavinck, *Reformed Dogmatics*, 3:366–67.

91. Letham, *The Work of Christ*, 24.

the dependence of the prophetic and kingly works upon the priestly work of atonement.

However, the Holy Scriptures distinguish prophet, priest, and king as distinct offices under the old covenant, which highlights their distinct functions. The priestly office is especially Godward, being "ordained for men in things pertaining to God, that he may offer both gifts and sacrifices for sins" (Heb. 5:1). If we collapse Christ's priesthood into his kingship, then we run the risk of losing the doctrine of atonement by the satisfaction of God's justice (Rom. 3:24–26). Salvation ceases to be salvation from divine judgment; it becomes merely help to bring wandering sinners back to God.[92] And if we merge Christ's prophetic work with his royal work, then we may lose sight of the fact that man needs more than just knowledge—he needs power to deliver him from the enslaving forces of sin and Satan (Luke 11:20–22). The doctrine of the threefold office constantly reminds us of the complete sufficiency of Christ. Wellum says that Christ's threefold office "shows us the comprehensive nature of both sin's corruption and Christ's salvation," and "summarizes and integrates the rich and far-reaching biblical data on all that Christ has done to fulfill God's plans and purposes."[93]

Practical Implications of Christ's Covenantal Office

Each of Christ's offices has massive implications for the Christian life, which we will explore in future chapters. Here we consider some practical implications of the general doctrine of Christ's office that this present chapter has outlined.

First, since Christ is the one Mediator, we must have Christ to save us. Flavel said, "It is a dangerous thing to reject Jesus Christ the only Mediator betwixt God and man. Alas! There is no other to interpose and screen thee from the devouring fire, the everlasting burnings!"[94] To trust anyone else to be our mediator or intercessor before God, be it even Mary herself, is "a horrid sin" that "pours the greatest contempt upon Christ." How will we escape God's wrath for so dishonoring his Son? On the other hand, Flavel said that those who are reconciled to God through the Mediator

---

92. In Socinianism, Christ's priesthood was debased into a metaphor for his kingship, which itself was merely his power to help those who followed his prophetic teaching. See Owen, *Vindiciae Evangelicae*, in *Works*, 12:397, 400–403; and Bavinck, *Reformed Dogmatics*, 3:347–48. The Socinians also deemed Christ's priestly work of sacrifice unnecessary for God to forgive sins. See Alan W. Gomes, "Faustus Socinus' *De Jesu Christo Servatore*, Part III: Historical Introduction, Translation and Critical Notes" (PhD diss., Fuller Theological Seminary, 1990).

93. Wellum, *Christ Alone*, 129.

94. Flavel, *The Fountain of Life*, in *Works*, 1:114.

"should thankfully ascribe all the peace, favours, and comforts they have from God, to their Lord Jesus Christ."[95]

Second, the knowledge of Christ's office brings "great joy" and "peace" to his people (Luke 2:10–14).[96] Their joy and peace are solidly grounded in the fact that Jesus did not come of his own will, but was chosen, anointed, and sent by God for this great work (John 5:30; 6:27, 38; 10:36). Christ comes to us as the One fully authorized by the Father to save sinners and bring them to God. We are, therefore, warranted to fully trust in him and freely rejoice that salvation and glory belong to us, for we belong to him.

Third, this doctrine encourages us to seek our all in all in Christ, for his threefold office suits the threefold need of mankind since our fall in Adam.[97] Whatever we need to live unto God and enjoy him forever is found in Christ. We by nature are "ignorant and blind," but "he is a prophet to teach us . . . not only the outward, but the inward man." We are powerless before "the rebellion and sinfulness of our dispositions," but "he is a king to subdue whatsoever is ill in us, and likewise to subdue all opposite power without us." We are "cursed by reason of our sinful condition, so he is a priest to satisfy the wrath of God for us."[98] Christ is the answer.

Consequently, the doctrine of Christ's threefold office is very experiential and practical. It is not merely a convenient way to analyze Christ's work. It is the offer of the all-sufficient Christ to needy sinners. In him, we find all the fullness of what we need, and in him we are complete (Col. 2:9–10).

Fourth, the doctrine of the one Mediator performing a threefold office greatly enriches preaching. Preachers are often told that they must preach Christ. However, this can become repetitive and formulaic if their view of Christ is limited to a particular facet of his work. The preaching of Christ may then seem artificial and not grounded upon a faithful exegesis of the Scripture passage being preached. By contrast, this doctrine opens up a wealth of ways to preach the grace of Christ from various texts of the Bible.

Furthermore, the threefold office highlights the necessity of preaching Christ in his full mediatorial office. Ralph Erskine (1685–1752) said,

---

95. Flavel, *The Fountain of Life*, in *Works*, 1:115–16.
96. Olevianus, *An Exposition of the Apostles' Creed*, 56–57.
97. Ames, *The Marrow of Theology*, 1.19.10–11 (132); Turretin, *Institutes*, 14.5.8 (3:393); and Vos, *Reformed Dogmatics*, 3:88.
98. Sibbes, *A Description of Christ*, in *Works*, 1:16.

No light, no hope, no strength for duties spring,
Where Jesus is not Prophet, Priest, and King.
No light to see the way, unless he teach,
No joyful hope, save in his blood we reach,
Nor strength, unless his royal arm he stretch. . . .
The gospel preacher, then, with holy skill,
Must offer Christ to whomsoever will.[99]

Finally, we should consider that Christ intervened at his great expense to save us from sin and wrath, and out of grateful love, we should intervene when wicked men attack Christ's holy name and kingdom in this world, regardless of what it costs us. Flavel said that it is better that the wicked would turn their weapons upon us than that they should attack the holy name of our Mediator and no one stand to vindicate him. Christ is the holy Servant of the Lord, the great office bearer of the covenant, and we must be zealous for his honor.[100]

Sing to the Lord

Praising Christ for His Threefold Office

Great prophet of my God,
My tongue would bless thy name:
By thee the joyful news
Of our salvation came;
The joyful news of sins forgiven,
Of hell subdued, and peace with heaven.

Be thou my counselor,
My pattern and my guide,
And through this desert land
Still keep me near thy side.
O let my feet ne'er run astray
Nor rove, nor seek the crooked way.

Jesus, my Great High Priest,
Offered his blood, and died;
My guilty conscience seeks

---

99. Ralph Erskine, *Gospel Sonnets, or Spiritual Songs* (Edinburgh: by J. Ruthven and Sons, for J. Ogle et al., 1812), 1.5 (74, 76).
100. Flavel, *The Fountain of Life*, in *Works*, 1:117–18.

No sacrifice beside:
His pow'rful blood did once atone,
And now it pleads before the throne.

My Advocate appears
For my defense on high;
The Father bows his ears,
And lays his thunder by:
Not all that hell or sin can say
Shall turn his heart, his love away.

My dear Almighty Lord,
My Conqueror and my King!
Thy scepter and thy sword,
Thy reigning grace I sing:
Thine is the pow'r; behold I sit
In willing bonds beneath thy feet.

Now let my soul arise,
And tread the tempter down;
My Captain leads me forth
To conquest and a crown:
A feeble saint shall win the day
Though death and hell obstruct the way.

Isaac Watts
Tune: Bevan or Darwall (*Trinity Hymnal—Baptist Edition*, No. 222
or 441)
Isaac Watts, *Psalms, Hymns, and Spiritual Songs* (London: Thomas Nelson, 1849), 1.150 (452–53).

Questions for Meditation or Discussion

1. What are several inadequate approaches to Christ's work?
2. What is the 1-2-3 pattern that Reformed theology employs to summarize the work of Christ?
3. What is an "office"? Why is it appropriate to speak of the "office" of Christ?
4. What did Paul mean when he said there is "one mediator" (1 Tim. 2:5)?

5. What are some examples of the threefold office in the teaching of early and medieval Christianity? When and how did the doctrine blossom and bear fruit?

6. How is Christ's threefold office revealed in the Old Testament? Address:
   - Adam's activity in paradise
   - fallen mankind's spiritual needs
   - the angel of the Lord
   - the officers of the old covenant
   - the promises of the coming Christ

7. How is Christ's threefold office of Prophet, Priest, and King revealed in the New Testament?

8. What objections can be raised against the doctrine of the threefold office? How can we answer them?

9. Which of the practical implications of Christ's office is most relevant to your ministry in the church right now? What should you do about it?

Questions for Deeper Reflection

10. As you consider inadequate approaches to Christ's work, which have you encountered most often in your experience? How was it imbalanced? What impact did this imbalance have on people's lives?

11. What arguments could be presented for saying that Christ is the Mediator according to his human nature alone? What arguments support his mediation according to both natures? Which is the better position? Why?

12. Which is most biblical and theologically helpful for presenting Christ's work: a threefold office, a twofold office (priest-king), or a singular office? Why?

44

The Two States of Our
Prophet, Priest, and King

The redemptive work of Christ is not an eternal set of principles or ideas, or merely an inner experience, but the fact of divine intervention in human history.[1] All of history since the fall of man may be regarded as redemptive history, for the preexistent Christ mediated saving grace to sinners through the ages by faith in the promise of his coming (Gen. 3:15; John 8:56).[2] The earthly ministry of Jesus Christ was the climax of redemptive history. For this reason, the Holy Scriptures indicate that Christ came in "the fullness of time" (Gal. 4:4 ESV), and his coming initiated the "last days" (Acts 2:17; Heb. 1:2).

Furthermore, the incarnate Lord's work was not done in a day, but has its own historical narrative that continues even now. Although this narrative consists of many steps, it may be summarized in two states: humiliation and exaltation. By "state" (or "estate"), theologians mean the low or high condition in which the incarnate Mediator performs his office.[3]

Historically, the doctrine of Christ's two states appears in seed form in the Apostles' Creed, which summarizes the historical narrative of Christ's work from his conception through his death, and from his resurrection

---

1. On theological liberalism's "flight from history to the heights of ideas . . . or to the depths of the human soul as the places to find and meet the living God," see G. C. Berkouwer, *The Work of Christ*, Studies in Dogmatics (Grand Rapids, MI: Eerdmans, 1965), 43–44, 49, 51–52.
2. See chap. 29.
3. Wollebius, *Compendium*, 1.18.(1).1 (98).

through his coming to judge the world.[4] Augustine and Thomas Aquinas distinguished between Christ's humility and the glory or exaltation he earned by his humility.[5] The doctrine of the two states was further developed in early Lutheran theology, where it functioned to explain the weakness of the incarnate Lord prior to his resurrection.[6] Reformed theologian Zacharias Ursinus took it up and refocused it upon Christ's saving office.[7] Amandus Polanus (1561–1610) and William Perkins integrated it into John Calvin's doctrine of Christ's threefold office as Prophet, Priest, and King.[8] Consequently, Reformed orthodox theology spoke of one Mediator acting in two incarnate states according to his threefold office, a doctrinal structure that has borne much good fruit in promoting faith and piety.

Biblical Testimony to Christ's Two States

God testified to the humiliation and exaltation of his Son in various ways in the Old Testament. He revealed it in types, such as the enslavement, imprisonment, and elevation of Joseph to be the lord of Egypt; by the pilgrimage of the tabernacle succeeded by the established glory of the temple; and by David's sufferings followed by his enthronement. God also revealed the humiliation and exaltation of the Christ in promises. He is the "stone" that the builders rejected, but that God made the cornerstone of his glorious, living temple.[9] God revealed it perhaps most clearly in the prophecy of the suffering and exalted Servant of the Lord (Isa. 52:13–53:12). Though he would be a "man of sorrows" (53:3), he would "be exalted and extolled, and be very high" (52:13).[10]

God's Son taught his disciples that the great theme of the Holy Scriptures is the humiliation and exaltation of the Christ: "Ought not Christ to have suffered these things, and to enter into his glory? And beginning at Moses and all the prophets, he expounded unto them in all the scriptures the things concerning himself" (Luke 24:26–27). Later, Jesus addressed the apostles and "opened their minds to understand the Scriptures, and

---

4. *The Three Forms of Unity*, 5.
5. Augustine, *Tractates on the Gospel of St. John*, 104.3, in *NPNF*[1], 7:395. On Christ's exaltation, see Aquinas, *Summa Theologica*, Part 3, introductions to Q. 27 and Q. 53; on his meritorious lowliness, see Q. 46, Art. 1, Answer; Q. 48, Art. 1, Contrary; Q. 49, Art. 6, Answer; Q. 53, Art. 4, Obj. 2; Q. 54, Art. 2, Answer; Q. 59, Art. 3, Answer; Q. 59, Art. 6, Answer.
6. Formula of Concord (Solid Declaration, 8.26), in *The Book of Concord*, 620–21; Schmid, *The Doctrinal Theology of the Evangelical Lutheran Church*, 382–413.
7. Ursinus, *The Summe of the Christian Religion*, 488 [Q. 37].
8. Muller, *Christ and the Decree*, 135–49, 172.
9. Ps. 118:22; cf. Mark 12:10; Acts 4:11; 1 Pet. 2:4–7.
10. Turretin, *Institutes*, 13.9.2 (2:333).

said to them, 'Thus it is written, that the Christ should suffer and on the third day rise from the dead, and that repentance for the forgiveness of sins should be proclaimed in his name to all nations, beginning from Jerusalem'" (vv. 45–47 ESV). The word translated as "ought" and "should" (*dei*) means "it was necessary," indicating that God's decree had fixed these things and tied them inseparably to the identity and mission of his Anointed.[11]

The apostles of Christ also bore witness to his two states. Peter summarizes the teachings of the ancient prophets about the Savior as "the sufferings of Christ, and the glory that should follow" (1 Pet. 1:11). Paul says of Christ that "being found in fashion as a man, he humbled himself. . . . Wherefore God also hath highly exalted him" (Phil. 2:8–9).[12] Humiliation and exaltation correspond to the biblical theme of Christ's descent and ascent.[13]

Steps in the State of Humiliation

When we consider Christ's state of humiliation, we must not view it merely as a situation to which he had to resign himself. Christ is God the Son, and as such, he could not suffer any abasement that he did not choose (Matt. 4:3; 26:53; John 10:17–18). Paul says, "He humbled himself" (Phil. 2:8). John Flavel wrote, "The voluntariness of his humiliation made it most acceptable to God, and singularly commends the love of Christ to us, that he would choose to stoop to all this ignominy, suffering, and abasement for us."[14]

We may consider the progress of Christ's humiliation in several steps: incarnation, being made under the law, the circumstances of his conception and birth, childhood and early adulthood, public ministry, passion and death, burial, and descent into hell.

Reformed theologians differ on how to relate the *incarnation* to Christ's humiliation. Some theologians favor counting the incarnation as the first step of humiliation.[15] In favor of this position, it may be said that Christ

---

11. On the use of *dei* and similar words to express the results of God's decree, see *RST*, 1:960.
12. See the discussion of Phil. 2:6–11 in the paradigm for Christology presented in chap. 36.
13. John 3:13; 6:33, 38, 62; Eph. 4:8–10; 1 Tim. 3:16.
14. Flavel, *The Fountain of Life*, in *Works*, 1:225.
15. Amandus Polanus, *Partitiones Theologicae*, 2nd ed. (Basel: Conrad Waldkirch, 1590), 58; *Substance of the Christian Religion*, trans. E. W. (London: by R. F. for John Oxenbridge, 1595), 64; Westminster Larger Catechism (Q. 46–47), in *Reformed Confessions*, 4:308; Flavel, *The Fountain of Life*, in *Works*, 1:226–29; Watson, *A Body of Divinity*, 192; Boston, *An Illustration of the*

took "the form of a servant" (Phil. 2:7), humbled himself to take a creaturely nature infinitely lower than his deity (cf. Ps. 113:6), and came down from heaven (John 3:13; 6:38). Other theologians favor counting Christ's incarnation as the foundation or preparation for his humiliation.[16] In favor of the latter position is Paul's order: "Being found in fashion as a man, he humbled himself, and became obedient unto death, even the death of the cross" (Phil. 2:8).[17] It seems difficult to speak about the humiliation of a person whose only nature is immutable. Furthermore, Christ's humiliation is reversed in his exaltation, but he remains incarnate. How we resolve this matter depends on whether we consider Christ's human nature concretely, for it was actually in a state of humiliation from the moment he assumed it, or abstractly, for human nature can be humiliated or exalted.[18]

In any case, Christ's incarnation certainly involved an "infinite, unspeakable, inconceivable condescension of the Son of God," as John Owen said, for one equal to God chose "to take our nature into union with himself."[19] Bonaventure (1221–1274) exclaimed, "What greater act of benevolence than for the Master to redeem the slave by taking the nature of a slave?"[20] The incarnation exhibited the same willingness on Christ's part to embrace our lowliness that ultimately took him to the cross. Isaac Ambrose marveled "that the Word should be an infant not able to speak a word; that Life should be mortal; that Power should be subject to a poor carpenter . . . that Wisdom should be instructed, Infiniteness should grow in stature; that the Feeder of all things should be fed, that all these are preludes, and but beginnings of his sufferings. O wonderful condescension! O admirable patience! O rare humility!"[21]

The humiliation of Christ required that he be *made under the law*. As God, he was not subject to the law (Matt. 17:24–27), but was the Law-

---

Doctrines of the Christian Religion, in *Works*, 1:491; Gill, *Body of Divinity*, 390; and Hodge, *Systematic Theology*, 2:611.

16. Ursinus, *The Summe of the Christian Religion*, 488 (Q. 37); Perkins, *An Exposition of the Symbol*, in *Works*, 5:137; Ames, *The Marrow of Theology*, 1.20.3–4 (135); Willard, *A Compleat Body of Divinity*, 349–50; Brakel, *The Christian's Reasonable Service*, 1:575–76; and Brown, *Systematic Theology*, 316. This position is consistent with, though not required by, the Westminster Shorter Catechism (Q. 27), in *Reformed Confessions*, 4:356–57.

17. In the Greek text of Phil. 2:7–8, only two verbs are in the indicative mood: "made himself of no reputation" (*ekenōsen*) and "humbled himself" (*etapeinōsen*). The others are participles. This may suggest two main actions in view, incarnation and humiliation.

18. Vos, *Reformed Dogmatics*, 3:184–85; and Berkhof, *Systematic Theology*, 336.

19. Owen, *An Exposition of the Epistle to the Hebrews*, 4:526.

20. Bonaventure, *Breviloquium*, 4.1.2, in *The Works of Bonaventure*, trans. Jose de Vinck, 3 vols. (Paterson, NJ: S. Anthony Guild Press, 1963), 2:144.

21. Ambrose, *Looking unto Jesus*, 191. We have capitalized some of the words referring to Christ for consistency.

giver (James 4:12) and the Lord of the law (Matt. 12:8). For the sake of his redeeming mission, God the Son became man and was "made under the law" (Gal. 4:4), taking on the obligation to keep the whole law of Moses and accepting the curse that his lawbreaking people had earned (3:10, 12). Louis Berkhof said, "The essential and central element in the state of humiliation is found in the fact that He who was the Lord of all the earth, the supreme Lawgiver, placed Himself under the law, in order to discharge its federal and penal obligations on behalf of His people."[22] All of the degradations and difficulties that the incarnate Son experienced sprang from this root: he was under the law for us.

Christ's humiliation appears in the *circumstances of his conception and birth*. His conception took place in the womb of a woman from Nazareth (Luke 1:26), no royal city but a town of poor reputation (John 1:46). He was of the flesh of the line of David, but David's house was greatly humiliated by that time, like the stump of a once great tree.[23] Though his conception in a virgin's womb was a miracle, it brought difficulty upon his mother and him (Matt. 1:18–20), a stigma of illegitimate birth that may have lasted into his adulthood (John 8:41, 48). Yet he was the holy Son of God (Luke 1:35).

Christ's birth took place "in a low condition."[24] The Roman census caused much hardship for Joseph, the very pregnant Mary, and her un-born child, requiring them to travel from Nazareth to Bethlehem (Luke 2:4), a journey of eighty or ninety miles (about 140 km) through difficult and dangerous territory. Bethlehem was a "little" place (Mic. 5:2). The joy of Jesus's birth was overshadowed by the unpleasant reality that due to overcrowding "there was no room for them in the inn" (Luke 2:7). Luke tells us three times that the infant was laid not in a crib but "in a manger" (vv. 7, 12, 16), a feeding trough for livestock. Angels announced his birth not to high officials but to shepherds (vv. 8–14). At the tender age of eight days, Jesus suffered the bloody cutting of circumcision as the covenant with Abraham and the law of Moses required (v. 21). After thirty-three days, his parents brought him to Jerusalem, but they were so poor they could only afford two little birds for an offering (vv. 22–24; cf. Lev. 12:1–8). Though Jesus was "Christ the Lord" from his birth (Luke 2:11), his circumstances starkly contrasted with the glory of "Caesar Augustus" (v. 1).

---

22. Berkhof, *Systematic Theology*, 332.
23. Gill, *Body of Divinity*, 391. See Isa. 11:1.
24. Westminster Shorter Catechism (Q. 27), in *Reformed Confessions*, 4:356.

How unspeakably humble was Christ's birth! Henry Law (1797–1884) said, "What see you there? A lowly babe lies in the lowly cradle of a lowly town, the offspring of a lowly mother. Look again. That child is the eternal 'I am.' . . . Wherefore is eternity's Lord a child of time? He thus stoops, that He may save poor wretched sinners, such as we are."[25]

The *childhood and early adulthood* of Jesus were neither easy nor elegant. He experienced the trauma of fleeing with his family to a foreign land in order to escape a violent death (Matt. 2:13–15). Later, his family returned to Nazareth. Though quite literate (Luke 4:16–20), Jesus did not have the benefit of higher education (John 7:15). Yet he devoted himself to learning God's Word, so much so that by age twelve he amazed the teachers in the temple with his understanding (Luke 2:42–47). Though he knew God as "my Father," he submitted himself to the parental authority of Joseph and Mary, even when they misunderstood and rebuked him (vv. 48–51). Jesus grew up as the "carpenter's son" (Matt. 13:55). He took up the same manual trade as his earthly father (Mark 6:3) and ate his bread in the sweat of his face (Gen. 3:19).[26]

Carpentry is a worthy trade by which people created in God's image may fulfill the mandate to subdue the earth (Gen. 1:27–28), but it was a humble vocation for the King of kings. Thomas Goodwin remarked, "Now for him to be hid under chips, who was born to sit upon the royal throne of Israel; for those hands to make doors and hew logs that were made to wield the sceptre of heaven and earth; and that he who was the 'mighty counsellor' [cf. Isa. 9:6] should give his advice only about squaring of timber; what an indignity, what a cross is this!"[27]

When Christ was "about thirty years of age" (Luke 3:23), he initiated his *public ministry* in the threefold office. Thirty was the age of Joseph, the Levites, and King David when they entered public service.[28] Jesus was baptized by John (Luke 3:21); since this was a baptism of repentance for the forgiveness of sins (v. 3), the sinless Christ was humbling himself to identify with the sinners he came to save. Thus, his baptism was a sign of his sacrificial suffering and death (12:50). The Holy Spirit descended upon him and led him into the wilderness to fast for forty days and suffer the

---

25. Henry Law, *"Christ Is All." The Gospel of the Pentateuch: Exodus* (London: The Religious Tract Society, 1867), 10.
26. Ames, *The Marrow of Theology*, 1.21.29 (140).
27. Goodwin, *Of Christ the Mediator*, in *Works*, 5:195.
28. Gen. 41:46; Num. 4:3; 2 Sam. 5:4.

Devil's temptations, from which Jesus emerged proven as a fully obedient Son (4:1–13). His absolute purity would have made the temptation all the more vexing. Flavel said, "A chaste woman would account it no common misery to be dogged up and down, and solicited by some vile ruffian, though there were no danger of defilement."[29]

Christ undertook a rigorous ministry of preaching, teaching, praying, healing, working miracles, and training apostles and evangelists—a ministry that brought him into direct conflict with the evil powers of this world. He grieved over the hardness of men's hearts (Mark 3:5). He suffered rejection from the people of his hometown (Luke 4:16–30) and bitter opposition from Pharisees (5:17–6:11). Men viciously accused him of being a sinner (John 9:16); deceiver (Matt. 27:63; John 7:12); blasphemer (Matt. 9:3; 26:65); Sabbath breaker (Luke 13:14); rebel against civil government (23:2); glutton, drunkard, and friend of sinners (7:34); indeed, a servant of Satan (11:15).[30]

Yet Jesus cast out demons, demonstrating that in Christ the kingdom of God had come and one stronger than Satan had arrived to conquer his evil kingdom (Luke 11:14–22). However, Christ's kingdom is not of this world (John 18:36). Though large crowds followed him, he accumulated no personal wealth and had nowhere to lay his head (Luke 9:58). As a real human being, he felt "the miseries of this life,"[31] being "a man of sorrows, and acquainted with grief" (Isa. 53:3). Sometimes he was weary; sometimes he wept (John 4:6; 11:35). The world hated him without cause (15:18, 25). Always he did his Father's will, which he cherished more than his daily food (4:34; 6:38). Consequently, Christ knew the joy of keeping his Father's commandments and abiding in his love (15:9–11). He rejoiced in his worship of the sovereign God (Luke 10:21) and pressed on, hoping in joy to come beyond this world (Heb. 12:2).[32]

The humiliation of Christ intensified greatly in his *passion and death*. While he celebrated his last Passover with his disciples, he taught them that his blood would be shed to ratify the new covenant with many sinners when God himself would strike him (Mark 14:24, 27). Great distress and anguish seized him in the garden of Gethsemane, casting him down on the ground and threatening to end his life, yet as he prayed he submitted

---

29. Flavel, *The Fountain of Life*, in *Works*, 1:239.
30. Gill, *Body of Divinity*, 394–95.
31. Westminster Shorter Catechism (Q. 27), in *Reformed Confessions*, 4:356.
32. Kelly, *Systematic Theology*, 2:347.

himself to his Father's will (vv. 32–36). One of the twelve apostles betrayed him to his enemies with a kiss, and another denied that he knew him (vv. 43–45, 66–72). False witnesses accused him before the Jewish Sanhedrin, and the council condemned him to death for claiming to be the Christ, spat on him, struck him, and mocked him (vv. 57–65). They took him to the Roman governor, whose soldiers scourged him, put a crown of thorns on his head, mocked him, and struck him (John 19:1–5). Pilate found no fault in him, but nevertheless handed him over to be crucified (vv. 4, 6, 16).

The Roman soldiers hanged him like a criminal on a cross between two robbers while people taunted him in his agony (Mark 15:25–32). The innocent one was suffering as a transgressor (Luke 22:37). To perish on a "tree," or wooden pole, was a public sign of dying as a lawbreaker under God's curse.[33] All these things took place, Jesus said, to fulfill the Scriptures.[34] A strange darkness fell on the land, and Christ called out, "My God, my God, why hast thou forsaken me?" (Mark 15:33–34). He descended into hellish horror. Instead of the Father's love, there was wrath. Instead of affection, there was coldness. Instead of support, there was opposition. Instead of nearness, there was distance. The sinless Son of God was forsaken by his holy Father as he gave his life as a "ransom for many" (10:45). Yet even in the darkness, Christ continued to cling to God in covenant faithfulness, praying, "Father, into thy hands I commend my spirit" (Luke 23:46). When his redemptive work was accomplished, he cried out, "It is finished" (John 19:30). And Jesus, the Son of God, died. He who is "the life" (John 14:6) was dead. "The light of the world" (8:12) was eclipsed by darkness.

The conclusion of Christ's humiliation was his *burial*. His lifeless body was taken down and buried in a tomb (Acts 13:49; 1 Cor. 15:4), which was closed and sealed by a large stone (Mark 15:42–47). Christ was buried to demonstrate that he truly was dead, and thus all that was foretold concerning his redemptive work was fulfilled (Acts 13:29).[35] Herman Bavinck said, "It is not only proof that he really died and hence rose from the dead but particularly that Christ . . . spent three days in the state of death, belonging to the realm of the dead, and thus fully bore the

---

33. Deut. 21:22–23. See the references to the cross as a "tree" in Acts 5:30; 10:39; 13:29.
34. Matt. 21:42; 26:24, 31, 54, 56; Mark 9:12; 14:21, 27, 49; 15:28; Luke 18:31; 20:17; 22:37; 24:25–27, 44–46; John 2:22; 12:16; 13:18; 15:25; 17:12; 19:24, 28, 36–37.
35. See Heidelberg Catechism (LD 16, Q. 41), in *The Three Forms of Unity*, 81.

punishment of sin (Gen. 3:19)."[36] By entering into death for his redeemed people, Christ removed the curse of the grave for them. Consequently, he overcame the terror of the grave (Heb. 2:14–15), so that it is now a holy resting place for the saints (Isa. 57:1–2). His descent into the place of the dead prepared for his resurrection as "the firstborn from the dead" (Col. 1:18).

Thus, we may say with the Apostles' Creed that Christ's humiliation culminated in his *descent into hell*[37]—not that his spirit went down to a place of separation from God after he died, but that he experienced the utmost humiliation in soul and body, bearing the blazing fire of divine wrath in his holy heart upon the cross, giving up his life under the divine curse, and lying dead in a tomb while his enemies rejoiced.[38] That God the Son would descend to such depths of suffering is astonishing. As Irenaeus said, during Christ's humiliation, "the Word rested," patiently concealing his divine glory so that his redemptive work would be accomplished.[39]

Yet even in Christ's death, God showed signs of his favor toward his Son that anticipated his exaltation. His body was not left exposed to scavengers or dumped into a mass grave, but was lovingly taken down and honorably buried in a rich man's tomb (Isa. 53:9; Matt. 27:57–60). Neither did God allow the corpse of Jesus to decay, but preserved it from corruption as was prophesied of the Holy One whom God would raise from the dead (Acts 2:27, 31–32; 13:34–35). And while Christ's body rested in the tomb, his spirit was received by his Father into the joys of paradise to rejoice with the spirits of those whom he had saved (Luke 23:43, 46).

Steps in the State of Exaltation

Christ's exaltation involved the steps of his resurrection from the dead, ascension into heaven, session at God's right hand, effusion of the Holy Spirit, and coming in glory.

The state of exaltation began with Christ's *resurrection* from the dead. An angel rolled away the stone, and Jesus left the tomb (Matt. 28:1–7). The living Lord first appeared to women at the tomb (vv. 9–10). Christ then made a series of appearances, at one point to more than five hundred

---

36. Bavinck, *Reformed Dogmatics*, 3:410.
37. *The Three Forms of Unity*, 5.
38. On the meaning of the descent into hell, see the excursus following this chapter.
39. Irenaeus, *Against Heresies*, 3.19.3, cited in Perkins, *A Golden Chain*, chap. 18, in *Works*, 6:58. This does not mean that the Word was inactive during Christ's state of humiliation, but that he did not act to manifest his divine glory in his human nature at that time.

of his disciples (1 Cor. 15:4–7), demonstrating to his astonished friends that he had truly, physically risen from the dead (Luke 24:36–43; Acts 1:3). Jesus insisted that he was not a ghost, but a living man risen bodily from the dead: "Behold my hands and my feet, that it is I myself: handle me, and see; for a spirit hath not flesh and bones, as ye see me have. And when he had thus spoken, he shewed them his hands and his feet" (Luke 24:39–40). He then ate some food with them to further prove his resurrection (vv. 41–42).

The resurrection constituted Christ's complete victory over death (Rom. 6:9; Rev. 1:18). It demonstrated divine and supernatural power (2 Cor. 13:4; Eph. 1:19–20). It was an act of the triune God, engaging the one power of the Father (Acts 3:26; 13:33), the Son (John 2:19; 10:18), and the Holy Spirit (Rom. 1:4; 8:11).

Christ's conquest of death confirmed his complete victory over sin and guilt (Rom. 4:25; 1 Cor. 15:17, 57), for "the wages of sin is death" (Rom. 6:23) and "the sting of death is sin" (1 Cor. 15:56). Caspar Olevianus said, "For since He died not in His own sins but in ours, which had been laid on Him; and since He rose again out of them to a life that will never die, a wonderful light shines on the minds of all believers: not even one of all their sins remains unatoned for. For if even one of all their sins . . . had remained . . . then Christ could not have arisen as our Surety and Guarantor of the covenant." Thus, Olevianus noted, Paul says that the incarnate God was "justified in the Spirit" (1 Tim. 3:16)—that is, "justified not for His own sins but for ours" in his resurrection.[40] Our Surety was condemned before the world, but now he is justified and vindicated as righteous (Isa. 50:8), and the vindication of the risen Lord Jesus is our justification (Rom. 8:34).[41]

The resurrection of Jesus Christ from the dead is the fountainhead of all spiritual blessing.[42] From Christ's resurrection springs the spiritual resurrection of his people from the death of sin to the life unto God by faith and hope.[43] From his resurrection springs their resurrection from physical death on the last day.[44] Therefore, Christ's resurrection launches the new creation that begins with inner regeneration and will

---

40. Olevianus, *An Exposition of the Apostles' Creed*, 94–95.
41. Goodwin, *Christ Set Forth*, in *Works*, 4:7.
42. For a list of twenty glorious blessings arising from Christ's resurrection, see MacArthur and Mayhue, eds., *Biblical Doctrine*, 320.
43. Rom. 6:4, 11; Eph. 1:19–20; 2:4–5; Col. 2:13; 1 Pet. 1:3, 21.
44. John 11:23–25; Rom. 8:11; 1 Cor. 6:14; 15:20–23; Col. 1:18.

culminate in the glorification of God's children in the new heaven and new earth.[45]

What a glorious message the empty tomb conveyed! "The Lord is risen indeed!" (Luke 24:34). All the promises and blessings of salvation lie wrapped in this wonderful news. The best news ever heard came from a graveyard! Oh, victorious resurrection—death is disarmed, sin is subdued, the world is overcome, Satan is trodden underfoot, the grave is sanctified, hell is conquered, and the old man is mortified. Do you see it and embrace it? Redemption is accomplished! Eternal life is secured! Justice is satisfied! The curse of the law is buried! Guilt is paid! Debt is cancelled! God's amen on the all-sufficient work of Christ is loudly declared! All of salvation is verified! Christianity is true! Jesus is alive! Hallelujah!

Forty days after Christ's resurrection, his disciples observed his *ascension* into heaven (Mark 16:19; Heb. 4:14), when he rose into the sky and disappeared in the clouds (Luke 24:51; Acts 1:9). He "ascended up far above all heavens" (Eph. 4:10; cf. Heb. 7:26) to be glorified in the manifest presence of the Father (John 17:5; 20:17). He is now the preeminent citizen of the heavenly city and the Mediator of all its blessings (Heb. 12:22–24). He has entered God's holy presence as "the forerunner . . . for us" to secure the future position of his people (6:20; cf. John 14:2), who by union with him are also raised up with him (Eph. 2:6). The ascension of Christ brought new splendor to the heavenly Jerusalem, for its light and glory are God and the Lamb, and its life flows from his throne (Rev. 21:23; 22:1). The ascended Christ now awaits his return, for "the heaven must receive [him] until the times of restitution of all things" (Acts 3:21). Robert Peterson calls the ascension "the linchpin of Christ's other saving works," saying that it "confirms the authenticity of Christ's previous works [such as his teaching about himself and his reconciling death] and is a prerequisite for the subsequent works [such as his intercession and sending of the Holy Spirit]."[46] Indeed, as Robert Letham says, "The ascension bridges our present world and that of the age to come."[47]

Christ's ascension led to his *session* (being seated) at God's right hand, as prophesied by David: "The LORD said unto my Lord, Sit thou at my right hand, until I make thine enemies thy footstool" (Ps. 110:1). This

---

45. Wellum, *Christ Alone*, 149.
46. Robert A. Peterson, *Salvation Accomplished by the Son: The Work of Christ* (Wheaton, IL: Crossway, 2012), 179.
47. Letham, *Systematic Theology*, 577.

may be the Old Testament text most frequently cited or alluded to in the New Testament.[48] Sitting down signifies that the painful labors of Christ's humiliation are finished (Heb. 10:11–14). Although "right hand" can be a figure of speech for power,[49] it also symbolizes honor and blessing (Gen. 48:18; Ps. 16:11). Sitting at a ruler's right hand is an idiom for a position of privilege and influence second only to that ruler (1 Kings 2:19–20; Matt. 20:21, 23; cf. Ps. 45:9).[50] Perkins said, "His sitting at the right hand of God the Father . . . metaphorically signifies that Christ hath in the highest heavens actually all glory, power and dominion."[51] On the one hand, Christ's human body and soul are really located in the highest heaven. On the other hand, we should avoid any notion of the Father as a glorified man sitting on a throne with Jesus to his right. The Father is not incarnate, but absolute and infinite spirit (John 4:24). Hence, we may speak of Christ sitting at God's right hand "metaphorically."[52]

Christ's session at the right hand of God honors him as the divine Mediator and initiated his ministry as the glorified Priest-King (Ps. 110:2–4). He is enthroned with supreme authority (Eph. 1:20–21; 1 Pet. 3:22), by which he will one day judge the world (Ps. 110:5–7) and visibly establish God's kingdom (Matt. 26:64; cf. Dan. 7:13–14). His sitting as Lord at God's right hand demonstrates that he is more than the Son of David (Matt. 22:41–45); he is the Son of God, greater than any angel or mere man (Acts 2:34; Heb. 1:3–5, 13). From that heavenly position, Christ gives repentance and forgiveness to sinners (Mark 16:19–20; Acts 5:31) and preserves his saints to the end despite all their trials and temptations (Rom. 8:34–35; Heb. 7:25; 8:1).

The first public act of the glorified and enthroned Lord was the *effusion* (outpouring) of the Holy Spirit upon his people at Pentecost (Acts 2:4, 32–36). The Spirit extends Christ's prophetic ministry to all his people (vv. 17–18) so that they receive power to be his witnesses to all nations (1:8; 2:4–11; 4:8; 5:32). The Spirit's descent in power depended upon Christ's ascent to glory (John 7:39; 16:7). When the Spirit came, Christ himself came to give life to his people and manifest God's presence in them, for the Son and the Spirit are one God in the Trinity (14:16–23). The Spirit comes

---

48. Matt. 22:44; 26:64; Mark 12:36; 14:62; 16:19; Luke 20:42; 22:69; Acts 2:33–34; 5:31; 7:55–56; Rom. 8:34; Eph. 1:20; Col. 3:1; Heb. 1:3, 13; 8:1; 10:12; 12:2; 1 Pet. 3:22.

49. Ex. 15:6, 12; Deut. 33:2; Pss. 17:7; 18:35; 20:6; 21:8; 29:9; 44:3; 45:4; 60:6; 63:8; 74:11; 77:10; 78:54; etc.

50. Wollebius, *Compendium*, 1.19.(5).i (113).

51. Perkins, *A Golden Chain*, chap. 18, in *Works*, 6:62.

52. See Watson, *A Body of Divinity*, 205.

in Jesus's name in order to powerfully advance the progress of the word of Christ in the world (14:26; 15:26–27). Hence, the Holy Spirit acts as the divine agent of the glorified Lord Jesus to build God's kingdom on earth. Although the outpouring at Pentecost was a unique redemptive-historical event in the narrative of Christ's exaltation, the Spirit's continued work of filling God's people daily manifests the activity of the Lord seated at God's right hand. Just as Christ brought his kingdom during his days of humiliation by "the Spirit of God" (Matt. 12:28), so his kingdom today consists of "righteousness, and peace, and joy in the Holy Ghost" (Rom. 14:17). From beginning to end, the work of God's Servant is by God's Spirit.[53]

The final step of Christ's exaltation is his *coming in glory*. Just as he ascended bodily into heaven, so he will descend bodily to earth again (Acts 1:9–11). The heavenly Priest who bore the sins of many will return to give complete salvation to those who hope in him (Heb. 9:28). The supreme revealer of God will himself be fully revealed: "He cometh with clouds; and every eye shall see him" (Rev. 1:7). His glory, presently hidden with God in heaven, will be openly manifest in all creation (Col. 3:3–4). The great King will appear in his beauty (Isa. 33:17). By his power to subject all things to himself, he will glorify his saints (Phil. 3:20–21), judge the world in righteousness (Acts 17:31), and regenerate creation (Matt. 19:28) as a "new heavens and a new earth, wherein dwelleth righteousness" (2 Pet. 3:13). Ambrose said that when Christ and his saints meet on that day, it will be "as when two admirable persons, two lovers meet together, their eyes sparkle, they look on, as if they would look through one another." They will look upon his glory, shine with his glory, and "admire at the infinite glory, and beauty, and dignity, and excellency that is in Christ."[54]

The Meaning of Christ's Two States

We may consider the significance of Christ's two states with respect to his incarnation and his work of salvation.

The Incarnation and Christ's Two States

Christ was the God-man in both his humiliation and his exaltation. However, the manifestation of his divine nature varied according to his state.

---

53. Isa. 11:1–10; 32:1–2, 15–17; 42:1; 59:21; 61:1. On the messianic reference in Isa. 59:21, see the biblical exposition of the new covenant in chap. 32.

54. Ambrose, *Looking unto Jesus*, 619.

Owen explained that in Christ's incarnate humiliation, "He veiled himself, he shadowed himself, he hid his divine nature, he eclipsed the glory of it. Not absolutely . . . [but] as to himself and his interest in it; for upon his taking our nature upon him, men were so far from looking on him as God, that they did not look on him as a good man."[55] Though rays of his divine glory shown out in his miracles (John 2:11), and those who believed in him recognized his glory as the only begotten Son of the Father, Christ "consented to have his divine glory covered and veiled, as to the ordinary manifestation of it," as John Gill said.[56]

As to Christ's exaltation, Johannes Wollebius explained, "In the human nature, he was exalted by the removal of the weakness he had assumed, and by receiving gifts which he had not formerly possessed; he attained, both in body and in soul, the maximum perfection of which a creature is capable. In the divine nature, he was exalted not by the addition of anything to this nature as such, but by the revelation of his majesty, formerly hidden under the form of a servant."[57]

Consequently, the two states of Christ reflect two modes of manifesting his deity while he is incarnate as the God-man. Christ's humiliation was a state of "hiddenness" (*krypsis*), in which God's wisdom and power were concealed in the humanity of Jesus, though fully present and active to accomplish our salvation.[58] Though "the arm of the Lord" had come in Christ, to whom was it revealed except through faith (John 12:38)? Christ's state of exaltation is a state of "revelation" (*apokalypsis*) in which the divine glory is openly made known through his humanity, though not by changing his humanity into divinity. This revelation dawned when Christ by his resurrection "abolished death, and . . . brought life and immortality to light" (2 Tim. 1:10). It shines in heaven even now where Christ sits in glory. It will reach its pinnacle in this age at Christ's return, "the day when the Son of man is revealed" (Luke 17:30).

The Work of Salvation and Christ's Two States

The significance of Christ's two states is grounded upon the necessity of the incarnation for him to fulfill his saving work. Christ's mission re-

---

55. Owen, "The Humiliation and Condescension of Christ," in *Works*, 16:498.
56. Gill, *Body of Divinity*, 395.
57. Wollebius, *Compendium*, 1.19.(1).iv–v (110).
58. See the discussion of *kenōsis* versus *krypsis* in the section on whether Christ set aside his divine attributes in chap. 42.

quired that he suffer our temptations and die the death we deserved. Yet it also required that he rise again to bring many sons with him to the glory that God had foreordained for his elect and creation as a whole (Heb. 2:6–18).[59] The state of humiliation was necessary for the accomplishment of salvation. The state of exaltation was necessary for the full application of salvation, though the Son had been applying salvation through the ages before his death and resurrection on the basis of the covenant of redemption. Greg Nichols writes, "His humiliation features his representative obedience and vicarious sin bearing. His exaltation features his effective application of redemption by his prayers and the power of the Holy Spirit, his righteous rule, and his ultimate victory over every foe, all unto God's praise and glory."[60]

Therefore, the threefold office requires the two states for Christ to perform his assigned task and receive his promised reward. Francis Turretin said, "The priestly consists of two parts: satisfaction on earth; intercession in heaven. As to the kingly, he must first by a struggle acquire for himself a people before he can be carried to the throne and take the reins of government. As a prophet, he must first be a minister of circumcision among his brethren before he can be raised to heaven as the light of the Gentiles and the teacher of the world."[61] Flavel noted that Christ's exaltation fulfilled the promise of God's covenant that Christ's obedient humiliation would gain for him a glorious reward (Isa. 49:5–7; 53:10–12), as he was lifted up in union with his people so that they too would be lifted up to glory (Eph. 2:6; Col. 3:1), and all this to the glory of God the Father (Phil. 2:11).[62]

Christ's mediatorial works in his states of humiliation and exaltation were all performed in union with his people. Union with Christ is the great bridge by which God saves his people and brings them to his glory. As we have seen, events such as Christ's death and resurrection have saving significance because Christ acted for his people and as one with them.[63]

The Importance of the Doctrine of Christ's Two States

The doctrine of the two states forms an important nexus in systematic theology. It holds together the historical Jesus with the exalted Lord of the

---

59. See the section on the incarnate Lord's unique necessity in chap. 39.
60. Nichols, *Lectures in Systematic Theology*, 3:565.
61. Turretin, *Institutes*, 13.9.3 (2:333).
62. Flavel, *The Fountain of Life*, in *Works*, 1:483–84.
63. See the chapters on union with Christ in *RST*, vol. 3 (forthcoming).

Spirit as one person, the God-man, both in humiliation and exaltation. It offers a narrative of the works of God's Servant, who does God's saving will both in his obedient suffering on earth and in his glorious ministry in heaven. This narrative links the once-for-all accomplishment of redemption to the present application of redemption to the nations. It stands as a reminder to us that Christ fulfilled his threefold office as Prophet, Priest, and King both in the course of events culminating in his death and in the events flowing from his resurrection. Consequently, the doctrine of Christ's two states greatly helps us to maintain a balanced, holistic Christology for the faith of God's people.

Practical Applications of Christ's Two States

Since the steps of Christ's humiliation and exaltation form the backbone of the gospel, it should not surprise us that they have many practical applications.

First, the most important application of this doctrine pertains to our salvation: *trusting the gospel of Christ humiliated and exalted.* The center of the gospel is "Christ died for our sins" and "he rose again" (1 Cor. 15:3–4). We must not be slow to believe that Christ suffered and entered his glory (Luke 24:25–26). Do you believe in the incarnate Lord Jesus, trusting that he lowered himself to the deepest abyss of abasement and rose up to the highest glory in order to save lost sinners? Have you trusted in him to save you by his humiliation and exaltation?

Second, the doctrine of Christ's two states reminds us that Christianity requires *following Christ in the lowly path to glory* (Luke 9:20–23; Heb. 12:1–2). Perkins said, "The same which was true in Christ, the Head, must be verified in all His members. They must all have their twofold estate— first, in this life the estate of humiliation; secondly, after this life the estate of glory. . . . He that will reign with Christ and be exalted must first suffer with Him and be humbled." This can bring great comfort to humbled, persecuted Christians, "because the state of humiliation in this life is a sign that they are in the plain and right way to salvation and glory."[64]

Gregory of Nazianzus said that Christ "by his passion taught us how to suffer, and by his glorification grants us to be glorified with him." Gregory exhorted, "Let us accept anything for the Word's sake. By sufferings let us imitate his passion: by our blood let us reverence his blood. . . . Sweet are

---

64. Perkins, *An Exposition of the Symbol*, in *Works*, 5:137–38.

the nails, though they be very painful. For to suffer with Christ and for Christ is better than a life of ease with others."[65]

Third, Christ's two states should also teach us the necessity of *evaluating people by obedience, not circumstances* (John 8:15; 2 Cor. 5:12, 16). When godly people suffer extraordinary troubles, Christ's example of humiliation should encourage them. Flavel said, "From . . . Christ's humiliation, I infer, that such as are full of grace and holiness, may be destitute and empty of creature-comforts."[66] We should learn from our Lord's abasement to count it "a very small thing" how people judge us (1 Cor. 4:3). Some of those most despised by the world have been people "of whom the world was not worthy" (Heb. 11:38). Flavel reminded us, "The judgment the world gives of persons, and their worth, is little to be regarded."[67]

Fourth, Christ's humiliation and exaltation call us to be daily *rejoicing in Christ's triumphant victory*. Wilhelmus à Brakel said, "He for our sake became poor, was a man of sorrows, and endured the contempt of men, has conquered all and triumphantly ascended into heaven." All Israel rejoiced when the ark was brought to Mount Zion (1 Chron. 15:28; Ps. 68:24–26) and again when Solomon was made king (1 Kings 1:40). Brakel said, "With how much more glory and joy the Lord Jesus made His entry into heaven! With what joy the heavenly legions must have accompanied Him upon His entry! With what joy the glorified saints must have beheld Him! With what delight the Father must have received Him!"[68] Therefore, let us join the heavenly celebrators in rejoicing in the Lord. No matter how low or sorrowful God's people may be on earth, their Savior is in heaven. Jesus is Lord! Let Christians say with joy, "Who is this King of glory? The LORD strong and mighty, the LORD mighty in battle" (Ps. 24:8).

Sing to the Lord

Rejoicing in Christ's Ascension into Heaven

What man shall stand before the Lord
On Zion's holy hill?
The clean of hand, the pure of heart,
The just who do His will.

---

65. Gregory of Nazianzus, *Orations*, 45.21, 23, in *NPNF*², 7:431.
66. Flavel, *The Fountain of Life*, in *Works*, 1:242.
67. Flavel, *The Fountain of Life*, in *Works*, 1:245.
68. Brakel, *The Christian's Reasonable Service*, 1:642.

Ye everlasting doors, give way,
Lift up your heads, ye gates!
For now, behold, to enter in
The King of glory waits.

Who is this glorious King that comes
To claim his sov'reign right?
It is the Lord omnipotent,
All conqu'ring in His might.

Who is this glorious King that comes
To claim His rightful throne?
The Lord of Hosts, He is the King
Of glory, God alone.

Psalm 24
Tune: Jazer
The Psalter, No. 59
Or Tune: Mirfield
Trinity Hymnal—Baptist Edition, No. 66

Questions for Meditation or Discussion

1. What Scripture passages show us that Christ's saving work involved two states?
2. How is Christ's incarnation a remarkable demonstration of his condescension?
3. What does it mean that Christ was "made under the law"?
4. How is Christ's humiliation evident in the following events?
   - his conception and birth
   - his childhood and early adulthood
   - his public ministry
   - his passion and death
   - his burial
5. How should we understand Christ's "descent into hell"? (For more information, see the excursus after this chapter.)
6. How do each of these events in Christ's exaltation contribute to our salvation?
   - resurrection
   - ascension into heaven

- session at God's right hand
- effusion of the Holy Spirit
- coming in glory

7. What practical implications do Christ's humiliation and exaltation have for the patience and hope of Christians? How does that help you in your present trials and temptations?

Questions for Deeper Reflection

8. What do Christ's two states mean with regard to his incarnation as the God-man? How do the Holy Scriptures testify to that?
9. Why were Christ's two states each necessary for the work of salvation? What would be the result if he had never passed through a state of humiliation? What if he had never been exalted?

Excursus

"He Descended into Hell"

In the previous chapter, we noted that the Apostles' Creed summarizes the historical narrative of Christ's work. The creed says that Jesus Christ "suffered under Pontius Pilate; was crucified, dead and buried; He descended into hell; the third day He rose again from the dead."[1] A similar statement is found in the Athanasian Creed (sec. 38), which says that Christ "suffered for our salvation, descended into hell, rose again the third day from the dead."[2]

What does it mean to confess that Christ "descended into hell"? The origin and meaning of this clause is surrounded by mystery and controversy.[3] It

1. *The Three Forms of Unity*, 5.
2. *The Three Forms of Unity*, 11.
3. For recent articles on the descent, see Dewey D. Wallace Jr., "Puritan and Anglican: The Interpretation of Christ's Descent into Hell in Elizabethan Theology," *Archiv für Reformationsgeschichte* 69 (1978): 248–87; John Yates, "'He Descended into Hell': Creed, Article and Scripture, Part 1," *Churchman* 102, no. 3 (1988): 240–50; "'He Descended into Hell': Creed, Article and Scripture, Part 2," *Churchman* 102, no. 4 (1988): 303–15; Ronald E. Otto, "*Descendit in Inferna*: A Reformed Review of a Creedal Conundrum," *Westminster Theological Journal* 52, no. 1 (January 1990): 143–50; Wayne Grudem, "He Did Not Descend into Hell: A Plea for Following Scripture instead of the Apostles' Creed," *Journal of the Evangelical Theological Society* 34, no. 1 (March 1991): 103–13; David P. Scaer, "He Did Descend to Hell: In Defense of the Apostles' Creed," *Journal of the Evangelical Theological Society* 35, no. 1 (March 1992): 91–99; Adrienne L. Jervis, "O Death, Where Is Thy Victory? A Study of Christ's *Descensus ad Inferos* in the Odes of Solomon" (PhD diss., University of Edinburgh, 1995); David V. N. Bagchi, "Luther versus Luther? The Problem of Christ's Descent into Hell in the Long Sixteenth Century," *Perichoresis* 6, no. 2 (2008): 175–200; Daniel R. Hyde, *In Defense of the Descent: A Response to Contemporary Critics* (Grand Rapids, MI: Reformation Heritage Books, 2010); Elikana Asheri Lova and Elia Shabani Mligo, *He Descended into Hell: A Christological Study of the Apostles' Creed and Its Implications to Christian Teaching and Preaching in Africa* (Eugene, OR: Wipf and Stock, 2015); Matthew Y. Emerson, "'He Descended to the Dead': The Burial of Christ and the Eschatological Character of the Atonement," *Southern Baptist Journal of Theology* 19, no. 1 (2015): 115–31; J. H. Charlesworth, "Exploring the Origins of the *Descensus ad Inferos*," in *Earliest Christianity within the*

does not appear in the earliest forms of the Apostles' Creed.[4] It is not found in the Nicene Creed, which has formed the basis of orthodox Christology for many centuries. Augustine omitted the descent clause in his treatment of the Apostles' Creed,[5] though he believed that Christ descended literally into hell.[6]

We find the earliest extant appearance of the descent clause in an orthodox creed in the writings of Rufinus (345–410), who said, "It should be known that the clause, 'He descended into Hell,' is not added in the Creed of the Roman Church, neither is it in that of the Oriental Churches. It seems to be implied, however, when it is said that 'He was buried.'"[7] Rufinus further said that Christ's descent "is also evidently foretold in the Psalms," which speak of descending into death and corruption (Pss. 22:15; 30:3, 9; 69:2), and in Peter's statement that Christ "preached unto the spirits in prison; which sometime were disobedient, when once the longsuffering of God waited in the days of Noah" (1 Pet. 3:19–20).[8]

Hence, Rufinus wove together two ideas in his understanding of the descent. On the one hand, he indicated that it was virtually synonymous with Christ's death and burial. On the other hand, he apparently included in its meaning a visit to the realm of "spirits in prison." However, the meaning of Peter's words is contested.

Given the descent clause's relatively late appearance, divergent interpretations of it, and its debatable biblical basis, Reginald Pecock (d. c. 1461) and some modern evangelical and Reformed theologians have proposed that the church remove it from its articles of faith.[9]

We do not count any writings outside of the Holy Scriptures to be divinely inspired, infallible, and inerrant. However, we should be very slow to change a creed that has unified professing Christians for many centuries. Furthermore, it should be considered whether the descent clause and the

---

Boundaries of Judaism: Essays in Honor of Bruce Chilton, ed. Alan J. Avery-Peck, Craig A. Evans, and Jacob Neusner (Leiden: Brill, 2016), 372–95.

4. *The Creeds of Christendom*, ed. Schaff, 2:11–55. The lack of testimony to the descent clause in the earliest creeds and church fathers was well known in early Reformed theology. See Calvin, *Institutes*, 2.16.8; Perkins, *An Exposition of the Symbol*, in *Works*, 5:229–30; Polyander, Walaeus, Thysius, and Rivetus, *Synopsis Purioris Theologiae*, 27.24 (2:147); and Turretin, *Institutes*, 13.16.2 (2:362).

5. Augustine, *On Faith and the Creed*, 6.11–12, in *NPNF*[1], 3:326; *On the Creed*, secs. 9–10, in *NPNF*[1], 3:372–73.

6. Augustine, Epistle 164.3, to Evodius, in *NPNF*[1], 1:515–16.

7. Rufinus, *A Commentary on the Apostles' Creed*, sec. 18, in *NPNF*[2], 3:550.

8. Rufinus, *A Commentary on the Apostles' Creed*, sec. 28, in *NPNF*[2], 3:553–54.

9. John Lewis, *The Life of the Learned and Right Reverend Reynold Pecock*, new ed. (Oxford: Oxford University Press, 1820), 145, 152–53, 179–80; Erickson, *Christian Theology*, 706–9; Grudem, *Systematic Theology*, 583–94; and Otto, "*Descendit in Inferna*," 143–50.

tradition behind it contain some biblical truth worthy of our confession. William Perkins wrote, "Considering that this clause has long continued in the Creed, and that by common consent of the catholic church of God, and it may carry a fit sense and exposition, it is not, as some would have it, to be put forth [removed]."[10]

In this excursus, we will review the main interpretations of Christ's descent and examine the passages of the Holy Scriptures relevant to it. In the process, we will argue that some traditional teachings about the descent into hell should be discarded, but there is a biblical sense in which it can be confessed.

Different Interpretations of the Descent

Widely different perspectives have been taken on this creedal phrase; here we survey six basic approaches to interpreting the meaning of "he descended into hell."

1. Rescuing the Ancient Fathers from Limbo

The most ancient view involves a literal descent of Christ after his crucifixion into the realm of the dead in order to rescue Old Testament saints and bring them to heaven.[11] A well-developed form of this view appears in the theology of Thomas Aquinas. Aquinas distinguished the afterlife into five regions: the upper region of heaven and the lower region of the place of the damned (hell proper), the limbo of unbaptized children (*limbus infantum*), purgatory for Christians who must suffer more before entering heaven due to their need for cleansing from personal demerit, and the limbo of the fathers (*limbus patrum*)—that is, the Old Testament saints.[12] The Latin word *limbus* means "border, edge," and thus describes places on the borders of hell.[13] The inhabitants of limbo are excluded from enjoying

---

10. Perkins, *An Exposition of the Symbol*, in *Works*, 5:230.

11. J. N. D. Kelly, *Early Christian Creeds*, 3rd ed. (London: Routledge, 1950), 379–81. For examples, see Ignatius, *Epistle to the Trallians*, chap. 9 (long version), in *ANF*, 1:70; Irenaeus, *Against Heresies*, 4.27.2; 5.31.1, in *ANF*, 1:499, 560; Tertullian, *On the Soul*, chap. 55, in *ANF*, 3:231; the Odes of Solomon, especially Ode 42:10–20, discussed in Charlesworth, "Exploring the Origins of the *Descensus ad Inferos*," in *Earliest Christianity within the Boundaries of Judaism*, ed. Avery-Peck, Evans, and Neusner, 379–80; and the semi-Arian council of Sirmium (359), in *Documents of the Christian Church*, ed. Henry Bettenson, 2nd ed. (Oxford: Oxford University Press, 1963), 43–44. Irenaeus partly based this doctrine upon a quotation that he mistakenly attributed to the Hebrew prophets. See Irenaeus, *Against Heresies*, 3.20.4, in *ANF*, 1:499; and Justin Martyr, *Dialogue with Trypho*, chap. 72, in *ANF*, 1:235.

12. Aquinas, *Summa Theologica*, Part 3, Supplement, Q. 69, Art. 7, Answer.

13. Muller, *Dictionary of Latin and Greek Theological Terms*, 203; and Aquinas, *Summa Theologica*, Part 3, Supplement, Q. 69, Art. 5.

God's glory because of their original sin. After Christ's death, his human soul descended into the limbo of the fathers to deliver them from original sin by his passion and bring them to glory. Though he did not enter the other regions, the glory of his descent shamed the wicked and gave hope to those in purgatory.[14] The Roman Catholic Church today confesses, "In his human soul united to his divine person, the dead Christ went down to the realm of the dead. He opened heaven's gates for the just who had gone before him."[15]

The traditional Roman Catholic doctrine of limbo has no biblical support. Believers in God's promise in ancient times were forgiven and justified just as we are (Gen. 15:6; Ps. 32:1–2).[16] Enoch and Elijah were caught up to heaven to be with God (Gen. 5:24; 2 Kings 2:11). Asaph said that while he lived, God would guide him with counsel and "afterward receive me to glory" (Ps. 73:24). Christ depicted the state of deceased believers prior to his death not as the fringes of hell, but as the very opposite of hell, a place of fellowship and comfort (Luke 16:22–26). Jesus also taught that God remains in covenant with Abraham, Isaac, and Jacob, and therefore they live in fellowship with him: "For he is not a God of the dead, but of the living: for all live unto him" (20:38). Furthermore, Peter's reference to "spirits in prison" cannot refer to the patriarchs, for he speaks of the "disobedient" (1 Pet. 3:19–20).[17] Therefore, despite its widespread support in the early church, the idea that Christ descended to deliver the saints from the *limbus patrum* is not part of biblical faith.

2. Giving the Unconverted Dead a Second Chance

The idea of Christ preaching to the dead suggests for others an evangelistic mission to the departed, offering them a second chance for salvation. Some church fathers, such as Clement of Alexandria and Augustine, speculated that Christ might have delivered everyone from hell in his descent, or at least the ancient people outside of Israel who had lived virtuous lives.[18] E. A. Litton (1813–1897) argued that Christ's descent is best understood to refer to an event following his resurrection, when he visited the spirits

---

14. Aquinas, *Summa Theologica*, Part 3, Q. 52, Art. 2, Answer; Art. 5–7.
15. *Catechism of the Catholic Church*, sec. 637.
16. Olevianus, *An Exposition of the Apostles' Creed*, 86–87.
17. Turretin, *Institutes*, 12.11.4–5, 8, 15 (2:258–59, 261).
18. Clement of Alexandria, *Stromata*, 6:6, in *ANF*, 2:490–92; and Augustine, Epistle 164.4, 8, to Evodius, in *NPNF¹*, 1:516–17.

of the deceased who "through no fault of their own, had lived and died without ever having had the opportunity of hearing of the Saviour." He further surmised that Christ might visit the realm of the dead more than once.[19] Somewhat similarly, Wolfhart Pannenberg took the descent as a metaphor for the wideness of God's saving mercy.[20]

While Christians should long for the gospel to be preached to every person, this view also lacks biblical support. The only texts that could possibly be rallied to support an evangelistic mission to hell are 1 Peter 3:18–20 and 4:6, which we will examine later in this excursus. However, Augustine recognized that Peter's words do not prove this doctrine: "If the Lord when He died preached in hell to spirits in prison, why were those who continued unbelieving while the ark was a preparing the only ones counted worthy of this favour, namely, the Lord's descending into hell? . . . Or if he preached to all, why has Peter mentioned only these, and passed over the innumerable multitude of others?"[21]

3. Suffering in Hell for Our Sins

The modern reader might assume that "he descended into hell" means Christ went to the place of the damned in order to suffer punishment to complete his atonement for the sins of his people. This idea has been taught as a minority viewpoint in the Roman Catholic tradition by Nicholas de Cusa (1401–1464) and Hans Urs von Balthasar (1905–1988),[22] and from a different perspective by Word of Faith teachers such as Kenneth Copeland, Fred Price, and Joyce Meyer.[23]

Against this doctrine, the Holy Scriptures teach that Christ completed his atoning work by his death on the cross: "We are sanctified through the offering of the body of Jesus Christ once for all. . . . For by one offering he hath perfected for ever them that are sanctified" (Heb. 10:10, 14). The Scriptures never attribute the forgiveness of sins and justification to Christ's descent, but to his blood.[24]

---

19. E. A. Litton, *Introduction to Dogmatic Theology*, ed. Philip E. Hughes (London: James Clarke, 1960), 194–95.

20. Pannenberg, *Jesus—God and Man*, 272.

21. Augustine, Epistle 164.2, to Evodius, in *NPNF*[1], 1:515.

22. Hans Urs von Balthasar, *Mysterium Paschale: The Mystery of Easter*, trans. Aidan Nichols (San Francisco: Ignatius Press, 1990), 168–88.

23. D. R. McConnell, *A Different Gospel: A Historical and Biblical Analysis of the Modern Faith Movement* (Peabody, MA: Hendrickson, 1988), 119–20; and Joyce Meyer, *The Most Important Decision You Will Ever Make* (New York: Warner Faith, 2003), 31–33.

24. Matt. 26:28; Rom. 3:24–25; 5:9; Eph. 1:7; Col. 1:14, 20; Heb. 9:14; 1 John 1:7, 9.

4. Conquering Satan after Dying on the Cross

Another view of Christ's descent takes it literally but assigns it the purpose of breaking the power of hell and Satan. The Lutheran Formula of Concord states, "The entire person [of Christ], God and human being, descended into hell after his burial, conquered the devil, destroyed the power of hell, and took from the devil all his power."[25]

This view of Christ's descent is commendable in that it avoids the unbiblical doctrine of a limbo for the deceased Old Testament saints. However, it, too, is speculative, for the Holy Scriptures nowhere teach that Christ went to hell to attack Satan and take away his power. Rather, the Bible teaches that Christ's death on the cross broke the power of Satan (Col. 2:14–15; Heb. 2:14).[26] Christians overcome the Devil not by Christ's descent but by his blood (Rev. 12:11).

5. Suffering Spiritual Anguish on the Cross

Some medieval theologians reportedly interpreted Christ's descent into hell in terms of "a punishment, and not a place."[27] Martin Luther, in addition to identifying the descent as a victorious visit to the underworld, also taught that Christ descended into hell spiritually at Gethsemane and Golgotha as he bore the divine wrath merited by the damned.[28] John Calvin wrote that "He descended into hell" means "that He not only suffered natural death, which is the separation of the body from the soul, but also that His soul was pierced with amazing anguish, which St. Peter calls the pains of death (Acts 2:24)."[29] Calvin also said that the creed first presents Christ's visible sufferings and then, in speaking of his hellish descent, describes "that invisible and incomprehensible judgment which he underwent" on the cross, namely, "suffering in his soul the terrible torments of a condemned and forsaken man."[30] The Heidelberg Catechism (LD 16, Q. 44) interprets Christ's descent as the "inexpressible anguish, pains, terrors, and hellish agonies, in which He was plunged during all His sufferings, but especially on the cross."[31]

---

25. Formula of Concord (Solid Declaration, 9.2–3), in *The Book of Concord*, 635.
26. Olevianus, *An Exposition of the Apostles' Creed*, 87. See chap. 53.
27. Yates, "'He Descended into Hell': Creed, Article and Scripture, Part 1," 245; and editorial note in Calvin, *Institutes*, 2.16.10 (1:515n23).
28. Bagchi, "Luther versus Luther?," 191–93. See Luther, *Sermons on the Gospel of St. John*, in *LW*, 22:325; *A Sermon on Preparing to Die*, in *LW*, 42:105.
29. Calvin's Catechism of 1545 (Q. 65), in *Reformed Confessions*, 1:477.
30. Calvin, *Institutes*, 2.16.10.
31. Heidelberg Catechism (LD 16, Q. 44), in *The Three Forms of Unity*, 81. See Ames, *A Sketch of the Christian's Catechism*, 84.

6. Dying and Dwelling in the State of Death

Other Reformed theologians have taken the descent as a metaphorical expression for dying, being buried, and becoming subject to a state of death for a time.[32] Perkins argued that the descent into hell means that "when He was dead and buried, He was held captive in the grave and lay in bondage under death for the space of three days." This, Perkins said, was the lowest point in his humiliation.[33] William Ames clarified that this hellish bondage "under the reign of death" was the "lowest humiliation," but it did not involve "affliction," which was finished on the cross.[34] This view is also endorsed by the Westminster Larger Catechism (Q. 50), which says,

> Q. Wherein consisted Christ's humiliation after his death?
> A. Christ's humiliation after his death consisted in his being buried (1 Cor. 15:3–4), and continuing in the state of the dead, and under the power of death till the third day (Ps. 16:10; Acts 2:24–27, 31; Rom. 6:9; Matt. 12:40); which hath been otherwise expressed in these words, *He descended into hell.*[35]

It is possible to combine the fifth and sixth interpretations, both accepted by Reformed theologians, into a holistic descent into the power of death in both its spiritual and physical aspects, as we find in the Leiden *Synopsis* and the theology of Herman Witsius.[36] Francis Turretin said, "If it is asked which of these two opinions ought to be retained, we answer both can be admitted and be made to agree perfectly with each other. Thus by descent into hell may be understood the extreme degree of Christ's suffering and humiliation, both as to soul and body; and as the lowest degree of humiliation as to the body was its detention in the sepulcher, so as to the soul were those dreadful torments he felt."[37]

We have surveyed six approaches to Christ's descent into hell, offering some critique of non-Reformed positions along the way. However,

---

32. Martin Bucer, *Enarrationes in Evangelia* (1536), 511–12, 792–94, cited in editorial note in Calvin, *Institutes*, 2.16.8 (1:513n18). The note also mentions Theodore Beza as a possible advocate of this view.
33. Perkins, *An Exposition of the Symbol*, in *Works*, 5:234.
34. Ames, *The Marrow of Theology*, 1.22.28–29 (144).
35. *Reformed Confessions*, 4:308.
36. Polyander, Walaeus, Thysius, and Rivetus, *Synopsis Purioris Theologiae*, 27.31–32 (2:155); and Witsius, *Sacred Dissertations on the Apostles' Creed*, 18.9–12, 18–19 (2:141–43, 147–48).
37. Turretin, *Institutes*, 13.16.8 (2:363).

the great question still remains: What does God's Word reveal about this matter?

Biblical Texts Relevant to the Descent

The Bible says very little about a descent of Christ or his state after his death and burial but prior to his resurrection. The Scriptures never say explicitly that Christ "descended into hell,"[38] but they do say that Christ "descended" and sometimes describe his condition as "hell."[39] It also should be noted that in the Bible, "hell" often translates terms in Hebrew (*sheol*) or Greek (*hadēs*) that can refer either generally to death and the grave[40] or, more specifically, to the realm to which the wicked go when they die under God's wrath.[41] Connected to the latter is the idea of the loss of all honor and total humiliation.[42] The meaning of humiliation is connected to the use of *sheol* or *hadēs* for the polar opposite of heaven, the lowest extreme versus the highest.[43] We must bear in mind the ambiguity of these words when interpreting the following Scripture passages.

First, Christ said that just as Jonah spent three days and nights in the "belly" of a great fish, so he would be "in the heart of the earth" (Matt. 12:40) for a similar period. However, this was likely an idiom for Christ's physical burial and need not imply a descent into the underworld.[44] In the book of Jonah, "the belly of the fish" (Jonah 1:17) has parallels in the expressions "the belly of hell" (2:2), or "death" (*sheol*), and "the heart of the seas" (v. 3 ESV), where Jonah nearly drowned and was imprisoned (v. 6) as a sinner "cast out of thy sight" (v. 4). Christ's allusion to Jonah suggests that Jesus would die and be buried as one under God's judgment against sinners. Interpreting Christ's words as a reference to his burial fits his calling this a "sign" (Matt. 12:39), for his death, burial, and empty

---

38. However, the Bible does speak of the wicked descending or going down into "hell" (*sheol* or *hadēs*). See Ps. 55:15; Prov. 5:5; 7:27; Isa. 5:14; 14:15; Ezek. 31:16–17; 32:21–22; Matt. 11:23; Luke 10:15.

39. Witsius, *Sacred Dissertations on the Apostles' Creed*, 18.2 (2:137).

40. Gen. 37:35; 1 Sam. 2:6; Ps. 89:48; Hos. 13:14; Hab. 2:5; 1 Cor. 15:55; Rev. 1:18; etc.

41. Deut. 32:22; Pss. 9:17; 49:14–15; Prov. 5:5; 7:27; 9:18; 23:14; Matt. 11:23; Luke 10:15; 16:23; etc.

42. Isa. 14:11, 15–17; Matt. 11:23. See Olevianus, *An Exposition of the Apostles' Creed*, 88; and Turretin, *Institutes*, 13.16.3 (2:362).

43. Job 11:8; Ps. 139:8; Amos 9:2.

44. The similar expression translated as "in the heart of the sea[s]" (Hebrew *beleb yam/yamim*) can refer to being surrounded by water while on the surface of the sea (Prov. 23:34; 30:19; Ezek. 27:4). Thus, "heart" need not refer to the utter depths.

tomb were widely known, and his resurrection was publicly testified by witnesses, but how could a secret descent into hell have been a sign to the scribes and the Pharisees?[45]

Second, another relevant text is the Gospel record that after Christ died, "the graves were opened; and many bodies of the saints which slept arose" (Matt. 27:52). This could be taken as a sign that Christ descended into the realm of the dead and released his saints from its imprisonment. However, the text does not report the release of dead spirits to go to heaven, but the bodily raising of people from the dead. Furthermore, while the breaking open of the graves took place in the earthquake at Christ's death (v. 51), the rising of these saints did not take place until "after his resurrection" (v. 53). Therefore, this passage does not teach us anything about Christ's activity between his death and resurrection.

Third, Paul writes, "Now that he ascended, what is it but that he also descended first into the lower parts of the earth?" (Eph. 4:9). The ascent is into heaven (v. 10). Paul says nothing more here about the descent. In other biblical texts, the verb translated as "descend" (*katabainō*) is used of Christ's incarnation, his coming down from heaven to earth (John 3:13; 6:33, 38). The phrase "the lower parts of the earth" (*ta katōtera merē tēs gēs*) could mean "the lower regions, that is, the earth," in contrast to the upper regions, which are the heavens (cf. Isa. 44:23).[46] It especially refers to death,[47] as in Psalm 63:9–10: "But those that seek my soul, to destroy it, shall go into the lower parts of the earth [*ta katōtata tēs gēs*, LXX]. They shall fall by the sword: they shall be a portion for foxes."[48] Paul's words, then, do not support a literal descent into hell, but are best interpreted as a figure of speech for Christ's humiliation unto death.[49]

Fourth, Luke reports Peter's Pentecost sermon (Acts 2) in terms relevant to the descent into hell. Peter says that when God raised Christ, he "loosed the pains of death [*tas ōdinas tou thanatou*]" (v. 24). This might

---

45. Perkins, *An Exposition of the Symbol*, in *Works*, 5:231.

46. Turretin, *Institutes*, 13.15.10 (2:359); and Witsius, *Sacred Dissertations on the Apostles' Creed*, 18.3 (2:138).

47. Witsius, *Sacred Dissertations on the Apostles' Creed*, 18.3 (2:138–39); cf. Ezek. 26:20; 31:14.

48. Though death is associated with the earth through burial, in Ps. 63:9–10, those who descend into the lower parts of the earth become food for scavengers, which implies that their bodies are not buried. This illustrates the extent to which the lower parts of the earth are associated with death even apart from interment in a grave. Perhaps death is viewed as inherently earthy because it is a return to the dust from which man was made (Gen. 3:19).

49. John Chrysostom, *Homilies on Ephesians*, hom. 11, in *NPNF*[1], 13:103–4; and Baugh, *Ephesians*, 327–28.

suggest a tormented afterlife. However, this phrase appears in the Psalms, where it refers to death itself as a powerful and painful danger threatening God's servant.[50] The word translated as "pain" (*ōdin*) is often used for the anguish of God's judgment.[51] Calvin linked Peter's statement with Christ's forsakenness on the cross (Matt. 27:46), which itself is expressed in terms of the Psalter (Ps. 22:1).[52]

Citing Psalm 16:10, Peter also says that Christ's "soul [*psychē*] was not left in hell [*hadēs*], neither did his flesh see corruption" (Acts 2:31; cf. v. 27). This could be interpreted as implying that Christ's soul was in "hell" until the resurrection (v. 32). However, in the Psalms, the language of delivering someone's "soul" from "hell" refers to rescuing the whole person from death, not releasing his spirit from the underworld.[53] The context of such statements is the danger presented by one's enemies or God's wrath. Peter applies Psalm 16:10 to Christ's resurrection from the dead, as does Paul (Acts 13:34–35). Therefore, rather than teaching a literal descent into hell, Peter's words far more likely imply that Christ's "hell" consisted of suffering and dying under God's judgment while being humiliated by his enemies.

Fifth, Peter also writes that Christ was "put to death in the flesh, but quickened by the Spirit: by which also he went and preached unto the spirits in prison; which sometime were disobedient . . . in the days of Noah" (1 Pet. 3:18–20). This is the Scripture passage most likely to support the doctrine of a literal descent into the spirit world. However, the text is extremely difficult to interpret and thus serves as a doubtful basis for this doctrine.

Two interpretations commend themselves as most likely in our view. One understands Peter to say that the preexistent Christ preached by his Spirit through Noah to wicked men in the days before the worldwide flood.[54] When the text says that Christ was made alive in the "spirit" (*pneuma*), in or by which he went and preached to those in prison, it refers

---

50. Pss. 17:5–6 (18:4–5); 114:3 (116:3) LXX.
51. Deut. 2:25; Job 21:17; Ps. 47:7 (48:6); Isa. 13:8; 26:17; Jer. 6:24; 13:21; 22:23; 27:43 (50:43); Ezek. 7:4 (7); Hos. 13:13; Mic. 4:9; Nah. 2:11 (10) LXX; Matt. 24:8; Mark 13:8; 1 Thess. 5:3. The literal meaning of *ōdin* is "labor pain" or "birth pang."
52. Calvin, *Institutes*, 2.16.11.
53. Pss. 29:4 (30:3); 48:16 (49:16); 85:15 (86:13); 88:49 (89:48) LXX. The word translated as "soul" (*psychē*) can refer to the whole person (Gen. 2:7 LXX; Rom. 13:1). Perkins, *An Exposition of the Symbol*, in *Works*, 5:232. On the wide range of meanings for "soul" (*nephesh, psychē*), see chap. 12.
54. Grudem, *1 Peter*, 165–70, 211–48.

to the divine Spirit, not Christ's human spirit, for it pertains to Christ's resurrection ("quickened" or "made alive").[55] "The Spirit of Christ" inspired the ancient prophets (1:10–11), including Noah, who was "a preacher of righteousness" to the wicked before God destroyed them in the flood (2 Pet. 2:5).

Another interpretation of 1 Peter 3:18–20 takes Peter's words as a revelation of a post-resurrection triumph of Christ over evil spirits imprisoned by God for their sins.[56] This interpretation follows the order of Peter's presentation: death, resurrection, and proclamation (vv. 18–19). A variation of this interpretation sees the preaching to these spirits as a way of describing the effect of Christ's ascension (v. 22)—his exaltation is itself a proclamation of victory over the evil spirits.[57] Peter uses the same Greek participle that means "having gone" (*poreutheis*) to say that Christ, literally, "having gone," preached to the spirits (v. 19) and that he, "having gone into heaven," now "is on the right hand of God; angels and authorities and powers being made subject unto him" (v. 22).

In either interpretation, both of which are plausible, Peter makes no reference to Christ's soul descending into hell. Therefore, this text offers little support for such a doctrine.

Sixth, Peter says, "The gospel [was] preached also to them that are dead" (1 Pet. 4:6). However, it seems best to interpret this text as saying not that the dead were evangelized, but that people were evangelized in their lifetime but now are dead.[58] In the same way, Naomi said that her daughters-in-law had dealt kindly "with the dead" (Ruth 1:8), referring to their acts of love for her deceased sons when the men were still alive.[59] Peter's point is probably that those who heard the gospel and believed it when they were alive in this world, though "judged" by wicked persecutors and now "dead," nevertheless still "live according to God in the spirit" (1 Pet. 4:6).

Seventh, we have a clear statement from our Lord Jesus concerning his spirit's location immediately after his death. Christ promised to the

55. Perkins, *An Exposition of the Symbol*, in *Works*, 5:232; and Turretin, *Institutes*, 13.14.12 (2:360–61).

56. Schreiner, *1, 2 Peter, Jude*, 184–90.

57. Bavinck, *Reformed Dogmatics*, 3:480–81; Andrew J. Bandstra, "'Making Proclamation to the Spirits in Prison': Another Look at 1 Peter 3:19," *Calvin Theological Journal* 38 (2003): 120–24; and Karen H. Jobes, *1 Peter*, Baker Exegetical Commentary on the New Testament (Grand Rapids, MI: Baker Academic, 2005), 242–43.

58. Schreiner, *1, 2 Peter, Jude*, 205–10.

59. Grudem, "He Did Not Descend to the Dead," 111n10.

repentant thief dying beside him, "Today shalt thou be with me in paradise" (Luke 23:43). "Paradise" refers to heaven.[60] Christ's promise that the thief would be "with me in paradise" answers the thief's request, "Lord, remember me when thou comest into thy kingdom" (v. 42). Turretin observed, "Fellowship with Christ in his kingdom is promised"—that is, his kingdom as the incarnate Mediator.[61] Thus, Christ committed his human "spirit" into the Father's hands shortly before died (Luke 23:46; cf. Ps. 31:5). Therefore, Christ's promise to the repentant thief teaches us that Christ's spirit entered triumphantly into heaven immediately after his death to fellowship with the Father and the spirits of believers who had died before him.

Concluding Thoughts on Christ's Descent

In conclusion, the Holy Scriptures give us no divinely revealed basis to believe in a literal descent of Jesus Christ into hell between his death and resurrection. Paul summarizes the gospel as Christ's death, burial, resurrection, and appearances, but says nothing of a descent into hell (1 Cor. 15:1–5).[62] Not one of the four Gospels narrates a descent of Christ's soul into hell. Each gives us a detailed account of Christ's earthly ministry, sufferings, death, burial, and resurrection, but is silent about any literal descent. It is unlikely that they would have omitted such an event, especially if it played a significant role in redemptive history.[63] Instead, the Scriptures use the language of "descent" and "hell" figuratively to describe Christ's sufferings, death, and burial as the nadir of his rejection under God's wrath and humiliation before his enemies, from which God delivered him in his resurrection. The word *hell* vividly communicates the sorrows inflicted upon Christ as he died in the place of his people.

Therefore, the Holy Scriptures warrant the adoption of a combination of the fifth and sixth interpretations listed above: Christ's descent into hell consists of his extreme humiliation in both soul and body, climaxing for his soul in the suffering of God's wrath on the cross and for his body in death under God's curse, burial, and continuation in death for a time.

---

60. 2 Cor. 12:2, 4; Rev. 2:7; cf. 22:1–3. The Greek word translated as "paradise" (*paradeisos*) means a garden and is used of the garden of Eden (Gen. 2–3; 13:10; Isa. 51:3; Ezek. 28:13 LXX).
61. Turretin, *Institutes*, 13.15.5 (2:357).
62. Turretin, *Institutes*, 13.16.4 (2:362).
63. Perkins, *An Exposition of the Symbol*, in *Works*, 5:230.

This integrated Reformed doctrine of the descent draws from the best in the historical tradition, such as Rufinus's statement that the descent is implied by Christ's death and burial.[64] Furthermore, we observe that in some ancient creeds, the descent appears to function as a substitute for the burial, which is then omitted.[65] Therefore, we argue that this view is a reformation of the ancient perspective. Its metaphorical interpretation of "descended into hell" is consistent with the biblical use of these terms and with the creed's later metaphorical (and biblical) language of Christ sitting at the "right hand" of God. Furthermore, coming at the end of the creed's sequence of Christ's humiliation, the descent aptly summarizes his passion, death, and burial without being redundant, for in it we confess that Christ experienced the greatest degree of humiliation in both soul and body.

When Christians recite the Apostles' Creed, the clause "he descended into hell" may cause confusion and raise concern among those who have not been taught its biblical meaning. However, the descent of Christ and his suffering of the pains of hell are biblical themes, which, when rightly interpreted, point to his complete experience of death as the curse of God upon sinners. Therefore, while the tradition of Christ's descent must be reformed by the Word of God, we need not cast aside the tradition entirely, for it contains strands of important biblical truth. This means that Christians can confess, with good conscience, that Christ "descended into hell" and bless God for it. At the very least, Christians should affirm the biblical teachings of Christ's utter humiliation in his soul's spiritual anguish prior to death and in his body's death, burial, and continuance in the grave until the third day.

The doctrine of the descent should make us marvel at the depths of humiliation to which Christ voluntarily went for us. Furthermore, it should make us willing to follow him in sharing his humiliation. Perkins said that Christ's descent into hell should teach "every one of us that profess the name of Christ that if it please God to afflict us either in body or in mind or in both, though it be in most grievous and tedious manner, yet must we not think it strange." Christ suffered "the pangs of hell" on the cross, and then death seized him and triumphed over him for a time. If God lays a heavy affliction upon us, let us not despair, Perkins said, but

---

64. Rufinus, *A Commentary on the Apostles' Creed*, secs. 18, 28, in *NPNF*², 3:550, 553–54.
65. Athanasian Creed (sec. 38), in *The Three Forms of Unity*, 11; Creed of Venantius Fortunatus (c. 570), in *The Creeds of Christendom*, ed. Schaff, 2:49. See Turretin, *Institutes*, 13.16.2 (2:362).

realize that God is making us like Christ so that we may live as his true children.[66] Furthermore, no matter how low God may humble his children, he will never send them into the hellish depths to which Christ went to redeem us when he died under God's curse, was buried, and abode in death for our sake.

---

66. Perkins, *An Exposition of the Symbol*, in *Works*, 5:234–35.

45

Christ's Prophetic Work, Part 1

Introduction and Typology

The Lord Jesus Christ said, "I am the way, the truth, and the life" (John 14:6). Christ is the Mediator of "the truth" by which we know God and his will for our salvation. In other words, Christ is the Prophet of his people; he fulfilled the prophetic office by which God reveals himself and his saving will to sinners.[1]

Christ is the living, personal revelation of God. He is more than a prophet; he is Lord of the prophets. He is more than a messenger; he is the Message. Robert Letham says, "As the incarnate Son of God, he was infinitely greater than any of the prophets of the Old Testament." They were sinners; he is the Holy One. They were God's servants; he is God's Son. He was "the focus of all the prophets"; indeed, he is "the truth" itself.[2]

In this chapter, we address five introductory matters that lay a foundation for our study of Christ's prophetic work. How is Christ's person uniquely suited to be the revealer of God? What role does Christ play in general revelation? Why is Christ's work of special revelation important? What did God reveal through Moses concerning Christ's coming ministry of revelation? Lastly, looking beyond Moses, what does the full ministry of the Prophet entail?

---

1. For biblical evidence that Christ fulfilled the threefold office of Prophet, Priest, and King, see chap. 43. For official titles given to Christ that pertain to his work of revelation, see chap. 37.
2. Letham, *The Work of Christ*, 91–92.

The Perfection of Christ's Prophetic Person

Christ's work as the Prophet depends upon his unique person as God the Son incarnate. His two natures and his relations as the Son in the Trinity qualify him to serve as the ideal divine revealer. We see this in three ways that the Bible describes Christ.

First, Christ is *the Word of God*. Unlike the Hebrew prophets, we never read of Christ that "the word of the Lord came unto him."[3] Rather, he is the Word. John begins his Gospel by saying, "In the beginning was the Word, and the Word was with God, and the Word was God" (1:1). It was through this Word that God made "all things"; indeed, "without him was not any thing made that was made" (v. 3). Hence, Christ is called "the Word" not merely because of his work in salvation, but because of his eternal relation to the Father and participation in the work of creation. The term translated as "Word" (*logos*) means a person's speech or rational thought. Christ is "the Word of God" (Rev. 19:13), not merely a temporal means of doing God's will, but the Father's eternal self-expression: "In the beginning was the Word." This "divine self-expression"[4] is so perfect that he is a distinct person from the Father ("with God") and yet shares the same deity as the Father ("was God").[5] Consequently, when "the Word was made flesh" (John 1:14), the perfect self-expression of God became truly human so that we could know him and relate to him on our level. Carl Henry (1913–2003) wrote, "The Logos of God—preincarnate, incarnate, and now glorified—is the mediating agent of all divine disclosure. He is the unique and sole mediator of the revelation of the Living God."[6]

Second, Christ is *the Son of God*.[7] This title implies, among many things, that Christ knows the Father in a unique manner. This qualifies Christ above all others to reveal God. John 1:18 says, "No man hath seen God at any time; the only begotten Son, which is in the bosom of the Father, he hath declared him." Jesus said, "No man knoweth the Son, but the Father; neither knoweth any man the Father, save the Son, and he to whomsoever the Son will reveal him" (Matt. 11:27). Who could better give us the knowledge of God than his Son?

---

3. For examples of this common expression, see Gen. 15:1, 4; 2 Sam. 7:4; 24:11; 1 Kings 13:20; 17:2, 8; 2 Kings 20:4; 1 Chron. 22:8; Jer. 1:2; Ezek. 1:3; Jonah 1:1; 3:1; Hag. 2:20; Zech. 4:8.
4. Carson, *The Gospel according to John*, 116.
5. On the eternal generation of the Son, see *RST*, 1:933–40.
6. Carl F. H. Henry, *God, Revelation and Authority*, 6 vols. (Waco, TX: Word, 1976), 3:203. See the discussion of special revelation's mediatorial, Trinitarian character in *RST*, 1:265–68.
7. On Christ's name "the Son of God," see the discussion of his names of deity in chap. 37.

Third, Christ is *the Image of God*. Paul says that Christ "is the image of the invisible God" (Col. 1:15). To see Christ is to see God (John 12:45; 14:9). One might think that Paul refers to Christ merely as a man here, for Adam was created "in the image of God" (Gen. 1:27), and Christ is "the last Adam" (1 Cor. 15:45; cf. Rom. 5:14). However, this Image transcends Adam, for Paul goes on to say, "For by him were all things created, that are in heaven, and that are in earth, visible and invisible, whether they be thrones, or dominions, or principalities, or powers: all things were created by him, and for him" (Col. 1:16). Therefore, Christ is God's Image not only in his humanity but in his eternal deity as Creator. John Owen said, "He is the essential image of the Father" due to "the unity or sameness of their nature."[8] Yet the Father is never called the image of Christ, though identical to him in attributes, for the idea of "image" derives from Christ's sonship: the Son is the Image of the Father. Owen explained, "Whatever belongs to the person of the Son, as the person of the Son, he receives it all from the Father by eternal generation: 'For as the Father hath life in himself, so hath he given unto the Son to have life in himself' (John 5:26)."[9] Thus, Owen said, "In his incarnation, the Son was made the representative image of God unto us—as he was, in his person, the essential image of the Father, by eternal generation."[10] This divine Image, now ascended into heaven, appears to us in the written Word. When people perceive the meaning of the gospel of Jesus Christ, they perceive the shining of God's glory, for Christ "is the image of God" (2 Cor. 4:4).

The connection between divine revelation and Christ as God's Son and Image also appears in Hebrews 1:3, which says that the Son of God is "the brightness of his glory, and the express image of his person." Here again, Christ's whole person as God and man is in view, for the context refers to Christ's participation in the works of creation and providence, and his atoning for sins by his death (vv. 2–3). William Gouge wrote, "As he is the Son of God, the second person of the Trinity, the whole divine essence, and all the divine properties are communicated to him."[11] The Son not only resembles the Father but is the very same in nature. Gouge also said, "As Christ's human nature is hypostatically united to the divine nature, Christ

---

8. Owen, *Christologia*, in *Works*, 1:71.
9. Owen, *Christologia*, in *Works*, 1:71.
10. Owen, *Christologia*, in *Works*, 1:72.
11. William Gouge, *Commentary on the Whole Epistle to the Hebrews*, 3 vols. (Edinburgh: James Nichol, 1866), 1:16.

is visibly the character or express image of God." In the incarnate Son, the divine properties, such as "almighty power, infinite wisdom, truth, justice, mercy, and the like," are visibly seen, like an image of a person stamped upon a coin.[12]

These three titles call us to trust in the great Prophet as the God-man.[13] Owen pointed out that those who praise Christ as a teacher but deny his deity lack the "holy qualifications" needed to receive Christ's teachings with spiritual benefit, for they do not regard their Teacher as God. Owen said, "For hence do reverence, humility, faith, delight, and assurance, arise and flow. . . . And the want of these things is the cause of much of that lifeless, unsanctified knowledge of the doctrine of the Gospel which is amongst many."[14] At the same time, the Prophet is truly human, a man who communicates to us on our level, having received "the divine thoughts" first in "his own human consciousness," as Henri de Vries (1847–1932) said.[15]

Christ the Revealer and General Revelation

Christ's involvement in God's works of creation and providence shows us that Christ is also directly involved in God's general revelation to all mankind (John 1:1–3; Col. 1:16; Heb. 1:2–3).[16] God's world reveals his glory because it is the work of God's essential Word and Image.

That is not to confuse general revelation with special revelation. Although God's creation continually testifies to his glory and goodness (Ps. 19:1; Acts 14:17), the gospel of salvation is unknown to man apart from special revelation from God (Rom. 1:16–17; 1 Cor. 1:20–21; 2:9–10).[17] George Stevenson (1771–1841) wrote, "The plan of mercy for the recovery of fallen man is supernatural, and could be known only by supernatural revelation."[18] Christ's official work as Prophet pertains to special revelation, for it is embedded in the covenant of grace. People cannot call upon the Mediator if they have never heard of him (Rom. 10:14). Therefore, Christ is the Mediator of truth.

---

12. Gouge, *Commentary on Hebrews*, 1:16–17.
13. On Christ as the God-man, see the discussion of the incarnate Lord's unique identity in chap. 39.
14. Owen, *Christologia*, in *Works*, 1:96.
15. Henri de Vries, *The Lord's Anointed Prophet, Priest and King: A Series of Devotional Studies on the Redemptive Work of Christ* (London: Marshall Brothers, 1925), 56.
16. On general revelation, see *RST*, 1:184–86, 195–263.
17. On the necessity of God's Word, see *RST*, 1:353–59. Against the error of religious pluralism that God has revealed many ways to himself through various religions, see *RST*, 1:299–304.
18. George Stevenson, *Treatise on the Offices of Christ*, 2nd ed. (Edinburgh: W. P. Kennedy, 1845), 17.

However, there is continuity and consistency between general and special revelation, for both come through Christ. Herman Bavinck wrote that though general revelation is "insufficient for salvation," it is still "a witness of the Logos" as "by various ways and means, Christ lays the groundwork for his own work of grace."[19] Therefore, those who love Christ should also value the general revelation of God's glory in his world. Yet they must cherish special revelation all the more. Though the cosmos is a theater for God's glory, if we seek God apart from Jesus Christ, we "must wander," John Calvin said, "in a labyrinth."[20] However, Calvin added, "since, when we wish to rise to God, all our senses immediately fail, Christ is placed before our eyes as a lively image of the invisible God."[21]

The Importance of Christ's Special Revelation

Christ came to deliver the truth of God to the minds of perishing men, women, and children. We should treasure his ministry of truth and look to him daily to teach us and guide us.

The Priority of Christ's Ministry of Truth

Some people might be inclined to pass quickly over Christ's prophetic ministry. Perhaps they would do so in reaction against theological liberalism, which so emphasizes Christ's teaching that it neglects his other saving works. Or they might think that our Lord's instruction is relatively unimportant compared to his atonement for sin and his return to reign in glory.

Christ, however, saw his ministry of preaching and teaching as essential to his mission. He announced his ministry in Nazareth by reading from the prophecy of Isaiah that God "hath anointed me to preach the gospel" (Luke 4:18; cf. 7:22). When his teaching stirred interest in Capernaum, people tried to persuade him to stay there. Jesus replied, "I must preach the good news of the kingdom of God to other towns as well; for I was sent for this purpose" (4:43 ESV). Hence, he "went throughout every city and village" preaching the gospel (8:1). When he came to Jerusalem, knowing that the time of his death drew near, he taught the people daily in the temple (19:47–48; 20:1; 21:37–38).

19. Bavinck, *Reformed Dogmatics*, 4:34.
20. Calvin, *Commentaries*, on John 8:19. See Edmondson, *Calvin's Christology*, 176–81.
21. Calvin, *Commentaries*, on John 5:22.

When Jesus reviewed his life's work just before he surrendered himself to those who would murder him, he prayed to the Father, "I have finished the work which thou gavest me to do. . . . I have manifested thy name unto the men which thou gavest me out of the world. . . . I have given unto them the words which thou gavest me. . . . I have declared unto them thy name, and will declare it" (John 17:4, 6, 8, 26). Christ said to Pilate, "To this end was I born, and for this cause came I into the world, that I should bear witness unto the truth" (18:37).

The Necessity of Christ's Ministry of Truth

Christ said, "I am the light of the world: he that followeth me shall not walk in darkness, but shall have the light of life" (John 8:12). Darkness vividly describes the spiritual ignorance of mankind: "The one who walks in the darkness does not know where he is going" (12:35 ESV; cf. 1 John 2:11). People go blindly to their own destruction. Yet their ignorance is culpable, for "men loved darkness rather than light, because their deeds were evil" (John 3:19).

The prophet Isaiah taught that those without God's Word have "no light," but dwell in "trouble and darkness, dimness of anguish" (Isa. 8:20, 22). This darkness was not peculiar to the ancient Jewish people, but has enveloped all nations in all ages until God's light has come to them (60:1–3). We see an example of this when Christ began preaching in Galilee: "The people that walked in darkness have seen a great light" (9:1–2; cf. Matt. 4:12–17).

The darkness that engulfs mankind is not merely around us as a lack of knowledge, but also within us as a lack of understanding. Jeremiah lamented, "They know not me, saith the LORD. . . . Through deceit they refuse to know me" (Jer. 9:3, 6). Paul says, "No one understands; no one seeks for God" (Rom. 3:11 ESV). The peoples walk "in the vanity of their mind, having the understanding darkened, being alienated from the life of God through the ignorance that is in them, because of the blindness ["hardness," KJV mg.] of their heart" (Eph. 4:17–18). It is not merely that people dwell in darkness, but they *are* darkness (5:8).[22]

The answer to man's inner darkness is inner illumination by union with Christ. Believers are "light in the Lord" (Eph. 5:8), for those who have learned differently from the unbelievers of this world "have heard him, and have been taught by him, as the truth is in Jesus" (4:21). Hence, God says

---

22. On human depravity and inability, see chap. 21.

to the perishing, "Awake thou that sleepest, and arise from the dead, and Christ shall give thee light" (5:14). Only then are the blinded minds of sinners opened to see and receive the truth that God reveals in Christ (2 Cor. 4:4, 6).

Now we can understand and appreciate the absolute necessity of Christ's ministry of communicating truth, both objectively and subjectively, to mankind. Salvation is by faith in Christ (Gal. 2:16; Eph. 2:8). The Lord Jesus would have died for our sins in vain if we had never heard his gospel and had our eyes opened to turn to God and receive his forgiveness (Acts 26:18). Thanks be to God for the Light of the World!

Christ's Prophetic Office Foretold and Foreshadowed by Moses

The prophets of the Old Testament prepared the way for the great messianic Prophet. Although the Bible identifies Abel (Luke 11:50–51), Enoch (Jude 14), and Abraham (Gen. 20:7) as prophets, the foundational figure for the prophetic office was clearly Moses. He was the "prophet" by whom "the LORD brought Israel out of Egypt" (Hos. 12:13). The old covenant rested upon revelation granted through Moses, just as the new covenant rests upon revelation through the incarnate Lord Jesus Christ (John 1:17). Moses was a type of Christ.

As his death drew near, Moses spoke of the officers through whom God would administer his covenant: priest and Levite, judge and king, and prophet (Deut. 17–18). In the latter part of that text (18:15–22), Moses described the prophetic office in a manner that the New Testament applies to Christ (Acts 3:22–23; 7:37). These words of Moses provide a focused description of Christ's prophetic work. We will study them according to four themes evident in the parallelism of the text (Deut. 18:15–19), as presented in Table 45.1 below.

Theme	Deuteronomy 18:15–16	Deuteronomy 18:17–19
Spokesman Called by God	[Moses said,] The LORD thy God will *raise up* unto thee a *Prophet*	And the LORD said unto me, They have well spoken that which they have spoken. I will *raise* them up a *Prophet*
Brother Sent in Condescending Mercy	from the midst of thee, of thy *brethren*,	from among their *brethren*,

Theme	Deuteronomy 18:15–16	Deuteronomy 18:17–19
Like Moses in Priestly Access and Kingly Power	*like unto* me [Moses];	*like unto* thee,
Mediator of God's Authoritative Words	unto him ye shall *hearken*; according to all that thou desiredst of the LORD thy God in Horeb in the day of the assembly, saying, Let me not *hear* again the *voice* of the LORD my God, neither let me see this great fire any more, that I die not.	and will put *my words in his mouth*; and he shall speak unto them all that I shall command him. And it shall come to pass, that whosoever will not *hearken* unto *my words* which he shall speak in my name, I will require it of him.

Table 45.1. Parallelism in Moses's Promise of a Prophet (Deut. 18:15–19)

The Spokesman Called by God

Who is the "Prophet" foretold by Moses? The prophet in view "has both a corporate and individual significance," as Meredith Kline commented. The collective reference to the whole prophetic office in Israel is evident in the contrast between a faithful prophet and a false prophet (vv. 20–22), and in the larger context, which "deals with the several theocratic offices."[23] However, the text highlighted a single "Prophet."[24] Deuteronomy said that God had not yet raised up anyone "like unto Moses" (Deut. 34:10). The promise had a singular, extraordinary Prophet ultimately in view, the second and greater Moses.[25]

The promise of Deuteronomy 18:15, then, while introducing "the prophetic institution," is "a Messianic promise,"[26] as the apostle Peter indicated when he quoted it (Acts 3:22–23). Christ called himself a "prophet" in continuity with the old covenant prophets (Luke 4:24) and anticipated that, as such, he would share the bloody persecution suffered by the prophets in Jerusalem (13:33–34). On the Mount of

---

23. Kline, *Treaty of the Great King*, 101.

24. The singular "prophet" (*nabi'*) is pushed to the front of the Hebrew text for emphasis in both Deut. 18:15 and 18.

25. Poole, *Annotations upon the Holy Bible*, 1:372, on Deut. 18:15. For arguments that the Prophet in Deuteronomy 18 is Christ, see Michael Rydelnik, *The Messianic Hope: Is the Hebrew Bible Really Messianic?*, NAC Studies in Bible and Theology (Nashville: B&H Academic, 2010), 56–64; and Yoon-Hee Kim, "'The Prophet like Moses': Deut. 18:15–22 Reexamined within the Context of the Pentateuch and in Light of the Final Shape of the TaNaK" (PhD diss., Trinity Evangelical Divinity School, 1995).

26. Edward J. Young, *My Servants the Prophets* (Grand Rapids, MI: Eerdmans, 1952), 29–35.

Transfiguration, Moses and Elijah, both prophets of major significance, appeared with Christ in glory and spoke with him about his "exodus" (9:30 KJV mg.), suggesting that he is the reality of which Moses was a type.

What does the word translated as "prophet" (*nabi'*) mean?[27] Etymology is not helpful here, for the Hebrew word is of uncertain derivation.[28] However, the Lord made his meaning clear by analogy when he said to Moses, "I have made thee a god to Pharaoh: and Aaron thy brother shall be thy prophet. Thou shalt speak all that I command thee: and Aaron thy brother shall speak unto Pharaoh" (Ex. 7:1–2). In a previous encounter, the Lord said to Moses, "You shall speak to him and put the words in his mouth, and I will be with your mouth and with his mouth and will teach you both what to do. He shall speak for you to the people, and he shall be your mouth, and you shall be as God to him" (4:15–16 ESV). Hence, a prophet is a divine spokesman, God's "mouth," someone appointed by God to declare the words God gives to him (Jer. 15:19).[29] As Calvin said, a prophet is God's "ambassador," commissioned to authoritatively speak his Lord's message.[30]

Other terms for a prophet also emphasize his divine calling to receive and proclaim God's word. A prophet is the Lord's "messenger," God's "servant," and a "man of God."[31] A prophet could also be called a "seer" because he sees the visions given to him by the Lord.[32] Due to his responsibility to keep watch over Israel's covenant keeping and to sound the alarm against covenant breaking, a prophet was also called a "watchman."[33]

In the Greek Septuagint Old Testament and the New Testament, the word used to render "prophet" (*prophētēs*) means one who speaks pub-

---

27. On Old Testament terms for a prophet, see *NIDOTTE*, 4:1068.

28. Young, *My Servants the Prophets*, 56–57.

29. Young, *My Servants the Prophets*, 58; Allan M. Harman, *Deuteronomy: The Commands of a Covenant God*, Focus on the Bible (Fearn, Ross-shire, Scotland: Christian Focus, 2001), 192; and Belcher, *Prophet, Priest, and King*, 21.

30. Calvin, *Commentaries*, on John 1:21. See also *Commentaries*, on Jer. 23:21; Ezek. 3:18; John 1:6, 15. Christ himself is called the Father's ambassador. *Commentaries*, on John 3:32; 8:14, 47.

31. Messenger (*mal'ak*): 2 Chron. 36:15–16; Isa. 44:26; Hag. 1:13; Mal. 3:1 (cf. *angelos* in Matt. 11:10; Mark 1:2; Luke 7:27). Servant (*'ebed*): 2 Kings 9:7; 14:25; 17:13; Isa. 20:3; 44:26; Dan. 9:6, 10; etc. Man of God: Deut. 33:1; Josh. 14:6; 1 Sam. 2:27; 9:6–10; 1 Kings 12:22; 13:1; 17:18; 20:28.

32. Seer (*roeh*): 1 Sam. 9:9, 11, 18–19; 2 Sam. 15:27; 1 Chron. 9:22; 26:28. 29:29; 2 Chron. 16:7, 10; Isa. 30:10. Seer (*khozeh*): 2 Sam. 24:11; 2 Kings 17:13; 1 Chron. 21:9; 25:5; 29:29; 2 Chron. 9:29; 12:15; 19:2; 29:25, 30; 33:18; 35:15; Isa. 29:10; 30:10; Amos 7:12; Mic. 3:7. See also Num. 12:6; 2 Chron. 18:18.

33. Watchman (participle of *tsapah*): Isa. 52:8; 56:10; Jer. 6:17; Ezek. 3:17; 33:2, 6–7; Hos. 9:8; Mic. 7:4.

licly or proclaims.[34] In pagan Greek culture, the term could refer to a man or woman who declared an oracle supposedly revealed by a god.[35] The New Testament reaffirms the same core idea of prophecy as the reception and proclamation of supernatural knowledge revealed by God. We read of the men who arrested Christ, that "when they had blindfolded him, they struck him on the face, and asked him, saying, Prophesy [*prophēteuō*], who is it that smote thee?" (Luke 22:64). Here prophecy does not necessarily pertain to prediction, but to the declaration of knowledge that a man could not naturally possess.[36] Paul says that "the prophets speak" things "revealed" by God (1 Cor. 14:29–30). Here again, prophecy is not primarily about predicting the future, but addressing the present: "He that prophesieth speaketh unto men to edification, and exhortation, and comfort" (v. 3). Thus, the New Testament also portrays a prophet as a spokesman for God.

Moses's words emphasized the divine initiative in choosing the spokesman: the Lord "will raise up" the Prophet (Deut. 18:15, 18). That is, God will call and ordain him to this office.[37] Edward Young said, "The institution of prophecy, therefore, is to be regarded as a gift of God. It is He who raised up the prophets and gave them their messages."[38] This is evident in the life of Moses (Ex. 2–4) and in the sending of Christ to be the light of the world (Isa. 42:1, 6).

Christ repeatedly indicated his dependence upon God for his mission and message. Jesus said, "My doctrine is not mine, but his that sent me" (John 7:16; cf. 8:28; 14:10, 24). However, Christ's ministry transcends a God-prophet relationship and manifests the Father-Son relationship (Luke 10:22). Accordingly, Jesus said, "I have not spoken of myself; but the Father which sent me, he gave me a commandment, what I should say, and what I should speak" (John 12:49). Christ is a "seer" not merely in the sense of a recipient of visions, but as the Son who sees the Father's glory and knows his mind (3:31–32; 5:19–20; 6:46). As the Son, his ministry surpasses that of all other prophets, for "God, who . . . spake in time past unto the fathers by the prophets, hath in these last days spoken unto us by his Son" (Heb. 1:1–2).

---

34. *TDNT*, 6:783.
35. *TDNT*, 6:791.
36. Nichols, *Lectures in Systematic Theology*, 3:663.
37. The same expression (*hiphil* of *qum*) is used of the Lord raising up judges to deliver Israel (Judg. 2:16, 18; 3:9, 15), raising up the Davidic king (Jer. 30:9; Ezek. 34:23), and raising up prophets (Amos 2:11).
38. Young, *My Servants the Prophets*, 36.

The Brother Sent in Condescending Mercy

The second theme appears in Moses's statement that God would raise up this Prophet from the Israelites' "brethren" (Deut. 18:15, 18). The Lord could send his word through a Gentile (Num. 22–24), but the prophetic office resided among the blessed seed of Abraham, Isaac, and Jacob. The repeated use of "brethren" or "brothers" suggests the committed compassion that arises from belonging to one family. Moses, though raised by Pharaoh's daughter, chose to identify with his enslaved Jewish "brethren" (Ex. 2:11; Acts 7:23–26). Office bearers in Israel were not to be foreigners, but brothers who would not despise their brethren (Deut. 17:15, 20). Deuteronomy presented an ethic of brotherhood among God's people that was designed to moderate their dealings with kindness.[39] Thus, Christ relates compassionately to God's people, for "he is not ashamed to call them brethren, saying, I will declare thy name unto my brethren" (Heb. 2:11–12; cf. Ps. 22:22).

The brotherly affection of the prophet is especially significant in light of the Israelites' terror when God spoke directly to them at Mount Sinai. The people feared that God's fiery glory and thunderous voice would slay them, so they asked that Moses mediate God's words to them (Deut. 5:23–31; 18:16–17). In Moses, God gently permitted the people to hear his word from a human mouth (Ex. 4:12, 14) and to see his glory shining in a human face (34:29).

In Christ, the greater Moses, God communicates to mankind in a truly human form. The unspeakably brilliant light of God, who dwells in unapproachable glory (1 Tim. 6:16), shines upon us not in searing holiness but in "tender mercy" (Luke 1:78–79) to bring healing and rejuvenation to weary sinners (Mal. 4:2). God calls us to listen to his Son, whose face shines with glory (Matt. 17:2, 5; 2 Pet. 1:16–18; cf. 2 Cor. 4:4–6). Stevenson said, "Our instructor is not only our God, but also our brother; and while his instructions, coming from the lips of God incarnate, are sanctioned by all the authority of the Son over his own house, they are at the same time softened and sweetened by the mild graces of human nature."[40]

When the Word clothed himself in flesh, divine glory came to mankind full of grace and truth (John 1:14). Our Prophet is no docetic Christ. He performs his prophetic ministry as a man among men. Douglas Kelly

---

39. Deut. 15:1–12; 22:1–4; 23:19–20; 25:3.
40. Stevenson, *Treatise on the Offices of Christ*, 19.

writes, "He speaks with a human voice that can be understood by other humans. He shares our experiences; he uses our thought-forms, linguistic conventions, and grammar. He is so truly human that nearly always he did not appear to be divine; he could be passed by on the road as any other man. . . . His full humanity welcomes us to come."[41]

Let this be an encouragement to you as you consider your sins. God comes to you as the humble and gentle Prophet, clothed in your own flesh and blood. Hear him call you to learn from him and enjoy his rest (Matt. 11:28–30). Listen to him announce God's blessing on the poor in spirit and those who mourn (Isa. 61:1–3; Matt. 5:3–4). This is no severe Master, but a good and kind Lord who leads the humble in the way. Humble yourself, therefore, and be led.

The One Like Moses in Priestly Access and Kingly Power

In the third theme, the Lord said he would raise up a Prophet "like" Moses (Deut. 18:15, 18). We do not need to guess at the main points of this comparison, for Deuteronomy later says, "There arose not a prophet since in Israel like unto Moses, whom the LORD knew face to face, in all the signs and the wonders, which the LORD sent him to do in the land of Egypt to Pharaoh, and to all his servants, and to all his land, and in all that mighty hand, and in all the great terror which Moses shewed in the sight of all Israel" (34:10–12). This Prophet is like Moses in that he enjoys remarkable intimacy with God and wields miraculous power from God.

Moses had an intimacy with God that surpassed even most of the prophets, for God spoke "mouth to mouth" with Moses, and Moses saw the likeness of the Lord (Num. 12:6–8). "The LORD spake unto Moses face to face, as a man speaketh unto his friend" (Ex. 33:11). This does not mean that Moses could gaze directly upon God's "face" or unmediated glory (v. 20), but rather that God and Moses communicated in a clear and intimate manner that was "up close and personal," or "heart to heart," as Douglas Stuart comments.[42] This divine communion was likely presented as Moses having priestly fellowship with God (cf. Ps. 99:6–7), for it took place at the temporary "tent of meeting" (Ex. 33:7 ESV) that Moses set up outside the camp—the same term used for the sacred tabernacle soon to

---

41. Kelly, *Systematic Theology*, 2:189.
42. Douglas K. Stuart, *Exodus*, The New American Commentary 2 (Nashville: Broadman & Holman, 2006), 698n. On friendship with the Lord, see 2 Chron. 20:7; Isa. 41:8; Luke 7:34; 12:4; John 15:13–15; James 2:23.

be erected for the rituals of the priests (29:44). Yet the purpose of Moses's priestly access was not to make atonement, but to receive divine revelation (33:9; cf. 25:22). Thus, it was priestly access for prophetic ministry.

When the great Prophet came, he was no less than the Son of God, which, as we saw earlier in this chapter, implies that Christ has unparalleled intimacy with the Father (John 1:18) and unique knowledge of him (Luke 10:22). The Son and the Father indwell each other, and the Son speaks out of this Trinitarian communion (John 14:10).[43] As the God-man, Jesus often drew near to God in prayer to receive strength and guidance in his ministry of revelation (Mark 1:35–39; Luke 6:12–13; 9:18–23). Christ is the priestly Prophet who brings his divine revelations from the highest and most holy place to the lowliest people on earth.

God worked amazing miracles through Moses to demonstrate his sovereign lordship over every element of creation.[44] These miracles climaxed at the Red Sea, where the Lord proved that he is the great Warrior-King (Ex. 15:3, 18). Moses functioned as the King's lieutenant, through whom God exercised his power. However, this kingly power did not establish a kingdom for Moses, but confirmed his prophetic word (4:1–9).

Christ's prophetic ministry was also marked by great miracles. Through his miracles, people recognized that he was a prophet sent by God (John 6:14; 9:17). However, whereas most of Moses's miracles engaged God's power to judge and destroy, Christ's miracles displayed God's power to save and heal. Thus, "Jesus went about all Galilee, teaching in their synagogues, and preaching the gospel of the kingdom, and healing all manner of sickness and all manner of disease among the people" (Matt. 4:23). Rather than drowning his enemies under the waves of the sea, Jesus calmed the stormy waters (8:26). When Christ raised the only son of a widow from the dead, "there came a fear on all: and they glorified God, saying, That a great prophet is risen up among us; and, That God hath visited his people" (Luke 7:16). These miracles confirmed his divine commission, for they showed that God was with him (Acts 10:38). Jesus said, "I told you, and ye believed not: the works that I do in my Father's name, they bear witness of me" (John 10:25).

We must receive Christ's teachings with reverence, admiration, and awe, for he is an extraordinary person. He is the friend of God, his beloved

---

43. On the mutual indwelling or perichoresis in the Trinity, see *RST*, 1:891–92.
44. Ex. 7:5, 17; 8:10, 22; 9:14, 16, 29; 10:2.

and favored Son. When he speaks of God, he speaks not as someone who has done research about God, but as one who knows him in the most intimate and personal way. Furthermore, God has shown that he is with Christ by his astonishing works of power. Yet his miracles are healing and saving works, which encourages us to listen to him with anticipation that his teachings will bless sinners.

The Mediator of God's Authoritative Words

We see the fourth theme when Moses said of the Prophet, "To him you shall listen" (Deut. 18:15 ESV). To "listen" ("hearken," KJV) is a key term in this context (vv. 14, 15, 16, 19) and in Deuteronomy as a whole.[45] It refers not just to the hearing of the ears, but to the faith of the heart and the obedience of the whole life. Moses repeatedly called Israel to listen to his message (4:1; 5:1; 6:3–4; 9:1) and warned against listening to false prophets (chap. 13).

The reason why we must listen to the divine spokesman is that God said, "[I] will put my words in his mouth"; it is "my words which he shall speak" (Deut. 18:18–19). This is a quality of every true prophet: God is not merely with the prophet's mind to reveal truth, but also with the prophet's "mouth" to guarantee that he speaks truth.[46] When a prophet speaks, it is the human equivalent of "the voice of the LORD" (Deut. 18:16; cf. 15:5; 28:1; 30:10). God authorizes prophets as the "divinely approved substitute for the divine voice," so that what the prophet says is no less the powerful and authoritative word of God than God's living voice.[47]

Christ is pure and absolute divine revelation, the living Word. Letham writes, "Since he was God incarnate, all his words were at the same time human and divine."[48] Christ is the standard of all, and he is judged by none. Maximus the Confessor (d. 662) said, "Christ is the measure of all persons and of all things, and one must neither measure nor explain Christ by anything whatsoever or by anyone whatsoever, but only by Christ himself, who is the measure of all and the explanation of all."[49]

---

45. Deuteronomy contains ninety-one uses of the verb that means "listen" (*shama'*). Only Isaiah (106) and Jeremiah (184) contain more.

46. Ex. 4:12, 15–16; Num. 22:38; 23:5, 12, 16; Isa. 51:16; 59:21; Jer. 1:9; 5:14; Acts 1:16; 3:18, 21; 4:25.

47. John M. Frame, *The Doctrine of the Word of God*, A Theology of Lordship (Phillipsburg, NJ: P&R, 2010), 89–90. On Scripture as the divinely approved substitute for God's "lively voice," see Rollock, *A Treatise of Effectual Calling*, in *Select Works*, 1:64–77, 274–87.

48. Letham, *The Work of Christ*, 94.

49. Maximus the Confessor, *Questions and Responses to Thalassius*, 60, cited in Kelly, *Systematic Theology*, 2:190.

The Lord promised, "He shall speak unto them all that I shall command him" (Deut. 18:18). Thus, the Prophet would be obedient to his calling to communicate God's word, in contrast to those who used magic and divination to seek supernatural knowledge (vv. 9–14) and false prophets who represented false gods or misrepresented the Lord (v. 20). Christ said, "I have not spoken of myself; but the Father which sent me, he gave me a commandment, what I should say, and what I should speak" (John 12:49). The Lord also promised through Moses, "He shall speak in my name" (Deut. 18:19), which meant that he would act as God's representative and messenger (cf. 1 Sam. 25:5). Jesus said, "I seek not my own will but the will of him who sent me. . . . I have come in my Father's name" (John 5:30, 43 ESV). Christ came so that we might know the true God and escape idolatry (1 John 5:20–21).

Christ's prophetic work, like every aspect of his mediatorial office, was essentially obedience to the will of his Father for the glory of the Father. G. C. Berkouwer demonstrates how the Gospel of John testifies abundantly to Christ's prophetic obedience:

> The Messiah radiates the full light of prophecy. . . . As the One sent by God, he speaks the words of God (John 3:34). . . . Whatever he speaks is free from arbitrariness and selfwilledness. He is the Dependent One. . . . His doctrine is not his own, but his that sent him (John 7:16). . . . He speaks as the Father has taught him (John 8:28) and he keeps *his* word (John 8:55). He received a commandment, what he should say and what he should speak (John 12:49, 50), so that the word which had been heard was not his but the Father's who had sent him (John 14:24; 17:14, "I have given them *thy* word").[50]

Christ's obedience radiates the glory of God the Son. The Lord said, "My servant Moses . . . is faithful in all mine house" (Num. 12:7). This is a high commendation. The writer of Hebrews uses the faithfulness of Moses, however, to highlight the superiority of Christ, for Moses was faithful "as a servant," but Christ "as a son over his own house" (Heb. 3:5–6). Christ's obedience is all the more glorious because he is not a subordinate worker, but the heir and owner with the Father. Christ is God and was "counted worthy of more glory than Moses, inasmuch as he who hath builded the

---

50. Berkouwer, *The Work of Christ*, 66–67.

house hath more honour than the house" (v. 3).[51] For God the Son to become the obedient Prophet shows both the amazing condescension of his love and the perfect excellence of his righteousness. Both invite us to trust him.

To refuse to hear a faithful prophet is to incur God's judgment. Moses reports the Lord's statement, "Whoever will not listen . . . I myself will require it of him" (Deut. 18:19 ESV). That is, God will call that person to account for his failure to hear and obey the prophet's words, and will judge him for it.[52] Richard Belcher says, "The prophets became covenant prosecutors sent by God to bring a complaint against the people for their disobedience and to hold out blessings if they repented."[53] Israel rejected its great Prophet just as it resisted all the prophets and the Spirit who spoke through them (Acts 7:37, 51–52). The result was disastrous (Matt. 21:43; 24:2).

However, the prophetic warning applies not merely to the Hebrew nation but to each hearer of the Word. Christ said that the person who hears his words but does not obey them is like a foolish man who builds his house on sand, with the result that it is easily destroyed by a storm (Matt. 7:26–27). The storm is the day of the Lord, when the Lord Jesus will reject the workers of iniquity and exclude them from God's kingdom (vv. 21–23). When Peter quotes the words of Moses, he says, "Every soul, which will not hear that prophet, shall be destroyed from among the people" (Acts 3:23), consigning him to the doom of brazen covenant breakers.[54] Thus, when Christ appeared in glory, flanked by Moses and Elijah, the Father said, "This is my beloved Son, with whom I am well pleased; listen to him" (Matt. 17:5 ESV). He teaches with astonishing authority (7:28–29; Luke 4:32). John Flavel said, "His commands are to be obeyed, not disputed."[55]

The only proper response to Christ is faith and obedience. Speaking of his disciples, Christ said to the Father, "I have given unto them the words which thou gavest me; and they have received them, and have known

---

51. The King James Version reads "this *man* was counted worthy" (Heb. 3:3), but the Greek text is more precisely rendered "this one" (*houtos*). Verse 4 makes it clear that Christ, the builder of the house, is God.

52. The verb translated as "require" (*darash*) has the general meaning of "seek." To "seek from" (*darash min*) means to ask a question (1 Kings 14:5; 2 Chron. 18:6) or to hold someone accountable or responsible (Gen. 9:5; Ezek. 33:6; Mic. 6:8).

53. Belcher, *Prophet, Priest, and King*, 25.

54. See the use of "be destroyed" (*exolethreuetai*) from God's people in Gen. 17:14; Ex. 12:15, 19; 30:33; 31:14; Lev. 17:4, 9, 14; 18:29; 19:8; 20:17–18; 22:3; 23:29; Num. 9:13; 15:30; 19:20 LXX.

55. Flavel, *The Fountain of Life*, in *Works*, 1:120.

surely that I came out from thee, and they have believed that thou didst send me" (John 17:8). Can you say the same of yourself? Have you recognized that Christ's words are God's words and received them as the rule of your life? Have you humbled yourself to be a disciple of this Master? Do his words govern your heart and behavior?

Or do you pretend to stand above Christ and judge his teachings? Beware of taking a noncommittal or independent position toward anything that Christ or his servants revealed in the Holy Scriptures. John Brown of Haddington warned that our hatred against Christ's prophetic office shows itself in our confidence in our own wisdom and in our despising of the teachings of Christ.[56] Believe all that Christ says in the Word.

The Word of God cannot fail; this was the test of a true prophet. Moses said, "When a prophet speaketh in the name of the LORD, if the thing follow not, nor come to pass, that is the thing which the LORD hath not spoken, but the prophet hath spoken it presumptuously: thou shalt not be afraid of him" (Deut. 18:22). All that God spoke through Moses came to pass (1 Kings 8:56). The words of a true prophet cannot fall to the ground (Josh. 21:45; 1 Sam. 3:19); they are inerrantly true (Prov. 30:5–6).[57]

Christ spoke the word of God with complete confidence that it was true. He regarded the Scriptures as possessing eternal truth in every part (Matt. 5:17–18) and put his own teachings in the same category, saying, "Heaven and earth shall pass away, but my words shall not pass away" (24:35). He prayed to the Father, "I have given them thy word. . . . Thy word is truth" (John 17:14, 17). Those who continue to believe and practice Christ's words "know the truth" (8:31–32), for Christ told "the truth" in the face of human opposition and demonic deception (vv. 40, 45). Christ said, "I am . . . the truth" (14:6).

Christ has been faithful even to declare difficult doctrines. His teachings have often struck his hearers as hard sayings (John 6:60). Many people have shown an initial interest in Christ, only to turn away from him later. Some have abandoned Christianity. Others have modified the biblical faith to make it more palatable to the tastes of fallen mankind, in the end becoming the followers of mere men instead of Christ. It may be that as you study theology and meditate on God's Word, you will see ways in which the Bible contradicts the teachings of your church, your favorite

---

56. Brown, *Questions and Answers on the Shorter Catechism*, 79.
57. On the inerrancy of the Holy Scriptures, see *RST*, 1:371–94.

teacher, or your own mind. Will you follow Christ or man? Knowing that Christ is the great Prophet of God enables us to say with Peter, "Lord, to whom shall we go? Thou hast the words of eternal life. And we believe and are sure that thou art that Christ, the Son of the living God" (vv. 68–69).

The Twofold Ministry of the Great Prophet

Moses is a type of Christ, but Moses fell short of the full prophetic ministry that sinners need. As the foundational prophet of the old covenant, Moses's task was to declare to Israel "the words of the covenant" that God had revealed to him and to urge the people to "keep therefore the words of this covenant, and do them" (Deut. 29:1, 9). However, the Lord also revealed to Moses that the Israelites would break the covenant and fall under its curses because of their stubborn rebelliousness (31:16, 27). Moses recognized that something was missing to make his prophetic ministry effective for the nation's repentance: "The LORD hath not given you an heart to perceive, and eyes to see, and ears to hear, unto this day" (29:4). God would supply this heart work in the future after Israel returned from exile (30:3–6). Moses looked forward to what Jeremiah would call the new covenant (Jer. 31:31–34), which is fulfilled in Christ's ministry of writing the law upon the heart (2 Cor. 3:3, 6; Heb. 8:6–12). In Christ, God has provided the Prophet who brings revelation and applies it to the heart.

Therefore, Christ's prophetic work involves two dimensions. Flavel said, "His prophetical office consists of two parts; one external, consisting of a true and full revelation of the will of God to men. . . . The other in illuminating the mind, and opening the heart to receive and embrace that doctrine."[58] We see these two in the ministry of the risen Lord, who said to his disciples, "These are the words which I spake unto you," and "then opened he their understanding, that they might understand" (Luke 24:44–45). Both dimensions are necessary to overcome man's ignorance of God.

We will examine how Christ fulfills these two tasks in the next two chapters. For now, let us rejoice that in Jesus Christ we have the complete prophetic work, both external and internal. God's saved people through the ages, including Moses himself, have received the truth into their

---

58. Flavel, *The Fountain of Life*, in *Works*, 1:118–19. See also Turretin, *Institutes*, 14.7.12.2 (2:400).

hearts (Ps. 37:30–31; Isa. 51:7). Therefore, they too enjoyed the prophetic ministry of Christ, even if before his incarnation, for Christ is the Mediator of all the salvation bestowed through the eternal covenant of grace: "No man cometh unto the Father, but by me" (John 14:6).[59]

Sing to the Lord

Praising Christ for His Revelation of Divine Truth

> O Word of God Incarnate, O Wisdom from on high,
> O Truth unchanged, unchanging, O light of our dark sky;
> We praise thee for the radiance that from the hallowed page,
> A lantern to our footsteps, shines on from age to age.
>
> The church from her dear Master received the gift divine,
> And still that light she lifteth o'er all the earth to shine.
> It is the golden casket, where gems of truth are stored;
> It is the heav'n drawn picture of Christ, the living Word.
>
> It floateth like a banner before God's host unfurled;
> It shineth like a beacon above the darkling world.
> It is the chart and compass that o'er life's surging sea,
> 'Mid mists and rocks and quicksands, still guides, O Christ, to thee.
>
> O make thy church, dear Saviour, a lamp of purest gold,
> To bear before the nations thy true light, as of old.
> O teach thy wand'ring pilgrims by this their path to trace,
> Till, clouds and darkness ended, they see thee face to face.

William Walsham
Tune: Munich
Trinity Hymnal—Baptist Edition, No. 267

Questions for Meditation or Discussion

1. How do each of these descriptions of Christ show that he is the perfect revealer of God: (1) the Word of God, (2) the Son of God, and (3) the Image of God?
2. What is Christ's relationship to God's general revelation through creation and conscience? What does this imply about Christ's work of special revelation through the Word?

---

59. On the new covenant, see chap. 32. On the eternal covenant of grace, see chaps. 30 and 33.

3. How do the Gospels display the high priority Christ put on his ministry of teaching and preaching?

4. Why is Christ's ministry of truth necessary for our salvation?

5. What four themes do the authors observe in Deuteronomy 18:15–19?

6. What does the word "prophet" mean?

7. How is the prophetic ministry an example of God's accommodation to fearful sinners?

8. What are two major ways that Deuteronomy indicates that the coming Prophet is like Moses?

9. What measure of authority do a prophet's words have? Why?

10. How does the work of salvation require Christ's prophetic ministry to surpass that of Moses?

Questions for Deeper Reflection

11. Someone tells you, "I agree that Christ is our Teacher, but your view of Christ is just too limited. Christ is Lord of the cosmos and teaches us through all things. The Bible is helpful, but it is not the only way to know God; Christ speaks to us through the stars, the seas, and the trees." How do you respond in a winsome and evangelistic manner?

12. Imagine you are attending a seminar in which the leader says, "It is plain from the text and context of Deuteronomy 18:15–22 that 'a prophet' refers collectively to the many prophets to come and not to a single person such as Christ. Only later in the tradition did the messianic interpretation of the text arise, on account of which the early church applied the text to Christ in Acts 3:22–23 and 7:37." How do you respond?

46

Christ's Prophetic Work, Part 2

Revelation by the Word

The great theme of the Bible is the gospel (Luke 24:44–47). We need the revelatory work of Christ because we need the gospel of salvation.[1] We are saved by faith (Eph. 2:8), and faith is not merely an experience of God, but trust grounded in knowledge (Ps. 9:10).[2] Francis Turretin said, "There can be no knowledge of God and divine things without a revelation . . . and no saving revelation is given except through Christ (John 1:18; Matt. 11:27). Nor could reason or the law disclose to us the mystery of piety, but Christ alone in the gospel."[3]

Christ's prophetic task presupposes that God has willed to save some sinners, and to save them only in a certain way. The way of salvation, being part of God's secret decree, is not known to men apart from divine revelation. But the Son of God is intimately and eternally acquainted with God's decree, so we can depend on him to know it.[4]

Therefore, Christ's work as the Prophet centers upon the Word. The Westminster Shorter Catechism (Q. 24) says, "Christ executeth the office of a prophet, in revealing us, by his word and Spirit, the will of God for

---

1. On the necessity of God's Word and its great unifying theme, see *RST*, 1:353–63.
2. On special revelation as verbal and propositional, see *RST*, 1:271–72, 276–79. For a summary and critique of the neoorthodox view of revelation as holy encounter, see *RST*, 1:304–9.
3. Turretin, *Institutes*, 14.7.3 (2:397–98).
4. Boston, *An Illustration of the Doctrines of the Christian Religion*, in *Works*, 1:413–14.

our salvation."[5] Hence, in this chapter, we will trace Christ's objective revelatory work from the fall of man through his second coming.[6] We will see that two great fruits of Christ's prophetic office are the Bible and the church's ministry of the Word.

The Preincarnate Mediator of God's Truth

We might think that Christ gives us only the words attributed to him in the Gospels, or at most the New Testament. However, Christ executes the office of a prophet "in all ages," albeit "in divers ways of administration."[7] John Flavel said, "Christ is the original and fountain of all that light which guides us to salvation."[8] Before our Lord came in the flesh, his mediatorial activity was not as open, for it took place in the era of shadows and types. However, God the Son was present with his people throughout history. Henri de Vries stated, "The Messiah Himself is the Predicting and the Predicted One. . . . What He had foretold He also fulfilled."[9]

The Only Revealer of God

Christ was the "Word" (*logos*) already "in the beginning" (John 1:1), an allusion to the first chapter of Genesis. The Gospel of John often speaks of the "word" (*logos*) of God and Christ as the message by which God saves people through faith.[10] John also calls Christ "the true Light" (v. 9; cf. vv. 4–5). He is "the light of the world" (8:12; 9:5), the only Mediator between man and the God who dwells in absolute light (1 John 1:5; 1 Tim. 6:16).[11] Therefore, John's designation of Christ as the Word and the Light implies that whenever God's word illuminates men, Christ is present. George Stevenson wrote, "All that we know of God as a God of grace is through Christ as a prophet."[12]

John concluded the introduction to his Gospel by writing, "No man hath seen God at any time; the only begotten Son, which is in the bosom of the Father, he hath declared him" (John 1:18). The divine nature is

---

5. *Reformed Confessions*, 4:356.

6. On the continuity of the gospel from its first revelation to fallen Adam and Eve, see chap. 29.

7. Westminster Larger Catechism (Q. 43), *Reformed Confessions*, 4:307.

8. Flavel, *An Exposition of the Assembly's Catechism*, 24.2, in *Works*, 6:182.

9. De Vries, *The Lord's Anointed Prophet, Priest and King*, 71–72.

10. See "word" or "saying" (*logos*) in John 2:22; 4:41, 50; 5:24, 38; 6:60; 7:36, 40; 8:31, 37, 43, 51–52, 55; 10:19, 35; 12:38, 48; 14:23–24; 15:3, 20, 25; 17:6, 14, 17, 20.

11. Calvin, *Institutes*, 3.2.1.

12. Stevenson, *Treatise on the Offices of Christ*, 18.

invisible (1 John 4:12, 20),[13] but God reveals himself through his Son, who dwells in his "bosom," a metaphor for close friendship and fellowship (John 13:23). A similar text, John 6:46, says, "Not that any man hath seen the Father, save he which is of God, he hath seen the Father." John's meaning in these texts is that the Son alone has direct knowledge of God, so the Son alone can reveal God to men (cf. Matt. 11:27).[14] John Calvin said, "The knowledge of God is the door by which we enter into the enjoyment of all blessings; and as it is by Christ alone that God makes himself known to us, hence too it follows that we ought to seek all things from Christ."[15]

If Christ is the only way to know God, then all who knew God prior to Christ's incarnation must have received revelation through Christ as well. Therefore, every special revelation of God through the ages has been through Christ. It might be objected that John contrasts Christ's revelation with that of previous ages: "For the law was given by Moses, but grace and truth came by Jesus Christ" (John 1:17). However, the contrast between Moses and Christ is not between no grace and grace, but "an early stage" of grace and "the final stage" of grace.[16] Both Abraham (8:56–58) and Moses (1:45; 5:46) knew Christ. Christ was "that spiritual Rock" who traveled with Israel in the wilderness (1 Cor. 10:4)—that is, Christ is the covenant God of Israel (Deut. 32:4).

Christ was able to perform the office of the Mediator throughout the ages because God had established his office before time began (2 Tim. 1:9).[17] Christ is the eternal Son, the "I Am" who was already alive in Abraham's time (John 8:58), who was, in fact, active "from of old, from everlasting" (Mic. 5:2). If someone asks how Christ could have been the Prophet of his people before his incarnation, then we answer that he was so in the same way that he is the Prophet after his ascension: by his word revealed by the Spirit working through his servants. Let us beware, lest in confining Christ's prophetic work to his ministry on earth, we slide into a practical denial of Christ's eternal deity and unique office as the sole Mediator of God's grace.[18]

---

13. On God's invisibility, see *RST*, 1:613–15.

14. William Hendriksen, *The Gospel of John*, New Testament Commentary, 2 vols. in 1 (Grand Rapids, MI: Baker, 1953), 1:90. To "see" often refers to knowledge, experience, and perception. John 1:14; 3:11, 32; 4:19, 35; 5:37–38; 6:40, 46; 8:38, 51; 12:19, 45; 14:7, 9, 17, 19; 15:24; 16:16; cf. 1 John 3:6; 4:14.

15. Calvin, *Commentaries*, on John 1:18.

16. Borchert, *John 1–11*, 123.

17. See the discussions of the counsel of peace in chap. 30 and Christ's preexistence in chap. 38.

18. Owen, *Christologia*, in *Works*, 1:88–90.

The Lord of the Ancient Prophets

God the Son exercised his prophetic ministry through the prophets who went before him. As the God of Israel and mediatorial Lord of the covenant, he acted through his covenantal officers to bring the word of God to the people. We have noted previously that the angel of the Lord was a manifestation of the preexistent Christ to his people.[19] This angel acted as the Lord of the prophets[20] and the Mediator of the prophets' mission and message. God the Son is also the Lord of the created angels, whom he sent to reveal truth to men.[21]

The prophet Isaiah recounted his call into ministry through a vision when he said, "In the year that king Uzziah died I saw also the LORD sitting upon a throne, high and lifted up" (Isa. 6:1). This person was none other than the thrice holy "LORD of hosts" (v. 3). However, John quoted Isaiah 6 and 53, and said, speaking of Jesus Christ, that Isaiah "saw his glory, and spake of him" (John 12:37–41). The person whose glory Isaiah saw (Isa. 6:3), the Lord who commissioned the prophet, was the preincarnate Christ. John wrote this immediately after saying that Jesus is "the light" (John 12:35–36). Flavel said, "All the prophets of the Old, and all the prophets, pastors, and teachers of the New Testament, have lighted their candles at his torch."[22]

It might be objected that the prophets were directed by the Holy Spirit (Num. 11:29; Neh. 9:30), not by Christ. However, Peter says that "the prophets" prophesied by "the Spirit of Christ" (1 Pet. 1:10–11). Just as the Holy Spirit is called "the Spirit of God" because he comes from God (1 John 4:2), so Peter calls him "the Spirit of Christ" to indicate that the Son sent the Spirit to give God's word to the prophets.[23] Therefore, Christ has ever been the Mediator of the prophetic word. De Vries said, "He is our chief Prophet, really our only Prophet. All other true prophets before and after Him were His mouthpieces."[24]

The Wisdom of the Wise

The Mediator not only granted prophecy to the prophets, but also wisdom to the sages of Israel.[25] The New Testament tells us that Christ is the

---

19. On the divine angel, see the section on Christ's preexistence in chap. 38.
20. Exodus 3; 1 Kings 19:4–8; 2 Kings 1:3, 15. On the angel of the Lord's prophetic office, see the discussion of Christ's threefold office in the Old Testament in chap. 43.
21. On revelation granted through angels, see Gen. 19:1, 15; Dan. 8:16; 9:21; Acts 7:53; Heb. 2:2; Rev. 1:1; 22:16. On Christ's lordship over the angels, see *RST*, 1:1125.
22. Flavel, *The Fountain of Life*, in *Works*, 1:123.
23. Schreiner, *1, 2 Peter, Jude*, 73; cf. Rom. 8:9; Gal. 4:6; Phil. 1:19.
24. De Vries, *The Lord's Anointed Prophet, Priest and King*, 38.
25. This section is adapted from "Introduction to the Book of Proverbs," in *The Reformation Heritage KJV Study Bible*, ed. Beeke, Barrett, Bilkes, and Smalley, 884. Used by permission.

reservoir of all God's saving wisdom (Col. 2:3). In Christ, God's "wisdom" has come (Luke 7:34–35), a "greater" revelation of wisdom than "the wisdom of Solomon" (11:31).[26] Christ even personified wisdom: "Therefore also said the wisdom of God, I will send them prophets and apostles, and some of them they shall slay and persecute" (v. 49). The parallel text in Matthew says nothing of wisdom; rather, Christ says, "I send" (Matt. 23:34). In this way, Christ taught that he is the Wisdom of God.[27] The background to Christ's identification of himself as Wisdom is the book of Proverbs, which presents Wisdom as a living person who preaches to people and sends out messengers to invite people to receive her benefits (Prov. 1:20–33; 8:1–36; 9:1–12).

Christ is the personal divine Wisdom who revealed himself in part to the wise men of ancient Israel. This comports with the qualities of personified Wisdom in Proverbs. She is the source of all human wisdom, power, justice, and glory (Prov. 8:14–19; cf. 1 Cor. 1:30). She cooperates with God in the divine work of creating the world and mankind (Prov. 8:27–31; cf. Col. 1:16; Heb. 1:2). Yet Wisdom is a distinct person in relationship to God (Prov. 8:22, 30), just as John later said that the Word was God and yet was with God (John 1:1).

Therefore, Wisdom in Proverbs is not Christless pragmatism, but Christ himself, the great Evangelist. Wisdom preaches the gospel, calling sinners to repent, receive God's Spirit of wisdom, learn his ways, escape his judgment, and enjoy his peace (Prov. 1:20–33; cf. Matt. 4:17; Acts 2:38). Proverbs teaches, "He that covereth his sins shall not prosper: but whoso confesseth and forsaketh them shall have mercy" (Prov. 28:13). Whoever finds Wisdom finds life (8:35; cf. 1 John 5:12, 20). Wisdom invites people to the banquet of life (Prov. 9:1–6; cf. Matt. 22:1–14; Luke 14:16–24).

When we read the Wisdom Literature of the Old Testament (Job, various psalms, Proverbs, Ecclesiastes, and the Song of Solomon), we may do so believing that we are reading the words of God's Son as he taught the saints in previous ages. Far from being empty of Christ, those books bring us into an encounter with Christ in his prophetic office. He was their Wisdom, and he is ours. The "words of the wise" are "given from one

---

26. Luke 11:31 literally says that "something greater [neuter *pleion*] than Solomon is here." The neuter indicates that the comparison is not between Christ and Solomon so much as Christ's wisdom and that of Solomon.

27. Stein, *Luke*, 343.

shepherd" (Eccl. 12:11), the Mediator who came as the "one shepherd" of his flock (Ezek. 34:23; 37:24; John 10:16).[28]

The Incarnate Prophet in His State of Humiliation

Just as the moon reflects the light of the sun to illuminate our night, so God's ancient prophets and sages reflected Christ's light to lost sinners. However, when Christ came in the flesh, the "Sun of righteousness" (Mal. 4:2) dawned upon this dark world (Luke 1:78–79) so that "the glory of the LORD" shown upon his people and the nations came into his light (Isa. 60:1–3).

The Incarnate Son of the Father

The arrival of the incarnate Son brought God's final word to this age, initiating the last days. Hebrews 1:1–2 says, "God, who at sundry times and in divers manners spake in time past unto the fathers by the prophets, hath in these last days spoken unto us by his Son, whom he hath appointed heir of all things, by whom also he made the worlds." This unique revealer is "the brightness of [the Father's] glory, and the express image of his person" (v. 3). Stephen Wellum says, "Jesus is the prophet par excellence in bringing God's word to man because he is the Son incarnate."[29]

God the Son incarnate is the supreme revelation of God.[30] John wrote, "The Word was made flesh, and dwelt among us." He then immediately noted, "And we beheld his glory, the glory as of the only begotten of the Father" (John 1:14). Christ is the living tabernacle of divine glory with his people, where God meets man.[31] In the old covenant, the cloud of glory descended to the tabernacle so that the glory of the Lord appeared to the people of Israel, and God spoke to them (Ex. 25:22, 40:34–38). In Jesus Christ, God has come to mankind to display his glory and commune with us in human form and speech. Thomas Watson said, "If you have been taught by Christ savingly, be thankful. It is your honour to have God for your teacher."[32]

---

28. The specific reference to the "one shepherd" in Eccl. 12:11 is somewhat mysterious, but the Old Testament uses the term translated as "shepherd" (the verb *ra'ah* or as a participle, *ro'eh*) to refer to both the Lord (Gen. 48:15; 49:24; Pss. 23:1; 80:1; Isa. 40:11) and the anointed king (2 Sam. 5:2; 1 Kings 22:17; 2 Chron. 18:16; Ps. 78:71–72). In God the Son, both aspects of the shepherd theme converge (Ezek. 34:12–15, 23–24; 37:23–24; Mic. 5:4).

29. Wellum, *Christ Alone*, 133.

30. On Christ as the consummate source of special revelation, see *RST*, 1:275–76.

31. See the discussion of how God dwelt among us in Christ in chap. 39.

32. Watson, *A Body of Divinity*, 171.

By his incarnation, God the Son became the object of human senses. Christ is "the Word" who "was from the beginning," but having come in the flesh, he is now also the One "which we have heard, which we have seen with our eyes, which we have looked upon, and our hands have handled," the apostle John said (1 John 1:1). The marvel is that when they heard, saw, and touched Jesus, they heard, saw, and touched God.[33]

Christ fellowships in human thoughts and feelings, entering our human psychological experience (Heb. 4:15).[34] He mediates to us the thoughts of God as received by his human mind and heart, and expressed in his human thoughts and words. De Vries said, "The chief function of the prophet is to receive the thoughts of God in his human consciousness in order to impart the same to the people. Hence the Son of God in order to be our Prophet must first of all assume our human consciousness, i.e. become man."[35] Yet the person expressing these human words remains God the Son. Consequently, by the incarnate "Word," we have fellowship "with the Father, and with his Son Jesus Christ" (1 John 1:1, 3).

The Spirit-Anointed Son

The Lord Jesus Christ initiated his public ministry by submitting to baptism at the hands of John, though he was John's Lord (Matt. 3:13–16). Since John was a prophet, and the greatest of the old covenant prophets (11:9–11), Christ thereby honored the prophetic office and showed his continuity with it. John called Israel to repentance in preparation for the imminent arrival of the promised Lord and Christ who would pour out the Spirit (3:1–12). After Christ's baptism, the Holy Spirit descended visibly upon him, and the Father announced his pleasure in his beloved Son (vv. 16–17). This remarkable theophany and special verbal revelation identified Christ as the God-pleasing, Spirit-empowered Servant (Isa. 42:1) and anointed royal Son (Ps. 2:2, 6–7).

The ministry of the Spirit is wedded to the Servant's speaking of the word: "For he whom God has sent utters the words of God, for he gives the Spirit without measure" (John 3:34 ESV). This is because Christ

---

33. We may say that people touched God (though we may not say that they touched the divine nature), for the person whose human body they touched is God the Son. See the discussion of the *communicatio idiomatum* in chap. 42.

34. See the discussion of Christ's human spirit in chap. 40.

35. De Vries, *The Lord's Anointed Prophet, Priest and King*, 38.

is more than a servant; he is God's Son upon whom God's revelation centers. "The Father loveth the Son, and hath given all things into his hand" (v. 35). This fullness of the Spirit "without measure," John Owen observed, distinguishes Christ from all previous prophets, for the complete wisdom of God, insofar as he willed to reveal it, has a permanent and constant home in Christ's mind (Col. 2:3), whereas Moses and the other prophets received revelation "by transient irradiations of their minds," so that they understood some particular truths according to "a measure of light accommodated unto the age in which they lived (1 Pet. 1:11–12)."[36]

One implication of the Son's incarnation is that he is the last Adam, who was also a son of God (Luke 3:22, 38). Adam served God as a prophet, receiving God's word and being called to proclaim it to others, such as his wife, who was not present to hear God's revelation (Gen. 2:15–17).[37] His temptation by Satan was a test of his faithfulness in the prophetic office, for the Devil attacked Eve's faith in God's word; however, Adam remained silent (3:1–6). Whereas Adam fell in a lush garden, God's Son was led by the Spirit to fast in a harsh wilderness, for the last Adam had to save a fallen race in a cursed world. Our great Prophet overcame the Devil by believing and speaking God's Word, three times parrying Satan's thrusts with "It is written" (Luke 4:1–13). In all this, Christ was "led by the Spirit" (v. 1), an allusion to God leading Israel in the wilderness by the Holy Spirit's prophetic ministry through Moses (Isa. 63:11–14).[38] Therefore, God's Son fulfilled the prophetic calling of Adam and Israel, so that he could say, "I do nothing of myself; but as my Father hath taught me, I speak these things. And he that sent me is with me: the Father hath not left me alone; for I do always those things that please him" (John 8:28–29). He is the faithful Son.

The Spirit-Empowered Teacher of Israel

The Lord Jesus engaged in public ministry for about three years, primarily in the capacity of a preacher and teacher. During this period, Christ was in particular "a minister of the circumcision"—that is, the Jewish people, to confirm "the truth of God" (Rom. 15:8). Christ emerged from the

---

36. Owen, *An Exposition of the Epistle to the Hebrews*, 3:32.
37. On Adam's office, see the discussion in chap. 14 of common covenantal elements in Genesis 2.
38. Belcher, *Prophet, Priest, and King*, 10–11, 47.

wilderness "in the power of the Spirit" and went to Galilee, where "he taught in their synagogues, being glorified by all" (Luke 4:14–15). As the Prophet to Israel, his ministry began in the "synagogues" (cf. v. 44), the local Jewish meeting houses.

Christ announced that he fulfilled the prophecy of Isaiah 61:1–2: "The Spirit of the Lord is upon me, because he hath anointed me to preach the gospel to the poor; he hath sent me to heal the broken-hearted, to preach deliverance to the captives, and recovering of sight to the blind, to set at liberty them that are bruised, to preach the acceptable year of the Lord" (Luke 4:18–19). Christ's focus on the poor, brokenhearted, captives, blind, and bruised shows that he came as the Prophet of grace, revealing God's saving mercy to sinners in their physical and spiritual misery. Christ said, "This day is this scripture fulfilled in your ears" (v. 21). Thus, Christ is the "eschatological" Prophet, for his ministry inaugurates the last days and the arrival of the promised "era of salvation."[39] The response to which he calls people is faith and repentance from sin toward God (5:20, 32; cf. Mark 1:15). The good news of salvation to sinners is grounded upon Christ's teaching about the necessity, merit, and power of his death,[40] themes expanded by further revelation after his resurrection.

Christ's prophetic ministry was holistic, authoritative, frank, trustworthy, affectionate, and skillful.[41] He practiced a holistic ministry of the word to mind, heart, and life. What Luke called "teaching" (*didaskō*) he also called "preaching the gospel" or "evangelizing" (*euangelizomai*) and "preaching" or "proclaiming as a herald" (*kēryssō*, Luke 4:15, 18; cf. Matt. 4:17; Mark 1:14).[42] Those who heard Christ "were astonished at his teaching, for his word possessed authority" (Luke 4:32 ESV; cf. Matt. 7:29; Mark 1:22). He spoke "openly" or "with frank boldness" (*parrēsia*) in his preaching to the world (John 18:20). He spoke the plain truth, even when addressing the rich and powerful.[43] Christ emphasized the absolute trustworthiness of his teachings with the frequent use of "verily" (*amēn*), or "truly," and, in the Gospel of John, the double "verily, verily" (*amēn*

39. I. Howard Marshall, *The Gospel of Luke*, New International Greek Testament Commentary (Grand Rapids, MI: Eerdmans, 1978), 178.
40. Matt. 16:21; 17:12, 22; 20:18, 28; 26:28; Mark 8:31; 9:12, 31; 10:33, 45; 14:24; Luke 9:22, 34; 22:19–20, 37; John 3:14–16; 6:51; 10:11, 17–18; 12:31–33.
41. See Turretin, *Institutes*, 14.7.13 (2:401); and Boston, *An Illustration of the Doctrines of the Christian Religion*, in *Works*, 1:419–23.
42. Marshall, *The Gospel of Luke*, 177.
43. Matt. 19:21–22; 22:16; 23:13; 26:63–64.

amēn). The Greek term, from which we derive our word *amen*, transliterates a Hebrew root often used of God's truth, trustworthiness, and faithfulness.[44] Yet Jesus was not a cold dispenser of truth; he spoke affectionately and warmly to sinners with grace upon his lips (Ps. 45:2; Luke 4:22). Flavel said, "This Prophet, Jesus Christ, taught the people the mind of God in a sweet, affectionate, and taking manner: his words made their hearts burn within them (Luke 24:32)."[45] Christ often skillfully illustrated his teaching with parables, metaphorical images, or stories that both concealed truth from the uncommitted and revealed it in a more penetrating manner to those with "ears to hear" (Mark 4:9–12).

No preacher has ever walked upon this earth who could compare to the Lord Jesus. In every respect, the Christ is the Master Teacher. The people "heard him gladly" (Mark 12:37). His insight is without equal, and his understanding penetrates the deepest subjects. Watson said, "He can untie those knots which puzzle angels."[46] Those who sought to confute and confound him found themselves silenced by his wisdom (Matt. 22:46; Luke 14:6). Even Christ's enemies had to confess, "No one ever spoke like this man!" (John 7:46 ESV). Truly was it prophesied that his "mouth" would be "like a sharp sword" (Isa. 49:2). Therefore, cherish the teachings of Christ recorded in the Gospels. Isaac Ambrose said, "Read and peruse those sermons he hath left on record, yea, ruminate and meditate on them in order to piety and holy life."[47]

Faith in Christ means submitting to him as our Master and Teacher. Christ's call is, "Come unto me. . . . Take my yoke upon you, and learn of me" (Matt. 11:28–29). The Father loves the Son, and says, "Listen to him" (17:5 ESV). Christianity requires us to be disciples of Christ—that is, people who submit our minds to his instruction and conform our conduct to his character.[48] His teaching in the Gospels is the bread and butter of the church.

The Sender of Apostles, Prophets, and Evangelists to Israel

Christ is not only the Master Teacher, but also the Master of all teachers of God's Word. He preached, but he also trained and authorized other people

---

44. On the Hebrew root *'aman* as a term for God's faithfulness, see *RST*, 1:806–8.
45. Flavel, *The Fountain of Life*, in *Works*, 1:125.
46. Watson, *A Body of Divinity*, 170.
47. Ambrose, *Looking unto Jesus*, 292.
48. See the section titled "Be a Disciple of Christ," in *RST*, 1:146.

to take his message throughout the land. In this manner, Christ instituted an organic structure that would be foundational for the instruction of all who would believe in him in the future (John 17:20).

After the teachers of Israel set themselves against Christ,[49] he "ordained twelve, that they should be with him, and that he might send [*apostellō*] them forth to preach, and to have power to heal sicknesses, and to cast out devils" (Mark 3:14–15). After being with him for a time to observe his ministry and hear his teaching, the apostles were deployed into ministry under Christ's supervision: "He called unto him the twelve, and began to send them forth by two and two" (6:7). The number of the apostles corresponded to the tribes of Israel, and he promised them, "In the regeneration when the Son of man shall sit in the throne of his glory, ye also shall sit upon twelve thrones, judging the twelve tribes of Israel" (Matt. 19:28). Thus, the apostolate was the seed of the spiritual Israel that Christ called out of physical Israel.

Christ sent not only the apostles but other messengers of his word: "prophets, and wise men, and scribes" (Matt. 23:34). After Christ sent out the twelve apostles, "the LORD appointed other seventy[50] also, and sent them two and two before his face into every city and place, whither he himself would come," to heal, speak the word, and cast out demons (Luke 10:1, 9, 17). These men were not merely preachers but extraordinary officers invested with supernatural gifts.

The Exemplary Image of God among Men

Christ's prophetic office centers upon his words, but we should not neglect his actions as revelations of God, for everything Christ did was an act of God the Son. Christ is the Image of God both in his eternal deity and in his assumed humanity (2 Cor. 4:4; Col. 1:15).[51] This accords with God's purpose: "For whom he did foreknow, he also did predestinate to be conformed to the image of his Son, that he might be the firstborn among many brethren" (Rom. 8:29).

Christ's prophetic revelation through his human example is an important part of the renewal of God's image in us (Eph. 4:20–24), and thus

---

49. Mark 2:6, 16, 18, 24; 3:6.
50. Some Greek manuscripts read "seventy-two," but the majority of manuscripts, including some significant uncials (Aleph, L, Delta, Lambda, Xi) and groups (families 1 and 13), read "seventy."
51. On Christ as the Image of God, see the discussion of the perfection of his prophetic person in chap. 45.

an important part of our salvation. We must be imitators of the Lord (1 Thess. 1:6). Bonaventure said, "The most perfect way for man to be raised out of this misery was for [God] to come down on man's level, offering Himself to him as an accessible object of knowledge, love, and imitation. . . . So, in order to raise man out of this state, the Word was made flesh; that He might be known and loved and imitated by man who was flesh."[52] William Perkins rightly said that while we are not called to imitate Christ in his divine miracles or in his unique mediatorial work, we are called to learn from his life and imitate him as the perfect man, "as, his obedience, his zeal, his patience, his humility, and all other virtues."[53] Ambrose said, "We must conform to Christ's life . . . in respect of all his . . . moral obedience. . . . In those things which he did, but commands not, we need not to conform; but in those things which he both did, and commanded, we are bound to follow him."[54]

The moral character of Christ should play a formative role in our ethics. We need the incarnation to fully know and appreciate the depths to which God has called us to bear his image. Irenaeus said, "For in no other way could we have learned the things of God, unless our Master, existing as the Word, had become man. For no other being had the power of revealing to us the things of the Father, except His own proper Word. . . . Again, we could have learned in no other way than by seeing our Teacher, and hearing His voice with our own ears, that, having become imitators of His works as well as doers of His words, we may have communion with Him."[55]

The imitation of Christ is a great and profound topic, but we can only briefly note some ways in which the Holy Scriptures call us to receive Christ's life as a revelation of God's will for us to obey by imitation. In general, Christ's example "magnified the law and made it honorable" (cf. Isa. 42:21); "his holy life and his cheerful obedience set forth in the clearest light . . . the excellence of the law . . . as worthy of all honor," as Charles Boothe said.[56]

More specifically, Christ's life reveals God's will that

- we must deny ourselves for him (Matt. 16:24);
- we must humbly obey God, even unto death (Phil 2:5, 8);

52. Bonaventure, *Breviloquium*, 4.1.3, in *Works*, 2:144–45.
53. Perkins, *A Cloud of Faithful Witnesses, Leading to the Heavenly Canaan: or, A Commentary upon the Eleventh Chapter to the Hebrews*, on Heb. 11:5–6, in *Works*, 3:59.
54. Ambrose, *Looking unto Jesus*, 314–15.
55. Irenaeus, *Against Heresies*, 5.1.1, in *ANF*, 1:526.
56. Boothe, *Plain Theology for Plain People*, 47.

- we must live for God's glory (1 Cor. 10:31; 11:1);
- we must serve one another in love (John 13:15; Eph. 5:2);
- we must bear with one another in meekness and forgiveness (Col. 3:12–13); and
- we must endure unjust suffering patiently (1 Pet. 2:21–23).

We do not imitate Christ's example for our justification, but the imitation of Christ is a crucial aspect of our sanctification. Perkins said that Christian conduct consists of "such a course of life, whereby we following Christ's example do by Him perform new obedience to God."[57] Meditation on Christ's conduct can increase our assurance of salvation, for one form of evidence that we truly abide in Christ is "to walk, even as he walked" (1 John 2:6).

The Crucified Glory

The greatest revelatory action that Christ performed in his state of humiliation was his passion and death for our sins. Christ was our Prophet on the cross, preaching by his wounds and blood. The cross is a beacon of divine glory. When Christ considered his impending death, he exclaimed, "Father, glorify thy name," and a voice from heaven replied, "I have both glorified it, and will glorify it again" (John 12:28; cf. vv. 24, 33). When Judas left to betray Jesus, Christ said, "Now is the Son of man glorified, and God is glorified in him" (13:31).

Every sparkling facet of truth about Christ's redeeming work reveals something glorious about God. We will explore the meaning of Christ's death in more detail under the topics of Christ's priesthood and kingship. Here we can but summarize. In his passion and death, Jesus Christ revealed the priceless worth of God's will, that it is so valuable it was worthy of sacrificing the very Son of God (Mark 14:36). Christ also revealed our total inability to justify ourselves, for would God have sent his Son to the cross if we could have been saved by doing works of obedience to the law (Gal. 2:21)?

At Calvary, Christ made known God's righteousness and justice, for his blood declared how God is both "just, and the justifier of him which believeth in Jesus" (Rom. 3:25–26). Owen wrote, "To see him who is the wisdom of God, and the power of God, always beloved of the Father; to see him, I say, fear, and tremble, and bow, and sweat, and pray, and die

---

57. Perkins, *A Golden Chain*, chap. 39, in *Works*, 6:190.

. . . and all this because our sins did meet upon him;—this of all things doth most abundantly manifest the severity of God's vindictive justice."[58]

The death of Christ was also the greatest demonstration of God's love for man (John 3:16; Rom. 5:6–8). What love is this, when God did not spare his own Son but gave him up to save his enemies (8:32)! It appeared to be a tragic display of foolishness (1 Cor. 1:18), the waste of the best of lives, but in fact it revealed God's wisdom and power to save sinners through the most amazing means (vv. 23–25).

Furthermore, Christ spoke prophetic words in his passion, including his seven words, or sayings, from the cross, which revealed the following:

- *God's grace to forgive sinners through Christ*: "Father, forgive them; for they know not what they do" (Luke 23:34).
- *God's salvation through Christ for the repentant*: "Verily I say unto thee, Today shalt thou be with me in paradise" (Luke 23:43).
- *God's creation of a new spiritual family in Christ*: "He saith unto his mother, Woman, behold thy son! Then saith he to the disciple, Behold thy mother! And from that hour that disciple took her unto his own home" (John 19:26–27).
- *God's abandonment of Christ to suffer divine judgment as he bore our sins*: "My God, my God, why hast thou forsaken me?" (Mark 15:34).
- *God's fulfillment of his promises and prophecies in Christ*: "Jesus knowing that all things were now accomplished, that the scripture might be fulfilled, saith, I thirst" (John 19:28).
- *God's complete accomplishment of salvation by Christ*: "It is finished" (John 19:30).
- *God's acceptance of Christ's spirit because he completed his work, in anticipation of his resurrection*: "Father, into thy hands I commend my spirit" (Luke 23:46).

Christ's greatest revelation of God took place when his deity was most hidden in suffering and shame. This hidden revelation can be accessed only by faith, a faith that humbles our pride "that no flesh should glory in his presence," but "he that glorieth, let him glory in the Lord" (1 Cor. 1:29, 31). Christ is the Prophet of the cross, and we can receive his revelation by the way of the cross.

---

58. Owen, *Communion with God*, in *Works*, 2:85.

The Incarnate Prophet in His State of Exaltation

When we think of Christ's prophetic work, we tend to think of his earthly ministry. However, Christ's work of mediating God's word to men continues with his exaltation.

The Resurrection as an Act of Revelation

The resurrection of Jesus Christ reveals many things, including:

- *God's faithfulness to his promises,* for Christ rose in accordance with the Scriptures (1 Cor. 15:4; cf. Acts 2:25–32).
- *Christ's reliability as a true prophet,* for he rose from the dead "as he said" (Matt. 28:6; cf. 16:21; 17:23; 20:19).
- *God's power,* "the exceeding greatness of his power . . . which he wrought in Christ, when he raised him from the dead" (Eph. 1:18–20; cf. Rom. 1:4).
- *Christ's mediation of eternal life and inauguration of the new creation,* for his resurrection vindicated his claim "I am the resurrection, and the life" (John 11:25; cf. 1 Cor. 15:45).
- *Believers' possession of life by union with the Son,* who himself is one with the Father: "Because I live, ye shall live also. At that day ye shall know that I am in my Father, and ye in me, and I in you" (John 14:19–20; cf. 1 Cor. 15:21–22).
- *Christ's unique position as the Cornerstone,* apart from whom no one can be saved (Acts 4:10–12).
- *Christ's appointment by God* to "judge the world in righteousness" (17:31; cf. 10:39–42).
- *Christ's vindication* (1 Tim. 3:16) as the perfect righteousness of his people for their justification by faith alone (Rom. 4:23–25). Robert Peterson says, "Christ's resurrection testifies to the efficacy of his death."[59]

It might be objected that while Christ's resurrection does reveal much, it cannot be viewed as an act of his prophetic office because Christ was merely passive in his resurrection. In response, we answer that Christ in his divine nature was an active agent in his resurrection (John 2:19–21). He said, "I lay down my life, that I might take it up again. . . . I have power to lay it down, and I have power to take it up again" (10:17–18). The

---

59. Peterson, *Salvation Accomplished by the Son,* 140. Peterson offers an excellent survey of biblical texts about the saving significance of Christ's resurrection (117–50).

Son is one with the Father in divine power (v. 30), and all that the Father does the Son does also (5:19). Therefore, the revelation radiating from his resurrection is truly Christ's work as our Prophet.

The Risen Lord of the Apostolic Mission and Message

What Christ began by sending his messengers through Israel, he expanded after his resurrection by initiating the mission to the whole world (Matt. 28:18–20; Mark 16:15). Christ addressed this Great Commission to the eleven apostles (Matt. 28:16), who represented the church to the end of the age (v. 20; cf. 24:14). The success of this mission hinges on the lordship of Christ (v. 18). Jesus said, "As the Father has sent me, even so I am sending you" (John 20:21 ESV).

From the day of his resurrection, the living Lord engaged in a ministry of teaching, opening up the Scriptures to his disciples so that they might see how the entire Old Testament witnessed to his suffering, glory, and mission to the nations (Luke 24:25–27, 44–47). For forty days, Jesus Christ appeared to his apostles and taught them many things about himself and his kingdom (Acts 1:1–3). His prophetic office had not ceased, but had entered into a new phase of glory. His post-resurrection teachings formed the basis of the apostles' preaching of Christ from the Old Testament, as the rest of the book of Acts attests.

The Ascended Mediator of the Spirit of Truth

Before Christ ascended into heaven, he told his disciples to wait in Jerusalem until the promised Holy Spirit came upon them and clothed them with power to be Christ's witnesses, beginning in Jerusalem but extending to all the earth (Luke 24:47–49; Acts 1:8). Then he was taken up into heaven (Luke 24:50–51; Acts 1:9). Seated at God's right hand, Christ received the Spirit in all his fullness so that Jesus could pour him out upon the church (Acts 2:33). This is "the Spirit of truth," whom Christ said he would obtain by interceding with the Father (John 14:16–17), so named because "he shall teach you all things, and bring all things to your remembrance, whatsoever I have said unto you" (v. 26). While these promises have some application to all believers, Christ spoke them specifically to the apostles, the primary Spirit-empowered witnesses to him (15:26–27).[60] Christ had "many things" to say to them after he died and rose again; hence, he gave

---

60. Bavinck, *Reformed Dogmatics*, 3:475. See *RST*, 1:284–85, 325–26.

them the Spirit of truth to guide them into all the truth granted to the Son by the Father (16:12–15). Robert Letham says, "Thus, the apostles' teaching was to be derived from the Holy Spirit and, in consequence, from Christ himself."[61]

The abiding fruit of Christ's sending the Spirit of truth to the apostles is the New Testament.[62] The apostles taught that their message was revealed to them by Christ (Gal. 1:12; Rev. 1:1). Christ's apostles and new covenant prophets were foundational to the new covenant church by their preaching and writing the riches of Christ revealed by the Spirit (Eph. 2:20; 3:1–8). God had used the prophetic office to set down the old covenant in written documents; with the revelation of new truth and ratification of the new covenant, "the expectation would have been for further written documents," as Richard Belcher says.[63] Therefore, the whole Bible comes to us through the Mediator, Jesus Christ.

Furthermore, the ascended Christ is the Lord of the church's present ministry of the Word. Paul writes, "He that descended is the same also that ascended up far above all heavens, that he might fill all things. And he gave some, apostles; and some, prophets; and some, evangelists; and some, pastors and teachers; for the perfecting of the saints, for the work of the ministry, for the edifying of the body of Christ" (Eph. 4:10–12). The words "he gave" root the entire ministry of the church in the activity of her great Prophet. Perkins said, "Christ is ascended to this end to teach the ignorant, to give knowledge and wisdom unto the simple, and to give gifts of prophecy unto His ministers, that they may teach His people."[64] Whenever we hear a faithful preacher explain and apply God's Word, we are experiencing the work of the ascended Lord Jesus. Richard Sibbes said, "The greatest gift Christ in triumph will scatter to his church is . . . men furnished with gifts for the service of his church."[65]

Gospel preachers are "ambassadors for Christ," so that Paul says, "God is making his appeal through us" (2 Cor. 5:20 ESV). Those who reject the messengers of Christ reject Christ himself, who speaks through

---

61. Letham, *The Work of Christ*, 97.
62. Kelly, *Systematic Theology*, 2:517.
63. Belcher, *Prophet, Priest, and King*, 56n30.
64. Perkins, *An Exposition of the Symbol*, in *Works*, 5:264. Perkins considered "prophecy" to broadly include all teaching and preaching gifts, not just the extraordinary gift of receiving and proclaiming divine revelation.
65. Sibbes, *An Exposition of Second Corinthians Chapter 4*, in *Works*, 4:353.

them insofar as they faithfully preach God's Word (Luke 10:16). Fearful sinners outside of God's kingdom may rejoice that the gospel invitation comes not from a mere man, but from Jesus Christ. We know this to be so because Paul said to the Ephesians that Christ himself "came and preached peace to you" (Eph. 2:17); though Jesus never visited Ephesus, he did preach there through the faithful gospel ministers who proclaimed God's Word. Charles Hodge said, "He is with the church always, even to the end of the world; and it is his annunciation of peace which is made, by word and Spirit, through the church."[66]

On the one hand, there is a finished aspect of Christ's prophetic work: the completed canon of God's Word. On the other hand, Christ continues to work through pastors and teachers to proclaim the faith once revealed to the saints. Calvin said, "He received anointing, not only for himself that he might carry out the office of teaching, but for his whole body that the power of the Spirit might be present in the continuing preaching of the gospel. This, however, is most certain: the perfect doctrine he has brought has made an end to all prophecies."[67] We need add no new revelations to the Word; what we need today is pastors and teachers filled with the Spirit of Christ to explain and apply the truths already revealed by God.

The Messianic Voice in the Scriptures

The Bible has many human authors, but one divine Author speaks through them all: the triune God who draws near to us in the Mediator. Though Paul wrote his letters, he insists, "Christ is speaking in me" (2 Cor. 13:3 ESV), and, "The things that I write unto you are the commandments of the Lord" (1 Cor. 14:37). Therefore, in the Bible, we continue to hear the voice of Christ today. In a manner of speaking, the whole Bible comes to us in red letters.[68]

This makes reading the Bible and hearing it preached a wonderfully personal encounter with Christ. Christ said that the Good Shepherd calls his sheep, and "the sheep hear his voice . . . and the sheep follow him: for they know his voice" (John 10:3–4). Christ did not refer here merely

---

66. Hodge, *Ephesians*, 96.
67. Calvin, *Institutes*, 2.15.2. On the cessation of special revelation, see *RST*, 1:409–57 (chaps. 23–24).
68. The practice of printing the words of Christ in red in some English Bibles started in 1899. See "The Origins of the Red-Letter Bible," *Crossway*, March 23, 2006, https://www.crossway.org/articles/red-letter-origin/.

to his earthly ministry to Israel, when people literally did hear his human voice. He included the calling of Gentiles: "Other sheep I have, which are not of this fold: them also I must bring, and they shall hear my voice; and there shall be one fold, and one shepherd" (v. 16). This is the assurance of Christ's people: "My sheep hear my voice, and I know them, and they follow me: and I give unto them eternal life; and they shall never perish, neither shall any man pluck them out of my hand" (vv. 27–28). Whenever we prepare to read or hear God's Word, we should say to ourselves, "I am about to hear the voice of Jesus." Calvin said, "When the pure doctrine of the gospel is preached, it is just as if he himself spoke to us and were living among us."[69]

If you are not converted, then realize that Christ is speaking to you personally in the gospel. Thomas Hooker wrote, "The Lord proclaims his mercy openly, freely offers it, heartily intends it, waits to communicate it. . . . He freely invites, fear it not, thou mayest be bold to go. He intends it heartily, question it not. Yet he is waiting and wooing, delay it not therefore, but hearken to his voice."[70] If you are not yet a Christian, then the voice of Jesus Christ rings out from the gospel in this very book, even now as you read it, and calls you to come to him and be saved.

Whether it is the gospel or the most profound doctrine, whatever the Bible teaches, Christ says, and therefore you must believe it. John Brown of Haddington said, "Being absolutely infallible, being truth itself, the faithful and true witness, he can neither deceive nor be deceived (John 14:6; Rev. 1:5; 3:14)."[71] Do not be swayed by your opinion, by mere men, or by tradition, but submit to Christ alone. Do not let any pastor or pope take Christ's place as your Lord. Perkins wrote, "The sovereign Judge of all questions and controversies in religion, is Christ alone. . . . The principal voice of the Judge, and the definitive sentence, is the written word. And the office of the church, is no more but to gather, declare, testify and pronounce this sentence."[72]

Someone might object that giving so much authority to the Bible is to turn a mere book into an idol instead of following Christ. Letham antici-

---

69. Calvin, *Sermons on the Epistle to the Ephesians*, 201.
70. Thomas Hooker, *The Application of Redemption by the Effectual Work of the Word, and Spirit of Christ, for the Bringing Home of Lost Sinners to God. The First Eight Books* (London: Peter Cole, 1656), 362–63.
71. Brown, *Systematic Theology*, 285.
72. Perkins, *Galatians*, 67.

pates this objection, saying, "Is not the Bible then seen as a competitor to Christ?" We must never isolate the Bible from Christ himself. However, to trust in the Bible is to trust in Christ, for the Bible is the Word of God revealed through Christ. Letham concludes, "Thus the word of the Spirit to us, as found in the Old and New Testaments, is Christ's own word to us."[73] There is no real dilemma.

By trusting the Word as the truth of Christ, we strengthen our faith with divine confidence and hope in the promises of God so that we are ready to obey his every command. The Bible's authority, inerrancy, and sufficiency arise from the authority, inerrancy, and sufficiency of Christ. Owen wrote, "All these are absolutely secured in the divine person of the great prophet of the church. His infinite wisdom, his infinite goodness, his essential veracity, his sovereign authority over all, give the highest assurance . . . that there is no possibility of error or mistake in what is declared unto us."[74] It is crucial for believers to see that the Word is the revelation of none other than God the Son, for it calls them to venture all for his sake.

The Coming Glory

Just as we tend to associate Christ's death with his priestly work, so we associate his second coming with his kingly work. However, just as Christ acted as a revealing prophet in his death, so he will also reveal God in his second coming. On that day, "the Lord Jesus shall be revealed from heaven with his mighty angels" (2 Thess. 1:7–8). The "blessed hope" of the saints is "the glorious appearing of the great God and our Saviour Jesus Christ" (Titus 2:13). They endure the fiery trials that test their faith in anticipation of "praise and glory and honor at the revelation of Jesus Christ" (1 Pet. 1:7 ESV; cf. 4:13).

For the unrepentant sinner, the day of Christ will be "the day of wrath and revelation of the righteous judgment of God; who will render to every man according to his deeds. . . . The day when God shall judge the secrets of men by Jesus Christ" (Rom. 2:5–6, 16). The divine Warrior riding upon a white horse to slaughter his enemies is named "the Word of God" (Rev. 19:13). His coming will answer the cry of the righteous: "Let them

---

73. Letham, *The Work of Christ*, 102.
74. Owen, *Christologia*, in *Works*, 1:94.

be confounded and troubled for ever; yea, let them be put to shame, and perish: that men may know that thou, whose name alone is JEHOVAH, art the most high over all the earth" (Ps. 83:17–18).

For the repentant and righteous children of God, Christ's coming will not cause them to "be ashamed" (1 John 2:28), but instead, "we shall be like him; for we shall see him as he is" (3:2). The glory of God in Jesus Christ irradiates the heavenly city (Rev. 21:23). In the new creation, special revelation will permeate general revelation. The saints will enjoy the unhindered sight of God's glory: "There shall be no more curse: but the throne of God and of the Lamb shall be in it; and his servants shall serve him: and they shall see his face" (22:3–4).

Consequently, Christ, the Lamb of God, will ever be the centerpiece of God's radiant glory shining upon his people. Owen said, "All communications from the Divine Being and infinite fulness in heaven unto glorified saints, are in and through Christ Jesus, who shall for ever be the medium of communication between God and the church, even in glory." By our vision of his glory, we will receive "eternal springs of life, peace, joy, and blessedness."[75]

All of Christ's work aims to impart to those whom God gave him the knowledge of God, which is eternal life (John 17:2–3). Christ's prayer for his people is, "Father, I will that they also, whom thou hast given me, be with me where I am; that they may behold my glory" (v. 24). Is this your great desire, to be with Christ and see his glory? David said, "One thing have I desired of the LORD, that will I seek after; that I may dwell in the house of the LORD all the days of my life, to behold the beauty of the LORD" (Ps. 27:4). Make this your prayer, too.

Sing to the Lord

A Prayer for the Lord to Graciously Teach Us

> Lord, to me Thy ways make known,
> Guide in truth and teach Thou me;
> Thou my Saviour art alone,
> All the day I wait for Thee.
>
> Lord, remember in Thy love
> All Thy mercies manifold,

---

75. Owen, *The Glory of Christ,* in *Works,* 1:414.

Tender mercies from above,
Changeless from the days of old.

Just and good the Lord abides,
He His way will sinners show,
He the meek in justice guides,
Making them His way to know.

Grace and truth shall mark the way
Where the Lord His own will lead,
If His word they still obey
And His testimonies heed.

Psalm 25
Tune: Seymour
The Psalter, No. 67
Trinity Hymnal—Baptist Edition, No. 583

Questions for Meditation or Discussion

1. What does John 1:1, 18 imply about all of God's self-revelations through history?
2. What biblical evidence is there that God the Son gave the word to prophets and wise men in the Old Testament?
3. How is God the Son incarnate the ultimate revealer of God?
4. If Jesus Christ was filled by the Holy Spirit to speak God's words, then what distinguishes his prophetic ministry from that of the prophets before him who also had the Spirit?
5. How did Christ exercise his prophetic ministry in Israel during his humiliation?
6. What are some ways in which Christ's example teaches us what it means to be God's human image bearers?
7. How did Christ reveal God's glory at the cross?
8. How was Christ's resurrection an act of revelation?
9. Why can we attribute the New Testament writings to Christ when he wrote nothing himself?
10. How will the Son of Man reveal God when Christ returns?
11. Did anything in this chapter move you to love Jesus more? If so, what and why? If not, then what might that suggest about your spiritual condition? What should you do?

Questions for Deeper Reflection

12. What arguments could be made for and against interpreting personified Wisdom in Proverbs as God the Son? What is the best interpretation of Wisdom? Why?

13. How should knowing that Christ's voice speaks to us in all the Bible affect how preachers and teachers go about their ministry?

47

Christ's Prophetic Work, Part 3

Illumination for His Prophetic People

One of the most curious of Jesus's miracles was his healing of a blind man in two stages. After the first healing, the man said, "I see men as trees, walking." Christ touched his eyes again, and then he "saw every man clearly" (Mark 8:22–25). This healing illustrates spiritual blindness and its cure.[1] Christ's disciples were not completely blind, for they knew Jesus to be the Christ (v. 29) and received the word of the kingdom (4:11–12). But just before this man's healing, we read that Christ rebuked his disciples, saying, "Do you not yet perceive or understand? Are your hearts hardened? Having eyes do you not see, and having ears do you not hear?" (8:17–18 ESV). The disciples still needed more healing from the spiritual doctor, for their perception of spiritual truth was weak and distorted.

Our study of the doctrine of sin showed us that sin has corrupted not only our actions but also our minds, which have become dark and futile in their thinking.[2] Mankind is spiritually blind to the glory and goodness of God (2 Cor. 4:4). By nature, we are unable to see, hear, or receive spiritual truth, even if our minds can understand the words that communicate it.[3] The natural man, who does not have God's Spirit, cannot spiritually discern

---

1. Edwards, *The Gospel according to Mark*, 243–44.
2. Rom. 1:21; 3:11; 1 Cor. 1:18–21; Eph. 4:17–18; 5:8. See chap. 21 on total depravity and total inability.
3. Jer. 6:10; John 8:43; 12:39–40.

the truths of divine revelation (1 Cor. 2:14). Samuel Willard said, "Though a natural man may understand the grammatical and logical meaning . . . yet they are foolish things to him."[4] Without the Spirit of Christ, theological discussion is like a debate about color among people blind from birth.

Thanks be to God, the Mediator provides not only the Word of God, but also the inward work of illumination so that our blindness is healed. Thomas Boston said, "Christ teaches his elect . . . by his Spirit, who joins inward illumination to external revelation." Through Christ's mediation, the Word of God "enlightens the mind, awakens the consciences, convinces of sin, and can effectually convert and change them," but only "by the Spirit," for "all its power and efficacy is from him."[5] Contrary to what some have thought, it is not true that Christ "entirely fulfilled his prophetic ministry" in his earthly life, teachings, and miracles.[6] Christ the Prophet continues both to present the truth and to heal the eyes of the heart to see it.

The Effectual Illuminator of Men by the Spirit

Illumination is a work of the Trinity: the glory of God the Father shining through the mediation of God the Son, Jesus Christ, by God the Holy Spirit, who is the divine agent of it. It is supernatural light from God's Spirit producing experiential knowledge of God in Christ.[7] Paul prayed "that the God of our Lord Jesus Christ, the Father of glory, may give unto you the spirit of wisdom and revelation in the knowledge of him: the eyes of your understanding being enlightened" (Eph. 1:17–18).

The Converting Light of the Nations

Isaiah prophesied that the Lord would give Christ "for a light of the Gentiles; to open the blind eyes" (Isa. 42:6–7). To close a person's eyes is a divine judgment that gives him over to spiritual blindness and hardness.[8] To open a person's eyes is to heal his blindness[9] or to grant him the ability to see some hidden or spiritual reality he previously could not see.[10] In Isaiah's prophecy, God's people are afflicted with blindness to the things

---

4. Willard, *A Compleat Body of Divinity*, 326.
5. Boston, *An Illustration of the Doctrines of the Christian Religion*, in *Works*, 1:418.
6. *The Arminian Confession of 1621*, trans. and ed. Mark A. Ellis (Eugene, OR: Pickwick, 2005), 8.5–6 (70–71).
7. These two sentences are adapted from Joel R. Beeke, "The Illumination of the Spirit," in *The Holy Spirit and Reformed Spirituality*, 54, 63. Used by permission.
8. Isa. 6:10; 29:10; 44:18; Jer. 5:21; Matt. 13:14–15; Acts 28:27; cf. Ps. 69:23; Rom. 11:10.
9. 2 Kings 6:20; Isa. 35:5; Matt. 9:30; 20:33; John 9:10, 14, 17, 21, 26, 30, 32; 10:21; 11:37.
10. Gen. 21:19; Num. 22:31; 2 Kings 6:17; Ps. 119:18; Luke 24:31; Acts 26:18.

of God.[11] God's messianic Servant illuminates sinners internally to see the realities of which the Word of God speaks so that they know and believe. John Flavel said, "The opening of the mind and heart, effectually to receive the truths of God, is the peculiar prerogative and office of Jesus Christ."[12]

This inner illumination has always been the need of sinful men, women, and children (Deut. 29:4). God gave this grace of Christ to his people through the ages so that they might spiritually perceive his glory in his word (Ps. 119:18). When Christ came in the flesh, his light broke forth with new brilliance to enlighten people in Israel and throughout the nations (Luke 1:78–79; 2:30–32). John Calvin said, "Teachers would shout to no effect if Christ himself, inner Schoolmaster, did not by his Spirit draw to himself those given to him by the Father."[13]

By God's sovereign creative power, the light of his glory shines in our hearts "in the face of Jesus Christ" (2 Cor. 4:6). Richard Sibbes said, "God can create a new spiritual eye to discern of spiritual things. . . . God, and only God, that created light out of darkness, can create light in the soul."[14] When Paul compares salvation to the time when God "commanded the light to shine out of darkness" (v. 6), he indicates that saving illumination is a work of new creation (cf. 5:17). Sibbes wrote, "There is no less work to shine in that dark heart of man, than to create the world, to create light out of darkness."[15] Therefore, Christ mediates effectual calling.[16]

There is a kind of illumination that does not result in salvation and spiritual fruit, but only temporary effects (Heb. 6:4–8). Flavel said that such light is "common, and intellectual only, to *conviction*," in contrast to the "special and efficacious light" that shines in the soul, "bringing the soul to Christ in true *conversion*."[17] Though this light issues from the prophetic ministry of Christ, it does not change the fundamental commitments of the heart, but convicts sinners of their guilt, provoking them to greater hatred toward God and Christ (John 3:19–20).[18]

There is another kind of illumination that saves people. We find an example of Christ's saving illumination in the conversion of Lydia, "whose heart the Lord opened, that she attended unto the things which were

---

11. Isa. 42:16–19; 43:8; 56:10; 59:10.
12. Flavel, *The Fountain of Life*, in *Works*, 1:133.
13. Calvin, *Institutes*, 3.1.4.
14. Sibbes, *The Glorious Feast*, in *Works*, 2:464.
15. Sibbes, *An Exposition of Second Corinthians Chapter 4*, in *Works*, 4:320.
16. See the chapters on effectual calling in *RST*, vol. 3 (forthcoming).
17. Flavel, *The Method of Grace*, in *Works*, 2:440–41, emphasis original.
18. See the chapter on preparatory grace in *RST*, vol. 3 (forthcoming).

spoken of Paul" (Acts 16:14). The "Lord" may here refer specifically to the Lord Jesus (v. 31; cf. 11:20–21). His opening of Lydia's heart resulted in her giving careful and thoughtful attention to God's word,[19] with the result that she was converted and baptized. Sibbes said, "As the minister speaks to the ear, Christ speaks, opens, and unlocks the heart at the same time; and gives it power to open, not from itself, but from Christ."[20]

Christ controls the results of ministry, not the minister. The examples of holy prophets such as Noah, Isaiah, and Ezekiel show that "a man may be a true and sincere minister, lawfully called by God and his church, and yet not turn many unto God," as William Perkins said. Such a response grieves ministers, yet it teaches them that "the power and virtue is not in them, but God." Therefore, they must serve knowing that whether their ministry is a savor of life or death to men, to God it is the sweet savor of Christ (2 Cor. 2:15–16).[21]

Christ does save sinners, however. When Christ commissioned Paul to his work, the Lord Jesus said, "Now I send thee, to open their eyes, and to turn them from darkness to light, and from the power of Satan unto God, that they may receive forgiveness of sins, and inheritance among them which are sanctified by faith that is in me" (Acts 26:17–18). Christ works through the apostolic word to heal sinners "from natural blindness, and worldly ignorance."[22] One result of this illumination is repentance unto life, for the text may be translated, "to open their eyes so that they turn from darkness to light."[23] Another result is saving faith: "that they may receive forgiveness of sins, and inheritance . . . by faith."[24] Wilhelmus à Brakel said, "In order to be delivered from your darkness and to be illuminated with spiritual light, the Lord Jesus, this great Prophet, must take the task in hand to instruct you. . . . He does this very thing, not only by giving His Word . . . but also, by His Spirit, illuminating His own."[25]

---

19. See the uses of the verb translated as "attend" (*prosechō*) in Acts 5:35; 8:6, 10, 11; 20:28.

20. Sibbes, *Bowels Opened*, in *Works*, 2:63.

21. Perkins, *A Cloud of Faithful Witnesses*, on Heb. 11:7, in *Works*, 3:108–9.

22. *The Dutch Annotations upon the Whole Bible*, on Acts 26:18.

23. The word "and" prior to "to turn" in Acts 26:18 (KJV) is in italics to show that it does not appear in the Greek text, which simply reads "the turning" (*tou hypostrepsai*). The genitive articular infinitive often denotes purpose or result. F. Blass and A. Debrunner, *A Greek Grammar of the New Testament and Other Early Christian Literature*, trans. and rev. Robert W. Funk (Chicago: University of Chicago Press, 1961), 400.5 (206–7).

24. Again, "that they may receive" translates a genitive articular infinitive "the receiving" (*tou labein*), which appears to modify "to open" in a manner parallel to "the turning," noted above. Both infinitives are in the aorist aspect.

25. Brakel, *The Christian's Reasonable Service*, 1:526.

Charles Spurgeon said,

> What a difference is made by Divine illumination! A moment ago the man was in the dark, but now he is brought into marvellous light! He was not in the dark because the sun was set or the shutters were closed, but because he was blind. What matters how bright the day when the eyes are sealed? . . . Jesus came on purpose to give eyes to the blind, and by a single word of the preacher, or a text of Scripture, or a verse of a hymn, the Lord can cause the darkened mind to enter upon the life of light and discernment.[26]

Therefore, let sinners seek Christ for sight. John Cotton advised lost sinners, "Cry after wisdom (Prov. 2:3). . . . The blind man cried after our Savior (Mark 10:51), and though the people rebuked him, yet he cried until he received sight. What though others should rebuke you and say, 'You have knowledge enough, will you be a fool now?' But alas, you are a poor ignorant creature; cry hard that you may receive sight."[27]

The Internal Instructor of God's People

The Lord Jesus Christ continues to exercise his work of illumination among those who have been saved. After Christ rose from the dead, he appeared to his disciples and "opened their minds to understand the Scriptures" (Luke 24:45 ESV). Though they were already believers, there remained in their hearts foolishness and resistance to believing God's word (v. 25). Christ overcomes this inner darkness by causing his light to increase in believers' hearts. No human teacher can do that. Flavel wrote, "It is one thing to open the Scriptures, that is, to expound them, and give the meaning of them . . . and another thing to open the mind or heart."[28]

Christ's saving illumination transforms his people progressively. Paul says, "We all, with open face beholding as in a glass the glory of the Lord, are changed into the same image from glory to glory, even as by the Spirit of the Lord" (2 Cor. 3:18). Through Christ, God causes his glory to shine within our hearts, illuminating our thoughts and warming

---

26. C. H. Spurgeon, *The Metropolitan Tabernacle Pulpit*, 57 vols. (Edinburgh: Banner of Truth, 1969), 30:199–200.

27. John Cotton, *The Way of Life, or, Gods Way and Course, in Bringing the Soule into, and Keeping It in, and Carrying It on, in the Wayes of Life and Peace* (London: by M. F. for L. Fawne, and S. Gellibrand, 1641), 185.

28. Flavel, *The Fountain of Life*, in *Works*, 1:131.

our affections toward him (4:6). Flavel said, "The light of Christ is powerfully transformative of its subjects. . . . All saving light endears Jesus Christ to the soul; and as it could not value him before it saw him, so once he appears to the soul in his own light, he is appreciated and endeared unspeakably."[29] This light creates a new spiritual sense, as Edward Reynolds said, a "taste and relish of the sweetness of spiritual truth."[30] Illumination thus brings an experiential knowledge, "a spiritual sense of the power and reality of the things believed," that the Bible compares to "acts of sense, as tasting, seeing, feeling," as John Owen wrote.[31]

Christ dwells in his people by his Spirit, and by that Spirit he leads them (Rom. 8:9–10, 14). Believers remain limited human beings with fallible minds that cannot fully understand God, but they do have communion with Christ in his revealed, human knowledge of God. Paul says, "For who hath known the mind of the Lord, that he may instruct him? But we have the mind of Christ" (1 Cor. 2:16). The mind of Christ is ours by the Spirit of God, whom "we have received . . . that we might know the things that are freely given to us of God" (v. 12). Yet this mind is not nurtured in us by new special revelations by the Spirit, but by the Word and wisdom that the Spirit has already revealed by the apostles, especially the gospel of Christ crucified (1:18, 23; 2:2, 6–10). All Christians have the Spirit, but there are degrees of this illumination, for some are as "babes in Christ" who must be fed "with milk, and not with meat" (3:1–2). Christians receive greater illumination from Christ as they obey his will insofar as they understand it (John 14:21).

We should pray for increased illumination. If we need understanding, Perkins said, "we must pray to Christ for it, and because we have so excellent a teacher, we must pray unto Him that He would give unto us hearing ears, that is, hearts tractable [teachable] and obedient to his word."[32] Like the psalmist, we should prepare to read or hear God's Word with the petition "Open thou mine eyes, that I may behold wondrous things out of thy law" (Ps. 119:18). As the disciples said to Jesus, so we should pray: "Lord, teach us" (Luke 11:1).

---

29. Flavel, *The Fountain of Life*, in *Works*, 1:142.

30. Cited in Flavel, *The Fountain of Life*, in *Works*, 1:133. See Reynolds, *Animalis Homo*, in *Works*, 4:368.

31. Owen, *The Reason of Faith*, in *Works*, 4:64; cf. Calvin, *Institutes*, 3.2.34. On experiential knowledge, see *RST*, 1:125–28, 463–64. See also the chapter on faith in *RST*, vol. 3 (forthcoming).

32. Perkins, *Commentary on Galatians*, on Gal. 1:12, in *Works*, 2:44.

The Glorious, Invisible Content of Christ's Illumination

The content of Christ's prophetic illumination has the same scope as the content of the Holy Scriptures. Christ's inward illumination does not reveal new truth, but applies truth already revealed: "He opened their minds to *understand the Scriptures*" (Luke 24:45 ESV). Brakel wrote, "When the Lord Jesus teaches sinners internally, He does not address Himself differently to them than He does to others. The same Word, the same sermons heard simultaneously by many, some only hear with the ear and understand the truth in a natural sense without their hearts being renewed by it. That same Word affects others internally, enlightening and renewing the heart."[33]

It is a delusion to claim the light of Christ in spiritual experience detached from the Holy Scriptures. The same prophet who foretold that Christ would be the light of the world (Isa. 9:2; 42:6) also warned, "To the law and to the testimony: if they speak not according to this word, it is because there is no light in them" (8:20). Gerard Wisse (1873–1957) said, "This inner, prophetical ministry of Christ is under no circumstances to be divorced from the Word."[34] Flavel warned that the illumination of Christ and his Spirit was "never designed to take men off from reading, and studying, and searching the scriptures . . . but to make their studies and duties the more fruitful, beneficial, and effectual to their souls."[35]

Paul's prayers for the saints reflect our need for increasing illumination concerning God's Word: to receive from God "the spirit of wisdom and revelation in the knowledge of him: the eyes of your understanding being enlightened; that ye may know" the hope, inheritance, and power God has for us; to abound "in knowledge and all judgment; that ye may approve the things that are excellent"; to "be filled with the knowledge of his will in all wisdom and spiritual understanding"; and to be "increasing in the knowledge of God."[36] Divine illumination enables believers to perceive with greater clarity and effect the unseen spiritual realities of God, salvation in Christ from sin, and the kingdom of glory. Let us consider each of these three focal points of revelation and how Christ illuminates people to see their unseen reality.

---

33. Brakel, *The Christian's Reasonable Service*, 1:522.
34. Gerard Wisse, *Christ's Ministry in the Christian: The Administration of His Offices in the Believer* (Grand Rapids, MI: Free Reformed Publications, 2013), 18.
35. Flavel, *The Fountain of Life*, in *Works*, 1:132.
36. Eph. 1:15–20; Phil. 1:9–11; Col. 1:9–14.

First, Christ reveals the glory of God to the soul. As we read, study, and hear the Word of God, we must depend upon the Son to reveal God to us (Matt. 11:27). The knowledge of God is the most important gift our Prophet can give us, for it is the very essence of eternal life (John 17:2–3). Ignorance of God destroys people (Hos. 4:1, 6); the knowledge of God is their only real wisdom, power, and wealth (Jer. 9:23–24). John writes, "We know that the Son of God is come, and hath given us an understanding, that we may know him that is true, and we are in him that is true, even in his Son Jesus Christ," and so only through Christ can we know "the true God" and avoid "idols" that misrepresent him (1 John 5:20–21).

Second, Christ reveals the glory of salvation in him. This focal point of revelation has three parts. The Heidelberg Catechism (LD 1, Q. 2) speaks of those things "necessary for thee to know, that thou . . . mayest live and die happily," namely, "the first, how great my sins and miseries are; the second, how I may be delivered from all my sins and miseries; the third, how I shall express my gratitude to God for such deliverance."[37] Gratitude includes obedience to God in response to his love. Here the catechism follows the pattern of Paul's epistle to the Romans.[38]

Regarding sin and misery, the exalted Prophet sends the Spirit of conviction to reveal sin, righteousness, and judgment (John 16:7–11). Though conviction often starts before conversion, it continues in an evangelical way after conversion to promote godly sorrow and repentance in believers (cf. 2 Cor. 7:10–11). Wisse said that Christ causes God's Word to give us a new perspective on God and ourselves. We once were "so enamored of ourselves that we hated God," but now we esteem him as delightful and worthy of being served, and hate our sinful hearts and ways. Furthermore, by Christ's illumination, "we will discover that we do not only have an aversion for the law, but also for the gospel." Thus, Christ's light kills our pride and self-righteousness, but "there is always some sweetness in being thus uncovered," for "the soul begins to appraise God . . . as being delightful and desirable to the superlative degree."[39]

Regarding deliverance, in Christ, believers have the Spirit of life by whom they gain experiential knowledge of their salvation from condemnation, sin, and death (Rom. 8:1–2). This is the Spirit of Christ (v. 9). How-

---

37. *The Three Forms of Unity*, 68.
38. Romans reveals man's sin and misery (1:18–3:20), deliverance or redemption in Christ (3:21–11:36), and the response of gratitude for God's mercies (12:1–15:13).
39. Wisse, *Christ's Ministry in the Christian*, 9–12.

ever, as Wisse pointed out, believers still want to do something to make themselves worthy of grace. We secretly doubt that Christ will bless us if we are spiritually bankrupt and worthy of damnation. We are constantly "in need of the internal ministry of Christ as prophet in order to overcome this skeptical opposition within us." Christ "lets us see that we have nothing, but also that we need not have anything in order to be objects of free grace. In Christ there is an all-sufficiency."[40]

Regarding gratitude and sanctification, believers have the Spirit of adoption, who leads them to live as faithful sons of their loving Father (Rom. 8:12–15). The Spirit of adoption is the Spirit of God's Son (Gal. 4:6). Wisse said that Christ the Prophet instructs his people for holiness in the following ways. Christ continues to reveal their sinfulness in a manner that drives them to prayer, which produces "spiritual growth," "fellowship with the Lord," and "heavenly-mindedness." Christ teaches them to see their afflictions as God's fatherly training, so that they learn to say, "It is good for me that I have been afflicted; that I might learn thy statutes" (Ps. 119:71). Christ grants them a deepening experiential knowledge of biblical doctrines about the triune God and his covenant. As a result, they rejoice and exult in their spiritual treasures in Christ and increase in godliness. Christ instructs them in the loveliness of God's law as the expression of God's own beauty. With great reverence, they come to see that "to be obedient is to love," indeed, to love God "in an absolute, unbounded, very special, incomparable, and entirely unique manner." In short, Christ teaches us "that God is . . . God!"[41]

Third, in addition to revealing God's glory and salvation's glory, Christ reveals to his people the glory of the coming kingdom. This is what Paul prayed: "that ye may know what is the hope of his calling, and what the riches of the glory of his inheritance in the saints" (Eph. 1:18). As in John Bunyan's allegory, Christ grants believers to look through his spiritual telescope to glimpse the Celestial City from afar and see "some of the glory of the place."[42] This illumination regarding the future hope greatly strengthens believers in their present sufferings, so that they can say, "Though our outward man perish, yet the inward man is renewed day by day. For our light affliction, which is but for a moment, worketh for us a far more exceeding and eternal weight of glory; while we look not

---

40. Wisse, *Christ's Ministry in the Christian*, 18, 20–21.
41. Wisse, *Christ's Ministry in the Christian*, 27–37.
42. Bunyan, *The Pilgrim's Progress*, in *Works*, 3:145.

at the things which are seen, but at the things which are not seen: for the things which are seen are temporal; but the things which are not seen are eternal" (2 Cor. 4:16–18).

Christ's Prophetic People

Great are the benefits of Christ's threefold office, not least of which is the believer's right to exercise some of the privileges of those offices by union with Christ. It should not surprise us that Christians are also prophets, priests, and kings, for the threefold office is rooted in God's calling and covenant with Adam, and believers live in Christ, the last Adam. God called Israel to the threefold office in the Mosaic covenant, as exemplified in the nation's covenantal officers. Now, in the new covenant, believers in Christ "are a chosen generation, a royal priesthood, an holy nation, a peculiar people; that ye should shew forth the praises of him who hath called you out of darkness into his marvellous light" (1 Pet. 2:9).

Christians share in Christ's anointing by the Holy Spirit and hence also serve God as prophets, priest, and kings. Paul says, "Now he which stablisheth us with you in Christ, and hath anointed us, is God; who hath also sealed us, and given the earnest of the Spirit in our hearts" (2 Cor. 1:21–22). John Chrysostom commented,

> What does that mean, "He has anointed and sealed us?" He has given us the Spirit, by whom he has done both things, making us at once prophets, priests, and kings, for these three kinds were in former times anointed. We however, have not received just one dignity, but all three at once, and that in a superior way. We taste the kingdom; we become priests, offering our bodies as a sacrifice, for it says, "Present your members as living sacrifices, acceptable to God" [cf. Rom. 12:1]; moreover, we are made prophets, for "what eye has not seen, nor ear heard, this has been revealed to us" [cf. 1 Cor. 2:9].[43]

Christians follow Christ in the threefold office in a subordinate and dependent manner. We are not the Lord, but are subordinate to the Lord. Therefore, our authority as prophets, priests, and kings is merely human, whereas God the Son exercises divine authority in his office. We are not the Mediator, but are dependent on the Mediator. Therefore, our ministry

---

43. John Chrysostom, *Third Homily on Second Corinthians*, cited in Wainwright, *For Our Salvation*, 112.

as prophets, priests, and kings adds nothing to Christ's work and is merely instrumental in blessing others, whereas Christ mediates salvation to us and through us with infinite merit and sovereign efficacy.

Nevertheless, the church's participation in some privileges of the three-fold office is an amazing grace and blessing. The Heidelberg Catechism (LD 12, Q. 32) queries, "But why art thou called a Christian?" and answers, "Because I am a member of Christ by faith, and thus am partaker of His anointing; that so I may confess His name, and present myself a living sacrifice of thankfulness to Him; and also that with a free and good conscience I may fight against sin and Satan in this life, and afterwards reign with Him eternally, over all creatures."[44]

Therefore, we will conclude our treatment of Christ's prophetic work by a practical consideration of how Christians also serve in that capacity. (We will do the same for Christ's priestly and kingly work at the conclusion of chap. 52 and in chap. 55).

The Promise of Christ's Prophetic People

In order to fulfill their calling, all of God's people must be prophets in some sense. Moses perceived this when he earnestly wished, "Would that all the LORD's people were prophets, that the LORD would put his Spirit on them!" (Num. 11:29 ESV).

The desire of Moses found divine sanction in the promise of Joel: "It shall come to pass afterward, that I will pour out my spirit upon all flesh; and your sons and your daughters shall prophesy, your old men shall dream dreams, your young men shall see visions: and also upon the servants and upon the handmaids in those days will I pour out my spirit" (Joel 2:28–29). The pairs of opposites in this text communicated that God would universally distribute the prophetic Spirit among all classes of his people.

On the day of Pentecost, Peter announced that Joel's prophecy had come true (Acts 2:17–18), for Christ's disciples "were all filled with the Holy Ghost, and began to speak with other tongues, as the Spirit gave them utterance" (v. 4). This supernatural phenomenon, Peter explained, signaled that the promised Son of David had died, risen from the dead, ascended into heaven, taken his throne at God's right hand, received the

---

44. *The Three Forms of Unity*, 78. See also Perkins, *An Exposition of the Symbol*, in *Works*, 5:105; *Commentary on Galatians*, on Gal. 4:19–20, in *Works*, 2:292.

Holy Spirit in his immense fullness, and poured out the Spirit on his church (vv. 22–36). The promised Holy Spirit is granted to everyone who repents of sin and receives baptism in Christ's name (vv. 38–39).

What does it mean that God has poured out the Spirit of prophecy on all in Christ? It does not mean that every Christian is a "prophet" in the sense of a spokesman authorized by God to receive and declare new special revelation. There were such prophets in the early church, but they could preface their prophesying with the words "Thus saith the Holy Ghost."[45] Even in the apostolic age, Paul says, "Are all prophets?" (1 Cor. 12:29). With the apostles, the prophets laid the foundation of truth for the new covenant (Eph. 2:20; 3:5), but the prophetic office has ceased because Christ's coming brought the full and final revelation of God (Heb. 1:1–2).[46]

The promise that "your sons and your daughters shall prophesy" (Acts 2:17) had a limited fulfillment in the gifts of tongues and prophecy to various people in the apostolic age. It will have a complete fulfillment in the future glory, when all Christians will see God "face to face" (1 Cor. 13:12), an allusion to the intimate knowledge that Moses, the foundational prophet of the old covenant, enjoyed with God.[47] However, in this present time, Joel's prophecy has an expansive though partial fulfillment in the indwelling of the Holy Spirit in every believer to anoint him to know God and speak his Word. Joel's promise looks forward to the universal blessing of the new covenant, for the Lord said, "They shall all know me, from the least of them unto the greatest of them" (Jer. 31:34; cf. Heb. 8:11). They are "all . . . taught of the LORD" (Isa. 54:13; cf. John 6:45). All are office bearers because all are truth bearers.

The Privileges of Christ's Prophetic People

Christ's prophetic grace confers great prophetic privileges to the people of God, which obligates them, as Brakel wrote, "to be conformed to Him in His prophetic office, since believers are named Christians after Christ, being partakers of His anointing."[48]

First, Christians are *anointed to know the truth of Christ*. John says of the true church, in distinction from those who depart to follow anti-

---

45. Acts 11:27–30; 13:1–4; 15:32; 21:9–11.
46. On the cessation of special revelation and prophecy in particular, see *RST*, 1:409–57 (chaps. 23–24).
47. Ex. 33:11; Deut. 34:10; cf. Num. 12:8.
48. Brakel, *The Christian's Reasonable Service*, 1:529.

Christian doctrine, "Ye have an unction from the Holy One, and ye know all things" (1 John 2:20). The word translated as "unction" or "anointing" (*chrisma*) is closely related to "Christ" or "anointed one" (*christos*, v. 22). John explains that this unction preserves believers in the knowledge of true doctrine and protects them from receiving heresy (vv. 21–22). He says, "The anointing which ye have received of him abideth in you, and ye need not that any man teach you: but as the same anointing teacheth you of all things, and is truth, and is no lie" (v. 27). John alludes to the new covenant ("they shall teach no more every man his neighbor," Jer. 31:34)[49] and to Christ's promise that he would send the Holy Spirit to "abide with" his disciples, "be in" them, and "teach" them "all things" (John 14:16–17, 26). Therefore, this "unction" is anointing by the Spirit.[50] Just as Christ is anointed by the Spirit, so he shares his anointing with his disciples so that we have a spiritual knowledge of the truth revealed in God's Word and cling to it.

As Christians, we must respond to this great privilege by clinging to the truth of Christ, studying it, and giving it a position of ruling influence in our thoughts and affections. John says, "Let that therefore abide in you, which ye have heard from the beginning" (1 John 2:24). Perkins said, "Whereas all Christians receive anointing from the Holy One, Christ Jesus, to become prophets in a sort, we must do our endeavors that the word of God may dwell plentifully in us. And for that cause we must search the Scriptures, even as hunters seek for the game and as men seek for gold in the very mines of the earth."[51]

Second, Christians are *empowered to witness for Christ*. Christ anticipated the fulfillment of Joel's promise regarding the outpouring of the prophetic Spirit, saying, "Ye shall receive power, after that the Holy Ghost is come upon you: and ye shall be witnesses unto me both in Jerusalem, and in all Judaea, and in Samaria, and unto the uttermost part of the earth" (Acts 1:8). Peter said on Pentecost, "We all are witnesses" (2:32). In the book of Acts, the "witnesses" of Christ are primarily his apostles.[52]

---

49. This did not make the teaching ministry obsolete, for John still wrote to these believers to teach them (1 John 2:21, 26; 5:13). Rather, it indicated that the true knowledge of God would no longer belong merely to a remnant among God's people that must call the larger community to know God, but to all true members of the church.

50. Stephen S. Smalley, *1, 2, 3 John*, Word Biblical Commentary 51 (Waco, TX: Word, 1984), 107.

51. Perkins, *An Exposition of the Symbol*, in *Works*, 5:105; cf. Brakel, *The Christian's Reasonable Service*, 1:531.

52. Acts 3:15; 4:33; 5:32; 10:39, 41; 13:31; 22:15, 18; 23:11; 26:16, 22.

However, the church's witness is not confined to the apostles. Stephen is also a "witness" (22:20 ESV). The book of Revelation also refers to Antipas as Christ's "witness" (Rev. 2:13 ESV).[53] Witness language in the New Testament alludes to God's call upon the people of Israel to be his witnesses and servants, which required the nation to know and believe that he alone is God, the Lord, the only Savior (Isa. 43:10–11).[54]

Although not all Christians are called to be preachers, all are called to speak God's Word to unbelievers around them as they have opportunity. Paul writes, "Walk in wisdom toward outsiders, making the best use of the time. Let your speech always be gracious, seasoned with salt, so that you may know how you ought to answer each person" (Col. 4:5–6 ESV). Brakel offered weighty motives for believers to talk to unbelievers about Jesus Christ. Whatever knowledge we possess is given to us to share with others, and God will call us to account for our faithfulness. Our love for Christ should move us to desire that all people would honor him. Our love for people should compel us to speak to sinners headed for hell. It is a great joy to see a lost sinner saved. And God uses our witness to build up the church.[55]

People raise a number of objections to personal evangelism, which Brakel addressed. If you are a poor speaker, then begin with people who do not intimidate you, such as children, and improve by practice. If you know little, at least say what you know. Simply saying, "We are going to die, which will be followed by eternity," might be used by God. If you feel powerless, remember that God will not hold you accountable for fruitfulness, but faithfulness. If you think your sins disqualify you, then include yourself among sinners (as Brakel said, "do not say *you*, but *we*") and let people know that you grieve over your sins and are battling against them. If you feel ashamed of spiritual things, repent of your shame and press on to do your duty regardless of how you feel. If you are spiritually lazy, consider what an important task this is and be diligent. If you fear that you are seeking your own honor, remember that silence is another way of

---

53. The KJV reads "martyr" in Acts 22:20 and Rev. 2:13, basically transliterating the Greek word *martys*, which has the core meaning of "witness" (Matt. 18:16; 26:65; Mark 14:63; Luke 24:48; Rom. 1:9; etc.). Where acting as a witness cost one's life, we find "a preliminary step toward the martyrological concept of the witness (*martys* = martyr) which emerged at once in the early church." *TDNT*, 4:502.

54. On the link between knowing God and witnessing for God, see John N. Oswalt, *The Book of Isaiah, Chapters 40–66*, The New International Commentary on the Old Testament (Grand Rapids, MI: Eerdmans, 1998), 146–47.

55. Brakel, *The Christian's Reasonable Service*, 1:532–33.

guarding your honor among men, and be a witness for Christ while praying for greater purity of motive.[56]

Brakel concluded his call to personal evangelism with principles for
how to do it. First, be "discreet." There are times when it is best to speak
only of earthly matters, lest our constant pressing of spiritual things provoke a bad reaction. Second, Brakel said, "be watchful against pride and
an air of superiority." We must conduct ourselves "in an amiable, loving
and humble manner," and yet show "we are serious about our intentions,
have great reverence for God, and greatly esteem spiritual truths." Third,
we must "often be engaged in private prayer." Pray before speaking and
pray while speaking. Pray for "enabling grace" and pray for "fruits in
others." Afterward, "we ought to again lift up our hearts to God with
thanksgiving for having received proper motivation and for the fact that
we were able to say something."[57]

The Christian's responsibility to witness for Christ begins with his own
family, especially if he is the head of the household.[58] Fathers and mothers
must teach future generations the things of God so that they might know
the Lord, repent of sin, believe the gospel, and obey his commandments.[59]
Perkins said that parents must teach "their whole household the doctrine
of the true religion, that they may know the true God and walk in all his
ways in doing righteousness and judgment [justice]." Parents must also
"prepare their families" before they come to church meetings so that gospel ministers may "see far more fruit of their ministry."[60] A central means
of raising one's family in the Lord is family worship.[61] This involves brief
daily reading and teaching in the Word of God (Deut. 6:6–7), prayer and
thanksgiving (1 Thess. 5:17–18; 1 Tim. 4:4–5), and singing God's praise
(Ps. 118:15). The saying is true: "A family without prayer is like a house
without a roof. It is uncovered and exposed."[62]

Third, Christians are *equipped to edify Christ's body.* The ascended
Christ works through pastors and teachers to build up his body, the

---

56. Brakel, *The Christian's Reasonable Service*, 1:534–36, emphasis original.

57. Brakel, *The Christian's Reasonable Service*, 1:536–37.

58. On Christian parenting from the Reformed perspective, see Joel R. Beeke, *Parenting by God's Promises: How to Raise Children in the Covenant of Grace* (Lake Mary, FL: Reformation Trust, 2011).

59. Gen. 18:19; Deut. 6:6–7; Ps. 78:2–8; Eph. 6:4.

60. Perkins, *An Exposition of the Symbol*, in *Works*, 5:105–6.

61. Joel R. Beeke, *Family Worship*, Family Guidance Series (Grand Rapids, MI: Reformation Heritage Books, 2009). See Beeke and Jones, *A Puritan Theology*, 864–76.

62. William Jay, *Morning Exercises for Every Day in the Year* (New York: American Tract Society, 1828), 14, for January 1.

church, in sound doctrine and mature godliness (Eph. 4:10–14). Christ's ministry through the Word does not stop with pastors and teachers; he uses those leaders to equip all the members of the church to serve each other. Paul says, "Speaking the truth in love, we are to grow up . . . into Christ, from whom the whole body . . . when each part is working properly, makes the body grow" (vv. 15–16 ESV). By Christ's ministry to fill his people with grace "through the power of the Holy Ghost," believers are "full of goodness, filled with all knowledge, able also to admonish one another" (Rom. 15:13–14).

If you are a believer in Christ, then you have a prophetic responsibility to encourage other believers in their walk with God. The Lord places upon all the requirement to "consider one another to provoke unto love and to good works . . . exhorting one another" (Heb. 10:24–25). The Holy Scriptures charge Christians to exhort each other daily to beware of sin (3:13), to give and receive painful rebuke in faithful love when needed (Ps. 141:5), and to encourage one another, saying, "Let us go" to meetings for worship and prayer (Isa. 2:3; Zech. 8:21).[63]

This does not mean that every Christian is gifted to be a teacher of doctrine (1 Cor. 12:29) or called to exercise the authority of an elder to teach the church and refute false teachers (1 Tim. 3:2; Titus 1:9). However, all Christians should use the basic truths of God's law and gospel to encourage one another in the practical duties of the Christian life, for we are a family.

Fourth, Christians are *illuminated to praise the God of Christ*. We think of prophets as preachers, but they also serve in the public worship of God. This is preeminently the case with Jesus Christ. In Psalm 22, he who says, "My God, my God, why hast thou forsaken me?" (v. 1), also says, "I will declare thy name unto my brethren: in the midst of the congregation will I praise thee" (v. 22), and forecasts that as a result all nations will turn to God and worship him (v. 27). This psalm was fulfilled in Jesus Christ (Heb. 2:12). William Gouge said, "Christ's prophetical office tended to the setting forth of the praise of God, as well as to the instructing of men in God's will. . . . These two duties, of instructing man, and praising God, belong to all faithful prophets of the Lord."[64] Christ is the worship leader of the church.

---

63. Perkins, *An Exposition of the Symbol,* in *Works,* 5:105–6; and Brakel, *The Christian's Reasonable Service,* 1:531–32.

64. Gouge, *Commentary on Hebrews,* 1:151.

Not only is our praise the fruit of Christ's prophetic work, but our praise is itself a prophetic act. Some of the Levites "prophesied" regularly when leading the music in temple worship (1 Chron. 25:1–3). The ministry of prophets was sometimes associated with musical instruments, probably used to praise the Lord.[65] Furthermore, worshiping the Lord is a declaration of his glory, name, and praise.[66] Therefore, God's people are never more prophetic than when they "shew forth the praises" of the God who saved them (1 Pet. 2:9).[67]

Christ's work of revelation obligates us to offer public worship to the Lord. Christ came so that the nations would sing God's praises (Rom. 15:8–12). One reason why Christ reveals God is so that we may worship him rightly. Therefore, we must turn Christ's Word into worship.

We must never break the link between our prophetic worship and Christ's prophetic Word. The Father seeks people to worship him "in spirit and in truth," and that truth is not of our own making but is the revelation of our Prophet, the Christ (John 4:19–26). Therefore, let us not offer anything to God except what he has revealed through Christ. Then the church worships God with prophetic praise that honors him, edifies the body, and evangelizes the world.

Sing to the Lord

Praying for Christ's Illumination

Blessed Jesus, at thy word
We are gathered all to hear thee;
Let our hearts and souls be stirred
Now to seek and love and fear thee,
By thy teachings, sweet and holy,
Drawn from earth to love thee solely.

All our knowledge, sense, and sight
Lie in deepest darkness shrouded
Till thy Spirit breaks our night
With the beams of truth unclouded.

---

65. 1 Sam. 10:5–6; 2 Kings 3:15; 1 Chron. 25:1, 3.

66. Pss. 79:13; 96:3; 102:21; Isa. 43:21.

67. The word *exangellō*, which means to proclaim or publish abroad, is translated as "shew forth" in 1 Pet. 2:9, but it is used for the praise of God in Pss. 9:15(14); 70:15(71:15); 72:28(73:28); 78:13(79:13); 106:22(107:22) LXX. "Praises" (plural *aretē*), which can also mean "excellency," is used for the praise of God in Isa. 42:8, 12; 43:21; 63:7 LXX.

Thou alone to God canst win us
Thou must work all good within us.

Glorious Lord, thyself impart,
Light of Light, from God proceeding;
Open thou our ears and heart,
Help us by thy Spirit's pleading;
Hear the cry thy people raises,
Hear and bless our prayer and praises.

Father, Son, and Holy Ghost,
Praise to thee and adoration!
Grant that we thy Word may trust
And obtain true consolation
While we here below must wander,
Till we sing thy praises yonder.

Tobias Clausnitzer, trans. Catherine Winkworth et al.
Tune: Liebster Jesu
Trinity Hymnal—Baptist Edition, No. 220

Questions for Meditation or Discussion

1. Why do people need Christ to illuminate their hearts by his Spirit? Why is it not sufficient to just teach them the Word?
2. How does the Bible show us that there are two kinds of illumination, one resulting in conviction and the other in conversion?
3. How does union with Christ contribute to the inward illumination of believers? Prove your answer with Scripture.
4. What is the relationship between Christ's inward illumination and the truths revealed in the Bible?
5. What are some major focal points of Christ's illumination?
6. Regarding the three categories of sin and misery, deliverance and redemption, and gratitude and holiness, for which do you most need more illumination from Christ? Why? Pray for God to give you this grace.
7. How did God foretell that he would create a prophetic people? How is that promise fulfilled in Christ?
8. What does it mean to be God's prophetic people with regard to (1) knowledge of the truth, (2) witness to the world, (3) edification in the church, and (4) praise to God?

9. How has reading this chapter caused you to see the prophetic calling of all Christians more clearly? How does this encourage you? What changes does this call require in your own life?

Questions for Deeper Reflection

10. Why is Christ's work of illumination necessary for people to know and experience the unseen realities of God, salvation, and the glory to come? How is this work crucial for experiential Christianity versus mere intellectual belief?

11. What are the dangers of separating Christ's inner illumination from the written Word? What are the dangers of studying God's written Word apart from Christ's illumination?

12. Some people from your church come to you in concern and confusion because they heard someone say that according to Jeremiah 31:34 and 1 John 2:27, Christians need no teachers, but should just follow the Bible and the Spirit who indwells them. How do you help them?

48

Christ's Priestly Work, Part 1

Introduction to Christ's Priestly Office

It may seem strange to call Jesus Christ a priest, for he was of the tribe of Judah, not Levi, and he did not wear special robes and perform sacred rituals, but worked as a carpenter and then as a preacher. However, Christ fulfilled the function of the high priest in Israel. Irenaeus said, "For He did not make void, but fulfilled the law, by performing the offices of the high priest, propitiating God for men . . . suffering death, that exiled man might go forth from condemnation, and might return without fear to his own inheritance."[1]

Jesus Christ, God the Son incarnate, is the great Priest.[2] Zechariah foretold that the Christ would serve as both King and Priest (Zech. 6:12–13).[3] David prophesied that Christ was appointed "a priest for ever" (Ps. 110:4). The book of Hebrews cites this prophecy several times regarding Christ's priesthood.[4] Paul says, "Christ . . . hath given himself for us an offering and a sacrifice to God" (Eph. 5:2). More than two dozen texts in the New Testament refer to Christ's sacrificial "blood," often with respect to forgiveness or cleansing from sin.[5] Jesus laid down his life as

---

1. Irenaeus, *Against Heresies*, 3.8.1, in *ANF*, 1:471.
2. See the section on Christ's threefold office in the New Testament in chap. 43.
3. On Zech. 6:12–13, see the section on the counsel of peace with the messianic Branch in chap. 30.
4. Heb. 5:6, 10; 6:20; 7:11, 17, 21.
5. Matt. 26:28; Mark 14:24; Luke 22:20; John 6:53–56; Acts 20:28; Rom. 3:25; 5:9; 1 Cor. 10:16; 11:25, 27; Eph. 1:7; 2:13; Col. 1:14, 20; Heb. 9:14; 10:29; 12:24; 13:12, 20; 1 Pet. 1:2, 19; 1 John 1:7; 5:6, 8; Rev. 1:5; 5:9; 7:14; 12:11.

"the Lamb of God, which taketh away the sin of the world" (John 1:29; 10:17).

The priesthood of Christ is Godward in its acts and effects. Hugh Martin (1822–1885) said, "It propitiates God; it intercedes to God. It satisfies God's justice; it pacifies God's wrath; it secures God's favour; it seals God's covenant love; and gives effect to God's eternal purpose and grace. Herein it is conspicuously distinguished from the prophetic and kingly offices of our Lord. These, in their several actings, have not God for their immediate object, but mainly the souls of His people."[6]

Christ's priesthood is foundational to all other aspects of his mediatorial work. If Christ were a revealing Prophet and a conquering King but not a merciful Priest to bring forgiveness and grace, then there would be no gospel for sinners, but only a revelation of justice and execution of wrath. His priesthood fills his whole office with tender mercies for those who deserve the fires of hell.

Biblical Terms and Concepts of the Priestly Office

The Hebrew word translated as "priest" (*kohen*) occurs 750 times in the Old Testament. It means a person consecrated to serve a deity. Predictably, the most occurrences of *kohen* in the Old Testament are in Leviticus (194 times). The related Hebrew verb that means "to serve God as a priest" (*kahan*) appears twenty-three times, of which half are in the Lord's instructions for consecrating and ordaining the sons of Aaron in the latter part of Exodus.[7]

Closely associated with priests in the Old Testament are Hebrew words related to "holiness" and those related to "altar" and "sacrifice." We see both in Exodus 29:44: "I will sanctify the tabernacle of the congregation, and the altar: I will sanctify also both Aaron and his sons, to minister to me in the priest's office [*kahan*]." To "sanctify" (*piel* of *qadash*) means to set apart as "holy" (*qadosh*). High concentrations of holiness language appear in biblical chapters pertaining to the institution and exercise of the priestly office.[8] To be holy is to be set apart from what is ordinary and set against what is unclean.[9] In distinction from ordinary people, a priest is

---

6. Hugh Martin, *The Atonement: In Its Relation to the Covenant, the Priesthood, the Intercession of Our Lord* (Edinburgh: James Gemmell and George Bridge, 1887), 59; cf. Vos, *Reformed Dogmatics*, 3:94.

7. Ex. 28:1, 3, 4, 41; 29:1, 44; 30:30; 31:10; 35:19; 39:41; 40:13, 15.

8. Exodus 28–30; Leviticus 10, 16, 22; 2 Chronicles 29; Ezekiel 44, 48.

9. On God's holiness, see *RST*, 1:566–83 (chap. 30).

"holy" and "chosen" by God "to come near unto him" (Num. 16:5).[10] A priest mediates between "the divine and the ordinary," bridging the gap between the holy and the common.[11]

The word translated as "altar" (*mizbakh*, Ex. 29:44) refers to an elevated structure on which people present the flesh, or sometimes just the blood (30:6; Lev. 16:18), of a "sacrifice" (*zebakh*) to God. An "offering" (*qarban*) is a gift that a priest "brings near" (*hiphil* of *qarab*) to the Lord.[12] A. A. Hodge said, "The priest's grand distinction was, that he had a right to draw near to God. Hence the common designation of priests was 'those who draw near to Jehovah' (Ex. 19:22; Num. 16:5; Ezek. 42:13; 44:13). The distinctive priestly act which marked his great function was to bring near (*hiqrib*), translated habitually *to offer* (Lev. 16:6, 9, 11, 20, etc.)."[13]

In the Greek Septuagint translation of the Old Testament and in the New Testament, priestly terminology is associated with the same themes that are evident in the Hebrew terms. The Greek word translated as "priest" (*hiereus*, or for "high priest," *archiereus*) is related to the words translated as "sacred" (*hieros*) and "sacred place" or "temple" (*hieron*, 1 Cor. 9:13). The New Testament associates the priesthood with that which is "holy" (*hagios*) and with "sacrifice" (*thysia*, Heb. 8:1–3; 1 Pet. 2:5).

The necessity of the priestly office arises from the grave offense that man's sin and uncleanness present to God's holy presence.[14] The Lord consecrates the priest to remedy this problem by sacrifices for sin and uncleanness. On the Day of Atonement, "he shall make an atonement for the holy place, because of the uncleanness of the children of Israel, and because of their transgressions in all their sins: and so shall he do for the tabernacle of the congregation, that remaineth among them in the midst of their uncleanness" (Lev. 16:16). Alec Motyer (1924–2016) wrote, "Holiness bars the way, but mercy opens it. . . . Everything ultimately rested on the work of the priest . . . and on the divine provision of sacrifice."[15]

---

10. Archibald A. Hodge, *The Atonement* (repr., London: Evangelical Press, 1974), 151.

11. *NIDOTTE*, 2:600.

12. In older literature and theological discourse, an offering is also called an "oblation" (Latin *oblatio*).

13. Hodge, *The Atonement*, 152–53.

14. Lev. 15:31; 20:3; 22:3–4, 6; Isa. 6:3, 5; Ezek. 5:11.

15. J. Alec Motyer, *The Message of Exodus: The Days of Our Pilgrimage* (Downers Grove, IL: InterVarsity Press, 2005), 265. See also Calvin, *Commentaries*, on Ex. 28, introduction.

Types of Christ's Priestly Office

God foreshadowed Christ's priesthood through two orders of priests that ministered to the true God, one consisting of Aaron and his sons, and the other represented in an ancient king named Melchizedek.

The Priestly Order of Aaron

Although God promised that Israel would be "a kingdom of priests, and an holy nation" if the people kept his covenant (Ex. 19:5–6), the Lord instituted an official priesthood in Israel for Aaron and his sons (28:1), which he later established in a covenant (Num. 25:11–13; Jer. 33:21).

The Aaronic priesthood revealed *a priest's qualifications*. No man appointed himself to this office; he had to be selected by God (Ex. 28:1; 1 Sam. 2:28). Intruders into the sacred work of the priesthood had to die (Num. 3:10; 18:7). Christ's priesthood is not a mere metaphor, but a definite office that God authorized Christ to perform (Heb. 5:1, 4–5).[16] John Calvin said, "God would only have those accounted lawful priests whom He had selected at His own sole will. . . . Not even Christ Himself would have been sufficient to propitiate God, unless He had undertaken the office by the decree and appointment of His Father." The reason is that "the priesthood depended on His authority, just as reconciliation flows from His mere mercy."[17]

Though appointed to a sacred and heavenly task, a priest was not an angel from heaven but a man taken from the people whom he served (Ex. 28:1). As one "taken from among men," he could be gentle with sinners, for he felt their weakness (Heb. 5:2). Yet he had to be a man without "blemish" (Lev. 21:16–24)—a bodily symbol of moral excellence.[18] The "holy" priestly garments depicted a person of "glory" and "beauty" (Ex. 28:2, 40), terms for the majesty and wealth of a great king (Est. 1:4). The colors of his clothing—gold, blue, purple, and scarlet—were the colors of the tabernacle, which was embroidered with images of heavenly cherubim (Ex. 26:1, 6; 28:5–6). Hence, Motyer calls the high priest "the heavenly man."[19] The high priest wore on his head a golden plate inscribed with the words "Holiness to the Lord" (vv. 36–38). Philip Ryken says, "If this is what God is like—beautiful in his holiness and glorious in his splendor—

---

16. Martin, *The Atonement*, 51–53.
17. Calvin, *Commentaries*, on Ex. 28:1.
18. Keach, *Preaching from the Types and Metaphors of the Bible*, 364.
19. Motyer, *The Message of Exodus*, 269.

then the only way to approach him is to be adorned with holiness, glory, and beauty."[20]

Christ is the true Priest. He is God's Son, the living radiance of his glory (Heb. 1:3). Christ embodies God's holiness among men. Hebrews 7:26 says, "For such an high priest became us, who is holy, harmless, undefiled, separate from sinners, and made higher than the heavens." John Owen commented, "He was every way, in the perfect holiness of his nature and his life, distinguished from all sinners; not only from the greatest, but from those who ever had the least taint of sin."[21] Yet Christ is the brother of his people, having taken their nature (2:11, 14, 18). Owen wrote, "He lived not in a wilderness, nor said unto the children of men, 'Stand off, I am holier than you.' . . . No; but as he was meek and lowly . . . so he did by all ways and means invite and encourage all sorts of sinners to come unto him."[22]

The Aaronic priesthood also revealed *a priest's work*. It was ministry unto God: "that he may minister *unto me* in the priest's office" (Ex. 28:1, 4). "For every high priest taken from among men is ordained for men in *things pertaining to God*, that he may offer both gifts and sacrifices for sins" (Heb. 5:1).

The first and fundamental work of a priest was to offer sacrifices to God (Ex. 29:38–42; Heb. 5:1; 8:3) to atone for the sins of his people (Lev. 1:4; 9:7). Owen said, "A priest is a sacrificer."[23] Unlike the ceremonial priests who offered up animal sacrifices, the true Priest presented a far greater sacrifice: "He offered up himself" (Heb. 7:27; cf. Eph. 5:2). Augustine said, "For us was He unto Thee both Priest and Sacrifice, and Priest as being the Sacrifice."[24]

The second and derivative work of a priest was to intercede for God's people by appearing in God's presence as their representative.[25] This task was derivative because the high priest could enter the Most Holy Place on behalf of Israel only with the blood of the sacrifice (Lev. 16:12–19; Heb. 9:7, 25). The Aaronic high priest wore on his shoulders two onyx stones engraved with the names of the tribes of Israel so that he might

---

20. Philip Graham Ryken, *Exodus: Saved for God's Glory*, Preaching the Word (Wheaton, IL: Crossway, 2005), 871.
21. Owen, *An Exposition of the Epistle to the Hebrews*, 5:558.
22. Owen, *An Exposition of the Epistle to the Hebrews*, 5:557.
23. Owen, *An Exposition of the Epistle to the Hebrews*, 2:14; cf. 4:449.
24. Augustine, *Confessions*, 10.43.69, in NPNF[1], 1:162.
25. Belcher, *Prophet, Priest, and King*, 64–65.

"bear their names before the LORD" (Ex. 28:6–12). Motyer said, "He was known before the Lord not by his own name but by their names." He was "responsible for securing their entrance into the Lord's presence (cf. Heb. 9:24; 10:19–20). They could enter only because they rested on him (Heb. 10:21–22)."[26] The high priest also wore a breastplate bearing twelve precious gems, each inscribed with a tribe's name (Ex. 28:15–21). Calvin wrote, "When our heavenly Father regards us in Him, He esteems us above all the wealth and splendor of the world."[27] Aaron bore these names "upon his heart" (v. 29), a sign of the high priest's compassion for his people (Heb. 2:18; 4:14–16).

The priest also invoked God's blessing of grace and peace upon the people.[28] This may be considered a third priestly work, or an aspect of the priestly intercession.

Therefore, we learn from the Aaronic priesthood that Christ's priestly work consists of two great parts, sacrifice and intercession, the latter of which includes or comes to fruition in blessing. The Westminster Shorter Catechism (Q. 25) says, "Christ executeth the office of a priest, in his once offering up of himself a sacrifice to satisfy divine justice (Heb. 9:14, 28), and reconcile us to God (Heb. 2:17); and in making continual intercession for us (Heb. 7:24–25)."[29] These will be the topics of coming chapters in which we consider Christ's work as Priest in more detail.

The Priestly Order of Melchizedek

After Abraham's victory in battle against the armies of several kings, "Melchizedek king of Salem brought forth bread and wine: and he was the priest of the most high God. And he blessed him, and said, Blessed be Abram of the most high God, possessor of heaven and earth: and blessed be the most high God, which hath delivered thine enemies into thy hand. And he gave him tithes of all" (Gen. 14:18–20). David said that God had sworn an oath that the Lord at his right hand is a priest forever "after the order of Melchizedek" (Ps. 110:4).

In the New Testament, the epistle to the Hebrews expounds the meaning of Melchizedek as a type of Christ, illuminated by David's words in Psalm 110. The divine oath shows that Christ is a priest by God's appointment

---

26. Motyer, *The Message of Exodus*, 270.
27. Calvin, *Commentaries*, on Ex. 28:4–8.
28. Lev. 9:22–24; Num. 6:24–26; Deut. 10:8; 21:5; 2 Chron. 30:27.
29. *Reformed Confessions*, 4:356.

(Heb. 5:4–6, 10). As Melchizedek blessed Abraham, the recipient of God's covenant promises, so Christ mediates the covenant blessing to his people (6:14; 7:1, 6). Just as Melchizedek was the king of Salem and a priest of the Most High God (7:1), so Christ is the great Priest-King, combining atoning mercy with infinite power for effectual grace (10:12–17). The author of Hebrews notes that in Genesis, a book of many genealogies, Melchizedek is mentioned "without father, without mother, without descent, having neither beginning of days, nor end of life" (7:3), so that he resembles the eternal Son of God.[30]

Christ is the supreme and final Priest. Abraham's paying of tithes to Melchizedek and Melchizedek's blessing of Abraham show that Christ is superior to the Levitical priests, Abraham's descendants (Heb. 7:4–10). Psalm 110:4 implied that God would abolish the Levitical priesthood and replace it with another Priest—one who proved to be from Judah, not Levi (Heb. 7:11–14). Christ alone has the perfect priesthood, not by "a carnal commandment," but by "the power of an endless life" (vv. 15–17). The types of the old covenant were annulled, proving that they were not effective in themselves for salvation, "for the law made nothing perfect" (vv. 18–19). Insofar as its ceremonies were a temporary administration of God's grace, the old covenant gave way to the new covenant, "a better testament" (vv. 20–22), and its always-dying priests were superseded by Christ, who lives forever and can save his people completely (vv. 23–26).

Basic Biblical Perspectives on Christ's Priestly Sacrifice

The primary purpose of a priest's sacrifice was to "make atonement."[31] The Hebrew verb translated as "make atonement" (*piel* of *kapar*) means to appease the wrath of an offended party by a gift that rectifies an injustice done in order to restore a broken relationship, as is illustrated in Jacob's gifts to appease Esau (Gen. 32:20).[32] God appointed the priest to offer a gift to him that appeased his wrath by rectifying the wrong done to him by the sins of the people he willed to save. By this payment offered to God, his relationship with sinners was restored to one of peace.

---

30. Owen, *An Exposition of the Epistle to the Hebrews*, 5:517.
31. Lev. 1:4; 4:20, 26, 31, 35; 5:6, 10, 13, 16, 18; 6:7, 30; 7:7; 9:7; 10:17; 12:7, 8; 14:18–21, 29, 31, 53; 15:15, 30; 16:6, 10, 11, 16–18, 20, 24, 27, 30, 32–34; 19:22.
32. See the extensive study of *kipper* (*piel* of *kapar*) in Leon Morris, *The Apostolic Preaching of the Cross*, 3rd ed. (Grand Rapids, MI: Eerdmans, 1965), 161–70.

The New Testament gives us three complementary perspectives on what Christ accomplished by his sacrifice, summarized in the words *propitiation*, *redemption*, and *reconciliation*.

Propitiation

According to the doctrine of propitiation, Christ offered himself as a sacrifice to appease the anger of God against sinners by bearing that wrath himself. The Greek words translated as "propitiate" (*hilaskomai*) or "propitiation" (*hilasmos, hilastērion*) appear only a few times in the New Testament.[33] Yet they summarize the crucial biblical teaching that salvation is deliverance from the wrath of God, who is offended at our sins. Owen wrote, "In the use of this word, then, there is always understood: first, an offense, crime, guilt, or debt, to be taken away; secondly, a person offended, to be pacified, atoned, reconciled; thirdly, a person offending, to be pardoned, accepted; fourthly, a sacrifice, or some other means of making atonement."[34]

The root word of "propitiate" had the common meaning in Greek of appeasing anger and was often used of appeasing angry gods.[35] In the Greek translation of the Old Testament, it can refer to winning over an angry man (Prov. 16:14). We have already noted a classic example of propitiation when Jacob sent gifts to his offended and vengeful brother Esau, thinking, "I will appease [*exilaskomai*] him with the present that goeth before me, and afterward I shall see his face; peradventure [perhaps] he will accept of me" (Gen. 32:20). When God was propitiated (*hilaskomai*), he relented from his furious anger (Ex. 32:12, 14; Ps. 77[78]:38 LXX).

When Paul writes of Christ's death as a "propitiation" (*hilastērion*, Rom. 3:25), he does so in a context of warning that the wrath of God is against sinners.[36] Similarly, after writing that Christ came to "make propitiation" (Heb. 2:17 ESV), the writer to the Hebrews warns of God's wrath and burning anger against unbelievers (3:11; 10:27). John calls Christ our "propitiation" (*hilasmos*, 1 John 2:2; 4:10) with regard to our need for a righteous Advocate when we sin against the God who is

---

33. Rom. 3:25; Heb. 2:17; 1 John 2:2; 4:10. *Hilastērion* also appears in Heb. 9:5 of the "mercy seat" on the ark of the covenant in the tabernacle.

34. Owen, *An Exposition of the Epistle to the Hebrews*, 3:476.

35. Morris, *The Apostolic Preaching of the Cross*, 145.

36. Rom. 1:18; 2:5, 8; 4:15; 5:9. See James Denney, *The Christian Doctrine of Reconciliation* (London: Hodder and Stoughton, 1917), 157.

absolute light (1:5; 2:1). Leon Morris wrote, "If we sinners need an advocate with God, then obviously we are in no good case."[37] While we may feel squeamish about God's wrath (it is surely a frightening idea), we must not deny Christ's propitiation or we abandon the doctrine that Christ suffered the penalty of our sins. John Murray said, "Christ vicariously bore God's judgment against sin," and "the essence of the judgment of God against sin is his wrath, his holy recoil against what is the contradiction of himself."[38]

It might be objected that God is not angry with sinners but loves them, for God is love (John 3:16; 1 John 4:8–10). The propitiation of God's wrath, we are told, is a pagan idea; the Christian God is gracious and needs no propitiation. C. H. Dodd asserted that references in the Bible to God's "wrath" speak not about divine anger but about an impersonal process of cause and effect by which sin brings negative consequences.[39]

In reply, we answer that the Bible pervasively testifies to God's anger against sin, not as a sinful passion or emotional perturbation, but as an expression of his perfect justice (Rom. 2:5–6) and infinite love for righteousness (Ps. 11:5–7). Real love cannot be indifferent to sins and lies, but abhors them (Rom. 12:9; 1 Cor. 13:6). Therefore, God's wrath must be propitiated, for he cannot deny his own goodness and righteousness.[40]

Furthermore, the biblical doctrine of propitiation does not hold that God's wrath was appeased by someone outside of himself, but that God himself satisfied the righteous demands of his wrath by sending his Son to be the sacrifice for sin: "Herein is love, not that we loved God, but that he loved us, and sent his Son to be the propitiation for our sins" (1 John 4:10). Morris writes, "It is to God himself that we owe the removal of God's wrath."[41] When God was angry enough against us to send us to hell, he also loved us so much that he sent his Son to bear that wrath for our salvation. Martyn Lloyd-Jones (1899–1981) wrote, "Why has God had anything to do with such creatures as men and women, dead in trespasses and sins, rebels—hating Him, being against Him, turning His world into a living hell? . . . 'Not that we loved God, *but that he loved us*,' moved by nothing but His own self-generated love. Though we are what we are,

---

37. Morris, *The Apostolic Preaching of the Cross*, 206.
38. Murray, "The Atonement," in *Collected Writings*, 2:145.
39. C. H. Dodd, *The Epistle of Paul to the Romans* (London: Fontana, 1959), 50, cited in *RST*, 1:857.
40. On God's wrath and its relation to his other attributes, see *RST*, 1:852–61.
41. Morris, *The Apostolic Preaching of the Cross*, 207.

'God is love,' and His great heart of love, in spite of all that is in us, unmoved by anything save itself, has done it all."[42]

The means of propitiation is the sacrifice of God's Son. When John speaks of Christ's "propitiation" (1 John 2:2; 4:10), he uses the exact word used of the Day of "Atonement" (Lev. 25:9 LXX). In context, John also speaks of cleansing by Christ's "blood" (1 John 1:7), an allusion to sacrificial atonement (Lev. 16:19 LXX; cf. Heb. 9:22). The verb translated as "make propitiation" (*hilaskomai*) in Hebrews 2:17 (ESV) is the root of the word used often in the Septuagint for the work of priests in making atonement through blood sacrifices.[43] Of course, this text in Hebrews has priestly sacrifice in view. Similarly, the word translated as "propitiation" (*hilastērion*) in Romans 3:25, which also mentions "blood," is the term for the golden cover of the ark of the covenant, where the priests made atonement by blood on the Day of Atonement.[44]

Therefore, Christ made propitiation by blood sacrifice. Though in himself he was God's beloved Son who always pleased his Father, Christ bore the wrath and curse of the righteous Judge (Mark 14:35–36; 15:34; Gal. 3:10, 13). Christ is our propitiation as "a sacrifice that bears God's wrath to the end and in so doing changes God's wrath toward us into favor," Wayne Grudem writes.[45] John Piper says, "The substitute, Jesus Christ, does not just cancel the wrath; he absorbs it and diverts it from us to himself. God's wrath is just, and it was spent, not withdrawn."[46] Augustine said, "Now, as men were lying under this wrath by reason of their original sin, and as this original sin was the more heavy and deadly in proportion to the number and magnitude of the actual sins which were added to it, there was need for a Mediator, that is, for a reconciler, who, by the offering of one sacrifice, of which all the sacrifices of the law and the prophets were types, should take away this wrath."[47]

The result of Christ's propitiation is God's pleasure in those whom Christ saves. By satisfying God's holy displeasure against sinners, Christ also extends God's approval to them, so that the Father delights in them. The prophets often spoke of God's anger, wrath, and fury against sinners

---

42. Martyn Lloyd-Jones, *Life in Christ: Studies in 1 John, Volume 4: The Love of God* (Wheaton, IL: Crossway, 1994), 60, emphasis original.
43. Lev. 1:4; 4:20, 26, 31, 35; 5:6, 10, 13, 16, 18; etc. LXX (forty-nine times in Leviticus in the LXX).
44. Ex. 25:17–22; Lev. 16:2, 13–15 LXX.
45. Grudem, *Systematic Theology*, 575.
46. John Piper, *The Passion of Jesus Christ* (Wheaton, IL: Crossway, 2004), 21.
47. Augustine, *Enchiridion*, chap. 33, in *NPNF*[1], 3:248–49.

(Isa. 63:3–6; Zeph. 1:15, 18), but also recorded remarkable promises that God would rejoice in his redeemed as a bridegroom delights in his bride (Isa. 62:4–5; Zeph. 3:17). By Christ's sacrifice, we can genuinely please God with who we are and what we do.[48] This is a wonderfully liberating truth for God's children: the Father is pleased with them.[49]

Redemption

In biblical usage, the Greek words translated as "redeem" (*lytroomai, apolytroō*), "redemption" (*lytrōsis, apolytrōsis*), and "ransom" (*lytron, antilytron*) refer to rescuing people from loss, slavery, or death by the payment of a price or ransom. Slaves were set free by being "redeemed" by the payment of a price (Ex. 21:8; Lev. 19:20; 25:47–55). A ransom released a criminal from the death he deserved by satisfying the offended party for his loss (Ex. 21:29–30; cf. Num. 35:31; Prov. 6:35). The law allowed for land that was sold to be bought back ("redeemed") by the family (Lev. 25:23–34). The New Testament also uses words translated as "buy" or "purchase" (*agorazō, exagorazō*) in a similar fashion.[50]

Redemption aims at liberating those who have brought themselves into loss, enslavement, or death due to their financial debts or criminal activities. Glorious types of Christ's redemption appear in the Lord's deliverance of the people of Israel from their slavery in Egypt and from their later exile in Babylon.[51] Redemption involves an exercise of power to save from oppressors.[52] Our "redemption" in Christ means that God "delivered us from the power of darkness, and hath translated us into the kingdom of his dear Son" (Col. 1:13–14).

However, as noted above, redemption also involves the payment of a price. This was foreshadowed in the types. Israel could not be redeemed from Egypt without the sacrifice of the Passover lamb, which died as a substitute to deliver Israel's households from God's wrath (Ex. 12:12–13).[53]

---

48. Matt. 25:21; 2 Cor. 5:9; Eph. 5:10; Phil. 4:18; Col. 1:10; 3:20; 1 Thess. 2:4; 4:1; 1 Tim. 5:4; 2 Tim. 2:4; Heb. 11:6; 13:16, 21; 1 John 3:22.
49. We will explore pleasing God in the discussion of the privileges of God's priestly people in chap. 52.
50. 1 Cor. 6:20; 7:23; Gal. 3:13; 4:5; 2 Pet. 2:1; Rev. 5:9; 14:3–4.
51. Ex. 6:6; 15:13; Deut. 7:8; 9:26; 13:5; 24:18; Isa. 41:14; 43:1, 14; 44:6, 24; 47:4; 48:17, 20; 49:7, 26; 54:5, 8; 59:20; 60:16; 63:16.
52. Neh. 1:10; Pss. 77:14–15; 78:42; Prov. 23:11; Isa. 50:2; Jer. 50:34; Luke 1:68–71.
53. On redemption as "not simply deliverance by power but deliverance by price as well," see Reymond, *A New Systematic Theology of the Christian Faith*, 520, 652–53.

Without blood sacrifice, God's righteous judgment on Egypt would justly have fallen on Israel as well. Shortly after the exodus, the Lord required the payment of a half shekel of silver per man, called "ransom for his soul," or life, so "that there be no plague among them" and "to make an atonement for your souls" (Ex. 30:11–16). Moses used the silver collected in this tax to make the bases of the tabernacle (38:25–28), linking the ransom and atonement price to the ministry of the priests. Similarly, God's redemption of Israel from exile was said to be at the price of other nations and peoples (Isa. 43:3–4).

Christ's obedience unto death was the price of our redemption. Jesus explained the meaning of his death as his voluntary laying down of his life as a "ransom" (*lytron*) for many (Matt. 20:28; Mark 10:45). B. B. Warfield said that "the essential meaning of the term" is "the price paid as a ransom in order to secure release."[54] This is the same term used for the price paid to rescue a lawbreaker from punishment (Ex. 21:29–30 LXX). Paul likewise says Christ gave himself as a "ransom" (*antilytron*, 1 Tim. 2:6). This is why Paul also tells Christians that they have been "bought with a price" (1 Cor. 6:20; 7:23). The word translated as "price" (*timē*), which also can mean "honor" or "value," is used of money to buy services or property (Matt. 27:9; Acts 4:34; 7:16). Peter identifies the price by which believers were "redeemed" as not "silver and gold," but "the precious [*timios*] blood of Christ" (1 Pet. 1:18–19).

If Christ's death was a redemption price, to whom was this price paid? Some theologians have taught that Christ paid a ransom to the Devil in order to release us from his bondage.[55] Gregory of Nyssa said, "In order to secure that the ransom in our behalf might be easily accepted by him who required it, the Deity was hidden under the veil of our nature, that so, as with ravenous fish, the hook of the Deity might be gulped down along with the bait of flesh," so that Satan would be caught and destroyed by his own devices.[56] However, as Gregory of Nazianzus said, it is an outrage to give "the robber . . . payment for his tyranny."[57] Anselm of Canterbury noted that "even though it was just for man to be tormented by the devil, it was unjust for the devil to torment him." He added, "God owed nothing to the

54. Warfield, "The New Testament Terminology of Redemption," in *The Person and Work of Christ*, 434.
55. See the survey in H. D. McDonald, *The Atonement of the Death of Christ: In Faith, Revelation, and History* (Grand Rapids, MI: Baker, 1985), 141–46.
56. Gregory of Nyssa, *The Great Catechism*, sec. 24, in *NPNF²*, 5:492–94.
57. Gregory of Nazianzus, *Orations*, 45.22, in *NPNF²*, 7:431.

devil but punishment, and man owed him nothing but retaliation . . . but whatever was required from man was due unto God, not to the devil."[58]

Christ offered the ransom to God. Redemption from sin brings forgiveness from God (Ps. 130:3–4, 7–8; Isa. 44:22) by the offering of Christ's sacrificial blood to him (Eph. 1:7; Col. 1:14). God's law places "under a curse" all who break it, but "Christ hath redeemed us from the curse of the law, being made a curse for us: for it is written, Cursed is every one that hangeth on a tree" (Gal. 3:10, 13). The price of redemption was substitution, the law's curse falling upon Christ instead of us. Murray wrote, "He became so identified with the curse resting on his people that the whole of it in all its unrelieved intensity became his. That curse he bore and that curse he exhausted. That was the price paid for this redemption and the liberty secured for the beneficiaries is that there is no more curse."[59]

Christ's crucifixion publicly displayed him as the bearer of God's wrath against lawbreakers in order to redeem them from what they deserved. Paul's quotation of Deuteronomy 21:22–23 in Galatians 3:13 indicates that Christ's death on a "tree" signified the curse of God.[60] Criminals and enemies in the ancient world were often hung on wooden poles before or after their death as a sign of public condemnation.[61] William Perkins wrote that Christ "entered . . . into the apprehension and feeling of the wrath and indignation of God due to man's sin. . . . He did not only in mind see it before His eyes, but also He felt it. It was laid and imposed on Him, and He encountered with it."[62] This was the price of our redemption.

Redemption restores a family from loss and enslavement to enjoy its inheritance (Lev. 25:23–55). The Lord typologically redeemed Israel, his "son," to be his people and enjoy priestly access to him in the Promised Land (Ex. 4:22; 6:6–8). When Christ redeemed his people with a true and eternal redemption, he accomplished their adoption as sons of God, bearers of the Spirit of the Son, and heirs of God (Gal. 4:4–7). He suffered their curse so that they would receive the blessing of God in the Holy Spirit (3:13–14). The blessing of the covenant is that God gives them himself to

---

58. Anselm, *Why God Became Man*, 1.7, 2.19, in *A Scholastic Miscellany*, ed. Fairweather, 108, 181.

59. Murray, *Redemption Accomplished and Applied*, 44.

60. The word for "tree" in both Greek and Hebrew could be used of logs, lumber, and articles of wood. Gen. 22:6–7; Ex. 7:19; Lev. 1:7–8; Num. 15:33; Matt. 26:47; Acts 16:24; 1 Cor. 3:12; Rev. 18:12. "Tree" is used of Christ's cross in Acts 5:30; 10:39; 13:29; 1 Pet. 2:24.

61. Gen. 40:19; Josh. 8:29; 10:26.

62. Perkins, *Commentary on Galatians*, on Gal. 3:13–14, in *Works*, 2:181.

be their God, their inheritance. They will experience the full measure of their redemption when they enter glory as "joint-heirs with Christ" (Rom. 8:17, 23; cf. Eph. 1:14; 4:30).

Reconciliation

Reconciliation involves a change of attitude and relationship from enmity and estrangement to friendship and harmony. Three Greek words that appear in the New Testament may be translated as "reconcile" or "reconciliation" (*katallassō, katallagē, apokatallassō*).[63] Closely related are the words rendered as "peace" (*eirēnē*) and "make peace" (*eirēnopoieō*) when used with respect to Christ's saving work.[64] The priests blessed Israel with the shining of God's "face" and the gift of his "peace" (Num. 6:22–27), the blessing of the reconciled God.[65]

Reconciliation refers to the deliverance of sinners from God's righteous enmity against them for their sins. Sinners are God's enemies (Rom. 5:10; Col. 1:21). However, the problem is not merely that sinners need to change their attitude toward God. Paul contrasts "enemies" of God with "beloved" of God (Rom. 11:28), and so "enemies" implies divine offense and hostility. In other words, God is the enemy of sinners (Lev. 26:28, 30). The accent of the New Testament regarding reconciliation falls upon the removal of God's offense against those who sinned against him: "not imputing their trespasses unto them" (2 Cor. 5:19). When Paul says, "Be ye reconciled to God" (2 Cor. 5:20), he uses the same syntax our Lord Jesus used when he said, "Be reconciled to your brother" (Matt. 5:24 ESV). In that situation, "your brother has something against you" (v. 23 ESV). Therefore, "be ye reconciled to" means to seek forgiveness from someone offended by your sins so that your relationship is restored. The invitation "Be ye reconciled to God" means trusting in Christ so that God will not count your trespasses against you (2 Cor. 5:19–20).[66]

Herman Ridderbos (1909–2007) wrote, "This reconciliation is qualified above all by the fact that God is its Author and Initiator."[67] Paul

---

63. Rom. 5:10–11; 2 Cor. 5:18–20; Eph. 2:16; Col. 1:20–21. A related word translated as "reconcile" (*diallassō*) appears only in Matt. 5:24, which does not pertain to the atonement.

64. Rom. 5:1; Eph. 2:14, 15, 17; Col. 1:20; Heb. 13:20. Note, too, the frequent epistolary greetings involving "peace."

65. For God's "face" to "shine" meant that God smiled upon people with favor and saved them from their enemies (Pss. 31:16; 67:1; 80:3, 7, 19; 119:135; Dan. 9:17).

66. Murray, *Redemption Accomplished and Applied*, 33–36, 40.

67. Herman Ridderbos, *Paul: An Outline of His Theology*, trans. John Richard de Witt (Grand Rapids, MI: Eerdmans, 1975), 182.

writes, "God was in Christ, reconciling the world unto himself" (2 Cor. 5:19). He adds in Romans 5:10–11, "For if, when we were enemies, we were reconciled to God by the death of his Son, much more, being reconciled, we shall be saved by his life. And not only so, but we also joy in God through our Lord Jesus Christ, by whom we have now received the atonement," literally, "the reconciliation" (*katallagē*).

God accomplished reconciliation by Christ's priestly sacrifice for sinners. The invitation to "be ye reconciled to God" is grounded upon the news that "he hath made him to be sin for us, who knew no sin" (2 Cor. 5:20–21). This is not about transformation, but imputation (v. 19). We were reconciled "by the death of his Son" (Rom. 5:10), "by the cross" (Eph. 2:16), or "through the blood of his cross" (Col. 1:20). Consequently, even before sinners are forgiven and restored to friendship with God, the divine reconciliation is "finished."[68] The "ministry of reconciliation" proclaims the good news that God accomplished reconciliation in Christ and calls sinners to trust in Christ to receive the forgiveness that God offers them (2 Cor. 5:19–21). Truly, the Lord is the God of peace and the great Peacemaker. Thomas Manton said, "When we had alienated our hearts from God, refused his service, and could expect nothing but the rigour of his law and vindictive justice, then he spared not his own Son to bring about this reconciliation for us."[69]

The opposite of "enemy" is "friend" (James 4:4). Therefore, the fruit of reconciliation is God's friendship. Irenaeus said, "In the last times the Lord has restored us into friendship through His incarnation, having become 'the Mediator between God and men'; propitiating indeed for us the Father against whom we had sinned."[70] The division between God and the reconciled is healed. "But now in Christ Jesus you who once were far off have been brought near by the blood of Christ" (Eph. 2:13 ESV). God reconciled the fallen world, "making peace by the blood of his cross" (Col. 1:20 ESV; cf. Rom. 5:1; Eph. 2:14–17). Peace with God means more than a feeling of security; peace is relational harmony as opposed to conflict. Consequently, believers have access to God (v. 18) and rejoice in God (Rom. 5:11).

The goal of reconciliation is not merely release from God's judgment, but restoration to God's friendship. This is the delight of the true Chris-

---

68. Morris, *The Apostolic Preaching of the Cross*, 228.
69. Manton, *Christ's Eternal Existence*, in *Works*, 1:498.
70. Irenaeus, *Against Heresies*, 5.17.1, in *ANF*, 1:544.

tian, but not good news to worldly people, who may rejoice at the thought of escaping hell but have no interest in God himself. Piper asks, "If you could have heaven, with no sickness, and with all the friends you ever had on earth, and all the food you ever liked, and all the leisure activities you ever enjoyed, and all the natural beauties you ever saw, all the physical pleasures you ever tasted, and no human conflict or any natural disasters, could you be satisfied with heaven, if Christ was not there?"[71] If you could, then you are not yet reconciled with God and do not desire to be. Awake, O sinner! You are still an enemy of God, and he is the Holy One, the majestic and righteous Lord. Manton said, "Consider what it is to be at odds with God, and how soon and how easily he can revenge his quarrel against you, and how miserable they will be for ever that are not found of him in a state of peace."[72] Consider, too, how willing God is to make peace on such reasonable terms. He has done all the work of reconciliation; what he calls you to do is to trust in his Son.

Faith in Christ's Priestly Sacrifice

The gospel of Christ's sacrifice calls us to faith in him. This is evident in each of the three depictions of Christ's sacrifice that we examined. God set Christ forth as "a propitiation through faith in his blood" (Rom. 3:25). Christ "redeemed us from the curse of the law . . . that we might receive the promise of the Spirit through faith" (Gal. 3:13–14). "Therefore, since we have been justified by faith, we have peace with God through our Lord Jesus Christ . . . through whom we have now received reconciliation" (Rom. 5:1, 11 ESV).

Faith must grasp hold of Christ's sacrifice as our only and perfect propitiation, redemption, and reconciliation. Faith lets go of every other means by which men try to accomplish what Christ alone can do. Yes, faith not only lets them go but casts them away as trash and dung (Phil. 3:4–9). John Brown of Haddington asked how our natural opposition to Christ's priestly office shows itself, and answered, "In our high esteem of our own righteousness, and seeking salvation by it in whole or in part; in men's strong opposition to the doctrine of God's free grace, and refusing to receive Christ as their only righteousness; and frequent rushing themselves upon eternal damnation, rather than be

---

71. John Piper, *God Is the Gospel* (Wheaton, IL: Crossway, 2005), 15.
72. Manton, *Christ's Eternal Existence*, in *Works*, 1:502.

saved by him alone (Rom. 9:31–32; 10:3)."[73] As Brown noted, though our most open opposition to Christ lies against his office as King, our "strongest secret enmity" against his saving office is to his priesthood, because "it most clearly displays the glory of God, and the vileness of our own righteousness."[74] Secret self-righteousness is a clinging vine that entangles all our souls.

Casting aside our pride and unbelief, we must rest our entire trust upon Christ's great work. Do we sense God's anger speaking through our consciences against our sins? Let us repent of sin and put no trust in our remorse and repentance to atone, but instead rest in the propitiation of Christ to exhaust the wrath of God against sinners. Do we long for God's smile and approval? Let us ground all our good works in utter reliance on Christ's obedience and death.

Does your sin place you under a terrible burden of guilt, binding and enslaving you to the Devil and the powers of corruption? Find hope in the cross of Jesus Christ. He is the Redeemer and has paid a price worth more than all the angels of heaven in order to liberate lost souls. Lay yourself down at his pierced feet, and he will remove your chains, embrace you as his brother or sister, and bring you home to the Father to feast forever.

Sing to the Lord

Trusting in the Lord for Redemption

From out the depths I cry to Thee;
O let Thy ear attentive be,
Hear Thou my supplicating plea,
Have mercy, Lord.

If marked by Thee our sin appeared,
Who, Lord, could stand in judgment cleared?
Forgiveness, that Thou mayst be feared,
There is with Thee.

I wait for Thee, my soul doth wait,
Thy word my hope in ev'ry strait;
None watch, O Lord, at morning's gate
As I for Thee.

---

73. Brown, *Questions and Answers on the Shorter Catechism*, 79.
74. Brown, *Questions and Answers on the Shorter Catechism*, 79.

O Israel, hope thou in the Lord,
His mercy will thy faith reward,
He full redemption will accord
From all thy sin.

Psalm 130
Tune: Hanford
The Psalter, No. 363

Questions for Meditation or Discussion

1. With what two word groups is the priesthood associated in the Bible? How do those word groups help us understand the office of a priest more clearly?
2. What can we learn from the Aaronic priesthood about (1) a priest's qualifications and (2) a priest's work?
3. How did Melchizedek foreshadow Christ's priesthood?
4. What does *propitiation* mean?
5. How can you prove from the Bible that Christ accomplished propitiation?
6. What answer can be given to the objection against propitiation that God is not angry with sinners but loves them?
7. What does *redemption* mean?
8. How do the Holy Scriptures testify that Christ accomplished redemption?
9. What does *reconciliation* mean?
10. Does being "reconciled to God" in the New Testament (Rom. 5:10; 2 Cor. 5:20) refer to a change in how we relate to God or in how God relates to us? Prove your answer from Scripture.
11. What does faith in Christ require people to embrace regarding his sacrifice? What does it require them to reject? Do you have faith in Christ?

Questions for Deeper Reflection

12. C. H. Dodd argued that God's "wrath" in the Scriptures refers to an impersonal process of consequences for sin, not his personal anger against sinners. How would you prove Dodd wrong?
13. Someone says to you, "It's barbaric to say that Christ died to appease God's wrath. That's a pagan view of God, not the Christian God of love." How do you respond?

14. Imagine that you are talking to a friend who says she trusts in Christ but feels oppressed by guilt and a sense that God is angry with her and distant from her. Write a letter to her explaining how she can make experiential use of the doctrines of propitiation, redemption, and reconciliation to overcome these oppressive feelings.

49

Christ's Priestly Work, Part 2

Penal Substitution for the
Satisfaction of God's Justice

Paul warns that there are other messages in the world that claim to be the gospel but are really no gospel at all, for they are false teachings that bring God's curse and damnation (Gal. 1:6–9). We must, therefore, beware of false gospels and reject those who bring them, even if they are angels from heaven. At the heart of the true gospel is the fact that Christ "gave himself for our sins" (v. 4). On that basis, we are justified by faith in Christ alone (2:16).

Paul wrote similarly to the Corinthians that the saving gospel that he "delivered unto you first of all" begins with the announcement that "Christ died for our sins" (1 Cor. 15:1, 3). It is his death *for our sins* that gives his resurrection its character of total victory over death, for the power of death is the law's condemnation of sinners (v. 56; cf. Rom. 6:23). Peter likewise proclaims that "he himself bore our sins" and "by his wounds you have been healed" (1 Pet. 2:24 ESV), alluding to Isaiah's prophecy that Christ would suffer because of our sins and bear our iniquities (Isa. 53:4–6, 12). From this substitutionary death flows our death to the power of sin, our turning to God, and our new life of righteousness (1 Pet. 2:24–25).

The Belgic Confession (Art. 20) says,

> We believe that God, who is perfectly merciful and just, sent His Son to assume that nature in which the disobedience was committed, to make satisfaction in the same and to bear the punishment of sin by His most bitter passion and death. God therefore manifested His justice against His Son when He laid our iniquities upon Him and poured forth His mercy and goodness on us, who were guilty and worthy of damnation, out of mere and perfect love, giving His Son unto death for us and raising Him for our justification, that through Him we might obtain immortality and life eternal.[1]

While the cross is the root of every spiritual blessing, the central meaning of Christ's sacrifice is penal substitution for the satisfaction of God's justice on behalf of those whom Christ redeemed. Tom Schreiner says, "Penal substitution is the heart and soul of an evangelical view of the atonement."[2]

Priestly Atonement through Penal Substitution by God

Christ's sacrifice unto God was his offering of himself in the place of his people under God's law and judgment. This doctrine is called "penal substitution," and for centuries it has been the standard evangelical and Reformed understanding of Christ's sacrifice, though not without its detractors and critics.[3]

Penal Substitution Defined and Explained

This view of the atonement is called "substitution" because Christ lived and died as his people's representative before God, offering himself in their place. Clement wrote in the late first century, "Jesus Christ our Lord gave His blood for us by the will of God; His flesh for our flesh, and His soul for our souls."[4] It is called "penal" because the substitution pertained to God's legal judgment. Edward Polhill (c. 1622–c. 1694) said, "Thus as a priest he gave himself an offering and sacrifice for us (Eph. 5:2), as a Redeemer he

---

1. *The Three Forms of Unity*, 37.
2. Thomas R. Schreiner, "Penal Substitution View," in *The Nature of the Atonement: Four Views*, ed. James Beilby and Paul R. Eddy (Downers Grove, IL: InterVarsity Press, 2006), 67.
3. For an overview of the controversy, see Steve Jeffrey, Michael Ovey, and Andrew Sach, *Pierced for Our Transgressions: Rediscovering the Glory of Penal Substitution* (Wheaton, IL: Crossway, 2007), 21–30.
4. Clement, *First Epistle*, chap. 49, in *ANF*, 1:18.

was made a curse for us (Gal. 3:13), as a Mediator and Redeemer he gave himself a ransom for all (1 Tim. 2:5–6), in each of which the substitution comes in. . . . His sufferings were properly penal, such as were not inflicted by sovereignty, but justice. . . . Christ was so far made one with us, as to render his sufferings penal and satisfactory."[5] The idea of substitution is sometimes communicated by saying Christ's atonement was "vicarious" (from Latin *vicarius*, "substitute, proxy, deputy"). However, the word *vicarious* can also be used in a weaker sense of acting on behalf of another for his benefit without meaning penal substitution.[6]

Theologians present different "theories of the atonement."[7] Some theologians argue that Christ saves us by the *moral influence* of his revelation of God's love and justice. Other theologians say that Christ's atonement consists primarily of *victory over evil powers*, such as the Devil.[8] We do not deny these aspects of Christ's saving work and discuss them under Christ's work as the crucified Prophet and King.[9] However, to insist that either moral influence or victory is a fully adequate description of Christ's atonement is to deny Christ's priesthood, for the ministry of a priest is toward God, to offer a sacrifice for sins (Heb. 5:1).[10]

J. I. Packer says that the doctrine of penal substitution "denies nothing asserted by the other two views save their assumption that they are complete," for man's bondage to sin and Satan arises from his standing "under divine judgment," so that Christ's death primarily aimed at God and our relation to him and his justice.[11] The salvation of sinners by penal substitution, Packer rightly asserts, is not merely a rationalistic theory that tries to explain the biblical data in a way our minds can fully comprehend. Rather, this doctrine is the good news that God's Word preaches to sinners so that they can know with certainty that they will never be punished for

---

5. Edward Polhill, *A View of Some Divine Truths, Which Are Either Practically Exemplified in Jesus Christ, Set Forth in the Gospel, or May Be Reasonably Deduced from Thence*, in *The Works of Edward Polhill* (1844; repr., Morgan, PA: Soli Deo Gloria, 1998), 79.

6. Hodge, *The Atonement*, 39. For an example of a weak sense of *vicarious*, see Horace Bushnell, *The Vicarious Sacrifice, Grounded in Principles of Universal Obligation* (London: Strahan & Co., 1871), 6–7.

7. See Warfield, "The Chief Theories of the Atonement," in *The Person and Work of Christ*, 351–69.

8. Two other "theories" of the atonement are the ransom to the Devil (addressed in chap. 48 under the topic of redemption) and the governmental view (addressed later in this chapter under the necessity of satisfying justice).

9. See the sections on the crucified glory in chap. 46 and the victory of the crucified King in chap. 53.

10. Martin, *The Atonement*, 66–71.

11. J. I. Packer, "What Did the Cross Achieve? The Logic of Penal Substitution," *Tyndale Bulletin* 25 (1974): 19–21 (full article, 3–45).

their sins, "and thus to evoke faith, hope, praise and responsive love to Jesus Christ."[12]

Penal Substitution Prophesied in the Old Testament

The ancient sacrifices portrayed Christ's saving work.[13] The daily duty of a priest was to sacrifice burnt offerings (Ex. 29:38–42) for God's pleasure and sin's atonement (Lev. 1:4, 9). The killing of sacrifices revealed the principle of substitution.[14] As John Owen said, why would people kill good and useful animals and offer them to God except to acknowledge their own worthiness of death and need for a substitute to receive punishment in their place?[15]

The ritual of sacrifice vividly pictured substitution when the sinner touched the sacrificial animal before it was killed: "He shall put his hand upon the head of the burnt offering; and it shall be accepted for him to make atonement for him" (Lev. 1:4).[16] The law said that on the Day of Atonement, "Aaron shall lay both his hands upon the head of the live goat, and confess over him all the iniquities of the children of Israel, and all their transgressions in all their sins, putting them upon the head of the goat," which then suffered the penalty of banishment that sinners deserve, for "the goat shall bear upon him all their iniquities" (16:21–22).[17]

Noah presented "burnt offerings on the altar" to the Lord after departing from the ark, and God responded with pleasure to the "sweet savour" and promised never again to destroy all living creatures by a flood, even though man's heart remained evil (Gen. 8:20–22), a promise later sealed in a covenant (9:8–11) that foreshadowed God's everlasting covenant of peace (Isa. 54:9–10). Hence, sacrifice aims to avert God's wrath against sinners and gain God's favor.[18]

After the Lord tested Abraham by demanding his son as a burnt offering, God directed Abraham to sacrifice "a ram . . . in the stead of his son" (Gen. 22:13). The location, Moriah (v. 2), is later identified with the temple mount and the area where Christ was crucified.[19] There the divine

---

12. Packer, "What Did the Cross Achieve?," 26–27.
13. For an overview of ancient sacrifices as types of Christ, see chap. 29.
14. Belcher, *Prophet, Priest, and King*, 76.
15. Owen, *An Exposition of the Epistle to the Hebrews*, 2:20.
16. See also Ex. 29:10, 15, 19; Lev. 3:2, 8, 13; 4:4, 15, 24, 29, 33.
17. Schreiner, "Penal Substitution View," in *The Nature of the Atonement*, 84; and John R. W. Stott, *The Cross of Christ* (Downers Grove, IL: InterVarsity Press, 1986), 144.
18. Gordon J. Wenham, "The Theology of Old Testament Sacrifice," in *Sacrifice in the Bible*, ed. Roger T. Beckwith and Martin J. Selman (Grand Rapids, MI: Baker, 1995), 80–81.
19. Kidner, *Genesis*, 154.

Father did not spare his only begotten Son, but gave him to die in place of his people (Rom. 8:32).[20] William Bates (1625–1699) said, "Many endearing circumstances made Isaac the joy of his father . . . yet at best he was an imperfect, mortal creature." However, God the Father gave his "only begotten Son, which title signifies his unity with him in his state and perfections; and according to the excellency of his nature, such is his Father's love to him."[21]

The Lord further foreshadowed Christ in the Passover. God's final plague upon Egypt, by which he redeemed Israel from slavery, came as death for the firstborn sons (Ex. 11:4–5). This plague was God's "judgment" (12:12), the climactic blow of "the fierceness of his anger, wrath, and indignation" (Ps. 78:49–51). However, God did not automatically exempt Israel from this death; the people had to kill a "lamb" as a "sacrifice" and put its blood on their doorposts so that the Lord would "pass over" them (Ex. 12:3–7, 13, 27). In later years, anyone refusing to eat the lamb of the Passover meal was cut off from the people (Num. 9:13). As scholars have noted, "At the first Passover, the Jewish people were delivered not only from the tyranny of Pharaoh, but also from the judgment of God on their idolatry," and that "through the substitutionary death of a lamb."[22]

The Passover lamb aptly foreshadowed Christ (1 Cor. 5:7), for it is meek like Christ in his suffering (Isa. 53:7); it was "without blemish" (Ex. 12:5), just as Christ was sinless (1 Pet. 1:19); it was to be roasted in fire (Ex. 12:8), a sign of God's holiness and wrath against lawbreakers (19:18; 24:17); none of its bones could be broken (12:46; John 19:31–36); and with its death, God "broke the chains of their slavery," just as Christ's death delivered his people from Satan's oppression and launched their journey to their inheritance (Col. 1:12–14).[23] Just as the people of Israel ate the Passover lamb and consumed all of its meat (Ex. 12:8–10), Benjamin Keach observed, so "Christ is spiritually to be received, and fed upon (John 6:55)," and that in his whole person and saving office, for "in Christ nothing is unprofitable, or to be rejected."[24] Let us, therefore, receive Christ as

20. God "spared not his own Son" (*tou idiou huiou ouk epheisato*, Rom. 8:32) alludes to what God said to Abraham: "You did not spare your beloved son" (*ouk epheisō tou huiou sou tou agapētou*, Gen. 22:12, 16 LXX).

21. William Bates, *The Harmony of Divine Attributes in the Contrivance and Accomplishment of Man's Redemption*, intro. Joel R. Beeke (1853; repr., Homewood, AL: Solid Ground, 2010), 150–51.

22. Jeffrey, Ovey, and Sach, *Pierced for Our Transgressions*, 41.

23. Charnock, *A Discourse of Christ Our Passover*, in *Works*, 4:511–14.

24. Keach, *Preaching from the Types and Metaphors of the Bible*, 640.

our penal substitutionary atonement and feed upon him regularly as the means of our entire salvation.

Substitutionary atonement is prophesied in Isaiah 53.[25] The prophet writes, "He was wounded for our transgressions, he was bruised for our iniquities" (v. 5). The preposition translated as "for" (*min*) means "from" or "because of"; he suffered punishment on account of our sins.[26] Hence, this is substitution, indeed, *penal* substitution.[27] Substitution appears again later in the text: "For [*min*] the transgression of my people was he stricken" (v. 8).[28]

It might be objected that Christ was stricken by sinful men, not God. However, the prophet said, "the LORD hath laid on him the iniquity of us all" (Isa. 53:6). This explains how Christ "hath borne our griefs" and "bare the sin of many" (vv. 4, 12). Sin involves corruption and guilt; one cannot carry another's corruption (sin is not a material object), and to bear the guilt of another implies suffering the punishment he has earned— "and that is to say that he was our substitute."[29] Verse 6 demonstrates that Christ did not suffer merely because people sinned against him, but because God judicially counted the sins of others as his own. "It pleased the LORD to bruise him" as "an offering for sin" (v. 10).

Penal Substitution Performed in the New Testament

Christ said, "The Son of Man came . . . to give his life a ransom for many [*lytron anti pollōn*]" (Matt. 20:28; Mark 10:45).[30] A "ransom" (*lytron*) was the price paid to redeem someone, such as to deliver a criminal from his punishment (Ex. 21:29–30 LXX). The preposition translated as "for" (*anti* with the genitive) often means "in the place of" or "in exchange for."[31] Leon Morris wrote that these are the characteristic meanings of the preposition and noted an example in the histories of Josephus: when a Roman plunderer threatened to rob the temple of its treasures, a priest gave him a bar of gold instead as a "ransom for all" (*lytron anti pantōn*)—

---

25. On penal substitution in Isaiah 53, see Jeffrey, Ovey, and Sach, *Pierced for Our Transgressions*, 52–67.

26. Poole, *Annotations upon the Holy Bible*, 2:448, on Isa. 53:5.

27. Motyer, *Isaiah*, 378.

28. Young, *The Book of Isaiah*, 3:352.

29. Young, *The Book of Isaiah*, 3:347–48.

30. On the context, background, authenticity, and meaning of this statement, see S. Page, "Ransom Saying," in *Dictionary of Jesus and the Gospels*, 660–62. For its substitutionary meaning, see also Peterson, *Salvation Accomplished by the Son*, 372–74.

31. For example, see Matt. 2:22; Luke 11:11; Rom. 12:17; 1 Thess. 5:15; Heb. 12:16; 1 Pet. 3:9. Compare "in the stead of his son Isaac" (*anti Isaak tou huiou autou*, Gen. 22:13 LXX).

deliverance by substitution.[32] John Murray said that Christ's "ransom was substitutionary in its nature."[33]

Substitutionary atonement involves an exchange of sin and righteousness. Paul says, "For he hath made him to be sin for us, who knew no sin; that we might be made the righteousness of God in him" (2 Cor. 5:21). Augustine explained that Christ was "made sin, not His own, but ours, not in Himself, but in us," and we are made righteousness, "our righteousness being not our own, but God's, not in ourselves, but in Him."[34] David Clarkson said, "He was made sin for us, as we are made the righteousness of God in him; his righteousness being imputed to us, the Lord rewards us as those that are righteous; and our sins being imputed to him, the Lord punished him as a sinner. Not for his own guilt, but for ours, was he punished; as not for our righteousness, but for his, are we saved."[35]

We can further demonstrate substitutionary atonement by the three great perspectives that the New Testament gives us on Christ's sacrifice.[36] First, he brought *redemption* to his people, which required that he take their place "under the law" and suffer the curse of that law for them (Gal. 3:13; 4:4–5). Robert Peterson observes, "Paul specifies what he means by the curse. It is the threat of the punishment that all lawbreakers deserve" (cf. 3:10).[37] Second, he is their *propitiation* by his "blood" (Rom. 3:25), the sacrifice that appeased God's wrath against sinners by receiving that wrath upon himself. Third, he is their *reconciliation* to God, for by the transfer of their sins to him and his righteousness to them, they are no longer counted as guilty but as forgiven (2 Cor. 5:18–20) and enjoy peace with God (Eph. 2:14–17). All three perspectives require penal substitution.

This substitution is the greatest exchange of history and the song of the redeemed through the ages. An anonymous Christian wrote in the early second century,

> When our wickedness had reached its height, and it had been clearly shown that its reward, punishment and death, was impending over us . . . He Himself took on Him the burden of our iniquities. He gave

32. Morris, *The Apostolic Preaching of the Cross*, 34, 36, citing Josephus, *Antiquities*, 14.107.
33. Murray, *Redemption Accomplished and Applied*, 42–43.
34. Augustine, *Enchiridion*, chap. 41, in NPNF¹, 3:251.
35. Clarkson, "Christ's Dying for Sinners," in *Works*, 3:68.
36. See the discussion of propitiation, redemption, and reconciliation at the end of chap. 48.
37. Peterson, *Salvation Accomplished by the Son*, 386.

His own Son as a ransom for us, the holy One for transgressors, the blameless One for the wicked, the righteous One for the unrighteous, the incorruptible One for the corruptible, the immortal One for them that are mortal.

For what other thing was capable of covering our sins than His righteousness? By what other one was it possible that we, the wicked and ungodly, could be justified, than by the only Son of God? O sweet exchange! O unsearchable operation! O benefits surpassing all expectation! That the wickedness of many should be hid in a single righteous One, and that the righteousness of One should justify many transgressors![38]

Priestly Atonement for the Satisfaction of God

What was the purpose of penal substitution? What did it accomplish? Out of his great love, God sent Christ to satisfy his justice as the substitute for his people under the law, voluntarily receiving on himself the violent penalty for their sins, according to the eternal covenant of the triune God, by which the Son was appointed to become a man and act as their surety.

The Meaning of the Satisfaction: Divine Payment

The theological term *satisfaction* (Latin *satisfactio*) refers to the fulfilling of an obligation or removal of an offense by payment. As God's "servants," our best obedience is simply doing "that which was our duty to do" (Luke 17:10), literally, "that which we owe." Jesus taught us to call our sins "debts" (Matt. 6:12; Luke 7:41–43). By not rendering the obedience that we owe to God, we aggravate our debt and earn punishment. The guilt of our sins is so great that Jesus compared it to a financial debt that would take us thousands of *lifetimes* to pay off ("ten thousand talents," Matt. 18:24). Christ must pay the debt to release his people. His sacrifice is the "ransom" (Mark 10:45; 1 Tim. 2:6) or "price" (1 Cor. 6:20; 7:23).[39]

Gregory the Great said in the sixth century that Christ, "being made incarnate, had no sins of His own, and yet being without offense took upon Himself the punishment of the carnal." Gregory added, "For our Mediator deserved not to be punished for himself, because he never was guilty of any defilement of sin. But if he had not himself undertaken a death not due

---

38. Anonymous, *Epistle to Diognetus*, chap. 9, in *ANF*, 1:28, paragraph break added.
39. See the discussion of Christ's redemption in chap. 48.

to him, he would never have freed us from one that was justly due us." Therefore, God "condemns him who is without sin; that all the elect might rise up to the height of righteousness, in proportion as he who is above all underwent the penalties of our unrighteousness."[40]

Anselm of Canterbury explained, "Every inclination of the rational creature ought to be subject to the will of God." To fail to give God this subjection and obedience is to rob him of the honor due to him. As a thief owes restitution to the one from whom he stole, so the creature who sins against his Creator owes God payment for what he stole and more: "In view of the insult committed, he must give back more than he took away."[41] This corresponds to the biblical principle of restitution (Ex. 22:1–6; Num. 5:7). John Calvin wrote that Christ "made satisfaction for our sins," "paid the penalty owed by us," and "appeased God by his obedience"—this is what it means that the Righteous One died for the unrighteous.[42]

The effect of Christ's satisfaction is sometimes called *expiation* (from Latin *expiatus*, "having made satisfaction, amends, atonement for a crime"), which means the removal of objective guilt under the law.[43] Though our sins remain a cause of shame and grief in our souls even after we are forgiven, all our legal liability to rejection and punishment is removed.[44] In the language of ritual sacrifice, his blood washes away our sins and makes us clean in God's sight.[45] "Blessed is he whose transgression is forgiven, whose sin is covered" (Ps. 32:1)! Do you know this blessedness? Do you have redemption in Christ, the forgiveness of all your sins by his blood (Eph. 1:7)? If so, then rejoice that your guilt is taken away and you are clean in God's sight. If not, then why not go to Christ in prayer even now and ask him to save you from your sins?

The Source of the Satisfaction: Divine Love

If a Christian is asked why he expects to go to heaven and not to hell, he will probably say something like "Christ died for my sins." However,

---

40. Gregory the Great, *Morals on the Book of Job*, 3 vols. (Oxford: John Henry Parker, 1844), 1.3.26–27, on Job 2:3 (1:148–49). We have modernized the capitalization of some words.

41. Anselm, *Why God Became Man*, 1.11, in *A Scholastic Miscellany*, ed. Fairweather, 119.

42. Calvin, *Institutes*, 2.17.3.

43. From the same Latin root comes the adjective *piacular*, meaning "appeasing, making/requiring atonement."

44. Ps. 103:12; Isa. 44:22–23; Mic. 7:19. On our remaining shame, see Ezek. 16:63; Rom. 6:21.

45. Lev. 16:30; Ps. 51:2, 7; Heb. 1:3; 9:13–14; 1 John 1:7.

why did Christ die for our sins? The answer is simple but stupendous: "For God so loved the world, that he gave his only begotten Son" (John 3:16). The source of the atonement is God's goodness, not our goodness. A. A. Hodge said, "The ultimate reason and motive of all God's actions are within himself. . . . The infinite justice and love of God both find their highest conceivable exercise in the sacrifice of his own Son as the Substitute of guilty men."[46]

Christ loves his church (Eph. 5:25). Clarkson wrote of "the ardency of this all-governing affection," saying, "He had thoughts of love to us from eternity, and we were never one moment out of his mind since then. . . . We are his jewels . . . his treasure . . . and where his treasure is, there will his heart be also."[47] He laid down his life voluntarily (John 10:17–18): he "gave himself for us" (Titus 2:14; cf. Gal. 1:4). No one has loved us more (John 15:13). William Perkins said, "The work of redemption exceeds the work of creation. For in the creation, Christ gave the creatures to man; in redemption He gave Himself, and that as a sacrifice."[48] Truly "the love of Christ . . . passeth knowledge" (Eph. 3:19). This is the personal assurance that every Christian may enjoy: "I live by faith in the Son of God, who loved me and gave himself for me" (Gal. 2:20 ESV).

However, in tracing the source of the atonement, we may go one step further, for all that the only begotten Son is and does is from the Father (John 1:14; 5:19). "Herein is love, not that we loved God, but that he loved us, and sent his Son to be the propitiation for our sins" (1 John 4:10). Though we were neither "righteous" nor "good," God demonstrated his love for us in that "Christ died for us" (Rom. 5:8). God sent Christ when "we were enemies" (v. 10), provokers of God's just anger. The Father was active in the Son during his passion, placing sin upon him (Isa. 53:6, 10; 2 Cor. 5:21) and reconciling sinners to himself through him (vv. 18–19).[49]

Stephen Charnock said that fallen man is so blind and perverse that instead of desiring pardon from the Judge, he either runs from his justice or, when that does not work, defends himself against God, "adding one provocation to another, as if he had an ambition to harden the heart of

---

46. Hodge, *The Atonement*, 48–50.
47. Clarkson, "The Love of Christ," in *Works*, 3:3–5.
48. Perkins, *Commentary on Galatians*, on Gal. 1:4–5, in *Works*, 2:24.
49. Murray, "The Atonement," in *Collected Writings*, 2:148–49.

God against him," but God acts "in immense love and grace" to make a way of salvation at Christ's expense.[50] Therefore, the doctrine of substitution for the satisfaction of God's justice is a doctrine that magnifies God's love. Robert Letham says, "Rather than presenting a cruel and distorted picture of God, what penal substitution shows us is that God's love for us is such that he was prepared to pay the ultimate price that love can pay."[51] Murray said that our proper response to the cross is to be "captivated by the Father's love."[52]

The cross underlines the great disparity between God's love and man's lovelessness (1 John 4:10). John Stott (1921–2011) said, "In order to save us in such a way as to satisfy himself, God through Christ substituted himself for us."[53] He concluded, "The concept of substitution may be said, then, to lie at the heart of both sin and salvation. For the essence of sin is man substituting himself for God, while the essence of salvation is God substituting himself for man. Man asserts himself against God and puts himself where only God deserves to be; God sacrifices himself for man and puts himself where only man deserves to be."[54]

Recognizing the divine love for sinners behind the death of Christ should move us to repent of our sins. Sinners often harden themselves with thoughts that God does not love sinners and will only punish them— so why not sin all the more? The prodigal son returned home when he realized, "I have squandered the marks of a son; he has not lost the characteristics of a father," as Peter Chrysologus wrote.[55] The cross confronts us with the God who loves sinners and is willing to receive them when they repent. Bates wrote, "What stronger evidence can there be of God's readiness to pardon, than sending his Son into the world to be a sacrifice for sin?"[56]

Furthermore, our trust in God's love should be as a channel through which his love flows to others. Christ said, "A new commandment I give

50. Charnock, *A Discourse of the Knowledge of Christ Crucified*, in *Works*, 4:496–97.
51. Letham, *The Work of Christ*, 137.
52. Murray, "The Atonement," in *Collected Writings*, 2:144.
53. Stott, *The Cross of Christ*, 159.
54. Stott, *The Cross of Christ*, 160.
55. Peter Chrysologus, *Selected Sermons*, and Saint Valerian, *Homilies*, trans. George E. Ganss, The Fathers of the Church 17 (Washington, DC: The Catholic University of America Press, 1953), 31.
56. Bates, *The Harmony of Divine Attributes*, 175. Bates also cited the statement of Chrysologus quoted above, paraphrasing the Latin, "*Ego perdidi quod erat filii; ille quod patris est non amisit,*" as, "Though I have neglected the duty and lost the confidence of a son, he hath not lost the compassion of a father."

unto you, That ye love one another; as I have loved you, that ye also love one another" (John 13:34). Perhaps you find love too costly. But what is love, if not the giving of ourselves? "By this we know love, that he laid down his life for us, and we ought to lay down our lives for the brothers. But if anyone has the world's goods and sees his brother in need, yet closes his heart against him, how does God's love abide in him? Little children, let us not love in word or talk but in deed and in truth" (1 John 3:16–18 ESV).

The Necessity of the Satisfaction: Divine Justice

We need Christ's sacrifice in order to be forgiven of our sins and escape God's punishment. If God could have forgiven sin by any means he chose, then why do the Scriptures say that "it is not possible that the blood of bulls and goats should take away sins" (Heb. 10:4)? Why do they teach that if we reject Christ "there remaineth no more sacrifice for sins," but only "judgment and fiery indignation, which shall devour the adversaries" (vv. 26–27)? Texts such as these imply that salvation from divine judgment required a sacrifice for sins that only Christ could supply.[57]

We argued in a previous chapter that there is a "consequent absolute necessity" to Christ's atoning work. Consequent upon God's free choice to save sinners, it was absolutely necessary for Christ to make atonement for their sins (Heb. 2:10, 17; 9:23; 10:22).[58]

The question of what Christ accomplished on the cross "is really a debate about the nature of God."[59] Atonement was necessary because of the offense of sin against God's righteousness. Sin in its essence is hatred of God and rebellion against his law (Rom. 8:7; 1 John 3:4).[60] Therefore, God's righteousness, which is inherently legal (Ps. 119:137–38), demands the just punishment of all who break his law (Ex. 23:7; Ps. 11:6–7). Owen said, "Sin is contrary to the nature of God," and "it is inconsistent therewith to pass by it unpunished," not because God is bound by "any external rule or law," but because "his law and rule is the holiness and righteousness of his own nature."[61] Hodge wrote, "God is determined, by the immutable holiness of his nature, to punish all sin because of its intrinsic guilt or demerit."[62] If God

---

57. Witsius, *The Economy of the Covenants*, 2.8.12, 15 (1:251–52).
58. See the discussion of the necessity of the incarnation at the end of chap. 39.
59. Adonis Vidu, *Atonement, Law, and Justice: The Cross in Historical and Cultural Contexts* (Grand Rapids, MI: Baker Academic, 2014), 236.
60. On the core meaning of sin, see chap. 17.
61. Owen, *An Exposition of the Epistle to the Hebrews*, 2:110–11.
62. Hodge, *The Atonement*, 53.

failed to be the fire of wrath against sinners, then he would not be the pure light of righteousness.[63]

Substitutionary atonement makes sense only if we believe in God's retributive justice against sinners. Letham notes, "This is hardly a popular message and many have been the attempts to evade it. The whole concept of retributive justice is unacceptable in the Western world. In our criminal law, we have laid emphasis either on deterrence or on reforming the offender."[64] However, God "will render to every man according to his deeds . . . indignation and wrath, tribulation and anguish, upon every soul of man that doeth evil" (Rom. 2:6–9).

This is not to propose a conflict between God's attributes, as people sometimes do when they speak about God's mercy arguing with his justice until his wisdom provided a solution that satisfied both. God is simple in his essence: he "is light" and "is love" (1 John 1:5; 4:8).[65] Consequently, in the perfect oneness of his essence, God always acts according to all his attributes. Herman Witsius said, "Some, when they consider the power of God alone, affirm every thing about it: not reflecting, that God can do nothing but consistently with his justice, holiness, veracity, wisdom, immutability, in a word, with all his other perfections."[66]

Though some people say that the doctrine of satisfaction is an invention of the medieval Latin church, it is rooted in the biblical concept of law and justice. We cannot understand the reason for Christ's death unless we perceive that his death was God's punishment for sin (Gen. 2:17; 3:19; Rom. 6:23). Christ had to die for sinners to save them, for God's law decrees that sinners are worthy of death (Rom. 1:32). This was recognized by ancient Christians. Athanasius said, "For God would not be true, if, when He said we should die, man died not." It is not sufficient that sinners repent, for delivering people merely upon their repentance would "fail to guard the just claim of God." Therefore, Christ, "taking from our bodies one of like nature, because all were under penalty of the corruption of death He gave it over to death in the stead of all, and offered it to the Father." In this way, Christ was offered "for the life of all"—literally, "as a substitute" (*antipsychon*)—and "satisfied the debt

---

63. Polhill, *A View of Some Divine Truths*, in *Works*, 11.
64. Letham, *The Work of Christ*, 125.
65. On God's simplicity, see *RST*, 1:624–37 (chap. 33).
66. Witsius, *The Economy of the Covenants*, 2.8.1 (1:245). See *RST*, 1:773–75.

by His death."[67] Chrysologus said that God sent Christ to die because "he would abrogate in an even more just manner the sentence of death, which he had imposed with justice. God wanted to fulfill his own statute by suffering."[68]

Some theologians argue that Christ's sacrifice publicly honored God's moral government, not to satisfy his retributive justice but to prove that God rules the world with justice.[69] This "governmental" view of the atonement has been particularly popular among Arminians and Wesleyans,[70] though John Wesley did not hold it.[71] Hugo Grotius (1583–1645) said, "God was unwilling to pass over so many sins, and so great sins, without a distinguished example. . . . The omission of punishment almost always detracts from the authority of the law among the subjects. . . . In his most perfect wisdom he chose that way by which he could manifest more of his attributes at once, viz. both clemency and severity, or his hate of sin and care for the preservation of his law."[72] However, Grotius still allowed a place for just "retribution" and "punishment" in Christ's death.[73] Jonathan Edwards Jr. (1745–1801) said, "Why is an atonement necessary in order to the pardon of the sinner? I answer, it is necessary . . . to maintain the authority of the divine law. If that be not maintained, but the law fall into contempt, the contempt will fall

---

67. Athanasius, *On the Incarnation of the Word*, secs. 6–8, in *NPNF²*, 4:39–40. See also *On the Incarnation of the Word*, secs. 20, 25, in *NPNF²*, 4:47, 49; *Four Discourses against the Arians*, 1.60, in *NPNF²*, 4:341. The word translated as "just claim" (*eulogos*) means that which is "rational," "fair," or "right." Lampe, *A Patristic Greek Lexicon*, 570. The word translated as "under penalty" (*hypeuthynos*) means "liable" or "guilty" (1443). The word *antipsychos* means "substitute" and refers to "the vicarious nature of atonement" (161). The relevant Greek text (with English translation) is published in Athanasius, *Contra Gentes and De Incarnatione*, ed. and trans. Robert Thomson (Oxford: Oxford University Press, 1971), 146–54.

68. St. Peter Chrysologus, *Selected Sermons, Volume 3*, trans. William B. Palardy, The Fathers of the Church 110 (Washington, DC: The Catholic University of America Press, 2005), 10.

69. For a historical review and analysis of the governmental view, see Oliver D. Crisp, "Penal Non-Substitution," *The Journal of Theological Studies* NS 59, no. 1 (April 2008): 140–68.

70. John Miley, *Systematic Theology*, 2 vols. (New York: Eaton & Mains; Cincinnati: Curts & Jennings, 1894), 2:168–69.

71. John Wesley held to the medieval/Reformation view of satisfaction by substitution. John Wesley, "The Lord Our Righteousness," I.6–9, in *John Wesley's Sermons: An Anthology*, ed. Albert C. Outler and Richard P. Heitzenrater (Nashville: Abingdon, 1991), 386–87; and Thomas C. Oden, *John Wesley's Scriptural Christianity: A Plain Exposition of His Teaching on Christian Doctrine* (Grand Rapids, MI: Zondervan, 1994), 183, 187.

72. Hugo Grotius, *A Defence of the Catholic Faith Concerning the Satisfaction of Christ, against Faustus Socinus*, trans. Frank Hugh Foster (Andover, MA: Warren F. Draper, 1889), 106–7. See Hugo Grotius, *Defensio Fidei Catholicae de Satisfactione Christi*, in *Operum Theologicorum*, 3 vols. (Amsterdam, Joannis Blaev, 1679), 3:316.

73. Grotius, *A Defence of the Catholic Faith Concerning the Satisfaction of Christ*, 33–35. He commented on Isa. 53:5, "Through his punishment is our exemption from punishment" (40). See Grotius, *Defensio Fidei Catholicae de Satisfactione Christi*, in *Operum Theologicorum*, 3:303–4.

equally on the legislator himself; his authority will be despised and his government weakened."[74]

However, the governmental view fails to reckon with the Godward thrust of Christ's sacrifice to propitiate his wrath, pay the redemption price to his justice, and reconcile sinners to himself so that he no longer counts their sins against them.[75] While this doctrine affirms God's sovereign authority and goodness, it denies the retributive justice of the righteous Judge. A merely governmental atonement does not involve "the *exercise* of divine justice upon Christ, but an *example* of punishment," as Hodge observed, which amounts to little more than moral influence upon those who hear the gospel.[76] How could Christ be an example of God's justice, however, if he were not suffering as the substitute bearing the penalty of God's justice? This doctrine implies an arbitrariness or even injustice in God, for he is said to have afflicted Christ as an example of divine punishment, even though Christ was not suffering punishment as the substitute for sinners. A *merely* governmental atonement would not remove sinners from the curse of God's personal holy displeasure against sin.

It should be noted, however, that a theologian may rightly use governmental language while affirming the satisfaction view of the atonement, which is a sound and biblical formulation.[77] Christ's death did publicly display God's "righteousness" and established his "law," but it did so precisely because his blood was the "redemption" that paid the price required by God's justice and the "propitiation" that satisfied the just demands of his holy wrath (Rom. 3:24–26, 31). God's "righteousness" here must have involved his retributive justice, or there would have been no need

---

74. Jonathan Edwards Jr., "The Necessity of Atonement," in *The Atonement: Discourses and Treatises by Edwards, Smalley, Maxcy, Emmons, Griffin, Burge, and Weeks*, ed. and intro. Edwards Amasa Park (Boston: Congregational Board of Publication, 1859), 6. The view of the atonement presented by Jonathan Edwards Jr. (son the more famous theologian by the same name) represents the "New England theology," a modification of historic Reformed theology.

75. See the treatment of propitiation, reconciliation, and redemption in chap. 48.

76. Hodge, *The Atonement*, 338, emphasis original. The governmental view of the atonement tends to reduce God's justice and righteousness to mere benevolence. See Edwards, "The Necessity of Atonement," and Nathanael Emmons, "Two Sermons on the Atonement," in *The Atonement: Discourses and Treatises*, ed. Park, 20–24, 116.

77. Manton, *Christ's Eternal Existence*, in *Works*, 1:420, 532–34. Thus, Jonathan Edwards (the elder) said that Christ's sacrifice satisfied God's justice because Christ suffered the penalty of judgment and wrath that sinners deserved. Edwards, *A History of the Work of Redemption*, in *WJE*, 9:331; "Christ's Sacrifice," in *WJE*, 10:598. However, Edwards also taught that Christ died to honor God's authority and majesty. Edwards, "Miscellanies," no. 449, 451, 452, 483, in *WJE*, 13:496–8, 526; "The Free and Voluntary Suffering and Death of Christ," in *WJE*, 19:503–4. The latter is biblical and sound when grounded upon the former. See Brandon James Crawford, *Jonathan Edwards on the Atonement: Understanding the Legacy of America's Greatest Theologian*, foreword Joel Beeke (Eugene, OR: Wipf and Stock, 2017), 112–22.

for Christ's blood so that God would be "just" and the "justifier" of the ungodly (4:5).[78] Douglas Moo writes, "Christ, in his propitiatory sacrifice, provides full satisfaction of the demands of God's impartial, invariable justice."[79]

The Scriptures present Christ's sacrifice as a satisfaction offered to the just God. Isaiah 53:10 says that Christ gave his life as "an offering for sin" (*'asham*). This word means the compensation or restitution one pays to the wronged party to cancel one's guilt (Num. 5:6–8) or the "trespass offering" or "guilt offering" that obtains forgiveness for one who has become guilty before the Lord, especially by desecrating his holy things (Lev. 5:14–6:7). This sacrifice of atonement went hand in hand with the payment of compensation or restitution to the temple or to a private individual for his losses (5:16; 6:2–7). Alec Motyer said, "It could well be called the 'satisfaction-offering.'"[80] Thus, God was pleased with the death of Christ because he gave his life as a payment to compensate for the offense of his people's sins against divine holiness.

Christ "hath given himself for us an offering and a sacrifice to God for a sweetsmelling savour" (Eph. 5:2), literally, "an aroma of fragrance" (*osmē euōdias*). This figure of speech often appears in the Bible to indicate God's pleasure in an offering and acceptance of those for whom it is offered, as we noted earlier regarding Noah's burnt offerings (Gen. 8:20–21).[81] S. M. Baugh comments, "The point is that this sacrifice pleases God in fulfillment of his commands and satisfies his justice."[82] Charnock said, "There was a complete satisfaction made to God, the supreme Judge offended, pleasing to him, and effectual to free the guilty party from the obligation to the deserved punishment."[83]

Paul teaches in Colossians 2:13–14 that God has "forgiven you all trespasses" by "blotting out the handwriting of ordinances that was against us, which was contrary to us, and took it out of the way, nailing it to his cross." God had to deal with the "ordinances," or legal demands, that stood against us as sinners. The word "handwriting" (*cheirographon*) refers to a

---

78. Witsius, *The Economy of the Covenants*, 2.8,11 (1:250–51). On God's justice, see *RST*, 1:814–16, 819–23.

79. Moo, *The Epistle to the Romans*, 242. See also Polhill, *A View of Some Divine Truths*, in *Works*, 13.

80. Motyer, *Isaiah*, 382; cf. Murray, "The Atonement," in *Collected Writings*, 2:142.

81. See also Ex. 29:18, 25, 41; Lev. 1:9, 13, 17; 2:2, 9, 12; 3:5, 11; 4:31; etc. LXX; cf. Ezek. 20:41 LXX.

82. Baugh, *Ephesians*, 405.

83. Charnock, *A Discourse of the Acceptableness of Christ's Death*, in *Works*, 4:552.

legal paper of financial obligation.[84] At the cross of Christ, God cancelled the debt, nailing the paper to the cross, as it were. Peterson calls this "a dramatic picture of legal substitution."[85] Hence, we conclude with Perkins that "Christ died to be a payment and satisfaction to God's justice for our sins."[86]

The cross teaches us how much God loves justice. God's insistence upon justice in penal substitution should motivate us to love and seek justice as well. Steve Jeffrey, Michael Ovey, and Andrew Sach say, "God is passionately concerned about justice, so we must be too. It will not do for us to ignore oppression in the world as if it does not matter. . . . Penal substitution provides a moral foundation for working for justice." It also "reminds us that God will one day put an end to injustice, for the crucial conflict with evil has been fought and won."[87]

The Agent of the Satisfaction: Divine Surety

Christ is the "surety of a better testament" (Heb. 7:22). The word "surety" (*enguos*) means a person who pledges himself to take on the legal obligations of another, whether paying his debts or suffering his punishment.[88] Proverbs warns against becoming a surety (using the Hebrew verb *'arab*), even if a person is motivated by "compassion, generosity, and neighborliness," because of "the grave dangers involved in gambling one's financial security by pledging to cover another's possible business losses."[89] A vivid picture of suretyship that foreshadows Christ appears in Judah's taking responsibility to guarantee Benjamin's safety to the point of suffering his brother's punishment in his place (Gen. 43:9; 44:32–33).[90]

Christ is the "surety" (Heb. 7:22) of his "brethren" (2:11–12, 17) in that he has undertaken to pay the debts of his people to God's law so that God's covenantal promises of grace will be fulfilled. Perkins said that the Son of God subjected himself to the law as "our pledge and surety"—that

---

84. The word translated as "handwriting" (*cheirographon*) appears in the apocryphal book of Tobit, where Tobit gives Tobias a "receipt" by which he can claim ten talents of silver held in trust by another man (Tobit 4:20–5:3).

85. Peterson, *Salvation Accomplished by the Son*, 390.

86. Perkins, *An Exposition of the Symbol*, in *Works*, 5:395.

87. Jeffrey, Ovey, and Sach, *Pierced for Our Transgressions*, 157.

88. "Surety" (*enguos*) is *hapax legomenon* in the canonical Greek Scriptures, but see *enguaō* in Prov. 6:1, 3; 17:18 LXX and *enguēs* in Prov. 22:26 LXX, which render forms of the Hebrew root *'arab*. See also Owen, *The Doctrine of Justification by Faith*, in *Works*, 5:182–87; *An Exposition of the Epistle to the Hebrews*, 5:501.

89. *NIDOTTE*, 3:513. See Prov. 6:1; 11:15; 17:18; 20:16; 22:26; 27:13.

90. *NIDOTTE*, 3:515. The Septuagint does not use *enguos* or its cognates in Gen. 43:9; 44:32, but the Hebrew text uses *'arab*.

is, "one that stands in our place, room, and stead, and before God represents the person of all the elect."[91] Owen wrote, "He is to pay that which they owe."[92] Hebrews 7:22 identifies the surety emphatically as "Jesus,"[93] likely highlighting Christ's humanity by which he was able to represent his people and stand in their place. His office as surety of the covenant "guarantees that that covenant will be honoured."[94] His role as guarantor is significant in light of Israel's failure to keep its covenant with the Lord (8:9): Christ takes responsibility himself to fulfill the requirements so that the new covenant (and the salvation it promises) cannot fail, but is eternal (9:12, 15; 13:20).[95]

The context in Hebrews 7 implies that Christ's suretyship consists of his priesthood.[96] God appointed Christ as surety by the divine "oath" (reported in Ps. 110:4) that Christ is a "priest" forever (Heb. 7:20–22). Christ acts as surety by his perpetual, heavenly intercession (vv. 23–26) and once-for-all sacrifice of himself (v. 27). Therefore, Christ's priestly work of accomplishing and applying atonement is the work of a covenantal surety. By his sacrifice, Christ paid the obligations of his people. By his intercession, Christ stands before God as the surety who has completed his task. Consequently, he rightly petitions for the benefits promised in the covenant to be granted to his people (8:10–12; 10:12–17).

Therefore, Christ's office as surety means that he stands as the covenantal representative of God's people before God, having pledged himself to fulfill their legal obligations so that they will escape God's curse and receive God's blessing. He is not a surety to persuade us of God's trustworthiness; he is a surety to satisfy God by fulfilling our legal requirements to be acceptable to him.[97]

Christ is the last Adam of the new creation, the Son who obeyed where Adam disobeyed (Luke 3:22, 38; Rom. 5:12–19). Calvin said, "Our Lord came forth as true man and took the person and the name of Adam in order to take Adam's place in obeying the Father, to present our flesh as the price of satisfaction to God's righteous judgment, and, in the same flesh,

---

91. Perkins, *Galatians*, 251.

92. Owen, *The Doctrine of Justification by Faith*, in *Works*, 5:187.

93. In the Greek text of Heb. 7:22, *Iēsous* is the last word of the sentence.

94. Donald Guthrie, *Hebrews: An Introduction and Commentary*, Tyndale New Testament Commentaries 15 (Downers Grove, IL: InterVarsity Press, 1983), 168.

95. Hughes, *A Commentary on the Epistle to the Hebrews*, 267–68.

96. Owen, *An Exposition of the Epistle to the Hebrews*, 5:503.

97. Witsius, *The Economy of the Covenants*, 2.5.1 (1:202). It was the Socinians who took "surety" to mean that Christ merely confirmed the promises and denied that he represented us toward God in paying our debts.

pay the penalty that we had deserved."[98] Charnock explained, "As Adam and all mankind were as one person . . . so Christ and believers are as one person, and what he did, is as if a believer himself did it, as the suffering of our sacrifice was accepted in lieu of the life of the sinner."[99] Christ satisfied God's justice by taking our place as our legal and judicial representative.

The Objections to the Satisfaction: Divine Violence

The opponents of the doctrine of penal substitutionary atonement argue that it was neither necessary nor right for God to place our sins on Christ. Therefore, substitutionary atonement would be an act of violence against justice itself and against Christ the victim.[100]

First, some object that God can simply forgive our sins. If a mere human being can choose not to take revenge, much more the sovereign Lord, "whose will alone is law in everything," has the right and authority to forgive without receiving any satisfaction to his justice, as Faustus Socinus said.[101] To insist that God must receive substitutionary satisfaction in order to accept sinners, Mark Baker and Joel Green tell us, is to "picture a God who has a vindictive character, who finds it much easier to punish than to forgive."[102]

In reply, we answer that, as we said earlier regarding the satisfaction of God's righteousness, our sins place us in criminal debt. While a financial creditor may choose to release a debtor without doing anything ethically wrong, a judge may not do so with a debt of justice from criminal activity. God is the righteous Judge, and his justice is "founded in his very nature," as Francis Turretin said.[103] "Shall not the Judge of all the earth do right?" (Gen. 18:25). When just punishment does not fall on the wicked, the righteous feel the tension: "Righteous art thou, O LORD, when I plead with thee: yet let me talk with thee of thy judgments: Wherefore doth the way of the wicked prosper? Wherefore are all they happy that deal very treacherously?"

---

98. Calvin, *Institutes*, 2.12.3.

99. Charnock, *Christ Our Passover*, in *Works*, 4:533.

100. Responses to several objections against satisfaction through penal substitution may be found in Jeffrey, Ovey, and Sach, *Pierced for Our Transgressions*, 205–328; Peterson, *Salvation Accomplished by the Son*, 396–407; and William Symington, *The Atonement and Intercession of Jesus Christ* (1863; repr., Grand Rapids, MI: Reformation Heritage Books, 2006), 20–47.

101. Socinus, *De Jesu Christo Servatore*, 3.1, in Gomes, "Faustus Socinus' *De Jesu Christo Servatore*," 61–62. Socinus regarded mercy and punitive justice not as attributes of God but mere effects of his sovereign will (63).

102. Mark D. Baker and Joel B. Green, *Recovering the Scandal of the Cross: Atonement in the New Testament and Contemporary Contexts*, 2nd ed. (Downers Grove, IL: InterVarsity Press, 2011), 174. Note their criticism of the idea "that God must punish Jesus on the cross in order to forgive" (178).

103. Turretin, *Institutes*, 14.10.25 (2:425).

(Jer. 12:1). In the last day, the godly will say, "Thou art righteous, O Lord . . . because thou hast judged thus. . . . Even so, Lord God Almighty, true and righteous are thy judgments" (Rev. 16:5, 7; cf. 15:3–4; 19:2).

Anselm said, "Nothing is less tolerable in the order of things, than for the creature to take away the honor due to the Creator and not repay what he takes away. . . . Again, if nothing is greater or better than God, then the highest justice, which is none other than God himself, maintains nothing more justly than his honor, in the ordering of things."[104] He exclaimed that it would be better for the entire universe to be destroyed than for us to commit the smallest act against God's will.[105] Since fallen mankind owes to God satisfaction for an offense greater than the value of the entire universe, only God can pay the debt. However, it is man who owes the debt to God. Anselm concluded that since "no one save God can make it and no one save man ought to make it, it is necessary for a God-Man to make it."[106]

Second, some object that the crucifixion is an act of horrendous violence, but the Lord is the God of peace and life. For the Father to inflict such evil upon his Son, we are told, would be nothing less than "cosmic child abuse"—inconceivable for the God who is love.[107]

In reply, we answer the charge of violence according to the doctrines of God's providence over sin and punishment for sin. The doctrine of providence teaches that God sovereignly rules over the sins of men, but is not the author of sin and does not approve of it.[108] The murder of Jesus Christ was a crime abhorrent to God, though God executed his plan for salvation through wicked men (Luke 22:23; Acts 2:22; 4:27–28). Therefore, the cross can never be taken as a justification for any form of sinful violence or abuse. We may not measure God's character or law by the acts of sinners. Rather, we must remember Joseph's words to his brothers regarding their cruel abuse of him: "But as for you, ye thought evil against me; but God meant it unto good, to bring to pass, as it is this day, to save much people alive" (Gen. 50:20).

But how, the objector might ask, could God ever ordain such an act of violence as Christ's cross? The answer arises from the doctrine of divine

---

104. Anselm, *Why God Became Man*, 1.13, in *A Scholastic Miscellany*, ed. Fairweather, 122.
105. Anselm, *Why God Became Man*, 1.21, in *A Scholastic Miscellany*, ed. Fairweather, 138.
106. Anselm, *Why God Became Man*, 2.6, in *A Scholastic Miscellany*, ed. Fairweather, 151.
107. Brad Jersak, "Nonviolent Identification and the Victory of Christ," in *Stricken by God? Nonviolent Identification and the Victory of Christ*, ed. Brad Jersak and Michael Hardin (Grand Rapids, MI: Eerdmans, 2007), 32–34. The phrase "cosmic child abuse" that Jersak quotes (34) is from Steve Chalke and Alan Mann, *The Lost Message of Jesus* (Grand Rapids, MI: Zondervan, 2003), 182.
108. On the doctrine of providence, see *RST*, 1:1031–1106 (chaps. 52–53).

punishment for sin.[109] God has no pleasure in death itself (Ezek. 18:32), but he ordained death as the penalty of sin (Gen. 2:17). In his wrath, God has swept billions of people into death over the millennia (Ps. 90:3–7). Sometimes he ordains a violent, gruesome death to punish a particular sinner (1 Kings 21:23; 2 Kings 9:33–37). All sinners who die unrepentant in their sins will suffer the torments of the second death, the fires of hell (Rev. 21:8). In order to save sinners, God decreed that Christ would suffer a violent, hellish death by the "sword" of his wrath (Zech. 13:7; Mark 14:27).

When we speak of Christ's violent death satisfying God, we must be clear that we mean satisfying God's justice, not satisfying a bloodthirsty "desire of revenge . . . for a pleasing one's self in the evils which another suffers," for such vindictiveness is not "to be ascribed unto God," as Clarkson said.[110] Augustine wisely distinguished between God's "righteous retribution" and the "love of violence, revengeful cruelty, fierce and implacable enmity, wild resistance, and the lust of power" that motivates much human killing and warfare.[111] God's violence is pure justice, and his violence toward Christ was tender mercy toward favored sinners.

If the objector argues that we cannot conceive of God acting with tender love and terrible justice in the same event, then we must plead the incomprehensible glory of God in Christ crucified. Paul Wells says, "The paradoxical nature of penal substitution is that it joins, in one divine act, expressions of justice and love, wrath and approbation, judgment and grace, and death and life. . . . Penal substitution does not pretend to explain the *how*, but only the *fact* of atonement. Mystery surrounds atonement, as in all the works of God."[112] Our response is not to demand a full explanation, but to bow in adoration and wonder at the cross of our Lord.

Third, some object that it would be unjust and oppressive for God to punish one man for the sins of other people.[113] God reveals that it is contrary to his justice that a person should suffer for the sins of another, even for a family member.[114]

---

109. On God's punishment of sin, see chap. 24.

110. Clarkson, "Christ's Dying for Sinners," in *Works*, 3:67.

111. Augustine, *Reply to Faustus the Manichaean*, 22.74, in *NPNF*[1], 4:301. Augustine was not addressing the atonement, but God's sending people to fight in war for a just cause.

112. Paul Wells, *Cross Words: The Biblical Doctrine of Atonement* (Fearn, Ross-shire, Scotland: Christian Focus, 2006), 139.

113. For examples, see the sources cited in Jeffrey, Ovey, and Sach, *Pierced for Our Transgressions*, 241.

114. Deut. 24:16; 2 Kings 14:6; Ezek. 18:20.

In reply, we appeal to the doctrines of Christ's deity and the covenant of grace. Regarding Christ's deity, he is no mere man compelled to die, but God the Son, equal to the Father in eternal glory. Charnock said, "He could not be constrained by his Father to undertake it; his will was as free in consenting, as his Father was in proposing. . . . If you consider Christ as one God with the Father, there is but one and the same will in both."[115] Hence, the Son freely entered into the work of the Mediator and freely executed it (John 10:17–18). Owen said, "The Son loved us, and gave himself for us. . . . These things proceeded from and were founded in the will of the Son of God; and it was an act of perfect liberty in him to engage into his peculiar concernments in this covenant. What he did, he did by choice, in a way of condescension and love." Therefore, there was "no injustice in God to lay it on him."[116]

The answer to this charge of injustice also draws from the Bible's covenant theology, which brings us to the next point in our exposition of Christ's atonement.

The Framework of the Satisfaction: Divine Covenant

The doctrine of Christ's priestly atoning work is firmly embedded in the covenant. God authorized Christ's priesthood by a covenantal oath (Ps. 110:4; Heb. 7:21–22). Christ's sacrifice involved the shedding of the blood of the covenant.[117] He is the Mediator of the covenant because he died and shed his blood to cleanse sinners, and God remembers their guilt no more (Heb. 8:6, 12; 9:14–15; 12:24). Just as the Mosaic covenant was not "inaugurated without blood," so the new covenant "takes effect only at [Christ's] death" (Heb. 9:17–18 ESV). Atonement is covenantal: the Lord says, "Gather my saints together unto me; those that have made a covenant with me by sacrifice" (Ps. 50:5). Hugh Martin said, "The doctrine of the atonement ought to be discussed and defended as inside the doctrine of the covenant of grace."[118]

God's covenants form the broader context in which Christ's atoning work has meaning. In the eternal counsel of peace, God federally united the elect with Christ so that he would redeem them by his blood. The

---

115. Charnock, *A Discourse of the Voluntariness of Christ's Death*, in *Works*, 4:543. See *RST*, 1:897.
116. Owen, *An Exposition of the Epistle to the Hebrews*, 2:87.
117. Zech. 9:14; Matt. 26:28; Mark 14:24; Luke 22:20; 1 Cor. 11:25; Heb. 10:29; 13:20.
118. Martin, *The Atonement*, 9.

broken covenant with Adam, which plunged mankind into guilt and corruption, established the need for Christ's work and foreshadowed the last Adam. In the historical covenants with Noah, Abraham, Israel, and David, the Lord gave many promises and types that Christ would fulfill in his sacrificial death. In the new covenant, God's covenant of grace is fully revealed through Christ's once-for-all accomplishment of redemption.[119]

The covenant, especially in its eternal aspect as the will of the triune God, guarantees that Christ's atonement is completely acceptable to God and effective in saving God's elect from their sins. Charnock said, "If it were according to the tenor of the covenant of redemption, it could be not refused by God, being consequent to his decree and promise. But if we consider it in itself, God was not bound to accept it for us, though he might have had an high esteem of it; for, according to the tenor of his law, he might have demanded a compensation from the person of the sinner, and laid the punishment upon the person upon whom he found the guilt."[120]

Covenant theology answers the objection of injustice because the Father constituted his Son as the covenantal representative of his people, just as Adam stood as the covenantal representative of all descended from him by natural generation (Rom. 5:12–19). Perkins said,

> How can it stand with God's justice to lay punishment upon the most righteous man that ever was, and that for grievous sinners, considering that tyrants themselves will not do so? Answer. In the passion, Christ must not be considered as a private person—for then it could not stand with equity that He should be plagued and punished for our offences— but as one in the eternal counsel of God set apart to be a public surety or pledge for us [Heb. 7:22] to suffer and perform those things which we in our own persons should have suffered and performed.[121]

The key to covenant theology is union with Christ.[122] The key to penal substitution is the same.[123] As Martin explained, the force of the objection of injustice dissipates once we recognize "the covenant oneness of Christ and His members," for in the covenant God ordained that Christ be "the last Adam," and "teaches us to regard Christ and the Church collectively

---

119. On these covenants, see chaps. 14–15, 30–33.
120. Charnock, *A Discourse of the Acceptableness of Christ's Death*, in *Works*, 4:553.
121. Perkins, *An Exposition of the Symbol*, in *Works*, 5:140.
122. Martin, *The Atonement*, 29.
123. Jeffrey, Ovey, and Sach, *Pierced for Our Transgressions*, 243.

in their relation to God, as virtually one and indivisible, so far as regards their legal standing and responsibilities."[124] Herman Bavinck said that even before there is the "mystical union between Christ and believers," there is "the federal relation: Romans 6–8 follows Romans 3–5." Bavinck added, "Vicarious satisfaction has its foundation in the counsel of the Triune God, in the life of supreme, perfect, and eternal love, in the unshakable covenant of redemption. Based on the ordinances of that covenant, Christ takes the place of his own and exchanges their sin for his righteousness, their death for his life."[125] Martin said, "Let Christ and His people be federally one, by the sovereign authority and love of the Father, and by the voluntary covenanted acceptation of the Son. In that case, legal fiction, make-believe, arbitrariness and caprice, are at the furthest possible remove from the divine covenant transaction of our redemption."[126]

The doctrine that Christ satisfied God's justice by penal substitution is a declaration of God's faithfulness to his promises. Chrysologus said Christ had to die for sinners because "God's promise of good things for good people is unreliable, if what has been established by God for the wicked comes to nothing."[127] Since God was unwilling that even the dread word of death to sinners would go unfulfilled, how much more can we trust him to keep his promises of mercy, grace, and glory to those who believe in Christ alone for salvation?[128]

The cross of Christ proves the unshakeable trustworthiness of our God. Let us, therefore, rest our whole confidence upon him, even though the circumstances of our lives may scream at us that God is unjust and unworthy of our trust. The God who sacrificed his Son to uphold his justice in salvation will not fail to keep his word.

By the Spirit's grace, trust him first and foremost for the forgiveness of your sins by the blood of Christ. Trust him to give you eternal life and glory on the basis of what Christ has done. And trust him to care for you through all of life and to use the worst of evils for your good. The more you live by faith in Christ crucified, the more you will be able to confess with confidence, "The LORD is upright: he is my rock, and there is no unrighteousness in him" (Ps. 92:15).

---

124. Martin, *The Atonement*, 14–15.
125. Bavinck, *Reformed Dogmatics*, 3:405–6.
126. Martin, *The Atonement*, 47.
127. Chrysologus, *Selected Sermons, Volume 3*, 10.
128. Jeffrey, Ovey, and Sach, *Pierced for Our Transgressions*, 155–56.

Sing to the Lord

Glorifying God for Penal Substitutionary Atonement

Man of Sorrows! What a name
For the Son of God, who came
Ruined sinners to reclaim:
Hallelujah! What a Saviour!

Bearing shame and scoffing rude,
In my place condemned he stood,
Sealed my pardon with his blood:
Hallelujah! What a Saviour!

Guilty, vile, and helpless, we;
Spotless Lamb of God was he;
Full atonement! Can it be?
Hallelujah! What a Saviour!

Lifted up was he to die,
"It is finished!" was his cry:
Now in heav'n exalted high:
Hallelujah! What a Saviour!

When he comes, our glorious King,
All his ransomed home to bring,
Then anew this song we'll sing:
Hallelujah! What a Saviour!

Philip Bliss
Tune: Man of Sorrows
Trinity Hymnal—Baptist Edition, No. 175

Questions for Meditation or Discussion

1. What does "penal substitution" mean?
2. How does this view of the atonement relate to the "moral influence" and "victory over evil powers" views?
3. How is the doctrine of penal substitution foreshadowed in the following types: (1) the sacrifices, (2) the Lord's testing of Abraham (Gen. 22), and (3) the Passover lamb?
4. How does Isaiah 53 reveal Christ's penal substitution?

5. How is the doctrine of penal substitution revealed in the New Testament?

6. What does Christ's "satisfaction" mean?

7. How does Christ's work of satisfaction by substitution relate to God's love and to his justice? Prove your answers from the Holy Scriptures.

8. What is a "surety"? How does Christ fulfill this role?

9. How has this chapter helped you to see God's moral attributes of love, righteousness, and faithfulness more clearly? How should you respond in trust, love, and imitation?

Questions for Deeper Reflection

10. What would happen to the doctrine of the atonement if we neglected or denied God's love? God's retributive justice? How does the atonement help us to glorify God in both attributes?

11. Someone says, "I could never believe in a God who tortured his Son because otherwise he could not forgive people of their sins. My father physically abused me as a child, and I want nothing to do with a God like him. I believe in a God of love." How do you respond?

12. How does covenant theology both illuminate and protect the doctrine of divine satisfaction by penal substitution? If we reject covenant theology, what implications could that have for our view of Christ's atoning work?

50

Christ's Priestly Work, Part 3

Christ's Sacrificial Obedience

The core of Christ's redeeming accomplishment is his obedience to the Father's will. Just as it was disobedience to God's command that cast down the human race into sin and misery, so it is obedience that saves sinners—not their obedience, but the obedience of Jesus Christ. As Martin Luther said, God justifies us by faith because faith grasps hold of Christ—so it is on the basis Christ's works, not ours, that we are justified.[1]

John Calvin said, "How has Christ abolished sin, banished the separation between us and God, and acquired righteousness to render God favorable and kindly toward us?" He answered that "in general" the answer is "by the whole course of his obedience," yet more precisely it is "Christ's death." Calvin said, "Even in death itself his willing obedience is the important thing because a sacrifice not offered voluntarily would not have furthered righteousness."[2] When John Murray sought some "comprehensive category" under which we could summarize all that the Bible teaches about Christ's atonement for sins, he concluded, "The Scripture regards the work of Christ as one of obedience."[3]

---

1. Luther, *Lectures on Galatians*, in *LW*, 26:130–32; and *The Judgment of Martin Luther on Monastic Vows*, in *LW*, 44:286–87.
2. Calvin, *Institutes*, 2.16.5.
3. Murray, *Redemption Accomplished and Applied*, 19.

A servant does his master's will. At the heart of God's justification of his people is the one whom he calls "my righteous servant," whose work greatly pleases the Lord (Isa. 53:10–11). Murray said, "He was the Lord's servant. . . . This office implies commission by the Father, subjection to, and fulfilment of, the Father's will. All of this involves obedience."[4] Paul writes of Christ's incarnation in the same terms: he "took upon him the form of a servant" (Phil. 2:7). Though Christ's servanthood culminated in his death on the cross (v. 8; Matt. 20:26–28), he acted as God's Servant throughout the days of his humiliation, including his public ministry before his death (Matt. 12:17–18; Luke 22:27). Girolamo Zanchi said, "We believe that Christ by his perfect obedience deserved eternal life not only for himself, but also for us. By his passion and death he satisfied for our sins in his flesh."[5]

Christ's Obedience as the Center of His Priestly Work

The work of the Priest, like every aspect of Christ's office, was essentially obedience. God foreshadowed this in the old covenant. The Aaronic priest did not try to convince God to do man's will, but implemented what "the LORD commanded" (Lev. 9:6–10). Richard Belcher says, "The salvation of the people of God depends on the priest being obedient to God's commands."[6] Only by obedience to God's will does a priest honor God's holiness (10:1–3).

Christ's fundamental work as Priest, his offering of himself as a sacrifice to God, revolved around his obedience. The typical sacrifices portrayed the total giving of oneself to God (cf. Rom. 12:1). The burnt offering especially pictured total dedication, for ordinarily the whole animal was offered up to God by fire (Ex. 29:18; Lev. 1:3–9, 13). However, God never sought external rituals, no matter how costly (Ps. 50:7–13), but the inward sacrifice of obedience, for "to obey is better than sacrifice" (1 Sam. 15:22). Murray noted, "To be an act of obedience . . . motive, direction, and purpose must be in conformity to the divine will."[7] David wrote that God did not desire "sacrifice and offering," but instead the heart attitude that says, "I delight to do thy will, O my God; yea, thy law is within my heart" (Ps. 40:6–8).

---

4. Murray, "The Obedience of Christ," in *Collected Writings*, 2:151.
5. Girolamo Zanchi, *De Religione Christiana Fides—Confession of Christian Religion*, ed. Luca Baschera and Christian Moser, Studies in the History of Christian Traditions (Leiden: Brill, 2007), 11.15 (1:223).
6. Belcher, *Prophet, Priest, and King*, 101.
7. Murray, "The Obedience of Christ," in *Collected Writings*, 2:152.

That psalm was fulfilled in Jesus Christ, whose obedience to God's will culminated in the offering of his body once for all for our sins (Heb. 10:4–12).

Christ's priesthood is closely related to his divine sonship (Heb. 4:14; 5:5, 8). As God's Son, Christ perfectly represents God's nature (1:3). He is faithful in all that the Father entrusts to him (3:6). He is the priestly Son who "was in all points tempted like as we are, yet without sin" (4:14–15). Our High Priest at God's right hand is the perfect Son (7:28–8:1).

God's incarnate Son obeyed him, whereas Adam, God's first created son, failed. Christ and Adam stand as the heads of the old and new humanity.[8] Paul says, "For as in Adam all die, even so in Christ shall all be made alive" (1 Cor. 15:22). Douglas Kelly writes,

> In the beginning, God created Adam to be a loving son, and love is always shown by obedience (cf. John 15:10, 14). Adam failed to render loving obedience. . . . So, 'in the fullness of time' (cf. Gal. 4:4), God sent his own Son to live a life of deepest and fullest loving obedience. In so doing, the incarnate Son of God obeyed from the heart, in every thought, word and action, all the holy will of the Father, thereby fulfilling the original intentions of God in his creation of Adam and his posterity.[9]

Therefore, Christ's offering as our Priest entailed not only suffering but being an obedient Son who did all that the Father commanded him. Like the burnt offering, he gave himself totally in devotion to God. As God's Son and our Adam, Christ not only suffered the penalty of the law but fulfilled its precepts in his holy life. Adam and Christ acted not only as private individuals but as public representatives of the people given to them by God (Rom. 5:12–19). Christ obeyed for us as our covenantal representative before God.

Christ, the End of the Law

God did not set aside his law when he saved sinners, but through Christ he satisfied its demands—the demands of his own justice. Paul concisely states Christ's relation to the law when he writes, "For Christ is the end of the law for righteousness to every one that believeth" (Rom. 10:4). The word translated as "end" (*telos*) could mean "result" (6:21–22), "termination"

---

8. Ridderbos, *Paul*, 61. See Beeke, "Christ, the Second Adam," in *God, Adam, and You*, ed. Phillips, 141–68.

9. Kelly, *Systematic Theology*, 2:317.

(1 Cor. 1:8), or "goal" (1 Tim. 1:5).[10] Christ is not the "result" of the law. We cannot regard Christ to be the "termination" of the law in the authority of its moral precepts for godly living, for Christians keep the commandments (1 Cor. 7:19; cf. Eph. 6:2) and fulfill the moral law through love (Rom. 13:8–10).[11] We could regard Christ as the "termination" of the Mosaic law in its function to maintain a dividing wall between Jews and Gentiles, for Christ reconciles both to God (Eph. 2:13–16)—a key turning point in redemptive history. However, it is best to understand "end of the law" as the law's "goal."

Paul's focus in the context of Romans 9:30–10:5 is not redemptive history, but the application of salvation to individuals. Paul wrote of Israel's zealous pursuit to attain righteousness by the law (9:30–31; 10:2–3).[12] The Jews of whom Paul spoke misunderstood the purpose of the law. The law aggravates our sin and misery under God's wrath, pressing sinners to find the solution that only the gospel provides (4:15; 5:19–20; 7:8).[13] Christ is the "goal" of the law because its aim of "righteousness" is granted to every believer (10:4) through Christ alone. This gospel is not a new development in redemptive history, but the testimony of God's word through the ages, as Paul notes throughout Romans.[14] Paul says that the "righteousness" that the law demands is obedience: doing what the law says (v. 5). By implication, Christ has fulfilled the law by his obedience. This interpretation well suits Paul's use of the prophetic image of Christ as the "stone" on which believers trust and are not disappointed (9:33; 10:11), for Christ is the solid rock perfectly true to the standard of righteousness by which God judges men (Isa. 28:16–17).[15] Built on him by faith, Christians pass the divine test, for Christ is righteous.

---

10. Moo, *The Epistle to the Romans*, 638.

11. John Murray takes "end" to mean "termination," so that "the end of the law" indicates "every believer is done with the law as a way of attaining to righteousness." *The Epistle to the Romans*, 2:49–50. This interpretation may correspond somewhat to Paul's doctrine of the believer's having died to the law (Rom. 7:4; Gal. 2:19). However, Paul does not say in Rom. 10:4 that Christ is the end of a believer's pursuit of righteousness by works, but the end of the law itself. In other words, if we followed this line of interpretation, the *telos* in Rom. 10:4 would not be the Christian's death, but the law's death, which is another matter.

12. Moo argues for a combination of "termination" and "goal," rendering *telos* as "culmination." *The Epistles to the Romans*, 639–41. His argument has merit, but though the idea of "termination" may be present, for it is part of Pauline redemptive-historical theology, it is in the background here, whereas the context highlights "goal."

13. We are indebted for this point to Greg Nichols (personal conversation).

14. Rom. 1:1–2; 3:21; 4:1–22; 9:4, 33; 10:6–8, 11, 13, 15; 11:27; 15:8–12; 16:25–26.

15. On the stone/rock image for God or Christ, see Gen. 49:24; Deut. 32:4; Ps. 118:22; Isa. 8:14–15; Dan. 2:34–35, 44–45; Zech. 3:9; Matt. 21:42–44; Rom. 9:33; 10:11; 1 Cor. 3:10–11; 10:4; Eph. 2:20; 1 Pet. 2:4–8.

Therefore, Christ is the end of the law because in him the law's goal of righteousness has been accomplished for every believer by his mediatorial work. Matthew Poole said, "Whatever the law required that we should do or suffer, he hath perfected it on our behalf."[16] Stephen Charnock said, "Since the law is not abrogated, it must be exactly obeyed, the honour of it must be preserved; it cannot be observed by us, it was Christ only who kept it, and never broke it, and endured the penalty of it for us, not for himself."[17]

The Two Dimensions of Christ's Obedience: Passive and Active

To appreciate the full-orbed obedience that our redemption required of God's Son, it is helpful for us to distinguish Christ's obedience into its passive and active aspects.[18] The Savoy Declaration (11.2) and the Second London Baptist Confession (11.2) state that God counts believers righteous "by imputing Christ's active obedience unto the whole law, and passive in his death for their whole and sole righteousness."[19]

The Distinction between Christ's Passive and Active Obedience

The term *passive obedience* refers to Christ's submission to God's purpose that he suffer and die for our sins. The word *passive* should not be misunderstood to imply that Christ was a helpless victim, for he voluntarily offered himself to atone for sin.[20] Rather, *passive* means that Christ willingly received and endured the punishment for sin upon himself. The word is used in a similar sense to Christ's *passion*—his sufferings, crucifixion, and death (from Latin *passio*, "suffering, enduring"). The term *active obedience* refers to Christ's keeping of the commandments of God revealed in his Word.

16. Poole, *Annotations upon the Holy Bible*, 3:513, on Rom. 10:4.
17. Charnock, *A Discourse of the Cleansing Virtue of Christ's Blood*, in *Works*, 3:519.
18. On this distinction, see Heber Carlos de Campos Jr., *Doctrine in Development: Johannes Piscator and Debates over Christ's Active Obedience*, Reformed Historical-Theological Studies (Grand Rapids, MI: Reformation Heritage Books, 2017); and R. Scott Clark, "Do This and Live: Christ's Active Obedience as the Ground of Justification," in *Covenant, Justification, and Pastoral Ministry: Essays by the Faculty of Westminster Seminary California*, ed. R. Scott Clark (Phillipsburg, NJ: P&R, 2007), 229–65.
19. *Reformed Confessions*, 4:470, 546. The Westminster Confession (11:2) simply says, "imputing the obedience and satisfaction of Christ unto them," a compromise statement that allowed some Westminster divines to subscribe though they objected to the imputation of Christ's active obedience. *Reformed Confessions*, 4:247.
20. Murray, *Redemption Accomplished and Applied*, 20.

Though some divines have rejected the doctrine that both Christ's obedience and death are imputed to his people, such as Georg Karg (1512–1576) among the Lutherans[21] and Johannes Piscator (1546–1625) among the Reformed,[22] it was accepted by the mainstream of seventeenth-century Lutheran and Reformed theologians.[23] Johannes Wollebius said, "Just as the passion of Christ is necessary for the expiation of sin, so his active obedience and righteousness are necessary for the gaining of eternal life." This is because "the law binds us both to punishment and to obedience. To punishment, because it places a curse on anyone who does not perform all the words of the law. To obedience, because it promises life only to those who keep it completely." Wollebius reminded us, "Righteousness, in the true and accurate meaning of the word, consists of actual obedience," citing Deuteronomy 6:25, "And it shall be our righteousness, if we observe to do all these commandments before the LORD our God, as he hath commanded us."[24]

Francis Turretin pointed out that the law has two aspects: "precepts, which prescribe duties," and "sanctions, which ordain rewards to those who keep the law and punishments to its violators." The first binds people as God's creatures according to their moral obligation to their Lord (cf. Luke 17:10). The second imprisons people as sinners according to their guilt against God. The payment of the second debt does not remove our natural obligation to obey God perfectly; that too must be satisfied, especially if we are to enjoy the reward he freely offers to the obedient.[25] Another way to look at this is that Christ's passive obedience removes the negative demerits of the guilt of our sin, but his active obedience adds the positive merits of obedience. Turretin said, "A righteousness of innocence (when one is accused of no fault) differs

---

21. Robert Kolb and Timothy Wengert note "the position of George Karg [aka Parsimonius], the leading theologian of Brandenburg-Ansbach, who taught that the active obedience of Christ had no vicarious value since Christ was obligated to keep the law." *The Book of Concord*, 564. See Erik H. Herrmann, "Conflicts on Righteousness and Imputation in Early Lutheranism: The Case of Georg Karg (1512–1576)," in *From Wittenberg to the World: Essays on the Reformation and Its Legacy in Honor of Robert Kolb*, ed. Charles P. Arand, Erik H. Herrmann, and Daniel L. Mattson, Refo500 Academic Studies 50 (Göttingen: Vandenhoek & Ruprecht, 2018), 93–108.

22. On Piscator's arguments against the imputation of Christ's active obedience, see de Campos, *Doctrine in Development*, 107–75.

23. Formula of Concord (Solid Declaration, 3.15), in *The Book of Concord*, 564; and Turretin, *Institutes*, 14.13.1 (2:445).

24. Wollebius, *Compendium*, 1.18.(2).4.i (106–7). The (2) to designate the second series of points in this chapter is missing in the text.

25. Turretin, *Institutes*, 14.13.14–15 (2:449). See Owen, *The Doctrine of Justification*, in *Works*, 264–65.

from a righteousness of perseverance (to which a reward is due for duty performed)."[26]

Obedience is submission to God's will. Christ expressed the heart of obedience by praying, "Thy will be done" (Matt. 6:10; 26:42). The passive and active aspects of Christ's obedience relate to God's decretive and preceptive will.[27] The law reveals God's decretive will that the punishment for sin is death (Gen. 2:17; Rom. 6:23). God's law threatens pain and destruction upon the wicked, a sovereign curse against each individual who breaks the law (Deut. 27:26). This divine curse is nothing less than the word of God executing the wrath of God (29:20, 27). The law's condemnation will be publicly executed when Christ says to the wicked, "Depart from me, ye cursed, into everlasting fire" (Matt. 25:41). His passive obedience meets the demand of God's decretive will in the law, for he suffered the curse of the law.

The commandment of the law is God's preceptive will, a revelation of what he loves and what he hates, which he gave to define man's duty and the path to blessing. The Mosaic covenant of law, which was a gracious arrangement, said, "If thou shalt hearken diligently unto the voice of the LORD thy God, to observe and to do all his commandments . . . all these blessings shall come on thee" (Deut. 28:1–2). The law, taken as an absolute requirement for righteousness in the covenant of works, requires obedience for life and blessing. Christ summarized the absolute demands of the law in the phrase "This do, and thou shalt live" (Luke 10:28). His active obedience met the demands of God's preceptive will in the law, for he kept the law.

The Holy Scriptures reveal a twofold gift in our justification. Christ came "to make reconciliation for iniquity, and to bring in everlasting righteousness" (Dan. 9:24). God does not impute our sins to us, but he does impute righteousness to us (Rom. 4:6–8). Through Christ, God both redeems us from the curse and gives to us the blessing (Gal. 3:13–14). Believers receive forgiveness of sins and a right to the inheritance (Acts 26:18). To use the imagery of the prophet Zechariah, the Lord removes the filthy garments of our guilt, then clothes us with the beautiful robes of righteousness (Zech. 3:1–5; cf. Isa. 61:10).[28]

---

26. Turretin, *Institutes*, 14.13.28 (2:453). See figures 36.1 and 36.2 in Grudem, *Systematic Theology*, 725.

27. On God's decretive and preceptive will, see the discussion of God's sovereign will in *RST*, 1:764–66.

28. Owen, *The Doctrine of Justification by Faith*, in *Works*, 5:267–68.

However, we cannot divide Christ's obedience into two parts, and neither should we think of Christ performing active obedience in one stage of his earthly work and passive obedience in another. Bernard of Clairvaux said that the mingling of labor and sorrow that flowed from Adam's sin made Christ's life "passive action" and his death "active passion" while he worked out salvation in our fallen world.[29] Turretin said, "The Scripture nowhere appears to distinguish the obedience of Christ into parts, but sets it before us as a unique thing by which he has done everything which the law could require of us."[30] The purpose of the passive/active distinction is not to separate the passive from the active, but to express the holistic fullness of righteousness that God imputes to his people; in the words of Cornelis Venema, it is "to underscore the richness of Christ's seamless life of obedience 'under the law' (Gal. 4:4)."[31] Christ offered, as Wollebius said, "the single and absolutely perfect satisfaction" by which "we have been both set free from punishment . . . and given the privilege [*ius*, or right] of eternal life."[32]

The Heidelberg Catechism (LD 23, Q. 60) expresses it well: "God, without any merit of mine, but only of mere grace, grants and imputes to me the perfect satisfaction, righteousness and holiness of Christ; as if I never had had, nor committed any sins; yea, as if I had fully accomplished all that obedience which Christ has accomplished for me."[33]

Christ's Passive Obedience to the Father's Decretive Will

Christ's sufferings for the sins of others began from the moment of his incarnation as a human being, for he did not deserve the least suffering that touches every human being in this fallen world. In all the afflictions, rejections, bruises, and wounds he suffered from the beginning of his life to his burial in the ground, the "man of sorrows" was bearing the sins of his people (Isa. 53:1–9).[34] Brakel pointed out that Christ was "despised and rejected of men" and received "stripes," or bruises and wounds, long before he was crucified (Isa. 53:3, 5).[35] The Gospels also suggest that

---

29. Bernard of Clairvaux, "Sermon on the Passion," sec. 11, cited in James Cotter Morison, *The Life and Times of Saint Bernard* (London: Macmillan and Co., 1894), 336; cf. Owen, *The Doctrine of Justification*, in *Works*, 5:271.

30. Turretin, *Institutes*, 14.13.12 (2:448).

31. Cornelis P. Venema, *The Gospel of Free Acceptance in Christ: An Assessment of the Reformation and New Perspectives on Paul* (Edinburgh: Banner of Truth, 2006), 247.

32. Wollebius, *Compendium*, 1.18.(1).8 (99).

33. *The Three Forms of Unity*, 87.

34. See the survey of Christ's afflictions in his state of humiliation in chap. 44.

35. Brakel, *The Christian's Reasonable Service*, 1:585.

Christ "carried our sorrows" (Isa. 53:4) as he healed the sick and raised the dead.[36] The Heidelberg Catechism (LD 15, Q. 37) says that Christ "suffered" in that "He, all the time that He lived on earth, but especially at the end of His life, sustained in body and soul the wrath of God against the sins of all mankind."[37]

We can appreciate the wonder of Christ's passive obedience all the more when we consider that he was not a helpless pawn shuffled about by the powers that be, but the sovereign Lord fully in control of the situation. He said, "Therefore doth my Father love me, because I lay down my life, that I might take it again. No man taketh it from me, but I lay it down of myself. I have power to lay it down, and I have power to take it again. This commandment have I received of my Father" (John 10:17–18). The One who has the power to raise the dead (5:21, 28–29) chose to give himself over to death out of obedience to his Father. He "gave himself" (Titus 2:14). He made himself a "servant" and gave "his life a ransom for many" (Matt. 20:27–28). Though capable of summoning a great army of angels to defend himself, he lived and died to see the Holy Scriptures fulfilled (26:53–54). Therefore, Christ's passion was the greatest act of obedience the world has ever seen. Hugh Martin said that "the Cross" must be seen as "an altar of priestly agency, a throne of powerful action, and a chariot of victory and triumph."[38]

Christ's Active Obedience to the Father's Preceptive Will

We must never consider Christ's sufferings apart from his obedience to God's commands. Paul writes that the law, considered as an absolute principle of righteousness by works in contrast to salvation by faith, curses everyone who breaks any of its precepts, and promises, "The man that doeth them shall live in them" (Gal. 3:12). Christ redeemed us from the curse (v. 13) and granted to us the blessing (v. 14), which implies that he suffered the curse and performed the obedience in our place. Calvin explained, "We obtain through Christ's grace what God promised in the law for our works. . . . For if righteousness consists in the observance of the law, who will deny that Christ merited favor for us when, by taking that burden upon himself, he reconciled us to God as if we had kept the law?"[39]

---

36. Matt. 8:17; cf. Christ's sighing and groaning in Mark 7:34; John 11:33, 35, 38. See Morris, *The Gospel according to Matthew*, 198–99.
37. *The Three Forms of Unity*, 80.
38. Martin, *The Atonement*, 82. On Christ's victory in his death, see chap. 53.
39. Calvin, *Institutes*, 2.17.5.

Later Paul writes that God's Son was "made under the law, to redeem them that were under the law," so that they would be heirs of God (Gal. 4:4–5, 7). Christ took upon himself the full obligations of obeying the law of Moses so that we might gain the blessing and inheritance that he earned. Christ had no need in himself to go through the excruciating process of obeying the law in order to gain eternal life. He was holy from the moment of his conception (Luke 1:35). He who was worthy of the praise of angels when he first came into the world was surely worthy of heaven (Heb. 1:6). Therefore, his earthly course of obedience was not for himself, but for our righteousness.[40]

Consider the life of Christ. The gospel narratives indicate that Christ did not start his public ministry until he was about thirty years old (Luke 3:23). The Son of God spent three decades without preaching or working a miracle, but simply obeying the precepts of the Mosaic law as a child under his parents' authority (2:51) and as a young man who followed his father's vocation in the manual trades (Matt. 13:55; Mark 6:3). Was this wasted time? No, for Christ was forging a truly human righteousness in the trials of ordinary life so that God could impute it to us and Christ could sympathize with us in our temptations.

When Christ inaugurated his public ministry by receiving baptism, the Father declared, "Thou art my beloved Son; in thee I am well pleased" (Luke 3:22). God's Son had already proven himself to be God's Servant whose obedience delighted his Lord (Isa. 42:1). His baptism, like his whole life and death, aimed "to fulfill all righteousness" (Matt. 3:15). At the same time, Christ's baptism was a public sign of identifying with repentant sinners (Luke 3:3) and thus submitting to God's plan that he suffer for their sake, which was to be a kind of "baptism" (12:50).

The obedience of God's Son is crucial for our salvation. The Gospel of Luke links Christ to Adam by calling Adam "the son of God," presenting Christ as the last Adam (Luke 3:22, 38). Just as Adam and Eve faced the Devil's temptations in the garden of Eden, so Christ had to face the Devil's temptations in the wilderness (4:1–13). Adam, God's first son, failed to resist temptation in paradise, and Israel, God's firstborn son (Ex. 4:22; Hos. 11:1), failed under testing in the wilderness, but Christ, God's eternal and incarnate Son, succeeded in obeying God and defeating Satan by the Word of God. Christ's active obedience to God's Word required him to choose

---

40. Owen, *The Doctrine of Justification*, in *Works*, 5:262.

suffering instead of worldly glory. Only after proving his obedience did Christ go out in the power of the Holy Spirit to preach, heal, and deliver people from demons (vv. 14–18, 33–44). He was able to set people free from sin because he was the Son who could say, "The Father hath not left me alone; for I do always those things that please him" (John 8:29–36). The holiness and righteousness of Christ is a key part of the apostolic gospel, as we see in several texts in the book of Acts.[41]

As Luke does in the third and fourth chapters of his Gospel, so also Paul frames Christ's obedience according to the contrast between Adam and Christ. Adam's sin brought "condemnation" to all in him, but Christ's righteousness brought "justification of life" to all in him (Rom. 5:18). Paul then says, "For as by one man's disobedience many were made sinners, so by the obedience of one shall many be made righteous" (v. 19). Calvin said, "As by the sin of Adam we were estranged from God and destined to perish, so by Christ's obedience we are received into favor as righteous."[42] He added, "The obedience of Christ is reckoned to us as if it were our own."[43] While Christ's death is certainly in the foreground in the context of Romans (3:25; 4:25; 5:6–10), Paul does not limit Christ's obedience to his passion, but views it as a process that culminated in "the death of the cross" (Phil. 2:8). Thus, his obedience spanned his whole state of humiliation.[44] Just as Adam's disobedience in the original covenant of works determined the status of mankind before God, so Christ's obedience in the covenant of grace determined the status of those in him, to their justification and life (Rom. 5:12–17).[45] Jonathan Edwards said that, according to Romans 5, "as what Adam did brought death, as it had the nature of disobedience, so what Christ did brought life, not only as a sacrifice, but as it had the nature of meriting obedience." He added, "Christ's active obedience was as necessary to retrieve the honor of God's law and authority as his suffering."[46]

Reflecting upon Paul's Adam-Christ teaching (Romans 5; 1 Corinthians 15), Thomas Goodwin said, "He speaks of them as if there had never been any more men in the world, nor were ever to be for time to come,

41. Acts 2:27; 3:14; 4:27, 30; 7:52; 22:14.
42. Calvin, *Institutes*, 2.17.3.
43. Calvin, *Institutes*, 3.11.23.
44. Turretin, *Institutes*, 14.13.18 (2:450).
45. On the covenant of works, see chaps. 14–16.
46. Edwards, "The Threefold Work of the Holy Ghost," in *WJE*, 14:398, cited in Craig Biehl, *The Infinite Merit of Christ: The Glory of Christ's Obedience in the Theology of Jonathan Edwards* (Jackson, MS: Reformed Academic Press, 2009), 180, 134.

except these two. And why? But because these two between them had all the rest of the sons of men hanging at their girdle."[47]

Objections to the Doctrine of Christ's Active Obedience

When people object to the doctrine of Christ's active obedience, often they do so because they reject the imputation of Christ's active obedience to believers. A fuller treatment of that subject is reserved for the topic of justification.[48] Here, however, we must somewhat anticipate our treatment of justification as we consider the topic of Christ's saving obedience.

First, the objection is made that Christ, in his human nature, owed his obedience to God. Therefore, his obedience could not justify others, but was necessary for his own righteousness.[49]

In reply, we answer that the law treats us not as abstract natures but as people, and the person of our Lord Jesus is both God and man. The Son of God is not under the law's authority, for he is the Lawgiver and the authority behind the law.[50] What he undertook to do as our Mediator was not for his sake, but for ours, and he undertook it freely in the eternal counsel of peace.[51] Even as an incarnate man, and that during the days of his humiliation, Jesus Christ remained the "Lord of the law,"[52] not one necessarily subject to it (Matt. 12:8; 17:24–27). His obedience was an act of humbling himself to do his Father's will rather than demanding and exploiting the glory that was rightfully his (Phil. 2:8). Hence, his becoming "under the law" (Gal. 4:4) meant his voluntary taking up of the obligations of the law for our sake.[53] Calvin commented,

> Christ the Son of God, who might have claimed to be exempt from
> every kind of subjection, became subject to the law. Why? He did so

---

47. Goodwin, *Christ Set Forth*, in *Works*, 4:31.

48. On imputation and its detractors, see the chapters on justification in *RST*, vol. 3 (forthcoming).

49. Socinus, *De Jesu Christo Servatore*, 3.5, in Gomes, "Faustus Socinus," 190–201. See Owen, *The Doctrine of Justification*, in *Works*, 5:253–55.

50. Note Christ's summary of traditional interpretations of the law followed by his remarkable "But I say" responses (Matt. 5:22, 28, 32, 34, 39, 44), an instance of his teaching with astonishing authority (7:29).

51. On the counsel of peace or covenant of redemption, see chap. 30.

52. Formula of Concord (Solid Declaration, 3.15), in *The Book of Concord*, 564.

53. Owen, *The Doctrine of Justification*, in *Works*, 5:255–56. On this argument as used by French Reformed theologians, see de Campos, *Doctrine in Development*, 184. This is not to communicate divine properties to the human nature of Christ, as the Lutherans did, but to recognize that the law relates to Christ as a whole person, and his relationship to the law must therefore account for both his deity and humanity.

in our room [place], that he might obtain freedom for us. A man who was free, by constituting himself a surety, redeems a slave: by putting on himself the chains, he takes them off from the other. So Christ chose to become liable to keep the law, that exemption from it might be obtained for us.[54]

Second, the objection is made that Christ's obedience is necessary for our salvation only as an essential prerequisite to his atoning death, but it does not constitute our righteousness before God. Christ's death does not supply us with imputed obedience, but only forgiveness of sins (Eph. 1:7), which is said to be all the righteousness we need.[55] Alternatively, it is said that Christ's death takes away the guilt of our sins, and faith is now our righteousness before God.[56]

In reply, we note that the Scriptures do indicate that Christ's sacrificial death required that he be without sin, like the ancient sacrifices that had to be without blemish.[57] However, this does not exhaust the centrality of his obedience in our salvation, which we see even more clearly when we consider the Pauline doctrine of justification. In justification, God not only grants forgiveness of sins, but counts believers to be righteous in his sight as a gift apart from their works (Rom. 4:4–8, 22–25). To be "righteous" in God's sight is to be counted as one who has obeyed God's law (Deut. 6:25; 24:13).

What is the basis of this righteousness that God credits to believers? We must frankly grapple with the fact that if Christ's righteousness is not imputed to us, then our righteousness must stand upon something in ourselves, whether our good works, love, or faith. However, though it is received by faith, our righteousness is not anything in us, for Paul writes of "not having mine own righteousness, which is of the law, but that which is through the faith of Christ, the righteousness which is of God by faith" (Phil. 3:9). This righteousness is imputed to us not on the basis of the value of our faith or any exercise of godliness on our part, but as a gift to those who in themselves are ungodly (Rom. 4:4–5).[58]

---

54. Calvin, *Commentaries*, on Gal. 4:4.

55. Richard Watson, *Theological Institutes*, 2 vols. (New York: Lane and Scott, 1851), 2:241.

56. Robert H. Gundry, "The Nonimputation of Christ's Righteousness," in *Justification: What's at Stake in the Current Debate*, ed. Mark Husbands and Daniel J. Treier (Downers Grove, IL: InterVarsity Press, 2004), 25.

57. Lev. 1:3, 10; 3:1, 6; 4:3, 23, 28, 32; 5:15, 18; 6:6; Heb. 9:14; 1 Pet. 1:19.

58. John Piper, *Counted Righteous in Christ: Should We Abandon the Imputation of Christ's Righteousness?* (Wheaton, IL: Crossway, 2002), 59–60.

As we argued earlier, the righteousness credited to believers is the obedience of Christ (Rom. 5:19). Christ stands as their representative before God, interceding for them not only on the basis of his death, but also his perfect righteousness (Heb. 7:25–26). When Paul writes, "For he hath made him to be sin for us, who knew no sin; that we might be made the righteousness of God in him" (2 Cor. 5:21), the parallel makes it clear that God makes an exchange by imputation: he causes believers to become "righteousness" by the legal reckoning of Christ's obedience to them, just as he made Christ to become "sin for us" not by being changed into an actual sinner, but by having the guilt of our disobedience reckoned to him.

In the words of the Belgic Confession (Art. 22), faith is "only an instrument with which we embrace Christ our Righteousness," so that God imputes "to us all His merits and so many holy works which He hath done for us and in our stead."[59] The Canons of Dort (Head 2, Rej. 4) affirm that we are justified by faith "inasmuch as it accepts the merits of Christ," and wisely reject the doctrine "that God having revoked the demand of perfect obedience of faith, regards faith itself and the obedience of faith, although imperfect, as the perfect obedience of the law, and does esteem it worthy of the reward of eternal life through grace."[60] Faith is not our righteousness; Christ is.

Third, opponents of this doctrine also object that if Christ's active obedience is counted to Christians, then they no longer need to obey God's commandments. Therefore, we are told that this doctrine feeds antinomianism, but its denial promotes holiness.[61]

In answer to this objection, we affirm that there is more than one reason why people must obey God's commandments. One reason is that they must obey in order to be counted righteous before God and inherit eternal life. Truly this reason no longer binds those in Christ: they do not obey, nor should they obey, for the purpose of becoming worthy of eternal life. This truth releases them from slavish fear of condemnation. However, there are other reasons to obey as those already counted righteous for Christ's sake. The Westminster Confession of Faith (16.2) says,

> These good works, done in obedience to God's commandments, are
> the fruits and evidences of a true and lively faith: and by them believ-

---

59. *The Three Forms of Unity*, 39–40.
60. *The Three Forms of Unity*, 138.
61. John Wesley, *Thoughts on the Imputed Righteousness of Christ*, in *The Works of John Wesley*, 10 vols., 3rd ed. (1872; repr., Grand Rapids, MI: Baker, 1979), 10:312–15; and Gundry, "Nonimputation," in *Justification: What's at Stake in the Current Debate*, 44.

ers manifest their thankfulness, strengthen their assurance, edify their brethren, adorn the profession of the gospel, stop the mouths of the adversaries, and glorify God, whose workmanship they are, created in Christ Jesus thereunto, that, having their fruit unto holiness, they may have the end, eternal life.[62]

We can see the wrongness of this objection if we apply its argument to Christ's passive obedience. By the same logic that says, "Since Christ obeyed for us, we no longer need to obey," we may also say, "Since Christ suffered for us, we no longer need to suffer." That, of course, is nonsense. While it is true that we do not need to suffer the punishment for our sins, Christians still must suffer in order to put sin to death, grow toward mature godliness, serve those around them, and spread the gospel through the world. In the same way, we who are Christians must still obey even though we are justified by Christ's active obedience, for our obedience serves many good purposes for God's glory.

Christ's Active and Passive Obedience United in His Life and Death

Though sometimes the Holy Scriptures focus on one or the other, the whole counsel of God reveals the necessity of Christ's active and passive obedience in order to save his people from their sins. In Isaiah's prophecy of the suffering Servant, we read, "By his knowledge shall my righteous servant justify many; for he shall bear their iniquities" (Isa. 53:11). Our justification depends both on Christ's bearing our sins and on his being God's "righteous servant"—that is, the One who perfectly obeyed his will.

John encourages believers that though they must strive not to sin, when they do sin, they can trust that "we have an advocate with the Father, Jesus Christ the righteous: and he is the propitiation for our sins" (1 John 2:1–2). Our confidence before God rests upon both Christ's personal righteousness and his suffering to propitiate God's holy wrath against sinners.

The active and passive dimensions of Christ's obedience are inseparably and organically related. The Son who devoted his whole existence to obeying his Father's laws most certainly also submitted to God's specific calling for him to suffer. The calling to suffer for the sins of his people could not have been fulfilled unless he had performed it in perfect love for God and man (Eph. 5:2)—that is, perfect obedience to God's great commandment

---

62. *Reformed Confessions*, 4:251–52.

and the second greatest commandment, upon which hang the whole law (Matt. 22:37–40). Furthermore, Christ could not have avoided suffering when he kept God's commandments, for every step of doing his Father's will defied the opposition of Satan and this wicked world. His righteous human character could develop into full maturity only by the strenuous, agonizing exercise of obedience in the midst of suffering (Heb. 5:8–9). All of Christ's active obedience was passion, and all of his passive obedience was action.

However, the distinction remains important and helpful "to emphasize the two distinct aspects of our Lord's vicarious obedience," Murray said, for "the law of God has both penal sanctions and positive demands."[63] Luther said that God gives to believers "the righteousness of another," so that each Christian can say, "'Mine are Christ's living, doing, and speaking, his suffering and dying.' . . . Through faith in Christ, therefore, Christ's righteousness becomes our righteousness and all that he has becomes ours; rather, he himself becomes ours."[64]

Christ's Climactic Obedience in His Passion

Though all of Christ's human life during his state of humiliation involved obedience through suffering, he exercised new heights of obedience as he entered new depths of sorrow. Shortly after his triumphal entry at Jerusalem, Christ said, "Now is my soul troubled; and what shall I say? Father, save me from this hour: but for this cause came I unto this hour. Father, glorify thy name" (John 12:27–28). Later that week, as he celebrated the Passover with his disciples, again "he was troubled in spirit" (13:21). However, Christ's resolve to lay down his life remained firm. He handed a piece of bread to his satanic betrayer in fulfillment of prophecy (vv. 18, 26). The sovereign Lord said to Judas, "What you are going to do, do quickly" (v. 27 ESV). Then, after Judas went out into the night, Christ said, "Now is the Son of man glorified, and God is glorified in him" (v. 31). For the glory of God, Christ did not shrink back from his passion.

Christ's Obedience at Gethsemane

After Christ celebrated the Passover with his disciples, they left Jerusalem, crossed the Kidron Valley, and went up a hill called the Mount of Olives,

---

63. Murray, *Redemption Accomplished and Applied*, 21.
64. Luther, *Two Kinds of Righteousness*, in *LW*, 31:297–98.

where they arrived at a garden called "Gethsemane," which means "oil press" (Mark 14:26, 32; John 18:1). By this path, Christ retraced the steps of the weeping David as he departed Jerusalem before his murderous son Absalom arrived (2 Sam. 15:23, 30). Yet Christ was not driven away, but purposefully advanced to face the death ordained for him and foretold by the prophets (Mark 14:21, 27).

In Gethsemane, the unseen darkness pressed yet more forcefully on Christ's soul. He "began to be greatly distressed and troubled" and said to Peter, James, and John, "My soul is very sorrowful, even to death" (Mark 14:33–34 ESV). The word translated as "greatly distressed" (*ekthambeo-mai*) means to "be astonished" or "amazed" (9:15; 16:5–6). Emotional anguish so shocked and pierced Jesus that it could have killed him. "His sorrow was as great as a man could bear, his fear convulsive, his astonishment well-nigh paralyzing."[65] He "fell on the ground" as under crushing weight and prayed, "Abba, Father, all things are possible unto thee; take away this cup from me: nevertheless not what I will, but what thou wilt" (14:36).

What could have affected God's Son with such horror? What was this cup? In the Scriptures, a "cup" often symbolizes the judicial wrath of God against sinners.[66] It is "the cup of his fury" (Isa. 51:17). The cup that will be the portion of the wicked is "fire and brimstone" (Ps. 11:6; Rev. 14:10). In Gethsemane, this wrath drew near to Christ, and he was already "feeling the terrible punishment which our sins had merited."[67] Murray said, "There now invaded his consciousness such increased understanding and experience . . . that amazement filled his soul. Our Lord was now looking into the abyss. . . . Here was the unrelieved, unmitigated judgment of God against sin. It filled him with horror and dread." Yet it was precisely here that he submitted himself to God's will.[68]

Christ grappled with the terror of this burning divine indignation without the support of his friends, for his disciples had fallen asleep and left him to pray by himself (Mark 14:37, 40). However, he overcame this fear, submitted to his Father, and received the cup of fury for our sakes. Calvin said, "Here was no common evidence of his incomparable love toward us:

---

65. Macleod, *The Person of Christ*, 174.
66. Pss. 11:5–6; 75:8; Isa. 51:17, 21–23; Jer. 25:15–18, 27–29; 49:12; Ezek. 23:31–34; Zech. 12:2; Rev. 14:10; 16:19.
67. Belgic Confession (Art. 21), in *The Three Forms of Unity*, 38.
68. Murray, "The Obedience of Christ," in *Collected Writings*, 2:155.

to wrestle with terrible fear, and amid those cruel torments to cast off all concern for himself that he might provide for us."[69]

Behold the marvelous obedience of Christ! He willingly embraced and drank into himself the most painful of dooms, the flaming wrath of almighty God against sinners. He chose submission to his Father's command and love for his fellow men and women at the highest cost to himself. Here we see penal substitution for the satisfaction of divine justice, not as an abstract doctrine, but as the personal experience of Jesus as sweat poured off him "like great drops of blood falling to the ground" (Luke 22:44). When he went out to meet those who came to arrest him, he was resolute: "The cup which my Father hath given me, shall I not drink it?" (John 18:11).

Christ was always sinless, but here we observe a major step in the development of his human obedience.[70] Murray said, "His obedience was forged in the furnace of trial, temptation, and suffering."[71] The author of Hebrews explains, "When he had offered up prayers and supplications with strong crying and tears unto him that was able to save him from death . . . though he were a Son, yet learned he obedience by the things which he suffered" (Heb. 5:7–8). This perfect obedience, heated in the fires of affliction and beaten out upon the anvil of his determination to do God's will, made Christ the perfect source of "eternal salvation unto all them that obey him" (v. 9).

It was no accident that Gethsemane was called a "garden" (John 18:1, 26), for there Christ worked to undo what Adam had done in another garden. The first Adam was surrounded by pleasure, but disobeyed God in the garden of Eden; the last Adam was pressed by sorrow, but obeyed God in the garden of Gethsemane. The first Adam was conquered by Satan; the last Adam conquered Satan. The first Adam reached out to take the fruit that God had forbidden; the last Adam received the cup that the Father had commanded. The first Adam tried to hide himself from the penalty of his sin; the last Adam voluntarily exposed himself to the penalty of our sins. The first Adam was driven out of Eden by the holy God; the last Adam willingly allowed sinners to lead him out of Gethsemane so that he would lead sinners into a better paradise. Outside of the first garden,

---

69. Calvin, *Institutes*, 2.16.5.

70. On Christ's sinlessness and development in obedience, see the discussion of his mediatorial relation to the Father in chap. 40.

71. Murray, "The Obedience of Christ," in *Collected Writings*, 2:155–56.

the burning sword of divine wrath was unsheathed; outside of the latter garden, the sword of divine wrath struck down Christ for our salvation. Praise be to God! Christ has regained all that Adam lost, and more.

Christ's Obedience at Gabbatha

After Christ's arrest, he was taken to the high priest, where he was accused of many things by false witnesses before the priests, elders, and scribes of Israel (Mark 14:53–59). When the high priest interrogated him, asking him if he was the Christ, he faithfully confessed, "I am: and ye shall see the Son of man sitting on the right hand of power, and coming in the clouds of heaven" (Mark 14:62). The men charged to render judgment according to God's law condemned Christ to death (Deut. 17:8–13). They proceeded to spit upon him, slap him, and mock him (Mark 14:63–65). Nearby, Peter denied three times that he knew him (vv. 66–71). The authorities then brought Jesus to Pilate, the Roman governor, who also interrogated him and finally passed judgment upon him at the place called "the Pavement," or, in Aramaic, "Gabbatha" (John 19:13).

Ironically, Pilate repeatedly declared Christ's innocence (John 18:38; 19:4, 6), but handed him over to death to appease the priests and scribes of God's law who had condemned him (v. 16)—and God permitted it. Robert Rollock noted that the narrative of Christ's passion shows us paradoxically that Christ was both vindicated as righteous and condemned as if a violator of God's law: "in himself the most innocent man, and in us the most guilty man in the world."[72] Man's injustice was God's justice executed against the righteous Surety of his people. Calvin said, "When our Lord Jesus Christ is judged before an earthly judge . . . it was in order that we might be exempt and absolved from the condemnation that we deserved before the heavenly Judge."[73]

The soldiers under Pilate's command "scourged" Christ, giving him a severe flogging (Mark 15:15).[74] James Brooks comments, "It was a Roman punishment and must be distinguished from the much milder synagogue beatings of forty lashes less one. Bits of metal, bone, or glass were imbedded in leather thongs; and the flesh of the victim was shredded, sometimes

---

72. Rollock, *Lectures upon the History of the Passion, Resurrection, and Ascension of Our Lord Jesus Christ*, in *Select Works*, 2:98.
73. John Calvin, *The Deity of Christ and Other Sermons*, trans. Leroy Nixon, foreword by Richard C. Gamble (Audubon, NJ: Old Paths, 1997), 115.
74. On flogging as a precursor to crucifixion, see Josephus, *Wars of the Jews*, 2.306, in *Works*, 617.

until bones or entrails appeared."[75] The soldiers gathered around Christ, mocked him, struck him, and spat upon him (vv. 16–19). When they crowned him with "thorns" (*akantha*, Matt. 27:29; John 19:2), they unwittingly marked him with the sign of God's curse on the earth for man's sin (Gen. 3:17–18 LXX). Friedrich Wilhelm Krummacher (1796–1868) said, "What befalls Christ befalls us in Him, who is our representative. . . . Our hell is extinguished in Jesus' wounds; our curse is consumed in Jesus' soul; our guilt is purged away by Jesus' blood."[76]

Jesus endured these insults and injustices from sinners meekly (Isa. 53:7) and "committed himself to him that judgeth righteously" (1 Pet. 2:23). At any moment, he could have but spoken a word and summoned an army of angels to defend him and destroy his foes (Matt. 26:53). Instead, he submitted to God's will, silently enduring the abuse of men (v. 63; 27:12–14). Christ faithfully confessed before Pilate that he was indeed a king but ruled over a spiritual kingdom (John 18:33–37; cf. 1 Tim. 6:13). When Pilate "released Barabbas," a man guilty of insurrection and murder, but "delivered Jesus . . . to be crucified" (Mark 15:7, 15), Christ accepted this remarkable exchange of "the just for the unjust" (1 Pet. 3:18), for he had come to give his life as "a ransom for many" (Mark 10:45).

Christ's Obedience at Golgotha

The Roman soldiers took Jesus to a location outside of the gates of Jerusalem (Heb. 13:12) but near the city (John 19:20). The place was known as "Golgotha," or "skull" (Matt. 27:33),[77] traditionally "Calvary" (Latin *calvaria*, "skull"). There they "crucified" (*stauroō*) him (v. 35)—that is, executed him by lifting him up on the "cross" (*stauros*, vv. 40, 42).

The Gospels pass over the details of crucifixion in reverent silence, but they would have been familiar to many people in the Roman Empire. The condemned criminal carried the horizontal bar of the cross to the place of his death. Then, forcing him onto his back, his executioners stretched his arms on the wooden beam and tied or nailed them in place. They then lifted him and fastened the crossbeam to a vertical pole already fixed in the ground. The criminal's feet were tied or nailed to the pole or to a wooden

---

75. James A. Brooks, *Mark*, The New American Commentary 23 (Nashville: Broadman & Holman, 1991), 252.

76. F. W. Krummacher, *The Suffering Saviour* (Edinburgh: Banner of Truth, 2004), 284–85.

77. Compare the Hebrew word translated as "skull" (*gulgolet*) in Judg. 9:53; 2 Kings 9:35.

board projecting from it.[78] In Christ's case, the soldiers nailed his hands to the cross (John 20:25, 27), probably at the wrists, and likely nailed his feet as well (Luke 24:39). Then commenced the slow process of dying in agony, as Christ struggled to breathe in that contorted position while suffering from his multiple bloody wounds.[79] Cicero (106–43 BC) said that crucifixion was "a most cruel and ignominious punishment . . . the most miserable and most painful punishment appropriate to slaves alone."[80]

The Gospels emphasize two factors that multiplied Christ's sorrows upon the cross, both of which were prophesied in Psalm 22. First, Jesus experienced rejection and abandonment by men. The crowds around the cross insulted and reviled him, mocking his faith in God and claim to be God's Son (Matt. 27:39–44; cf. Ps. 22:7–8). Their scorn did not fall on deaf ears; it broke Christ's heart to suffer so without comforter or pity (Ps. 69:20).[81]

Second, Christ experienced rejection and abandonment by God: "Jesus cried with a loud voice, saying, Eli, Eli, lama sabachthani? That is to say, My God, my God, why hast thou forsaken me?" (Matt. 27:46; cf. Ps. 22:1). To "forsake" is to abandon or leave. God forsakes those who forsake him, break his covenant, and provoke his wrath (Deut. 31:16–17; 2 Chron. 15:2; 24:20). Christ uttered this cry of desolation while supernatural darkness fell upon the land (Matt. 27:45), a sign that God was executing judgment as in the day of his anger.[82] The cross itself was a sign that Christ suffered and died under God's curse against lawbreakers, for he whose body was hung on a wooden pole was considered "accursed of God" (Deut. 21:22–23; cf. Gal. 3:13). Therefore, God placed his wrath and curse on Christ for the sins of his people.

The Gospels record Christ's cry of dereliction in his native language of Aramaic ("Eli, Eli, lama sabachthani"). Thabiti Anyabwile says, "There are some traumas so deep only your mother tongue will do."[83] Christ cried out to God in his deepest distress, but the Father remained silent. On the

---

78. Carson, *The Gospel according to John*, 608.

79. Gerald L. Borchert, *John 12–21*, The New American Commentary 25B (Nashville: Broadman & Holman, 2002), 264.

80. Marcus Tullius Cicero, *Against Verres*, 2.5.64, 66, in *The Orations of Marcus Tullius Cicero*, trans. C. D. Yonge, 2 vols. (London: Henry G. Bohn, 1856), 1:536–37.

81. Note that the next verse, Ps. 69:21, is fulfilled in the Gospel accounts of the crucifixion (Matt. 27:34, 48).

82. Ex. 10:21–23; Isa. 13:9–13; Joel 3:14–15; Amos 8:9; Zeph. 1:14–15.

83. Thabiti M. Anyabwile, *Captivated: Beholding the Mystery of Jesus' Death and Resurrection* (Grand Rapids, MI: Reformation Heritage Books, 2014), 27. Mark 14:36 similarly records Christ's prayer with the Aramaic "Abba."

cross, Christ experienced the agony of seemingly unanswered supplication: "How long, LORD? Wilt thou hide thyself for ever? Shall thy wrath burn like fire?" (Ps. 89:46). Jesus felt his soul crushed by seemingly unbearable stress. John Flavel said, "And it is as much as if Christ had said, O my God, no words can express my anguish: I will not speak, but roar, howl out my complaint; pour it out in volleys of groans."[84] Christ received the unmitigated guilt and condemnation due to all his people's sins, compressed into a crushing weight upon his soul. God "made him to be sin for us" (2 Cor. 5:21). And Christ bore this weight in absolute solitariness, without the slightest comfort from God or man.

Christ "was numbered with the transgressors; and he bare the sin of many" (Isa. 53:12), and he did so willingly and obediently (Luke 22:37). Calvin said, "He did not refuse to bear the agonies which are prepared for all those whose consciences rebuke them and who feel themselves guilty of eternal death and damnation before God. . . . He willed in full measure to appear before the judgment seat of God His Father in the name and in the person of all sinners, being then ready to be condemned, inasmuch as He bore our burden."[85]

In the midst of such devastating darkness, Christ honored his Father. The words "my God, my God" were not a cry of unbelief, but of trust in God's faithfulness to his covenant (Ps. 22:1–5, 10; cf. 25:2; 31:14). Christ's use of the words of Psalm 22 from the cross publicly declared that God can be trusted to do what he says in the Scriptures. Christ did not die merely as a passive victim, but as an active priest offering to God his body and soul. Consequently, for his piety and godly fear, he "was heard" by God (Heb. 5:7). God raised him from the dead and exalted him to the highest place because he "became obedient unto death, even the death of the cross" (Phil. 2:8–9). Therefore, we conclude that God was pleased with his Son upon the cross. God did not reject his Son, but poured out upon him the rejection that we deserve. In Christ's crucifixion, we see the pinnacle of his obedience in both its active and passive glory. And that is all our salvation.

Practical Implications of Christ's Sacrificial Obedience

The doctrine of Christ's active and passive obedience has massive implications both for becoming a Christian and living the Christian life.

---

84. Flavel, *The Fountain of Life*, in *Works*, 1:412. "Volleys" was originally spelled "vollies."
85. Calvin, *The Deity of Christ and Other Sermons*, 52.

First, recognize that God will glorify his righteousness and his law. Do not fall prey to the false teaching that since God is love, he cheerfully overlooks matters of obedience. God cannot deny himself. Know him for who he is, namely, the God of righteousness and the Lord of law. Rejoice and delight in his just and upright character. It is the very essence of his love.

Second, rely upon Christ alone to deliver you from the punishment that you deserve. Your sins have merited damnation and eternal death in the lake of fire. God's law and his very being demand that your sins receive their just punishment. There is no other way of escape than through Jesus Christ. He is the Lamb of God, without spot or blemish, who died not for his own sins but for the sins of his people. Trust him to save you from hell.

Third, rest your hope in Christ's perfect obedience as your righteousness. Do not rest upon your good works, your sincere love, or your faith. Faith is an empty hand to receive Christ. Do not dare to add something to what Christ has done in an effort to make yourself acceptable to God. Is the life and death of God's Son not enough? Embrace Jesus Christ as your only righteousness, your perfect righteousness, your unchanging righteousness, your heavenly righteousness, your eternal righteousness, and your effective righteousness to bring you to glory.

Fourth, resist the temptation to judge yourself by the strictness and severity of the law. Reject perfectionism. If you have trusted in Christ and are a justified child of God, then the law is your friend, guide, and helper. However, you no longer need to meet its absolute demands for righteousness in order to be welcomed by the Father. God is pleased with you because of Christ, and he takes pleasure in your sincere but imperfect works.

Fifth, reckon the high value of obedience in the sight of God. The lack of obedience cast the entire human race into slavery and death. The salvation of sinners required nothing less than the obedience of God's Son even unto the death of the cross. God treasures obedience because he treasures his glory as God. Practice a new accounting in your mind: learn to value the treasures of this world lightly, but to see that nothing is more precious than the will of God.

Sixth, run the race of obedience in imitation of Christ. Focus your mind and engage your energies to this great aim: to obey the will of God. Meditate upon God's Word as you face temptation. Make the doing of your Father's will to be your meat and drink. Follow Christ in loving God and loving your neighbor—not to save yourself, but because he has saved you.

Seventh, remain patient and faithful through suffering, even unto death. Do not shrink back from sorrow when it lies in the path of duty. Do not grumble and grow bitter when life pierces you. Count the cost and press on to glory. The One who saved you by his obedient sufferings waits for you at the end of your journey. He can grant you strength to do all seven of these things by his amazing, superabounding grace.

Sing to the Lord

Glorifying God for Christ's Atoning Work

And can it be that I should gain
An interest in the Saviour's blood?
Died He for me, who caused His pain?
For me, who Him to death pursued?
Amazing love! How can it be
That Thou, my God, shouldst die for me? (repeat last two lines)

He left His Father's throne above
(So free, so infinite His grace!)
Humbled himself because of love,
And bled for all His chosen race:
'Tis mercy all, immense and free,
For, O my God, it found out me. (repeat last two lines)

Long my imprisoned spirit lay
Fast bound in sin and nature's night;
Thine eye diffused a quick'ning ray,
I woke, the dungeon flamed with light;
My chains fell off, my heart was free,
I rose, went forth, and followed Thee. (repeat last two lines)

No condemnation now I dread;
Jesus, and all in Him, is mine!
Alive in Him, my living Head,
And clothed in righteousness divine,
Bold I approach th'eternal throne,
And claim the crown, through Christ my own. (repeat last two lines)

Charles Wesley, with alterations
Tune: Sagina
Trinity Hymnal—Baptist Edition, No. 731

Questions for Meditation or Discussion

1. How do the Holy Scriptures show us that obedience is the heart and soul of Christ's saving work as the Priest?

2. What does Paul mean by saying, "For Christ is the end of the law for righteousness to every one that believeth" (Rom. 10:4)?

3. What do theologians mean by Christ's "active" and "passive" obedience?

4. Why is it important for us to make the active/passive distinction regarding Christ's obedience?

5. What three objections are often raised against the doctrine of Christ's active obedience? How can we answer these objections?

6. How did Christ exercise his saving obedience at (1) Gethsemane, (2) Gabbatha, and (3) Golgotha?

7. How has meditating upon Christ's obedience at Gethsemane, Gabbatha, and Golgotha affected your soul? What does that imply about your spiritual state? What would be an appropriate response for you to give to God and to Christ for what he has done?

8. Which of the practical implications listed at the end of this chapter is most urgent for you to put into practice right now? Why? What will you do about it?

Questions for Deeper Reflection

9. How does Christ's obedience show us the glory of the love between God the Father and God the Son? What does it teach us about living as adopted sons of God?

10. You have an opportunity to teach an hour-long Sunday school class for college students on the subject of Christ's active obedience: what it means, why it is important in the gospel, and how it should affect our lives. Using these as your main points, develop a detailed outline of what you will present to the class.

11. Is it better to speak of Christ's obedience in two parts (active and passive) or to speak of Christ's single obedience as having two dimensions? Why?

51

Christ's Priestly Work, Part 4

The Perfections of Christ's Sacrificial Accomplishment

Christ's sacrifice is perfect. The Westminster Confession of Faith (8.5) says, "The Lord Jesus, by His perfect obedience, and sacrifice of Himself, which He through the eternal Spirit, once offered up unto God, hath fully satisfied the justice of His Father; and purchased, not only reconciliation, but an everlasting inheritance in the kingdom of heaven, for all those whom the Father hath given unto Him." Hence (8.8), "to all those for whom Christ hath purchased redemption, He doth certainly and effectually apply and communicate the same."[1]

There are several doctrinal approaches to the perfection of Christ's sacrifice.[2]

1. *Universal Redemption.* Christ effectively reconciled all to God. This position is the tendency of the theology of Karl Barth, Jürgen Moltmann, and open theists.[3]

2. *Potentially Universal Redemption.* Christ made possible the salvation of all people, and all can be reconciled to God if they meet

---

1. *Reformed Confessions*, 4:245.

2. Andrew David Naselli and Mark A. Snoeberger, eds., *Perspectives on the Extent of the Atonement: Three Views* (Nashville: B&H Academic, 2015), 143–94, henceforth cited as *Perspectives*, ed. Naselli and Snoeberger.

3. Barth, *Church Dogmatics*, II/2, sec. 35.3 (422); IV/3.1, sec. 70.3 (477); Jürgen Moltmann, *The Crucified God*, 194–95; and Fritz Guy, "The Universality of God's Love," in *The Grace of God and the Will of Man*, ed. Pinnock, 45.

God's conditions. This is the teaching of Roman Catholicism,[4] Lutheranism,[5] and Arminianism.[6]

3. *Hypothetically Universal Redemption.* Christ made redemption potential for all but effectual only for the elect. This doctrine has appeared in various forms within Reformed theology, most famously in Amyraldianism.[7]

4. *Particular or Definite Redemption.* Christ redeemed his people, and all of them will be brought to God by the Spirit through the gospel. This is the mainstream Reformed position, which we advocate.[8]

As Anne Dutton (1695–1765) wrote, the doctrine of particular redemption brings together God's election in "his great love" to "save a certain number of fallen men"; "the covenant of redemption," in which the Father and Son eternally pledged to redeem them by the Son becoming their Mediator; penal substitution, in which "he substituted him in their room . . . to bear their sin, to be made their curse, to endure their hell, to obey and suffer, to live and die, and rise again for them"; and effective satisfaction, for "such is the justice and faithfulness of God, that Christ's full payment must needs be the sinner's full discharge for whom it was given."[9]

In order to show the biblical basis and theological beauty of particular redemption, we will examine the following perfections of Christ's sacrifice: sufficiency, finality, efficacy, universality, and particularity. The

---

4. *Catechism of the Catholic Church*, sec. 605.

5. Formula of Concord (Solid Declaration, 11.28), in *The Book of Concord*, 645; and David Scaer, "The Nature and Extent of the Atonement in Lutheran Theology," *Bulletin of the Evangelical Theological Society* 10, no. 4 (Fall 1967): 179–87.

6. Arminian Remonstrance of 1610 (Art. 2), in *Reformed Confessions*, 4:43; and Terry L. Miethe, "The Universal Power of the Atonement," in *The Grace of God and the Will of Man*, ed. Pinnock, 71–72.

7. Jonathan D. Moore, *English Hypothetical Universalism: John Preston and the Softening of Reformed Theology* (Grand Rapids, MI: Eerdmans, 2007); and John S. Hammett, "Multiple-Intentions View of the Atonement," in *Perspectives*, ed. Naselli and Snoeberger, 143–94. On Moïse Amyraut or Amyraldus, see *RST*, 1:1024, 1026.

8. The classic Reformed work on particular redemption is Owen, *Salus Electorum, Sanguis Jesu: or, the Death of Death in the Death of Christ*, in *Works*, 10:139–424. Henceforth cited as *The Death of Death*. An excellent shorter treatment may be found in Hodge, *The Atonement*, 399–429. For more recent works, see Lee Gatiss, *For Us and For Our Salvation: 'Limited Atonement' in the Bible, Doctrine, History, and Ministry* (London: The Latimer Trust, 2012); and David Gibson and Jonathan Gibson, eds., *From Heaven He Came and Sought Her: Definite Atonement in Historical, Biblical, Theological, and Pastoral Perspective* (Wheaton, IL: Crossway, 2013), henceforth cited as *From Heaven*, ed. Gibson and Gibson. Brief treatments include Joel R. Beeke, *Living for God's Glory: An Introduction to Calvinism* (Lake Mary, FL: Reformation Trust, 2008), 89–100; Carl R. Trueman, "Definite Atonement View," in *Perspectives*, ed. Naselli and Snoeberger, 19–61; and the literature cited in *RST*, 1:124n40.

9. Anne Dutton, *A Letter to the Reverend Mr. John Wesley*, in *Selected Spiritual Writings of Anne Dutton, Volume 1: Letters*, ed. JoAnn Ford Watson (Macon, GA: Mercer University Press, 2003), 51–52.

doctrine of particular redemption asserts that Christ's sacrifice is sufficient to save all who believe because of its infinite worth; final in accomplishing redemption once for all without need for any supplement; efficacious to satisfy God's justice and obtain all the blessings of God's covenant; universal in its salvation of people from all nations and classes, and in its proclamation of the free offer of the gospel to everyone; and particular in its penal substitution to redeem a definite people chosen by God.

The Sufficiency of Christ's Perfect Sacrifice

For thousands of years, men offered to God the blood of animals, but those sacrifices could never make atonement for them and served only as shadows by which faith grasped hold of Christ before he came (Heb. 10:1). Millions of beasts, rivers of drink offerings, or even the deaths of our children could never atone for sin (Mic. 6:6–7). However, Christ "obtained eternal redemption for us," not "by the blood of goats and calves, but by his own blood" (Heb. 9:12).

Many theologians have said that Christ's sacrifice was sufficient for all men and efficient for the elect. Peter Lombard wrote that Christ "offered himself . . . for all with regard to the sufficiency of the price, but only for the elect with regard to its efficacy, because he brought about salvation only for the predestined."[10] The Canons of Dort (Head 2, Art. 3) say, "The death of the Son of God is the only and most perfect sacrifice and satisfaction for sin, and is of infinite worth and value, abundantly sufficient to expiate the sins of the whole world."[11]

The worth of Christ's sacrifice transcends the value of the universe. God's chosen people "were not redeemed with corruptible things, as silver and gold," but "with the precious blood of Christ, as of a lamb without blemish and without spot" (1 Pet. 1:18–19). Gold does not rust or tarnish, but Peter calls it "corruptible" because it is part of this creation in contrast to the eternal heavenly world (vv. 4, 23). Christ's blood was corruptible, being the bodily fluid of a true man, but was more precious than all the gold and silver on earth because he is an eternal person, the divine rock,

---

10. Lombard, *The Sentences*, 3.20.5, cited in Hogg, "Sufficient for All, Efficient for Some," in *From Heaven*, ed. Gibson and Gibson, 81. On Calvin's qualified use of this formula, see Richard A. Muller, *Calvin and the Reformed Tradition: On the Work of Christ and the Order of Salvation* (Grand Rapids, MI: Baker Academic, 2012), 93, 103, 105. See also Perkins, *An Exposition of the Symbol*, in *Works*, 5:361.

11. *The Three Forms of Unity*, 134.

God himself (2:8).[12] Paul exhorted elders to care for "the church of God, which he hath purchased with his own blood" (Acts 20:28).[13] Though the divine nature does not have blood, the person who died on the cross was both man and God. He is "our great God and Savior Jesus Christ, who gave himself for us to redeem us" (Titus 2:13–14 ESV).[14] The person who became incarnate and died for sins is the radiance of God's glory, the Son of God whom the angels worship, the unchanging and eternal Creator of the universe (Heb. 1:3, 6, 10–12). This fact gave his sufferings "a divine value and virtue," resulting in "the invaluable price of our redemption."[15] Consequently, his sacrifice accomplished "eternal redemption" and obtained an "eternal inheritance" for many (9:12, 15). Christ will receive unending worship for the unspeakable worth of his sacrifice that redeemed countless people (Rev. 5:9–14; 7:9, 13–14).

Stephen Charnock explained that we must reckon the value of Christ's sacrifice according to the "union of the divine with the human nature," for "by the personal union, the dignity was conferred upon the sufferings of his human nature." He added, "It was not necessary his deity should suffer to make the sacrifice infinite, and indeed it was impossible. The divine nature is as impassible as it is immutable; yet in regard of the strait [close] union of the two natures, his mediatory actions and sufferings, being the actions and sufferings of the person, may be counted as the sufferings of the Deity itself, in a moral way, and by legal estimation."[16] Christ's sufferings were "finite in regard of the time of duration" and "in regard of the immediate subject wherein he suffered, his human nature; which, being a creature, could no more become infinite, than it could [become] omnipotent, omniscient, or eternal." However, "as the greatness of an offence is to be measured by the greatness of the person whose honour is invaded; as the striking a king is capital . . . so the value of a satisfaction is to be measured by the excellency of the person satisfying." Thus, "the sacrifice of Christ deserves an infinite acceptation [approval], because it is offered by an infinite person."[17]

This is not to say that because of the infinite dignity of Christ's person, he could have redeemed sinners by a prick of a thorn that shed one drop

---

12. In 1 Pet. 2:8, Peter applies to Christ the "rock" prophecy of Isa. 8:14, originally spoken of the Lord God (v. 13).

13. On the words translated as "his own" in Acts 20:28, see the discussion of Christ's unique person in chap. 39.

14. On the translation of Titus 2:13, see *RST*, 1:641n18.

15. Gouge, *Commentary on Hebrews*, 1:20.

16. Charnock, *A Discourse on the Acceptableness of Christ's Death*, in *Works*, 4:571–72.

17. Charnock, *A Discourse on the Acceptableness of Christ's Death*, in *Works*, 4:570.

of his blood. As William Bates said, Christ had to bear the full curse of the law (Gal. 3:13) and pay our debt to propitiate God's offended justice (Rom. 3:24–26).[18] The Canons of Dort (Head 2, Art. 4) say that Christ's death "derives its infinite value and dignity" from the fact that he is "the only begotten Son of God, of the same eternal and infinite essence with the Father and the Holy Spirit," and he suffered "the wrath and curse of God due to us for sin."[19]

John Owen concluded, "It was, then, the purpose and intention of God that his Son should offer a sacrifice of infinite worth, value, and dignity, sufficient in itself for the redeeming of all and every man, if it had pleased the Lord to employ it to that purpose; yea, and of other worlds also, if the Lord should freely make them, and would redeem them."[20] We do not say that Christ's sacrifice is simply sufficient to redeem everyone—for a sufficient cause produces its effect, and all would be redeemed.[21] Rather, Christ's sacrifice is of infinite worth, and hence is sufficient to save all whom God might choose to save—even the people of a thousand worlds.

Therefore, let us never think that our good works, or the works of any mere man or woman, can atone for our sins. If such an infinitely precious ransom price was required for our forgiveness, then shall we think our pitiful works will save us? We must trust in Christ alone. John Calvin said, "Wherefore, whenever we intend to seek God's favour and mercy, let us fasten the whole of our minds on the death and passion of our Lord Jesus Christ, that we may there find the means by which to appease God's wrath. And, further, seeing that our sins are done away by such payment and satisfaction, let us understand that we cannot bring anything of our own by which to be reconciled with God."[22]

Do not insult God by bringing your works to try to satisfy divine justice after Christ has paid so precious a price. Instead, come to Christ freely, though you are the worst sinner on earth. Are your sins of greater weight than the death of God's Son? Here is a ransom payment for you, sinner. Though the debt of your sins would cast you into hell for unending ages,

---

18. Bates, *The Harmony of the Divine Attributes*, 217.

19. *The Three Forms of Unity*, 134–35.

20. Owen, *The Death of Death*, in *Works*, 10:295.

21. Henry A. G. Blocher, "Jesus Christ *the* Man: Toward a Systematic Theology of Definite Atonement," in *From Heaven*, ed. Gibson and Gibson, 574–75. Blocher notes Blaise Pascal's criticism of "sufficient grace" that fails to produce its effect. Blaise Pascal, *The Provincial Letters*, ed. M. Villemain (London: Seeley, Burnside, and Seeley, 1847), letter 2 (18–19).

22. Calvin, *Sermons on the Epistle to the Ephesians*, 52.

the blood of God the Son has worth enough to save you. Honor him by coming to him with full confidence in the infinite sufficiency of his sacrifice.

The Finality of Christ's Perfect Sacrifice

The worth and sufficiency of Christ's redemption implies that he has completed the work of atonement, and nothing more need be added. Just before Christ died, "knowing that all things were now accomplished [*tetelestai*]," he declared, "It is finished [*tetelestai*]" (John 19:28, 30). This verb is in the perfect tense, indicating completed action or a state resulting from completed action. The verb itself (*teleō*) means to achieve, perform, accomplish, perfect, fulfill, finish, or bring to completion. Hence, with the words "It is finished," Christ was not resigning himself to death but declaring triumphantly that he had completed the work given him by the Father.[23] John next relates how Christ fulfilled the type of the Passover lamb (v. 36; cf. v. 14).[24] Therefore, Christ finished the work of offering himself as a sacrifice for sins to deliver people from God's judgment. The redemption price was paid in full (Mark 10:45).[25]

It directly contradicts the sufficiency and finality of Christ's sacrifice for people to seek to make satisfaction to God for their own sins or to depend upon earthly priests to do so. This is one of the grave errors of the Roman Catholic Church. The Roman Eucharist is seen as "a sacrifice," and whenever it "is celebrated on the altar, the work of our redemption is carried

---

23. Carson, *The Gospel according to John*, 621. The only other instance in the New Testament where *teleō* appears in the perfect tense is in Paul's statement "I have finished my course" (2 Tim. 4:7), referring to the faithful completion of his earthly calling and mission just before he died. A very similar verb (*teleioō*) is used in John's Gospel for Christ performing and completing the work given to him by the Father (4:34; 5:39; 17:4) in fulfillment of the Scriptures (19:28; cf. *teleō* in Luke 18:31; 22:37; Acts 13:29).

24. "A bone of him shall not be broken" (*ostoun ou syntribēsetai autou*, John 19:36) is nearly an exact quotation of two texts about the Passover lamb, Ex. 12:46 and Num. 9:12 LXX (*ostoun ou syntribēsetai ap' autou*).

25. Though "it is finished" implies that Christ completely paid the price to redeem sinners, we should be cautious about assertions that *tetelestai* is a technical term meaning "paid in full." The verb *teleō* does sometimes take the sense to "pay" a financial obligation such as a tax (Matt. 17:24; Rom. 13:6), though this sense does not appear in the Septuagint except in the cognate noun *telos* for "tax." See *TDNT*, 8:52, 57–58. James H. Moulton and George Milligan said, "Receipts are often introduced by the phrase *tetelestai*." *Vocabulary of the Greek Testament* (London: Houghton and Stoughton, 1929), 630. They cited fourteen papyri that are tax receipts, published in Bernard P. Grenfell and Arthur S. Hunt, eds., *New Classical Fragments, and Other Greek and Latin Papyri*, Greek Papyri, Series II (Oxford: Oxford University Press, 1897), papyrus group 50 (78–84). However, these papyri are dated from the mid-second to third century AD and do not bear directly on the use of the term at the time of the New Testament's writing. John 19 does not seem to make any other reference to Christ's death as a payment of a debt. Instead, it presents Christ's declaration of *tetelestai* as his triumphant announcement that he had completed the work assigned to him by the Father and foretold by the prophets—the accomplishment of salvation.

out."[26] According to Roman Catholic teaching, "the sacrifice of Christ and the sacrifice of the Eucharist are one single sacrifice: 'The victim is one and the same: the same now offers through the ministry of priests, who then offered himself on the cross; only the manner of offering is different.'"[27] By this sacrifice for sins, they attempt to render God "favorable" toward the living and those dead who still suffer in purgatory.[28] Thus, the Roman Mass "is nothing else than a denial of the one sacrifice and sufferings of Jesus Christ."[29]

Furthermore, in the Roman Catholic sacramental system, sinners perform penance in order to "make satisfaction for" their sins by their prayers, good works, and self-inflicted sufferings offered "through Jesus Christ" to the Father.[30] The goal of these satisfactions for sin is "reconciliation" with God and "peace and serenity of conscience."[31] The Roman Catholic Church also grants "indulgences" to sinners, the "remission before God of the temporal punishment due to sins," including the punishment of dead Christians suffering in purgatory.[32] Through indulgences, the church says that it dispenses the merits of Christ and the merits that the Virgin Mary and the saints obtained through him by their holy lives.[33] How have Roman theologians twisted Christ's perfect satisfaction for our sins into the idea that he gives us the power to make satisfaction for ourselves?[34] John Murray said, "In opposition to every such notion of human satisfaction Protestants rightly contend that the satisfaction of Christ is the only satisfaction for sin and is so perfect and final that it leaves no penal liability for any sin of the believer."[35] We may imitate the saints, but must not look to them for expiation and merit. As Thomas

---

26. *Catechism of the Catholic Church*, secs. 1364–65, in the latter quotation citing Pope Paul VI, *Lumen Gentium*, sec. 3, November 21, 1964, The Vatican, https://www.vatican.va/archive /hist_councils/ii_vatican_council/documents/vat-ii_const_19641121_lumen-gentium_en.html.
27. The Council of Trent, cited in *Catechism of the Catholic Church*, sec. 1367.
28. Cyril of Jerusalem, *Catech. Myst.* 5, 9, 10, cited in *Catechism of the Catholic Church*, sec. 1371.
29. The Heidelberg Catechism (LD 30, Q. 80), in *The Three Forms of Unity*, 95.
30. *Catechism of the Catholic Church*, secs. 1459–60.
31. *Catechism of the Catholic Church*, sec. 1468.
32. *Catechism of the Catholic Church*, sec. 1471.
33. *Catechism of the Catholic Church*, secs. 1476–77. In 1998, the pope of Rome offered indulgences for faithful Roman Catholics who engaged in works of piety, including making significant financial gifts—"donating a proportionate sum of money to the poor" and "supporting by a significant contribution works of a religious or social nature." John Paul II, *Incarnationis Mysterium: Bull of Indication of the Great Jubilee of the Year 2000*, and *Conditions for Gaining the Jubilee Indulgence*, The Vatican, November 29, 1998, http://www.vatican.va/jubilee_2000/docs/documents /hf_jp-ii_doc_30111998_bolla-jubilee_en.html.
34. Turretin, *Institutes*, 14.12.12 (2:441).
35. Murray, *Redemption Accomplished and Applied*, 51.

Aquinas rightly said, Christ alone is properly called our Redeemer, and "the sufferings of the saints are beneficial to the Church, as by way, not of redemption, but of example and exhortation."[36]

The glory of Christ's priesthood is that he has offered the full and final sacrifice for sins. Under the old covenant, the sacrifices were never done (Heb. 10:1–3, 11). However, Christ offered himself "once" (*ephapax*, 7:27; 9:12; 10:10), where the Greek word means "once for all." Christ has not needed to suffer repeatedly for sinners (9:26). He is not suffering now for our sins, but "after he had offered one sacrifice for sins for ever, [he] sat down on the right hand of God" (10:12). "For by one offering he hath perfected for ever them that are sanctified" (v. 14). Thus, no more offering for sin is necessary (v. 18). Hugh Martin wrote, "It is one solitary, matchless, Divine transaction—never to be repeated, never to be equaled, never to be approached."[37] Christ's redemption results in riches of forgiveness (Eph. 1:7), not a partial forgiveness limited to some sins or some aspects of punishment, but total, permanent forgiveness of all sins.[38]

Evangelical Christians might not look to the Eucharist or penance to satisfy for their sins, but they, too, can fall into the error behind those practices. Whenever they depend on having said a prayer (such as the "sinner's prayer"), on having performed a work of devotion (such as tithing or having their "quiet time"), or on having done good works (such as helping someone in need) in order to obtain reconciliation with God and a good conscience, they dishonor the finished work of Christ. The "altar call" has become for many the Protestant version of penance, and the same people may go forward in meetings again and again to quiet their guilty consciences. Rather, let us rest entirely upon Christ's perfect sacrifice and walk in the liberty of the gospel.

"It is finished" should fly like a banner over Christians with respect to satisfying God's justice, rescuing them from God's wrath, and forming the basis of their justification and acceptance by God. "The blood of Christ" is all that you need to "purge your conscience from dead works to serve the living God" (Heb. 9:14). Only by faith in Christ's satisfaction can we walk in true repentance, which is not a fearful attempt to atone for our sins, but a bittersweet turning from sin in penitent sorrow toward God in

---

36. Aquinas, *Summa Theologica*, Part 3, Q. 48, Art. 5, cited in Turretin, *Institutes*, 14.12.17 (2:442).
37. Martin, *The Atonement*, 241.
38. Brakel, *The Christian's Reasonable Service*, 1:595–96. See Ps. 103:3, 12; Col. 2:13; 1 John 1:7; Heb. 10:17.

joyful love.[39] Then we will be prepared to submit to God's painful discipline, for we will know that it is not our well-deserved punishment for sin, but the training that our loving Father has ordained to bring his children to glory (12:5–11).

We should often meditate on the finished work of Christ. Wilhelmus à Brakel said that the Christian who by faith is "more occupied with a quiet and sweet meditation upon the suffering of Christ" will better appreciate the depth of the Savior's sorrows, "have a deeper insight into the abominable nature of sin and the sublime nature of God's righteousness . . . rejoice more in the truth and perfection of the satisfaction accomplished by that suffering . . . love Christ more, hate sin more, have a heart more steadfast in the practice of godliness, and proceed with more courage, comfort, and peace." Such meditation will "yield strong consolations," including the grace to "perceive the perfect satisfaction of divine justice and how perfect the sinner is before God in Christ . . . [and] how certainly and truly salvation has been merited." This will bring "peace of conscience in God and free access to the Father." Furthermore, "when considering His passion, all the suffering of this life becomes light."[40]

The Efficacy of Christ's Perfect Sacrifice

The Bible represents the sacrifice of Christ not as accomplishing a potential salvation if we meet certain conditions, but as actually and effectively accomplishing the salvation of those for whom he died. Two thousand years ago, God blotted out his people's legal debt, "nailing it to his cross" (Col. 2:14). Christ has "obtained eternal redemption" (Heb. 9:12). He "bought" us with a price (1 Cor. 6:20). The Lamb of God "redeemed" people of every nation before they even heard the gospel (Rev. 5:9; cf. Gal. 3:13). "After making purification for sins, he sat down at the right hand of the Majesty on high" (Heb. 1:3 ESV).

The "efficacy" of Christ's sacrifice has to do with its power to produce its intended effect. If people for whom Christ died forever remain sinners under God's wrath, condemned prisoners and slaves, enemies outside of God's friendship, objects of his judicial punishment, and offenders against his righteous justice, then how can we say that Christ accomplished propitiation, redemption, reconciliation, penal substitution, and satisfaction for

---

39. Heidelberg Catechism (LD 33, Q. 88–90), in *The Three Forms of Unity*, 99.
40. Brakel, *The Christian's Reasonable Service*, 1:613–15.

them? Owen said, "When a ransom is paid for the liberty of a prisoner, is it not all the justice in the world that he should have and enjoy the liberty so purchased for him?"[41]

Isaiah prophesied, "He shall see of the travail of his soul, and shall be satisfied: by his knowledge shall my righteous servant justify many; for he shall bear their iniquities. Therefore will I divide him a portion with the great, and he shall divide the spoil with the strong; because he hath poured out his soul unto death: and he was numbered with the transgressors; and he bare the sin of many, and made intercession for the transgressors" (Isa. 53:11–12). This text grounds Christ's certain victory upon his finished work. Isaiah said, "He shall bear their iniquities. *Therefore* will I divide him a portion," and, "He shall divide the spoil with the strong; *because* he hath poured out his soul." Charles Spurgeon observed, "The whole of this victory results from Christ's own work. . . . Why, then, will Christ win the victory? The answer is, 'Because he hath poured out his soul unto death.' . . . He must, he shall, he will win that for which he died."[42] The victory in view in Isaiah's prophecy was not just that Christ would be exalted, but that he would effectively save and "justify" the spiritual family ("seed") assigned to him by the Lord (v. 10). Herman Witsius wrote, "Christ by his satisfaction, obtained for himself, as Mediator, a right to all the elect: which the Father willingly and deservedly bestows on him."[43]

It might be objected that some people for whom Christ died may perish forever in their sins, as several Scripture passages seem to warn.[44]

In reply, we argue that these texts do not teach the damnation of those redeemed by Christ. When Paul warns believers not to "destroy" a brother "for whom Christ died" (Rom. 14:15; 1 Cor. 8:11), the verb translated as "destroy" (*apollymi*) can mean to perish or die (physically or spiritually), but can also mean to lose or suffer loss.[45] The context speaks of someone being "grieved" and "made weak" (Rom. 14:15, 21). Though we should not underestimate the spiritual harm we can do to a brother in Christ, these texts need not refer to eternal destruction.

Peter's condemnation of false teachers who deny "the Lord that bought them" (2 Pet. 2:1) uses a word (*despotēs*) translated as "Lord" or "Master"

---

41. Owen, *The Death of Death*, in *Works*, 10:261.
42. C. H. Spurgeon, "Even This Our War Cry—Victory! Victory!," in *Spurgeon's Expository Encyclopedia*, 14 vols. (Grand Rapids, MI: Baker, 1996), 4:481.
43. Witsius, *The Economy of the Covenants*, 2.7.1 (1:234).
44. Rom. 14:15; 1 Cor. 8:11; Heb. 10:29; 2 Pet. 2:1.
45. Luke 15:4, 8, 32; John 6:12, 39; 18:9; 2 John 8.

(ESV) that is relatively rare in the New Testament, and nowhere used directly of Christ.[46] In the Old Testament, the word often refers to the Lord God of Israel,[47] and Peter is comparing the false prophets of his day to the false prophets in Israel (v. 1) and other ancient rebels against God (vv. 5–6, 15). Perhaps being "bought" by the "Lord" does not refer to Christ's redemption, but to God's national deliverance of Israel (cf. Deut. 15:15; 32:6).[48] In any case, Peter describes them ironically: they claim to be "bought" by the "Master," but they show by their lives that they are "slaves of corruption" (v. 19 ESV). Peter compares these false teachers to dogs and swine that show their true nature by returning to their filth (v. 22).[49] Whatever effect the gospel had on them, it did not change the basic orientation of their hearts.

In the warning of Hebrews 10:29,[50] it is not clear that the phrase "the blood of the covenant by which he was sanctified" (ESV) indicates that the apostate was once saved by Christ. First, it is possible to translate "he was sanctified" as "one was sanctified," meaning that it does not refer to the person rejecting Christ, but to a general principle of salvation by Christ's blood that the apostate rejects.[51] Second, the person "sanctified" by the blood may be the apostate, but his sanctification could refer to outward consecration as a professing member of the "saints" (6:10; 13:24), not inward sanctification.[52] Third, it may be that "he was sanctified" refers to "the Son of God" (10:29).[53] It could refer to Christ's consecration as a priest, for priests were consecrated with blood (Ex. 29:20–21).[54] Or it could refer to Christ's consecration as the true and living sanctuary that unbelievers "trampled underfoot" just as the Gentiles did to the blood-

---

46. Luke 2:29; Acts 4:24; 1 Tim. 6:1–2; 2 Tim. 2:21; Titus 2:9; 1 Pet. 2:18; 2 Pet. 2:1; Jude 4; Rev. 6:10. The passage in Jude, which parallels 2 Peter 2, uses *despotēs* of God in distinction from Christ.

47. Gen. 15:2, 8; Isa. 1:24; Jer. 1:6; Dan. 9:8, 15–19 LXX.

48. Grudem, *Systematic Theology*, 600.

49. Schreiner, *1, 2 Peter, Jude*, 364–65.

50. On the warnings against apostasy in Heb. 6 and 10, see the first chapter on preservation and perseverance in *RST*, vol. 3 (forthcoming).

51. George H. Guthrie, *Hebrews*, The NIV Application Commentary (Grand Rapids, MI: Zondervan, 1998), 230, 357. In the Greek text, "he was sanctified" is simply a third-person singular verb (*hēgiasthē*) with no explicit subject. The aorist tense could be global or gnomic in significance, which fits a generalization or principle.

52. Hughes, *A Commentary on the Epistle to the Hebrews*, 422–23. The "blood of the covenant" (10:29) alludes to the ceremonial initiation of the old covenant by the sprinkling of the people of Israel with blood (9:19–21; cf. Ex. 24:6–8), corresponding to the outward consecration of people through covenantal rites such as baptism and the Lord's Supper.

53. The second and third interpretations are in Poole, *Annotations upon the Holy Bible*, 3:857, on Heb. 10:29.

54. Owen, *An Exposition of the Epistle to the Hebrews*, 6:545.

consecrated sanctuary.[55] In any of these interpretations, it is not a person redeemed by Christ's blood who falls away, and so the text is consistent with the efficacy of his sacrifice.

It is highly unlikely that Hebrews 10:29 indicates that Christ's blood consecrates some who will perish, for earlier in the same chapter we read that Christ accomplished the work to fulfill the promises of complete salvation: "For by one offering he hath perfected for ever them that are sanctified. Whereof the Holy Ghost also is a witness to us: for after that he had said before, This is the covenant that I will make with them after those days, saith the Lord, I will put my laws into their hearts, and in their minds will I write them; and their sins and iniquities will I remember no more" (10:14–17, citing Jer. 31:33–34). Christ's sacrifice secures all grace for his people, including the sovereign grace that achieves their inward transformation so that they meet the conditions of the covenant and, unlike many in old covenant Israel, will not be rejected as covenant breakers.[56]

Therefore, if Christ died for us, we will be saved. The death of Christ for us demonstrates God's absolute intention to save us: "What shall we then say to these things? If God be for us, who can be against us? He that spared not his own Son, but delivered him up for us all, how shall he not with him also freely give us all things?" (Rom. 8:31–32). What does "all things" include? In the context, it means that God grants effectual calling, justification by faith, growing conformity to Christ's image, and glorification with Christ to all for whom he died (vv. 29–30). God causes "all things" to "work together for good" for the redeemed, so that they inherit glory as "joint-heirs with Christ" (vv. 17, 28). It is impossible for them to be condemned or separated from the love of Christ because Christ died for them and is their living Savior (vv. 34–35). The "us all" for whom God gave his Son (v. 32) is not all without exception, but all whom God foreknew and predestined to glory (v. 30), "God's elect" (v. 33), those whom God effectively brings through all their trials to glory.[57]

---

55. The "blood of the covenant" (Heb. 10:29) was applied by Moses to Israel *and the altar* (Ex. 24:6–8). The verb translated as "trample under foot" (*katapateō*) is used of the Gentiles trampling God's holy places (Isa. 63:18; 1 Macc. 3:45, 51; 3 Macc. 2:18 LXX; cf. Dan. 8:13 [*katapatēma*]; Luke 21:24 [*pateō*]; Rev. 11:2 [*pateō*]). These Gentiles came against Israel in "insolence" (*hybris*, 1 Macc. 3:20; 3 Macc. 2:3, 21 LXX), just as the apostate has "done despite unto" (*enybrizō*) or "insolently mocked" the Spirit (Heb. 10:29). Applied to Christ, this trampling suggests that he is the sanctuary (cf. 10:20; 13:10), consecrated by God's glory (1:3; cf. Ex. 29:43) and his blood (Heb. 9:21; cf. Ex. 29:12, 36; Lev. 8:15), but disdained by those who prove to be outsiders to Israel.

56. See Owen, *The Death of Death*, in *Works*, 10:237.

57. Murray, *Redemption Accomplished and Applied*, 65–69.

What God accomplished for sinners in Christ, God must also apply to sinners through Christ by the work of the Holy Spirit. Witsius said, "True saving benefits are bestowed on none of the elect, before effectual calling, and actual union with Christ by a lively faith."[58] However, by offering himself as a sacrifice, the Lord Jesus accomplished the unfailing salvation of those for whom he died. Witsius added, "The Lord Jesus obtained for the elect, by his satisfaction, an immunity from all misery, and a right to eternal life, sanctification, conservation, and glorification."[59] Charnock said, "The sacrifice of Christ was acceptable to God, and efficacious for men. There was a complete satisfaction made to God, the supreme Judge offended, pleasing to him, and effectual to free the guilty party from the obligation to the deserved punishment."[60] If we doubt it, we may look to Christ's resurrection, ascension, and session at God's right hand as the Father's vindication of the completed work of our Surety (Heb. 10:12), whom he raised by "the blood of the eternal covenant" (13:20).[61]

Therefore, Christ's sacrifice calls for rejoicing and praise for our certain hope of salvation from divine wrath. Greg Nichols says, "This blessed truth gives every Christian solid ground for confidence and assurance. It calls every Christian to stand fast, with one mind and heart striving for the faith of the gospel. It calls every Christian to sing the praises of the Lamb, for he is worthy, for his blood accomplished and obtained redemption (Rev. 5:9–10)."[62]

The Christian's peace and contentment must rest upon Christ and his finished work. In the midst of great sorrows of his own, Horatio Spafford (1828–1888) wrote,

> Though Satan should buffet, though trials should come,
> Let this blest assurance control,
> That Christ has regarded my helpless estate,
> And has shed his own blood for my soul.
> It is well with my soul; it is well, it is well with my soul.
>
> My sin—O the bliss of this glorious thought!—
> My sin, not in part, but the whole,

---

58. Witsius, *The Economy of the Covenants*, 2.7.8 (1:237).
59. Witsius, *The Economy of the Covenants*, 2.7.3 (1:235). "Immunity" here refers to legal exemption from liability to judicial prosecution and punishment (as in "diplomatic immunity").
60. Charnock, *A Discourse on the Acceptableness of Christ's Death*, in *Works*, 4:552.
61. Charnock, *A Discourse on the Acceptableness of Christ's Death*, in *Works*, 4:559–60.
62. Nichols, *Lectures in Systematic Theology*, 3:696–97.

Is nailed to the cross and I bear it no more;
Praise the Lord, praise the Lord, O my soul!
It is well with my soul; it is well, it is well with my soul.[63]

The Universality of Christ's Perfect Sacrifice

Our consideration of the perfect sufficiency, finality, and efficacy of Christ's sacrifice leads us to also consider its extent. "Extent" refers to its intended scope: Whom has Christ redeemed? The Holy Scriptures speak of Christ's mission and death in order to save "the world," "all," "the whole world," and even "all things."[64] In our interpretation of these texts, we begin with the meaning of the terms. The Greek word translated as "all" (*pas*) has a variety of meanings; it can refer to everything without exception (John 1:3), but it can also mean "all kinds of" (1 Tim. 6:10).[65] For example, Paul exhorts us to pray "for all men" (2:1); however, we are not obligated to pray for every single person who has ever lived, but rather for all kinds of people, including "kings" and those "in authority" (v. 2).[66] "All" can mean many, as when people said of Christ, "All men come to him" (John 3:26), or when Christ said that "every man" presses into the kingdom (Luke 16:16).

The Greek term translated as "world" (*kosmos*) can refer to the created universe (John 17:5), the earth (13:1), the human race in general (17:6), or mankind in rebellion against God (3:19; 14:17, 30; etc.).[67] It is often used in a plainly limited sense, such as those who heard Christ's words (8:26), celebrated his coming to Jerusalem (12:19), or rejoiced at his death (16:20), even though most of humanity had never heard of Jesus at the time. Paul wrote that the gospel was bearing fruit "in all the world" (Col. 1:6) and that the faith of the Roman saints was discussed "throughout the whole world" (Rom. 1:8). He also said that in God's purposes, the unbelief of many Israelites toward Christ had served to propagate the gospel among the Gentiles so that Israel's fall meant "riches for the world" and "the reconciliation of the world" (11:12, 15 ESV), referring to the salvation

---

63. Horatio G. Spafford, "When Peace Like a River," in *Trinity Hymnal—Baptist Edition*, No. 580.
64. Isa. 53:6; John 1:29; 3:16–17; 12:32; Rom. 5:18; 1 Cor. 15:22; 2 Cor. 5:14, 19; Col. 1:20; 1 Tim. 2:5; Heb. 2:9; 1 John 2:2.
65. The KJV rightly translates as "all manner of" a number of texts in which the Greek text simply reads "all" (*pas*), such as Matt. 4:23; 5:11; Acts 10:12; Rom. 7:8; Rev. 21:19.
66. Knight, *The Pastoral Epistles*, 115.
67. See Leon Morris, *The Gospel according to John*, rev. ed., The New International Commentary on the New Testament (Grand Rapids, MI: Eerdmans, 1995), 111–13.

of many Gentiles, but certainly not everyone.[68] The New Testament often uses universal language to emphasize the salvation of sinners from all nations, both Jews and Gentiles.[69]

Let us now consider the texts that assert Christ's redemption for the "world" and "all." Sometimes "world" is an indefinite term for sinners, without specifying who or how many. God loved "the world" and sent Christ to save "the world" (John 3:16–18). In context, this means that God loved sinners who hated him, as we see from the next verse: "And this is the condemnation, that light is come into *the world*, and men loved darkness rather than light, because their deeds were evil" (v. 19). This is the wonderful message of the gospel, that God loved sinners who did not love him (1 John 4:9–10). As B. B. Warfield said, the wonder of God's love for the world in John 3:16 is not that "the world is so big," but that "the world is so bad."[70]

"World" and "all" can also reveal the expansiveness of Christ's work to redeem people from all nations and groups. Christ "gave himself a ransom for all" (1 Tim. 2:6)—that is, for all kinds of people, from the mightiest kings to the lowest men and women (vv. 1–2; cf. Titus 2:1–14).[71] Hence, we should preach the gospel indiscriminately and without boundaries in order to reflect God's desire and delight in saving all kinds of people (1 Tim. 2:4). Christ is the propitiation for "the whole world" (1 John 2:2), not just our little group. Paul uses this same expression when he says, "Your faith is spoken of throughout the whole world [*holos ho kosmos*]" (Rom. 1:8); not every individual in the world was speaking about the Romans' faith, but many people in many places were. In the same way, John is saying that Christ is the propitiation not for one nation or people, but for "all who by faith embrace the gospel . . . scattered through various parts of the world," as Calvin said.[72] This interpretation well suits the purpose of 1 John 2:1–2, which aims to comfort believers that God will not reject them when they sin. Francis Turretin said, "For what solace can a man receive from that grace which is

---

68. Brakel, *The Christian's Reasonable Service*, 1:607; and Murray, *Redemption Accomplished and Applied*, 59–60.

69. Matt. 24:14; 28:19; Mark 16:15, 20; Luke 24:47; Acts 1:8; 17:30; 22:15, 21; Eph. 2:11–17; Rev. 5:9; etc.

70. Benjamin B. Warfield, *Biblical and Theological Studies* (Philadelphia: Presbyterian and Reformed, 1952), 516. This quotation is drawn from a piece that was originally published as Benjamin B. Warfield, "God's Immeasurable Love," in *The Saviour of the World* (New York: Hodder and Stoughton, 1913), 120–21.

71. Thomas R. Schreiner, "'Problematic Texts' for Definite Atonement in the Pastoral and General Epistles," in *From Heaven*, ed. Gibson and Gibson, 376–79.

72. Calvin, *Commentaries*, on 1 John 2:2.

common to the elect and the reprobate, if he knows that Christ in dying has done nothing more for him than for the unbelieving and the reprobate?"[73]

Often "all" is used of Christ's redemption to refer to the whole people saved by union with him. Christ's death is said to be for the justification and life of "all men" in contrast to the condemnation that fell on "all" because of Adam's sin (Rom. 5:18), but "all men" must be understood to refer not to everyone without exception but to all "in Christ," just as the "all" who die because of Adam are all people "in Adam" (1 Cor. 15:22). As Nichols observes, "Just as there are two Adams, two representative heads, even so there are two human races, two humanities."[74] "One has died for all," but this "all" refers to those who "died" with Christ and, as a consequence of Christ's death, "no longer live for themselves but for him who for their sake died and was raised" (2 Cor. 5:14–15 ESV). Thus, the "all" is everyone who died and rose in union with Christ (Rom. 6:8).[75] When Paul writes that "God was in Christ, reconciling the world unto himself, not imputing their trespasses unto them," he is not saying that everyone is already forgiven, but that "the word of reconciliation" calls everyone to be "reconciled to God" (2 Cor. 5:19–20).[76] Hebrews 2:9 says that Christ was humbled below the angels "so that by the grace of God he might taste death for everyone" (ESV). However, the context makes it clear that the "everyone" consists of all the "sons," "brethren," and "children" of the covenantal "seed" (vv. 10–16). The word "all" may emphasize the comprehensiveness of the new humanity (vv. 6–8) and serve to repel any notion that salvation is limited to the Jews.

Isaiah 53:6 says, "All we like sheep have gone astray; we have turned every one to his own way; and the LORD hath laid on him the iniquity of us all." The argument is made that just as the "all we" at the beginning of this text refers to every human being's sinfulness, so too the "us all" at the end refers to Christ's bearing the sin of every human being.[77] However, this argument, if valid and applied to other texts, would prove that all mankind is justified, for Paul says, "all have sinned, and come

73. Turretin, *Institutes*, 14.14.40 (2:474).

74. Nichols, *Lectures in Systematic Theology*, 3:705.

75. Murray, *Redemption Accomplished and Applied*, 69–71.

76. Jonathan Gibson, "For Whom Did Christ Die?: Particularism and Universalism in the Pauline Epistles," in *From Heaven*, ed. Gibson and Gibson, 306.

77. Grant R. Osborne, "General Atonement View," in *Perspectives*, ed. Naselli and Snoeberger, 107.

short of the glory of God; being justified freely by his grace" (Rom. 3:23–24). While it is true that all people have sinned, the "all we" must be understood in context, where the "we" identifies people who once did not trust in Christ (Isa. 53:4) but have recognized their transgressions (vv. 5–6) and God's saving power in Christ (v. 1).[78] Hence, the "us all" (v. 6) is God's people: "for the transgression of my people was he stricken" (v. 8). Christ bore the sins of all his people, the "many" who are justified (v. 11).

Paul's statement that God in Christ worked "to reconcile all things unto himself" (Col. 1:20) is more difficult to understand, because it includes "all things" in the created universe (vv. 16–17). It may be best to interpret "reconcile" as meaning the restoration of cosmic peace by subjecting creation, disordered by the fall (Rom. 8:19–22), to Christ the Lord and his redeemed and forgiven people in union with him (Eph. 1:10–11)—not as the universal restoration of all demons, sinful men, and other creatures to right relationship with God.[79] Paul's theme in this part of the epistle to the Colossians is the supremacy and lordship of God's Son over all things, grounded upon creation and reasserted in the messianic kingdom (Col. 1:13–20). Christ reigns not by saving the demonic powers but by conquering them at the cross (2:15).[80]

Therefore, we can draw some conclusions about how Christ's sacrifice is not universal and how it is. Christ's sacrifice is *not* universal in the sense that he died to save all individual people without exception. There is nothing in these texts with universalistic language about actual or potential salvation for every individual, only the effectual salvation of those united to Christ by a Spirit-worked faith. These Scripture passages are quite consistent with Christ's redemption of his elect people from all nations. It might be objected that "world" (*kosmos*) does not mean "the elect."[81] However, as Owen said, the doctrine of particular redemption does not require that "world" have this lexical meaning, but merely that it is an indefinite term

---

78. J. Alec Motyer, "'Stricken for the Transgression of My People': The Atoning Work of Isaiah's Suffering Servant," in *From Heaven*, ed. Gibson and Gibson, 260–61.

79. Melick, *Philippians, Colossians, Philemon*, 226–28.

80. Douglas J. Moo, *The Letters to the Colossians and to Philemon* (Grand Rapids, MI: Eerdmans, 2008), 134–37. For an alternative interpretation, where "all things" refers to the new creation from which the wicked are excluded, see John Piper, "'My Glory I Will Not Give to Another': Preaching the Fullness of Definite Atonement to the Glory of God," in *From Heaven*, ed. Gibson and Gibson, 652–56.

81. Miethe, "The Universal Power of the Atonement," in *The Grace of God and the Will of Man*, ed. Pinnock, 77.

that does not designate every individual in the world.[82] Therefore, these texts provide no basis for potentially universal redemption.

If our understanding of the texts with universalistic language is correct, it also undermines the exegetical basis for hypothetically universal redemption. This view pits God's will against itself, engaging God in an internal contradiction of two contrary purposes: to possibly save all and to actually save only some.[83] It posits "disruption in the Trinity," Robert Letham writes, for "the electing purpose of the Father and the work of the Spirit are in conflict with the intention in the death of the Son on the cross."[84] Furthermore, Carl Trueman says, "if Christ has died in the same substitutionary way for the one who dies in Christ and the one who dies outside of Christ, has Christ really substituted in any meaningful, saving way for anyone?"[85]

There are significant ways in which Christ's redemptive accomplishment is universal. His sacrifice is universal in that he redeems people from *all* nations. Revelation 5:9 says, "Thou art worthy to take the book, and to open the seals thereof: for thou wast slain, and hast redeemed us to God by thy blood out of every kindred, and tongue, and people, and nation." People of every color, from the darkest black to the palest white, are redeemed by the red blood of the Savior. There is one Mediator between God and man, who gave himself a ransom for all peoples (1 Tim. 2:5–6). Therefore, we must love people of all ethnic and national backgrounds, welcome them into the church when they trust in Christ, and rejoice in the international, multicolored people whom Christ has reconciled to God.

Christ's sacrifice is also universal with respect to God's offer of salvation to *all* who hear the gospel. The gospel reveals our duty to repent and believe the promise that everyone who comes will be welcomed and saved. Revelation 22:17 says, "The Spirit and the Bride say, 'Come.' And let the one who hears say, 'Come.' And let the one who is thirsty come; let the one who desires take the water of life without price" (ESV). God

---

82. Owen, *The Death of Death*, in *Works*, 10:325–26.

83. Hammett, "Multiple-Intentions View of the Atonement," in *Perspectives*, ed. Naselli and Snoeberger, 149, 169–70. See Hodge, *The Atonement*, 416; Trueman, "Definite Atonement View," in *Perspectives*, ed. Naselli and Snoeberger, 30; and Thomas H. McCall with Grant R. Osborne, "Response" to Hammett, "Multiple-Intentions View of the Atonement," in *Perspectives*, ed. Naselli and Snoeberger, 197.

84. Robert Letham, "The Triune God, Incarnation, and Definite Atonement," in *From Heaven*, ed. Gibson and Gibson, 440.

85. Trueman, "Response" to Hammett, "Multiple-Intentions View of the Atonement," in *Perspectives*, ed. Naselli and Snoeberger, 204.

"commandeth all men every where to repent" (Acts 17:30), and this call to repentance is grounded upon Christ's death and resurrection, and the promise of forgiveness of sins in the gospel (Luke 24:46–47).[86]

The Particularity of Christ's Perfect Sacrifice

Christ died to redeem a particular people, those chosen from every nation by God for salvation. The Canons of Dort (Head 2, Art. 8) say, "It was the will of God, that Christ by the blood of the cross, whereby He confirmed the new covenant, should effectually redeem out of every people, tribe, nation, and language, all those, and those only, who were from eternity chosen to salvation and given to Him by the Father; that He should confer upon them faith, which together with all the other saving gifts of the Holy Spirit, He purchased for them by His death."[87] Christ's redeeming sacrifice is not to be abstracted from the other parts of God's saving grace, but was offered in perfect harmony with the election and effectual calling of a particular people.

The Scriptural Evidence for Particular Redemption

In the types of the old covenant, atonement was made for the covenant people. The blood of the Passover lamb was shed for individual households (Ex. 12:4), not for people in general, and certainly not for Egyptians. Only the circumcised could participate in the Passover (vv. 43–49). When the Lord took the Levites in place of the firstborn sons delivered by the Passover, a redemption price (*lytron*, LXX) was required for every Levite who exceeded their number (Num. 3:46–50). The Day of Atonement made atonement for Israel, not for the whole world.[88]

Christ died in order to save "many," who are identified in context as those whom he justifies, redeems, gives forgiveness of sins, and brings to glory.[89] The purpose of Christ's saving mission into this world was to "save his people from their sins" (Matt. 1:21). Christ said, "I came down from heaven" to do "the will of him that sent me," which was that he would save all those "which he hath given me" (John 6:38–39).[90]

---

86. Murray, "The Atonement and the Free Offer of the Gospel," in *Collected Writings*, 1:59–62.

87. *The Three Forms of Unity*, 136.

88. Paul R. Williamson, "'Because He Loved Your Forefathers': Election, Atonement, and Intercession in the Pentateuch," in *From Heaven*, ed. Gibson and Gibson, 232, 234.

89. Isa. 53:11; Matt. 20:28; 26:28; Mark 10:45; Heb. 2:10.

90. Trueman, "Definite Atonement View," in *Perspectives*, ed. Naselli and Snoeberger, 24.

The Lord Jesus Christ said, "I am the good shepherd, and know my sheep, and am known of mine. . . . I lay down my life for the sheep" (John 10:14–15). A few verses later, Christ said to certain people, "But ye believe not, because ye are not of my sheep" (v. 26). Augustine said, "He saw that they were predestined to eternal destruction, not secured for eternal life by the price of his blood."[91] The sheep of Christ are those whom the Father "gave" him (v. 29), people entrusted to him so that not one would perish but all would enjoy life forever (6:39; 17:2). Many of the sheep had not yet heard the gospel (10:16). George Smeaton (1814–1889) said, "They were already called His sheep, because they were given to Him in the divine decree, and known as His own."[92] Later in the same Gospel, we read that Christ died "that he should gather together in one the children of God that were scattered abroad" (11:52).

Christ died to save "the children," that is, those whom he calls "my brethren" and "the children which God hath given me" (Heb. 2:11–18). This refers to the covenant family of Christ, the spiritual "seed of Abraham" (v. 16). In this context, we see again that Christ's propitiatory sacrifice is an act of his priesthood (v. 17). Priesthood is a covenantal office. Christ is the Mediator and Surety of the new covenant people (7:22; 9:15).[93] They are the members of "the heavenly Jerusalem," both the saints of old who have entered heaven and those who live by faith on earth (12:22–24).

Isaiah foretold that Christ would die "for the transgression of my people" (Isa. 53:8). Paul writes that Christ "gave himself for us, that he might redeem us from all iniquity, and purify unto himself a peculiar people, zealous of good works" (Titus 2:14). The Lamb "redeemed us to God . . . out of every kindred, and tongue, and people, and nation" (Rev. 5:9), where "out of" (*ek*) means he bought some people from every group.[94] God purchased his "church" with "his own blood" (Acts 20:28). Therefore, Gottschalk of Orbais (d. 869) wrote, "The body and blood of Christ were handed over and shed for the church of Christ alone."[95]

---

91. Augustine, *Tractates on the Gospel of St. John*, 48.4, in NPNF[1], 7:267. See Michael A. G. Haykin, "'We Trust in the Saving Blood': Definite Atonement in the Ancient Church," in *From Heaven*, ed. Gibson and Gibson, 71.

92. George Smeaton, *Christ's Doctrine of the Atonement* (repr., Edinburgh: Banner of Truth, 1991), 368.

93. Nichols, *Lectures in Systematic Theology*, 3:701.

94. Gatiss, *For Us and For Our Salvation*, 24–25.

95. Cited in Hogg, "Sufficient for All, Efficient for Some," in *From Heaven*, ed. Gibson and Gibson, 79.

Paul writes, "Husbands, love your wives, even as Christ also loved the church, and gave himself for it" (Eph. 5:25). God has a universal love, a love by which he shows kindness and goodness to all creation.[96] However, the love that moved Jesus to die on the cross was a special, unique love reserved for his church, his people.[97] It would be nonsense to say that Christ loved the church just as he loved all people, for he is set forth as an example to husbands regarding their special love for their wives. Therefore, Christ gave his life out of his loving intention to save his church, which consists of those chosen by God (1:4; cf. Rev. 13:8).[98] A. A. Hodge said, "Redemption is in order to accomplish the purpose of election."[99]

The particularity of Christ's sacrifice is also established by the unity of Christ's priestly work.[100] He both gives himself as a sacrifice for his people and intercedes for them (Isa. 53:12; 1 John 2:1–2). These are the two inseparable functions of a priest for the covenant people.[101] Those for whom Christ died and intercedes cannot be damned in the end (Rom. 8:34). However, Christ does not intercede for all people, but only for those whom the Father has given him (John 17:9, 20). Now, as their exalted Priest-King, he will surely save them. Dutton said, "His boundless love, in which he once died for them, to give them a right to glory, is still as great towards them now as ever, to give them the enjoyment of it: and having engaged so to do, both his love and faithfulness employ his power on their side."[102] Therefore, he died for his elect.

Objections to Particular Redemption

Several objections are raised against this doctrine.[103] Three we have already addressed.

---

96. Ps. 145:8–9; Matt. 5:44–45; Acts 17:25, 30.

97. Rom. 1:7; Eph. 2:4; 1 Thess. 1:4.

98. Paul links Ephesians 1:4 and 5:25–27 by means of phrases translated as "holy and without blame" (*hagious kai amōmous*) in the former and "holy and without blemish" (*hagia kai amōmos*) in the latter.

99. Hodge, *The Atonement*, 370.

100. See Stephen J. Wellum, "The New Covenant Work of Christ: Priesthood, Atonement, and Intercession," in *From Heaven*, ed. Gibson and Gibson, 517–39.

101. Perkins, *An Exposition of the Symbol*, in *Works*, 5:361; and Owen, *The Death of Death*, in *Works*, 10:179–87.

102. Dutton, *A Letter to the Reverend Mr. John Wesley*, in *Selected Spiritual Writings*, 1:57.

103. See Robert P. Lightner, *The Death Christ Died: A Case for Unlimited Atonement* (Des Plaines, IL: Regular Baptist Press, 1967); Norman F. Douty, *The Death of Christ: A Treatise which Answers the Question: "Did Christ Die Only for the Elect?"* (Swengel, PA: Reiner, 1972); and Miethe, "The Universal Power of the Atonement," in *The Grace of God and the Will of Man*, ed. Pinnock, 71–96.

First, it is objected that particular redemption *contradicts Christ's sacrifice for the "world" and "all."* As we have argued, these texts refer to his redemption of many sinners from all nations, not to the redemption of every person who will ever exist.[104]

Second, it is objected that particular redemption *fails to account for the perishing of some of the redeemed.* We have argued that the Scripture passages quoted in this regard refer to Christians who are spiritually harmed but not eternally destroyed, or to people who were never saved.

Third, it is objected that particular redemption, or "limited atonement," *limits the value of what Christ has done* and so dishonors God.

In response, we acknowledge that the term "limited atonement" is open to misunderstanding and is not the language historically used in early Reformed Christianity for particular or definite redemption.[105] We have argued that Christ's satisfaction is infinite in value, which glorifies God as the all-sufficient Savior. However, unless Christ's sacrifice will save everyone, then it must be limited in some respect, either its extent (being made only for some) or its efficacy (being ineffective to save all for whom he died).[106]

Fourth, it is objected that particular redemption *discourages evangelism and missions* because we cannot assure unbelievers that "Christ died for you."

In response, we say that the assurance that Christ "loved me, and gave himself for me" belongs to those who have died with him and risen with him to a new life (Gal. 2:20). In the New Testament, evangelism is preaching Christ and calling sinners to him—not telling unbelievers that "Christ died for you." We may proclaim that there is all-sufficient grace for all who come to Christ in repentance and faith.[107] Christ says, "All that the Father gives me will come to me, and whoever comes to me I will never cast out" (John 6:37). We can preach this promise "to all nations and to all persons promiscuously and without distinction."[108] Indeed, we may preach the gospel with great confidence, knowing that Christ has redeemed his sheep throughout the world, and they will hear his voice and follow him (John 10:11, 16, 27).

---

104. Lightner also includes in this category texts that speak of Christ dying for the "lost" (Luke 19:10) and the "ungodly" (Rom. 5:6), arguing that they must refer to all lost, ungodly sinners. *The Death Christ Died*, 64, 68. However, if "ungodly" necessarily means all sinners, then we would have to conclude that all sinners are justified, for God "justifieth the ungodly" (Rom. 4:5).

105. See *RST*, 1:116–17; and Muller, *Calvin and the Reformed Tradition*, 60–61, 74–77.

106. Murray, *Redemption Accomplished and Applied*, 64.

107. Owen, *The Death of Death*, in *Works*, 10:297–98.

108. Canons of Dort (Head 2, Art. 5), in *The Three Forms of Unity*, 135.

Fifth, it is objected that particular redemption *is inconsistent with God's sincere gospel call* that everyone should repent and believe in Christ for salvation.

In response, we rejoice that God's general goodness toward all his creatures (Ps. 145:9) calls every sinner to turn back to him and escape the judgment he deserves (Ezek. 18:23; Rom. 2:4–5). However, Christ's redemption springs from God's special love for his particular people, by which he wills to redeem, purify, and bring them to glory (Titus 2:13–14).[109] Unbelievers hearing the gospel do not know yet whether they are the objects of God's redeeming love, but the gospel reveals to them the goodness of God in the free offer of Christ.

We also note that other views of redemption face similar theological tensions. Hypothetically universal redemption involves the tension between God's free offer of Christ in the gospel to all who hear and God's election and effectual calling of only some. Potentially universal redemption (as in Arminianism) implies that God sacrificed Christ for every individual when God knows for certain that many will not trust in Christ. Indeed, how is it consistent with God's wisdom that Christ should die to save millions of people who rejected God and perished in their sins during the ages prior to Christ's coming? Whatever our theological position, we cannot fully comprehend the perfect ways of the infinite God as he sincerely invites all sinners to come to Christ and yet knows in his eternal plan that only some will be saved.[110]

Sixth, it is objected that particular redemption *ignores God's common grace* (Matt. 5:44). Some, if not all, of these benefits come to the world by Christ's redemption.

In reply, we recognize that Christ's obedience unto death has brought many common, temporal benefits to the world.[111] It may well be that God preserves the universe and humanity from total destruction because of his election and redemption of the elect by Christ's blood.[112] Furthermore, God patiently manifests his general goodness to all his creation. However, common grace is not the question before us. Murray said, "The question is: on whose behalf did Christ offer himself a sacrifice? On whose behalf

---

109. See *RST*, 1:846, 1033–35; see also the chapter on the general call of the gospel in *RST*, vol. 3 (forthcoming).

110. Hodge, *The Atonement*, 420–23.

111. Nichols, *Lectures in Systematic Theology*, 3:700–701.

112. Dutton, *A Letter to the Reverend Mr. John Wesley*, in *Selected Spiritual Writings*, 1:64.

did he propitiate the wrath of God? Whom did he reconcile to God in the body of his flesh through death? Whom did he redeem from the curse of the law, from the guilt and power of sin, from the enthralling power and bondage of Satan?"[113] The answer, the Bible says, is the people whom the Father chose and gave to Christ, those individuals whom Christ actually saves.

Seventh, it is objected that particular redemption *hinders assurance of salvation*. How can a believer in Christ have a settled assurance if he cannot know whether Christ died for him?

In response, we point out that assurance is not based on the reasoning "Christ died for each and every man; therefore, also for me." Does it help assurance to tell ourselves that Christ did no more for us than for Judas? The Holy Spirit applies God's promises to the peace and joy of the Christian through this biblical logic: "Christ died for all who believe and repent . . . I believe and repent; therefore he died for me also."[114] Faith rests in the perfection of Christ's work, and assurance arises in faith by seeing the fruits of his work in us.

Eighth, it is objected that particular redemption *implies that God elected only some to salvation*. If God saves some and not others, we are told, it is only because of our choices.

This is an objection not against particular redemption as much as against the doctrine of election, a biblical teaching that we explained and defended in the section of this work on theology proper.[115] The doctrine of particular redemption fits into a network of other biblical truths to form a beautiful and coherent, though incomprehensible, system of truth. Jonathan Gibson says, "The saving work of God is indivisible." Though the Bible distinguishes "the moments of redemption predestined, accomplished, applied, and consummated," they are "integrally connected" as "cause and effect" (cf. Rom. 5:9–10; 8:29–34).[116] In eternity, the Father chose some people in Christ (Eph. 1:3–4). In history, the Son redeemed them with his blood (v. 7). In individual experience, the Holy Spirit applies that redemption to the chosen through the gospel (v. 13).

---

113. Murray, *Redemption Accomplished and Applied*, 62.
114. Turretin, *Institutes*, 14.14.51 (2:480).
115. On the doctrine of election, see *RST*, 1:979–1057 (chaps. 49–51).
116. Jonathan Gibson, "The Glorious, Indivisible, Trinitarian Work of God in Christ: Definite Atonement in Paul's Theology of Salvation," in *From Heaven*, ed. Gibson and Gibson, 336–43.

The redemption of Christ is the most exquisite love story ever told. From among fallen, corrupt, God-hating mankind, the Father chose a bride for his Son, a church selected from all nations. Christ accepted his Father's heavenly matchmaking, though he knew the terrible price it would cost him. At the appointed time, the Bridegroom became one of us. He obeyed God's laws without flaw, though severely tempted by the Devil, and embraced the very curse of God upon the cross. Yet he scorned its agony and shame for the joy that was set before him. He knew that by his death he paid the full ransom price to redeem his bride. When Jesus rose, he did so to take his bride by the hand and lead her to glory, one person at a time, as the gospel is preached. Amazing love!

The Argument from Efficacy to Particularity

Since Christ effectively accomplished propitiation, redemption, and reconciliation for those for whom he died, and only some will be saved from divine wrath, redeemed, and reconciled, therefore Christ died as the substitute only for some people.

The doctrine that Christ died for everyone, but everyone will not be saved, is inconsistent with the doctrine of penal substitution for the satisfaction of God's justice.[117] Indeed, the doctrine of potentially universal redemption implies that Christ might have offered his sacrifice and it might have "never in fact been applied to any person," which contradicts the perfection of his work.[118] Hodge said, "The very conception of substitution necessarily involves definite, personal relations. . . . The work of Christ as our Substitute was a complete Satisfaction, fully discharging all the demands of the law. . . . It hence follows, that all of those for whom Christ has in this sense made a perfect satisfaction must be saved."[119]

At the center of the doctrine of penal substitution is the truth that Christ has made a full satisfaction to divine justice for the redeemed (Col. 2:13–14). Ambrose of Milan wrote, "Can he damn you, whom he has redeemed from death, for whom he offered himself, whose life he knows

---

117. Owen, *The Death of Death*, in *Works*, 10:288–90. Arminian theologian John Miley said, "The Wesleyan soteriology, taken as a whole, excludes the satisfaction theory." *Systematic Theology*, 2:168. Clark Pinnock chronicled his movement away from penal substitutionary atonement because of his belief in God's will to save all mankind. "From Augustine to Arminius," in *The Grace of God and the Will of Man*, ed. Pinnock, 22–23.

118. Canons of Dort (Head 2, Rej. 1), in *The Three Forms of Unity*, 137.

119. Hodge, *The Atonement*, 400.

is the reward of his own death?"[120] This is not a fabrication of minds influenced by a strong view of divine predestination. As Dutton pointed out, one of John and Charles Wesley's own hymns said, "But if he paid my utmost pain, Thou canst not ask the debt again."[121]

It is objected that Christ made satisfaction for the sins of all people, but not for their unbelief. Thus, Christ is said to have atoned universally for sin, leaving a man's eternity hinged on his faith. Lutheran theologian Jakob Andreae (1528–1590) said, "Those assigned to eternal destruction are not damned because they sinned . . . but they are damned for this reason, because they refuse to embrace Jesus Christ with true faith."[122]

In response, we answer with Theodore Beza, "Sin is the sole cause of eternal damnation."[123] God will judge and damn the wicked for their wicked works, not merely their unbelief.[124] Paul says, "For you may be sure of this, that everyone who is sexually immoral or impure, or who is covetous (that is, an idolater), has no inheritance in the kingdom of Christ and God. Let no one deceive you with empty words, for *because of these things* the wrath of God comes upon the sons of disobedience" (Eph. 5:5–6 ESV; cf. Col. 3:5–6). Christ has not washed away or cancelled the sins of all men by his blood. He died to redeem his people, and upon faith they—and they alone—are forgiven and justified (Acts 13:38–39; Gal. 2:16).

It is further objected that if Christ's death is effectual for all whom he redeemed, then they all must be forgiven and counted righteous even before faith in the gospel.

In response, we acknowledge that the Scriptures distinguish between redemption accomplished and redemption applied. However, the delay in justification until a person trusts in Christ alone for salvation does not break the covenantal link between perfect redemption and effectual salvation. Owen said that Christ's satisfaction and the salvation that

---

120. Cited in Haykin, "We Trust in the Saving Blood," in *From Heaven*, ed. Gibson and Gibson, 70.

121. Dutton, *A Letter to the Reverend Mr. John Wesley*, in *Selected Spiritual Writings*, 1:53. See John and Charles Wesley, *Hymns on God's Everlasting Love* (Bristol: S. and F. Farley, 1741), 17. Ironically, this hymnal attacks particular redemption.

122. Cited in Garry J. Williams, "Punishment God Cannot Twice Inflict," in *From Heaven*, ed. Gibson and Gibson, 513.

123. Cited in Williams, "Punishment God Cannot Twice Inflict," in *From Heaven*, ed. Gibson and Gibson, 513.

124. Jer. 17:10; 32:19; Matt. 7:23; 13:41; 16:27; 25:26, 41–46; Rom. 2:5–9; Rev. 21:8; 22:11–12.

followed "depended on a previous compact and agreement," the eternal counsel of peace. Owen concluded, "Deliverance, therefore, doth not naturally follow on this satisfaction . . . but in the way and order disposed in that covenant."[125] God's eternal plan designated both Christ's atonement for the elect and the time and means of its application to them. God's covenant promises both justification and sanctification by Christ's redemption (Heb. 10:14–17). As Thomas Hooker said, "Christ hath purchased all spiritual good for his," that they would "partake of his Spirit in effectual vocation and faith," and thus, "Christ died for none but the elect."[126]

In the end, we must regard Christ's accomplishment of redemption as either particular and effectual or universal and only potential. If redemption is incomplete, then it requires that we add something to it in order for salvation to take place. As Roger Nicole (1915–2010) quipped, redemption is then like the famous Pont Saint-Bénézet in Avignon, France, a bridge that goes only partway across the river.[127] An atonement like that, though pleasing to men, fails to save. Spurgeon said, "They believe that Judas was atoned for just as much as Peter; they believe that the damned in hell were just as much an object of Jesus Christ's satisfaction as the saved in heaven . . . in the case of multitudes, Christ died in vain."[128] However, God's Word reveals that Christ completed the work of redemption, and his sacrifice is effectual because of God's faithfulness to his covenant. He "once suffered for sins," and his cross bridges the gap to "bring us to God" (1 Pet. 3:18). Hence, salvation is by grace alone through Christ alone to the glory of God alone.

If we would receive Christ as the perfect and effectual sacrifice, then we must renounce all our own righteousness as unfit to save us or please God. Hooker wrote, "All that he looks for is mere poverty and emptiness. If thou hast nothing, then he will have thee with thy nothing; provided that thou wilt have him."[129]

As Christians, we can put the doctrine of particular redemption to practical use to attack the wickedness of our pride, for it is of sover-

---

125. Owen, *An Exposition of the Epistle to the Hebrews*, 2:129.
126. Hooker, *The Application of Redemption . . . The First Eight Books*, 12–13.
127. Roger R. Nicole, "Particular Redemption," in *Our Savior God: Man, Christ, and the Atonement*, ed. James M. Boice (Grand Rapids, MI: Baker, 1980), 168–69.
128. C. H. Spurgeon, *New Park Street Pulpit*, 6 vols. (Pasadena, TX: Pilgrim Publications, 1975), 4:70.
129. Thomas Hooker, *The Poor Doubting Christian Drawn to Christ* (Hartford: Robins and Smith, 1845), 28.

eign grace alone that Christ died for any individual. As Brakel said, we should ask ourselves, "Why is Jesus my Surety? Why does Jesus love me with an everlasting love, considering that so many millions go to hell?"[130]

William Perkins said, "The cause that moved Christ to give Himself is the will of God. Hence it appears that God gives Christ to no man for his foreseen faith or works. For there is no higher cause of the will of God." And Christ died that "so often as we remember the work of our redemption by Christ, so often must we give praise and thanks to God. Yea all our lives must be nothing else but a testimony of thankfulness for our redemption." This Godward life must engage "the serious affection of the heart," so that we may truly give our "amen" to the glory of God.[131] For the Father to give his only Son to be our Savior should provoke us to say, "What shall I render unto the LORD for all his benefits toward me?" (Ps. 116:12). Perkins said, "We should give unto God both body and soul in token of our thankfulness for this wonderful blessing that He has given His only Son to be our Savior."[132]

Sing to the Lord

Glorifying God for Perfect Redemption

> To God be the glory, great things he hath done!
> So loved he the world that he gave us his Son,
> Who yielded his life an atonement for sin,
> And opened the life-gate that we may go in.
>
> *Refrain*:
> Praise the Lord, praise the Lord,
> Let the earth hear his voice!
> Praise the Lord, praise the Lord,
> Let the people rejoice!
> O come to the Father, through Jesus the Son,
> And give him the glory—great things he hath done!
>
> O perfect redemption, the purchase of blood!
> To ev'ry believer the promise of God;

130. Brakel, *The Christian's Reasonable Service*, 1:617.
131. Perkins, *Commentary on Galatians*, on Gal. 1:5, in *Works*, 2:26.
132. Perkins, *An Exposition of the Symbol*, in *Works*, 5:115.

The vilest offender who truly believes,
That moment from Jesus forgiveness receives.

Great things he hath taught us, great things he hath done,
And great our rejoicing through Jesus the Son;
But purer, and higher, and greater will be
Our wonder, our transport, when Jesus we see.

Fanny J. Crosby, with alterations
Tune: To God Be the Glory (Doane)
Trinity Hymnal—Baptist Edition, No. 667

Questions for Meditation or Discussion

1. What four major approaches to the perfection of Christ's sacrifice do the authors list?

2. What gives the sacrifice of Christ its infinite value? Support your answer from Scripture.

3. What practical effect should the sufficiency of Christ's sacrifice have on us?

4. What did Christ mean when he said, "It is finished" (John 19:30)? How is this great declaration also revealed in the book of Hebrews?

5. What is the error of the Roman Catholic Church by which it denies the finality of Christ's sacrifice? How might evangelical Christians fall into similar errors?

6. How do the following factors show the efficacy of Christ's sacrifice?
   - the accomplishment of propitiation, redemption, and reconciliation
   - the promises of the new covenant, of which Christ is the Priest and Mediator (Heb. 10:14–17)
   - the expectation of those for whom God has already given his Son (Romans 8)

7. How can the efficacy of Christ's sacrifice strengthen the believer's hope and confidence?

8. In what senses is Christ's sacrifice universal, and in what senses not? How should that affect the church's practice of evangelism?

9. What are the objections often raised against the doctrine of particular redemption?

10. What are the arguments and evidences used to prove the doctrine of particular redemption?

11. After reading this chapter, which of the four approaches to Christ's sacrifice (see question 1) best describes your own belief? What are the decisive reasons why you hold that view?

Questions for Deeper Reflection

12. How might each of the four major approaches to Christ's sacrifice listed at the beginning of this chapter make use of the phrase "sufficient for all, effective for the elect"? How would you clarify or explain the phrase in its proper biblical sense?

13. How should we best interpret each of the Scripture passages that may indicate the final damnation of someone for whom Christ died (Rom. 14:15; 1 Cor. 8:11; Heb. 10:29; 2 Pet. 2:1)? Justify your answer by briefly exegeting each text in its context.

14. How would you critique the doctrine of hypothetically universal redemption held by some people in the Reformed tradition?

15. Sometimes the debate over the extent of Christ's redemption degenerates into Arminians quoting Scripture passages about "world" and "all" and Calvinists quoting Scripture passages about "sheep" and "church." How do Calvinists typically handle the "world" and "all" texts? How do Arminians typically handle the "sheep" and "church" texts? How do we discern what is the best way to interpret the *whole* witness of the Holy Scriptures?

52

Christ's Priestly Work, Part 5

Intercession for a Priestly People

The saving work of Jesus Christ did not end with the cross and the tomb. Christ rose from the dead as the triumphant Priest and is active even now in heaven. Though his sacrifice is the foundation of our salvation, his intercession is central to its application, for Christ ever lives as the Mediator of the new covenant, and all grace comes to us through him.

The doctrine of Christ's intercession is one of the most comforting and encouraging doctrines of the Christian faith. John Owen wrote, "The actual intercession of Christ in heaven . . . is a fundamental article of our faith, and a principal foundation of the church's consolation."[1] Robert Murray M'Cheyne (1813–1843) resolved, "I ought to study Christ as an Intercessor. . . . If I could hear Christ praying for me in the next room, I would not fear a million of enemies. Yet the distance makes no difference; He is praying for me."[2]

The Biblical Testimony to Christ's Intercession

God foreshadowed Christ's intercession through *the old covenant types*.[3] When Israel provoked God's wrath by making and worshiping

---

1. Owen, *An Exposition of the Epistle to the Hebrews*, 5:538.
2. Robert Murray M'Cheyne, "Reformation," in *Memoir and Remains of Robert Murray M'Cheyne*, ed. Andrew Bonar (1892; repr., Edinburgh: Banner of Truth, 1966), 154.
3. Clarkson, "Of Christ's Making Intercession," in *Works*, 3:144–45.

a golden calf, the people were delivered and restored to God's presence by Moses's prayers (Ex. 32:9–14, 30–32; 33:12–17). The Aaronic high priest carried the names of Israel's tribes on his shoulders and over his heart as he entered the holy places to represent Israel (28:6–21).[4] When the priest killed the sacrifice and offered it on the bronze altar outside the tabernacle, he then brought blood into the holy places to apply to the golden altar of incense (30:1–10; Lev. 4:7; 16:18–19)—a type of Christ's ascension and intercession (Heb. 9:6–12, 24–26). The ministry of the same priest with the same blood at two altars shows the inseparable unity of sacrifice and intercession in the one priestly office.[5] No one but the priest could burn the holy incense specially made for this altar— a sign of the uniqueness of priestly intercession.[6] The rising smoke of the incense served as a kind of shield to preserve sinners from death (Lev. 16:12–13; Num. 16:48). The Bible compares prayer to incense,[7] implying that the holy incense symbolized the priest's prayerful intercession to God.[8]

The interceding Christ was not only pictured in the Old Testament, but was also present. We get a glimpse of him interceding as *the angel of the Lord* in a prophetic vision: "Then the angel of the LORD answered and said, O LORD of hosts, how long wilt thou not have mercy on Jerusalem and on the cities of Judah?" (Zech. 1:12). Matthew Poole commented, "Christ speaks to his Father, speaks as one much affected with the state of his afflicted church."[9] In answer to the angel's petition, the Lord promises the restoration of the exiles (vv. 14, 16). In another vision, the angel of the Lord stands in God's presence, the accusations of Satan against God's people are thwarted, the uncleanness of their sins is not counted against them, and they are clothed in perfect righteousness (3:1–5).

God revealed the intercession of Christ in *the promise of the suffering Servant*. Isaiah designated intercession as one of the two parts of his atoning work: "He bore the sin of many, and makes intercession for the transgressors" (Isa. 53:12 ESV). His finished work of substitution

---

4. See the section on the Aaronic priesthood in chap. 48.
5. Martin, *The Atonement*, 117.
6. Ex. 30:34–38; Num. 16:1–40; 2 Chron. 26:16–21.
7. Ps. 141:2; Rev. 5:8; 8:3–4, cf. Luke 1:10.
8. Charnock, *A Discourse of Christ's Intercession*, in *Works*, 5:100.
9. Poole, *Annotations upon the Holy Bible*, 2:991, on Zech. 1:12. On the divine angel of the Lord as the preincarnate Christ, see chaps. 38 and 43, and *RST*, 1:273.

issued in his continuing work of intercession.[10] The Hebrew verb translated as "make intercession" (*hiphil* of *pagʻa*) has the sense of intervening on someone's behalf (59:16) or making an appeal (Jer. 36:25).[11] God's Servant "pleads before God the merit and virtue of his atoning work as the only ground of acceptance of the transgressors for whom he dies."[12]

Our Lord Jesus Christ interceded for his people in his *prayers during his state of humiliation*. The Gospels often tell us that Christ prayed.[13] His mediatorial intercession was particularly in focus when Jesus foretold that Satan would severely tempt Peter and said, "But I have prayed for thee, that thy faith fail not" (Luke 22:32). An entire chapter records Christ's magnificent intercession to his Father for his people (John 17).

After Christ's resurrection, ascension, and the commencement of his session at God's right hand, we read of his *intercession as the exalted High Priest*. John says that Christ is the sinning Christian's "advocate with the Father, Jesus Christ the righteous" (1 John 2:1). Paul says, "Who is he that condemneth? It is Christ that died, yea rather, that is risen again, who is even at the right hand of God, who also maketh intercession for us" (Rom. 8:34). We also read in the epistle to the Hebrews, "Wherefore he is able also to save them to the uttermost that come unto God by him, seeing he ever liveth to make intercession for them" (7:25). The Greek verb translated as "make intercession" (*entynchanō*) in these last two texts means to petition, make an appeal to authority, or pray to God.[14] Douglas Kelly observes that Christ's intercession at God's right hand "is not a continuation of the purging of our sins, but rather a consequence of this completed work."[15] It is written, "After making purification for sins, he sat down at the right hand of the Majesty on high" (Heb. 1:3 ESV; cf. 10:12). Herman

---

10. The past and present tenses of "bore" and "makes intercession" (Isa. 53:12 ESV) reflect the perfect and imperfect tenses of the two Hebrew verbs that they translate. See Peterson, *Salvation Accomplished by the Son*, 231.

11. In the *qal binyan*, the verb translated as "make intercession" (*pagʻa*) means to "meet" or "encounter," sometimes in making a request or prayer (Gen. 23:8; Ruth 1:16; Job 21:15; Jer. 7:16; 27:18).

12. Young, *The Book of Isaiah*, 3:359.

13. Matt. 11:25–26; 14:23; 15:36; 19:13; 26:27, 36–44; 27:46; Mark 1:35; 6:46; 8:6; 14:23, 32–39; 15:34; Luke 3:21; 5:16; 6:12; 9:18, 28–29; 10:21; 11:1; 22:17, 19, 32, 41–45; 23:34, 46; John 6:11, 23; 11:41–42; 12:28; 17:1–26.

14. Dan. 6:13(12) LXX; Acts 25:24; Rom. 8:27; 11:2. A related noun, *enteuxis*, means "prayer" (1 Tim. 2:1; 4:5).

15. Kelly, *Systematic Theology*, 2:517. See Owen, *An Exposition of the Epistle to the Hebrews*, 3:117.

Bavinck said, "In this intercession his sacrifice continues to be operative and effective."[16]

The Perfections of Christ's Heavenly Intercession

What is Christ's heavenly intercession? What does it do for his people? The Westminster Larger Catechism (Q. 55) says, "Christ maketh intercession, by appearing in our nature continually before the Father in heaven, in the merit of his obedience and sacrifice on earth, declaring his will to have it applied to all believers; answering all accusations against them, and procuring for them quiet of conscience, notwithstanding daily failings, access with boldness to the throne of grace, and acceptance of their persons and services."[17] The Holy Scriptures, especially the epistle to the Hebrews, reveal the following perfections of Christ's priestly intercession.

First, Christ's priestly intercession is *holy*. The Mediator has "holiness to the LORD" engraved, as it were, upon his very person (Ex. 28:36), for he is "without sin" (Heb. 4:15) and is "holy, harmless, undefiled, separate from sinners" (7:26). Consequently, the intercession of Christ glorifies God's holiness, for God wills to be honored by those who draw near to him (Lev. 10:3). The holiness of our Intercessor also invites our absolute confidence, for he intercedes with perfect love and purity of motive, unlike corrupt religious leaders on earth.

Second, Christ's priestly intercession is *heavenly*. "We have a great high priest, that is passed into the heavens, Jesus the Son of God" (Heb. 4:14), "set on the right hand of the throne of the Majesty in the heavens" (8:1). Owen commented, "Higher expression there cannot be used to lead us into a holy adoration of the tremendous invisible glory which is intended . . . a state of inconceivable power and glory."[18] William Gouge noted that this position at God's side reveals the High Priest's "divine dignity" as God the Son (1:2–3).[19]

Third, Christ's priestly intercession is *perpetual*. He ministers by "the power of an endless life," just as God the Father promised: "Thou art a priest for ever" (Heb. 7:16–17). The Aaronic priests had to be constantly replaced as each generation died (v. 23). In the same way, everyone on

---

16. Bavinck, *Reformed Dogmatics*, 3:478.
17. *Reformed Confessions*, 4:310.
18. Owen, *An Exposition of the Epistle to the Hebrews*, 6:10.
19. Gouge, *Commentary on Hebrews*, 1:18.

earth who has prayed for us eventually dies. However, Christ "holds his priesthood permanently, because he continues forever. . . . He always lives to make intercession" (vv. 24–25 ESV). Christ remains "the same yesterday, and to day, and for ever" (13:8).

Fourth, Christ's priestly intercession is *authoritative*. We must not imagine the heavenly Priest as prostrate before the Father, pleading for mercy for his people.[20] Our Lord Jesus intercedes as the covenantal officer appointed by God to this very work and exalted to sit at God's right hand (Heb. 5:4–6; 7:21; 8:1). He mediates to sinners the graces that God solemnly promised to give them in his covenant (8:6–12). Furthermore, he intercedes as one who has already accomplished redemption by his blood (9:12). Stephen Charnock said, "He is our advocate, because he was our propitiation [1 John 2:1–2]; the efficacy of his plea depends upon the value and purity of his sacrifice."[21] He is able to say, "Deliver him from going down to the pit: I have found a ransom" (Job 33:24). This "official and authoritative intercession" before God distinguishes Christ from all other intercessors, as Ezekiel Hopkins said, for Christians intercede for others as mere friends (Eph. 6:18; 1 Tim. 2:1).[22]

Fifth, Christ's priestly intercession is *legal*. It averts the condemnation of those charged with breaking the law and establishes their justification (Rom. 8:33–34). Our Surety had been "delivered for our offences" and now is "raised again for our justification" (Rom. 4:25), which manifests "that his death was a full satisfaction to divine justice, or else our sins should have kept him in the grave still," as Richard Sibbes said.[23] John writes, "If any man sin, we have an advocate with the Father, Jesus Christ the righteous" (1 John 2:1). The word translated as "advocate" (*paraklētos*) refers to a person called in to help in a legal case, perhaps not a lawyer but certainly a witness or representative in court.[24] Owen said, "He is gone into heaven . . . to make a legal appearance for our defence before the judgment-seat of God."[25] The Advocate's "righteous" life and "propitiation for our sins" obtain favor from the divine Judge (2:1–2).

---

20. Owen, *The Death of Death*, in *Works*, 10:177.

21. Charnock, *A Discourse of Christ's Intercession*, in *Works*, 5:102.

22. Ezekiel Hopkins, "The All-Sufficiency of Christ to Save Sinners with the Prevalency of His Intercession," in *The Works of Ezekiel Hopkins*, 3 vols. (Philadelphia: The Leighton Publications, 1874), 2:367.

23. Sibbes, *Christ's Exaltation Purchased by His Humiliation*, in *Works*, 5:329.

24. *TDNT*, 5:800–803. As to the same word *paraklētos* being used for the Holy Spirit (John 14:16, 26; 15:26; 16:7), Louis Berkhof said, "Christ pleads our cause with God, while the Holy Spirit pleads God's cause with us." *Systematic Theology*, 401.

25. Owen, *The Doctrine of the Saints' Perseverance*, in *Works*, 11:366.

Sixth, Christ's priestly intercession is *protective*. It defeats the saints' great "accuser," Satan, "who accuses them day and night before our God" (Rev. 12:10 ESV; cf. Zech. 3:1–5).[26] Louis Berkhof said, "Satan the accuser is ever bent on bringing charges against the elect; but Christ meets them all by pointing to His completed work."[27] The saints conquer the Devil by humble reliance on "the blood of the Lamb," who has been "caught up unto God, and to his throne" (Rev. 12:5, 11). Charnock said, "As he was a priest upon the cross to make an expiation for us, so he is our priest in the court of heaven, to plead this atonement, both before the tribunal of justice and the throne of mercy, against the curses of the law, the accusations of Satan, and indictments of sin, and to keep off the punishment which our guilt had merited."[28]

Seventh, Christ's priestly intercession is *personal*. He has entered heaven as the priestly "forerunner" of his people (Heb. 6:20). "By his own blood he entered in once into the holy place, having obtained eternal redemption for us" (9:12). He entered "into heaven itself, now to appear in the presence [literally, "to the face"] of God for us" (v. 24). Perkins said, "As on the cross He stood in our room, so in heaven He now appears as a public person in our stead, representing all the elect that shall believe in Him."[29] Christ is in heaven as the Lamb that was slain (Rev. 5:6), the Priest who made propitiation for sins in the very body in which he appears as our Advocate (1 John 2:1–2).[30] Owen explained, "The safest conception and apprehension that we can have of the intercession of Christ, as to the manner of it, is his continual appearance for us in the presence of God, by virtue of his office as the 'high priest over the house of God,' representing the efficacy of his oblation [offering], accompanied with tender care, love, and desires for the welfare, supply, deliverance, and salvation of the church."[31] We do not exclude prayer (verbal or mental) from Christ's intercession, for as we noted above, the very word translated as "make intercession" (*entynchanō*, Rom. 8:34; Heb. 7:25) means to pray or petition. However, he intercedes not merely by petitions but by the presence of his incarnate person before God.

---

26. The verb translated as "accuses" (*katēgorōn*) is in the present tense, implying a continuing action. On Satan's accusations against God's children, see *RST*, 1:1134, 1146, 1152.

27. Berkhof, *Systematic Theology*, 402–3.

28. Charnock, *A Discourse of Christ's Intercession*, in *Works*, 5:101.

29. Perkins, *An Exposition of the Symbol*, in *Works*, 5:274. See also William Bridge, *The Great Gospel Mystery of the Saints' Comfort and Holiness Opened and Applied from Christ's Priestly Office*, in *Works*, 1:25–28.

30. Owen, *An Exposition of the Epistle to the Hebrews*, 6:383–84.

31. Owen, *An Exposition of the Epistle to the Hebrews*, 5:541.

Eighth, Christ's priestly intercession is *effectual*.[32] Jesus warned Peter that Satan aimed to sift him "like wheat," a violent trial, but said, "I have prayed for you that your faith may not fail. And when you have turned again, strengthen your brothers" (Luke 22:31–32 ESV). Christ did not say "if" Peter would turn back to him, but "when" (*pote*). No one can condemn "God's elect" when Christ "is interceding for us," for "who shall separate us from the love of Christ?" (Rom. 8:33–35 ESV). "For if, when we were enemies, we were reconciled to God by the death of his Son, much more, being reconciled, we shall be saved by his life" (5:10). The writer to the Hebrews says, "He is able also to save them to the uttermost that come unto God by him, seeing he ever liveth to make intercession for them" (7:25). The phrase translated as "to the uttermost" (*eis to panteles*) could be rendered as "to the all-completion."[33] William Symington (1795–1862) said, "The intercession of Christ secures the complete salvation of the chosen of God, their entrance into heaven, and their everlasting continuance in a state of perfect blessedness."[34]

Ninth, Christ's priestly intercession is *particular*. The Aaronic high priest bore the names of the tribes of Israel into the sanctuary, not the names of all nations (Ex. 28:29). Just as Christ offered himself as a sacrifice for a particular people, so he intercedes for the blessings gained by his sacrifice to be applied to those people.[35] His intercession secures the salvation of "God's elect" (Rom. 8:33–34). Jesus said to the Father, "I pray not for the world, but for them which thou hast given me; for they are thine" (John 17:9; cf. 6:39). When Christ assured Peter that he had prayed for Peter's faith not to fail, Christ used singular pronouns to indicate he was praying for Peter in particular (Luke 22:32).[36] David Clarkson said, "Every [one] of them in particular is in his mind and heart while he is interceding. There is in heaven a special, personal regard of all that come unto God by him, as if their names were there recorded (Luke 10:20; Rev. 21:12). . . . Their names are written in the Lamb's book, that was slain, that was sacrificed, and he that was sacrificed is the same who intercedes (Rev. 13:8)."[37]

---

32. For more arguments for efficacy, see Charnock, *A Discourse of Christ's Intercession*, in *Works*, 5:116–27.

33. The term translated as "uttermost" (*panteles*) is part of a word group (*teleioō, teleiōsis, synteleia, teleiōtēn*, etc.) used for the perfection of Christ to save his people and bring them into the glory of the new creation, as opposed to the old ceremonies (Heb. 2:10; 5:9; 7:11, 19, 28; 9:9, 11, 26; 10:1, 14; 11:40; 12:2, 23).

34. Symington, *The Atonement and Intercession of Jesus Christ*, 282.

35. See chap. 51 on the particularity of Christ's sacrifice.

36. "I have prayed for thee [*sou*, singular], that thy [*sou*, singular] faith fail not" (Luke 22:32).

37. Clarkson, "Of Christ's Making Intercession," in *Works*, 3:162–63.

Tenth, Christ's priestly intercession is *comprehensive*. His intercession obtains for his people all the grace that they need for a complete salvation from beginning to end.[38] Christ makes intercession for the "transgressors" (*poshe'im*, Isa. 53:12), a term that denotes those presently unconverted (Ps. 51:13).[39] Regeneration is granted "through Jesus Christ our Saviour" (Titus 3:5–6). Christ looks upon the elect yet dead in their sins and intercedes for them before the Father, and the Spirit of the new birth goes forth to turn them from darkness to light.[40] Christ's prayer in John 17 shows the breadth of his intercession for the converted, for Christ asked the Father to grant his people spiritual preservation (vv. 11–16), sanctification (vv. 17–19), unity (vv. 20–23), and glorification (v. 24).[41] The merciful and faithful High Priest helps the tempted (Heb. 2:17–18), obtaining for them hatred of sin and love for holiness.[42] Justification is complete at the first moment of saving faith, but Christ's intercession preserves believers in a state of justification despite their culpable slips and falls, so that no one can condemn them before God (Rom. 8:33–34; 1 John 1:7–2:2).[43] Preservation from fully and finally falling away from God is granted through Christ's intercession (Luke 22:31–32; Heb. 7:25). Nothing can separate believers from the love of Christ, who intercedes for them (Rom. 8:34–35).[44] When Christ judges the world, he will confess their names before the Father (Rev. 3:5). Anthony Burgess said that "the matter of Christ's prayer for his children . . . is for the accomplishing of all grace here and glory hereafter. There is no heavenly or spiritual mercy but Christ hath prayed for it."[45]

Eleventh, Christ's priestly intercession is *compassionate*. He took "flesh and blood" like ours "that he might be a merciful and faithful high priest," and since "he himself hath suffered being tempted," he is able to help his tempted, suffering people (Heb. 2:14, 17–18). "For we have not an high priest which cannot be touched with the feeling of

---

38. Bunyan, *Christ a Complete Saviour: or, The Intercession of Christ, and Who Are Privileged in It*, in *Works*, 1:203–5.

39. See also "transgressors" (*poshe'im*) in Ps. 37:38; Isa. 1:28, 46:8; 48:8; 53:12 (twice); Hos. 14:9.

40. Owen, *Communion with God*, in *Works*, 2:198; *The Death of Death*, in *Works*, 10:236; and Symington, *The Atonement and Intercession of Jesus Christ*, 274.

41. Nichols, *Lectures in Systematic Theology*, 3:721.

42. Symington, *The Atonement and Intercession of Jesus Christ*, 279.

43. Perkins, *A Golden Chain*, chap. 18, in *Works*, 6:60.

44. Owen, *The Doctrine of the Saints' Perseverance*, in *Works*, 11:371.

45. Anthony Burgess, *CXLV Expository Sermons Upon the Whole 17th Chapter of The Gospel According to St. John: or Christs Prayer Before his Passion Explicated, and Both Practically and Polemically Improved* (London: Abraham Miller, 1656), Sermon 2 (9). See John 17:11, 15, 17, 20–21, 24.

our infirmities; but was in all points tempted like as we are, yet without sin" (4:15). Clarkson said, "He took our infirmities, and bare them; and so knows how heavy they are by his own feeling. . . . He knows what it is to be in pain. . . . He knows what it is to be despised and set at nought [treated as worthless], to be abused and reproached, to be hated, and persecuted, and despitefully [contemptuously] used. He knows the sorrows of life, and pangs of death."[46] Now, as he looks upon our sorrows and temptations, Christ "recalls how himself was once affected, and how distressed whilst on earth, under the same or the like miseries," Thomas Goodwin said.[47] He relates to his people as a friend (John 15:14–15), brother (Heb. 2:11–12), and Husband (2 Cor. 11:2); indeed, as a head to a body (Eph. 1:22–23).[48] John Murray said that through Christ's intercession, God relates to us with "nothing less than omnipotent compassion."[49]

Twelfth, Christ's priestly intercession is *unique*. While others may pray for us, Christ alone intercedes as the Mediator who gave himself as the ransom for our sins (1 Tim. 2:5–6).[50] This follows from all the perfections of his intercession: he alone presents intercession that arises from an absolutely holy life without sin, is authorized by God for a mediatorial office and presented at his right hand, and obtains effectual results. It is an error of Roman Catholicism to say, "Those who dwell in heaven . . . do not cease to intercede with the Father for us, as they proffer the merits which they acquired on earth through the one mediator between God and men, Christ Jesus."[51] Charles Hodge noted that multiplying mediators and intercessors "leads to practical idolatry," for they are regarded as always present, aware, and able to help those who pray to them.[52] But why would we desire other heavenly intercessors? As the Belgic Confession (Art. 26) says, "Whom could we find who loved us more than He who laid down His life for us, even when we were His enemies? And if we seek for one who hath power and majesty, who is there that hath so much of both as

---

46. Clarkson, "Christ Touched with the Feeling of Our Infirmities," in *Works*, 3:83–84.

47. Goodwin, *The Heart of Christ in Heaven unto Sinners on Earth*, in *Works*, 4:141–42. See Beeke and Jones, *A Puritan Theology*, 387–99; and Clarkson, "Christ Touched with the Feeling of Our Infirmities," in *Works*, 3:86.

48. Clarkson, "Christ Touched with the Feeling of Our Infirmities," in *Works*, 3:87.

49. Murray, "The Heavenly, Priestly Activity of Christ," in *Collected Writings*, 1:50.

50. See Calvin, *Institutes*, 3.20.20–27.

51. *Catechism of the Catholic Church*, sec. 956.

52. Hodge, *Systematic Theology*, 2:595.

He who sits at the right hand of His Father, and who hath all power in heaven and on earth?"[53]

The Objections to Christ's Intercession

It might be objected, first, that the doctrine of Christ's intercession is either superfluous or suggests a failing on God's part. Why does God the Father need to be reminded and petitioned to bless his people if Christ finished the work of redemption?

John Brown of Haddington said, "If God's justice be satisfied, and all blessings purchased by his sacrifice, what need is there of Christ's intercession? That he may procure the possession of these blessings to the elect in such a way as best secured the glory of God, his own honour, and our welfare."[54] Christ's intercession magnifies God's holiness and love, honors Christ by fostering our constant dependence on him, and grants us great boldness and security as believers.

We gain a deeper appreciation for Christ's intercession when we consider the Trinitarian economy of salvation and Christ's union with his people. Christ does not intercede in order to convince the Father to love believers, for the Father already loved them when he sent Christ to accomplish their redemption (John 3:16; 16:26–27). The Father then exalted the Son to glory to apply redemption to his body, the church (Eph. 1:19–23). When God seated his incarnate Son at his right hand, he also raised and seated all those in union with Christ (2:6; Col. 3:1). Murray said, "The active and abiding intercession of Christ is engaged with the permanency of the bond that unites the people of God to Christ in the efficacy of his death, in the power of his resurrection, and in the security of his exalted glory."[55] Since Christ's intercession especially consists of his personal presence before the face of God, his intercession saves because God accepts and approves him as the representative of his people.

Second, it might be objected that the intercession of Christ cannot be effectual, because on the cross Christ prayed, "Father, forgive them" (Luke 23:34), but some of them perished.

In reply, we observe that Christ said in his prayer, "for they know not what they do" (Luke 23:34). Either those words limited the scope

---

53. *The Three Forms of Unity*, 44–45.
54. Brown, *Questions and Answers on the Shorter Catechism*, 116.
55. Murray, "The Heavenly, Priestly Activity of Christ," in *Collected Writings*, 1:55.

of his prayer to some people, such as the Gentile soldiers who crucified him (vv. 33–34), or they referred to his enemies in general.[56] If the
scope of the prayer was limited, then the Gospels suggest that it was
heard and answered, beginning with the centurion (Mark 15:39; Luke
23:40–43, 47). On the other hand, if his prayer was general, then we
observe that there is a distinction between Christ's official intercession
for his people and his prayers in general during his state of humiliation,
in which he expressed his human desires in submission to the Father's
will (Matt. 26:39). As a man under God's law of love, Christ was required to pray for his enemies (5:44), though not all of them were saved
(Mark 14:21). Such prayers are distinct from his effectual intercession
for God's elect.[57]

The efficacy of Christ's official intercession is established on strong
exegetical and theological grounds. Christ "is able to save to the uttermost
those who draw near to God through him" (Heb. 7:25 ESV). He is God's
appointed Priest doing God's will (v. 21) and the Surety who has fulfilled
the legal obligations of his people and now asks that God do what he
bound himself to perform in his covenant (v. 22).[58] Christ intercedes perpetually for each of his people (vv. 23–25) and in perfect holiness (v. 26),
so that God is always completely pleased to bless those whom Christ represents. He already has offered himself as the sacrifice for their sins once
for all (v. 27) and now intercedes with the authority of one already exalted
to the right hand of God (vv. 28–8:1). Therefore, God the Father hears his
intercession, and Christ saves his people without fail.

Third, it might be objected that according to this doctrine, Christ's
priestly intercession supplants his offices as Prophet and King, making
them redundant.

In reply, we assert the centrality of Christ's priesthood in the unity
of his work—what Murray called "an inter-permeation of the various
offices."[59] Just as Christ's sacrifice accomplished our entire redemption, so
his intercession obtains every grace needed to apply our redemption. What
Christ applies as Prophet and King, he first receives as interceding Priest.

The Aaronic priesthood foreshadowed the grounding of the prophetic
and kingly offices in the priesthood. Just as the high priest bore the reve-

---

56. See Acts 3:17; 13:27; 17:30; Rom. 10:3; 1 Cor. 2:8.
57. Manton, *Sermons upon John XVII*, in *Works*, 10:242.
58. Flavel, *The Fountain of Life*, in *Works*, 1:171.
59. Murray, "The Heavenly, Priestly Activity of Christ," in *Collected Writings*, 1:47.

latory Urim and the Thummim over his heart as he interceded for God's people,[60] so Christ's priestly work secures for us his prophetic ministry to reveal God's secret will. A priest was a teacher of God's Word.[61] The high priest wore a "crown" (*nezer*), a term also used of kings' crowns.[62] The priests and Levites exercised regal and military functions in ruling and guarding God's holy things.[63] Consequently, when Jesus Christ came in the flesh, his prophetic and kingly work flowed out of his priestly redemption, and his greatest accomplishments of revelation and conquest took place on the cross. William Bridge said, "Whatever comfort we have in the other offices of Christ, namely his kingly and his prophetical offices, it is all originated and principiated [founded] in this: the priestly office of Jesus Christ, it does give a life, and being, and efficacy to those other offices."[64]

The Blessing of Christ's Intercession

One of the great functions of a priest was to pronounce God's blessing, or benediction, upon his people. Melchizedek, "the priest of the most high God," blessed Abraham, the covenantal father of all the faithful (Gen. 14:18–20), and did so as a type of Christ (Ps. 110:4; Heb. 7:1, 6–7) The Lord chose the Aaronic priests to bless Israel in his name (Deut. 10:8; 21:5), saying, "The LORD bless thee, and keep thee: the LORD make his face shine upon thee, and be gracious unto thee: the LORD lift up his countenance upon thee, and give thee peace" (Num. 6:22–26). The core elements of this priestly blessing, "grace" and "peace," now flow from the Father and the Son to his people, as the greetings in the New Testament Epistles abundantly affirm.[65]

Some theologians have considered blessing to be a distinct third function of priests after sacrifice and intercession.[66] Aaron blessed the people after making sacrifices and again after going into the tabernacle to intercede (Lev. 9:22–23). Other theologians have seen the priestly blessing to be

60. Ex. 28:30; 1 Sam. 28:6; Ezra 2:63; Neh. 7:65.
61. Lev. 10:11; Deut. 17:9–11; 33:10; Mal. 2:6–7.
62. Ex. 29:6; 39:30; Lev. 8:9; 2 Sam. 1:10; 2 Kings 11:12; 2 Chron. 23:11; Pss. 89:39; 132:18; cf. Thomas Godwyn (or Goodwin), *Moses and Aaron: Civil and Ecclesiastical Rites Used by the Ancient Hebrews*, 12th ed. (London: for R. Scot et al., 1685), 16. This author (1587–1642) is not to be confused with the Puritan Thomas Goodwin.
63. See Belcher, *Prophet, Priest, and King*, 90–94.
64. Bridge, *The Great Gospel Mystery*, in *Works*, 1:5.
65. Rom. 1:7; 1 Cor. 1:3; 2 Cor. 1:2; Gal. 1:3; Eph. 1:2; Phil. 1:2; Col. 1:2; 1 Thess. 1:1; 2 Thess. 1:2; 1 Tim. 1:2; 2 Tim. 1:2; Titus 1:4; Philem. 3; 1 Pet. 1:2; 2 Pet. 1:2; 2 John 3; Rev. 1:4.
66. Witsius, *Sacred Dissertations on the Apostles' Creed*, 10.22 (1:269); and Gill, *Body of Divinity*, 430, 435–38.

an aspect of intercession.[67] The blessing was a prayer that invoked God's name upon his covenant people so that God would bless them (Num. 6:27). "The priests the Levites arose and blessed the people: and their voice was heard, and their prayer came up to his holy dwelling place, even unto heaven" (2 Chron. 30:27).

What is clear is that Christ blesses his people as their Priest. Just before Christ ascended into heaven, "he lifted up his hands, and blessed" his disciples (Luke 24:50–51), just as formerly "Aaron lifted up his hand toward the people, and blessed them" (Lev. 9:22). Peter, citing God's promise to bless all nations by Abraham's seed, says, "God, having raised up his Son Jesus, sent him to bless you, in turning away every one of you from his iniquities" (Acts 3:25–26).

God's blessing through Christ is covenantal.[68] Sinners are under God's curse for breaking the commandments of his law (Gal. 3:10). In his redeeming sacrifice, Christ received the curse of God's law, absorbing its full fury in his sufferings while perfectly obeying the law, so that his believing people are delivered from the curse (v. 13; 4:4). They receive the blessing promised in the covenant with Abraham "through Jesus Christ" by faith (3:14).

God's curse against lawbreakers hangs over all the good things that they receive in this world (Deut. 28:15–19), mingles sorrow into all good (Gen. 3:17–19), and one day will take all good away from unrepentant sinners (Luke 6:24–25; 16:24–25). However, Christians may pray to their Father for their "daily bread" (Matt. 6:11), "that of God's free gift we may receive a competent portion of the good things of this life, and enjoy his blessing with them."[69] The ability of believers to enjoy earthly goods with God's blessing presupposes that he is pleased with them (Eccl. 9:7–9). Therefore, the goodness of all God's providences toward his elect comes to them through Christ's intercession (Rom. 8:28, 34). Paul says, "My God shall supply all your need according to his riches in glory by [or "in"] Christ Jesus" (Phil. 4:19).[70]

---

67. Brakel, *The Christian's Reasonable Service*, 1:539. See the twofold analysis of the priestly function as sacrifice and intercession in the Westminster Shorter Catechism (Q. 25), in *Reformed Confessions*, 4:356.

68. Gen. 9:1, 9; 12:2–3; 17:2, 16; 18:18; 22:17–18; 24:1; 26:3–4, 24; 27:26–29; 28:3–4, 14; 35:9–12; 48:3–4, 16; Deut. 11:26–29; 27:1–28:68; 30:19; 33:1; Josh. 8:33–34; 2 Sam. 7:29; 1 Kings 2:45; Pss. 21:1–6; 72:17; Prov. 3:33.

69. Westminster Shorter Catechism (Q. 104), in *Reformed Confessions*, 4:368.

70. Benjamin Beddome, *A Scriptural Exposition of the Baptist Catechism, by Way of Question and Answer* (Richmond, VA: Harrold & Murray, 1849), 261, on the Shorter Catechism question cited above.

The core of God's blessing is justification and the grace of the Holy Spirit (Gal. 3:8, 14).[71] Owen observed that the work of the Spirit is the "purchased grace" that Christ won by his obedience and sufferings.[72] Christ obtains the Spirit for his people by his intercession: "I will pray the Father, and he shall give you another Comforter, that he may abide with you for ever" (John 14:16). The fullness of the Spirit's new-covenant ministry depends on the glorification of the Son (7:39). Christ himself sends us the Spirit from the Father's side (16:7).

By these spiritual graces, the reality and efficacy of Christ's invisible intercession in heaven is demonstrated on earth, for we have received the Holy Spirit and know the fruit of Christ's intercession in our lives, as Perkins said.[73] The best evidence that Christ prays for us in heaven is the Spirit's work to make us pray on earth.[74]

The exaltation of our great High Priest signals the fulfillment of the covenant of grace and the inauguration of the last days (Heb. 1:2–3; 9:26). Murray said, "Jesus as high priest is the surety and mediator of the new and better covenant. . . . The new covenant brings to its consummation the communion which is at the heart of all covenant disclosure from Abraham onwards: 'I will be your God, and ye shall be my people.' . . . The heavenly high priesthood of Christ, means, therefore, that Christ appears in the presence of God . . . to plead on the basis of what he has accomplished the fulfilment of all the promises."[75] Therefore, Christ's intercession unlocks all grace and glory for his people. In union with Christ, they are blessed by the Father with "all spiritual blessings" (Eph. 1:3).

The Applications of Christ's Intercession

The intercession of our Lord Jesus is a boundless field full of flowers from which we may draw sweet nectar for our souls. Let us consider some of the riches of knowing our Intercessor by God's grace.

First, we must allow this doctrine to form in us *constant reliance on the exalted Christ.* We must run the race set before us, "looking unto Jesus" (Heb. 12:2; cf. Col. 3:1). Brown said that Christ's intercession glorifies

---

71. On the Holy Spirit as the sum of blessings purchased by Christ, see Bridge, *The Great Gospel Mystery*, in *Works*, 1:69–70; and Edwards, *An Humble Attempt*, in *WJE*, 5:341.
72. Owen, *Communion with God*, in *Works*, 2:168.
73. Perkins, *Commentary on Galatians*, on Gal. 4:6, in *Works*, 2:258, 262.
74. Perkins, *An Exposition of the Symbol*, in *Works*, 5:277.
75. Murray, "The Heavenly, Priestly Activity of Christ," in *Collected Writings*, 1:47–48.

him, for "in this way believers have an immediate dependence on Christ for ever."[76] Let us look to him for every grace.

Second, Christians may find here *strong consolation and hope.* Christ's entrance into heaven as our forerunner confirms the unbreakable promise of God that he will bless his people (Heb. 6:17–20). If Christ's death reconciled us to God when we were his enemies, much more will his living ministry deliver us from the wrath of God (Rom. 5:10). We can exult in hope.

Third, believers should look to Christ's intercession for *confidence in our justification.* Christ was raised for our justification and intercedes to deliver us from condemnation (Rom. 4:25; 8:33–34). His appearing before the face of God confirms that his blood sacrifice has expiated the guilt of our sins once for all (Heb. 9:24). We should assure our consciences with this doctrine.

Fourth, knowing Christ as the Intercessor can encourage *quickness to confess sin to God.* Rather than remaining silent when God convicts us of sin (Ps. 32:3–5), let us immediately confess our sins with faith in Christ's propitiation and intercession, for God "is faithful and just to forgive us our sins, and to cleanse us from all unrighteousness" (1 John 1:9, 2:1–2).

Fifth, the doctrine of Christ's intercession increases *expectation and comfort in prayer.* What is more comforting in trials than to go to a friend who knows how we feel and how to help us? Christ sympathizes with us perfectly. "Let us therefore come boldly unto the throne of grace, that we may obtain mercy, and find grace to help in time of need" (Heb. 4:15–16).

Sixth, given that all spiritual blessings come to us through Christ's intercession, we should learn to exercise *trust in Christ for the grace of the Holy Spirit.* Let us never separate the Spirit from Jesus Christ, for he is the Spirit of God's Son (Gal. 4:6). Whether we need the Spirit's power to mortify sin (Rom. 8:13), his fruit for works of love and self-control (Gal. 5:22–23), or his gifts to serve the church effectively (1 Cor. 12:7, 11), let us drink of his living water by exercising faith in the exalted Christ (John 7:37–39). Believers overcome trials, even unto martyrdom, by "the supply of the Spirit of Jesus Christ" (Phil. 1:19). Owen said, "The great duty of tempted souls, is to cry out unto the Lord Christ for help and relief."[77]

Seventh, the more God's children meditate upon Christ's intercession, the more they will increase in *assurance of ultimate salvation and blessed-*

---

76. Brown, *Questions and Answers on the Shorter Catechism,* 116.
77. Owen, *An Exposition of the Epistle to the Hebrews,* 3:486.

ness. We will be purged of legalistic perfectionism and rest in his perfection. We will learn to recognize all our good desires and good works as fruit of his priestly work. Then we will be able to rejoice and exult, for our Intercessor is able to save us completely (Heb. 7:25). As long as this Intercessor stretches out his hands of blessing, we may be sure that the true Israel will prevail over its enemies (Ex. 17:8–13).

Christ's Priestly People

In union with their living High Priest, Christians are also an anointed priesthood. They cannot and need not repeat his work of redemption, but they share many priestly privileges by union with the Redeemer. Martin Luther said that the Christian has a "royal marriage" with Christ as the heavenly Bridegroom, so that the believer may say, "All his is mine and all mine is his."[78] As we noted in our study of Christ's prophetic work,[79] each believer may confess with the Heidelberg Catechism (LD 12, Q. 32) that he is "called a Christian" because he shares in Christ's anointing. Thus, he may present himself "a living sacrifice of thankfulness to Him."[80]

This sharing in our High Priest's anointing confers *the priesthood of believers in Christ*. Isaiah says, "Ye shall be named the Priests of the LORD" because he has clothed you "with the robe of righteousness" (Isa. 61:6, 10). Paul says that Christ made reconciliation and peace by his blood, so that "through him we both [believing Jews and Gentiles] have access by one Spirit unto the Father" (Eph. 2:18). Peter says, "Ye also, as lively stones, are built up a spiritual house, an holy priesthood, to offer up spiritual sacrifices, acceptable to God by Jesus Christ" (1 Pet. 2:5; cf. v. 9). This is possible because Christ saved us from our sins by his blood, redeeming a people from all nations to be "priests unto God" (Rev. 1:5–6; 5:9–10). Calvin said, "Christ plays the priestly role, not only to render the Father favorable and propitious toward us by an eternal law of reconciliation, but also to receive us as his companions in this great office."[81]

Our priesthood encourages *the simplicity and spirituality of worship in Christ*. The church of Jesus Christ is "the temple of God" (1 Cor. 3:16; cf. 2 Cor. 6:16). Physical holy places are abolished in the new covenant

---

78. Luther, *The Freedom of a Christian*, in *LW*, 31:352.
79. See the section on Christ's prophetic people in chap. 47.
80. *The Three Forms of Unity*, 78.
81. Calvin, *Institutes*, 2.15.6. See Bavinck, *Reformed Dogmatics*, 3:479.

and replaced by worship "in spirit and in truth" (John 4:19–24).[82] It is misguided to re-create the obsolete system of sacred buildings, garments, and rituals of the old covenant (Heb. 8:13). Robert Godfrey explains the classic Reformed principle: "Simplicity meant the removal of physical symbolism and ceremonies not instituted in the Bible. Simplicity is closely linked to spirituality. In the simplicity of the Spirit's power, Christ is present among his people in the preaching and sacrament. . . . Worship draws the Christian into heaven in communion with the ascended Christ. . . . A visually elaborate context would interfere with our spiritual ascent, binding our minds too much to earth."[83]

The priesthood of believers includes *the access of the saints to God's holy presence.* Hebrews 10:19–22 says, "Having therefore, brethren, boldness to enter into the holiest by the blood of Jesus, by a new and living way, which he hath consecrated for us, through the veil, that is to say, his flesh; and having an high priest over the house of God; let us draw near." God's priestly people have access to God's heavenly presence through Jesus Christ, whose blood cleanses us from guilt and whose living intercession as our High Priest secures our welcome. Kelly notes that the incarnate Son of God is the perfect worshiper, and "God accepts all true worshipers as His crucified, risen Son now represents them in the heavenly sanctuary."[84] We may come with boldness in Christ, for, as Luther wrote, "as priests we are worthy to appear before God. . . . Therefore we may boldly come into the presence of God in the spirit of faith and cry 'Abba, Father!'"[85] Hebrews 10:22 continues, "Let us draw near with a true heart in full assurance of faith, having our hearts sprinkled from an evil conscience, and our bodies washed with pure water." We must have "a true heart," a heart made faithful to God by his covenantal grace (v. 16). The priests were washed with water,[86] a type of regeneration by the Holy Spirit through the Word, symbolized in baptism.[87] We must also have "full assurance of faith," not necessarily full assurance of our own salvation, but confident trust in

---

82. Although Christians often refer to the room where they worship as a "sanctuary," which means "holy place," the new covenant temple is the people of God and not a building (Eph. 2:20–22; 1 Pet. 2:5).

83. W. Robert Godfrey, "Calvin and the Worship of God," in Terry L. Johnson et al., *The Worship of God: Reformed Concepts of Biblical Worship* (Fearn, Ross-shire, Scotland: Christian Focus, 2005), 40–41.

84. Kelly, *Systematic Theology*, 2:337.

85. Luther, *The Freedom of a Christian*, in *LW*, 31:355.

86. See Ex. 29:4; 30:18–21; 40:7, 12, 30–32.

87. Ezek. 36:25–27; 1 Cor. 6:9–11; Eph. 5:25–26; Titus 3:5; 1 Pet. 1:22–23; cf. Acts 22:16.

the blood of Christ that cleanses the conscience from guilt (v. 17) so that the believer can "serve the living God" (9:14). The sons of Aaron were "sprinkled" with sacrificial blood to consecrate them for priestly service.[88] Thomas Manton summarized, "Now, then, if we come aright, we must come with a true heart, and in full assurance of faith (Heb. 10:22). With an assurance of faith, that God will be as good as his word, pardoning, sanctifying, blessing, and that he will keep us to everlasting glory; and with a true heart bind ourselves to a return to our duty, depending on the Redeemer's sacrifice, and to walk in all new obedience."[89]

As priests in God's presence, we may enjoy *the satisfaction of communion with God*. People often seek satisfaction through the sensory experiences of external religion, but "it is good for the heart to be strengthened by grace, not by foods, which have not benefited those devoted to them. We have an altar from which those who serve the tent have no right to eat" (Heb. 13:9–10 ESV). The Aaronic priests ate portions of the sacrifices offered to God, a kind of shared meal in fellowship with the Lord.[90] Christ is "the bread of life" on whom we feed by faith to the satisfaction of our deepest needs and desires (John 6:35). The sacrifice of his "flesh" and "blood" nourishes our souls, not by a bodily eating but in spiritual communion with his living person (vv. 54–56). This eating and drinking, outwardly represented in the elements of the Lord's Supper (1 Cor. 10:16–18), takes place through faith as the glorified Christ pours out upon his people the living waters of the Holy Spirit to satisfy them forever (John 4:14; 7:37–39). What joys believers may partake of in their communion with God each Lord's Day and every day!

Christ makes priestly worship and communion possible by *the pleasure of God in the redeemed*. Though the Lord knows our sins (Rev. 2–3), there is a great difference between those in a state of sin who "cannot please God" and those in Christ who have his Spirit (Rom. 8:8–9). People who live by faith please God (Heb. 11:5–6), and that by their good works.[91] This is not legalism or merit, but the result of God's grace, by which he is "working in you that which is wellpleasing in his sight, through Jesus Christ; to whom be glory for ever and ever" (13:21). We offer our good works to God through Christ's mediation (vv. 15–16), so that "the defect

---

88. Ex. 29:21; Lev. 8:30; cf. Isa. 52:15; Heb. 9:19; 11:28; 12:24; 1 Pet. 1:2.
89. Manton, "A Sermon on the Ends of the Sacrament," in *Works*, 15:494.
90. Lev. 2:3, 10; 6:14, 18, 26, 29–30; 7:6–10, 14–15, 19–21, 31–36.
91. Eph. 5:10; Phil. 4:18; Col. 3:20; 1 Thess. 4:1; 1 John 3:22; cf. Matt. 25:21.

of our works is covered" and God will "embrace them in Christ."[92] Christ's intercession is like a mother who takes the flowers that her children gathered for their father, picks out the ugly weeds, and mingles flowers of her own to make a beautiful bouquet for the father's pleasure.[93]

The priesthood of believers as God's pleasing children undergirds *the freedom of Christian prayer.* God answers the prayers of his priests (Ps. 99:6). Christ's exaltation as the High Priest paves the way for our welcome by the Father: "We have a great high priest, that is passed into the heavens, Jesus the Son of God. . . . Let us therefore come boldly unto the throne of grace, that we may obtain mercy, and find grace to help in time of need" (Heb. 4:14–16). God's "throne" symbolizes his supreme power, authority, righteousness, and justice by which he reigns over all things,[94] but for those in union with the Son of God, it is "the throne of grace." Therefore, we may pray with "boldness," which Owen explained as "our spiritual liberty and freedom, attended with holy confidence, in our access unto God, to make our requests known unto him, expressing our condition, our wants, our desires."[95]

Furthermore, God's priests are called to engage in *the offering of spiritual sacrifices.* Believers are a "holy priesthood, to offer up spiritual sacrifices, acceptable to God by Jesus Christ" (1 Pet. 2:5). The word translated as "acceptable" (*euprosdektos*) means more than tolerable or meeting minimal standards; it means "pleasing."[96] The wonder of the priesthood of believers is that all our lives can be a sacrifice pleasing to God if lived with faith and love. The Christian longs to offer all he has to God in response to his mercies. Christians offer:

- *The sacrifice of repentance*: "The sacrifices of God are a broken spirit: a broken and a contrite heart, O God, thou wilt not despise" (Ps. 51:17).
- *The sacrifice of self*: "Present your bodies a living sacrifice, holy, acceptable unto God, which is your reasonable service. And be not conformed to this world: but be ye transformed by the renewing of

---

92. Perkins, *An Exposition of the Symbol,* in *Works,* 5:277; and Calvin, *Institutes,* 3.17.5.

93. Isaac Ambrose, *Media: The Middle Things . . . The Means, Duties, Ordinances, Both Secret, Private, and Publick; For Continuance, and Increase of a Godly Life* (Glasgow: Archibald Ingram et al., 1737), 12.

94. Pss. 93:1–2; 97:1–2; 103:19.

95. Owen, *An Exposition of the Epistle to the Hebrews,* 4:430.

96. Cf. Balz and Schneider, eds., *Exegetical Dictionary of the New Testament,* 2:82; and Johannes P. Louw and Eugene Albert Nida, *Greek-English Lexicon of the New Testament: Based on Semantic Domains* (New York: United Bible Societies, 1996), 25.86 (298).

your mind, that ye may prove what is that good, and acceptable, and perfect, will of God" (Rom. 12:1–2).

- *The sacrifice of praise*: "By him therefore let us offer the sacrifice of praise to God continually, that is, the fruit of our lips giving thanks to his name" (Heb. 13:15).
- *The sacrifice of care and companionship*: "To do good and to communicate forget not: for with such sacrifices God is well pleased" (Heb. 13:16).[97]
- *The sacrifice of missions*: Paul was "a minister of Christ Jesus to the Gentiles in the priestly service of the gospel of God, so that the offering of the Gentiles may be acceptable, sanctified by the Holy Spirit" (Rom. 15:16 ESV). Financial support for his mission was "a sacrifice acceptable, wellpleasing to God" (Phil. 4:18).
- *The sacrifice of martyrdom*: "For I am already being poured out as a drink offering, and the time of my departure has come" (2 Tim. 4:6 ESV).

The calling to offer spiritual sacrifices requires following Jesus in *the pattern of the cruciform life*. The cross must mark us with the sorrows of persecution (Gal. 6:17). The remains of the sacrifices were burned outside the camp, and Christ suffered outside the city as one rejected by men. Thus, we must follow Christ, "bearing his reproach, . . . for here we have no continuing city, but we seek one to come" (Heb. 13:10–14). The gospel of Christ crucified provokes hostility because it overthrows human systems of righteousness (Gal. 6:12, 14–15). The cross must also mark us with the sacrifices of love. Paul says, "Walk in love, as Christ also hath loved us, and hath given himself for us an offering and a sacrifice to God" (Eph. 5:2). Though we cannot offer sacrifices for sin, love still requires our sweat, tears, and perhaps blood.

As God's holy priests offer up costly sacrifices to him, they can do so joyfully because of *the priority of the divine inheritance*. Christians are pilgrims; they do not count this world their home, but live by faith in "the promise of eternal inheritance" that Christ obtained by redeeming them (Heb. 9:15; 11:13–16). Wilhelmus à Brakel wrote, "The priests

---

97. The word translated as "to communicate" (*koinōnia*) or "fellowship" in Heb. 13:16 can refer to practical, financial help (2 Cor. 8:4; 9:13), but also suggests friendship, such as when we become "companions" (*koinōnoi*) with the suffering to support them (Heb. 10:33). John Calvin said, "It embraces all the duties by which men can mutually assist one another; and it is a true mark or proof of love." Calvin, *Commentaries*, on Heb. 13:16.

had no inheritance in Canaan, but God was their portion. They [believers] must likewise also turn away from all that is of the earth, leaving this for the men of the world, and look not at the things which are seen (2 Cor. 4:18), but rather delight themselves in the Lord who is their portion (Lam. 3:24)."[98] Heaven would be no heaven if God were not there. Believers' glory, inheritance, and happiness will be the enjoyment of God.[99] This is one reason why God's priests relish public worship on earth—the church militant already participates in "the heavenly Jerusalem," joining with "an innumerable company of angels" and "the spirits of just men made perfect" to worship "the living God" through "Jesus the mediator of the new covenant" (Heb. 12:22–24). What an amazing privilege it is to be God's priestly people with Jesus Christ as our heavenly Priest!

Sing to the Lord

Praising the Living Savior at God's Right Hand

O the deep, deep love of Jesus!
Vast, unmeasured, boundless, free;
Rolling as a mighty ocean
In its fullness over me.
Underneath me, all around me,
Is the current of thy love;
Leading onward, leading homeward,
To thy glorious rest above.

O the deep, deep love of Jesus!
Spread his praise from shore to shore;
How he loveth, ever loveth,
Changeth never, nevermore;
How he watches o'er his loved ones,
Died to call them all his own;
How for them he intercedeth,
Watcheth o'er them from the throne.

O the deep, deep love of Jesus!
Love of ev'ry love the best:

98. Brakel, *The Christian's Reasonable Service*, 1:559. On the inheritance of the Aaronic priests, see Num. 18:20; Deut. 10:9; 12:12; 14:27; 18:1–2; Josh. 13:33; 14:3; 18:7.
99. Flavel, *The Fountain of Life*, in *Works*, 1:189–90.

'Tis an ocean vast of blessing,
'Tis a haven sweet of rest.
O the deep, deep love of Jesus!
'Tis a heav'n of heav'ns to me;
And it lifts me up to glory,
For it lifts me up to thee.

Samuel Trevor Francis
Tune: Ebenezer
Trinity Hymnal—Baptist Edition, No. 453
Or Tune: Bunessan ("Morning Has Broken")

Questions for Meditation or Discussion

1. How does the Old Testament reveal Christ's intercessory ministry?
2. What texts of Scripture explicitly say that Christ "intercedes" for people? According to these texts, what is the intercession of Christ?
3. What are the twelve perfections of Christ's intercession? Give a brief explanation and proof of each.
4. Which of the perfections of Christ's intercession are most comforting to you? Why?
5. What objections are raised to Christ's intercession? How can these be answered?
6. What is the relationship between Christ blessing his people and the Holy Spirit?
7. Based upon the authors' discussion of the applications of Christ's intercession, how might a Christian be affected if he loses sight of Christ's present priestly ministry?
8. What is the doctrine of the priesthood of believers? How can Christians offer spiritual sacrifices to God through Christ?

Questions for Deeper Reflection

9. If Christ's sacrifice made atonement for sins once and for all, then why does Christ continue to intercede with the Father in heaven? Explain how your answer is consistent with God's omniscience, love, and righteousness, and the unity of the Trinity.
10. Consider the Roman Catholic doctrine that the angels and saints in heaven intercede for and mediate grace to Christians on earth. What implications would that have for theology? Faith? Worship?

11. What are the advantages of considering Christ's priestly work of blessing as distinct from intercession? What are the advantages of considering it an aspect of intercession?

12. How might the doctrine of the priesthood of all believers be abused to the harm of Christians and churches? What would Christianity lose if this doctrine were neglected or denied?

53

Christ's Kingly Work, Part 1

Introduction, Victory, and Triumph

Even in modern societies where kings are merely figures of ceremony or legend, many people still have a fascination with royalty. The opulence of royal weddings attracts numerous viewers. People love stories of kings, warriors, and heroes with unusual powers, whether those of ancient mythology, medieval folklore, or modern popular entertainment media. Though such stories often reflect an unbiblical worldview, they show mankind's hunger for a mighty leader who will deliver people from evil and inaugurate an age of peace and prosperity.

Compared to legendary figures of power, wealth, and beauty, Jesus Christ seems like a strange candidate for kingship. He himself acknowledged, "My kingdom is not of this world" (John 18:36). His title "King of the Jews" was not displayed on a throne or battle chariot, but on a bloody cross where he died (19:19–22). Even now, long after Christ was raised from the dead and seated at the right hand of God, no one on earth can see his heavenly majesty (Col. 3:1–3). Hence, there is a mystery about the kingdom of Christ that can be penetrated only by faith.

However, Christ is indeed the King. He is more worthy of that title than any other man who will ever exist. He was King with his ancient people before his incarnation and has been the King of his people since becoming a man.[1] He is "King of kings and Lord of lords" (Rev. 19:16), and his kingdom is the joy and treasure of his people (Matt. 13:44).

Introduction to Christ's Kingly Office

The Gospel of Matthew summarizes the content of Christ's preaching in a single sentence: "Repent: for the kingdom of heaven is at hand" (Matt. 4:17; cf. Mark 1:15). The "kingdom of heaven" or "kingdom of God" (the terms are synonymous[2]) represents a central theme of Christianity. What does it mean? In what sense is Christ a king?

The Kingdom of God

The Bible is full of accounts of kings.[3] A "king" (Hebrew *melek*, Greek *basileus*) could rule over a domain as small as a city (Gen. 14:1–2; Ezek. 28:12) or as large as an empire encompassing many nations (Est. 1:2; 1 Pet. 2:13–14). The term did not designate the size of his dominion, only the fact that he reigned over his people (1 Sam. 8:11). The Lord is often described as the "King" in the Bible, especially in the Psalms.[4] He is said to "reign" (Hebrew *malak*, Greek *basileuō*)[5] and to "rule" or "have dominion" (Hebrew *mashal*).[6] He has a "kingdom" (Hebrew *malkut* or *mamlakah*; Aramaic *malku*; Greek *basileia*)[7] and a "dominion" (Hebrew *memshalah*).[8]

---

1. Ex. 23:20–22; Josh. 5:14–15; Judg. 2:1–5; 2 Kings 19:34–35; Matt. 2:2; 16:18–19; 21:5; 25:31, 34; Mark 14:61–62; Luke 1:32–33; 19:38–40; Acts 2:25–36; Rev. 17:14; 19:16. See chap. 43.

2. The phrase "kingdom of heaven" appears thirty-two times in the New Testament (KJV), always and only in the Gospel of Matthew. The same Gospel also refers to the "kingdom of God" (Matt. 6:33; 12:28; 19:24; 21:31, 43). Christ used the two terms with the same meaning in Matt. 19:23–24: "A rich man shall hardly enter into the kingdom of heaven. . . . It is easier for a camel to go through the eye of a needle, than for a rich man to enter into the kingdom of God." Note also the synoptic parallels in Matt. 4:17 and Mark 1:15; Matt. 13:11 and Mark 4:11; Matt. 19:14 and Mark 10:14; etc. "Heaven" may be a pious circumlocution for "God" (Matt. 5:34; 16:1; 18:18; 21:25; 23:22; Luke 15:18). See Geerhardus Vos, *The Teaching of Jesus Concerning the Kingdom of God and the Church* (New York: American Tract Society, 1903), 31–37.

3. The Bible contains 2,526 uses of the Hebrew term translated as "king" (*melek*) and 118 of the Greek (*basileus*).

4. Deut. 33:5; 1 Sam. 12:12; Pss. 5:3; 10:16; 24:7, 8, 9, 10; 29:10; 44:5; 47:3, 8; 48:3; 68:25; 74:12; 84:4; 95:3; 98:6; 145:1; 149:2; Isa. 41:21; 43:15; 44:6; Jer. 10:7, 10; 46:18; 48:15; 51:57; Zeph. 3:15; Zech. 14:9, 16, 17; Mal 1:14; Matt. 5:35; 1 Tim. 1:17; 6:15; Rev. 15:3.

5. *Malak*: Ex. 15:18; 1 Sam. 8:7; 1 Chron. 16:31; Pss. 47:9; 93:1; 96:10; 97:1; 99:1; 146:10; Isa. 24:23; 52:7; Ezek. 20:33; Mic. 4:7. *Basileuō*: Rev. 11:15, 17; 19:6.

6. *Mashal*: Judg. 8:23; 1 Chron. 29:12; 2 Chron. 20:6; Job 25:2; Pss. 22:28; 59:13; 66:7; 89:9; 103:19; Isa. 40:10; 63:19.

7. *Malkut*: 1 Chron. 28:5; Pss. 45:6; 103:19; 145:11–13. *Mamlakah*: Ex. 19:6; 1 Chron. 29:11; 2 Chron. 13:8. *Malku*: Dan. 2:44; 4:3, 34. *Basileia*: Matt. 6:33; 12:28; Mark 1:14–15; 1 Thess. 2:12; Rev. 12:10; and many other texts.

8. *Memshalah*: Pss. 103:22; 114:2; 145:13.

In the Old Testament, God's kingdom sometimes referred to his reign over all creation, what we call his sovereign providence (Pss. 103:19; 145:9–15; Dan. 4:34–35). At other times, however, God's kingdom referred to the nation of Israel (Ex. 19:6; Ps. 114:2), especially as it was ruled by the descendants of David (1 Chron. 28:5; 2 Chron. 13:8). The Lord was "the King of Israel" (Isa. 44:6; Zeph. 3:15). Though this kingdom often appeared weak and imperiled by the sins of men, the good news is that God will establish his reign in Zion, indeed over all nations (Isa. 24:23; 52:7; Zech. 14:9, 16–17). George Ladd (1911–1982) said, "While God is the King . . . he must manifest his kingship in the world of human beings and nations."[9] Theologians distinguish between God's essential kingdom, which is his omnipotence over all creatures, and his reign by his Word and Spirit in his elect.[10]

Therefore, in Scripture, God's kingdom may refer to his sovereignty over all things by virtue of his divine nature or to his reign in people who obey his will as his royal servants. This dual kingdom is rooted in the doctrine of creation. God's creation of all things demonstrates his sovereign kingship over them all (Ps. 95:3–5). However, God created mankind, his image bearers, to "have dominion" over the fish, birds, and land animals (Gen. 1:26, 28).[11] God created Adam to serve him as his servant-king over the world.

Adam fell from his high position, but God worked to restore his kingdom in Israel through the line of David.[12] David was chosen by God after the first king of Israel failed to obey the Lord (1 Sam. 13:13–14; 15:23; 16:1), like a second Adam after the first Adam. God promised that the Son of David would reign over God's people with an eternal kingdom according to God's covenant (2 Sam. 7:12–16) and over all nations for the peace of man and the glory of God.[13] Parallels between Solomon and Adam suggest that David's seed is a kind of second Adam, culminating in Jesus Christ, the last Adam.[14] David marveled that God remembered

---

9. Ladd, *A Theology of the New Testament*, 58.
10. Bullinger, *The Decades*, 2.1:276.
11. The verb translated as "have dominion" (*radah*) is used of the reign of a king (1 Kings 4:24; Ps. 72:8) and his officers (1 Kings 5:16; 9:23), but not of God's reign.
12. Note how 1 Chronicles 1–3 moves from Adam to David and his offspring.
13. Pss. 2:6–8; 72:8–11, 18–19; Isa. 9:6–7; Zech. 9:9–10.
14. Note the following parallels between Solomon and Adam. Solomon was anointed as king at the spring "Gihon" (1 Kings 1:33, 38, 45), also the name of a river issuing from Eden (Gen. 2:13). Solomon was charged to "keep" (*shamar*) God's commands (1 Kings 2:3); Adam was charged to "keep" the garden according to God's commands (Gen. 2:15–17). Solomon prayed for wisdom to "discern between good and evil" (1 Kings 3:9 ESV); Adam was tested

"man" and the "son of man," granting him glory, honor, and dominion over the creatures for God's glory (Ps. 8:4–8)—a look back at creation and forward to restoration (Heb. 2:5–9). Daniel saw a vision of the "Son of man" receiving "dominion, and glory, and a kingdom, that all people, nations, and languages should serve him: his dominion is an everlasting dominion" (Dan. 7:13–14). God establishes this human kingdom; by his power, it conquers all other kingdoms and is conquered by none (2:44). Thus, the kingdom is God's victory over the evil powers of this age and his reign in the age to come.

Jesus Christ came to fulfill the ancient prophecies of the Davidic king (Luke 1:31–33). At the heart of Christ's message was the kingdom.[15] His gospel was the "gospel of the kingdom" (Matt. 4:23; 9:35; 24:14). The kingdom in view was not God's essential sovereignty, but his reign through his servants that must be restored, for Christ taught his disciples to pray, "Thy kingdom come, Thy will be done in earth, as it is in heaven" (6:10). The kingdom of which Christ spoke is no mere earthly political power, but "the kingdom of God" (6:33; 12:28; etc.), "my Father's kingdom" (Matt. 26:29). Yet Christ also called it "my kingdom" (Luke 22:30; John 18:36); it belongs to the "Son of man" as "his kingdom" (Matt. 13:41; 16:28; cf. Luke 1:33). Thus, Christ is the divine King, God the Son incarnate (Isa. 9:6–7).

Just as we may speak of God's kingdom in a double sense, so we may speak of the Son's kingdom in two ways. Since Christ is God the Son, the second person of the Trinity, he shares in God's essential or natural providential reign over all creation. The Father "made the worlds" through the Son, and Christ is constantly "upholding all things by the word of his power" (Heb. 1:2–3). We may also speak, however, of Christ's mediatorial kingdom over all things for the church. As the Mediator and for our sake, Christ was "appointed heir of all things" (v. 2). He has been

---

with the tree of "the knowledge of good and evil" (Gen. 2:17). Solomon in his wisdom "spake of trees . . . also of beasts, and of fowl, and of creeping things, and of fishes" (1 Kings 4:33), an allusion to creation (Gen. 1:11–12, 24–26, 29; 2:9), and particularly to Adam naming the beasts and birds (2:19–20). Solomon built the temple adorned with gold, trees, and cherubim (1 Kings 6:14–38), more allusions to the garden of Eden (Gen. 2:9, 11–12; 3:24). Solomon was promised the continuance of his throne and temple conditioned upon his obedience to God's commands (1 Kings 9:1–9), which he disobeyed (11:1–13), just as was the case with Adam (Gen. 2:16–17; 3:6). See Belcher, *Prophet, Priest, and King*, 124; and G. K. Beale, *A New Testament Biblical Theology: The Unfolding of the Old Testament in the New* (Grand Rapids, MI: Baker Academic, 2011), 65–73.

15. For Christ's many references to the "kingdom" in only one of the four Gospels, see Matt. 3:2; 4:17, 23; 5:3, 10, 19–20; 6:10, 13, 33; 7:21; 8:11–12; 9:35; 10:7; 11:11–12; 12:28; 13:11, 19, 24, 31, 33, 38, 41, 43–45, 47, 52; 16:19, 28; 18:1, 3–4, 23; 19:12, 14, 23–24; 20:1; 21:31, 43; 22:2; 23:13; 24:14; 25:1, 34; 26:29.

"crowned with glory and honour" in order to bring "many sons unto glory" (2:9–10).[16]

Christ's mediatorial "kingdom" refers to the active reign of God through Christ by the Spirit to deliver people from Satan's dominion and bring them to grace and glory. Christ said, "If I cast out devils by the Spirit of God, then the kingdom of God is come unto you" (Matt. 12:28). In context, Christ's words refer to the invasion of God's power into this present age to break the power of Satan and rescue his captives (vv. 25–27).[17] Christ said, "How can one enter into a strong man's house, and spoil his goods, except he first bind the strong man?" (v. 29). The kingdom of God has entered this world in a hidden manner like a seed (13:11, 19–23), though it will appear in glory when the Son of man comes to judge the world (vv. 41–53).

The kingdom of God and Christ continued to be a significant theme in the preaching and writing of the apostles, though not as prominently as in the Gospels.[18] Like his Master, Paul taught that the kingdom of God and Christ is a present reality by the Holy Spirit (Rom. 14:17) as people are brought into union with Christ the Redeemer and delivered from Satan's dominion (Col. 1:12–14), and that the kingdom will be a future reality when Christ returns to judge the world (Eph. 5:5–6; 2 Tim. 4:1). As Geerhardus Vos said, the "age to come" has already broken into "this age" through the incarnation, death, and resurrection of God's Son, who sits at God's right hand in the heavenly places.[19] Christians live in the overlap of the ages, not yet fully delivered from the influences of this present evil age (Titus 2:12) but already participating in the kingdom in their union with Christ (Eph. 2:6; Col. 3:1).

Why is the term *kingdom* less prominent in the New Testament Epistles than in the Gospels? Robert Letham suggests that it is because "the kingdom of God is embodied in the risen Christ, who has been given plenipotentiary powers over the entire universe," and he is the center of the apostolic message.[20] It is not that the kingdom of God has vanished or been postponed, but that the messianic King now reigns.

---

16. Owen, *An Exposition of the Epistle to the Hebrews*, 3:40–42; and Turretin, *Institutes*, 14.16.2 (2:486).

17. Ladd, *A Theology of the New Testament*, 63.

18. Acts 14:22; 19:8; 20:25; 28:23, 31; Rom. 14:17; 1 Cor. 4:20; 6:9–10; 15:24, 50; Gal. 5:21; Eph. 5:5; Col. 1:13; 4:11; 1 Thess. 2:12; 2 Thess. 1:5; 2 Tim. 4:1, 18; Heb. 1:8; 12:28; James 2:5; 2 Pet. 1:11; Rev. 1:9; 12:10; cf. *basileuō* in Rom. 5:17, 21; 1 Cor. 4:8; 15:25; Rev. 5:10; 11:15, 17; 19:6; 20:4, 6; 22:5.

19. Geerhardus Vos, *The Pauline Eschatology* (Princeton, NJ: Geerhardus Vos, 1930), 38–39.

20. Letham, *Systematic Theology*, 585.

The Messianic Typology of the Davidic Kingdom

The Davidic kingship revealed that the king was God's chosen, anointed, beloved, and covenantal servant. He did not attain kingship by his own initiative or effort, but was chosen by God.[21] David was anointed with oil ceremonially and with the Spirit effectually (1 Sam. 16:13).[22] As a result, "the LORD was with him" to give him power and victory (18:12, 14).[23] David won the love of Jonathan (vv. 1–4), who made a covenant with David because he recognized that the Lord would make him the victorious king (20:13–17; 23:16–18). Indeed, "all Israel and Judah loved David" (18:16), and entered a covenant with him to be their king (2 Sam. 5:2–3). God loved Solomon and adopted him as his son (12:24–25; 1 Chron. 28:6), as promised in the covenant he made with David (2 Sam. 7:12–14).[24] David and his seed reigned as the Lord's "servant."[25] Likewise, Christ is God's chosen, anointed, beloved, and covenantal Servant-King.[26]

The lives of David and Solomon showed that obedience to God and wisdom from God characterized the ideal king. The distinguishing characteristic of God's king was not "the outward appearance," for "the LORD looketh on the heart" (1 Sam. 16:7). David loved God (Ps. 18:1) and generally walked with God in faithfulness, righteousness, and uprightness of heart.[27] David was also known as a king of remarkable wisdom (2 Sam. 14:17, 20). Solomon also loved the Lord, especially in his early reign, and received unparalleled wisdom from God (1 Kings 3:3, 12). He demonstrated his wisdom by his discernment in executing justice (v. 28). Similarly, Christ is characterized by righteousness, justice, and wisdom (Isa. 11:2–5; Jer. 23:5–6).

David's kingship involved three primary functions. First, David subdued Israel's enemies (2 Sam. 8:1–6, 13–14), for "the LORD gave victory to David wherever he went" (vv. 6, 14 ESV). Second, David accumulated treasures through his conquests, which he dedicated to the Lord

---

21. 1 Sam. 16:1–12; 2 Sam. 6:21; 1 Kings 8:16; 11:34; 1 Chron. 28:4–5; 2 Chron. 6:6; Pss. 78:70; 89:3, 19.

22. The expression that the Spirit "came upon" (*tsalakh*) him refers to supernatural empowerment for service. See Judg. 14:6, 19; 15:14; 1 Sam. 10:6, 10; 11:6.

23. Compare "The Spirit of the LORD came upon David. . . . But the Spirit of the LORD departed from Saul" (1 Sam. 16:14) with "The LORD was with him [David], and was departed from Saul" (18:12).

24. See the exposition of the covenant of the kingdom in chap. 32.

25. 1 Sam. 23:10–11; 25:39; 2 Sam. 3:18; 7:5, 8, 19–21, 25–29; 1 Kings 3:6–9; 8:23–30, 66; 11:13, 32, 34, 36, 38; 14:8; 2 Kings 8:19; 19:34; 20:6.

26. Isa. 42:1, 6; Mark 1:10–11; John 8:42; 14:23; Acts 10:38.

27. 1 Kings 3:6; 9:4; 11:4, 6, 38; 14:8; 15:5, 11; 2 Kings 14:3; 16:2; 18:3; 22:2.

(vv. 7–12) to be used to construct, adorn, and fill the temple that Solomon built (1 Chron. 18:8; 29:1–5; 2 Chron. 5:1). Third, "David reigned over all Israel; and David executed judgment and justice unto all his people" through various leaders in his administration (2 Sam. 8:15–18). These functions foreshadowed the kingly work of Christ, who rules over his people through his chosen officers, leads his people in spiritual warfare, and builds his church.[28] Greg Nichols says, "Scripture identifies three overarching functions of Christ's kingship. Christ rules God's people, fights God's enemies, and builds God's temple."[29]

David and Solomon performed these kingly functions according to the varying states of the kingdom. David was anointed king in a state of humiliation. Although he won decisive victories for Israel (1 Sam. 17:48–53; 18:5–7; 19:5), he was scorned by friend and foe alike (17:26–28, 33, 43–44) and persecuted almost to death by Saul. However, David's kingdom entered a state of militant exaltation when he was anointed king by Judah and later by all Israel, was established by the Lord in Jerusalem, and continued to wage war against his enemies (2 Sam. 2:4; 5:3, 11–12). After David died and Solomon ascended to the throne, God gave the kingdom an unprecedented degree of majesty, stability, peace, and wealth.[30] In this manner, David and Solomon foreshadowed the humiliation of Christ the King, his exaltation to heaven while yet engaged in spiritual warfare by his grace, and his open glory at his coming.

The Victory of the Crucified King

With respect to each aspect of Christ's threefold office, we may speak of his finished and continuing work—redemption accomplished and applied. The Prophet of God's people has completely revealed God's Word and presently illuminates people to understand and believe it by the Spirit. The great High Priest has finished offering a sacrifice for sins and now intercedes for the redeemed. The King has accomplished victory and now reigns to apply it to his people. Jesus Christ fully accomplished this victory on the cross.[31] John Calvin said, "On the cross, as in a magnificent chariot, he triumphed over his enemies and ours."[32]

---

28. Matt. 16:18; 18:15–20; Eph. 4:10–16; Rev. 17:14.
29. Nichols, *Lectures in Systematic Theology*, 3:612. Nichols later expounds these functions (3:630–38).
30. 1 Kings 2:12, 45–46; 4:20–25; 8:1–66; 2 Chron. 1:1; 9:1–31.
31. On the Christian's reliance on Christ's victory over Satan, see *RST*, 1:1147–48.
32. Calvin, *Commentaries*, on Luke 23:16.

The Priority of Victory

The first promise of salvation given to fallen mankind consisted of a proclamation of conflict and victory (Gen. 3:15).[33] Victory is one of the great purposes for which Christ came: "He that committeth sin is of the devil; for the devil sinneth from the beginning. For this purpose the Son of God was manifested, that he might destroy the works of the devil" (1 John 3:8).

Gustaf Aulén (1879–1977) asserted that the classic doctrine of the atonement taught by the early church was one of "divine conflict and victory," in which "Christ—Christus Victor—fights against and triumphs over the evil powers of this world, the 'tyrants' under which mankind is in bondage, and in Him God reconciled the world to Himself."[34] Aulén asserted that this is "the dominant idea in the New Testament," in contrast to the theory of satisfaction logically developed in the medieval period by Anselm of Canterbury.[35]

We have argued, contrary to Aulén, that the foundational doctrine of atonement in the Holy Scriptures is the satisfaction of divine justice by penal substitution, described biblically as propitiation, redemption, and reconciliation.[36] We cited several church fathers to demonstrate that the early church taught satisfaction by substitution.[37] However, the fathers also saw the multidimensional richness of Christ's office, involving reconciliation, revelation, and victorious reign. Irenaeus said, "For it was incumbent upon the Mediator between God and men, by His relationship to both, to bring both to friendship and concord, and present man to God, while He revealed God to man." Christ came "that He might kill sin, deprive death of its power, and vivify man."[38] Hence, Aulén's historical analysis is reductionistic and his theological criticism oversimplified. Still, his book serves to highlight a neglected biblical theme and counter a tendency toward reductionism among those who emphasized other views of the atonement,[39]

---

33. See the last part of chap. 18.

34. Gustaf Aulén, *Christus Victor: An Historical Study of the Three Main Types of the Idea of the Atonement*, trans. A. G. Hebert (New York: Macmillan, 1969), 4.

35. Aulén, *Christus Victor*, 6.

36. See chaps. 48–49.

37. Clement, *First Epistle*, chap. 49, in ANF, 1:18; Anonymous, *Epistle to Diognetus*, chap. 9, in ANF, 1:28; Irenaeus, *Against Heresies*, 3.8.1; 5.17.1, in ANF, 1:471, 544; Athanasius, *On the Incarnation of the Word*, secs. 6–8, 20, 25, in NPNF², 4:39–40, 47, 49; *Four Discourses against the Arians*, 1.60, in NPNF², 4:341; Augustine, *Enchiridion*, chaps. 33, 41, in NPNF¹, 3:248–49, 251; Chrysologus, *Selected Sermons, Volume 3*, 10; and Gregory the Great, *Morals on the Book of Job*, 1.3.26–27, on Job 2:3 (1:148–49).

38. Irenaeus, *Against Heresies*, 3.18.7, in ANF, 1:448.

39. Stott, *The Cross of Christ*, 228–30; and Jeremy R. Treat, *The Crucified King: Atonement and Kingdom in Biblical and Systematic Theology* (Grand Rapids, MI: Zondervan, 2014), 169–72, 177–81.

including some Reformed theologians.[40] Victory over evil is a central aspect of Christ's work, built upon the foundation of substitutionary atonement. When Christ suffered and died as the Priest offering himself as a sacrifice for sins, he was also conquering and achieving victory as the King.

A Picture of Victory

When we go to the Holy Scriptures to discover how "the Lion of the tribe of Judah, the Root of David, has conquered," we find "a Lamb standing, as though it had been slain" (Rev. 5:5–6 ESV). Just as the Passover lamb was central to Israel's exodus and victory over Egypt, so Christ crucified is central to the spiritual exodus of God's saints from all nations and their victory over Satan and this world (12:11).[41]

We have already noted that the Passover pictured salvation by penal substitution—Christ's sacrificial work as our only High Priest.[42] The same type foreshadowed his kingly victory, for redemption is not just by the payment of a price but also by means of power. The Lord said, "For I will pass through the land of Egypt this night, and will smite all the firstborn in the land of Egypt, both man and beast; and against all the gods of Egypt I will execute judgment: I am the LORD" (Ex. 12:12). The judgments of God in the form of the plagues, Vos wrote, broke Israel's "enslavement to an alien power" and effected "a deliverance from an objective realm of sin and evil."[43] Stephen Charnock said, "God's greatest mercies to his church are attended with the greatest plagues upon their enemies. The salvation of man is the destruction of sin and the devil; the Passover was the salvation of Israel and the ruin of Egypt."[44]

The ultimate target of God's paschal judgment was "all the gods of Egypt" (Ex. 12:12). Through Moses, the Lord had initiated a conflict or contest between spiritual powers (7:11–12, 22) so that all people would

---

40. Sinclair B. Ferguson, "*Christus Victor et Propitiator*: The Death of Christ, Substitute and Conqueror," in *For the Fame of God's Name: Essays in Honor of John Piper*, ed. Sam Storms and Justin Taylor (Wheaton, IL: Crossway, 2010), 172. Ferguson notes the relative neglect of this topic by Francis Turretin, Charles Hodge, and Louis Berkhof. Note, however, the treatments of Christ's victory over Satan in Goodwin, *Of Christ the Mediator*, in *Works*, 5:295–337; and Owen, *An Exposition of the Epistle to the Hebrews*, 3:54–55, 447–53.

41. On Revelation's allusions to Exodus, see *The Reformation Heritage KJV Study Bible*, ed. Beeke, Barrett, Bilkes, and Smalley, on Rev. 1:5–6; 5:9–10; 7:9–14; 8:6–12; 15:2–3; 16:1–7, 10–11 (1867–87). See also Richard Bauckham, *The Theology of the Book of Revelation* (Cambridge: Cambridge University Press, 1993), 70–72.

42. See the section on penal substitution as prophesied in the Old Testament in chap. 49.

43. Vos, *Biblical Theology*, 110.

44. Charnock, *Christ Our Passover*, in *Works*, 4:508.

know that he, and he alone, is the Lord.[45] Vos wrote that there was a "demonic background" to this conflict, explaining, "The plagues . . . are inextricably mixed up with the Egyptian idolatry. This idolatry was nature-worship, embracing the good and beneficent as well as the evil and baneful aspects of nature. Jehovah, in making these harm their own worshippers, shows His superiority to this whole realm of evil."[46] By this means, God broke the enslaving power of these false deities over his people, who had joined in the worship of these gods (Josh. 24:14).

This typical deliverance of Israel foreshadowed the spiritual deliverance of the elect accomplished by Christ's victorious death. Peter calls believers to pursue holiness, quoting God's words to Israel, "Be ye holy; for I am holy" (1 Pet. 1:16, citing Lev. 11:44). Moses had based this exhortation to Israel on the Lord's bringing them out of Egypt (v. 45). Peter says, "You were ransomed from the futile ways inherited from your forefathers, not with perishable things such as silver or gold, but with the precious blood of Christ, like that of a lamb without blemish or spot" (1 Pet. 1:18–19 ESV). Charnock said, "The efficacy of this divine Passover delivers men from a spiritual captivity, under the yoke of sin and the irons of Satan, instates them in the liberty of the children of God, whereby they become a holy nation, a royal priesthood."[47] Just as the firstborn sons saved by the Passover lambs became God's special possession (Ex. 13:1–2), so Christ "gave himself for us, that he might redeem us from all iniquity, and purify unto himself a peculiar people, zealous of good works" (Titus 2:14).

The Price of Victory

Christ overcame Satan by purchasing his people with his blood (Rev. 5:5, 9; 12:11). Christians are no longer to live in sin because they were "bought with a price" (1 Cor. 6:20). Our deliverance "from the power of darkness" is inseparable from our "redemption through his blood, the forgiveness of sins" (Col. 1:13–14; cf. Eph. 1:7).[48]

Peter says that Jesus "bare our sins in his own body on the tree, that we, being dead to sins, should live unto righteousness: by whose stripes ye were healed. For ye were as sheep going astray; but are now returned unto the Shepherd and Bishop of your souls" (1 Pet. 2:24–25). Peter's allusion

---

45. See Ex. 7:5, 17; 8:10, 22; 9:14, 16, 29; 10:2.
46. Vos, *Biblical Theology*, 111.
47. Charnock, *Christ Our Passover*, in *Works*, 4:514.
48. On redemption, see the basic biblical perspectives on Christ's priestly sacrifice in chap. 48.

to Isaiah 53 places this statement in the context of penal substitution,[49] but the apostle highlights the practical fruit of Christ's death in the repentance and righteous living granted to his redeemed people. Sinclair Ferguson says, "The altar of propitiation of God is at one and the same time the arena of conflict against and victory over Satan."[50]

Why was Christ's satisfaction to justice necessary for the deliverance of his elect from the Devil? Though Satan has no right to lead people in rebellion against God, God justly gave sinners over to the power of sin when they rejected him (Rom. 1:24, 26, 28). The penalty of Adam's sin and our sins is death (5:12; 6:23), which includes a mindset of hostility against God that renders people unwilling and unable to submit to his law (8:6–8).[51] It is only by the curse of justice against sinners that sin and Satan have ruling power.[52] Augustine said, "By the justice of God in some sense, the human race was delivered into the power of the devil. . . . For when He [God] abandoned the sinner, the author of the sin immediately entered."[53]

The good news is that Christ has saved his people from the powers of evil by paying their debt to God's justice. Paul says that God has "forgiven you all trespasses; blotting out the handwriting of ordinances that was against us, which was contrary to us, and took it out of the way, nailing it to his cross; and having spoiled principalities and powers, he made a shew of them openly, triumphing over them in it" (Col. 2:13–15). Christ's death satisfies God's justice toward sinners, canceling their liability to punishment.[54] Consequently, he has "spoiled," or stripped away, the great weapon that Satan and his demons had against people—the death they deserve (Heb. 2:14–15). John Owen said, "He died for their sins, took that death upon himself which was due unto them; which being conquered thereby, and their obligation thereunto ceasing, the power of Satan is therewith dissolved."[55] Augustine said that Christ's blood delivers us from Satan's power because it "was poured out for the remission of our sins," and Satan has power to hold people captive only because they are "guilty

---

49. See the section on penal substitution prophesied in the Old Testament in chap. 49.

50. Ferguson, "*Christus Victor et Propitiator*," in *For the Fame of God's Name*, ed. Storms and Taylor, 181.

51. On original sin and total depravity, see chaps. 19–21.

52. Thomas Hooker, *The Application of Redemption, The Ninth and Tenth Books* (Ames, IA: International Outreach, 2008), 429.

53. Augustine, *On the Trinity*, 13.12.16, in *NPNF*[1], 3:175–76.

54. On Col. 2:13–14, see the section on the necessity of the satisfaction to divine justice in chap. 49.

55. Owen, *An Exposition of the Epistle to the Hebrews*, 3:450. See Goodwin, *Of Christ the Mediator*, in *Works*, 5:304.

of sin."[56] Ironically, Satan's putting Christ to shame and death was the very means by which God put Satan "to open shame" (Col. 2:15 ESV). As Peter Lombard said, Christ "set a mouse-trap for Satan, which was his own cross, and he set his own blood as if bait for him."[57]

William Perkins said, "Christ did triumph when He was upon the cross."[58] The cross was a spiritual battlefield where Christ, like an "emperor," faced "the world, the flesh, hell, death, damnation, the devil, and all his angels," and conquered them. Our "surety" fulfilled the "obligation" by which "Satan might have accused and condemned us before God." The cross was "a chariot of triumph" where "principalities and powers, that is, the devil, and his angels, hell, death, and condemnation," are stripped of their "armor and weapons," chained, bound, and led in defeat by the victorious Christ.[59]

The sacrifice of Christ the Priest paid the price of the victory achieved by Christ the King. Jeremy Treat calls this doctrine "*Christus Victor* through penal substitution," explaining, "Jesus' conquest of the devil was not just a victory; it was a just victory."[60] John Eadie (1810–1876) said, "Redemption is a work at once of price and power, of expiation and conquest. On the cross was the purchase made; on the cross was the victory gained. The blood that wipes out the sentence was there shed, and the death which was the death-blow of Satan's kingdom was there endured."[61] On the basis of his death, Christ now effectually works the conversion of the lost. Thomas Hooker said, "The Lord says to sin, hands off, that soul is mine. . . . So that when Christ, as the second Adam, and head of the covenant, comes to take a soul, and to bring him from sin to God the Father, look by what irresistible power he acts."[62]

This truth gives strong hope and spiritual vigor to the Christian. John Brown of Wamphray wrote that when a Christian considers the power of sin, he "may now look on that enemy, however fearful it may appear, as condemned and killed in the death of Christ." The Christian is "to look to Christ hanging on the cross and there vanquishing and overcoming this archenemy—as a public person, representing the elect who died in

56. Augustine, *On the Trinity*, 13.15.19, in *NPNF*[1], 3:177.
57. Cited in Kelly, *Systematic Theology*, 2:68.
58. Perkins, *An Exposition of the Symbol*, in *Works*, 5:210.
59. Perkins, *An Exposition of the Symbol*, in *Works*, 5:221.
60. Treat, *The Crucified King*, 208.
61. John Eadie, *A Commentary on the Greek Text of the Epistle of Paul to the Colossians*, ed. W. Young, 2nd ed. (Edinburgh: T&T Clark, 1884), 169.
62. Hooker, *The Application of Redemption, The Ninth and Tenth Books*, 429.

Him. . . . From hence, even while fighting, the believer may account himself a conqueror, indeed more than a conqueror, through Him that loved him."[63]

The Power of Victory

Christ's crucifixion displays "the power of God" (1 Cor. 1:18, 24), a hidden power known only by faith but divine power nonetheless, for "the weakness of God is stronger than men" (v. 25). By Christ's passion and death, "the Son of man [is] glorified, and God is glorified in him" (John 13:31). Jesus said, "Now is the judgment of this world: now shall the prince of this world be cast out. And I, if I be lifted up from the earth, will draw all men unto me" (12:31–32); with these words, he was "signifying what death he should die" (v. 33). Therefore, Christ's death glorified God, struck down Satan, defeated Satan's kingdom, and accomplished the conversion of people from all nations.[64]

How did Christ glorify God and conquer Satan by his passion? He did so by completing the work God had given him to do (John 17:4), obeying his will (4:34; 5:30; 6:38). Christ laid down his life in obedience to the Father's commandment (10:18). Christ went to his passion crying out, "Father, glorify thy name" (12:23, 28). Owen spoke of the "unspeakable zeal for and ardency of affection unto, the glory of God" that energized Christ's obedience.[65] Satan, "the prince of this world," had nothing in Christ, for Christ loved the Father and went to the cross in obedience to his commandment (14:30–31). Therefore, Christ overcame the Devil by obedience to God. By his obedience unto death, Christ became like a seed buried in the soil to reproduce himself in many others who also would lose their lives in obedient service (12:24–26).

Christ saved us by his obedience as he increasingly sanctified his holy human nature, not from the presence of sin, but to attain deeper levels of consecration to God's will. This was a process spanning Christ's incarnate life in his state of humiliation. God's incarnate Son was born in holiness, yet he increased in wisdom and piety (Luke 1:35; 2:52).[66] Christ battled against Satan's temptations in the wilderness and overcame by

---

63. Brown, *Christ the Way, the Truth, and the Life*, 100.
64. To "draw [*helkuō*] all men" (John 12:32) signifies the effectual calling of sinners to Christ: "No man can come to me, except the Father which hath sent me draw [*helkuō*] him: and I will raise him up at the last day" (6:37). The "all" in this context refers to "all kinds of people," including the "Greeks" seeking Jesus (12:20).
65. Owen, *Pneumatologia*, in *Works*, 3:178.
66. On the human development and sinlessness of God the Son incarnate, see chap. 40.

obedience to God's Word (4:1–13). In so doing, he further subdued his natural human desires for food, wealth, and honor. Ferguson says that these temptations "are not merely personal," but "constitute the tempting of the last Adam." He adds, "His testing was set in the context of a holy war in which he entered the enemy's domain, absorbed his attacks and sent him into retreat."[67] Jesus emerged victorious and began teaching, healing, and casting out demons (vv. 14–19, 35–36, 41; cf. Acts 10:38).

Christ's obedience came to a climax in his passion, when he "became obedient unto death, even the death of the cross" (Phil. 2:8). As we discussed earlier, he pressed his humanity into the deepest submission to God's will at Gethsemane when he said, "Abba, Father . . . not what I will, but what thou wilt" (Mark 14:36).[68] On the basis of the Son's victorious obedience, "the Spirit of Christ" now works in those in Christ to lead them to live as "the sons of God" and cry out in persevering faith, "Abba, Father," just as Christ did, for they "suffer with him" so that they "may be also glorified together" with him (Rom. 8:9–17).

At Gabbatha and Golgotha, the Scriptures portray Christ as the suffering "King," even on the cross.[69] Christ exercised regal power in his passion. True kingship begins with ruling oneself: "He that is slow to anger is better than the mighty; and he that ruleth his spirit than he that taketh a city" (Prov. 16:32). John Stott said, "By his obedience, his love and his meekness he won a great moral victory over the powers of evil. He remained free, uncontaminated, uncompromised. The devil could gain no hold on him, and had to concede defeat."[70]

Paul explains that when Christ became incarnate in his state of humiliation, he came "in the likeness of sinful flesh" (Rom. 8:3), where "flesh" refers to humanity under the power of sin (vv. 5–9). Though he was the sinless Son of God, Christ entered a world of sin, suffered temptation to sin, and was capable of sin in his human nature.[71] He conquered the power of sin and entered a new state by his death and resurrection. Paul says, "For in that he died, he died unto sin once: but in that he liveth, he liveth unto God" (Rom. 6:10). Christ left behind sin as a "ruling power" and made a "final

---

67. Ferguson, *The Holy Spirit*, 48.
68. See the discussion of Christ's climactic obedience in his passion in chap. 50.
69. John 18:33, 37, 39; 19:3, 12, 14–15, 19–21. See Perkins, *An Exposition of the Symbol*, in *Works*, 5:210–11.
70. Stott, *The Cross of Christ*, 235.
71. On Christ's human ability to sin but divine impeccability, see the section on his sinlessness in chap. 40.

and definitive" transition into a state of life for the glory of God, as Douglas Moo comments.[72] Jesus entered that state of perfect freedom for man, of which Augustine said, "In the future life it shall not be in [man's] power to will evil; and yet this will constitute no restriction on the freedom of his will. On the contrary, his will shall be much freer when it shall be wholly impossible for him to be the slave of sin."[73] Consequently, John Murray said, "It is because Christ triumphed over the power of sin in his death that those united to him in his death die to the power of sin (vv. 2, 11)."[74] Those in vital union with Christ cannot live in the state of sin (v. 14), and one day they all will join Christ in the state in which it is impossible for them to sin.

Christ defeated the power of sin once for all by exercising perfect obedience to God in the most extreme sorrow.[75] Enduring suffering while persevering in obedience to God's will strengthens any man in his rejection of sin and performance of righteousness (1 Pet. 4:1–2). Much more the last Adam forged a new, righteous humanity in the fiery furnace of human rejection, Satanic temptation, and divine wrath. Calvin said, "By his wrestling hand to hand with the devil's power, with the dread of death, with the pains of hell, he was victorious and triumphed over them, that in death we may not now fear those things which our Prince has swallowed up."[76] Christ now imparts by his Spirit the human holiness he perfected in his own human nature. By the Spirit, "we have the mind of Christ" (1 Cor. 2:16), the mindset of self-denial that Christ exercised when he became "obedient unto death" (Phil. 2:5, 8).

The Perfection of Victory

The epistle to the Hebrews uses a group of related words (*tel-* or *telei-*) to reveal the perfection of Christ's unique accomplishment.[77] The idea of

---

72. Moo, *The Epistle to the Romans*, 379.

73. Augustine, *Enchiridion*, chap. 105, in *NPNF*[1], 3:271. On the fourfold state of man, see chap. 22.

74. Murray, *The Epistle to the Romans*, 1:225.

75. "The Apostle believed that Christ 'knew no sin' (2 Cor. 5:21), and cannot have supposed that he had ever lived in subjection to sin, from which he was released only by death. But he may have believed that 'the man Jesus Christ' had real spiritual struggles, that he had painfully to repress the claims of self, of the wearied body and the anxious brain, that his exalted life required a voluntary conquest of opposing forces, and a clinging in faith to God . . . and the death on the cross, which was the final and complete abnegation [denial] of self, was also a dying once and forever to sin, and entering upon that life where sin has no more power." James Drummond, *The Epistles of Paul the Apostle to the Thessalonians, Corinthians, Galatians, Romans and Philippians*, International Handbooks to the New Testament (New York; London: G. P. Putnam's Sons, 1899), 298.

76. Calvin, *Institutes*, 2.16.11.

77. See *telos* (Heb. 3:6, 14; 6:8, 11), *teleios* (5:14), *teleiotēs* (6:1), *teleiōsis* (7:11), *teleioō* (7:19; 9:9; 10:1–2, 14; 11:40; 12:23), *teleioteros* (9:11), *synteleia* (v. 26), and *pantelēs* (7:25).

perfection in Hebrews pertains to being fully qualified for the new, heavenly order that Christ alone inaugurated. What is especially relevant to the theme of victory is that Hebrews also speaks of Christ being "made perfect" in a manner related to his suffering and obedience (*teleioō*, Heb. 2:10; 5:9; 7:28). By his perseverance unto death on the cross, he became "the author and finisher [*teleiōtēs*] of our faith" and attained glory at God's right hand (12:2). In other words, Christ won the victory by perfecting his human faith and obedience through trials.

The incarnate Son "learned . . . obedience by the things which he suffered" (Heb. 5:8); that is, he experienced obedience by patiently submitting himself to God's will, though it was extremely hard.[78] By this experience, Christ was "made perfect" (*teleioō*, v. 9) as the cause of eternal salvation for his people. There was no moral imperfection in Jesus (4:15). Rather, the text means that by enduring suffering, Christ attained greater maturity and, in the fires of sorrow, forged proven character.[79] Philip Hughes commented, "What was essential was that, starting, like Adam, with a pure human nature, he should succeed where Adam had failed. His sufferings both tested and, victoriously endured, attested his perfection, free from failure and defeat."[80]

God found it fitting, "in bringing many sons unto glory, to make the captain of their salvation perfect [*teleioō*] through sufferings" (Heb. 2:10). The word translated as "captain" (*archēgos*) could mean "author," "originator" or "founder,"[81] or, as was often the case in the Septuagint, "leader" or "ruler" over a family, people, or military unit.[82] In this context, Christ is portrayed as the One who leads a new family ("many sons") into "glory" or "the world to come" by virtue of his suffering and death, and being "crowned with glory and honour" to take up the status of dominion over creation for which God first made mankind (2:5–10). The last Adam founded a new humanity to rule over a new creation. Owen said that the "captain of salvation leads on the sons of God" in that "he goes before them in the whole way"—in "their obedience," "their sufferings," and "their entrance into glory."[83]

As Christians, we must "run with endurance the race that is set before us, looking to Jesus, the founder [*archēgos*] and perfecter [*teleiōtēs*] of our

78. Owen, *An Exposition of the Epistle to the Hebrews*, 4:524.
79. Leon Morris, *The Cross in the New Testament* (Grand Rapids, MI: Eerdmans, 1965), 281.
80. Hughes, *A Commentary on the Epistle to the Hebrews*, 188.
81. *TDNT*, 1:487–88.
82. Ex. 6:14; Num. 10:4; 1 Chron. 5:24; 12:21; 26:26; etc. LXX; cf. "prince" in Acts 3:15; 5:31.
83. Owen, *An Exposition of the Epistle to the Hebrews*, 3:387.

faith, who for the joy that was set before him endured the cross, despising the shame, and is seated at the right hand of the throne of God" (Heb. 12:1–2 ESV). Christ has completed the race that all his people must run through sorrow and shame to reach glory. He is "the founder and perfecter of our faith" because he perseveringly exercised faith (2:12–13)[84] in "the joy that was set before him" so that he could be "the supplier and sustainer of the faith of his followers."[85] We look to the Son and endure as sons under our Father's loving discipline to train us in holiness (12:3–11).

Christ's victory on the cross secured the liberty of Christians from all that would tyrannize over them.[86] Irenaeus said, "He has therefore, in His work of recapitulation, summed up all things, both waging war against our enemy, and crushing him who had at the beginning led us away captives in Adam, and trampled upon his head" (cf. Gen. 3:15).[87] Thus, believers in Christ have liberty from:

- the condemning tyranny of the rigor of the law (Gal. 5:1–3);
- the legalistic tyranny of man's judgments (Col. 2:14–23);
- the enslaving tyranny of sin (John 8:34–36);
- the satanic tyranny of evil spirits (Eph. 6:10–13);
- the persecuting tyranny of the world (John 16:33); and
- the fear-driven tyranny of death (Heb. 2:14–15).

Whatever our social or economic status, whether we are at liberty or behind bars, if we are in Christ then we are truly free because Christ won the victory over all that would attack and oppress us. This victory is the basis of Christian courage and the many commands in Scripture that we should not fear. As Calvin said, strong fears arise from ignorance of the grace of Christ.[88] No power of earth or hell can conquer you if Christ died for your sins. Be encouraged, Christian, and lift up your head, for the day is coming soon when the God of peace will crush Satan under your feet by the grace of Jesus Christ (Rom. 16:20). He achieved perfection as the new Adam and has made you perfect by his atoning and

---

84. Christ did not exercise faith in the gospel for justification and sanctification, for he was holy from birth (Luke 1:35). He is the content of the gospel, the object of our faith. However, he did trust in God and put confidence in his promises (Heb. 2:13). "Christ himself, being man, rested on God to be supported in all his weaknesses, and to be enabled to go through all his undertakings, and well accomplish them." Gouge, *Commentary on Hebrews*, 1:155.

85. Hughes, *A Commentary on the Epistle to the Hebrews*, 522–23.

86. Stott, *The Cross of Christ*, 241–43.

87. Irenaeus, *Against Heresies*, 5.21.1, in *ANF*, 1:548.

88. Calvin, *Commentaries*, on Heb. 2:15.

sanctifying death so that you most certainly will attain the perfection of the heavenly city of God.

The Triumph of the Risen King

In the ancient world, when a ruler won a great military victory, he would return home in a triumphal procession to receive honor, glorify his gods, and often to consolidate his power.[89] The exaltation of Jesus Christ is his heavenly triumph for the glory of God the Father and salvation of his people.[90] His triumph began with his resurrection, which itself was a mighty act of Christ the King (John 10:17–18). Christ is "the firstborn from the dead; that in all things he might have the preeminence" (Col. 1:18). "Firstborn" refers not only to chronological order (1 Cor. 15:23) but more especially to his "rank and privilege" as the supreme King (Ps. 89:27; Rev. 1:5).[91]

Christ's resurrection was *his glorification for eternal life* (Luke 24:26; Rom. 6:4, 9). His resurrection was of one piece with his ascension and session at God's right hand (Rom. 8:34), when he was invested with universal power (Matt. 28:18). His resurrection was his triumph over sin and death, for, as Thomas Goodwin noted, "the resurrection of Christ was not an ordinary resurrection, for it was not an ordinary death."[92] Christ died for our sins (1 Cor. 15:3) under the curse of God's law (Gal. 3:13) and rose as the victor over the power of sin and death to receive God's blessings for us in the Spirit in the heavenly places (Eph. 1:3).[93]

Christ arose as the last Adam to rescue his people from the death that sin deserves and to give them eternal life by God's Spirit (1 Cor. 15:21–22, 45). Paul prays for believers to know "what is the immeasurable greatness of his power toward us who believe, according to the working of his great might that he worked in Christ when he raised him from the dead and seated him at his right hand in the heavenly places" (Eph. 1:19–20 ESV). Paul Bayne wrote, "The selfsame power which raised Christ to be a second Adam, and quickening spirit to all who belong to him, that is the power

---

89. On the Roman *triumphus*, see William Smith, ed., *A Dictionary of Greek and Roman Antiquities* (London: Taylor and Walton, 1842), 1005–9.
90. Pss. 24:7–10; 68:18; Eph. 1:19–23; 4:7–10; Phil. 2:9–11. On Christ's exaltation, see chap. 44.
91. Peterson, *Salvation Accomplished by the Son*, 133, 135.
92. Goodwin, *Exposition of the First Chapter of the Epistle to the Ephesians*, in *Works*, 1:430.
93. "The eschatological significance of Christ's resurrection is determined by the special character of his death. . . . For Paul Christ's death is determined primarily by its connection with the power and guilt of sin." Ridderbos, *Paul*, 55.

which doth cause us in our time [to] receive this supernatural life and being from him. For Christ's resurrection is both the resurrection of our souls and bodies, inasmuch as he is raised up, that he may be a fountain and root of all supernatural life."[94]

Christ's resurrection inaugurated *his supremacy over all*. In him was fulfilled the prophecy of Psalm 110:1: "The LORD said unto my Lord, Sit thou at my right hand, until I make thine enemies thy footstool." For King David to call Christ "my Lord" implies that he is the King of kings, not merely the heir of an earthly throne (Matt. 22:41–45). To sit at God's right hand is the highest honor. However, it is not merely an honor, but the position from which Christ actively reigns to govern his willing people and destroy his enemies (Ps. 110:2–3, 5–7).

Such glory and supremacy over all things are fitting only for the God-man, God the Son incarnate.[95] However, to have such honor *given* to him implies that he received it not in his divine nature but as the incarnate Mediator who was humiliated but is now exalted (Phil. 2:6–11). Christ was raised from the dead and enthroned as the promised Son of David (Acts 2:29–31; 13:33). Though God the Son was always Lord (Luke 2:11), God the Father "hath made" him "Lord" by his resurrection and session at his right hand (Acts 2:36). Christ died and rose again "that he might be Lord both of the dead and living" (Rom. 14:9). This mediatorial lordship conferred upon Christ at his exaltation does not deny his eternal deity, but displays a greater manifestation of his deity than was done previously. Christ's resurrection initiated a new phase in his mediatorial kingship.[96]

Christ's resurrection displayed *his conquest over the powers of evil*. Paul says that God raised Christ and seated him "far above all principality, and power, and might, and dominion, and every name that is named, not only in this world, but also in that which is to come" (Eph. 1:21). Christ won the victory over the corrupt human authorities who condemned him to death and continue to persecute his people (Ps. 2:1–7; Acts 4:24–28), and over the evil spiritual "principalities" and "powers" that war against the church (Eph. 6:12; cf. Rev. 12:5, 17). Satan is the ruler of this world, but believers have been raised with Christ out of the Devil's dominion (Eph. 2:1–6). Calvin wrote, "Our Lord Jesus Christ is set at the right hand

94. Bayne[s], *An Entire Commentary upon . . . Ephesians*, 104. "Christ's" was originally "Christ his."

95. Hodge, *Ephesians*, 49.

96. Sibbes, *Christ's Exaltation Purchased by His Humiliation*, in *Works*, 5:329.

of God his Father . . . so that if we are under his protection, we may defy the devil and all our enemies."[97]

When Paul speaks of "every name that is named" (Eph. 1:21), he alludes to the pagan practice of calling on the name of a god or spirit to seek its power and wisdom, a common exercise of worship and sorcery.[98] The exaltation of Jesus Christ above all such beings shows us that the only name on which we need call for salvation is that of the Lord Jesus (Rom. 10:9, 13). This exclusive dependence on Christ characterizes the true church (1 Cor. 1:2). Calvin said, "We shall find in him all things needful."[99]

Christ's resurrection inaugurated *his restoration of man*. Paul says that God "hath put all things under his feet" (Eph. 1:22). Here he quotes David's celebration of God's purpose for mankind when God made us in Adam: "to have dominion over the works of thy hands; thou hast put all things under his feet" (Ps. 8:6). God fulfilled this purpose of man's delegated dominion in Christ's exaltation (cf. 1 Cor. 15:27; Heb. 2:5–10).

Christ's suffering and death for our sins and his resurrection from the dead initiated the dawn of a new creation in which man is restored to his original glory. His resurrection on the first day of the week was "the real beginning of the new spiritual world in which we are made the sons of God," Perkins said.[100] The new creation that has begun in believers (2 Cor. 5:17; Eph. 2:10) will one day transform the whole universe when God's children enter Christ's glory (Rom. 8:17–23). Richard Belcher writes, "In Jesus' exaltation there is a reinstatement of the originally intended divine order for the earth, with a human being properly situated as God's viceregent"; this is "the restoration of our rule over creation."[101]

Christ's resurrection inaugurated *his enrichment of the church*. God gave the risen Christ "to be the head over all things to the church, which is his body, the fulness of him that filleth all in all" (Eph. 1:22). Christ's kingship is highlighted with the title "head over all things" (cf. Col. 2:10). His universal mediatorial lordship is God's gift to the church, those united

97. Calvin, *Sermons on the Epistle to the Ephesians*, 111.
98. Josh. 23:7 (LXX); Acts 19:13; cf. Gen. 4:26; Ex. 23:13. See Lincoln, *Ephesians*, 65, citing C. E. Arnold, *Ephesians: Power and Magic* (Cambridge: Cambridge University Press, 1989), 54–55.
99. Calvin, *Sermons on the Epistle to the Ephesians*, 112.
100. Perkins, *An Exposition of the Symbol*, in *Works*, 5:241.
101. Belcher, *Prophet, Priest, and King*, 155, 157.

to Christ as members of his body. The church is his "fullness"—not that we fill him, but that he fills us until we reach the full measure of his glorified humanity in union with God by the Spirit (Eph. 3:19; 4:15; 5:18).[102] As Christ fills the church through the ministry of the Word, so the church fills "all things" with Christ's manifest glory (4:10–13). Christians are representatives and servants of the King, working to establish God's kingdom over every aspect of life in every place of his world.

Calvin wrote, "If we have and possess his only Son, Jesus Christ, we have the full perfection of all good, so that if we cast our eye upon him, we may see all that can be desired." The righteousness and power of our risen Lord is greater than all our sin and weakness. Calvin concluded, "Although there are many blameworthy things in us, and even though we find nothing but frailty in ourselves, yet we have a good, firm support to lean on, in that our Lord Jesus Christ calls us to him and tells us that the things he has received from God his Father are for us all, and that although we do not yet enjoy them to the full, we cannot come short of them."[103]

Consequently, we may say not only that Christ gives us life but that he is our life (John 11:25; Col. 3:4). As Hooker said, Christ "is the life of the soul."[104] Douglas Kelly writes, "From that honored seat of mediatorial victory, he is continually pouring his resurrection life into the souls and bodies of his people on earth, thus enabling them to live as Christians in union with him."[105]

The victory and triumph of Christ gives believers strong warrant for solid hope. Truly did our Lord declare, "It is finished!" (John 19:30). Anne Dutton said,

> Christ is such a glorious leader, that none under the banner of his dying love can possibly fall short of endless life! This Captain of salvation went into the field of battle to fight single-handed with all the powers of darkness, to rescue all those which his Father gave him, to be brought to glory, out of the hands of all their enemies. He won the victory, took the spoil, trampled down the powers of darkness, led captivity captive, triumphing over them in it. He in his mighty love by the merit of his death and the power of his resurrection brought away his ransomed ones, from out of their enemies' hands, with amazing triumph! He had

---

102. Lincoln, *Ephesians*, 73–75. Contra Hodge, *Ephesians*, 54–55.
103. Calvin, *Sermons on the Epistle to the Ephesians*, 111.
104. Thomas Hooker, *The Soul's Humiliation* (Ames, IA: International Outreach, 2000), 57.
105. Kelly, *Systematic Theology*, 2:520.

them all mystically in himself when he rose and carried them up to heaven with him, and there they sit in him! . . . And who or what shall pluck them from God's right hand? Who shall separate them from the love of God in Christ?[106]

Christ's triumph does not produce proud triumphalism, but confident dependence on him. In ourselves, we do not yet reign in glory as kings, but remain weak, poor, mortal, and despised men (1 Cor. 4:8–13). Our souls are battlegrounds between sin and righteousness (Gal. 5:17; 1 Pet. 2:11). Richard Sibbes said, "The life of Christ is but now begun in us, and it is very little at the first."[107] Yet Christ is sufficient, for he is King. William Mason (1719–1791) said, "Quickened souls see their sinfulness, know their poverty, feel their misery and wretchedness, and groan . . . but here is there glory, joy and comfort, they are one with Christ. His life is theirs, his death is theirs, his righteousness is theirs, his holiness is theirs, his fullness is theirs."[108]

Sing to the Lord

Praise God for the Victorious King

Now the King in Thy strength shall be joyful, O Lord,
Thy salvation shall make Him rejoice;
For the wish of His heart Thou didst freely accord,
The request of His suppliant voice.

All the blessings of goodness Thou freely didst give;
With the purest of gold He is crowned;
When He asked of Thee life Thou hast made Him to live
While the ages shall circle around.

Through salvation from Thee hath His fame spread abroad,
Thou didst glory and honor impart;
Thou hast made Him most blessed forever, O God,
And Thy presence hath gladdened His heart.

For the King in the strength of Jehovah Most High
Did unwavering confidence place;

---

106. Dutton, *A Letter to the Reverend Mr. John Wesley*, in *Selected Spiritual Writings*, 1:56–57.
107. Sibbes, *The Hidden Life*, in *Works*, 5:211.
108. William Mason, *A Spiritual Treasury for the Children of God* (1834; repr., Grand Rapids, MI: Reformation Heritage Books, n.d.), 569 (reading for the evening of Sept. 9).

On the Name of Jehovah He still will rely,
And shall stand evermore in His grace.

Psalm 21
Tune: Latakia
The Psalter, No. 45

Questions for Meditation or Discussion

1. How do people think about kings today? How might that attitude influence their understanding and feelings about Christ as the King?
2. In what two senses may we speak of God's "kingdom"? Show both from the Holy Scriptures.
3. What can we learn from David and Solomon about the ideal messianic King?
4. What claim did Gustaf Aulén make regarding the doctrine of the atonement? How should we respond to it?
5. How does the Passover picture redemption by price and power?
6. What is the relationship between Christ's victory over Satan and penal substitution?
7. The authors say, "The last Adam forged a new, righteous humanity in the fiery furnace of human rejection, Satanic temptation, and divine wrath." What does this mean, and how is it taught in the Bible?
8. What is the significance of Christ's resurrection regarding the following (see Eph. 1:19–23)?
   - His glorification for eternal life
   - His supremacy over all
   - His mastery over the powers of evil
   - His restoration of man
   - His enrichment of the church
9. How are you in conflict with the evil powers of this world? How does the doctrine of Christ's victory over those powers encourage you? How can you draw upon his victory?

Questions for Deeper Reflection

10. Someone comes to you and tells you that she is confused by statements in the Bible that Jesus was "made perfect" (Heb. 2:10; 5:9). How do you explain such statements to her? How does this truth show us something of the wonder and glory of the gospel?

11. A missionary gives a talk in your church, in which he says, "The people group that I serve are not concerned with whether or not they are guilty before God. They live in terror of the spirits and demons. Therefore, when I preach the gospel, I preach Christ's victory, not substitution." Afterward, you have an opportunity to talk to him. What do you say?

12. Prepare a twenty-minute devotional to share with your small group on what it means that Christians are "more than conquerors through him that loved us" (Rom. 8:37). Make use of the doctrine in this chapter and add experiential and practical applications.

54

Christ's Kingly Work, Part 2

Power, Grace, and Glory

One of the ironies of the modern era is that in our rush to escape God's sovereignty we have cast ourselves into the iron jaws of secular fatalism. In the name of liberty, people have sacrificed freedom on the altar of determinism and declared the secular "gospel" that life is nothing more than the mindless reactions of atoms. Bertrand Russell (1872–1970) said,

> Brief and powerless is man's life; on him and all his race the slow, sure doom falls pitiless and dark. Blind to good and evil, reckless of destruction, omnipotent matter rolls on its relentless way; for man, condemned today to lose his dearest, tomorrow himself to pass through the gates of darkness, it remains only to cherish, ere yet the blow fall, the lofty thoughts that ennoble his little day . . . to worship at the shrine his own hands have built.[1]

In warm contrast to this ideology of despair, the Holy Scriptures reveal that history pulses with God's wise and loving purposes in Christ. God the Father has made a covenant with God the Son that Christ will rule a mediatorial kingdom (Luke 22:29). This kingdom cannot fail: "Of

---

1. Bertrand Russell, *A Free Man's Worship* (Portland, ME: Thomas Bird Mosher, 1923), 27.

the increase of his government and peace there shall be no end, upon the throne of David, and upon his kingdom, to order it, and to establish it with judgment and with justice from henceforth even for ever. The zeal of the LORD of hosts will perform this" (Isa. 9:7). Jonathan Edwards said, "God the Father had committed the whole affair of redemption, not only the purchasing of it but the bestowment of the blessings purchased, that he should not only purchase it as priest but actually bring it about as king, and that he should do this as God-man."[2]

Christ's kingdom is different from merely human kingdoms. Jesus refused to be made an earthly king (John 6:15). He said, "My kingdom is not of this world: if my kingdom were of this world, then would my servants fight, that I should not be delivered to the Jews: but now is my kingdom not from hence" (18:36). Christ's mediatorial kingdom is also different from a purely divine reign. The triune God—the Father, Son, and Holy Spirit—exercises sovereign providence at all times and in all places of creation.[3] However, God has also set up a messianic kingdom entrusted to the Mediator.[4] John Dick (1764–1833) said that we may "consider his mediatorial kingdom as being his original kingdom, invested with a new form, wearing a new aspect, administered for a new end." In it, the Mediator is appointed to exert "the power which he always possessed, for a specific purpose, namely, the salvation of the church."[5]

Christ's Threefold Kingdom

Reformed theologians have often spoken of Christ's kingdom of *power*, his kingdom of *grace*, and his kingdom of *glory*.[6] More precisely, the one mediatorial kingdom "may be considered in a threefold view," as Herman Witsius said.[7] These three dimensions are not three different kingdoms, but the one kingdom of Christ viewed according to its three modes of operation. Christ reigns through his universal power, spiritual grace, and heavenly glory.

---

2. Edwards, *A History of the Work of Redemption*, in *WJE*, 9:358.

3. On the doctrine of providence, see *RST*, 1:1058–1105 (chaps. 52–53).

4. Flavel, *The Fountain of Life*, in *Works*, 1:211; Witsius, *Sacred Dissertations on the Apostles' Creed*, 10.32 (1:277); Turretin, *Institutes*, 14.16.2 (2:486); Gill, *Body of Divinity*, 439; and William Symington, *Messiah the Prince: The Mediatorial Dominion of Jesus Christ* (Pittsburgh: Crown and Covenant, 2012), 3, 33–34, 52–54. For biblical evidence for this distinction, see the section on the kingdom of God in chap. 53.

5. John Dick, *Lectures on Theology*, 2 vols. (Philadelphia: F. W. Greenough, 1840), 2:132.

6. Samuel Rutherford, *Rutherford's Catechism: or, the Sum of Christian Religion* (Edinburgh: Blue Banner, 1998), chap. 17 (37–38); and Brown, *Systematic Theology*, 313–15.

7. Witsius, *Sacred Dissertations on the Apostles' Creed*, 10.33 (1:277–78).

The Universal Power of Christ's Kingdom

God's King reigns over all (Matt. 28:18). The nations "rage" and "the kings of the earth set themselves . . . against the LORD, and against his anointed," but God says, "I have set my king upon my holy hill of Zion," and he grants to him sovereignty over the nations (Ps. 2:1, 6, 8). The Lord's king "shall have dominion from sea to sea, and from the river unto the ends of the earth" (72:8). He sits at God's right hand and will rule until all his enemies are made a footstool for his feet (110:1–2). He is the "Son of man" who receives from God "dominion, and glory, and a kingdom" over "all people, nations, and languages" (Dan. 7:13–14).[8]

The Lord Jesus Christ demonstrated his universal dominion even during his state of humiliation by working miracles. When Christ healed the sick, gave sight to the blind, calmed the stormy sea, cast out demons, and raised the dead, he not only showed that God himself had come to save his people (Isa. 35:1–6), but also revealed his power to deliver people from all the forces that threatened them.

Universal sovereignty was delegated to the incarnate Son after he completed his earthly mission. Christ prayed to the Father, "Father, the hour is come; glorify thy Son, that thy Son also may glorify thee: as thou hast given him power over all flesh, that he should give eternal life to as many as thou hast given him" (John 17:1–2). Here we see the universal scope of Christ's power over the entire human world ("all flesh") and its particular intent: to give salvation to the elect ("as many as thou hast given him"). Therefore, the mediatorial dominion of God the Son incarnate is universal; he submits to no authority other than God the Father. "For he hath put all things under his feet. But when he saith, all things are put under him, it is manifest that he is excepted, which did put all things under him" (1 Cor. 15:27), that is, "the Father" (v. 24).

The exalted Christ reigns as Lord of all (Acts 10:36; Phil. 2:9–11). He is "the head of all principality and power" (Col. 2:10). John says, "He that cometh from heaven is above all. . . . The Father loveth the Son, and hath given all things into his hand" (John 3:31, 35). He is crowned with glory and honor, and reigns over all things, including all livestock, wild animals, birds, and fish (Ps. 8:4–8; Heb. 2:5–9).

---

8. It is sometimes argued that the figures of Daniel's vision represent peoples and that the "Son of man" represents all the "saints," for later in the prophecy the kingdom is said to be given to them (Dan. 7:27). However, individual "kings" are also in view (vv. 17, 24). Christ applies the prophecy to himself individually (Matt. 24:30; 26:64).

Christ's reign from God's right hand ensures the success of the gospel and the ultimate triumph of the church. James Ussher said, "Hereby we are assured, that by this kingly power we shall finally overcome the flesh, the world, the devil, death and hell."[9] John Owen said, "Though our persons fall, our cause shall be as truly, certainly, and infallibly victorious, as that Christ sits at the right hand of God. . . . The cause in which we are engaged shall surely conquer as Christ is alive and shall prevail at last.[10]

All Christians hope in Christ's future reign, but we do not think often enough of his present reign as the Lord of heaven and earth. Meditating on Christ's universal sovereignty brings joy, sober-mindedness, and reverence to believers. Wilhelmus à Brakel said,

> Wherever love for this King is active, there will be exceptional light, clarity, and delight within the soul. The soul looks to Him, beholds Him, and meditates and reflects upon His glory and preciousness, rejoicing that Jesus is so highly exalted and is crowned with honor and glory. Such a soul wholeheartedly desires this to be so, and delights to see how all the angels bow before Him and worship Him; how all the godly in radiating their love end in Him as their focal point; how the devils tremble before Him; and how all things are in His hand and must be subservient to Him.[11]

The Spiritual Grace of Christ's Kingdom

Christ reigns in grace, as John Flavel said, in a manner "spiritual and internal, by which he subdues and rules the hearts of his people," whereas he reigns in power in a manner "providential and external, whereby he guides, rules, and orders all things in the world, in a blessed subordination to their eternal salvation."[12] Thus, we now consider the "kingdom of grace," in which, as Thomas Hooker said, "Christ, by his Spirit and his grace, by the ministry of the Word, takes [his] place in the hearts of his [people] . . . by overpowering and casting down all other things which are opposite thereunto, all the power of sin and Satan . . . [and] he sets up that frame of the Spirit, whereby it is subject to grace."[13]

---

9. Ussher, *A Body of Divinity*, 14th head (162).
10. Owen, "The Use of Faith, If Popery Should Return Upon Us," in *Works*, 9:507–8.
11. Brakel, *The Christian's Reasonable Service*, 1:570.
12. Flavel, *The Fountain of Life*, in *Works*, 1:199.
13. Thomas Hooker, *A Briefe Exposition of the Lords Prayer* (London: by Moses Bell for Benjamin Allen, 1645), 20.

God the Son incarnate reigns by God the Holy Spirit. Isaiah said that a branch would spring from David's house, "and the spirit of the LORD shall rest upon him, the spirit of wisdom and understanding, the spirit of counsel and might, the spirit of knowledge and of the fear of the LORD" (Isa. 11:1–2). The "king shall reign in righteousness" and would be "as rivers of water in a dry place" when the Spirit would be "poured upon us from on high (32:1–2, 15). John Calvin wrote, "Christ's kingdom lies in the Spirit, not in earthly pleasures or pomp." The Spirit resides in Christ, "that from him might abundantly flow the heavenly riches of which we are in such need."[14] The kingdom of the great Son of David coincides with the gift of life by the indwelling Spirit and the salvation of his people from sin to walk in God's commandments (Ezek. 37:14, 23–24).

Our Lord Jesus Christ certainly proclaimed a future kingdom coming into this world (Matt. 25:34; 26:29), but also said that the kingdom is already the possession of people characterized by inward poverty, mourning, meekness, hunger for righteousness, mercy, purity, peacemaking, and persecution (5:3–10).[15] He taught that entrance into the kingdom is obtained through the new birth by the Holy Spirit (John 3:3, 5). Thus, Christ's kingdom has a spiritual dimension pertaining to the work of God's Spirit in the human spirit. This spiritual kingdom has already arrived in "seed" form to exert a hidden but powerful influence (Mark 4:26–32) upon those who receive God's Word (Matt. 13:19–23). In this sense, Jesus told the Pharisees, "The kingdom of God is within you" (Luke 17:21) or possibly "in the midst of you" (ESV). The kingdom is already present in Christ and his disciples.[16]

The spiritual nature of Christ's kingdom does not divorce it from the kingdom of David, but brings David's kingdom to a greater fulfilment, just as Christ, the Son of David (Matt. 1:1), is the supernatural Lord far greater than David ever was (22:41–46). The kingdom of the Son of David will never end (Luke 1:32–33). The risen Lord who is proclaimed in the gospel is "the seed of David" (2 Tim. 2:8). The prophets link Christ's kingdom of righteousness to God's covenant with David, implying that the greater "David" brings true righteousness.[17] Christ's resurrection fulfills promises

---

14. Calvin, *Institutes*, 2.15.5.
15. Note that Christ did not say, "Theirs *shall be* the kingdom of heaven," but that it "is" (*estin*) theirs (Matt. 5:3, 10).
16. Vos, *The Teaching of Jesus Concerning the Kingdom of God and the Church*, 51–58.
17. Isa. 9:7; 16:5; 55:1–3; Jer. 23:5–6; 33:15–26; Ezek. 37:24; Hos. 3:5.

given to David concerning his seed (Acts 2:30–31). The "grace" that is operative in the apostolic mission to the nations fulfills God's covenant regarding "the seed of David" (Rom. 1:3–5), for God is raising up the house of David by gathering the Gentiles to himself by faith in Christ (Amos 9:11–12; Acts 15:14–17). As Christ reigns over his churches among the nations, he does so by his authority as the Davidic King (Rev. 3:7). Therefore, the kingdom promised to David consists not merely in the earthly dominion of national Israel, but in the kingdom of God now being fulfilled in Christ's spiritual kingdom and yet to be fulfilled in the glory to come.

Christ's spiritual kingship is covenantal, for he is the royal administrator of the covenant of grace. In the new covenant, the promises of the covenant of grace come to their clearest and highest expression: God will overcome the covenant breaking of his people by writing his law on their hearts, causing them all to know him, and forgiving their sins (Jer. 31:31–34). Christ is the Mediator of the new covenant. He purchased these graces by his priestly sacrifice and obtains them by his intercession.[18] Christ administers these covenantal graces as the King. The Son of Man has the authority to grant divine forgiveness and does so as the Prince at God's right hand (Luke 5:20–26; Acts 5:31).[19] This King writes his laws "not with ink but with the Spirit of the living God, not on tablets of stone but on tablets of human hearts" (2 Cor. 3:3). By his power, his people are willing to serve him (Ps. 110:3). Flavel wrote, "He rules not by compulsion, but most sweetly. His law is a law of love, written upon their hearts. . . . For he delighteth in free, not in forced obedience. He rules children, not slaves; and so his kingly power is mixed with fatherly love. His yoke is not made of iron, but gold."[20]

Though Paul generally uses "kingdom" (*basileia*) to refer to the future inheritance of Christ's people,[21] the apostle repeatedly uses the language of kingdom, mastery, and lordship to describe the grace of Christ.[22] Whereas Adam broke the first covenant in the garden and his disobedience cast mankind into sin and death, Christ came as the last Adam to conquer the reign of sin and bring the reign of righteousness, that "as sin hath reigned

---

18. Heb. 8:1, 6–12; 9:12, 15, 24; 10:12–17.
19. Owen, *An Exposition of the Epistle to the Hebrews*, 3:60–61.
20. Flavel, *The Fountain of Life*, in *Works*, 1:206.
21. 1 Cor. 6:9–10; 15:50; Gal. 5:21; Eph. 5:5; 1 Thess. 2:12; 2 Thess. 1:5; 2 Tim. 4:1.
22. *Kyrieuō*: Rom. 6:9, 14; 7:1; 14:9. *Douloō*: Rom. 6:18, 22. *Doulos*: Rom. 6:16–20. *Basileuō*: Rom. 5:14, 17, 21; 6:12; 1 Cor. 15:25. *Basileia*: Rom. 14:17; Col. 1:13. Note also the references to Christ's sitting at God's right hand in Rom. 8:34; Eph. 1:20; Col. 3:1; and the risen Christ's title *Kyrios* (Rom. 4:24; 5:21; 6:11; 10:9; etc.).

unto death, even so might grace reign through righteousness unto eternal life by Jesus Christ our Lord" (Rom. 5:21). By Christ's victorious death and triumphant resurrection, those in vital union with him have died to sin and live to God, and sin cannot reign over them anymore (6:1–11, 14). Flavel said, "When Christ takes the throne, sin quits it. It is true, the being of sin is there still; its defiling and troubling power remains still; but its dominion is abolished. O joyful tidings! O welcome day!"[23]

In Christ's kingdom, the Spirit produces abundant fruit. Christians have died to the law as a righteous but condemning power that could only further agitate their rebellion against God, and have been married spiritually to Christ to bear fruit by the Spirit (Rom. 7:4–6). Formerly they hated God and could not submit to his law, but now, by the power of Christ's death for their sins, they keep the law by the life-giving Spirit of Christ dwelling in them (8:1–10). Christ died and rose again that he would be the Lord of the people who live for him (14:8–9).[24] "The kingdom of God" is among them, not in merely external regulations such as the dietary laws of Israel's theocracy, but in "righteousness, and peace, and joy in the Holy Ghost" (v. 17).

All our holiness comes by union with Christ through the Spirit. Owen said that the main difference between mere morality and "evangelical holiness" is that the latter comes only by union with Christ—both through the first principle of holiness that regeneration plants in us and by the daily supplies of grace Christ sends to preserve and grow our holiness.[25] All goodness, life, and power in the new creation originate in God, who gave people to Christ the Mediator as the treasury of grace.[26] He is the Head, and they are members of the body who receive life from him (Eph. 1:22–23; 4:15–16; Col. 2:19). Because he lives, they live also (John 14:19). He is the Vine, and they are his branches (15:4–5). The incarnate Christ is "full of grace and truth" (1:14), and they receive "of his fulness" (v. 16)—that is, the fullness of grace granted to him by union of his two natures in the one person of the God-man.[27] Christ sends the Holy Spirit in order to glorify Christ and bring the things of Christ to the people of Christ (16:13–15).[28] Owen rightly concluded that the Holy

---

23. Flavel, *The Fountain of Life*, in *Works*, 1:207.
24. Sibbes, *Christ's Exaltation Purchased by His Humiliation*, in *Works*, 5:338–39, 350.
25. Owen, *Pneumatologia*, in *Works*, 3:513–14.
26. Owen, *The Glory of Christ*, in *Works*, 1:362.
27. Owen, *Pneumatologia*, in *Works*, 3:518–23.
28. Owen, *Pneumatologia*, in *Works*, 3:516; cf. *The Glory of Christ*, in *Works*, 1:365.

Spirit is Christ's representative on earth, so the Spirit's work is "the work of the Son, by whom he is sent, in whose name he doth accomplish it."[29]

Therefore, the spiritual grace of Christ's kingdom springs from the redemptive work that his Father sent him to do and flows to his people through their union with him by the Holy Spirit. The kingdom of God is a present reality for believers on earth, though they yet await its glory.

The Heavenly Glory of Christ's Kingdom

Though we tend to think of the kingdom of glory as future, Christ has already entered his glory by his resurrection from the dead, ascension into heaven, and session at God's right hand.[30] He has inaugurated the glory of his kingdom, though it remains hidden from earthly eyes.

Christ reigns in the glory of his resurrected humanity. Though he appeared to his disciples after his resurrection in a body that was clearly human (Luke 24:39–40), he manifested himself to Saul of Tarsus in blinding, glorious light from heaven that shone brighter than the sun (Acts 9:3, 17; 22:6, 14; 26:13). Thus, Jesus Christ has already received the future glory belonging to the saints in his Father's kingdom (Matt. 13:43; Phil. 3:20–21). Christ's humanity is now immortal (Rom. 6:9). Like the bodies of his people, Christ's body "is sown in corruption; it is raised in incorruption: it is sown in dishonour; it is raised in glory: it is sown in weakness; it is raised in power: it is sown a natural body; it is raised a spiritual body"—that is, a body fully vivified and energized by the Holy Spirit (1 Cor. 15:42–44). Yet his is the unique glory of God the Son incarnate (Rom. 1:4), and even in his humanity he received preeminent glory above all men and angels, for he created them all and they exist for him (Col. 1:16–18). In heaven, Christ is the great manifestation of the divine King to his creatures (Rev. 21:22–23; 22:3–4).[31]

Christ reigns in the glory of his exalted position. He is seated at God's right hand (Ps. 110:1), which is "far above all principality, and power, and might, and dominion" (Eph. 1:21). God the Father has "given him a name which is above every name" to express his pleasure in his Son's obedience unto death (Phil. 2:8–9). He is "the head of all principality and power"

---

29. Owen, *Pneumatologia*, in *Works*, 3:193, 195.
30. Luke 24:26; Acts 7:55; 1 Pet. 1:11.
31. Revelation 22:3–4 says, "The throne of God and of the Lamb shall be in it; and his servants shall serve him: and they shall see his face; and his name shall be in their foreheads." Note how God and the Lamb share one "throne," and the singular pronouns "him" and "his" refer to both God and the Lamb as the focal point of heaven's worship and the beatific vision.

(Col. 2:10). It is from this position especially that Christ displays the glory of his deity as he reigns over all the universe with infinite power, wisdom, and goodness. Both in rendering judgment and giving life, the Father does all things through the Son so that the Son is honored to the glory of the Father (John 5:19–30). Thereby, the Father displays his eternal and infinite love for his Son before the eyes of his marveling people (17:24).

The Royal Acts of Christ's Present Reign

Christ's kingly office involves his regal functions to reign in righteousness over God's people, build the temple of God's presence, and conquer the enemies of the Lord.[32]

Christ Reigns in Righteousness over God's People

Christ employs his power over all things for the church while working in the church by his resurrection life. God "put all things under his feet, and gave him to be the head over all things to the church" (Eph. 1:21–22). All of Christ's work in the church aims at establishing his kingdom of righteousness. The Son of David and the Son of God, Christ is building an everlasting kingdom of peace, righteousness, and justice (Isa. 9:6–7). This King is "THE LORD OUR RIGHTEOUSNESS," and his righteous reign is the salvation of his people (Jer. 23:5–6). To attain this goal, Christ engages in the following acts.

Christ *appoints ministers in the church*. Ministers of the Word are gifts from the ascended Christ. Paul says, "He that descended is the same also that ascended up far above all heavens, that he might fill all things. And he gave some, apostles; and some, prophets; and some, evangelists; and some, pastors and teachers; for the perfecting of the saints, for the work of the ministry, for the edifying of the body of Christ" (Eph. 4:10–12). Through the Holy Spirit, God the Son appoints overseers to shepherd the church that he bought with his blood (Acts 20:28).

Christ *directs the church's worldwide mission*. The risen Lord says, "All power is given unto me in heaven and in earth. Go ye therefore, and teach all nations . . . and, lo, I am with you alway, even unto the end of the world" (Matt. 28:18–20). Whenever a missionary goes to a nation or people to preach Christ, he goes "for his name's sake" (3 John 7). Gospel

---

32. On these functions, see the discussion of the messianic typology of the Davidic kingdom in chap. 53.

ministers are authorized "ambassadors" of Christ the King (2 Cor. 5:20; cf. Eph. 6:20). William Symington said, "What they are doing may be unauthorized by man, may be contrary even to the will and command of the rulers of those regions of the earth into which they have gone: but they proceed in the name of One whose authority extends over all nations."[33]

Christ *sends heavenly protectors to the church.* The Son of God was the Lord of the angelic armies even in his state of humiliation (Matt. 26:53). Much more does he actively exercise command of them now that he "is gone into heaven, and is on the right hand of God; angels and authorities and powers being made subject unto him" (1 Pet. 3:22). They are "his angels" (Matt. 13:41; 16:27; 24:31). The angels are "all ministering spirits, sent forth to minister for them who shall be heirs of salvation" (Heb. 1:14). Therefore, Christ continually cares for his people by sending his angels to be their protectors and rescuers (Ps. 91:11; Acts 12:11).[34]

Christ *liberates his disciples by the truth.* Jesus says, "If ye continue in my word, then are ye my disciples indeed; and ye shall know the truth, and the truth shall make you free. . . . Whosoever committeth sin is the servant of sin. . . . If the Son therefore shall make you free, ye shall be free indeed" (John 8:31–32, 34, 36). Christ's kingdom does not depend on military power, but advances by the power of the truth working in people's lives (18:36–37; cf. Rom. 1:16; 1 Thess. 2:13). Therefore, Christ is the Prophet-King, who rules the subjects of his kingdom through the influences of his Word.[35] William Ames said that in Christ's state of exaltation, "the kingly glory of Christ overflows into his other offices so that he exercises a kingly priesthood and kingly prophecy."[36] However, Witsius explained that Christ's prophetic office is distinct from his kingly office through the Word: "In the one, he enlightens our minds by his Spirit to understand the truth; in the other, he bends our hearts, and causes all our faculties, both of soul and body, to yield a prompt obedience."[37]

Christ *renews the image of God.* He is the ideal and eternal Image of God, for he is God's Son (Col. 1:13, 15–16). Christ's identity as God's image is central to the gospel and God's glory revealed in it (2 Cor. 4:4).

---

33. Symington, *Messiah the Prince*, 152.
34. On angels, their service to God's Son, and their ministry to believers, see *RST*, 1:1109–32 (chap. 54).
35. Bullinger, *The Decades*, 2.1:277; and Perkins, *An Exposition of the Symbol*, in *Works*, 5:167.
36. Ames, *The Marrow of Theology*, 1.23.32 (148).
37. Witsius, *Sacred Dissertations on the Apostles' Creed*, 10.36 (1:279).

Athanasius said, "The Word of God came in His own person, that, as He was the Image of God, He might be able to create afresh the man after the image."[38] As the incarnate Mediator, Christ is also the perfect human image of God, the last Adam in whom his people are re-created in God's image by the life-giving Spirit (1 Cor. 15:45, 49). God predestined his chosen people "to be conformed to the image of his Son, that he might be the firstborn among many brethren" (Rom. 8:29). Paul is speaking here of union with Christ in suffering, obedience, and glory through the Holy Spirit (vv. 1–17, 23, 26–27). Irenaeus said that the Son of God became man "so that what we had lost in Adam—namely, to be according to the image and likeness of God—that we might recover in Christ Jesus."[39] Christ has "become what we are, that He might bring us to be even what He is Himself."[40] This he does by the Spirit.[41] By the Holy Spirit, God enables people to see the glory of his image in Jesus Christ and to be transformed into the same likeness (2 Cor. 3:3, 18; 4:4, 6).

Therefore, the presence of Christ in his people by the Spirit is their sanctification and hope of glory (Rom. 8:9–10; Col. 1:27). His human obedience to God won the victory that enables their practical holiness.[42] Richard Sibbes said, "The same Spirit that sanctified . . . the human nature of Christ . . . doth sanctify the mystical body of Christ" so that the church gains "a holy and humble and meek nature . . . altering our natures and working in our hearts a disposition like Christ's: that we judge as Christ judgeth, and choose as Christ chooseth, and aim at God's glory as Christ did."[43] Therefore, the renewal of God's image in Christians "is the same grace, in the kind thereof, which is in the holy nature of Christ," Owen said.[44] He added, "It is not enough for us that he hath taken our nature to be his, unless he gives us also his nature to be ours—that is, implants in our souls all those gracious qualifications, as unto the essence and substance of them, wherewith he himself in his human nature is endued."[45] Believers, regardless of their ethnic background or social status in this world, are

---

38. Athanasius, *On the Incarnation of the Word*, sec. 13, in *NPNF²*, 4:43.
39. Irenaeus, *Against Heresies*, 3.18.1, in *ANF*, 1:446. On "recapitulation," see 3.21.10, in *ANF*, 1:454.
40. Irenaeus, *Against Heresies*, preface to book 5, in *ANF*, 1:526.
41. Irenaeus, *Against Heresies*, 5.9.2–3, in *ANF*, 1:535.
42. See the discussion of the power of Christ's victory in chap. 53.
43. Sibbes, *The Spiritual Jubilee*, in *Works*, 5:243.
44. Owen, *Pneumatologia*, in *Works*, 3:478. See Goodwin, *The Work of the Holy Ghost in Our Salvation*, in *Works*, 6:217–20.
45. Owen, *The Glory of Christ*, in *Works*, 1:366.

all "renewed in knowledge after the image of him that created him," for "Christ is all, and in all" (Col. 3:10–11).

Christ *loves the church as his bride*. He is the Bridegroom of his people (Mark 2:19–20). Though he reigns over them as their authoritative Head, he does so as the spiritual Husband who loved them so much that he died for them (Eph. 5:23, 25). Indeed, he does not love them because of their beauty and goodness; rather, because of his love, he died to make them beautiful and good (vv. 26–27). He rules his church as his own body and flesh, tenderly nourishing and cherishing her (vv. 28–30). Therefore, Sibbes said, we must see Christ's kingdom as "a sweet lordship," for "he is not only a king, but a husband."[46] We must not only obey Christ, but love him and delight in his loveliness (Ps. 45:1–2). By the power of his death and resurrection, we no longer live for ourselves, but for him (2 Cor. 5:14–15). Gerard Wisse said, "Here it will become evident that we, by grace and in the exercise of grace, do not belong to ourselves, but to *Another*—another who will exercise His authority and supremacy toward us and over us."[47] Let us, therefore, resolve to be his alone and guard our devotion to Christ with holy jealousy (2 Cor. 11:2–3).

Christ *reigns over his righteous people in heaven* at this very moment. The Lord, the King of Israel, promised that he would dwell with his people for their mutual delight (Zeph. 3:15–17; Rev. 21:2–3). This was the prayer of Christ on earth: "Father, I will that they also, whom thou hast given me, be with me where I am; that they may behold my glory, which thou hast given me" (John 17:24). The last phrase reminds us that Jesus was referring to his mediatorial glory by which he reveals God to the elect (v. 22). Seeing his glory and being with him forever are the blessed hope of Christ's people (1 Thess. 4:17–18; Titus 2:13). They are the present experience of those who have died in Christ (2 Cor. 5:8; Phil. 1:21–23). With Christ and the angels in the heavenly Jerusalem, "the spirits of just men made perfect" dwell in the kingdom of absolute righteousness (Heb. 12:23). No Christian should fear to die when death will usher him into the presence of such a glorious King.

Christ Builds the Temple of God's Presence

The King greater than Solomon also engages in constructing God's temple on earth. His construction project is more glorious than any undertaken

---

46. Sibbes, *Christ's Exaltation Purchased by His Humiliation*, in *Works*, 5:334.
47. Wisse, *Christ's Ministry in the Christian*, 89.

by an earthly monarch, for Christ builds people from all nations into a living temple indwelt by the Holy Spirit (1 Cor. 3:16–17).

Christ *constructs God's temple on earth* not only by giving leaders to the visible church as an organization, but also by breathing the Spirit of life into the church as an organism. When a person is united to Christ by the Spirit, his "body is the temple of the Holy Ghost" (1 Cor. 6:15–19). Christ is the temple of God (John 2:19–21) and the cornerstone of the larger spiritual edifice where God dwells, for "through him" we have access to God (Eph. 2:18–22). Believers are "living stones" in God's "spiritual house, an holy priesthood, to offer up spiritual sacrifices, acceptable to God by Jesus Christ" (1 Pet. 2:4–5). We should not misinterpret the term "cornerstone" to imply that Christ is passive in this construction project. Christ said, "I will build my church; and the gates of hell shall not prevail against it" (Matt. 16:18).

Therefore, the ministry and worship of the church depend completely on the Spirit of Christ. Owen said, "The kingdom of Christ is spiritual. . . . It is not an outward visible ordination by men—though that be necessary, by rule and precept—but Christ's communication of that Spirit, the everlasting promise whereof he received of the Father, that gives being, life, usefulness, and success, to the ministry."[48] He said that the sending of the Holy Spirit is "the hinge" on which the whole ministry of the church turns, and he went so far as to declare, "He that would utterly separate the Spirit from the word has as good burn his Bible."[49] The church of Christ must pray for the work of the Spirit, or all our work and worship are in vain.

Christ *establishes the ordinances of God's temple with his Word.* Just as King David ordained and organized the duties of the Levites in God's temple,[50] so our Lord Jesus Christ ordains the sacred practices of his living temple, the church. In his capacity as Prophet, Christ reveals all of God's will to us. However, Christ's kingly authority particularly shines in his institution of the ordinances of his church. For example, it was the risen Christ, invested with mediatorial authority over all heaven and earth, who ordained the church's evangelism, baptism, and instructional ministry (Matt. 28:18–20). It was Christ who ordained the Lord's Supper as a sign of the new covenant in anticipation of the coming kingdom (26:26–29). Christ gave to the church's officers, beginning with the apostles, "the keys

---

48. Owen, *Pneumatologia,* in *Works,* 3:191.
49. Owen, *Pneumatologia,* in *Works,* 3:192.
50. 1 Chron. 23:25–27; 24:3; 25:1; 2 Chron. 8:14; 29:25; Neh. 12:24.

of the kingdom" to admit or exclude members of the church as God's saved society per Christ's instructions (16:18–19; 18:15–18). Christ ordained the financial support of gospel ministers (1 Cor. 9:14). Even Paul's commands for the regulation of tongues and prophecy in the church were "the commandments of the Lord" (14:34). Greg Nichols says, "The Christian church is Christ's ecclesiastical kingdom, his Messianic theocracy."[51] No pastor or bishop is king in Christ's church. Neither is the church a democracy ruled by its people's wishes or an aristocracy ruled by a group of leaders.[52] Perkins wrote, "Christ alone is the Head of the catholic church" (cf. Eph. 5:23). He has the authority to "prescribe laws properly binding the consciences of all His members." The word "alone" especially aimed at the claims of the papacy of Rome. Christ needs no human deputy on earth, "for He is all-sufficient in Himself and always present with His church" (cf. Matt. 18:20).[53]

Christ *equips the servants of God's temple with spiritual gifts*. He poured out the Holy Spirit at Pentecost after he had ascended into heaven and sat down at God's right hand (Acts 2:32–33). Though the gifts of the Spirit are common blessings possessed by the unconverted (Matt. 7:22–23; 1 Cor. 13:1–2), they are still graces from Christ. Paul says, "Unto every one of us is given grace according to the measure of the gift of Christ. Wherefore he saith, When he ascended up on high, he led captivity captive, and gave gifts unto men" (Eph. 4:7–8). The Holy Spirit comes to glorify Jesus as Lord, and though he produces a variety of ministries, all are of the same Lord (1 Cor. 12:3, 5–6). Christ's distribution of spiritual gifts to church members is the foundation of all the ministries of the church and the spring of all its edification.[54] Therefore, we should neither be proud of our gifts nor envy others for theirs, for all gifts are from Christ and for his glory.

Christ *purifies God's temple with discipline*. It was prophesied of him, "The Lord, whom ye seek, shall suddenly come to his temple. . . . And he shall sit as a refiner and purifier of silver: and he shall purify the sons of Levi, and purge them as gold and silver, that they may offer unto the Lord an offering in righteousness" (Mal. 3:1). He demonstrated his kingly

---

51. Nichols, *Lectures in Systematic Theology*, 3:633.

52. This is not to deny that Christ rules the church through officers (1 Tim. 3:1–13) or that its officers should seek the consent of the church in some decisions (Acts 6:3, 5). However, it is to assert that no officer or congregation has any authority independent of Christ and his Word. On the government of the church, see *RST*, vol. 4 (forthcoming).

53. Perkins, *An Exposition of the Symbol*, in *Works*, 5:372.

54. Owen, *An Exposition of the Epistle to the Hebrews*, 3:64.

zeal for God's worship when he drove merchants and money-changers out of the temple in Jerusalem (John 2:14–17). Christ instituted the practice of mutual admonition and church discipline among his people, and he is present among them in the process (Matt. 18:15–20; 1 Cor. 5:4). The Lord Christ himself disciplines the visible church, sometimes visiting people with sickness and death as he calls his churches to repent.[55]

Christ *reigns over God's temple in heaven*. Just as Solomon built and dedicated the house of God on earth, leading Israel in worship there (1 Kings 8), so our Lord Jesus Christ reigns over the glorious temple of God in heaven. He is the "high priest over the house of God" (Heb. 10:21). In the visions of Revelation, the city of God is made of gold and constructed of equal length, width, and height (Rev. 21:16–21), like the Most Holy Place in Solomon's temple (1 Kings 6:20). However, John does not refer to the city as a great temple, but says, "I saw no temple therein: for the Lord God Almighty and the Lamb are the temple of it" (Rev. 21:22). Therefore, at the center of heaven's worship stands the Lion-Lamb, the King-Priest who has overcome and shown himself worthy (5:5–14).

Christ Conquers the Enemies of God

The great King fights against the enemies of God (Ps. 110:2, 5–6). While victory was won at the cross and open battle waits for the day of the Lord, Christ is fighting now to conquer his foes. No one else can overcome the evils of this world but Christ, and so he comes in righteousness, salvation, and vengeance to glorify the name of the Lord (Isa. 59:16–20).

Christ *restrains the powers of evil*. Even before Christ's coming in the flesh, Satan could do nothing to God's servants without his permission (Job 1:12, 21; 2:6; 10).[56] When Christ walked the earth, a "legion," or army of thousands, of demons cowered before him and begged for clemency (Mark 5:1–20). By his death, Christ accomplished victory over the Devil (Col. 2:14–15; Heb. 2:14–15).[57] Now the risen Lord Jesus reigns "far above" all such powers (Eph. 1:21). The forces of hell and the wicked men who serve them are restrained and limited by what God wills to grant them (Rev. 9:3–5; 17:17). Flavel said, "The Lord Jesus providentially protects his people amidst a world of enemies and danger."[58] He added, "Even

---

55. 1 Cor. 11:27–32; Rev. 2:5, 16, 22–23; 3:3, 19.
56. On Satan and the sovereignty of God, see *RST*, 1:1141–42.
57. See chap. 53.
58. Flavel, *The Fountain of Life*, in *Works*, 1:215.

those that fight against Christ and his people, receive both power and permission from him. . . . As he permits no more than he will overrule to his praise, so that very permission of his, is holy and just."[59] The Shepherd is with his people in the presence of their enemies (Ps. 23:5). Those called by God are "preserved in Jesus Christ" (Jude 1). His strength prevails despite our weakness. Watson said, "Christ preserves his church as a spark in the ocean, as a flock of sheep among wolves."[60]

Christ also *judges the nations*. He is "the prince of the kings of the earth" (Rev. 1:5). "Prince" here refers not to a male child of a king, but to a "ruler" (ESV), one "first" (*archōn*) in rank.[61] All men, including kings, presidents, and prime ministers, are obligated to glorify and obey God insofar as he reveals himself to them (Rom. 1:19–22, 32; 2:14–16). Like Nebuchadnezzar, they should give God public praise, repent of their sins, and govern with justice and mercy (Dan. 4:27, 34). If they hear the gospel, they are accountable to serve Jesus Christ: "Be wise now therefore, O ye kings: be instructed, ye judges of the earth. Serve the LORD with fear, and rejoice with trembling. Kiss[62] the Son, lest he be angry, and ye perish from the way, when his wrath is kindled but a little. Blessed are all they that put their trust in him" (Ps. 2:10–12). Furthermore, the Father has entrusted all divine judgment to the mediation of the Son (John 5:22). Christ's judgment need not wait until judgment day. He who will come with the clouds (Rev. 1:7) has already come "upon a swift cloud" against Egypt and judged that nation in its power and prosperity so that Egyptians might serve the Lord (Isa. 19). As a result, the gospel penetrated Egypt, bore fruit in such notable servants of God as Athanasius, and continues to bear fruit despite the rigors of Islamic rule over the church. The Lord sent an angel to strike Herod dead for persecuting the church and boasting as if he were a god (Acts 12:1–2, 21–23). When war, famine, or some other deadly disaster strikes a nation, we may be sure that this event comes from the Lamb at God's throne and that he is working in the world to save his redeemed and execute upon the wicked "the wrath of the Lamb" (Rev. 5:9–10; 6:1–8, 16).[63]

---

59. Flavel, *The Fountain of Life*, in *Works*, 1:214.
60. Watson, *A Body of Divinity*, 188.
61. In current English usage, "prince" often refers to a son of a monarch, but in older usage, it was a term for the monarch himself.
62. "Kiss" may express submission to an authority or worship given to a deity. See Gen. 41:40 [Hebrew text]; 1 Sam. 10:1; 1 Kings 19:18; Job 31:26–27; Hos. 13:2.
63. Symington, *Messiah the Prince*, 149–52.

Christ *converts the lost and rescues Satan's captives.* Those whom the Father gave to Christ to save are rebels against God, spiritually dead slaves of Satan (Eph. 2:1–3). Therefore, Christ must deliver them from the Devil and exercise resurrection power to give them life and subdue them to his service. Though Satan was like a strong warrior who captured people and held them securely in his house, Christ conquered Satan, bound him, and plunders his treasures (Mark 3:27).[64] Flavel said, "Christ obtains a throne in the hearts of men . . . by conquest, for though the souls of the elect are his by donation and right of redemption (the Father gave them to him, and he died for them), yet Satan hath the first possession."[65] Christ wars with spiritual weapons of divine power—especially his mighty, soul-piercing Word—to capture his enemies and make them obedient to him (2 Cor. 10:4–5).[66] God sends the Spirit of regeneration through Christ (Titus 3:5–6), and Christ's resurrection life becomes the life of his people so that they are born again (Eph. 2:4–6; 1 Pet. 1:3).[67] The risen King gives conversion and justification to sinners: "Him hath God exalted with his right hand to be a Prince and a Saviour, for to give repentance to Israel, and forgiveness of sins" (Acts 5:31).

Christ *leads God's army into spiritual battle.* Having defeated the spiritual Goliath, the Son of David now leads his people to overcome the spiritual forces of wickedness (Rev. 5:5; 12:10–11; 17:14). Indeed, Christ is not only our Captain but our strength, our armor and equipment, and our all. The first lesson of spiritual warfare is, "Be strong in the Lord, and in the power of his might" (Eph. 6:10). The spiritual soldier must "put on the whole armour of God, that ye may be able to stand against the wiles of the devil" (v. 11). The church walks in "the armour of light" when it obeys this injunction: "Put ye on the Lord Jesus Christ" (Rom. 13:12, 14). William Gurnall said, "Till Christ be put on, the creature is unarmed."[68] However, clothed with Christ as our armor in justification and sanctification, we are able to overcome all the forces of hell (Eph. 6:13).

Christ *will execute final judgment.* The presently hidden glory of the King will appear in open majesty when Christ comes (Col. 3:3–4). At that time, grace will find fruition in glory and patience will give way to

---

64. On Christ's victory over Satan, see chap. 53.
65. Flavel, *The Fountain of Life*, in *Works*, 1:201. The punctuation has been modernized.
66. Isa. 11:4; 49:2; Heb. 4:12; Rev. 1:16.
67. Peterson, *Salvation Accomplished by the Son*, 145.
68. Gurnall, *The Christian in Complete Armour*, 1:45. On spiritual warfare, see *RST*, 1:1146–55.

judgment. Christ will return as the conquering Warrior-King to destroy all who oppose his reign and persecute his people (Rev. 19:11–16). He will raise the dead by the power of his voice, and judgment day will commence (John 5:28–29). Jesus says, "When the Son of man shall come in his glory, and all the holy angels with him, then shall he sit upon the throne of his glory," and "the King" will judge men by their works, welcoming those characterized by Christian love into the kingdom and casting the wicked into "everlasting fire" (Matt. 25:31–46). In that judgment, Christ will show his infinite divine knowledge of all people and events; his perfect divine justice in administering the proper punishment or reward to each person; his absolute divine power over all beings; and his supreme divine authority as he calls each of his intelligent creatures to account as their Lord and Master.[69] Then Christ will subdue all his enemies—even the "last enemy," death itself (1 Cor. 15:26)—under his feet for the sake of his people.[70]

The Everlasting Kingdom of Christ in Glory

The returning King is the Son of God and "heir of all things" (Heb. 1:2). Christ's coming will begin the inheritance of his people in the new heaven and new earth, a new and renewed creation characterized by joy (Isa. 65:17–19), righteousness (2 Pet. 3:13), God's manifest presence, and the end of all suffering and death (Rev. 21:1–4). Whatever authorities we may serve on earth, if we serve the Lord Christ when serving them, we will receive his royal reward in the coming inheritance (Matt. 25:23; Col. 3:23–24).

Although Christ's great work of saving his people will be done, he will abide as the last Adam and Mediator of his people, for God has raised them up with Christ "that in the ages to come he might shew the exceeding riches of his grace in his kindness toward us through Christ Jesus" (Eph. 2:7). Then the righteous will rejoice, saying, "The kingdoms of this world are become the kingdoms of our Lord, and of his Christ; and he shall reign for ever and ever" (Rev. 11:15).

It might be objected that Christ's kingdom will end at the consummation of all things, for Paul says, "Then cometh the end, when he shall have delivered up the kingdom to God, even the Father; when he shall have put

---

69. Manton, *Several Sermons upon Matthew 25*, in *Works*, 10:16–21.
70. On Christ's return, see the locus of eschatology in *RST*, vol. 4 (forthcoming).

down all rule and all authority and power. . . . And when all things shall be subdued unto him, then shall the Son himself be subject unto him that put all things under him, that God may be all in all" (1 Cor. 15:24, 28).

In reply, we point out that the Holy Scriptures indicate that Christ will reign as King forever.[71] Theodoret (393–c. 458) said, "In handing over the kingdom to the God and Father he is not himself stripped of the kingdom; rather, he brings into subjection the tyrannical devil and his assistants, and forces all to do obeisance and acknowledge the God of all."[72] The delivery of the kingdom to the Father and the subjection of the Son may be understood, as Francis Turretin said, "not as to the very essence of the kingdom, but only as to the mode of its administration."[73]

The key to understanding Paul's words is the fact that Christ always acts according to the Father's will and for his glory. Roy Ciampa and Brian Rosner comment,

> To understand Paul we will return to the analogy of a Roman emperor who sends out his top military general to quash a rebellion in the empire. . . . While the general is out executing the war, he is surrounded by the symbols and instruments of power, and it is he who serves as the physical expression of the power of the empire in his battles against the rebels. Once he has accomplished his mission, however, he is expected to return to Rome, acknowledge that he is in submission to the emperor, and show that he does not intend to use the power of his armies to take over the empire by force. He does not cease to be a general or to have great power and influence, but the mission for which he was commissioned has been accomplished.[74]

Christ's kingdom will then enter a new state of established glory, for the time of its militant struggle against the powers of evil will be done. However, Christ's threefold office must continue forever in some sense,

---

71. 2 Sam. 7:13; Pss. 45:6; 89:4, 29, 36–37; Isa. 9:6–7; Dan. 2:44; 7:14; Luke 1:33; Heb. 1:8; Rev. 11:15. See Symington, *Messiah the Prince*, 227.

72. Theodoret of Cyrus, *Commentary on the Letters of St. Paul*, trans. Robert Charles Hill (Brookline, MA: Holy Cross Orthodox Press, 2001), 1:228, cited in Roy E. Ciampa and Brian S. Rosner, *The First Letter to the Corinthians*, The Pillar New Testament Commentary (Grand Rapids, MI: Eerdmans, 2010), 766.

73. Turretin, *Institutes*, 14.17.10 (2:493). The Socinians used 1 Cor. 15:24 to argue that Christ was not God. See Turretin, *Institutes*, 14.17.1 (2:490). Leon Morris said, "Paul is not speaking of the essential nature of either the Son or the Father. He is speaking of the work that Christ has accomplished and will accomplish." *1 Corinthians*, Tyndale New Testament Commentaries (Downers Grove, IL: InterVarsity Press, 1985), 208.

74. Ciampa and Rosner, *The First Letter to the Corinthians*, 776.

because "Christ is the bond of our perpetual union with God." As Prophet, he will forever illuminate the saints with God's glory (Rev. 21:23). As Priest, his presence before God will continually represent the basis of our enjoyment of God in the kingdom (5:6). As King, he will perpetually reign as the Head of his people—God the Son incarnate, our everlasting Prince of Peace (Isa. 9:6–7).[75]

We should view the kingdom of God and Christ as the greatest treasure. The world seeks after earthly goods and the life of the body. Christ says, "Seek ye first the kingdom of God, and his righteousness; and all these things shall be added unto you" (Matt. 6:33). Jesus compares the kingdom to a treasure hidden in a field, which, when discovered, is worth selling all one has in order to get it (13:44). For when we gain the kingdom, we gain the King. When God's kingdom purposes come to complete fulfillment, God will be "all in all" (1 Cor. 15:28). Therefore, make Christ's kingdom the supreme object of your personal pursuit.[76] Seek Christ's grace as your riches on earth and his eternal glory as your inheritance forever.

Sing to the Lord

Glorifying God for the Reign of Christ

> Christ shall have dominion
> Over land and sea,
> Earth's remotest regions
> Shall His empire be;
> They that wilds inhabit
> Shall their worship bring,
> Kings shall render tribute,
> Nations serve our King.

> *Refrain*:
> Christ shall have dominion
> Over land and sea,
> Earth's remotest regions
> Shall His empire be.

> When the needy seek Him,
> He will mercy show;

---

75. Turretin, *Institutes*, 14.17.7–8 (2:492).
76. Vos, *The Teaching of Jesus Concerning the Kingdom of God and the Church*, 87.

Yea, the weak and helpless
Shall His pity know;
He will surely save them
From oppression's might,
For their lives are precious
In His holy sight.

Ever and forever
Shall His Name endure,
Long as suns continue
It shall stand secure;
And in Him forever
All men shall be blessed
And all nations hail Him
King of kings confessed.

Psalm 72
Tune: St. Gertrude (the tune used for "Onward Christian Soldiers")
The Psalter, No. 200
Trinity Hymnal—Baptist Edition, No. 678

Questions for Meditation or Discussion

1. What are the three dimensions or modes of Christ's kingdom?
2. What does John 17:1–2 teach about the scope and the purpose of Christ's kingdom?
3. Someone says to you, "Christ's kingdom is his reign when he returns to earth. That is a different thing from his saving grace at work in the church today." How do you reply?
4. In what sense has Christ's kingdom of glory already begun?
5. What are the three functions of Christ's reign?
6. How does Christ the King lead his churches today?
7. How is Christ the King involved in the sanctification of his people?
8. How does Christ work in the building, direction, equipping, and purifying of the church?
9. Why can the knowledge of Christ's kingship give Christians confidence as they face their enemies—both human persecutors and the demons of Satan?
10. Why should the truths of this chapter increase our fear and joy toward Christ? How has reading this chapter affected your attitude

toward the Lord Jesus? What is one specific way the doctrine of Christ's kingship is calling you to change?

Questions for Deeper Reflection

11. How does Christ's present kingdom fulfill God's promises to Abraham and David?

12. What is the relationship between the image of God and the kingdom of God and Christ?

13. Why is it crucial for the church to order its worship and other activities only according to the ordinances of the Lord Jesus Christ? What might happen to a congregation that forgets that Christ alone is King of the church?

14. How should Christians honor and serve Christ in their political activities as voting citizens of democratic republics? How should a Christian holding office in the civil government honor and serve Christ?

55

Christ's Kingly Work, Part 3

Christ's Kingly People

Christ's kingly office aims at creating a kingly people, renewed in the image of God to reign as his servant-kings in the new creation. Christ "made us kings" by the saving power of his blood (Rev. 1:5–6). The Heidelberg Catechism (LD 12, Q. 32) reminds us that those in union with Christ share in his anointing as the King, so that every Christian may say, "I am a member of Christ by faith . . . that with a free and good conscience I may fight against sin and Satan in this life, and afterwards reign with Him eternally, over all creatures."[1]

Therefore, it is the highest honor to be called a "Christian," for we bear the very name of Jesus Christ. If we share in his sufferings, then we also share in his Spirit and will share in his glory (1 Pet. 4:13–16). Johannes VanderKemp (1664–1718) said, "Rejoice and glory in a holy manner on account of your name. The great Theodosius esteemed it a greater honor to be a Christian than an emperor."[2]

In order to fuel the joy that flames from this privilege and to stir up Christians to exercise their kingship in Christ, we will examine the royal calling that belongs to everyone in Christ.

---

1. *The Three Forms of Unity*, 78.
2. Johannes VanderKemp, *The Christian Entirely the Property of Christ, in Life and Death, Exhibited in Fifty-Three Sermons on the Heidelberg Catechism*, trans. John M. Harlingen, 2 vols. (repr., Grand Rapids, MI: Reformation Heritage Books, 1997), 1:271.

The Gracious Reign of God's Sons and Daughters

Salvation is our deliverance from one kingdom and transfer into another, where God reigns over us and we conquer and reign over our spiritual enemies through Jesus Christ. Sin and death reign over mankind because of the disobedience of Adam, but Christ by his obedience has delivered us from sin's dominion (Rom. 5:12, 14, 21; 6:14). The result is not merely that we have freedom, but we also reign in Christ. Paul says, "For if by one man's offence death reigned by one; much more they which receive abundance of grace and of the gift of righteousness shall reign in life by one, Jesus Christ" (5:17). The full glory of this reign will be in the future kingdom, but God's grace is reigning even now through Christ (v. 21). Once slaves of sin, we are now obedient to the truth of God (6:17). We have the power to give our bodies to righteousness instead of sin (v. 13). Therefore, by God's sovereign grace, "we are more than conquerors through him who loved us" (8:37). "All things," even sorrow and death, serve to bring us into the fullness of God's "image" in the Son (vv. 28–29). We are kings now in grace, though we wait for our enthronement in glory.

This is the liberty of God's children. Martin Luther said, "With respect to the kingship, every Christian is by faith so exalted above all things that, by virtue of a spiritual power, he is lord of all things without exception, so that nothing can do him any harm. As a matter of fact, all things are made subject to him and are compelled to serve him in obtaining salvation."[3]

Therefore, Christians should not concern themselves with worldly glory, but with humble service (Matt. 20:20–28), for they already reign over all things. Paul writes, "Therefore let no man glory in men. For all things are yours; whether Paul, or Apollos, or Cephas, or the world, or life, or death, or things present, or things to come; all are yours; and ye are Christ's; and Christ is God's" (1 Cor. 3:21–23). Zacharias Ursinus commented, "We are, therefore, kings, because we are lords over all creatures in Christ."[4] VanderKemp said, "They have also kingly riches, although they may be the poorest in the world; for they have a true title to whatsoever exists."[5] As William Perkins explained, in "union with Christ every

---

3. Luther, *The Freedom of a Christian*, in LW, 31:354.

4. *The Commentary of Dr. Zacharias Ursinus on the Heidelberg Catechism*, trans. G. W. Williard (repr., Phillipsburg, NJ: Presbyterian and Reformed, 1985), 180.

5. VanderKemp, *The Christian Entirely the Property of Christ*, 1:266.

believer comes to have interest and recover his title in the creatures of God," Christ having come as "Lord and King over all" to recover what Adam lost.[6]

The kingship of Christians is theirs by right as adopted sons and heirs of God.[7] Divine sonship stands at the heart of God's covenant to give David's seed an everlasting kingdom (2 Sam. 7:13–14; Pss. 2:6–7; 89:26–27). God's Son is the mediatorial heir of all things (Matt. 21:38; Heb. 1:2). He has purchased an "eternal inheritance" by his redeeming death (9:15). Those in Christ are also sons by adoption and therefore heirs with Christ (Rom. 8:16–17; Gal. 4:7). By faith they are heirs of the blessing promised in the covenant with Abraham, which includes the whole world (Rom. 4:13–14; Gal. 3:29; cf. Matt. 5:5). They inherit the kingdom and eternal life,[8] unlike those under the power of sin and death in Adam.[9] God says, "He that overcometh shall inherit all things; and I will be his God, and he shall be my son" (Rev. 21:7).

However, we must distinguish between Christ's reign at God's right hand and the reign of the church militant on earth. First, there is a distinction in persons. Ursinus said, "He is the natural Son of God, whilst we are the sons of God by adoption." Therefore, "he alone is king over all creatures, and especially over the church; but we are kings and lords, not of angels and the church, but only of other creatures."[10]

Second, there is a distinction of states. The Corinthian church was confused on this matter, prompting Paul to write sarcastically, "Now ye are full, now ye are rich, ye have reigned as kings without us: and I would to God ye did reign, that we also might reign with you" (1 Cor. 4:8). Perkins said, "In this life we have no more but right unto the creature [*jus ad rem*] and right in it [*jus in re*]—that is, actual possession—is reserved for the life to come. Therefore, we must content ourselves with our allowed portions given unto us by God, by His grace using them in holy manner, expecting by hope the full fruition of all things till after this life."[11]

Therefore, we must not confuse the saints' spiritual reign with earthly riches and political power. Luther qualified the statement "all things are yours" (1 Cor. 3:21) by explaining,

---

6. Perkins, *An Exposition of the Symbol*, in *Works*, 5:370.
7. Perkins, *A Golden Chain*, chap. 37, in *Works*, 6:184.
8. Matt. 19:29; 25:34; Titus 3:7; James 2:5.
9. 1 Cor. 6:9–11; 15:49–50; Gal. 5:21; Eph. 5:5.
10. Ursinus, *Commentary on the Heidelberg Catechism*, 180.
11. Perkins, *An Exposition of the Symbol*, in *Works*, 5:370.

This is not to say that every Christian is placed over all things to have and control them by physical power—a madness with which some churchmen are afflicted—for such power belongs to kings, princes, and other men on earth. Our ordinary experience in life shows us that we are subjected to all, suffer many things, and even die. As a matter of fact, the more Christian a man is, the more evils, sufferings, and deaths he must endure, as we see in Christ the first-born prince himself, and in all his brethren, the saints.[12]

The paradox of a Christian's present reign is the paradox of Christ's cross—we conquer by suffering and overcome through death. Luther wrote, "The power of which we speak is spiritual. It rules in the midst of enemies and is powerful in the midst of oppression. This means nothing else than that 'power is made perfect in weakness' [2 Cor. 12:9] and that in all things I can find profit toward salvation, so that the cross and death itself are compelled to serve me and to work together with me for my salvation." Luther said that this "truly omnipotent power" and "spiritual dominion" is possible only through faith, but "this is the inestimable power and liberty of Christians."[13] Christians must constantly tell themselves that they are already conquerors in grace though not yet crowned in glory.

The Noble Faith of God's Righteous People

Slavery to sin degrades humanity, but serving Christ ennobles God's children with true liberty (Gal. 5:13; 1 Pet. 2:16). Paul exhorts us, "Stand fast therefore in the liberty wherewith Christ hath made us free, and be not entangled again with the yoke of bondage," but instead devote yourself to "faith which worketh by love" (Gal. 5:1, 6). God's children are heirs of liberty (Rom. 8:21), a liberty that the Spirit already manifests among them (2 Cor. 3:17).

A good conscience washed in Christ's blood, restored through repentance, and fortified through proven obedience makes the Christian intrepid and fearless. "The wicked flee when no man pursueth: but the righteous are bold as a lion" (Prov. 28:1). God's adopted children need not cringe and cower before their Father (Rom. 8:15), and if not before God, then not before anyone.

---

12. Luther, *The Freedom of a Christian*, in *LW*, 31:354–55.
13. Luther, *The Freedom of a Christian*, in *LW*, 31:355.

Living by faith forms within us what VanderKemp called "a kingly spirit" or "an elevated mind" with "a free and good conscience" that is not enslaved to men or earthly things. By this kingly spirit, Paul pursued Christ wholeheartedly and counted all other things as worthless in comparison to him (Phil. 3:7–10). Faith lifted Moses above the visible things of this world, so that he "refused to be called the son of Pharaoh's daughter; choosing rather to suffer affliction with the people of God, than to enjoy the pleasures of sin for a season; esteeming the reproach of Christ greater riches than the treasures in Egypt . . . not fearing the wrath of the king: for he endured, as seeing him who is invisible" (Heb. 11:24–27).[14]

The wicked are easily corrupted and turned aside by influential leaders, but "the people that do know their God shall be strong, and do exploits" (Dan. 11:32). Wilhelmus à Brakel said that God's children have "a royal heart" and "an excellent spirit" that empower them to be "courageous" and to "persevere" with "great and lofty things in view," namely, the invisible, eternal kingdom of Christ.[15] Even in this life, if you examine a true believer, you can see "the radiance of the image of God," which is his "majesty and glory."[16]

Therefore, VanderKemp wrote, "conduct yourself with a holy, but humble greatness of mind, as kings, 'who will not be brought under the power of any[thing],' as that great man [Paul] said (1 Cor. 6:12). Ye are too noble, and of too high a condition to suffer yourself to be enslaved to any sin, or to any creature, without and contrary to the will of God."[17] Brakel said, "They are not to allow anyone to control them by either favor or disfavor, or out of love or fear for them, and thus be drawn away from obedience to our sovereign King."[18]

The faith of God's righteous children is a strenuous exercise of spiritual conflict against our unbelief and Satan's lies. The believer often can sympathize with the man who said to Jesus, "Lord, I believe; help thou mine unbelief" (Mark 9:24). We should not be discouraged if we find much cowardice remaining in our hearts, though we sincerely trust in Christ. Instead, we should press on in the battle. Remind yourself and your brethren of God's promises. Pray without ceasing. Train your conscience

---

14. VanderKemp, *The Christian Entirely the Property of Christ*, 1:265.
15. Brakel, *The Christian's Reasonable Service*, 1:572.
16. Brakel, *The Christian's Reasonable Service*, 1:573.
17. VanderKemp, *The Christian Entirely the Property of Christ*, 1:271.
18. Brakel, *The Christian's Reasonable Service*, 1:573.

to follow the Word of God and not your experiences and feelings. Develop spiritual nobility by defying your fears and disciplining yourself to practice righteousness despite the opposition of earth and hell. When you follow Peter in cowardice, follow him also in tearful repentance and restoration. By God's grace, you may become like John Knox, "who in his life never feared the face of man."[19]

The Overcoming Power of God's Spiritual Warriors

In Ezekiel's vision of the valley of dry bones, when the Spirit came to give life, there arose a "great army" (Ezek. 37:10). God's Spirit-vivified people are indeed an army; however, it is an army outfitted not with swords and spears, but "by purity, knowledge, patience, kindness, the Holy Spirit, genuine love; by truthful speech, and the power of God; with the weapons of righteousness for the right hand and for the left" (2 Cor. 6:6–7 ESV). Our principal enemies are not people, but the Devil and his demons (Eph. 6:12). The Heidelberg Catechism (LD 12, Q. 32) says that we share in Christ's anointing "that with a free and good conscience I may fight against sin and Satan in this life."[20]

Christians are overcomers. John says that they "have overcome the wicked one" (1 John 2:13–14). He writes, "For whatsoever is born of God overcometh the world: and this is the victory that overcometh the world, even our faith. Who is he that overcometh the world, but he that believeth that Jesus is the Son of God?" (5:4–5). Ursinus said, "The kingly office of Christians is to oppose and overcome, through faith, the devil, the world, and all enemies."[21]

John Calvin said,

[Christ's] manner of rule is not so much for his advantage as for ours. For he arms and fortifies us with his power, he decks us with his splendor, he enriches us with his gifts; in short, he raises us up and exalts us with the majesty of his kingdom. For through that fellowship by which he is joined to us he makes us kings, equipping us with his strength to do battle with the devil, sin and death, clothing and adorning us with the dress of his righteousness, and in hope of immortality filling us

---

19. David Laing, preface to *The Works of John Knox*, ed. David Laing, 6 vols. (Edinburgh: Thomas George Stevenson, 1864), 6:lii.
20. *The Three Forms of Unity*, 78.
21. Ursinus, *Commentary on the Heidelberg Catechism*, 179.

with the riches of his holiness that we may bear fruit for God through good works.[22]

Here again, we must distinguish between the only Mediator-King and the people he redeemed to reign with him. Ursinus said, "Christ conquers his enemies by his own power, but we overcome our foes in and through him—by his grace and assistance." Yet we do have an obligation to imitate our Warrior-King if we intend to follow in his footsteps to glory. Ursinus said, "Since we are kings it becomes us to fight manfully against sin, the world, and the devil, that we may reign with Christ."[23]

The Christian's greatest battles are within his own soul (Rom. 7:20). Perkins taught that as "spiritual kings even in this life," Christians must rule over their own thoughts and feelings, "over-mastering them as much as we possibly can by God's Word and Spirit, withal maintaining and proclaiming continual war against our corrupt natures, the devil, and the world." Perkins remarked that the one who can rule his own heart is a "king indeed."[24] This is not a proud kingship, but the likeness of Christ that lifts up a man's head in hope while inculcating lowliness of mind. It produces humble warriors of love: "Be watchful, stand firm in the faith, act like men, be strong. Let all that you do be done in love" (1 Cor. 16:13 ESV).

Jonathan Edwards explained,

Many persons seem to be quite mistaken concerning the nature of Christian fortitude [strength]. 'Tis an exceeding diverse thing from a brutal fierceness, or the boldness of beasts of prey. True Christian fortitude consists in strength of mind, through grace, exerted in two things; in ruling and suppressing the evil, and unruly passions and affections of the mind; and in steadfastly and freely exerting, and following good affections and dispositions, without being hindered by sinful fear, or the opposition of enemies. . . . The strength of the good soldier of Jesus Christ, appears in nothing more, than in steadfastly maintaining the holy calm, meekness, sweetness, and benevolence of his mind, amidst all the storms, injuries, strange behavior, and surprising acts and events of this evil and unreasonable world.[25]

---

22. John Calvin, *Institutes of the Christian Religion: Translated from the First French Edition of 1541*, trans. Robert White (Edinburgh: Banner of Truth, 2014), 235.
23. Ursinus, *Commentary on the Heidelberg Catechism*, 180.
24. Perkins, *An Exposition of the Symbol*, in *Works*, 5:107.
25. Edwards, *Religious Affections*, in *WJE*, 2:350.

Thus, we conquer through self-denial. The royal church of Christ does not overcome Satan by the sword, but by suffering and sanctification. Revelation 12:11 (ESV) says, "They have conquered him by the blood of the Lamb and by the word of their testimony, for they loved not their lives even unto death." They surely conquer, for the Lamb is with them (17:14).

Christ's advice to his sleepy disciples remains very applicable today: "Watch and pray, that ye enter not into temptation" (Matt. 26:41). Be on the alert for ways that Satan is quietly infiltrating your life to draw you into sins such as pride, unbelief, prayerlessness, bitterness, or worldliness. Engage every temptation head on and fight to mortify every inward lust with the confidence that Christ came to destroy the works of the Devil.

The Purposeful Stewardship of God's Royal Servants

Another aspect of Christians' kingship with Christ is how it empowers their obedience to the creation mandate. God created man in his image in order to rule as his servant-kings on earth—God's stewards managing, enjoying, and caring for his creation.[26] Furthermore, all human beings bear the responsibility to labor as they are able to provide for their households and help those in need.[27] The kingdom of Christ is spiritual, heavenly, and eternal in its aims, not earthly, but our kingship in Christ does provide new motives for Christians to fulfill their vocations in this world.

Christ the King subdues people to God's authority. Redemption restores them to the humble posture of stewardship that is theirs by creation. Instead of vainly attempting to throw off God's reign by their power and intelligence, by Christ's kingship they are converted to serve the Lord with joyful fear (Ps. 2:1–6, 11). Bought with a price, they know that they do not belong to themselves but to God, whom they must glorify (1 Cor. 6:19–20). They are being renewed in God's image (Col. 3:10), which equips and empowers them to rule as God's representatives.

The Christian view of work and possessions is profoundly shaped by the knowledge that Christ is the Lord and Heir of all things (Matt. 28:18; Heb. 1:2). Whether we labor in the home, agriculture, transportation,

---

26. See the section on the practical implications of the image of God in chap. 10.

27. Eph. 4:28; 1 Thess. 4:11–12; 2 Thess. 3:10, 12; 1 Tim. 5:4, 8. On the doctrine of labor, see William Perkins, *A Treatise of the Vocations* (London: John Legat, 1603); Richard Steele, *The Religious Tradesman* (1823; repr., Harrisonburg, VA: Sprinkle, 1989); Nichols, *Lectures in Systematic Theology*, 2:238–69; and Daniel M. Doriani, *Work: Its Purpose, Dignity, and Transformation* (Phillipsburg, NJ: P&R, 2019).

financial services, the military, law enforcement, medicine, music, the arts, science, engineering, education, civil government, church ministry, construction, mining, computer programming, advertising, sales and marketing, information technology, plumbing, athletics, food preparation, the automotive industry, retail, or some other field, every object and person falls under Christ's sovereignty and exists for his glory (Col. 1:16–17). Abraham Kuyper (1837–1920) said, "Oh, no single piece of our mental world is to be hermetically sealed off from the rest, and there is not a square inch in the whole domain of our human existence over which Christ, who is Sovereign over all, does not cry: 'Mine!'"[28]

Consequently, all work may and should be done for the Lord. Paul could say to Christian slaves, "Whatsoever ye do, do it heartily, as to the Lord, and not unto men; knowing that of the Lord ye shall receive the reward of the inheritance: for ye serve the Lord Christ" (Col. 3:23–24). For a slave to receive the inheritance implies that he is really no slave but a son. Serving Christ grants nobility to all work and fundamental equality to all workers, for with Christ "there is no respect of persons" (v. 25)—he judges all by the same law. Both slave and master have one "Master in heaven" (4:1; cf. Eph. 6:8–9). The Christian with little political and societal freedom is still "the Lord's freeman," and the believer with much earthly freedom is "Christ's servant" (1 Cor. 7:22). The Lord has given to everyone his "talents," all the resources of his person and possessions, and will reward the "good and faithful servant" (Matt. 25:14–30).

However, it is precisely here that the kingship of Christians exhibits its otherworldly focus. Christians serve Christ in this world but do not seek this world; instead, they seek "treasures in heaven" in "the kingdom of God" (Matt. 6:19–20, 33). Their inheritance is not here, for they are "pilgrims on the earth" on their way to the heavenly city (Heb. 11:13–16). They do not love this world or lust after its pleasures and honors, for "the world passeth away . . . but he that doeth the will of God abideth for ever" (1 John 2:15–17). Here they are uncrowned princes sojourning in a strange land soon to be destroyed; there they will reign as kings in their own palatial estates, having received their Lord's reward on judgment day for deeds done in this life.

---

28. Abraham Kuyper, "Sphere Sovereignty," in *A Centennial Reader*, ed. James D. Bratt (Grand Rapids, MI: Eerdmans, 1998), 488. A "hermetic seal" makes a container airtight.

The Glorious Hope of God's Deputy Rulers

The Christian's kingship in Christ is a present reality that will find its fulfillment in the age to come. The Lamb receives this praise: "Thou art worthy . . . for thou wast slain, and hast redeemed us to God . . . and *hast made* us unto our God kings and priests: and we *shall reign* on the earth" (Rev. 5:9–10).[29] In the new heaven and new earth, "they shall reign for ever and ever" (22:5). Yet they shall reign as "his servants" (v. 3).

Therefore, in the new creation, God's children will exercise a dominion similar to that granted to man in the first creation (Gen. 1:26–28; Ps. 8:4–8), but with far greater glory, for they shall reign in union with God the Son incarnate (2 Tim. 2:12). Christ says, "To him that overcometh will I grant to sit with me in my throne, even as I also overcame, and am set down with my Father in his throne" (Rev. 3:21).

What this means exactly is not revealed to us, but it involves authority to rule the new world. In the parable of the talents, the master says, "Well done, thou good and faithful servant: thou hast been faithful over a few things, I will make thee ruler over many things: enter thou into the joy of thy lord" (Matt. 25:21). In a similar parable, a king rewards a faithful servant by granting him "authority over ten cities" (Luke 19:17). The dominion granted is certainly "a reward . . . not of merit, but of grace," far out of proportion to the servant's work.[30] Furthermore, our reward in the new creation will be "an inheritance incorruptible, and undefiled, and that fadeth not away" (1 Pet. 1:4). Best of all, reigning with Christ will lift us up into a higher experiential knowledge of God, for Christ is God's Image, and we will reign in Christ as God's image bearers. Whether we gaze upon the incarnate Lord, our fellow saints, the angels, or the wonders of the new heaven and new earth, we will see the radiance of God's glory (Rev. 21:23; 22:4). God has so ordered our salvation and glorification "that God may be all in all" (1 Cor. 15:28).

Therefore, the consummation of Christ's kingdom will bring the full fruit of Christ's threefold office. The Priest will bring us to God as his reconciled children. The Prophet will reveal God to us face-to-face. The King will lead us to reign in divine glory so that God's glory will be increasingly manifested to his creatures in the ages to come.

---

29. The Greek verb translated as "hast made" is in the aorist tense; "shall reign" is in the future tense. The change of tense suggests a past endowment of royal status that will come to fruition in the future. See also the future tense of "reign" in Rom. 5:17; 2 Tim. 2:12.

30. Heidelberg Catechism (LD 24, Q. 63), in *The Three Forms of Unity*, 88.

The knowledge of Christ's coming in glory should stir and warm the hearts of Christians to serve the Lord in a lively manner. As Richard Sibbes said, this doctrine should move believers to serve Christ *sincerely*, for Christ will judge them; *constantly*, for Christ will reward them; *abundantly*, for Christ will make sure their labor is not in vain; and *cheerfully*, for Christ will come in glory to crown every good work, down to the least act and cup of cold water given in his name.[31] In light of all that Christ is for us as our life, "our whole life should be spent in thankfulness to God." In Christ, Sibbes said, "the life of heaven is begun on earth. We are kings now; we are priests now; we are conquerors now; we are new creatures now. We must praise God, and begin the employment of heaven now; for what they do perfectly, that we begin to do."[32]

Sing to the Lord

Christ the Victorious King and Our Victory in Him

As Thou, O Lord, hast made me strong
To overcome my mighty foe,
So now to fight against the wrong
And conquer in Thy Name I go.

Jehovah lives, and blest is He,
My rock, my refuge and defense,
My Saviour Who delivers me,
And will the wicked recompense.

For grace and mercy ever near,
For foes subdued and victories won,
All nations of the earth shall hear
My praise for what the Lord has done.

To David, His anointed king,
And to his sons upon his throne,
The Lord will great salvation bring
And ever make His mercy known.

Psalm 18
Tune: Mozart
The Psalter, No. 36

---

31. Sibbes, *The Hidden Life*, in *Works*, 5:215.
32. Sibbes, *The Hidden Life*, in *Works*, 5:216.

Questions for Meditation or Discussion

1. Why are Christians kings and queens?
2. How do Christians already reign in grace?
3. How must we distinguish between Christ's reign at God's right hand and the reign of Christians on earth?
4. How does faith in Christ give Christians a strong and noble spirit?
5. To what warfare is every Christian called?
6. What is the difference between the strength of a spiritual warrior in Christ and what Jonathan Edwards called the "brutal fierceness" of a worldly person?
7. How should the believer's kingship in Christ affect how he views earthly possessions and work?
8. How should the believer's kingship in Christ have an otherworldly focus?
9. What privilege will believers enjoy in the new creation as kings in Christ?
10. What is one way that this chapter has increased your confidence and hope? What is one way that it has challenged you to follow Christ more faithfully?

Questions for Deeper Reflection

11. What is the proper balance in the Christian life between optimism and realism, so that we fall into neither spiritual defeatism nor triumphalism?
12. What is the relationship between the creation mandate for mankind to "have dominion" over the earth (Gen. 1:28) and Christ's kingdom by the Holy Spirit (Rom. 14:17)?
13. How does a good conscience promote courage? How can a Christian grow in boldness before God and men by cultivating a good conscience?

56

Practical Conclusion to Christology

The Centrality of Christ

When Jesus was teaching in Jerusalem in the days before his crucifixion, the Herodians, the Pharisees, and the Sadducees all tested him with difficult questions in attempts to make him appear foolish or dangerous. They all failed, for they were no match for the wisdom of God's Son. Then Christ asked them a question: "What do you think about the Christ?" (Matt. 22:42 ESV). He challenged their messianic understanding by quoting Psalm 110:1: "The LORD said unto my Lord, Sit thou on my right hand, till I make thine enemies thy footstool" (Matt. 22:44).

There is no more important question in theology than "What do you think about the Christ?" Over the course of our study of this locus of systematic theology, we have argued that the great promises of God's covenants with his people reach their fulfillment in the mediatorial work of God the Son incarnate as their Prophet, Priest, and King. In him, all God's promises find their climactic *yes* to the glory of God (2 Cor. 1:20). Nothing can compare to "the excellency of the knowledge of Christ Jesus my Lord" (Phil. 3:8). "Christ is all" to the believer (Col. 3:11).

Therefore, we conclude our study of Christology with practical reflections on the uniqueness, fullness, and supremacy of Christ.

Uniqueness: Christ Alone

One of the aspects of Christianity that the world finds most offensive is its singularity: the Bible insists that there is only one man in all of human history who can reconcile us to God.[1] The people of ancient Israel lived in a world of many gods and religions, but the Lord said, "Look unto me, and be ye saved, all the ends of the earth: for I am God, and there is none else" (Isa. 45:22). Christ tells us, "No one knows the Father except the Son and anyone to whom the Son chooses to reveal him" (Matt. 11:27 ESV). He also says, "I am the way, the truth, and the life: no man cometh unto the Father, but by me" (John 14:6). Heinrich Bullinger commented, "Hath he not in these few words rejected and utterly excluded all other means of salvation, making himself alone our life and salvation?"[2]

The apostles also testify to salvation in Christ alone. Peter and John proclaimed, "Neither is there salvation in any other: for there is none other name under heaven given among men, whereby we must be saved" (Acts 4:12). Paul writes, "For there is one God, and one mediator between God and men, the man Christ Jesus; who gave himself a ransom for all" (1 Tim. 2:5–6). John says, "Whosoever denieth the Son, the same hath not the Father: but he that acknowledgeth the Son hath the Father also," and, "He that hath the Son hath life; and he that hath not the Son of God hath not life" (1 John 2:23; 5:12).

The uniqueness of Christ runs contrary to the popular perspectives of relativism, religious pluralism, and postmodernism. *Relativism* refers to the skeptical denial that moral and spiritual claims can bear absolute truth.[3] According to *religious pluralism*, God reaches out to humanity in many ways, so that the various religions all present valid paths to knowing him.[4] In *postmodernism*, we find universal, radical relativism and pluralism; there is no absolute truth of any kind, but each person has his own knowledge determined by his personal context, knowledge that is merely a reflection of himself.[5] To say that Christ is the only way to God in such a cultural milieu is to be held guilty of intolerance because of a failure to appreciate that all sincerely religious or spiritual people can be close to God (or however one describes ultimate reality). The only permissible intoler-

---

1. See the section on salvation always through the one Mediator in chap. 29.
2. Bullinger, *The Decades*, 2.1:30.
3. On relativism, see *RST*, 1:136–37.
4. For a summary and critique of religious pluralism, see *RST*, 1:299–304.
5. On postmodernism and its effects on Christology and biblical hermeneutics, see Wellum, *God the Son Incarnate*, 67–76. For a summary, see Wellum, *Christ Alone*, 298–301.

ance is intolerance toward people who teach only one way of salvation, no matter how kind and gentle they may be.[6]

Biblical Christology equips us to answer the charge of intolerance by presenting a coherent explanation of why Christ alone brings people to God. The claim of the uniqueness of Christ does not arise from pride, divisiveness, fear of those different from us, judgmentalism, or hatred. Instead, it arises inevitably from the worldview revealed by God's Word. The Bible teaches that there is only one God who created all things and thus is Lord of all. It also teaches that mankind has fallen into a state of sin, enmity against God, spiritual death, and total inability to know God or rescue itself from its predicament. Only a divine Savior can help us.

The doctrine of the covenant of grace teaches us that Jesus Christ is the One to whom God's promises and works throughout history have pointed. Therefore, he is unique, the promised one. He is not so merely for Israel; the Abrahamic promises encompass all nations.

The Bible's doctrine of Christ's person also establishes his uniqueness. Whatever claims may have been made by great leaders of other religions, they could not claim to be the one God. There are many avatars of the divine in Hinduism, but their bodies either only appear to be real or are perfect and without suffering.[7] The Bible indicates that Christ alone is the Word become flesh. He is God the Son. Therefore, he is uniquely qualified to reveal the Father. Christ alone is God and man. In his deity, he has all the attributes of God to save his people. In his humanity, he has the capacity to substitute for them and sympathize with them.

The doctrine of Christ's work also demonstrates that he is the only Mediator between God and men. As the great Prophet, Christ is the only revealer through whom sinners may know the Father. As the High Priest, Christ alone obeyed God to the point of death on the cross in order to offer himself as the penal substitute to satisfy God's justice on behalf of his people. Furthermore, Christ our High Priest alone intercedes in heaven as the Mediator of the new covenant. As the King of kings, Christ rules over all men and angels in order to give eternal life to his elect through the Spirit. He is the life of his people, and apart from him we can do nothing.

---

6. Marilyn Sewell, "Saying Goodbye to Tolerance," *Huffington Post*, October 19, 2012, https://www.huffpost.com/entry/saying-goodbye-to-tolerance_b_1976607.

7. See Noel Sheth, "Hindu Avatāra and Christian Incarnation: A Comparison," *Philosophy East and West* 52, no. 1 (January 2002): 109 (full article, 98–125). Sheth (1943–2017), a Jesuit scholar, downplayed the differences between the Hindu avatar and the Christian incarnation, seeking to promote dialogue between the two religions.

This is what the Bible tells us it means for him to be Jesus (the Savior) and Christ (the anointed Prophet, Priest, and King).[8]

To sum up, the uniqueness of Christ is essential to the gospel of Christ. It is not the invention of human bigotry, but the revelation of God for our salvation. Neither it is merely the teaching of a few statements of the Bible, but a truth woven into the very fabric of the Bible's message. Unless we truncate Christianity to some of its ethical teachings, we cannot accommodate it to pluralism. If Christ is who the Bible says he is and does what the Bible says he does, then it is entirely justifiable, indeed necessary, to assert that he is the only Mediator of salvation.[9]

The reason why it may seem necessary to deny Christ's uniqueness is that modern secularism has rejected the biblical worldview and replaced it with an alien worldview that denies the doctrines of creation, the fall, the revelation of God's promises, the incarnation of God's Son, and the saving work of Christ. Instead, this worldview asserts the sovereignty of the physical world independent of divine activity, the goodness of human nature, and the supremacy of human reason and feeling, while it skeptically views Jesus and the Bible as merely human phenomena on the same level as ourselves.[10] To fit the gospel into that perspective is to destroy it. Rather, the church must challenge the false assumptions of our day with the Word of God.

Therefore, the faithful preacher of God's Word and the faithful Christian witness must not flinch on this crucial point, but state it boldly. The eternal destiny of precious human beings hinges upon the true doctrine of Jesus Christ. Furthermore, we must be zealous for the glory of God the Son. If, in order to avoid offending the world, we recoil from the clear declaration that Christ alone saves sinners, then we offend God the Father. Indeed, the uniqueness of Christ is not merely an intellectual truth for assertion and argument, but the foundation of our complete devotion to the Lord Jesus. We must love Christ and lean on him completely.

Fullness: The Whole Christ

In God the Son incarnate, we find all that we need for life and godliness (1 Pet. 1:1–3). John says, "The Word was made flesh, and dwelt among us

---

8. See Theodore Beza's Confession at Poissy (1561), in *Reformed Confessions*, 2:414.
9. Macleod, *The Person of Christ*, 240.
10. Wellum, *Christ Alone*, 277–95.

... full of grace and truth" (John 1:14). Paul says, "In him dwelleth all the fulness of the Godhead bodily. And ye are complete in him, which is the head of all principality and power" (Col. 2:9–10). The play on words between the noun translated as "fulness" (*plērōma*) and the verb translated as "are complete" (*plēroō*) links Christ's sufficiency and our need. His fullness for us implies both that we should not look to any other source of spiritual wisdom and power (v. 8), and that we should draw from Christ all that he is for us in order to be stable and growing Christians (vv. 6–7, 19).

John Calvin celebrated the fullness of grace in our Lord Jesus:

> We see that our whole salvation and all its parts are comprehended in Christ. We should therefore take care not to derive the least portion of it from anywhere else. If we seek salvation, we are taught by the very name of Jesus that it is "of him." If we seek any other gifts of the Spirit, they will be found in his anointing. If we seek strength, it lies in his dominion; if purity, in his conception; if gentleness, it appears in his birth. For by his birth he was made like us in all respects that he might learn to feel our pain.
>
> If we seek redemption, it lies in his passion; if acquittal, in his condemnation; if remission of the curse, in his cross; if satisfaction, in his sacrifice; if purification, in his blood; if reconciliation, in his descent into hell; if mortification of the flesh, in his tomb; if newness of life, in his resurrection; if immortality, in the same; if inheritance of the Heavenly Kingdom, in his entrance into heaven; if protection, if security, if abundant supply of all blessings, in his Kingdom; if untroubled expectation of judgment, in power given to him to judge. In short, since rich store of every kind of good abounds in him, let us drink our fill from this fountain, and from no other.[11]

Relying upon the sufficiency of Christ guards us from the errors of legalism and antinomianism. People sometimes use the term *legalism* as if it referred to any serious insistence on obedience to law, but a more biblical view of legalism sees it as the addition of man-made requirements to God's law (1 Tim. 4:3) or gospel (cf. Rom. 3:28). Subtle forms of legalism may use theological orthodoxy to cloak selfish pride, judgmentalism, and hypocrisy (Matt. 7:1–5; 23:25–28). Steven Lawson says, "Legalism erects an artificial façade that religious people hide behind, but it never changes

---

11. Calvin, *Institutes*, 2.16.19, paragraph break added.

the heart of man."[12] The term *antinomianism* (Greek *anti*, "against," and *nomos*, "law") refers to a perspective that regards efforts to obey God's law as unimportant or even contrary to the gospel (Rom. 3:8; 6:1, 15). Blatant antinomianism, the plain denial that Christians must obey God's commandments, is rare. Ordinarily the word is used to describe a theological or practical imbalance that tends toward an accommodating approach to sin.

Contrary to what most people believe, legalism and antinomianism are not opposites, but fruit that spring from one bitter root: rebellion and unbelief against the goodness of God.[13] Like Adam and Eve yielding to the Serpent's temptations, we mistrust the goodness of our Lawgiver and Lord, scorn his power and resolution to judge sin, rebel against his commandments (antinomianism), and seek to cover our shame with the "fig leaves" of our works and by wrongly judging one another and God (legalism).[14]

The only weapon with which to slay this two-headed monster is the gospel of Christ, for, as Mark Jones says, "in essence, the mistakes of legalism and antinomianism are Christological errors."[15] By faith in Christ the Prophet, we repent of our tendency to add human regulations to God's Word and submit ourselves to the Scriptures as the only divine rule of faith and obedience. By faith in Christ the Priest, we reject our own works as means of gaining righteousness before God and receive Christ alone as our justification. By faith in Christ the King, we gain the power to overcome Satan and keep God's commandments with desire, delight, and determination while we hope in the gracious reward of the everlasting kingdom. And as we meditate on the Father's love in sending his Son to be such a perfect Mediator, we taste his goodness and our hearts warm to love him and gladly obey him. We obey increasingly with a spirit characterized not by a proud, legalistic, "metallic spirit . . . unyielding and sharp edged,"[16] but eager desire to do God's will completely because of his love and grace. This desire, however, is attained not merely by embracing right doctrines in the mind, but by embracing the truth with the faith, hope, and love supplied by the Spirit of Christ.

---

12. Steven J. Lawson, "Truth vs. Tradition," in *Law and Liberty: A Biblical Look at Legalism*, ed. Don Kistler (Orlando, FL: The Northampton Press, 2014), 19.

13. Sinclair B. Ferguson, *The Whole Christ: Legalism, Antinomianism, and Gospel Assurance—Why the Marrow Controversy Still Matters* (Wheaton, IL: Crossway, 2016), 82–88, 155–58.

14. For an exposition of Gen. 3, see chap. 18.

15. Mark Jones, *Antinomianism: Reformed Theology's Unwelcome Guest?* (Phillipsburg, NJ: P&R, 2013), 3.

16. Ferguson, *The Whole Christ*, 71–72.

Supremacy: To Live Is Christ

Knowing Christ's uniqueness and sufficiency establishes his experiential and practical supremacy in the hearts of his people. Paul writes, "For whether we live, we live unto the Lord; and whether we die, we die unto the Lord: whether we live therefore, or die, we are the Lord's. For to this end Christ both died, and rose, and revived, that he might be Lord both of the dead and living" (Rom. 14:8–9). All true Christians "live unto the Lord" as the people who "are the Lord's." Furthermore, it was "to this end" or for this purpose that Christ died and rose again: "that he might be Lord" of his people. Similarly, Paul says, "For the love of Christ controls us, because we have concluded this: that one has died for all, therefore all have died; and he died for all, that those who live might no longer live for themselves but for him who for their sake died and was raised" (2 Cor. 5:14–15 ESV). Thus, the believer can confess with Paul, "To live is Christ, and to die is gain" (Phil. 1:21).

The Heidelberg Catechism (LD 1, Q. 1) beautifully links belonging to Christ the Mediator to living in worshipful communion with the whole Trinity:[17]

> I with body and soul, both in life and death, am not my own, but belong unto my faithful Savior Jesus Christ; who, with His precious blood, hath fully satisfied for all my sins, and delivered me from all the power of the devil; and so preserves me that without the will of my heavenly Father, not a hair can fall from my head; yea, that all things must be subservient to my salvation, and therefore, by His Holy Spirit, He also assures me of eternal life, and makes me sincerely willing and ready, henceforth, to live unto Him.[18]

The supremacy of Christ delivers his people from the errors of nihilism and existentialism. The perspective of *nihilism* (from Latin *nihil*, "nothing"), as Friedrich Nietzsche (1844–1900) explained, is that "everything lacks meaning." In other words, "The aim is lacking; 'why?' finds no answer."[19] This is the logical consequence of atheism, both the theoretical

---

17. Living unto Christ is not a denial of the Trinity leading to the neglect of the Father and the Holy Spirit, but an assertion of the centrality of the Mediator to our knowledge of the Trinity. Christians belong to Christ so that they might belong to the triune God. The doctrine of the Trinity guards *solus Christus* from becoming Christomonism.

18. *The Three Forms of Unity*, 68.

19. Friedrich Nietzsche, *The Will to Power*, trans. Walter Kaufmann and R. J. Hollingdale, ed. Walter Kaufmann (New York: Random House, 1967), 7, 9.

atheism that explicitly denies God's existence and the practical atheism so common in secular societies, in which people live as if God is nonexistent for all practical purposes. However, life without meaning is intolerable. Therefore, nihilism often leads to *existentialism*: though life is meaningless and absurd, each individual must create his own meaning and significance, and pursue the ideal of being authentic to himself. Jean-Paul Sartre (1905–1980) said, "Man is nothing else but that which he makes of himself. That is the first principle of existentialism."[20] In a world without God, transcendent values, or good in any absolute sense, man bears the responsibility to use his freedom to create his future. We see this man-centered approach to life advocated and embraced throughout society today. It is a major factor in the moral confusion and social fragmentation that afflicts our families, communities, and nations.

When Christ saves us, he reorients our entire lives toward him. Consequently, if anyone loves the Lord Jesus, he is the recipient of God's grace (Eph. 6:24); if anyone does not love the Lord Jesus, he is the object of God's curse (1 Cor. 16:22).

What does it mean to live unto the Lord Jesus? Richard Sibbes wrote a very profitable little book on this subject, and we close this volume by listening as Sibbes preaches to us about living to the Lord (Rom. 14:7–8).[21]

Living for Christ requires turning away from living for ourselves.[22] Sibbes said that people without the Spirit of Christ "live within that circle, *self*. The devil keeps them that they go not out of it; so that self doth run through all their actions . . . yea, their religious actions."[23] The Christian says to himself, "I am not my own, for I was bought at a price" (cf. 1 Cor. 6:19–20). This teaches us "to live to Christ in a way of humility and self-denial" (cf. Luke 9:23).[24]

To live to the Lord positively means, Sibbes said, "to acknowledge the Lord in all our ways to be our Lord, to whom we owe ourselves."[25] The Christian "liveth to none but Christ," and the Christian life is "to go on in a constant tenor of the whole course of our lives aiming at Christ."[26] "The reason is, Christ hath redeemed our persons, and our times, and all that

---

20. Jean-Paul Sartre, *Existentialism Is a Humanism*, trans. Carol Macomber, ed. John Kulka (New Haven, CT: Yale University Press, 2007), 22.
21. Sibbes, *The Christian's End*, in *Works*, 5:287–322.
22. Rom. 14:7; 2 Cor. 5:15; Phil. 2:4, 21.
23. Sibbes, *The Christian's End*, in *Works*, 5:293, emphasis added.
24. Sibbes, *The Christian's End*, in *Works*, 5:299.
25. Sibbes, *The Christian's End*, in *Works*, 5:292.
26. Sibbes, *The Christian's End*, in *Works*, 5:297.

we are, or have, or can do; all our ability, our whole [power], is Christ's, and not our own. . . . Myself, my time, my advantages, my calling, and all, are his."[27]

Sibbes wrote, "We will never give ourselves to the Lord, till we consider what he hath done for us. He hath given himself wholly for us . . . made himself of no reputation for us [Phil. 2:7]; became a worm and no man [Ps. 22:6], a curse for us [Gal. 3:13]."[28] In response, the Christian should be single-minded in living to the Lord (Ps. 27:4; Luke 10:41–42). Sibbes said, "He will use the world as if he used it not, will buy as if he possessed not, will marry as if he married not. Not that he will be slight or superficial in these things; but he will do them no further than they be advantageous to the enjoying of Christ here . . . and for ever hereafter."[29]

Such a life is not possible for fallen human nature without the Spirit of God. Therefore, Sibbes wrote, to live to Christ "we must have spiritual life from him. . . . We must live by faith, from union with Christ by faith, and then live to Christ."[30] Only by faith can we live from his death and resurrection (Gal. 2:20). Only by faith can we count the reproach of Christ greater riches than the treasures of this world (Heb. 11:24–26).

Living unto the Lord involves the surrender of ourselves in all our conduct to obey his commands and submit to his providence as he does with us as he pleases.[31] Sibbes said, "They must be directed by his will, and not their own," and "his will is in the Scriptures."[32] When Satan tempts and corruptions stir, we must say, "My body is not mine, it is the Lord's. . . . I am his, my thoughts are his."[33] Keeping this great goal in view makes everything that helps us to attain it lovely, no matter how hard. Sibbes says, "Welcome is poverty, or disgrace, or whatsoever that maketh a man live more to Christ, and die to himself." We also should be heartbroken over the sad fact that "we have let so much precious time, and strength, and dear advantages be lost" that we could have used to seek Christ and his kingdom.[34]

To live to the Lord Jesus means to aim at his glory as our ultimate goal "and to endeavor that God and Christ may be known and magnified in the

---

27. Sibbes, *The Christian's End*, in *Works*, 5:301. "Power" was originally "*posse*."
28. Sibbes, *The Christian's End*, in *Works*, 5:305.
29. Sibbes, *The Christian's End*, in *Works*, 5:301.
30. Sibbes, *The Christian's End*, in *Works*, 5:303.
31. Sibbes, *The Christian's End*, in *Works*, 5:292.
32. Sibbes, *Christ's Exaltation Purchased by His Humiliation*, in *Works*, 5:338–39.
33. Sibbes, *The Christian's End*, in *Works*, 5:312.
34. Sibbes, *The Christian's End*, in *Works*, 5:301–2.

world."[35] Thus, when Paul said "to live is Christ," he did not have in view an experience of Christ's closeness so much as his resolution and earnest desire that "Christ shall be magnified in my body, whether it be by life, or by death" (Phil. 1:20–21).

Finally, the person who lives to the Lord lives by the comfort that Christ knows him and cares for him in life and death.[36] Perhaps he will lose his friends and be counted a fool. Maybe he will lose earthly wealth and suffer persecution. However, Sibbes asked, "what is all pleasure here to the pleasure of a good conscience? What is friendship here to communion with God, and friendship with Christ?" The Christian can say, "I have God, that is all-sufficient for all turns, that is near to me," and "a man hath never more of God than when he denieth himself most for God."[37]

Sibbes said, "We are all travelers in the way to heaven, and every step of our life should be to that end." It is a great tragedy that creatures come into this world, live for some decades, and then depart it without knowing why they lived.[38] How happy is the Christian, however, for "heaven is always before him, because his way is to God and to Christ." The sweet irony of the Christian's life is that in turning away from self to live for the Lord, he aims at both God's glory and his own eternal happiness: "one chief end and good." Sibbes said, "Our salvation and happiness is within the glory of God, and we live to Christ, not only in serving him, but in seeking our own souls; and what a sweetness is this in God, that in seeking our own good we should glorify him."[39]

The Mediator restores us to our purpose as human beings. Calvin said, "What is the chief end of human life? To know God. Why do you say that? Because He created us and placed us in this world to be glorified in us." And that, Calvin said, is our supreme good.[40] Sibbes said, "Man is not for himself . . . all things below are for him, but he is for something above himself. He is not of himself, and therefore not to himself. God only is of himself, by himself, and to himself. Everything under God is of God, and by God, and therefore to God. As Saint Augustine saith, 'Thou has made us for thee, and our hearts rest not till we come

35. Sibbes, *The Christian's End*, in *Works*, 5:292.
36. Sibbes, *The Christian's End*, in *Works*, 5:293.
37. Sibbes, *The Christian's End*, in *Works*, 5:304.
38. Sibbes, *The Christian's End*, in *Works*, 5:296–97.
39. Sibbes, *The Christian's End*, in *Works*, 5:298–99.
40. Calvin's Catechism of 1545 (Q. 1–3), in *Reformed Confessions*, 1:469.

to thee.'" Man's "wisdom" is to aim primarily at "that which is his last and best and main end, which is God, and union and communion with God in Christ, who is God in our nature, God-man, the best of all."[41] And that is a fitting way to conclude our weak attempts to describe our Lord Jesus Christ: "the best of all."

Sing to the Lord

Living unto the Lord Alone

> My soul in silence waits for God,
> My Saviour He has proved.
> He only is my rock and tow'r;
> I never shall be moved.
>
> My enemies my ruin seek,
> They plot with fraud and guile;
> Deceitful, they pretend to bless,
> But inwardly revile.
>
> My honor is secure with God,
> My Saviour He is known;
> My refuge and my rock of strength
> Are found in God alone.
>
> On Him, ye people, evermore
> Rely with confidence;
> Before Him pour ye out your heart,
> For God is our defense.
>
> For God has spoken o'er and o'er,
> And unto me has shown
> That saving power and lasting strength
> Belong to Him alone.

Psalm 62
Tune: Sawley
The Psalter, No. 161
Or Tune: Howard
Trinity Hymnal—Baptist Edition, No. 571

---

41. Sibbes, *The Christian's End*, in *Works*, 5:300.

Questions for Meditation or Discussion

1. What Scripture passages explicitly teach that Christ alone is the Mediator of salvation?
2. Define the following terms: (1) relativism, (2) religious pluralism, and (3) postmodernism.
3. How do the biblical doctrines of Christology prove that Christ is the only way to God?
4. How does the Bible show us that Christ has the fullness of all grace in himself?
5. Define the following terms: (1) legalism and (2) antinomianism.
6. How is the gospel of Christ the answer to both of the errors mentioned above?
7. What Scripture passages teach that Christ died and rose again to create a people who live for him?
8. Define the following terms: (1) nihilism and (2) existentialism.
9. What is one point that Richard Sibbes makes that is especially relevant to you? Why? How do you need to act upon that point in order to live wholly and solely for Christ?

Questions for Deeper Reflection

10. What is one thing that you learned from your study of Christology in this volume that has increased your faith and love toward the Lord Jesus? How has it affected your life?
11. How does living unto the Lord Jesus also glorify God the Father and God the Holy Spirit?

Bibliography

Works Cited in This Volume

For abbreviations such as *ANF*, *LW*, etc.,
see the list in the front matter.

* Denotes a frequently consulted work or series.

Creeds and Confessions

The Arminian Confession of 1621. Translated and edited by Mark A. Ellis. Eugene, OR: Pickwick, 2005.

* *The Book of Concord: The Confessions of the Evangelical Lutheran Church.* Edited by Robert Kolb and Timothy J. Wengert. Translated by Charles Arand et al. Minneapolis: Fortress, 2000.

Catechism of the Catholic Church. New York: Doubleday, 1995.

A Confession of Faith, Put Forth by the Elders and Brethren of Many Congregations of Christians, (Baptized upon Profession of Their Faith) in London and the Country. With an Appendix Concerning Baptism. London: for John Harris, 1688.

* Dennison, James T., Jr., comp. *Reformed Confessions of the 16th and 17th Centuries in English Translation: 1523–1693.* 4 vols. Grand Rapids, MI: Reformation Heritage Books, 2008–2014.

The Racovian Catechism. Translated and introduced by Thomas Rees. London: Longman, Hurst, Rees, Orme, and Brown, 1818.

Schaff, Philip, ed. *The Creeds of Christendom.* 3 vols. New York: Harper and Brothers, 1877.

* *The Three Forms of Unity.* Introduction by Joel R. Beeke. Birmingham, AL: Solid Ground, 2010.

Westminster Confession of Faith. Glasgow: Free Presbyterian Publications, 1994.

Psalms and Hymns

Havergal, Frances. *The Poetical Works of Frances Ridley Havergal*. New York: E. P. Dutton & Co., 1888.

Manly, Basil, and Basil Manly Jr., eds. *The Baptist Psalmody: A Selection of Hymns for the Worship of God*. New York: Sheldon & Co., 1850.

* *The Psalter, with Doctrinal Standards, Liturgy, Church Order, and Added Chorale Section*. Preface by Joel R. Beeke and Ray B. Lanning. 1965. Reprint, Grand Rapids, MI: Eerdmans for Reformation Heritage Books, 2003.

Rippon, John. *A Selection of Hymns from the Best Authors*. New York: William Dursell, 1792.

* *Trinity Hymnal—Baptist Edition*. Edited by David Merck. Suwanee, GA: Great Commission Publications, 1995.

Trinity Psalter Hymnal. Willow Grove, PA: The Committee on Christian Education of the Orthodox Presbyterian Church and the Psalter Hymnal Committee of the United Reformed Churches in North America, 2018.

Watts, Issac. *Psalms, Hymns, and Spiritual Songs*. London: Thomas Nelson, 1849.

Language and Writing Resources

Balz, Horst Robert, and Gerhard Schneider, eds. *Exegetical Dictionary of the New Testament*. 3 vols. Grand Rapids, MI: Eerdmans, 1990.

Blass, F., and A. Debrunner. *A Greek Grammar of the New Testament and Other Early Christian Literature*. Translated and revised by Robert W. Funk. Chicago: University of Chicago Press, 1961.

Brown, Francis, Samuel Rolles Driver, and Charles Augustus Briggs. *Enhanced Brown-Driver-Briggs Hebrew and English Lexicon*. Oxford: Clarendon, 1977.

Gibson, J. C. L. *Davidson's Introductory Hebrew Grammar*. 4th ed. Edinburgh: T&T Clark, 1994.

Kittel, Gerhard, Geoffrey W. Bromiley, and Gerhard Friedrich, eds. *Theological Dictionary of the New Testament*. 10 vols. Grand Rapids, MI: Eerdmans, 1964.

Lampe, G. W. H., ed. *A Patristic Greek Lexicon*. Oxford: Oxford University Press, 1961.

Liddell, Henry George, Robert Scott, et al. *A Greek-English Lexicon*. Oxford: Clarendon, 1996.

Louw, Johannes P., and Eugene Albert Nida. *Greek-English Lexicon of the New Testament: Based on Semantic Domains.* New York: United Bible Societies, 1996.

Merriam-Webster's Collegiate Dictionary. 11th ed. Springfield, MA: Merriam-Webster, 2003.

Moulton, James H., and George Milligan. *Vocabulary of the Greek Testament.* London: Houghton and Stoughton, 1929.

Silva, Moisés, ed. *The New International Dictionary of New Testament Theology and Exegesis.* 5 vols. Grand Rapids, MI: Zondervan, 2014.

VanGemeren, Willem A., ed. *The New International Dictionary of Old Testament Theology and Exegesis.* 5 vols. Grand Rapids, MI: Zondervan, 1997.

Waltke, Bruce, and M. O'Connor. *An Introduction to Biblical Hebrew Syntax.* Winona Lake, IN: Eisenbrauns, 1990.

Theological, Historical, Philosophical, and General Works

Albrecht, Andreas, and João Magueijo. "A Time Varying Speed of Light as a Solution to Cosmological Puzzles." November 2, 1998. Revised January 5, 1999. Cornell University, https://arxiv.org/abs/astro-ph/9811018.

Alexander, Archibald. *Thoughts on Religious Experience.* 1844. Reprint, Edinburgh: Banner of Truth, 1967.

Allberry, Sam. *Is God Anti-Gay? And Other Questions about Homosexuality, the Bible and Same-Sex Attraction.* Epsom, Surrey, UK: The Good Book Company, 2013.

Allen, David L. *Hebrews.* The New American Commentary. Nashville: Broadman & Holman, 2010.

Allison, Gregg R. *Roman Catholic Theology and Practice: An Evangelical Assessment.* Wheaton, IL: Crossway, 2014.

———. "Toward a Theology of Human Embodiment." *Southern Baptist Journal of Theology* 13, no. 2 (2009): 4–17.

Ambrose. *Saint Ambrose: Theological and Dogmatic Works.* Translated by Roy J. Deferrari. Fathers of the Church 44. Washington, DC: The Catholic University of America Press, 1963.

Ambrose, Isaac. *Looking unto Jesus: A View of the Everlasting Gospel; or, the Soul's Eyeing of Jesus, as Carrying on the Great Work of Man's Salvation, from First to Last.* Philadelphia: J. B. Lippincott and Co., 1856.

———. *Media: The Middle Things . . . The Means, Duties, Ordinances, Both Secret, Private, and Publick; For Continuance, and Increase of a Godly Life.* Glasgow: Archibald Ingram et al., 1737.

American Psychological Association. *Answers to Your Questions: For a Better Understanding of Sexual Orientation & Homosexuality.* Washington, DC: American Psychological Association, 2008), https://www.apa.org/topics /lgbt/orientation.pdf.

* Ames, William. *The Marrow of Theology.* Translated by John Dykstra Eusden. Grand Rapids, MI: Baker, 1968.

———. *Medulla Theologica.* New ed. Amsterdam: Ioannem Iansonium, 1634.

———. *A Sketch of the Christian's Catechism.* Translated by Todd M. Rester. Grand Rapids, MI: Reformation Heritage Books, 2008.

———. *The Works of the Reverend and Faithfull Minister of Christ William Ames.* 2 books in 1 vol. London: John Rothwell, 1643.

Anonymous [Westminster divines]. *Annotations upon All of the Books of the Old and New Testament.* London: Evan Tyler, 1657.

Anonymous [Evangelical theologians]. The Chicago Statement on Biblical Inerrancy. Alliance of Confessing Evangelicals, http://www.alliancenet.org /the-chicago-statement-on-biblical-inerrancy.

Anonymous ["Fidus"]. "Commentary on the Epistles to the Seven Churches in the Apocalypse." *The Morning Watch; or Quarterly Journal on Prophecy, and Theological Review* 2 (1830): 510–18.

Anonymous [Dutch divines]. *The Dutch Annotations upon the Whole Bible.* Translated by Theodore Haak. 1657. Facsimile reprint, Leerdam, The Netherlands: Gereformeerde Bijbelstichting, 2002.

Anonymous. "Hematohidrosis." October 31, 2016. National Institutes of Health: Genetic and Rare Diseases Center. https://rarediseases.info.nih.gov /diseases/13131/hematohidrosis.

Anonymous. "Humanism and Its Aspirations: Humanist Manifesto III, a Successor to the Humanist Manifesto of 1933." American Humanist Association. https://americanhumanist.org/what-is-humanism/manifesto3/.

Anonymous [OPC theologians]. "Report of the Committee to Study Republication" (2016). The Orthodox Presbyterian Church. https://www.opc.org /GA/republication.html.

Anonymous [Dutch divines]. *Statenvertaling* [States Translation Dutch Bible with annotations]. Leiden: Paulus Aertsz van Ravesteyn, 1637.

Anonymous. *The Upanishads.* Translated by F. Max Müller. 2 vols. Oxford: Oxford University Press, 1884.

Anyabwile, Thabiti M. *Captivated: Beholding the Mystery of Jesus' Death and Resurrection.* Grand Rapids, MI: Reformation Heritage Books, 2014.

* Aquinas, Thomas. *Summa Theologica.* Translated by Fathers of the English Dominican Province. 22 vols. London: R. & T. Washbourne, 1914.

Arand, Charles P., Erik H. Herrmann, and Daniel L. Mattson, eds. *From Wittenberg to the World: Essays on the Reformation and Its Legacy in Honor of Robert Kolb*. Refo500 Academic Studies 50. Göttingen: Vandenhoek & Ruprecht, 2018.

Aristotle. *De Anima (On the Soul)*. Translated and edited by Hugh Lawson-Tancred. Penguin Classics. London: Penguin, 1986.

———. *Ethics*. Translated by J. A. K. Thomson. Revised by Hugh Tredennick. London: Penguin, 1976.

Arminius, Jacob. *Articuli nonnulli diligenti examine perpendi* (c. 1620). https://reader.digitale-sammlungen.de/resolve/display/bsb10945232.html.

Aristotle. *De Anima (On the Soul)*. Translated and Edited by Hugh Lawson-Tancred. Penguin Classics. London: Penguin, 1986.

———. *The Works of James Arminius*. Translated by James Nichols (vols. 1–2) and W. R. Bagnall (vol. 3). 3 vols. Auburn: Derby and Miller, 1853.

Arrowsmith, John. *Theanthropos; or, God-Man: Being an Exposition upon the First Eighteen Verses of the First Chapter of the Gospel According to St John*. London: for Humphrey Moseley and William Wilson, 1660.

Asimov, Isaac. *The Foundation Trilogy: Three Classics of Science Fiction*. Garden City, NY: Doubleday, 1951–1953.

Athanasius. *Contra Gentes and De Incarnatione*. Edited and translated by Robert Thomson. Oxford: Oxford University Press, 1971.

Augustine. *The Enchiridion on Faith, Hope, and Love*. Translated by J. B. Shaw. Washington, DC: Regnery, 1961.

———. *Expositions on the Book of Psalms*. Translated by H. M. Wilkins. 6 vols. Oxford: John Henry Parker, 1847–1857.

———. *The Works of Saint Augustine: A Translation for the Twenty-First Century*. 42 vols. Hyde Park, NY: New City Press, 1995–2015. Citations from this source take the form *Works*, part/volume: page, such as *Works*, 1/13: 351.

Aulén, Gustaf. *Christus Victor: An Historical Study of the Three Main Types of the Idea of the Atonement*. Translated by A. G. Hebert. New York: Macmillan, 1969.

Avery-Peck, Alan J., Craig A. Evans, and Jacob Neusner, eds. *Earliest Christianity within the Boundaries of Judaism: Essays in Honor of Bruce Chilton*. Leiden: Brill, 2016.

Bagchi, David V. N. "Luther versus Luther? The Problem of Christ's Descent into Hell in the Long Sixteenth Century." *Perichoresis* 6, no. 2 (2008): 175–200.

Bainton, Roland. *Here I Stand: A Life of Martin Luther*. New York: Abingdon, 1950.

Baker, J. Wayne. *Heinrich Bullinger and the Covenant: The Other Reformed Tradition*. Athens, Ohio: Ohio University Press, 1980.

Baker, Mark D., and Joel B. Green. *Recovering the Scandal of the Cross: Atonement in the New Testament and Contemporary Contexts*. 2nd ed. Downers Grove, IL: InterVarsity Press, 2011.

Ball, John. *A Treatise of the Covenant of Grace*. London: by G. Miller for Edward Brewster, 1645.

Balthasar, Hans Urs. *Mysterium Paschale: The Mystery of Easter*. Translated by Aidan Nichols. San Francisco: Ignatius Press, 1990.

Bandstra, Andrew J. "'Making Proclamation to the Spirits in Prison': Another Look at 1 Peter 3:19." *Calvin Theological Journal* 38 (2003): 120–24.

Barcellos, Richard C. *The Covenant of Works: Its Confessional and Scriptural Basis*. Recovering Our Confessional Heritage 3. Palmdale, CA: Reformed Baptist Academic Press, 2016.

———. *Getting the Garden Right: Adam's Work and God's Rest in Light of Christ*. Cape Coral, FL: Founders, 2017.

———. *In Defense of the Decalogue: A Critique of New Covenant Theology*. Enumclaw, WA: Winepress, 2001.

———, ed. *Recovering a Covenantal Heritage: Essays in Baptist Covenant Theology*. Palmdale, CA: Reformed Baptist Academic Press, 2014.

Barker, Kenneth L. *Micah, Nahum, Habakkuk, Zephaniah*. The New American Commentary 20. Nashville: Broadman & Holman, 1999.

Barrett, Matthew, ed. *Reformation Theology: A Systematic Summary*. Wheaton, IL: Crossway, 2017.

———. *Salvation by Grace: The Case for Effectual Calling and Regeneration*. Phillipsburg, NJ: P&R, 2013.

Barrett, Matthew, and Ardel B. Caneday, eds. *Four Views on the Historical Adam*. Grand Rapids, MI: Zondervan, 2013.

Barrett, Michael P. V. *Beginning at Moses: A Guide for Finding Christ in the Old Testament*. Rev. ed. Grand Rapids, MI: Reformation Heritage Books, 2018.

Barth, Karl. *Against the Stream: Shorter Post-War Writings, 1946–52*. Edited by Ronald Gregor Smith. New York: Philosophical Library, 1954.

———. *Christ and Adam: Man and Humanity in Romans 5*. Translated by T. A. Smail. Eugene, OR: Wipf and Stock, 2004.

———. *Church Dogmatics*. Edited by G. W. Bromiley and T. F. Torrance. 4 vols. in 14. Edinburgh: T&T Clark, 1960.

———. *The Epistle to the Romans.* Translated by Edwyn C. Hoskyns. London: Oxford University Press, 1933.

Bates, William. *The Harmony of Divine Attributes in the Contrivance and Accomplishment of Man's Redemption.* Introduction by Joel R. Beeke. 1853. Reprint, Homewood, AL: Solid Ground, 2010.

Batka, L'ubomir. "Martin Luther's Teaching on Sin." December 2016. *Oxford Research Encyclopedias: Religion.* http://religion.oxfordre.com/view/10.1093/acrefore/9780199340378.001.0001/acrefore-9780199340378-e-373.

Bauckham, Richard. *Jesus and the God of Israel: God Crucified and Other Studies on the New Testament's Christology of Divine Identity.* Grand Rapids, MI: Eerdmans, 2008.

———. *The Theology of the Book of Revelation.* Cambridge: Cambridge University Press, 1993.

Baugh, S. M. *Ephesians.* Evangelical Exegetical Commentary. Bellingham, WA: Lexham Press, 2015.

Baum, Wilhelm, and Dietmar W. Winkler. *The Church of the East: A Concise History.* Translated by Miranda G. Henry. London: RoutledgeCurzon, 2003. http://www.peshitta.org/pdf/CoEHistory.pdf.

Bavinck, Herman. *Foundations of Psychology.* Translated by Jack Vanden Born, Nelson D. Kloosterman, and John Bolt. *Bavinck Review* 9 (2018): 1–244.

———. *Reformed Dogmatics.* Edited by John Bolt. Translated by John Vriend. 4 vols. Grand Rapids, MI: Baker Academic, 2003–2008.

Bayes, Jonathan F. *The Threefold Division of the Law.* Salt and Light Series. Newcastle upon Tyne, England: The Christian Institute, 2017. https://www.christian.org.uk/wp-content/uploads/the-threefold-division-of-the-law.pdf.

Bayne[s], Paul. *A Commentarie upon the First and Second Chapters of Saint Paul to the Colossians.* London: by Richard Badger, for Nicholas Bourne, 1634.

———. *An Entire Commentary upon the Whole Epistle of St Paul to the Ephesians.* 1866. Reprint, Stoke-on-Trent, England: Tentmaker, 2007.

Beach, J. Mark. "Christ and the Covenant: Francis Turretin's Federal Theology as a Defense of the Doctrine of Grace." PhD diss., Calvin Theological Seminary, 2005.

Beale, G. K. *The Erosion of Inerrancy in Evangelicalism: Responding to New Challenges to Biblical Authority.* Wheaton, IL: Crossway, 2008.

———. *A New Testament Biblical Theology: The Unfolding of the Old Testament in the New.* Grand Rapids, MI: Baker Academic, 2011.

———. *The Temple and the Church's Mission: A Biblical Theology of the Dwelling Place of God.* New Studies in Biblical Theology. Downers Grove, IL: InterVarsity Press, 2004.

———. *We Become What We Worship: A Biblical Theology of Idolatry.* Downers Grove, IL: InterVarsity Press, 2016.

Beckwith, Roger T., and Martin J. Selman, eds. *Sacrifice in the Bible.* Grand Rapids, MI: Baker, 1995.

Beddome, Benjamin. *A Scriptural Exposition of the Baptist Catechism, by Way of Question and Answer.* Richmond, VA: Harrold & Murray, 1849.

Beeke, Joel R., ed. *The Beauty and Glory of the Father.* Grand Rapids, MI: Reformation Heritage Books, 2013.

———. *Debated Issues in Sovereign Predestination: Early Lutheran Predestination, Calvinian Reprobation, and Variations in Genevan Lapsarianism.* Göttingen: Vandenhoek and Ruprecht, 2017.

———. *Family Worship.* Family Guidance Series. Grand Rapids, MI: Reformation Heritage Books, 2009.

———. *Friends and Lovers: Cultivating Companionship and Intimacy in Marriage.* Adelphi, MD: Cruciform Press, 2012.

———. *How Should We Consider Christ in Affliction?* Grand Rapids, MI: Reformation Heritage Books, 2018.

———. *Living for God's Glory: An Introduction to Calvinism.* Lake Mary, FL: Reformation Trust, 2008.

———. *The Lord Shepherding His Sheep.* Welwyn Garden City, England: Evangelical Press, 2015.

———. *Parenting by God's Promises: How to Raise Children in the Covenant of Grace.* Lake Mary, FL: Reformation Trust, 2011.

———. *Puritan Reformed Spirituality.* Darlington, England: Evangelical Press, 2006.

———. *Revelation.* The Lectio Continua Expository Commentary on the New Testament. Grand Rapids, MI: Reformation Heritage Books, 2016.

———. *What Did the Reformers Believe about the Age of the Earth?* Petersburg, KY: Answers in Genesis, 2014.

Beeke, Joel R., Michael P. V. Barrett, Gerald M. Bilkes, and Paul M. Smalley, eds. *The Reformation Heritage KJV Study Bible.* Grand Rapids, MI: Reformation Heritage Books, 2014.

Beeke, Joel R., and Mark Jones. *A Puritan Theology: Doctrine for Life.* Grand Rapids, MI: Reformation Heritage Books, 2012.

Beeke, Joel R., and Paul M. Smalley. *One Man and One Woman: Marriage and Same-Sex Relations*. Grand Rapids, MI: Reformation Heritage Books, 2016.

———. *Reformed Systematic Theology, Vol. 1: Revelation and God*. Wheaton, IL: Crossway, 2019.

Beeke, Joel R., and Derek W. H. Thomas, eds. *The Holy Spirit and Reformed Spirituality: A Tribute to Geoffrey Thomas*. Grand Rapids, MI: Reformation Heritage Books, 2013.

Behe, Michael J. *Darwin's Black Box: The Biochemical Challenge to Evolution*. New York: Simon and Schuster, 1996.

Beilby, James, and Paul R. Eddy, eds. *The Nature of the Atonement: Four Views*. Downers Grove, IL: InterVarsity Press, 2006.

Belcher, Richard P., Jr. *Genesis: The Beginning of God's Plan of Salvation*. Focus on the Bible. Fearn, Ross-shire, Scotland: Christian Focus, 2012.

———. *Prophet, Priest, and King: The Roles of Christ in the Bible and Our Roles Today*. Phillipsburg, NJ: P&R, 2016.

Bell, Thomas. *A View of the Covenants of Works and Grace; and a Treatise on the Nature and Effects of Saving Faith. To which Are Added, Several Discourses on the Supreme Deity of Jesus Christ*. Glasgow: by Edward Khull and Co. for W. Somerville et al., 1814.

Bellarmine, Robert. *Disputationum Roberti Bellarmini . . . De Controversiis Christianae Fidei, Tomus Quartus*. Milan: Edente Natale Battezzanti, 1862.

* Berkhof, Louis. *Systematic Theology*. Edinburgh: Banner of Truth, 1958.

Berkouwer, G. C. *Man: The Image of God*. Studies in Dogmatics. Grand Rapids, MI: Eerdmans, 1962.

———. *Sin*. Studies in Dogmatics. Grand Rapids, MI: Eerdmans, 1971.

———. *The Triumph of Grace in the Theology of Karl Barth*. Translated by Harry R. Boer. Grand Rapids, MI: Eerdmans, 1956.

———. *The Work of Christ*. Studies in Dogmatics. Grand Rapids, MI: Eerdmans, 1965.

Bernard of Clairvaux. *Concerning Grace and Free Will*. Translated by Watkin W. Williams. London: Society for Promoting Christian Knowledge, 1920.

Berry, R. J. "Adam or Adamah?" *Science and Christian Belief* 23, no. 1 (2011): 23–48.

Bethune-Baker, J. F. *Nestorius and His Teaching: A Fresh Examination of the Evidence*. Cambridge: Cambridge University Press, 1908.

Bettenson, Henry, ed. *Documents of the Christian Church*. 2nd ed. Oxford: Oxford University Press, 1963.

Beza, Theodore. *A Booke of Christian Questions and Answers*. Translated by Arthur Golding. London: by William How, for Abraham Veale, 1572.

———. *A Little Book of Christian Questions and Answers*. Allison Park, PA: Pickwick, 1986.

———. *Sermons upon the Three First Chapters of the Canticle of Canticles*. Translated by John Harmar. Oxford: Joseph Barnes, 1587.

Biddle, John. *A Twofold Catechism*. London: J. Cottret, for Ri. Moone, 1654.

Biehl, Craig. *The Infinite Merit of Christ: The Glory of Christ's Obedience in the Theology of Jonathan Edwards*. Jackson, MS: Reformed Academic Press, 2009.

Bierma, Lyle D. *The Covenant Theology of Caspar Olevianus*. Grand Rapids, MI: Reformation Heritage Books, 2005.

Bilezikian, Gilbert. *Beyond Sex Roles: A Guide for the Study of Female Roles in the Bible*. Grand Rapids, MI: Baker, 1985.

Billings, J. Todd. "The Problem with 'Incarnational Ministry.'" *Christianity Today*, July/August 2012: 58–63. Also available at http://jtoddbillings.com /2012/12/the-problem-with-incarnational-ministry/.

Blackburn, Earl M., ed. *Covenant Theology: A Baptist Distinctive*. Birmingham, AL: Solid Ground, 2013.

Blacketer, Raymond A. "Arminius' Concept of Covenant in Its Historical Context." *Nederlands archief voor kerkgeschiedenis (Dutch Review of Church History)* 80, no. 2 (2000): 193–220.

Blaising, Craig A., and Darrell L. Bock. *Progressive Dispensationalism: An Up-to-Date Handbook of Contemporary Dispensational Thought*. Wheaton, IL: Victor, 1993.

Blake, Thomas. *Vindiciae Foederis, or, A Treatise of the Covenant of God Entered with Man-Kinde*. London: for Abel Roper, 1653.

Blenkinsopp, Joseph. *Wisdom and Law in the Old Testament: The Ordering of Life in Israel and Early Judaism*. Oxford: Oxford University Press, 1995.

Bloesch, Donald G. *Jesus Christ: Savior and Lord*. Christian Foundations. Downers Grove, IL: InterVarsity Press, 1997.

Blomberg, Craig L. *The Historical Reliability of John's Gospel: Issues and Commentary*. Downers Grove, IL: InterVarsity Press, 2001.

Boardman, Henry A. *The "Higher Life" Doctrine of Sanctification, Tried by the Word of God*. Philadelphia: Presbyterian Board of Publication, 1877.

Boff, Leonardo. *Jesus Christ Liberator: A Critical Christology for Our Time.* Translated by Patrick Hughes. Maryknoll, NY: Orbis, 1978.

Boice, James M., ed. *Our Savior God: Man, Christ, and the Atonement.* Grand Rapids, MI: Baker, 1980.

Bolton, Samuel. *The True Bounds of Christian Freedom.* Puritan Paperbacks. Edinburgh: Banner of Truth, 1964.

Bonar, Horatius. *Earth's Morning: or Thoughts on Genesis.* New York: Robert Carter and Brothers, 1875.

Bonaventure. *The Works of Bonaventure.* Translated by Jose de Vinck. 3 vols. Paterson, NJ: S. Anthony Guild Press, 1963.

Boothe, Charles Octavius. *Plain Theology for Plain People.* Introduction by Walter R. Strickland II. Bellingham, WA: Lexham Press, 2017.

Borchert, Gerald L. *John 1–11.* The New American Commentary 25A. Nashville: Broadman & Holman, 1996.

———. *John 12–21.* The New American Commentary 25B. Nashville: Broadman & Holman, 2002.

* Boston, Thomas. *The Complete Works of the Late Rev. Thomas Boston, Ettrick.* Edited by Samuel M'Millan. 12 vols. 1853. Reprint, Stoke-on-Trent, England: Tentmaker, 2002.

———. *Human Nature in Its Fourfold State.* Edinburgh: Banner of Truth, 1964.

Bowman, Robert M., Jr., and J. Ed Komoscewski. *Putting Jesus in His Place: The Case for the Deity of Christ.* Grand Rapids, MI: Kregel, 2007.

Boyce, James P. *Abstract of Systematic Theology.* 1887. Reprint, Cape Coral, FL: Founders, 2006.

Boys, John. *An Exposition of the Several Offices Adapted for Various Occasions of Public Worship.* New York: Stanford and Swords, 1851.

Bradford, John. *The Writings of John Bradford, Volume 1, Sermons, Meditations, Examinations, Etc.* Edited by Aubrey Townsend for the Parker Society. Cambridge: Cambridge University Press, 1848.

* à Brakel, Wilhelmus. *The Christian's Reasonable Service.* Edited by Joel R. Beeke. Translated by Bartel Elshout. 4 vols. Grand Rapids, MI: Reformation Heritage Books, 1992–1995.

Brett, Murray G. *Growing Up in Grace: The Use of Means for Communion with God.* Grand Rapids, MI: Reformation Heritage Books, 2009.

Bridge, William. *Christ and the Covenant.* London: for Thomas Parkhurst, 1667.

———. *The Works of the Rev. William Bridge.* 5 vols. London: Thomas Tegg, 1845.

Bridges, Charles. *A Commentary on Proverbs*. Geneva Series of Commentaries. 1846. Reprint, Edinburgh: Banner of Truth, 1968.

Bright, Pamela, ed. and trans. *Augustine and the Bible*. Notre Dame, IN: University of Notre Dame Press, 1999.

Brinkman, Martien E. *The Tragedy of Human Freedom: The Failure and Promise of the Christian Concept of Freedom in Western Culture*. Translated by Harry Flecken and Henry Jansen. Amsterdam: Rodopi, 2003.

Brock, Sebastian P. *Fire from Heaven: Studies in Syriac Theology and Liturgy*. Aldershot, England: Ashgate, 2006.

Brooks, James A. *Mark*. The New American Commentary 23. Nashville: Broadman & Holman, 1991.

Brooks, Thomas. *London's Lamentations: or, a Serious Discourse Concerning that Late Fiery Dispensation that Turned Our (Once Renowned) City into a Ruinous Heap*. London: for John Hancock and Nathaniel Ponder, 1670.

———. *The Works of Thomas Brooks*. 6 vols. Edinburgh: Banner of Truth, 1980.

Brown, Charles J. *The Divine Glory of Christ*. Edinburgh: Banner of Truth, 1982.

Brown, John. *Expository Discourses on the First Epistle of the Apostle Peter*. New York: Robert Carter, 1855.

Brown, John, of Haddington. *A Dictionary of the Holy Bible*. 3rd ed. 2 vols. Edinburgh: W. Anderson and J. Fairbairn, 1789.

———. *Questions and Answers on the Shorter Catechism*. 1846. Reprint, Grand Rapids, MI: Reformation Heritage Books, 2006.

———. *Systematic Theology: A Compendious View of Natural and Revealed Religion*. 1817. Reprint, Grand Rapids, MI: Reformation Heritage Books, 2015.

Brown, John, of Wamphray. *Christ the Way, the Truth, and the Life*. Grand Rapids, MI: Soli Deo Gloria, 2016.

Brown, Michael L. *Can You Be Gay and Christian? Responding with Love and Truth to Questions about Homosexuality*. Lake Mary, FL: Charisma House, 2014.

Bruce, A. B. *The Humiliation of Christ*. 5th ed. Edinburgh: T&T Clark, 1900.

Bruce, F. F. *Hebrews*. New International Commentary on the New Testament. Grand Rapids, MI: Eerdmans, 1964.

Brueggemann, Walter. "Of the Same Flesh and Bone (Gn 2, 23a)." *The Catholic Biblical Quarterly* 32, no. 4 (October 1970): 532–42.

Brunner, Emil. *The Christian Doctrine of Creation and Redemption, Dogmatics, Volume 2*. Translated by Olive Wyon. Philadelphia: Westminster, 1952.

———. *Man in Revolt*. Translated by Olive Wyon. London: RTS-Lutterworth Press, 1939.

———. *The Mediator: A Study of the Central Doctrine of the Christian Faith*. Translated by Olive Wyon. Philadelphia: Westminster, 1947.

———. *Revelation and Reason: The Christian Doctrine of Faith and Knowledge*. Translated by Olive Wyon. Philadelphia: Westminster, 1946.

Bulkeley, Peter. *The Gospel-Covenant or the Covenant of Grace Opened*. London: by M. S. for Benjamin Allen, 1646.

Bullinger, Heinrich. *The Decades of Henry Bullinger*. Edited by Thomas Harding. Translated by H. I. 4 vols. in 2. 1849–1852. Reprint, Grand Rapids, MI: Reformation Heritage Books, 2004.

———. *De Testamento Seu Foedere Dei Unico et Aeterno*. English translation in *Fountainhead of Federalism: Heinrich Bullinger and the Covenantal Tradition*, by Charles S. McCoy and J. Wayne Baker, 99–138. Louisville: Westminster/John Knox, 1991.

Bultmann, Rudolf. *Theology of the New Testament, Volume 1*. Translated by Kendrick Grobel. New York: Charles Scribner's Sons, 1951.

Bunyan, John. *Doctrine of the Law and Grace Unfolded*. London: for M. Wright, 1659.

———. *The Works of John Bunyan*. Edited by George Offor. 3 vols. 1854. Reprint, Edinburgh: Banner of Truth, 1991.

Burgess, Anthony. *CXLV Expository Sermons Upon the Whole 17th Chapter of the Gospel According to St. John: or Christs Prayer Before His Passion Explicated, and Both Practically and Polemically Improved*. London: Abraham Miller, 1656.

———. *The Doctrine of Original Sin, Asserted and Vindicated against the Old and New Adversaries Thereof, Both Socinians, Papists, Arminians, and Anabaptists. And Practically Improved for the Benefit of the Meanest Capacities*. London: by Abraham Miller for Thomas Underhill, 1658.

———. *Faith Seeking Assurance*. Edited by Joel R. Beeke. Puritan Treasures for Today. Grand Rapids, MI: Reformation Heritage Books, 2015.

———. *Vindiciae Legis: or, A Vindication of the Morall Law and the Covenants*. Westminster Assembly Project. 1647. Facsimile reprint, Grand Rapids, MI: Reformation Heritage Books, 2011.

Burgon, John William. *The Revision Revised*. London: John Murray, 1883.

Burk, Denny. "Is Homosexual Orientation Sinful?" *Journal of the Evangelical Theological Society* 58, no. 1 (2015): 95–115.

Bushnell, Horace. *The Vicarious Sacrifice, Grounded in Principles of Universal Obligation*. London: Strahan & Co., 1871.

Butterfield, Rosaria Champagne. *Openness Unhindered: Further Thoughts of an Unlikely Convert on Sexual Identity and Union with Christ.* Pittsburgh: Crown and Covenant, 2015.

———. *The Secret Thoughts of an Unlikely Convert: An English Professor's Journey into Christian Faith.* Expanded ed. Pittsburgh: Crown and Covenant, 2015.

Calamy, Edmund. *Two Solemne Covenants Made Between God and Man: viz. The Covenant of Workes, and the Covenant of Grace.* London: for Thomas Banks, 1647.

Calvin, John. *The Bondage and Liberation of the Will.* Edited by A. N. S. Lane. Translated by G. I. Davies. Texts and Studies in Reformation and Post-Reformation Thought. Grand Rapids, MI: Baker, 1996.

* ———. *Commentaries.* Reprint, Grand Rapids, MI: Baker, 2003.

———. *The Deity of Christ and Other Sermons.* Translated by Leroy Nixon. Audubon, NJ: Old Paths, 1997.

* ———. *Institutes of the Christian Religion.* Edited by John T. McNeill. Translated by Ford Lewis Battles. Philadelphia: Westminster, 1960. Cited as *Institutes.*

———. *Institutes of the Christian Religion: 1536 Edition.* Translated and edited by Ford Lewis Battles. Rev. ed. Grand Rapids, MI: H. H. Meeter Center for Calvin Studies/Eerdmans, 1986.

———. *Institutes of the Christian Religion: Translated from the First French Edition of 1541.* Translated by Robert White. Edinburgh: Banner of Truth, 2014.

———. *Letters of John Calvin.* Edited by Jules Bonnet. Translated by Marcus R. Gilchrist. 4 vols. Philadelphia: Presbyterian Board of Publication, 1858.

———. *Sermons on 2 Samuel, Chapters 1–13.* Translated by Douglas Kelly. Edinburgh: Banner of Truth, 1992.

———. *Sermons on the Epistle to the Ephesians.* Edinburgh: Banner of Truth, 1973.

———. *Sermons on Genesis: Chapters 1:1–11:4.* Translated by Rob Roy McGregor. Edinburgh: Banner of Truth, 2009.

———. *Tracts Relating to the Reformation.* Translated by Henry Beveridge. 3 vols. Edinburgh: Calvin Translation Society, 1844–1851.

Carlson, Richard F., and Tremper Longman III. *Science, Creation, and the Bible: Reconciling Rival Theories of Origins.* Downers Grove, IL: IVP Academic, 2010.

Carson, D. A. *The Gospel according to John*. The Pillar New Testament Commentary. Grand Rapids, MI: Eerdmans, 1991.

Cartwright, Thomas. *A Treatise of Christian Religion*. London: Felix Kyngston for Thomas Man, 1616.

Cave, Stephen. "There's No Such Thing as Free Will: But We're Better Off Believing in It Anyway." *The Atlantic* (June 2016). https://www.the atlantic.com/magazine/archive/2016/06/theres-no-such-thing-as-free-will /480750/.

Chafer, Lewis Sperry. *Systematic Theology*. 8 vols. Dallas, TX: Dallas Seminary Press, 1947.

Charles, R. H., ed. *The Apocrypha and Pseudepigrapha of the Old Testament*. 2 vols. Oxford: Oxford University Press, 1913.

* Charnock, Stephen. *The Works of Stephen Charnock*. 6 vols. Edinburgh: Banner of Truth, 2010.

Chemnitz, Martin. *The Two Natures in Christ*. Translated by J. A. O. Preus. St. Louis, MO: Concordia, 1971.

Chou, Abner, ed. *What Happened in the Garden: The Reality and Ramifications of the Creation and Fall of Man*. Grand Rapids, MI: Kregel, 2016.

Christopher, Mark. *Same-Sex Marriage: Is It Really the Same?* Leominster, UK: Day One, 2009.

Chrysologus, Peter. *Selected Sermons, Volume 3*. Translated by William B. Palardy. The Fathers of the Church 110. Washington, DC: The Catholic University of America Press, 2005.

———. *Selected Sermons*. And Saint Valerian, *Homilies*. Translated by George E. Ganss. The Fathers of the Church 17. Washington, DC: The Catholic University of America Press, 1953.

Chrysostom, John. *Homilies on Genesis, 1–17*. Translated by Robert C. Hill. The Fathers of the Church 74. Washington, DC: The Catholic University of America Press, 1986.

Ciampa, Roy E., and Brian S. Rosner. *The First Letter to the Corinthians*. The Pillar New Testament Commentary. Grand Rapids, MI: Eerdmans, 2010.

Cicero, Marcus Tullius. *The Orations of Marcus Tullius Cicero*. Translated by C. D. Yonge. 2 vols. London: Henry G. Bohn, 1856.

Clark, R. Scott, ed. *Covenant, Justification, and Pastoral Ministry: Essays by the Faculty of Westminster Seminary California*. Phillipsburg, NJ: P&R, 2007.

Clarkson, David. *The Works of David Clarkson*. 3 vols. Edinburgh: Banner of Truth, 1988.

Clines, D. J. A. "The Image of God in Man." *Tyndale Bulletin* 19 (1968): 53–103.

Cobb, John B., Jr., and David Ray Griffin. *Process Theology: An Introductory Exposition.* Philadelphia: Westminster, 1976.

Cocceius, Johannes. *The Doctrine of the Covenant and Testament of God.* Translated by Casey Carmichael. Grand Rapids, MI: Reformation Heritage Books, 2016.

Collins, C. John. *Did Adam and Eve Really Exist? Who They Were and Why You Should Care.* Wheaton, IL: Crossway, 2011.

———. "A Syntactical Note (Genesis 3:15): Is the Woman's Seed Singular or Plural?" *Tyndale Bulletin* 48, no. 1 (1997): 139–47.

Collins, Francis S. *The Language of God: A Scientist Presents Evidence for Belief.* New York: Free Press, 2006.

Colquhoun, John. *A Treatise on the Covenant of Works.* Edinburgh: Thomsons Brothers, 1821.

———. *A Treatise on the Law and the Gospel.* Introduction by Joel R. Beeke. Edited by Don Kistler. Grand Rapids, MI: Soli Deo Gloria, 2009.

Cooper, John W. *Body, Soul, and Life Everlasting: Biblical Anthropology and the Monism-Dualism Debate.* Grand Rapids, MI: Eerdmans, 1989.

———. *Panentheism—The Other God of the Philosophers: From Plato to the Present.* Grand Rapids, MI: Baker Academic, 2006.

Copan, Paul. "Is *Creatio ex Nihilo* a Post-Biblical Invention? An Examination of Gerhard May's Proposal." *Trinity Journal* 17NS (1996): 77–93.

Copan, Paul, and William Lane Craig. *Creation Out of Nothing: A Biblical, Philosophical, and Scientific Exploration.* Grand Rapids, MI: Baker, 2004.

Corey, David Munro. *Faustus Socinus.* 1932. Reprint, Eugene, OR: Wipf and Stock, 2009.

Cotton, John. *The Way of Life, or, Gods Way and Course, in Bringing the Soule into, and Keeping It in, and Carrying It on, in the Wayes of Life and Peace.* London: by M. F. for L. Fawne, and S. Gellibrand, 1641.

Coxe, Nehemiah. *A Discourse of the Covenants that God Made with Men before the Law.* London: J. D. for Nathaniel Ponder and Benjamin Alsop, 1681.

Coxe, Nehemiah, and John Owen. *Covenant Theology from Adam to Christ.* Edited by Ronald D. Miller, James M. Renihan, and Francisco Orozco. Palmdale, CA: Reformed Baptist Academic Press, 2005.

Crawford, Brandon James. *Jonathan Edwards on the Atonement: Understanding the Legacy of America's Greatest Theologian.* Foreword by Joel Beeke. Eugene, OR: Wipf and Stock, 2017.

Crisp, Oliver D. "Penal Non-Substitution." *The Journal of Theological Studies* NS 59, no. 1 (April 2008): 140–68.

Crockett, William, ed. *Four Views on Hell*. Grand Rapids, MI: Zondervan, 1992.

Cross, Richard. *The Metaphysics of the Incarnation: Thomas Aquinas to Duns Scotus*. Oxford: Oxford University Press, 2002.

Cummings, Asa. *A Memoir of the Rev. Edward Payson*. 3rd ed. Boston: Crocker and Brewster, 1830.

Cunningham, William. *Historical Theology*. 2 vols. Edinburgh: T&T Clark, 1863.

———. *The Reformers and the Theology of the Reformation*. Edinburgh: T&T Clark, 1866.

Currid, John D. *A Study Commentary on Genesis: Genesis 1:1–25:18*. EP Study Commentary. Darlington, England: Evangelical Press, 2003.

Custance, Arthur C. *Without Form and Void*. Brockville, Canada: n.p., 1970.

Cyril of Alexandria. *A Commentary upon the Gospel According to S. Luke, Part 2*. Translated by R. Payne Smith. Oxford: Oxford University Press, 1859.

Dales, Douglas. *Alcuin: Theology and Thought*. Cambridge: James Clarke and Co., 2013.

Dallimore, Arnold. *Forerunner of the Charismatic Movement: The Life of Edward Irving*. Chicago: Moody, 1983.

Darby, John Nelson. *The Collected Writings*. Edited by William Kelly. Reprint, Oak Park, IL: Bible Truth Publishers, 1962.

Darwin, Charles. *On the Origin of Species by Means of Natural Selection, or the Preservation of Favoured Races in the Struggle for Life*. London: John Murray, 1859.

Davids, Peter H. *The Letters of 2 Peter and Jude*. The Pillar New Testament Commentary. Grand Rapids, MI: Eerdmans, 2006.

Davies, Brian. *Aquinas*. Outstanding Christian Thinkers. London: Continuum, 2002.

Davis, Dale Ralph. *2 Samuel: Out of Every Adversity*. Focus on the Bible. Fearn, Ross-shire, Scotland: Christian Focus, 1999.

Davis, John D. "The Semitic Tradition of Creation." *Presbyterian and Reformed Review* 3 (1892): 448–61. At Princeton Theological Seminary Library. http://journals.ptsem.edu/id/BR1892311/dmd004.

de Beauvoir, Simone. *Le Deuxième Sexe*. Paris: Gallimard, 1949. English translation, *The Second Sex*. Translated by Howard M. Parshley. London: Jonathan Cape, 1953.

de Campos, Heber Carlos, Jr. *Doctrine in Development: Johannes Piscator and Debates over Christ's Active Obedience.* Reformed Historical-Theological Studies. Grand Rapids, MI: Reformation Heritage Books, 2017.

Denault, Pascal. *The Distinctiveness of Baptist Covenant Theology: A Comparison between Seventeenth-Century Particular Baptist and Paedobaptist Federalism.* Birmingham, AL: Solid Ground, 2013.

Denlinger, Aaron C. *Omnes in Adam ex Pacto Dei: Ambrogio Catarino's Doctrine of Covenantal Solidarity and Its Influence on Post-Reformation Reformed Theologians.* Göttingen: Vandenhoek and Ruprecht, 2011.

Denney, James. *The Christian Doctrine of Reconciliation.* London: Hodder and Stoughton, 1917.

de Vries, Henri. *The Lord's Anointed Prophet, Priest and King: A Series of Devotional Studies on the Redemptive Work of Christ.* London: Marshall Brothers, 1925.

DeYoung, Kevin. *What Does the Bible Really Teach about Homosexuality?* Wheaton, IL: Crossway, 2015.

Dick, John. *Lectures on Theology.* 2 vols. Philadelphia: F. W. Greenough, 1840.

Dickson, David. *Select Practical Writings of David Dickson.* Edinburgh: The Committee of the General Assembly of the Free Church of Scotland for the Publication of the Works of Scottish Reformers and Divines, 1845.

———. *Therapeutica Sacra; Shewing Briefly the Method of Healing of Diseases of Conscience, Concerning Regeneration.* Edinburgh: Evan Tyler, 1664.

Diodati, John (Giovanni). *Pious and Learned Annotations upon the Holy Bible.* 3rd ed. London: by James Flesher, for Nicholas Fussell, 1651.

Dodd, C. H. *The Epistle of Paul to the Romans.* London: Fontana, 1959.

Doriani, Daniel M. *Work: Its Purpose, Dignity, and Transformation.* Phillipsburg, NJ: P&R, 2019.

Douty, Norman F. *The Death of Christ: A Treatise which Answers the Question: "Did Christ Die Only for the Elect?"* Swengel, PA: Reiner, 1972.

Downame, John. *The Christian Warfare against the Devill, World and Flesh: Wherein Is Described Their Nature, the Maner of Their Fight and Meanes to Obtaine Victorye.* London: William Stansby, 1634.

Drummond, James. *The Epistles of Paul the Apostle to the Thessalonians, Corinthians, Galatians, Romans and Philippians.* International Handbooks to the New Testament. New York; London: G. P. Putnam's Sons, 1899.

Dryden, John. *The Conquest of Granada by the Spaniards.* London: by T. N. for Henry Herringman, 1672.

Dumbrell, William J. *Covenant and Creation: An Old Testament Covenantal Theology*. Nashville: Thomas Nelson, 1984.

Duncan, J. Ligon, III. "The Covenant Idea in Ante-Nicene Theology." PhD diss., University of Edinburgh, 1995. https://www.era.lib.ed.ac.uk/bit stream/handle/1842/10618/Duncan1995.pdf.

Dunn, James D. G. *Christology in the Making: A New Testament Inquiry into the Origins of the Doctrine of the Incarnation*. 2nd ed. Grand Rapids, MI: Eerdmans, 1989.

———. *The Theology of Paul the Apostle*. Grand Rapids, MI: Eerdmans, 1998.

Dutton, Anne. *Selected Spiritual Writings of Anne Dutton, Volume 1: Letters*. Edited by JoAnn Ford Watson. Macon, GA: Mercer University Press, 2003.

Dyer, William. *Christ's Famous Titles, and a Believer's Golden Chain*. London: n.p., 1663.

Eadie, John. *A Commentary on the Greek Text of the Epistle of Paul to the Colossians*. Edited by W. Young. 2nd ed. Edinburgh: T&T Clark, 1884.

Ebied, Ry, A. van Roey, and L. R. Wickham. *Peter of Callinicum: Anti-Tritheist Dossier*. Louven, Belgium. Departement Orientallstlek, 1981.

Eddy, G. T. *Dr. Taylor of Norwich: Wesley's Arch-Heretic*. Eugene, OR: Wipf and Stock, 2003.

Eddy, Mary Baker. *Miscellaneous Writings, 1883–1896*. Boston: Allison V. Stewart, 1917.

Edmondson, Stephen. *Calvin's Christology*. Cambridge: Cambridge University Press, 2004.

Edwards, James R. *The Gospel according to Mark*. The Pillar New Testament Commentary. Grand Rapids, MI: Eerdmans, 2002.

Edwards, Jonathan. *The Great Christian Doctrine of Original Sin Defended . . . A Reply to the Objections and Arguings of Dr. John Taylor*. Boston: S. Kneeland, 1758.

* ———. *The Works of Jonathan Edwards*. 26 vols. New Haven, CT: Yale University Press, 1957–2008.

Eichrodt, Walther. *Theology of the Old Testament*. Translated by J. A. Baker. Old Testament Library. Philadelphia: Westminster, 1961–1967.

Eldredge, Niles, and Stephen Jay Gould. "Punctuated Equilibria: An Alternative for Phyletic Gradualism." In *Models in Paleobiology*, edited by Thomas J. M. Schopf. San Francisco: Freeman, Cooper, 1972. Available at http://www.blackwellpublishing.com/ridley/classictexts/eldredge.asp.

Elwell, Walter A., ed. *Evangelical Dictionary of Theology*. Grand Rapids, MI: Baker, 1984.

Emerson, Matthew Y. "'He Descended to the Dead': The Burial of Christ and the Eschatological Character of the Atonement." *Southern Baptist Journal of Theology* 19, no. 1 (2015): 115–31.

Engelbrecht, Edward A. *Friends of the Law: Luther's Use of the Law for the Christian Life*. St. Louis, MO: Concordia, 2011.

English, Donald. *The Message of Mark: The Mystery of Faith*. The Bible Speaks Today. Leicester, England: Inter-Varsity Press; Downers Grove, IL: InterVarsity Press, 1992.

Enns, Paul P. *The Moody Handbook of Theology*. Rev. ed. Chicago: Moody, 2008.

Enns, Peter. *The Evolution of Adam: What the Bible Does and Doesn't Say about Human Origins*. Grand Rapids, MI: Brazos, 2012.

———. *Inspiration and Incarnation: Evangelicals and the Problem of the Old Testament*. Grand Rapids, MI: Baker Academic, 2005.

Erasmus, Desiderius. *A Diatribe or Sermon Concerning Free Will*. In *Discourse on Free Will*, translated and edited by Ernst F. Winter. New York: Continuum, 1989.

* Erickson, Millard J. *Christian Theology*. 3rd ed. Grand Rapids, MI: Baker, 2013.

———. *The Word Became Flesh: A Contemporary Incarnational Christology*. Grand Rapids, MI: Baker, 1991.

Ernesti, Johannes Augustus. *Opuscula Theologica*. Leipzig: Caspar Fritsch, 1773.

Erskine, Ralph. *Gospel Sonnets, or Spiritual Songs*. Edinburgh: by J. Ruthven and Sons, for J. Ogle et al., 1812.

Evans, C. Stephen, ed. *Exploring Kenotic Christology: The Self-Emptying of God*. Oxford: Oxford University Press, 2006.

Evans, Robert F. *Pelagius: Inquiries and Reappraisals*. New York: Seabury, 1968.

Fairweather, Eugene R., ed. and trans. *A Scholastic Miscellany: Anselm to Ockham*. Library of Christian Classics, Ichthus Edition. Philadelphia: Westminster, 1956.

Fee, Gordon D. *The First Epistle to the Corinthians*. The New International Commentary on the New Testament. Grand Rapids, MI: Eerdmans, 1987.

———. *Pauline Christology: An Exegetical-Theological Study*. Peabody, MA: Hendrickson, 2007.

Feinberg, John S. *No One Like Him: The Doctrine of God.* Foundations of Evangelical Theology. Wheaton, IL: Crossway, 2001.

Fenner, Dudley. *Sacra Theologia.* 2nd ed. Apud Eustathium Vignon, 1586.

Ferguson, Sinclair B. *The Holy Spirit.* Contours in Christian Theology. Downers Grove, IL: InterVarsity Press, 1996.

———. *The Whole Christ: Legalism, Antinomianism, and Gospel Assurance— Why the Marrow Controversy Still Matters.* Wheaton, IL: Crossway, 2016.

Ferguson, Sinclair B., and Derek W. H. Thomas. *Ichthus: Jesus Christ, God's Son, the Saviour.* Edinburgh: Banner of Truth, 2015.

Fergusson, James. *A Brief Exposition of the Epistles of Paul to the Galatians, Ephesians, Philippians, Colossians, and Thessalonians.* 1841. Reprint, Edinburgh: Banner of Truth, 1978.

Fesko, J. V. *The Covenant of Redemption: Origins, Development, and Reception.* Göttingen: Vandenhoek & Ruprecht, 2016.

———. *Death in Adam, Life in Christ: The Doctrine of Imputation.* Reformed, Exegetical and Doctrinal Studies. Fearn, Ross-shire, Scotland: Christian Focus, 2016.

———. *The Trinity and the Covenant of Redemption.* Fearn, Ross-shire, Scotland: Christian Focus, 2016.

Fields, Weston W. *Unformed and Unfilled: A Critique of the Gap Theory.* 1976. Reprint, Green Forest, AR: Master Books, 2005.

Finney, Charles G. *Lectures on Systematic Theology: Embracing Ability, (Natural, Moral, and Gracious,) Repentance, Impenitence, Faith and Unbelief, Justification, Sanctification, Election, Reprobation, Divine Purposes, Divine Sovereignty, and Perseverance.* Oberlin, OH: James M. Fitch, 1847.

———. *Lectures on Systematic Theology: Embracing Lectures on Moral Government, Together with Atonement, Moral and Physical Depravity, Regeneration, Philosophical Theories, and Evidences of Regeneration.* Oberlin, OH: James M. Fitch, 1846.

Fiorenza, Francis Schüssler, and John P. Galvin, eds. *Systematic Theology: Roman Catholic Perspectives.* Minneapolis: Fortress, 1991.

Fisher, Edward. *The Marrow of Modern Divinity.* Introduced by Philip Graham Ryken and William VanDoodewaard. Fearn, Ross-shire, Scotland: Christian Focus, 2009.

Fisher, James et al. *The Assembly's Shorter Catechism Explained.* Stoke-on-Trent, England: Berith, 1998.

Fitzmyer, Joseph. *Romans: A New Translation with Introduction and Commentary.* The Anchor Bible 33. New York: Doubleday, 1993.

Fitzpatrick, Elyse M. *Idols of the Heart: Learning to Long for God Alone.* Rev. ed. Phillipsburg, NJ: P&R, 2016.

* Flavel, John. *The Works of John Flavel.* 6 vols. 1820. Reprint, Edinburgh: Banner of Truth, 1968.

Ford, Paul Leicester, ed. *The New England Primer: A Reprint of the Earliest Known Edition, and Many Facsimiles and Reproductions, and an Historical Introduction.* New York: Dod, Mead, and Co., 1899.

Forsyth, P. T. *The Person and Place of Jesus Christ.* 1909. Reprint, Grand Rapids, MI: Eerdmans, 1964.

Foulkes, Francis. *Ephesians: An Introduction and Commentary.* Tyndale New Testament Commentaries 10. Downers Grove, IL: InterVarsity Press, 1989.

Frame, John M. *The Doctrine of God.* A Theology of Lordship. Phillipsburg, NJ: P&R, 2002.

———. *The Doctrine of the Word of God.* A Theology of Lordship. Phillipsburg, NJ: P&R, 2010.

Freud, Sigmund. *A General Introduction to Psychoanalysis.* Translated by G. Stanley Hall. New York: Horace Liveright, 1920.

Friedan, Betty. *The Feminine Mystique.* New York: Dell, 1964.

Fudge, Edward William, and Robert A. Peterson. *Two Views of Hell: A Biblical and Theological Dialogue.* Downers Grove, IL: InterVarsity Press, 2000.

Fulgentius of Ruspe. *Selected Works.* Translated by Robert B. Eno. Fathers of the Church 95. Washington, DC: The Catholic University of America Press, 1997.

Gagnon, Robert A. J. *The Bible and Homosexual Practice: Texts and Hermeneutics.* Nashville: Abingdon, 2001.

Garland, David E. *1 Corinthians.* Baker Exegetical Commentary on the New Testament. Grand Rapids, MI: Baker Academic, 2003.

———. *2 Corinthians.* The New American Commentary 29. Nashville: Broadman & Holman, 1999.

Garner, Paul A. *The New Creationism: Building Scientific Theories on a Biblical Foundation.* Darlington, England: Evangelical Press, 2009.

Garrett, Duane A. *Hosea, Joel.* The New American Commentary 19A. Nashville: Broadman & Holman, 1997.

Gasque, W. Ward, and Ralph P. Martin, eds. *Apostolic History and the Gospel: Biblical and Historical Essays Presented to F. F. Bruce on His 60th Birthday.* Grand Rapids, MI: Eerdmans, 1970.

Gathercole, Simon J. *The Preexistent Son: Recovering the Christologies of Matthew, Mark, and Luke.* Grand Rapids, MI: Eerdmans, 2006.

Gatiss, Lee. *For Us and For Our Salvation: 'Limited Atonement' in the Bible, Doctrine, History, and Ministry.* London: The Latimer Trust, 2012.

Gentry, Peter J., and Stephen J. Wellum. *Kingdom through Covenant: A Biblical-Theological Understanding of the Covenants.* Wheaton, IL: Crossway, 2012. 2nd ed., 2018.

George, Timothy, ed. *Reformation Commentary on Scripture, Old Testament.* 15 vols. Downers Grove, IL: IVP Academic, 2012–.

Gerhard, Johann. *On the Person and Office of Christ.* Translated by Richard J. Dinda. Edited by Benjamin T. G. Mayes. St. Louis, MO: Concordia, 2009.

Gibson, David, and Jonathan Gibson, eds. *From Heaven He Came and Sought Her: Definite Atonement in Historical, Biblical, Theological, and Pastoral Perspective.* Wheaton, IL: Crossway, 2013.

Gielen, Steffen, and Neil Turok. "Perfect Quantum Cosmological Bounce." *Physical Review Letters* 117, no. 2 (July 8, 2016). http://journals.aps.org/prl/abstract/10.1103/PhysRevLett.117.021301.

* Gill, John. *A Complete Body of Doctrinal and Practical Divinity.* Paris, AR: The Baptist Standard Bearer, 1995.

———. *Gill's Commentary.* 6 vols. 1852–1854. Reprint, Grand Rapids, MI: Baker, 1980.

Gillespie, Patrick. *The Ark of the Covenant Opened, or, A Treatise of the Covenant of Redemption between God and Christ.* London: for Tho. Parkhurst, 1677.

———. *The Ark of the Testament Opened.* London: by R. C., 1661.

Gitt, Werner. *In the Beginning Was Information.* Green Forest, AR: Master Books, 2005.

Godwyn (or Goodwin), Thomas. *Moses and Aaron: Civil and Ecclesiastical Rites Used by the Ancient Hebrews.* 12th ed. London: for R. Scot et al., 1685.

Gomes, Alan W. "Faustus Socinus' *De Jesu Christo Servatore*, Part III: Historical Introduction, Translation and Critical Notes." PhD diss., Fuller Theological Seminary, 1990.

Gonzales, Robert, Jr. "The Covenantal Context of the Fall: Did God Make a Primeval Covenant with Adam?" *Reformed Baptist Theological Review* 4, no. 2 (2007): 5–32.

* Goodwin, Thomas. *The Works of Thomas Goodwin.* 12 vols. 1861–1866. Reprint, Grand Rapids, MI: Reformation Heritage Books, 2006.

Gootjes, Nicolaas H. "Calvin on Epicurus and the Epicureans: Background to a Remark in Article 13 of the Belgic Confession." *Calvin Theological Journal* 40 (2006): 33–48.

Gordon, Bruce, and Emidio Campi, eds. *Architect of Reformation: An Introduction to Heinrich Bullinger, 1504–1575*. Texts and Studies in Reformation and Post-Reformation Thought. Grand Rapids, MI: Baker Academic, 2004.

Gossett, Thomas F. *Race: The History of an Idea in America*. New ed. Oxford: Oxford University Press, 1997.

Gouge, William. *Building a Godly Home, Volume 1, A Holy Vision for Family Life*. Edited by Scott Brown and Joel R. Beeke. Grand Rapids, MI: Reformation Heritage Books, 2013.

———. *Commentary on the Whole Epistle to the Hebrews*. 3 vols. Edinburgh: James Nichol, 1866.

———. *Of Domestical Duties*. 1622. Reprint, Pensacola, FL: Puritan Reprints, 2006.

Gould, Stephen Jay. *The Structure of Evolutionary Theory*. Cambridge, MA: Harvard University Press, 2002.

Green, Joel B., Scot McKnight, and I. Howard Marshall, eds. *Dictionary of Jesus and the Gospels*. Downers Grove, IL: InterVarsity Press, 1992.

Greenham, Richard. *The Workes of the Reverend and Faithfull Servant of Jesus Christ M. Richard Greenham*. Edited by H. H. 5th ed. London: William Welby, 1612.

Greenhill, William. *An Exposition of the Prophet Ezekiel*. Edited by James Sherman. Edinburgh: James Nichol, 1864.

Gregory the Great. *Morals on the Book of Job*. 3 vols. Oxford: John Henry Parker, 1844.

Greidanus, Sidney. *Preaching Christ from Genesis: Foundations for Expository Sermons*. Grand Rapids, MI: Eerdmans, 2007.

Grenfell, Bernard P., and Arthur S. Hunt, eds. *New Classical Fragments, and Other Greek and Latin Papyri*. Greek Papyri, Series II. Oxford: Oxford University Press, 1897.

Gribben, Crawford. *Evangelical Millennialism in the Trans-Atlantic World, 1500–2000*. New York: Palgrave Macmillan, 2011.

Gribben, Crawford, and Timothy C. F. Stunt, eds. *Prisoners of Hope? Aspects of Evangelical Millennialism in Britain and Ireland, 1800–1880*. Studies in Evangelical History and Thought. Eugene, OR: Wipf and Stock, 2004.

Grillmeier, Aloys. *Christ in the Christian Tradition, Volume 1: From the Apostolic Age to Chalcedon (451)*. Translated by John Bowden. 2nd ed. Atlanta: John Knox, 1975.

Grillmeier, Aloys, with Theresia Hainthaler. *Christ in the Christian Tradition, Volume 2: From the Council of Chalcedon (451) to Gregory the Great (590–604), Part 2: The Church of Constantinople in the Sixth Century*.

Translated by Pauline Allen and John Cawte. Louisville: Westminster John Knox, 1995.

Grotius, Hugo. *A Defence of the Catholic Faith Concerning the Satisfaction of Christ, against Faustus Socinus*. Translated by Frank Hugh Foster. Andover, MA: Warren F. Draper, 1889.

———. *Operum Theologicorum*. 3 vols. Amsterdam: Joannis Blaev, 1679.

Grudem, Wayne. *1 Peter: An Introduction and Commentary*. Tyndale New Testament Commentaries 17. Downers Grove, IL: InterVarsity Press, 1988.

———. *Evangelical Feminism and Biblical Truth: An Analysis of More than 100 Disputed Questions*. Sisters, OR: Multnomah, 2004.

———. "He Did Not Descend into Hell: A Plea for Following Scripture instead of the Apostles' Creed." *Journal of the Evangelical Theological Society* 34, no. 1 (March 1991): 103–13.

———. *Systematic Theology: An Introduction to Biblical Doctrine*. Grand Rapids, MI: Zondervan, 1994.

Gundry, Robert H. *Sōma in Biblical Theology: With Emphasis on Pauline Anthropology*. Grand Rapids, MI: Zondervan, 1987.

Gurnall, William. *The Christian in Complete Armour*. 2 vols. in 1. 1662–1665. Reprint, Edinburgh: Banner of Truth, 2002.

Guthrie, Donald. *Hebrews: An Introduction and Commentary*. Tyndale New Testament Commentaries 15. Downers Grove, IL: InterVarsity Press, 1983.

Guthrie, George H. *2 Corinthians*. Baker Exegetical Commentary on the New Testament. Grand Rapids, MI: Baker Academic, 2015.

———. *Hebrews*. The NIV Application Commentary. Grand Rapids, MI: Zondervan, 1998.

Gutiérrez, Gustavo. *A Theology of Liberation*. Maryknoll, NY: Orbis, 1973.

Haga, Joar. *Was There a Lutheran Metaphysic? The Interpretation of Communicatio Idiomatum in Early Modern Lutheranism*. Göttingen: Vandenhoek & Ruprecht, 2012.

Hagopian, David G., ed. *The Genesis Debate: Three Views on the Days of Creation*. Mission Viejo, CA: Crux Press, 2001.

Hall, Francis J. *The Kenotic Theory: Considered with Particular Reference to Its Anglican Forms and Arguments*. New York: Longmans, Green, and Co., 1898.

Hamilton, Victor P. *The Book of Genesis, Chapters 1–17*. The New International Commentary on the Old Testament. Grand Rapids, MI: Eerdmans, 1990.

———. *The Book of Genesis, Chapters 18–50*. The New International Commentary on the Old Testament. Grand Rapids, MI: Eerdmans, 1995.

Hanna, William. *Memoirs of the Life and Writings of Thomas Chalmers.* Edinburgh: Thomas Constable, 1842.

Hansen, G. Walter. *The Letter to the Philippians.* The Pillar New Testament Commentary. Grand Rapids, MI: Eerdmans, 2009.

Harman, Allan M. *Deuteronomy: The Commands of a Covenant God.* Focus on the Bible. Fearn, Ross-shire, Scotland: Christian Focus, 2001.

Harnack, Adolf. *History of Dogma.* Translated by Neil Buchanan. 7 vols. Boston: Roberts Brothers, 1895–1900.

———. *Marcion: The Gospel of the Alien God.* Translated by John E. Steely and Lyle D. Bierma. Durham, NC: Labyrinth, 1990.

———. *What Is Christianity? Lectures Delivered in the University of Berlin During the Winter-Term 1899–1900.* Translated by Thomas Bailey Saunders. Rev. 2nd ed. New York: G. P. Putnam's Sons, 1902.

Harris, Robert. *A Brief Discourse of Mans Estate in the First and Second Adam.* London: by J. Flesher for John Bartlet, the elder, and John Bartlet, the younger, 1653.

Haugaard, William P. "Arius: Twice a Heretic? Arius and the Human Soul of Christ." *Church History* 29, no. 3 (September 1960): 251–63.

Havergal, Frances R. *Under the Surface.* 3rd ed. London: J. Nisbet and Co., 1876.

Haykin, Michael A. G., and Mark Jones, eds. *Drawn into Controversie: Reformed Theological Diversity and Debates within Seventeenth-Century British Puritanism.* Reformed Historical Theology 17. Göttingen: Vandenhoeck & Ruprecht, 2011.

Helm, Paul. *Human Nature from Calvin to Edwards.* Grand Rapids, MI: Reformation Heritage Books, 2018.

———. *John Calvin's Ideas.* Oxford: Oxford University Press, 2004.

Hendriksen, William. *The Gospel of John.* New Testament Commentary. 2 vols. in 1. Grand Rapids, MI: Baker, 1953.

Henry, Carl F. H. *God, Revelation and Authority.* 6 vols. Waco, TX: Word, 1976.

Henry, Matthew. *Matthew Henry's Commentary on the Whole Bible: Complete and Unabridged in One Volume.* Peabody, MA: Hendrickson, 1994.

Henry, Philip. *Christ All in All: What Christ Is Made to Believers.* Grand Rapids, MI: Soli Deo Gloria, 2016.

Herder, J. G. *The Spirit of Hebrew Poetry.* Translated by James Marsh. 2 vols. in one. Burlington: Edward Smith, 1833.

Herodotus. *Herodotus, Volume 1.* Translated by A. D. Godley. Loeb Classical Library. London: William Heinemann, 1946.

Hick, John, ed. *The Myth of God Incarnate*. London: SCM, 1977.

Hicks, John Mark. "The Theology of Grace in the Thought of Jacobus Arminius and Philip van Limborch: A Study in the Development of Seventeenth-Century Dutch Arminianism." PhD diss., Westminster Theological Seminary, 1985. http://evangelicalarminians.org/wp-content/uploads/2013/07/Hicks.-The-Theology-of-Grace-in-the-Thought-of-Arminius-and-Limborch.pdf.

Hodge, Archibald A. *The Atonement*. Reprint, London: Evangelical Press, 1974.

———. *Outlines of Theology*. 1879. Reprint, Grand Rapids, MI: Zondervan, 1973.

Hodge, Charles. *A Commentary on 1 & 2 Corinthians*. Edinburgh: Banner of Truth, 1974.

———. *Discussions in Church Polity*. Edited by William Durant. Preface by Archibald Alexander Hodge. New York: Charles Scribner's Sons, 1878.

———. *Ephesians*. The Geneva Series of Commentaries. Edinburgh: Banner of Truth, 1964.

* ———. *Systematic Theology*. 3 vols. Peabody, MA: Hendrickson, 1999.

* Hoekema, Anthony A. *Created in God's Image*. Grand Rapids, MI: Ferdmans, 1986.

Hoenecke, Adolf. *Evangelical Lutheran Dogmatics*. Translated by James Langebartels. 4 vols. Milwaukee, WI: Northwestern Publishing House, 1999–2009.

Honey, Charles. "Adamant on Adam: Resignation of Prominent Scholar Underscores Tension over Evolution." *Christianity Today* (June 2010): 14.

Hooker, Thomas. *The Application of Redemption by the Effectual Work of the Word, and Spirit of Christ, for the Bringing Home of Lost Sinners to God. The First Eight Books*. London: Peter Cole, 1656.

———. *The Application of Redemption, The Ninth and Tenth Books*. Ames, IA: International Outreach, 2008.

———. *A Briefe Exposition of the Lords Prayer*. London: by Moses Bell for Benjamin Allen, 1645.

———. *The Poor Doubting Christian Drawn to Christ*. Hartford: Robins and Smith, 1845.

———. *The Soules Exaltation*. London: by Iohn Haviland, for Andrew Crooke, 1638.

———. *The Soul's Humiliation*. Ames, IA: International Outreach, 2000.

Hooper, John. *Early Writings*. Edited by Samuel Carr. Cambridge: Cambridge University Press, 1843.

Hoover, Roy W. "The Harpagmos Enigma: A Philological Solution." *Harvard Theological Review* 64 (1971): 95–119.

Hopkins, Ezekiel. *The Doctrine of the Two Covenants.* London: Richard Smith, 1712.

———. *The Works of Ezekiel Hopkins.* 3 vols. Philadelphia: The Leighton Publications, 1874.

Horner, Tom. *Jonathan Loved David: Homosexuality in Biblical Times.* Philadelphia: Westminster, 1978.

Horton, Michael. *The Christian Faith: A Systematic Theology for Pilgrims on the Way.* Grand Rapids, MI: Zondervan, 2011.

Howe, John. *The Works of the Rev. John Howe.* London: Henry G. Bohn, 1846.

Howell, Robert Boyte C. *The Covenants.* Charleston, NC: Southern Baptist Publication Society, 1855.

Huber, Karen C. "The Pelagian Heresy: Observations on Its Social Context." PhD diss., Oklahoma State University, 1979.

Huey, F. B. *Jeremiah, Lamentations.* The New American Commentary 16. Nashville: Broadman & Holman, 1993.

Hughes, Philip E. *A Commentary on the Epistle to the Hebrews.* Grand Rapids, MI: Eerdmans, 1977.

———. *Paul's Second Epistle to the Corinthians.* The New International Commentary on the New Testament. Grand Rapids, MI: Eerdmans, 1962.

Hurley, James B. *Man and Woman in Biblical Perspective.* Grand Rapids, MI: Zondervan, 1981.

Hurtado, Larry W. *Lord Jesus Christ: Devotion to Jesus in Earliest Christianity.* Grand Rapids, MI: Eerdmans, 2003.

Husbands, Mark, and Daniel J. Treier, eds. *Justification: What's at Stake in the Current Debate.* Downers Grove, IL: InterVarsity Press, 2004.

Hutchinson, George P. *The Problem of Original Sin in American Presbyterian Theology.* Nutley, NJ: Presbyterian and Reformed, 1972.

Hyde, Daniel R. *In Defense of the Descent: A Response to Contemporary Critics.* Grand Rapids, MI: Reformation Heritage Books, 2010.

Innes, Stephen. *Creating the Commonwealth: The Economic Culture of Puritan New England.* New York: W. W. Norton, 1995.

International Theological Commission [of the Vatican]. *Communion and Stewardship: Human Persons Created in the Image of God.* http://www.vatican.va/roman_curia/congregations/cfaith/cti_documents/rc_con_cfaith_doc_20040723_communion-stewardship_en.html.

Ironside, H. A. *The Great Parenthesis.* Grand Rapids, MI: Zondervan, 1943.

Isbell, R. Sherman. "The Origin of the Concept of the Covenant of Works." ThM thesis, Westminster Theological Seminary, 1976.

Jackson, Samuel Macauley, ed. *The New Schaff-Herzog Encyclopedia of Religious Knowledge*. 12 vols. New York; London: Funk & Wagnalls, 1908–1914.

Jay, William. *Morning Exercises for Every Day in the Year*. New York: American Tract Society, 1828.

Jeffrey, Steve, Michael Ovey, and Andrew Sach. *Pierced for Our Transgressions: Rediscovering the Glory of Penal Substitution*. Wheaton, IL: Crossway, 2007.

Jennings, David. *A Vindication of the Scripture-Doctrine of Original Sin, from Mr Taylor's Free and Candid Examination of It*. London: R. Hett and J. Oswald, 1740.

Jeon, Jeong Koo. *Covenant Theology: John Murray's and Meredith G. Kline's Response to the Historical Development of Federal Theology in Reformed Thought*. Lanham, MD: University Press of America, 1999.

Jersak, Brad, and Michael Hardin, eds. *Stricken by God? Nonviolent Identification and the Victory of Christ*. Grand Rapids, MI: Eerdmans, 2007.

Jervis, Adrienne L. "O Death, Where Is Thy Victory? A Study of Christ's *Descensus ad Inferos* in the Odes of Solomon." PhD diss., University of Edinburgh, 1995.

Jobes, Karen H. *1 Peter*. Baker Exegetical Commentary on the New Testament. Grand Rapids, MI: Baker Academic, 2005.

John Paul II. *Incarnationis Mysterium: Bull of Indication of the Great Jubilee of the Year 2000*, and *Conditions for Gaining the Jubilee Indulgence*. The Vatican. November 29, 1998. http://www.vatican.va/jubilee_2000/docs/documents/hf_jp-ii_doc_30111998_bolla-jubilee_en.html.

John Paul II and Dinkha IV. *Common Christological Declaration between the Catholic Church and the Assyrian Church of the East*. November 11, 1994. http://www.vatican.va/roman_curia/pontifical_councils/chrstuni/documents/rc_pc_chrstuni_doc_11111994_assyrian-church_en.html.

Johnson, Dennis E. *Him We Proclaim: Preaching Christ from All the Scriptures*. Phillipsburg, NJ: P&R, 2007.

Johnson, Phillip E. *Darwin on Trial*. Downers Grove, IL: InterVarsity Press, 1991.

Johnson, Terry L. et al. *The Worship of God: Reformed Concepts of Biblical Worship*. Fearn, Ross-shire, Scotland: Christian Focus, 2005.

Jones, Mark. *Antinomianism: Reformed Theology's Unwelcome Guest?* Phillipsburg, NJ: P&R, 2013.

———. *A Christian's Pocket Guide to Jesus Christ: An Introduction to Christology.* Fearn, Ross-shire, Scotland, Christian Focus, 2012.

Josephus, Flavius. *Flavia Josephi Opera.* Edited by Benedictus Niese. Berolini: Weidmannos, 1888.

———. *The Works of Josephus.* Translated by William Whiston. Peabody, MA: Hendrickson, 1987.

Junius, Franciscus. *Opuscula Theologica Selecta.* Edited by Abraham Kuyper. Bibliotheca Reformata 1. Amsterdam: Fredericum Muller cum Soc. Et Joannem Hermannum Kruyt, 1882.

———. *A Treatise on True Theology: With the Life of Franciscus Junius.* Translated by David C. Noe. Grand Rapids, MI: Reformation Heritage Books, 2014.

Karlberg, Mark W. *Covenant Theology in Reformed Perspective.* Eugene, OR: Wipf and Stock, 2000.

Kassian, Mary A. *The Feminist Mistake: The Radical Impact of Feminism on Church and Culture.* Wheaton, IL: Crossway, 2005.

Kaufmann, Matthias, and Alexander Aichele, eds. *A Companion to Luis de Molina.* Leiden: Brill, 2014.

Keach, Benjamin. *The Ax Laid to the Root: or, One Blow More at the Foundation of Infant Baptism, and Church-Membership . . . Part I.* London: for the Author, 1693.

———. *The Display of Glorious Grace, or, The Covenant of Peace Opened.* London: by S. Bridge, for Mary Fabian, Joseph Collier, and William Marshall, 1698.

———. *The Everlasting Covenant, a Sweet Cordial for a Drooping Soul: or, the Excellent Nature of the Covenant of Grace Opened.* London: for H. Barnard, 1692.

———. *Preaching from the Types and Metaphors of the Bible.* 1855. Reprint, Grand Rapids, MI: Kregel, 1972.

Kelly, Douglas F. *Creation and Change: Genesis 1.1–2.4 in the Light of Changing Scientific Paradigms.* Fearn, Ross-shire, Scotland: Christian Focus, 1997.

* ———. *Systematic Theology: Grounded in Holy Scripture and Understood in the Light of the Church, Volume 2, The Beauty of Christ: A Trinitarian Vision.* Fearn, Ross-shire, Scotland: Christian Focus, 2014.

Kelly, J. N. D. *Early Christian Creeds.* 3rd ed. London: Routledge, 1950.

———. *Early Christian Doctrines.* 5th ed. London: Bloomsbury, 1977.

Keown, Gerald L., Pamela J. Scalise, and Thomas G. Smothers. *Jeremiah 26–52*. Word Biblical Commentary 27. Nashville: Thomas Nelson, 1995.

Kersten, G. H. *Reformed Dogmatics: A Systematic Treatment of Reformed Doctrine*. 2 vols. Grand Rapids, MI: Netherlands Reformed Book and Publishing Committee, 1980.

Kidner, Derek. *Genesis*. Tyndale Old Testament Commentaries. Downers Grove, IL: InterVarsity Press, 1967.

———. *Psalms 73–150: An Introduction and Commentary*. Tyndale Old Testament Commentaries. Downers Grove, IL: InterVarsity Press, 1975.

Kim, Chankyu. *Balthasar Hubmaier's Doctrine of Salvation in Dynamic and Relational Perspective*. Eugene, OR: Pickwick, 2013.

Kim, Yoon-Hee. "'The Prophet like Moses': Deut. 18:15–22 Reexamined within the Context of the Pentateuch and in Light of the Final Shape of the TaNaK." PhD diss., Trinity Evangelical Divinity School, 1995.

Kistler, Don, ed. *Justification by Faith Alone*. Morgan, PA: Soli Deo Gloria, 1995.

———. *Law and Liberty: A Biblical Look at Legalism*. Orlando, FL: The Northampton Press, 2014.

Klein, George L. *Zechariah*. The New American Commentary 21B. Nashville: Broadman & Holman, 2008.

Kline, Meredith G. *By Oath Consigned: A Reinterpretation of the Covenant Signs of Circumcision and Baptism*. Grand Rapids, MI: Eerdmans, 1968.

———. *Glory in Our Midst: A Biblical-Theological Reading of Zechariah's Night Visions*. Eugene, OR: Wipf and Stock, 2001.

———. "Gospel until the Law: Rom 5:13–14 and the Old Covenant." *Journal of the Evangelical Theological Society* 34, no. 4 (December 1991): 433–46.

———. *Kingdom Prologue: Genesis Foundations for a Covenantal Worldview*. Overland Park, KS: Two Age Press, 2000.

———. *Treaty of the Great King: The Covenantal Structure of Deuteronomy*. Eugene, OR: Wipf and Stock, 1963.

Knight, George W., III. *The Pastoral Epistles: A Commentary on the Greek Text*. The New International Greek Testament Commentary. Grand Rapids, MI: Eerdmans, 1992.

Knox, John. *The Works of John Knox*. Edited by David Laing. 6 vols. Edinburgh: Thomas George Stevenson, 1864.

Kolb, Robert. *Bound Choice, Election, and Wittenberg Theological Method*. Lutheran Quarterly Books. Edited by Paul Rorem. Grand Rapids, MI: Eerdmans, 2005.

Kolb, Robert, Irene Dingel, and L'Ubomír Batka, eds. *The Oxford Handbook of Martin Luther's Theology*. Oxford: Oxford University Press, 2014.

Köstenberger, Andreas J., and Margaret E. Köstenberger. *God's Design for Man and Woman: A Biblical-Theological Survey*. Wheaton, IL: Crossway, 2014.

Kremer, F. W. "The Impeccability of the Lord Jesus Christ." *The Reformed Theological Review* 26 (April 1879): 258–77.

Krummacher, F. W. *The Suffering Saviour*. Edinburgh: Banner of Truth, 2004.

Kruse, Colin G. *The Letters of John*. The Pillar New Testament Commentary. Grand Rapids, MI: Eerdmans, 2000.

Kuyper, Abraham. *A Centennial Reader*. Edited by James D. Bratt. Grand Rapids, MI: Eerdmans, 1998.

[Lacunza, Manuel] Ben-Ezra, Juan Josafat. *The Coming of the Messiah in Glory and Majesty*. Translated by Edward Irving. 2 vols. London: L. B. Seeley and Son, 1827.

Ladd, George E. *A Theology of the New Testament*. Rev. ed. Grand Rapids, MI: Eerdmans, 1993.

Laidlaw, John. *Bible Doctrine of Man, or The Anthropology and Psychology of Scripture*. Rev. ed. Edinburgh: T&T Clark, 1895.

Lane, Eric. *Psalms 1–89: The Lord Saves*. Focus on the Bible. Fearn, Ross-shire, Scotland: Christian Focus, 2006.

Lane, W. L. *Hebrews*. Word Biblical Commentary. Dallas, TX: Word, 1991.

Lang, U. M. "Anhypostatos-Enhypostatos: Church Fathers, Protestant Orthodoxy and Karl Barth." *Journal of Theological Studies* NS 49, pt. 2 (October 1998): 630–57.

Lange, John Peter. *A Commentary on the Holy Scriptures*. Translated by Tayler Lewis and A. Gosman. Bellingham, WA: Logos Bible Software, 2008.

Large, James. *Sunday Readings for a Year: or, Two Hundred and Eighty Scripture Titles and Symbols of Christ*. London: Hodder and Stoughton, 1879.

Lavallee, Louis. "Augustine on the Creation Days." *Journal of the Evangelical Theological Society* 32, no. 4 (December 1989): 457–64.

Law, Henry. *"Christ Is All." The Gospel of the Pentateuch: Exodus*. London: The Religious Tract Society, 1867.

Lea, Thomas D., and Hayne P. Griffin. *1, 2 Timothy, Titus*. The New American Commentary 34. Nashville: Broadman & Holman, 1992.

Lehner, Ulrich L., Richard A. Muller, and A. G. Roeber, eds. *The Oxford Handbook of Early Modern Theology, 1600–1800*. Oxford: Oxford University Press, 2016.

Leigh, Edward. *A Treatise of the Divine Promises*. London: George Miller, 1633.

Leighton, Robert. *A Commentary upon the First Epistle of Peter*. In *The Whole Works of Robert Leighton*. New York: Robert Carter and Brothers, 1859.

Leith, John H., ed. *Creeds of the Churches: A Reader in Christian Doctrine from the Bible to the Present*. 3rd ed. Louisville: Westminster/John Knox, 1982.

Lerner, Eric. "Bucking the Big Bang." *New Scientist*. May 22, 2004. https://www.newscientist.com/article/mg18224482-900-bucking-the-big-bang/.

Letham, Robert. "Baptism in the Writings of the Reformers." *The Scottish Bulletin of Evangelical Theology* 7, no. 1 (Spring 1989): 21–44. http://www.biblicalstudies.org.uk/articles_sbet-01.php.

———. *The Message of the Person of Christ*. The Bible Speaks Today, Bible Themes. Nottingham, England: Inter-Varsity Press, 2013.

———. *Systematic Theology*. Wheaton, IL: Crossway, 2019.

———. *The Work of Christ*. Contours of Christian Theology. Downers Grove, IL: InterVarsity Press, 1993.

Levering, Matthew. *The Theology of Augustine. An Introductory Guide to His Most Important Works*. Grand Rapids, MI: Baker Academic, 2013.

Lewis, C. S. *The Problem of Pain*. New York: HarperCollins, 2001.

Lewis, John. *The Life of the Learned and Right Reverend Reynold Pecock*. New ed. Oxford: Oxford University Press, 1820.

Lightfoot, J. B. *Saint Paul's Epistle to the Philippians*. London: Macmillan and Co., 1903.

Lightner, Robert P. *The Death Christ Died: A Case for Unlimited Atonement*. Des Plaines, IL: Regular Baptist Press, 1967.

Lillback, Peter A. *The Binding of God: Calvin's Role in the Development of Covenant Theology*. Texts and Studies in Reformation and Post-Reformation Thought. Grand Rapids, MI: Baker Academic, 2001.

Lim, Won Taek. *The Covenant Theology of Francis Roberts*. Chungnam, South Korea: King and Kingdom, 2002.

Lincoln, Andrew T. *Ephesians*. Word Biblical Commentary 42. Dallas, TX: Word, 1990.

Lincoln, Charles Fred. "The Development of the Covenant Theory." *Bibliotheca Sacra* 100 (1943): 134–63.

Lints, Richard. *Identity and Idolatry: The Image of God and Its Inversion*. New Studies in Biblical Theology. Downers Grove, IL: InterVarsity Press, 2015.

Litton, E. A. *Introduction to Dogmatic Theology.* Edited by Philip E. Hughes. London: James Clarke, 1960.

Livy. *Livy, Volume 4.* Translated by B. O. Foster. Loeb Classical Library. London: William Heinemann, 1926.

Lloyd-Jones, Martyn. *Life in Christ: Studies in 1 John. Volume 4: The Love of God.* Wheaton, IL: Crossway, 1994.

Lohse, Bernhard. *Martin Luther's Theology: Its Historical and Systematic Development.* Translated and edited by Roy A. Harrisville. Minneapolis: Fortress, 1999.

* Lombard, Peter. *The Sentences.* Translated by Giulio Silano. 4 vols. Toronto: Pontifical Institutes of Mediaeval Studies, 2007–2010.

Longenecker, Richard N. *Galatians.* Word Biblical Commentary 41. Dallas, TX: Word, 1990.

Longenecker, Richard N., and Merrill C. Tenney, eds. *New Dimensions in New Testament Study.* Grand Rapids, MI: Zondervan, 1974.

Longman, Tremper, III, and David E. Garland, eds. *The Expositor's Bible Commentary, Revised Edition.* 13 vols. Grand Rapids, MI: Zondervan, 2006–2012.

Lova, Elikana Asheri, and Elia Shabani Mligo. *He Descended into Hell: A Christological Study of the Apostles' Creed and Its Implications to Christian Teaching and Preaching in Africa.* Eugene, OR: Wipf and Stock, 2015.

Love, Christopher. *The Naturall Mans Case Stated: or, an Exact Mapp of the Little World Man, Considered in Both His Capacities, Either in the State of Nature, or Grace.* London: by E. Cotes, for George Eversden, 1652.

———. *The Natural Man's Condition.* Edited by Don Kistler. Orlando, FL: Northampton Press, 2012.

Luther, Martin. *The Bondage of the Will.* Translated by James I. Packer and O. R. Johnston. Grand Rapids, MI: Baker, 1957.

* ———. *Luther's Works.* Edited by Jaroslav Pelikan et al. 79 vols. St. Louis, MO: Concordia, 1958–2016.

———. *Sermons of Martin Luther.* Edited and translated by John Nicholas Lenker. 8 vols. Grand Rapids, MI: Baker, 1989.

MacArthur, John, and Richard Mayhue, eds. *Biblical Doctrine: A Systematic Summary of Bible Truth.* Wheaton, IL: Crossway, 2017.

Macedo, Breno L. "The Covenant Theology of Robert Rollock." ThM thesis, Puritan Reformed Theological Seminary, 2012.

Machen, J. Gresham. *Christianity and Liberalism.* 1923. Reprint, Grand Rapids, MI: Eerdmans, 1992.

———. *The Virgin Birth of Christ.* New York: Harper, 1930.

Mackay, John L. *Haggai, Zechariah, Malachi: God's Restored People*. Focus on the Bible. Fearn, Ross-shire, Scotland: Christian Focus, 2003.

———. *Jeremiah: An Introduction and Commentary, Volume 1, Chapters 1–20*. Mentor Commentary. Fearn, Ross-shire, Scotland: Christian Focus, 2004.

———. *Jeremiah: An Introduction and Commentary, Volume 2: Chapters 21–52*. Mentor Commentary. Fearn, Ross-shire, Scotland: Christian Focus, 2004.

———. *Jonah, Micah, Nahum, Habakkuk and Zephaniah*. Focus on the Bible. Fearn, Ross-shire, Scotland: Christian Focus, 1998.

Macleod, Donald. *The Person of Christ*. Contours of Christian Theology. Downers Grove, IL: InterVarsity Press, 1998.

Madueme, Hans, and Michael Reeves, eds. *Adam, the Fall, and Original Sin: Theological, Biblical, and Scientific Perspectives*. Grand Rapids, MI: Baker Academic, 2014.

Magueijo, João. "New Varying Speed of Light Theories." October 15, 2003. Cornell University. https://arxiv.org/pdf/astro-ph/0305457v3.pdf.

Manton, Thomas. *The Complete Works of Thomas Manton*. 22 vols. London: James Nisbet, 1871.

Mariña, Jacqueline, ed. *The Cambridge Companion to Friedrich Schleiermacher*. Cambridge: Cambridge University Press, 2005.

Marshall, I. Howard. *The Gospel of Luke*. New International Greek Testament Commentary. Grand Rapids, MI: Eerdmans, 1978.

Martin, Hugh. *The Atonement: In Its Relation to the Covenant, the Priesthood, the Intercession of Our Lord*. Edinburgh: James Gemmell and George Bridge, 1887.

———. *Christ's Presence in the Gospel History*. 2nd ed. Edinburgh: John MacLaren, 1865.

Martin, Ralph P. *Carmen Christi: Philippians ii.5–11 in Recent Interpretation and in the Setting of Early Christian Worship*. Society for New Testament Studies Monograph Series 4. Cambridge: Cambridge University Press, 1967.

———. *Philippians: An Introduction and Commentary*. Tyndale New Testament Commentaries 11. Downers Grove, IL: InterVarsity Press, 1987.

Mason, William. *A Spiritual Treasury for the Children of God*. 1834. Reprint, Grand Rapids, MI: Reformation Heritage Books, n.d.

Mathews, Kenneth A. *Genesis 1–11:26*. The New American Commentary 1A. Nashville: Broadman & Holman, 1996.

———. *Genesis 11:27–50:26*. The New American Commentary 1B. Nashville: Broadman & Holman, 2005.

May, Gerhard. *Creatio ex Nihilo: The Doctrine of "Creation Out of Nothing" in Early Christian Thought*. Translated by A. S. Worrall. Edinburgh: T&T Clark, 1994.

McCall, Thomas H. *Against God and Nature: The Doctrine of Sin*. Foundations of Evangelical Theology. Wheaton, IL: Crossway, 2019.

McComiskey, Thomas E. *The Covenants of Promise: A Theology of the Old Testament Covenants*. Grand Rapids, MI: Baker, 1985.

McComiskey, Thomas E., ed. *The Minor Prophets: An Exegetical and Expository Commentary*. 3 vols. Grand Rapids, MI: Baker, 1992–1998.

McConnell, D. R. *A Different Gospel: A Historical and Biblical Analysis of the Modern Faith Movement*. Peabody, MA: Hendrickson, 1988.

McCoy, Charles S., and J. Wayne Baker. *Fountainhead of Federalism: Heinrich Bullinger and the Covenantal Tradition*. Louisville: Westminster/John Knox, 1991.

McCree, Walter T. "The Covenant Meal in the Old Testament." *Journal of Biblical Literature* 45, no. 1/2 (1926): 120–28.

McDonald, H. D. *The Atonement of the Death of Christ: In Faith, Revelation, and History*. Grand Rapids, MI: Baker, 1985.

McElrath, Damian, ed. *Franciscan Christology: Selected Texts, Translations, and Introductory Essays*. St. Bonaventure, NY: Franciscan Institute of St. Bonaventure University, 1980.

McGinn, Bernard. *Anti-Christ: Two Thousand Years of the Human Fascination with Evil*. San Francisco: HarperCollins, 1994.

McGrath, Alister E. *Iustitia Dei: A History of the Christian Doctrine of Justification*. 3rd ed. Cambridge: Cambridge University Press, 2005.

———. *The Making of Modern German Christology*. Oxford: Basil Blackwell, 1986.

M'Cheyne, Robert Murray. *Memoir and Remains of Robert Murray M'Cheyne*. Edited by Andrew Bonar. 1892. Reprint, Edinburgh: Banner of Truth, 1966.

McKelvey, R. J. "Christ the Cornerstone." *New Testament Studies* 8 (1962): 352–59.

Meade, John D. "The Meaning of Circumcision in Israel: A Proposal for a Transfer of Rite from Egypt to Israel." *Southern Baptist Journal of Theology* 20, no. 1 (2016): 35–54.

Melick, Richard R. *Philippians, Colossians, Philemon*. The New American Commentary 32. Nashville: Broadman & Holman, 1991.

Merrick, J., and Stephen M. Garrett, eds. *Five Views on Biblical Inerrancy*. Counterpoints: Bible and Theology. Grand Rapids, MI: Zondervan, 2013.

Merrill, Eugene H. *Deuteronomy*. The New American Commentary 4. Nashville: Broadman & Holman, 1994.

Meyer, Joyce. *The Most Important Decision You Will Ever Make*. New York: Warner Faith, 2003.

Mickelsen, Alvera, ed. *Women, Authority, and the Bible*. Downers Grove, IL: InterVarsity Press, 1986.

Migne, J. P., ed. *Patrologiae Graeca*. 161 vols. Paris: Imprimerie Catholique, 1857–1866.

Miley, John. *Systematic Theology*. 2 vols. New York: Eaton & Mains; Cincinnati: Curts & Jennings, 1894.

Miller, Hugh. *The Testimony of the Rocks: Or, Geology in Its Bearings on the Two Theologies, Natural and Revealed*. Boston: Gould and Lincoln, 1857.

Miller, J. R. *Week-Day Religion*. Philadelphia: Presbyterian Board of Publication, 1880.

Moffat, J. W. "Superluminary Universe: A Possible Solution to the Initial Value Problem in Cosmology." Revised November 14, 1998. Cornell University. https://arxiv.org/abs/gr-qc/9211020. Originally published in *International Journal of Modern Physics* D, 2, no. 3 (1993): 351–65.

Mohler, R. Albert, Jr., ed. *God and the Gay Christian? A Response to Matthew Vines*. Louisville: SBTS Press, 2014. http://sbts.me/ebook.

———. *We Cannot Be Silent: Speaking Truth to a Culture Redefining Sex, Marriage, and the Very Meaning of Right and Wrong*. Nashville: Thomas Nelson, 2015.

Mollenkott, Virginia R. *Omnigender: A Trans-Religious Approach*. Cleveland: Pilgrim Press, 2001.

Moltmann, Jürgen. *The Crucified God: The Cross of Christ as the Foundation and Criticism of Christian Theology*. New York: Harper & Row, 1974.

———. *The Way of Jesus Christ: Christology in Messianic Dimensions*. Translated by Margaret Kohl. San Francisco: HarperCollins, 1990.

Moo, Douglas J. *The Epistle to the Romans*. The New International Commentary on the New Testament. Grand Rapids, MI: Eerdmans, 1996.

———. *The Letter of James*. The Pillar New Testament Commentary. Grand Rapids, MI: Eerdmans, 2000.

———. *The Letters to the Colossians and to Philemon*. Grand Rapids, MI: Eerdmans, 2008.

Moore, Jonathan D. *English Hypothetical Universalism: John Preston and the Softening of Reformed Theology*. Grand Rapids, MI: Eerdmans, 2007.

Moreland, J. P., and William Lane Craig. *Philosophical Foundations for a Christian Worldview*. 2nd ed. Downers Grove, IL: InterVarsity Press, 2003.

Moreland, J. P., Stephen C. Meyer, Christopher Shaw, Ann K. Gauger, and Wayne Grudem, eds. *Theistic Evolution: A Scientific, Philosophical, and Theological Critique*. Wheaton, IL: Crossway, 2017.

Morison, James Cotter. *The Life and Times of Saint Bernard*. London: Macmillan and Co., 1894.

Morris, Desmond. *The Naked Ape: A Zoologist's Study of the Human Animal*. London: Jonathan Cape, 1967.

Morris, Leon. *1 Corinthians*. Tyndale New Testament Commentaries. Downers Grove, IL: InterVarsity Press, 1985.

———. *The Apostolic Preaching of the Cross*. 3rd ed. Grand Rapids, MI: Eerdmans, 1965.

———. *The Cross in the New Testament*. Grand Rapids, MI: Eerdmans, 1965.

———. *The Epistle to the Romans*. The Pillar New Testament Commentary. Grand Rapids, MI: Eerdmans, 1988.

———. *The Gospel according to John*. Rev. ed. The New International Commentary on the New Testament. Grand Rapids, MI: Eerdmans, 1995.

———. *The Gospel according to Matthew*. The Pillar New Testament Commentary. Grand Rapids, MI: Eerdmans; Leicester, England: Inter-Varsity Press, 1992.

———. *Luke: An Introduction and Commentary*. Tyndale New Testament Commentaries 3. Downers Grove, IL: InterVarsity Press, 1988.

Motyer, J. Alec. *Isaiah: An Introduction and Commentary*. Tyndale Old Testament Commentaries. Downers Grove, IL: InterVarsity Press, 1999.

———. *The Message of Exodus: The Days of Our Pilgrimage*. Downers Grove, IL: InterVarsity Press, 2005.

———. *The Prophecy of Isaiah*. Downers Grove, IL: InterVarsity Press, 1993.

Muller, Richard A. *Calvin and the Reformed Tradition: On the Work of Christ and the Order of Salvation*. Grand Rapids, MI: Baker Academic, 2012.

———. *Christ and the Decree: Christology and Predestination in Reformed Theology from Calvin to Perkins*. Durham, NC: Labyrinth, 1986.

———. "The Covenant of Works and the Stability of Divine Law in Seventeenth-Century Reformed Orthodoxy: A Study in the Theology of Herman Witsius and Wilhelmus à Brakel." *Calvin Theological Journal* 29 (1994): 75–101.

———. *Dictionary of Latin and Greek Theological Terms: Drawn Principally from Protestant Scholastic Theology*. 2nd ed. Grand Rapids, MI: Baker Academic, 2017.

———. *Divine Will and Human Choice: Freedom, Contingency, and Necessity in Early Modern Reformed Thought.* Grand Rapids, MI: Baker Academic, 2017.

———. "The Federal Motif in Seventeenth Century Arminian Theology." *Nederlands archief voor kerkgeschiedenis (Dutch Review of Church History)* Nieuwe Serie 62, no. 1 (1982): 102–22.

———. "Toward the *Pactum Salutis*: Locating the Origins of a Concept." *Mid-America Journal of Theology* 18 (2007): 11–65.

Murray, David P. *Christians Get Depressed Too: Hope and Help for Depressed People.* Grand Rapids, MI: Reformation Heritage Books, 2010.

———. *Jesus on Every Page: Ten Simple Ways to Seek and Find Christ in the Old Testament.* Nashville: Thomas Nelson, 2013.

* Murray, John. *Collected Writings of John Murray.* 4 vols. Edinburgh: Banner of Truth, 1977.

———. *The Covenant of Grace.* 1953. Reprint, Phillipsburg, NJ: Presbyterian and Reformed, 1988.

———. *The Epistle to the Romans.* The New International Commentary on the New Testament. Grand Rapids, MI: Eerdmans, 1968.

———. *The Imputation of Adam's Sin.* Grand Rapids, MI: Eerdmans, 1959.

———. *Principles of Conduct: Aspects of Biblical Ethics.* Grand Rapids, MI: Eerdmans, 1957.

———. *Redemption Accomplished and Applied.* Grand Rapids, MI: Eerdmans, 1955.

Musculus, Wolfgang. *Common Places of Christian Religion.* London: n.p., 1563.

Myers, David G., and Letha Dawson Scanzoni. *What God Has Joined Together? A Christian Case for Gay Marriage.* New York: HarperCollins, 2005.

Naselli, Andrew David, and Mark A. Snoeberger, eds. *Perspectives on the Extent of the Atonement: Three Views.* Nashville: B&H Academic, 2015.

Nestlehutt, Mark. "Chalcedonian Christology: Modern Criticism and Contemporary Ecumenism." *Journal of Ecumenical Studies* 35, no. 2 (Spring 1998): 175–96.

Nestorius. *The Bazaar of Heracleides.* Translated and edited by G. R. Driver and Leonard Hodgson. Oxford: Oxford University Press, 1925.

Neusner, Jacob. *The Rabbis and the Prophets.* Studies in Judaism. Lanham, MD: University Press of America, 2011.

Nevin, Norman C., ed. *Should Christians Embrace Evolution? Biblical and Scientific Responses.* Phillipsburg, NJ: P&R, 2011.

Newton, John. *Twenty-Six Letters on Religious Subjects . . . To Which Are Added, Hymns, Etc. by Omicron.* London: W. Oliver, 1777.

Nicholl, W. Robertson, ed. *The Expositor's Greek Testament.* New York: George H. Doran, n.d.

Nichols, Greg. *Covenant Theology: A Reformed and Baptistic Perspective on God's Covenants.* Birmingham, AL: Solid Ground, 2011.

* ———. *Lectures in Systematic Theology.* 7 vols. Seattle: CreateSpace Independent Publishing Platform, 2017–.

Niebuhr, Richard. *The Kingdom of God in America.* 1937. Reprint, New York: Harper & Row, 1959.

Nietzsche, Friedrich. *The Will to Power.* Translated by Walter Kaufmann and R. J. Hollingdale. Edited by Walter Kaufmann. New York: Random House, 1967.

Norris, Richard A., Jr., ed. and trans. *The Christological Controversy.* Sources in Early Christian Thought. Philadelphia: Fortress, 1980.

Núñez C., Emilio A. *Liberation Theology.* Translated by Paul E. Sywulka. Chicago: Moody, 1985.

Oberman, Heiko A. *The Dawn of the Reformation: Essays in Late Medieval and Early Reformation Thought.* Edinburgh: T&T Clark, 1986.

———. *The Harvest of Medieval Theology: Gabriel Biel and Late Medieval Nominalism.* Durham, NC: Labyrinth, 1983.

O'Brien, Peter T. *The Epistle to the Philippians.* The New International Greek Testmament Commentary. Grand Rapids, MI: Eerdmans, 1991.

Oden, Thomas, ed. *Ancient Christian Commentary on Scripture, Old Testament.* 15 vols. Downers Grove, IL: InterVarsity Press, 2001–2005.

———. *John Wesley's Scriptural Christianity: A Plain Exposition of His Teaching on Christian Doctrine.* Grand Rapids, MI: Zondervan, 1994.

Oecolampadius, Johannes. *In Iesaiam Prophetam Hypomnematon.* Basle: n.p., 1525.

O'Leary, Denyse. "Stasis: Life Goes On but Evolution Does Not Happen." *Evolution News and Views.* October 12, 2015. http://www.evolutionnews .org/2015/10/stasis_when_lif100011.html.

Olevianus, Caspar. *An Exposition of the Apostles' Creed.* Translated by Lyle D. Bierma. Grand Rapids, MI: Reformation Heritage Books, 2009.

Oord, Thomas Jay, ed. *Theologies of Creation: Creatio Ex Nihilo and Its New Rivals.* London: Routledge, 2014.

Oswalt, John N. *The Book of Isaiah, Chapters 40–66.* The New International Commentary on the Old Testament. Grand Rapids, MI: Eerdmans, 1998.

Otto, Ronald E. "*Descendit in Inferna*: A Reformed Review of a Creedal Conundrum." *Westminster Theological Journal* 52, no. 1 (January 1990): 143–50.

Ovid. *Metamorphoses*. Translated by Frank Justus Miller. Loeb Classical Library. Cambridge, MA: Harvard University Press, 1921.

Owen, John. *Biblical Theology: The History of Theology from Adam to Christ*. Translated by Stephen P. Westscott. Orlando, FL: Soli Deo Gloria, 1994.

* ———. *An Exposition of the Epistle to the Hebrews*. 7 vols. Reprint, Edinburgh: Banner of Truth, 1991.

———. *Theologoumena Pantodapa: Sive de Natura, Ortu, Progressu, et Studio Verae Theologiae*. Oxford: Henry Hall, 1661.

* ———. *The Works of John Owen*. Edited by William H. Goold. 16 vols. 1850–1853. Reprint, Edinburgh: Banner of Truth, 1965–1968.

Packer, J. I. *Knowing God*. Downers Grove, IL: InterVarsity Press, 1973.

———. *Knowing Man*. Westchester, IL: Cornerstone Books, 1979.

———. "What Did the Cross Achieve? The Logic of Penal Substitution." *Tyndale Bulletin* 25 (1974): 3–45.

Pannenberg, Wolfhart. *Jesus—God and Man*. Translated by Lewis L. Wilkins and Duane A. Priebe. 2nd ed. Philadelphia: Westminster, 1977.

Park, Edwards Amasa, ed. and intro. *The Atonement: Discourses and Treatises by Edwards, Smalley, Maxcy, Emmons, Griffin, Burge, and Weeks*. Boston: Congregational Board of Publication, 1859.

Parsons, Michael, ed. *Reformation Faith: Exegesis and Theology in the Protestant Reformation*. Eugene, OR: Wipf and Stock, 2014.

Pascal, Blaise. *The Provincial Letters*. Edited by M. Villemain. London: Seeley, Burnside, and Seeley, 1847.

Pausanias, *Description of Greece*. Translated by W. H. S. Jones and H. A. Ormerod. Cambridge, MA: Harvard University Press; London: William Heinemann Ltd., 1918.

Payne, J. Barton. "Theistic Evolution and the Hebrew of Genesis 1–2." *Bulletin of the Evangelical Theological Society* 8, no. 2 (Spring 1965): 85–90.

Pearse, Edward. *The Best Match, or the Soul's Espousal to Christ*. London: for Jonathan Robinson and Brabazon Aylmer, 1673.

———. *The Best Match: The Soul's Espousal to Christ*. Edited by Don Kistler. Grand Rapids, MI: Soli Deo Gloria, 1994.

Pelagius. *The Christian Life and Other Essays*. Translated by Ford Lewis Battles. Pittsburgh: s.n.: 1972.

Perdue, Leo G. *Proverbs.* Interpretation: A Bible Commentary for Teaching and Preaching. Louisville: John Knox, 1989.

Perkins, William. *A Treatise of the Vocations, or, Callings of Men.* London: John Legat, 1603.

* ———. *The Works of William Perkins.* 10 vols. Series edited by Joel R. Beeke and Derek W. H. Thomas. Grand Rapids, MI: Reformation Heritage Books, 2015–2020.

Peterson, Robert A. *Salvation Accomplished by the Son: The Work of Christ.* Wheaton, IL: Crossway, 2012.

Petit, Jean-Pierre. "An Interpretation of Cosmological Model with Variable Light Velocity." *Modern Physics* Letters A, 3, no. 16 (Nov. 1988). https://www.jp-petit.org/science/f300/modern_physics_letters_a1.pdf.

Petry, Ray C., ed. *Late Medieval Mysticism.* The Library of Christian Classics 13. Philadelphia: Westminster, 1957.

Petto, Samuel. *The Difference between the Old and New Covenant Stated and Explained: with an Exposition of the Covenant of Grace in the Principal Concernments of It.* London: Eliz. Calvert, 1674.

———. *The Great Mystery of the Covenant of Grace: or the Difference between the Old and New Covenant Stated and Explained.* Stoke-on-Trent, England: Tentmaker, 2007.

Phillips, Richard D., ed. *God, Adam, and You: Biblical Creation Defended and Applied.* Phillipsburg, NJ: P&R, 2015.

Philo. *The Works of Philo: Complete and Unabridged.* Edited by Charles Duke Yonge. Peabody, MA: Hendrickson, 1995.

Pink, Arthur W. *Practical Christianity.* Grand Rapids, MI: Guardian, 1974.

Pinnock, Clark H., ed. *The Grace of God and the Will of Man.* Minneapolis: Bethany House, 1989.

Piper, John. *Counted Righteous in Christ: Should We Abandon the Imputation of Christ's Righteousness?* Wheaton, IL: Crossway, 2002.

———. *God Is the Gospel.* Wheaton, IL: Crossway, 2005.

———. *The Passion of Jesus Christ.* Wheaton, IL: Crossway, 2004.

Piper, John, and Wayne Grudem, eds. *Recovering Biblical Manhood and Womanhood: A Response to Evangelical Feminism.* Wheaton, IL: Crossway, 1991.

Plato. *Plato, Volume 1, Euthyphro, Apology, Crito, Phaedo, Phaedrus.* Translated by H. N. Fowler. Loeb Classical Library. New York: Macmillan, 1908.

———. *The Republic.* Translated and edited by Desmond Lee. Revised ed. Penguin Classics. London: Penguin, 1974.

Polanus, Amandus. *Partitiones Theologicae*. 2nd ed. Basel: Conrad Waldkirch, 1590.

———. *Substance of the Christian Religion*. Translated by E. W. London: by R. F. for John Oxenbridge, 1595.

Polhill, Edward. *The Works of Edward Polhill*. 1844. Reprint, Morgan, PA: Soli Deo Gloria, 1998.

Polman, A. D. R. *The Word of God according to St. Augustine*. Translated by A. J. Pomerans. Grand Rapids, MI: Eerdmans, 1961.

* Polyander, Johannes, Antonius Walaeus, Antonius Thysius, and Andreas Rivetus. *Synopsis Purioris Theologiae, Synopsis of a Purer Theology: Latin Text and English Translation, Volume 1, Disputations 1–23*. Translated by Riemer A. Faber. Edited by Dolf te Velde, Rein Ferwerda, Willem J. van Asselt, William den Boer, Riemer A. Faber. Leiden: Brill, 2014.

———. *Synopsis Purioris Theologiae, Synopsis of a Purer Theology: Latin Text and English Translation, Volume 2, Disputations 24–42*. Translated by Riemer A. Faber. Edited by Henk van den Belt. Leiden: Brill, 2016.

Poole, Matthew, *Annotations upon the Holy Bible*. 3 vols. New York: Robert Carter and Brothers, 1853.

Powlison, David. "Idols of the Heart and 'Vanity Fair.'" *Journal of Biblical Counseling* 13, no. 2 (1995): 35–38, https://www.ccef.org/resources/blog/idols-heart-and-vanity-fair.

Poythress, Vern S. "Kinds of Biblical Theology." *Westminster Theological Journal* 70, no. 1 (Spring 2008): 129–42.

———. *Understanding Dispensationalists*. 2nd ed. Phillipsburg, NJ: P&R, 1994.

Pratt, Richard L., Jr. *1 and 2 Chronicles*. Fearn, Ross-shire, Scotland: Christian Focus, 1998.

———. "Reformed Theology Is Covenant Theology." *Reformed Perspectives Magazine* 12, no. 20 (May 16–22, 2010). http://thirdmill.org/articles/ric_pratt/ric_pratt.RTiscovenant.html.

Preston, John. *The New Covenant, or, the Saints Portion: A Treatise Unfolding the All-Sufficiencie of God, and Mans Uprightnes, and the Covenant of Grace*. London: by J. D. for Nicolas Bourne, 1629. Reprinted in 1630.

Pronk, Cornelis. *No Other Foundation than Jesus Christ: Pastoral, Historical, and Contemporary Essays*. Mitchell, ON: Free Reformed, 2008.

Pronk, Pim. *Against Nature? Types of Moral Argumentation regarding Homosexuality*. Translated by John Vriend. Grand Rapids, MI: Eerdmans, 1993.

Purnell, Robert. *A Little Cabinet Richly Stored with All Sorts of Heavenly Varieties, and Soul-Reviving Influences.* London: by R. W. for Thomas Brewster, 1657.

Ramm, Bernard. *The Christian View of Science and Scripture.* Grand Rapids, MI: Eerdmans, 1954.

Reisinger, John G. *Abraham's Four Seeds: A Biblical Examination of the Presuppositions of Covenant Theology and Dispensationalism.* Frederick, MD: New Covenant Media, 1998.

Reymond, Robert L. *A New Systematic Theology of the Christian Faith.* Nashville: Thomas Nelson, 1998.

Reynolds, Edward. *The Whole Works of Right Rev. Edward Reynolds.* 6 vols. 1826. Reprint, Morgan, PA: Soli Deo Gloria, 1996.

Rhodes, Ron. *Christ before the Manger: The Life and Times of the Pre-incarnate Christ.* Grand Rapids, MI: Baker, 1992.

Ridderbos, Herman. *Paul: An Outline of His Theology.* Translated by John Richard de Witt. Grand Rapids, MI: Eerdmans, 1975.

Riker, D. B. *A Catholic Reformed Theologian: Federalism and Baptism in the Thought of Benjamin Keach, 1640–1704.* Studies in Baptist History and Thought. Eugene, OR: Wipf and Stock, 2009.

Ritschl, Albrecht. *The Christian Doctrine of Justification and Reconciliation.* Edited by H. R. Mackintosh and A. B. Macaulay. 2nd ed. Edinburgh: T&T Clark, 1902.

* Roberts, Alexander, and James Donaldson, eds. *The Ante-Nicene Fathers.* Revised by A. Cleveland Coxe. 9 vols. New York: Charles Scribner's Sons, 1918. Includes cited works written by Clement of Alexandria, Hippolytus, Ignatius, Irenaeus, Justin Martyr, Novatian, Origen, Papias, and Tertullian.

Roberts, Francis. *Mysterium et Medulla Bibliorum. The Mysterie and Marrow of the Bible: Viz. God's Covenants with Man.* London: by R. W. for George Calvert, 1657.

Robertson, O. Palmer. *The Christ of the Covenants.* Phillipsburg, NJ: Presbyterian and Reformed, 1980.

Robinson, J. A. T. *The Body: A Study in Pauline Thought.* Studies in Biblical Theology 5. London: SCM, 1952.

Rollock, Robert. "Robert Rollock's Catechism on God's Covenants." Translated and introduced by Aaron C. Denlinger. *Mid-America Journal of Theology* 20 (2009): 105–29.

———. *Select Works of Robert Rollock.* 2 vols. Grand Rapids, MI: Reformation Heritage Books, 2008.

Ross, Hugh. *Creation and Time: A Biblical and Scientific Perspective on the Creation-Date Controversy.* Colorado Springs: NavPress, 1994.

Rousseau, Jean-Jacques. *The Collected Writings of Rousseau, Volume 9, Letter to Beaumont, Letters Written from the Mountain, and Related Writings.* Translated by Christopher Kelly and Judith R. Bush. Edited by Christopher Kelly and Eve Grace. Hanover, NH: University Press of New England, 2001.

———. *The Social Contract, or Principles of Political Right.* Translated by H. J. Tozer. Wordsworth Classics of World Literature. Ware, Hertfordshire, England: Wordsworth, 1998.

Rowdon, Harold H., ed. *Christ the Lord: Studies in Christology Presented to Donald Guthrie.* Downers Grove, IL: InterVarsity Press, 1982.

Russell, Bertrand. *A Free Man's Worship.* Portland, ME: Thomas Bird Mosher, 1923.

Rutherford, Samuel. *The Covenant of Life Opened: or a Treatise of the Covenant of Grace.* Edinburgh: by Andre Anderson, for Robert Broun, 1655.

———. *Letters of Samuel Rutherford.* Edited by Andrew A. Bonar. Reprint, Edinburgh: Banner of Truth, 1984.

———. *Rutherford's Catechism: or, the Sum of Christian Religion.* Edinburgh: Blue Banner, 1998.

Rydelnik, Michael. *The Messianic Hope: Is the Hebrew Bible Really Messianic?* NAC Studies in Bible and Theology. Nashville: B&H Academic, 2010.

Ryken, Philip Graham. *Exodus: Saved for God's Glory.* Preaching the Word. Wheaton, IL: Crossway, 2005.

Ryrie, Charles. *Dispensationalism.* Rev. ed. Chicago: Moody, 1995.

Sagan, Carl. *Cosmos.* 1980. Reprint, New York: Ballantine Books, 2013.

Salkeld, John. *A Treatise of Paradise.* London: by Edward Griffin for Nathaniel Butter, 1617.

Sartre, Jean-Paul. *Existentialism Is a Humanism.* Translated by Carol Macomber. Edited by John Kulka. New Haven, CT: Yale University Press, 2007.

Saucy, Robert L. *The Case for Progressive Dispensationalism.* Grand Rapids, MI: Zondervan, 1993.

Scaer, David P. "He Did Descend to Hell: In Defense of the Apostles' Creed." *Journal of the Evangelical Theological Society* 35, no. 1 (March 1992): 91–99.

———. "The Nature and Extent of the Atonement in Lutheran Theology." *Bulletin of the Evangelical Theological Society* 10, no. 4 (Fall 1967): 179–87.

Scanzoni, Letha Dawson, and Virginia Ramey Mollenkott. *Is the Homosexual My Neighbor? A Positive Christian Response*. Rev. ed. New York: Harper-Collins, 1994.

Schaeffer, Francis A. *Genesis in Space and Time*. Downers Grove, IL: Inter-Varsity Press, 1972.

Schaff, Philip. *Christ and Christianity*. New York: Charles Scribner's Sons, 1885.

————. ed. *A Select Library of Nicene and Post-Nicene Fathers of the Christian Church, First Series*. 14 vols. New York: Christian Literature Co., 1888. Includes cited works written by Augustine and John Chrysostom.

* Schaff, Philip, and Henry Wace, eds. *A Select Library of Nicene and Post-Nicene Fathers of the Christian Church, Second Series*. 14 vols. New York: Christian Literature Co., 1894. Includes cited works written by Ambrose, Athanasius, Basil, Cyril of Alexandria, Eusebius, Gregory of Nazianzus, Gregory of Nyssa, Gregory the Great, Hilary of Poitiers, John of Damascus, Leo the Great, Rufinus, Scholasticus, Theodoret, and various councils.

Schleiermacher, Friedrich. *The Christian Faith*. Edited by H. R. Mackintosh and J. S. Stewart. 2 vols. New York: Harper and Row, 1963.

Schmid, Heinrich. *The Doctrinal Theology of the Evangelical Lutheran Church, Verified from the Original Sources*. Translated by Charles A. Hay and Henry E. Jacobs. 2nd ed. Philadelphia: Lutheran Publication Society, 1889.

Schortinghuis, Wilhelmus. *Essential Truths in the Heart of a Christian*. Translated by Harry Boonstra and Gerrit W. Sheeres. Edited by James A. De Jong. Grand Rapids, MI: Reformation Heritage Books, 2009.

Schreiner, Susan E. *The Theater of His Glory: Nature and the Natural Order in the Thought of John Calvin*. Grand Rapids, MI: Baker Academic, 1991.

Schreiner, Thomas R. *1, 2 Peter, Jude*. The New American Commentary 37. Nashville: Broadman & Holman, 2003.

————. *Romans*. Baker Exegetical Commentary on the New Testament. Grand Rapids, MI: Baker Academic, 1998.

Schreiner, Thomas R., and Bruce A. Ware, eds. *The Grace of God, the Bondage of the Will*. 2 vols. Grand Rapids, MI: Baker, 1995.

Schuller, Robert H. *Self-Esteem: The New Reformation*. Waco, TX: Word, 1982.

Schweitzer, Albert. *The Quest of the Historical Jesus: A Critical Study of Its Progress from Reimarus to Wrede*. Translated by W. Montgomery. London: Adam and Charles Black, 1910.

Scofield, C. I., ed. *The New Scofield Reference Bible*. New York: Oxford University Press, 1967.

———. *The Scofield Reference Bible*. New York: Oxford University Press, 1909.

Sedgwick, Obadiah. *The Bowels of Tender Mercy Sealed in the Everlasting Covenant*. London: by Edward Mottershed, for Adoniram Byfield, 1660.

Seeberg, Reinhold. *Text-Book of the History of Doctrines*. Translated by Charles E. Hay. Philadelphia: Lutheran Publication Society, 1905.

Seneca. *Ad Lucilium Epistulae Morales*. Translated by Richard M. Gummere. Loeb Classical Library. Cambridge, MA: Harvard University Press, 1917.

Sewell, Marilyn. "Saying Goodbye to Tolerance." *Huffington Post*. October 19, 2012. https://www.huffpost.com/entry/saying-goodbye-to-tolerance _b_1976607.

Shaw, George Bernard. *Back to Methuselah: A Metabiological Pentateuch*. New York: Brentano's, 1921.

Shaw, Robert. *An Exposition of the Confession of Faith*. 2nd ed. Edinburgh: John Johnstone, 1846.

Shedd, William G. T. *Dogmatic Theology*. 2 vols. New York: Charles Scribner's Sons, 1888.

Shelley, Bruce. *Church History in Plain Language*. Revised by R. L. Hatchett. 4th ed. Nashville: Thomas Nelson, 2013.

Sheth, Noel. "Hindu Avatāra and Christian Incarnation: A Comparison." *Philosophy East and West 52*, no. 1 (January 2002): 98–125.

Shults, F. LeRon. "A Dubious Christological Formula: From Leontius of Byzantium to Karl Barth." *Journal of Theological Studies 57* (1996): 431–46.

Sibbes, Richard. *The Works of Richard Sibbes*. Edited by Alexander Grosart. 7 vols. Reprint. Edinburgh: Banner of Truth, 1973.

Silliman, Benjamin. *Outline of the Course of Geological Lectures Given in Yale College*. New Haven, CT: Hezekiah Howe, 1829.

Silva, Moisés. *Philippians*. 2nd ed.. Baker Exegetical Commentary on the New Testament. Grand Rapids, MI: Baker Academic, 2005.

Simons, Menno. *The Complete Works of Menno Simons*. 2 parts in 1 vol. Elkhart, IN: John F. Funk and Brother, 1871.

Smalley, Stephen S. *1, 2, 3 John*. Word Biblical Commentary 51. Waco, TX: Word, 1984.

Smeaton, George. *Christ's Doctrine of the Atonement*. Reprint, Edinburgh: Banner of Truth, 1991.

Smith, Christian, with Melina Lundquist Denton. *Soul Searching: The Religious and Spiritual Lives of American Teenagers.* Oxford: Oxford University Press, 2005.

Smith, Gary V. *Hosea, Amos, Micah.* The NIV Application Commentary. Grand Rapids, MI: Zondervan, 2001.

———. *Isaiah 40–66.* The New American Commentary 15B. Nashville: Broadman & Holman, 2009.

Smith, Morton H. *Systematic Theology.* 2 vols. Greenville, SC: Greenville Seminary Press, 1994.

Smith, Robert Pearsall. *"Walk in the Light." Words of Counsel to Those Who Have Entered into "the Rest of Faith."* London: Morgan and Scott, n.d.

Smith, William, ed. *A Dictionary of Greek and Roman Antiquities.* London: Taylor and Walton, 1842.

Snelling, Andrew A. *Earth's Catastrophic Past: Geology, Creation, and the Flood.* 2 vols. Petersburg, KY: Answers in Genesis, 2010.

Snyder, James. "Meaning of the 'Maiestas Domini' in Hosios David." *Byzantion* 37 (1967): 143–52.

Sobrino, Jon. *Jesus the Liberator: A Historical-Theological Reading of Jesus of Nazareth.* Translated by Paul Burns and Francis McDonagh. Maryknoll, NY: Orbis, 1993.

Sproul, R. C. *The Gospel of God: An Exposition of Romans.* Fearn, Ross-shire, Scotland: Christian Focus, 1994.

———. *Willing to Believe: The Controversy over Free Will.* Grand Rapids, MI: Baker, 1997.

Spurgeon, C. H. *The Metropolitan Tabernacle Pulpit.* 57 vols. Edinburgh: Banner of Truth, 1969.

———. *New Park Street Pulpit.* 6 vols. Pasadena, TX: Pilgrim Publications, 1975.

———. *Sermons on Christ's Names and Titles.* Edited by Chas. T. Cook. Greenwood, SC: Attic Press, 1961.

———. *Spurgeon's Expository Encyclopedia.* 14 vols. Grand Rapids, MI: Baker, 1996.

Starke, John. "The Incarnation Is about a Person, Not a Mission." The Gospel Coalition. May 16, 2011. https://www.thegospelcoalition.org/article/the-incarnation-is-about-a-person-not-a-mission/.

Steele, Richard. *The Religious Tradesman.* 1823. Reprint, Harrisonburg, VA: Sprinkle, 1989.

———. *The Tradesman's Calling.* London: for J. D. by Samuel Spring, 1684.

Stein, Robert H. *Luke.* The New American Commentary 24. Nashville: Broadman & Holman, 1992.

Stephen, W. P. *The Theology of Huldrych Zwingli.* Oxford: Clarendon, 1986.

Stevenson, George. *Treatise on the Offices of Christ.* 2nd ed. Edinburgh: W. P. Kennedy, 1845.

Stoever, William K. B. "The Covenant of Works in Puritan Theology: The Antinomian Crisis in New England." PhD diss., Yale University, 1970.

Storms, Sam, and Justin Taylor, eds. *For the Fame of God's Name: Essays in Honor of John Piper.* Wheaton, IL: Crossway, 2010.

Stott, John R. W. *The Cross of Christ.* Downers Grove, IL: InterVarsity Press, 1986.

———. *The Message of Romans.* Downers Grove, IL: InterVarsity Press, 1994.

Strong, Augustus H. *Systematic Theology.* 3 vols. Philadelphia: Griffith and Rowland, 1909.

Strong, William. *A Discourse of the Two Covenants.* Westminster Assembly Project. 1678. Facsimile reprint, Grand Rapids, MI: Reformation Heritage Books, 2011.

Stuart, Douglas K. *Exodus.* The New American Commentary 2. Nashville: Broadman & Holman, 2006.

Stuckenberg, J. H. W. "The Theology of Albrecht Ritschl." *The American Journal of Theology* 2, no. 2 (April 1898): 268–92.

Swanson, Dennis M. "Introduction to New Covenant Theology." *The Master's Seminary Journal* 18, no. 1 (Fall 2007): 149–63.

Swinnock, George. *The Works of George Swinnock.* 5 vols. Edinburgh: James Nichol, 1868.

Symington, William. *The Atonement and Intercession of Jesus Christ.* 1863. Reprint, Grand Rapids, MI: Reformation Heritage Books, 2006.

———. *Messiah the Prince: The Mediatorial Dominion of Jesus Christ.* Pittsburgh: Crown and Covenant, 2012.

Synod of the Reformed Presbyterian Church in North America. *The Gospel and Sexual Orientation.* Edited by Michael Lefebvre. Pittsburgh: Crown and Covenant, 2012.

Taylor, John. *The Scripture-Doctrine of Original Sin Proposed to Free and Candid Examination.* London: for the author, by J. Wilson, 1740.

Teellinck, Willem. *The Path of True Godliness.* Translated by Annemie Godbehere. Edited by Joel R. Beeke. Classics of Reformed Spirituality. Grand Rapids, MI: Reformation Heritage Books, 2003.

Templeton, Julian, and Keith Riglin, eds. *Reforming Worship: English Reformed Principles and Practices.* Eugene, OR: Wipf and Stock, 2012.

Teresa of Avila. *The Collected Works of St. Teresa of Avila.* Translated by Kieran Kavanaugh and Otilio Rodriguez. Washington, DC: ICS Publications, 1980.

Theodoret of Cyrus. *Commentary on the Letters of St. Paul.* Translated by Robert Charles Hill. Brookline, MA: Holy Cross Orthodox Press, 2001.

Thiselton, Anthony C. *First Epistle to the Corinthians.* New International Greek Testament Commentary. Grand Rapids, MI: Eerdmans, 2000.

Thompson, Mark D., ed. *Engaging with Calvin.* Nottingham, England: Apollos, 2009.

Tillich, Paul. *Systematic Theology.* 3 vols. Chicago: University of Chicago Press, 1957.

Torrance, Thomas. *Incarnation: The Person and Life of Christ.* Edited by Robert T. Walker. Downers Grove, IL: InterVarsity Press, 2008.

Traill, Robert. *The Works of the Late Reverend Robert Traill.* 4 vols. Edinburgh: J. Ogle et al., 1810.

Trapp, John. *A Commentary on the Old and New Testaments.* Edited by Hugh Martin. 5 vols. London: Richard D. Dickinson, 1867–1868.

Treat, Jeremy R. *The Crucified King: Atonement and Kingdom in Biblical and Systematic Theology.* Grand Rapids, MI: Zondervan, 2014.

Tregelles, S. P. *The Hope of Christ's Second Coming: How Is It Taught in Scripture? And Why?* London: Houlston & Wright, 1864.

Trinterud, Leonard J. "The Origins of Puritanism." *Church History* 20, no. 1 (March 1951): 37–57.

* Turretin, Francis. *Institutes of Elenctic Theology.* Translated by George Musgrave Giger. Edited by James T. Dennison Jr. 3 vols. Phillipsburg, NJ: P&R, 1992–1997.

Udemans, Godefridus. *The Practice of Faith, Hope, and Love.* Translated by Annemie Godbehere. Edited by Joel R. Beeke. Classics of Reformed Spirituality. Grand Rapids, MI: Reformation Heritage Books, 2012.

Underhill, Evelyn. *Mysticism: A Study in the Nature and Development of Man's Spiritual Consciousness.* 12th ed. London: Methuen & Co., 1930.

Ursinus, Zacharius. *The Commentary of Dr. Zacharias Ursinus on the Heidelberg Catechism.* Translated by G. W. Williard. Reprint, Phillipsburg, NJ: Presbyterian and Reformed, 1985.

———. *The Larger Catechism.* Translated by Lyle D. Bierma, Fred Klooster, and John Medendorp. In *An Introduction to the Heidelberg Catechism.* Texts and Studies in Reformation and Post-Reformation Thought. Grand Rapids, MI: Baker Academic, 2005.

————. *The Summe of the Christian Religion.* Translated by Henry Parry. London: James Young, 1645.

Ussher, James. *A Body of Divinity: Being the Sum and Substance of the Christian Religion.* Edited by Michael Nevarr. Birmingham, AL: Solid Ground, 2007.

Vail, Isaac N. *The Waters above the Firmament: or, The Earth's Annular System.* 2nd ed. Philadelphia: Ferris and Leach, 1902.

van Asselt, Willem J., J. Martin Bac, and Roelf T. te Velde, eds. *Reformed Thought on Freedom: The Concept of Free Choice in Early Modern Reformed Theology.* Texts and Studies in Reformation and Post-Reformation Thought. Grand Rapids, MI: Baker Academic, 2010.

VanderGroe, Theodorus. *The Christian's Only Comfort in Life and Death: An Exposition of the Heidelberg Catechism.* Translated by Bartel Elshout. Edited by Joel R. Beeke. 2 vols. Grand Rapids, MI: Reformation Heritage Books, 2016.

VanderKemp, Johannes. *The Christian Entirely the Property of Christ, in Life and Death, Exhibited in Fifty-Three Sermons on the Heidelberg Catechism.* Translated by John M. Harlingen. 2 vols. Reprint, Grand Rapids, MI: Reformation Heritage Books, 1997.

VanDoodewaard, William. *The Quest for the Historical Adam.* Grand Rapids, MI: Reformation Heritage Books, 2015.

VanGemeren, Willem A. *The Progress of Redemption: The Story of Salvation from Creation to the New Jerusalem.* Grand Rapids, MI: Baker, 1988.

van Genderen, J., and W. H. Velema. *Concise Reformed Dogmatics.* Translated by Gerrit Bilkes and Ed M. van der Maas. Phillipsburg, NJ: P&R, 2008.

van Limborch, Philipp. *Compleat System, or Body of Divinity, Both Speculative and Practical, Founded on Scripture and Reason.* Translated by William Jones. London: for John Taylor and Andrew Bell, 1702.

van Mastricht, Petrus. *Theoretical-Practical Theology.* Translated by Todd M. Rester. Edited by Joel R. Beeke. 7 vols. Grand Rapids, MI: Reformation Heritage Books, 2018–.

Venema, Cornelis P. *Christ and Covenant Theology: Essays on Election, Republicationism, and the Covenants.* Phillipsburg, NJ: P&R, 2017.

————. *The Gospel of Free Acceptance in Christ: An Assessment of the Reformation and New Perspectives on Paul.* Edinburgh: Banner of Truth, 2006.

————. *Heinrich Bullinger and the Doctrine of Predestination: Author of "the Other Reformed Tradition"?* Texts and Studies in Reformation and Post-Reformation Thought. Grand Rapids, MI: Baker Academic, 2002.

Venema, Dennis R., and Scot McKnight. *Adam and the Genome: Reading Scripture after Genetic Science*. Grand Rapids, MI: Baker, 2017.

Venning, Ralph. *Sin, the Plague of Plagues; or, Sinful Sin the Worst of Evils*. London: John Hancock, 1669.

———. *The Sinfulness of Sin*. Puritan Paperbacks. Edinburgh: Banner of Truth, 1965.

Vermigli, Peter Martyr. *The Peter Martyr Library, Volume 4, Philosophical Works*. Translated and edited by Joseph C. McLelland. Sixteenth Century Essays and Studies. Kirksville, MO: Thomas Jefferson University Press and Sixteenth Century Journal Publishers, 1996.

Via, Dan O., and Robert A. J. Gagnon. *Homosexuality and the Bible: Two Views*. Minneapolis: Augsburg Fortress, 2003.

Vidu, Adonis. *Atonement, Law, and Justice: The Cross in Historical and Cultural Contexts*. Grand Rapids, MI: Baker Academic, 2014.

Vines, Matthew. *God and the Gay Christian: The Biblical Case in Support of Same-Sex Relationships*. Colorado Springs: Convergent Books, 2014.

Voorwinde, Stephen. *Jesus' Emotions in the Gospels*. London: T&T Clark, 2011.

Vos, Geerhardus. *Biblical Theology: Old and New Testaments*. Edinburgh: Banner of Truth, 1948.

———. *The Pauline Eschatology*. Princeton, NJ: Geerhardus Vos, 1930.

———. *Redemptive History and Biblical Interpretation: The Shorter Writings of Geerhardus Vos*. Edited by Richard B. Gaffin Jr. Grand Rapids, MI: Baker, 1980.

* ———. *Reformed Dogmatics*. Translated and edited by Richard B. Gaffin et al. 5 vols. Bellingham, WA: Lexham Press, 2012–2016.

———. *The Teaching of Jesus Concerning the Kingdom of God and the Church*. New York: American Tract Society, 1903.

Wainwright, Geoffrey. *For Our Salvation: Two Approaches to the Work of Christ*. Grand Rapids, MI: Eerdmans, 1997.

Wallace, Dewey D., Jr. "Puritan and Anglican: The Interpretation of Christ's Descent into Hell in Elizabethan Theology." *Archiv fur Reformationsgeschichte* 69 (1978): 248–87.

Wallace, Ronald S. *Calvin's Doctrine of the Christian Life*. Tyler, TX: Geneva Divinity School Press, 1982.

Walton, John H. *The Lost World of Adam and Eve: Genesis 2–3 and the Human Origins Debate*. Downers Grove, IL: IVP Academic, 2015.

Ward, Rowland S. *God and Adam: Reformed Theology and the Creation Covenant*. Wantirna, Australia: New Melbourne Press, 2003.

Ware, Bruce A. "Human Personhood: An Analysis and Definition." *Southern Baptist Journal of Theology* 13, no. 2 (Summer 2009): 18–31.

Warfield, Benjamin B. *Biblical and Theological Studies*. Philadelphia: Presbyterian and Reformed, 1952.

———. "Jesus' Mission, According to His Own Testimony." *Princeton Theology Review* 13, no. 4 (October 1915): 513–86.

———. *The Lord of Glory: A Study of the Designations of Our Lord in the New Testament with Especial Reference to His Deity*. 1907. Reprint, Grand Rapids, MI: Zondervan, n.d.

———. *The Person and Work of Christ*. Edited by Samuel G. Craig. Philadelphia: Presbyterian and Reformed, 1950.

———. "Professor Henry Preserved Smith on Inspiration." *The Presbyterian and Reformed Review* 5, no. 4 (October 1894): 600–653. Reprinted as *Limited Inspiration*. Philadelphia: Presbyterian & Reformed, 1962.

———. *The Saviour of the World*. New York: Hodder and Stoughton, 1913.

———. *Selected Shorter Writings*. Edited by John E. Meeter. Nutley, NJ: Presbyterian and Reformed, 1970.

———. *Two Studies in the History of Doctrine*. New York: Christian Literature Co., 1897.

Watson, Richard. *Theological Institutes*. 2 vols. New York: Lane and Scott, 1851.

Watson, Thomas. *All Things for Good*. Puritan Paperbacks. Edinburgh: Banner of Truth, 1986.

———. *A Body of Divinity*. Edinburgh: Banner of Truth, 1965.

———. *A Divine Cordial; or, the Transcendent Priviledge* [sic] *of Those That Love God, and Are Savingly Called*. London: Thomas Parkhurst, 1663.

———. *The Ten Commandments*. Edinburgh: Banner of Truth, 1965.

Watts, Isaac. *The Ruin and Recovery of Mankind: or, an Attempt to Vindicate the Scriptural Account of These Great Events upon the Plain Principles of Reason*. London: R. Hett and J. Brackstone, 1740.

Weinandy, Thomas. "The Soul/Body Analogy and the Incarnation: Cyril of Alexandria." *Coptic Church Review* 17, no. 3 (Fall 1996): 59–66.

Weinandy, Thomas G., Daniel A. Keating, and John P. Yocum, eds. *Aquinas on Scripture*. London: T&T Clark, 2005.

Weir, David A. *The Origins of the Federal Theology in Sixteenth-Century Reformation Thought*. Oxford: Oxford University Press, 1990.

Wells, David F. *The Person of Christ: A Biblical and Historical Analysis of the Incarnation*. Foundations for Faith: An Introduction to Christian Doctrine. Alliance, OH: Bible Scholar Books, 1984.

Wells, Paul. *Cross Words: The Biblical Doctrine of Atonement.* Fearn, Rossshire, Scotland: Christian Focus, 2006.

Wells, Tom, and Fred Zaspel. *New Covenant Theology.* Frederick, MD: New Covenant Media, 2002.

Wellum, Stephen J. *Christ Alone: The Uniqueness of Jesus as Savior: What the Reformers Taught . . . and Why It Still Matters.* The Five Solas Series. Grand Rapids, MI: Zondervan, 2017.

———. "Editorial: The Urgent Need for a Theological Anthropology Today." *Southern Baptist Theological Journal* 13, no. 2 (Summer 2009): 2–3.

* ———. *God the Son Incarnate: The Doctrine of Christ.* Foundations of Evangelical Theology. Wheaton, IL: Crossway, 2016.

Wellum, Stephen J., and Brent E. Parker, eds. *Progressive Covenantalism: Charting a Course between Dispensational and Covenant Theologies.* Nashville: B&H Academic, 2016.

Wenham, John. *Christ and the Bible.* 3rd ed. Grand Rapids, MI: Baker, 1994.

Wesley, John. *The Doctrine of Original Sin According to Scripture, Reason, and Experience.* Bristol: E. Farley, 1757.

———. *John Wesley's Sermons: An Anthology.* Edited by Albert C. Outler and Richard P. Heitzenrater. Nashville: Abingdon, 1991.

———. *The Works of John Wesley.* 10 vols. 3rd ed. 1872. Reprint, Grand Rapids, MI: Baker, 1979.

Wesley, John, and Charles Wesley. *Hymns on God's Everlasting Love.* Bristol: S. and F. Farley, 1741.

Whitcomb, John C., and Henry M. Morris. *The Genesis Flood: The Biblical Record and Its Scientific Implications.* Philadelphia: Presbyterian and Reformed, 1961.

White, James R. *The King James Only Controversy: Can You Trust the Modern Translations?* Minneapolis: Bethany House, 1995.

White, James R., and Jeffrey D. Niell. *The Same Sex Controversy.* Bloomington, MN: Bethany House, 2002.

Wiggers, G. F. *An Historical Presentation of Augustinism and Pelagianism from the Original Sources.* Translated and edited by Ralph Emerson. Andover: Gould, Newman, and Saxton, 1840.

Wiley, Tatha. *Original Sin: Origins, Developments, Contemporary Meanings.* New York: Paulist, 2002.

* Willard, Samuel. *A Compleat Body of Divinity in Two Hundred and Fifty Expository Lectures on the Assembly's Shorter Catechism.* Boston: by B. Green and S. Kneeland for B. Eliot and D. Henchman, 1726.

——. *The Doctrine of the Covenant of Redemption.* Boston: Benj. Harris, 1693.

Williams, Carol A. "The Decree of Redemption Is in Effect a Covenant: David Dickson and the Covenant of Redemption." PhD diss., Calvin Theological Seminary, 2005.

Williamson, Paul R. *Sealed with an Oath: Covenant in God's Unfolding Purpose.* New Studies in Biblical Theology. Downers Grove, IL: InterVarsity Press, 2007.

Wisse, Gerard. *Christ's Ministry in the Christian: The Administration of His Offices in the Believer.* Grand Rapids, MI: Free Reformed Publications, 2013.

Wisse, Maarten, Willemien Otten, and Marcel Sarot, eds. *Scholasticism Reformed: Essays in Honour of Willem J. Van Asselt.* Leiden: Brill, 2010.

* Witsius, Herman. *The Economy of the Covenants between God and Man.* 2 vols. 1822. Reprint, Grand Rapids, MI: Reformation Heritage Books, 2010.

* ——. *Sacred Dissertations on the Apostles' Creed.* Translated by Donald Fraser. 2 vols. 1823. Reprint, Grand Rapids, MI: Reformation Heritage Books, 2010.

Wold, Donald J. *Out of Order: Homosexuality in the Bible and the Ancient Near East.* Grand Rapids, MI: Baker, 1998.

* Wollebius, Johannes. *Compendium Theologiae Christianae.* In *Reformed Dogmatics*, edited and translated by John W. Beardslee III. A Library of Protestant Thought. New York: Oxford University Press, 1965.

Woolsey, Andrew A. *Unity and Continuity in Covenantal Thought: A Study in the Reformed Tradition to the Westminster Assembly.* Reformed Historical-Theological Studies. Grand Rapids, MI: Reformation Heritage Books, 2012.

Wright, David F. "Homosexuals or Prostitutes? The Meaning of ΑΡΣΕΝΟΚΟΙΤΑΙ (1 Cor. 6:9, 1 Tim. 1:10)." *Vigiliae Christianae* 38, no. 2 (June 1984): 125–53.

Yates, John. "'He Descended into Hell': Creed, Article and Scripture, Part 1." *Churchman* 102, no. 3 (1988): 240–50.

——. "'He Descended into Hell': Creed, Article and Scripture, Part 2." *Churchman* 102, no. 4 (1988): 303–15.

Young, Edward J. *The Book of Isaiah.* 3 vols. Grand Rapids, MI: Eerdmans, 1969.

——. "The Days of Genesis: Second Article." *Westminster Theological Journal* (May 1963): 143–71.

———. *In the Beginning: Genesis 1–3 and the Authority of Scripture.* Edinburgh: Banner of Truth, 1976.

———. *My Servants the Prophets.* Grand Rapids, MI: Eerdmans, 1952.

———. *Studies in Genesis One.* Phillipsburg, NJ: Presbyterian and Reformed, 1964.

Zalta, Edward N., ed. *The Stanford Encyclopedia of Philosophy.* https://plato .stanford.edu/.

Zanchi, Girolamo. *De Religione Christiana Fides—Confession of Christian Religion.* Edited by Luca Baschera and Christian Moser. Studies in the History of Christian Traditions. Leiden: Brill, 2007.

Zaspel, Fred G. "A Brief Explanation of 'New Covenant Theology.'" Unpublished paper.

Zwingli, Ulrich. *Of Baptism.* In *Zwingli and Bullinger.* Edited and translated by G. W. Bromiley. The Library of Christian Classics XXIV. Philadelphia: Westminster, 1953.

———. *The Latin Works and the Correspondence of Huldreich Zwingli Together with Selections from His German Works, Volume 1.* Edited by Samuel M. Jackson. Translated by Henry Prebel, Walter Lichtenstein, and Lawrence A. McLouth. New York: G. P. Putnam's Sons, 1912.

———. *The Latin Works of Huldreich Zwingli, Volume 2.* Edited by William J. Hinke. Philadelphia: Heidelberg Press, 1922.

General Index

patriarchs, 571–76, 594, 670
patristic theology, 285–87
Paul, 565
　on Abraham, 525–26
　on Adam, 153, 156, 280
　on covenant of works, 292–93,
　　527–29
　on creation, 116
　on the fall, 151–52
　on gender, 150
　on image of God, 169, 172–73, 181
　on Old Testament, 533
　on seed, 360
　on wrath of God, 454
Paul of Samosata, 830
Pausanias, 38n3
Payne, John Barton, 133, 135
Payson, Edward, 485
Peacocke, Arthur, 84n33
Pearse, Edward, 309, 714
Pecock, Reginald, 913
Pederson, Randall J., 546n74
Pelagianism, 152, 188, 286, 297, 366,
　367, 368, 370, 371, 375, 381,
　383, 407, 420
Pelagius, 178, 367
penal substitution, 1008–14, 1082,
　1118, 1119, 1122
penance, 1064, 1065
Pentecost, 770, 883, 904–5, 979, 981,
　1148
Pentecostalism, 823
Pentecost, Dwight, 557–58
people of God, 658–61, 978–85,
　1143–46, 1162–64
Perdue, Leo G., 687n35
perfection, 1125–28
perichoresis, 938n43
Perkins, William, 55, 68, 86n49,
　182nn41–42, 233–34, 246n4,
　268n11, 289, 293n58, 340,
　351, 352n21, 396n47, 401,
　413, 462, 463, 527, 530, 545,
　566, 567, 596, 711n36, 741,
　742n18, 759n7, 762n23, 775n79,
　777, 778, 779, 784n5, 791n43,
　793, 795n68, 836n84, 858,

860, 862, 876, 877n39, 894,
　896n16, 901n39, 904, 904n51,
　908, 913n4, 914, 918, 920n45,
　922n55, 923n63, 924–25, 957,
　958, 962, 964, 972, 974, 979n44,
　981, 983, 1000, 1016, 1023–24,
　1029, 1078n101, 1085, 1095n43,
　1101, 1106n92, 1122, 1124n69,
　1130, 1144n35, 1148, 1158–59,
　1163, 1164n27
persecution, 460
perseverance, 317, 429n67, 491–92
personality, 163, 199, 253
personhood, 252–53
Peter, 442, 813
Peterson, Robert A., 250n11, 903,
　960, 1013, 1023, 1025n100,
　1090n10, 1128n91, 1151n67
Petit, Jean-Pierre, 110n11
Petto, Samuel, 546n69, 598, 602n80
Pharaoh, 454–55
Philo of Alexandria, 220n38, 881
Philoponos, John, 822, 830
philosophical idealism, 43
philosophy, 43, 84, 107, 164, 252,
　256, 367, 420–23, 729
Phinehas, 270, 359, 642n28
Photinus, 825, 830
physical death, 358
Pianka, Eric, 148n23
piety, 262, 281, 412, 491
Pighius, Albertus, 373
Pink, Arthur, 471, 474
Pinnock, Clark H., 249n11, 404n16,
　1082n117
Piper, John, 997, 1003, 1045n58,
　1074n80
Piscator, Johannes, 1038
"plant of the field," 132n31
Plato, 43, 83, 249n10, 253n16, 256,
　259
Platonism, 83, 86, 253n16
pleasure, 42
Plotinus, 58
pluralism, 929n17, 1170, 1172
Plymouth Brethren, 555, 556
poetry, 80, 144

Scripture Index